MW00816546

THE OFFICIAL HISTORY OF THE FALKLANDS CAMPAIGN

Volume II: War and Diplomacy

In the second volume of his official history of the Falklands Campaign, Lawrence Freedman provides a detailed and authoritative account of one of the most extraordinary periods in recent British political history and a vivid portrayal of a government at war.

After the shock of the Argentine invasion of the Falklands in April 1982, Margaret Thatcher faced the crisis that came to define her premiership as she determined to recover the Islands. The book covers all aspects of the campaign – economic and diplomatic as well as military – and demonstrates the extent of the gamble that the Government took. There are important accounts of the tensions in relations with the United States, concerns among the military commanders about the risks they were expected to take, the problems of dealing with the media and the attempts to reach a negotiated settlement. *War and Diplomacy* describes in dramatic detail events such as the sinking of the *Belgrano*, the battle of Goose Green and the final push to Stanley. Attention is also paid to the aftermath of the war, including the various inquiries, and the eventual restoration of diplomatic relations with Argentina.

This paperback edition of Lawrence Freedman's acclaimed study is updated, corrected and contains some new material.

Lawrence Freedman is Professor of War Studies at King's College London where he is currently Vice-Principal. He has written extensively on military strategy, cold war history and contemporary conflict and is a regular newspaper columnist.

WHITEHALL HISTORIES: GOVERNMENT OFFICIAL HISTORY SERIES

ISSN: 1474–8398

The Government Official History series began in 1919 with wartime histories, and the peacetime series was inaugurated in 1966 by Harold Wilson. The aim of the series is to produce major histories in their own right, compiled by historians eminent in the field, who are afforded free access to all relevant material in the official archives. The Histories also provide a trusted secondary source for other historians and researchers while the official records are not in the public domain. The main criteria for selection of topics are that the histories should record important episodes or themes of British history while the official records can still be supplemented by the recollections of key players; and that they should be of general interest, and, preferably, involve the records of more than one government department.

THE UNITED KINGDOM AND THE EUROPEAN COMMUNITY:
Vol. I: The Rise and Fall of a National Strategy, 1945–1963
Alan S. Milward

SECRET FLOTILLAS:
Vol. I: Clandestine Sea Operations to Brittany, 1940–1944
Vol. II: Clandestine Sea Operations in the Mediterranean, North Africa and the Adriatic, 1940–1944
Brooks Richards

SOE IN FRANCE
M. R. D. Foot

THE OFFICIAL HISTORY OF THE FALKLANDS CAMPAIGN:
Vol. I: The Origins of the Falklands War
Vol. II: War and Diplomacy
Lawrence Freedman

THE OFFICIAL HISTORY OF BRITAIN AND THE CHANNEL TUNNEL
Terry Gourvish

CHURCHILL'S MYSTERY MAN:
Desmond Morton and the World of Intelligence
Gill Bennett

THE OFFICIAL HISTORY OF THE FALKLANDS CAMPAIGN

Volume II: War and Diplomacy

Lawrence Freedman

Routledge
Taylor & Francis Group

LONDON AND NEW YORK

First published 2005
by Routledge
2 Park Square, Milton Park, Abingdon, Oxon OX14 4RN

Simultaneously published in the USA and Canada
by Taylor & Francis Inc
711 Third Avenue, New York, NY 10017, USA

This edition published in paperback 2007

Routledge is an imprint of the Taylor & Francis Group, an informa business

© 2005, 2007 Crown Copyright

Typeset in Times by
Taylor & Francis Books

British Library Cataloguing in Publication Data
A catalogue record for this book is available from the British Library

Library of Congress Cataloging in Publication Data
A catalog record for this title has been requested

*Published on behalf of the Whitehall History Publishing Consortium. Applications
to reproduce Crown copyright protected material in this publication should be
submitted in writing to: HMSO, Copyright Unit, St Clements House, 2-16 Colegate,
Norwich NR3 1BQ. Fax: 01603 723000. E-mail: copyright@hmso.gov.uk*

ISBN10: 0–415–41911–5

ISBN13: 978 0–415–41911–6

CONTENTS

ILLUSTRATIONS

MAPS

ILLUSTRATIONS

TABLES

ABBREVIATIONS

AAA	Air Defence Artillery
AAM	Air-to-Air Missile
AAR	Air-to-Air Refuelling
AAW	Anti-Air Warfare
AAWC	Anti-Air Warfare Controller
AD	Air Defence
ADS	Advanced Dressing Station
AEW	Airborne Early Warning
ALADI	Latin American Integration Association
AOA	Amphibious Operations Area
AOC	Air Officer Commanding
APC	Armoured Personnel Carrier
ASW	Anti-Submarine Warfare
ATGW	Anti-tank guided weapons
AVCAT	Aviation Fuel
BAS	British Antarctic Survey
BBC	British Broadcasting Corporation
BFSU	British Forces Support Unit
BMA	Brigade Maintenance Area
CAP	Combat Air Patrol
CATF	Commander Amphibious Task Force
CBFFI	Commander British Forces Falkland Islands
CBFSU	Commander British Forces Support Unit (Ascension Island)
CDS	Chief of the Defence Staff
CIA	Central Intelligence Agency
C-in-C	Commander-in-Chief
CINCFLEET	Commander-in-Chief, Fleet
CLFFI	Commander Land Forces Falkland Islands
CO	Commanding Officer
COMAW	Commodore, Amphibious Warfare
COREPER	Committee of Permanent Representatives (EC)

COS	Chiefs of Staff
C/S	Call-Sign
CTF	Commander Task Force
CTG	Commander Task Group
CTU	Commander Task Unit
CVA	Aircraft Carrier
CVBG	Carrier Battle Group
CVRT	Combat Vehicle Reconnaissance (Tracked)
DCDS(I)	Deputy Chief of Defence Staff (Intelligence)
DSCS	Defence Satellite Communications System
DIS	Defence Intelligence Staff
DSSS	Defence Secure Speech System
EC	European Community
ECGD	Export Credit Guarantee Department
ECM	Electronic Counter-Measures
EDATS	Extra Deep Armed Team Sweep
ELINT	Electronic Intelligence
ENG	Electronic News Gathering
EOD	Explosive Ordnance Disposal
ESM	Electronic (Warfare) Support Measure
EZ	Exclusion Zone
FAC	Forward Air Controller
FAO	Food and Agriculture Organisation (UN)
FBMA	Forward Base Maintenance Area
FCDT	Fleet Clearance Diving Team
FCO	Foreign & Commonwealth Office
FI	Falkland Islands
FICZ	Falkland Islands Conservation and Management Zone
FIDA	Falkland Islands Development Agency
FIGAS	Falkland Islands Government Air Service
FIPZ	Falkland Islands Protection Zone
FOF1	Flag Officer, First Flotilla
FOF3	Flag Officer, Third Flotilla
FOSM	Flag Officer Submarines
FRG	Federal Republic of Germany
GDP	Gross Domestic Product
GMT	Greenwich Mean Time
GPMG	General Purchase Machine Gun
HE	High Explosive
HF	High Frequency
HFDF	High Frequency Direction Finding
HMG	Her Majesty's Government
HQ	Headquarters

IAEA	International Atomic Energy Agency
ICJ	International Court of Justice
ICRC	International Committee of the Red Cross
IFF	Identification Friend or Foe
IMF	International Monetary Fund
INMARSAT	International Maritime Satellite Organisation
ITN	Independent Television News
ITV	Independent Television
JIC	Joint Intelligence Committee
JSIW	Joint Services Interrogation Wing
LADE	Líneas Aéreas del Estado
LANDSAT	Environmental resource satellite series
LCU	Landing Craft Utility
LCVP	Landing Craft, Vehicles and Personnel
LFFI	Land Forces Falkland Islands
LPD	Landing Platform (Dock)
LPH	Landing Platform (Helicopter)
LSL	Landing Ship Logistic
LST	Landing Ship Tank
M&AW	Mountain & Arctic Warfare
MARISAT	Maritime Satellite (commercial satellite company)
MAT	Media Assessment Team
MCM	Mine Counter-Measures
MCMV	Mine Counter-Measure Vessels
MEZ	Maritime Exclusion Zone
MFA	Ministry of Foreign Affairs (Argentina)
MoD	Ministry of Defence
MP	Member of Parliament
MPA	Maritime Patrol Aircraft
MRR	Maritime Radar Reconnaissance
MSA	Auxiliary Minesweeper
MV	Merchant Vessel
NAAFI	Navy, Army and Air Force Institutes
NASA	National Aeronautical and Space Agency (US)
NATO	North Atlantic Treaty Organisation
NCO	Non-Commissioned Officer
NGS	Naval Gunfire Support
OAS	Organisation of American States
OD(SA)	Defence and Oversea Policy Committee, Sub-Committee on the South Atlantic and Falkland Islands
OD(FAF)	Defence and Oversea Policy Committee, Sub-Committee on Future Arrangements for the Falkland Islands

PNG	Passive Night Goggles
POL	Petrol, Oil, Lubricants
POW	Prisoner-of-War
PR	Public Relations
PSA	Property Services Agency
PTSD	Post-Traumatic Stress Disorder
QE II	Queen Elizabeth II
R of A	Radius of Action
RAF	Royal Air Force
RAMC	Royal Army Medical Corps
RAP	Regimental Aid Post
RAS	Replenishment at Sea
RE	Royal Engineers
RFA	Royal Fleet Auxiliary
RHG/D	The Royal Horse Guards/Dragoons (Blues and Royals)
RM	Royal Marines
RMAS	Royal Maritime Auxiliary Service
RN	Royal Navy
ROE	Rules of Engagement
RRS	Royal Research Ship
SAM	Surface-to-Air Missile
SAPU	South Atlantic Presentation Unit
SAR	Search and Rescue
SAS	Special Air Service
SBS	Special Boat Service
SCOT	Satellite Communications Terminal
SCR	Security Council Resolution
SELA	Latin American European System
SF	Sustained Fire
SHAR	Sea Harrier
SIGINT	Signals Intelligence
SPG	Special Projects Group
SSBN	Ballistic Missile Nuclear-powered Submarine
SSK	Submarine-Killer Submarine
SSN	Nuclear-powered Submarine
SST	Surgical Support Team
STUFT	Ships Taken Up From Trade
TEZ	Total Exclusion Zone
TG	Task Group
TML	Twelve Mile Limit [ex-Three Mile Limit]
TQ	Tactical Questioners
UHF	Ultra High Frequency
UK	United Kingdom

UN	United Nations
US	United States
USAF	United States Air Force
USN	United States Navy
VCDS (P&L)	Vice Chief of Defence Staff (Personnel and Logistics)
VCNS	Vice Chief of the Naval Staff
VHF	Very High Frequency
VMC	Visual Meteorological Conditions
WMR	War Maintenance Reserve

INTRODUCTION TO THE
FIRST EDITION

As the month of March 1982 drew to a close it dawned on the British Government that an incident in the South Atlantic, initially thought to be rather trivial, was turning into a major crisis. The incident had begun with the discovery on 19 March of a number of Argentine scrap metal merchants who had landed without authorisation on the island of South Georgia. South Georgia, significant largely as a base for the British Antarctic Survey (BAS), was then a Dependency of the Falkland Islands. On 31 March information was received confirming not only that Argentina had switched its attention to the Falkland Islands but also that it had put to sea a substantial task force with the intention of occupying the colony. Diplomatic attempts to get the invasion called off using the United States soon failed and on 2 April the invasion took place.

In the first volume of this Official History I described the history of the dispute with Argentina over the ownership of the Falkland Islands, the years of negotiations that had failed to produce a resolution and the dynamics of the South Georgia incident. This second volume picks up the story with the invasion of the Falklands. It then describes the despatch of a Task Force to the South Atlantic capable of repossessing the Falklands and the intense political activity surrounding attempts to get Argentina to withdraw. The failure of these attempts resulted in a British landing and a tough fight for the Islands. This volume therefore covers the two and a half months of intense activity, leading to the recapture of the Falklands, and then considers the aftermath, up to the restoration of diplomatic relations in 1990. I have also looked at some of the post-war investigations into its origins, including the Franks Report and the controversy surrounding the sinking of the *Belgrano*. The benefits of hindsight should never be underestimated, but it can distort historical interpretation. I have therefore tried to avoid the tendency to start with what is known and work backwards. In the process I have sought to open a window on the decision-making process to reveal the expectations and anxieties of the time, the options that were discussed but not pursued, and the pressures weighing down upon those responsible for advising upon and reaching decisions. The focus is on British policy and strategy. I have tried to treat the Argentine position fairly and report what is known about Argentine attitudes and behaviour as is relevant to the main thrust of my narrative. I have been interested to compare what was thought by British policy-makers and commanders at the time with what later appeared to have been the case.

I have already written two books on this topic, one with an Argentine academic. I am therefore more than aware that I am passing here over some very familiar ground and telling a story that, in broad terms, is already well known. What then can an Official History add? Most importantly, it provides an account grounded in the documentary record. As official historian I have had privileged access to all archived material, including briefing notes and official submissions, diplomatic telegrams, boxes of military signals and raw intelligence reports. The privilege is a very real one, and this opportunity to explore such a major event in all its dimensions has been quite marvellous.

Although the war in the Falkland Islands lasted only ten weeks, the material available for research in government files is quite staggering. Senior officials at the time, particularly within the Ministry of Defence (MoD), often put in requests for 'Paper Minimise', while on other occasions the amount of signal traffic significantly slowed the transmission of signals. Although Volume One was perhaps dominated by research into Foreign & Commonwealth Office (FCO) files, this is not the case for Volume Two and research is spread far more evenly between military, political, economic and intelligence resources. I was also assisted by the invaluable in-house staff histories of the campaign by the Naval, Air and Army Historical Branches.

This book makes use throughout of papers and signals in the files of the Office of the Prime Minister, the Cabinet Secretariat, Foreign & Commonwealth Office, Ministry of Defence, Chief of the Defence Staff and Chiefs of Staff, Secretary of State for Defence, and Joint Intelligence Committee. I have consulted Cabinet minutes and memoranda, including those of the two key committees of the Defence and Oversea Policy Committee (OD) – the War Cabinet (OD(SA)) and that considering the post-war future for the Islands (OD(FAF)). Among the key documents on the campaign are the war diaries of CINCFLEET (Admiral Fieldhouse), FOF1 (Admiral Woodward), Flag Officer Submarines (Admiral Herbert) and Brigadier Thompson, the post-war Reports of Proceedings by the Commodore of Amphibious Warfare (Commodore Clapp), the Commander Land Forces (Major General Moore), and Captain Young (Commander of the PARAQUET Task Force). I have consulted the Boards of Inquiry into those ships lost during the campaign, plus the war diaries and signal logs produced by the various participating units (2 Para, 3 Para, 1 WG, 2 SG, 40 Cdo, 42 Cdo and 45 Cdo), as well as those from the Commanders of 5 Infantry Brigade and 3 Commando Brigade, and Headquarters Land Forces Falkland Islands. I was also able to look at the files connected to the Franks Report, including transcripts of their interviews with participants. I have also spoken with many of those involved in the war. I am also grateful to the Ronald Reagan Presidential Library and the US National Archives for the provision of documents relevant to the deliberations of the Reagan Administration.

I was fortunate enough to discuss the campaign with Admirals Lewin and Fieldhouse before they died for my earlier books on the subject. For this research I have conducted many other interviews, and these have been helpful to varying degrees. It is unreasonable to expect too much from memories after two decades, and for this reason I have put much more weight on the archive material. It is also the case that many participants wrote up their own accounts, including the Prime Minister of the time, her Secretary of Defence and many of the senior commanders. They and others also gave interviews to those who wrote the earlier histories. In addition individual soldiers, sailors and airmen have told their stories. I have had no hesitation in drawing on these accounts, especially when they could fill in gaps left in the archives.

It has expressly not been my task to highlight the failures of individuals, sensationalise events, or take the opportunity to get as many secrets as possible into the public domain. With regard to intelligence, a variety of sensitive and delicate sources were tapped, providing materials that contributed at all levels. Even if I had wanted to do so it would have been impossible to provide a comprehensive declassified evaluation of the performance of the intelligence community, or even credit many of the contributions. I did, however, believe it to be essential to describe the impact of intelligence reports and assessments on decision-making, and I am grateful to the mature attitude shown by the relevant agencies in accepting the importance of this task.

This resulting account is official to the extent that it has been built up from primary sources. Official in this context does not mean an officially sanctioned history, so that only safe or agreed opinions are expressed. No attempt has been made to steer my account of events in one direction or another. If I had been inclined to provide an approved governmental interpretation of the conflict, and had been able to identify the form it might take, the existence of so many other independent histories of the campaign would soon test the credibility of any account that diverged markedly from the ample evidence already in the public domain or ducked the obvious areas of controversy.

From almost every comment that has been made to me since I started work on this project I am well aware that this is seen as an opportunity to explore with the best possible information the lingering controversies left over from the Falklands. It might be too optimistic to hope that I can bring some of these controversies to closure, at least in respect of the claims that have been made as to what 'really happened', and in some respects it would be a shame if I did. It will not be long before many, although not all, of the files that I have consulted will be opened up and others will be able to form their own judgements. Undoubtedly they will find materials that I have missed or with meaning and significance that I failed to appreciate. Although this may be considered to be a rather long book with which to cover such a short war, in many areas I have managed only a limited exploration of a wealth of material that has been stored away, and in other areas the documentary record remains frustratingly sparse. I look forward to the new analyses to come: that is how history stays fresh.

Space imposes its own limitations. I have not begun to do justice to the many acts of bravery, comradeship and sacrifice that marked combat in the Falklands, though I hope that I have been able to give some indication of where the course of the campaign depended on the efforts of individuals. This was a war fought with a small margin of error. More so than was perhaps realised by those not directly involved at the time, final success could by no means be taken for granted. Ministers and commanders-in-chief could only take matters so far before handing over the burden down the chain of command to the point where everything depended on the courage and professionalism of a few individuals. So while from a top-down perspective battles can be described with some confidence, because their material consequences can usually be measured and some rough sequence of events identified, this cannot begin to do justice to the dramas of battle. Campaigns such as this, let alone the particular military engagements of which they are composed, can be turned by moments of heroism or losses of nerve or acts of will or tactical errors.

For the historian, official or otherwise, the story of the fighting itself is always problematic. In part this is because so much disparate and often disconnected activity is compressed in time and space that unpacking the story is bound to require more words than can realistically be made available, especially in a history that is bound to look at the 'big picture'. In addition the detail also gets confused and it can be surprising how many differences still persist on questions of timings and casualties. The problem, however, goes deeper. Precisely because of the intensity and confusion of battle there is rarely an agreed account. Some records of some signals are kept. Others are discarded almost immediately. Owing to the lack of secure communication means, most situation reports (Sitreps) went back and forth along the command structure by word of mouth. Only in exceptional circumstances were messages sent by radio and they were recorded even more rarely due to a lack of administrative back-up. During the Battle of Mount Tumbledown, for example, a long Sitrep was sent by radio but no paper record of it was maintained.

Responsible officers write up accounts, normally in a highly abbreviated form, after the event. Journalists, and then historians, interview participants. Their task is to extract memories from blurred impressions, made up of a succession of images and noises, of shouted commands, incoming fire, desperate runs, anxious waiting, intense violence, the calls of the scared and the dying, of friends and foe. Inevitably some incidents, though not necessarily the most important, will stand out and be readily recalled. Other memories will be less reliable, refashioned through constant retelling, consultation among friends, and even cues from the first circulated chronicles of the events.

With most of the battles I describe there are already many accounts in place. At the very least they normally achieve what I do not attempt, which is to recreate the sounds, sights, smells and pain of battle. That these accounts still often contradict each other may in some instances be the result of poor research, but it is as likely to be the result of attempts to record events which by their nature generate fallible records, suspect memories and partial perceptions, leaving aside any deliberate distortion and myth-making. Many veterans have recounted to me tales of operational confusion, the failings of those above them in the hierarchy and surprising behaviour by colleagues, regularly described as the 'real story' of the Falklands. These were often as plausible as they were impossible to corroborate.

It is therefore frustrating, and contrary to what is often claimed to be the arbitrative role of an official historian, to be unable to settle authoritatively many of the disagreements in the accounts of particular battles, particularly those on land. Where possible I have drawn on materials that were unavailable to earlier historians, but as often as not I have had to draw on those who got to the participants while their memories were still fresh and uncluttered. I have done my best to provide the best account I can manage, but it must be recognised that often here I am synthesising and assessing the research of others rather than providing the definitive account.

Pressures of space mean not only that I have had to exclude many anecdotes and vignettes that would have provided a degree of colour to what may be seen at times as a dry account, but also that I have been unable to acknowledge the achievements of many people who played important roles in the campaign. To all those disappointed by their non-inclusion I apologise. Whatever one may think of the wisdom of embarking on Operation CORPORATE or its political and military direction over those ten weeks in 1982 it is hard not to be impressed, and at times moved, by the commitment and fortitude shown by the members of the armed forces as they took on hazardous tasks in less than optimum conditions. In addition, behind those on the front line was an extraordinary effort to keep their equipment serviceable and to provide emergency improvements, to keep them supplied with armaments, fuel and the essentials of survival in inhospitable conditions. At the same time the diplomatic service was stretched to the full, explaining the policies of the United Kingdom to often sceptical interlocutors, working on votes in the United Nations, keeping up the pressure on Argentina. There is not space here to describe in detail all that was achieved but there is a responsibility to all the men and women involved to acknowledge these efforts and explain their context.

The organisation of this book is not straightforward. The simplest approach would have been strictly chronological. This would have the advantage of conveying, on an almost daily basis, the competing pressures and the variety of issues faced by ministers. It would throw into relief the distinctive mind-sets and time horizons of those planning and conducting military operations and those holding the diplomatic line. By the same token this approach would convey rather than explain the complexity of policy-making, while some of the smaller but still significant issues could get lost altogether. So although the organisation is largely chronological, I have sought to disentangle the strands of policy so that each can be explored in their own terms as well as in the context of the wider conflict. This means at times the narrative may seem to be getting ahead of itself. This is particularly true with the sub-themes of economic pressures and media relations, and at times even with the core themes of diplomatic negotiations and military operations. The strengths and limitations of this approach will become apparent in the earlier sections, where I describe how the Government organised itself during the campaign, the extent of the logistics effort, some legal and economic dimensions, and issues connected with the islanders and British nationals in Argentina. These may lack the drama of the more highly-charged arguments over the possibility of a peaceful settlement or the military engagements, and some readers may even find them tedious, but along with the background discussions of designs for a settlement and alternative military options, they help make sense of these extraordinary months.

INTRODUCTION TO THE
SECOND EDITION

Since the publication of the first edition of the Official History I have been grateful not only for the many positive reviews, but also to the number of individuals who have got in touch with material which they think I have missed or got wrong. One objective of this second edition is to integrate some of this new material as well as to correct those errors that have been drawn to my attention. Accuracy is a core requirement for an Official History. As it was impossible to give the text wide circulation prior to publication, to some extent it is inevitable that some issues have only come to light afterwards, which is not the most desirable sequence. At the same time it has been fascinating as well as salutary to have been contacted by so many people since publication, offering additional detail.

It is normally unwise to dwell too long on points raised in reviews. There are, however, a number of issues that have been raised with sufficient regularity that it may be sensible to use this opportunity to address them. From my perspective the most insidious of these is that this was somehow a 'New Labour' or 'Blairite' history. For the record, I was approached in 1996 by the Cabinet Office to undertake this work. The topic and my potential commission were discussed by a committee of Privy Counsellors set up to oversee the Official History series. My contract was agreed by the time of the 1997 general election. Whether Tony Blair or John Major won they would have been asked to approve my commission. At no stage was the content of my book officially controlled or subject to political influence. The judgements contained within are entirely my own.

Second, and despite many offers of help from Buenos Aires, this had to be a British history. My task was to explain British policy and decisions and not those of Argentina (or the US or France) except to the extent where it was necessary, as was often the case, for purposes of context and evaluation. I had neither the space nor the time for more. My focus was to be on the way the Government as a whole addressed the developing dispute with Argentina, and then how it responded to the sudden Argentine occupation of sovereign territory. This required exploring sets of complex relations such as those between the civil and the military spheres, the executive and Parliament, domestic considerations and foreign policy, officials and the media, the War Cabinet and commanders in the field. I found this a rich area for study and I think this is where the strength of the book is to be found. Of course that means that other aspects of the episode are less well covered. I would have felt guiltier about that had there not been a vast literature already on the Falklands, to which I had already contributed, dealing with these other aspects and to which I referred where appropriate. This includes some professional studies, for example relating to such issues as post-traumatic stress disorder as well as the more familiar accounts of battle.

A third criticism is that far more time is spent on the diplomacy, covered in minute detail, than on the various military engagements, covered with irritating brevity. There is, I confess, a personal preference in this. I am more at home discussing policy-making and diplomacy than military operations and I lacked the material to improve much on many of the first-hand accounts of the land battles. The balance of material was, however, determined by another factor. Whitehall and Parliament spent most of their time on the diplomacy and very little on military operations. The Prime Minister's files have numerous reports from embassies about the problems of convincing other governments of the rightness of the British cause — or at least on why armed force was being used in the name of this cause — and very little on how armed force might be used, especially once the extensive discussions of rules of engagement were largely over. Moreover, the land battles took up very little time. Other than Goose Green, which was a complicated, and controversial, encounter, they were not drawn out. The bulk of the major land force engagements were concentrated in the last few days of the war. In terms of activity, therefore, days were spent on negotiation compared with the hours that were spent in battle. Of course a lot of time was spent in thinking about battle and preparing for it, and I hope I have done justice to the strategic and tactical planning as well as to the logistical aspects of the war. For those involved in the battles they were intense and complex affairs but their basic form and development were relatively straightforward.

Fourth, and where I have the greatest regret, is that I do not spend much time on individual exploits. It is extraordinary how busy many people get during intense periods of national emergency, and how many small experiences can throw light on the larger questions connected with the big decisions on diplomacy and war. One criticism, for example, which I take seriously, is that the daily experiences of islanders under occupation are not fully explored and the contributions made by islanders to the military campaign are not described in detail. Unfortunately the same criticism holds true when it comes to the many cases when it would have been appropriate to tell of the bravery of young soldiers, sailors and airmen or even the intrigue of covert agents. That was not the history I was commissioned to write. I could not tell the story at the level of the individual although there are many extraordinary individual stories that could be told. This was partly also why I did not name individuals who might be blamed for particular mishaps, such as *Sheffield* or *Sir Galahad*.[1] Apart from a natural disinclination to censure someone operating under pressures and in circumstances of which I have no experience, I also felt it unfair to pick on people with no right of reply in a publication that was not the result of a formal commission of inquiry but did carry an official title.

By and large my basic account of events has not been challenged. Even where reviewers disagreed with my analysis they tended to recognise that I had made an effort to provide the evidence upon which alternative interpretations might be built. In some cases particular judgements of mine have been challenged, and in some cases I think the challenge is right. Where possible I have tried to correct accordingly. It is fair to say that the bulk of the challenges of this sort, and concerns about inaccuracies, have come in the maritime area. In part this may reflect the considerable interest, and therefore expertise, generated by the naval dimensions of the conflict. I am at any rate very grateful to those who obviously took pity on my own lack of naval experience and have put in a considerable effort to identify errors. I am sure it was galling for those who had been neglected in earlier studies and reports to find that this omission was continued. An example of this is the Fleet Clearance Diving Teams whose role I am now pleased to acknowledge.

A second edition provides an opportunity to draw upon new literature, and some which should have been considered in the first place, and also consider new revelations. One of the more newsworthy disclosures in the first edition concerned the British nuclear depth charges that had been taken to the South Atlantic, not because they might be required but because there was no satisfactory way of removing them safely without delaying the journey of the Task Force. At the same time I had dealt with, and dismissed, the notion that some preparations had been made, in the deployment of a Polaris submarine, to use submarine-launched missiles if things had been going badly. Not long after publication some support to this idea came from an unexpected source, the diaries of François Mitterrand's psychiatrist, which suggested that after HMS *Sheffield* had been sunk by an Exocet missile, Margaret Thatcher was threatening to unleash an atomic weapon against Argentina 'if I don't provide her with the secret codes that will make the missiles we sold the Argentinians deaf and blind'.[2] Mrs Thatcher would not have been the first political leader to have seen advantage in the appearance of being potentially crazy with nuclear weapons, but whatever the nature of her conversation with the French president, it is clear that the nuclear option was never seriously discussed in the War Cabinet, nor were preparations made for its implementation by the Royal Navy. Usefully this story prompted a welcome clarification from Toby Elliot, the then Commanding Officer of the boat that was at sea during the war, HMS *Resolution*. He reports being told about the Argentine seizure of the Falklands 'some few weeks into a routine national deterrent patrol'. He adds:

> During the weeks that followed I have to say that at no time did I ever get the feeling that we were going to be needed. We remained well out of maximum strike range. We did not even feel the urge to break out the charts which we would have been required for the long voyage south.[3]

An important question, which has not been so much picked up by reviewers but has led to some fascinating discussions with some of the senior commanders, concerns the nature of the formal command structure and the informal relationships between the commanders, especially Admiral Sandy Woodward, in charge of the Carrier Battle Group, Commodore Michael Clapp, who had specific responsibility for the amphibious landing, and Brigadier Julian Thompson, who was in charge of the landing force. The individual memoirs by all three personalities have addressed these issues and they confirm that there were – to say the least – different understandings of how well this worked and what was appropriate. This mattered because there were at times real differences over strategy and tactics, which often reflected distinctive concerns.

I outlined these disagreements and what seemed to me to be some of their causes in the first edition. It is of course a problem when trying to record any dispute that the historian can appear to be taking sides, merely by repeating the criticisms one officer has made of another, or in trying to assess the validity of particular criticisms. It was always likely that the Official History would open up some of the old disputes but less likely that the three commanders would find ways of discussing these issues that allowed them to agree on many of their sources and understand better how they arose. It was my privilege to be part of these discussions.[4] While where possible I have tried to incorporate the fruits of these discussions in the text, there are also some larger themes that are relevant to the overall course of the Falklands campaign. Many of these are already present in the text but they are worth setting out in a more systematic form in this introduction.

There were certain features of the military campaign that shaped its conduct and the nature of the command relationships. Any major military operation at this time would have been experimental because it was bound to be fought with equipment and concepts that had not been properly tested in battle. Only the most senior commanders were veterans of the Second World War; experience elsewhere was largely confined to low-intensity operations. For some operations contingency plans existed: recovering the Falklands was not amongst them. The limited military analysis of the problem had been confined to demonstrating just how difficult, and probably foolhardy, such an operation might be. As the commanders first tried to make sense of what actually would be required to retake the Falklands after the Argentine occupation, elements of the operation were understood but only in a quite different context. Fighting the Warsaw Pact, the Navy would have had more to fear from submarines and long-range air-to-surface missiles in open water than directly from aircraft with iron bombs and guns. An amphibious landing in the context of reinforcing a NATO country assumed a host nation able to provide escorts and air cover and transports from the beach rather than from an offshore battle group.

Any command structure will find the transition from peace to war difficult. Numerous decisions have to be taken in a great hurry, with incomplete information. Each decision is potentially extremely serious. The number and frequency of individual decisions mean that the orders that flow from them often arrive without great clarity or full explanation and those whose activities might be affected are left out of the loop. A further factor in this case, adding to the improvised quality of the operation, was the backdrop of intense diplomatic activity, geared to producing a peaceful solution which could have produced an abrupt conclusion to the military preparations at any time. Even in the absence of a settlement the diplomacy always had the possibility of influencing the speed and focus of military activity. To the time pressures created by diplomacy could be added those resulting from the limited durability of the Task Force in the face of continuing operations in harsh conditions, likely to become even harsher with the arrival of the South Atlantic winter. Vital strategic decisions were being taken in London well after the Task Force had set sail, on rules of engagement, reinforcements and ultimate objectives. Because of the long logistics line, resources were scarce and there were many competing tasks for which they might be allocated. Officers would find themselves ordered to undertake tasks for reasons that remained obscure and rarely with enough capabilities.

With the Task Force hurriedly put together for Operation Corporate these problems were aggravated. There was no joint headquarters, and air and land advice had to be drawn into the naval headquarters at Northwood. There were command procedures that might have been expected to be followed in defining individual areas of responsibility, particularly with regard to the conduct of an amphibious landing. Not everyone appeared aware of them. Different branches of each service had their own culture and expectations which might not always have been appreciated elsewhere. Submariners, for example, are bound to use their initiative for tactical decisions because of the problems of communicating with a higher command. This may help explain why Fieldhouse and Woodward were more comfortable with what to others seemed to be a loose command structure.

Many of the key commanders did not know each other and there was little opportunity for them to get acquainted. They did not have a chance to explore their differences or develop plans together through regular meetings. Once they were dispersed into their separate task groups, combining the everyday burdens of command with the detail of their own particular next steps, then it was even harder to appreciate the distinctive problems being faced elsewhere. Voice communications were through the unsatisfactory Defence Secure Speech System (DSSS), which often left meanings unclear and could only involve two people, so there was no possibility of conference calls. Woodward and Clapp, for example, could have their own separate conversations on the same issue with Sir John Fieldhouse, the overall commander of the task force at the Northwood HQ, without being aware that he had spoken to the other. While the carrier battle group, led by Woodward, had the latest communications equipment, the amphibious force led by Clapp did not. Some modern satellite communications had been fitted to Clapp's command ship, *Fearless*, but he was unsure of its reliability and many of the ships under his command, such as the RFAs and merchant ships, had very basic kit. Even ship-to-shore communications were problematic, which created difficulties between Clapp and Thompson once the latter had joined troops on the beachhead, though they had worked closely together on *Fearless*. Woodward had to concern himself with the interaction of a large number of demands with a wide geographic spread; Clapp was focused more narrowly on the dangers that his ships would face in the rather confined Amphibious Operations Area (AOA) for which he had to prepare. When General Jeremy Moore arrived to lead land operations different problems developed. Although Clapp shared *Fearless* with Moore and had regular personal contact, he was not part of the discussions that Moore had with the other land commanders, even though he would somehow have to support them. At the same time, Moore did provide information on the wider concerns that were current in London.

Against this background it is not surprising or indeed unusual that relations between the various commanders were at times tetchy. So the well-publicised tensions between Woodward, in charge of the carrier battle group, and Thompson and Clapp, preparing for the amphibious landing, were largely a function of the circumstances in which they found themselves as much as personality clashes or even the formal command structure, although ambiguities here certainly did not help. The major ambiguity in the arrangements concerned Woodward's relationship with Clapp, in charge of the amphibious landing, and Thompson, in charge of the landing force. Woodward was the more senior and the initial command arrangements put him in charge of all three Task Groups heading south. There was concern about the geographic spread of the forces notionally under Woodward's command and their disparate roles, especially once a further task group was created to retake South Georgia. Clapp believed that he needed a direct relationship with Fieldhouse. Fieldhouse agreed and by 10 April a new arrangement was in place that had all four Task Group Commanders reporting directly to him.

However Woodward was then made *primus inter pares* which did create an ambiguity, as it suggested that there would be circumstances when he would be more overtly in charge. The main idea on the part of Fieldhouse's staff, it would appear, was that Woodward was to have a superior co-ordinating role, particularly with regard to shared assets, such as escorts, and, crucially, to make it clear that Woodward had to be able to defend his main assets, and especially carriers, before anything else, because if one of those was lost so too would be the campaign. Yet this approach raised questions about the standing of Woodward's views on matters that appeared to be squarely the responsibility of Clapp and Thompson, such as the choice of where to land on the Falklands, yet where Woodward also had an interest because of its direct relevance to his ability to sustain air support over an extended period, including after the successful completion of a land campaign. Moreover, because of the wider range of Woodward's responsibilities and the fact that he was in charge of the engagements with Argentine forces prior to the landing, Fieldhouse did tend to treat him as the senior commander. Although undoubtedly those engaged in the South Atlantic made their own organisational charts to remind them who they needed to talk to, Northwood did not send out a detailed chart of its own. The one reproduced in this volume, at use in Northwood in early June, does not appear to have been widely circulated.

Of the various difficulties experienced, it is probably the case that problems of poor communications caused far more problems than ambiguity in command. The consequences of both were illustrated when the three men met on board *Fearless* on 16 April. After this there were a number of occasions for mutual irritation, at times vigorously expressed. Yet despite this the relevant commanders largely respected each other's professional judgements and, of course, the overall campaign objectives were achieved. Where misapprehensions had emerged, with regard to the capabilities of Rapier or the advisability of a feint to draw out Argentine forces, the hurried and unsatisfactory nature of the conversations seems to be largely to blame. This is not to deny the importance of personality and the fact that given the stakes for all involved it would have been surprising, even alarming, if the key commanders lacked a tough-minded and stubborn streak.

This remains a long book – now a bit longer than before. Many issues are still imperfectly addressed. To be frank I now look forward to the progressive opening of the Falklands files with a degree of apprehension because I know this is bound to lead to further correction of my account and new interpretations. Yet I also know that it is this constant challenge that keeps history fresh. I am well aware that no history is definitive and that even on this subject, on which I have written excessively, there is still much for me to learn.

ACKNOWLEDGEMENTS

My research assistant Christopher Baxter has made an immense contribution to this and the previous volume. To say that I could not have managed without him would be a major understatement. He has been assiduous in seeking out files and identifying the critical material for me. I have also been extremely fortunate in being able to work closely with Tessa Stirling of the Cabinet Office's Histories, Openness and Records Unit. She has done everything she can to ensure that relations with the key government departments were smooth and efficient. In this she was ably assisted by first Richard Ponman and then Sally Falk. Members of the steering group from the various departments involved have always been helpful. I was able to visit the Falklands in March 2000 and was very grateful to the warm welcome shown to me by the Governor and his staff, and by the islanders. Many people offered themselves as 'sources'. They are too numerous to mention by name, especially as a number spoke to me in confidence, but they know who they are and I hope that they will recognise where I have been able to make use of the evidence they provided. Special mention is due to Chris Collins who provided me with some material that I would not have been able to get otherwise, Jean Seaton and Simon Wessely for advice on the BBC and psychiatric issues respectively, the Lewin family for permission to see Lord Lewin's papers, and Peter Freeman for his wise suggestions after reading an early draft of the manuscript. My thanks are due to Mark Lacey of Picture This for the artwork.

After the publication of the first edition I received a number of points from individuals which where possible I have tried to take into account. I am particularly grateful to James McCoy for the many points of detail he picked up, which proved to be invaluable in correcting errors that had slipped into the first edition, and to Sandy Woodward, Julian Thompson and Michael Clapp for both their lively conversations on issues raised by the first edition and their clarification of many specific aspects of the campaign. I hope they agree that the second edition has benefited from their contributions.

TIMINGS

All accounts of the Falklands have difficulty with timing. The campaign headquarters at Northwood insisted at Admiral Woodward's request that the campaign be fought in 'Zulu' time (suffix 'Z'), that is GMT. A standard time meant that there was no need to rely on hasty mental arithmetic to reconcile orders, reports and actions. This was neither the time in London (which was British Summer Time, which started on 28 March, and so one hour ahead), nor that in the Falklands, which was four hours behind. Taking account of the diplomacy it becomes apparent that many of the principal participants spread across six time zones (France and West Germany, in which some important discussions and meetings were held, were, at GMT+2hrs, a further hour ahead of London). To complicate matters further, Argentine time was only three hours behind Zulu, and during the occupation this was imposed on the Falklands, although this was ignored by the residents, and the British troops as they re-captured the Islands. In normal times the Falklands was four hours behind.

By and large I have used Zulu time, because that is how timings appeared in many of those documents I have consulted and cited. It is also important to note that is how the members of the Task Force lived. That is they began their day three hours before their Argentine counterparts. On occasion, however, when attempting to give a sense of how matters appeared to the participants I have used the relevant local time and have tried to make this clear when doing so. It is also relevant that in the South Atlantic dawn was about 1030 Zulu and dusk about 2015. Readers can make the necessary calculations to note that as dawn broke in the Falklands, at 0630 local time, it was already 1130 in London. The following tabulation shows the relationships between the main areas involved:

Table 1 Timings

		Local time at GMT noon
Lima	GMT-5hrs	0700
Santiago, New York, Washington, Falklands	GMT-4hrs	0800
Buenos Aires, S. Georgia, *Falklands under occupation	GMT-3hrs	0900
	GMT (Z)	1200
London	GMT+1hr	1300

*During the occupation the Argentines introduced Buenos Aires time in the Falklands

I have used the local time without elaboration for both precise timings and in such general references as 'later in the morning' or 'that night' when this introduces no uncertainties, as is generally the case when describing geographically limited incidents or diplomatic discussions such as those at the UN. When necessary I have made explicit reference to the time zone in use when describing incidents or actions which crossed time zones, such as long-range telephone calls or other exchanges involving participants in different time zones. For military engagements I have used the GMT time provided by British military records (often with the suffix 'Z' to make that explicit). Where Argentine sources also contribute precise times (as in the case of the sinking of the *Belgrano*) I have quoted them as local, usually accompanied by a GMT translation.

With regard to distances and speeds, I have generally used miles, although I have followed the sources using kilometres in one or two cases, though ships' speeds are in knots. The ratio is about five nautical miles to six statute miles. Thus while the Falklands are normally put at 8,000 statute miles from the United Kingdom, they are 6,761 nautical miles.

I have also, after some deliberation, written of Argentina and the Argentines, rather than the Argentinians (although I have kept the original in quotes).

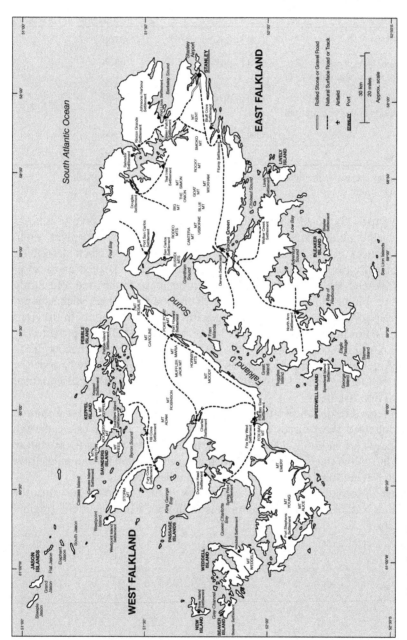

Map 1 The Falklands

SECTION ONE

1

AT WAR

During the late afternoon of 31 March 1982, ministers received an intelligence report indicating that an Argentine Task Force expected to reach Stanley, the capital of the Falkland Islands, in the early hours of Friday 2 April. Admiral Sir Henry Leach, the First Sea Lord, told them that little could be done to prevent the Argentine occupation but that with sufficient effort repossession was possible. This would require as powerful a force as Britain could muster, with both available aircraft carriers, a full complement of escorts, an amphibious capability and a commando brigade. If it could be despatched within a few days, after three weeks it would reach the Falkland Islands. The Government decided to send such a force.

Up to this moment the only available naval unit in a forward position was HMS *Endurance*, the patrol ship that had been supposed to provide the main British presence in the South Atlantic. This had been sent to South Georgia to deal with the scrap metal merchants whose unauthorised arrival had triggered the latest incident. Then it had been held back to avoid escalating this incident; now it was told to disembark its Marines to defend South Georgia and get back to the Falklands to do what it could there, although it was almost bound to arrive after the Argentines. Available to greet the Argentine force on the Falklands were 69 Royal Marines. The only additional moves that had been made thus far were to instruct two nuclear-powered submarines (SSNs) to sail, and consideration was to be given to the possibility that they might be joined by a third. A Royal Fleet Auxiliary (RFA), *Fort Austin*, had been tasked to replenish *Endurance*, and could stock up with extra personnel and supplies for the new contingency when it reached Ascension, the Atlantic island that served as a valuable mid-way point between the UK and the Falklands. Once it was determined to put together a Task Force, ships that had been exercising off Gibraltar began to move south in order to meet up with a force assembling in British ports. In addition, 3 Commando Brigade was brought to short notice to move to the South Atlantic. The developing military operation was now known as CORPORATE.

The Argentine invasion

It was not until 1 April that Sir Rex Hunt, Governor of the Falkland Islands, received warning of 'apparently reliable evidence that an Argentine Task Force will gather off Cape Pembroke early tomorrow morning 2 April'. He had, however, already decided that something strange was going on, because a Polish supply ship heading for Stanley had been stopped by an Argentine warship some 110 miles north and told not to proceed further. At a meeting in Downing Street the possibilities for more detailed instructions for Hunt had been considered, but it had proved hard to draft anything sensible. Neither assertions of confidence nor exhortations to glory quite seemed appropriate. The prospect of sending the Governor vague instructions largely composed of platitudes filled Leach with dismay. If he was in Hunt's position, he explained to the Prime Minister, on receipt of such a message, he would 'put it straight in the wastepaper bin and lose my remaining confidence in Whitehall.' His view was that at such a late stage matters should be left to the man on the spot.[1]

This view prevailed, and it might have spared Hunt some additional aggravation. On the other hand, having been given no advice other than to dispose his meagre forces and do what he could, Hunt might have appreciated a bit more information. No guidance was given on how the Argentine forces might arrive, including their likely use of amphibious personnel carriers, though this might have helped when choosing which beach to defend. The only suggestion received was to crater the runway, but there was no time to do this properly: it would have involved drilling holes in order to insert dynamite. All that was possible was to attempt to block the runway with vehicles. The late warning also meant that there was not time to evacuate out of Stanley old people and children, who were at a boarding school.

Defence was the responsibility of the small Royal Marines detachment, NP 8901. Major Gary R H Noott, the outgoing commanding officer, and his replacement, Major Mike J Norman, were halfway through the administrative handover when the first hints of the impending invasion were received. The handover meant that the defending force was about twice what might otherwise have been expected, but it was still only 69 all ranks, together with 11 Royal Navy personnel from HMS *Endurance's* survey parties and one ex-Royal Marine then living on the Falklands who re-enlisted. Their firepower consisted of a few rocket launchers (Carl Gustav and 66mm). In addition, twenty-three men from the Falkland Islands Defence Force did report for duty and they were sent to observation posts. These were stationed on Sapper Hill and in Cape Pembroke Lighthouse, and a reaction section was held at immediate notice at Moody Brook by day, and deployed to the airport at night. At 0900 local time on 1 April, Norman assumed operational command.

The war role of NP 8901, was laid down as:

4

1. To enable the seat of government to be maintained in the event of armed incursions.
2. To provide a covert alternative means of communication between the UK and the seat of government.
3. To impede and, if possible, contain any incursion which might affect the maintenance of an effective government or endanger the life of the community.
4. To maintain a cohesive identity in the event that government can no longer continue.

Hunt had recently described this latter role as taking to the hills in the hope that the Marines would be difficult to winkle out. They would then be able to broadcast to the outside world to let them know of the existence of a token resistance.

Norman's plan was to hit the invading force as hard as possible at the outset, inflicting maximum casualties and forcing it to deploy, thus delaying its advance and gaining time for possible negotiations. Hunt was keen to avoid house-to-house fighting in Stanley and so sections were in prepared positions on the narrow approach route from the beach/airfield area into Stanley. Norman based one third of his small force in and around Government House, and the remainder he split into sections to cover the airport peninsula and the approaches to the harbour and the town. He himself set up his Tactical Headquarters (HQ) with the section at Lookout Rocks at the southeast edge of Stanley. The airport runway was blocked with vehicles and oil drums. Overnight the Falkland Islands Company coaster, Merchant Vessel (MV) *Forrest*, made two sorties in order to carry out radar sweeps.

Meanwhile the Councillors and senior civil servants were summoned to Government House and told what to expect. At approximately 2015 local time, the Governor went on the local radio and warned the islanders of the situation.[2] Members of the Falkland Islands Defence Force were asked to report to the drill hall, but everyone else was to remain calm, stay at home and avoid the airport roads. At 0400 local time the next morning Hunt was on the radio again explaining that there was little hope of a peaceful solution and declaring a state of emergency. Half an hour later he warned that unless the Argentine Task Force changed course it would be off Cape Pembroke by first light.[3] A few hours later, in case there was a saboteur squad around, he ordered the police chief to round up and intern about 30 Argentine nationals living in Stanley, including a suspicious group of 'oil workers' that had arrived for a holiday at the start of the week. They were to be held in the town hall.

The invading force

While this was going on the Argentine forces were preparing to land. The original Argentine intention had been to land on the night of 31 March/1 April,

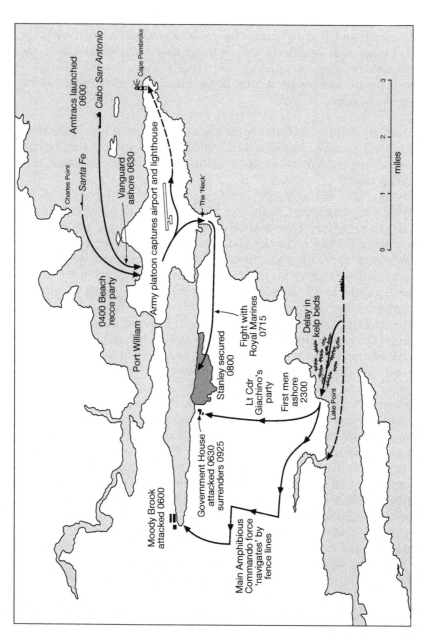

Map 2 Battle for Stanley

but bad weather caused a 24-hour delay. In addition, the two senior commanders, General O. Garcia, the Army Commander, embarked in the destroyer *Santisima Trinidad* with the Naval Commander, Rear Admiral G. Allara, were aware that there was a double complement of Royal Marines at Stanley, and also that Hunt had broadcast to the islanders that an invasion was imminent. This intelligence presumably came from the office of the Argentine airline, Líneas Aéreas del Estado (LADE). Its local representative, Vice-Comodoro Hector Gilobert, had left Stanley in February but returned suddenly to Stanley on 31 March. With the element of surprise now lost, a new plan was concocted which saw the main landing beach switched to a more westerly point at Yorke Bay. A direct flight from the mainland to Stanley airport was aborted. The army platoon that was detailed for the capture of Government House was switched to capturing the airport and Government House was now allocated to a small and ill-prepared amphibious commando party.[4]

Early in the morning of 2 April the *Santisima Trinidad* put 90 Marines in inflatables in the water off Seal Point. The Marines split into two groups, the larger making for the Royal Marine barracks at Moody Brook, and the smaller for Government House. The submarine *Santa Fe* launched special force swimmers east of Cape Pembroke, bound for Yorke Bay. The other ships of the amphibious landing force, the Landing Ship Tank (LST) *Cabo San Antonio*, the transports *Almirante Irizar* and *Isla de los Estados*, the destroyer *Hercules*, and the corvettes *Drummond* and *Granville*, were to the northeast off Stanley. Warships prepared to protect the *Cabo San Antonio* and provide supporting gunfire for the landing force if required. The aircraft carrier, *25 de Mayo*, escorted by the destroyers *Hipolito Bouchard*, *Piedra Buena*, *Segui* and *Comodoro Py*, was well to the north in support. Some 1,000 troops were available – largely Marines but with some Army. Such a large force against such a puny enemy suggested that the main purpose was to make a show of overwhelming strength.

The British were not aware of the Argentine presence until well after the first marines had landed. Stanley received its first report of Argentine activity at 0230 local time from the MV *Forrest* on radar watch in Port William. A large contact had been detected five miles off Mengeary Point. Then, at 0430, as the state of emergency was declared, the observation post on Sapper Hill reported what was thought to be helicopter activity in Port Harriet, followed by more reports of shipping approaching and entering Port William. An attempt was made at this point to get back a message to London that Argentine forces were landing but Cable and Wireless were facing problems with their emergency circuits. At 0600 firing was heard as the Moody Brook barracks, fortunately empty, was attacked in such a way as to contradict the view that the primary objective was to keep casualties down to the minimum. Shortly afterwards movement was reported from behind Government House. As his residence came under fire, Hunt was told of landing craft coming ashore at Yorke Bay. Norman ordered two of his forward sections back to cover Government House, and retired there himself. There was now no way of resisting the landing, and soon the airport buildings were in Argentine hands. A large Argentine force drove across the isthmus down the four and half mile stretch of road to Stanley. After being temporarily held up at the edge of the town, the bulk continued towards Government House. The Marines, who had been trying to delay this advance, now fell back towards the outskirts of Stanley and then to Government House as the final redoubt.

At Government House, the initial assault was repulsed, leaving one Argentine dead and three wounded, although the Marines believed that they had inflicted much greater casualties. Later three commandos who had got into the servants' quarters were disarmed and taken prisoner. As dawn broke, it was relatively quiet, but the local radio transmitter was off the air and some 120 Argentine troops were on the hillside overlooking them. Reports had come in of Armoured Personnel Carriers coming ashore. There was an exchange of fire when a column of these vehicles was challenged with rocket fire from a small Royal Marine party, who then had to fall back in the face of Argentine fire. More troops landed at the cleared airport in C-130 Hercules transports of the Argentine Air Force. Meanwhile a group of Royal Marines, who knew the Islands well and who had been charged with staying behind, were prevented from taking off on motorcycles into the hills. Argentine Special Forces who had landed two miles south of Stanley blocked their way. An attempt was made to send out another section, which did get away, but these men were new to the Falkland Islands and they gave up after 48 hours. Hunt spoke dramatically to Patrick Watts at the local radio station who asked him: 'are you going to hang on and keep them back for as long as possible, or are you going to surrender?' Hunt replied that 'We are not surrendering, we are resisting'. But he added that the group with him 'were pinned down. We can't move'.[5]

Argentine fire was limiting the options for those in Government House. Norman advised the Governor that the options were either for them all to break out and establish a seat of government elsewhere, continue to resist until overrun or else negotiate a truce. The prospect of unnecessary loss of life among local civilians as well as service personnel weighed heavily on Hunt's mind, and he decided to start negotiations. He rang Gilobert, the LADE representative, who professed ignorance of the operation. Hunt encouraged him to leave his house, which he was reluctant to do, and act as intermediary. Gilobert went with Dick Baker, the Chief Secretary to the Falkland Islands Government, to meet Rear Admiral C. Busser, the Commander of the Argentine Marines, at the Town Hall. Busser made it clear that he already had some 800 men ashore with more to come, and that the British position was hopeless. He came to Government House himself at 0920, and at 0925 (or 1225 London time (BST)) the Governor ordered

Norman to instruct his men to cease firing and lay down their arms. The attitude of the Marines to this order was later described as generally 'fed up' but they accepted, at least in retrospect, that the Governor's decision was a sound one. The British had suffered no casualties. Many of NP 8901, led by Major Norman, volunteered, after repatriation, to return to the Falkland Islands in Operation CORPORATE, and formed the nucleus of J Company, 42 Commando Royal Marines.

At 1315 General Garcia informed Hunt that he had taken over as Governor of Las Malvinas. Hunt told him that he had landed unlawfully and should leave with his troops forthwith. Garcia said he had no intention of doing so and that now that the Argentines had regained what was right-fully theirs they would stay forever. Hunt was told that he would be flown out of the Falkland Islands that evening. It was agreed that he could broad-cast to the islanders so long as he also contacted the Royal Marines at Grytviken in South Georgia to tell them of the position in Stanley. Hunt refused to ask them to surrender without resistance. He drove to the airport in ceremonial uniform in his official taxi flying the Falklands' flag. Through all these events the local radio station had been broadcasting, picking up calls from islanders reporting on what they saw with occasional comments from the Governor and even, when he was trying to arrange the ceasefire, Gilobert. Patrick Watts, Director of Broadcasting, kept the station going after Argentine officers arrived with tapes to broadcast with instructions for the population and did much to sustain morale.

At 0945 in London on 2 April (0645 in Stanley), the Ministry of Defence (MoD) reported to Admiral Sir John Fieldhouse, CINCFLEET, that all communications with Stanley had been lost: 'Reason not known but not due to evident communication equipment fault'. This was around the time when Hunt had been trying to get back the message that Government House was surrounded. At 1235, with still no radio link, London ordered *Endurance* to remain covert and not to get any closer to the Falkland Islands in the hope that it could discover what was going on. Twenty minutes later, it was told to attempt to make contact with Stanley despite the breaching of High Frequency (HF) silence. This enabled it to confirm the news of the Argentine invasion, which was already being broadcast by the Argentine media. Intelligence from the Master of the British Antarctic Survey (BAS) ship, Royal Research Ship (RRS) *Bransfield*, reported that he had picked up a Falkland Islands radio station broadcast that 200 Argentine Marines with armoured vehicles had landed and were moving towards Stanley. It was also reported that three warships were anchored in the Port William area and there had been considerable helicopter activity. At 2155 BST on 2 April, *Endurance* reported to London that a local radio operator had reported Stanley quiet with no injuries to British troops. As far as was known there were no civilian casualties either. Captain Nick Barker of the *Endurance* signed off 'This has been a humiliating day'.

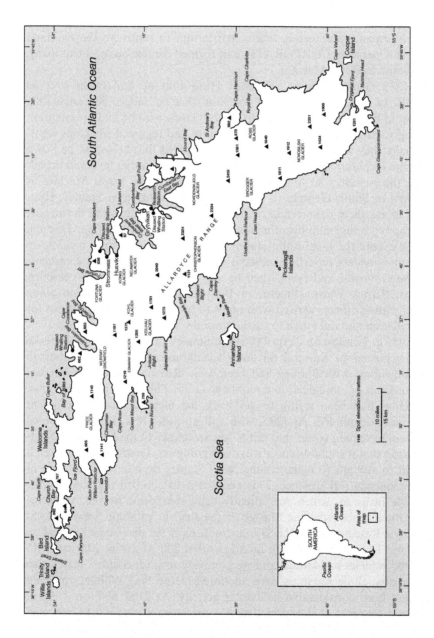

Map 3 South Georgia

The humiliation was soon reinforced by images of the Argentine flag being raised and of the Royal Marines as prisoners. The photographs of the surrender of the Royal Marines had been taken by Simon Winchester of the *Sunday Times*, and were smuggled out by Rex Hunt's son, Tony. (Winchester went to Argentina where he was later arrested, with two colleagues, for spying.) Soon the invading forces had consolidated their hold on the Falklands with units moved to Goose Green and Fox Bay on West Falkland.

The invasion of South Georgia

Some 800 miles away, the defence of South Georgia depended on the 22 Royal Marines landed from *Endurance* on the evening of 31 March, commanded by Lieutenant K Mills. His small force occupied the BAS base at King Edward Point, on the northern side of the entrance to King Edward Cove, at the end of which lies Grytviken Whaling Station. His orders were:

1. To provide a British military presence on South Georgia.
2. To protect the BAS personnel at Grytviken in the event of an emergency.
3. To maintain surveillance over the Argentine scrap metal merchants at Leith Whaling Station.

It was the landing of the scrap metal merchants at Leith in the middle of March in such a way as to defy British sovereignty that had set in motion this chain of events. Mills did receive warning of a likely Argentine assault. He was told to 'open fire without warning on any Argentinian landing in South Georgia, provided you are certain they are armed'. No attempt was to be made to arrest the Argentine party at Leith Harbour, whose arrival had caused all the trouble in the first place. This was just as well as the British still had no idea exactly how many Argentine personnel were at the old whaling station, and would have been surprised at the resulting confrontation.

At first light on 1 April a four-man observation team was sent by boat to Jason Ridge overlooking Leith Harbour to try to see what if anything the Argentine group was up to. The rest of that day passed uneventfully, until about 2000 local time when the Governor's broadcast on Falklands Islands Radio was picked up, warning that the invasion of the Falklands was imminent. The next day Mills heard through the BBC World News what was happening on the Falklands, and he therefore expected some kind of Argentine presence to arrive. He knew of the *Bahia Paraiso* and the Argentine party at Leith and so assessed that he might be attacked by up to 50 Marines, probably in small landing craft or boats, since the *Bahia Paraiso*'s helicopter lift was insufficient to land a substantial number of troops at one time. On 2 April therefore the beach and jetty at King Edward

Point were obstructed with wire and improvised explosive and incendiary devices, and defensive positions were prepared protecting the BAS Base. Mills's intention was 'to hit the enemy as hard as possible and then to withdraw through Grytviken up into the mountains and mount subsequent attacks from there'.

That morning MoD had signalled *Endurance* warning of 'strong possibility of assault on Grytviken by 40 Argentine Marines from destroyer/*Paraiso*. Possible time 021300 local'. All forces were ordered to concentrate at Grytviken immediately. Previous rules of engagement (ROE) were to be cancelled and 'you are to open fire without warning on any Argentine party landing on South Georgia provided you are certain they are armed'. In difficult communication conditions *Endurance* passed the information to Mills, using 'guarded English and a very cumbersome Slide Code', since there was no cypher facility at the BAS Base. Slidex, the army code, was of Second World War vintage.

Barker had proposed that his orders to make for the Falkland Islands should be reconsidered. He wanted to get *Endurance* to South Georgia to support the force ashore: 'If *Bahia Paraiso* is only escorted by one small frigate, then using South Georgia terrain which I know well as cover I could carry out series of AS12 [air-to-surface missile] attacks on both ships'. Fieldhouse, with MoD approval, ordered a return to South Georgia, but not offensive action. *Endurance*'s orders were to 'hold in maximum concealment to act as afloat covert intelligence platform'. The ship was to return round the south of the island, and be within helicopter range of Grytviken the following afternoon, 3 April. On the erroneous assumption that there had been no serious resistance in Stanley to avoid loss of life, another change in the rules of engagement (ROE) was passed to Mills: 'Do not (R) not fire without warning'. This was a reversion to the rules issued on 23 March.

The *Bahia Paraiso* had already entered Cumberland Bay East as predicted at approximately 1325 (1625Z) to check on whether *Endurance* was present. The weather over South Georgia was particularly severe which led the *Bahia Paraiso*, after it had contacted the Grytviken Base, to state that contact would be made again the next morning. This information was passed to *Endurance*, who told London that 'it is assumed that this message will ask Grytviken to surrender the Base as South Georgia is in Argentine hands'. As Hunt could not issue orders, Barker asked London 'what instructions do you wish to be passed to Base Commander?' Prime Minister Margaret Thatcher's first view, and that of the FCO, was that the Base Commander should be instructed not to resist. Henry Leach and John Nott, the Defence Secretary, disagreed, taking the view that they should not surrender but should keep to the ROE agreed by the Cabinet (fire in self-defence, after warning). The Foreign Secretary, Lord Carrington, agreed with them and spoke to the Prime Minister early on the morning of 3 April. She accepted that, in light of Nott's views, minimum force should be used. Instructions reached the *Endurance* in time to be passed to Grytviken before the next Argentine move. The text read:

If statement from *Bahia Paraiso* at 031000Z asks for base to be surrendered, Base Commander should not comply. He should make clear that any attempted landing will be resisted. If Argentines then invade RM detachment is to resist invasion using force in accordance with ROE laid down ... but they should not resist beyond point where lives might be lost to no avail.

However, the ROE referred to were those that had been superseded on 31 March, causing some confusion. In the event Mills acted exactly as Whitehall intended.

At dawn on 3 April the weather had improved markedly, and at 1030Z, as expected, the *Bahia Paraiso* came up on Very High Frequency (VHF) and demanded the surrender of the base. 'I have important message for you involving the successful operation by Argentine Forces at Malvinas,' stated Captain C. Trombetta, Commander Antarctic Naval Squadron, 'the ex-Governor has surrendered the Islands and the Dependencies unconditionally and I suggest you do the same'.

Apparently under the misapprehension at this point that, in the absence of *Endurance*, he was dealing only with the civilian BAS party, Trombetta ordered the corvette *Guerrico* to close the shore, sent his Alouette helicopter to reconnoitre, and loaded the first group of Marines into his other helicopter, a Puma. Mills read back the surrender demand on HF, much to Argentine irritation, so that this transmission would be heard by *Endurance*. His objective at this time was to get into some sort of negotiation to provide time for *Endurance* to get back. This was not successful, and after five minutes the Argentines demanded that all personnel assemble on the beach in the open. By this time the *Guerrico* was approaching and there was a helicopter overhead. In the words of Mills' report:

I then tried to stall the Argentines further. I informed the officer on board the *Bahia Paraiso* that there was ambiguity between what he had told us and what our orders were. I suggested that the corvette should hold back until this ambiguity could be cleared up. The Argentines ignored this demand and the corvette continued towards the harbour. As a final attempt to stall the Argentines I told them that there was a British military force on the island whose orders were to prevent them from landing. The Argentines ignored this statement also.

Mills then told the BAS Commander to go to the church for safety, where the rest of his team was sheltering, as there was little else he could do. He then walked down to the jetty, assuming that the corvette would send a boat ashore. He intended to meet any landing party and persuade the officer in charge not to land his troops. However, the *Guerrico* was already turning in King Edward Cove and retiring to seaward, while a small party of troops were landed by helicopter on the point only some 30 yards from the jetty. Mills moved quickly back to rejoin his detachment in their defensive position.

Under fire from the newly landed Argentine group, and threatened by the Puma helicopter about to land more troops on King Edward Point, Mills ordered his men to open fire. The Puma was repeatedly hit by small arms as it flew across the British positions and crash-landed across the cove. The battle then went on for some two hours. The small Argentine group on King Edward Point was pinned down, but the Alouette continued to land troops across the cove. The *Guerrico* again closed and was effectively engaged with anti-tank rockets and small arms, inflicting substantial damage, so she withdrew off-shore to where she could shell the defensive positions without reply. Eventually Mills realised that, outnumbered and outgunned, his position was precarious. His retreat was cut off by enemy troops moving round to Grytviken and darkness was still some hours away. Having achieved his aim of compelling Argentina to use military force and faced with the likelihood of losing lives to no avail, he decided to surrender, even though his men still had the Argentines pinned down on the beaches. One Royal Marine had been wounded while the Argentines had suffered several killed (*Endurance* later reported three) and wounded, lost a helicopter, and had the *Guerrico* extensively damaged. Soon 100 Argentine Marines and 10 Special Forces were gathered on the foreshore where they took the Royal Marines prisoner and searched them.

The Argentines left a garrison of about 55 Marines in South Georgia, based at Grytviken and Leith, and the 39 civilian scrap metal workers also remained at Leith. In remote locations away from the main base there were still four BAS field parties, who stayed in South Georgia until it was recaptured three weeks later. The questioning of Mills and his group seemed to be largely geared to finding out why the Argentine operation to take South Georgia had been so badly handled. The RM detachment eventually returned to Britain on 20 April.

Endurance rounded Cape Disappointment, the southern tip of South Georgia, about midday on 3 April, and flew off a Wasp reconnaissance sortie at maximum range in the afternoon (approx. 1903Z). The helicopter landed on the ridge to the east of Cumberland East Bay, and shut down. The pilot and observer saw the two Argentine ships in the bay and some boat and helicopter activity, but the battle was over. *Endurance* remained in South Georgia waters for another two days, providing intelligence and giving what comfort was possible to the few BAS people still on the island. On 5 April *Endurance* headed north.

2

RESPONSE

The Cabinet met on the morning of 2 April to hear of the imminent invasion and the preparations that had been set in motion to provide a
diplomatic and military response. With little hard information, the Cabinet
'parted in some gloom'.[1] Cecil Parkinson, Conservative Party Chairman and
soon member of the War Cabinet, recalls his despondency at the timing. The
party had survived a deep economic recession and the day before had
regained its lead in the opinion polls for the first time in eight months. His
reaction to the news of the Argentine invasion was that 'this was really
deadly'.[2] Margaret Thatcher was not at this stage the formidable political
force she later became (in part because of the Falklands) but presided over a
Cabinet which was by no means wholly loyal. By upping the ante and
deciding to take on Argentina, rather than accepting the loss of a piece of
distant land of limited value, she was taking an enormous gamble. She had
no military background herself and could be presented as clutching at
straws presented to her by self-serving admirals. If it all went badly and
concluded with heavy casualties and the Falklands still in Argentine hands,
her premiership would be over.

But it could well be over if nothing was done. Already the Government
was on the defensive. Explanations for its surprise at the turn of events were
being rehearsed: this invasion might have taken place at any time over the
previous fifteen years; the present crisis had begun only twelve days earlier.
The quality of the explanations, however, soon seemed to be overshadowed
by evidence of the extent of the surprise. When at 1100 a statement was
made in the Commons by Sir Humphrey Atkins, the Lord Privy Seal and
the second minister in the Foreign Office, the communications problems
meant that he was unable to confirm the Argentine landing but, he informed
the Commons, it appeared that regrettably the Islands had fallen. He indicated, incorrectly, that the Governor had been in touch with the FCO. The
lack of information added to the Government's embarrassment. Opposition
and Conservative backbenchers alike were outraged.

Around lunchtime the Government heard via the BAS vessel that the
Islands had been occupied. By this time the BBC was already reporting the

15

story from Buenos Aires. When the Cabinet met again at 1930 on 2 April there was still no confirmation of the invasion, let alone information on the degree of resistance, or the extent of any damage or casualties, though enough was known about the situation by mid-afternoon to instruct Sir Anthony Parsons to launch the Security Council debate on the British emergency resolution which was to become Resolution 502. The Chiefs of the Air and Naval Staffs gave their appreciation of the military situation and described the Task Force that would set sail in three days. There was nervousness about encouraging any belief that a military solution could be easily accomplished as well as sensitivity to the criticisms already being levelled at the Government for acting too slowly, and looking after nuclear forces at the expense of conventional.

That evening the Cabinet agreed to send the Task Force. This decision was assumed as much as taken, a reflection of genuine indignation at the Argentine act of aggression and a determination to demonstrate that the Government was not completely helpless. Once it became apparent that a Task Force could be sent there was never any doubt that it would be sent. There may have been much shaking of heads that the decision had been impetuous, taken without due consideration of the consequences, and without really knowing where it might all lead, but if such thoughts were harboured at the senior levels of government they were barely articulated. With only John Biffen (Lord President of the Council) raising any doubts, backing was given to the despatch of the Task Force.

The mood was not helped that evening when the first full report on the Argentine invasion, from Buenos Aires via the US State Department, suggested that the Royal Marines at Stanley had not offered any resistance and had surrendered. It was understood that this was on the orders of Hunt to avoid unnecessary loss of life. This impression was only corrected when Hunt and Majors Norman and Noott were released and were able to provide their own accounts. When they met the Prime Minister on their return to the UK on 5 April 1982, she was able to congratulate them on their courage, but was still perplexed by the breakdown in communications.

The morning papers of 3 April were full of this unanticipated humiliation. In order to cope with the anger in Parliament an emergency debate had been promised and it took place that day, though it was Saturday. Members of Parliament met with the country in shock. The debate did not in itself shape policy. The Task Force was already being assembled. But the fact that the Prime Minister could announce this made the occasion more bearable for the Government. The speed of events meant that her speech had been written by her two private secretaries – Clive Whitmore and John Coles – the previous night. The key phrase 'restore British administration' came from Whitmore, who felt this sounded less provocative than the restoration of British rule. There was no time to see what other government departments felt. The draft was reviewed by the Prime Minister and then typed out by late Friday and by the time it was sent out around Whitehall the Prime Minister was almost ready to speak in the Commons. Yet the tone was crucial to calming parliamentary nerves. If the speech had appeared equivocal on whether British administration could or should be restored then the Government might have fallen. Even with action in hand, however, the experience was a painful one. MPs from all parties spoke of their anger and disbelief. For a Government that was so avowedly patriotic it was galling to be castigated by an Opposition that was so clearly to its left for losing sovereign British territory to a military dictatorship in such a surprising and convincing manner. The Prime Minister's personal vulnerability was evident in Enoch Powell's reference to the 'Iron Lady' sobriquet, which though provided by the Soviet Union she rather liked. In the coming weeks, Powell warned, the Prime Minister would 'learn of what metal she is made'. When she returned to her private office after the debate it was this remark more than any other which had made the greatest impression.

The debate was wound up for the Government by John Nott. His speech was truncated because the Whips wanted more time for backbench speeches. During his remarks, he was caught off balance by former Foreign Secretary David Owen, who remarked on the importance of backing negotiations with force. At this point Nott began to attack the Opposition, at a time when his own Party was not in its most authoritative position, leading, as he later recalled, to 'uproar and calls for my resignation'. The Conservative MP Alan Clark wrote a vivid account in his diary:

> Poor old Notters on the other hand was a disaster. He stammered and stuttered and garbled. He faltered and fluttered and fumbled. He refused to give way; he gave way; he changed his mind; he stood up again; he sat down again. All this against a constant roaring of disapproval and contempt.[3]

As the debate had ended in a bad way for the Government, the Chief Whip, Michael Jopling, urged that Nott and Carrington attempt to calm backbenchers.[4]

Carrington had not been unduly troubled by the parallel debate to that of the Commons in the Lords, but when he spoke to the Party meeting, with up to 200 Members present, he was 'met by an element of cat-calling, derision and jeers from the assembled members.' Nott was able to sound tougher in the Commons by emphasising the Government's readiness to use the Task Force. Carrington meanwhile was coping not only with the debacle over the Falklands but past resentments, including over the recently negotiated settlement leading to transition to black majority rule in Rhodesia (Zimbabwe), and a general dislike of the Foreign Office.[5] After this Carrington decided to resign. Nott began the effort immediately to prevent this, but he was not to be dissuaded. The press was also clamouring for ministerial blood. The Defence and Foreign Secretaries were described as 'Thatcher's Guilty Men' by the *Express*. The *Daily Mail* wrote that Carrington should be sacked if he did not 'have the grace to resign'. Particularly influential was a tough leader in the *Times* asserting that he 'should do his duty'. Carrington was convinced not only that a senior resignation was necessary to take the heat off the Government as a whole but also that a Foreign Secretary could not perform effectively in the Lords at a time of such crisis.[6] On 6 April, the other senior members of his team – Atkins and Richard Luce – resigned with him.

When Nott heard of these resignations he was anxious that he would now be depicted as the 'dishonourable' man, who had clung to office while the 'honourable man' resigned. Nott decided that he had no choice but to follow suit and went back to MoD to write his letter of resignation. For the Government, already in dire straits, the simultaneous loss of both the Foreign and Defence Secretaries at the start of a major conflict would have been a devastating blow. Moreover, Nott's own position had recovered from the Saturday debate as a result of an extended interview on Sunday's leading current affairs programme, *Weekend World*, where he had effectively talked up the Task Force and the Government's readiness to use it. Now the Prime Minister refused to let him go. Eventually the matter was resolved by Nott's letter of resignation and Thatcher's fulsome rejection both being published.[7] Carrington was replaced by Francis Pym, a former Defence Secretary and then Leader of the Commons and with a strong position in the Conservative Party independent of the Prime Minister. All this was symptomatic of a government rocked by crisis. Margaret Thatcher's administration was only just recovering from two years of harsh economic conditions. She was aware that her position – and that of her Government and Party – had suddenly become more fragile and that it was to be severely tested in the coming weeks.

Why resist?

The incident was shocking in part because the Falklands had not loomed large in the national consciousness. The country was suddenly locked in an intense dispute over a distant territory that few could find without consulting a map. Britain had spent the previous decades divesting itself of its imperial responsibilities and many were surprised to find that there were any colonies left, especially one situated so precariously. There were rumours of great oil wealth to be unlocked from the waters around the Falklands, and claims of strategic importance in the light of Soviet encroachments into the South Atlantic, but it was hard to build a case that a great national interest was at stake here. The marginality of the Falklands was underscored by the distinct lack of resources devoted to them by successive British governments, who had only paid attention when trying to find ways out of the sovereignty dispute with Argentina. If the Falklands had mattered so little to Britain in the past, and had been noted in Whitehall largely for their nuisance value, why should they matter now?

In building a case that could settle nerves and point the way forward, the Government pointed to the two principles at stake in the conflict. Scholars of international relations are often sceptical when it is suggested that countries can go to war for the sake of principle – but democracies find it difficult to go to war for anything else, especially when national survival is not directly threatened. The first principle, and one that provided an important continuity with the history of the dispute, was that of self-determination. The small size of the population and the anomaly of their circumstances only made the principle appear more pure, while the evident Britishness of the people and the obnoxious nature of the Argentine regime made its relevance even more evident. To this was added a second principle: aggression must not be rewarded. The Junta may have hoped that a relatively bloodless occupation of what they anyway considered to be their own territory would avoid international condemnation, resulting in little more than a public display of dismay in London, probably combined with private relief. If so, they were mistaken.

The Commons debate of 3 April was therefore of particular importance in putting these two principles to centre stage and forging a bipartisan consensus behind them. They were summed up by the Prime Minister as: 'We cannot allow the democratic rights of the islanders to be denied by the territorial ambitions of Argentina'.[8] Much credit for the bipartisanship went to the Leader of the Opposition, Michael Foot, who had no problem denouncing the Argentine action as that of a ruthless dictatorship acting against a small democracy. He had made his name in the 1930s as a campaigner against appeasement and more recently as a campaigner for disarmament. He stood for high principle in international affairs. His speech demanded action on this basis:

> The rights and circumstances of the people in the Falkland Islands must be uppermost in our minds. There is no question in the Falkland Islands of any colonial dependence or anything of the sort. It is a question of people who wish to be associated with this country and who have built their whole lives on the basis of association with this country. We have a moral duty, a political duty and every other kind of duty to ensure that is sustained.[9]

With the Labour leadership's support, and support from the centre parties as well, there was no serious organised opposition in Parliament to the sending of the Task Force. There was strictly speaking no vote. A motion to continue the debate beyond the planned adjournment time was defeated 204 to 115.

There was, as some commentators observed, a uniquely cultural aspect to the ease with which the British accepted a case for the use of armed force. One less than enchanted commentator, Anthony Barnett, listed the 'essential symbols' that were to be found in the fate of the Falkland islanders:

> an island people, the cruel seas, a British defeat, Anglo-Saxon democracy challenged by a dictator, and finally the quintessentially Churchillian posture – we were down but we were not out. The parliamentarians of right, left and centre looked through the mists of time to the Falklands and imagined themselves to be the Grand Old Man. They were, after all, his political children and they too would put the 'Great' back into Britain.[10]

The positive aura surrounding World War II, combined with the negative connotations of appeasement, the presumed folly of putting a yearning for peace above all other values, allowed the Government to draw deep on national experience and symbols in setting out the case for the Task Force. Yet, at the same time, it had been many years since Britain had mounted a conventional military campaign. The dominant memory remained the Suez fiasco of 1956, when an attempt, in collusion with France and Israel, to topple Nasser's Government in Egypt had been thwarted by a painfully slow military build-up and then economic pressure from the US. In 1967 when Britain decided to abandon its military presence 'East of Suez,' there was a presumption that the time had passed when the country would engage in military operations in areas distant from the European continent, and this judgement had apparently been confirmed in the 1981 Defence Review. Sending a naval Task Force had once been the sort of thing British Governments did regularly: but it was a long time since anything like this had been attempted, and even longer since an attempt had been successful.

The Task Force was sent before the Government had the measure of the risks it was taking. For many sending the fleet made sense as an instrument of crisis diplomacy, but only on the supposition that it would be able to turn back and come home as soon as a political settlement had been agreed. Others, including the Prime Minister, suspected that there would be a fight. 'I knew, as most MPs could not,' she later recalled, 'the full extent of the practical military problems. I foresaw that we could encounter setbacks that would cause even some of the hawkish disposition to question whether the game was worth the candle. And how long could a coalition of opinion survive that was composed of warriors, negotiators and even virtual pacifists?'[11]

Organising Government

As the Task Force prepared and set sail the Government reorganised itself to cope with the rigours of the coming weeks. Initially the Cabinet itself had managed the crisis, meeting twice on 2 April. The immediate economic response was arranged through an ad hoc meeting of economic Ministers, chaired by the Chancellor, meeting the next day, and this led to a special official committee, under the Cabinet Office Secretariat – ODO(SA) – to manage the range of economic measures taken against Argentina. The ad hoc character of the process at this time reflected the lack of any previous formal planning on the organisation of government for crises short of a major confrontation with the Warsaw Pact. The Transition to War Committee was convened, but the sets of issues that such a group might expect to address, relating to national mobilisation and emergency powers, were not for the moment relevant.

Mrs Thatcher was revealed as 'a punctilious traditionalist in her dealings with both her Cabinet and with Parliament even when her Boadicea qualities were most in demand'.[12] She had spoken with Sir Frank Cooper, Permanent Under Secretary (PUS) at MoD, over lunch on 4 April. Cooper, one of the senior civil servants most admired by Thatcher, emphasised the importance of a small War Cabinet meeting regularly and taking decisions, with a simple chain of command responsible for implementation. Cooper later recalled that Thatcher had already decided that the Chancellor should not be included because finances could not be overriding in such a situation. This view is normally attributed to former Prime Minister Harold Macmillan whom she saw on 6 April, and who certainly confirmed this preference. His advice was similar to Cooper's, except harking back more to Churchill's success rather than to Eden's failure with Suez in 1956, which Cooper (and many others) had in mind. She still consulted the Chancellor, Sir Geoffrey Howe, her neighbour in Downing Street, often after returning from Chequers on Sunday evenings.

When on 6 April the Cabinet met again, the Prime Minister explained that day-to-day political oversight was to be provided by a special Ministerial Sub-Committee of the Defence and Oversea Policy Committee (OD) on the South Atlantic and Falkland Islands (OD(SA)), which came to be known as the War Cabinet. This became the critical instrument of crisis management. Its terms of reference, as set down that day, were 'to keep under review political and military developments relating to the South Atlantic and the Falkland Islands, and to report as necessary to the Defence and Oversea Policy Committee'. It contained the Prime Minister, Home Secretary (Sir William Whitelaw), Foreign Secretary (Francis Pym), Defence Secretary (John Nott), the Chancellor of the Duchy of Lancaster and Paymaster General (Cecil Parkinson), with support provided by the Cabinet Office. Parkinson had been brought in as a result of Nott's concern that he was bound because of his departmental role on occasion to oppose Pym, and that Whitelaw would be inclined to support Pym, leaving a War Cabinet of four divided. Parkinson was seen as a natural loyalist. In the event Whitelaw always supported the Prime Minister, so the combination tended to isolate

Pym. The effect was accentuated because Pym disliked rows, especially in the presence of others, and so he would tend to back off. While the Prime Minister may have been unsure when it came to challenging military judgements, she had no hesitation in challenging diplomatic judgement, and it was Pym's misfortune to be representing a strand in the debate about which she was naturally wary.

Because Parkinson lacked a departmental role he was available to do more media work. He was also the only member of the War Cabinet who had made regular visits to Latin America, including Argentina, although on a variety of trade missions. The Attorney General (Sir Michael Havers) was also a regular as a result of the large number of legal matters that had to be addressed, although his war-time service in the Fleet Air Arm appears to have been a larger influence on his thinking. The exclusion of the Chancellor was understandably against the wishes of the Treasury. Economic issues did not loom large again until the later stages of the campaign, largely in connection with post-war reconstruction of the Falklands. On 22 June, after the fighting, a new Committee – OD(FAF) – was convened.

Over the subsequent weeks the Prime Minister took care to keep the full Cabinet informed, especially when critical decisions, such as the authorisation of the landing on the Islands, were involved, although in this case, and others, questions of timing and secrecy meant that the Cabinet was being associated with decisions already effectively taken. Until the crisis machinery was wound down on 15 July, the Cabinet reviewed the Falklands situation on 20 occasions, sometimes in meetings solely convened for this purpose, and was therefore meeting as a group far more often than in normal times – on average twice a week. In this way the constitutional proprieties could be honoured, but also some real meaning could be given to the concept of collective responsibility. On the other hand, the OD(SA) did not, contrary to its terms of reference, report directly to the Defence and Oversea Policy Committee. OD met only once, the day after the loss of HMS *Sheffield* to an Exocet missile on 4 May. In general its slightly larger membership than OD(SA) offered no advantages. A post-war assessment still described the 'invisibility' of OD as 'remarkable' given that it was supposed to be the senior ministerial sub-committee on defence and foreign affairs and all other committees created were in the OD series.

Until it was dissolved on 12 August, OD(SA) met at least daily. By that time it had held 67 meetings, and considered 70 notes, papers and memoranda on all aspects of the campaign. It was judged to have been a success, to the extent that after the war, on 12 August 1982, a new OD Sub-Committee on the Management of Political and Military Emergencies Overseas (OD(EM)) was created, with precisely the same powers. By starting their meeting between 0900 and 1000, Ministers may not have left quite enough time before they gathered to take stock with their senior officials, but it did allow time for the minutes to be circulated by mid-afternoon. These carried the conclusions of the meetings but, for pressures of time, made no attempt to convey the substance of the discussions.[13] Sufficient officials were also present, including the Chiefs of Staff Secretary, to ensure that decisions were communicated and followed up immediately. There were at times sharp disagreements but the recollection of those involved is that the seriousness of the situation kept the meetings calm and productive. Nott later recalled 'There was none of the hectoring or personal antipathy which had characterised our debates on domestic economic policy.'[14] Initially it had been assumed that the political line-up within the War Cabinet would have Pym and Whitelaw as doves and Nott and Parkinson as hawks. In practice the relationships were much more complex.

Thatcher dominated the War Cabinet. This was not through failing to consult or ignoring opposition. One, who watched her closely during this period, recalls that the Prime Minister would 'fret away' while arriving at a decision, 'discussing the options endlessly with different people'. She liked to canvass a range of views before making up her own mind. Once it was made up and the decision was taken she 'did not look back'. It was not only force of will that kept the Prime Minister going, but also an extraordinary work rate, that meant that she kept on top of the issues and was often better briefed than her colleagues. Her ability to keep up with other policy issues was also remarked upon. Requiring only four hours sleep a night, she worked through her 'red boxes', on all other Government business, every night. Another official, however, suggested that the boxes were relatively empty. Other departments refrained from loading her with non-Falklands work. Certainly another senior policy-maker recalled days waiting for news from the South Atlantic with little else to do because routine matters were being handled elsewhere.

Macmillan had also told the Prime Minister that she needed a Lord Ismay figure (Military Secretary to the Cabinet) close at hand. Her staff searched, in vain, for a retired officer to provide independent advice on operational issues. None appeared to combine sufficient seniority with probable sympathy with her political objectives and the appropriate personal chemistry. The campaign itself forged close and warm links between the armed forces and the Prime Minister but at the start they were not at all good. Initially Thatcher was seen to have been as culpable as Nott for the 1981 defence review and guilty of not paying attention to what was going on in the forces, evident in her ignorance of the scrapping of *Ark Royal*, the large carrier which would have been very useful in 1982 had it still been in one piece. Her comments on military matters during the first few days of the conflict did not inspire confidence. Yet she was a quick learner. In this she was supported by Clive Whitmore in her private office, who came from the Ministry of Defence, and was able to interpret much of the information she was receiving. She was also fortunate in the Chief of the Defence Staff

(CDS), Admiral Sir Terence Lewin. His own political and personal skills were considerable and he conveyed a confidence and clarity of purpose to which she warmed. Also fortunate was the fact that his position had been enhanced by a reform instigated by Lewin and instituted as late as February 1982. The essential principle was that the CDS became 'the principal military adviser to the Secretary of State and to the Government in his own right, and no longer as chairman of a committee with collective responsibility.' As a result 'the Chiefs of Staff Committee would become the forum in which the Chief of Defence Staff sought the advice of his colleagues. No longer would it become the fulcrum of collective responsibility.'[15] In this reinforced position Lewin became in many respects one of the critical members of the War Cabinet.

Lewin had been in New Zealand when the crisis broke. He had been kept in touch with the developing crisis but also discouraged from flying home while there was still hope of peaceful solution, on the grounds that his recall would soon become known.[16] As a result his return had been a rush. To many in Whitehall this was not before time. Relations among the Chiefs of Staff were uneasy, largely as a result of the previous year's defence review, which had been widely assumed to be anti-Navy. The active role of the First Sea Lord in persuading the Government that there was a serious military option available had inevitably been assessed by the other services in the light of the defence review. Henry Leach was seen to have seized the opportunity to demonstrate the Royal Navy's continued worth to the United Kingdom, with a degree of confidence that even senior members of his own service did not share. The Chief of Air Staff (Air Chief Marshal Sir Michael Beetham) and the Chief of the General Staff (General Sir Edwin Bramall) understood why the Government needed to act, and the diplomatic advantages of an early show of resolve, but they were uneasy about where it might all lead.[17] The fact that the Task Force was, in the first instance, largely configured as a naval operation did not encourage great activism on their part. Later Bramall commented that he was not 'bubbling over with enthusiasm for the operation, because first of all I thought we needn't have got ourselves into this muddle. And I resented the casualties that I knew would be inevitable in order to recover from the mistakes we'd made.'[18]

For all these reasons the initial Chiefs of Staff meetings, in the absence of Lewin, had not gone well. Lewin's return made a substantial difference. His own relations with the other Chiefs had been bruised by the defence review, including with Leach, but as an Admiral he understood the immediate operational issues in a way that a CDS from another service would not. The other Chiefs were brought in to the War Cabinet as and when required, and they met daily to discuss the developing situation, but the views offered by Lewin were his own, and while taking care to consult he did not always attempt to fashion a consensus. He later described the regular Chiefs' meetings as having taken up 'too much time of too many people', with a 'tendency towards post-operational arguments'. His position was strength-ened during the course of the campaign as ministerial confidence grew in his ability to deliver the results he promised. One official noted after the conflict that one of the 'political imperatives for the Prime Minister' was that the politicians should support the military, although she sensed at times that she was being provided with a cleared military position without much indication of the alternative views that lay behind it. Only on one occasion was a request for a particular military action turned down. Lewin 'developed an effective technique of obtaining the Prime Minister's approval by making requests orally at OD (SA), often to the extreme annoyance of the FCO'.

Lewin's day would begin at 0600, with the latest signals read through breakfast, and MoD reached by 0715. After an intelligence and operational briefing he would talk to Fieldhouse, and this would take him up to the War Cabinet's 0930 meeting. The Chiefs of Staff would meet later in the morning.[19] Although Nott would attend the Chiefs of Staff meeting for the first few items on the agenda, and in particular the intelligence briefing, he would be briefed later by Lewin on the overall outcome. The relationship between Lewin and Fieldhouse was close. They had been together on *Hermes* and had a close mutual understanding. While Lewin could manage the Government, Fieldhouse could manage the Task Force. In part because he took strenuous steps to avoid direct contact with ministers, including the Prime Minister, Fieldhouse never felt under political pressure on how to run the war. He nonetheless regularly reported, though inevitably on a piecemeal basis, to the commanders in the South Atlantic what he knew to be the concerns of the politicians.

The military chain of command passed directly from the Prime Minister to the Chief of the Defence Staff and then on to the Task Force Commander. Nott took the view that in 'time of war there is no room for the post of Defence Secretary', except he suspected as scapegoat if things went wrong. This meant that junior MoD ministers had even less of a role and generally felt excluded for much of the crisis. In key respects, the Prime Minister had to be her own Defence Secretary and so Nott confined himself to being a participant in the War Cabinet and, often by playing devil's advocate, 'ques-tioning but not overly influencing the decisions of the military.'[20] He also took the view that while other government departments needed to be kept informed about military thinking, it was essential that the decision-making process was not hampered by strictly military decisions having to be cleared with the Foreign Office in advance. He judged it important that military requirements be assessed independently of immediate diplomatic exigencies. As a result operational military matters were not divulged to or processed through any formal interdepartmental mechanism. Political control was largely exercised through discussions of rules of engagement (ROE) rather than specific operational plans. John Weston of the FCO developed the proposals on these with Moray Stewart of MoD and the Assistant Chief of

Staff (Operations). This made possible a full review of large changes in military practice, but there were still occasions when the Foreign Office had real anxiety that critical decisions had been taken without a full appreciation of their political impact.

Partly for reasons of personality and the sudden elevation of Pym as Secretary of State following Lord Carrington's resignation the diplomatic input was not always forcefully presented. The Foreign Office team always had the handicap of the Prime Minister's instinctive distrust of proposals which were bound to explore possibilities for compromise and conciliation. Moreover, while the Prime Minister tended to display a certain diffidence when dealing with the military, this was not at all the case with the diplomats, whose expertise she felt able to challenge. Within the Foreign Office, an Operational Emergency Group was established to handle the day-to-day requirements of the emergency and produce regular Situation Reports (Sitreps). The Information Policy department produced 90 guidance telegrams for missions abroad as well as a number of background papers on controversial topics. After the Falklands a proper situations room would be available for a future emergency. For this crisis the group had to make do with minimal facilities. A Strategy Group was established to consider the military issues and future diplomatic action at the UN and elsewhere, while a Parliamentary and Press Group was responsible for the preparation of future parliamentary and press statements and for the public relations aspect generally. These groups reported to a steering group, which included the Private Secretaries from the appropriate ministerial offices. The appointment of Sir Michael Palliser, who had been until 1 April the Permanent Under Secretary at the FCO, as the Prime Minister's Special Adviser on the Falklands, added an independent viewpoint based on considerable experience, and a specific remit to think about the longer term. The appointment was something of a surprise because Palliser, as a result of his pro-European views, had never been one of the Prime Minister's favourites.

Unlike Suez, the constant reference point on how not to manage great crises, the senior members of Government were not engaged in a grand act of deception, requiring excessive secrecy. In this case the demands for secrecy reflected the extreme delicacy of the military situation. Moreover, much of the coordination was bilateral – between the FCO and MoD – and the role of other departments was marginal, and in many respects largely over early in the conflict once the Treasury and the Department of Trade had sorted out sanctions, the Home Office the handling of Argentine nationals, and the Law Officers possible emergency legislation.

Real difficulties were experienced in the organisation of interdepartmental coordination at the official level, with the need for the bureaucracy to function being set against a disinclination to allow the wide circulation of sensitive material. The official group – ODO(SA) – began by ensuring distribution of key papers on the key issues, but had only met three times by 13

April and did not meet again until 2 June when, now renamed ODO(SA)(FE), it began to address the issues of post-war reconstruction. It was later supplanted by MISC 82, a group to consider the future administration of the Islands, which reported to OD(FAF). The organisational problem was that the sensitivity of the issues meant that they had to be handled at a senior level, but the senior figures were extremely busy. By 5 April the Permanent Secretary at MoD was observing that staff in some key divisions had been on a 24 hour basis for several days and it was important that they should not become exhausted. The same day steps were taken to minimise the circulation of paper. All non-Falklands business that would normally go to the Secretary of State was to go to the relevant junior minister.

In the end it was the most senior civil servants who had to prepare the ground for War Cabinet meetings. The Cabinet Secretary, Sir Robert Armstrong, saw his role as being to ensure that OD(SA) was properly serviced and that decisions were communicated quickly, and that the interests of the wider cabinet were not overlooked. He chaired the ad hoc and informal Mandarins Group, or 'Armstrong group', which met to consider the politico-military aspects of the conflict, in order to identify the decisions that would need to be taken and communicate those that had been taken, as well commission any necessary papers. It included the Permanent Secretaries of the FCO and MoD (Sir Anthony Acland and Sir Frank Cooper respectively) as well as Lewin and Palliser and the Deputy Secretary in the OD Secretariat (Robert Wade-Gery) who acted as de facto secretary. Unfortunately it operated wholly by word of mouth, with no notices of meetings issued and no minutes taken, so its role is now difficult to assess. Lewin's biographer suggests that this was the most draining and exhausting of all the CDS's meetings. The question most frequently asked was 'where do we go from here?' The questioning and probing from the substantial figures in this group meant that Lewin felt that if he could win over this group 'he would most likely be able to carry his proposals in OD(SA) itself.'[21] An official commenting at the time, however, suggested that Lewin limited this restraint by working on his direct relationship with the Prime Minister.

The informality and inability to draw on staff resources in the normal Whitehall way was later criticised, as the process meant that some problems were missed. Against this had to be put the Government's anxiety that the constant demands for information from the media, backbench MPs and foreign governments would result in damaging and potentially fateful leaks. It was probably also the case that there simply was not the time for lower level preparation given the intense pressure of events. At times such as these the most senior civil servants have to act as their own desk officers. Some extra support was provided through the direct liaison between MoD and FCO, with a senior FCO representative attending the Chiefs of Staff meeting and the defence desk in the FCO's own Emergency Unit providing a permanent point of contact with MoD. For many, the crisis conditions were something of a liberation. Nott describes the Whitehall system 'hit below the solar plexus':

> A great tangled mass of co-ordinating committees, Cabinet sub-committees, the great panoply of bureaucratic checking and double-checking had been completely flattened. The horrendous way in which Whitehall ensures that it retains control through an excess of co-ordination means that nothing happens with any kind of urgency. The whole system had been caught with its trousers down. It was partly due to the fact that Whitehall was virtually in suspense, shell-shocked and useless, that no obstacles arose in getting the Fleet to sea.[22]

Another input that was problematic was intelligence. The key provider to the War Cabinet was the Joint Intelligence Committee (JIC), based in the Cabinet Office, chaired by a senior FCO figure, and including representatives of all the key ministries as well as the security and intelligence agencies. It could use secret reports as well as publicly available information and diplomatic telegrams. Assessments would come forward from the Current Intelligence Groups (CIG), of which there were eight organised on a regional basis (in this case Latin America). They would be prepared by the Assessment Staff, largely seconded from FCO and MoD. On 4 April the JIC decided that a daily intelligence briefing had to be produced, and that it should contain sections on the Argentine military dispositions and intentions, Latin American and other international reactions, cease-fire negotiations and the reaction and involvement of the Soviet Union. In all 75 daily assessments were issued between 4 April and 18 June, together with 23 more detailed notes. The JIC met twice a week during the crisis, but the main work was done by the CIG. The problem came not with the substance of the assessments but the timing. With Buenos Aires four hours behind, an assessment composed in the early morning in London could seldom take account of events that took place after South Atlantic midnight. At the same time, news of American assessments, which continued to influence the British, would only come in during the afternoon.

Because the preparation of the daily assessment normally took about five hours, if it was to be ready for the normal start of the War Cabinet at 0900, the drafting process would normally have had to begin about 0400. It was decided that this would be impractical. Instead the CIG met at 1100 to consider a draft that was normally issued as early as possible after lunch, between 1430 and 1500. The War Cabinet received some full intelligence assessments, and after 6 May, following the stormy first days of that month, their meetings were opened by Lewin with a briefing on the latest military situation, pulled together from the latest signals. In addition there was a regularly updated basic military intelligence summary (INTSUM), the first of which was available at 0600 each morning. Ministers who had the requisite access undoubtedly looked at any raw intelligence prior to War Cabinet meetings, and would probably have done so even if there was an up-to-date JIC assessment on their desks.

The Deputy Chair of the JIC was the Director General Intelligence, a retired 3-star officer serving as a civilian, in charge of the Defence Intelligence Staff (DIS). While the DIS contributed to the wider assessments they also produced material directly for their MoD customers. Responsible for this task was General Glover, the Deputy Chief of Defence Staff Intelligence (DCDS(I)), who pursued this task with the support of CDS, while the Chief concentrated on JIC and relations with the US. The DIS had barely a person working on the South Atlantic before April, and a number of the first team set up to deal with the crisis to meet the demands of the campaign had to be replaced. It required a drastic shift in resources to meet the insatiable demand for information and analysis. The FCO also had to reorganise itself. It took until 10 May before it began to produce a daily Sitrep on diplomatic developments.

Command structure

The Commander-in-Chief Fleet (CINCFLEET), Admiral Sir John Fieldhouse, became the overall commander of the Task Force. Operational Control was vested in Flag Officer First Flotilla, Rear Admiral John 'Sandy' Woodward, who became Combined Commander of the expeditionary force (CTG 317.8) including all surface ships, land and air forces. There were alternative candidates for the role, notably Rear Admiral D Reffell, The Flag Officer, Third Flotilla (FOF3), who had considerable amphibious experience, but he had not been in post long. Although the Prime Minister was anxious that command was being entrusted to a man that neither she nor Nott knew, they accepted Lewin's and Leach's view that it was important to stick in war with those who had been designated for particular roles in peacetime. In addition there were four Commanders Task Units (CTUs). One, the Carrier Battle Group, Woodward also commanded (TU 317.8.1). Commodore Amphibious Warfare (COMAW), Commodore Michael C Clapp, was in charge of the Amphibious Task Force (TU 317.8.3) while Brigadier Julian H A Thompson, Brigade Commander No 3 Commando Brigade, was in charge of the landing group (TU 317.8.4). A fourth group, destined for South Georgia, was soon commanded by Captain Brian Young (TU 317.9).

Two key figures in Woodward's team were the Captains of the two carriers – Jeremy Black of *Invincible* and Lin Middleton of *Hermes*. Their individual styles were quite different. Black as a gunnery officer delegated to his aviators; Middleton, an aviator himself, sought tight control. Their Sea

Harrier squadrons – *Invincible*'s 801 and *Hermes*' 800 – also followed distinctive approaches. Woodward does not appear to have had full confidence in Middleton, the Captain of his Flagship, and this may have contributed to an occasional sense of isolation.

The amphibious group became TG 317.0 under Commodore Clapp. The landing force became TG 317.1 under the command of Brigadier Thompson. The Commanding Officer, HMS *Antrim*, Captain Brian Young, was designated CTG 317.9, in charge of the group for South Georgia comprising the *Antrim*, *Plymouth*, *Endurance* and *Tidespring*. On 10 April, CINCFLEET signalled that M Company, 42 Commando and one SSN (with 6 SBS embarked to launch reconnaissance if possible) would join these ships. CINCFLEET, as Commander Task Force (CTF) 317, retained operational control of TG 317.0 and TG 317.9, intending that it should later be delegated to Commodore Clapp for the amphibious group and to Woodward for any other ships operating with or supporting him once they went south from Ascension. The combat ships from Young's group eventually reverted back to Woodward's battle group, although it was reconstituted as TG 317.9, commanded by Captain Barker of *Endurance*, to remain in charge of all operations in and around South Georgia.

The two charts below show, first, the early arrangement for the command structure and, second, the amended version as promulgated by Fieldhouse on 9 April. In the first all four groups appeared as separate but equal, but with Woodward doubling as Commander Task Group. In the second the four units appeared as equal. After 17 April Woodward was considered *primus inter pares*. This reflected the range of tasks with which Woodward already had to cope, and the fact that Clapp and Thompson needed their own direct line to Northwood. Woodward, however, was still described as 'Senior Task Group Commander', and was a Two Star officer while the

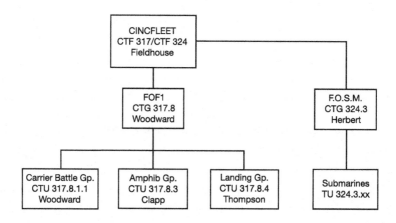

Figure 1 Initial Command Structure

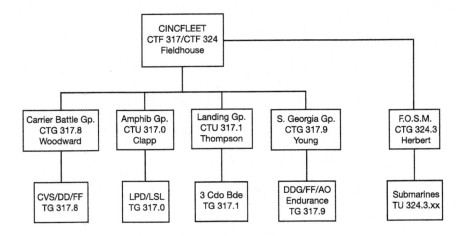

Figure 2 Command Structure after 9 April

others were One Star. This created an ambiguity that soon caused difficulties, as will be discussed later. When General Jeremy Moore arrived in San Carlos on 30 May the position changed again, for Clapp now had no direct line to Thompson but instead had to work through Divisional HQ.

The third, and larger, chart was prepared by Northwood on 2 June, when two brigades were now on the Falklands with Moore in charge. Its actual status is unclear as it was never promulgated, but it tells us something of the prevailing assumptions at Northwood. Notably, in addition to its complexity, it does not follow the 'separate-but-equal' assumption with which the task group commanders (who did not see this chart) were operating, but instead puts Woodward above Clapp, just as Moore was now above Thompson and Brigadier Wilson of 5 Infantry Brigade. When the war came to a close Moore became Commander British Forces Falkland Islands, with Clapp his Chief Staff Officer (Navy) and Rex Hunt, the former Governor, returning as Commissioner.

If there was a gap it was the lack of a Three-Star commander to be in theatre, capable of assessing priorities on the spot and dealing directly with Northwood. Thompson, who felt the absence of such a figure more than most, expressed this view strongly after the war. Woodward might have been able to play this role if he had felt able to leave *Hermes*. Moore was able to support Thompson when he eventually reached the South Atlantic. Either way the separation of sea and land operations would always have caused problems.[23]

The submarines taking part in CORPORATE formed TG 324.3, under the Flag Officer Submarines (FOSM), Vice Admiral Peter G M Herbert,

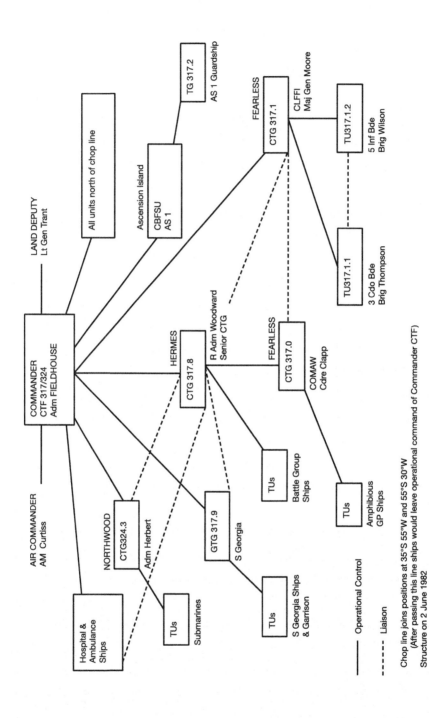

Figure 3 Operation CORPORATE: Command Structure

based at Northwood and reporting directly to Fieldhouse rather than Woodward. Woodward, a submariner himself, knew the boats and their senior officers, and believed he had the wherewithal to exercise effective operational control. If he had been given appropriate communications he would have been able to get orders immediately to submarines, rather than the three cycles of broadcasts it took to be sure they had received messages from Northwood, and they would not have needed to be kept so tightly in separate boxes during operations. There were a number of times during the campaign when he regretted the lack of this direct control. In part Northwood kept control because that is how the headquarters expected to operate in the Cold War and there was no expectation that a battle group commander would play that role. There was the additional thought that any use of a nuclear submarine, Britain's most lethal weapon, was replete with possibilities for political controversy, which is how it turned out. It was therefore deemed essential to keep them under central control.

Once British troops were firmly established ashore operational control of the landed force would be transferred to Brigadier Thompson as Commander Land Forces. When it was decided to send 5 Brigade, commanded by Brigadier Tony Wilson, a divisional command structure was required, and General Jeremy Moore transferred into this role, with his position at Northwood being taken over by Lieutenant General Richard Trant, General Officer Commanding South East District. Brigadier John Waters accompanied Moore as his Deputy. Moore's appointment was logical, because he had been working closely with Fieldhouse up to this point. There were some later Army complaints, when it was providing five battalions to the three RM Commandos, about a chain of command that went through an Admiral and then a Royal Marine General, but generally the arrangement worked.[24]

The media

As the war progressed, the handling of media relations appeared as the most evident area of weakness in the political and military management of the campaign. It was the first war-related issue to be addressed by the House of Commons Defence Committee.[25] Operational plans lacked a media dimension, and issues concerning the accreditation and handling of correspondents dogged the campaign, aggravated in this case by scarce and limited communications facilities as well as the standard issues of the balance between withholding information to protect operations while releasing it to ensure the most positive public presentation of the military and diplomatic effort.

The novelty, after so many years, of Britain sending a substantial force to a remote part of the world in such strange circumstances naturally encouraged enormous media interest. To be able to satisfy public curiosity the media expected to be able to travel with the Task Force, have their material cleared with the minimum delay, without any interference with style or content unless it compromised security, and opportunities to move between force units as often as the opportunity permitted. The politicians and senior commanders were all well aware of the need to maintain a high level of public support for, and understanding of, the Task Force's role, and so dare not take the media for granted. As Cooper put it, 'keeping the media and public opinion with us here is absolutely crucial'. Yet there was no serious information policy in place that would help them work their way through the unavoidable tensions resulting from the twin policies of keeping the media happy and supportive while at the same time protecting information according to the demands of operational security. The tensions between military and media operations were never resolved and while all agreed the need for an information policy, it was widely confessed after the conflict that nobody with the requisite combination of time and authority worked one out.[26]

There were a number of reasons for this. The factors of distance that made this campaign special in so many respects had a critical influence on information policy. There were severe practical as well as operational reasons why it was difficult to satisfy media demands for material commensurate with the importance of the event. There was not much space for correspondents to travel with the Task Force and those that did were wholly dependent upon Task Force facilities to transmit copy back to Britain. This made censorship possible but it also meant that media copy was competing for time on the ships' military communications system with operational traffic. Another problem was a lack of coordination. There were a number of information policies in circulation at the same time; Northwood, MoD and the Prime Minister's office all had distinctive interests and approaches. None of these made much impact on senior officers. Nor had the military much experience in dealing with journalists. The Army understood the public relations aspect of contemporary conflict better than the other services because of Northern Ireland but initially this was largely a naval operation, and many in the RN did not welcome the presence of journalists on the ships. Only the Royal Marines took their own public relations team.

The Navy's view tended towards the more traditional: an active information policy could appear as an imposition on busy people, who had a war to fight. Feeding a media frenzy seemed an absurd distraction when preparing for battles in which lives were at stake. When helicopters were scarce and communications were overloaded with vital signals, was it not odd to give any sort of priority to ferrying reporters around and dispatching their reports? Yet at the same time they were disappointed when there was criticism or misrepresentation of British strategy. They found it difficult to envisage that this might be a matter of give and take. The country was at war and they expected the media to play their part in the national effort.

As it was assumed that the main flow of information would be emanating

34

from the accredited journalists with the Task Force then that is where any controls would have to be exercised, especially as the media would be relying on military means of communication to get their material back to Britain. The tightness of Britain's military position meant that the controls would have to be severe. Giving intelligence to the enemy seemed foolhardy when the margin of error was so slight, and almost any operational detail could soon be characterised as vital intelligence. To exclude anything containing hard information or speculation on plans and capabilities, the disposition of units and almost anything to do with intelligence necessarily meant only allowing through trivial, colour stories, describing personalities sailing with the Task Force and how they were spending their time. These, however, could hardly appear serious enough for scarce communication facilities. Captain Jeremy Black of *Invincible* later explained the problems this created in terms of priorities, by citing the traffic for 19 April. He needed to exchange data and programming information to update his electronic warfare equipment, yet had to use up 30 per cent of his outgoing traffic on the journalists' copy, including an item about how 'page 3 girls' were going to war, in the form of 'outsize pin-up pictures' that had been airlifted to the Task Force.[27] It was thought that two journalists on *Invincible* were interested in no issue other than what Prince Andrew, a helicopter pilot as well as the Queen's son, was up to.[28]

It was space limitations, as well as an inherent wariness, that encouraged the Navy at first to resist the media clamour to send their correspondents with the Task Force. Though applications from the press to join the ships were pouring in, Northwood initially only allocated six places on ships. There then followed 'violent lobbying of Downing Street.' MoD soon doubled this to twelve, who were to fly to Ascension and join the force there. It was then agreed to increase the number of correspondents to fifteen, embarking them in ships sailing from the UK. Finally, because of the impossibility of rationing such a small number of places sensibly, and the Newspaper Publishers' Association's shrewd exclusion of the *Times*, *Sun* and *Guardian* from their original list, as well as the need to include the broadcasting media, a total of 29 was settled upon (17 newspapermen, two photographers, two radio reporters and three television reporters supported by five technicians) and they were divided between the carriers and the amphibious ships. This still left disappointed some 160 organisations. Applications from the foreign press were not accepted. Later complaints were received from the regional press over their poor representation and allocation of facilities they had received.

The speed of departure meant that the journalists sent were often those that happened to be available rather than those with experience of war, while many lacked appropriate kit. Press identification documents dated from the 1956 Suez operation, and therefore contained passages in Arabic. The Deputy Fleet Public Relations Officer, CINCFLEET Staff, was the principal public

35

relations adviser to Northwood. He had overall professional charge and direction of all MoD public relations staff embarked and was the liaison officer for civilian journalists. The six MoD public relations officers (known as 'minders') who were sent to work with the journalists had, like the journalists, been sent without proper preparation or briefings, and also found themselves caught between the need to support the work of the journalists and preventing the wrong sort of disclosure. They reviewed all materials before transmission, although further vetting took place in London. However unpopular overt censorship might be, MoD was confident that so long as the restricted areas were defined and implemented in a reasonable way they would be accepted without too much fuss. The media and the military soon displayed different views about what was reasonable. During the course of the campaign there were numerous complaints about inconsistency and small-mindedness in some of the censorship, and generally that good news came out quicker than bad news. When the assets of the Task Force were so limited, however, news of equipment losses in accidents, even when there had been no casualties, provided Argentina with valuable intelligence, and when there had been casualties then some sensitivity had to be shown to the next of kin.

On 9 April, instructions were sent to the Task Force on the need for tight security when talking with the press, or even where they might be overheard. The press would be looked after by information officers who would remind them of the need for responsible reporting. It was important, Fieldhouse told Woodward, that all correspondents on board should continue to feel free to file their stories and material. 'We rely on public opinion in UK being kept informed but it is also vital that nothing is published which puts at risk lives or success of operation'. In principle there was very little of interest that did not come into that category, and the list of topics to be avoided was long:

> Operational plans, which would enable a potential enemy to deduce details of our intentions; Speculation about possible courses of action; State of readiness and detailed operational capability of individual units or formations; Location, employment and operational movements of individual units; Particulars of current tactics and techniques; Operational capabilities of all types of equipments; Stocks of equipment and other details of logistics; Information about intelligence (especially communications intelligence) on Argentinian dispositions or capabilities; Communications; Equipment or other defects.

Woodward later summarised his instructions as 'Co-operation, yes; information, no.'[29] While there was an effort to exercise tight control over the contact between senior officers and the press, junior officers and NCOs often felt less constrained.

A number of ships with the Task Force, although no warships, had terminals for INMARSAT (a commercial maritime satellite system), and this allowed for voice reports to be transmitted back. There were no good means available for getting pictures of any sort back to London. Still pictures were transmitted using four facsimile transmission machines, initially on *Canberra* but later transferred to other ships, which worked in conjunction with the *Inmarsat* facility. During the conflict 202 pictures taken by Service and press photographers were transmitted from the Task Force, very few by any standards. It took until the middle of May before still photographs could be transmitted from the South Atlantic to the UK. While for a brief time TV pictures could be sent back by direct transmissions from Electronic News Gathering systems while the ships were in the Channel, this rapidly became impossible. As early as 3 April an investigation was initiated by MoD into the possibility of embarking a portable satellite television transmitter on *Hermes* to send pictures from a ship back to Britain using the American Defence Satellite Communications Systems (DSCS) satellite on which the RN had leased channels, but there were two problems with this. The RN channels were standard military audio ones, but TV pictures required a bandwidth 1000 times greater; and no higher-capacity channels could be made available. For pictures to pass through the narrow military channel they would have to be sliced, but this would take 20 minutes to pass a single picture and would require the Americans to tilt their communications DSCS satellite, or a wider channel would need to be provided. At most poor-quality black and white pictures could be transmitted via this route. Informal approaches to the US resulted in a negative response: with their load the satellites could be put at risk by the manoeuvre. The broadcasters suspected that if the military had not been so reluctant to have television pictures of the fighting, on the grounds that images of blood and gore might sap the nation's will and distress the families of those doing the fighting, they might have pushed harder. There is no direct evidence for this but the consequential media frustration is not hard to understand. Video film had to be sent to Ascension Island, from where it could be fed by satellite to BBC or ITN using the specially adapted Cable and Wireless facility, or brought by air to the United Kingdom. This could mean that it could take as much as three weeks from filming to transmission. For all these reasons this was a radio rather than a television war.

The media made proposals for improving the Ascension facility, but the military did not want any correspondents based in a place where so many sensitive activities were underway. Fieldhouse did not want the importance or the vulnerability of the facilities at Ascension to be publicised. The Americans were already embarrassed enough by the British use of their facilities at the airport there and although this was now firmly in the public domain every effort was being made not to draw further attention to it. Nonetheless, two journalists (BBC and Reuters freelance) appeared on Ascension without anyone being aware how they had got there. The bulk of journalists who sailed on *Canberra* were effectively locked up on board for six weeks, with the added frustration of watching troops go ashore at Ascension while being unable to do so themselves, and then later hearing reports on the World Service of action that they themselves were unable (and despite their editors' urgings) to report.

This difficult relationship had to be managed in London as well as on the Task Force. Peace-time planning for war had never contemplated the imposition of press censorship but relied on the voluntary co-operation of the press and broadcasting authorities connected with a system of intensive and continuous guidance operated by both Ministers and the Government's press relations machinery. Imposition of censorship would require Emergency Powers. A draft Defence Regulation did exist but in order for it to be legally enforced, an enabling Bill was required to be passed by Parliament. Short of this the only other method available under current legislation would be to issue D notices and enforce them by prosecution under the Official Secrets Act. There was therefore no formal censorship regime in London. Instead editors were briefed on the principles upon which the Ministry expected the media to operate. There was also some awareness of traditional sources of leakage – letters home from the Task Force and informal conversations between the media and senior officers and officials – but little idea what to do about it other than issue firm guidance. Although the Prime Minister expressed anxiety to the Home Secretary about the problem of armchair strategists, there was little grasp of the unavoidability of informed speculation in an open democracy.

On 6 April a South Atlantic Presentation Unit (SAPU) was set up within the Cabinet Office, consisting of a First Secretary from the FCO and a Principal from MoD, and tasked with providing Ministers and relevant Press Officers material for public use to counter what were believed to be false and potentially damaging media assessments of the military situation or diplomatic developments. It was initially to be responsible to Cecil Parkinson but soon Michael Palliser took it over. All Departments were required to inform the unit immediately of any such assessments, even if they were still no more than subjects of discussion or rumour among opinion formers, journalists, and Members of Parliament. To ensure reliable responses Departments were asked to give a high priority to answering queries from the unit. It produced 32 papers on aspects of policy. This worked well initially in helping establish a consistent line but was less suitable as events began to move faster.

The main channels to backbench Conservative Party opinion were established through the Chief Whip's Office and the Ministers' Parliamentary Private Secretaries (John Wilkinson for Nott, Spencer le Marchant for Pym and Ian Gow for Thatcher) who met daily to coordinate strategy. Gow was particularly active in getting key Conservative MPs in to meet with the Prime Minister. Northwood saw Parliament as one of the main sources of leaks. Nott believed that Northwood had little understanding of the need to maintain parliamentary morale. While the Defence Secretary did not see it as his business to brief the press, in the Commons 'I was very concerned to bring into my confidence the defence buffs, as I called them, the defence specialists who felt that they knew what was going on.' Suspicions of how much backbenchers were being told, and how much they then passed on to journalists, was one reason why Northwood became sparing when it came to passing information to MoD.[30]

Although consideration was given to establishing a formal Press Working Party, in the event daily co-ordination of the press line was handled by a less formal Information Group on the Falklands (IGF), which met 53 times between 8 April and 25 June. It was chaired by the Prime Minister's Press Secretary (Bernard Ingham) and normally met at 1000. The daily round of press briefings, which started with Ingham's meeting with lobby correspondents at 1100, dictated the timing but this meant that he could not attend War Cabinet meetings. For the same reason Parkinson could not attend IGF, and so there was no ministerial input. This underlined the basic problem that those talking to the press were not always au fait with the thinking at the highest level of government, while the highest level did not always appreciate the presentational issues and possibilities raised by the items they were addressing.

As the fighting began the burden for the presentation of military news, good, bad and often sparse, fell to MoD, although an Emergency Press Centre was not opened in MoD until 2 May. The conflict began with the Ministry's Public Relations Department lacking a permanent professional head and this situation was not remedied until 18 May 1982, when Neville Taylor took over, who had been appointed before the conflict but was serving out his notice at another ministry. Until that time the Deputy Chief of Public Relations, Ian MacDonald, acted as Chief even though his civil service background was in policy rather than public relations. This lack of background was apparent in his public performances, although their distinctive style did result in a sort of following for MacDonald. He later recalled how he sat down 'for five minutes' during the first days of the conflict to try to establish some sort of information policy.[31] The quality of his performance became a matter of debate, illustrated by the divergent assessments provided by Leach and Nott. According to Leach:

> Unfortunately he had not the prudent advice proffered in the naval parade training manual for those responsible for conducting a Service funeral: 'assuming an aspect cheerful but subdued ...' Weighed down by the solemnity of what he was about to reveal to an expectant public, MacDonald's otherwise handsome face assumed an aspect of stark tragedy bordering on abject horror and his voice was matchingly sepulchral.[32]

Nott acknowledges that the Americans found MacDonald 'strange' and that 'PR smoothies worldwide, including Ingham at No. 10,' wanted a more professional style:

Frank Cooper, in one of his better moves, said that he thought the way around the problem was to send Ian up to Glasgow for a weekend with his mum. In his place we put on parade a number of polished young officers to do the job. Sure enough, as soon as Ian was gone there was a surge of demand for us to reinstate him. Ian Macdonald was borne back to the world's screens in triumph. There he remained to the end.[33]

In addition to his sense of public tastes, Nott's preference may also reflect his desire to have someone in a key position who understood the policy priorities. He later commented: 'Mr. MacDonald was my man.'[34]

3

RESOLUTION 502

The first task was to establish Britain's case internationally. If any practical support was going to be garnered from allies and partners it was first necessary to confirm that the country was justified in its deep sense of grievance. This provided an opportunity for the FCO to redeem itself at a time when it was in some disarray.

The Argentine invasion had come at the exact moment when the Head of the Diplomatic Service was changing, although the retiring Sir Michael Palliser was soon asked to continue to advise the Government for the duration of the crisis. The two Cabinet Ministers from the FCO, Lord Carrington and Sir Humphrey Atkins, both resigned, as did Richard Luce, the Minister who had been dealing with the Falklands. Senior diplomats who had been handling the issue believed themselves to have been discredited, even though they were not sure what else they might have done, given the approach to the issue taken by the Government as a whole. The new Foreign Secretary, Francis Pym, was a figure respected in the Conservative Party and the Commons, and he made a particular effort to keep Parliament informed about the diplomacy. His instincts were in line with the FCO: 'the fact that people should die for an issue of this kind seemed to me to be wrong, unless absolutely no alternative presented itself.'[1] He was however being thrown in at the deep end and was not notably close to the Prime Minister. In her memoirs she described him as 'a good tactician but no strategist.' She had reason later, she confided, to question the common judgement that this was a man who would be 'just right in a crisis.'[2]

Nor was the Prime Minister enamoured of the Foreign Office as an institution. Its standing had not been helped by a paper prepared as the crisis broke by the Defence Department in the FCO, which had been asked about the political costs of military action. These were: a backlash against the 17,000 British subjects in Argentina and possibly formal action, if a state of war was declared; the lack of international support if it appeared that Britain was exacting retribution rather than exercising a legitimate right to self-defence; unreliable allies with their own interests to protect with Argentina; an ambivalent US; a Soviet Union fishing in troubled waters; and then, even if action were successful, the problem of 'sustaining a viable British position in the face of much compounded Argentine antagonism and without severe prejudice to our interests in that country.' In addition, the effort to 'many of our friends ... will also seem disproportionate to their stake involved.' Thatcher later recalled receiving advice 'which summed up the flexibility of principle characteristic of that department.'[3] Nott added in his own memoir:

> It might have been the duty of the Foreign Office to warn of all these obstacles, which were very clear to all of us, but it is the never-ending feebleness of the institution and its demeaning role as a spokesman for foreign interests that rankles so deeply with Tories like myself.[4]

Yet this was to be an unusually testing time for British diplomacy. Few other governments, even amongst the most friendly, were quite sure why Britain was putting in such an effort and accepting such high risks to retake an asset with so little real value, and less sure why they should put themselves out to help. Whatever Britain wanted – from access to facilities en route to the South Atlantic, to information on arms supplied to Argentina, to adherence to economic sanctions – the case had to be compelling and tenaciously argued. Ambassadors and High Commissioners around the world became overnight experts on the dispute and its ramifications. At the same time as the FCO became bound up with the many practical demands of the crisis, it had to keep a close eye on the political implications of every military move being planned at Northwood. It expected to be to the fore in the search for a negotiated outcome to the crisis, but here the Prime Minister was very much in charge, aware that any apparent concession to Argentina was political dynamite at home.

The critical advice on the diplomatic strategy to be adopted if compromises on the core issues of principle were to be avoided, while entreaties for moderation were respected, was provided largely from the two Ambassadors at the most important posts in Washington and New York. The handling of the American Government was going to be crucial in arranging any political settlement and to gain access to military support. Here the Ambassador was Sir Nicholas Henderson, an unusually experienced and independent-minded diplomat, with a personality admirably suited to making a mark in Washington. The most vital diplomatic battles would be fought in and around the UN, where Britain's Ambassador was Sir Anthony Parsons, a shrewd and popular diplomat, on the rebound from a difficult period as Ambassador to Iran during the time of the Islamic revolution. He understood the culture of the UN and the conflicting pressures that would influence the collective response to the unfolding crisis.[5] Henderson and Parsons together had a clear sense of the amount of flexibility it was appropriate and necessary to show as they faced the unusually demanding audiences of the Security Council and the American media.

Sir Anthony helped redeem the FCO in the Prime Minister's eyes by securing a notable victory in the Security Council, pushing through a resolution, which put the onus on Argentina to withdraw. Institutionally Britain had an advantage as a Permanent Member of the Security Council, working from the commanding heights of the organisation and with the capacity to veto any unfavourable resolution. Yet while it had reason to expect solidarity from fellow members of the western alliance and from Commonwealth countries, the UN had been a difficult arena for some time because of the strength of third world opinion with its strong anti-colonial sentiment. The more the Falklands could be presented as a matter of colonialism, which is how it had previously been developed in the General Assembly, the more awkward Britain's position could become. It did not help that it so happened that the two European non-Permanent Members of the Security Council at this time – Spain and Ireland – were the only two with their own territorial disputes with Britain. Moreover, while normally Britain would expect vital support from its closest ally, the US Ambassador to the UN, Jeanne Kirkpatrick, was closely associated with the Reagan Administration's Latin America policy and led the pro-Argentina camp in Washington. Argentina's Ambassador, Eduardo Roca, who had only arrived in late March to take up his position in New York, could take Latin American support for granted, hope for a helpful response from the Soviet bloc by opposing a leading member of NATO, make the most of the UN's devotion to anti-colonialism, while at the same time relying on a sympathetic hearing from Kirkpatrick.

The fact that the new Secretary-General of the UN was from Latin America – the Peruvian Javier Perez de Cuellar – might also have been expected to work against Britain. Perez de Cuellar was fully aware, however, of the need for impartiality and was cautious when it came to launching initiatives that had scant chance of success. As the crisis developed on 31 March he was about to leave for a tour of Europe. He summoned both Roca and Parsons successively to express concern at the rising tension and urge a diplomatic resolution of the dispute, followed by a public appeal for restraint.[6] By this time Roca was already preparing the diplomatic ground for the invasion, circulating a letter to the President of the Security Council, referring to the South Georgia incident and the dispatch of British warships to the area, and complaining about Britain's 'obstinately negative' approach to Argentina's efforts to find a peaceful resolution to the illegal occupation of the Islands:

It is appropriate for me to emphasise in the clearest possible terms that the means employed by the British Government and their unilateral acts have created a situation of serious tension whose continuation could jeopardise the maintenance of international peace and security.

On the afternoon of 1 April the FCO warned Parsons of the 'mounting evidence' that an invasion was imminent and he was instructed to seek immediately an emergency meeting of the Security Council. A draft statement had already been prepared by the UK Mission, which rehearsed the history of the dispute from a UK perspective, examined the events in South Georgia, and noted the latest exchanges in Buenos Aires between British Ambassador Anthony Williams and the Argentine Foreign Minister Nicanor Costa Mendez. To bring home to the Council the seriousness of the situation reference was made to Argentine naval movements, and Argentine press references to these being 'in readiness for operations in the South Atlantic,' leave being cancelled, and C130 transport aircraft departing from their bases.

Parsons contacted the Security Council President, Ambassador Kamanda of Zaire, to ask that the Council meet in emergency session. Kirkpatrick, the previous month's President, was less than pleased, having told Roca that such a move was unlikely, and warned Parsons that she would 'block' any call for such a session. Parsons warned in return that if she did then he would demand a 'procedural vote on whether we actually discussed the problem. She would have to oppose me on the vote, in public, underneath the television cameras and the rest of it.' Kirkpatrick backed down.[7] Parsons was suspicious of Kirkpatrick's 'close and sympathetic relationship with Roca.' He suspected that she had given the Argentine Ambassador to understand that, if Argentina could support the US over Nicaragua, she would return the compliment over the Falklands.

From Kamanda then came a second appeal to the two parties. He expressed concern and urged the two to 'exercise the utmost restraint at this time and in particular to refrain from the use or threat of force in the region and to continue the search for a diplomatic solution.' Parsons accepted this language in full. By the end of 1 April, Parsons' view was that as much as possible had been extracted from the Council in one day and that 'the sympathy of the majority of the Council is undoubtedly with us and the Argentines are on the wrong foot.' Assuming that an invasion was imminent Parsons now sought from London not only discretion to make an immediate call to the Council and work for an early resolution, but also to be allowed the 'maximum latitude' in the drafting of this resolution. His problem was to prepare London for language that might not fully reflect the strength of public and parliamentary opinion. Careful drafting would be needed to secure the necessary nine out of fifteen possible votes, which would be required for a positive result or force the Russians to veto.[8] He had in mind a resolution that would call for an immediate cessation of hostilities and immediate withdrawal of all Argentine forces. The 'traffic would bear,' he warned, only so much in terms of 'deploring, condemning and so on.' The standard references to Charter principles and the need to resume peaceful negotiations would have to be included. Carrington gave him the discretion he needed. The next day the invasion took place.

When Resolution 502 was passed on 3 April it took the following form:

> The Security Council, recalling the statement made by the President of the Security Council at the 2345th meeting of the Security Council on the 1 April 1982 calling on the Governments of Argentina and the United Kingdom of Great Britain and Northern Ireland to refrain from the use or threat of force in the region of the Falkland Islands (Islas Malvinas),
> Deeply disturbed at reports of an invasion on 2 April 1982 by armed forces of Argentina,
> Determining that there exists a breach of the peace in the region of the Falkland Islands (Islas Malvinas),
>
> 1. Demands an immediate cessation of hostilities;
> 2. Demands an immediate withdrawal of all Argentine forces from the Falkland Islands (Islas Malvinas);
> 3. Calls on the Governments of Argentina and the United Kingdom to seek a diplomatic solution to their differences and to respect fully the purposes and principles of the Charter of the United Nations.

The strategy behind the resolution was straightforward. It put Argentina in the dock by drawing attention to its failure to respond to the appeal by the President of the Security Council for restraint and linked the existence of the breach of the peace with the Argentine invasion. It did not, however, go so far as to denounce Argentina as an aggressor. This would have implied an expectation of a collective response, in the form of economic sanctions if not military action. This could not have been extracted from the Council at that time. The objective was therefore more modest: to put the onus on Argentina to withdraw its forces after the cessation of the current hostilities but then respond to inevitable Security Council concerns by suggesting a peaceful, negotiated route out of the dispute.

The text of the resolution was not very different from Parsons' first draft. As will be discussed below, for tactical reasons, 'Islas Malvinas' was introduced after the Falkland Islands. It was recognised that the first demand could be problematic. The original version, drafted before the actual invasion, referred to 'cessation of operations', which could include the eventual British response to the invasion, and so was replaced by the more definite 'cessation of hostilities' once news came that the invasion was actually underway. A later Argentine attempt to turn this resolution round against Britain depended on separating this first operative paragraph from the second, which called for an Argentine withdrawal.

With a resolution drafted to put the maximum pressure on Argentina consistent with the political realities of the Security Council, Parsons' tactics depended on quick movement. He persuaded Kamanda to allow him to introduce the resolution at a meeting called for another purpose at 1030 New York time on 2 April. As it began London – where it was now the middle of the afternoon – flashed Parsons, informing him he should 'go ahead' in the Security Council on the basis that the Falklands had been invaded. In his speech the Ambassador observed, to dramatic effect, that: 'As we sit here, a massive Argentine invasion of the Falkland Islands is taking place.' He described this as:

> an attempt to impose by force a foreign and unwanted control over one thousand nine hundred peaceful agricultural people who have chosen in free and fair elections to maintain their links with Britain and the British way of life.

Roca's reply stressed the British failure to address the issue of sovereignty of the Islands, which had nothing to do with the wishes of the inhabitants. This sovereignty had been taken unjustly from Argentina but had now been recovered. Roca reported that in this recovery there had been no deaths among the civilian population, that an Argentine Governor had been appointed and that Argentine administration had been established throughout the Falkland Islands. The Security Council should be pleased that a dispute, which had been a constant threat to peace and security in the region, had now been resolved. The Argentine delegation, however, had been given no advance warning of the invasion and were slow off the mark in mobilising support, relying largely on Cuba and Panama to appeal on their behalf to the UN's substantial anti-colonial bloc.

After the initial speeches and the introduction of the draft resolution Parsons found that he was unable to get it carried that day. The Soviet delegation was unhappy that there had been no prior consultations on the issue. A number of delegations were unsure how to vote and needed to get back to their capitals for instructions. There were other pressing issues – on Nicaragua and Israel – that others wanted to discuss. Nicanor Costa Mendez, the Argentine Foreign Minister, was on his way to New York and would not arrive until the next day. For all these reasons Parsons decided to bow to the inevitable and agree on the resumption of the debate that evening. He insisted that there must be a vote the next day.

Parsons argued against a British minister rushing out to New York simply because Costa Mendez was coming. He had thought that there might be a case for a high-profile presentation on the legal and historical aspects of the dispute, but now the situation was becoming more fluid and messy. The Russians, he reported, were suggesting that, as there was a fait accompli, there was no need to hurry. Others saw Britain doing no more than looking for a face-saving resolution. If these sentiments led to delay then pressure would grow for Britain to water down the resolution to meet Argentine concerns. So sympathy was beginning to ebb, and he was by no means sure of getting the necessary nine votes. It was better, he thought, that a rebuff be inflicted upon an Ambassador than a Minister.

The possible outcomes he considered began with the most positive, at least nine votes in favour and no Soviet veto, and then got steadily worse, taking in a Soviet veto, then less than nine votes and then not even being able to bring the resolution to a vote as the result of the loss of a procedural motion. He saw little to choose between the third and fourth of these outcomes. Given the state of opinion in Britain he judged that it was better to refuse to accept any softening amendments and press for a vote.[9] Failing would still be better than acquiescing in a heavily watered down draft that might not reach a vote for another two to three days. At worst he might have to withdraw if he was not getting any support, even from Britain's friends. At any rate a fall-back position had to be prepared, accepting that there was no useful action to be taken in the UN, and to re-iterate, in the words of Sir Humphrey Atkins' statement on the Friday to the Commons, that Britain would take:

> appropriate military and diplomatic measures to sustain our rights under diplomatic law and in accordance with the provisions of the UN Charter.

Even if the current round went well, he was coming to the view that the UN might best be avoided in the future. He feared that 'the Argentines will get us embedded in the substance of sovereignty dispute where they have the votes and we do not'. Carrington agreed that if the effort was to fail, then it was 'better to fail on a good text,' although he was reluctant to rule out future recourse to the UN.

Proceedings on other issues went on until quite late in the evening of 2 April. When debate on the Falklands resumed France, Ireland, Australia, Canada and New Zealand all spoke in favour of the draft resolution. Further discussion was then postponed until the next morning, when Costa Mendez would arrive from Argentina. Now was the time for intense lobbying to secure the votes. Not all those inclined to vote in favour could be taken for granted. France and the US would vote with Britain, as probably would Ireland, Jordan, and Uganda. France was asked to encourage Zaire and Togo to vote the right way, while the US also worked on Zaire as well as Japan. Into the camp of potential opponents or abstainers were put the Soviet Union, Poland, and China because of general opposition to Britain, Spain because of its close connections with Argentina and its own quarrel over Gibraltar, and Panama and Guyana as Latin Americans. The British Embassy in Madrid applied pressure for a positive vote, warning about the implications of Argentina's use of force, while it was soon recognised that Guyana was by no means a lost cause, for its own dispute with Venezuela gave it a stake in the proposition that these matters should never be resolved by force.

At the start of the debate on 3 April, Costa Mendez spoke, in more careful and moderate terms than had Roca the previous day. He described the Falklands as a classic colonial problem, which had now been terminated. The rights and way of life of the islanders would be respected and troops would be used only as strictly necessary. In the ensuing debate, by and large the Latin Americans supported the Argentine case, Jordan (as it later turned out, without instructions) opposed Argentina as did Japan in cautious terms and the United States in a brief statement. Kirkpatrick absented herself from the UN during the course of the debate, while, according to Parsons' sources, her deputy watered down the text of the statement supporting Britain that the State Department had instructed him to deliver. Britain's most strident opponent on the Security Council was Panama. Foreign Minister Illueca, whose statement was described by Parsons as 'long and vicious,' introduced his own draft resolution which went through all past UN and non-aligned resolutions on the topic and called upon Britain 'to cease its hostile conduct, refrain from any threat or use of force and co-operate ... in the decolonization of the ... islands.' Illueca proposed suspending the meeting so that a draft could be prepared in all working languages for tabling. He lost the vote with seven against, three for and four abstaining. Later Illueca attempted to deprive Britain of its vote under Article 27 (3). This move had been anticipated, and could be dealt with because, although the resolution was being submitted under Chapter 7 (Article 40) no sanctions were being proposed and therefore 27 (3) did not apply. This time even Spain supported Britain.

At this point the British learned that Ambassador Nuseibeh of Jordan had been told by Amman to abstain. Time was needed to reverse this instruction, and to gain it Parsons sought an adjournment that the Latin Americans could not oppose. With a straight face he explained that time was needed to reprint the resolution correctly with the addition of 'Islas Malvinas' after the Falklands. This allowed the Prime Minister to contact King Hussein to get Jordan's vote moved from abstention to support. The conversation was extremely short. The Prime Minister explained the line-up at the Security Council and how Jordan's vote would make a difference. The King said he would be in touch right away, and Mrs Thatcher expressed gratitude to a 'very kind and a wonderful ally.'[10] While this was going on it was learned that, with French help, Zaire and Togo were both now in favour. In the resumed debate, these countries indicated that while they supported Argentina's case they strongly deplored the use of force and the rejection of the President's appeal. This was the basic thrust of the remarks from Ambassador Dorr of Ireland. Then Ambassador Troyanovsky of the Soviet Union made a standard anti-colonialist speech, apparently preparing the ground for a veto.

Then came the vote – without a Soviet veto. The Soviet Ambassador apparently justified his abstention to Costa Mendez by reference to problems in consulting Moscow at that time,[11] but the real reason was probably a sense that third world countries were not overwhelmingly with Argentina. When the vote came he leaned over and congratulated Parsons, suggesting (according to an aide who overheard) that he 'should get the garter'. Only Panama voted against. The three communist states and Spain abstained. Illueca spoke again in heated tones but did not insist on a vote on his resolution. Later he attempted, unsuccessfully, to extract from Parsons a promise that Britain would not use force. Costa Mendez spoke again to maintain Argentina's rights and express disappointment without explicitly rejecting the resolution. Parsons reminded him of Argentina's obligations under Article 25 to carry out the decisions of the Security Council. Given his pessimism of the previous evening Parsons was delighted – he 'could not have got a better result.' He still sounded a clear note of caution back to the FCO:

It became only too clear that, as I have consistently reported, we have virtually no support on the substance of the problem. We must bear this closely in mind for the future in the UN context.

4

THE TASK FORCE

The successful passage of Resolution 502 was an unexpected diplomatic triumph but there was no optimism that it might lead to an Argentine withdrawal. It was assumed from the start that diplomacy and military pressure were not alternatives but complementary. Until Buenos Aires appreciated that it could not hold onto the Falklands in the face of superior force it was unlikely to contemplate abandoning the long-coveted Malvinas. It was necessary at all times to demonstrate that Britain was offering Argentina a diplomatic way out, largely for international benefit, but without a display of coercive force Argentina would not accept the offer. The second achievement of the first days of the crisis, after 502, was to generate an immediate and conspicuous military response.

Argentina had not been expecting such a response, and was obliged to come to terms with the prospect of a prolonged conflict instead of its intended *coup de main*. Speed was important because of the anticipated deterioration in conditions in the South Atlantic as its winter drew closer. The speed achieved astonished even those who depended upon the First Sea Lord's promises being met. The mobilisation was immediate and ungrudging. Out came the army, including the territorials, to get equipment and stores to the dockyards. Visiting Portsmouth on the Monday, Nott later described as one of his 'most poignant memories' the 'dignity and restraint' with which dockyard workers greeted him despite the fact that under his defence review many would be put out of work.[1] At the same time, assembling a Task Force at speed had its costs. The Task Force sailed without an agreed operational plan.

On 3 April, the Navy Department at the MoD signalled to Fieldhouse the ships to be nominated for Operation CORPORATE. The ships were to be sailed 'as soon as they are fully prepared for the operation' and Task Force (TF 317) was, as laid out in CINCFLEET's initial directive, 'to proceed for such operations in the South Atlantic as may be ordered'. There was no time to consider, except in the broadest terms, what might be done on arrival in the South Atlantic. There was a widespread hope that there would be no need to complete the journey, as the search for a negotiated settlement was

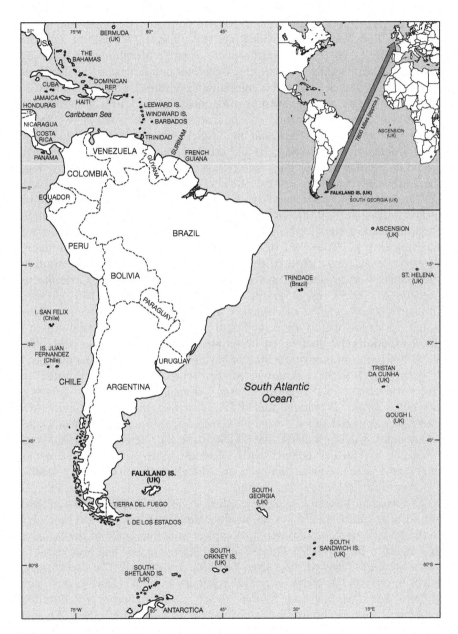

Map 4 The Logistics effort

launched at the same time. Should this search fail it was presumed that somehow the Argentine garrison on the Falkland Islands would have to be kept isolated and denied effective air and sea support, and that at some point an amphibious landing might have to be mounted. This presumption led to the Task Force being divided into two. First to go would be a carrier battle group led by *Hermes* and *Invincible*, capable of enforcing a blockade and coping with whatever forces the Argentines could muster (the details of which were still unclear). Later an amphibious landing force would follow.

Prior to the Argentine invasion some measures had already been taken with a view to reinforcing the Falklands, notably the despatch of two SSNs, HMS *Spartan* and HMS *Splendid* on 1 April. These were later followed by HMS *Conqueror*. On 31 March it had become apparent that these measures would be pointless unless they were part of a full Task Force. At this stage the force was comprised of two carriers, one Landing Platform (Dock) (LPD), at least four destroyers/frigates and appropriate support. It was to be tasked to transport all three RM commando battalions and the Commando Brigade Headquarters to the South Atlantic. The Army were to provide two Landing Ship Logistics (LSLs). This response to the crisis was ineffectual in deterrent terms, but it ensured that there was now sufficient momentum in the mobilisation process to provide the visible effort that the Government needed. At 0227Z on 2 April, CINCFLEET warned HMS *Hermes*, *Invincible*, *Fearless*, *Alacrity*, *Antelope* and RFA *Resource* to come to four hours' notice for operations in the South Atlantic. At 0240Z Woodward got his instructions. He had sailed his group of ships on exercise SPRING-TRAIN from Gibraltar on 29 March, having been warned that he may need to go south. Now he was instructed 'to proceed at economical speed' to Ascension Island with HMS *Antrim, Glamorgan, Glasgow, Coventry, Brilliant, Arrow, Plymouth,* and RFA *Appleleaf* and *Tidespring*. HMS *Sheffield* was also detailed for the Falklands operation, provided Woodward was content with her material state. Fieldhouse considered it 'vital that your force has no further contact with Gibraltar since for political reasons impression is to be given that you are already well on your way south'. Woodward was told to move covertly.

The remaining surface ships were either in need of repair or ill-equipped and so, after transferring stores, ammunition and key equipment and personnel to the Task Force ships, they were to complete what they could of the exercises and return to Britain. HMS *Broadsword* and *Yarmouth* who had been about to go to the Gulf followed them from Gibraltar on 8 April. The two carriers, HMS *Hermes* and *Invincible,* were at Portsmouth with main leave parties away and their Sea Harriers ashore. *Hermes*, as well as the LPD *Fearless*, had started a maintenance period but this was not too far advanced. Both the LPDs had only recently been reprieved from disposal as proposed under the 1981 Defence Review. The other LPD, HMS *Intrepid,* was not quite available, and it would be challenging to get it ready to sail before 14 April. In addition to *Fearless*, the amphibious lift was to be provided by five LSLs, including *Sir Galahad, Sir Geraint, Sir Lancelot,* and *Sir Percivale,* plus *Sir Tristram,* then in Belize, which would sail directly for Ascension Island. RFA *Stromness,* at Portsmouth having been stripped of sensitive facilities prior to being laid up and then disposed of in some way, was now given the order to reactivate and be at readiness to deploy by 6 April. It was required to carry 350 Royal Marines and 7,500 man months of provisions.

Not only ships but also personnel had to be assembled in a hurry. In the early hours of 2 April, 3 Commando Brigade RM was brought to 72 hours' notice to move. The Brigade was kept permanently at seven days' notice to move in emergency, but the few days' warning were of little help in reducing notice, since no overt action could be taken nor information be passed on. Units were widely spread. 40 Commando was completing personal weapon training near Liverpool; 42 Commando was on leave having just returned from Norway; 45 Commando in Scotland was about to go on leave; with Y Company in Hong Kong en route from Brunei. Many of the key staff officers of the Brigade Headquarters, together with most of the staff of COMAW, were at a NATO planning meeting in Denmark. The Commando Logistics Regiment was due to go on leave on 3 April. At 0400 on 2 April its Commanding Officer, Colonel I J Hellberg, heard that 3 Commando Brigade was to be sent to the Falklands and within three hours the first trucks were on their way to collect ammunition. Because British Rail was unable to reposition their rolling stock, all the war maintenance reserve (WMR) stocks from the major depots had to be moved by road. By 12 noon on 5 April most stocks had been loaded. The Brigade's WMR consisted of 30 days' stocks of Combat Supplies at Limited War rates with 60 days' stocks of technical and general stores. A quick decision was taken to supplement the Brigade's inadequate air defence capability with a Royal Artillery Rapier Battery and also to add two troops of armoured reconnaissance vehicles (four each of Scimitar and Scorpion plus a Samson recovery vehicle) from the Blues and Royals. Taken together the enhanced 3 Commando Brigade would total some 3,500 men with large quantities of weapons, stores, equipment and vehicles.

On 3 April, the Third Battalion of the Parachute Regiment (3 Para) was added. This had important consequences. *Hermes* had been initially tasked, with *Invincible,* in an anti-submarine role and ordered to 'embark the maximum number of Sea Harrier and Anti-Submarine Warfare (ASW) Sea King aircraft commensurate with air operations'. Then, during the morning of 2 April, the requirement was changed so that helicopters able to land troops and 800 marines could be accommodated. The decision to take 3 Para confirmed what was already becoming apparent: the RN would not be able to carry the whole amphibious force. Some 2,000 troops and most of the vehicles and equipment would have to be sent in merchant ships. So *Hermes* was confirmed again in the anti-submarine role, with nine Sea Kings

Mk5 (826 Squadron), although some operational flexibility was retained by embarking 120 Marines together with nine troop-carrying Sea King Mk4 (846 Squadron). *Invincible* took eleven Sea Kings Mk5 (820 Squadron). After searching for all available Sea Harriers and pilots, including some involved in training and trials and in the reserve, sufficient were found for twelve aircraft (800 Squadron) to travel with *Hermes* and eight (801 Squadron) with *Invincible*. Meanwhile, the current dispositions of Sidewinder air-to-air missiles read *Hermes* (30), *Invincible* (40) and RFA *Resource* (33). The Navy urgently requested from the US a further 70 for *Hermes* and 30 for *Invincible*, asking that if possible these should be of the improved AIM-9L version (the UK's current equipment was of the older AIM-9G variant). The Captain aboard *Hermes* felt that in assessing the likely air threat: 'urgent procurement of these missiles with their significantly greater capability is highly desirable'.

The lack of clear operational directives aggravated those problems that resulted simply from haste. Commodore Clapp complained on 7 April that he had not had the opportunity to assess a concept of operations in any depth. He explained that: 'Because the speed of mounting, type of STUFT (Ships Taken up from Trade) allocated and lack of a clear amphibious objective has meant we have basically managed to squeeze what we considered essential into the given space'. He worried about the re-loading problem, which could occur 'once we get enough hard intelligence to allow C-in-C and MoD to state clear objective'. On 9 April, he discussed with Fieldhouse the need to carry out military training at Ascension Island. Clapp also reiterated by signal that because of the hurried loading there would be considerable 'shuffling' of personnel/stores during the stay at Ascension. The lack of clarity about what would be the priority items for offloading led to arbitrariness to the initial loading. The next day it was agreed that once ashore the landing force would best be supported directly from ships using helicopters. At the time it was assumed that it would be safe to do so, on the grounds that without air and sea superiority the landing would not be authorised in the first place. This concept required two LSLs (*Sir Galahad* and *Sir Percivale*) each loaded with the requisite stocks. To get the correct split of stocks, so that the Brigade would not be dependent upon the survival of a particular LSL, as well as ensuring that stocks could be unloaded according to tactical priorities, there had to be a major ship restow in Ascension Island. So while the political logic for getting the carrier task group on its way was unassailable, whether this need have been carried through to the amphibious force is more debatable. Major General Moore later took the view that the landing force could have sailed 'better briefed and loaded tactically up to two weeks later and still have achieved the landing on 21 May, having avoided the wasted effort entailed in the complete re-stow at Ascension'.

There were no contingency plans in existence for the Falkland Islands or indeed for anywhere else outside the NATO area to support any deployment much larger than a brigade, and there was neither the time nor the hard information to form detailed plans now. The nearest thing to the current activity for which detailed plans existed, a major deployment to north Norway, was the best available guide on what to take and how much, so long as allowances were then made for an extra 7,000 miles. What was clear was that there was no risk of taking excessive supplies – leading to the principle that all available stowage space must be used. The Falklands was known to lack roads so few vehicles were taken. For the most part only tracked or very lightly loaded four-wheel drive vehicles could move across country. Helicopters, by contrast, would be at a premium, both for moving men and equipment from shipping standing offshore and then taking them forward on land.

The process was hectic and often chaotic. There were regular changes of orders, uncertainties over available space, manning arrangements and communications fits. For most of the first week of April supplies were being moved by road, with the Royal Corps of Transport having to bring in Territorial Army vehicles and drivers, and charter about 100 40ft flat-bed trucks. Some 39,108 tons of freight were moved by road. Rail was also important, but problems were encountered in getting vital equipment and stores to the loading areas, often dependent on the availability of appropriate British Rail rolling stock. By the second week 44 special trains had been hired. Key items had to be found from around the country and so arrived piecemeal.

Of the 4,350 men to be carried, service transport could accommodate all but 1,700 men, 150 tons of stores and some 60 vehicles. By 3 April the P&O cruise liner SS *Canberra* had been identified as a ship that could embark approximately 1,400 Royal Marines and 600 Paras while the P&O ferry MV *Norsea* could take the Paras' vehicles and equipment. After further investigation the P&O roll on/roll off ferry *Elk* was chosen instead of *Norsea*. It took 100 vehicles, 2,000 tons of ammunition, and hundreds of tons of stores. The Navy Department explained to CINCFLEET that:

> it is not intended that either ship should be placed unnecessarily at risk on entering a hostile environment. The men will it is planned be transferred to RN ships for assault operations on the Falklands and the equipment on *Elk* will not be landed until safe to do so.[2]

Plans were still being laid with the optimum – rather than the most likely – operational environment in mind.

While the merchant tankers could be taken up on charter, for the P&O ships insurance issues arose because of the possible need to carry troops and military equipment right into the combat area. For this reason, and also to avoid claims for breach of existing contracts, P&O and some other companies insisted on requisition. There was some political sensitivity about this, as it required an Order in Council, for the first time since Suez, and could be presented as a conspicuous demonstration of the inability of the RN to carry British troops. On the other hand the blue ensign would be flown under the command of a captain in the RN Reserve and as a consequence of well-established emergency plans. Nott wanted to get the order signed 'while the nation and Parliament is still in a highly bellicose mood.' This was done on the evening of 4 April. Discussions with the companies and unions established appropriate bonus rates, conditions of service and disciplinary regimes for the merchant seamen in STUFT. Non-British seamen would not be employed, so the *Canberra* was obliged to land some 400 Asian crew members. While the master retained responsibility for the safety of his ship, a senior naval officer and a naval party were appointed to each, responsible through the naval chain of command for her employment.

As *Canberra* steamed home with cruise passengers on board, she was inspected to see if she would serve as a troopship and then hospital ship, while preparations began to turn her sundeck and swimming pool areas into two helicopter flight decks. Although not requisitioned until 10 April, the P&O ship *Uganda* (which normally took school children on educational cruises) was chosen to serve as a hospital ship. By the time that it sailed on 19 April, it had acquired a helicopter platform, a refuelling point and 83 naval medical staff. Small naval survey vessels, *Hecla*, *Herald* and *Hydra*, would serve as ambulance ships.

In addition to troop carrying, fuel supplies were the other reason for acquiring STUFT. RFA *Appleleaf* and *Tidespring* were tankers with the SPRINGTRAIN contingent; while RFA *Pearleaf* and *Olmeda* were topped up to accompany the ships leaving Britain. RFA *Blue Rover*, returning from SPRINGTRAIN, was ordered to Portsmouth to load aviation fuel and petrol for vehicles. RFA *Brambleleaf* in the Indian Ocean was released on 3 April from her assignment in the Persian Gulf, and ordered to the South Atlantic via the Cape of Good Hope. Fieldhouse had also been encouraged by the news that the Chileans had offered to make RFA *Tidepool* available for the Task Force. *Tidepool* had been sold to Chile, and on 2 April was off Peru heading south, when the Chileans were asked if she could be promptly returned. CINCFLEET requested that this 'be pursued with the utmost vigour'. The additional tanker would give the Task Group Commander 'greater flexibility of operations and endurance'. The next day the Chileans made *Tidepool* available. The ship was turned round and ordered back through the Panama Canal, to load and prepare at Curacao before joining the Task Force at Ascension. Over such long distances, more tankers would inevitably be needed. Two British Petroleum tankers, *British Esk* and *British Tamar,* were the first STUFT. They were already fitted with equipment to act as escort oilers so they were ready for their new role in a day. A third, *British Tay*, was soon added.

As the ships were made ready, so they sailed, singly and in groups. The

SSNs, having received their orders before the invasion, were the first to go. On 3 April the carrier group and the amphibious ships were ordered to gather before heading south. On the morning of 5 April HMS *Hermes* and *Invincible* and RFA *Olmeda* sailed from Portsmouth, waved off by vast crowds ashore. Earlier HMS *Alacrity* and *Antelope* had sailed quietly from Devonport to join the carriers. Even as they sailed from Britain, aircraft and stores continued to be embarked.

At 14 knots they would not arrive at Ascension Island until 17 April, especially as *Invincible* soon experienced a mechanical failure. There they would meet up with Woodward's group. He had intended to arrive by 10 April, but as he would have to wait for the carriers his group now proceeded at a more leisurely pace. The Government, however, wanted ships as far south as possible as early as possible, and the carrier group was ordered to make haste, as soon as the *Invincible* defect permitted, to get to Ascension by 15 April.

Although unable to meet the 5 April target, the amphibious group still managed to sail early with *Fearless*, four LSLs, RFA *Pearleaf* and *Stromness* setting off from Portsmouth on the evening of 7 April. *Resource*, which had anchored off Portland to embark a large quantity of last minute stores by helicopter, set out to overhaul the *Fearless* group a day's steaming ahead. The *Elk* sailed on 9 April after a hectic two days in Southampton. That evening it was followed by *Canberra*, with much excitement ashore and Vosper Thorneycroft personnel still working on her forward flight deck.

Sustaining the Task Force

Fieldhouse had in mind from the start a 90 days campaign, with the weather, wear and tear and declining public support all likely to be limiting factors. There could be no question of a minimum force. He needed to get out the maximum possible. He told the officer getting ships from trade that 'If you think you need four, order eight'. As soon as the ships set sail consideration was given to what might need to follow. A fourth SSN was soon sent. It was assumed that extra escorts would be needed and early preparations were made to put together the group that was eventually led by the Type 82 Destroyer, HMS *Bristol*, which left Portsmouth on 10 May with the Type 21 frigates, *Active* and *Avenger*, along with the Leander frigates, *Andromeda*, *Minerva* and *Penelope*, and was soon joined by the Type 42 HMS *Cardiff*. They eventually joined the Task Force on 26 May and were able to provide some relief to what was by then a very battered fleet.

The first tentative consideration of the Argentine mining threat made the case for a Mine Counter-Measures (MCM) force, which would require the MCM support ship HMS *Abdiel*, one RFA, five Hunt or Ton Class Mine Counter-Measure Vessels (MCMVs), and five Extra Deep Armed Team Sweep (EDATS) fitted trawlers as auxiliary minesweepers (MSAs). Argentine mine stocks were known to be well maintained but there was no intelligence to suggest that mines had yet been laid. However, a high-localised threat could exist if the choice of landing beach were correctly anticipated by the Argentines. Clapp's concerns about mines led him to acquire three Fleet Clearance Diving Teams (FCDT) who later played an invaluable role in bomb disposal.

Other options were examined. Would it be possible to get another carrier to the South Atlantic if needed? HMS *Illustrious* was some way from completion on Tyneside while HMS *Bulwark* was at Portsmouth awaiting disposal. What about the three ships built for the Shah of Iran's Navy but not delivered after he had been overthrown? These had potential value for the amphibious operation but it was diplomatically too complicated to take over Iranian assets. One of the early departures, in fact the first Task Force ship to leave Britain, was a rescue tug, Royal Maritime Auxiliary Service (RMAS) *Typhoon,* and it was decided that three more were needed, so the *Salvageman, Irishman* and *Yorkshireman* of the United Towing Company were selected and requisitioned.

There was also the issue of casualties, a problem that was logistical as well as being highly political. If losses were sustained, and the Government expected the Task Force to continue with its mission, then not only would casualties have to be evacuated but also replacements would have to be sent. The most hazardous time would be during the initial assault of a landing force and then the establishment of a beachhead. Casualties could be as high as 20 per cent of the landing force over the first seven days of operation, or a total of over 900 men. Of this number about three quarters would need to be evacuated: the others either killed or able to return to their units, giving an evacuation requirement averaging 100 per day, with about 40 of this number put as the more severe, priority one and two cases. After seven days the casualty rates would be expected to reduce. The Royal Marines earmarked 500 men from their training organisation as battle casualty replacements. A provisional plan was agreed to fly 171 Royal Marines to Ascension on 11 May and use an RFA to reach the Falklands about 24 May. Others could be held in Britain until needed. Leach argued that all the services should make similar preparations once the main Task Force had sailed from Ascension Island. The Chiefs agreed this on 18 April.

The surge of activity and the need to prepare for a long haul created pressure on manpower, but no emergency measures, such as recalling reservists, seemed necessary initially. Training was curtailed, leave restricted, and service extended. The initial planning assumptions were that forces would have to be sustained for three months, and that there would be military action, with losses of men and equipment. Later this was raised to six months. Even with local superiority there could be up to 25 per cent attrition of ships and aircraft. This required consideration of replacement ships, the loading of dockyards, the eventual need for extra troops, heavy demands on fuel, rations and ammunition, where it might be necessary to order extra stocks in anticipation or re-open production lines. If necessary, extra helicopters could be found. Extra Sea Harriers would require bringing forward reserve aircraft and re-deploying aircrew, although the Royal Air Force's Harrier GR3 squadrons provided an obvious source of extra aircraft. The container ship *Atlantic Conveyor* after four days' work could hold 15 Harriers, with a fly on/fly off capability. Extra effort was put into bringing forward the delivery of weapons already on order, such as Sub Harpoon, Sidewinder AIM9L and Sea Skua.

The sudden emergency in the South Atlantic did not bring to an end all other commitments. The ships participating in operation ARMILLA in the Persian Gulf were told that they would not be relieved and had to accept a further patrol. There was a risk that Guatemala might decide to make an opportunistic move against Belize and so HMS *Exeter* stayed on station in the West Indies and the Chiefs of Staff recommended that the planned withdrawal of British forces from Belize should be postponed for at least three months. A significant reduction in the United Kingdom's maritime and air assets committed to NATO was unavoidable, including almost half of Britain's ship declarations, all Sea Harriers and one third of Britain's maritime helicopters. Naval war reserve fuel stocks would be reduced by one third in the first 20 days and one half of the afloat war reserve back stock of ammunition was going 'out of area.' There could be permanent shortfalls in ammunition stocks and deficiencies in many specialist areas. It was assumed that British forces would not be considered so critical to the balance of power that the Warsaw Pact would suddenly see an attractive opportunity for aggression.

A further factor to be taken into account was the position of Gibraltar, in dispute with Spain, a country well disposed towards the Argentine case. Because of a possible threat from Argentine sympathisers in Spain against Gibraltar, a frigate was assigned to a guardship role. Certain precautionary and low-key measures were taken in response to a request from the Governor, including additional radar and air defence capability, with a plan for further reinforcement if necessary. By and large intelligence assessments were relaxed about the risk of any Spanish action against Gibraltar, while unauthorised small-scale action by individual elements of the Spanish Armed Forces was not thought to represent a serious military threat.[3] Routine movements of ships and aircraft were used to avoid attracting undue publicity that could inflame Spanish nationalist sentiment and make it harder to make political progress on the wider Gibraltar issue.

The nuclear complication

Brilliant and *Broadsword* joined the Task Force each carrying two MC (600) nuclear depth charges, suitable for delivery by Lynx and Wasp helicopters. The two carriers were already carrying similar weapons. Also at sea were training rounds (which though empty carcasses appeared as accurate replicas of the live rounds, and were intended for training in ground and flight handling and loading), and surveillance rounds, which were also inert and used to monitor the wear and tear on the weapons. These inert rounds were also held on three destroyers and three RFAs.

Even taking nuclear weapons into the South Atlantic could appear as a violation of the Treaty of Tlatelolco (1967), which had established Latin America and surrounding waters (including the Falkland Islands and the Dependencies) as a nuclear weapon free zone. Strictly speaking there could be no violation because not all states had signed and ratified the Treaty, while extra-continental states with responsibilities for territories within the intended zone of application were required to sign and ratify Additional Protocol I, with nuclear weapon states also acceding to an Additional Protocol II. Argentina had signed the Treaty in 1967 and while it had publicly announced its intention to ratify it had not yet done so. The United Kingdom had signed both protocols in 1967 and ratified them in 1969. This meant that had the Treaty been in force, the presence of nuclear weapons or warheads or nuclear materials which were not for peaceful purposes and under International Atomic Energy Agency (IAEA) safeguards, within the Falklands, their Dependencies, surrounding waters and air space, was prohibited, but the prohibition did not apply to UK nuclear weapons elsewhere in the South Atlantic, including in Argentine territorial waters. The presence of a nuclear-powered warship in Falkland Islands territorial waters would not contravene the Treaty as it was so clearly unrelated to nuclear weapons.[4]

A further factor was that Britain had issued a Negative Security Assurance in June 1978, in connection with the United Nations' Special Session on Disarmament, which applied to non-nuclear weapon states. The assurance involved an undertaking 'not to use nuclear weapons against such states *except* in the case of attack on the UK, its dependent territories, its armed forces or its allies by such a state in association or alliance with a nuclear weapons state.' But to be considered a non-nuclear weapons state, Argentina would have had to have ratified either the nuclear non-proliferation treaty or the treaty of Tlatelolco and it had done neither, so in principle it was *not* protected by the Negative Security Assurance, and nuclear weapons could be used (subject to provisions of the law of armed conflict regarding proportionality, discrimination etc.) against Argentine vessels or territory *provided* the weapons used were not in the Falklands or territorial waters.[5]

After the conflict there were suggestions that the nuclear option had been seriously considered. It was claimed in one report that it was raised in early internal studies, with one source quoted as saying that: 'Certainly the nuclear option was one of the options studied on 2 April ... part of the work done that day involved examining the possibility of retargeting Polaris against Argentina.'[6] When this report was first made public an official investigation could find no trace of such study. It probably was the case that nuclear use appeared in a very early draft of the main options paper, only to be taken out almost immediately. I have found no references to any consideration of nuclear employment. This was never taken seriously as a realistic possibility.[7] Nor is there any archival evidence to support a story that also appeared in the *New Statesman* that an SSBN (Polaris ballistic missile-carrying submarine) went as far south as Ascension Island in order to threaten or have a demonstrative nuclear attack against Cordoba in northern Argentina in the event of the loss of a major capital ship. The source was a senior Conservative backbench MP in conversation with Labour MP, Tam Dalyell, so this may just have been a mischievous test of the latter's gullibility. It was claimed that the details of the deployment 'were given in a series of highly classified telegrams sent to the British Embassy in Washington'. I have found no such telegrams.[8]

While there was never any thought of strategic nuclear use the possibility of tactical nuclear use was less readily dismissed. Lewin had not asked for nuclear depth charges, and had no plans to use them, but he was inclined to take them to the South Atlantic, just in case. The scenario he had in mind involved Russian submarines getting involved on the Argentine side. This scenario did not in itself calm those MoD civilians aware of the issue. As they began to press for urgent action to get the weapons away from the Task Force this began to develop, at least in the minds of some Admirals, as a test case as to whether their operational judgement was to be overruled. Thus while the main influences on decision-making were essentially logistical and political, an admittedly far-fetched operational possibility was also in play.

The politicians were unimpressed by these possibilities and shared their officials' anxiety about the conflict developing any nuclear connections. Indeed they had not appreciated the routine nature of nuclear deployments at sea and as a result of this experience revisited the matter after the war. They did not want to take nuclear weapons to the South Atlantic and how to prevent this was one of the issues to confront the War Cabinet when it met for the first time on 7 April. The immediate reaction was that some way must be found to offload them before they were involved in any combat, but without attracting any publicity. If the issue was raised in Parliament, the whereabouts of the depth charges was to be kept a secret but there would be an unequivocal affirmation that nuclear weapons would not be used in the present context. The MoD would never confirm or deny the presence of nuclear weapons in any particular location and never had done so.

It might have been possible to remove at least some of the weapons at Portsmouth before the Task Force set sail. This was considered but it could not have been undertaken in even a semi-covert manner, and would have added four to 16 hours to the preparations at the docks, during which time no other major activity would have been permitted in the ships involved or within a 300 yard radius. This would have led to considerable delays at a time when none could be countenanced. On 8 April the War Cabinet backed the Foreign Secretary's proposal that the depth bombs be off-loaded. A range of options was then considered. At a minimum it was possible, using a heavy jackstay, to transfer the weapons from the frigates to the carriers or the RFAs, where they could be more safely stored. Because an RFA could not be spared to get the weapons back to the UK there was no point in them taking on the weapons from the carriers. The alternative was to transfer the weapons to Ascension Island, but there was a lack of suitable storage. Furthermore, any activity at Ascension carried a risk of publicity: reducing this by disembarking by night would increase the more serious risk of accident. Most seriously, taking off the weapons at Ascension Island might have delayed the planned deployment by 36 hours, by taking the helicopters away from the demanding duties to which they had already been assigned in sorting out the stowage on the amphibious force.

In the event and with enormous reluctance Ministers decided that there was little choice but for them to stay with the carriers. They agreed on 11 April that the effort to remove the weapons would introduce an unacceptable delay to the Task Group getting to the Falkland Islands and initiating operations there. The decision was to concentrate the weapons in the carriers, where the safest stowage could be found. Initially the weapons were transferred to RFAs before being taken to the carriers, in order to get them off the frigates as quickly as possible. This meant that *Hermes* was carrying 40 percent and *Invincible* 25 percent of the total UK stockpile of MC(600)s into the South Atlantic. The surveillance rounds that were carried on *Sheffield* and *Coventry* were also transferred to an RFA. In no circumstances, insisted the Prime Minister, would ships carrying nuclear weapons enter the 3-mile territorial waters zone round the Falkland Islands, which would be a potential breach of the Treaty of Tlatelolco. After the losses of ships to Argentine air attacks in late May, the thought of the consequences if they had been carrying nuclear weapons led to a decision to bring the depth charges back from the South Atlantic. On 28 May it was decided that the depth bombs, plus the training and surveillance rounds, should be removed from ships and brought back to the UK. *Invincible*'s load was brought back in *Fort Austin*. In the event, not all could be quickly carried, because this would delay the ships' return. It took until 26 June before *Hermes* could 'disembarrass' itself of the depth charges to *Resource* which returned to Plymouth on 20 July.

While they were still at sea, the weapons were placed where they could be stored with added security. If there was a problem the carriers were more robust than the frigates and had more resources with which to cope with any damage. Analyses were undertaken of the worst case attacks, for example direct Exocet hits, which led to the conclusion that there was no risk of a nuclear explosion, that the weapons were not vulnerable to fire or the detonation of high explosives in the magazines. The Explosive Ordnance Disposal (EOD) teams with the Task Force had no real experience of nuclear systems - the only expertise was at Aldermaston. On the other hand an incident at sea would not carry the same risk to centres of population as would one in a home port. As a quick response would be impossible the greatest concern was in ensuring an accurate assessment before any action was taken, initially handled by those on a strictly need to know basis. If the accident came under the most serious 'category three', leading to radioactive contamination, then embarrassing publicity could not be avoided even if the effects were modest.

Another question was how this issue was to be handled should questions be asked. At one level this was straightforward. There was a standard formula to the effect that the presence of nuclear weapons at a particular location would never be confirmed nor denied. The Government would therefore avoid even getting into a discussion on the matter. The only further clarification believed to be required, provided in the form of a parliamentary answer, was that there was no intention to use nuclear weapons in the Falklands context. On 27 April Viscount Trenchard stated in the Lords 'categorically that there is no question at all of our using nuclear weapons in this dispute.'[9] There was occasional speculation – for example the German *Der Spiegel* carried a story that US enquiries had led to a British confirmation that not only were nuclear weapons being carried but that Woodward had permission to defend himself with them in very difficult circumstances. They would be used only if massive air attacks threatened the fleet (an unlikely role for depth charges).

After the sinking of the Type 42 destroyer *Sheffield* there was some speculation, encouraged by the Soviet Union, that the ship had been carrying nuclear weapons and indeed had been scuttled deliberately to prevent radioactive contamination. Allegations were also made that nuclear depth charges had to be recovered from the sunk *Coventry* as well as *Sheffield*.[10] Officials in the Soviet embassy in Buenos Aires were reported to have spread this canard, with the appearance of a number of dead penguins being cited as evidence of the spread of nuclear contamination.[11] *Sheffield*'s surveillance round had in fact been removed in mid-April and *Coventry*'s before the San Carlos landing. The diving activity noted around the wreck of the *Coventry*, which encouraged speculation, was the result of its accessibility and the consequent need to remove classified equipment. *Sheffield* sank at a depth well beyond diving range.

Attention was drawn again to the nuclear issue in November 1982 with the publication of a collection of letters from an RN Officer, David Tinker, who was killed during the last days of the war. He referred to what he presumed to be a dummy nuclear depth charge on RFA *Fort Austin* (which was quite possible). This led at least one journalist to obtain confirmation that nuclear depth charges reached the South Atlantic, and that *Fort Austin* had collected them to get them back to Britain. The main effect of this story, however, was to revive the mistaken speculation about *Sheffield*.[12]

When asked about the presence of nuclear weapons, British officials stuck to the standard line of 'neither confirm nor deny'. The *Sheffield* question did lead to a modification of this policy, after the war, and to a parliamentary statement, requested by the FCO, to the effect that there had never been any incident involving a British nuclear weapon leading to its loss or to the dispersal of radio-active contamination.[13] In December 2003, after repeated requests by Rob Evans of the *Guardian* for information about nuclear accidents under the Code of Practice on Access to Government Information, MoD acknowledged that nuclear depth charges had been taken to the South Atlantic, and returned, and that at some point the door housing to one container had received some damage.[14]

Ascension Island

In planning for Falklands contingencies, the lack of an airhead either on or close to the Falklands had always been seen as a major impediment to appropriate reinforcement but the availability of Ascension Island helped considerably. Ascension Island is situated over 3,700 nautical miles from the UK and 3,300 miles from the Falkland Islands. This British Dependency, devoid of native population, was used on leasehold terms by various authorities including Cable and Wireless, the BBC, the United States Air Force (USAF) and the United States National Aeronautical and Space Agency (NASA). Including a local labour force brought in from St Helena, there were some 1,100 inhabitants. Its most vital facility was Wideawake airfield (named after a local species of bird). This had no port and one unreliable landing bay, capable of taking one LCU, subject to weather, but it did boast a 10,000 ft runway, built by the Americans during the Second World War and operated by Pan-American Airways, under an agreement with the US Government.

In principle the 1962 agreement allowed British military use at any time required.[15] It did not take much contemplation of a map to realise the potential importance of Ascension Island. It was the only possible option as a forward mounting base. Here the ships of the Task Force could be replenished and provided with the stores, equipment and men that could not be embarked before their hurried departure from Britain.[16] The value of Ascension was enhanced by access to facilities at Dakar in Senegal on the west coast of Africa. By refuelling at Dakar Hercules could carry heavier loads on their way to Ascension.

Ensuring constant and unimpeded access to the facilities at Ascension was one of the first priorities, once it was decided that the Task Force should set sail. One sensitive area was that replenishment of bulk fuel on the Island was an American responsibility. The fuel demands were about to rise steeply and this would require special efforts by the American side that arguably would go well beyond the expectations of impartiality. Fuel storage did not allow for much more than weekly transport to service the US satellite tracking station and further replenishment was not due until 14 April. The US Admiral in charge of logistics at the Pentagon was told that Britain needed an eight-million-gallon tanker full of aviation fuel within the next seven days – and would need this regularly. By 13 April the US had agreed that 950,000 US gallons of fuel could be used by British forces out of the 1.2 million gallons that remained in Ascension. There was also the possibility that the British could use the US reserve fuel stockpile in an emergency. At one stage this was permitted because of a problem with a tanker.[17] On 19 April stocks were reported as 700,000 gallons; by 25 April – when a re-supply tanker with 2.4 million gallons began to unload – it was down to 120,000 gallons. At this point the Americans agreed to make available all fuel on Ascension, including their own reserve. Eventually, the British provided their own fuel but its storage required American facilities. There was a shortage of water, which had to be rationed, sewerage, accommodation and other basic facilities. For reasons of basic safety it was necessary to build an ammunition store well away from the runway.

Wideawake was only accustomed to dealing with three movements each week. Its facilities were limited and its technical and domestic back-up were totally inadequate. Suddenly it became an extraordinarily busy base. The necessary engineering, freight handling, weapon loading and administrative support brought the establishment from nothing to over 800 officers and men of all three services within three weeks. Just before the Argentine invasion, units sent to Ascension included an RM Blowpipe detachment, airfield enhancement units, Lynx and Wessex helicopters and their flight personnel. Soon men and equipment were arriving at the rate of about five RAF transport flights each day: RN and RAF personnel to manage the logistics, detachments of the Special Air Service (SAS) and Special Boat Service (SBS), a mass of stores, equipment and men for Task Force ships, as well as two Wessex for work on the island. An RAF complement of about 180 dealt with six Hercules and two VC10 transport flights each day as well as operating between two and four Nimrods stationed at Wideawake. The arrival of five Victors would more than double the personnel numbers. The RN party of about 50 had one Sea King and two Wessex. In addition, there were usually men waiting to join ships. Eventually Ascension's role became much more than logistic support, as preparations had to be made to mount RAF operations from the island. It came to support up to 17 Victors, three Vulcans, four Hercules, four Nimrods, two air defence aircraft and two support helicopters.

The management of the limited facilities at Ascension became a challenge. Aircraft not required for the moment often had to be parked back in the UK or Gibraltar. Furthermore, the RAF had to relearn the conduct of long distance operations. The service had increasingly become geared to the demands of the European cold war. Only Victor aircraft were fitted for air-to-air refuelling and long-distance flights tended to be no more than crossing the Atlantic to exercises in North America. Within a few weeks aircraft were modified to take extra fuel while Vulcan and Nimrod aircraft were fitted so that they could refuel in air. The Hercules aircraft became adept at dropping critical spares into the water close to the Task Force ships and then fishing them out.

As the various components of the Task Force reached Ascension – the *Antrim* group on 10 April, the SPRINGTRAIN ships on 12 April, the *Hermes* group on 16 April, *Invincible* and *Fearless* on 17 April – stores and personnel transfer flights among the ships grew accordingly, reaching a peak of several hundred each day on 17 and 18 April. It was of particular importance for the Amphibious re-load although this was hampered by the lack of suitable beaches, limited by their steep gradients, soft sand, heavy surf, and their use as a turtle breeding ground!

To start with Fieldhouse was largely concerned about the potential for difficulties with the Americans. Too much was dependent upon the goodwill of the USAF Commander and a handful of Pan Am employees, although so far there had been no complaints about their responsiveness to the tremendous pressure they suddenly faced. When the issue arose over the potential use of the Island as a base for Vulcan raids against Stanley airfield, which the USAF Base Commander believed might fall outside of the Anglo-American agreement, Fieldhouse argued that the time had come to re-examine the lease as a matter of urgency to ensure Britain had full control of the facilities for the duration of the operation. He wanted to make the senior naval officer, who had arrived on 8 April, overall commander of the Island base and the senior RAF officer the airfield commander. The view in MoD was that the rapid build-up on the Island had led to inevitable problems but that the position should stabilise. The preference was to sort out difficulties with the Americans rather than renegotiate the agreement, especially as the arrangements were generally working well.

The real problems lay in managing the pressures on the Island's limited facilities as it became the hub of the British logistics operation. Captain McQueen, Commander British Forces Support Unit (CBFSU), had under his command all British forces stationed on the Island in the logistic and administrative support of CORPORATE. He was responsible for the effective and efficient operation of all the facilities and also their security. In this role he was answerable to the Vice Chief of Defence Staff (P&L), not CINCFLEET. He also had the delicate job of liaising with the Commander United States Forces Ascension Island. Beneath him there was a rather complex command structure. There were three single-service commanders on Ascension Island, each responsible to McQueen but accountable to their own commanders-in-chief who all had their own views of priorities. From the vantage point of Northwood, the Air Commander, Air Marshal Curtiss, for example, felt that it was incorrect to see Ascension Island purely in terms of naval logistics. In command terms, the focus on logistics, which was organised through MoD, took Ascension Island out of Northwood's direct control. It was true that Northwood could barely cope with existing demands, but real problems were bound to arise under this arrangement, as they did as Ascension became a base for large-scale air operations. In a directive to Group Captain M F J Tinley, the senior RAF officer, Ascension Island, on 14 April, Curtiss stressed that he was to 'ensure that any matters which you are unable to resolve and/or which significantly detract from the efficient and effective employment of RAF resources located at Ascension Island are immediately brought to the attention of the Air Commander'. This officer was not responsible for operations of the Air Transport Force which would continue to be tasked and controlled under normal arrangements.

There could never be a neat division between operations, for which Tinley was responsible to Curtiss, and administration, for which he was responsible to McQueen, and as the operational requirements changed dramatically so did the issues that had to be resolved. It could be hard to extract quick and appropriate decisions from the Central Staff in London, at the same time as having to cope with numerous requests for information and apparently irrelevant communications coming back in the other direction. McQueen later observed that there was a problem with too much command and too little control. He had gained a right of veto over who could stay on the base and a commitment to keep numbers at around 200, a limit that did not last long. The problem was that 'there was only one war and an oversupply of people who wanted to be part of it'. As a result, working closely with Tinley, he was constantly urging units coming to Ascension to trim their numbers, and then sending excess people back to the UK. He became known as 'Captain One in, One out'. This was not always appreciated. (Brigadier Thompson was particularly irked when an ordnance team he had especially requested was sent back.)[18]

There were particular problems with the RAF because of the constant pressure to send more aircraft and personnel beyond the base's already remarkably expanded capacity. In these circumstances McQueen had little choice but to exercise somewhat arbitrary authority because there was no other means of preventing the base being swamped. The problems, particularly with the RAF, grew as their role expanded.

From the air perspective the Island's role as a forward logistics base for the forces heading south was given priority over its operational role as an RAF base. This was seen as following naturally from McQueen's responsibility to VCDS (P&L). Accepting that there was not enough space to do either the logistics or the operational job properly, the RAF became frustrated that the decisions were being made at their expense by a local commander with a logistical remit who was, in practice, exercising judgements about another service's missions.

Because McQueen was still working through VCDS (P&L), the RAF suspected he was not getting advice from his immediate superiors on the operational demands because they too lacked the full picture. The airmen saw themselves as improvising unusual and demanding operations, as ordered by Northwood, well outside their normal training and experience. To McQueen the purposes of the Vulcan and Nimrod operations, with their heavy use of tankers, seemed disproportionately expensive in terms of

Ascension's scarce resources – elaborate but uneconomic.[19] He would not have been alone in the RN if he felt that the RAF were desperate to get into the Falklands act in some way, and that this had clouded their collective judgement about the real value of the Vulcan operation in particular. Nor was he convinced that the RAF had made much effort to trim where possible, particularly in deploying personnel to the Island, or in sorting out their own command arrangements. As far as the RAF was concerned these were not McQueen's judgements to make. Their core missions, including the Vulcan raids, had been approved by the Chiefs of Staff and ordered by the Task Force command at Northwood. They found it increasingly exasperating that such missions could be frustrated by the base commander, especially when they had to be undertaken in short order.

Another indication of anxiety was concern that Argentina might try to disrupt the British operation at Ascension Island. When, on 17 April, Northwood asked MoD for an assessment of the threat to Ascension, the reply was 'negligible'. Then on 25 April the Argentine merchant ship *Rio de la Plata* was identified a few miles off shore, and there was a concern that it might have been monitoring communications for a couple of days or even infiltrating saboteurs. There were also indications, probably spurious, of underwater attack. Nothing was found, but the result was a much higher state of alert ashore and in the anchorage. On 29 April another Argentine merchant ship, the *Glaciar Perito Moreno*, was detected to the north. After being shadowed by *Antelope* it passed clear and continued south. On the same day there was a report that a Soviet intelligence-gathering vessel, *Primorye* was approaching from the north. This vessel remained off Ascension for the duration of the conflict. The Argentine effort, such as it was, was devoted to intelligence gathering rather than any disruptive activity.

The appearance of the *Rio de la Plata* nonetheless led to a reassessment of the threat. On 27 April the Chiefs of Staff had a short discussion of the issue, leading to a request for an assessment from the DIS. In addition to the visit by the *Rio de la Plata* one source had also mentioned a possible covert Argentine attack on Ascension, probably making use of a 707 aircraft. If successful this could be a major propaganda coup as well as potentially causing sufficient physical damage to interfere with British operations. Possible targets included the airfield and the parked British aircraft, water and power supplies, and, if relations between Argentina and the US broke down, the fuel storage sites. More daring still would be an attack from the sea, using Special Forces, or midget submarines deployed from Argentina or neutral merchant ships.

The risk was small. McQueen was sceptical that the Argentines would risk a direct attack on a base widely assumed to be American. Argentine Special Forces had scant opportunity to deploy covertly into appropriate ships, which would then have to reach Ascension undetected and disembark on a rocky coast. It was highly unlikely that the aircraft carrier would be risked on such a mission, which meant that no Argentine combat aircraft would be within range. Even air-to-air refuelling would not allow for a return journey to Argentina. There were some 14 civil and military aircraft (747 and 707) with sufficient range which could land an attack force, but this would have to be a small force at risk to changes in weather and inaccurate drops. To get surprise an aircraft might be disguised as neutral, simulating an emergency that called for a diversion into Ascension, or operating at night. This risk could not quite be ruled out, especially if the 'Junta wanted a propaganda coup that could also severely damage our lines of communication'. In addition Ascension would be presented as an exclusive military target. Small as it was, when the Chiefs discussed this risk on 29 April, they decided that it had to be addressed, and that this would best be achieved by early warning radar, and some troops for ground defence. A reconnaissance team was sent to Ascension, as were small arms for about 400 of the 600 British servicemen there. For the moment RN ships provided adequate air defence but an early warning radar detachment was placed at 48 hours' notice to move. In addition, the Sea Harriers flying out to join the *Atlantic Conveyor* were put at air defence readiness on arrival.

In early May it was agreed that a Wing Headquarters and one Flight of the RAF Regiment and an air defence early warning radar should be sent to Ascension Island as soon as possible. By this time there were sufficient small arms for two thirds of British forces at Ascension, a Guardship had been sent, three GR3 Harriers had been made available and Nimrod flights were providing cover of the area around Ascension. On 10 May, ROE for Harrier GR3 aircraft in the air defence of Ascension Island were signalled. These required that aircraft approaching Ascension by day or night had to be identified by any means available and that any aircraft committing a hostile act or visually identified as Argentine combat aircraft could be destroyed. 'Aircraft Captains' were 'authorised to destroy without warning aircraft operating within 100nm radius of Ascension Island'.

Fieldhouse remained concerned: it was not that he was worried by a Hercules unloading Argentine troops at Ascension, it was more that it might drop incendiary devices which could be devastating against Britain's tightly packed aircraft parking facilities at Ascension. He wanted an air defence aircraft such as Lightning, but the Air Commander on Ascension warned that this would cause too many operating difficulties. Instead three Phantoms were to be made available for the air defence of Ascension. They took over from the Harrier GR3s on 24 May. At least one senior naval officer felt that Fieldhouse 'was slightly piling on the threat to Ascension Island but nonetheless supported his general approach'. He was not alone. Nott was also concerned that not enough was being done, to the point that Lewin had to reassure him privately that sufficient protection was now in place.

5

FIRST ASSESSMENTS

On 5 April, Woodward wrote that this had been 'the first day since leaving Gibraltar that there has been sufficient time to look much more than one day ahead! Not short of ideas: very short of answers.' Two days later he was 'particularly keen that everyone should face up to the real possibility of war and the way that most habits will have to change'. He had emphasised that whatever happens, 'we have a very long haul ahead and that our ships are our homes and they need tender loving care if they are ever to get us home'.

Those involved with CORPORATE, military and civilian alike, hoped that the military effort could produce a diplomatic solution before more blood had been shed. At the same time, if in the end it all came down to the quality of the military operation, then diplomatic considerations could come to be seen as the source of unnecessary constraints. From the moment the first ships set sail the requirements of the military tasks ahead had to be met within the terms set by prevailing political circumstances. These were military tasks that had barely been taken at all seriously in earlier analyses. Plans for retaking the Falkland Islands had never progressed beyond sketch form, sufficient to make the point that this would be a deeply unattractive operation to undertake, bordering on the hopeless. Such entirely hypothetical ventures were not deemed worth more than a few paragraphs. Officials who had recently been expressing doubts about the wisdom of expending any resources on the Falklands did not turn into sudden enthusiasts. They remained convinced that even success would mean a bothersome, expensive commitment, lasting as long as the Argentine conviction that the Falklands were theirs, that is indefinitely.

When the question of whether the Falklands could be retaken was posed seriously within MoD on 2 April 1982, the answer therefore was inevitably discouraging. If war began there was no certain conclusion. Much of course would depend on Argentina, and in particular the size of the force it was able to establish on the Islands, its disposition and its ability to re-supply and reinforce that force from the mainland. It was also a matter of the reliability of British intelligence on all of this. At the time the data bank of material on Argentine forces was virtually empty, with no information on even the details of Argentina's most recent arms acquisitions. If the Argentine concept of operations to hold on to the Malvinas had been known, it might have been consoling that this was in as sketchy a form as was Britain's to recapture them. Argentine planners had rarely thought much beyond the initial occupation of the Malvinas and had never supposed that they would have to be defended.

The margins were tight. In the first rush a naval force large enough to defend itself and defeat the enemy in air and sea engagements had been sent, backed up by a land force able to mount an amphibious assault. If the naval force had to stay in position for an extended period then elements of it would need at some point to be replaced; if the land force was to do more than establish a presence then it was probably too small; if more troops were to be sent then that would impose extra demands on the already stretched sea lift capabilities of the UK. With every one of these issues questions of time and distance loomed large. It was not possible just to wait and see how events unfolded before deciding whether to move the amphibious force into position, or to send extra reserves. If they were to be there on time the conditions they would face on arrival had to be anticipated. This required identifying the optimum dates for a landing and, working back, by which time the amphibious force would have to arrive and when, therefore, it would have to leave Ascension Island. That decision would also be influenced by the ease with which it could be accommodated at Ascension. A judgement also had to be made about the durability of the force. For how long could effective operations be sustained, in the face of wear and tear, the consumption of resources and Argentine attacks, requiring the effort to be scaled down or even abandoned? The military planning that went on for much of April was dominated by these questions. Even as the Task Force steamed towards the first engagements with Argentine forces the military strategy to be advanced was still being clarified. Decisions had yet to be taken on how the Government proposed to bring the fighting to a satisfactory conclusion in the absence of a negotiated agreement.

Assessing Argentina

The early state of knowledge about the enemy was reflected in the first briefing to the Chiefs of Staff Committee on 2 April 1982. Three days later, on 5 April, the first full assessment of Argentine capabilities was published by the Chiefs of Staff. The next day the JIC published its own estimate. Yet a further assessment was prepared by the DCDS(I) on 7 April. Thereafter this was regularly updated. On 14 April the available intelligence was brought together on all aspects of Argentine activity. This served as the basis for a major briefing of the War Cabinet on 15 April and also for the development of the operational plans.

It did not take a military genius to recognise that, as the Falkland Islands were 300 miles from the mainland, the critical intelligence issue was the extent of Argentina's ability to project its military power into the South Atlantic. Only if the Argentine Navy and Air Force failed to prevent the Task Force from getting close enough to the Falkland Islands to enforce a blockade and attempt a landing, would the ability of their Army to defend the Islands be properly tested. On 5 April, Woodward signalled Fieldhouse, stating that:

> my operational plans will be critically dependent on top grade information from manufacturers, delicate sources, wherever on the following: A. USA and German built submarines B. Submarine anti-ship torpedo capability C. Exocet – ship fitting/numbers. Radar parameters D. Details of any Exocet air launch capability E. Mirage 3 and 5: R of A [Radius of Action], night/all weather capability F. Canberra R of A, and armament G. CVA [aircraft carrier] carried Super Etendard capability and R of A H. Lynx: Numbers delivered, equipment fitted, training levels I. Information gleaned from exercises, particularly with USN of CVA operations, ASW, RAS [Replenishment at Sea].

The next day Fieldhouse noted how much would also be needed about the garrison on the Falklands. He considered 'every scrap of information gleaned from Falkland Islands, especially of troop movements locations etc will be of vital importance in the future'. He believed that radio hams currently operating in the Falklands might be a good source, but could dry up.

To start with the available information was limited, indeed sufficiently so for the lack of knowledge almost to be a military secret in itself. When talking about Argentine capabilities in public care had to be taken to avoid betraying the extent of British ignorance. Prior to 2 April, collection of Falklands-related intelligence had been set at level four, the lowest in the scale of priorities. There was material in the public domain, including such standard reference works as the *Janes'* publications on weapons systems and *The Military Balance*, the annual inventory of international forces published by the International Institute for Strategic Studies. These sources in themselves were not to be lightly dismissed as they reflected excellent contacts with a number of governments, so while not of the highest-grade intelligence nor were they the lowest. Meanwhile, the DIS scoured their archives and made contact with any person or organisation who might have useful information. One of the most significant early inputs came from a serving RN officer who collected unclassified information on foreign air forces, including Argentina's, as a hobby. He provided detailed material on the order of battle.

The initial rush and limited capacity meant that the first papers on Argentine capabilities contained several errors and misleading statements.

The analyses were thereafter refined regularly as the quality of information improved, but there remained many gaps, for example coverage of the Argentine mainland bases. Contrary to much speculation there was no satellite imagery, except for the retaking of South Georgia, which was reportedly photographed in April.[1] Another potential source of information was communications intercepts. These could often provide useful tactical intelligence, but were of less strategic value. As Woodward's signal indicated, one of the most useful sources of information might flow from the fact that Argentina's military capability owed its origins and its equipment to three countries – primarily the US and France but also the UK.

The British looked to the US for help. The Americans could boast the largest intelligence-gathering machinery in the world and their military had been in regular touch with their Argentine counterparts. There was some relief when it became apparent that the even-handedness being displayed at the political level was having little impact on intelligence co-operation, and then when it transpired that American assessments had reached broadly similar conclusions to those of the British, although there were real differences, particularly with regard to the capabilities of the Argentine Air Force. As early as 8 April, Lewin was thanking his American counterpart, General D C Jones, Chairman of the US Joint Chiefs of Staff, 'for all the help we have already had from your people over our problem in the South Atlantic,' before firing off a range of questions on Argentine capabilities, especially those of the Argentine Navy. The replies came back quickly, after what had been clearly a hard weekend's work in Washington. The British Defence Staff at Washington reported back to Lewin that: 'The co-operation we are getting from the Americans is truly marvellous.'

In addition, the French Foreign Minister, Charles Hernu, had promised Britain complete information as 'we are side by side with you'. This was particularly important given France's role as an arms supplier to Argentina, notably of air systems. Using the Defence Attaché in Paris as a conduit, the British sought lists of military sales to Argentina, details of any imposed modifications/limitations to systems, precise capabilities of key aircraft as well as serviceability rates, spares consumption and known shortages, and proficiency of those Argentine pilots trained by the French. The French even sent over some aircraft to conduct mock dogfights against British pilots. Detailed technical information on the Exocet was also provided. Nott later observed that: 'In so many ways Mitterrand and the French were our greatest allies.'[2]

It took time before the improved information was available. During that first week after the invasion the British intelligence community might have preferred to concentrate on assembling and collating raw data prior to the careful preparation of sensible and reliable assessments but they had to respond to the urgent demands for whatever assessments could be put together as a basis for planning. The uncertainties on the British side were not simply about the raw military power at Argentina's disposal, but also about the country's strategic culture and the fighting spirit of its armed forces.

The Defence Attaché, on his return from Argentina, warned in his debrief against underestimating the Argentine armed forces. He pointed to the quality of the Air Force and the danger posed by the two German-built diesel submarines, the rapid build-up of the Argentine garrison on the Islands and the possibility that this could be re-supplied by air, even if sea supplies were cut. He also however drew attention to a brittle national pride that might be damaged by reverses, such as the loss of their carrier or Britain retaking South Georgia. Argentina would find a protracted conflict problematic: the fleet was neither used to long periods at sea nor the army to winter conditions. He reported the apparent significance attached by Argentines to the fact they had not killed anyone yet and claims that they gave their own forces instructions to shoot to miss (although this hardly seemed consistent with the attack on Moody Brook barracks during the invasion). This suggested that they would be very reluctant to be the first to open more serious hostilities by attacking elements of the British Navy. However, there was still almost total public support, and a feeling of national solidarity.

This popular support, even for an initiative taken by an unpopular military government, was also the starting point for the first JIC assessment. Again it was suggested that this support would inevitably wane over time, especially if Argentina were to suffer a military setback or the economic crisis continued to worsen as a result of a prolonged military confrontation. Another factor would be the extent of wider diplomatic support. Neighbouring countries generally backed Argentina's case on the transfer of sovereignty over the Falkland Islands but were concerned about the use of force. Only Brazil had expressed unreserved political support for Argentina but that was unlikely to be translated into making available their facilities to assist Argentina's defence of the Islands. At most, other Latin American countries were expected to offer diplomatic assistance and possibly some economic sanctions against British interests. There was little likelihood that Argentina would secure overt military support, especially given the influence of the United States within the Rio Treaty, although covert military supplies might be obtained.

Another uncertainty was how the Argentine Government would view the population of the Falkland Islands. They might constrain a British assault, especially if directed against the airfield or Stanley itself. The 'kelpers' might also be used in some way as effective hostages in diplomatic negotiations. Yet at the same time Argentina must regard them as a security problem. Some pre-invasion intelligence indicated that the possibility of serious local resistance had been judged to be one of the main difficulties of the operation. Now the occupation forces would be aware of the provision of intelligence to British forces: action had already been taken to seize the equipment of the radio hams on the Islands. As the Task Force drew closer, policy towards the islanders might become harsher, including even interning some or all of the population, or removing them to Argentina.

Against this background, two basic questions had to be addressed. How vulnerable would the Task Force be to the Argentine Navy and Air Force as it sought to cut the Falklands off from the Argentine mainland? How strong a defence would the Argentine Army be able to mount to a British landing force, both at the point of landing and as it then moved to retake the Islands?

The threat to the Task Force

The Argentine surface fleet was not a major concern, other than the sea-launched version of Exocet it carried. It was an effective seagoing force, the best in South America, but should not be a match for a Western force using advanced tactics and modern weapons systems. The information from the US Navy suggested technical proficiency, high levels of training and professionalism to be set against a relatively small size, ageing and obsolescent equipment and deficiencies in command, control, and communications. Fleet training tended to be tailored to existing capabilities and familiar tactics and was not particularly innovative. Officers had not generally shown much adaptability or creativity when faced with unfamiliar tactical situations.

Of the Argentine Navy's thirteen major surface units, most were elderly, although recently two British Type 42 and three French A69 frigates had entered service. One of these had been damaged during the occupation of South Georgia. Otherwise, all ships were operational. There were some doubts about the 44 year old cruiser, the *General Belgrano,* which was thought close to the end of her seagoing life until an American source reported it to be in good order, though with serious boiler problems and a tendency, shared with the aircraft carrier, to limp back from exercises. The main problem for Argentina if it was to deploy its fleet was the threat posed by Britain's SSNs. Here Argentina would depend on the ability of Trackers and Sea Kings, combined with ship-based sonars, to detect the SSNs, which might then be attacked with torpedoes and depth charges. Capabilities had been enhanced with the acquisition of Sea Lynx and Alouette helicopters, but little information was available on their tactical employment. Their own submarines were estimated to provide only a minimal additional benefit to the overall (ASW) capability, though there was concern that a possible sonar advantage and the quality of their German torpedoes might mean that the Type 209s could pose dangers to the SSNs should they get to close quarters. While there was some evidence that the Argentine Navy had a good understanding of basic ASW procedures, they would probably be extremely wary about their ability to cope with nuclear submarines, of which they had negligible experience. In addition waters off the Argentine coast were among the worst in the world for surface ASW operations, as they tended to be shallow, and were not helped by the weather and other complications such as a large fish population.

The Argentine surface fleet would also be vulnerable to air attack. The most modern air defence system available was the Sea Dart fitted on the

Type 42 destroyers, but this was a well understood British system and the problems the Argentines had suffered were known, including defects which caused excessive miss distances in trials. The *Santisima Trinidad*'s Sea Dart system suffered from a major defect and the Naval Staff believed that *Hercules* could not fire Batch 2 missiles because of Missile Tuning Unit incompatibility. It was known that up to nine warships had been fitted with the Exocet MM38 anti-ship missile, with a stand-off range of some 24 miles. This was similar to the RN version but with a less sophisticated homing head. None of this suggested that the Argentine surface fleet would be any match for the RN in any encounter on the high seas. With only one large and two small tankers, and no other fleet stores ships available, general re-supply could prove difficult and would require merchant shipping or naval transports.

There were, however, still significant areas of concern. In terms of harming the Task Force early on, much would depend on Argentina's ability to find the Task Force and then attack individual ships. As with the RN, the Argentine Navy lacked an airborne early warning capability and so detection was always going to be difficult. Surface surveillance was provided by a small number of P2E Neptune, of which probably no more than two were available because of maintenance problems, S2E Tracker aircraft, and radar fitted in surface ships and submarines, while air surveillance was entirely dependent on ship and shore radar, which were generally poor. It was not known whether any air surveillance radar had been installed in the Falkland Islands.

If the Task Force could be found it was most likely to be attacked from under the sea or from the air. There were four conventional diesel submarines, of which two were ex-US Guppy Class and now 38 years old, suitable only for reconnaissance rather than offensive roles. One had been in harbour for some time and might not be operational. Little information was available about the two modern German Type 209 diesel submarines, but what was known suggested that they should be taken seriously. They could pose a major and continuing threat for Britain's ASW capabilities, particularly due to their small size. However, the Argentines would have difficulty positioning their patrol areas effectively, given their slow speed and the short detection range of their sonar. They would not present easy targets in an engagement. The Americans did not expect them to be used far away from shore, being held back to clear and protect sea-lanes.

The Argentine Navy's other prospect of getting at the Task Force depended on the ability of its single carrier to get close. The *25 de Mayo* had originally been built for the RN in 1945. Her normal complement of aircraft was eleven A-4Q Skyhawks, six Trackers and four Sea Kings. The key to the role to be played by the carrier, and the vulnerability of British ships, was whether or not 14 Super Etendards, recently purchased, were operational at sea, and whether Exocet AM39 missiles had been acquired from France for these aircraft. This will be examined in detail in a later chapter. For the moment we need only note that the carrier air group could conduct at most limited air-to-air and air-to-surface operations in good weather conditions. On the critical question of the status of the Super Etendard aircraft and the Exocet AM39s missiles that they might carry, the balance of information tended towards the view that five of each were operational, but that they were probably not deployed on the carrier.

The main threat to the Task Force was therefore likely to come from shore-based aircraft. Not a lot was known about the Argentine Air Force. It consisted of 20,000 men, half of whom were conscripted for 12 months. Information on their training, proficiency and operational readiness was sparse, but there was believed to be a general shortage of spares that restricted aircraft availability and financial constraints had limited flying training. There was little serious night flying and few intensive operations. Nevertheless, it appeared that within these limitations, pilots flew with dash and flair, sufficient to be formidable adversaries, especially if they could sustain their confidence and enjoyed good weather. There were some 300 aircraft of which only 175 had a combat capability. Most of these were old and equipped with simple weapons systems that limited their effectiveness at night and in poor weather. In the earlier estimates it was assumed that only just over 60 had any realistic capability to conduct operations at the range of the Falkland Islands.

The Air Force's airfields were concentrated in the northern half of the country, orientated towards the potential threat from Chile. With few suitable airfields in southern Argentina, and transport aircraft re-supplying the Falklands garrison making their own demands, options for re-deployment of aircraft for operations over the Falkland Islands would be limited, although still probably just about adequate. It was initially assumed, incorrectly, that most airfields had little more than a runway with a marked absence of hard-standings, approach aids and technical support facilities. There were even doubts about whether the most suitable airfield, Rio Gallegos, some 400 miles due west of the Falklands, could handle the much larger numbers of aircraft required for offensive operations.

It was also, again incorrectly, assumed that the nearest mainland base, Rio Grande, housed all 57 of the Skyhawk A4 fighter-bombers. These aircraft were believed to have a combat radius of 500nm so they should be able to reach the Falklands comfortably using external tanks and carrying 1,500lb to 2,000lb bombs. They would be handicapped by simple navigation aids and reliance on visual weapons delivery. On the basis of this inadequate data, it was estimated that 60–80 sorties per day might be mounted from Rio Grande. The Argentines might also bring forward the small force of Canberra light bombers from its current base, which left them out of range. From Rio Grande their combat radius of about 800nm would put the Islands in range, but these aircraft were obsolescent and had limited navigational abilities. The most modern and effective combat aircraft available to the Argentine Air Force were the eleven Mirage IIIs and 24 Mirage Vs (Israeli

Daggers) of the Air Defence Command. They faced severe range problems, and the French suggested that these were unlikely to be overcome using in-flight refuelling. The British had already come to this conclusion because Argentina only possessed two KC-130 Tankers. Argentine pilots were not thought to be effective in poor weather conditions because of lack of practice.

The assumption that the Mirage V was dedicated to air defence was erroneous. Its primary role was ground attack. It had two integral 30mm cannon and could carry two 1,000lb. bombs or two Sidewinder missiles. Six Mirage Vs were believed to be based at Rio Gallegos and could provide some air defence cover over the Falklands. After their journey from base they would have about 40 minutes on task but they would then be constrained by the lack of an all-weather capability and the absence of radar control (although some, albeit rudimentary, was available). The other 18 Mirage Vs were based at Moreno (Buenos Aires) and could be re-deployed to Rio Gallegos, from where it would be possible to maintain a Combat Air Patrol (CAP) over the Stanley area, though this would be a very inefficient use of resources that might quickly affect serviceability rates. They would be restricted to daylight and visual conditions, and constrained by the lack of a modern navigation attack system when on offensive operations. Only the Mirage IIIs had an all-weather capability, as well as a better fire control radar and serviceability than the Mirage V, but they had a shorter combat radius; the Falklands would be out of range from their bases at Tandil and Mariano, and they could only just reach the Stanley area from Rio Gallegos.

It was unlikely that attack aircraft would be based on the airfield at Stanley since the pressing need there would be for air defence and the ground facilities would be critically over-stretched by a mixture of air defence, attack and transport aircraft. DCDS(I) assessed that the best form of air defence for Stanley would be afforded by stationing, say, four Mirage aircraft on the airstrip there. Because of the lack of night operating facilities and as it was the simpler as well as the lighter of the two types, these would probably be Mirage V. There was some intelligence suggesting an intention to extend the runway at Stanley by the 19 April to 4,000 metres using 'fulminated concrete' and if this were achieved it would open the possibility of operating 10 Mirage Vs, 58 Pucaras, and Super Etendards (with Exocet capability) from the airfield, as well as four S2s (mid-1960s ASW technology). The best estimate, however, was that only a limited air defence capability was likely to be available to the Argentines at Stanley, and even then only in daylight and good weather.

Against the Argentine air threat, the Naval Staff were reasonably confident that there was sufficient defensive capability, provided the Task Group was not too widely scattered. Exocet was the most serious prospect, although that was vulnerable to decoy chaff, which was readily available. The Sea Harrier should be more than a match for Argentine aircraft in air-to-air combat, although the advantage would decline should there be dogfights closer to the mainland and in clear weather. The French had supplied air-to-air missiles for the Mirage and estimated the probability of destruction to be high. If the Argentine aircraft reached their targets then a high number of successful hits would have to be anticipated.

Given that it was difficult at the best of times to detect and attack surface ships, the Chiefs' initial assessment was that the Falkland Islands themselves were comfortably within the radius of action of Argentine land-based offensive aircraft, but that a combination of range limitations and inadequate navigational aids would leave British ships reasonably secure so long as they kept their distance. This view was supported by the first Naval Staff study, produced on 7 April, which reported that so long as RN units remained over 700nm from Argentine-held airfields, the air-to-surface threat should be negligible. It was only as RN ships moved to within 300nm that the threat increased greatly, notably from the Super Etendard/AM39 Exocet combination.

By the time the DIS came up with their 15 April assessment, the basis for the War Cabinet briefing, the headlines remained the same. In a naval battle the Argentine Type 209 submarines might be difficult to find and attack and could threaten surface units if they got close enough, but in surface engagements the RN would have the edge because of superior tactics with their Exocets and more modern gunnery systems. The Task Force ought to be able to defend itself, so long as it kept beyond the limits of Argentine land-based air cover, while the Argentine fleet was vulnerable to air attack. Argentine in-flight refuelling capabilities were (incorrectly) believed to be limited as were improvements to Stanley airport, which for the moment could only accommodate Tracker and Pucara aircraft for maritime surveillance and close air support and was anyway vulnerable to British air attack. The Argentine aircraft carrier posed the major danger, especially if it had embarked Exocet-armed Super Etendard aircraft.

Those listening to the briefing would have come away concluding that the Argentine Navy could hurt the Task Force but only by taking substantial risks itself. In addition, the air threat was judged to be 'only moderate. The Argentines will need luck on their side if they are to inflict substantial damage on the Task Force.' This assessment of the air threat was seriously contested at the time, especially by those thinking about an amphibious landing. One factor to which not enough attention had been paid was Argentine aerial refuelling, using KC-130s. In the event these made a significant difference to the Argentine campaign, most notably in permitting the Super Etendards to reach British ships. They also made a difference to the A4s although the gap between the assessment and the actuality was less marked because the maximum unrefuelled radius of action of the A4s, which was about 380nm, was regularly overstated in British estimates.[3]

The optimistic assessment about the air threat did not only depend on technical assumptions, about basing and range, but also on assumptions about the conduct of the landing. The further east the landing, the tougher it would be for the Argentine Air Force but also the easier for the defending garrison. The further west the landing site the more grave the air threat. This might be tolerable if there were ways of reducing this threat prior to the landing, but would be less so if the Argentine commanders decided, as they did, to conserve their forces precisely for this contingency. Presumably the Argentine commanders knew they could not shirk battle once a landing began but equally they were under no obligation to accept it before then, especially if they agreed that unit for unit British forces were superior.

If air and sea dominance could not be achieved a landing could be hazardous, and more than just reputation and ownership of the Falklands were at stake if the Government pushed ahead with a calamitous operation. Regardless, this option could not be relinquished without a loss of face and bargaining position. An alternative strategy was to plan for a prolonged blockade in order to break the Argentine hold on the Falklands. It was by no means clear, however, that Argentina would break first. As winter weather approached, and with the defender's advantage, the Junta might be able to sit it out. Britain would be under counter-pressure out of concern for the condition of the islanders. A third strategy might therefore be to put the landing on hold, by retaining the amphibious force at Ascension Island until the conditions had been created for a successful operation or else moving it on to the South Atlantic but requiring it to loiter before it could be safely employed. If there was a landing, and it was successfully executed, there were further questions about what the landed force would then do. Would a mere presence on Falklands territory be sufficient even if the main – the only – town was in Argentine hands? If an assault on Stanley was unavoidable how could the safety of the local population be guaranteed? Any reoccupation of the Islands would be progressive, and would depend on the strength of the resistance and the ability to sustain operations. If it were well defended would the landing force be sufficient? What about the need for reinforcements?

The defending force

The Argentine amphibious force that had taken the Falkland Islands was built around the Marine Corps, or Naval Infantry, which numbered about 7,000 and had a seaborne force comprising a variety of landing ships. It was believed to be efficient, with high morale and equipment well balanced for its mission. The US Navy confirmed that they were disciplined, well trained and well led. Their capacity to plan and conduct amphibious assaults had been amply demonstrated. The issue now was their ability to defend against a British assault. In this units of the Argentine Army would support them.

The total strength of the Army was put at some 85,000, with about 20,000 regular officers and senior NCOs. Of the 65,000 in the junior ranks, the majority were conscripts. Its equipment had improved significantly over the last five years. It was a heterogeneous collection of weapons and vehicles from the US, Western Europe and some of local design and manufacture. The obvious weaknesses were in artillery and air defence and it was assumed only a portion of Argentina's sophisticated artillery would be deployed to the Falkland Islands. The Army was also expected to face significant logistical problems. The diversity of equipment created difficulties with maintenance while the lack of adequate railway networks in the south and a shortage of mechanical transport meant that movement might depend on civilian vehicles.

The only heavy equipment believed to be on the Falklands were 22 Armoured Personnel Carriers (APCs) – the LVTP-7 amphibious tracked armoured car with turret-mounted twin 12.8mm machine gun. These had in fact been withdrawn along with part of the invading maritime force. The existence of 105mm artillery pieces was correctly assumed. The estimate was that the Argentines probably intended the final strength of their occupying force to be that of an expanded brigade group, possibly five to six regiments (each approximately equivalent to a British infantry battalion) totalling between 5,000 and 8,000 men drawn from their elite units. When the estimate was made it was probably broadly correct in terms of Argentine intentions. Later Buenos Aires added a third brigade, making for nine regiments in total. Of the initial deployment it was assumed that at least three regiments would occupy the area to the north of East Falkland, including Stanley, its port facilities and the airport as the most vital ground. One further regiment could be then deployed to Lafonia and another to West Falkland.

The terrain would force the Argentines to adopt a static defence posture. There was little natural cover and the ground was both soggy and stony, making the preparation of defensive positions difficult and requiring considerable engineer stores. But there would be enough time before the arrival of Britain's Task Force for these to be prepared. They should also be able to reconnoitre and improve routes for moving reserves and building helicopter pads. Once battle was joined the movement of reserves would be difficult unless they had use of helicopters. It was unlikely that many of these would be deployed on the Islands because of the high fuel and servicing penalties that they would incur. For the same reasons it was unlikely that more than a few tanks would be deployed. With helicopters there was an underestimate. The deployed capability was of high quality, allowing for flights in foul weather and by night, when necessary, and was sufficient to lift one regiment. It did, however, suffer severe attrition.

Fire support would be provided by artillery and each battalion's own mortars. Missile-armed helicopters based on one or more of the grass strips on the Falklands could be used. These helicopters might be used in ground support, or even to attack surface units at sea. Argentina's 40 Pucara twin turboprop aircraft with a radius of 500nm would be ineffective against defended maritime targets. These had, however, been designed for counter-insurgency purposes and with two 20mm cannon, four machine guns and a 3,500lb. weapon load they could be used against any landings on the Falkland Islands, and especially against helicopters.

For air defence a proportion of Argentine holdings of Blowpipe (120 missiles/20 launchers), Roland and Tiger Cat (150/6) would probably be deployed and they might sea-lift some of their 20mm Oerlikon air defence artillery (AAA) guns (240) to the Islands. Their effectiveness would be limited to daylight visual engagements in good weather. They would, however, be very effective against helicopters. In the event a comprehensive mix of air defence weapons was deployed: 35mm with Skyguard, 30mm, 20mm, Tiger Cat and one Roland. Blowpipe deployment was very limited, probably due to the dearth of trained operators.[4] The Argentine garrison would have ample time to stockpile sufficient combat supplies for a brief defensive operation, although they could have difficulties with artillery ammunition. To reinforce the Islands there were 23 transport aircraft (seven C130 and sixteen Fokker 27/28) but if they were used at a high rate their serviceability would drop rapidly as there was a shortage of skilled maintenance and spares. A blockade could soon lead to shortages of food (other than meat) and water. Similar conditions would apply also to the civil population, except that they were accustomed to making the best use of incidental sources of water.

In terms of tactics and organisation the Argentine Army followed the US model but with local variations. A major issue was the extent to which the dependence upon one-year conscripts constituted a serious weakness. The initial inclination was not to make too much of this. The Chiefs of Staff assumed that training was generally effective, although its scope was limited by the turnover of conscripts to company and platoon level. Formation exercises were infrequent and there was little evidence of joint training of any sort. The units involved in the initial occupation did not contain a high proportion of conscripts. Nor, it was assumed, did those sent as reinforcements. In the event many conscripts were sent. The elite units, such as the Airborne Brigade and Marines, were probably trained to a high standard. Morale was high, especially while the population was imbued with an intense spirit of nationalism and this could encourage a determined fight to hold on to the Falklands.

The question was whether it could remain effective under testing conditions and after one or two reverses. As Argentine forces had not seen active service for over 60 years, if they were exposed to a protracted blockade or started to doubt their ability to defend successfully, their performance could be less than staunch. The optimistic view was that Argentine morale would be brittle. Isolated troops would face worsening weather, with deficient equipment and the approach of a strong, well trained, well equipped, British Task Force. Their apprehension should only grow if the military pressure could be sustained right up to the landings. This might argue for delay, on the assumption that the longer the delay the greater the deterioration in Argentine morale. Against this, delay would also affect British morale.

Rather than depending on a collapse in Argentine morale it seemed more sensible to plan to land as soon as sufficient intelligence had been acquired and a reasonable level of attrition achieved. This latter condition depended on the choices made by Argentina, which might include deciding to keep its Navy clear of the Task Force until the last minute, when a landing appeared imminent. Even so, the Chiefs of Staff were confident that the inhospitable and rugged terrain and the size of both islands coupled with the problems of establishing and maintaining logistic re-supply would probably preclude a strong Argentine defence in all good landing areas.

The 15 April assessment took the view that on the ground the Argentine forces enjoyed numerical superiority, but their air defences would only have a daylight, fair weather capability, most effective against helicopters, and would probably only be deployed, along with heavy artillery, in support of Argentine concentrations in the Stanley area. Inadequate numbers of helicopters and of aviation fuel would hamper their mobility. British training standards, tactics, equipment reliability and tactical mobility should be superior. The main Argentine advantage lay in the time available to reinforce and prepare forward positions, defences, shelters and internal lines of communication. The Task Force should be able to retake South Georgia without too much difficulty and then secure a bridgehead on the Falklands. With local air and sea superiority, good tactical intelligence and adequate softening up of the enemy, an amphibious and/or heliborne landing could be achieved with minimal casualties if mounted away from Stanley. To prevent Britain from landing forces on the Islands, the Argentines might resort to defensive minefields – they had a capacity and the waters around the Falkland Islands were suitable – and this could impose disproportionate constraints on the Task Force's tactical options.

Argentine naval units acting in close support of the garrison were likely to be used to attack British ships engaged in an amphibious assault. They could provide some shore bombardment, though at risk to themselves. Carrier-borne fighters would provide the greater part of the airborne air defence of the Malvinas and some fighters based in Argentina, although they would be operating at an extreme range. For the moment an effective airborne defence seemed unlikely, but this could change if the Argentines were able to improve the airfield over the coming weeks. The Argentine Army's close-range surface-to-air missiles, which had little or no effectiveness at night or in bad weather, would be concentrated for the defence of the Falkland Islands, placing some limits on the use of the Task Force aircraft, particularly helicopters. Regardless of the final size of the reinforced garrison, in addition to the defence of key installations, particularly the airfield, the Argentine command might decide to hold a sizeable force in reserve to react to an assault wherever it took place.

As the British planners worked through Argentine capabilities and likely strategies the real problem began to revolve around the conduct of land operations against a well dug-in Argentine garrison at Stanley. By mid-April the total size of the Argentine garrison was put at around 7,000 men, which could possibly be raised to 10,000. Britain's troops and supporting arms then en route totalled 4,600. It was presumed that the Argentines would consider Stanley, its airport and harbour of vital strategic and tactical importance. It would also be essential to hold the high ground overlooking Stanley to prevent the British gaining observation over it. Other areas that the Argentines could consider to hold were Darwin, Port Howard and Fox Bay, the latter two settlements situated in West Falkland. They would be defending what they regarded with deep conviction to be their own soil, with the whole world watching and at least rhetorical support from most other Latin American countries. So while the Task Force would hold the balance of military power at sea, and had the capability to repossess South Georgia with minimal risk as well as secure a bridgehead on the Falklands, the Argentine garrison would be hard to dislodge, and this would be particularly so if local air superiority was not achieved.

6

RULES OF ENGAGEMENT

The political momentum created by the decision to send the Task Force and the enthusiastic national backing that it had received swept up officials and officers alike, no longer advising on the wisdom of setting a challenging strategic objective but obliged instead to work out how it could be met. The doubts and uncertainties could not, however, be wholly suppressed. The basic operational requirements were clear enough: Argentine forces on the Falklands would have to be cut off from the mainland; then naval and air supremacy would have to be established; lastly, if possible, a force would have to be landed in order to move to retake Stanley. Each step seemed fraught: the logistical issues nightmarish. Lesser options, from covert operations to a partial blockade and occasional attacks on Argentine vessels by SSNs, did not change the big picture. Politics added further complications. The UK depended on international support not only in its diplomatic efforts but also in logistics and material support. So even if a military conclusion was assumed, the political dimension could not be disregarded. Some actions might therefore have to be eschewed because their political impact would outweigh their military impact. Early in the discussions, the Secretary to the Cabinet, Sir Robert Armstrong, identified for the Prime Minister examples of such actions, of which the most obvious was directing British military power in some way against the Argentine mainland, with air raids against military targets, such as airbases, ships in harbour, military infrastructure, or even civil targets. Such operations would not only be politically unacceptable but also unusually demanding, not least because they would require the carriers, and their escorts, getting into positions well in range of Argentine forces. Similar problems would accompany an attempt to impose a full blockade of Argentina.

Even more straightforward operations carried political risks. For example, when considering the role to be played by the SSNs, which would soon be on station, Armstrong raised the possibility that they should be confined to a reconnaissance role rather than be authorised to attack Argentine naval units. His concern was that an attack would lead to reprisals against the Falkland Islanders and also international opinion turning against Britain, leading to resolutions in the Security Council calling upon a disavowal of force, and possibly to the withdrawal of logistic support by some of those countries now providing it. It is striking in retrospect just how unsure policy-makers were of where limits could be drawn, of what opinion – domestic and international – could stand, of how difficult it would be to explain military imperatives and the potentially shocking effect of casualties. Suez was always in the background, warning of how apparently resolute action could rebound leaving the country isolated. There was a keen sense of the possible fragility of support, ready to turn against Britain almost as soon as military muscles were flexed. In a post-colonial world, and with normal strategic priorities geared to deterrence and avoiding major war, any assertive military action had a retrograde feel.

The military were also aware of these concerns, and feared that rather than test the political tolerances the Government would be inhibited by them, making a difficult task almost impossible. There was a widespread view that the Task Force had been sent just to make a show to support diplomatic attempts to extricate the country from an embarrassing situation. Many in Government and the military were nervous that those who assumed that it was worth sending the Task Force to make a political point were not ready to face the consequences if this political point failed to have an effect. If the attempts to solve the problem politically failed then there would be no choice but to press forward. Bringing the fleet home with Argentina still holding the Falklands would compound the original humiliation. Any sign of hesitation, of second military thoughts, of gearing up for a stalemate rather than victory, would ease the pressure on Argentina just when this might produce the concessions that would provide a real reason for not going to war. If no concessions were obtained then attempting liberation but then failing because of hesitation and restraint at crucial moments would add to the humiliation. The military scrutinised the politicians for signs that they would lose their nerve when it came to the crunch; the politicians sought reassurance that if they kept their nerve, and the crunch was reached, then the military could deliver.

The medium through which the civil-military interface was managed was discussions on the rules of engagement. These provided the means by which ministers could exercise some political control over complicated and hazardous military operations being conducted 8,000 miles away. Three broad princi-ples reflected the attempt to reconcile the conflicting pressures on strategy. First, sufficient military pressure had to be exerted on Argentina to create the conditions for either successful diplomacy or else a successful reoccupa-tion of the Falklands. Second, military action that might be judged excessive or in violation of international law had to be avoided – both because of regard for the principles at stake and the need to sustain the support of allies. This principle generally acted as a restraint on the offensive operations implied by the first. The third principle complicated the first two. This was to keep to a minimum the Task Force's losses. This might seem to imply a further restraint on offensive operations, by requiring close attention to the defensive needs of the forces. In some circumstances this is what happened. In other cases, however, this defensive principle served to ease the restraints, for it added to the importance of attacking certain targets and encouraged reliance on surprise when mounting the attacks.

Early in the conflict Lewin explained to Nott how the ROE should 'define with precision the limits of the action authorised and, at the same time, allow the commander on the spot the maximum freedom to achieve the aim encompassed by the rules.' Reviewing the situation after the war, one senior officer said that the ROEs were often 'difficult to understand' and 'logically tortuous'. 'Some are restrictive with permissive exception', he noted, while 'others the other way round. Certain rules are intended to stand alone, some qualify all other rules – the difference is not always easy to discern in the wording.' As with any 'indistinct order' these features would invite interpretation.

This was relevant to the most important function of the ROEs, which was to send signals to the commanders about the limits within which they were able to conduct their operations. The question of what might be said to Argentina about these limits was a quite different matter. Private warnings via the Swiss (responsible for British interests in Buenos Aires after the breaking of diplomatic relations) or public statements had the advantage of inhibiting Argentine operations as well as furnishing rationales for later British actions when they had to be explained to the international community. They could indicate in advance the geographical areas in which Argentine forces would be most at risk, and also the activities that would invite a British response. For the same reasons, a warning might help Argentine forces avoid traps being set for them. In addition public statements had to be framed with multiple audiences in mind – not only the Junta and its military commanders, but also domestic public opinion, allies and neutrals. This required a certain ambiguity and for this reason, as well as the requirements of security, they could never be as full as the actual ROEs (which tended in practice to be much more restrictive).

The statements created expectations for Britain's future conduct of the war against which actions would later be judged. Yet the conduct of Britain's war would necessarily be influenced by the conduct of Argentina's. Britain could acknowledge this by adding provisos to the main public warnings. There was always the risk that as the conflict developed and Argentine forces became increasingly engaged, these provisos would become even more important than the main statements, as it would become increasingly difficult through public declarations to offer an open commentary on planned actions.

Maritime Exclusion Zone

These issues were first addressed following a proposal from the Chiefs of Staff, arising out of their meeting of 5 April, to establish an Exclusion Zone around the Falkland Islands. The FCO's Legal Adviser strongly advised against describing this as 'a blockade' in any public statements, as in international law this term was closely connected with a state of declared or acknowledged war.[1] He also stressed the importance of giving adequate notice in advance of the Zone, and distinguishing the positions of various types of vessel and aircraft. He proposed that:

1. All Argentine warships and military aircraft entering or found within the area would be treated as hostile and appropriate force would be used accordingly.
2. Other Argentine vessels or aircraft entering or found within the area would be deemed to be there for the purpose of supplying Argentine forces or warships.
3. With regard to the vessels or aircraft of any other State (whether military or civil), the Royal Navy would take all appropriate measures to ensure that they did not supply Argentine forces or warships.

No more force should be used than necessary to achieve the objectives. Unarmed merchant vessels or aircraft could only be attacked as a last resort and when all other means to persuade the vessel not to enter or leave the area had been exhausted.[2]

The zone was to be defined as a circle of 200 nautical miles from latitude 51° 41′ South and longitude 59° 39′ West, approximately the centre of the Islands. The advantage of a circle was precision, although it did mean that some parts of the Islands were only 100 miles from the edge. The awkward shape of a territorial zone would have led to ambiguities in interpretation.[3] The size was judged sufficient to provide enough room to be able to signal to a merchant ship to stop, chase it if it did not, and fire a shot across the bows if it continued to dash for a safe port. By giving warning of the risks that ships or aircraft would face while in the zone, Britain would provide an incentive for Argentine units not to try to reach the Falklands, and this would have many advantages in terms of cutting off the supply lines to the Argentine garrison. Any military action against units within the EZ would be demonstrably related to the political aim and should not jeopardise international support as well as put pressure on Argentina.

By the same token, however, an opportunity to inflict attrition on the Argentine Fleet would be lost if ships knew to stay clear. Also any accidental attack on neutral merchant shipping or indeed any non-naval vessel would attract widespread criticism, particularly in the UN. Freedom to conduct further operations could therefore be politically inhibited. Over time, as Lewin recognised, the EZ could cause problems, for 'the public perception would be that the zone was a sort of jousting area, within which battle would be joined but outside which there was sanctuary for all participants.' This perception was unavoidable, and was indeed reflected in the ROE, which gave far more latitude for the use of force within the zone than without.[4]

SSN ROE

From the start the special problems of SSNs were at the heart of the discussion over ROE. Not only would they be the first boats to arrive in the South Atlantic but they also represented Britain's most important comparative advantage in any naval battle. They lent themselves to surprise attack: indeed they would be very difficult to use in any other way as submarines could not easily fire warning shots or demand that a potential target identify itself. There was therefore a problem of how Britain should use its most offensive and lethal weapon at a time when political considerations weighed heavily on all considerations of the use of force. As the Task Force departed on 5 April, the First Sea Lord had stressed the importance of developing rules of engagement for SSNs over the next two days in order that *Spartan*, the first to arrive around 11 April, was fully prepared for any eventualities. By that afternoon he was able to tell his fellow Chiefs that, following their request, he had prepared draft ROE for SSNs operating in the South Atlantic.

In many ways the easiest approach would have been to adopt the ROEs developed and tested in exercises during the cold war. The political and military context was quite different however and so the Chiefs decided that quite tailored rules would be necessary. One consequence of this was that many rules applied exclusively to SSNs, reflecting their singular lethality, and would not necessarily be in harmony with those adopted for the surface fleet. In the first instance the priority targets for SSNs would be Argentine warships. Civilian targets would be left alone for it would be hard to start a campaign with unrestricted submarine attacks on merchant shipping. This meant that little could be done to cut the supply route to the Falklands. By themselves the SSNs could not identify and turn back merchant shipping in the zone. It would take until approximately 29 April, when the full Task Group was in place, before it would be possible to police the zone in a comprehensive fashion. Once air and sea control was established, merchant shipping could be intercepted, and turned back, and air supplies interdicted.

More positively, warships provided suitable targets because of the threat they posed to the Task Force, the effect of their loss on Argentina's efforts to reinforce and re-supply the Falkland Islands, or even mount a second invasion at a later date, and the boost that would be given to British diplomacy. The issue then became one of whether they could be attacked outside the EZ, which could be escalatory, especially if the relationship to the Falkland Islands was tenuous, and whether any warning should be given to Argentina. Warnings that warships might be attacked, but only in the EZ, would reduce the likelihood of being able to engage the Argentine Navy at all. Its warships could simply avoid the zone.

On 6 April Nott tabled a memorandum for the War Cabinet that tried to get round this problem. He proposed that as soon as possible an SSN would sink one or more Argentine warships, claiming action in self-defence. To achieve surprise no declaration would be made of either the presence of the SSNs or their readiness to use force. Only then would the EZ be declared, as an area within which SSNs could sink Argentine warships as well as any support vessels supplying the Falkland Islands. A third phase would begin once the Carrier Task Group arrived. This would carry out intensive operations to sink Argentine warships, shoot down Argentine military aircraft, and turn back or sink supply vessels, within the EZ. The idea that an SSN could attack a warship without warning as Britain's opening shot appeared too radical and, when the War Cabinet met on 7 April, it was dropped.

That day they considered pressures in the opposite direction: those that might be faced from Secretary of State Haig as he began his diplomatic initiative. Even with Nott's revised proposal to announce the 200-mile Maritime Exclusion Zone (MEZ) with effect from midnight 11/12 April, the FCO were anxious about the timing of the announcement. It would be sending a message to Haig as he arrived in London as well as to the Junta. It had been intended that Nott would announce the zone in his speech to the House that evening, but not long before he was due to speak it was made clear that the FCO was now quite opposed. Nott was furious at the change of plan and saw the whole credibility of the military operation at risk. Just when it was necessary to show resolve to both Haig and the Argentines, Britain would be holding back. There would never be a good time for such an announcement, or indeed any tough measures, because something diplomatic would always be underway.

Whatever the Prime Minister may have thought she was in a difficult position. Having just appointed Pym it was difficult to reject his deeply-felt advice the first time it was proffered. Joined by Whitelaw and Parkinson the argument continued in Thatcher's office in the Commons. In Nott's favour was the date. The next day, 8 April, was also Good Friday, not a good day for a bellicose announcement and, anyway, Parliament would not be sitting. By Saturday Haig could be in Buenos Aires and so the announcement could seem inappropriate then for quite different reasons. Eventually Pym came round. It was agreed that Haig would be informed in advance. Nott later described this as one of 'the most relieving moments of the crisis.' When he made the statement that evening, at the beginning of his speech, it was accepted without question by the Labour Party. Haig was notified in advance of the announcement, but with no time to develop any objections.[5] The MEZ would cover a circle of 200 nautical miles from the centre of the Islands and would take effect from 12 April:

> From the time indicated, any Argentine warships and Argentine naval auxiliaries found within this Zone will be treated as hostile and are liable to be attacked by British forces. This measure is without prejudice to the right of the United Kingdom to take whatever additional measures may be needed in exercise of its right of self-defence, under Article 51 of the United Nations Charter.

On 8 April the War Cabinet endorsed ROE for the SSNs. These had been developed by Lewin in consultation with officials of the Foreign and Commonwealth Office (including the Legal Adviser), MoD and Cabinet Office. On positive identification inside the EZ, Argentine warships, submarines and naval auxiliaries could be attacked. After the first successful attack, the SSN would withdraw from the scene of action and report. Having reported, or if unable to clear report after twelve hours, the SSN would be authorised to continue patrol. Situation Reports were to be made at the commanders' discretion as soon as possible after any subsequent successful attacks and on all Argentine units detected. If the SSNs were attacked, commanders were authorised 'to retaliate as necessary for your self defence both inside and outside the Exclusion Zone'.

The submariners judged the proposed rules to err excessively on the side of caution, most notably in the suggestion that SSN commanders should positively identify Argentine submarines before attacking. This carried very high risks of being spotted and attacked while still in the process of identifying the enemy. One difficulty here was the lack of intelligence about the submarines of other nations that might be in the area. If other South American states, as well as the Russians, could be persuaded to keep all conventional submarines out of the combat zone (and messages were sent to this effect) then it could be assumed that any conventional submarine detected could be presumed to be Argentine and so attacked. The rules were so amended by 10 April. Apart from a last minute problem related to the Haig mediation[6] they came into effect on 12 April when *Spartan* entered the EZ, soon to be followed by *Splendid* on 15 April. The SSNs were warned on 13 April that there could be requirements for early attacks if there was a political need to make a point to Argentina about the vulnerability of their warships. *Spartan* patrolled close to East Falkland while *Splendid* went to the northwest sector of the MEZ, between the main Argentine ports and the Falklands.

7

NON-MILITARY PRESSURE

While the knowledge that a Task Force was on its way put immediate, and unexpected, pressure on Argentina, the risks associated with military action encouraged the British to explore all other means of encouraging Buenos Aires to think again about the wisdom of violating sovereign British territory.

Declaration of war

On hearing of the Argentine occupation of the Falklands a natural reaction was that the proper response to such an act of aggression was a declaration of war. Even before the occupation was confirmed Carrington had asked for advice on the subject. According to the FCO's Legal Adviser, Sir Ian Sinclair, this was the most 'momentous' piece of advice he was ever asked to give but also the 'easiest'.[1] Any action Britain now took could depend on the 'inherent right of individual or collective self defence' as confirmed in Article 51 of the UN Charter. Not only was a firm declaration unnecessary, it would also attract considerable baggage in international law. States at war not only acquire a distinct legal status but so do states not at war, who become neutrals, a status with its own rights and duties. A British declaration of war in 1982, for example, would have had immediate implications for all Argentines resident in or carrying on business in British territory. They could be subjected to a variety of restrictions, up to internment, and the process could lead to the effective abrogation of all contracts involving Argentine nationals, and turn any trading with Argentina into a criminal offence, allowing for the seizure and requisitioning of Argentine merchant ships in British ports and the suspension of all bilateral treaties. There were about 1,000 Argentines with indefinite leave to stay in Britain and another 4,000 with limited leave, of whom about 1,000 were registered with the police. The best assessment was that there was no serious risk of acts of sabotage or terrorism and so there were no security reasons to intern or expel them as this would require emergency legislation as well as invite reciprocal action against British citizens in Argentina.

Because of these far-reaching implications the tendency, unsurprisingly, is to consider entry into a state of war as a technical legal matter rather than as a reasonable description of events. Indeed a state of war can be sustained even in the absence of actual hostilities while the use of force in itself does not necessarily give rise to a state of war. The absence of such a state might suit both parties to a conflict as a means of keeping it limited and avoiding difficult questions in relation to third parties. For a state of war to exist, one side would have to assert that this was so. Hence Sinclair's preference for Article 51 as sufficient legal cover. This could be extended to include any action necessary to repel or expel an invading force, while not precluding the introduction of other diplomatic or economic sanctions.

Britain deciding against declaring war on Argentina did not prevent Argentina declaring war on Britain. This would cause problems if countries that were generally neutral but in practice quite co-operative in helping Britain keep the fleet supplied took the view that their duties as non-belligerents required them to refuse British entry into their ports. One example might be Senegal, which had allowed Britain to use port facilities and overfly its territory. The possibility of an Argentine declaration became a live issue after the recapture of South Georgia, when Costa Mendez observed that technically war now existed between Britain and Argentina. This appeared to be an off-the-cuff remark and was not followed by any statement from the Junta so the inclination was to ignore it. Even so attention had to be given to getting any necessary legislation in place – an Emergency Powers (Falkland Islands) Bill had been drafted – and the policies that would be adopted in relation to Argentines resident in the UK. Given the substantial number of British nationals in Argentina, the Government wished to avoid provoking any retaliatory actions against them.

The 'Trading with the Enemy Act 1939' would automatically come into effect, making it an offence to have any commercial, financial or other intercourse or dealings with or for the benefit of an enemy. This would cover *inter alia* visible exports and imports, payment of royalties, shipping and aviation, banking, consultancy and the provision of all other services. Branches and subsidiaries of British companies operating in Argentina would be defined as 'enemies' for the purpose of the Act, requiring the Boards of the parent UK companies ceasing to have any dealings with them. The Department of Trade considered the Act to be too all-embracing, going much further than Ministers had agreed. It was therefore proposed to include a provision in the draft Emergency Powers Bill making the operation of the Act subject to an Order in Council.

A statement was drafted for the Prime Minister:

We have no quarrel with Argentinians living in this country. We do not propose to intern them. Many have lived here for some time and they are welcome to stay, provided of course that they stay within the law. We trust that our people in Argentina will enjoy similar protection.

Reference would then be made to a statement from the Argentine Minister of the Interior of 25 April that its obligations to British citizens would be honoured. It was further proposed that some statement be made looking forward to the restoration of normal relations and promising to take appropriate actions to safeguard long-standing commercial and personal ties from the effects of the hostilities, but that was thought to set an inappropriate tone. Neither side did declare war.

Without having to go so far as declaring war, there are a number of standard options for a state to follow when falling out with another. They reflect the impossibility of doing business with a country behaving in an outrageous manner but are often also claimed to be carrying some hope of changing the offending behaviour. Because of the severity of the Argentine crime there was never any doubt that there would be a break in economic and cultural as well as diplomatic relations between the two countries. At the cultural level this would only be of marginal relevance. Although an Anglo-Argentine Cultural Convention was in place, implemented by the British Council, there was minimal academic interchange (there were no government-supported British students in Argentina and only 10 Argentine scholars in Britain with British Council support), no cultural events planned on either side and few sporting events, other than a fencing team in Argentina and a Roller Hockey team with a fixture planned at the world championships at the end of April in Portugal. At the end of June the football World Cup was due to start in Spain with both England and Argentina competing.

Economic relations were more substantial. On 2 April, even before the Argentine invasion had been confirmed, the MoD and the Department of Trade sought to establish the position on military equipment and spares awaiting shipment to Argentina, and halted all processing of export licence applications. Yet here also the prior relations between the two countries were not sufficiently close for Britain to exert great pressure on Argentina to mend her ways by disrupting them. Any serious pressure would depend on drawing more countries into the dispute, so increasing Argentina's sense of diplomatic isolation and economic vulnerability. At the same time Argentina would be looking for ways to discomfort Britain. When the FCO worried about international perceptions of intransigence in negotiations or recklessness in military operations it was because of the potential impact on these tangible forms of international support. In seeking to keep up the pressure on Argentina, and deflecting it from Britain, the diplomats had to draw on reserves of political credit and claims of solidarity as well as more pragmatic arguments that suggested that sustaining tough economic sanctions might just make armed force unnecessary.

The credibility of such claims depended on the presumed vulnerability of the Argentine economy to sanctions. Britain also had to consider its own vulnerability. The Suez adventure in 1956 had come to an abrupt halt with the loss of American support and a run on sterling. In practice the extent to which other countries were prepared to implement economic sanctions would serve largely as a measure of general international support for Britain's policies, influencing the course of the conflict more through the indirect psychological effects than direct physical effects.

Argentine vulnerability

The initial assumption was that the Argentine economy was fragile and could be put into severe difficulties through sanctions. There had, after all, been large-scale demonstrations on 30 March against the harsh economic conditions under the Junta. The previous Junta's attempts to stabilise the economy and reduce the rate of inflation had led to a severe recession. Rising unemployment (particularly in the towns), wide income disparities and annual inflation at some 130 per cent at the end of 1981 (among the highest rates in the world) contributed to domestic unrest. This dismal condition was one reason why Galtieri had come to power, yet despite attempts at even stricter austerity measures, inflation had risen further as living standards had fallen.

At the same time the political consequences of increased economic pain were not self-evident. The reconquest of the Malvinas was a popular cause, and the Argentine Trade Union movement was unlikely to encourage action regarded as prejudicing national interests. Nor was there reason to suppose that denying it certain goods and sources of income would soon render it helpless. This was a large country of some 27 million, self-sufficient in energy and food, with adequate supplies of many industrial raw materials and with a quite diversified economy.

In 1980, exports represented eight per cent and imports 11 per cent of Gross Domestic Product (GDP). Over two-thirds of exports were of agricultural produce, with cereals, notably wheat and corn, predominating. Imports were mainly intermediate manufactured goods for the country's substantial industrial sector. The country was a small net oil importer, mainly of heavy crude and specialised products, at around $1 billion in 1981 (representing some 15 per cent of domestic consumption). Some $500 million of domestic lighter crudes were exported. In 1981, the US took an estimated 12 per cent of Argentina's exports while providing almost one-quarter of imports. The European Community was the source of 27 per cent of Argentina's imports and in 1981 provided a market for 23 per cent of the country's exports. In Latin America, Brazil was Argentina's major trading partner, taking 12 per cent of exports and providing nearly 10 per cent of imports. Politically the most intriguing feature of Argentina's trade was the sale of grain to the

Soviet Union. Argentina had stepped in following President Carter's grain embargo on the Soviet Union, imposed as a result of the invasion of Afghanistan. In 1981 a sale of at least 12 million tons of grain represented 36 per cent of Argentina's total exports, and three-quarters of its grain exports, and provided the Soviet Union with around a third of its grain shortfall. Soviet exports to Argentina, however, remained negligible.

Britain had a favourable trade balance with Argentina, with exports (predominantly machinery and power generation equipment) at around £160 million as against imports at £110 million (mainly beef and other food-stuffs). This represented just over three per cent of the Argentine market and of Argentine exports. It was Britain's third largest market in Latin America although only 42nd in Britain's world table. About 60 per cent of British exports were covered by the Export Credit Guarantee Department (ECGD) with firm commitments for business worth £290 million. Britain held about eight per cent of Argentina's direct foreign investment at a book value of up to £250 million and probably higher, representing about 15 per cent of Britain's total investment in Latin America.

The most drastic form of economic pressure that Britain could impose, a physical blockade of Argentina's ports, could create quite serious disruption of trade flows in the short term, but Argentina had extensive land borders with five countries, and so the re-routing of both imports and exports could be arranged quite quickly. It would also be unpopular with third countries trading with Argentina. Only with grain might there be some problems. This pointed to one of the main risks of a blockade, which was that it could involve the Soviet Union directly in the crisis. Action covering imports could result in the loss of essential semi-manufactures and spare parts, creating problems for Argentine industry within months. Argentina could find it difficult to replace some suppliers of high technology goods, but in general it could probably absorb quite large cuts in imports without suffering serious damage. Domestic industry could provide additional supplies of many consumer items.

Argentina's defence industry was fairly broadly based, but had a limited capability. Most major equipment and spares were imported and even local production was heavily dependent on foreign designs, components and technical expertise. Nonetheless, local capacity could sustain most of Argentina's existing equipment in operations short of full-scale hostilities for some weeks or even months. Only if there was extensive and protracted fighting would the loss of imports make a difference, especially with more advanced systems. Much of Argentina's military equipment was of American origin, although increasing amounts had come in recent years from Germany, France and Israel, as well as the UK. If regular suppliers and uncompleted contracts were cut, other sources, probably including neighbouring Brazil and the private arms market, would be sought. In the short term, smaller and simpler items could undoubtedly be provided in substantial quantities provided the finance was available. In the longer term the Soviet Union would be extremely interested in becoming a major arms supplier to Argentina.

An excellent grain harvest and a reduction in the overvalued exchange rate had led to a sharp improvement in Argentina's trade accounts during 1981. The current account deficit had fallen only slightly in 1981 to approximately $4 billion. In the early months of 1982 imports had fallen quite sharply so the deficit might have improved modestly in 1982 without the crisis. The real problem was that the invisibles account remained in substantial and growing deficit because of over $3 billion of interest payments on external debt. Here lay Argentina's most serious economic constraint. The external debt had increased from $12.5 billion at the end of 1978 by some $34 billion over three years, including nearly $10 billion in short-term loans. This debt was equivalent to about one-quarter of GDP. Around 70 per cent of the debt had been borrowed from commercial banks, many from the US but also from Europe and Japan. The claims of UK registered banks (British and foreign) on Argentina were $5.8 billion at the end of 1981. The claims of British banks alone were $2.9 billion in mid-1981, making Britain Argentina's second largest creditor after the US. The debt profile had been improved by replacing short-term with longer-term loans, but still $4.7 billion of medium and long-term debt was believed to fall due in 1982. Argentina could suffer if it could no longer obtain international credit.

From this two conclusions emerged. The first was that Britain acting in isolation could not have much effect on the Argentine economy and the second was that Argentina's greatest vulnerability lay in its dubious creditworthiness. Nonetheless, not too much should be expected here. Even a total collapse of credit would, according to the Treasury in an early assessment, 'not necessarily cut Argentina off from a flow of imports for cash payment out of export proceeds, and although the disruption of trade must begin to affect the population fairly soon, it might be tolerable for a period if morale were buoyed up from other causes'. Sanctions were not going to be decisive, even though the Treasury believed that the quick actions taken by Britain had left Argentina 'taken aback' and worried by the prospective international effects.

In a major assessment of 15 April, the JIC argued that:

> because of the near self-sufficiency of the Argentine economy in the critical areas of food and fuel, trade sanctions alone would not be expected to cause serious economic problems in the short-term. But the longer term effect of action by major trading partners would be of considerable concern to the regime.

So while the Argentine regime would be concerned about the impact of economic sanctions, their real impact would be long-term. The most immediate difficulties would be in raising new external loans against the relatively low level of foreign exchange reserves in an economy prone to capital flight. Imports would have to be reduced: domestic substitution was possible although also probably inflationary. Neither the lending banks nor the regime would wish to precipitate a default but that could not be ruled out. At most these were factors that 'the Argentine Government will have to weigh carefully in deciding whether to seek a negotiated settlement or risk military confrontation'.

Trade

Obtaining international support for trade sanctions was always going to take time and in the first instance depended on the stance Britain was prepared to take on its own. On 1 April, before the actual invasion, the ECGD suspended consideration of any new credit for exports to Argentina. The aim in confining the ban to exports not already shipped was to reduce the scale of problems that could arise with existing contracts. After the invasion the Department of Trade banned the direct export of all military equipment to Argentina.[2] Similar action was soon taken to ban the export of components or spares for military equipment being supplied by third parties wherever these could be identified. A complete ban on exports to Argentina was not introduced, as this would have raised awkward questions of compensation for British exporters. It was assumed anyway that the Argentines would retaliate against a ban on their exports by banning imports from the UK. An embargo on the import of all goods from Argentina was established from midnight on 6 April.

The Import, Export and Customs Powers (Defence) Act 1939 provided the powers to control by Order the export of goods from the UK. The current instrument of control was the Export of Goods (Control) Order 1981. The schedule in the order contained a list of goods, which were controlled for security or strategic reasons.[3] In effect once the Argentines decided to ban all imports from the European Community (EC) this problem largely resolved itself but it was still conceivable that they would wish to buy certain key components and spares, and so items of military potential to be denied to the Argentines were identified. On 23 April the Secretary of State for Trade wrote to colleagues drawing attention to this list but said that for political reasons he did not propose to proceed immediately with an Order to introduce licensing.

The ban on military and other strategic equipment was not without problems. Various anomalies soon emerged. While overseas branches of British companies could be required not to supply banned goods, for extra-territorial reasons this could not be required of subsidiaries. There were also uncertainties over the ultimate destination of goods, particularly components. These required a combination of direct discussions with companies, or in the case of onward sales, working with relevant allies to make sure that they had similar bans in place to those of Britain. In one important case, Rolls-Royce's Brazilian subsidiary, Motores Rolls-Royce, served the whole South American market for civil engine spares and overhauls. If Motores Rolls-Royce attempted to avoid trading with Argentina they might fall foul of local laws, but if no more spares were sent to Brazil for general distribution then this could eventually ground the airlines of other South American countries. In the end it had to be left to Motores Rolls-Royce to deal pragmatically with the matter, for example by obtaining from countries other than Argentina declarations that spares were for their own use.[4]

At the start of the conflict British ships were warned through the General Council of British Shipping not to enter Argentine territorial waters, and to keep clear of the Falkland Islands. Those in Argentine ports were advised to leave. At the time there was one ship up river from Buenos Aires and two further ships en route for Argentine ports. Britain did not have the formal powers to seize Argentine ships and aircraft, although this could be handled through emergency legislation and they could possibly prohibit them leaving UK ports. British Caledonian, the only British airline operating a scheduled service to Argentina, had cancelled the day flights and suspended further services. This made it easier to suspend formally all air services. Aerolineas Argentinas had also suspended its service. Any further action would therefore be largely presentational, although it was just possible that the Argentines might seek to embarrass Britain by sending a flight to London that the Government could legally not refuse. On 8 April the FCO recommended to the Prime Minister that the operating rights of Aerolineas Argentinas into London should be suspended. It was thought preferable to do this as part of the general package of economic measures against Argentina than risk having to do so later in isolation, which might draw attention to the use of air service agreements as a political weapon and set a damaging precedent for Britain in its relations with other countries.

Financial measures

The Cabinet decided on 2 April to explore freezing Argentine banking deposits in the UK. Quick action would be necessary to prevent their withdrawal for, if they could be removed, Buenos Aires would enjoy a free hand with British assets in Argentina. Even so, as Argentina was a substantial debtor of Britain, freezing bank deposits would not greatly damage its economy. A Statutory Instrument bringing into effect powers under Section 2 of the 1964 Emergency Laws (Re-enactments and Repeals) Act was laid before Parliament during its session of 3 April.[5]

The value of the Argentine assets involved was estimated to be approaching $1.5 billion, almost one-quarter of Argentine total liquid assets in all financial centres. They would remain frozen except in the rare cases where the Treasury might grant permission for release.[6] Only later, after the higher figure had been given to journalists, was it realised that in the first few days of April substantial sums were transferred from London to New York, meaning that the actual amount frozen was closer to $900 million. The Chancellor, Sir Geoffrey Howe, also noted that there was evidence that the total of UK claims on Argentina had fallen by some $500 million between the end of 1981 and the close of business on 2 April. No attempt was made to interfere with normal transactions of bank branches of financial centres outside the UK, or with the entrepot handling by London agents of syndicated international loans, or with roll-over of normal Euro-dollar loans provided no net new resources or shift of resources was involved. Not only would this have had minimal effect on Argentina, it might also have generated conflicts of interest with other financial centres

This action against Argentine assets had an immediate impact on Argentina's standing in capital markets worldwide. A British bank withdrew from a loan about to be placed in which it was a leader. Other countries soon showed themselves unwilling to contemplate new commitments toward Argentina. 'The focus on the very poor underlying economic position of the Argentine economy is strong', noted the Treasury, 'and the massive external borrowing requirement of Argentina during 1982, much of it to service existing debt, has been widely quoted.' Argentina's borrowing requirement for 1982 was estimated at $17.4 billion to finance short and long-term loans, mainly from commercial banks. Yet there was an issue about how far this could be pushed. If Argentina was driven into formal default there could be serious implications for the international banking system, whereas the additional strain on Argentina would for some time be quite small. Argentina was soon blocking the transfer of payments to the UK to service debt and could well be short of immediate funds owed to other countries. The Treasury judged that Argentina could fall significantly further into arrears before the international banking community, or individual members of it, would decide that the time had come to declare default.

Appeals were made to friendly governments to match Britain's actions. It was unclear how successful this effort would be, given that Britain had not always responded to similar appeals by others in the past and in many countries the banking systems were quite independent of government. No other European country, for example, had been prepared to freeze Iranian assets when the Americans had asked Britain to do so during the hostage crisis of 1980. Furthermore, the claims by international banks against Argentina exceeded the assets they held by about four to one. Nevertheless, Argentina could still be damaged if states gave guidance to their banks to make no loans to Argentina. This would make it hard for them to finance their external deficit and counter the outflow of capital. Britain could also hamper any application Argentina might make to the International Monetary Fund (IMF), although there were strong policy objections to opposing a first tranche application by Argentina. Only if a subsequent application was made to the IMF, would it be worth considering mobilising EC opposition.

In its 15 April assessment, the JIC identified the financial side as the most immediately worrying aspect of the crisis for the Argentines. The loss of market confidence could restrict the amount of short-term money on offer, and they would be forced to take action to improve their balance of payments position, notably by restricting imports. Strict exchange control measures had been implemented but there remained the possibility of further capital flight, putting pressure on the reserves. Faced with a growing inability to raise funds in international markets, the Argentines might consider repudiating existing debt, but default would not be an easy option. Argentina would be excluded from international capital markets for a number of years and, more importantly, few countries would be prepared to trade with them on anything other than a cash basis. The result could be a very serious dislocation of their trade. Even so, if servicing the existing debt became increasingly problematic a default could be triggered within a matter of weeks. As a result of cross-default clauses, much of Argentina's outstanding debt could fall due for immediate payment.

As Argentina was one of the largest debtors in the world (larger even than Poland), such a default would have very serious international effects. Given the very low levels of Argentine assets held in most Western banks, the JIC was sure that: 'most creditors would be extremely unwilling to consider such a course of action'. The War Cabinet recognised the danger. While any decision to declare Argentina in default lay in the hands of its creditors there was no advantage in precipitating one. This might hurt creditors more than the Argentines and have harmful consequences throughout the international banking system.[7]

International support

In terms of extracting the maximum political benefit from economic sanctions, much depended on getting wider international support. Lord Carrington, just prior to his resignation on 5 April, sent a long minute on the matter to the Prime Minister, taking as his starting point Britain's inability itself to inflict severe damage to the Argentine economy and the need to involve Britain's partners in Europe and beyond. The best assumption was that they would be 'sympathetic but reluctant to take action damaging to their own interests.' Somehow, therefore, early action must be made 'as easy for them as possible'. Here there was an advantage in Britain's membership of the European Community.[8] In addition to the flagrant violation of international law and Security Council Resolution 502, the Falklands was also covered by Part 4 of the Treaty of Rome as a dependent territory of a Member State. The first task was to line up Britain's European partners behind sanctions. In 1980 EC trade with Argentina totalled about $4 billion, with a $460 million surplus.

While there were limits on how far they would be prepared to go they would at least impose an arms embargo. The Germans, for example, reported that they would stop the building of submarines and frigates in German yards, although these would in any case not be completed for another few months. Some other limited trade measures might also be implemented, notably banning selected agricultural imports from Argentina, consisting mainly of beef (to Germany and the UK) and cereals. Several EC members might welcome this action on Common Agricultural Policy grounds, in effect to protect their domestic producers, and for similar reasons they might take action on other 'sensitive' products such as textiles, footwear, clothing and steel. The list of items, which it was proposed that EC partners should be urged to stop importing from Argentina, was later extended to include sheep meat and vegetable oil, even though the impact of these would be slight. Argentine leather was not added to the list in view of its importance to the German and Italian shoe-making industries.

Other possibilities would be withholding guarantees on export credits to Argentina, especially as the blow to international confidence in the Argentine economy as a result of the decision to invade cast further doubt on its credit-worthiness. Argentina could also be struck from the list of beneficiaries under the Generalised Preference Scheme, which had given it, along with other developing countries, preferential access to the EC's market. Seeking a complete embargo, however, would be problematic. There was a risk of long drawn out discussions if Britain pressed its partners to go much further. It might be best to get a quick decision on initial measures, leaving open the possibility of additional measures for later.

Supporting action should be taken under Article 224 of the Treaty of Rome, and should be implemented nationally but co-ordinated as to timing and extent. Britain called for an immediate meeting of the Permanent Representatives (COREPER) on 6 April, before the Easter Holiday. Member countries would be invited to take the same action as Britain, with the fall-back position of selective measures against certain Argentine exports. On the financial side the objective was to get guaranteed exports credit to Argentina withheld, exclusion from the Generalised Preference Scheme and banks to be discouraged from further lending. The Prime Minister sent messages, covering the substance of the various proposals, to Community Heads of Government urging their support and providing some indication of the fallback. On 10 April Community members agreed a total ban on Argentine imports, excluding those under existing contracts, along with an embargo on arms exports. As the Prime Minister acknowledged, this decision 'cannot have been very easy for our partners, given the commercial interests at stake.'[9] As it took time to sort out all the legal aspects of the ban, the sanctions did not come into effect until 17 April, and were to last, initially, for four weeks. Most member states were unlikely to authorise further export credits under the circumstances. The provision of new loans was also unlikely.

In addition, the old Commonwealth was extremely supportive. Canada, Australia and New Zealand banned imports from Argentina and agreed to grant no new export credits. New Zealand also banned exports and, with Canada, embargoed military supplies. Hong Kong, the only Dependent Territory with significant trade links with Argentina, banned imports. The Japanese Government took no action, other than warn that economic relations with Argentina could be affected if the dispute continued. Eventually it issued advice to Japanese firms designed to prevent any actions that would undermine trade sanctions by other countries. It was also disinclined to issue new official credits for exports to Argentina. This position, as much for reasons of prudence as politics, was adopted by a number of countries. Other countries were generally supportive. Norway banned imports, while Switzerland, Portugal, Sweden and Austria banned arms exports. Korea cancelled a trade mission to Argentina.

The biggest gap in all of this was the US. The FCO view was that the shock effect to the Argentine Government of trade measures by the United States would be as important as any direct economic damage. The US took some $744 million of imports from Argentina (compared with the UK's $251 million), nine per cent of total Argentine exports but less than one per cent of US trade. The most telling measure, as with the EC, would be a ban on food and animal imports, accounting for over three per cent of total Argentine exports. The Americans would have no trouble finding alternative sources of supply. A ban on petroleum products (around one per cent of total Argentine exports) would also have a significant effect. Argentina owed some $7.5 billion dollars to the US, as against American liabilities of $2.4 billion. Direct investment by the United States in Argentina was now assumed to be near $3 billion. Export credit exposure totalled $1.8 billion in September 1980. There was already a ban on military supplies, imposed by Congress in 1978 on human rights grounds. Contracts in the pipeline for spare parts for US equipment currently held by Argentina (notably helicopters, armed personnel carriers and carrier-borne aircraft) remained frozen although some spares were believed to be 'trickling' through. As this was fairly old equipment, Argentina could probably obtain spares from dealers and possibly neighbouring countries quite easily.

While American mediation was underway the US was unwilling to take any action on trade. In addition to the problems posed by these efforts, the Americans were also wary of imposing sanctions because of the consequences for their relations with Latin America, their obligations as a member of the Organisation of American States (OAS) and a party to the Rio Treaty. All that was done by Washington was to opt for a prudent course on Government Credit Insurance, by avoiding new commitments until the policy was clarified, and taking a defensive line on banking credit, with some readiness to roll over existing credits if past ones were repaid. The FCO view was that even if the US Government did no more than advise banks in America not to undertake new lending, this could have a 'serious impact'. About half of the $10 billion of short-term Argentine loans maturing in 1982 was owed to the US. When American mediation eventually failed, the US suspended new export/import bank credit and guarantees, and commodity credit guarantees.

The Treasury became progressively unsure about the wisdom of Washington freezing Argentine assets, on the grounds that this might do more damage to the international banking community generally than to Argentina, now severely isolated. Banks were already not issuing new loans. Having used its influence to discourage new credits, especially in the first couple of weeks, there was soon 'little or no need for discouragement. Overall, we reckon that Argentina is now effectively denied international financial help.' A formal default would give Buenos Aires some temporary alleviation with an excuse to suspend servicing of existing debt, and get Britain blamed for creating a difficult situation for the banking community. The MoD was less inclined to let Argentina off the hook, wondering whether more could be done to hinder access to short-term loans that could be used to finance arms purchases. Where they agreed with the Treasury was in seeking to dispel any notion that financial sanctions would do the political trick. Part of the case of those opposed to military action was that sanctions could serve as an alternative by bringing Argentina 'to her knees' and the unreality of this position had to be made clear.

8

AGAINST BRITAIN

The possibility of pressure was not just one-way. The Government was aware of a number of means by which Argentina could make life uncomfortable. In particular there were grounds to be concerned about the position of the group whose fate had prompted the crisis in the first place – the Falkland Islanders.

Islanders

The original Argentine plan was to establish an administration in the Falklands with a normal garrison of about 500 troops. An army battalion was flown in on 2 April, and most of the assault force was withdrawn. The warships under Rear Admiral Allara returned to the mainland while the transports completed the unloading of heavy equipment. Stanley airport became Base Aerea Militar Malvinas, and four Pucara aircraft flew in on 2 April. General Garcia and Rear Admiral Busser returned to the mainland, and a few days later Brigadier General M Menendez arrived as Garrison Commander and Military Governor. To support him in the latter role he had a forty strong civil affairs team staffed by military officers and non-commissioned officers (NCOs). He saw his main task as looking after the islanders. Only as news came through of London's decision to send a Task Force did he have to give thought to the problems of defence and of managing a garrison that would exceed 10,000.

As the Governor and the Royal Marines left, the civilian population at Stanley was allowed to carry on 'as usual'. By and large Argentine forces behaved properly towards the islanders. There were some exceptions. Major Patricio Dowling soon got a reputation for being tough and threatening. On 13 April the Chief Secretary, Dick Baker, and his wife were deported along with Ronnie Lamb, the Chief Police Officer, Ray Checkley, the Magistrate, and Bill Luxton, a leading figure in local politics. On 27 April 14 islanders, including members of the Falkland Islands Committee and the Defence Force, some with their children, were moved to Fox Bay. The Senior Medical Officer was also detained, largely because he opposed the use of the hospital for Argentine troops.[1] There they stayed with the local manager, keeping up with events using a hidden radio, and finding shelter from British shells and bombs by spending the nights under the floorboards.[2] For most of May the population of Goose Green was confined to a meeting hall in unpleasant conditions. As the fighting touched the Islands it produced its own dangers and anxieties, and eventually counted for the lives of three islanders. Daily life under occupation, with uncertainty about the long term, was inevitably difficult. The islanders were, at least in Stanley, able to talk to each other and even hold meetings in the West Store.

As in Britain, the critical factor in terms of popular attitudes and morale was the knowledge that a Task Force had been assembled so quickly and was on its way. This meant that the islanders knew that liberation was possible. Nonetheless, it could be hard to sustain hopes of liberation as more Argentine troops and equipment were brought ashore. Most civilian Land Rovers had been requisitioned. There was little for people to do, although colour television sets had been made available. The telephone system was jammed with military traffic and the local radio was treated warily as a source of news because of its controlled content. On 6 April, in addition to demanding that all civilians must carry identification documents, the military government required that all HAM radios and 2-metre transmissions were to cease forthwith and the equipment had to be handed in to the military.[3] Not surprisingly, compliance with this order was modest. For the coming weeks, the ability to get news through the BBC World Service became critical in sustaining morale. The audibility of the BBC's special services to the Falkland Islands was good. They were broadcast daily for 35 minutes. The reports of the progress of the Task Force encouraged the islanders and helped them keep up their spirits.[4]

The occupying forces put their own personnel into government departments such as the Secretariat, Education, Public Works, Post Office and eventually the Medical Department (where an Argentine doctor was inserted to run the hospital alongside an islander doctor).[5] Financial Secretary, Harold Rowlands, the most senior member of the former government left, had initially also considered leaving rather than work closely with Argentines in the civil administration but relented, at least for an interim period, to be able to do his best for the local people. He resisted requests for information of strategic interest, notably about South Georgia and the British Antarctic Territory.

Argentine preparations for the civil administration had been rushed and were inadequate. Comodoro Carlos Bloomer-Reeve was appointed Head of the Secretariat and acted as a liaison between the civilian population and military administration. He was an Air Force officer who had spent time in the Falklands some years previously and was well known to and respected by many islanders. During the occupation he managed to retain that respect by being fair and considerate in his dealings with the islanders, in contrast to

Dowling. Bloomer-Reeve changed the road traffic code, but the result was chaos, and the Argentines were obliged to put up signs in English, saying 'Keep Right', and to paint large white arrows on the road surfaces. The Post Office 'Royal Mail' sign and cipher soon had a twin sign in the Spanish language. Argentine stamps were issued. Mail services continued to the UK and other parts of the world but only letters and postcards were accepted (parcels could be sent only to the mainland). There were suspicions that some mail was censored and towards the end of the conflict large amounts of mail were held up both in the Islands and Argentina, but fears that stamp stocks and other postal matter would be disposed of proved to be unfounded.[6] At the same time much of the mail intended for the Argentine conscripts did not reach them. The Falklands were also put on the same time zone as Argentina.

The Argentines wanted schools to continue but, despite concerns about the effect on education, the islanders decided that they did not want to hand Argentina a propaganda coup. Many children had also been moved to the Camp, the area outside Stanley. The Falkland Islands Government Air Service (FIGAS) was also told to stay operational, but this was judged to be far too dangerous. The islanders were anxious about the possible behaviour of the Argentine soldiers, especially in the event of an imminent defeat, a concern that was apparently shared by some of the senior officers. The Argentine Military Police were active, increasingly so as the conflict developed, as conscripts became cold, wet and hungry and were reported to have broken into houses and stolen food. On the whole, civil-military relations remained correct and there were only a few minor incidents.

Evacuation

One issue of immediate relevance that came through from a BBC report, on 9 April, was of a letter received in London from the Falklands signed by several people, including the Chief Constable, saying that they wished for a ship to be sent to evacuate the civilian population. Rex Hunt had stated that 90 per cent of the islanders wished to stay, and it was noticeable that the letter did not include the signature of any of the elected members of the Falklands Government. As one islander, Ian Strange, noted in his diary: 'We have heard talk of the letter, but no one seems to have actually seen it or to know who has signed it. Hope the community is not going to split into sections acting independently for their own safety. Now is the time for unity not fragmentation.'[7]

In London news of the conditions of the islanders was sparse. The concern about how they would cope under Argentine occupation was compounded by the risks they would face when it came to liberating them by military means. It was part of the instructions to the Task Force commander that the safety of the islanders should be a critical restraint on any plans for the re-occupation of the Islands. In a blockade the islanders could be expected to suffer shortages along with the Argentines. One way of keeping the islanders out of harm's way was to evacuate them all from the Falklands. This raised practical problems, in terms of finding them all and, with Argentine co-operation, getting them to Uruguay and thence on to the UK, but these were manageable. There were larger issues of principle. A territory without British inhabitants was exactly what Buenos Aires had been after: it would take away the justification from the Task Force and undermine the claim for sovereignty. Argentina might not want to lose potential hostages but they might also be tempted to encourage islanders to leave and replace them with its own nationals, thereby altering the complexion of the population. Yet if the Government failed to respond to requests for evacuation and islanders were subsequently hurt then, to use the dry language of official submissions, 'there could be presentational difficulties.'

According to the 1981 census, before the crisis 1,813 islanders had been distributed between 1,050 in Stanley, 441 in the rest of East Falkland and 322 in West Falkland. By 26 April ninety people had been evacuated, but these were largely UK citizens on contract work and had not been included in the census. It was known that substantial numbers of people from Stanley had left to go into the 'Camp' where it would be safer. Those returning to Britain reported that 'up to 50% of the Port Stanley residents had left the town and gone to live on the Camp,' which would put the remaining number at around 500, but defence intelligence thought this too high and took 'recent press reports' to indicate that even more civilians had left. They later took the number down to as low as 180 in Stanley, with the rest in home-steads in East Falkland, of which the largest group of some 150, including many children, had gone to Darwin/Goose Green. Those staying in Stanley had moved to stone houses in the centre of the town. The FCO tended to use a figure of 300 as the maximum still in Stanley. In fact the numbers staying were significantly higher than this. A report based on a count by the local civil defence warden put the number at 500, and there were also reports that civilians who had gone to the Camp were returning because of over-crowding and difficulties with the water supply.

The evacuees suggested a lowering of morale in Stanley, with sterner Argentine attitudes. 'Military hygiene standards are low with clear signs of dysentery.' Roadsides had been mined, some bridges prepared for demolition and areas close to town and airport declared closed:

> There appears to be general non-co-operation by the islanders with
> the force of occupation but no open hostility. The Argentines seem
> to have been well prepared for the occupation, with lists of person-
> alities etc. They also seem to have appointed an Argentine Officer as
> Police Chief (Intelligence), who is not making himself popular with
> the Islanders; and could be a 'hard-liner'. Outside Stanley there are

currently no restrictions on civilian movement by foot or vehicle and ID checks and body searches are not being made.

From late April to early June, with the exception of a letter dated 7 May, virtually no first-hand reports of life under Argentine rule became available. The DIS estimate from 27 April was that about 545 civilians were in Stanley, accepting that some who had fled immediately after the Argentine invasion had returned, probably because of a shortage of supplies elsewhere and worry about the safety of empty property. Cold and tired troops were believed to be sleeping in vacated property, resulting in some pilfering, but the Argentine authorities had paid compensation in such cases. This was reasonably accurate, yet as late as 11 June the FCO was still using an estimate of only 200 islanders in Stanley.

The Chairman of the Falkland Islands Company, C Needham, visited the Prime Minister on 15 April. He was still receiving telexes from his manager on the spot, and this was one of the few means available of passing messages as well as gauging the mood among the islanders. At this time he seemed to think that a number wished to leave to somewhere safer, and his Company was prepared to help finance their departure. He even raised the issue of a more general evacuation. When he probed further, however, he did not find evidence of islanders anxious to leave, except for some concerns about older people and children. Most were waiting to see what happened. The Government tended to assume, although without much evidence, that those in the Camp were more likely to want to stick it out while those in Stanley were more likely to want to leave. Communications were certainly difficult with the Camp and so whatever their preferences people outside of Stanley would probably have to stay put. The DIS assessment was that more would leave now if they could, although the evidence for this was contradictory. Some of those that had left believed that others would follow: the evidence from those who had stayed, such as employees of the Falkland Islands Company, was that they had not changed their minds.

At most it was assumed by late April that between 100 and 200 would wish to leave temporarily. Their conditions were unlikely to improve. If the blockade was successful, shortages in food and other essentials could be expected and fighting would put civilians at risk. Meanwhile if the blockade was properly enforced aircraft would not be able to get in and out. The Argentines would probably not want to risk aircraft for the sake of civilians and might prefer to keep them on the Islands as effective hostages. If they wanted to leave this would probably then depend on an evacuation ship arranged by the International Committee of the Red Cross (ICRC). The ICRC had offered good offices to both sides on 2 April and London had accepted at once. It had been trying, with British encouragement, to gain access to the Islands to check the state of affairs. Initially this was turned down by Argentina but they later accepted the idea in principle, although they were still not offering an early presence. It was assumed that one reason why Argentina had repatriated British prisoners so quickly was to frustrate ICRC attempts to get to the Islands. The British were anxious that something should be done before the Exclusion Zone began to be fully enforced. On the other hand it could not be seen to be pushing the issue, as this might appear to be colluding with the ICRC. Efforts by the Red Cross to get a representative into Stanley to assess the local situation were repeatedly rebuffed by Argentina. Later, despite British promises that Red Cross flights would be allowed, Argentina used the EZ as an excuse.

The Government was certainly not anxious to encourage people to leave and there was concern that even raising the issue publicly could send quite the wrong signals to the islanders. The FCO took the view that no assurances could be given to the Falkland Islands Company or to the islanders about financial loss: 'The question of reparations for losses resulting from the Argentine invasion or subsequent hostilities' would have to be part of a larger long-term settlement. If they offered what would amount to 'a blank cheque to the Islanders for their evacuation, reception and eventual return, it seems likely that very many would opt to leave':

> It would need to be made clear to the Islanders that they are not being offered compensation or indemnification, and they will be expected to return to the Falkland Islands when it becomes possible.

The implication of the stance was that if any islanders arrived at Montevideo and in need of help from the Government, unless deported by Argentines, they should only get the normal provisions for distressed British subjects and would have to sign an undertaking to repay the costs of fares. In the circumstances this sounded harsh. There were no indications that the islanders were rushing to leave: just understandable anxieties about being caught in cross-fire and, if the guidance from London was to get out, a lack of resources with which to do so.

The eventual position taken was that the Government would pay the return fares of islanders who wished to leave temporarily but would not push the point. 'It would be a mistake at the moment to encourage departures.' Pym set the line on 19 April when he said in the House that sympathetic consideration would be given to the question of temporary evacuation of islanders who wished to leave. If they did decide to leave the issue was neither money nor a problem of absorbing a sudden flow of refugees. The numbers were small and most had families in the UK. The Home Office considered how to cope with a small number of effectively destitute families without loss of dignity or unseemly arguments with local authorities responsible for their care. It was then decided that a fuller statement was needed. The Governor argued that a public announcement that return fares would be paid would 'create consternation among remaining islanders', and might build up more pressures to evacuate than currently existed. The statement generally was to be presented as a response to requests for guidance rather than as a British attempt in some way to encourage people to leave. It confirmed the Government's concern for the safety of islanders and that if any wished to 'leave temporarily until the immediate crisis is past, we will give sympathetic help to ensure that they are not prevented from doing so by lack of means.' It was broadcast by the BBC on 26 April and was repeated by the Prime Minister in the Commons.

The Anglo-Argentines

The total number of Anglo-Argentines was put at 100,000. These were largely people of British descent who had settled in Argentina, the vast majority taking out Argentine citizenship. There were about 17,000 UK passport-holders with another 30,000 who might be entitled to passports. The large majority of these were firmly established in Argentina in the professional and commercial sectors. The initial estimates were that perhaps 7,500 short stay British citizens might wish to get out. From 5 April the BBC transmitted advice to British citizens in Argentina to make plans to leave the country by normal commercial means unless they had a pressing need to stay. With the Embassy closed, four British officials remained behind to man a British Interest Section in the Swiss Embassy in Buenos Aires.

On 9 April a telegram came from the Chairman of the British Community Council to the Prime Minister, recording the respect shown for the British way of life in the Argentine Republic and the lack of animosity shown over the days of the conflict. The telegram requested no more than a search for a peaceful solution and consideration of the position of the Anglo-Argentine community. A firm but courteous reply was sent back, regretting the anxieties caused to British people in Argentina but stressing the importance of the rule of law.

On 10 April it was learned in Britain that a number of prominent Anglo-Argentines were planning to go to the Islands to meet with the Executive Council. A six-member delegation arrived on 16 April. It appeared their task was to allay the fears of the islanders about becoming part of Argentina and perhaps suggest some solution to the problem. Strange, who met two of the delegation, concluded that they were genuine in their concerns and anxious about the repercussions if fighting was to break out in the Falklands. It was, as Strange noted, 'in effect ... a form of plea to the Islanders to accept what had happened and try and make a new life out of the situation.' He explained that 'Their own acceptance of Argentine customs, language and politics had been their choice; we had suddenly had this thrust upon us, which was a very different situation indeed.'

The group returned on 23 April, following a meeting with Galtieri, at which time they had submitted a proposal for a settlement of the issue. At the core of the proposal was the maintaining of the 'way of life', which they understood to be the most important thing to the islanders. This led to the suggestion that Stanley should remain as it was, and that Argentina would build a new town elsewhere. Strange queried what 'would happen about our currency, laws, export of our main produce, our stamps and postal system, none of which was mentioned and of course could not remain remotely the same under an Argentine regime.' He saw the proposal as indicative of how the islanders were viewed, 'a simple, camp community, which in the eyes of the generals, wanted nothing other than a "superficial" existence.' The visitors were allowed to hold a public meeting at Stanley, but all this produced were some bitter exchanges.[8]

A reflection of islander views comes from the diary of one islander on West Falkland:

> This afternoon a group of two-faced Anglo-Argies talk on Stanley radio and suggest that they don't want war & neither do we so suggest we accept Arg sovereignty and the Argies will leave us alone and just build their own town with Governor etc. and we can have our own 'committees' and ask for our views – they get them from all farms which can still call up Stanley. BALLS! We don't want a war and people getting killed but look who started it – now they can accept the consequences. We heard on the grapevine that they got the same unanimous reply in Stanley as well. There is no creature worse than an Anglo-Argie – their loyalty is purely to their pocket and the country which best suits their pocket at the time and NOTHING else.

That things could look different in Buenos Aires even from the perspective of the senior British diplomat left there, in charge of the British Interests Section in the Swiss Embassy, can be illustrated in a telegram sent on 30 April. This considered the consequences of Galtieri's fall. No scenarios 'give much confidence that Argentina will be any easier to deal with after Galtieri than now. The Falklands will be ours, but for what purpose, at what national cost, and for how long?' He spoke of a healing time dependent upon the magnitude of the casualties. His preference would be for a surgical victory and then the Islands 'handed promptly over to UN or US or joint administration as a magnanimous gesture of victory. It will have been worth making our points against the use of force and for democracy.' The alternative was a 'pyrrhic victory, bringing chaos in this country and irreparable long term damage to our interest on this continent, if not wider afield.' On 6 May Murchison of the Anglo-Argentine community sent another telegram warning that 'There is a growing feeling of indignation in this country which is serving to unite Argentina and preparing it to face a bitter struggle.'

On 13 May Murchison arranged a meeting involving Moya, an Admiral close to the Junta, and the head of the British Interests Section. His ideas now involved offering Argentina a base on the Falklands in return for the status quo ante in everything else, and negotiations over sovereignty, but only the idea of a base was passed to Moya who did not comment. The British diplomat was also not prepared to express a view. Neither side appears to have taken the effort very seriously. By the end of May, Murchison was putting his efforts into reporting back to London on the well-being of the islanders and looking forward to eventually being able to establish a 'cordial and beneficial relationship' between the two countries.

While undoubtedly anxious, the Anglo-Argentine community was well embedded in the Argentine establishment and not too vulnerable. Bank accounts could be frozen but that would not be so simple as those involved were residents of Argentina, not of the UK, and also long practised in moving their money around to mitigate the effects of inflation and devaluation. Other possibilities, but also problematic in practice, would be to target institutions such as the British Community Council and the English/Spanish bilingual schools. The Argentine authorities behaved properly both to the British in Argentina and to the islanders. Yet there were sinister reports during the course of April that a unit of the Argentine Army Intelligence Service had orders to 'remove' (i.e. probably kill) a number of British and Argentine citizens believed to be British agents. Perhaps as many as 500 individuals were on the list. Blame would be assigned to the Montoneros guerrillas, who had been largely beaten in the 1975–8 'War against Subversion' but whose leader, exiled in Cuba, had offered to co-operate with the Argentine Government in mounting attacks on British citizens and property anywhere in the world. It was also known that plans existed to expropriate British-owned land and possessions following any hostilities. It was hard to assess these claims. They could be disinformation, designed to deter.

With the start of serious hostilities in May reports grew in number of various plans for private enterprise terrorism or assassination plots, including against British officials in neighbouring countries. One was viewed sufficiently seriously for measures to be taken to protect a named person at the Montevideo Embassy from a naval intelligence hit squad. As the Uruguayan Government did not think the threat serious, and there was a risk that exaggerated publicity could lead to a mass exodus of British citizens, there was some debate about the wisdom of publicising the danger. The Argentine Government was still clearly reluctant to sanction any acts of terrorism abroad or violence against British citizens in Argentina, lest it damage attempts to create a public image of acting entirely correctly at all times.

Economic measures

On the economic side the first and unsurprising measures taken were to ban payment for imports of goods and services from the United Kingdom (including payment of dividends on British investments) and suspend repayments of loans. The Argentine authorities set up an escrow account in New York in which payments due to the UK would be held. The repudiation of Argentine debts to British banks (worth $3.6 billion) would be extremely serious, but Argentina had strong reasons for avoiding this, even after hostilities had begun. Even so the FCO warned that: 'in the emotional climate which fighting would generate, such a step cannot be ruled out'. On 13 April Argentina also imposed a formal ban on imports from those countries that had taken economic sanctions against it. These actions seemed to be geared to matching those taken against Argentina, which gave grounds for hope that anything more, such as the confiscation of British assets, would not be implemented short of further escalation. Several companies with significant investments in Argentina, including Unilever, Shell and Pilkingtons, were registered in countries other than Britain, notably the Netherlands. In these cases, confiscation seemed less likely. In no case did companies' investments in Argentina appear to be significant in relation to their global operations. Within the banking sector, Barclays Bank and Lloyds Bank International lent on the domestic Argentine market and were rumoured to have lost deposits, but not to unmanageable levels.

The restrictions on exports to Argentina were unlikely to have a significant impact on Britain's trading position worldwide or have major industrial or employment consequences. The one exception was John Brown Engineering, involved in two power generation contracts, both nearing completion. Nor was it expected that confiscation of British assets would have serious consequences for the British economy or even for the majority of companies involved, except in the banking sectors. The Bank of London and South America had a particularly important stake with 37 branches in Argentina. This was the third largest foreign-owned bank in Argentina with deposits totalling the equivalent of $315 million. About 60 per cent of British exports were covered by ECGD, who had firm commitments for business worth £290 million, of which £72 million related to payments due to be made in 1982. There was also some £8 million at risk under ECGD Investment Insurance facilities, which could be the subject of claims when, and if, Argentina retaliated against UK investments. While it was tempting to suppose that the Argentine bank deposits in the UK would be available to cover these potential bad debts, these assets had been frozen, not expropriated.[9]

A decree blocking the transfer by British residents of share holdings in Argentine companies was published on 10 May. The measure was reportedly introduced to comply with the Presidential decree issued on or around 5 April that temporarily froze Argentine payments to the UK. The Argentine Government also published on 19 May a law prohibiting the sale or transfer of British assets, including property, in Argentina. Details of all assets and of those involved in transactions since 2 April had to be notified to the Ministry of the Interior. This would enable the Ministry to compile a register of British assets, making possible the introduction of confiscatory measures at short notice. There were exemptions for permanently resident British citizens providing they did not involve themselves in any activity endangering the national economy or Argentina's productive capacity. This did not lead to any take-over of the administration of British interests in Argentina.

Latin America

There were 32,000 British citizens elsewhere in Latin America. Britain had embassies in 13 capitals (with 136 members of the diplomatic service in post), plus the Interest Section in Buenos Aires and a First Secretary at the Swiss Embassy in Guatemala and two Consulates-General. There was a risk of violence or demonstrations and all posts were urged to prepare for such eventualities. By 14 May there had been anti-British demonstrations in Venezuela, Peru and Ecuador but nothing unmanageable.

Brazil and Mexico were Britain's most important Latin American markets, taking 20 per cent and 15 per cent respectively of exports to the area. This was also reflected in investment in these countries although at 50 per cent of total investment in Latin America, Brazil had far and away the largest amount. British bank claims amounted to some US$32.5 billion with offsetting liabilities of US$13 billion. The largest amounts were for Mexico, Brazil and Venezuela: in the case of Venezuela liabilities (i.e. assets in London) exceeded claims. Similarly most of the ECGD liability was concentrated in Mexico and Brazil.

Imports from Latin America as a whole were £1,016 million in 1980, about two per cent of imports from all sources. The area was not an important supplier, although Bolivia and Peru provided quantities of tin and zinc. With the world market depressed there would be no difficulty in obtaining supplies of these metals elsewhere. There was little therefore in economic terms to fear from a Latin American export embargo while an import embargo would affect only a few companies, if any. There was a much greater exposure through investment in, and loans to, the area. The most likely form of action would be discrimination against British companies in public sector project business, but there was initially little sign of this. In Mexico and Brazil, for example, negotiations appeared to be progressing smoothly on major contracts, including one with Brazil on the supply of equipment and armament for Brazilian corvettes. When the Secretary of Trade met the Brazilian Planning Minister on 15 April 1982, the Brazilian side demonstrated continued enthusiasm for new business with the UK. Other countries might be disposed to take punitive actions. Panama, the only country to vote against UN Resolution 502, might discontinue negotiations with a British company on a public transport contract worth £70 million. Peru might break off negotiations on the construction of naval port facilities at Chimbote, although it was less likely that civil contracts would be affected. A £200 million contract, signed on 26 March, for the supply of Hawk aircraft to Venezuela could yet be jeopardised. For the moment, however, all such actions were hypothetical.

Any action against Britain in accordance with the Rio Treaty required a two-thirds majority. This was unlikely to be obtained for joint military action.[10] Economic actions under the Treaty (which would be mandatory) could range from a call for total severance of economic relations to the more moderate option of an embargo on all new government contracts going to Britain. The other Latin American countries might judge that while an embargo on exports to them would not have a severe impact on Britain, by the same token it would not harm their own economies much. They would have little difficulty in replacing the UK as a supplier while Britain would find it much harder to acquire new markets. Halting loan repayments would be too risky as this would make banks much more cautious in lending to them and raise the cost of loans. So any collective action from Latin America would probably not extend beyond trade.

Even this seemed unlikely given the evident differences among these countries. The Mexican Foreign Minister, for example, had said privately that he did not think that the Argentines would get very far in the OAS and that anyway Mexico would not support sanctions against Britain. The Brazilians were more disposed to lean towards Argentina but they would not want to affect their international credit-worthiness. At a time when oil prices were very weak, this concern would also affect Venezuela, the country most supportive of Argentina. An illustration of the ambiguities in the situation was the situation with lending to Venezuela. There were erroneous reports that the authorities had refused to invite British banks to a meeting in Caracas on 30 April, to consider Venezuela's borrowing needs. In fact they had been invited but had decided not to attend as, with other international banks, they were nervous about future lending to Venezuela. Standard Chartered Bank had withdrawn from a $200 million syndicated loan to Venezuela and Lloyds Bank International was possibly considering the same move. The Swiss bank organising this loan had reported a general lack of support. In the end the British Ambassador in Caracas had to be instructed to issue a firm denial that Britain was using these negotiations to take economic measures against Venezuela.

Radical measures were occasionally mentioned, such as banning imports, breaking existing contracts, or restricting the operations of locally established British companies, but during the first weeks of April it was 'business as usual.' Reports from Latin American embassies suggested that while other countries might feel obliged to go along with economic measures to show political solidarity with Argentina, especially after hostilities had begun, they would be very aware of the damage they could do to their important economic relations with Britain and the EC. Any implementation was likely to be unenthusiastic. In mid-April the FCO concluded that:

the balance which South American countries will have to strike in deciding on whether to adopt economic or other measures is between, on the one hand, popular pressures to take action in support of Argentine claims to sovereignty over the Falkland Islands and, on the other hand, the implications of supporting the unprovoked aggression undertaken by an unpopular regime.

On 17 April declarations supporting Argentina and deploring the EC import ban were issued by the Andean Pact, the Latin American Integration Association (ALADI) and the Latin American European System (SELA). The Andean Pact also offered assistance on trade. These were apparently achieved with ease and the moderates – even Chile – were unwilling to swim against the tide. This reflected, the FCO observed, 'considerable readiness to give verbal support to Argentina; and adverse reactions to the measures taken by other Community countries who are seen as not directly involved in the dispute'. Yet, these statements had no economic impact.

Anything more substantial required a meeting of 'the Organ of Consultation' of the Rio Treaty. One was convened on 26 April. Speculation beforehand was that Argentina might seek a Resolution imposing a range of measures, including diplomatic and economic action, against the UK, under Article 8 of the Treaty.[11] This would require a two-thirds majority, or 14 out of 21. The FCO lobbied moderate members of the OAS to oppose this, as did the United States. In the event the resolution adopted made no reference to economic measures, though it did deplore the import ban introduced by the EC and called for its early removal. The FCO reported that: 'Many delegations concealed behind extravagant statements of solidarity their reluctance to take practical action.' The US, Colombia, Chile and Trinidad abstained on the resolution. Mexico and Brazil shared their views on Argentina's illegal action but sought to avoid confrontation.

It was never likely that economic measures would decide the dispute either way. Any punitive sanctions would take too long to have an effect, especially as their application was always likely to be limited. Along with degrees of diplomatic assistance in the various international fora in which the dispute was discussed and resolutions were passed, they were important largely as a means of demonstrating wider support for what might otherwise appear to be rather narrow national aspirations. On this basis the British could take some comfort from what was achieved during April. Not only did they have far less trouble convincing their allies to adopt sanctions against the Argentines than did the Argentines against them, but also the value of 'hemispheric solidarity' to the Argentine cause appeared to be quite marginal.

SECTION TWO

9

OPTIONS FOR A SETTLEMENT

Even as the dust was still settling after the Argentine invasion the FCO began to think about the options for a settlement should the pressure to compromise turn out to be irresistible. A number were identified along with a set of criteria against which to judge them. The obvious preference was for an unconditional withdrawal of Argentine forces and the re-establishment of British administration. Next best would be the same outcome but achieved by negotiations through an intermediary (UN or US). To start with the prospect of the International Court of Justice (ICJ) loomed large, either in the form of an advisory opinion or a referral by the two parties for a binding decision. Coming well down the original list, but nonetheless soon in play, was the prospect of a temporary administration of the Islands by a neutral authority (UN or US or other Administrator or Commissioner). From there the really difficult options started to develop: perhaps ceding dependent territories but keeping the Falklands or a lease-back arrangement. Most humiliating of all would be withdrawal of Argentine forces, combined with a continuing Argentine administration and the probable departure of many islanders to Britain, other Commonwealth countries or dependent territories.

From one perspective the crisis provided a means by which the problem might be sorted out once and for all, which meant that diplomacy offered a real chance for an internationally backed settlement. The corollary of this was that a comprehensive military victory would not be an unalloyed blessing. An early paper in the FCO set as an objective the need:

> to ensure that not only the immediate problem is resolved but that the position of the Falkland Islands is not left in a manner which requires either a costly and permanent defence commitment and which does not leave the Falklands as a source of future instability and crisis.

This argued for a serious diplomatic settlement, one that would secure the early withdrawal of Argentine forces and administration, and provide long-term international guarantees for the islanders, but at the same time 'save at least sufficient Argentine face to prevent it becoming a permanent historical sore in Argentine politics.' This would render the immediate re-imposition of British administration problematic. Preferable might be an administration neither Argentine nor British but 'under international auspices or by a third country.' The natural outcome would be a UN administration with a Security Council mandate, endorsed by the General Assembly, preferably with 'a clear and not too narrow time limit.' There would need to be some sort of British office to deal with islanders' views and problems. A less satisfactory alternative would be an American administration.

Such thoughts were very much in the minority within Government circles. British policy had been set as the restoration of British administration and there was no indication of Prime Ministerial interest in anything less. Even if the advantages of a lasting settlement were accepted it was unclear how this could be achieved. The resumption of direct talks with Argentina would soon become a sterile exercise, with lease-back still the only possible basis for a compromise.[1] The known gap between British and Argentine views on an acceptable period for such an arrangement was hardly going to be bridged with national passions running so strong. Mediation posed considerable risks if one assumed, as did Sir Anthony Parsons, little sympathy for Britain's sovereignty claim. Once negotiations began it would be hard for Britain to keep control of the process, but it was clear that the international community was expecting negotiations.

International Court of Justice

It was in this context that reference to the ICJ seemed to hold some advantages. The idea was not new. It had been considered in detail in 1966 with the conclusion that, while the British case was strong enough to withstand a reference, it was still possible that the ICJ might find against Britain. As the Court had no attraction for Argentina and its membership was becoming less favourable to Britain, the matter was not pursued. The same view had been taken in 1981. In March 1982, in the light of the growing Argentine pressure, the Buenos Aires Embassy suggested that it might be worth offering to submit the Falklands to the court 'as a last resort if things really turn nasty.' If the offer was refused, which was quite likely given the Argentine attitude, then Britain would have gained moral support; if accepted then the whole matter would be put on ice for a considerable period. If the ICJ ruled in Britain's favour its moral position would be strengthened even more; a ruling against would at least provide an escape route from the issue that did not involve bloodshed or political humiliation. In March the FCO saw insufficient merit in adopting this strategy, but it was agreed that it might be reviewed in the light of the new circumstances.

As the new circumstances arose the option loomed large. It was raised in one of the first meetings to discuss the crisis on 2 April by a group of

Permanent Under-Secretaries. One idea was that a friendly member of the Security Council might propose an arrangement whereby if Argentina withdrew, the question of sovereignty would be referred to the ICJ for an advisory opinion, the two sides undertaking to abide by the opinion. Would this work? It might be that the ICJ would consider it inappropriate to give an opinion on a territorial dispute but, on the whole, it was unlikely that such a request would be declined. The Security Council could also request an advisory opinion from the ICJ as a procedural matter (i.e. not subject to veto). Alternatively it would be possible to get the Security Council to call on the UK and Argentina under Article 36 of the Charter to refer the sovereignty dispute to the ICJ, but this would be less likely given the sensitivities of the Soviet Union about the Court's role.

Even assuming that a call could be made it was unlikely that Argentina would consent, at least for the moment, to ICJ proceedings (or to arbitration or to other forms of peaceful settlement procedure). Parsons discouraged any mention of the ICJ during the drafting of Resolution 502, largely because of France's known dislike of the Court. He was given discretion to encourage a friendly state to make the suggestion so long as it would not prejudice the nine votes needed to get the resolution passed.[2] The issue did not arise and by 4 April the problems were beginning to impress themselves on the Government. Whatever the procedure adopted an essential condition would still have to be that Argentina withdrew her forces and that some suitable arrangements were made for the interim administration of the Islands. Britain would be unable to take any military action while the court was considering the case. Nor was there any reason why Argentina would entrust the issue to international arbitration, let alone agree to withdraw. It was not under sufficient pressure. Nobody was bound to accept an advisory opinion. A Security Council resolution calling for compliance would not be binding, although rejection of an ICJ opinion would incur some odium. The difficult area was the relationship between recourse to a court and the threat of force. Argentina had achieved its objectives and could count on the general level of opprobrium decreasing. They might be tempted to offer to withdraw forces, thereby allowing undisturbed occupation, while waiting for an opinion, a process which would take at least a year and which they could help prolong. Britain would have no recourse to other remedies, as the matter would be *sub judice*.

If Britain won, there could be no certainty that Argentina would accept the result. Its attitude to international arbitration had been demonstrated in the dispute with Chile: it would only accept a judgement in its favour. In 1947 and subsequently Britain had in fact offered to submit the dispute over the Dependencies, although not the Falklands themselves, to the Court in the face of Argentine and Chilean encroachments, and in 1955 had even approached the Court unilaterally on this matter. Then Argentina had refused to submit to the Court's jurisdiction. Yet even if Argentina was persuaded to go along there was a risk that Britain might lose. To reduce this risk, it would be essential that the reference should not be simply one related to historic title, but should encompass the applicability of the principal of self-determination. The advantage of self-determination was that it was a more modern concept: an obvious problem was that it was less relevant in relation to the Dependencies, which were uninhabited.

Of the fourteen members of the Court in addition to its own member, Argentina could rely on support from Brazil, Algeria, India, the Soviet Union, Syria, and probably but not definitely Poland. Britain had its own member plus likely support from France, the United States, West Germany, Italy and probably Japan. On this count Argentina could expect six to seven votes, and Britain five to six. That would leave two moderate Africans from Nigeria and Senegal in critical positions. They might support Britain but this could not be guaranteed and so the final vote would be too close to call. This reinforced the view that had developed prior to the invasion that while there might be political grounds on which to raise the issue, as part of some package deal, there could be no guarantee that a reference to the ICJ would 'be certain, or even more likely than not, to uphold our case.' This reflected more the 'political make-up of the Court' than 'the intrinsic merits of the case.'

Those in favour of defusing the issue for the long term did not consider these points to be decisive. There were clear immediate political advantages to be gained from recourse to the ICJ, as many countries, such as the Netherlands, were enthusiastic, and it would be difficult for Argentina to reject this procedure. One advantage of the protracted deliberations of the ICJ or any tribunal would be that this would 'allow domestic opinion to adjust to any outcome.' Nonetheless, Britain would still be obliged to commit itself to an outcome before it could consult islander opinion. An authoritative judgement 'would establish the status of the islands with both sides having to offer legal guarantees.' If all went well the Islands would be removed as a 'time bomb for future crises.'

The ICJ option remained on the table during April but elicited no great enthusiasm. The main consequence of having looked again at the basis for the British claim was to re-establish the importance of the principle of self-determination in governmental thinking. This was reflected in the Prime Minister's speech on 14 April. This made explicit reference to:

> another important factor which is nowadays recognised to be of fundamental importance and is indeed enshrined in the Charter of the United Nations – namely, the right of self-determination of peoples.

The UN: after 502

Another international organisation whose immediate relevance appeared less than initially supposed was the UN itself. Although Britain's position had just been strengthened with the passage of Resolution 502, Parsons expected this to be the peak of diplomatic success. Any further steps would require persuading the Security Council to increase the pressure on Argentina, and this was unlikely. Britain would also sound less than persuasive if calling for economic sanctions given its own past scepticism with regard to such measures, often professed for example in connection with Israel and South Africa. The Ambassador warned that to attempt such a call under Chapter 7 would be not so much 'going down fighting' as an invitation to humiliation: it would be 'regarded by all members as a ritual preliminary to military action by us.' Still in mind was the saga of the US diplomats being held hostage in Iran over 1979–80. The Americans' request for sanctions then was later seen as a preliminary to an attempt to extract the hostages by force rather than an alternative.

Even a further resolution merely deploring the Argentine failure to implement 502 (which 'would by itself be a bit wet') could court trouble, as Britain would be put under pressure to halt military preparations and refrain from use of force. To reject such calls explicitly would upset friends, and jeopardise the offers of facilities for the Task Force, which had already been received from certain third world countries. Argentina had not helped by refraining from rejecting Resolution 502 outright, preferring instead to attempt to re-interpret it as requiring Britain to cease its military preparations. Argentine lawyers were also said to be working on arguments that Britain had tied its hands by going into Chapter 7 because only the Council could take actions to enforce its resolutions thereunder. They were also seeking to argue that the Task Force would not be exercising the right of self-defence because the armed attacks by Argentina on the Islands had ceased and the UK representatives had surrendered. As a result any future military actions would constitute armed reprisals and so be illegal.

The prevailing atmosphere at the UN was anti-colonial and anti-force. With Resolution 502 Parsons was able to play on the anti-force theme while keeping the anti-colonial theme subdued. As Britain prepared to take the military initiative the anti-force sentiment could turn in its direction, and encourage a search for a negotiated solution that would inevitably bring in anti-colonial sentiment. To counter this, the British needed to take every opportunity to present the issue in terms of the islanders' right to self-determination. This could be done by presenting the country's case at various UN fora, and possibly issuing a press release about Argentine actions on the Falklands, though this idea was dropped when it became apparent that there was no evidence of gross violations of human rights. The Human Rights Division of the UN Secretariat at Geneva had received no complaints, although that was an organisation where Argentina had few friends because of the 'disappearances' in Argentina itself in recent years. For the moment the Foreign Office could only report back to New York that those acts by the Argentine administration on the Islands 'would be regarded by many UN members as reasonable steps to be taken in the initial phase of an armed occupation with a counter-attack in prospect.' Two days later the FCO confirmed that it was unable to 'substantiate accusations that the Argentinians are seriously violating the islanders' rights other than the right to self-determination.' Argentina's 'appalling domestic record' could, however, be used to justify concern. Even this area was problematic, as Galtieri was less hard-line than his predecessor and had made some tentative concessions on local human rights issues. There were other reasons to treat the human rights issue with caution:

> you will of course be aware of possible counter-allegations concerning Northern Ireland and of the doubtful human rights record of many other nations, including in South America, whose support we wish to obtain.

All possible options, from the introduction of a new Security Council Resolution to a dramatic statement preparing the way for military action, suffered from substantive and procedural problems. The procedural were often the more difficult because UN diplomacy could be so cumbersome and time-consuming and because of the opportunities presented to mischief-makers to seek to amend the substance, and so wrest control of the initiative from Britain. In the end Parsons envisaged that his inability to take the initiative might lead him to resort to procedural devices to delay or thwart the initiatives of others. He still had the ultimate weapon of the veto.

Only Panama was really pro-Argentine. Parsons' main concern was with those he described as the 'do gooders,' represented on the Council by Japan and Ireland, who felt obliged to seek any means of preventing further hostilities. Having abstained on 502, the Russians seemed likely to move to a more pro-Argentine and anti-colonial position. Parsons was still worried by the American Ambassador's sympathy with the Argentine regime, to the extent 'if and when we come back to the Council, she will not be actively helpful to us and that, behind the scenes, she may well work against us,' although Mrs Kirkpatrick did make some effort to repair relations to the point where Parsons observed that she was smothering him with 'olive branches.' This came after adverse publicity, and uproar in Britain, when it became known that she had attended a dinner in her honour given by the Argentine Ambassador to the US, Esteban Takacs, on the night of the Argentine invasion.[3] When the dinner became known, Henderson had compared it to him attending a dinner at the Iranian embassy as US hostages were being seized. Her reply was hardly calculated to mend fences: the analogy was false as the US had no position on the sovereignty of the Falklands. 'Armed aggression would take place in a clear-cut way against territory on which there was clear-cut ownership,' she observed. 'If the Argentines own the Islands then moving troops into them is not armed aggression.'

Now she was trying to make amends. According to Parsons:

> Using her best classroom manner, punctuated by expressions of affection for myself and Britain, she explained that the Soviet Union was busy dismantling the foundations of the inter-American system. The U.S. had to hold this system together at all costs. Argentina was a key element in it. Hence, the short term interests of the US were slightly different from ours, although successful US protection of the inter-American system would be in our long term interests. After a lot more in this vein I suggested that there was no particular point in holding a post mortem over her attendance at the dinner. It was not my habit to harp on what was past.

The Secretariat

An eye had to be kept on the UN Secretariat and other members of the Council. One of the advantages of 502 was that the Secretary-General could only take action within its terms, and the resolution had not actually called on him to do anything. Perez de Cuellar understood this and also the pointlessness of launching himself into any major effort without the consent of both parties. He was aware that, as a Latin American, some in Britain might doubt his credentials as an impartial negotiator. As it became apparent that the Americans were going to be leading the effort to get a negotiated settlement before further hostilities, Perez de Cuellar was quite content to use this as a good reason for his relative passivity.

From a variety of sources Parsons was reasonably well informed about the ideas circulating within the Secretariat, most of them revolving around the Secretary-General putting himself forward in a mediating role. This was, for example, the starting point for an options paper prepared by Under Secretary-General Rafeeudin Ahmad.[4] This was described by Parsons' deputy, Whyte, as a 'half-baked document which would be totally unacceptable to us.' It envisaged a military disengagement by both sides and an Interim Administration (possibly run by the Secretary-General under a Security Council mandate). Parsons told Ahmad that 502 remained the only basis for a settlement and that it was unwise to arouse expectations about a greater role for the Secretary-General. Perez de Cuellar himself was content to continue with his trip to Europe for the first week of the crisis. A message from Costa Mendez to the effect that Argentine sovereignty was non-negotiable and there could be no return to the status quo ante convinced him that for the moment he was better off leaving mediation to the US.

When US Secretary of State Alexander Haig launched his effort on 6 April he effectively precluded other would-be mediators from getting in on the act. The day before this the possibility of UN mediation was raised. Parsons was informed that the Argentine Foreign Minister had telephoned the Secretary-General in Rome that morning 'in a negotiating mood'. The Secretary-General now wanted to talk to the British to see if he could do anything. Parsons' immediate response was that the only action open to him at present was to urge the Argentine Government immediately to implement SCR 502 in all its parts. Perez de Cuellar did not see merit in making a move at this stage, whatever later role he might play, and had no intention of cutting short his trip lest he give the impression that he was seeking to mediate.

On 6 April Costa Mendez continued his own mini-initiative by contacting Kamanda, claiming that Argentina respected 502 and was prepared to negotiate, but Britain's Task Force was contrary to the call for a cessation of hostilities. He had in mind a deal for the islanders:

> If they wished to remain they would be free to do so. If they wished to leave, compensation would be paid them. Those who chose to stay would have all their rights safeguarded, including the right to their own language, their religion and even to participate in the local government. Argentina wished to proceed with the UK to negotiate such arrangements.

Parsons responded that the Task Force was not engaged in hostilities and that the resolution was all one piece. Britain would negotiate when Argentina withdrew. By the end of that day both Britain and Argentina had accepted the Haig mission and the pressure on the Secretary-General to act subsided.

10

HAIG'S FIRST VISIT

On 7 April it was announced that US Secretary of State Haig was coming to London to begin this mediation effort. From the start the Government was torn between its preference for an old ally as an intermediary and concern that performance of this role resulted in distance between the two, as the US sought to convince Argentina of its impartiality. Britain really wanted the US to become part of the campaign to secure an Argentine withdrawal from the Falklands. When Haig's visit was announced, the press line was 'that Haig was coming as a friend and ally to discuss ways in which the United States might most effectively support us ... and not as a mediator.' The official American announcement, however, suggested a different construction. This stated that the President had:

> directed Secretary of State Haig to continue consultations with the Governments of the United Kingdom and Argentina in the interests of assisting both parties in the search for a peaceful resolution of the dispute in the South Atlantic.

The British view was that this could best be achieved if the Americans geared their efforts to persuading Argentina to return to the position of 31 March. The issue was quite simple. An invasion had occurred despite a UN call for restraint and then a withdrawal had been refused despite the demands of a UN resolution. It was presumed that it was as much in American as in British interests that 'illegal and naked aggression of this kind should be firmly countered.' The remedy was equally simple: Argentine forces must now withdraw and British administration be restored. The US must understand that neither public nor parliamentary opinion would stand for anything less. If this could not be achieved by diplomatic means then Britain would be prepared to fight. The only possible concession was that Britain might resume talks about substance following the Argentine withdrawal. This could not be done while the Islands were occupied. Even then Britain would be guided by the wishes of the islanders, which were not accessible under the prevailing circumstances. It was not, of course, hard to imagine their contents. From this perspective the only real question for discussion was 'how to put continuing and increasing pressure on Argentina?' This would require American assistance, such as economic measures. Sir Nicholas Henderson had asked the US to recall its Ambassador from Buenos Aires, rally opposition to Argentina in the OAS, and impose an embargo on arms sales. He got a non-committal response.

Why did a different view emerge from Washington? It was not as if the British lacked grounds for expecting something positive. When Haig had called in Argentine Ambassador Takacs when he learned of the Argentine plans, he told him that if they went ahead: 'The reaction of the American people will be overwhelming, we will have to side with the British, and US-Argentine relations will be back to the worst days.' After his failed call with Galtieri, Reagan had promised Thatcher that: 'While we have a policy of neutrality on the sovereignty issue, we will not be neutral on the issue of Argentine use of armed force.' Both sides had reason to suppose that US support for Britain would be the clear result of any invasion.

The interests of the two allies were not wholly coincident. The Americans came sympathetic to Britain's predicament, and aware that Washington could not, in the end, condone such blatant aggression against the territory of its closest ally. But a lot of effort had gone recently into cultivating Argentina and those in Washington most committed to this effort, notably Jeanne Kirkpatrick and Thomas Enders, Assistant Secretary for Inter-American Affairs, argued vigorously for an 'even-handed' approach. They pointed out that the United States had always been neutral on the substance of the Falklands issue. There seemed to be a strong argument for sustaining this neutrality, given the valuable role that Argentina was now playing in supporting Washington in its anti-communist campaigns in Central America. In February 1981, for example, General Vernon Walters, who maintained contacts with the tougher Latin American regimes, was briefed by Galtieri as Army Commander-in-Chief on Argentine support for the anti-guerrilla campaigns of the Governments of El Salvador and Honduras. 'All we have to do,' he reported back to Haig, 'was to tell them what to do.' The 'Latinos' also argued the need to correct the hemispheric suspicion that when it came to the crunch the US would always support Europeans rather than its closest neighbours. Actually, in terms of distance, all the NATO capitals, except Rome, Athens and Ankara, were closer to the US than Buenos Aires. The view from the Buenos Aires Embassy was that the diplomatic pressure mounted by the British had made the Argentines more disposed to negotiate, but they would not wish to appear cowardly as the British fleet approached, and would not accept the US as a mediator 'if we participate in the British sanctions against them.'

The Europeanists, such as the Assistant Secretary for European Affairs, Laurence Eagleburger, were appalled by the very idea of failing to support a NATO ally in these circumstances, especially given the vigorous support that

Margaret Thatcher had provided President Reagan on a number of controversial matters. Anglo-American relations had taken time to recover from Suez in 1956, when the British had been in the wrong. It would be disastrous to abandon them now when they were clearly in the right. Already a comment from Haig's deputy, Walter Stoessel, that 'We are going to be right down the middle on this one' had left the British suspicious that they would be let down again. Hence Haig's promise to Henderson that there 'cannot be another Suez'. The political weight was on Britain's side, as a democracy that had been wronged by a dictatorship, and as a country which could call on close ties of affection and interest at all levels of the American political system. Britain received press coverage that remained favourable and 'well ahead of the Administration.'

Haig, however, thought the question for American policy to be more complex than a decision on who to back. Obviously Argentina could not be supported, but that did not mean that a more neutral stance should be ruled out, at least in the first instance. He was fearful that if the US turned against Argentina the main beneficiary would be Moscow. He tended to view most issues through the framework of the cold war, and was impressed by the opportunities the crisis presented 'for Soviet mischief-making, either directly, or through their Cuban proxies, in Argentina.'[1] To this concern was added some sense of British responsibility for its poor management of this issue in the past, but most of all a belief that the US was uniquely well placed to facilitate a negotiated settlement. The risk here, including for Haig personally, was that it would fail and this was understood to be the most likely outcome, given the past difficulties with this dispute and the added factor of military action by Argentina.[2] Any hope here relied on the uncertainty both sides must face when contemplating further hostilities. Meanwhile, the mediator role would at least allow Washington off the hook when it came to taking sides immediately. All lines of communication would need to be kept open and no unnecessary offence proffered.

With Vice-President George Bush having already been rejected by Buenos Aires, Haig was the only mediator available. While the previous Republican Secretary of State, Henry Kissinger, had seen his reputation grow with 'shuttle diplomacy', Haig was not so suited to this role. Henderson, in his many discussions with Haig, often found the Secretary of State discursive and ill-informed, developing ideas in rapid succession as he went along. On the one hand this provided a valuable insight, and opportunities to squash the more far-fetched ideas before they got too far. On the other hand Henderson was aware that his telegrams must make disturbing reading back in London and he urged that Haig's words not be analysed or criticised too severely. Henderson understood that the cross-cutting American interests in the dispute would create an incentive for Haig to try his hand at mediation before the British Task Force arrived and he warned London to be prepared.

It is important to keep in mind that the assessment of British prospects at this time in Washington was hardly rosy. On 6 April, for example, the State Department's Bureau of Intelligence and Research (INR) predicted that the Prime Minister would face great pressure to use military force if diplomatic efforts failed. It noted a leadership damaged first as a result of economic troubles, and now by this humiliation, that would be unable to survive a 'futile "voyage to nowhere"'. Thatcher was likely to fall if honour could not be redeemed yet military action was full of risks and, even if successful, might involve enormous human cost. While British optimism about military action was noted, so was the possibility that events could lead to the fall of Thatcher, new elections and Conservative defeat.

An analysis of military possibilities the next day, as the National Security Council (NSC) decided on the Haig mediation, observed that the British could recapture South Georgia 'with relative ease', but that the onset of winter would rule out a prolonged siege of the Falklands 'to starve out the invaders' and it would also add urgency to any operations to recapture the Islands. These could well be 'costly and bloody'. The 'outcome would be in doubt.' The only change here from the first appreciations for the US Joint Chiefs of Staff, was that the military had assumed a preference for a blockade. Another State Department report for that day, drawing on the views of the London Embassy, noted concern among Conservative moderates and the Foreign Office that Thatcher was listening too much to senior naval officers. The assessment by the US Minister in London, Ed Streator, on 6 April was that in approaching Britain it was fine to say that the US has to remain credible as mediators, but it would infuriate the British to say that the US attached 'equal importance to both sides'. He advised that it would be valuable to get the British to state clearly their diplomatic and military objectives, and 'think through their strategy in a way they have not done yet', and that any proposal should be dramatic and targeted:

> The Falklands are a searing political issue in Britain. And with the Prime Minister's future at stake, and bureaucracy shaken, we suggest it will be best to jump traditional channels and go right to the top with a proposal Mrs. Thatcher herself can judge politically.

There appears to have been another factor, which is a misapprehension of the Argentine position. On 7 April, after he had decided on mediation, Haig asked that Galtieri be told what he had told Costa Mendez:

> He would not put himself at the disposition of the parties if the sine qua non were instant solution of a 150 year old conflict, including sovereignty issues, but that we are sensitive to Argentine concerns to advance an issue which has been on dead center for so long. And hope we can be helpful to our two old friends in this regard.

He had concluded from his conversation with Costa Mendez that sovereignty would not be a sticking issue, that some form of words could be used to cover that, but that 'retention of an Argentine administrative presence on the islands is important, and of course, as much a sense of direction in the negotiations as possible.' If this was the case then he would assume that his hardest task was going to be the extraction of concessions from London. His notes for the NSC meeting on 7 April indicate the way the analysis was going.

Britain was in a 'warlike mood, high strung, unpredictable.' If the Government fell, then the beneficiaries would be the 'Labor opposition, no friend of ours on security issues'. It was not clear, however, if the Government could win. The Argentine Navy could be hurt and possibly some territory would be retaken but the recovery of the main island would be difficult. 'UK best option to block maritime commerce to Argentina.' At the same time Argentina could survive by pulling major ships to port. Meanwhile, he reported, Argentina appeared to be looking for a way out. They could not be given sovereignty but some way could be found to show that their efforts had not been in vain. Argentina would be more flexible, he supposed, if there is a little running room in Britain. Thus, he continued, he had deliberately put London on guard by going there first. The proposal he had in mind was to get all military forces on the Islands withdrawn, no additional military force within 200 miles, a consortium of nations with a small force to assume responsibility for local administration, with British and Argentine administrators attached, and negotiations on the ultimate disposition of the Islands within a framework of respect for sovereign rights and for the rights of the inhabitants of the Islands to self-determination. The British had taken the initiative and to stop war their fleet had to be stopped:

We should ask them to show first card. Question for Brits: 'if Argentines evacuate and there is an interim administration involving us, plus agreed negotiating scenario, will you hold up the fleet?'

He sought the President's authority to say, 'when talk gets tough in London, that we can't support a military solution if a reasonable political solution is available.' Such views exceeded Britain's worst fears, and, had they been known, would have made the early reassurances to London on the mediation process appear disingenuous and deceitful.

London's suspicions grew as the Americans asked that they should not be put on the spot with regard to requests for help, and seemed ready to describe the dispute in terms that equated Argentina with Britain. On 5 April the President had commented that:

It's a very difficult situation for the United States because we're friends with both of the countries engaged in this dispute and we stand ready to do anything we can to help them, and what we hope for and would like to help in doing is have a peaceful resolution of this with no forceful action or bloodshed.

On 6 April Henderson was told that the US dare not lose credibility with Argentina, even if this meant not tilting so far in Britain's direction as might be deserved. Only the US could 'exert influence in Buenos Aires.' Henderson acknowledged Argentine susceptibility to American influence, so long as it took the form of pressure rather than 'niceness'. Having been inclined to wait before getting a negotiating effort started, so as to let the implications of the British response to the occupation sink in on the Junta, Haig had decided that there was little time left. Thinking aloud, at least that is what Henderson hoped, he raised the possibility of a mixed Anglo-Argentine administration of the Islands. Henderson quickly disabused him of the idea that there could be any negotiations about the future until Argentine forces had been withdrawn and British administration had been restored. He stressed the strength of public opinion, explaining that it was possible to care for the fate of some 2,000 islanders just as in 1980 it had been possible for the Americans to care so deeply about 52 diplomatic hostages held by Iran. At stake was the principle of self-determination and whether differences were to be settled by force.

Haig would not give up on helping Argentina extricate itself from the conflict by means of a device that could not but appear to London as rewarding aggression. Still thinking aloud he came up with the idea of an impartial interim administration, perhaps including a Canadian and Latin American as well as an American. At most, Henderson thought, a group of wise men might come up with ideas for the future. Meanwhile rather than attempt to save Galtieri's face he judged that American efforts would be best put to persuading Galtieri to withdraw before he was defeated in battle. Haig came back with the idea of involving the OAS: deplorable countered Henderson, while further involvement of the UN would just invite a Soviet veto.

Having met with Costa Mendez, then in Washington, Haig reported back to Henderson on what sounded to the latter like Argentine intransigence, arguably confirming that pressure was needed. This led Henderson to suggest that Buenos Aires should be Haig's first stop, on the grounds that he already knew the British position and he needed to see whether there really was any Argentine room for manoeuvre. Haig took the view that he had to go to the ally first, if only to dispel any suggestion that he was colluding with Argentina. Henderson was unconvinced, although he noted that wherever Haig started he 'may well be embarking on a shuttle.' Pym later, in a telephone conversation, also sought to dissuade Haig from his visit, offering to visit Washington himself, but Haig was insistent. Britain was in a difficult tactical position. Haig could not be rebuffed but Pym did not welcome the mediating role, noting to Henderson that 'we must not seem to allow the Americans to sap our determination to reverse the Argentine fait accompli and to restore British Administration.'

On the tactics, the Ambassador did not think it wise for Pym to fly to Washington, as it would indicate anxiety on Britain's part, leaving aside Haig's concern about the appearance of collusion, and there was not much point in trying to stop Haig's visit. The exercise need not necessarily be harmful. Henderson doubted that Haig would press for major concessions while in London, such as joint administration of the Islands. He reported American concern about the ability of the British actually to recapture the Islands, and the requirement to continue to defend them if they did. So he had no doubt that the 'Americans are hankering after some kind of solution which would entail Argentinian withdrawal from the Islands and their return to British administration: but which would offer them some satisfaction in terms of an eventual solution on sovereignty.'

Haig in London[3]

When Haig arrived in London on 8 April, he was well aware of the challenge he faced. He wished to persuade his hosts that if they could provide some concessions he could support them by negotiating an Argentine withdrawal. Before he explained his position to the Prime Minister he tried out his arguments with the Foreign Secretary, while other members of his team met with senior FCO officials. In both meetings the American message was the same: the strength of feeling in Britain was understood; the US was in no sense 'even-handed'; the mediator role was the most useful way that they could support Britain for the moment and this would have been lost by a conspicuous tilt and the adoption of strong measures against Argentina; Argentina was in an uncertain mood but could be persuaded to withdraw; alternatively, if pushed too hard Buenos Aires could take a turn for the worse, with an even more hard-line government flirting with the Soviet Union.

Haig emphasised that the Americans had also been caught by surprise by the Argentine action even though it must have been under preparation for months. Even the Embassy in Buenos Aires had been completely in the dark. Now it was the Argentine turn to be surprised. Having expected an easy ride they had been taken aback by both the UN vote and the British military reaction. All this created a temporary weakness in the Argentine position. Britain's declaration of the MEZ provided a welcome source of additional pressure, even though it caused difficulties for Haig who was trying to calm down the conflict. He warned that if Britain pushed too hard now then uncertainty in Buenos Aires might be replaced with 'a new wave of macho.' Furthermore, unless he acted soon Argentina could turn to the OAS, and, if that was not enough, even to the Soviet Union. At the same time he was not convinced that Britain would find it at all easy to retake the Islands by force. There was a prospect of a long drawn-out and bitter conflict. Enders indicated another American worry: the invocation of the Rio Treaty as soon as British ships entered the relevant area. Whatever the legal case, hemispheric solidarity would mean that no Latin American country would oppose Argentina and this could trigger mandatory sanctions against Britain.

In this context Haig saw a fleeting opportunity for diplomacy, one sufficiently serious for it to be worth avoiding a 'high profile tilt' in Britain's direction. This window of opportunity might last for no more than 72 hours and so this time had to be used intelligently. Haig was looking for something to take to Buenos Aires, something more than 'a priori demands of sovereignty.' Thomas Enders asked point blank what way out the British were giving Argentina. Sir Antony Acland, Permanent Under-Secretary, following a ploy that would be used regularly by British diplomats, asked about the way out the US would give Cuba if it invaded Puerto Rico.

Haig sketched out his preliminary ideas for a settlement. These ideas, as with all those that followed, were based on three stages: withdrawal; interim administration; negotiations leading to a definitive settlement. As with subsequent discussions the most difficult stage was the one in the middle. This was because it raised all the issues connected with the outcome of the final negotiations. The British would want any interim administration to be as close as possible to the status quo ante; the Argentines would want this interim stage to represent a clear step on the route to a transfer of sovereignty.

Haig's ideas on this interim administration had yet to mature. He mentioned to Pym the possibility of a British and Argentine umbrella, with an administrative authority possibly comprising US and Canadian elements and perhaps elements from two Latin American states acceptable to both sides. There would need to be suitable guarantees of the rights of the population. Here was an issue that touched on the core and apparently conflicting issues of principle that had long dogged the dispute – self-determination and sovereignty. Pym listened but was non-committal. Haig must raise these matters with the Prime Minister. He was given no clue as to their likely reception.

Negotiations begin

The first full meeting took place at 1900 on 8 April. After describing the background to the crisis, the Prime Minister said that she wished to 'explain clearly the mood in Britain.' She described the country as 'deeply wounded.' Sovereign territory had been invaded and islanders whose only wish was to be British had not been effectively defended. In Parliament she had faced the charge that the Government had betrayed and humiliated the Falkland Islanders and the nation. If she had not been able to announce that the fleet was to sail, the Government might have fallen. Now the country was coming behind the action that had been taken. The preference was clearly for a diplomatic solution, but there was total determination that a dictator should not be appeased. 'If strength was the only language the Argentine regime understood, it would have to be exercised.'

She pointedly observed that Britain's key European allies, as well as the Commonwealth, were supporting Britain. 'It was impossible to be neutral as between unprovoked aggression and a people who just wished to live their lives in their own way.' The status of the Islands could not be changed by an act of aggression and there could be no question of a negotiation until Argentine forces were withdrawn. In this context she had been disturbed by President Reagan's reference to friendship with both the UK and Argentina, though it was an 'off the cuff' remark. Britain, she reminded the Secretary of State, had always tried to support the US.

Haig then attempted to explain the American stance: it was *not* impartial, certainly when it came to breaches of international law. It appreciated British concerns and past support for American policies. He developed for the Prime Minister his analysis of the shocked and uncertain state of Argentine opinion, now that they were faced with such a strong British reaction, and the risk that Galtieri would be replaced by someone even more intransigent, and that Argentina would resort either to the OAS or, worst of all, to the Soviet Union. He described the Argentine character as 'less than rational,' fearful lest they appear cowardly. As soon as the British fleet reached the fiftieth parallel, the Americans were convinced that Argentina would harden its stance and persuade the OAS to follow their 'anti-colonial stance.'

While Haig claimed that there was this brief but optimum time to hold rational discussions with Galtieri, he provided scant reason for optimism. He reported his conversations with Costa Mendez who had promised to negotiate everything – except sovereignty. According to Haig this position softened when he 'made it plain that America would only become involved if it was fully understood that they could not accept a change in the status quo brought about by force.' Before he went to Buenos Aires he knew he must first visit America's closest friend and ally so that he could acquire a 'fundamental understanding of the limits of our possibilities for negotiation.' He wished to be able to portray accurately the vigour of the British approach.

The discussion then moved to the strength of the respective bargaining positions. The Prime Minister was dubious about American fears of active Soviet involvement, while accepting that they might fish in troubled waters. As she was convinced that the Argentine Government had been using negotiations earlier in the year as a cover for military preparations there was no particular reason to suppose that they would take them any more seriously now, unless put under very severe pressure. Haig's portrait of Galtieri was of a man who was unlikely to respond well to pressure. He characterised him as religious, attending Mass every day, but also as one who 'drank, perhaps too often and too early.' He saw himself 'as a man of principle and strength' but also 'a poker player who doubled when he lost. He would up the ante if he decided force was inevitable.'

Haig also warned of the dangers for Britain with the military option:

> The United Kingdom could damage the Argentine fleet severely and could blockade the Islands fairly easily. But a landing on the Falklands would be very costly and would put the population in jeopardy. It would be very difficult at this time of the year and in high seas. The problems and burdens would grow. Questions and doubts would appear in the United Kingdom. American opinion was now much in favour of our principled stance. But he was not sure this would last long – he remembered Vietnam.

The US transcript has Haig saying:

> In the final analysis once engagement starts it will become an increasingly difficult burden to protect principle. People will begin to ask difficult questions like why are they making such a sacrifice for a thousand sheep herders. U.S. opinion now supports the principled position Britain has taken but we cannot be sure it will last too long if the issue is not settled.

He then moved to try to wean the British away from the idea that nothing could be agreed with Argentina until they left the Islands. The issue, argued Haig, was how to obtain withdrawal. This required some device to allow Argentina to claim that it had not lost face totally. The outcome had to appear to be less like total victory for Britain. This possibility had to be explored in connection with the three obvious areas for negotiation – the method of withdrawal, the immediate administration and the long-term status of the Islands. It might even be helpful to avoid 'a priori judgements about sovereignty.' It was possible to envisage different types of regime.

This seemed to the Prime Minister to be very dangerous ground. The islanders 'were British by choice and by allegiance' and their wishes had to be 'paramount.' When Haig responded that this stance would require Britain to use force she observed that force had already been used. More would be a tragedy but she was pledged to restore British administration and could not accept dictatorship being imposed on a people who would not be subjugated. Haig then tried a different tack, though not finding it expedient to pose the possibility of an interim administration to the same extent as he had posed it earlier when meeting with the Foreign Secretary. Perhaps, he suggested, a temporary arrangement, with some kind of US or Canadian presence, might be possible while negotiations with Argentina continued on a final settlement. Mrs Thatcher dismissed the possibility: this would mean Argentina would have gained from force.

Haig offered a more positive gloss. If his proposals were sufficient to get an Argentine withdrawal then the islanders' freedom and sovereignty could be guaranteed while the substantive negotiations continued. The Prime Minister returned to the standard formula: Britain would be guided by the islanders' wishes, and this meant, as with earlier schemes, proposals could founder. Britain would consider resumption of negotiations after Argentine withdrawal, though these would 'inevitably take a different course than previously.' The conversation proceeded inconclusively along these lines. The Americans had posed the question of an alternative to a straightforward return of a British administration, if only on a temporary basis. The British had not found this palatable.

The discussions continued over dinner and lasted until 2300. Again they concentrated on the American ideas for a three part process, beginning with an Argentine withdrawal, then moving on to the introduction of a local administration as close as possible to the one in place before the invasion and then a negotiating process between the two countries that was consistent with the islanders' right to self-determination. The British remained puzzled and uncertain about what Haig had in mind for the second stage and the role that an international group might play. The Secretary of State had no detailed formula in mind, but was building on an apparent readiness by Costa Mendez to 'let an autonomous government remain in hands of islanders.'[4] The group from third party countries, he explained, would:

provide an internationally recognised umbrella, which would prevent a war, safeguard the islanders, ensure the preservation of their traditions and their laws, and give international credibility to the agreed solution.

Haig explained that he was seeking an arrangement that had 'certain constructive ambiguities' but provided no real departure from the standards of administration, which would essentially be what they had always been. The Prime Minister could only envisage one function for an international body – 'to supervise a test of opinion among the islanders about their future' and see whether they wished 'to remain British, become Argentinian, or become independent.' Haig demurred. This body would guarantee that negotiations would still, nonetheless, take place even after British administration had been restored.

It was hard to see, the Prime Minister suggested, why these ideas should be at all acceptable to Argentina anyway. Haig accepted the point:

he did not want a situation to arise where the United States could be accused of having failed to seize an opportunity to resolve the problem. The very fact that the United States were ready to volunteer to be a member of the proposed international group showed how important they thought this issue. The scheme would engage the United States in the Falkland Islands in a way in which they had not been engaged before. They would be sharing the burden with the United Kingdom.

Given that under these proposals any agreement would contain language on self-determination when referring to the negotiations on the future status of the Islands, and that it was quite possible that these negotiations would go on without ever reaching a conclusion, the second stage of resumed British administration could continue indefinitely. This would give Britain virtually what existed before the invasion. How then to make it saleable to Argentina? Here Haig, tentatively, raised the possibility of an Argentine observer in the international group, only for it to be shot down by the Prime Minister. This was unacceptable, as would be any equality of treatment between Argentina and the UK, since Argentina was the aggressor. Enders pointed out that there would have to be some liaison between Argentina and the international group, if only because it would be supervising withdrawal.

In summing up Haig noted that they had agreed on the first stage of withdrawal, and the third stage of negotiations, but had not yet settled what was to happen between the two. The Prime Minister hoped that Haig would go to Buenos Aires to assess the situation there, but the line she intended to take with the press was that the two sides had agreed that Resolution 502 should be implemented as soon as possible and had discussed how the United States could help in the process. Haig should not give any impression that the British position had changed or that flexibility was being shown.

The British assessment after the meeting, confirmed in the American line to the press, was that Haig did now understand the strength of British feeling. Ideas on an interim administration were imprecise, and apparently largely geared to saving Argentine face. The Prime Minister saw already the challenge that was posed to her public pledge to restore British administration.[5] The only work that it seemed necessary to set in motion was on how an Argentine withdrawal could be organised and supervised, supposing it could actually be secured. The American assessment was slightly different. There was no doubting the Prime Minister's resolve, although one member of Haig's party, after recording the Prime Minister's barbed guide to the portraits in No. 10, wondered whether by pointing to Wellington as well as Nelson she was acknowledging that the conflict could be a 'close run thing'. Nor had she actually tried to persuade the Americans against going to Buenos Aires. By the end of the evening she was prepared to see advantages if Haig was able to bring home to the Argentines the potential consequences of their action and the strength of British feeling, and then to find out the conditions under which they might withdraw. The Americans had also been struck by the sharpness of Thatcher's exchanges with Pym, indicating that the British Cabinet was not of one mind (although they perhaps did not appreciate the Prime Minister's normal forms of discourse).

After the meeting, still presumably supposing that he was going to find some flexibility in Buenos Aires, Haig appreciated he had a serious difficulty with extracting any flexibility from the British. The problem, he surmised, was that the British, normally so good on cold war matters, did not realise quite what was at stake. Accordingly he concluded that the War Cabinet needed to be provided with a 'powerful, strong analysis of our shared interests, if Falklands dispute is not resolved peacefully and promptly.' This would be an 'analysis of the regional and global, strategic, political and economic dangers to the vital interests of the West.' For example, he noted, raising an issue that the British never took as seriously as he did, 'in our smaller and larger meetings, we did not sense that the British had sufficiently thought through that an Argentine-British military conflict might lead to a cementing of a Soviet-Argentine military relationship'. Haig's hope was that a satisfactory analysis would 'help the British focus on such considerations as they evaluate each step they take – and what most especially on what must be done if armed conflict is to be avoided.' They also need 'to recognize that the international support they now enjoy could evaporate if there is a diplomatic failure.'

When the document arrived it established a wholly negative framework for the evaluation of a British determination to press ahead regardless – while their leverage might grow as the fleet approached the South Atlantic thereafter it could 'fall precipitously, resulting in a situation in which mediation is impossible and in which the regional and global interests of the west are jeopardized'. NATO would be weakened through ship losses, while financial pressure might lead to cuts in British forces in Germany. London would lose sympathy if 'seen to be acting without regard for the consequences of violence'. The military action would hurt mediation while other measures would strain allies, and all of this could undermine cohesion in the Atlantic Alliance, encourage anti-colonialist feeling, and undercut efforts in Central America. It was as if US officials were scanning the nightmares of the FCO – that these things might happen, and, even worse, that London would be blamed.

Haig reported back to Reagan, with some admiration, that Thatcher had the 'bit in her teeth,' and was 'rigid in her insistence on a return to the status quo ante.' Nott, he judged to be 'squarely behind her', but less ideological, and apparently preferring a blockade rather than a landing. Pym had surprised Haig by his readiness to show his disagreements in the Prime Minister's presence, but it was not clear whether he could be a restraining influence. 'All in all,' he concluded:

We got no give in the basic British position, and only the glimmering of some possibilities, and that only after much effort by me with considerable help not appreciated by Mrs Thatcher from Pym.

Now moving on to Argentina, he reported to the President, he intended to 'draw a picture of total British resolve'. Only if the Argentines gave him something to work with would he return to London. 'It may then be necessary for me to ask you to apply unusual pressure on Thatcher.' Reagan took the message that there was no obvious basis for compromise – a deal that would give 'Maggie enough to carry on and at the same time meets the test of equity with our Latin neighbors.' He expressed no confidence that the British position would change quickly, and, if that was the case, then 'the closure of the British submarines is all the more worrisome'.

Haig in Buenos Aires

Haig arrived in Argentina late in the evening of 9 April to a mass demonstration organised for his benefit. The Argentine Government was determined that the United States should be aware not only of the strength of patriotic feeling in Argentina, but also the extent to which support for Britain would jeopardise its position in Latin America. They played on American fears that the Rio Treaty might be invoked and that Cuba might be approached for support. Haig later told the British that Galtieri had informed him of the Cuban Ambassador's return after a year's absence offering him everything he needed. Not only was this offer said to have the support of the Soviet Union, but Moscow had also offered to sink British vessels. Haig did not find this threat credible: Moscow would be well aware of the dreadful international consequences of such a move.

In his discussions with Galtieri, Haig explained that the British position was currently that there could be no negotiations without an Argentine withdrawal. In the face of Argentine scepticism, he warned that war was a real possibility. In his view Britain would win. He also stressed the strength of Britain's international support. On this basis Argentina could not expect the outcome demanded – a confirmation of sovereignty. The sovereignty issue was non-negotiable for the moment and was best not mentioned at all. He sought to sell his basic idea of the withdrawal of forces (including a zone from which British forces would be excluded) and then an interim administration with an international character. Admittedly Argentina would not be in direct control, but then nor would Britain. The response was tepid. Argentina expected to run the Malvinas, with some islander involvement and perhaps some external guarantees, until the negotiations on sovereignty concluded with a formal transfer.

Argentina had its own ideas for agreements with Britain on the basis of special rights to exploit any natural resources around the Islands and special privileges for the islanders. The Americans had seen little point in building upon any of these, as they offered no basis for a settlement. Instead they began to develop further their own ideas, concentrating on an interim administration, and the associated consortium of the US, Canada and two

Latin American countries to monitor demilitarisation. This interim administration would continue while the two sides negotiated a final settlement,
which they would undertake to achieve by the end of 1982. The Americans
had drafted treaty language for the interim administration. This read:

> The traditional local administration shall continue, including the
> executive and legislative councils. Argentina shall name a senior
> official as its co-ordinator on the islands to act as liaison with the
> consortium and to assist it in its tasks.[6]

As this was discussed the Argentine team indicated a preference for a
smaller consortium involving only Britain, Argentina and the US, and
pressed for representation on the islanders' councils. They were still unhappy
to concede any return of British administration, whatever the consequences
for Thatcher's political position. They also revived a long-standing demand
for an Argentine right to live, work and own property on the Islands if they
so desired.

As the discussions in Buenos Aires broke up before midnight, Galtieri
reported back to the Junta. They were still unimpressed with the American
ideas and wanted to reinstate the principle of a continuing Argentine administration. When this view was presented to Haig he asked to meet privately
with Galtieri, who was accompanied only by Costa Mendez and Rear
Admiral Moya. In the middle of a heated discussion, as the Argentine group
sought to impress upon the Secretary of State their exasperation with the
British and their unwillingness to back down in the face of threats, Haig
perceived a possible breakthrough.

He concluded that a problem for Galtieri might be the complete lack of
an Argentine presence on the Falklands once its forces had withdrawn.
Perhaps, he thought, allowing Argentine flags to fly on the Islands could fill
this gap. Although Argentina had not moved at all from the view that a
formal transfer of sovereignty had to occur, Haig now believed he could
obtain a withdrawal by offering it a more substantial presence during the
interim stage. His team now worked on a new draft of an agreement that
had been maturing since the London visit:

> Argentinian troops would leave the islands and the British adminis-
> tration would be restored. But economic and financial measures
> against Argentina would be terminated within two weeks, the flags of
> the six nations would be flown at the headquarters of the consortium,
> and, finally, national flags could be displayed at the residences and on
> the official automobiles of all countries represented on the islands.[7]

The Argentine side was ignorant of Haig's construction of their views and of
his draft. They were not aware that Haig thought he had a major concession.

To the extent Haig did think this he was soon disabused. As he left Buenos Aires on the morning of 11 April to return to London he met briefly with Costa Mendez who handed him a paper containing the official Argentine proposal that they hoped he would transmit to the British Government. The essence was that one way or another sovereignty must be transferred to Argentina.

11

HAIG'S SECOND VISIT

Before he departed from Buenos Aires, and before he received this final Argentine missive, Haig sent a message to Mrs Thatcher reporting that he had had 'lengthy and intensive' discussions and intended to arrive in London at 0630 on 12 April. He wanted to talk about 'a draft proposal and some additional ideas' that had come out of twelve hours of meeting with the Argentine leaders. Though serious problems remained some progress had been made. 'In the meantime,' he added, 'I am sure you would agree that any military confrontation must be avoided at all costs until you have been able to consider this draft proposal.'

Haig's request for restraint had in fact come at an awkward moment. As Haig well knew, the MEZ was about to come into force and in principle submarines might start attacking Argentine ships. The ROE were about to change from orders to 'fire merely in self-defence if attacked' to orders to attack any Argentine naval vessels or naval auxiliaries in the zone. If the new orders were implemented just as Haig was stepping off his plane, then it would appear, whatever the intention, as a serious rebuff and could have damaging political consequences internationally when it was known that a peace effort was underway. Yet suspending the enforcement of the MEZ, as Haig was apparently urging, might give him more time to search for a settlement but would also leave Argentina free to continue to strengthen and supply the occupation forces.

There was a further problem. It might seem the easiest thing to send an order to an SSN to hold fire, but when the FCO first made investigations in case Haig did ask that Britain should stay its hand for 48 hours, they were told that, unfortunately, it took some 30 hours to be sure of communicating with SSNs. If there were a decision to delay the MEZ's implementation, it would have to be taken before midnight on 10 April. After that ministers would have no flexibility. As a way round this, and to avoid being put in a situation where the Government was embarrassed by Haig making a request around the time of the effective deadline, it was proposed to arrange with the SSN Commander for a brief contact very shortly before his ROE became activated at 0400 GMT on Monday 12

April. This would provide a safety catch without affecting Argentine behaviour, for it would remain secret and their Navy would still behave as if the EZ was being enforced actively. Furthermore, in order to avoid an incident over this crucial period, ministers decided to revert to the previous, cautious rule: 'Remain covert. Carry out surveillance of area allocated. If detected evade. If unable to evade, prosecuting units may be attacked in self defence.'

Communication with submarines was not simple. In fact, according to Admiral Herbert, CTF 324.3, they were 'awful'. He noted the 'many excuses being offered, such as the novelty of the system, and the unfamiliarity of operations at sea' before concluding that 'it is simply proving too difficult to be 100% certain that any one signal has been received by any one unit'. Outgoing signals were transmitted in 'routines', which could contain a large number of messages for a number of different submarines. The routine was repeated a number of times at each broadcast and the broadcasts themselves were repeated at intervals of some four hours. Each submarine commander had instructions to listen for routines at a certain periodicity. Under the SSNs' current regime MoD would need to transmit a counter-holding order by noon on 11 April to be sure that it had been received. The alternative to this arrangement was simply to issue the revised ROE immediately, but this was deemed undesirable both politically, because it would convey the wrong message about the Government's resolve around the Ministry and to the submarine commander, and bureaucratically because it would require collective ministerial approval. So 1000Z on 11 April was accepted as the latest moment a holding order could be issued without asking the SSN to accept the delays and added vulnerability that would flow from having to come up too often to receive messages.

Although the FCO remained unhappy with this early deadline, the Prime Minister showed little interest in delaying the enforcement of the EZ. Lewin was also strongly opposed. He rehearsed his arguments in his notes for the War Cabinet on 11 April. Haig as 'a soldier ... will be expecting us to do something like this and will think us weak if we don't.' If it was done after Haig left it would look like his permission had been sought. In addition, enforcing the zone was not an undertaking to sink a ship. The clinching argument: 'the whole scheme' was in 'today's *Sun*'. The War Cabinet therefore decided that any proposal by Haig should be met by a request for counter-concessions – an agreement that Argentine naval vessels would leave the MEZ and none would enter, and that forces would not be supplied by air or sea. Merchant vessels of other nations would be allowed to go to the Islands with food and other essential supplies, under some kind of US verification of cargoes. Picking up on Chilean Government warnings that Argentina was playing for time, any such arrangement could only be for a limited period, while the Task Force was continuing its approach. The Prime Minister was disinclined to rely on bluff and felt that having announced the

EZ it should be implemented. As it happened there did not seem to be Argentine targets in the Zone so the risk of an early attack seemed small, while nothing from Buenos Aires indicated that Haig was on the verge of a diplomatic breakthrough. Accordingly the Prime Minister did not make any promises. She wrote to Haig:

> I should certainly prefer to avoid military confrontation. But Argentina is the aggressor, and is still trying to build up the occupying force in the Falklands. The right way to prevent naval incidents is therefore for Argentina to remove all her naval vessels from the Maritime Exclusion Zone. The Argentine Government has had plenty of warning. I am sure that you will have impressed this point upon the Argentine leaders. But if there is any doubt in your mind as to their intentions, you may wish to consider sending them a further immediate message.

While they waited for Haig to arrive British officials speculated on what his new ideas might involve. Parsons had flown over to talk over the negotiating strategy with the Prime Minister on 10 April (Good Friday) and she talked further with Pym, Nott and Lewin the next day. The second stage of interim administration had been identified as the area where major British concessions appeared to be expected, as this did not guarantee a transfer of sovereignty in stage three and might achieve withdrawal of Argentine forces as stage one. It was still difficult to imagine any language acceptable to both sides. A failure to restore British administration in stage two when stage three might drag on indefinitely would be bad enough, but would be even worse if Argentina were participants. The best that officials could manage in devising a possible agreement was encapsulated in a rather unpromising paragraph:

> a stand-off by the British Task Force while Argentina withdraws; non-British, probably US, administration of the islands for a finite period, probably confined to the time needed for Argentine withdrawal; American chairmanship of future negotiations about the Falklands; and an international method of ascertaining the future wishes of the Islanders after the re-establishment of British Administration.

It is, however, important to note that at this point the Prime Minister had accepted that if there were to be a negotiated settlement the Government would have to concede on the interim administration. When she was sent a draft of the line ministers should take in response to parliamentary and media questions, she amended paragraphs on objectives to exclude the restoration of British administration. The original stated:

There can be no negotiation about the future status of the Falkland Islands until the Argentine forces have withdrawn and British Administration has been restored. In any subsequent negotiations the wishes of the Islanders will remain dominant.

This became after her redrafting:

There can be no negotiation about the future status of the Falkland Islands until the Argentine forces have withdrawn. Then in any subsequent negotiations with Britain, the wishes of the Islanders will remain paramount.[1]

Haig returns

The British had asked for a description of Haig's discussions with the Junta, and prior to his arrival on the morning of Monday, 12 April they received a rather portentous message:

You may reveal in the strictest confidence that our conversations have revealed tentative cracks in the Argentine stone wall on the withdrawal of military forces and the restoration of British administration. But we still have a long way to go in very little time, and will need the highest statesmanship of both our governments. We are more than ever convinced that an Anglo-Argentine War would severely damage Western interests in containing Soviet expansionism.

They did not have long to wait for the meaning of this note to be explained, for at 0930 Haig brought his rather tired team to Downing Street. He began with a detailed account of his time in Buenos Aires, and insisted that he had been 'brutally frank' with Galtieri, telling him that 'the United Kingdom was ready militarily and psychologically for war and British people right behind the British Government.' 'War would be inevitable' if Argentina 'did not alter course.' Galtieri had not been as bellicose as expected though the demonstrations had almost got out of hand. His impression was that the Navy was looking for a fight, the Air Force did not want a war, with the Army somewhere in between. He had almost broken off the negotiations when it seemed that Argentine proposals essentially envisaged virtually complete capitulation by Britain, but this prospect had proved to be sufficiently alarming to persuade the Argentine Government to be more constructive.

Haig did not try to persuade Britain to relax its tough position. On the contrary he believed that it helped him in his search for a diplomatic solution, even though he did not believe that force alone would get Argentina off the Falkland Islands. He now felt that it was possible to structure a plausible settlement around the core British demands of the withdrawal of Argentine forces, the restoration of British administration, and respect for the islanders' right of self-determination. The proposal offered had seven elements:

1. Both agree to withdraw from the Islands and an agreed surrounding area, to be accomplished within two weeks.
2. The vacated zone would be demilitarised until a final settlement. Neither side would reintroduce military forces. The UK would not be expected to turn round its Task Force while it needed the leverage it provided, until London could 'announce unilaterally' its return 'when the crisis had been defused.' The forces would then return to 'normal duties.'
3. A commission made up of British, American and Argentine representatives would ensure compliance with the first two provisions. Argentina did not want UN, OAS or Canadian involvement.
4. Economic and financial sanctions would be lifted.
5. The traditional local administration of the Islands would be restored, but would submit acts and regulation to a special commission. They would need representatives of the Argentine community based in the Islands on the Councils (of which there were only some 40). They would oppose the return of the Governor, but were prepared to see senior officials return. The commission would not have any initiating powers.
6. The Commission would recommend ways to the two countries of promoting and facilitating communications, trade and transportation between the Islands and Argentina and Britain would have a veto here. 'The veto would be a protection against Argentina trying to populate the islands with settlers.' Nonetheless Argentina was still after an opportunity to get permission for their citizens to start up businesses or rent property.
7. There would be negotiations on a final settlement that must be consistent with the purposes and principles of UN Charter. Argentina wanted these completed by 31 December 1982. Although both sides would pursue their objective of establishing sovereignty, there should be no pre-conceived outcome of the negotiations.

Questioned by Thatcher, Haig agreed that Argentina probably was trying to seek practical arrangements that would enable them to change the character of the Falkland Islands, but he did not think that they could get very far by the end of 1982:

> It was important to emphasise that these proposals were not what the Argentines wanted. Rather, they were what the Americans had driven them to contemplate under threats to break off the talks and then go back to Washington.

He claimed that the draft language he showed the Prime Minister represented the absolute limit of Argentine toleration 'and a bit more'.[2] If he could reach an agreement with Britain then he proposed to fly back to Buenos Aires. The meeting ended at 1100 to enable the British Government to consider the American text.

The War Cabinet reconvened at 1545 to discuss the situation. In contrast to the rigidity of the previous visit, the Government was now inclined to accept the American proposals. They could be defended to Parliament, though there were some problems. In stage two, the powers of the proposed commission, and the nature of Argentine representation on the Councils, seemed limited.[3] This was not too much to concede in return for getting Argentine forces off the Islands. They set down their concerns, but took as a starting point that: 'With a few modifications this could be an acceptable agreement.' The modifications related to the need to define the areas to be demilitarised, the exclusion of the local police from this process, a limitation on the total number of each special commissioner's staff, and that the 'representation of the Argentine population on the Executive and Legislative Councils should be proportionate to their numbers, subject to their not having less than one representative on each council.' In addition they were also anxious to:

> preserve the principle that the Special Commissioner's proposals on travel, transportation, communications and trade would have the status of recommendations, on which decisions could not be taken without the agreement of the British and Argentine Governments or (as appropriate) the Executive and Legislative Councils.

The War Cabinet could not know whether or not these modifications were negotiable with Argentina but the basis for agreement appeared to be present. Turning to Stages One and Three other pitfalls became evident. In Stage One the British had no intention of holding back while waiting to see if Argentina honoured its pledges, nor could they then promise, as Argentina wanted, to stay out of the South Atlantic altogether. Haig was proposing instead a clause whereby British forces returned to 'normal' duties. Much would depend here on how 'normal' was interpreted: it was decided that this phrase need not preclude the Task Force from proceeding to or remaining in the South Atlantic if the Government so wished. This fed into Stage Three concerns on what would happen if the negotiations failed to produce a solution, quite likely if they were successful in insisting that the islanders' wishes were paramount. Would the Americans then provide a guarantee against Argentine re-invasion?

At 1755 they met again with Haig's team and went through the draft agreement in what turned into a serious drafting session. Nott later observed how the officials present (too many he thought) at last saw an opportunity to get an agreement. 'These civil servants ... started passing amendments up and down the table. We reached the point where they were trying to broker a drafting compromise between us and Haig.' Nott protested when 'with the assistance of these Whitehall draughtsmen, we had nearly reached a stage where we were being asked to withdraw 4,000 miles to Ascension whilst the Argentinians were withdrawing 400 miles to their mainland.'[4]

Haig did want the Task Force to stop and stand off, though not turn back, once the agreements were signed. The Prime Minister insisted that she would not survive in the Commons if the Task Force stopped before Argentina had completed its withdrawal. They could not rule out Argentina reversing its withdrawal or even re-invading. There was no basis of trust. The best that could be offered was that the Task Force would halt at the same distance from the Falkland Islands as Argentina. Haig said this position 'would not be understood publicly.' Once Argentina withdrew Britain would be seen to have won. The Task Force could be held in position until the withdrawal was completed. Nonetheless, Haig agreed to look at the original wording to see if this point could be finessed.

Britain agreed to drop the word 'interim' when describing the commission, and did not object to dropping a unanimity provision for the local administration, although this would leave the Americans in the position of referee. Argentina was apparently intending to keep Governor Menendez in place as a Commissioner: in that case, the Prime Minister replied, Rex Hunt would need to return as the British Commissioner. The British rejected any reference to immigration, a highly controversial subject since the position of the Falkland Islanders had been changed in the Nationality Act. There was also a discussion of the timing of the lifting of sanctions. Britain did not insist that these could only be lifted when the Argentine withdrawal was complete but wanted to be able to make a judgement on the progress of the Argentine withdrawal. The meeting ended at 2030. The next day Thatcher gave Parliament a moderately positive report. Ideas had been put forward by Haig concerning the withdrawal of troops and its supervision, and an interim period during which negotiations on the future of the Islands would be conducted:

> Some things we could not consider because they flouted our basic principles. Others we had to examine carefully and suggest alternatives. The talks were constructive and some progress was made.

The negotiations with the British had only progressed well, however, on the basis of setting to one side Argentine concerns, including those expressed by Costa Mendez in his parting note to Haig the previous morning.

A message came to Haig from the US Ambassador to Argentina indicating that Costa Mendez was not only trying to play up the message he had passed on to Haig on Sunday morning but also to play down the discussions Haig had had with Argentine negotiators on the Saturday evening. These had only been 'conversations'. The key position had been set down by

Galtieri and encapsulated in the paper from Costa Mendez. Do 'not discard the paper', the Argentine Foreign Minister urged, pointing out that he had not 'participated in the final drafting session at the palace.' He was anxious that 'some of the principles embodied in the paper he gave you should be incorporated in the proposal.'

During the day Haig was in intermittent telephone communication with Costa Mendez. The hardline position represented by the paper had appeared in that morning's *New York Times*. Just after lunch, at 1430 (1030 Buenos Aires), Haig rang the Argentine Foreign Minister to explain that little could be achieved on the basis of this paper, which is why he was still working with the ideas developed by his own team while in Buenos Aires. Costa Mendez insisted that the paper contained the true Argentine position, but agreed to talk with Haig again later in the day. Haig sent a message via the US Ambassador warning Costa Mendez that the negotiations were reaching a crisis point. It was hard enough with his draft but would be impossible with the Argentine draft. The Saturday evening proposals were the only ones worth working with. 'I am convinced that any substantial deviation by your government from the ideas discussed on Saturday night will doom this mission.'

Haig received a call from the Argentine Foreign Minister almost as soon as he had finished his last meeting with the British team.[5] There was no point in Haig returning to Buenos Aires, Costa Mendez said, unless he brought with him an agreement that provided for the Governor of the Islands to be appointed by Argentina and for the Argentine flag to continue to fly, or at least with assurances that at the end of the negotiations Britain would recognise Argentine sovereignty over the Islands. At 2155 Haig rang Thatcher with this news. She commented that such demands were unacceptable. Haig replied that he said the same to Costa Mendez and, after Haig reported how well things had gone in London, there had been some backpedalling. Accordingly Haig had instructed the US Ambassador in Buenos Aires to see Costa Mendez to ascertain if he still faced an ultimatum. The Prime Minister urged that, if the ultimatum was still in place, then Washington should let it be known publicly why the effort to find a diplomatic solution had collapsed. Haig agreed.

At 0115 (2115 Buenos Aires) Haig was back on the phone to Thatcher. He had spoken once again to Costa Mendez who was 'dissembling and quibbling,' demanding sovereignty on the one hand and asking for negotiations to continue on the other. Haig said he would not go back under present circumstances but would sleep on it, while Costa Mendez went back to talk to Galtieri. In order for it not to look as if the problems were with Britain he proposed to say to the press that they had arisen at the Argentine end. Because of this new development Haig and Thatcher agreed to meet again in the morning. At this point Haig revealed to Thatcher the existence of the letter that had been handed to him as he left Buenos Aires. He now accepted that the contents were more than the private thoughts of Costa Mendez. These were the demands of the Argentine Government.

In his conversations with Costa Mendez Haig described his role as not so much a negotiator as a 'transmitter of ideas between both parties that have profound differences,' who were still moving towards a war 'that will have very damaging consequences for all.' If his efforts were now concluded that would be his decision and not Britain's and the blame would be placed on Argentina's increasingly hard-line position. He warned that the White House had told him that everything must be placed 'in suspense' unless he could be sure that 'the talks are a help and not a hindrance or a commitment to the US.' Costa Mendez was anxious that the talks did not end on this basis, though he saw the problem as finding a formula that might make the Argentine position more acceptable to the UK. According to Haig, he concluded by telling the Argentine Foreign Minister to talk to Galtieri. 'Tell him we are close to a workable solution if we are not faced with these kinds of alternatives. I'll call you in the morning.'

On the morning of 13 April the British and American teams met again.[6] Haig had more unhelpful news from Argentina. Costa Mendez was saying that he 'needed' an outcome that embodied a de facto change in the administration of the Islands and a process leading to Argentine sovereignty. Haig handed over the paper embodying the five points that Costa Mendez described as being essential:

1. The governor of the islands must be appointed by the Argentine government. The Argentine flag should continue to be flown on the islands;
2. Assurances should be given to the Argentine Government that at the end of the negotiations there will be a recognition of Argentine sovereignty. Any formulation implying that sovereignty is being negotiated should be avoided;
3. Equal rights should be recognised for Argentines coming from the mainland as for the inhabitants of the islands;
4. The agreement on demilitarisation should be considered as complying with Resolution 502 of the United Nations Security Council;
5. The draft agreement should be made compatible with the above mentioned elements.

Costa Mendez had implied that the first two points were the most important, and Argentina needed at least one of them. The previous day's draft Anglo-US agreement arrangement blocked both: an interim commission did not represent enough movement towards de facto Argentine administration while the provision for negotiations on the definitive status was inadequate as a commitment. There appeared to be no point in Haig returning to Buenos Aires unless he could take assurances on these matters, yet he also did not want to break off talks. Thatcher did not push for an immediate break, although she had a strong case for doing so. Instead she asked for definite progress to be registered 'this week'.

All this undermined British confidence in the whole initiative. They had assumed that the document upon which they had been negotiating the previous day had a measure of Argentine agreement. It now turned out that this was not so. The arguments on the draft could well be to no purpose, and the whole exercise was doing little more than help Argentina buy time.[7] The more they drew attention to the total unreality of the Argentine proposals and unacceptability of attempts to claim victory by force of arms, the more Haig seemed to fret about the cold war implications of Argentina moving closer to the Soviet Union and the possible interference of other bodies such as the UN and the OAS. Evidence of Soviet fishing boats providing Argentina with intelligence suggested to the British that Argentina was already a less than deserving case, but led Haig to seek to keep the process going by making another effort at the 'evolution' of the document already agreed with Britain. The Prime Minister, despite her tough stance, was also worried that if negotiations broke down the public reaction in Britain might be that the Government had not tried hard enough to find a peaceful solution.

Much depended on whether the five points really represented the final position of the Junta. Haig expected to talk again to Costa Mendez. Meanwhile, in a gesture he hoped would have a sobering effect on the Argentine Government, he had instructed the American Ambassador in Buenos Aires to take all necessary precautionary measures for the protection of staff and the local American community. If there was any point in returning to the Argentine capital he was going to need more concessions from Britain, though the British thought that they had gone quite far enough with face-saving devices the previous day. Without more, an early return to Buenos Aires held open a possibly unreal prospect of further progress, especially as Argentina had yet to offer any serious concessions of its own. A later return would not necessarily help: as the Task Force approached its destination it might be even more difficult, psychologically, for Argentina to concede. None of this moved the British delegation: Haig had to understand that Britain would not hold back from further military measures if no progress was being made. Argentina was even less likely to budge if it assumed that Britain was unwilling to fight. This rather unsatisfactory discussion concluded at 1040.

Paragraph 8

There then followed what Thatcher would later describe as a 'bizarre turn.'[8] At 1240 Haig rang Pym, reporting that Costa Mendez had come back to him with a further compromise proposal:

The Argentine Government would in effect accept the reformulation in paragraph 5 of the Anglo/US paper, but in return insisted on language paralleling the 1964 UN Resolution on decolonization of the Islands. In that context, they would be willing to give the islanders local self-determination.

The Argentine Government had now apparently dropped their five demands and had moved considerably from their previous position. A breakthrough seemed to be at hand so long as the British did not reject this latest proposal out of hand. The key, he thought, lay in agreement on language about decolonisation, subject to the wishes of the islanders. This might make it possible for the Argentine Government to accept the Anglo/US paper, perhaps with one or two small changes to make it even more palatable. Pym promised to consider the matter carefully. This would need careful research. Haig acknowledged the point. The Americans also needed to do their homework, as well as get a more specific formulation from Argentina.

Haig was pushing the War Cabinet into yet more concessions. Having got them to acknowledge a role for Argentina in an interim administration he was now expecting them to acknowledge that final negotiations would not lead to a return to the status quo ante. Haig noted that the British position over sovereignty had been eroded over the years in the view of many other governments, and so it should not be too rigid now. The British observed this warily. A tendency to put a positive gloss on inconclusive conversations with the Junta had been observed and this might be more wishful thinking. Regardless, if the Secretary of State believed that the Argentine suggestion was an opportunity to keep the dialogue going it was difficult for them to call a halt.

Haig was putting a more positive construction on his conversation with Costa Mendez than it warranted.[9] The Foreign Minister had referred the previous night to the 1964 Declaration on Decolonisation, but largely to make the point that Britain had indicated in the past that the Falklands might be decolonised and that this declaration had led to the original negotiations on sovereignty between the two countries. The Falkland Islands was categorised as a non-autonomous territory. Ending this status did not, however, mean a transfer to Argentina. The alternative could be independence – which was the norm for territories in this category. The Declaration had led to the formulation of General Assembly Resolution 2065, which linked the broad principle of decolonisation with the particular case of the Falklands. The basis for a compromise might be in the language in the Declaration on self-determination. From the Argentine perspective, however, the key point was that Resolution 2065 stressed only the islanders' 'interests' rather than their 'wishes.' There was no basis for a real compromise here: at best there was an opportunity for a fudge.

Haig did not want to stay in London, lest he appear to be acting as Britain's agent, but nor was he ready to dash straight back to Buenos Aires. Instead he decided first to return to Washington. Before he left for the airport he wanted to leave the British with a specific proposal. His latest communications with Argentina had apparently convinced him that the Junta now realised what faced them and that they dare not be too intransigent. His mood was upbeat: 'the Argentines were now terrified. The climate was right for progress.' Pym and Haig met that afternoon.[10] The Americans handed over a new version of Paragraph 8 of their draft Treaty:

> December 31, 1982, will conclude the interim period and, during this period, the signatories shall negotiate the conditions of the decolonization and definitive status of the Islands, consistent with the purposes and principles of the UN Charter, United Nations General Assembly Resolution 1514 (XX), and the 1964 Report of the Special Committee of the General Assembly on the situation with regard to the implementation of the declaration on the granting of independence to colonial countries and peoples.

The Americans pressed this draft on the British: this was a step forward on the Argentine part and offered the possibility of a solution. The implications were not so serious. Resolution 1514 contained helpful references to self-determination and, while decolonisation might be a charged word in Britain, the proposed language must be preferable to a transfer of sovereignty. In return for accepting this paragraph 8 Argentina would be pressed to accept paragraph 5 of the existing draft, on the interim administration. It might also be possible to weaken language providing for a fixed end to the interim period. At the same time the Americans reported that the Argentines were producing their own version, due to be received that evening. The British were hardly dizzy with anticipation: 'the result is clearly unlikely to be any more palatable to us than the American cockshy.'

Haig insisted that he was looking for an arrangement whereby Argentina would live in hope for the next nine months that they would eventually get what they wanted. But it was vital to the British position that this remained no more than a hope. The Government had been careful not to oppose change, but had insisted that the choice in the end had to be left to the islanders, and the islanders had not chosen Argentina in the past for perfectly good reasons. Parliament certainly would not accept any attempt to push the islanders towards the Argentine embrace. The obvious problem with the formula now being proposed was that it would limit the islanders' right of self-determination if they were precluded from returning to the status quo ante. When pressed Haig promised that the American position at the end of the day would be to 'stick to the right of the individual,' but the British were nonetheless becoming nervous that the Argentines had made headway with their argument to Haig that self-determination was an artificial concept in this context because of restrictions on Argentine immigration and investment. Solace was only found in a couple of references from Haig to a referendum as part of a solution and an understanding that Britain could not sanction the Islands suddenly being swamped by Argentine immigrants.

The War Cabinet was left with some difficult questions. The Americans had been uncomfortably vague on the purpose behind the new Argentine ideas: did they truly represent a lowering of sights or did they simply offer different language within which they were seeking a commitment to sovereignty? Haig's insistence that he accepted the principles behind the British position had to be set against his constant reminders that Britain had been prepared to contemplate new arrangements for the Falklands in the past. He reported, for example, that Costa Mendez had claimed that Britain had previously accepted the Falkland Islands in a list of territories to be decolonised. He also sought to impress upon the British that they could not expect unlimited support from their allies if they appeared to be intransigent. From soundings among a number of Britain's 'European friends' he concluded that 'there won't be as much robustness on either side of the Atlantic when we get down to ground zero.' Most worrying was the thought that Haig was so determined to get an agreement that he would put great pressure on Britain to move away from its principles, almost forcing the Government to choose between a transatlantic and a parliamentary crisis.

The British did not feel it prudent to undermine Haig's mission at this time, but this was not the same as justifying the confident call Haig made to Costa Mendez, before he left for Washington on 13 April, to report that he had 'spoken to the highest figures in the British government', and saw 'grounds for a breakthrough' and that he would come to Buenos Aires from Washington.

American military support

Haig was not representing a united administration. On the one hand he was under pressure from the 'Latinos' and in particular the redoubtable Kirkpatrick. On the other hand, the American Secretary of Defense Caspar Weinberger was proceeding with his own policy of backing Britain strongly. Like Haig he feared Soviet influence in South America, but unlike Haig he saw Argentina as already in something of a Russian bear hug, because of the grain agreement. There was also some evidence that Moscow was providing intelligence on British fleet movements to Buenos Aires. His view was that if the British were going to retake the Islands then the US had to 'help them to the utmost of our ability'. He was ready to take full advantage of long-standing agreements between the two allies, and their close working relationships:

> I therefore passed the word to the Department that all existing UK requests for military equipment, and other requests for equipment or other types of support, short of our actual participation in their military action, should be granted immediately.[11]

The importance of Weinberger's stance is hard to overstate (and helps explains his honorary knighthood after the war). It was taken in the face of military advice in the Pentagon that the odds were against a British success and in knowing contradiction of Haig's public emphasis on impartiality. It would not have surprised the British if the American response to their requests for military assistance had been tardy: instead they were imbued with a sense of urgency. Weinberger had not sought backing for his position at the National Security Council and nor had he informed Haig just how much was going on.

The media, however, was informed. The first reports came out on 13 April, as Haig left London, referring to the provision of satellite communication links, weather forecasts, intelligence and jet fuel. The Argentines were furious. To them Haig's mission was now cast in a completely new light. Galtieri rang Reagan who blamed a Soviet fabrication and then said publicly that the British had not asked for help. The Pentagon having originally denied the reports soon opted for 'no comment' while Haig attempted to convince Buenos Aires that the stories were untrue and that he should still continue with his mediation.[12] To calm Costa Mendez down Haig promised a public denial. This required British co-operation.

At 1930 on 14 April Haig rang Thatcher. He described the reports and the problems that had been created. 'The Argentines had concluded that they could not proceed with negotiations unless the situation was rectified.' In addition they were not prepared to see him again without confirmation that the British would also be flexible, or at least that the US could table new proposals that were an advance on those last seen. Lastly, they wanted some (unspecified) assurance about 'The Fleet.' Then Haig read out his proposed statement:

> The dispute between Argentina and the United Kingdom was an exceptionally difficult and dangerous problem. The positions held by both countries were deeply felt and in many respects mutually contradictory. But the leaders of both countries had told him today that they were prepared to go on working to reach a political solution. That would require flexibility by both sides – not abandonment of principles but responsible and sensible adjustments. As a result of his discussions in London, in addition to telephone contacts today, he (Mr Haig) had developed new ideas which he had described to the Argentine Government. In the light of these new ideas, the Argentines had invited him to return to Buenos Aires. He proposed to do so and would go tomorrow or, if necessary, tonight.
>
> From the outset in this crisis the United States had viewed its role as one of assisting the two sides to find a peaceful solution. Its ability to do so was based on its longstanding relationships with both the United Kingdom and Argentina. The United States had been careful to maintain these relationships in order to preserve its

influence with both governments. Failure to live up to existing obligations or going beyond them would obviously jeopardise the United States ability to play the role which both countries had wished it to perform. Since the outset of the crisis the United States had not acceded to requests that would go beyond the scope of customary patterns of co-operation. That would continue to be its stand while peace efforts were under way. Britain's use of US facilities on Ascension Island had been restricted accordingly.

Thatcher was appalled. The Task Force was now gathering at Ascension and American assistance was more vital than ever. She warned Haig that many in Parliament that afternoon had expressed considerable disappointment about the US apparently taking a neutral position as between democracy and dictatorship. She said she wished to consult further before responding. After discussing the matter with Pym, Thatcher rang back and insisted that this statement, especially with the reference to Ascension Island, would cause adverse reaction in the UK. To say that the use of Ascension Island would be restricted but that customary patterns of co-operation would continue was a contradiction. 'There was already a feeling that the US was doing less for us than we deserved, given the support we had given to President Reagan and the help which Argentina seemed to be receiving from the Soviet Union.' (On which Haig reported an Argentine denial.) The British Government could not accept being placed 'on an equal footing with the Junta.'

After protesting the difficulty caused by the supply of fuel to British forces at Ascension Haig agreed to delete the reference to Ascension Island. He did however use the conversation to stress that there were only a couple of days left if he was to get a breakthrough, and to warn of the consequences should the Argentine Government find out what help the Americans were really giving to Britain.[13]

The press stories had been so unhelpful Haig was convinced that they had been 'encouraged, if not planted,' by the Soviets in the hope of derailing efforts at a peaceful solution. Yet, as Henderson observed, the leaks had come from within the Administration and their impact on Haig was the result, in addition to jet lag, of his conviction that his mediation depended on a credible appearance of impartiality and maintaining Galtieri in power. The argument that any successor regime to Galtieri's would be worse illustrated the familiar diplomatic tendency to prefer the status quo, no matter how awful. At any rate, having stopped over in Washington, and still convinced that he could extract a deal, Haig pressed on to Argentina.

While all this was going on the British had been labouring to improve the original text developed with Haig. Following his late conversations with Haig on 13 April, Pym had returned to consider the situation with his colleagues in the War Cabinet. He judged it to be good news that the mediation effort could continue and that, at least according to Haig, Argentina had dropped its unacceptable demands. The bad news was that the Americans were now pressing upon Britain an awkward new paragraph. The reference to decolonisation was difficult. Ministers certainly did not intend to share these ideas with the Commons.

Already reporting back to Parliament was becoming tricky, as now only a rather qualified form of restoration of British administration was anticipated, without a British Governor. In addressing Parliament that day, the Prime Minister had stressed her commitment to a 'peaceful solution by diplomatic effort,' and the importance of the withdrawal of the invaders' troops as the first stage, that the sovereignty of the Islands was not affected by the act of invasion and that when it came to future negotiations what would matter most would be what the Falkland Islanders themselves wished. This left open the nature of the administration of the Islands in the short-term and their long-term status. Lest this hint of compromise be detected she also reaffirmed the Government's readiness to use force:

> Our naval Task Force sails on towards its destination. We remain fully confident of its ability to take whatever measures may be necessary. Meanwhile its very existence and its progress towards the Falkland Islands reinforce the efforts we are making for a diplomatic solution.[14]

The American push threatened domestic political difficulties but its rejection out of hand threatened international difficulties. The only option appeared to be to continue to work on American drafts in the hope of making them just about acceptable. Accordingly the Prime Minister proposed redrafting the American paragraph to take account of the possibility that the proposed negotiations might fail to agree a definitive settlement by the end of the year. The Cabinet Office suggested two alternatives. Neither used the word 'decolonisation' and both kept in a reference to Resolution 1514 of 1960 but balanced it with a complementary reference to Resolution 2625 of 1970. The 1960 Resolution, on which Britain had abstained at the time, had proclaimed (1) the necessity of ending colonialism, (2) that peoples should not be subjected to 'alien subjugation,' (3) that they had a right to 'self-determination' and (4) that it was contrary to the UN Charter to disrupt 'the territorial integrity of a country.' In the present context, of these elements, (1) and (4) favoured Argentina, while (2) and (3) favoured the UK. The 1970 Resolution was more helpful to the British position. It contained a short paragraph referring to ending colonialism, but only 'having due regard to the freely expressed will of the peoples concerned.' There were also references to territorial integrity, but most welcome was a whole section devoted to the right to self-determination, including a provision that, in addition to independence, free association and integration, 'the emergence into any other political status freely determined by a people' shall constitute a mode of implementing the right of self-determination. In addition the document opposed 'alien subjugation' and the use of force to settle international disputes.

Of the two alternative drafts developed in London, the first referred to the possibility of sounding local opinion, picking up on the suggestion made by Haig, and also included provision for a limited extension of the interim period. The second alternative referred to Article 73 of the UN Charter that recognised the principle that 'the interests of the inhabitants' of such territories 'are paramount.' The eventual redraft was mainly based on Alternative 1, amended to deal with the problem of the different political position of each of the three sets of islands. South Georgia and the South Sandwich Islands had been administered as Dependencies of the Falkland Islands but should not necessarily be treated in the same way in any long-term settlement, since they had an importance of their own in relation to Antarctic claims. This clause now read as follows:

> December 31, 1982, will conclude the interim period. During this period, the signatories shall negotiate with a view to determining the future definitive status of each of the three groups of Islands, within the framework of the provisions of the UN Charter relating to non-self-governing territories, and consistently with the purposes and principles of the UN Charter, United Nations General Assembly Resolution 1514 (XX) and 2625 (XXV) and, so far as islands with a settled population are concerned, in accordance with their wishes and interests, which shall be ascertained by a sounding of local opinion to be supervised by the Special Commission. If it is not possible to complete the processes envisaged in this paragraph by December 31, 1982, the interim period may be extended for [three] months by agreement between the parties.

Work was also done to strengthen paragraphs 2 and 3 of the draft agreement relating to the withdrawal of forces. It was agreed that Pym would send Haig an urgent message covering the redrafting but also the need for the US to play a special role in both the enforcement of any proposed agreement during the interim period, for example excluding Argentine military forces, and the security of the Islands thereafter (with the airfield identified as the most likely point of entry for any second Argentine invasion). A focus on how the negotiations might conclude had raised the need to think about contingency plans should the crisis re-erupt. If the US was going to push for this agreement, then it should also be prepared to consider how it might be guaranteed, if necessary by armed force.

A telegram was drafted to Haig on these points:

> The conduct of the Argentines so far leaves us with no confidence that – if they are disappointed in the progress of negotiations

161

towards the end of the interim period – they may not disregard these provisions and attempt to re-occupy the Islands or Dependencies. Although our own naval forces would of course be outside the immediate area, we should nonetheless be in a position to ensure that the Argentines could not do this by sea without incurring heavy penalties. My anxiety relates to the airfield at Port Stanley. This is only 350 miles from the Argentine mainland and massive troop reinforcements could be quickly and easily introduced onto the Islands without our being in any position to prevent this. Indeed, the extension of the runway which we know to be taking place would increase the risk of this, since it could enable larger aircraft from more distant airfields to converge rapidly on Port Stanley. Having been the victim of surprise aggression once, we cannot risk it happening again.

Therefore some restraint must be devised on the Argentine use of the airfield. Proposals included a US Commissioner required to maintain control of the airfield, a US guarantee of its non-military use or a formal warning by the US to Argentina of the consequences of misusing it for aggressive purposes. Somehow the British were now looking to the Americans to fashion an effective deterrent to Argentina.[15]

In the Commons that day the Prime Minister had avoided mentioning the restoration of British administration as an immediate demand, but she gave little ground on the advance of the Task Force and Britain's readiness to use force until it was sure that the occupying forces had left. She also gave little ground on the future negotiations, stressing the principle of islanders' wishes remaining paramount. She doubted that they would prefer any alternative to the previous administration, but added:

> It may be that their recent experiences will have caused their views on the future to change, but until they have had the chance freely to express their views, the British Government will not assume that the islanders' wishes are different from what they were before.

The sentence had been carefully constructed. With information on conditions on the Islands limited, and the state of islander morale uncertain, with many possibly prepared to leave, there was a risk of being caught out by a change in islander views.[16] She had, however, received a letter from John Cheek, a member of the Falklands Council who had been expelled from the Falklands. He had written suggesting an Andorra type solution, but more importantly also explaining why lease-back and condominium had proved to be so unacceptable to the islanders, and why these views would have 'hardened following the Argentine invasion.'

The next day President Reagan sent a message, following a conversation with Galtieri who had claimed that he was anxious to avoid conflict and was prepared to deal 'honestly and seriously' with Haig. Responding, the Prime Minister took the opportunity to reply in terms of the general principles the President liked to espouse:

> Any suggestion that conflict can be avoided by a device that leaves the aggressor in occupation is surely gravely misplaced. The implications for other potential areas of tension and for small countries everywhere would be of extreme seriousness. The fundamental principles for which the free world stands would be shattered.[17]

Haig returns to Buenos Aires

By the time that Haig got back to Buenos Aires on 15 April he was in difficulty with both sides. The British Government accepted that some effort had to be made to broker an agreement, if only to show that every effort was being made to avoid bloodshed, but they could not help but be irritated at being asked by Washington to offer concessions to an aggressor, and could not help but wonder whether the American effort might have been better put into exerting pressure on Argentina to withdraw from an illegal occupation. For their part the Argentines felt that the Americans were not being open with them, neither communicating their views properly to London nor sending London's views back to them. The British Task Force had not been halted or even slowed while Thatcher's statements to the Commons provided them with little sense that she was preparing to back down. They understood as well as the British the potential political costs of appearing to be the cause of a breakdown in a peace process, and they realised that this would require some show of reasonableness, although they also did not want their public to believe that they had been prepared to water down their basic demands.

With this in mind the Argentines offered Haig their own draft, which saw the interim administration as an opportunity to increase and assert the Argentine presence while generous incentives would be offered for the current islanders to leave.[18] There was scant overlap with the concessions from Britain reported back to Galtieri when Haig met with him on the morning of 16 April. Haig still felt that he was showing significant progress: the British fleet stopping; the Argentine flag kept flying in the Islands; the Argentine role in the Islands to be expanded little by little during the period of the interim administration; a guarantee that the negotiations would finish by the end of the year; the process to be guided according to the principles of decolonisation; communications between the continent and the Islands to be normalised; sanctions to be lifted and US assistance in the Islands guaranteed during this process.

But the gap was still wide and it was not surprising that little further progress was made. The Argentine delegation judged that the American draft would leave them without a future military option, Britain in effective control of the Islands with only minimal Argentine representation, and the prospect of being outvoted in the negotiations by Britain and the US working in unison. There would not even be support from the UN. To improve the document the Argentine side decided to focus on the interim administration and the negotiating process. Their basic approach was to draw the UN much more into the scheme of things. They drafted a number of new clauses,[19] strengthening Argentine representation on any interim body, providing for full Argentine access to the Islands, and the conclusion of the final negotiations on the basis of the principle of Argentine territorial integrity.

When late that evening Costa Mendez showed Haig the draft clauses he replied 'I am sure that the British will shoot'. Again Costa Mendez urged him not to do anything hasty. Haig called Reagan who agreed that he should return to Washington the next day unless progress was made.[20] Reagan then telephoned the Prime Minister, at 2030 London time, on 16 April. He wished to reassure the Prime Minister that he understood the efforts she had made to reach a compromise and, in a point underlined by Thatcher, 'did not think she should be asked to go any further.' He reported that while Galtieri had adopted a more reasonable approach, the Junta had taken a harder stance.

Haig asked to see the Junta for one last effort. They met the next morning, 17 April, for some heated exchanges. Haig's strategy appears to have been to persuade the Junta that even if their core objectives were not embodied in the agreement they could still be achieved as a result of its implementation. This required that they should not assume that the US would side with Britain on all matters, and accept that once this immediate crisis was over Britain would be looking for ways to rid itself of this problem. What it could not do was to be seen to give way to force:

> I can't speak for Mrs Thatcher, at times I don't speak very well to her, but I know they don't care about the sovereignty of the islands. They are prepared to re-negotiate but we must permit her to do it gracefully and on honourable terms. But I can assure you we will drive it to a solution. Secondly, I personally am convinced that Britain wants this problem off the plate. They will never be able to face another crisis of this kind. They could not politically, and they could not by their own assessment of the cost.[21]

Haig was seeking to encourage the Junta to accept a formula that was sufficiently vague to allow the two sides to enter into an apparently open negotiation although all involved would know that it could only conclude with Argentine sovereignty. This argument initially made little impression. It sounded like so much wishful thinking, and contradicted Argentina's own experience of negotiating with Britain on this issue. The Junta was frustrated with this whole exercise and irritated by apparent American complicity with British military pressure. Nonetheless, they attempted to identify areas of potential flexibility. Considering the matter further, the Argentine team, following Haig's suggestion, decided to play down the interim administration while concentrating on the sovereignty clause.

Late that morning the two sides met again to work on the drafts. Turning to the sovereignty clause Haig sought to reduce its political impact by avoiding a firm deadline and leaving open the outcome. The less specific the language the better. Not surprisingly Argentina wanted something more concrete. The principle of territorial integrity had to be clearly taking precedence to that of self-determination. The arguments went back and forth but there was still deadlock when the meeting ended at 2200. Haig reported back to Pym that he had threatened to break off the negotiation but that the Junta had asked him to stay, leading to a ten-hour session during which the British language on future negotiations had been rejected out of hand. He described difficulties in all other areas. The situation was 'grim', he was waiting for the Argentine text before deciding whether to break off and come to London. He did not want to shift the pressure onto Britain if the Argentine text was unacceptable. 'If I suspend my mission tomorrow morning I will leave no doubt as to where lies responsibility for the impasse.' At this point Haig decided to play what he describes in his memoir as a 'wild card'. He had not been told Britain's military plans yet the Argentines assumed otherwise. He therefore called Judge Clark, Reagan's National Security Adviser, on an open line, knowing that the call would be picked up, and warned that British military action was imminent.[22] This, he believed, did the trick. Soon he received new Argentine proposals and an invitation to discuss them the following afternoon. There is no confirmation that the reference to British action made the difference: Argentine accounts refer to Haig making the same threats the next day (19 April), and by Haig's own account he openly spoke to the Argentines about the possibility of a British attack on South Georgia.[23]

The discussions on 17 April had left a reference in the negotiations clause to 'due consideration for the rights of the inhabitants as well as for the principle of territorial integrity applicable to this dispute', while the interim administration clause gave more weight to the existing arrangements, although still envisaging equal Argentine representation on the Island councils. After further deliberations on the Argentine side there was another marathon negotiating session from 1500 on 18 April until 0155 the next day. Haig now believed he was getting somewhere and praised the progress already made. But he needed more. For the Argentine team the problem was that they had no idea of whether or not Britain had shown any flexibility, whether their concessions were to be reciprocated. Moreover, they had interpreted Haig's encouraging views on the prospects for an eventual British climb-down on sovereignty as being somehow subject to an American guarantee, rather than just the quality of the Secretary of State's political analysis. Now Haig pressed them to modify the text – removing references to UN resolutions and to the name 'Malvinas,' while putting 'fundamental' in front of the 'rights of the inhabitants,' extending the interim period 'until a definite agreement is reached.' All the Junta could see was the creation of more opportunities for British procrastination.

Their response was to harden rather than soften further their position, reasserting their demand for the Argentine Government to appoint the Governor of the Islands during the interim period. Haig angrily rejected this position, warning again of the imminence of war and the downfall of the Junta. Eventually, by early morning, a text had been produced that gave the Argentine side more of what they wanted though it was unlikely to please the British. By the middle of the day it had been tidied up sufficiently for Haig to deem it worth sending off to the British Government for consideration. Haig planned to return to Washington, although he was prepared if necessary for another visit to London. He told the press that there had been a 'further refinement of the Argentine position' and the 'results were being made available to the British Government.' Once again Costa Mendez arrived to meet Haig at the airport and handed him a note to be read when airborne. 'It is absolutely essential and *conditio sine qua non*,' it read, 'that negotiations will have to conclude with a result on 31 December 1982. This result must include a recognition of Argentinian sovereignty over the islands.'[24] Haig was now convinced that the Junta were unreliable and incompetent interlocutors. Having promised to pass on new proposals to London Haig felt obliged to do so, but he did not even bother to send this latest Argentine addition knowing the response it would get and he sent word to Costa Mendez of this intention.

The unacceptable draft

For two days the British debated amongst themselves about how best to cope with a breakdown in negotiations. Then on 19 April Haig's document arrived. They were unprepared for a complete draft agreement, much more extensive than the last draft, and containing quite unacceptable material. There were some concessions. This draft required the withdrawal of Argentine forces in compliance with SCR 502 (although on terms which saved some face), no present recognition of sovereignty, the withdrawal of the Argentine Governor and no direct Argentine administration, the involvement of a third party in the running of the Islands and the absence of a veto in Special Authority, the acceptance of local islander administration and the lack of any definition of the status of the Islands at the end of the negotiating period, except that there was no allowance for a return to the status quo ante. There would, however, be two Argentine representatives on the Island Councils, an opportunity to bring in many more Argentine nationals, and a denial of self-determination.[25]

Haig's accompanying letter did not exactly endorse the new draft ('My own disappointment with this text prevents me from trying to influence you in any way') but he claimed that it would be acceptable to Argentina, even though this was no longer the case ('Costa Mendez has given [sic] me a letter saying that Argentina could accept it if the U.S. proposes it, and Britain accepts'). Moreover with each clause of the text that was short of the British position he sought to demonstrate that Britain could keep control of the process. 'Francis,' he wrote to Pym, 'I do not know whether more can be wrung out of the Argentines. It is not clear who is in charge here, as many as 50 people, including corps commanders, may be exercising vetos [sic]. Certainly I can do no better at this point.' He asked Pym to assess this imperfect outcome, which would at least bind Argentina, Britain and the United States together in the search for a solution, 'against the advantages and disadvantages of armed action.' He was now returning to Washington although if necessary he would happily divert to London.

British patience with the American effort was starting to run out. Leaving aside the very attempt to broker an agreement as if Argentine claims had any real legitimacy, and that somehow saving Galtieri's face was a matter of real strategic importance, the American determination to put on a show of impartiality had been a cause of incessant irritation in London. It had been bad enough that Haig had attempted, on 14 April, to cut back on the assistance at Ascension. There was now a growing list of other indications that the Americans were bending their principles even more just to get some sort of agreement. On 13 April, for example, the Washington Embassy was informed that, despite British objections, Air Force Chief General Allen would be attending a meeting of the Air Chiefs of the Americas in Buenos Aires, and that the US Trade Representative Bill Brock would also visit the Argentine capital during a planned tour of Latin America. The British found such displays of business as usual 'lamentable': the Americans saw them as essential to keeping the peace process on track. Then, after the leak on 14 April about the extent of American co-operation with Britain, Argentina put in a mischievous but legitimate request for the civilian LANDSAT satellite to provide images of the Falklands area.[26] The *New York Times* reported on 17 April how many in Britain were unhappy with the American stance, and that 28 per cent of Britons had a lower opinion of Reagan as a result.[27] The fact that a similar story appeared in the *Washington Post* that day indicated that the Embassy was engaged in some active briefing. Certainly, Henderson used these stories to impress upon Judge Clark, the President's National Security Adviser, that the bad press American policy was getting in London reflected real feeling. It was perhaps because of this that Reagan had reassured the Prime Minister in his telephone conversation later that day that he was 'deeply interested in keeping this great relationship we have.'

Now, unaware of the final twist in Haig's dealings with Argentina, the War Cabinet could see Britain being set up to be blamed if it refused to accept an unreasonable draft leading to the breakdown in negotiations. Nonetheless there seemed to be no alternative to a robust response. A message was sent to Haig, reminding him that Argentina was the aggressor; that the President had assured the Prime Minister that it would not be reasonable to ask Britain to move further, and that he had promised to consult fully on any new text. There seemed to be no point in the Secretary of State coming to London specially to discuss this text. Britain would send their comments to him in Washington.

The War Cabinet met again on 20 April in a slightly better mood. A long letter had been received from Haig, reassuring the Government that he had done no more than push Argentina as far as he could go, without associating the US with the position reached let alone the United Kingdom. He was also clearly aware of growing anger in London, reflected in the media, to the effect that he was too solicitous of Argentine concerns while not keeping Britain informed. He urged that this impression be corrected, for he understood the strength of feeling in Britain and welcomed sustained military pressure, but had to sustain credibility in Buenos Aires if war was to be averted. Rather than more detailed drafting proposals from London he urged that the Foreign Secretary should go to Washington on 22–3 April to discuss the evolving document. While the War Cabinet saw this as an opportunity to put British counter-proposals to him, and therefore supported the Foreign Secretary's view that he should accept the invitation with alacrity, they might also have noted his request to Pym 'that you limit your reformulations to the minimum essential points.'

The Prime Minister told the Commons:

> I cannot disguise from the House that the Argentine proposals at present before us fall far short in some important aspects of those objectives and of the requirements expressed in this House ... Among the many problems presented by the Argentine proposals is that they fail to provide that the Falkland Islanders should be able to determine their own destiny. The House has always said that the wishes of the islanders are paramount.

The negotiation was not, however, yet over:

> We are examining the proposals very closely and will seek to put forward our own proposals to Mr. Haig. With that in mind my Right Hon. Friend the Foreign Secretary plans to visit Washington on Thursday.

The War Cabinet had also concluded that in some way the negotiating outcome would be a function of the perceived balance of military strength. To put even more pressure on Argentina, they decided that the recapture of

South Georgia should go ahead and also that the quid pro quo of any pressure towards compromise from the US was an American agreement for a guarantee that they would prevent the airfield being used by Argentina for a re-invasion and of the security of the Islands thereafter. Other possibilities were a UN rather than US guarantee, which might involve the UN providing forces and conducting the test of local opinion.

12

THE HAIG MISSION
CONCLUDES

Preparatory work in London prior to Pym's trip was intensive and, at least as far as the FCO was concerned, this had to be constructive. The requirement to reach a position on counter-proposals obliged the Government to face questions of priorities. The US was not going to take seriously a paper that simply stressed the British position on every point: there had to be some sense of elements that were negotiable. If this was the only way to keep the process alive then authority was needed from the War Cabinet to develop proposals that displayed some flexibility. For each of the three elements of the package – withdrawal, interim administration and final negotiation – this was not at all straightforward. Something that might seem common sense internationally, such as the simultaneous withdrawal of Argentine and British forces, might raise objections at home.

Objections at home were going to count for most. The War Cabinet on 21 April decided that it was vital to resist unfair procedures for withdrawal, disproportionate weighting for Argentina in an interim administration, an influx of Argentine people and businesses, and the exclusion of the old arrangement as one possible outcome of the negotiations. Detailed proposals for amendments were made on these points. The Prime Minister also wanted to keep the Dependencies out of any agreement. Furthermore, if a weak Treaty was to be accepted then Britain wanted some sort of guarantee of Argentine implementation. The preference was for a straight bilateral agreement with the Americans, for which language was developed,[1] but as a fallback a draft clause was also prepared for a UN force with which the Americans might be associated. This was only a reserve because no excuse was to be provided to the Americans to use the UN to get themselves off the hook.[2] Some sort of guarantee was needed because it was hard to have confidence in any agreement signed by the Junta. From what Haig had said, the Argentine leadership was utterly chaotic, consumed by bitterness and historic frustration and incoherent in its decision-making. The only hope was that they were less confident on the military side and aware of the danger that the US would openly support Britain. There was no basis for confidence that they would accept a compromise proposal or would stick to it if they did.

Nor was there evidence that Haig was going to be responsive to British anxieties. Prior to his arrival Pym warned Haig that the draft he had sent would have the effect that:

> Argentine withdrawal would be delayed, the Argentine voice in the administration of the Islands would be disproportionate, Argentine influence and pressure in the Islands would be given free rein, and future negotiations would be organised in a way that could only prejudice the principles of sovereignty and self-determination.

Yet Haig told Henderson that he considered the developing positions on withdrawal satisfactory and a tripartite administration manageable, although on this latter point the British would be wholly dependent upon the US taking their side in any disputes, for example over Argentine immigration. The third stage remained problematic. Haig was referring to the 'rights' of the islanders as a compromise between the British 'wishes' and the Argentine 'interests.' As for the question of an American guarantee, also pressed on Haig in advance, the best on offer was a Presidential statement. This would emphasise the importance of the British and Argentine Governments showing good faith in implementing the agreement, and Reagan's confidence that they would:

> Just as the United States has played a role in arriving at this agreement, we will have important responsibilities in its implementation. Both parties have encouraged this. It is in keeping with the close relationship we have with both, as well as our own deep commitment to the peaceful settlement of disputes.

The statement would also mention the future American role in facilitating and encouraging negotiations. 'I am sure that both parties recognise that greater openness in the months ahead is essential if the negotiations are to result in a stable long-term solution.'

On his arrival in Washington on 22 April Pym soon was made aware of the deep tensions within the Reagan Administration, personal as much as philosophical. On the morning of 23 April he breakfasted with Judge Clark. The National Security Adviser raised the possibility of Argentine trusteeship, which was clearly a non-starter, and then the British asked about the possibility of American trusteeship, which elicited a surprisingly positive answer, including the intelligence that the President himself had been thinking along those lines. The matter was left for Clark to explore further with the possibility that Pym would meet Reagan. Haig was then called over to the White House, and soon after arrived for a consequently delayed meeting with Pym. Haig was furious that such an idea, clearly unacceptable to Argentina, had been floated without reference to him.[3]

Most of these two days was taken up with Pym's team going over the issues again with Haig and his officials. At first Haig was hoping to go once again to Buenos Aires to present 'reasonable proposals from London' but by the conclusion he had decided that the mediation role was not going to produce an agreement and this could only be achieved if he presented an American proposal to both sides. His approach was to concentrate on self-determination for the benefit of the British, as it seemed to be a higher principle than sovereignty. This meant that the possibility of a transfer of sovereignty should be held open for the benefit of Argentina, even though the final decision would have to be left to the islanders.[4] He intended to present the draft to both sides and then request an early answer.

A meeting of the OAS was taking place in Washington on 26 April and part of Haig's thinking was that it would be ideal to have a settlement before this organisation got involved, especially as its main contribution would probably take the form of berating the US for its lack of hemispheric solidarity. Also, on 24 April, Costa Mendez was arriving for this meeting and this would provide an opportunity to hand him the final proposal. He intended to send the text to Galtieri at the same time. The British would also be sent the text for form's sake 'to avoid giving an impression that they were an Anglo-US concoction.' Haig proposed to give Buenos Aires 48 hours to accept these proposals as they stood, Pym reported back, making it clear that no further delays or discussions were possible. 'He would add that if the Argentines rejected the proposals the US would consider its peace-making role to have ended and would from then on give political, economic and – he suggested – military support to the UK.' There now also seemed to be more of a guarantee of American involvement: any Argentine violation would leave them 'looking down the barrel of a US gun.'

Back to London

Haig's text was sent back to London, with an accompanying note from Pym indicating that 'his personal reaction was sympathetic.' He warned of the situation that could develop if the British failed to agree. Haig had then implied that 'we might be on our own.' The Secretary of State had warned that many in Washington still wanted the US to keep itself in reserve for a later peace-making effort, and also expressed his own scepticism about the prospects of Britain achieving a quick and satisfactory military solution. International support, he surmised, would start to evaporate quickly after any British military action and even victory would leave a requirement for either a permanent military presence in the area or else a political solution that would be no easier to achieve or more favourable than that currently proposed.

If the Argentines rejected the text Washington could blame them publicly for the failure of Haig's effort and the process would be at an end. The gamble was that they might not, in which case Britain would be in an awkward position. Haig had resisted any further amendments to his previous draft on the grounds that the US would work with the British to prevent Argentine mischief-making. Pym acknowledged the problem:

> Although I was able to persuade him to modify his position in some important respects during our two days of talks, his final draft still falls far short in several places of what we have regarded as acceptable, notably in respect of Argentine representation in the Islands Councils (para 6), Argentine scope for influence in the economic and related fields (para 7) and in precluding the continuation of the present colonial status (para 8).[5]

Nonetheless, according to the Foreign Secretary, the arrangement proposed by the US offered the best chance of a peaceful solution and was clearly preferable to the military alternative. He therefore recommended that subject to these changes and the suggested letter of assurance from Reagan he 'be authorised to inform Mr Haig that, having consulted my colleagues here, I can concur in the plan and draft which he put to me in Washington.'

Pym met with the rest of the War Cabinet when he returned from Washington on the Saturday morning. He recommended that Haig's 'new text' should be accepted as the best negotiated solution available.

The moment was a tense one: the outcome of the operation to retake South Georgia was still uncertain. Henderson's memoir suggests that Pym had been caught out by a change in sentiment while he was away. He later told the Ambassador that 'he failed to realise how feelings were hardening at home so that when he got back he felt light-years away from the sentiment there.'[6] To the Prime Minister Pym had come back with a document she saw as a 'conditional surrender.' In Stage One the British would soon lose all leverage if Argentina went back on its promise to withdraw, with the Task Force, including the SSNs, pulled back and the sanctions lifted. In Stage Two Argentina would have plenty of opportunity to change the character of the Islands. In Stage Three there was no possibility of a return to the status quo ante. She was prepared to resign rather than accept such ideas.[7] Nott later observed that because the deal did not actually concede sovereignty, the Cabinet as a whole and the Commons would have been inclined to accept the formulation.[8]

In the event the War Cabinet agreed with the Prime Minister's misgivings. During the course of the discussion, Nott suggested a way forward. Rather than send Haig an outright rejection, with all the political problems that would generate, he proposed that no comment be made on the draft, but instead request that it first be put to Argentina. If the Junta accepted it then all that could be done was to put it to Parliament for a decision. If, as was thought more likely, Argentina rejected it, then the Americans would have no excuse not to come down on Britain's side.[9] A message was drafted along these lines from the Prime Minister to Haig:

> Thank you for your message giving your comments on your long discussions with Francis Pym. My colleagues most closely concerned and I have now had a full report from him. We remain most grateful to you for your continuing efforts.
>
> You asked me to send you a reaction this evening. This whole business started with an Argentine aggression. Since then our purpose together has been to ensure the early withdrawal by the Argentines in accordance with the Security Council Resolution. We think therefore that the next step should be for you to put your latest ideas to them. I hope that you will seek the Argentine Government's view of them tomorrow and establish urgently whether they can accept them. Knowledge of their attitude will be important to the British Cabinet's consideration of your ideas.

The next day a satisfactory reply was received from Haig. In addition, South Georgia was recaptured. At last ministers were persuaded that the momentum was really on their side and that Britain's hand had been strengthened. Pym called Haig on 26 April, the day of the OAS meeting, with 'new ideas' that attempted to claw back some of the concessions he had accepted a few days earlier. With time now running out before the Task Force was in position, he proposed that the best way forward might be a simple approach that allowed for mutual withdrawal, and a traditional administration minus the Governor for the moment but plus an Argentine representative. The idea was that President Lopez Portillo of Mexico, who had been showing some sympathy with the British position, might put forward the proposal during the course of the OAS meeting and later host the conference on sovereignty. This was a curious intervention, reflecting a sudden surge of optimism in London yet calculated to irritate Haig, and possibly lead him to conclude that the British Government was more anxious for a compromise settlement than it had let on to him while remaining unappealing to Argentina. Haig replied that Argentina would view these ideas as 'surrender terms'.[10] Haig was not prepared to do more than put his package to Argentina, accepting that Britain was still reserving its position.

Denouement

Haig, like the British, believed that the successful action on South Georgia might encourage Argentina to seize an available diplomatic solution. Prior to the action he had been finding Argentina unresponsive. On 20 April, with Pym on his way Haig had written to Costa Mendez that contrary to what he might have read, the British had not rejected the last draft, and that he had urged that any amendments be kept to a minimum. 'I believe I am now fully sensitized to Argentine concerns', he reassured Costa Mendez, and would reflect them fully in later discussions. 'Some modification of the Buenos Aires paper is inevitable,' he acknowledged, 'but I continue to believe that it is the right framework in which to seek a solution.' Later, however, he had to report the British response of 'disappointment'. It was now 'clear to me that substantial further mutual adjustment will be necessary if war is to be avoided.' At the same time his Ambassador in Buenos Aires was reporting that the Argentine Government had continued 'to paint itself further into a corner from which explicit recognition of Argentine sovereignty in the Malvinas will be exceedingly difficult.' The capacity of the Foreign Ministry to influence events was waning, as they had failed to generate sufficient international support for the cause, while military assessments were becoming more confident. 'If Galtieri and his crowd get the impression that the British resolve has weakened – that a shooting war can be evaded without a settlement – they will scuttle rapidly away from the concession that they have already made.' By 23 April (prior to the recapture of South Georgia), Ambassador Shlaudeman was reporting that:

> The sense our military people are now getting from their contacts in the Army is one of increasing solidarity and a degree of cockiness about the outcome. The feeling at the moment appears to be that the Argentines have a good hand to play: a strong military presence on the Island with plenty of firepower and provisions; a questionable British capacity to maintain an effective blockade for very long, let alone land troops; and, in general, a strong military advantage in terms of weather, distance and the like. The conclusion is that Galtieri may well pull it off, and thus there is a rallying around him.

After concluding his discussions with Pym that day, Haig wrote to Costa Mendez:

> We have just ended our second day of tiring discussions with Francis Pym and his colleagues. As we had anticipated, the text that I brought with me from Buenos Aires is unacceptable to the British. We found strong resistance in those areas that I told you about.
>
> Nevertheless, we have made a serious effort and are trying to achieve some progress. Now I hope to have a new text soon that you and I can review when we meet on Sunday.

On the Sunday, 25 April, Haig was back in touch with the Argentine side, but relations were frosty because of the ongoing British action on South Georgia. Once this action had succeeded Haig decided that he should take the opportunity to visit Buenos Aires to press his proposals on them. He did not intend to spend an inordinate amount of time on the matter as he was still seeking a clear indication within a couple of days of whether a settlement could be reached. This appeared as a significant change of tactic, and posed serious difficulties to London given some impending operational decisions. As officials in London were discussing whether or not Haig should be advised not to make the trip, a message came in from Henderson saying that he was not now intending to go as he had decided to send his proposals straight to Galtieri. His intention to go to Buenos Aires to present the text himself had been discouraged by the Junta. As a show of good faith Henderson was authorised to tell Haig that he could assure Galtieri that the prisoners taken at South Georgia would be returned to Argentina in due course. Galtieri, according to Haig, was now less 'rumbus-tious' and appeared anxious to avoid a confrontation, and was complaining about America's inability to restrain Britain.

As far as the British understood, Argentina was being asked for a straight 'yes or no' answer by midnight on 27 April on a text that the Americans had put beyond alteration. This indeed was the case. In telling him that the new text was on its way Haig explained to Costa Mendez that 'We believe that full-scale conflict with the United Kingdom is imminent. This information comes from our own sources; the British do not consult with us on such matters; nor do we have any means of restraining them':

> Our proposal will enable you to set an entirely new direction for the Islands, one whose ultimate outcome cannot be in question even if it cannot be made fully explicit. You will have made your point. The course of Argentine history will have been irrevocably changed.

He also wrote to Galtieri that:

> During the present critical period as we make a final search for a peaceful solution to the current British-Argentine dispute it is important that both sides avoid any incidents in the maritime exclu-sion zone. I am therefore asking both parties to exercise restraint with regard to the exclusion zone for the time being. I do not ask for nor expect a response from either side to this suggestion.

To his Ambassador he added, 'in delivering this message please pass on orally that I do not know if the British will accede to this request and would not want the President to assume that Argentine forces can operate safely in the exclusion zone.' I have found no reference to a similar appeal being made to London. It would have received a dusty response.

Britain was sent the draft agreement as well. It was essentially the one seen the previous week. It would not be published unless there was an

Argentine rejection. At this point Haig seemed to think that South Georgia meant that Argentina could accept. Henderson reported back that 'Haig has hoisted in that there is not a lot of time, and I believe he thinks that he has at last persuaded the Argentinians that we mean business, or, to be more exact he believes that our action has done this.' Later in the House of Commons Thatcher explained her position:

> Mr Haig has put formal American proposals to the Argentine Government and requested an early response. I stress the status of those proposals. They are official American proposals. Mr. Haig judged it right to ask Argentina to give its decision first, as the country to which Security Council Resolution 502 is principally addressed. ... Mr. Haig has also communicated to us the text of his proposals.... The proposals are complex and difficult and inevitably bear all the hallmarks of compromise in both their substance and language. But they must be measured against the principles and objectives expressed so strongly in the debates in the House.

In the same debate, Pym outlined the central principles by which the American proposal might be judged and which might lead him to argue for acceptance:

> Our basic position is that Britain is ready to co-operate in any solution which the people of the Falkland Islands could accept and any framework of negotiation which does not predetermine and does not prejudice the eventual outcome.[11]

By 28 April there was still no word from Argentina. Pym and Henderson pressed Haig to acknowledge failure and blame Argentina. This he was reluctant to do, and anxiety about how far he might be prepared to go in search of a deal grew in London. Haig appeared to be expecting Argentine amendments and while he was prepared to dismiss most of their likely demands, he seemed to think that it might be possible to offer more on Argentine representation on the Legislative Council. He was even suggesting that midnight on 27 April had not been so much a deadline as a time when, absent an Argentine reply, the 'whole situation would change.' When pressed by Henderson on Argentine stalling tactics he said that he had 'to go right down to the end of the line before coming down on our side.' Haig was also looking for evidence of British hesitation: he noted a speech by opposition leader Michael Foot,[12] and the delay in establishing the Total Exclusion Zone (TEZ), which had in fact been solely for operational reasons. Nor were British nerves eased when an official from the National Security Council staff, with no Falklands responsibilities, told journalists, incorrectly on all counts, that US SR71 reconnaissance aircraft had been overflying the

Falklands for the British and that the British had been asked to delay military action for three days.[13]

Later that day, Haig received Costa Mendez, anxious for the negotiating process to continue, giving dark hints about bringing in the Russians, and raising the prospect of going to the UN. When asked if he would forward further proposals to London, Haig replied that the American draft already went further than the British wanted to go, but he could not refuse to pass them on. Costa Mendez did not make any proposals but went out and told the press that the American draft had not been rejected and negotiations continued. To Henderson's chagrin, Haig now seemed to be thinking of the morning of Friday, 30 April, when a new total Exclusion Zone would come into effect, as the deadline. The Ambassador was told that the effort had to continue and an ultimatum would be a bad idea.

Pym's brief for Cabinet on 29 April still argued that in the unlikely event that Argentina accepted the UK should also do so, despite unhappiness over the proposals on the withdrawal of forces, the Argentine presence on the Executive and Legislative Councils and the replacement of Governor by Special Commission. Though there would be no return to the status quo ante, the result would still be a reverse for the Argentines. But 'if they accept and we don't even friends and allies will wobble.' When the full Cabinet met that day, before notification of any Argentine reply, they were told of the objections to the American proposals:

- South Georgia was covered as well as the Falklands;
- Argentine representatives would be appointed to the Executive and Legislative Councils;
- Unsatisfactory provisions for the Special Interim Authority;
- No provision for a return to the status quo ante.

The last of these was of particular importance. Haig was ruling out the established political status of the Islands continuing, which meant that the alternatives were either a full merger with Britain or Argentina, independence or some sort of lease-back. There was unease also about the provision allowing for due regard of the rights of the inhabitants as this could be taken to refer only to basic human rights and not to self-determination. There was not even confidence that Haig would deny Argentina further concessions. He had promised a strict deadline and no amendments. Yet the deadline had passed without comment and it was now understood that what had been described as 'minor' amendments could be transmitted to London.

The prize was getting Argentina to withdraw without a fight, but that morning the Cabinet were being prepared for a possible situation in which it could no longer be assumed that Britain would retain American support, important though this was. This was why the Government was refraining from any comment until it was clear that, as hoped, Argentina rejected the proposals. No reason should be given to Argentina or the US for blaming Britain for the failure of the initiative. Nonetheless, if it did fail it was vital to ensure that there was no implication that the package was agreeable to Britain. The first priority was to ensure that the Americans would recognise that the refusal of Argentina to accept the proposal constituted rejection, and that the Administration must now honour its promise to come down firmly on the side of the UK.

The American effort to remain conspicuously neutral politically had taken its toll. There had been no economic measures taken by Washington, a refusal to take a stand on the sovereignty issue, and a readiness to conduct business as usual with Buenos Aires. After the Cabinet Pym wrote to Haig expressing the surprise of his colleagues that deadlines had passed without an American response, and that now Britain expected a public confirmation that Argentina had rejected the proposals. He also confirmed British reservations. The Prime Minister wrote to President Reagan along similar lines. The Argentine silence must be construed as a rejection. 'I cannot conceal from you how deeply let down I and my colleagues would feel if under these circumstances the US were not now able to give us its full support.'

Some comfort was drawn from evidence of public and Congressional support for Britain's cause. This had been building up for some time, with a number of senior Congressional figures writing to the President urging support for Britain as a close and loyal ally which, in this case, clearly was in the right. Henderson had been particularly active and had become something of a media celebrity. The Ambassador hit American television screens as if out of central casting: 'the perfect English country gentleman, honourable but slightly down-at-heel, reluctantly engaged in a disagreeable quarrel with unprincipled ne'er-do-wells'. His staff at the Embassy were organised to ensure that the Congress and the media not only understood the British view but were flattered through personal attention. The effort, to ensure that any administration tilt away from Britain would exact a high political price, paid off. A Harris poll on 29 April showed 60 per cent popular support for Britain as against 19 per cent for Argentina.[14] Late on 29 April the US Senate voted 79 votes to 1 (with Jesse Helms the dissenter) on a resolution supporting Britain, proposed by Democrat Senators Joe Biden and Daniel Moynihan and co-sponsored by Republican Charles Percy. This was drafted in close co-operation with the British Embassy and was matched in the House Foreign Affairs Committee with a pro-British resolution adopted by a voice vote.

Though the British had reason to suppose that there might be a body of civilian opinion within the Argentine Government prepared to accept the Haig proposals – in order to put pressure on the British to accept a settlement with which they fundamentally disagreed – the military were caught by their past promises and hopes that somehow casualties would force the British to concede. The Junta had in fact concluded on 27 April that Haig's proposals could not be accepted as they stood. The eventual response sent to Haig, delivered on 29 April, noted that the document fell short of Argentine demands. They argued that they could only be flexible on a provisional administration if there were confidence about an eventual transfer of sovereignty. They remained willing to consider further ideas, but in practice this particular mediating effort was now over.

Haig had another tough meeting with Costa Mendez at which he indicated what he considered to be the dire consequences of the Argentine position: war, during which the United States would have to back Britain, and the fall of the Argentine Government (a threat which went down badly with the Foreign Minister). When Costa Mendez asked whether the UK had rejected the American proposal, Haig replied that they did not like it all as the document offered a fundamental change in the status quo of the Islands. Yet if Argentina accepted it, he would force Britain into doing likewise. He would not contemplate further changes to the draft.

The Americans now accepted that this stage of their diplomatic effort had concluded and there was no choice but to back Britain. The President wrote to the Prime Minister about how this would be communicated. She found the terms satisfactory. Argentina would be blamed while the detailed US proposal would not be released because this would cause Britain problems. On 30 April Haig made a public statement, along lines agreed at a National Security Council meeting, describing the reasons for his attempt at mediation and the final proposal. As Britain had not exactly accepted his compromise he chose his words carefully:

> We had reason to hope that the United Kingdom would consider a settlement along the lines of our proposal, but Argentina informed us yesterday that it could not accept it.

This language had been carefully negotiated to avoid any suggestion that the British had either accepted or rejected the American proposal. 'Concrete steps' were now to be taken to demonstrate that the US 'cannot and will not condone the use of unlawful force to resolve disputes'. The steps took the form of limited economic sanctions and a Presidential directive 'to respond positively to requests for materiel support for British forces'. This was less than the British had been hoping for. The British saw an American commitment to serious sanctions, such as an import ban, as being helpful with other waverers such as Japan. The Americans had legal and administrative difficulties. This was regretted, but London was told that what was on offer was the maximum available. Reagan also concluded with a warning for London:

> A strictly military outcome cannot endure over time. In the end, there will have to be a negotiated outcome acceptable to the interested

parties. Otherwise, we will all face unending hostility and insecurity in the South Atlantic.

The President's own sense of what was at stake was indicated when, speaking to reporters, he explained how it was vital to oppose aggression even though the fight was over that 'little ice-cold bunch of land down there'.

13

AFTER HAIG

UN enthusiasm

As early as 14 April, when various communications suggested that the Haig mission was on the verge of failure, the FCO Planning Staff warned that any other negotiating method would be less favourable to Britain and so if Haig appeared to be about to give up, 'our first priority should be to try to persuade him not to do so.' This was so even if it required coming up with serious new proposals on the substance, for example a revival of lease-back, or the process, such as proximity talks with Costa Mendez and Pym. There was no reason to suppose that anybody else – a respected international figure, a group of states, or a special representative of the UN – could be more successful in mediation. Arbitration, such as a commission appointed by the Security Council, carried the obvious risk of a finding against Britain, especially if it included a large third world component. An even more legally binding process, such as a referral to the ICJ, carried the same risk. Of all the options this was probably the most favoured – because of the interest among some of the European allies, the presentational advantages in terms of showing a willingness to get a solution, as well as simplicity and maximum impact.

Within the UN three countries on the Council appeared to anticipate any failure of the Haig mission as an opportunity for the UN to step in: Ireland, Spain and Japan, along with Ahmad of the Secretariat. On 13 April Parsons briefed the representatives of European Community members, including Dorr, the Irish delegate, explaining that so long as Haig was still in business Britain could not entertain any other moves at the UN, although nothing was ruled out for later. He then quizzed Dorr about reports from Dublin suggesting an Irish initiative, involving proposals for a tripartite administration with the UN as the third party. Dorr protested that the Irish had no intention of wrong-footing Britain or of bringing anything into the Security Council that Britain might oppose. He reported that he had spoken to Roca, who had been 'casting about' for ideas to get Argentina off the hook but was inhibited in putting anything forward for fear of an adverse reaction from the military.

A different sort of problem came from Panama. An eight-page letter to the President of the Council 'set out the Argentine case at tedious length and in offensive terms.' It applauded the bloodless way in which the Argentines had recovered their territory and accused Britain of acting in a war-like manner. It was assumed that this was the initiative of Foreign Minister Illueca, whom Parsons considered to be a 'malicious and persistent operator.' To get Illueca restrained the British Ambassador spoke to Panama's President Roya who instructed his UN delegation not to press for an immediate discussion of this letter. Vernon Walters of Haig's team also spoke to Roya, urging Panama not to do anything while Haig was still at work. The Panamanians claimed that they had mistakenly believed Haig was on the verge of abandoning his mission. Argentina had, like Britain, taken the line that for the moment matters were best left to Haig. The President of the Council, Kamanda, conducted his own consultations at a suitably slow pace, and he was well aware of the hazards facing any attempt to put the UN back on to centre stage.

If Haig demonstrably failed and/or military action began, Britain expected strong calls for restraint and for it to accept either the appointment of a sub-committee of the Council to make contact with the two sides, or a request to the Secretary-General to use his good offices. Parsons was, however, now more confident 'that, even in the worst circumstances, we could make a good fight of it (perhaps for several days) before being driven into a corner and having to veto.' During the course of these tactical debates Parsons was asked about the possibility of raising the idea of a trusteeship for the Falklands. Under this proposal Argentina would withdraw and then the UN would sound out the islanders and others about the future. In the interim the administering authority would be either the US or UN, and would report via the Trusteeship Council to the General Assembly or Security Council. In the past territories had become independent or merged with neighbours, although other outcomes were not excluded (for example the US intended for Micronesia a 'status of free association'). UN plebiscites were the normal way of finding the 'freely expressed wishes' of the people. There would be no British administration, but Argentina would get neither sovereignty nor administration so its advantage would solely be as a face-saver based on the Charter. Would it be in the British interest, Parsons was asked, to propose such a trusteeship for, say, two years? During this time various possibilities for their future could be put to the islanders.

He was asked for his views as a contribution to a discussion of options at a meeting Pym was holding on the afternoon of 17 April. This was the point at which a failure of the Haig mission had first appeared imminent. The Ambassador saw this idea as posing in an acute form the problem with which he had been wrestling for a week:

how to retain the initiative in the Security Council without either getting bogged down in endless negotiations about UN mechanisms

... or having to veto such propositions because they were combined with calls on us to cease our military preparations.

Most forms of UN involvement, and certainly a formal proposal for UN Trusteeship, would result in a long period of drift during which Britain's hands would be tied militarily. If a demand for Britain to cease its military preparations were included in a Security Council resolution, so that it had to veto, this could possibly lead to an emergency special session of the UN general assembly. The country would be seen to be defying the international community if it subsequently took military action. Yet, on the other hand, a failure to take the initiative could lead to exactly the same scenario as a result of someone else's action.

Proposals for a new resolution

Parsons wanted instead to try a different approach: submitting a draft UK resolution as soon as it was known that Haig had failed. Up to this point he had been out of the decision-making loop on Haig, so he did not actually know what had been proposed. His own draft still followed the rather inevitable sequence of issues – immediate withdrawal, medium-term interim administration and long-term negotiations on sovereignty – but had its own spin on the detail. Thus in the withdrawal stage, the Argentine presence would be removed completely from the Islands by a week after the adoption of the resolution. Britain would abandon the MEZ and stop the fleet as soon as withdrawal began. He envisaged the interim administration lasting for five years, with the Islands governed by freely elected representatives (implying British administration but without a Governor) under the supervision of a UN administrator appointed by the Secretary-General with the approval of the Security Council. Only the UN flag would be flown. During this period each side would maintain its position on sovereignty and would engage in discussions designed to reach a final solution acceptable to all sides, including the islanders.

No amendments would be accepted, although this could mean rejecting proposals from the 'do gooders'. The resolution would be presented as 'a last ditch attempt by HMG, the wronged party, to find a way of avoiding force to defend our rights.' By keeping the initiative in this way, Parsons hoped to avoid drift and military constraints. By appearing reasonable Britain would be better placed even if it did not muster sufficient votes, or the Soviet Union vetoed, or Argentina rejected. There was certainly no guarantee of success. To get the maximum effect he would need immediate notice of Haig's failure and a green light to go to Council:

It will be a race between me, the Latin Americans, and the Do-Gooders, with the Secretary General pushing hard, as to who gets to the Council first, once the news of Haig's failure breaks.

Later he added the thought that Haig might be asked to put the proposed draft to Argentina, not so much to get a deal but to meet the objection that draft resolutions should not be introduced without some pre-negotiation with parties. Aware of the rumblings in the Council, Parsons was becoming even more convinced of the desirability of deterring other initiatives by letting Kamanda know that Britain was 'actively peddling a detailed proposal.'

This proposal reached the FCO on the morning of 17 April as officials were digesting the implications of Haig's stark warning that his talks might come to an end. They had taken on board the logic of Parsons' analysis of the likely development of the UN debate and the advisability of taking the initiative. Parsons was told to 'urgently make detailed preparations within the mission, on a basis of strict confidentiality.' Suggested FCO amendments appeared to move the draft more in the direction of making it acceptable to Argentina. Little could be done about the inevitable Argentine inclination to attempt to get a commitment to eventual sovereignty, but they might be mollified by an interim administration that lasted two rather than five years, and an allowance made in the resolution for the special representative of the Secretary General to be involved in the longer-term negotiations. It might also be wise to pre-empt the inevitable Argentine insistence on reference to favourable General Assembly resolutions by including them in Parsons' paragraph 5.

Parsons had no problems with the proposed amendments. He now started outlining more detailed plans, hoping that he would not have to act over the coming weekend. As he went into action at the UN there would need to be simultaneous lobbying at the highest level in all of the Security Council's member state capitals. The communist states must be encouraged not to procrastinate, the Spanish not to use procedural knowledge to wreck the initiative, the Panamanians not to throw a spanner in the works. The others must have it explained to them that there had been inadequate time to consult before taking action and that no progress at all would have been possible if there had been an attempt to clear the draft with Argentina.

That evening Ministers, including Thatcher, again discussed Parsons' proposals. Thatcher had already had some discussions and had criticised the plan because the arrangements proposed would not prevent a future Argentine invasion of the Falklands. She was also concerned about the potential role of a UN Interim Commissioner. Against the suggestion that this person might supervise the administration of the Islands she wrote a large 'No'. The Prime Minister was considering the resolution as a draft agreement as much as a diplomatic ploy. This led to a draft that became more a negotiating position than an attempt to see just how far Britain could go with the Security Council. She was reluctant to contemplate any military concessions until an Argentine withdrawal had been confirmed, and not inclined to put the Dependencies into the negotiations when there were hopes that South Georgia could soon be recovered. A singular UN role in administering the Islands was unacceptable. At most it could supervise the cease-fire and help with the negotiations. Even then there was still a long-term worry over a solution that emerged through the UN system rather than US mediation. With the latter it might be supposed that there would be some sort of American guarantee against the Argentines attempting to mount another invasion in the future; the existence of the Secretary-General's representative might not have the same deterrent effect. This approach would therefore only be tolerable if more guarantees were built in – preferably by the Americans.

The next day Pym's office took up the issue again with Number 10, explaining the rationale for this effort. The most optimistic view was that the 'atmosphere of crisis following Haig's failure,' combined with the prospect of American economic sanctions, might persuade Buenos Aires to accept Britain's text. If so an Argentine withdrawal would have been achieved without casualties and with the wishes of the islanders to be taken into account in any final negotiation. 'Argentina, by contrast, would have secured virtually nothing by means of her aggression and the British policy of military, diplomatic and economic pressure would be seen to have produced results.' If it did not pass then Britain could claim to have done everything necessary to achieve a peaceful solution. Britain should have the votes to prevent unacceptable amendments and in the end should be able to push through a vote on its own resolution. With the letter to the Prime Minister went a new draft text of a resolution. This required immediate Argentine withdrawal and the easing of military and economic pressure only to the extent this was taking place. The UN official role was reduced to ensuring demilitarisation. The FCO still believed that it was prudent to recognise the UN expectation that the Dependencies would have to be included by inserting a reference in the terms for the future negotiations, and sought to assure the Prime Minister that the resolution would not preclude getting US guarantees of some sort. Parsons was now warned of the tentative nature of this exercise. Contingency planning had to be confined to the Mission.

The Prime Minister remained unconvinced. That evening she and Pym spoke on the phone. The news from Haig in Buenos Aires did not suggest that he was achieving much. The Prime Minister was worried that he was discussing proposals with the Argentines that went well beyond anything to which the Government could agree. She retained an 'awful suspicion that compromise is going to be everything to him.' Pym was by now aware that the Prime Minister was unlikely to be won over to the latest UN strategy and so a discussion could wait – Thatcher promised that she would still be unhappy about the proposed draft the next day, especially as she thought she had disposed of much of it the previous day and the discarded text had now returned.

She then rang Parsons to explain her concerns. She was puzzled. When they had met in London he had told her not to go back to the UN because

Britain would never get such a good resolution as 502. This had 'become part of the Ten Commandments practically.' Now he seemed to be disobeying his own commandment. She explained:

> Last night when we discussed it, I took one look at it and said well I suppose this is Foreign Office. I really can't think Sir Anthony Parsons would have put this forward and they said, oh yes, this is his advice. What you are saying is that if you want us to take an initiative it's only that kind of thing that would succeed.

She had remarked to Pym about the 'devil's advocates' in his department, and now she observed to Parsons the problems she faced because she had no department of her own 'and therefore I have to rely on third-hand hearsay and I don't like it.'[1]

He sought to explain that what he had been trying to do was draft the sort of resolution that would allow the UK to keep the initiative in the Security Council. As they discussed the options he explained how almost anything that was submitted that offered few concessions would soon be covered with amendments. She explained how submitting a resolution in the proposed form would send all the wrong signals. If accepted the proposal 'would preclude us from really carrying out our duty to the Falkland Islanders.' Instead it would serve notice that Britain was washing its hands of them for the interim period, while relying on 'some United Nations guy there who will absolutely protect you from anyone landing, although everyone knows he can't possibly.' Interestingly she drew a parallel with the decision in 1981 to withdraw HMS *Endurance* from the South Atlantic, as giving 'notice that our resolution is not as good, our determination to look after them is not as great as they thought it was.'

The effort required to turn the draft resolution into something tolerable to the Government had left it unable to perform the role Parsons had in mind. His objective had been to design a resolution in order to keep the initiative, offer some realistic chance of success but not tie Britain's hands militarily. As it was it would take at least three or four days to get a resolution through from scratch. Time would be demanded to allow Costa Mendez to come to New York to state his position, and then an Argentine rejection might lead 'weak sisters' to abstain on the grounds that a substantive resolution would be pointless unless acceptable to both parties. The new draft text would not command general support because it left the future of the Task Force ambiguous. The absence of any reference to South Georgia would arouse suspicion that the intention was to seize this island as a base and then 'negotiate from strength with fleet hovering around the Falklands.'

He told the Prime Minister that he had already concluded that it was best not to bother. The idea was dropped. Better to wait for the proposals from others and then postpone and prolong discussion. It would be possible to hold out for a number of days before having to use the veto, and Parsons supposed that a really bad proposal might permit him to organise a triple veto, with American and French support. The next day he reported his growing confidence in the support and respect for Britain's position among the delegations, especially, he noted, those from the Commonwealth. 'The general view is that we have beaten the Argentines hands down in the diplomatic contest here and that our cause is just.' He was still bothered about how this was to be preserved, and if necessary translated into votes, as the conflict moved from a diplomatic to a military phase.

The issue had become largely presentational. Britain should be seen to be observing 'diplomatic proprieties here to the bitter end' and ensuring that Argentina was the side seen to have rejected the final diplomatic effort. So rather than move to yet another negotiating effort he now proposed calling a meeting of the Security Council and simply making a statement, without tabling a resolution. This would spell out how fully Britain had co-operated with the Security Council's efforts to prevent hostilities and with Haig's subsequent efforts to find a diplomatic solution. The punch line would be an assertion that as all diplomatic avenues had been explored, Britain now had no choice but to defend its rights under Article 51 of the Charter. The effect, he anticipated, would be like 'a bombshell.' It would 'provoke allegations of aggression from Argentina's supporters, alarm the non-aligned and panic the do-gooders.' There would be appeals to think again and it might be necessary to veto resolutions to that effect. Against this, Britain would have observed the proprieties and put Argentina on the wrong foot. Perhaps he was trying to bring home to London the implications of not being able to move forward with a credible, positive proposal in a draft resolution. At any rate, at face value, the new idea does not seem to have impressed London. While there was now understanding that any attempt to launch a pre-emptive draft resolution would get bogged down, it was not at all clear that Britain would want to draw a line under all diplomatic efforts or preclude a move to the UN.

By 24 April it was easier to see just how the Haig mission might break down and the move into the use of force begin. UN members were becoming 'conditioned to the likelihood that hostilities will break out piecemeal.' This reflected the speculation that had already developed around an assault on South Georgia and because of the evident logic of the situation. Given this logic, the 'bombshell' as previously proposed would not have the desired effect but would instead be seen as a transparent ploy. Parsons was also aware of the idea circulating at the OAS meeting that if Haig failed both parties should be invited to nominate a negotiator to hold talks with a neutral referee appointed by the Secretary-General, accompanied by the normal calls for restraint. His main worry was that the US might agree to an OAS consensus that was then tabled as a Security Council resolution. The actual attack on South Georgia reinforced the sense of a gradual move into hostilities and did not produce much of a clamour in the UN. There was little criticism of the action, although that probably had something to do with the lack of fatal casualties. It had, nonetheless, heightened the 'disposition of the do-gooders to think about fresh recourse to Council designed to prevent more military action.'

The Secretary-General's appeal

The retaking of South Georgia had one awkward consequence at the UN. Through his press office the Secretary-General issued an appeal:

> In view of the further armed exchange between Argentine and British forces which has taken place over South Georgia Island, it is imperative that the escalation of the situation be halted.
>
> In this critical situation, the Secretary-General therefore appeals to both parties to comply immediately with the provisions of Security Council Resolution 502 (1982) and to refrain from any action that would broaden yet further the conflict which threatens to have serious consequences for world peace.

Parsons immediately went to see the Secretary-General to explain that this suggested that Britain had failed to comply with SCR 502, yet only Argentina was in breach. Perez de Cuellar took the point and 'was most apologetic.' He had tried to produce a neutral text but now saw that it could be regarded as equivocal.

There the matter might have rested had it not been for the fact that the appeal was picked up by the Labour Opposition in London and endowed with considerable significance. Denis Healey, Shadow Foreign Minister, after his own talks with Perez de Cuellar, was expecting a formal appeal, comparable to that issued by an earlier Secretary-General, U Thant, to Kennedy and Khrushchev during the Cuban Missile Crisis, calling for restraint on both sides. From this perspective it could appear that Britain was in the parlous position of rejecting such a call just as it embarked on military action, requiring all the international support it could get. Though Parsons had disabused Healey of this notion this may not have been until after Healey had alerted Michael Foot, Leader of the Opposition, to the potential significance of the statement.

The easiest response would have been to leak the fact of Perez de Cuellar's apology to Parsons, but the British Ambassador was anxious that not be done, both because of the impact on his own relations with the Secretary-General and the subsequent clamour from the Latin Americans if it were known that an apology had been made to the British. Nor did Parsons want to make a formal response to what was understood in New York to be no more than a 'routine sort of statement' as this would encourage a rejoinder from Roca. All that could be done in London was to play down its significance, noting that the 'appeal' was only a press release without any formal status, not yet circulated to any of the UN bodies. It was stressed that Britain had explained that it had not failed to comply with Resolution 502.

After the Prime Minister sought to play down the issue in the Commons she received a letter from Foot in which he professed himself shocked by the fact that the Government did not attach as great an importance as he did to a statement issued by the Secretary-General. International support depended on allegiance to the UN Charter. 'If that great asset is destroyed or impaired at this moment, the responsibility will be yours.' The positive suggestion he made – that the Foreign Secretary should be despatched forthwith to New York to talk directly with the Secretary-General – did not commend itself as a response to the immediate non-crisis but it did have attractions as a possible response to the inevitable sense of crisis that would follow any announcement that the Haig mission was over without a result.

After having seen Foot's letter Parsons suggested that if the issue arose in the next House of Commons debate, it could be pointed out that he had been in daily touch with the Secretary-General since the crisis began. He had advised ministers that Perez de Cuellar was very conscious of the complexity of the problem and the need for careful preparation of any initiative that he might take. He could not act under Article 99 because the Security Council was already seized of the problem and would not wish to take any initiative not cleared in advance with the parties and while the Haig mission was alive. He would also require a clear mandate from the Security Council. Not even the OAS had yet asked him to get involved. Meanwhile he had advised that the only valid course for the Security Council was to stick to 502.

Alternatives

When the news came through at the end of April that Haig intended at last to make a statement announcing the failure of his mediation and the intention of the US Administration to come out against Argentina, work was underway on a full examination of Britain's negotiating options. Politically there seemed to be a need for some diplomatic activity if only to keep unacceptable initiatives out of play, to justify Britain's position at home and abroad, and to provide a mechanism for progress if Argentina cracked. On the basis that the British objective remained the return of the Falklands to British administration, if necessary through the use of force, the purpose of diplomatic activity was to put pressure on Argentina and not detract from other forms of pressure. The Haig mediation had worked in so far as it deflected any international clamour for Britain to promise not to use force or agree to a cessation of hostilities, at the price of immediate American pressure on Buenos Aires. Now that the Haig mediation was ending with the blame being directed firmly in Argentina's direction and a clear tilt in Britain's favour then its conclusion should not necessarily be mourned. Any new negotiating exercises had to be judged as opportunities for Britain to demonstrate its reasonableness, and to resist pressures for a cease-fire, as much as a means to a settlement.

Demonstrations of reasonableness, however, could not be too transparently cynical if they were to have the required political effect. If the exercise was not being taken at all seriously then the result could be to jeopardise US support or risk having to resort to the veto in the Security Council. Once any initiative was launched there would be the familiar pressures to hold back on military action. So it was unwise to assume that Britain could control any negotiating process so that it made just enough progress to enhance Britain's diplomatic standing but not so much that it created a momentum for an unacceptable solution. Merely restating the Government's requirements might not create the best political impression, but the alternative of putting forward proposals that might be negotiable, offering Argentina something short of humiliation, carried its own presentational difficulties. Moreover, many in the FCO and MoD did want to negotiate seriously, in the hope that Argentina could be persuaded to accept a settlement that caused only modest upset to the islanders. This would remove the Falklands as a burden on British foreign policy and military provision. There was a nagging worry that a military solution to the immediate crisis would leave Britain with a substantial long-term requirement. One of the advantages of a deal brokered by the US was that it might be persuaded to guarantee Argentine compliance.

As the Haig mission drew to its close, the FCO Planning Staff investigated the possibilities for a deal. Their new trawl threw up no surprises. If a deal was required most options fell because they could not be acceptable to one side or the other. Some arrangements would be unacceptable to both. These included partition, whereby Britain might keep West Falkland and Argentina would get East Falkland, and a condominium, putting sovereignty into suspense along the lines of the Antarctic treaty. Examining a variety of precedents did not help much. US sovereign rights in the Canal Zone had been ceded to Panama on 1 October 1979. Administration and operation were held initially in US hands but were to pass to Panama before the end of the century. Little account was taken of the residents in this process. It was similar to but worse than lease-back. The Aaland Islands model would lead to a transfer of sovereignty to Argentina, home rule for the Falklands, special guarantees of the islanders' way of life plus demilitarisation, but in the Aaland case, the populations of Finland, to whom sovereignty was ceded, and Sweden were not too dissimilar. It was unlikely to work for people as dissimilar as the Argentines and the Falkland Islanders. It would also be over-dependent on Argentine fair play. The precedent itself was not that promising. The Swedish-speaking population was conquered by Russia in the 19th century. Having spent the first half of the 20th century pleading, and voting, to be Swedish, they were retained by Finland.

Mr Cheek, a member of the Falkland Islands Legislative Council, raised the Andorran model. This would involve sovereignty and self-government for the Falklands with a guarantee of territorial integrity by the Permanent Five members of the Security Council, plus Argentina. Andorra was under the 'Suzerainty' of the President of France and the Palatine Bishop of Burgos. Neither France nor Spain interfered in Andorra's internal affairs. This was possibly acceptable to the islanders but not Argentina. The guarantee of territorial integrity would help to deter further Argentine aggression but a military guarantee – from US – would also probably be needed. There would also be practical problems in self-government for such a tiny territory. Argentina would fight islander independence 'tooth and nail.'

Of the familiar options only lease-back had any coherence. This would involve an immediate transfer of sovereignty with British administration for a substantial period (50 years) and a referendum before the package was implemented or towards the end of a period of administration. Although this had been found unacceptable in the past it was widely canvassed in the press as a way out of the dilemma, and was known to have been taken seriously by the Government in 1980. Could Argentina accept a sufficiently long period of British administration? Would this require relatively liberal arrangements for Argentine immigration and acquisition of property? Would it be necessary to arrange a US security guarantee?

The difficulties faced in coming up with credible methods for resolving the dispute through agreement rather than force highlighted the difficulties facing any diplomatic initiative. It was precisely because of the zero-sum quality of the dispute that Argentina sought a deal that would pre-judge the outcome of later negotiations. Anything else offered to Argentina to make something akin to the Haig package more palatable – on the manner of withdrawal, the interim administration, or arrangements for long-term negotiations – faced this problem. Nor was there much interest in trying to consider Argentina's difficulties. Haig's text had been awkward enough for Britain. Any attempt to improve on it would fail to satisfy Argentina while creating further pitfalls for Britain, especially if it was correct that Argentina would find it easier to accept new proposals rather than a variation of Haig's ideas. And then, why should Britain be more conciliatory when it was about to step up the pressure?

Any attempt to save Argentine face, if that really was worth saving, would have to be through a procedural device rather than more concessions of substance. Such procedural approaches, all following Argentine withdrawal, might involve referring the Islands or possibly just the Dependencies to the ICJ, or to an ad hoc arbitration tribunal or some conference under UN or US chairmanship. The UN Secretary-General was recognised to be the most natural alternative, but he was not long in office and there was little experience of his negotiating style. Other inducements might be a recognition of a legitimate Argentine interest in the future of the Falkland Islands, forces returning to normal duties during negotiations, Argentine and US official representation on the Islands in a consultative capacity. In all of this Britain would have to insist that the wishes of islanders would be taken into account and that the US would provide assurances about security of the Islands pending negotiation.

SECTION THREE

14

OPERATION SUTTON

The Haig mediation had kept diplomats and politicians busy during April. Meanwhile the military had to prepare for war, with a growing probability that it might actually happen. Many in the Task Force may have departed in the firm expectation that they would soon be home, as the fleet reversed course to the cheer of a diplomatic triumph. The expectation soon dimmed and planning was carried forward in earnest. The political imperatives behind the early despatch of the Task Force had taken account of military imperatives only to the extent that it was to take the maximum feasible load, but the precise form those imperatives might take remained hazy, and indeed had not been fully clarified by the time that the Haig mediation collapsed.

The Chief of Defence Staff, Sir Terence Lewin, was, like many of his generation, influenced by the 1956 Suez debacle, a powerful memory for all those contemplating the way in which such ventures can go horribly wrong. In 1956 Lewin had been in command of a destroyer, stuck in Malta. After Suez he had read up about the episode and concluded that the services had been let down by the politicians. He was, he later told his biographer, 'determined that this shouldn't happen again and that we should, right from the beginning, get a very clear statement of what it was the politicians wanted the services to do.' On his return to London from New Zealand he discussed the matter with his staff and had what he thought these objectives might be typed out. He then went to the War Cabinet. There he raised the issue. When he asked for a precise objective, he recalled, 'there was a bit of a silence and I said very well I have got one written out here, could I read it to you. And I read it out and everybody said that is what we want to do.'[1] The objectives were as follows:

The overall aim of Her Majesty's Government is to bring about the withdrawal of Argentine forces from the Falkland Islands and dependencies, and the re-establishment of British administration there, as quickly as possible. Military deployments and operations are directed to the support of this aim.

By 9 April the majority of Task Force ships were at sea and heading south. With a Maritime Exclusion Zone agreed, it was possible to start thinking seriously about future operations. The Chiefs requested a paper 'to assess the various military options for putting a force ashore in the Falkland Islands, with a view to repossessing the islands'. This operation was now known as SUTTON. The assumptions were that South Georgia had been re-taken and an effective sea/air EZ established around the Falkland Islands. Limitations to the aim were that civilian casualties had to be kept to a minimum (safeguarding property was a lesser but important consideration). The request was problematic in two respects. First it assumed what had yet to be achieved: that South Georgia had been re-taken and a protection force stationed there, that an effective sea/air EZ had been established around the Falkland Islands and that adequate intelligence would be available. Second it set a requirement to establish a bridgehead but not to consider the next steps; this limitation was reflected in the phrase 'with a view to'. It discouraged consideration of what a landed force might actually achieve. At the same time as this was being analysed in London, the issue was being addressed by the Amphibious Force commanders, Thompson and Clapp, as well as by Woodward.

The paper before the Chiefs of Staff on 14 April, that served as the basis for the planning directive sent to Fieldhouse the next day, argued that sea control and a reasonable degree of air superiority over the Falkland Islands could be established and also that the area close to Stanley was the most suitable landing spot in terms of early and decisive military results, and where tactical surprise might just be achieved. There was less concern about the problems involved in getting a brigade ashore to re-establish a British presence than about those connected with moving to a direct assault against the Argentine defences. This introduced new orders of risk. Landing too far from Stanley would not put the Argentine garrison under sufficient pressure; landing too close would leave the British force vulnerable to an early challenge by the Argentine defenders.

The three principal options for a landing were West Falkland, and either the south or north of East Falkland. Of these the West Falkland promised minimal opposition, good ground cover for deployed troops, distance from any mobile Argentine forces and minimal risk of civilian casualties. Against this was vulnerability to mainland-based air attacks, a lack of direct pressure on the main Argentine force and yet another move required to East Falkland, which would be exposed and hazardous and possibly on to unsuitable beaches. Analysis of East Falkland pointed to the advantages of the south where there would be light opposition and minimal risk of civilian casualties, but problems of inadequate cover and a difficult approach to Stanley. The north offered proximity to Stanley and immediate pressure on the Argentine force, but a greater risk of an opposed landing, a loss of tactical surprise and an early confrontation with Argentine quick reaction forces. The Chiefs' inclination was to look to the north of East Falkland, but they were also inclined to leave the choice of landing options until later when there might be better intelligence.

At this stage planners considered Stanley to be a challenging objective. The surrounding ring of hills would be a natural location for observation posts and defensive positions. A direct assault would also risk a major loss of life among the civilian population, and so operations subsequent to a landing might have to be confined to attacks on selected Argentine positions and to special force operations. There was no guarantee that the Argentine garrison would become hopelessly demoralised in the face of such attacks: they might become more entrenched. Of all these factors the main constraint was the risk of civilian casualties. For the moment the inclination was to think of alternatives to direct assault, including a long siege. The Chief of the General Staff, General Sir Edwin Bramall, was concerned about the lack of an adequate concept of land operations, but as he was still doubtful about even the feasibility and necessity of an amphibious landing he saw this as an issue that could be left until the basic strategy had been agreed.

Such thoughts discouraged proposals for sending additional troops to join 3 Brigade. They would not necessarily help but would only add to the logistic support and re-supply problems. Nonetheless, the difficulties surrounding an amphibious landing, never mind what followed, argued for some prudent augmentation. The Chiefs of Staff decided to ask the War Cabinet to take another 900 men from 5 Infantry Brigade, this time the 2nd Battalion of The Parachute Regiment (2 Para), and transfer them to 3 Commando Brigade. The Prime Minister reported this on 15 April, when it was also agreed to send appropriate additional ships, if possible including HMS *Intrepid*, which, with MV *Norland*, would carry 2 Para. The commanders were anxious to get *Intrepid* attached to the amphibious force as an additional helicopter operating deck as well as for its landing craft. The operation of Sea Harriers was too important a role for *Hermes* for it to be risked in the landing. *Intrepid*, however, would not be ready until 28 April and would not arrive until 18 May, which Lewin thought would be a 'bit late.' *Norland* had her drawbacks, a ramp that would not lower to the height of a Mexeflote,[2] limited water capacity, and a probable need for dedicated tanker support. There were, however, very few suitable commercial ships able to carry as many personnel.

Tensions on the Task Force

Woodward had picked up the caution in London. In a signal of 12 April he wondered whether Argentina had already been allowed so much time for consolidation that it might be impossible to take the heavily defended Stanley airstrip, except at high cost and collateral damage to Stanley. If so then there was no major advantage to hurrying to the Falklands:

Such a new approach could allow sea blockade to continue while the necessary equipment is assembled to provide us with our own airstrip on say West Falkland once landing is effected clear of Arg concentrations, it could also for instance allow us to ferry Harrier GR3 aircraft to the scene in Bulwark [a recently decommissioned carrier] or with in-flight refuelling from Ascension. This would greatly help to keep Stanley airstrip unavailable to Args while leaving our remaining Sea Harriers free for air defence.

This was not a cheap option, but neither were the alternatives:

At least the cost in lives might be markedly less since the very inevitability of the outcome should cause an early capitulation. Even the steady preparation should have its effects as the winter deepens in the Falklands. Hope this is not eggsucking but it is not a course I have so far considered.

Fieldhouse's response would not have led him to assume that he was wholly off beam:

We are thinking very much on the same lines. Above all I am convinced that the opportunity for a hasty landing operation is already past. 'Better walk across the meadow and take them all'.

His staff, the CINC reported, was working on a full-scale appreciation. 'We can talk about all this when we meet.' In fact Fieldhouse was convinced himself that it was necessary to plan for full repossession. Nonetheless, the Chiefs of Staff planning directive of 15 April notably refrained from a commitment to a full-scale land battle, and this encouraged the view that an enclave ashore might be sufficient.

On 16 April Woodward visited *Fearless* to prepare, with Thompson and Clapp, an agenda for a visit by Fieldhouse the next day. Woodward later commented that 'while discussion seemed amiable enough to me, others have reported it differently'[3]. Thompson's report was that Woodward's style was 'totally at odds with mine, and Clapp's'. According to Clapp, 'Trust was broken and it would take a long time to repair.'[4] To understand why these different perceptions emerged from that meeting it is necessary to note the influence of a variety of factors. These included the ambiguity in command arrangements. As noted earlier initially Woodward had been put in overall charge but after changes to the command structure he was now *primus inter pares* with the commanders of the task groups, all reporting directly to Fieldhouse. His seniority was relevant in this case because of the broader view he, as the Carrier Battle Group Commander, had of the range of strategic possibilities facing the Task Force.

Woodward, who had only moved his flag to HMS *Hermes* the previous day, was grappling with two conundrums set him by Fieldhouse. The first was that the conflict could last a long time, requiring him to look ahead to a point when he would be unable to rely on having two carriers on station, because of either wear and tear or enemy action. Without two decks (or landing strips on land) it would be unsafe to operate the Sea Harriers and the operation would have to be called off. If, as seemed likely, *Illustrious* would not be available for some time, the alternative would be a strip on the Falklands. He had in mind its use by Phantom air defence fighters, essential to reinforce the limited number of Sea Harriers for long-term air defence of the Task Force and the Islands. This was in itself an argument for moving ahead with some urgency and, at the very least, obtaining a relatively secure position on the Falklands. But if, at the same time, there was concern about the balance of forces on East Falkland then this was an argument for considering a landing on West Falkland where a defendable enclave might be found, thereby strengthening Britain's bargaining position in any negotiations. If West Falkland was unsuitable then Low Bay in Lafonia might be considered, for he believed it was defensible over the long term from sea and air attack. He had specifically been asked by Fieldhouse for a 'front-line' view on the possibility of an enclave, and had already indicated his own distaste for the idea. It was not inconceivable, however, that this would be the most that the British could achieve. In addition to this long-term contingency there was short-term pressure. Fieldhouse had told him that he must 'hurry south'. He had also been led to believe that he was to escort the amphibious group south, but he was unaware of Clapp's discussions with Fieldhouse about how much had to be accomplished at Ascension Island before the amphibious group could contemplate moving on.

Clapp and Thompson were not at all ready to travel south. They needed time for training and, above all, for restowing all the equipment that had hurriedly been packed into the ships so that they could leave their ports as quickly as possible. With regard to a site for the landing they believed that full repossession would in due course follow a landing. They therefore needed to get in the best position in relation to their ultimate target and reduce the sea and air threat they would face, particularly if they were ordered to wait before launching the final land attack. Clapp's main concern was to choose a place where there would be no chance of swell, critical if there was to be a continuous unloading of ships. Along with its rocky approaches and lack of beaches for vehicles and equipment, this was one reason why Low Bay had been discarded as an option. There was also a view that it would be less defensible against air attack because the adjacent coast would enable low-flying aircraft to arrive without warning. The Stanley area was ruled out as too dangerous for a landing, but they had also ruled out West Falkland because of its vulnerability from the air and the need for a later move across the Falkland Sound. After considering some fifty beaches, the choice had been narrowed down to two sites on East Falkland – San Carlos and Cow Bay/Volunteer Bay/Berkeley Sound (Port Louis).

The meeting on 16 April should have been a chance to explore the fact that, as Woodward later noted, all three commanders had been planning to different directives. When Woodward arrived, however, Thompson and Clapp were not expecting him and Clapp was unable to spend much time with him at all. Thompson reflected his concerns when he asked Major Southby-Tailyour, the Royal Marine expert on the Falkland Islands, to brief Woodward on the Islands' topography. This irritated Woodward because that was not what he needed to talk about and there was not much time. From this point on every issue raised suggested to Thompson and Clapp that Woodward had an agenda markedly different from their own. Although Woodward had already concluded that in practice he could not control the work of the amphibious task group and that it was probably best not to try, he believed the exception to this general rule would be the passage south, when he thought he was to be in overall charge, and that it would also be sensible for him to be so. Yet Clapp had been told that he was in charge of the amphibious group during this stage as well, and so became concerned that Woodward's expectation here might eventually extend to the actual amphibious assault. Clapp's concern about how Woodward might use these ships was further aggravated by the idea of a feint towards the Argentine mainland as a means of drawing out the Argentine air force. To Clapp and Thompson this seemed to require the use of *Fearless*, as the only ship that had the identifiable radio signatures to give the impression of an assault, and they were not enamoured with the idea of their command ship being used as a decoy. Woodward's recollection is that Clapp told him that the general idea had some merit and – after the campaign – that he had directed his own staff to look into it. Clapp's recollection is that he saw some value in a feint but that it would be hard not to use *Fearless* if the impression was to be created that something major was underway, and that he and Thompson were to move to another ship. Either way this was not an idea that survived very long.

The main issue was over the landing site. In his memoir Thompson described the notion of a landing on West Falkland as 'grotesque':

> Apart from the fact that the proposed site for the airstrip was about as close to the Argentine mainland airbases as it was possible to get without actually being in the sea, my engineers neither had the plant nor the numbers to carry out such an ambitious scheme. Landing on West Falkland would also necessitate another amphibious operation on East Falkland, if the Argentines refused to budge, and this itself was reason enough not to contemplate such a move. Had we been put into the picture on the West Falkland option from the outset, we might have been in a position to thrash it out together and give a reasoned response, instead of greeting the idea with scorn and

contempt [...] The responsibility for the ensuing acrimony rests largely with Northwood. It is simply not good enough to promulgate a structure of three co-equal commanders, and then arbitrarily, and without ever telling the other two, treat one of the commanders as if he was the overall boss on some occasions, which they did a number of times. Although to be fair, Northwood was faced at short notice with an amphibious landing followed by a land campaign, two phases of war of which they had no experience, even on exercises.[5]

As this quote makes clear Thompson was not blaming Woodward for the situation in which such disagreements could occur. The problem, however, went beyond that of the command structure. Clapp and Thompson were looking for the optimum landing site on the assumption that the next step was to repossess the Falklands; Woodward was sensitive to a broader range of possibilities – including a potential requirement from London for an enclave – and felt that in those circumstances it was not at all grotesque to consider West Falkland as one possible option, but the only responsible thing to do. His main interest was in a Phantom base and if that was not possible there would be no interest. In fact, as Thompson later confirmed, the Task Force lacked the capacity to construct such a base even if it had been possible.

The next day, 17 April, was the meeting with Fieldhouse on *Hermes*. Fieldhouse provided essential background on the developing political situation at home, including the level of national support behind the Task Force, and urged that planning move forward on the basis that there would be no reprieve from war. His team had brought with them all the material prepared over the previous few days on all aspects of the campaign. Having been through debates in London on the appropriate strategy, they now went through them again with the officers who would be responsible for implementing the plans. Woodward found this valuable: 'The need to clear minds and exchange views was considerable. For the first time a general plan and timetable emerged.' The timetable began with the departure the following day of the Carrier Battle Group. It ended in mid-June with the likely loss of effectiveness of the Battle Group as a result of enemy action, lack of maintenance and the time at sea in winter conditions. The intention was that it would arrive in the EZ by 29 April. The most relevant factor for timing the landing was the possible arrival of *Intrepid* on 16 May, from which Woodward constructed a bar chart, setting out a schedule. If 16 May was the earliest date, the latest would be 23 May, leaving some 15 days for intelligence gathering beforehand and three weeks after landing for the land operations.

The amphibious force was to reach Ascension on 19 April, from where it was due to sail on 29 April, once 2 Para had joined it, with a view to arriving at the Falkland Islands on 16 May. Clapp and Thompson were adamant that they needed those days just to sort out the stowage problems resulting from the hurried departure from Britain. The 16 May target date had emerged independently from Woodward's staff, the amphibious planning group on *Fearless*, as well as Northwood and MoD. Another uncontroversial conclusion was that there could be no waiting beyond May to attempt a landing. If the landing was delayed, the logistics, physical fitness and morale of the landing force would be severely tested, and the supporting ships of the carrier battle group would literally run out of steam. Thompson would have preferred longer for reconnaissance, but Moore wanted to aim for the earliest possible date. The landing site was not yet confirmed but San Carlos was already emerging as a strong contender. Everybody agreed that local air superiority was a prerequisite.

Lingering at Ascension

The *Hermes* meeting had been the first chance for those responsible for planning the campaign to address issues with those responsible for the implementation of their plans. Despite the points of agreement it left all involved more anxious and unsure. The size of the task ahead was becoming clearer as the diplomatic context was becoming daily more difficult. The military knew that they would need steady nerves to see the campaign through to the end but could they be sure that the political nerve would hold? Should they at least build into the plans opportunities for doubts and delay or must military and ministers alike accept that once they had agreed to prepare a force for a landing they had no choice but to commit it, and having landed they would have no choice but to follow it through to seize Stanley by force?

Back in London it was assumed that if there was to be hesitation it would be best if it occurred while the amphibious force was at Ascension Island. How well could the island cope with the extra inhabitants? Once 2 Para arrived, there would be 5,600 men in 3 Commando Brigade. Of these *Canberra* could accommodate and support some 2,100. The British Forces Support Unit (BFSU) Ascension, with a permanent staff of approximately 250, had accommodation under its control for up to 300 personnel in transit. There was no other permanent accommodation available on the Island, and other pressures were already building up, especially as RAF personnel were expected to increase from a little over 200 to about 450. So the extra 3,500 men ashore would have to be under canvas, for which there was just about enough space. The tentage and accommodation stores, a total of 150 tons, could be provided by the Army and could be delivered to Ascension Island within four days. The main problem areas would be water, which would have to be rationed initially until it was possible to install a water distilling plant or import it by tanker. Until this could be arranged men would need to stay on the amphibious ships and troop transports. Once drainage, sanitation and electricity had been provided, the major effort thereafter would be regular supplies of provisions by sea and air. There were further issues of local transport, where helicopters would have to be used intensively, as well as ensuring that the forces continued to exercise and train. There were also questions of American political sensitivities if the Island was turned into a large military base, even though it was sovereign British territory. In sum, the maintenance of the Landing Force at Ascension Island for up to two months was just about manageable.

Whether or not it was desirable was another matter. An opposed amphibious landing would require the highest level of operational effectiveness. If delays meant the equipment becoming less serviceable, and ships and aircraft crew less efficient, then the risk of battle casualties would grow. It might be argued that two months of training at Ascension would raise the physical standard of the whole force, but the climate would be extremely hot (Ascension is only 8 degrees from the Equator) and would hardly acclimatise the force for conditions akin to a harsh and unforgiving British winter, while the time spent ashore would take its toll in terms of motivation. Equipment would suffer because of limited servicing and maintenance. Ships would have to stay in unprotected anchorage facilities, helicopters and landing craft would be used intensively, and all this time the carrier battle group and the SSNs would have to work hard to conserve resources and maintain their operational effectiveness. The strain would probably be particularly severe on the Sea Harriers, and this could undermine their ability to provide adequate air defence and close air support both during and subsequent to the landing. So while, by itself, holding the Landing Force back would not prevent it being able eventually to mount an effective operation, given the logistic challenges, possible attrition and the onset of Antarctic winter, the longer the carrier force was operating alone the greater would be the reduction in the availability and effectiveness of the force at the time of the landing. If matters were not decided by mid-July the success of the operation would be severely prejudiced.

The issue of holding back the amphibious force was brought to the Chiefs of Staff on 19 April. Leach argued against any delay, largely out of concerns for the sustainability of the Carrier Battle Group. The efficiency of the force, if not committed, would begin to decline from about the end of May. The two carriers could not be relied upon beyond about August, and there were no comparable replacements. Adding more delay at Ascension, so that the date for a landing slipped, would add to all these problems. The First Sea Lord preferred the Task Force to sail as planned and then wait if necessary, so that any operation could then be executed when it suited the commander. The discussion identified more arguments against delay: the plight of the Falkland Islanders; the danger of a prolonged stay at Ascension Island being interpreted as a lack of resolution, sending the wrong signal in diplomatic negotiations. Against this was the possibility that letting the blockade of the Argentine garrison run on before any landing was attempted could be a tempting strategy. As a practical matter, there was no harm in having tentage and water supplies moved to Ascension Island, as these could also be needed on the Falkland Islands in due course. For the moment the timetable was to stay the same, but if the strategic view changed and the force was to stay longer at Ascension this could be managed.

Similar arguments also told against leaving on time from Ascension but then loitering in the South Atlantic. On arrival the Task Force's morale would be high, its training at a peak and its equipment fully operational. If this was then followed by a lengthy blockade with low intensity operations in mid-winter there could be a loss of motivation while the equipment would be in need of routine maintenance and replacement. Logistic support would also require a continuous cycle of RFAs and STUFT to be maintained in order to prevent interruptions in re-supply of ammunition, food, stores and fuel. The issue of the durability of the carriers would remain: by early August HMS *Illustrious* might be available to take over, but in an unworked-up condition without sea trials completed or a dedicated Air Group. She could not be counted upon to maintain the blockade or to support an opposed landing adequately. The Air Defence Ships and modern Anti-Submarine Frigates could not be replaced if sunk or sustained on a roulement basis. This might make no difference if the Argentines decided to engage in order to break the blockade, as then they would probably lose, and open up the possibility of a successful landing. The risks would come if the Argentines were patient.

The conclusion from these deliberations was that the blockade, now due to start on 29 April, could be sustained until August, although effectiveness would begin to decline from early June. The optimum date for the landing would be 16 May, although it could take place from as early as 7 May or be delayed until the end of the month. On that basis, given a 14-day passage, the amphibious force would need to leave Ascension by mid-May. If the landing was to be postponed to the end of May or later, many of the troops would have to stay on Ascension in tents, and early arrangements would be needed for this.

CINCFLEET's outline plan

On his return to the UK, Fieldhouse prepared his outline plan for SUTTON, based on the *Hermes* discussions, for consideration by the Chiefs of Staff on 20 April. None of the basic assumptions had been altered about the parameters of the operation and the nature of the Argentine threat. This summed up the position reached on how and when to 'land a force in the Falkland Islands with a view to repossessing the islands'. Fieldhouse was opposed to delay largely because of the likely weather conditions. Stormy weather was frequent in late April and winter set in by mid-May. There would be rain on fifteen days each month and gales on five. Long periods at sea would have a debilitating effect on embarked troops, particularly in rough weather. After a period of about a month south of

Ascension the Landing Force would require about a week of shore training to regain its fighting efficiency. The only place this might be possible would be South Georgia, only three days passage from the Falkland Islands and more suitable than Ascension for the acclimatisation of troops, but offering very hostile conditions. The deteriorating weather could make amphibious operations more difficult, particularly on exposed coasts, and severely inhibit parachute operations as well as limit daylight satellite and air reconnaissance. It also had implications for the next step. The weather would pose morale and survival problems for troops in the open, especially on high ground. On the other hand, once landed the weather could favour seasoned, well-trained British troops and lead the Argentine force to concentrate in the immediate area of settlements, particularly Stanley, where there would be accommodation for troops not deployed in the field.

Questions of morale, weather, troop fitness, political direction and military judgement all strongly combined to favour an early landing date. The only additional capabilities whose late arrival might influence the decision were the trawlers for minesweeping, but there was only a small chance that the selected beach approaches would have been mined and these vessels would anyway only be of limited value in reducing the probability that an assault vessel would be mined in shallow water. Their steel hulls and noisy engines put them at risk of being blown up themselves by magnetic or acoustic mines. Checking the shallow waters would be an important role for the Fleet Clearance Diving Teams. The relevant period for a landing was now narrowed down to 14–23 May, with 16 May still the optimum, as soon as practicable after *Intrepid*'s arrival with 2 Para on the ferry *Norland* and her preparation for landing operations. Operating difficulties would be most severe in the western sector of the EZ, because it was closer to the mainland, and so this would not be a good area to attempt an amphibious landing, but the eastern sector looked more promising, where the threat was more limited and hence more easily containable. No definite choice was offered on the landing beach: better intelligence and more study were required. To gain tactical intelligence, and perhaps to engage in advanced operations, Special Forces could be inserted onto the Falklands using Sea King helicopters and possibly submarines.

There was enough time between the arrival of the Battle Group and the earliest landing date for local sea control and air superiority to be gained and for the airfield to be neutralised. With additional helicopter support proposed, British forces should enjoy sufficient tactical mobility to counter any Argentine forces deployed forward. Once they had the bridgehead they would also be strong enough to sustain it. Argentine morale and ability to resist were likely to deteriorate as the blockade continued. The bridgehead should be close enough to exert direct military and psychological pressure against the main Argentine force in the Stanley area. This might convince the Argentines that their position was militarily untenable, and that they could honourably agree to withdraw, but the possibility that the enemy could advance for a decisive battle could be allowed for in selecting the position of the bridgehead.

The Navy commended the Outline Plan as 'confident in tone, robust in its approach and broadly consonant' with the appreciation that had been prepared by the Chiefs of Staff. Areas of concern were the playing down of the impact of Argentine shore-based air forces and Guppy-class submarines. There was some interest in whether more attention should have been given to the option of parachuting SAS intelligence-gathering patrols direct from Ascension and to the risks of waters being mined. The Army remained concerned about the lack of attention given 'to the development of subsequent land operations, the time they will take, the objectives to aim for and the problems involved'. Would the landing force be large enough both to make the assault and subsequently exploit it against determined opposition? Would ministers prefer to adopt other operations together with diplomacy to achieve their aim? With the proviso that these issues must be addressed, the general thrust of the plan was supported. The landing date should be as soon as possible; there was no military advantage in delay. The Army was also interested in the use of parachute-landed Special Forces, in this case to attack Port Stanley airfield to minimise civilian casualties.

The RAF shared the concern about the lack of attention to the follow-up operations but was more anxious about the critical assumption that an effective sea/air EZ could be established. The Chief of Air Staff argued for caution. He was in favour of delaying a landing until an effective blockade could be imposed and had time to demoralise the enemy. To this end he sought greater use of air reconnaissance and offensive air support, noting that the Sea Harrier would be the most effective means of putting Stanley airfield out of action and risked being wasted if employed solely for air defence. As an alternative he was already assessing the possible use of Vulcans. Cooper, PUS at MoD, drew attention to the potential consequences of any operations on world opinion. For example, bombing Stanley airfield might create such a backlash that Ministers might feel unable subsequently to authorise a landing. The worst outcome would be for the operation to be stopped after it had started but before it was complete. Any final plan therefore required a proper assessment of the possible political and diplomatic consequences of each step. The Chiefs agreed that the next step would be that the amphibious force should wait at Ascension Island until it could integrate 2 Para and then leave for the South Atlantic. Beyond that many uncertainties lingered.

Alternatives to a landing

It was by no means clear that a landing would be authorised. Politicians would be very cautious about authorising anything without a high assurance of eventual success. It was therefore important that the Government had to be offered options for military action short of an assault. All of these had to work on Argentine morale: if the garrison was not to be forcibly removed it had to decide on its own account that it had had enough. If morale was already low, surrender might come even before an assault but if it was high then the only alternative to an assault would be to wear the Argentine forces down in a long blockade, even though at this stage it was believed that the Argentines had sufficient supplies on the Falkland Islands to last over two months, including 30 days of combat.

On 22 April a paper was tabled to the Chiefs on the alternatives to SUTTON, all designed to obtain the withdrawal of Argentine forces through attrition and demoralisation. None appeared very promising. They were:

1. To land as presently planned but with the aim changed from the 'repossession of the Falklands' to 'establish a British presence'. A substantial part of the Falkland Islands would be occupied and secured but no attempt would be made to evict the main body of Argentine Forces from Stanley. One variant would be to land in West Falkland. This option offered a high chance of operational success and lower casualties, but would have the same planning constraints as SUTTON, leave Argentine forces as the gaolers of Stanley and might not produce the requisite diplomatic effects before the British military position became hard to sustain.

2. Continue to enforce the Exclusion Zone with the full Carrier Task Force without attempting a landing in order to isolate and weaken the garrison to the point where a negotiated withdrawal on British terms might be possible. Operations would be geared to attaining and maintaining air/sea superiority around the Falklands, with some attrition to Argentine forces. This would be achieved by stopping all traffic in and out of Stanley and harassment operations. The limiting factor would be the eventual need to withdraw a carrier for maintenance, which could be as early as late July. This option would tie up a considerable portion of the fleet but without necessarily sustaining sufficient pressure for a political result before it had to be drawn down, leaving Britain bereft of alternative ways of stepping up the pressure as the landing forces would have returned to Britain.

3. Addressing the problem of maintaining a blockade by first achieving sea/air superiority and then reducing the force to a level that could be sustained by roulement for at least six months. This would require concentrating on stopping air and sea traffic to Stanley. After some time harassing raids might be launched, geared in their timing and execution to the political

situation. This would have the political advantages of minimal force, but, with only one carrier, the risks to British forces would grow while little could be done for the civil population.

4. General offensive operations against the Argentine Navy on the high seas, with the aim of sinking sufficient units of the Argentine Navy to influence their Government to make substantial concessions in early negotiations. This would provide an improved military setting for any later British landing or blockade operations, and eventually for a smaller British re-occupation force. Operations using SSNs could commence immediately, at a variety of levels and did not preclude other options, but their decisive nature and high visibility could trigger a strong world reaction.

5. A supplementary option was to mount a series of raids using air, Special Forces or heliborne troops to weaken and wear down Argentine troops, with their timing and level tuned to the political setting. They could be aimed at key points such as communication centres, store dumps, strong points, airfield facilities, barracks, command facilities etc. With a steady attrition of men and material, a war of nerves could develop, exacerbating the already difficult conditions of weather, terrain and accommodation.

As these various options were addressed they dropped away. There were too many uncertainties and risks of stalemate, too great a dependence upon Argentina playing along, for example by not keeping their ships inshore. Decisive action soon seemed essential if Britain's determination was not to come into question at home and abroad. The full spectrum of operations had now been identified with measures tantamount to full-scale warfare at one extreme and an ultra-cautious and probably untenable strategy of delay at the other. In the middle of this range the options were not necessarily exclusive, as they could serve as graduated steps leading up to a landing.

Landing and post-landing

There was never any indication that the War Cabinet had any interest in delaying the departure of the amphibious Task Force or holding back in any respect. The problem was the opposite. To get the maximum political pressure on Argentina the War Cabinet wanted the military preparations to be as conspicuous and advanced as possible. One example of this came on 21 April, just two days after the force had arrived at Ascension, when ministers were looking for military means to improve Britain's bargaining position. South Georgia was vital to this but so was getting the amphibious force moving into position. Fieldhouse was warned on the morning of 22 April that the Government might demand that it sail either that day or the next 'for a further political demonstration of resolve.' Receipt of this news led to dismay at Ascension where the group was assembling and re-arranging its stores, leading to an uncompromising warning from Commodore Clapp, replete with references to Gallipoli, of the chaos and the severe, possibly catastrophic operational penalties that could ensue. Preparing to move, just in case the order was given, led to additional delay to the training. This included a planned firing of the Rapier missile.[6] One consequence of this cancellation was that the launchers remained in the LSL hold and so were not maintained satisfactorily.

On 23 April Thatcher received a personal briefing at Northwood. Fieldhouse appears to have taken the opportunity to explain the problems being caused by military considerations constantly being overruled by often passing political considerations. On 24 April, he signalled a reassurance that the Prime Minister understood the difficulties. The next day, Sunday 25 April, the Chiefs of Staff and the senior commanders met with the War Cabinet at Chequers. In the morning all members of the War Cabinet, other than the Prime Minister, together with the Chiefs of Staff had attended a briefing at Northwood. There were still uncertainties. This was the critical day in the battle for South Georgia. The Haig plan was on the table and the Argentine reaction was awaited, and there was anxiety about the extent of the American pressure Britain would face if Argentina replied positively. Nott considered the presentation to the War Cabinet 'very well done' in going through the military options, but too much was packed into too short a time: 'there was such a mass of information, the decisions were so difficult and so far-reaching, that the PM protested that she could not carry on the discussion at that time'. Thatcher recalled looking from the Chiefs of Staff to her colleagues. 'It was a lot for them to take in ... they seemed somewhat taken aback.'[7]

The paper presented to the Chequers meeting on 25 April did not explore the various alternatives to pressing on. It was made clear that once the amphibious force reached the Falklands it could not loiter for long and so the aim was to land on 16 May. 'Anyone,' noted Thatcher, 'who had harboured the idea that the Task Force could blockade the Falklands and mount raids in the case of the negotiations being successful was soon disabused.'[8] Exactly where the landing would take place had still not been decided but notably the assumption was still that this would be to the north of East Falkland, close to Stanley. The real difficulties appeared post-landing. Britain's force of some 5,500 troops would face up to 8,000 Argentine troops, largely concentrated in and around Stanley. It was hoped that Britain would enjoy the advantages that came from tactical mobility and a successful air and sea blockade, and the attrition of Argentine air assets. In weather likened to Dartmoor on a bad day, Britain's force would again have an advantage as it was trained and equipped for arctic and mountain warfare operations. Nonetheless, exactly what would happen once a bridgehead had been established was uncertain. The landing on its own might convince the Argentines that their own position was militarily hopeless and that they could honourably agree to withdraw; but the possibility that the enemy would fight fiercely had to be recognised. Rather than a major battle the Chiefs envisaged a series of damaging and demoralising attacks on outlying forces, headquarters and logistic installations separated from the civilian population. With so little to show on the diplomatic front and news coming in about the battle for South Georgia as the day progressed, the War Cabinet accepted that planning for a full-scale landing had to go ahead, even though this would probably lead to British casualties.

Exactly what casualties might be incurred was unclear. Some numbers had been used in planning for reserves but no estimates were put on paper. Right from the start of the campaign the risks to the Task Force had tended to be expressed in terms of numbers of ships lost – four to six escorts and an aircraft carrier. When Thatcher had been briefed at Northwood a couple of days earlier she had asked Fieldhouse for an estimate and he had replied 'anything up to 3,000 people', but this appears to have been off the top of his head.[9]

The result of the first Chequers meeting was essentially to line up the decisions that would have to be taken over the coming week: whether to impose a Total Exclusion Zone and whether to attack Stanley airport; whether to attack the Argentine fleet outside the Exclusion Zone; whether to mount special force reconnaissance and offensive operations; whether to sail the amphibious force and land 3 Commando Brigade.

5 Infantry Brigade

The first decision needed was for permission for the amphibious group to sail from Ascension Island. Nott had gained agreement, unusually against Lewin's advice, for a two-day delay out of concern that they might leave and then turn back because of negotiations.[10] On 27 April Fieldhouse signalled that the amphibious group should sail on 29 April as planned, allowing *Intrepid* and 2 Para to catch up before they reached the Falklands area. The *Intrepid* group were expected by 6 May, and the amphibious commanders wanted it to spend 24 hours at Ascension integrating with the rest of the amphibious force before sailing together on 7 May for a landing about 18 May. This allowed 2 Para and the crew of *Norland* to have their first and only practice in transferring to a landing craft (and that was in daylight). Again indicating the political sense that time was of the essence, ministers wanted an option for an earlier landing without these reinforcements should the diplomatic or military situation make it attractive.

The post-landing issue had not yet been resolved. There was a risk that the planned force would not only be insufficient to repossess the Falklands in the face of Argentine resistance, but that it also might be unable to defend itself in the face of an Argentine offensive. That a substantial augmentation might be necessary had been evident from the start of the planning process, as had been the identity of 5 Infantry Brigade as the natural accompaniment to 3 Commando Brigade. Moore had begun to press for the Brigade's participation as soon as he arrived at Northwood as Land Commander on 9 April and on 14 April it had been earmarked with the Army's agreement.

The Brigade's problem was that it had been depleted by the loss of first 3 Para and then 2 Para to 3 Commando Brigade. This left only 1/7 Gurkha Rifles (1/7 GR) of the original battalions. The use of Nepalese troops in such a British venture might be expected to raise eyebrows. According to Nott, when told by Bramall that the Gurkhas would be going he said this could not be done:

> We are having frightful trouble holding things together in the United Nations and it is more than likely that the Indians will kick up a frightful fuss. It is just too risky politically to send the Gurkhas in my view.

Bramall objected that if the Government recoiled from sending a designated part of the strategic reserve now 'there will always be some reason for not sending the Gurkhas on future operations'. As Nott acknowledged, as an ex-Gurkha, that they would 'be mortified if we spoilt their chances', Bramall pulled rank as 'Colonel of your Regiment' (the 2nd Gurkhas, with which Nott had served) and told the Secretary of State 'that they must go and I am requiring your support to fight our corner with the Foreign Office.'[11]

Even so Nott saw this as a delicate matter and wanted no 'opportunity for speculation about Gurkha involvement,' or anything that carried the slightest risk of upsetting world opinion, particularly in the non-aligned countries. This worked only so long as the role of 5 Infantry Brigade was hypothetical. Once the logic was accepted so must be the political fall-out. Otherwise it would be a Brigade without battalions. The numbers were to be made up by 2nd Battalion Scots Guards (2 SG) and 1st Battalion Welsh Guards (1 WG). In addition to the three battalions, the 4th Field Regiment was sent. 5 Infantry Brigade did not include artillery, and strictly speaking 4th Field Regiment was committed to NATO. One battery (29) had already gone with 3 Commando Brigade. After some lobbying it was agreed that 97 battery would travel with 5 Brigade. In addition, an engineer regiment, an Army Air Corps squadron and logistic support travelled with the Brigade. On 16 April they were also told to get prepared through intensive training while waiting for a decision on deployment. These battalions were neither trained nor equipped for an amphibious landing (which was true for all Army battalions), but they could reinforce 3 Commando Brigade once a suitable bridgehead had been established, as well as relieving it as a garrison force. The choice led to some queries, in terms of fitness and their ability to convert from ceremonial duties. They were immediately sent to Wales to exercise.

Although these preparations had been made, the ground reinforcements issue had not been addressed seriously during the deliberations leading up to the Chequers meeting on 25 April, and nor was it raised then. On 27 April Fieldhouse made his request for the extra Brigade. His case opened with the intelligence that the enemy now had up to seven battalions ashore. In order to defeat the main enemy positions and maintain a strong reserve, Moore had requested at least eight battalions, with the reinforcements arriving two weeks after the main landing. Moore's line, agreed with Fieldhouse, was that there was sufficient force to establish a beachhead and develop operations ashore. He was, however, apprehensive that he could find himself:

> with no better strength than the enemy, investing him on Port Stanley, where he has shelter, and I am faced with the alternatives of either:
> a   Sitting out an Antarctic winter in the hills, without shelter and unable to relieve troops for adequate rest and recuperation, or
> b   Having to carry out a costly and bloody assault on the main enemy position without adequate numerical superiority.

If it was decided to send another brigade, then it would be unwise to rely on ships released after the main landing picking up battalions flown in to Ascension. They would then not arrive in the Falkland Islands before mid-June, so the recommendation was that they be embarked in fresh ships that would leave Britain on 5 May. Following this request, Lewin raised the issue with the Chiefs of Staff when they met that day. Immediately there was resistance. Bramall observed that the case for extra forces, either to break out of any bridgehead or subsequently to repossess the Islands, had yet to be made: a relief garrison was a longer-term matter. The decision was left pending a paper that had already been commissioned on a concept for follow-up land operations.

The Army's view was quite political. With the major use of force now under consideration would it be possible to keep the support of parliamentary, public and international opinion? There was also concern that the Brigade was not battle ready. The three battalions had not trained together and helicopters and artillery support would be limited. Bramall's preference was for a more gradu-ated approach, starting with intelligence gathering followed by harassment operations. This would allow for another three to four weeks before deciding upon whether to deploy 5 Infantry Brigade. On 28 April Bramall minuted his concerns: an increase of this size would raise the scale of the operation well beyond the level which the Chiefs and the War Cabinet had so far envisaged, and could generate serious political doubts. The timing was difficult because the role of the extra battalions would depend on the impact of the softening-up operations, the success of the initial landing, as well as diplomatic manoeu-vring, while the logistic bill would certainly be large.

That afternoon the Chiefs met again with Fieldhouse to discuss the issue further. Part of the difficulty was that CINCFLEET's orders did not look beyond a successful landing, but he had to assume that his mission would be to repossess the Falkland Islands. His view was that he had to plan for a short, sharp decisive action because the Task Force was unlikely to win a campaign of attrition. The combined effects of enemy action, deteriorating weather and progressively unserviceable equipment would erode the capability of his forces in a prolonged campaign. Yet his present force was numerically too weak to ensure rapid success beyond the limited aim of Operation SUTTON: even with the additional three battalions he would only have a small margin of superiority. If the Argentines conserved their sea and air forces until a landing had been made and then launched a major attack when Britain's forces were ashore and at their most vulnerable, it was inevitable that some losses would be suffered, and so it was essential that a proper reserve was immediately available, either to reinforce the landing if that operation proved difficult, or to enable such a landing to be exploited rapidly. He could not afford a three-week delay in reinforcement.

Bramall remained unconvinced. He accepted the military logic of Fieldhouse's case but still doubted whether the situation merited a military operation on the scale now envisaged. It was possible that the operation could be contained within the scope of the forces that had already been allotted to it. This was a proposal for a major, high-profile and demanding effort when diplomacy, the weather or inadequate tactical reconnaissance might still mean that authority would be withheld from an early landing. Before looking at a full-scale repossession operation against determined defence forces he wanted to explore the alternatives of a blockade and harassing operations by air attack and special forces to achieve an Argentine surrender without a landing, or else SUTTON plus harassing operations to induce a quick surrender. Beetham was also doubtful. For him the key question was the reduction in Argentine air and sea capability and the enforcement of the blockade. If those could be achieved then a landing might not be necessary: if they could not then a landing might be too hazardous. He shared Fieldhouse's concern but questioned whether the reinforcements requested would be sufficient or appropriate: he would make extra aircraft a higher priority than troops. Leach agreed that Fieldhouse should have sufficient resources for the task he was set, and that the whole operation should be short and sharp. Again he was unsure whether, if further land operations were necessary, more important than extra troops would be extra aircraft and possibly naval resources as well as an easing of the constraints on civilian casualties and damage. He doubted whether one extra brigade would effectively increase the necessary pressure. The meeting was therefore inconclusive. They would return to it the next day.

Later that day Lewin, Cooper and Fieldhouse met with Nott without the Chiefs of Staff. The Secretary of Defence was warned that if this issue was to be taken forward the politicians would not have long for their decision, with the availability of sea lift the driving factor. The liner *Queen Elizabeth II (QEII)* had been identified as the likely carrier: her return from a cruise on 3 May provided the opportunity to take her up. Employing the country's best-known cruise liner added to the political sensitivity of the matter. With such a step change in military provision under consideration Nott warned that the Prime Minister would need to be alerted as soon as possible. She might yet have to respond to Haig's final proposals and the feasibility of the military options could play a critical role. If it all looked like getting difficult and dangerous then there might even be an argument for delaying the imminent departure of the amphibious force from Ascension. If it was necessary to stagger the departure, so as to give it a lower profile, then the slower LSLs could leave first and the rest of the amphibious force could wait another day, with scant delay to the timetable. Lewin and Cooper tentatively approached Clive Whitmore, the Prime Minister's Private Secretary, to ascertain how she would respond for a request to use the *QEII*. His view was that if the military case was made she would accept it. This turned out to be the case. The Prime Minister was surprised to receive such a substantial and politically sensitive request so late in the day although she was, as always, loath to deny the military what they said they needed. When the eventual announcement came there was no political storm.

When the Chiefs returned to the issue the next day they were informed that Thatcher as well as Nott were now aware of the possibility that 5 Infantry Brigade would need to be sent and that the War Cabinet had added it to the agenda for the next day. Even though the concept of follow-on operations had yet to be sorted out, the case for reinforcements now depended on the problems associated with establishing a beachhead, and the lack of any margin for set-backs. An extra Brigade, plus appropriate combat support and Harrier aircraft and helicopters, would provide a small margin of superiority. The Chiefs now agreed that Fieldhouse's request should be met, and soon, so that the extra forces would arrive some two to three weeks after the main landing. The discussion was short. The difficulty of the issue was underlined by the fact that it was not until 2 May, the last minute, that the War Cabinet actually authorised the extra Brigade. The public relations line was to be that the move was being made to position reserves nearer the operational area. The Defence Secretary's reinforcement proposals were approved and it was reluctantly accepted that these made the requisitioning of the *QEII* unavoidable.

The proposed order of battle for 5 Infantry Brigade would be 3,961 men, including 552 as third line support; 1,067 tons ammunition; 1,129 tons supplies (for 35 days); 205 vehicles; and 19 helicopters. The *QEII* and two Ro-Ro ships, *Baltic Ferry* and *Nordic Ferry*, were earmarked, together with RFA *Engadine* and the *Atlantic Conveyor*'s sister ship *Atlantic Causeway* to carry support helicopters. The *QEII*, with a troop capacity of 3,000, was the last large British passenger vessel available. The alternatives were either much smaller or in foreign ownership. Because only these ships were available 5 Infantry Brigade had to be slimmed down so that it could fit. This 'slimline' Brigade reduced the force by some 1,000 men and the quantity of vehicles and freight support. It was required to reach the Falkland Islands by 28 May.

By 8 May, the concept of air operations included a requirement for a further six Harrier GR3 to augment the six already embarked on the *Atlantic Conveyor*. They were required to provide close air support, reconnaissance and limited air defence. Because there was now a risk that the carriers would be overloaded these Harriers had to be able to operate from shore, and so with them would have to go point air defence and supporting ground equipment, along with 450 personnel.

The majority of the personnel would travel in the *QEII*, sailing on 12 May, with the bulk of support equipment, vehicles and stores travelling in *Atlantic Causeway*, sailing from Devonport on 13/14 May. Another vessel would have to be found for the aircraft, possibly one already deployed, unloaded at the Falkland Islands and then sailing to Ascension to pick up the Harriers. Every effort was being made to minimise the degradation of missile stocks pending the arrival of new missiles from America by flying them to Ascension as late as possible. Lewin sought Nott's immediate approval, and this was given on 10 May.

Although the decision had been to approve only a 'slimmed down' 5 Infantry Brigade, with a combat and logistic support element able to sustain the brigade for up to 14 days, on 10 May Lewin told Nott that Fieldhouse had requested that this element should be brought up to a level where it could support operations for up to 30 days. This would entail the additional movement of 355 soldiers, 200 tons of freight and up to 100 vehicles. All units of this 'follow-on' element were currently at seven days' notice to move and could embark in shipping provisionally earmarked to sail on 17 May. When giving his approval, Nott suggested that the public presentation of this further deployment should be low key, with the emphasis being that these additional elements were an integral part of 5 Brigade, and were not 'additional' reinforcements.

15

THREATS TO THE TASK FORCE

Argentine submarines

Attention had to be paid not only to preparing for British initiatives but also to guarding against those taken by Argentina. By Thursday 15 April the UK believed that three of the four Argentine submarines, though unlocated, had been at sea for several days, and at 1630 London time on that day Nott brought to an ad hoc group of ministers and senior officials meeting with the Prime Minister information that an Argentine submarine was probably already active in the MEZ and might shortly be relieved by another. They discussed varying the ROE for the British SSNs about to reach the area. MoD's initial proposal was that 'any submarine found within the MEZ should be presumed to be an Argentine submarine, and might be attacked.' The FCO was nervous that there might be other submarines in the MEZ – perhaps Soviet (which would be nuclear) or those of other nations (Brazil and Chile were the only possible candidates, both equipped with conventional submarines). FCO's principal motivation at this stage was to avoid the sinking of any Argentine ship while the Haig mission was still in progress, and both Pym and FCO officials were uneasy that 'there are those in MoD who will want to bounce us into over-hasty decisions.'

MoD's advice was that SSNs could distinguish between nuclear and conventional, but the 15 April meeting postponed making any change to the ROE pending demarches, which were made to both the USSR and Brazil (assurances from Chile may already have been received). Given the delicate stage of Haig's mediation it had been agreed following the ad hoc meeting that the Secretary of State should be informed of the British concerns about Argentine submarines; Nott therefore sent him an appropriate message, commenting that 'I felt that you should know this immediately as you will appreciate the very real dangers.' As soon as Nott's message was received the State Department checked with the Argentine Foreign Ministry, and through Costa Mendez received an assurance from Admiral Anaya that there were no Argentine submarines in the Exclusion Zone and that firm orders had been given to the submarines not to enter it. Neither the UK nor the US defence establishment accepted these bland assurances at face value.

MoD assessed that a submarine (tentatively identified as the *San Luis*) had intended to enter the MEZ, but was now holding some 60 km outside it; indeed Lewin minuted Nott that 'it would seem that your message to Al Haig and his approach to Costa Mendez has borne fruit'. The Americans did not seem to think that the submarine could have reached the MEZ by this time. Pym was concerned that MoD's original conclusion that a submarine was already in the MEZ had gone beyond the available evidence; he was also worried that Haig might feel that the British were deliberately exaggerating the issue in order to raise the temperature. He was re-assured that MoD had reached a fair conclusion on the evidence then available, and that the same evidence had subsequently reached the Americans whose analysis paralleled that of the British.

By 18 April, although no Argentine warships appeared to be testing the MEZ, three of Argentina's four submarines were believed to have been at sea for about a week. There was a disturbing lack of information on their precise whereabouts. Any one of them could be operating within the MEZ, and there were reports that the *Santa Fe* had been given orders for unspecified operations on 23 April. *Conqueror* reached the MEZ on 19 April, by which time there was evidence that the Argentine submarine *Santa Fe* had been despatched to conduct an (unknown) operation on 23 April (in fact in South Georgia). While these developments strengthened Leach's hand in pressing for the ROE to be altered to permit attack on any submarine identified as Argentine, on the other hand a report had come through that the two modern type 209 submarines (*Salta* and *San Luis*) had vibration problems with their periscopes and their torpedo tubes malfunctioned (though the JIC still judged them to be a 'moderate threat to British vessels in their close vicinity'). The FCO was still not keen, in part because 'present intelligence suggests that this is unlikely' but also because the sinking of any Argentine ship should be avoided if at all possible, so long as the Haig mission continued. ROE changes waited on the diplomatic enquiries. On 22 April the Embassy in Rio reported that all Brazilian submarines would be held within 200 miles of the Brazilian coast. The Embassy in Moscow had reminded the Soviet Union of the implications of the MEZ, though no similar guarantee was provided by the USSR. On this basis the rule was promulgated that 'any submarine detected, not classified nuclear, may be presumed to be Argentine and may be attacked'.

The possible presence of Argentine submarines kept the Task Force on its toes. Each day after the departure of the Carrier Group from Ascension there were three or four possible contacts with a submarine requiring investigation. On 25 April there were seven such detections, leading in one case to a Sea King dropping a Mk46 torpedo and one depth charge, although it was later assessed as probably being a whale. Indeed as a result of such anxieties the Atlantic whale population suffered badly during the course of the campaign. The news that day from South Georgia about the attacks on the

Santa Fe simplified the submarine intelligence picture. The *San Luis*'s general position north of the MEZ was known while the *Salta* was reported either in harbour or local waters.

Reconnaissance aircraft

The idea of a feint towards Buenos Aires, to persuade the enemy to react, reveal his battle plans, and provide an opportunity for the attrition of his forces had been raised by Woodward during the meetings of 16 April, with the possible inclusion of the amphibious group, much to the horror of Thompson and Clapp. The idea still lingered with a proposal that just the carrier group, comprising the *Hermes, Invincible, Glamorgan, Broadsword, Alacrity, Yarmouth, Olmeda* and *Resource*, should aim to become more overt on the later stages of its journey. This idea too did not last. On 19 April Woodward ordered a direct passage to the Falkland Islands. Politically an early presence in the Exclusion Zone was required and before the ships arrived it was important to avoid unnecessary mishap. In case the Argentines had anything planned Woodward signalled that it should be assumed that Argentine units 'are closing the CVBG (Carrier Battle Group)' and could reach it by 22 April. The task group was 'to be in all respects ready for action at this time'.

With this in mind, Woodward was unsurprisingly concerned when it became apparent that Argentina had managed to work out, earlier than anticipated, the location of the *Hermes* group. It had been assumed that Argentine surveillance aircraft would not pick the group up until 23 April at the earliest, but two days before that, at 1225Z on 21 April, an Argentine aircraft was detected on radar at 150 miles to the west closing the force. It may be that these flights were triggered by Haig's warnings to the Argentines on 18 and 19 April of imminent British action.[1] On 20 April the Argentines tasked Boeing 707s, designed for transport rather than reconnaissance, to search for the carrier battle group.[2]

A Sea Harrier was scrambled, and after the target had passed within 20 miles at over 25,000 feet and turned away to the south, it was intercepted and identified as a Boeing 707 with Argentine Air Force markings, carrying no weapons. The next day Boeing 707s twice came across the group. In each case they were intercepted and identified by Sea Harriers. After the first sighting, on 21 April, Woodward noted:

> The arrival of 707 recce aircraft gives me the feeling that the sooner
> I can concentrate my force, the better. ROE to deal with him
> woefully inadequate. Maybe it does not matter at this stage.

The sighting the following day, led him to request a 'leak' of an 'intention' to shoot if an aircraft got within 25 miles in future. He also began to wonder whether he might face air attack earlier than expected and wanted to get his ships together quickly so that they could work on preparations for air defence. A group, led by *Brilliant*, had been sent forward in order to ensure that there were units close to the EZ should any cease-fire be called. This group had not been detected and had been ordered to remain covert until the carrier group could join it on 25 April. Its commander, Captain John Coward, was inclined to continue south into the zone but Woodward instructed it to wait and 'stay out of trouble.' Now he wanted to bring it back for the air defence exercises. This was not agreed. A firm line went from MoD to Northwood on 23 April: 'for overriding political and presentational reasons the advanced group must not turn back'. Furthermore, at this point the South Georgia operation was at a delicate stage and Fieldhouse's main concern was that the *Brilliant* group get in position to provide support if necessary. Even with his group Woodward realised that it might be fatal to be caught in the middle of an air defence exercise by an Argentine carrier-launched raid: 'Nevertheless, we shall have to try since the Type 42s have never yet worked with *Invincible* and the Sea Harriers.' On 26 April, the Task Force managed an air defence exercise. Although 'fairly chaotic' many lessons were learnt. Admiral Woodward signed off his diary that day: 'Still have all too little intelligence on whereabouts of opposition surface forces. Uncomfortable.' The surveillance also stimulated a wider analysis about how best to clarify the ROE so as to avoid politically damaging incidents while being able to deal with attempted pre-emptive attacks. On 21 April Woodward had promulgated as a precautionary measure the codeword CONFISTICATE, which would give authority to open fire in extreme circumstances regardless of the ROE in force.[3]

The daily Argentine surveillance continued. Chaff was laid, to give an impression of a much larger force, and the intruders were intercepted but not attacked. Woodward observed that while it was true that 707s were not carrying weapons of their own, and that they would not normally be classed as long-range military patrol aircraft, if that was the role that they were effectively performing they should be treated as such in the rules of engagement (they were in fact equipped with Israeli-provided Sigint reconnaissance systems). He was assured that the Chiefs of Staff were taking up the issue for early decision by ministers: 'Pressures and potential dangers fully appreciated here'. Lewin made the point to the War Cabinet that by shadowing the Task Force, the 707s could direct combat units, including submarines, to attack positions. He proposed that all Argentine aircraft engaged in surveillance should be treated as combat aircraft. Their role could be verified by electronic means or by a Sea Harrier interception. If a 707 did not turn back after internationally accepted signalling, the Harriers should have authority to fire across its path and, if that had no effect, attack.

The issue raised, once again, the balance between potential military and political harm. The FCO was uncertain about the advantages this surveillance gave to Argentina but very clear politically about how the Argentines might exploit the downing of a civilian aircraft. They would undoubtedly claim this was on a normal transatlantic flight with a filed flight plan. At this sensitive moment, with Pym visiting Washington, the diplomats wanted a more cautious approach. Any suspicious aircraft could be harassed but not attacked, while the Argentines should be warned, through the Swiss, that surveillance aircraft would be treated as hostile and dealt with accordingly. The Attorney General, who was personally prepared to go further than harassment, also urged getting a warning out as soon as possible, irrespective of whatever ministers decided to do about authorising attacks on surveillance aircraft. This was agreed on the morning of 23 April by senior civil servants and the First Sea Lord. A submission to ministers on offensive action would have to be delayed until the legal position was clarified, but meanwhile it was hoped that the warning itself would serve to deter further flights. There is an interesting hint of dissatisfaction in the Prime Minister's annotations on the record of this decision, wondering who was representing her at the meeting and putting exclamation marks beside a note that she had been informed of the matter and was content. This indicates the difficulty she faced in keeping up with all the various aspects of the conflict with only a few civil servants working directly to her.

The announcement of 7 April had contained the critical rider that the measures described were 'without prejudice to the right of the UK to take whatever additional measures may be needed in exercise of its right of self-defence, under Article 51 of the United Nations Charter'. According to the FCO Legal Adviser, Article 51 provided sufficient legal cover for all likely contingencies, as Britain was now countering a blatant act of aggression. Any Argentine forces encountered en route by the Task Force could be presumed to be acting in support of the aggression, wherever they were encountered. There was then a separate question as to whether it was desirable to issue a warning designed to dissuade Argentine forces from approaching the Task Force. Although there was an argument that such an announcement might be taken as a dare by the Argentine Navy, then to be challenged out of national pride, the Naval Staff took the view that it would underline British resolve, provide a fillip to the morale of those serving with the Task Force, and might put Britain in a better position politically in the aftermath of any engagement. The FCO were happy with the principle of the announcement, but wanted the timing geared to the Haig mediation effort.

On 23 April a confidential warning was conveyed to the Argentines via the Swiss. This was delivered in Buenos Aires at 1720 (Local) on 23 April. Parsons recommended that the text should be circulated in the UN lest Argentina do so first, citing it as evidence of Britain's aggressive intentions. Whitehall followed this advice and at the same time announced in London the fact of the warning:

In announcing the establishment of a maritime exclusion zone around the Falkland Islands, HMG made it clear that this measure was without prejudice to the right of the UK to take whatever additional measures may be needed in the exercise of its right of self defence under Article 51 of the UN Charter. In this connection, HMG now wishes to make clear that any approach on the part of Argentine warships, including submarines, naval auxiliaries, or military aircraft which could amount to a threat to interfere with the mission of British forces in the South Atlantic will encounter the appropriate response. All Argentine aircraft including civil aircraft engaging in surveillance of these British forces will be regarded as hostile and are liable to be dealt with accordingly.

In connection with the South Georgia operation bolder ROE were also agreed: there the force commander had discretion to shoot down any Argentine surveillance flight over South Georgia waters. The political risks attached to a 707 being shot down over South Georgia were not so great, as the only possible explanation for it being in such a vulnerable position would be the ongoing military operation. It suited both the FCO and MoD if the policy was first put to the test over South Georgia. If the 23 April statement served to deter then that was also good to know and helpful operationally; if it failed to do so then action against a 707 might reinforce general deterrence against the use of these aircraft for surveillance elsewhere. It would still be a quite different matter to shoot down a 707 over the high seas, even after the warning had been issued, and so the FCO recommended against authorisation, although they would be prepared to reconsider if the flights became more regular.

That evening an incident occurred, or almost occurred, that had they known about it, would have reinforced the FCO's anxiety. On the basis of his discussions with Northwood on 22 April, conducted through the inadequate Defence Secure Speech System (DSSS) voice links, Woodward understood incorrectly that he had in fact received permission to attack an intruding aircraft so long as it came sufficiently close and could be positively identified. He was expecting the conversation soon to be confirmed by signals and was therefore fully prepared to engage as soon as the identification was made. Unsuccessful attempts were then made to intercept incoming 707s on the evening of 22 April and the next morning. On the evening of 23 April an aircraft was detected heading straight for the Task Force, with radars switched on, and was soon picked up by the Sea Dart air defence system on board *Invincible*. In the context Woodward was prepared to attack. He was told that there was no record of a scheduled commercial flight, but then it was noted that the aircraft appeared to be on a direct line from Durban to Rio de Janeiro. Barely a minute away from firing the missile, he held back to allow a Sea Harrier to make a visual identification: it was a Brazilian airliner.

Two days later, on 25 April, a concerned Fieldhouse signalled Woodward:

> Brazilian press report ... airlines DC10 intercepted by Sea Harrier ... Aircraft said to have approached from behind and above before overtaking and settling 50 metres to port. Passengers alleged to have been frightened. Request comments.

Woodward replied:

> Air radar contact detected 120 ZZ 250nm at 231910Z no IFF (Identification Friend or Foe) response. Contact closing force heading 290 at 485 kts Fl 350. Visident [Visual Identification] by SHAR [Sea Harrier] at 1930 as Brazilian Airlines DC10/30. SHAR hauled off after careful close look on parallel course to port in perfect VMC [Visual Meteorological Conditions]. Aircraft registration PP/VMD. Hence press report correct. Not enemy, not reported. Inconvenience to passengers underwear regretted unless any of them were Argentinian.

In his memoirs Woodward mused in a less relaxed manner about the dire political consequences if he had failed to hesitate.[4]

When Woodward's new instructions did arrive later that evening (23 April) they were not as expected. An Argentine civil or military aircraft positively identified as carrying out surveillance of the Task Force should be warned off by an intercepting Sea Harrier, including firing across the intruder's path, but in no circumstances should it be fired at even if it failed to clear the area (defined as radius 40 miles from the nearest British unit). The Admiral amended the detail of this instruction to substitute close harassment for firing across the intruder's path, which could be pointless because of the lack of tracer. The next day, 24 April, he signalled back to Fieldhouse that his new ROE had been received. They would be:

> correctly observed despite facts that lack of tracer ammunition renders shot across bows nugatory, 707 height pushes SHAR performance to limit and use of guns puts sidewinder at some risk of damage. I was taught however by uncomfortable experience as a prefect at prep school never to issue a threat unless I was prepared to carry it out immediately my bluff was called. Request permission to take final step to splash Arg recce if all previous warnings are ignored since I assess that the occasion that the recce finally does come on in could presage a carrier strike. 40nm is of course totally inadequate to stop effective TACDI : 140nm would be more suitable though still less than can be achieved. I am sure no one can have forgotten the maxim 'Hack the Shad'.

Some 12 hours after the warning had been given to Argentina on 24 April there was another overflight of the Task Force. This led to a proposal that the warning should be repeated to Buenos Aires, but it was also decided on 25 April, now that the Argentines had had time to absorb the initial warning, to change the ROE so that 'If an Argentine (surveillance) aircraft fails to depart after warning action ... has been taken it is to be destroyed.' It was later decided that a further warning, especially in the light of events in South Georgia, might seem feeble and unnecessary. It was also reported that the surveillance flights had stopped. The Argentines had been encouraged by the lack of attacks on their reconnaissance aircraft: once they realised that they could no longer be expected to have a free run they abandoned the flights.[5]

In addition to the Argentine overflights on occasion the Task Force was overflown by Soviet Naval BEAR maritime reconnaissance aircraft, operating out of Luanda, Angola. The Soviet deployments there were part of Soviet Cold War operations and were not especially associated with the Falklands. It was also assumed that British vessels were regularly monitored by Soviet reconnaissance satellites. With this in mind, the Task Force conducted anti-surveillance measures, including deceptive formations and decoys. Although there were occasional allegations, there was never any evidence that Soviet intelligence was passed to Argentina.

16

RETAKING SOUTH GEORGIA

While all this was going on, attitudes towards the use of force were being shaped and reshaped by the effort to retake South Georgia. This at first seemed to be surprisingly difficult and then, in the end, turned out to be surprisingly easy. The island had been identified as the first possible objective for the Task Force almost as soon as it set sail. Indeed some thought that this might be all that could be achieved militarily if the Falklands Islands themselves turned out to be beyond recovery. At least having South Georgia back in British hands would be an assertion of sovereignty and a bargaining chip for later negotiations. Even as a step on the way to the recovery of all the occupied British territory, a successful operation would boost morale and keep the pressure on Argentina. Nott later described the operation as 'pure politics'. The Naval Staff and Northwood, he recalled, saw the operation as a distraction. He credits Lewin as understanding the need of the War Cabinet to have some activity to fill the gap while waiting for the amphibious force to arrive.[1]

There was still a risk. If the operation turned out to be protracted and bloody then it could be counter-productive, undermining both morale and Britain's international position. Even if all went smoothly there was an argument that the effort would dissipate resources and delay the main Falklands operations. The map gave some comfort to those arguing that the diversion to South Georgia would repay the effort. Located 800 miles to the southeast of the Falklands, it was believed, not wholly correctly, to be out of range for Argentine aircraft. The small Argentine garrison ought not to be able to resist a party of Marines once landed. Alternatively, it could even be blockaded into surrender. So long as these conditions of a small enemy force lacking air support held then the pros of the operation outweighed the cons. As early as 7 April a special task group, TG 317.9, was formed. The frigate *Plymouth* and destroyer *Antrim* detached from the main task group to rendezvous with RFA *Tidespring,* a large tanker. *Endurance* would later attach itself as it headed up from the south. *Plymouth* and *Tidespring* sailed from Ascension on 11 April, while *Antrim* followed behind after embarking Arctic clothing and equipment flown in from the United

Kingdom. M Company, 42 Commando would provide the landing force. In charge was Captain B Young of *Antrim*, one of the Navy's most experienced officers. As designated Land Force Commander, Major G Sheridan of 42 Commando was also unusually experienced after ten winters spent in Arctic Norway in addition to mountaineering in the Himalayas. SSN *Conqueror* was detailed to reach the area before the task group and act independently. The code name for the operation was PARAQUET. This appears as a misspelling of the tropical bird, Parakeet (or Paroquet in French). Members of the Task Force soon corrupted it to PARAQUAT, a weed poison, although the original remained the official designation.[2] On 10 April a separate cell was established at Northwood charged with developing a plan. With all eyes on the main Task Force and diplomatic negotiations, South Georgia had yet to become the subject of much outside speculation. The preference was to keep it that way to deny Argentina any advance warning. The level of secrecy was such that discussions were confined to the Prime Minister, Defence Secretary and the most senior commanders.

The plan

The plan depended on Argentina failing to provide reinforcements or any other significant support to the small garrison left on South Georgia at the start of April. Two Argentine groups were believed to be on the island: the 'sizeable' party of mixed military and civilian personnel who had landed illegally in Leith Harbour and 54 Marines involved in the assault at Grytviken on 3/4 April. Of these the Marines represented the most serious proposition: they could be equipped with mortars, hand-held anti-tank weapons, night vision aids, possibly some vehicles and an A3 Alouette helicopter, in addition to small arms. They had probably not been reinforced. It was true that the Argentine ships involved in the occupation could have carried far more troops than those apparently landed. The *Bahia Paraiso* alone had space for at least 120 passengers, but this had now left as had all the original ships connected with the Argentine operation without apparently leaving any reinforcements.

An offensive air threat from the Argentine mainland was discounted while one from Stanley depended on the runway there being extended. If that were done Canberras, Skyhawks and Mirages might just reach South Georgia at the extreme limits of their radius of action, but then only in daylight and good weather. Skyhawk A4Qs launched from the *25 de Mayo* would need to be launched from within 300nm of South Georgia, which would mean deploying to an area with a high SSN threat. At any rate the carrier was currently believed to be under repair in Puerto Belgrano following engine trouble. Reconnaissance of South Georgia by P2 and C130 aircraft either from the mainland or Stanley was possible, especially if the Argentines suspected the presence of a surface force, although the C130s were more likely to be committed to the re-supply of forces in the Falkland Islands. They were unlikely to paradrop troops or supplies due to weather conditions and terrain. Lastly, it was feasible that enemy submarines could operate in the South Georgia area. Two were believed to be on base at Mar del Plata and one at Puerto Belgrano. It was believed that the fourth (probably ex-US Guppy Class 2 *Santa Fe*) might have deployed on 9 April (in fact it had). It would take seven or more days to reach the South Georgia area if that was indeed its destination. As noted earlier by 15 April there was evidence that it had moved out of port.

All this encouraged the view that South Georgia would probably not be heavily defended. An informed diplomatic source had suggested that, faced with superior force levels, the Argentine garrison in South Georgia would offer only token resistance knowing that they could not expect any reinforcements. When, on 8 April, the Chiefs of Staff agreed that South Georgia should be repossessed as soon as possible, they stipulated that only those forces already assigned should be used for the operation, while recognising that subsequent intelligence might require a reappraisal of force levels. On 9 April Fieldhouse was ordered to produce an outline plan, keeping civilian casualties on the island to a minimum and causing the least detriment to all other operations in the South Atlantic. Fieldhouse set out his Order 2/82 for the repossession of South Georgia on 12 April 1982. The next day Bramall, having been briefed on the order, wondered whether the RM force despatched was adequate. He made this point strongly at a Chiefs of Staff meeting that day. The problem, acknowledged by his colleagues, was the lack of hard intelligence. The assigned force level allowed no margin for error. The first operation would set the tone for all that followed, and so they dare not fail on South Georgia. If better intelligence pointed to the need for more forces then these would be difficult to provide. *Hermes*, carrying an RM company group, could be diverted. Otherwise the task group could wait for the LSLs carrying 45 Commando. In either case the operation would be delayed. Diverting *Hermes* would breach the integrity of the Carrier Battle Group with implications for sea and air control around the Falkland Islands.

In fact the remedy had already been found in the form of D Squadron SAS. The high reputation enjoyed by the Special Forces, especially after the 1980 siege at the Iranian Embassy in London, had led to a number of proposals for their immediate deployment right at the start of the crisis. Proposals for dramatic action ranged from blowing up Argentine aircraft on the ground to attacks on oil rigs. Nott was said on 3 April to be 'firmly of the view that SAS/SBS deployed from SSNs will be the answer to winning back the Falklands.' On this particular proposition the Navy view – that any diversion of SSNs would detract from their main role of preventing Argentina reinforcing the Falklands by sea – prevailed. Nonetheless, this enthusiasm for Special Forces combined with the evident need to get advanced reconnaissance forces on the ground as soon as possible encouraged their early and piecemeal deployment. The SAS would be responsible for intelligence-gathering on land; the SBS for reconnoitring the beaches. D Squadron on standby for worldwide operations did not wait for official authorisation but flew to Ascension on 5 April, ready to join the *Fort Austin*. The SAS would have their own communication nets, including their own secure High Frequency and satellite links to the Hereford base, as well as a range of means of tactical communication. SBS units also flew to Ascension as well as sailing in the *Conqueror* on 5 April, and plans were made to take them on other SSNs. As the SAS plans developed it was envisaged that D Squadron would support operations in South Georgia, before moving on to offensive operations in the Falklands. G Squadron, which followed, arriving in Ascension on 20 April, would be responsible for the main reconnaissance operations on the Falklands.[3]

Major C Delves, Officer Commanding, D Squadron 22 SAS, advised Captain Young on *Antrim* that the latest intelligence on Argentine strength in South Georgia argued that the whole of his Squadron should be embarked, in addition to 2 SBS. Land force commander, Major Sheridan, with his own experience in extremely cold conditions, saw no need for the SAS, but was not consulted. When Young discussed Delves's proposal with Northwood he received a positive response. The added numbers would meet Bramall's concerns about the size of the force. The Chief of the General Staff declared himself reassured. The Chiefs were now satisfied that the operation was feasible in general terms and that the diversion of forces required should not prejudice CORPORATE. CINCFLEET's Operation Order 2/82 was passed to *Antrim* by Nimrod airdrop at 0930Z on 15 April, a method chosen to avoid breaking the radio silence considered essential in maintaining the secrecy of the operation. (None of the RN communications systems, except those to submarines, could transmit 'in the blind'.)

The embarked force of some 150 Royal Marines and 70 SAS would be landed in the three available helicopters, (one WESSEX 3 on *Antrim* and two WESSEX 5s on *Tidespring*), supported if necessary by naval gunfire, in order to capture Leith and Grytviken, neutralise Argentine communications in the area, capture or kill Argentine armed forces personnel, and arrest and remove civilians. This was to be done with the minimum loss of life and damage to property. In practice, avoiding damage to property, necessary because of future accommodation requirements, would be more limiting than avoiding civilian casualties. Other than Davidoff's men, the BAS people on the island, plus Cindy Buxton and Annie Price, who had been making a documentary for Anglian Television, were well away from both settlements.[4] CTF 317 would order initiation of the landing of covert reconnaissance, using SBS and SAS, and assault operations. The codeword for initiation was DANDELION. Young would be in tactical operational control and could withdraw his forces at anytime he considered a successful landing to capture Leith and Grytviken could not be achieved in the circumstances prevailing. Sheridan was in charge of land forces, although the arrival of Delves, also a Major, complicated the command arrangements. The SAS had a tradition of independent action and had their own communications with their headquarters.

En route to South Georgia Captain Young's team discussed many options, from simply pounding the Argentine garrison with naval gunfire, which would have contradicted the injunction to preserve property, to a direct amphibious assault against the Argentine positions, which risked heavy casualties. Sheridan preferred to rely on RM M Company to lead an assault on the main Argentine defences, following covert gathering of intelligence. He judged the marines to have more relevant experience in Mountain and Arctic Warfare operations than D Squadron. The SAS, however, pushed successfully for a leading role. D Squadron SAS 19 Troop (Mountain and Arctic Warfare) would be inserted by helicopter on to the western edge of the Fortuna Glacier with reconnaissance objectives at Leith, Husvik and Stromness, while 2 SBS RM would be taken to Hound Bay by helicopter or boat to reconnoitre Cumberland Bay and the approaches to Grytviken. After the intelligence had been gathered and correlated, the main landing envisaged covert night insertion of the RM M Company Group while the remaining SAS would conduct a daylight assault on the main Argentine defensive position.

Into position

Young's force had been put together from what was available. *Antrim* and *Plymouth* had been with SPRINGTRAIN off Gibraltar and their supplies had been run down, and although some replenishment had taken place much more was needed, especially for an operation of uncertain duration which would require the accommodation of large numbers of Marines. The group now planning the operation had never worked together as a team before, and were uncertain what to expect when they arrived in South Georgia. As the planning progressed it also became apparent that the personnel and their supplies were not always embarked on the appropriate ships and so there would need to be substantial cross decking. There was, as so often with Britain's first forays into war, an improvised quality to the whole operation.

On 12 April the HQ/signals elements and two troops of D Squadron SAS, together with all SAS equipment/ammunition and the personnel of the surgical team, were transferred from *Fort Austin* to *Antrim*. One troop of SAS was also transferred to *Plymouth*, and the surgical team's stores and equipment to *Tidespring*. It was a complicated operation, with decent weather but poor aircraft availability, and was not finally completed until early the next morning, when *Fort Austin*, which had only stayed for replenishment, was detached to join the rest of the Task Force. The next day

Endurance rendezvoused with TG 317.9, in urgent need of fuel. Favourable weather conditions made it possible for it to be refuelled by *Tidespring*. Now complete, the task group proceeded south at *Endurance's* best speed of 13.5 knots.

Young was concerned about the dual role of *Tidespring*. Because it now carried the main landing force, helicopter and troop elements, it had an operational role that could require it to get close to South Georgia. If as a result of this role it was lost then the other ships would have no means of refuelling. Fuel might also become short if ships were held back during the initial stages of reconnaissance, and these became protracted, or if the landing had to be delayed because of bad weather. Sheridan's indication that up to five days might be needed for covert reconnaissance added to this concern. To Young this argued for the group topping up with fuel before action commenced and also for extra tanker support. He therefore proposed that *Brambleleaf* be diverted for pump-over to a waiting position 500 miles northeast of South Georgia. If his ships could refuel before the initial reconnaissance landings, *Tidespring* would not then be prevented from undertaking quick reaction operations if required. This seemed even more prudent when *Endurance* warned that the forecast weather en route and the presence of icebergs would severely limit the speed of advance. If the whole operation required at least a week, *Tidespring* might be caught with insufficient fuel.

On 16 April Young therefore recommended that the start of the reconnaissance operations be delayed from 21 April to 23 April. At first he appeared to have been granted his wish. *Brambleleaf* was diverted towards South Georgia, with its estimated time of arrival on 21 April so an early pump-over would delay the landings to first light on 23 April. CINCFLEET's signal of 17 April even spoke of 'capitalising on your later date of approach'. However, on 18 April, Sir David Hallifax, Fieldhouse's Chief of Staff, informed Young on the secure speech system that politically there was no scope for delay. Once again nervousness in Whitehall over the implications of Haig's efforts argued for pressing ahead. Young had to be in position for the original date of 21 April. The pump-over was now to take place as early as possible after the initial landings. *Brambleleaf* would then be released to support other elements of the Task Force.

The route to South Georgia had been governed by reference to the range of Argentine reconnaissance aircraft as well as any shore-based attack aircraft (Super Etendard, A4 and Canberras) presumably, but not necessarily, operating from Stanley, along with the need to avoid ice. Concerned now with fuel consumption, Young's group changed to the direct track for South Georgia, raising the risk of an earlier entry into Argentine air reconnaissance cover. Assuming favourable weather conditions, the group would arrive 30 miles north of Cumberland Bay on the morning of 21 April and after inserting the reconnaissance teams would conduct a pump-over with *Brambleleaf* the next day.

The following days were focused on detailed planning and briefing, and in completing a considerable inter-ship exchange of personnel and equipment 'to get the right people and things into the right places at the right time'. It was decided that the insertion of the SAS troop on the Fortuna Glacier would be conducted by Wessex 3/5 helicopters from *Antrim* and *Tidespring* from a position 10 miles north of Antarctic Bay. Meanwhile, *Plymouth* and *Endurance* would proceed to the east of the island to land 2 SBS by helicopter/boat into Hound Bay. During the latter stages of the approach on 20 April, the weather started to worsen with rapidly falling pressure and wind building to a northwesterly of 25 knots. Despite this, a sufficient speed of advance was maintained to reach the launch positions on time.

ROE

The recapture of South Georgia, as the first major operation of the British campaign, threw into relief many of the complex political and military issues inevitably raised by such an undertaking. These were addressed through considerations of ROE. On 15 April a paper was discussed at a Chiefs of Staff meeting on the three phases of the operation: transit toward South Georgia on the high seas; transit within the declared Argentine 'defence zone'; and execution of the operation. The next day a revised paper was put before the War Cabinet. There were no major issues with the first phase. Here the overriding concern was to avoid provocation but to respond to aggression with 'firmness'. Minimum force should be used by surface vessels in response to any clear intent to engage although all units could assist in the defence of any unit being attacked. Maritime international law was not to be infringed unless commanders deemed it necessary to achieve their stated goals. SSNs should remain covert, while reverting to evasion if detected, engaging with the enemy only if attacked first. Lewin felt this involved little risk, as an encounter on the high seas was inherently much less likely than one in the MEZ round the Falkland Islands.

The second set of instructions concerned transit within the declared Argentine 'Defence Zone' of 200nm around South Georgia. The aim here was to show sufficient force to dissuade Argentine units from enforcing this zone. Lewin amended the draft memorandum to allow surface vessels to take 'any necessary action against positively identified Argentine ships, whether naval or merchant, and Argentine combat aircraft'. Non-Argentine merchant ships should be warned off. Any hostile submarines could be attacked if they demonstrated hostile intent. Unless hostile intent had been demonstrated, no ship would be attacked without first being ordered to turn back, then being 'headed-off', and, only if that failed, being warned by a shot across the bows. The SSNs would be allowed to attack any positively identified Argentine submarine, warship or naval auxiliary showing hostile intent. Initially Leach had wanted all ships attacked without warning. Both the FCO and senior MoD civilians had been anxious that attacks on merchant shipping without warning might be construed as a war crime. Legal advice confirmed the potential criminality of attacks on merchant ships without warning, leaving aside the political risks. To Vice Admiral Herbert, in charge of the SSNs, these ROEs were therefore 'dove' not 'hawk'. To those in the Task Group, assuming only minutes' warning of attack with no more than fleeting opportunities for detection and neutralization in the prevailing weather and environmental conditions, these discussions on ROE carried with them a degree of unreality.

The final set of instructions concerned the execution of operation PARA-QUET. The aim was to repossess South Georgia. British surface vessels could take any action necessary to achieve this aim against ships and aircraft positively identified as Argentine. Any submarine, which demonstrated hostile intent, could also be attacked. The SSNs would observe the same rules as laid out in the second set of instructions. Lewin explained to the War Cabinet that an enemy adopting a firing position would clearly demonstrate 'hostile intent' and it would not therefore 'be obligatory for British ships to allow a potential enemy to fire first'. He was worried that surface ships, unlike submarines, would have difficulty assessing whether a submarine they encountered was nuclear or conventional or indeed Argentine. Hesitation, however, could put them at risk. This might be an acceptable risk for the time being but he warned that: 'if the diplomatic situation became less delicate he might wish to seek Ministerial authority for less restrictive rules of engagement in such cases'.

The War Cabinet approved the ROE for the first phase at once and they were implemented immediately. The second set would take effect when British forces entered the declared Argentine 'Defence Zone,' then expected to be on 20 April. The third set would apply if and when British forces began Operation PARAQUET, then projected for 21 April. MoD argued successfully for one revision to the established ROEs, as the advanced group of the Task Force got closer to Argentine waters. Since the Argentine fleet was now at sea in strength, the Chiefs of Staff, at the urging of the Navy, sought 'some enhancement' of the Rules to provide British forces with 'sufficient discretion to counter the threat'. Argentine warships, equipped with the 25-mile range Exocet surface-to-surface missile, could pick out targets with ordinary surveillance or navigational radar, giving no warning of the imminence of attack. There would be the same lack of warning if an Argentine submarine fired its torpedoes. It would only become known when the target was hit. The proposal was that when naval forces passed 35° south, the latitude of Buenos Aires, they would be allowed to:

> attack any positively identified Argentine naval ship, combat aircraft or submarine which demonstrates hostile intent by coming

within 25 miles of a British unit. All units of an Argentine force may be attacked if one of them initiates an attack on a British unit. Merchant ships may not be attacked. Maritime International Law is not to be broken unless necessary in order to achieve aim.

Naval forces north of 35° south should 'avoid provocation but ... respond to aggression with sufficient firmness to ensure safe transit'. To accomplish this, units could also attack any Argentine units that came within 25 miles, but minimum force was to be used. While the public warning to Argentina on 23 April had been prompted by the surveillance aircraft issue, it was also judged helpful in the context of South Georgia, that it had been stated that 'any approach on the part of Argentine warships, including submarines, naval auxiliaries, or military aircraft which could amount to a threat to interfere with the mission of the British Forces in the South Atlantic will encounter the appropriate response.'

Decision

The planning for PARAQUET took place against a backdrop of intense diplomatic activity. On 18 April the possibility of a breakthrough in the Haig mediation still seemed possible. The Chiefs of Staff recognised that in these circumstances the War Cabinet might wish to consider alternatives to an assault on the defended Grytviken, such as a landing at Leith or a remote part of the island to re-establish a British presence. Perhaps the 15 remaining BAS personnel on the island might suffice as evidence of Britain's continuing presence. The next day, 19 April, the War Cabinet met during the afternoon to consider the unacceptable document drawn up during Haig's discussions in Buenos Aires and, at the same time, whether to go forward with operation PARAQUET under agreed ROE. The decisions were to respond negatively to the latest proposals and that the operation should proceed, with the aim of minimum Argentine casualties to an extent consistent with the safety of British forces.

The decision was not straightforward. We have already noted some senior military concern that the operation represented a distraction from the main aim of getting as quickly as possible in strength to the Falklands. Within the FCO there were other objections. One official, in a less than accurate description, queried the value of an asset consisting of a 'string of volcanic islands, none longer than 10 miles across, most inaccessible from sea, no harbours, virtually useless.' It could not sustain human habitation and there was little possibility for economic development. There was minimal strategic interest and it was not even essential for the BAS's research. Preserving it would require the stationing of a land force. Recapturing it appeared to contradict the stress on self-determination in the negotiations:

It would be difficult to explain internationally why, when our public position is based primarily on self-determination for the Islanders, we were so intent on retaining a piece of uninhabited real estate. Ultimately, if South Georgia were the one remaining issue between us and the Argentines, we would not expect South American states to support Argentine pretensions as strongly over South Georgia as over the Falkland Islands themselves. But before that stage is reached our insistence on maintaining our position in South Georgia would introduce an element of puzzlement about our real objectives which would tend to obscure the simplicity of our self-determination argument. In UN terms any prejudice to our self-determination argument could cost us votes; how many we cannot forecast.

Hand-written comments reinforced the sceptical tone – 'virtually useless to HMG or anyone else apart from krill possibilities within 200nm if such could be established'. While such arguments carried little weight in the War Cabinet, there was a wider appreciation that this delicate diplomatic situation would not be helped by any loss of Argentine life and if the international community drew the conclusion that Britain was deliberately escalating the conflict.

The political anxieties gathering around the operation were reflected in instructions sent by the Chiefs of Staff to CTF 317 on 20 April:

While not overriding the primacy of military considerations and safety of our own forces, the Force Commander should know that the political needs of the present situation would best be served by a quick clean operation with maximum prisoners and minimum dead. If it comes to a conflict of priorities speed is secondary.

Fieldhouse took the view that this message was not helpful, and so it was not relayed to Young.

Politically therefore this was a delicate moment. So long as there was a possibility of a negotiated settlement there was considerable sentiment in Whitehall and Westminster (including in the Conservative Party) that nothing should be done to put it in jeopardy. The outcome of a war could not be known for certain, other than it was bound to be bloody for all concerned, and it was supposed that the more bloody it became the more public support would subside. Those of this view saw Pym as their champion, and were encouraged by his speech to the Commons on 21 April which stressed the Government's desire for a peaceful settlement, and even appeared to suggest that no shots would be fired until the hopes of such a settlement might be dashed.

There was, however, at least within the Governing party, an alternative view that there could be no compromises over substance with Argentina and that it was vital to prepare the country for war. Alan Clark MP wrote in his diary of how following Pym's statement 'groups of MPs were standing about in the lobby, grumbling and speculating about what all this meant.' Pym sought to calm nerves by returning to the Commons later to correct the impression he might have given. Shots might indeed have to be fired before negotiations were concluded. All this left the Conservative Party, Clark noted, 'very prickly and unsure of itself. I dread a sell out. I am sure we are being slowly set up for one.'[5] George Gardiner MP later recalled how a number of right-wing MPs met that evening and contemplated resigning the Tory whip 'if the merest fraction of sovereignty was to be ceded to the Argentinian aggressor'. A deputation went directly to Cecil Parkinson, as a member of the War Cabinet and Party Chairman, and warned him of 20 to 30 resignations. Parkinson promised to convey their warning to the Prime Minister.[6] Clark, who was part of the delegation, reports Parkinson 'more or less' saying to this group that the Task Force would be 'going into South Georgia in the next couple of days or so'.[7]

Nott's concern with Pym's speech was not that he feared a sell out but that the Government might be misleading the public, their supporters and possibly themselves by not drawing attention to the improbability of a settlement. Expressions of continuing interest in a settlement might allow the Government to hold the political high ground but, given what was known about the Argentine position, this was unrealistic. He was worried about the lingering impression that 'with a final heave' an agreement might be reached, so that the doves in the Cabinet, aware that Pym was due to travel the next day to Washington, would be disturbed if this visit might be undermined as a result of any military action, including on South Georgia, and were also anxious lest the country stray on to the wrong side of international law.[8] It was because of these concerns that in his own presentation to Cabinet two days later Nott talked about the military situation while seeking to dampen diplomatic expectations by reading from Henderson's latest report of Haig's adventures in Buenos Aires, including chaotic decision-making and Galtieri's apparent inebriation.[9]

This difficult political context appears to have added uncertainty to the operation as late as the evening of 21 April, after the House of Commons debate, when Pym, Nott and Thatcher met with officials to discuss the Foreign Secretary's trip to Washington. Pym remained uncomfortable about any military action while negotiations were still underway. Nott felt that having put *Antrim* into position it could not be left to 'hang around' and the operation, which had already been approved, had to go forward. When Whitelaw joined them he helped persuade Pym that they could not hold back.[10]

The most serious altercation, however, was not among War Cabinet members, but between Henderson and Haig. When suggesting to ministers that they needed to take a decision on 19 April, the Secretary to the War Cabinet had also raised the question of whether or not Haig should be informed.[11] The Prime Minister's view was that the Americans 'were well aware of the possibility of such an operation' and therefore need not be informed in advance. Previously Haig had implied that, although military action could have adverse consequences in the OAS, it was 'imperative' that Britain should maintain military pressure. Thatcher was convinced that this statement left it open for the British to proceed with PARAQUET. Even so she accepted that as a precaution Henderson's views should be sought about how well this really would be received in Washington. The Ambassador reported back that PARAQUET was unlikely to be opposed by the American public, Congress or Government. He did, however, urge that Haig be informed in advance. This was agreed. The Secretary of State's office did not open until 0800 Washington time (1200Z) on 21 April, four hours after the planned initial landings (in fact weather intervened and the landings did not begin until 1300Z). Haig could have no veto, nor details of the time factors involved, since these were unpredictable and would depend on decisions by local commanders. It was already too late to abandon the operation.

At first when so informed Haig claimed surprise, because his own intelligence was that British ships were holding back, and was disconcerted that he was being informed rather than consulted. He was concerned because he had hoped that military action would wait until after Pym's visit. By the end of the meeting, Henderson was more confident that the Secretary of State understood the merits of the British case. A few hours later, however, Haig recalled him, having been worrying about the implications of the British decision if the Argentines could then accuse Washington of colluding with London. As the Americans now had their own independent intelligence about the British operation (although it is unclear where this could have come from) he felt he should give the Junta advanced notice, although not so advanced that they could act on the information. This would help him maintain a display of even-handedness.

Henderson was aghast and warned of the ways in which the Argentines could take advantage and the adverse impact such an American act could have in London. Haig then assured him that no prior notice would be given. The fact that Haig even considered this move shook London's confidence in his judgement. That it should have even crossed his mind was considered 'amazing' enough. Ministers were also worried that any American statements that appeared to criticise a British use of force would have a detrimental effect at home. When Pym visited Haig on 22 April, he reported that the Government had been 'appalled' at the suggestion that such information be shared with Argentina. At this meeting Haig accepted the value of the military pressure but was concerned at the risk of a 'sharp emotional reaction' that would add to his problems in the OAS and the negotiations. He suspected that the Americans would have to make some statement 'about moderation'. It would be best if there were no casualties. The episode left the Prime Minister even more wary about American intentions: she even suspected that Task Force movements were getting through to the Argentines via the US authorities. Checks began to be made on what was being passed to the United States. 'It is a frightening thing,' Nott noted, 'that our greatest ally is not wholly on our side.'[12]

The curiosity of this is that Haig had warned the Argentines on 17 April of the possibility of imminent British action. This was the 'wild card', Haig's unprotected call back to Washington containing a warning of imminent British military action that he hoped would persuade the Argentines to take a more reasonable position.[13] The day after this Haig recalled the episode for Judge Clarke:

> I called you on open line with clear recognition that Argentines would monitor. In order to break impossible impasse this morning on force withdrawal modalities, I created impression that British military action was about to take place. While somewhat over-theatrical, it has the virtue of being true in the context of first British units steaming toward South Georgia island. Fortunately, the ploy worked and it is vital that I leave here with an assessment by the Argentines not only that the British are going to attack but we are only hours away from such an event. You handled it on the phone precisely as I had hoped.

So Haig already knew that the British were preparing for an assault on South Georgia and had knowingly shared this information with the Argentines, albeit as part of an effort to extract concessions from them. He continued to talk directly to the Argentines about imminent British military action over the next two days (18 and 19 April), and he even appears to have mentioned South Georgia.

Of course, it did not require extensive contemplation of a map to reveal this as a likely target for the British. Whether as a result of their own assessments or Haig's surmises, the Argentines began to press the Americans further about what they actually knew. On 21 April, the US Ambassador was reporting that the Argentine Navy 'expects an armed encounter next week at South Georgia Island,' and the next day, as Pym was complaining about the very suggestion that the US might discuss British plans with Argentina, Argentine Ambassador Takacs made contact with the State Department and asked whether the US had information on a possible British attack on South Georgia. As a result of this a letter was drafted from Haig to Costa Mendez:

> Regarding your judgement that any occurrences of military action would end efforts to achieve a diplomatic solution to the crisis, you will recall I indicated to you on Monday [19 April] that we should all be concerned about the possibility of imminent military action in the area of South Georgia.

This was why, Haig continued, a diplomatic solution was required. He continued:

> As I know you understand we have no influence with the British with regard to these matters. Any decision they might take would be theirs alone, without consulting us.

The obvious interpretation of this was that the Americans were expecting the British to attack.

The Junta had decided to make no serious effort to defend South Georgia in order to concentrate on the Falkland Islands. The naval units involved in its occupation had been withdrawn with a small number of troops left as a garrison. Air cover was impossible due to the distance from the Argentine mainland. Yet, contrary to this decision, Admiral Lombardo had decided to reinforce South Georgia after a request for reinforcements from Captain Trombetta soon after the occupation.[14] The submarine *Santa Fe* was sent with material and some 40 men from Mar del Plata on 9 April. It attempted to save batteries by travelling on the surface, though this resulted in a battering from strong wind and waves. The aim was to get to Grytviken without detection and then withdraw as soon as possible.

Haig's intimations while in Buenos Aires that some sort of military action might be imminent led the Junta to attempt to discover the whereabouts of the British fleet using aerial reconnaissance. We have already noted above the consternation this surveillance activity caused Woodward. A Boeing 707 encountered the main Task Force on 21 April, but withdrew when faced by a Sea Harrier. It observed that the fleet had divided into advanced force and amphibious elements south of Ascension. This was taken by Argentine commanders as evidence that Britain was planning to retake South Georgia, although actually the South Georgia force had detached long before. More reconnaissance was planned and thought began to be given to a possible air response.

17

PARAQUET IN TROUBLE

The British view up to 21 April was that Argentina had neither reinforced the garrison nor detected the Task Group. There was fluctuating intelligence on the strength of the Argentine garrison in South Georgia. As American sources warned of from 100 to 200 Argentine naval infantry, a Chilean report suggested that the Argentines had evacuated all military and civilian personnel from South Georgia. These reports were all treated with reserve. The British stuck to their view that the 50 Argentine Marines known to have landed at the start of hostilities were still there. Another 20 might be at Leith, along with some 15 'scrap metal workers'. On balance, it seemed unlikely that Argentine commanders would judge that they had spare resources, particularly naval, to devote to the defence of this remote acquisition and also that they would make much effort to contest any reoccupation by the United Kingdom. A landing at Grytviken might be stiffly defended but not 'to the death' if confronted by superior forces. Argentine press reports that its South Georgia garrison was as large as 350 were dismissed.

Young greeted this agreed assessment with some relief, as his own sources were rudimentary. 'Janes, the wardroom encyclopaedia and hearsay from Portland did not provide a reassuring basis for threat assessment during the initial planning stage.' The further south he moved towards his target, the more the surface threat receded. The Argentine Navy appeared to be fully committed to the defence of the Falkland Islands. Nor did the Argentine air force give cause for concern. The Task Group was out of range of land-based aircraft from the mainland and little progress had been made by the Argentines in improving airfield facilities at Stanley. In any case the weather pattern forecast for the South Georgia area militated against effective air operations. The Argentine carrier was still assumed to be unlikely to risk an encounter with an SSN. By keeping emissions to a minimum the task group's approach to and presence off South Georgia should be undetected until after the initial reconnaissance parties had been inserted. Indeed the Argentines seemed to be considering allowing *RRS Bransfield* (in fact no longer in the area) to evacuate the remaining BAS personnel from South Georgia instead of using one of their own vessels.

On 23 April the position changed. On board *Antrim* Young was alarmed to hear on the World Service that information had leaked to the press, possibly via sources in Washington, that a British force was close to South Georgia and that a landing was imminent.[1] The first public reference on the World Service to South Georgia came on 23 April, two days into the still-undetected reconnaissance operations, when an interview with Costa Mendez (putting the chances of war with Britain at 50–50) was followed by news that some British warships were in striking distance of South Georgia. The next day Argentine reports concerning two British warships and a troop carrier, were cited, confirming that they had been spotted. Galtieri had promised that his troops on South Georgia would 'fight on to the last drop of their blood'.[2]

The new assessment, backed up by these Argentine press reports, suggested that Argentina recognised that elements of the British Task Force were within 'helicopter and plane range' of South Georgia, and that an attempt to retake the island was imminent. That day the BAS party at Schlieper Bay reported an unidentified aircraft overhead – judged by Young to be a probable C130 Hercules. This aircraft, relieved by a second one, continued surveillance throughout daylight hours, closing *Plymouth* and the tanker group to visual identification range that morning. Little could be done to prevent this surveillance: the ships were not authorised to engage the aircraft, since (following the wording of the general warning issued by the UK that day) its presence could not be directly interpreted as a threat to the repossession of South Georgia. In any case the aircraft kept outside the engagement range. A combination of maintained radar silence and overcast weather gave some grounds for supposing that the enemy had not established with any accuracy the composition of CTG 317.9. The optimistic view, as put forward by the Defence Intelligence Staff, was that as this surveillance had followed a couple of days of press speculation the Junta could not be surprised by the loss of South Georgia, an event it now seemed too late for them to prevent, and they must have 'assessed that they could withstand the internal repercussions which might follow'.

This could not, however, be taken for granted. In the build-up to the operation, every means was sought to assess the state of readiness of Argentine forces on South Georgia. This was the one exceptional case during the whole Falkland campaign in which the United States passed on satellite images, in this case taken just over a week after the occupation. These images showed no signs of life at Grytviken, Stromness or Leith, although three small fishing vessels were in Grytviken Harbour, supporting the view that Argentina was not making much of an effort to hold South Georgia. The same conclusion was drawn from a sonar/electronic reconnaissance sweep conducted along the coastline by *Conqueror* prior to TG 317.9's arrival. There was still no activity or shipping to be seen.

Enormous efforts were made using a Victor aircraft supported by multiple air-to-air refuelling to obtain Maritime Radar Reconnaissance

(MRR) on the location of Argentine ground forces and whether any shipping was concealed in inlets and coastal waters. There were doubts within the Task Group about this approach, with some concern that a Victor flight might simply alert the enemy or that the aircraft might be obliged to divert to Brazil.[3] Taking account of these concerns Beetham and Nott concluded such a sortie was only to be mounted if this was the only way Young could get decent intelligence on South Georgia. Young, pleased to get whatever information was on offer, was keen and so, on 20 April, the first Victor MRR was flown. The aircraft was airborne for nearly 15 hours, requiring seven tankers, and became the first to overfly occupied British territory. Again no shipping was detected in the vicinity of South Georgia. Further sorties were planned for 22 and 24 April and in due course successfully completed.

Fortuna Glacier

More detailed information depended on landing Special Forces into the harsh South Georgian environment. Fortuna Glacier had been chosen by the SAS as a landing site. It was a compromise between the problems of moving any distance in this harsh environment against the need to land people without being spotted by Argentine observers or being given away by the noise of the helicopters. It was viewed with misgivings by the aircrew who would have to fly the missions and the officers of *Endurance* and members of BAS, who had not actually been up to this particular glacier. Sheridan advised 'to avoid glaciers like the plague'. When the SAS stressed the need for secrecy Barker is reported to have replied: 'It's not exactly as busy as Brighton beach out there, you know.'[4] One pilot, on being told that Argentines would not expect the SAS to come from that direction, observed, 'Well, they won't expect you to come by Polaris missile either, but that's no reason to do it!' Others believed the glacier manageable. The great explorer Shackleton had managed it in a weak physical state and without the training and equipment available to the SAS (although as it turned out with much better weather). By and large the SAS trusted their own counsel, and those who remained anxious that they were underestimating the hazards posed by South Georgia had to assume that they knew what they were doing.[5]

The authority to initiate landing operations was received in the afternoon of 20 April. *Antrim* and *Tidespring* were in position for the first reconnaissance insertion at 0800Z (the local time in South Georgia was 3 hours behind GMT), but the weather was unrelenting (45, gusting up to 70 knots of wind, patchy visibility and a rapidly falling pressure at 965 mb). *Antrim*'s Wessex 3 crew suggested and flew a weather reconnaissance at 0930Z, which found a weather window, but the aircrew thought that it would not last. The sortie also reported extremely challenging conditions on the glacier itself, with deep, multiple crevassing and violent katabatic winds. Even so, and after extensive debate, an insertion attempt was made at 1100Z using this aircraft and *Tidespring*'s two Wessex 5s. After several attempts by the Wessex 3 to find a way up onto the glacier, this was aborted in the face of severe icing, loss of visibility, high winds and a heavy snowstorm. In another Wessex 3 sortie Delves and Hamilton of the SAS checked for themselves, and despite misgivings of their own felt that they had to press on with their plan. Two hours later with the wind still at 40 knots gusting to 60 knots, but visibility improving, the three helicopters set out again. They flew from Possession Bay into Antarctic Bay and up over Fortuna Glacier. The landing was made in hazardous and near whiteout conditions caused by swirling snow and violent local winds. The helicopters returned safely, leaving the SAS troop and their equipment on the inhospitable glacier. *Antrim* and *Tidespring* retired to a holding position 30 miles off Cape Constancy from which SAS reconnaissance communications could be monitored. Unfortunately the weather rapidly deteriorated during the afternoon and evening with the wind backing south-west and increasing to a steady 70 knots, with gusts beyond that. Both ships had to heave to until the storm abated on the morning of 22 April.

Meanwhile, *Plymouth* and *Endurance* had proceeded to the east of the island during 21 April conducting ice and merchant ship reconnaissance during daylight hours. The *Endurance* also landed a senior rating by heli-copter to get to the BAS field party at St. Andrews Bay and brought off a scientist to help brief the SBS. The report was that there had been no Argentine movements since the day of the invasion. BAS personnel were warned that British warships were now in the vicinity and that, for security reasons, this should not be revealed in conversations on their field radio circuit. *Endurance* then proceeded into Hound Bay to land, at last light, the 2 SBS advance reconnaissance team first by Wasp and then the last wave, after appalling weather conditions, by Gemini boats while *Plymouth* remained covering seaward. The deployment was finally achieved at 0300Z on 22 April. The plan was that the SBS should cross the Barff Peninsula on foot, and the next evening a Wasp would deliver two Geminis for the approach to Grytviken across Cumberland Bay East.

Tidespring's planned rendezvous with *Brambleleaf* for pump-over on 22 April had to be postponed because of the weather. *Plymouth* and *Endurance* were ordered to remain in comparative shelter to the east of South Georgia, while *Antrim* and *Tidespring* remained to the north, with *Brambleleaf* holding in the rendezvous position. Then, at 1100Z, the Commander of the SAS reconnaissance troop on the Fortuna Glacier called for immediate evac-uation. The atrocious weather conditions and terrain had defeated these experienced mountain and arctic warfare specialists who had only been able to move some 500 metres in less than five hours. With the wind speed rising, in temperatures below −20°C, and whiteout conditions almost continuous, the Troop was forced to stop and try to make camp. They managed to erect two of the four tents, the others being damaged by the strong winds, so that only ten men could take shelter, the remainder seeking what protection they could outside. In the morning conditions had improved somewhat but immediate evacuation appeared prudent before further, serious cold weather casualties occurred. *Antrim*'s Wessex 3 and both Wessex 5s from *Tidespring* were launched at 1205Z, but, amid increasingly violent winds and continuous cloud down to the glacier surface, could not find the SAS who were enveloped in heavy snow showers. After refuelling the helicopters were re-launched for a further effort at 1330Z. The SAS were found and embarked, but on take-off one Wessex 5 ran into whiteout conditions and crashed. Its aircrew and passengers were transferred to the two remaining aircraft but, on re-launching, the surviving Wessex 5 hit a ridge in the gloom while following close behind the Wessex 3 and crashed. The Wessex 3, already overloaded, managed to return to *Antrim*, land its passengers and then return to the scene, with blankets, survival aids and medical supplies. It was unable to reach the crash area because of the conditions, but made contact with the survivors on emergency radio and established that there were no serious casualties. Having returned to *Antrim* and refuelled, the helicopter made two more aborted attempts before launching again at 1630Z on the last possible mission before night-fall. After packing everyone in and overloaded by about a ton, it successfully lifted the party back to *Antrim*.[6]

These dramatic events, on a faraway glacier, produced great anxiety in London. The first news reached London from Young at 1610Z:

> Regret both Wessex 5 crashed in whiteout conditions while attempting rescue SAS recce party from untenable position Fortuna Glacier. *Antrim* Wessex 3 conducting SAR (search and rescue) in marginal conditions. 4 SAS and one Wessex 5 pilot recovered so far.

Nott later recalled the gravity of this signal, fearing many fatalities. This was, he recalled, 'the worst moment of the war for all of us, for Thatcher, Lewin and myself.' The fact that this first landing of the campaign had gone so badly wrong was a 'terrible blow.' Nott and Lewin received the grim news first and decided immediately 'on the spur of the moment' to tell the Prime Minister. Lewin did not relish his task, but described what he knew, adding that 'in war things go wrong'. The Prime Minister made it clear that she did not expect things to go so wrong very frequently. Soon another signal came in stating that: 'WX3 established radio contact with second WX5. Remainder SAS troop, Wessex 5 pilot and 2 aircrewmen accounted for. No (R) no casualties. Whiteout conditions persist. Will attempt rescue ASAP.' CINCFLEET immediately passed on the headlines to MoD, and Downing Street was soon informed. At 1725Z on 22 April Captain Young reported to CTF 317: 'WX3 recovered all 12 survivors. Returned onboard 1715Z. All well.'[7]

News of a fumbled landing, equipment losses or just activity on South Georgia had enormous political as well as operational sensitivity. Very few people knew about this, and there was confidence that the Argentines were also ignorant. At least one senior member of the FCO was aware of what had transpired on Fortuna Glacier, as a result of a dinner with Admiral Hallifax, and believed strongly that Pym, then in Washington, should be given the full story. Neither No. 10 nor MoD wanted any more people to know the details. In the end the Foreign Secretary was told only that: 'The preliminary stages were proceeding more slowly than had been expected and the timetable as a whole was therefore shifting to the right by a few days.' Nonetheless the FCO was still demanding a detailed report by the next morning. The Prime Minister gave specific instruction that these events were not even to be mentioned during the 25 April meeting at Northwood for the War Cabinet, when Pym would also be present. The briefing was to be confined to where the operation stood at the time. It was not until 17 May that the loss of two helicopters was confirmed after an account of the episode had appeared in the press as a result of a letter written home by a member of the Task Force to his parents.

Meanwhile, Young was trying to return to his intelligence-gathering schedule. During the night of 22/23 April, *Plymouth* and *Endurance* were to land the back-up element of the SBS reconnaissance troop at Hound Bay, *Antrim* was to land an SAS reconnaissance troop in Stromness, while *Tidespring* and *Brambleleaf* held clear 35 miles north of Cumberland Bay. All ships were to rendezvous in position at 0900Z 23 April for replenishment at sea and pump-over. Once again the elements intervened. A Wasp from *Endurance* duly delivered two Geminis to the SBS at the agreed point on the foreshore at the south-east corner of Cumberland Bay in the later afternoon of 22 April, but one craft was damaged. After dark a small party, in the one serviceable boat, attempted the crossing to Dartmouth Point but was driven back by high wind (Force 11, gusting to 70 knots) and sea conditions of gathering ice from the Nordenskjold Glacier. Assessing the situation the next morning, the SBS leader decided that the mission must be abandoned and requested evacuation.

Similar problems threatened D Squadron SAS Boat Troop as *Antrim* entered Stromness Bay at 0400Z. They disembarked by Gemini to Grass Island. The craft was not helped by being put into extremely cold conditions after being held on a warm ship. Difficulties with starting the outboard engines, whose obsolescence was the source of many of the troubles of these few days, meant that at one stage the operation was close to being abandoned. Only three of the five craft managed the one-mile passage to Grass Island. Then, at 0800Z Young received a distress call informing him that one Gemini and crew were being swept out to sea from Stromness Bay. Consequently, Young closed the coast and launched his Wessex 3 to search, while *Plymouth* was ordered to take charge of the *Brambleleaf/Tidespring* pump-over. The Gemini, which had drifted in the high winds a considerable way out to sea (20 miles offshore and heading for South Africa) was located on the last leg of the helicopter's search and its exposed and exhausted occupants successfully recovered at 1000Z. The fifth Gemini beached on the Busen Peninsula: the occupants were picked up three days later. At least there were now some parties ashore and *Antrim* remained within 25 miles of the coast to monitor the communication nets.

The party on Grass Island was able to reconnoitre Stromness and Leith, reporting no signs of life at the former and almost no activity at the latter. An attempt next nightfall to cross Harbour Point, between the two old whaling stations, had to be abandoned when Gemini engines failed again but on the night of 24/25 April they reached the coast, checked that Stromness was deserted and climbed to Harbour Point to observe Leith. They reported back that the Argentine forces there spent most of the day indoors sheltering from the weather.

The *Santa Fe*

As early as 18 April the British had (correctly) concluded that the *Santa Fe* had departed the mainland on 9 April. On assumptions about what they would do if in the Argentines' shoes, they assessed that the submarine was on the way to South Georgia, and by 20 April it was estimated that she might arrive as early as 22 April; this suggested a purpose for the unknown operations which, according to a report, she was due to conduct on 23 April.[8] Although the British were concerned that the Argentine Navy might plan to pull some sort of stunt prior to the scheduled meeting of the OAS on 26 April, such as simulating evidence of an oil slick to claim a British attack against one of their submarines, it was also clear that by 23 April the *Santa Fe* would have been warned of British intentions to recapture South Georgia, and required to carry out its mission as soon as possible. It therefore constituted a threat. In fact papers subsequently captured in the submarine, and discussions with her officers, indicated that she had been instructed to sink any British ships that she found off South Georgia.

On 23 April *Endurance* picked up emissions from a submarine's radar, which though not precisely locatable enabled the warning to be issued that 'a submarine might be in or approaching the S Georgia area'. *Conqueror* was ordered to return to the area and to take up an ASW patrol 70 miles to the west of the island, to intercept the *Santa Fe*. Unfortunately a defect to *Conqueror*'s communications mast meant that it could not receive or transmit easily, and by the time it received this order it was 24 April and the *Santa Fe* was already past any line it could patrol. Young ordered *Plymouth*, about 60 miles to the east with the two tankers, and *Endurance*, to break off the pump-over and withdraw south to clear the area in which the *Santa Fe* might be operating. The Argentine air surveillance of 23 April was now seen in a new light, as possibly directing the submarine to engage with the Task Group.

Every aspect of PARAQUET now looked different. Disastrous reconnaissance insertions meant that no intelligence on enemy dispositions had been gained except at Leith. Both of the group's Wessex 5s had been lost, reducing Young's lift capacity drastically, the force was under surveillance from the air and now there was the *Santa Fe* threat. The group's ASW capability was very limited, particularly since the sonar equipment had been removed from *Antrim's* Wessex 3 in favour of troop lift capacity. *Brilliant*, commanded by Captain John Coward, with two Lynx helicopters was supposed to be providing reinforcement, and, though steaming as fast as possible, would not arrive until the morning of 25 April. On 23 April both Young and Sheridan received urgent communications from their superiors on the lack of progress. That afternoon they conferred on their options. Could they manage a landing before the *Santa Fe* was in threatening position the next morning? Their remaining helicopter lift was insufficient to enable them to re-dispose their forces in time to make a viable landing at Grytviken. With this in mind, on the night of 23/24 April, Young instructed *Plymouth*, *Brambleleaf* and *Tidespring* to clear the Falklands MEZ to the north-east overnight, complete pump-over during 24 April and rendezvous with *Brilliant*. *Antrim* was to enter Stromness Bay to land troops at first light to take Leith, to provide naval gunfire support as required and, on completion, withdraw at best speed to rendezvous with the main group. *Endurance* was to proceed to Hound Bay to recover the SBS reconnaissance party and then withdraw to the east and remain covert in the shelter of the ice. The group would then assume an ASW posture to detect and attack the *Santa Fe*.

Shortly before *Antrim* was to detach it appeared that it had again been spotted by an Argentine Hercules and its position might be passed to the *Santa Fe*. The risk of being trapped while conducting the landings was unacceptable and so this operation was cancelled. Instead *Antrim* proceeded north with the Replenishment at Sea group. By now Northwood was getting concerned at the complete lack of progress. The carrier battle group was ordered to hasten south and be prepared to support the PARAQUET force if required. There was now reason to suppose that not only was the *Santa Fe* operating off South Georgia, but that it would engage without warning. The *Santa Fe* captain later claimed to have had *Endurance* in his sights, but not to have attacked as this was not the destroyer he had been ordered to attack. (Those who have seen the positional data of the submarine question whether this was so.) The Argentine submarine, it was supposed, was either lurking in the South Georgia area to attack ships or else, possibly, preparing to disembark some personnel. The bad weather affecting British forces would undoubtedly also have had its effect on the Argentines.

London was reluctant to begin all-out submarine warfare, but with Pym having now left Washington without any diplomatic breakthrough in sight, and evidence of an Argentine readiness to attack British vessels, Nott instructed the SSN *Splendid*, then in the Falklands MEZ, to proceed in the direction of the area in which the main Argentine force was patrolling. This would create the option of being able to execute retaliation should ministers so decide following an attack upon a British ship in the South Georgia area. This indicates that politically the critical consideration was where, when and against whom the first shots were to be fired rather than the second shots.

By now Young accepted that, given the precautions that had been taken to remove all ships from the approaches to Grytviken and Leith, the *Santa Fe* would probably arrive unchallenged, possibly to land troops, perhaps even during daylight on 24 April. With Leith covered by the SAS reconnaissance team, Young ordered *Endurance*, recovering the SBS reconnaissance party from the Hound Bay area, to conduct covert surveillance of Cumberland Bay and Grytviken during daylight hours with his Wasp helicopters, armed with AS12 missiles. This would be in the hope of catching the submarine on the surface as it entered. Approval was given to attack a surfaced submarine, even though *Conqueror* was still in the same area. It was hoped that *Conqueror* did not have to surface in an emergency! Young was also wary about the possibility of mounting an attack on a friendly submarine, yet ASW capabilities would not improve until *Brilliant* arrived. He therefore decided to get the *Brambleleaf*/*Tidespring* pump-over out of the way and then to replenish *Antrim*, *Plymouth* and *Brilliant* on its completion, so that the warships could return south to carry out operations against *Santa Fe* on 25 April. The plan was to operate clear of, but adjacent to, *Conqueror*'s area in the hope of forcing *Santa Fe* to snort or provide other detection opportunities for the SSN. *Tidespring*, with the main elements of M Company RM embarked, would remain clear of the exclusion zone to the north, while *Endurance* would take shelter among the icebergs on completion of operations in Hound Bay.

18

THE BATTLE FOR SOUTH GEORGIA

During the afternoon of 24 April a Boeing 707 overflew *Endurance* while in Hound Bay. Captain Barker assessed that he had been detected. More disturbing news was then picked up from BAS personnel at Bird Island who reported sighting two warships (which were in fact British), two small jets as well as a Boeing 707 aircraft in their vicinity. In the face of possible multiple threats Barker requested support. When the Boeing passed over him, as he was on a secure line to Northwood, Barker asked for permission to attack as it was probably passing his position to the *Santa Fe*. The request was refused: the ROE were still that only aircraft posing a direct threat could be attacked.[1] The BAS intelligence was recognised to be anomalous: there was no other evidence that enemy warships were in the area, nor of an Argentine capability to get ground attack aircraft to South Georgia using in-flight refuelling. Intelligence indicated that there had been few improvements to the Stanley runway. Nonetheless Barker felt that the whole operation was losing momentum and proposed a plan for landing his small number of embarked SAS and SBS to take Grytviken. His force was judged insufficient to the task and his method too hazardous for his ship.

Young did not feel able to discount the BAS report, despite the doubts. He decided to speed up preparations. Following replenishment by *Tidespring*, *Brilliant* was to close South Georgia at 25 knots as *Antrim* and *Plymouth* proceeded at the same speed to join *Endurance*. Young was then informed that *Conqueror*'s areas were being extended to cover the whole of the north and northeast coasts of South Georgia, effectively closing the whole of these areas for ASW operations except against surfaced submarines. By now there was concern on *Antrim* that as long as the Argentine submarine was around the operation could not proceed. The ship's helicopter's aircrew suggested to Young that they should refit the radar to the aircraft (which had been removed for the Fortuna Glacier operation), and search for the *Santa Fe* on the assumption that its commander would approach at night on the surface, to avoid detection and icebergs, offload men and materiel and depart at or before dawn the following day on the surface. The analysis was not universally accepted but there seemed little to lose. Young therefore ordered his

249

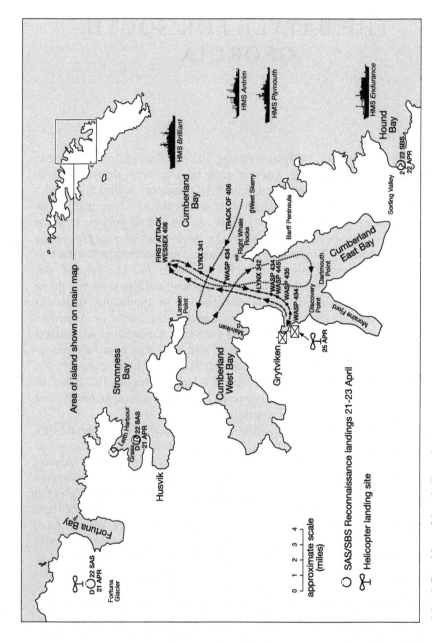

Map 5 Retaking of South Georgia

three frigates to rendezvous about 25 miles northeast of Cumberland Bay, clear of *Conqueror*'s expanded area at 0800Z on 25 April, while *Antrim*'s Wessex 3, armed with two MkII depth charges, was to launch, to be off the entrance to Cumberland Bay by first light, followed by a Lynx from *Brilliant* with Mk46 torpedoes to see if the assumptions were correct and the submarine could be caught on the surface. The Wasps from *Plymouth* and *Endurance* were to remain on alert, armed with AS12 in the anti-surface role.

The Wessex soon detected the *Santa Fe* five miles north of the entrance to Cumberland Bay on the surface, and it was positively identified at 0855Z. The *Santa Fe,* on sighting the helicopter, had decided to remain on the surface to avoid the torpedo threat but had not bargained on depth charges and air-to-surface missiles. The submarine was immediately attacked with two MkII depth charges both of which exploded very close (one bounced off the casing into the water). *Brilliant*'s Lynx, already airborne some 30 miles to the north-west, closed and dropped one Mk46 torpedo which ran harmlessly beneath the submarine. The Wasp from *Plymouth* was then vectored onto the submarine, but before it could engage was overtaken and preempted by a Wasp from *Endurance*, which had decided to join the fray. The action then became a free-for-all, with *Endurance*'s Wasps taking it in turns to take pot shots at the submarine as it attempted to reach Grytviken. The damage from the depth charges and several hits on the fin left the submarine effectively disabled, although it was kept under pressure until it berthed alongside the BAS jetty at King Edward Cove. By 1121Z news of the attack on the *Santa Fe* appears to have filtered through to London and the action had been heard on the main Task Force HF radios a thousand miles to the north-west. This was the first anti-submarine operation successfully conducted exclusively by helicopters.

As it was obvious that the Argentine garrison knew of his Task Group's presence, Young took the opportunity of having the helicopters in Cumberland Bay conduct reconnaissance of any military dispositions. There was no sign of any activity ashore, nor of distinct observation posts or defensive positions, although machine gun fire was reported. All agreed that the momentum must be maintained and the garrison attacked as soon as possible. Sheridan later observed that until that morning the Argentines on South Georgia:

> had not even known for certain that we were in the area. Then they suddenly saw their submarine being hammered, forced back to base, and abandoned by its crew. To them it must have seemed that the air was full of our helicopters and that we had overwhelming resources.

This argued for going straight in before the Argentines had time to catch their breath.[2]

Young agreed and decided to land troops to secure Grytviken as soon as possible. Preparations were immediately put in hand, with all available embarked forces being brought to one hour's notice for landing at 1040Z. Young also ordered *Tidespring*, with the main elements embarked, to close on South Georgia. With *Santa Fe* neutralised, Young requested CINCFLEET to clear *Conqueror* from the area.

The final plans and preparations took longer than Sheridan would have wished. It was decided to conduct the initial landing with the 79 troops available in *Antrim*, drawn from M Company Command element and Mortar Troop, D Squadron Command and Signals Troop and the Mountain & Arctic Warfare Troop, 2 SBS Command and Signals element, 148 Battery RA, and *Antrim's* RM detachment. The remaining SAS and SBS personnel and RM detachments onboard *Plymouth*, *Brilliant* and *Endurance*, a further 62 men, were to be held in reserve ready to conduct flanking landings if required. The Marines of 'M' Company were two hundred miles away on *Tidespring* and so could play no part in the operation they had expected to lead. The main landing was to be made on flat ground 1.5 miles south of Grytviken. After planning, briefing and preparations, at 1400Z *Antrim* and *Plymouth* began to bombard the landing zone and the related high ground, with spotting provided by an observer from one of *Endurance's* Wasps. *Antrim's* Wessex 3 and both of *Brilliant's* Lynxes were launched at 1430Z and 15 minutes later landed 19 men to secure the landing zone. Over the next 45 minutes these three aircraft landed all 79 men from a range of about eight miles in what Young described as 'a very creditable effort'.

The troops advanced north towards the Brown Mountain ridge-line, which hid them from Grytviken, with the SAS well in advance. General Purpose Machine Gun (GPMG) and Milan were fired at a suspected enemy position in the tussock grass but this turned out to be a group of elephant seals. *Antrim* and *Plymouth* continued to provide gunfire support ahead of the advancing troops. At 1640 *Antrim* entered Cumberland Bay to improve communications and to open arcs into the Grytviken/King Edward Cove area if necessary. The first troops moved forward cautiously, but when they got close to King Edward Point at 1705 they saw a white flag flying, which had in fact been raised soon after the start of the intense naval bombardment.

Captain Bicain, from the *Santa Fe*, was now the senior officer. Having just managed to get out of a submarine being circled by hostile helicopters, and with naval gunfire close by, he presumably calculated that the odds were very much against his men, although on land he still did have numerical superiority. Ten minutes later Bicain announced on the radio his wish to surrender. At the same time he also warned that the settlement and landing area at King Edward Cove was heavily mined so British forces should be led through by the Argentines. Delves had seen no disturbance to the ground and walked through to get to the Argentine garrison. The mines could only have been set off by command.[3] Sheridan followed in a helicopter. At 1729Z Captain Young signalled London: 'Argentinian Forces in Grytviken surrendered at 251715Z to British Forces'.

Antrim's Wessex 3 was launched immediately with a medical team to treat and evacuate any casualties. There was only one: a sailor from the *Santa Fe*, injured during the attacks on the submarine, whose right leg had been amputated above the knee by the Argentine medical team ashore. He was brought to *Antrim* for stabilising surgery and medical attention overnight, being transferred to the surgical unit in *Tidespring* the next morning. At 1730Z the Union Flag (which had been brought from Hereford by an SAS Sergeant-Major) and White Ensign flew together over Grytviken and the task of consolidation began. CINCFLEET sent *Antrim*'s signal back to the MoD: 'Be pleased to inform Her Majesty that the White Ensign flies alongside the Union Flag in Grytviken South Georgia. God save the Queen.' That evening, more relieved than the press could appreciate, the Prime Minister and Nott announced the successful recapture of South Georgia. Irritated at being pressed for information on the next steps, Thatcher stopped the questioning by stating: 'Just rejoice at that news and congratulate our forces and the marines ... Rejoice.'[4]

Argentina, on the basis of garbled reports of the initial attacks, was making its own protests to the UN about an 'aggressive escalation' and 'armed aggression' against Argentine territory. That evening Bicain and the Argentine garrison commander signed a formal surrender document onboard *Antrim*, to where they had been invited for dinner. The hospitality had an ulterior motive. Their acceptance would confirm that there were no plans to sabotage the ship through concealed swimmers or floating mines. *Antrim*, now anchored off King Edward Point, transferred equipment and stores to the troops ashore who had some 140 prisoners to secure and guard. Structurally the buildings and facilities were intact but there had been some looting/vandalism by the Argentines. A major cleaning-up operation was required as well as technical assistance to service the power and fresh water facilities, which were near breakdown because of neglect.

At 1815Z Young detached *Plymouth* and *Endurance*, with one of *Brilliant*'s Lynxes embarked, to secure Leith with their SAS and SBS troops. *Brilliant* was ordered to remain at sea to patrol the offshore areas overnight while *Tidespring*, closing from the north, was ordered to an area inshore of *Brilliant* to prepare to disembark the remainder of M Company and receive casualties. The Argentine Commander at Leith was Lieutenant Commander A Astiz, formerly in charge of the Argentine 'Dirty War' interrogation centre at the School of Naval Mechanics and wanted by several countries for the disappearance of their nationals. He was invited on the radio to surrender to far superior British forces following the capture of Grytviken. Later Barker made an attempt to persuade him. The reply came back that 39 civilians were willing to surrender but that the Argentine Marines were ready to fight.

One reason for this defiance might have been some hope of an Argentine air force attack in support. Over the previous few days the Boeing 707 surveillance had discovered a number of the Task Force ships. Three

Canberras, detailed to the Rio Grande airstrip in case targets for an attack were identified, took off at noon on 25 April with orders to attack British ships so long as they were isolated and away from Cumberland Bay. Just before they were due to arrive a KC-130 informed them that the meteorological conditions around the island were poor and that the British fleet was already inside the Bay, where the Canberras would be vulnerable to defensive fire. The aircraft therefore returned to base.[5] Further plans for sorties to South Georgia were abandoned because of the Argentine surrender.

The British made plans to land all troops by boat at 2300Z close in Stromness Bay, and for their attack to be preceded by a naval bombardment. Just as *Plymouth* was preparing for this, at 2245Z, Astiz reported to Barker that he was after all prepared to surrender. Barker, he proposed, should accept this the next day after landing by helicopter on the football pitch at Leith. Here a sizeable explosive charge had been concealed which would have been detonated as the Wasp touched down. Barker had initially agreed to the Astiz plan but fortunately had second thoughts. Instead Astiz was told that he would receive instructions for surrender at 0800Z the next day. *Plymouth* landed the remainder of D Troop SAS near Harbour Point while *Endurance* landed her 50 Special Force troops. The combined SAS/SBS detachments took up defensive positions overlooking Leith to await the Argentine surrender. On 26 April the white flag could be seen at the flagpole set before the only inhabitable building in Leith. Twelve Argentine Marines then moved in single file behind the buildings and made their way to Harbour Point. Two other Marines who had been 'missing' for some hours were later traced nearby. At 1100 Captain Astiz formally surrendered on board *Plymouth*. Together with the 39 scrap metal workers this now meant that the Task Group had nearly 200 detainees and prisoners of war.

Aftermath

The next few days were spent in complex and time-consuming transfers of personnel and equipment, hampered by gale force winds and snow showers, which made conditions very difficult, and complicated by the force continuing to be under surveillance by enemy reconnaissance aircraft. On the afternoon of 26 April CINCFLEET ordered Young to embark all Special Forces and Naval Gunfire Forward Support personnel and stores into *Brilliant* and *Plymouth* for transfer immediately to TG 317.8. In the prevailing conditions these transfers could not be completed until 1330Z on 28 April, at which time both ships detached. On 26 April, Young asked Coward to conduct a survey of the *Santa Fe*, assisted by technical officers from *Antrim*, while *Antrim* proceeded to the open sea to conduct anti-air defence in the event of Argentine reprisals. The submarine was found to be in an unstable state with obvious risks from its torpedoes and other stores and likely to sink alongside the BAS jetty, but there was a possibility of moving it across the bay to the old whaling station at Grytviken. Young agreed to this and accordingly Coward, assisted by the *Santa Fe*'s Commander and a number of Argentine ratings, moved the submarine under its own power later that day. On board was an RM Guard Party, briefed by British submariners about the risk of sabotage. The submarine was successfully started up but when it had got a few hundred yards from the jetty it suddenly lurched to port. The Argentine Commanding Officer shouted to a crew member, Chief Petty Officer Artuso, to pull a lever to blow more air into the submarine to keep it stable. Artuso moved to do this but a young Marine guard, apparently under strain in the wet, dark and dangerous conditions, believed that the man was about to pull another lever nearby that had been pointed out to him as one that could flood the submarine. So he shot Artuso to prevent the boat being scuppered.[6]

Tidespring completed disembarking M Company personnel and stores as the garrison for South Georgia, and embarked all the Argentine prisoners of war and detainees. *Endurance* started work at Leith, clearing a considerable amount of booby-trapping, explosives and ammunition, and contacted all twelve BAS and the two TV personnel on the island on the BAS radio net, briefing them of the situation, warning them to be ready to be collected at short notice. Young was less than pleased to be awoken in the middle of the night to receive a Prime Ministerial enquiry on behalf of Lord Buxton, who was concerned that no contact had been made with the BAS/TV personnel since the island had been re-captured.

Prisoners of war

On 21 April, the Chief of Defence Staff had prepared a paper on dealing with Argentine prisoners. Although the Prime Minister said that the Argentine prisoners were not 'of war' because the two countries were not at war, the four Geneva Conventions of 1949 (to which Britain and Argentina were parties) applied from the start of actual hostilities not only when at war but whenever an armed conflict could be said to exist, and in all cases of partial or total occupation of territory. As prisoners of war under the Conventions they had to be evacuated as soon as possible after their capture to camps situated in an area far enough from the combat zone for them to be out of danger. It was likely that the holding of prisoners on South Georgia would fit this requirement, if adequate accommodation could be provided. Yet it was also clear that it was in Britain's interest that prisoners should be repatriated to Argentina as soon as possible, thereby relieving the Task Force of the responsibility for guarding and accommodating them. The return of the small numbers of prisoners likely to arise from PARAQUET could also be presented as a humanitarian *quid pro quo* for the Argentine's treatment of the captured Royal Marines. However, if this was done, it had to be accepted that the Argentines could obtain a considerable amount of intelligence about Britain's own forces from returning prisoners unless they were held for a sufficient period to ensure that any information had become stale. This was an important consideration, as was the possible need to hold enemy prisoners as a bargaining counter for the return of any British prisoners of war or British citizens taken hostage in the Falkland Islands.

Prisoners could be repatriated either direct from the combat zone via a neutral third country (e.g. Uruguay or Brazil), through a suitable staging post such as Ascension Island or, in the event of large numbers being involved, possibly by either Argentine commercial shipping or an Argentine hospital ship direct from the Falkland Islands. It would be possible for prisoners to be staged through the United Kingdom but there was no particular reason to adopt what would be clearly a most expensive and unnecessary option and this was soon excluded. Subject to the provision of additional tentage, guards and administrative support, up to 150 prisoners could be staged through Ascension for up to a week, and this might be suitable for PARAQUET. Any risk of British vessels entering ports of neutral countries being harassed or even detained would largely be avoided if a nominated British ship conveyed prisoners from the combat zone either direct or via Ascension to either Uruguay or Brazil. Such action had been acceptable to the Uruguayans in the case of the repatriation of the Marines and civilians from the Falklands.[7]

The return of prisoners arising from PARAQUET was a matter of urgency and instructions had to be passed to the appropriate commanders as soon as possible. As the numbers were small the best course was to get them to Ascension and from there by air to either Uruguay or Brazil. It was, however, unlikely that any warship or RFA involved in PARAQUET could be spared to take prisoners to Ascension. The BAS ship RRS *Bransfield*, which had room for 40 additional passengers, was already too far north. It seemed as if the prisoners would have to be retained on the island for a limited period until an RFA or other suitable vessel could be spared for this task. It was eventually decided that there was little choice but to transport them to Ascension on *Tidespring*, which, by 29 April, had 155 Argentine naval and army personnel on board. Young shared the concern of *Tidespring*'s master at the conditions under which the prisoners had to be accommodated on the RFA. Severe overcrowding, discomfort, few sanitary facilities and the extreme cold, against which little protection could be provided, were thought to be a danger to health. Some unrest and defiance occurred, particularly in the Astiz group and, at the Master's request, Young transferred Astiz to *Antrim* where he was kept in close custody in the doctor's cabin, where despite its stripped-out state he still managed to manufacture, but not conceal, some improvised weapons.

The intention had been to wait until *Plymouth* could take over guardship duties at South Georgia on 7 May, but that might require the prisoners remaining in these poor conditions for nearly three weeks. Young therefore proposed on 30 April that they departed early, leaving only *Endurance* on guard until *Plymouth* arrived. In the circumstances, with the main group approaching the Falklands, Young considered this a justifiable risk. In all 151 Argentine prisoners taken on South Georgia were repatriated via Ascension. The ICRC agreed to provide three observers (including a doctor) to accompany the prisoners from Ascension. It had been hoped that the United States would provide an aircraft but in the end an aircraft was chartered from the Dutch firm Martinair. At Argentina's suggestion they were to go to Montevideo.

The group of 13 BAS and two TV personnel were picked up by *Endurance* on 30 April, as *Antrim* collected BAS stores from Lyell Glacier, and recovered SAS equipment from the crash site on the Fortuna Glacier. At 1300Z the next day (1 May) *Antrim* received an order from CINCFLEET to embark the BAS/TV personnel parties from *Endurance* and sail from South Georgia the next day. On Sunday 2 May *Antrim* and *Tidespring* departed South Georgia; they met *Plymouth* (which refuelled from *Tidespring*) on Monday 3 May, and then sailed north. On 7 May they rendezvoused with *Antelope*; Captain Astiz and the other prisoners, the BAS/TV personnel, mail and stores were transferred to the latter, which continued northwards to Ascension while *Antrim* returned to rejoin the Task Force. *Antelope* delivered its passengers to Ascension on 11 May; and the BAS/TV personnel arrived back at Brize Norton the next day, while the main body of Argentine prisoners left for Montevideo early on 13 May.

En route to Ascension came the opportunity for interrogation of Argentine prisoners.[8] Although the Geneva Convention provided that a prisoner of war was required only to give his number, rank, name and date of birth, experience suggested that many would be willing to do rather more than this and answer simple questions about the name and location of their unit and about their mission. Any information of value to the Task Force Commander yielded would probably be only of immediate tactical value and so would diminish should questioning be delayed. By the time it got underway, Young at least felt that 'a valuable opportunity' had already been lost.[9] Once captured many prisoners had been willing to talk, explain and justify themselves, 'whether through shock, natural disposition or lack of training', but permission was not granted for immediate questioning. By the time guidance had been received on interrogation procedures the prisoners had regained some of their confidence and became less likely to volunteer information. There were two qualified, Spanish-speaking interrogators with the Task Force Commander together with a number of Spanish-speaking linguists and interpreters who could assist with tactical questioning. There were plans to increase the number of trained interrogators to four and further support personnel could be made available if required. On 26 April, Nott commented that Britain had to veer on the side of extreme caution and treat prisoners with great care and respect. No pressure of any kind should be put on them and he asked that this guidance be passed directly to the Force Commander.

Of most interest were the *Santa Fe*'s crew. They were to be given simple interviews, without duress, on board *Tidespring*. In questioning any form of physical or mental ill-treatment, or the use of disorientation techniques such as stress positioning or white noise, was forbidden. Arrival at Ascension, by 8 May, could be delayed if necessary. An ambitious scheme to process large numbers of interviewees, involving a team of up to 10 non-linguist Tactical Questioners (TQ) supported by a similar number of interpreters and a few technical advisers (e.g. submarine specialists) was abandoned because of a shortage of interpreters and the practical difficulties that might be faced in *Tidespring*. Its high profile could cause political repercussions. The more modest plan adopted would cover fewer prisoners but involved only two TQ trained interpreters supported by technical advisers and commanded by an officer from the Joint Services Interrogation Wing (JSIW). Of the 150 prisoners held 26 were interviewed. Only four refused to co-operate. Once Captain Bicain realised that interviews were taking place, he registered complaints with representatives of the International Red Cross embarked, and then with the interrogation team, on the grounds that interviews were taking place without his knowledge and permission. He also directed that all prisoners be given immediate instruction in how to behave if interviewed. As a result of this, prisoners interviewed during the last ten hours of the operation were generally much more secure. It was of interest that none of those captured in South Georgia had served in the Falkland Islands, but this also resulted in a complete lack of new intelligence on Falklands forces, although information was gleaned on communication systems and night-fighting equipment. From the *Santa Fe*'s officers came some details on the SST-4 Torpedo (for anti-ship use only) and past mine-laying exercises. The strongest impression was of their professionalism and competence, and the high regard in which they held Bicain.

Lieutenant Commander Astiz was not repatriated after South Georgia. This followed representations from the Swedish and French Governments who wished to interview him. This was in connection with the wounding and disappearance of a Swedish woman in Buenos Aires in 1977, and the disappearance of two French nuns. The two Governments were asked to explain their concerns. The Prime Minister was very sympathetic and was inclined to hand him over to either France or Sweden. Her officials were less sure. This was a man who would require watching, because of his violent past, but picking on Astiz might violate obligations under the Geneva Conventions. There were no obligations to return him until hostilities were over, but he had to be accorded the treatment expected for POWs and Argentina had indicated through the ICRC that the treatment of Astiz would be considered when they were judging how to handle any British POWs. They now had one – Flt Lt Glover – in their hands. While held on the guard ship at Ascension, HMS *Dumbarton Castle*, Astiz again proved to be a difficult prisoner.

If Astiz was to be interviewed then he might have to be brought back to Britain, but he could not be held in prison and was not obliged to answer any questions. MoD soon came to the view that Astiz should be got 'off our hands as soon as possible.' It was decided on 21 May that he should be asked at Ascension by the Commander BFSU whether he was prepared to see Swedish and French representatives. If agreeable, he would then be taken to Britain and held at the Keep at Chichester, where he would be allowed the extensive privileges accorded to a POW. The ICRC refused to co-operate with this as they saw it outside the third Geneva Convention. Article 13 of this Convention required protection against public curiosity so there could be no media involvement. Unsurprisingly, neither the Argentine Government nor Astiz was prepared to agree to any sort of interrogation. Stockholm and Paris were both unhappy with this failure to move the issue forward and still demanded the opportunity to question him. The Swedish Foreign Minister appealed directly to Pym and offered his own interpretation of the Geneva Conventions. British legal advice still pointed to early repatriation. It would also be necessary to keep the goodwill and co-operation of the ICRC, who believed that they had lost credibility when Astiz was held back. If he were handed over to Sweden they would be bound to criticise Britain publicly. In the event he was repatriated.

South Georgia as a possible Forward Base

Exactly what was to be done with South Georgia once recaptured had been discussed prior to the event. One possibility was that it could serve as a Forward Operating Base in support of operations in the South Atlantic. It showed good potential but there were limitations, of which the most important was the lack of an airhead. A temporary airstrip could not be built and the range from Ascension was at any rate 3,400 miles. There were a number of places where ships could get alongside or anchor. Although the 'recreation' would be limited the weather should not inhibit personnel proceeding ashore. The island was a long way from the main operating area for minor war vessels such as the MCMVs and salvage tugs. It might be more use as a sheltered anchorage for the amphibious Task Force should any last minute maintenance to the ships and equipment be required, or if political circumstances meant that it was prudent to hold back. Limited training ashore could be carried out in terrain which was supposed (erroneously) to be similar to that which might be expected on the Falkland Islands. Another possible use was for damaged ships to effect temporary repairs before proceeding to a main base.

Most of these and other possible uses required that South Georgia have adequate defences against Argentine submarines and warships, in the form of surface ships, a submarine and ASW helicopters. These would not then be available for Falklands operations. The air threat was less worrisome unless the Argentine carrier moved to the area. The Director of Naval Plans felt that South Georgia could be useful if the Falkland Islands operation were prolonged for any length of time, and if bases in Chile could not be used for political reasons, and would be suitable as a base for a Forward Support Ship. After South Georgia had been retaken the issue was reappraised. Whatever the desirability of an airstrip it would take time and scarce resources and so made no sense in the context of the current operation. The view taken was that the only role for South Georgia was as a possible support base for the force and to provide secure moorings, and this is how it was eventually used. If the landing was delayed for some reason, then it could, if absolutely necessary, be used to allow the troops to come ashore. However, it was extremely unsuitable for the purpose.

19

THE CARRIER ISSUE

Total Exclusion Zone

As the Task Force approached the Falklands in late April it was time for the Maritime EZ to be turned into a Total EZ. There were a number of issues. The first concerned the extension to cover merchant shipping. The traditional view was that merchant ships should not be attacked so long as they were not active participants in the hostilities. During the course of two world wars this view had been undermined, not only because of the wholesale attacks on merchant shipping but also the tendency to arm merchant ships and integrate them with warships in convoys. In the prevailing circumstances where the UK was acting in self-defence, sinking an Argentine merchant ship could be justified if this was evidently part of the Argentine military effort at sea. This could be so whether the ship in question was operating in either the Argentine or British exclusion zones, and certainly if shown to be carrying supplies of arms or military materiel, or was itself armed.

On 27 April Leach reported to the Chiefs his concern about the activities of five Argentine fishing vessels that were known to be under Argentine naval control for surveillance and intelligence gathering purposes, yet there was a legal difficulty about adding them to the list of naval auxiliaries in the sense that they could not be 'seen' to be acting in support of the Argentine Navy. Nevertheless Leach took the view that they would become a 'thorn in the flesh' of the Task Force. It was agreed to look urgently into the possibility of issuing a warning through the Swiss that intelligence and surveillance activities by such Argentine merchant or fishing vessels would encounter an appropriate response. As to what action might be taken against such vessels, Leach wanted to treat them under the ROE applicable to merchant ships inside the MEZ, that is warning them off, but if necessary making an example of one such vessel by stopping, boarding and destroying relevant equipment as an exercise in minimum force.

The second issue was the extension to cover air activity. Initially it was intended to announce a separate air Exclusion Zone, but it soon seemed sensible for reasons of clarity for this to be merged into a total Exclusion Zone. This zone was described on 23 April, as potentially providing 'negotiating leverage while retaining a degree of international support for the United Kingdom's position'. If food and supplies could be denied to the Argentine garrison its morale and fighting capability would be weakened. Officials contended that: 'if the Argentines were unable or unwilling to break this blockade, internal pressure on their Government to negotiate a solution could mount'. All this depended on the Exclusion Zone being enforced, effectively requiring Stanley airfield to be neutralised. This could best be achieved by taking out the runway using either a Vulcan or Sea Harrier raid. If successful this would have the additional benefit of preventing the airport's use for fighter or ground attack aircraft. To rely instead on Harrier patrols intercepting Argentine aircraft would involve an intensive use of scarce resources, especially given the defensive needs of the Task Force, and would be inefficient, especially at night. It would also require direct attacks on transport aircraft, civil or military, with possibly a considerable loss of life.

The only amendments made by the War Cabinet to the proposals set before them stressed the importance of confining actions to within the TEZ. As Lewin had feared, the boundaries of this zone were acquiring a symbolic significance that put a premium on avoiding operations outside of this zone. Submarines, however, encouraged a blurring of the boundaries. New ROE were signalled to the Task Force on 26 April. Because of concerns about Argentine submarines, on 27 April it was decided that the SSNs could attack any conventional submarine they detected, 'whether or not it was itself inside the Zone'.

On 28 April, Thatcher told the War Cabinet that the projected announcement regarding the TEZ should be made immediately which would allow the enforcement of the TEZ to be established 48 hours later, i.e. on 30 April. The announcement stated that:

> From 11.00 GMT on 30 April 1982, a Total Exclusion Zone will be established round the Falkland Islands. The outer limit of this Zone is the same as for the Maritime Exclusion Zone established on Monday the 12 April 1982, namely a circle of 200 nautical miles radius from latitude 51 degrees 40 minutes South, 59 degrees 30 minutes West. From the time indicated, the Exclusion Zone will apply not only to Argentine warships and Argentine naval auxiliaries but also to any other ship, whether naval or merchant vessel, which is operating in support of the illegal occupation of the Falkland Islands by Argentine forces. The Exclusion Zone will also apply to any aircraft, whether military or civil, which is operating in support of the illegal operation. Any ship and any aircraft whether military or civil which is found within this Zone without due authority from the Ministry of Defence in London will therefore be regarded as hostile and liable to be attacked by British forces. Also

from the time indicated, Port Stanley airport will be closed; and any aircraft on the ground in the Falkland Islands will be regarded as present in support of the illegal occupation and accordingly is liable to attack. These measures are without prejudice to the right of the United Kingdom to take whatever additional measures may be needed in exercise of its right of self defence, under Article 51 of the UN Charter.

It was agreed, after the rather difficult experience over South Georgia, that at this stage of the conflict, the US would not be given any specific indication of British military plans beyond a general warning about the imminence of the next phase of operations.

As we have seen, the issue of operations outside of the TEZ had been dealt with in connection with South Georgia. While Article 51 of the UN Charter could provide sufficient legal cover for all likely contingencies, the statement on 23 April had also made it clear that:

any approach on the part of Argentine warships, including submarines, naval auxiliaries, or military aircraft which could amount to a threat to interfere with the mission of the British Forces in the South Atlantic will encounter the appropriate response. All Argentine aircraft including civil aircraft engaging in surveillance of these British Forces will be regarded as hostile and are liable to be dealt with accordingly.

The phrase 'could amount to a threat to interfere with the mission' covered a wide range of possibilities, although the word 'approach' suggested a more deliberate intent to seek out British forces. This question of approach was of particular relevance in regard to the Argentine carrier, the *25 de Mayo*, because of the potential range of its aircraft. This posed by far the greatest difficulties when it came to reconciling the conflicting political and military imperatives.

The threat from the *25 de Mayo*

Although elderly, having originally been built for the Royal Navy in 1945, and not in the best of condition, the aircraft carrier still provided Argentina with its most effective means of threatening the Task Force. In addition to its age there were reasons to qualify the threat. It would not wish to get too close to the Task Force for fear of presenting itself as too easy a target for SSNs. Its main air surveillance radars had suffered maintenance difficulties in the past and could be degraded. The critical issue concerned her ability to launch aircraft against the Task Force. Her normal complement of aircraft was eleven A4s, six Trackers and four Sea Kings. The Skyhawks were armed with two Sidewinder and 2 × 20mm cannon for the air defence role and could also be armed with bombs and the radio-controlled Pescador anti-ship missile with a range of 3.75nm. The Skyhawks, however, faced serious maintenance problems, aggravated by the American arms embargo. The Argentines had attempted to manufacture their own A4 parts: this was blamed for two known Argentine Air Force A4 losses in late 1981. One early analysis suggested that only about eight Skyhawks were probably operational at any given time and the Americans doubted that Air Force A4 pilots had been cross-trained on the carrier or in a naval strike mission. Some additional strike capability was provided by the Alouette helicopters, which could carry the French AS-11 and AS-12 air-to-surface missiles.

As things stood, therefore, the Carrier Air Group could conduct at most limited air-to-air and air-to-surface operations in good weather conditions. The helicopters lacked an effective anti-submarine capability while the fixed-wing elements were probably only capable of daylight operations. Six Tracker aircraft could carry out radar surveillance operations up to 500 miles from the carrier, enabling her to direct other air and naval units into attack positions. A more troubling possibility was that the most advanced Argentine aircraft, the Super Etendard, was operational at sea. Some 14 of the aircraft had been ordered from France, but only five to six had so far been delivered, in November 1981. This was a single-engined, single-seat aircraft fitted with modern avionics to give it a night and all-weather capability. It could carry a range of conventional attack weapons and also air-to-air missiles (AAM) for air defence. The possibility would be even more troubling if its most lethal weapon, the Exocet AM39 anti-ship missiles, with a 22nm range, had been acquired from France for these aircraft. Information obtained in early April tended to confirm that Exocets were operational. It appeared that the original American inertial guidance system fitted to the missiles had not worked properly but a new system developed by the French had been supplied for the Super Etendards. There was evidence that the French firm SNIAS was helping the Argentines and that five Super Etendards had been modified. Of the ten Exocet delivered to Argentina only five had been handed over so far for fitting, and France had undertaken to stop supplying military equipment to Argentina from 15 April.

Against this was a more reassuring suggestion that Super Etendards might not be able to operate from the carrier because of catapult limitations. Operating from a southerly shore base they had a radius of action of 350–400nm, depending on weapons fit. This could be a critical limitation. Initially the DIS was inclined to the view that Super Etendards could not reach the Falklands area with any effective weapons load; the Naval Staff also argued that the aircraft's operation and effectiveness would be limited by its targeting capability and also its vulnerability to decoy chaff.

These reassuring thoughts were contradicted by a US Naval assessment, which was that it should be assumed that when operating from land the aircraft would have full Exocet capability (including adequate targeting), and that they could also operate from the carrier although limitations in the alignment of inertial platforms would probably rule out effective use of Exocet in this role. On 8 April MoD's advice to CINCFLEET followed these lines. Information from the French, received on 12 April, and then confirmed, was that the Super Etendards could probably not operate from the carrier; this encouraging news was undermined by the warning that they were re-fuellable in flight using Argentina's two C130 tankers, although there was no evidence that this had been practised.

When the War Cabinet had its intelligence briefing on 15 April the doubt about whether the Super Etendard could be operated from the carrier was noted. The Americans still thought this to be possible while the French did not believe that the carrier had been fully modified to take the aircraft. For the moment the Navy Department were inclined to the American view, that modifications to the carrier catapult in 1977 were sufficient to enable the Super Etendard to be successfully launched. So while it was clear that the aircraft had not yet been flown from the carrier this future possibility could not be discounted.

The aircraft had insufficient range to operate effectively from a land base, unless it had acquired an aerial refuelling capability. This was noted as a technical possibility but there was little evidence one way or the other on whether the Argentines had made progress in this direction. There was also now reasonable confidence that each of the five aircraft was being fitted with one Exocet missile. Without refuelling, and with Exocet, it had a Hi-Lo-Hi radius of action of 375nm, just sufficient to reach East Falkland from Rio Grande. (In the event the use of KC-130 tankers made all the difference and the radius of action was extended significantly.) In mid-April the prudent intelligence estimate was that the Super Etendards fitted with Exocet would be operational by about 20 April, and that the carrier could operate the aircraft fully loaded but it had yet to do so. The carrier itself was described to the War Cabinet as a threat, quite serious if the Super Etendards were operating from it, but less so with the A4, and 'very vulnerable to counter action, especially Britain's SSNs'. As to what the 25 de Mayo was actually carrying, the best intelligence being distributed through JIC and to the Task Force on 19 April gave the aircraft embarked on the carrier as up to eight Skyhawk, six Trackers and five helicopters.

By now the weight of intelligence was that the Super Etendards would not be used on the carrier: if they could be used at all they would operate from land bases. Of particular concern was that, along with the A4s, they might operate from Stanley airfield. Acknowledging the conflicting reports, the intelligence summary of 23 April assessed that the Super Etendards were most likely to be operated from mainland air bases only. A full intelligence assessment of that day argued that, while these aircraft constituted the greatest threat, their limits could lie in the difficulties of identifying the highest value British units and their radius of action.

The carrier seemed less of a threat. It was thought unlikely that Argentina would raise more than about seven aircraft to fly from it. Further doubts about its capability surfaced on 27 April when uncorroborated reports suggested that it was suffering from a vibrating propeller shaft at speeds above 16 knots. This appeared the next morning as part of the JIC assessment. It was known that a couple of days earlier the carrier had been slowed down by a repair problem and bad weather. The speed restriction was significant, in that the fighter aircraft required a strong wind over the carrier's deck, in order to be able to operate at their maximum all up weights. As far as was known the carrier was in port for defect rectification, but would sail on 28 April. The continuing maintenance problems underlined the age of Argentina's Fleet and the difficulties the Navy had in keeping key ships at sea. By 29 April JIC was reporting further evidence that Argentina would not risk flying the Super Etendard from the carrier on operational sorties as their pilots were only half-trained on the aircraft.

A full report of 1 May pulled the various assessments together. This old ship, often suffering from mechanical failure, usually propulsion related, had spent ten days at sea and then back to home base on 25 April. If it went to sea again, its need to refuel regularly would be a constraint, as would be its limited ASW defence, largely dependent upon aircraft. Though capable of using Super Etendard this had never been attempted and there was no evidence that any were embarked. Moreover, arrester gear problems might affect its ability to operate its A4 aircraft. It rarely operated aircraft by night. No more than 75 per cent of its aircraft would be available at the start of operations and this would reduce to less than 60 per cent after any period of sustained operations, mainly because of spares problems. Another constraint would be the onboard stocks of fuel for the A4s. It was capable of a maximum radius of action of 500nm if conducting sustained flying operations and 900nm at economical speed. The maximum range for anti-ship strikes was put at 300–400nm, but this would be much reduced at night and in poor weather conditions. Furthermore, if two aircraft were being kept on combat air patrols, then only four would be available to mount an attack.

Targeting the carrier

This assessment came the day after new ROE had come into force, permitting a submarine to attack the carrier if it was found outside of the TEZ. This change followed days of intensive debate, and persistent pressure by the Royal Navy to get the rules relaxed. On the morning of 21 April the carrier's group was believed to be on a slow passage south. After the War Cabinet meeting that day Lewin told the Prime Minister that 'it had been possible to identify the location of the Argentine naval force including the aircraft carrier *25 de Mayo* in a patrol area between the Argentine coast and the

Falkland Islands Maritime Exclusion Zone,' and that he had ordered *Splendid*, which was some two days' sailing away from this area, to conduct surveillance operations in the carrier's likely vicinity and prepare for offensive operations against the group if so ordered. For the moment existing ROEs would be in effect: SSNs could not attack surface ships except in self-defence but could attack any conventional submarine detected. When the Foreign Secretary found out about this he was extremely concerned, not least because he had been left the impression at the War Cabinet meeting that day that no decisions had been taken on SSN operations outside the MEZ. There was a risk of a major incident once they began and he was just about to leave for sensitive negotiations in Washington. His main concern at this time was the possibility of an encounter with an Argentine submarine as under existing rules this could be attacked and sunk.

The War Cabinet was given a briefing on the morning of 22 April, during which it was explained that if it was decided to intercept the carrier group, then believed to be 90nm off Punta Delgado and some 480nm from the Falklands, it would take an SSN about 36 hours. The earlier an SSN could be despatched the sooner the carrier might be found. Nonetheless, as a result of the FCO position, the orders to *Splendid* were reversed. As an attack on the carrier would not be ordered in these circumstances there seemed to be little point in using up an SSN just on surveillance. Nevertheless, on 24 April further intelligence, and the imminent arrival of the Task Group into the Falklands area, led to the orders to *Splendid* to conduct surveillance and prepare for offensive operations against the carrier group being reinstated. By the next day there was intelligence that the *25 de Mayo* and the *Santisima Trinidad* had left Puerto Belgrano and moved south. The problem was now finding the group with sufficient accuracy to permit an attack and a day later *Splendid* was still being instructed to do so (in fact by then the carrier had put back into port for repairs).

The need to prepare specifically for an attack on the carrier was raised at Chequers the next day. There was considerable apprehension among ministers. All agreed that it was essential to protect the amphibious force at the moment of greatest danger, that the essential first step was to close down Stanley airport to all Argentine aircraft capable of interfering with a landing, and that dealing with the *25 de Mayo* might well be a sensible second step. Otherwise, as the First Sea Lord warned them, the British air defences might become just too stretched. If the Argentine Air Force was also close to the limits of its range over West Falkland, then the carrier provided Argentina's most likely means of mounting a serious threat to the Task Force. Yet sinking the carrier seemed a large step to take. Nott worried about a 'horrible logic' that would see the taking out of Argentine airfields as the move after that. Whitelaw wondered whether public opinion was ready for the sinking of a carrier. Thatcher took the view that it would find that more acceptable than attacks on their airfield, which might be understood as putting civilians at risk. Leach followed this by insisting that taking out the carrier was essential to the future security of the Falkland Islands and then Lewin came in arguing that it was essential for the security of the amphibious force, so much so that it needed to be taken out by 3 May. Then there was the question of whether a warning should be issued to the Argentines to stay clear of the zone of operations, but against this came the objection that this would merely encourage the Argentine Navy to hold the carrier close to the mainland until its aircraft were most needed. Given the uncertainties surrounding the Haig negotiations at the time, and in the light of South Georgia, a warning could appear provocative. Not issuing a warning and then sinking the carrier would be even more provocative. The decision was too momentous for the War Cabinet to take at that time. Ministers agreed that Nott should be invited to report further on the appropriate ROE if it did become necessary to attack the carrier outside the Exclusion Zone and on the possibility of issuing a warning.

It was recognised that this issue would raise all the difficult questions of military escalation. The military logic was pointing to taking every possible action to reduce the threat to the Task Force. For example, if, as was at times claimed, the operating distance of aircraft launched from the carrier was as much as 500nm, this was significantly greater than the distance between the Argentine mainland and the Falklands. This could lead to a case for attacking the carrier in port, where at least casualties could be kept down, and this could lead by extension into a case for attacking mainland bases. Yet the political logic stressed the need to avoid escalatory or provocative action, especially while negotiations were still underway, and to stay within the framework of international law. The FCO's Legal Adviser was clear that the carrier could be sunk on the high seas as soon as its aircraft were in range of the Task Force, especially if a clear warning had been given that if it moved beyond a certain point the carrier could expect to be attacked. Attacking without warning would be much more problematic. It would be appropriate to inform Argentina, through the Swiss, that if the carrier moved south or east over a designated boundary line this would be considered a hostile act.

The Chiefs of Staff, taking their cue from the Chequers meeting, began to review the carrier issue on 26 April. The First Sea Lord made the running. Once the *25 de Mayo* could sail with Super Etendards he argued, it would be hard for the Task Force to anticipate when an attack would materialise. He therefore judged it essential for the safety of Britain's own ships that pre-emptive action be taken as soon as an attack was threatened. It would not be safe to wait under such circumstances for decisions to be taken in London and then transmitted to the SSNs. He set a deadline for 3 May on how to deal with the carrier including the extent to which Argentina should be made aware of what had been decided. The Chief of the General Staff rejected the possibility of an attack without warning before a hostile act had been committed or the Task Force approached. The FCO representative also warned of legal problems if a presumed hostile intent was declared at ranges as great as 500nm. The Navy were unconvinced: at the carrier's operating range even declaring a zone out of which the carrier should not move could define a sanctuary from which it could present a constant threat. The inconclusive debate led to Lewin proposing the drafting of a paper for the next day addressing the nature, range and timing of the threat posed by the aircraft carrier; the options available to the Task Force Commander to protect the amphibious force; the means of reducing the threat either by authorising pre-emptive attacks or by declaring special zones; the advantages and disadvantages of giving a warning of Britain's intentions; and action to be taken in respect of survivors of any attack.

The same day, the Task Force commanders decided to approach the issue from another angle. The starting point was an anomalous situation that had arisen with regard to one of the critical rules of engagement, Rule 206, according to which authority would be delegated to assume that an attack by an enemy unit was the first in a set of pre-planned multiple attacks. In such circumstances the British would wish to strike all threatening units to reduce the further risk to ships of the Task Force. What might constitute a 'threatening unit' would vary but in almost all circumstances would include the carrier. This rule, however, only applied to RN aircraft or surface ships: the ROE for SSNs only permitted attacks outside the TEZ in self-defence or against a detected conventional submarine. Northwood therefore proposed that a new rule should be devised to cover a contingency, in which a multiple attack could be about to occur and an SSN was trailing the carrier. If Woodward then determined that the carrier was a threatening unit, Northwood would authorise an attack. Against the claim that the critical issue here was conformity between the SSNs and aircraft and surface ships, Sir Ian Sinclair, the FCO Legal Adviser, was dubious that this issue was really different from the general issue of when to attack the carrier.

On the evening of 27 April authority was requested for the ROE to be changed to allow for offensive action by SSNs outside of the TEZ should an attack be reported from any Argentine source. This was known when the Chiefs of Staff met on 27 April to address the paper on how to target the carrier. Leach expressed concern that the paper had not considered the full range of options. It had instead identified a fallback position, in line with the FCO view, based on a safe zone. He argued that monitoring the movement of the carrier within the proposed zone would lead to a large diversion of effort from the major task of enforcing the TEZ. His own preference was to sink the carrier without warning after other Argentine naval units had attacked, under the Rule of Engagement 206. This was also the option proposed by Northwood.

Alternatively Argentina should be given 48 hours' notice that the carrier should return to harbour and remain there, or it would be attacked as showing hostile intent. Lower down his order of preferences came a warning to Argentina that if the carrier was not kept within a 12 mile territorial limit, it would be attacked as demonstrating hostile intent. His least favourite option was to specify a range of 200 miles from the Task Force, within which it could be attacked. This was an extension of the existing ROEs, which allowed for warships to be deemed hostile and attacked once they were in Exocet range (about 25nm). He judged that only the first two options were feasible. The reiterated objections of Bramall to sinking the carrier without warning indicated the presentational problems posed by any decision to single out the carrier for special treatment. Again no decision was reached but the paper was to be revised for a further meeting the next day.

The likely reaction of the Argentine Navy if Britain issued a warning was examined. One possibility might be that obedience to British demands would offend the honour of this most hawkish of the Argentine services, while it might ignore a 12 mile limit because it did not recognise the concept. On the other hand they might decide that a designated boundary was easier to manage, for they could still claim to be operating as they wished. It was not wholly clear what would be the ideal response. Perhaps the optimum scenario would have Britain obtaining political cover by issuing a warning, and then this being ignored by Argentina so that there would be an opportunity to attack the carrier before it could cause too much trouble.

Leach was still unhappy the next day with the revised paper. The threat assessment now was more cautious – with the combat range of Skyhawks, and possibly Super Etendards, put at 400 miles from the carrier. As the options were now phrased he wanted a clear recommendation for sinking the carrier as soon as possible. Sinking it under Rule 206 was acceptable. Inducing the carrier to return to port or to stay within territorial waters and north of 43°S, were fallback positions. These had little military merit whatever their political and diplomatic attractions. In discussion, the possibility of a further option was identified, according to which Argentina would be warned that the aircraft carrier would be attacked if any British naval or air forces were engaged by any Argentine forces anywhere. This seemed to fit with setting a geographical limitation for SSN operations. The consensus was moving in this direction. A redraft of the paper was provided for a further meeting later that day. Another short meeting took the Chiefs towards an agreed paper to be passed on to the War Cabinet.

The paper that reached the War Cabinet described the threat:

> The Argentine has one old aircraft carrier. However, she can carry 7 to 9 Skyhawk and, possibly, up to 5 Super Etendard aircraft. Both types of aircraft are capable of mounting air-to-surface and air-to-air attacks at a distance of about 400 miles from the carrier. The 6 Tracker aircraft can carry out radar surveillance operations up to 500 miles from the carrier, giving her the capability to direct other

air and naval units into attack positions as well as using her own offensive aircraft.

Defence against carrier-based aircraft, it was explained, required the use of Sea Harriers, which at the same time were also required to deal with land-based aircraft and engage in offensive air operations. Ship air defences could well prove to be inadequate. So the best defence against the carrier would be 'to neutralise' it, preferably by attacking the carrier as soon as possible wherever she could be found on the high seas. Alternatively a warning could be given that the carrier would be attacked if British forces were attacked first, or else as soon as it left port, or its internationally recognised waters, or an area from which it could not mount damaging attacks. These other options became progressively difficult to enforce, as they became progressively easier to justify politically.

Whatever the policy the attack would best be undertaken with SSNs, which could be thwarted by shallow waters and fast movement, but would involve less risk and diversion of effort than attacks by surface ships or aircraft. The question of Argentine casualties was addressed. It was expected that if struck she would be disabled:

> It is possible that she might sink quickly, but this is unlikely given good damage control practices. An attack by gunfire, missiles or bombs would also result in severe damage to the carrier or loss of life. If the carrier did sink, it is probable that a large proportion of her crew numbering about 1,000 would have time to abandon ship with life rafts. Her escorting vessels should be able to pick up survivors.

The conclusion was clear. While attack without warning on the high seas provided the 'most economic and certain prospect of neutralising the threat', MoD recognised that 'the legal basis for such action could be difficult to establish, and that the political reaction to it could be damaging'. The recommendation was for a determination to sink the carrier once any Argentine unit made an attack. To reduce the risk that it might get into a position where an immediate threat might be posed to British forces before hostilities broke out elsewhere, there should also be a warning that the 25 de Mayo would be vulnerable once it moved into an area where it could in principle threaten the Task Force.

The deliberations within Government had been difficult. As late as the morning of 30 April it was still assumed that no decision could be taken until the next day. Nott had yet to make up his mind and was not prepared to give a firm recommendation. One senior civil servant observed that the Foreign Secretary was 'fussed' about the carrier issue, adding: 'He feels he is being bounced. He is.' There had been sharp disagreements among the

Chiefs. The War Cabinet addressed the issue on the morning of 30 April but failed to conclude their discussions. They met again in the afternoon, this time with an FCO Legal Adviser present. The Attorney General was not present at either session.[1] The FCO Legal Adviser had taken the position that the actuality of any threat must be demonstrable. Force could only be used if the carrier was close enough to mount an air attack. Lewin, whose view was close to Leach's, could argue that on the worst case, if the carrier could cover 500 miles in a day and carry aircraft with an operating radius of 500 miles, it was always able to threaten the Task Force. On that basis, the open warning of 23 April telling Argentina not to interfere with the mission of the Task Force was quite sufficient. In the end Lewin's view prevailed. On the Friday afternoon the War Cabinet decided to change the ROE to permit all forces to attack the carrier outside the TEZ, even if there had been no prior attack on the Task Force, except when it was north of 35°S and west of 48°W (a triangle off the Uruguay coast) or within 12nm of the Argentine coast.

As already noted, by the time the ROE was changed it was known that the *25 de Mayo* could have difficulty launching its Skyhawks, and that it was not carrying any Super Etendards and in all probability would not be able to do so. On this basis it is arguable that the Chiefs of Staff could have given the War Cabinet a more relaxed view of the carrier and the steps that were needed to neutralise it. This would have relieved the Foreign Secretary and the Attorney General of their anxiety, which lay not so much in the military merit behind the change in ROE but in its presentation should it be executed. A draft statement was prepared to deal with the uproar anticipated on the sinking of the carrier, explaining the danger it posed and the reasons why the 23 April statement covered it. No warning was to be issued in advance. Pym, about to leave for Washington, was worried about whether such a statement could be sufficient to defend an attack if there had been no prior warning. He wrote to the Prime Minister on 1 May. Having consulted with Havers, he argued that 'our position would be immeasurably strengthened if we had given a warning to the Argentine Government, requiring the aircraft carrier to stay within the narrow zone we discussed yesterday, or within territorial waters south of about 41 degrees South.' With this in mind, he attached the 'draft of a possible warning message, which we could ask the Swiss to convey urgently to the Argentine Government'.

The starting point of Pym's draft was an Argentine statement of 30 April. According to this, British vessels within 200 miles of the Argentine mainland, the Falklands and their Dependencies, would be considered hostile. While including the British TEZ, this unambiguous combat zone was much wider (and in fact included the area in which the *Belgrano* was eventually sunk). Pym's draft mentioned the *25 de Mayo* and warned that it would be at risk if it ventured beyond territorial waters. It went on to say that:

272

if any attack anywhere in the South Atlantic is made upon British naval or air forces by an Argentine unit, all other Argentine naval units operating on the high seas, including the carrier 'THE 25TH OF MAY', even if she is still inside the limits defined in this communication, and all Argentine military aircraft operating in air space over the South Atlantic will be regarded as hostile and are liable to be dealt with accordingly.

It is of note that while this warning was specific to the carrier it would also have indicated to Argentina that once British forces were attacked outside the TEZ all Argentine forces would then have become liable to attack, and no regard would have been paid to Argentina's 12 mile zone.

This proposal was not rejected. It was due to be discussed by the War Cabinet on 2 May, although by the time of the meeting events had moved on and so there is no record of any discussion. The clear evidence of Argentina's readiness to engage British forces, exhibited on 1 May, would have at the very least required substantial redrafting. In preparation for the decision, and in response to the Foreign Secretary's letter, Lewin did observe that if the warning was issued, and heeded, the carrier would remain a threat into the long term.

20

HOSTILITIES

As the first major military confrontations drew closer, the starting point for the military was that the Task Force was far from home and vulnerable to attack if the enemy could just get close enough. This was made very clear by Woodward in his 24 April signal to Fieldhouse:

> My unequivocal military advice from the sharp end is that while it suits the Args to continue talking as though we were at peace, their invasion of the Falklands, and all evidence since, demonstrates clear intention to fight wherever its suits unless totally outnumbered/ outgunned. Present ROE allow the battle to be fought in one area but not in another unless Args choose, thereby optimising their capability while minimising mine. This is military nonsense not least since loss of or serious damage to Hermes/Invincible in a pre-emptive attack completely spitchers any prospect of further UK ops. I assess this arguably small probability of a large military disaster has to offer substantial political advantage to be justified. If political pressures nevertheless demand, then TG 317.8 should be concentrated and fully prepared for bitter battle, not least because such concentration should also have maximum deterrent effect.

His signal concluded:

> If we wish to make a show of force we should do it in style. If we make a stylish show of force it should be in full acceptance of the possible need to fight. If we have to fight we should seek to engineer the best possible killing ground. If the killing starts in earnest we should recognise the political need to pursue the fight to the conclusion if lives are not to be needlessly wasted. If lives are not to be needlessly wasted we should first try the show of force, and so on again.

We have seen how this concern drove the Chiefs to press for less restrictive rules of engagement, even as the diplomats and lawyers insisted that no move should be taken that could not be fully justified internationally. By the end of April, after a lot of pressure, the major concession to the military view was that the carrier could be attacked in a designated area. We have noted that this pressure coincided with apparently greater clarity over the limited capabilities of the carrier, and in particular its inability to carry the Super Etendards and the restrictions on its ability to launch Skyhawk A4s.

Assessing the threat

Woodward's concern anticipated a definite trend in the assessments coming from the intelligence community to the effect that Argentina appeared prepared to act with massive force, and even some desperation, when the moment came. This analysis developed as part of an effort to understand the Junta's response to their frustration over the course of the Haig mediation and the manner in which the British had retaken South Georgia. Other than that this had left them smarting, the evidence was by no means clear-cut. Some Argentine sources still suggested a degree of complacency, as if Britain would be bound to seek new negotiations because of the suicidal consequences of attempting to retake the well-fortified Islands. Perhaps, it was argued, the Argentines might consider 'performing a mad dog act' with *kamikaze*-type attacks, as if Galtieri might lash out when backed into a corner. The thrust of most of the analysis was that Argentina was preparing for a British offensive, to which it intended to respond with large-scale air strikes against the Task Force. The Argentine fleet would be held back while the impact of the strikes was evaluated. As the British Task Force drew closer to the Islands, however, all forces would be fully committed to battle.

On 28 April one substantial analysis of likely Argentine strategy, emanating from Washington, made worrying reading. Although not based on any new evidence, it drew attention to the growing possibility of a high-risk Argentine pre-emptive strike. The Argentines were known to be readying contingency plans for a combined air and naval assault against British forces, and this included developing tactical plans to attack Britain's superior forces using anti-ship missiles from their own surface fleet. A readiness to take greater risks was already evident in the re-supply effort for their forces on the Falklands, which had led to efforts to run the MEZ with one or more cargo vessels. More seriously, on 27 April, following South Georgia, the *San Luis* was en route to the zone to sink enemy ships in what could well be an opening offensive action. It was intending to reach a patrol area just to the north of the Falkland Islands by the morning of 29 April, authorised to sink any enemy warship or merchant ship. As with the British ROE for SSNs, the Argentine ROE allowed *San Luis* to presume that any submarine contact was the enemy. In other respects this was more hawkish than the

British ROE, and indeed, represented what the Royal Navy was after. Furthermore, through aerial surveillance they were getting a reasonable idea of the disposition of British surface ships.

With details of the South Georgia defeat beginning to leak, and internal criticism growing, Galtieri was in even greater need than before of a military initiative. Anaya, the most hawkish member of the Junta, would be feeling particularly irritated by the loss of the *Santa Fe* and the surrender of special naval forces. He could be looking for retribution, even at great cost. If Argentina believed, as it well might, that it faced an imminent end to negotiations and a near-term British assault on the Falklands, the coming few days provided the best opportunity it might ever get to mount a substantial air attack on British units, especially if they started to move into the area between the mainland and the Falklands.

Press reports in Argentina and the United States drew attention to intensifying Argentine preparations and the possibility that Buenos Aires was considering a pre-emptive air strike on British units before the blockade was scheduled to go into effect. The key test for the Argentines, these reports suggested, was whether significant damage could be inflicted on a major British warship such as one of the carriers. A US report of 1 May of a conversation with the Argentine Air Force Chief of Staff noted his claim that Argentina would not open fire and that any response to a British attack would be graduated, depending on its nature and scale, but that 'an attack on Port Stanley airport would trigger a full-scale attack on the British fleet' and almost any engagement was likely to lead to a rapid escalation. The US Embassy in Buenos Aires commented that there was 'considerable pressure from the Argentinean Navy to attempt a major strike before all units of the British Task Force have reached the scene' and that they had been told that if British vessels came too close to the Islands, 'Argentina Would Open Fire.'

This changing intelligence assessment provides a part explanation for the toughening of the British position over the last few days of April and the anxiety over the American reluctance to declare the Haig mediation over. On the morning of 28 April the JIC could still contrast the hawkish intimations with the reality of the problems the Argentine surface fleet was experiencing as it spent more time at sea and attempted to move itself to a war-time footing. There had been many returns to port and reported defects: 'a prolonged period at sea is likely to degrade their condition even more'. By the next morning, however, the JIC was reporting that Argentina had reacted to Britain's declaration of the TEZ and was anticipating imminent military operations. The carrier was getting back to its operating area from Puerto Belgrano, the *San Luis* had no restrictions on the use of its armaments, and, after a lull from 24 April, maritime air reconnaissance had started again on 26 April. Probably as a result of the British warning, they were no longer overflying British units but relying on radar for contact reporting. The Argentine command on the Falklands was now expecting the British would be landing commando reconnaissance parties.

During 29 April it became clear that by the next day two of the three Task Forces of the Argentine Fleet would be en route to positions north-west of the MEZ, the third remaining in a position off the southern tip of Argentina. The Junta had responded to Britain's announcement about the TEZ with a declaration that it would consider hostile all British civil or military ships and aircraft within 200 miles of the Argentine mainland or within a 200-mile radius of the Falkland Islands, South Georgia and the Sandwich Islands. It seemed likely that until Buenos Aires knew more about the location of the British fleet and especially of the SSNs, it would keep its major surface forces on the periphery of the EZ under land-based air cover until general conflict broke out. It was doing its best to find out: over a 24-hour period there were at least three reconnaissance flights by 707s, including one intercepted by a Harrier.

During 30 April it became clear to the British that the Argentine fleet was divided into three task groups, two of which were apparently en route to positions off the southern tip of Argentina, although one was currently among the islands and the other was just to the south. In fact Allara, Commander TF79, was on the carrier. With four other warships and a tanker this composed TG79.1; together with the second group (TG79.4, of three A69 corvettes, all armed with Exocet), it was operating to the north of the EZ. To the south was TG79.3, comprising the *Belgrano* together with two Exocet-armed destroyers and a tanker. Reconnaissance had been stepped up as the Argentines looked out for support units behind the Task Force. From 29 April Argentine air and surface units could well be operating within the TEZ, moving to battle readiness, conducting anti-submarine operations and with relaxed ROE, geared largely to checking that it was the enemy in their sights while, if possible, not giving their positions away, and following an established battle plan. If any British ships were in the Argentine EZ – none actually were – they would also be attacked. The JIC now concluded that Argentina was 'planning for a pre-emptive air and naval attack on the United Kingdom Task Force.' In this they accepted the view that Galtieri's past record marked him out as a commander willing to act boldly or take risks, especially if backed into a corner.

So it seemed possible that Argentina would initiate large-scale air and naval assaults on the British forces, possibly as early as 30 April. That day the press was reporting that Argentine forces were on red alert as Britain's TEZ went into effect. One curiosity lay in the activity of the southern Argentine Task Force, composed of the *Belgrano* and two destroyers. A few days earlier it had appeared to be guarding against Chile, and was even believed to have infringed Chilean territorial waters by cruising as little as 8–10 miles off the coast, with maritime patrol aircraft in support, possibly trying to provoke the Chilean Navy. It might have been looking for British warships or the former, HMS *Norfolk* on the erroneous assumption that this ship had been handed back by Chile to Britain.

The continuing Argentine interest in South Georgia, including air surveillance, led to the possibility that it might be sent there to challenge the recently installed British garrison. By the evening of the 29 April the group was noted to be patrolling between the Isla de los Estados and the Burdwood Bank, in order to draw out British forces and test reactions within the TEZ. The cruiser took up a course that would take it into the southern edge of the TEZ early Sunday morning where it would remain for a limited period of time before withdrawing. There were also indications that both Argentine Navy 209 submarines were operating in the TEZ. Information on Argentina's offensive intent was distributed in intelligence summaries on the evening of 30 April, and provided the headline for the JIC assessment on the morning of 1 May. The JIC saw this as a high-risk strategy, probably reflecting an assumption that British SSNs would be patrolling in the northern half of the TEZ, so that the southern half was a less risky area for its own forces. Yet, as the JIC noted, 'the vessels in task group 79.3 are elderly and have a poor anti-submarine capability; and the area into which they have been ordered has deep water suitable for operations by British submarines'.

Woodward's plan

In some respects the gearing up of the Argentine Navy for battle was good news, for without engagement there could be no attrition. When the Argentine reconnaissance 707 had been watching the carrier group, chaff helped to give the impression that the amphibious group was there as well. On 30 April, Woodward wrote of his hope that he might 'convince Argentinians that we were the advance landing force. Thus they might be tempted to come out and fight on our terms (despite our difficulties with ROE).' Woodward's plan was to enter the Exclusion Zone by night and operate the carriers in the eastern sector. All available firepower, from air and sea, would be concentrated on Stanley airfield and the other Island airstrips would also be suppressed. The *25 de Mayo* would be neutralised by an SSN while offensive ASW action would be carried out in known Argentine submarine areas. By night the reconnaissance teams would be inserted. Between 30 April and 2 May eight patrols of G Squadron SAS and two SBS were landed on the Falklands by Sea King helicopters from 846 Naval Air Squadron.[1]

The analysis distributed to the Task Force during the evening of 30 April warned that Argentine units might be encountered in the TEZ, and were likely to have relaxed ROEs, and later, in a supplementary, that the *Belgrano* group could also be moving northwards in a probing sortie. Not until 0735Z on 1 May were the *Belgrano*'s likely movements reported, including its probable entry into the TEZ. By this time the SSN *Conqueror* was looking for the cruiser. On the morning of 29 April, it had been told of the likely assembly of the *Belgrano* group; by the afternoon of 30 April it had detected by sonar the oiler, *Puerto Rosales*. That evening it received instructions from Northwood to intercept and attack the *Belgrano* group, but only within the TEZ. The next morning, 1 May, it received the intelligence summary that anticipated a deliberate incursion into the TEZ taking place on 2 May between 0630Z and 0930Z. At 1400Z on 1 May *Conqueror* sighted the *Belgrano* group, and began to shadow. This was reported back to Northwood (1529Z) and then to MoD (1605Z).

By contrast *Splendid*, ordered to seek out the carrier, was having a much more frustrating time. On 29 April the SSN sighted at various times the three A69 frigates (or corvettes) – *Granville*, *Drummond* and *Guerrico*, and the two Type 42 destroyers, *Santisima Trinidad* and *Hercules*. But there was no sign of the carrier, which was now presumed to be back at port. *Splendid* decided to stick with the frigates, which were moving south possibly to rendezvous with the carrier close to the coast. As *Splendid* moved to periscope depth to transmit a situation report the frigates chose to accelerate south-west and so firm contact was lost. *Splendid* was encouraged to follow them south as that was where the carrier could be, and it also offered the SSN a good defensive position. It came across *Hercules* again and also the Gearing class destroyer, *Commodoro Py*. Now that it had some contacts *Splendid* was reluctant to move again, but there was still no sign of the carrier, though from the next morning it knew of the change in ROE allowing for an attack on the *25 de Mayo*. *Splendid* now had a position where it expected the *25 de Mayo* to rendezvous with its escorts, but when it arrived at 0800Z on 1 May, it found nothing. Several sonar contacts were made, including possibly some warships, but none that indicated the presence of an aircraft carrier. It went to periscope depth but failed to make a sighting and by 0900Z concluded that there were no contacts in its chosen area. It searched for some time and then went north on another fruitless journey to investigate possible signs of an Argentine submarine.

Vulcan raid

The start of renewed hostilities was marked by action not by the Royal Navy but by the Royal Air Force. The RAF had not envisaged carrying out offensive air operations in the South Atlantic and when the Task Force was constituted few of the roles that the RAF could play in its support were immediately apparent. Only the Nimrod Maritime Patrol aircraft of 18 Group were initially seen as having an operational task in addition to the transport aircraft required to supply the forward base at Ascension Island under the control of HQ 38 Group. Any independent operations against targets thousands of miles away would involve its long-range Vulcan bomber force. The possible use of the Vulcans occurred to RAF personnel as soon as the possibility of a campaign to retake the Islands arose in late

March, although this was not part of the original options papers, and initially was ruled out because of the amount of effort involved.

One difficulty was that this force was configured only for nuclear operations; another was that the remaining squadrons were due to be phased out by 30 June 1982. The phasing out could be delayed by a ministerial decision, although in agreeing to run on three squadrons until the end of the year, Nott asked that no impression should be given 'through MoD statements that the Vulcan Squadrons have been "reprieved"'. Reconnecting and proving the air-to-air refuelling capability and working up a conventional bombing capability required a considerable effort. It had been twenty years since Vulcan crews had required training in aerial refuelling. Soon ten aircraft were ready, backed by ample stocks of engines, other essential spares, and 1000-lb bombs.

On 11 April Woodward had requested plans for the best use of the Sea Harriers to attack targets on the Falklands, and this prompted a much more serious analysis of how Vulcans might be used. Even so it was still not part of the thinking among the Central Staff as they prepared analyses of the options for the Chiefs and Task Force commanders. Gradually thinking focused on a single Vulcan operation against the airfield at Stanley, discarding other vague ideas about the Argentine mainland or even shipping. A range of mainland targets, such as airfields and ports, which depended on use of Chilean airfields should the Vulcans need to divert, always seemed to be of questionable legality, provocative politically and probably doubtful operationally, given the known difficulties of putting such facilities out of action with anything other than massive raids. Yet because targets in Argentina could in principle be struck, and this would be understood as soon as it was known that Vulcans had been deployed to Ascension Island, there could be additional strategic benefits. For example, the Chief of Air Staff argued, Argentina would need to maintain or deploy some of their fighters to the country's north, in case they had to deal with an attack, so reducing the threat to the Task Force.

Whether it would be wise actually to mount an attack just against Stanley airport was another question. The initial briefing for Beetham had taken a 'robust approach' and made only a passing reference to the risks of causing civilian casualties or a great effort producing a very modest result. The initial plan was for a single Vulcan to carry seven bombs, thereby keeping down the refuelling requirements and the number of tankers involved, but this might not be enough to do the job. On Tuesday 20 April Beetham acknowledged to the other Chiefs the uncertainties, particularly with regard to civilian casualties, and promised a full assessment of the Vulcan's capabilities by the coming Friday.

The paper tabled on 23 April had raised the payload and the refuelling requirement. The bombing tests at the Garvie Island range had shown that seven 1,000-lb bombs were not enough but a full load of 21 should do the job. If they could be dropped at a low level on the Stanley runway, there would be a 90 per cent probability that this would cause one runway crater and a 75 per cent probability of causing two. The attack should also cause considerable damage to the parking area, and any parked aircraft. This would be a major effort. To get a single Vulcan to the Falkland Islands from Ascension Island, 3,350 miles away, would require a force of ten Victor tankers. As far as the risk to the local population was concerned the proposed direction of attack should keep Stanley itself and its outskirts outside the predicted impact area. The risks to the crews would be reduced by the lack of Argentine Air Defence aircraft deployed to the Falkland Islands, and they were unlikely to be intercepted by aircraft based on the mainland. The main threat would be anti-aircraft guns and surface-to-air missiles around Stanley, and related air defence radars. They would probably be defeated by flying at night, the likely bad weather and achieving surprise. In case the defences were more capable, the Vulcan's Electronic Counter-Measures (ECM) capability was being enhanced. One aircraft could be ready to conduct bombing operations on the second night after authority to deploy to Ascension Island was given. If the authority was given the next day, two aircraft would deploy to Ascension Island on Sunday of which one would be ready to make a first raid on Stanley airfield during the night of 26 April, three days before the Carrier Battle Group could be within range to carry out that operation with Sea Harriers. The advantages of an early raid would be in surprise and the basic advantage of stopping the re-supply operation as quickly as possible.

At the meeting on 23 April Beetham was 'an extremely hawkish proponent of the idea.' Against this was concern that the use of long-range bombers might cause presentational problems, as this would reinforce the sense of being in a state of war. The alternative, of using Sea Harriers to attack the airfield, had political advantages. They would also be better placed to prevent the runway being repaired and the airfield reopened. Lewin concluded by stressing the advantages of an early attack, before the carrier group arrived, and of conserving the Harriers for other activities. Some MoD civilians were sceptical about the effectiveness of the attack but the Chiefs were unanimous. Lewin reported that evening to Nott that: 'The Chiefs-of-Staff are confident that such an operation is militarily feasible and stands a good chance of success.' They were reluctant to leave the attack too long lest its demands start to clash with other operations out of Ascension, including flying in Harrier reinforcements. Deploying two Vulcans to Ascension would not in itself be a commitment to the operation, but might by itself have deterrent value.

The Prime Minister by this time was also well aware of the issues connected with the Vulcan raid, as she had been visiting Northwood on the afternoon of 23 April and Lewin briefed her on the proposal. Like everything else at this time it was caught up in the complex diplomatic end game surrounding the Haig mediation effort. There had already been evidence of

American concerns about more assertive British actions, including the wider use of Ascension. The USAF Base Commander had suggested that Vulcan operations would come outside the UK/US agreement. Pym was to have attempted to deal with US anxieties about the use of the airport as a base for offensive operations while in Washington.[2] Henderson and Haig would be concluding the discussions but until this was done, the War Cabinet decided on 22 April, no Vulcans could be deployed to Wideawake until it proved possible to dispose of American anxieties. However, the State Department confirmed that there would be no objection to Britain deploying Vulcan aircraft to Ascension, and the Pentagon was so informed. As problematic, as Lewin acknowledged, was that 'since the deployment would become known its effect on the diplomatic scene needs to be taken into account, particularly if Mr Haig were to return to Buenos Aires'. A further cause of delay was problems with Vulcan air-to-air refuelling, which were not sorted out until late on 26 April. So it was not until 27 April, by which time the British, if not yet the American, Government was convinced that the Haig plan had no future, that deployment of Vulcans to Ascension was authorised. A decision to mount the attack would have to wait. As the diplomatic fog cleared that was given.

While the strategic debate was decided in favour of the Vulcan raid (designated BLACK BUCK), an intensive tactical debate had developed between Northwood and the Task Force over the relationship between Vulcan and Sea Harrier operations. Outside of the RAF the Vulcan operation was considered by many to be an expensive and cumbersome effort to achieve an uncertain result that could probably be achieved much more easily through the use of Sea Harriers. Moreover, the clinching argument for the use of the Vulcan was that it would conserve Sea Harrier resources, yet the requirement for damage assessment meant that Harriers would have to be put in harm's way to take photographs after the Vulcan attack.

These views had been forcefully expressed to Woodward by the naval aviators with the Task Force and were made, equally forcefully, by Woodward in a signal on 27 April, as the War Cabinet was considering whether to deploy the Vulcans to Ascension. As he could not now get an early attack on the airport then at least it should be 'substantial and accurate'. While 'freely admitting total ignorance of Vulcan capability', he suspected that the attack he would now get from this source would be 'too little, too late.' He would therefore prefer to use Sea Harriers directly for the attack, rather than later reconnaissance, backed by naval gunfire support (NGS), while the Vulcans could be used to help in what was still a major concern, the location and shadowing of Argentine surface forces and the *25 de Mayo* in particular.

These concerns indicated the problems caused by Woodward not having his own RAF adviser, who would have been able to brief him on the respective capabilities of Vulcans and Sea Harriers. As later became apparent, Sea Harriers were not that suited to attacking runways. Post-attack reconnaissance would be, at a high altitude, a less demanding task than low-level attack but it would still have to be done, whether or not the Harriers had also mounted the main attack. Moreover, as Northwood pointed out, SSNs remained the best way to shadow the Argentine carrier. In this role both the Vulcan and the Victor tankers would be vulnerable to Argentine fighters, which they would find difficult to detect. The reply to Woodward the next day was therefore uncompromising. Considerable assets had now been devoted to mount this operation. The risks involved, particularly of a politically undesirable aircraft diversion to Brazil, meant that Fieldhouse was concentrating on the most valuable role for the Vulcans. Woodward was told that: 'On receipt codeword from Vulcan for successful attack you are to initiate target recce at earliest opportunity from organic air resources.'

Unfortunately the Sea Harriers were not particularly suited for the air reconnaissance role either. Their value lay in air defence. This had to be their priority role. This was confirmed in the concept of air operations agreed on 28 April, which also argued the importance of making the best use of assets other than Sea Harriers. This document raised again the possible role of the Vulcans not only in the neutralisation of Stanley airport, but also in attacking the mainland air bases, assuming that they participated in the conflict and 'political approval is obtained'. They would thereby inflict 'maximum damage and maximum effect on morale of Arg forces'. When the Victors were not required for air-to-air refuelling they would continue in a maritime reconnaissance role. Eventually, when it could cope with aerial refuelling, Nimrod would be used for surveillance as well as anti-submarine warfare and search and rescue. The delivery of the RAF's Harrier GR3 would add to the capability for ground attack and reconnaissance, allowing the Sea Harriers to concentrate even more on air defence.

In naval circles there was concern that the RAF were underestimating the Sea Harrier's offensive capabilities. Rear Admiral D Reffell, The Flag Officer, Third Flotilla (FOF3), argued that it would be possible to mount an attack on the airport using eight aircraft, leaving sufficient air defence cover for the Task Group, which would target aircraft on the ground, the radar, fuel, other facilities and the local air defence systems. By attacking the air bridge to the mainland in this way, Argentina could be forced to mount a continuous combat air patrol over the airport or provide fighter escort to transports. He proposed that a Sea Harrier attack on the airport should be carried out immediately before the Vulcan attack. This led to an amended air concept, including this prior attack to eliminate airfield fire control radars, with the Vulcans targeting the runway and dispersal area, followed by the Harriers carrying out the post-attack reconnaissance.

Woodward, advised by Captain Middleton of *Hermes*, was unimpressed. He would be delighted if the Vulcan attack could damage the runway and take out aircraft on the ground, fuel dumps and ground defences. But he could not see the point of the Harriers attacking in advance for purposes of fire suppression as this would not only put them at risk but, if they had to go, they might as well do the whole job, aided by naval gunfire support, and take out the runway. He had assumed that the Vulcans would fly at a sufficiently high level to stay outside of any ground defence cover. He also felt that he did not have enough information on the Vulcan's optimum attack method and the number of sorties planned to allow him to achieve effective co-ordination with his own assets. The final plan had the Sea Harriers following the Vulcan rather than preceding it. There was some debate between the commanding officers of the two Naval Air Squadrons on appropriate tactics for the Sea Harriers. One witness recalls most the contribution to the debate by Middleton: 'I know a bit about runway busting. Whatever you think you're going to achieve, divide it by ten and don't cry if you fail even that.'[3] The observation turned out to be prescient.

Woodward was told on 29 April that the Vulcan bombing run was timed for 1 May at 0700Z, and that Sea Harrier photo reconnaissance sorties should be attempted as soon as possible after the first Vulcan run as already tasked. Whether there would be further Vulcan sorties would depend on the success of the attack as revealed in these photos. It was also explained that the Vulcan had the advantage over the Sea Harrier of a blind capability if the weather was bad. Woodward was still unhappy. Instead of the Vulcan raid helping conserve Sea Harriers for air defence purposes the opposite now seemed likely. Daylight photographic reconnaissance, accompanied by 'defence suppression against alerted and possibly undiminished firepower', would put the Harriers at a severe risk and so would negate the aim. 'If photo recce essential to BLACK BUCK, cancel BLACK BUCK.' If it was not, he would cancel the photographic missions and trust in naval gunfire on 2 May to finish the job. On 30 April he was told that the BLACK BUCK raid had been approved. It was explained that at issue was not only the need for confirmation of the success or otherwise of the raid, but also a need to show that any damage was confined to the airfield in case Argentine propaganda claimed that Britain was indulging in indiscriminate bombing.

Operation BLACK BUCK came before dawn.[4] The initial wave from Ascension Island, consisting of 11 tankers, two reserves plus the Vulcan and a reserve, took off during the night of 30 April. With the first operation one plane had to return because a minor problem on a side window meant that it would not seal properly and so the aircraft would not pressurise. This left Flt Lt Martin Withers, an Australian serving in the RAF, in the reserve Vulcan to execute the mission. The raid was successful but the recovery phase became very critical due to excess fuel transfer time and a higher than estimated fuel consumption. In all 18 Victor sorties were flown in support of this mission. The attack was made at a height of 8,000 feet and a ground speed of 300 knots. Twenty-one 1000-lb bombs at approximately 48-yard spacing were delivered. Withers returned with barely enough fuel. The first attack was the most successful of all these raids, as it ensured that Skyhawks and Super

Etendards could not use the airfield. Later attacks made the airfield more difficult to use, to which was added all the other hazards of flying to Stanley. The raid was followed up by attacks from nine Sea Harriers, while three attacked targets at Goose Green, including the local airstrip. In the late afternoon warships began to bombard Stanley airfield. This prompted Argentine attacks against the ships by fighter and bomber aircraft.

The British Attack Sitrep 1 delivered by CINCFLEET to MoD at 1737Z on 1 May described the problems in assessing the effectiveness of the Vulcan attack. Photographic reconnaissance was difficult because of the need for AAA suppression before the low-level approach required by the Sea Harrier. The weather also did not permit easy damage assessment with rain under a 1200 ft cloud base. Visual assessment, however, was 'long scar 250m long 70m wide across the airfield straddling centre of runway north-east–south-west with three apparent craters one on runway, and one each side'. Follow-up Sea Harrier raids, which destroyed the two Falkland Islands aircraft that had been captured by the Argentines, were also difficult to assess due to bad weather, but the 'general observation was area devastated'. Bad weather also affected the Sea Harrier raid on Goose Green. Up to 12 aircraft were spotted on the airfield though some were suspected decoys. The runway was not clearly defined but bombed. The strike assessment was vague but recorded 'fires burning no secondary explosions'.

In a follow-up report the next day Woodward reported that photographic reconnaissance now showed that:

> Vulcan attack made single crater with first bomb halfway down runway just south of centre, remaining bombs landed over to SW over 1000m run without further damage. 3 × 1000-lb retard bombs laid down by one SHAR during suppression attack all hit runway centre line causing damage over 150m in area of Vulcan hit. Other damage done in stores and dispersal area at west end of runway by cluster bombs. Goose Green not known.

The Stanley runway had been cratered but after repairs were made this was not the main hindrance to re-supply operations. It took a few days before any further photographs could be taken and this showed three shallow craters in addition to the main crater. These were artificial, intended to encourage the British to believe that more had been achieved than was in fact the case. By the time it was possible to take another picture, on 16 May, the shallow craters were nowhere to be found.

The significance of the Vulcan raids remained controversial. It was an expensive and cumbersome way of delivering bombs but it reduced the demands on the Sea Harriers. The hole in the middle of the runway was probably as much as could have been achieved and it precluded Stanley's use by the more capable Argentine aircraft. Perhaps most importantly it drew

Argentine attention to the vulnerability of their mainland bases. This led to the redeployment of their Mirage III to the defence of the mainland bases and away from support of offensive operations against the Task Force. A factor in this decision on the Argentine side may well have been the revelation of the Mirage III's vulnerability in air combat on 1 May. The British did expect the Mirage III to escort Argentine air raids, flying high above them and adding to the risk facing the defending Sea Harriers, and were relieved when they did not.

The Argentine response

On 1 May the most immediate Argentine response was bound to take the form of an air attack against the Task Force. At the time the Argentine inventory was believed to include 33 A4B and 20 A4C Skyhawks, 36 Israeli Daggers (Mirage V), 14 Mirage IIIs and six Canberras operated by the Air Force with another 12 A4Q Skyhawks operated by the Navy along with its five Super Etendards. Not all of these would be in a decent operational state. Wear and tear, problems with spare parts and the limited attrition already achieved would reduce the numbers. In practice it seems that the Argentine Air Force had 82 serviceable combat aircraft with a few more held in reserve for training and other purposes. The best estimate is that this 82 was made up of six Canberra B62s, 14 A4Cs, 18 A4Bs, 24 Israeli Daggers and eight Mirage IIIs. There were twelve Pucara based on the mainland in addition to those that had been sent to the Falklands.[5] When the moment came the plan was to launch 14 A4B and 12 A4C sorties, six Canberra sorties, 12 Dagger and ten Mirage IIIs. The single Vulcan appears to have confused the Argentine air staff as they were expecting a mass assault on the airfield, and so the response was more cautious than intended. When they appreciated the role played by the Vulcan the Argentine commanders also had to contemplate the possibility that the same aircraft might be used against the mainland. The threat to the mainland became a theme in Argentine planning from this time.

Having misread the signs on 1 May, the Argentine air response was inadequate. There were 56 planned sorties but only 35 reached targets, and what they reached was irrelevant. The Mirage IIIs were the most recent acquisitions, had an all-weather capability, and were armed with Magic anti-aircraft missiles but the events of the day proved that neither they nor the Daggers could match the Harriers, and that the Canberra was hopelessly vulnerable. The British understood that one Mirage had been shot down by a Harrier, with another shot down by friendly gunfire from around the airport. A further bombing raid was mounted in the evening, leading to the loss of one Canberra to a Harrier, and another severely damaged. Woodward's damage assessment for the day had three Mirages destroyed as well as one, possibly two, Canberras. The MoD press release claimed that the Argentine air raids had been 'ineffective. Only one ship was damaged and that was only superficial splinter damage. The frigate is continuing to perform its operational task. A seaman sustained a splinter wound.' Although the damage was slight, the fact that it had been caught in daylight led to future NGS operations taking place at night. Furthermore, it had been an uncomfortable experience for other ships. Commander Craig of *Alacrity* later recalled how his crew had been so absorbed in the task of firing their shells that they had been unprepared for the sudden appearance of the Mirages. They had been able to fire cannon into the decks while the only response had been 'a few rounds of ill-directed light-calibre gunfire.' He described this as a result of the 'breathless freezing of existence that is the initial moment of combat'. It was a reminder that this was real war and that the Task Force's lack of airborne early warning made for great dependence on the Sea Harriers.[6]

At 2147Z, Woodward reported that:

> ships have been bombarding Argentinian positions ashore on Falkland West. In an air battle which has lasted most of daylight hours one Arg Mirage and one Arg Canberra have been splashed. Other Arg aircraft are known to have been damaged. None of our own aircraft are missing.

At 2335Z, in an updated report to MoD, Fieldhouse stated that despite damage to Stanley airfield, high-level photographic reconnaissance indicated five Pucara had returned to the airfield. For this reason *Glamorgan*, *Arrow* and *Alacrity* under a Sea Harrier Combat Air Patrol (CAP) conducted NGS against the airfield. The damage to the airfield was unknown. Woodward intended to withdraw the warships before daylight and had requested a further Vulcan strike.

Woodward had sought to put on a major demonstration of force, well inside the EZ. Given what was known about Argentine assessments he would have had some confidence that if they believed that landings were about to take place this would 'provoke a reaction that would allow me to conduct a major attrition exercise before the amphibious force actually arrived to complicate my problem. And at the very least, I might discover whether they had a coherent defensive plan.'[7] In addition to attrition his other objective for 1 May was to insert the first of many SAS and SBS reconnaissance patrols on the Islands. These were variously landed by helicopter, small boats and HMS *Onyx*.[8]

Everything was done to convince the Argentine command that this might be the real thing. In this he succeeded, and much was learned about how Argentine forces might respond to a landing. British units had performed well, and the Harriers had shown that they could get the better of the Mirages, although Woodward signalled Fieldhouse that: 'Mirage kills to date have been with AIM 9L with firings at extremities or outside expected

9G brackets. Live combat has proved that SHAR needs improved performance of AIM 9L to counter Mirage speed superiority. It is essential that further Sidewinders supplied are Lima variant.' Against this only modest attrition had been achieved. Woodward's signal back that evening to Fieldhouse indicated his satisfaction but also his concern. Argentina's air effort seemed 'confused and disorganised'. It was largely defensive and surprised by 'our robust start to TEZ operations':

> They had ample opportunity to welcome us with a large air attack, but they passed up the chance. Only towards the end of the day did the Canberras appear and turn this theory on its head. I believe the Canberra attack, abortive though it was, indicated the strength of their wish to bash us and the inadequacy of their landbased resources to do so. The maintenance of this situation is critically dependent on keeping Stanley airfield down, and I fear that continued daylight attacks by low level SHAR must sooner or later deplete our AD [Air Defence] force.

Indicating that he was now converted to the possibilities of Vulcan, he continued:

> I would prefer to rely on Vulcan high level work for this task, escorted by Harrier if needs be. Nevertheless the fact has to be faced that the Args have considerable land based air resources and we have only 20 SHAR; to gain control over the air, considerable risks will have to be taken.
>
> Meanwhile our only other real offensive capabilities lie in the SSN force and NGS. NGS is a high risk business in daylight but thoroughly good nuisance value at night, but on the other hand SSN attack on Arg HVUs [High Value Units] is relatively low risk. A badly damaged *Belgrano* or *25 de Mayo* would really set the Args back, and the SSNs can do it given the right ROE. We must do our best to be as offensive as possible while minimising the risks, but at the same time making the enemy expend his air resources by forcing them to operate at extended range.

He ended 'Hope SSNs hit *Belgrano* and *25 de Mayo*, who seem to becoming more adventurous'.

21

THE SINKING OF
THE *BELGRANO*

From this point events started to take on a more dynamic quality as the two forces engaged with each other. It is important to recognise that the same events could be interpreted in quite different ways from the distinctive national vantage points. The Argentine take on the events of 1 May varied considerably from that of the British. Unlike the British they knew that the damage to Stanley airfield was limited. They also believed that their air defences had shot down two Harriers during the dawn raids, and that they had inflicted serious damage on at least one warship. Woodward's ruse had therefore worked so well that when his units began to withdraw this was assumed by Argentine commanders to represent something of a British failure. A serious landing had been attempted to establish some sort of presence on the Islands but the attempt had been abandoned. If there had not been technical problems – with the *San Luis*'s torpedoes and the refuelling of Exocet-armed Super Etendards – they would have been able to achieve even more.[1]

As British ships moved away from around the Falklands, Argentine naval units sought to press home what they thought was an advantage and inflict more damage upon them. The carrier was much further east than *Splendid* had been led to expect, involved now in the search for the British fleet. During the evening of 1 May Admiral Allara was gearing up to mount his attack. He felt he understood where the British were and what they were up to. His Tracker aircraft had picked up signs of British warships 120 miles away as a result of aerial reconnaissance and he was aware of the reports from the Falklands of attempted British landings. Admiral Lombardo, Commander South Atlantic, had given him new rules of engagement, allowing for attacks on the British fleet without restriction. He moved towards the Task Force and, at 2007 local time (2307Z) ordered the initiation of offensive operations.

The subsequent events have become controversial, largely through suppositions about what was or was not known by the British about Argentine plans. The Task Force commanders responded to what was believed to be revealed about Argentine strategy and tactics by observable actions, what had been picked up by reconnaissance and tactical sensors, and by whatever became available through intelligence channels. Argentine communications, but by no means all, were intercepted, though there was often a delay of several hours between interception and dissemination of whatever could be discerned. This information was largely helpful as general guides to Argentine intentions, although on occasion it was of sufficient strength to enable British units to be better prepared than they might otherwise have been.

During the morning of 2 May the British assessed two Argentine orders sent on the previous day. The first, of 1855Z (1555L/South Atlantic), was from Lombardo to Allara, and appeared to assume that the British were static and gave Argentine forces complete freedom of action, presumably tough rather than soft. At any rate, it was soon superseded by what turned out to be the most important intercept of all. This was Allara's order sent at 2307Z, that is the evening of 1 May (2007 local time). According to these orders the carrier group was to deploy during the night hours to a spot which could not be clearly identified, then to find British units and launch air attacks against them at first light. The group would then remain at a safe distance so as not to be caught by any British air strikes.

The second group, TG 79.4, was to deploy well to the south of the Exclusion Zone, to get into position to attack any British units which had been dispersed or weakened as a result of the carrier group's air attacks. The *Belgrano* group, TG 79.3, which was then to the north of the Exclusion Zone, was to deploy south to Burdwood Bank, and then to close in on the British to deal with any surface units operating to the south of the Falklands, to the point where they could be attacked with Exocets. Conscious of the air threat, this group was cautioned only to attack under favourable conditions.

One final intercept fed into the critical intelligence reports for that morning. A signal sent at 2213 local time on 1 May (0113Z of 2 May) from Lombardo to all Argentine units described British warships, including a carrier, close to the Falklands providing naval fire support and landing troops on the Islands with helicopters, while a second substantial task group, also with a carrier, had been sighted by TG 79.1 to the south-east of the Islands. Lombardo urged an early reconnaissance followed by a massive attack on the British fleet before any units had a chance to withdraw.

It was the receipt of the detailed offensive plan that caused the most stir. Within a few hours of the order being issued by Allara, this was being relayed to the Task Force as an intelligence summary:

> it is believed that a major Argentine attack is planned for 2 May. *BELGRANO* is deploying to a position 54.00S 060.00W to attack targets of opportunity S of the Falkland Islands. The CVA group is believed to be deploying into the TEZ during darkness to launch air attacks against British Task Force at first light. A task group of 3 ×

A69 frigates and PUNTA MENDANOS deploying to attack any dispersed units of Task Force.

On board *Hermes*, Woodward received all this information with some anxiety. He had received no new information for some time on the Argentine carrier group, although at midnight there had been an indication that it might be about 100 miles north-west of the TEZ. His own group was then making ground to the north-east, to be rejoined by the ASW group coming from the north of East Falkland later that morning. The NGS group would come later still. It was continuing to bombard the Stanley area, and did not stop until 0137Z when *Glamorgan* reported that the last gun had been fired. The last Sea King inserting Special Forces was due back at about 0200Z. He decided to order the other groups to bring forward their rejoining time to 0900Z, intending to make ground to the south-east and concentrate his forces into defensive positions.

The supposed new location of the Argentine force was signalled to *Splendid* and *Spartan* but they were 100 miles distant, and there was always uncertainty as to whether these communications were properly received. Woodward's frustration was not helped by his belief that the system whereby each SSN had to stay in its own patch and not trespass into that of another was thwarting the search for the carrier.

There was a further critical piece of information. Reports came in just after 0300Z that the radar of an Argentine S-2E Tracker coming from the north-west had been detected by both *Invincible* and *Coventry*. At 0325Z a Sea Harrier was sent to investigate to see what it could find. Nothing was found but an hour later another Harrier came across several radar contacts, indicating a group of four to five ships, to the north-west at over 200 miles. It soon became apparent that at least one had a Sea Dart, leading the Harrier to leave quickly and report his finding. In the light of the latest intelligence on Argentine offensive plans, Woodward assumed that the contact might possibly be the Argentine carrier group preparing for a dawn strike. This location was again transmitted to the SSNs, at 0548Z, but they were still some distance away and there was no reason for confidence that the *25 de Mayo* would be found before it had a chance to launch its aircraft.

Woodward assumed that the attack would come at dawn. Sunrise was at 1040Z. His war diary noted that: 'The *Belgrano* group is moving west [actually it was moving east], south of the Falkland Islands shadowed by *Conqueror*, and may wish to effect a pincer movement from that direction.' At this point, this group was the only part of the Argentine fleet that he could locate with any accuracy. At 0500Z on the morning of 2 May, as Woodward was assessing his strategy, *Conqueror* reported *Belgrano*'s position along with its course of 90° back to Northwood. The destroyers accompanying *Belgrano* were known to carry Exocets, and while it was not known if the cruiser had the missile, its 6in guns outranged the 4.5in guns used by the British. Woodward was concerned that should the *Belgrano* move across the submerged ridge known as the Burdwood Bank, as it had been ordered to do, *Conqueror* would be hard-pressed to stay in contact, particularly so if it wanted to remain undetected. In exercises the previous year Woodward had shown that it was possible to get a destroyer close enough to a fully-prepared American carrier to fire four Exocets. He did not want his own carrier to suffer the same fate.

Changing the ROE

At 0700Z the Task Force was all together again, and Woodward began to feel a bit less exposed. Yet there were grounds for frustration. To the north he had permission to attack the carrier but no contact, while to the south he had a contact with no permission. The situation, he noted, was unsatisfactory 'particularly in view of the SSNs inability to contribute at all for lack of suitable ROE'. At issue was not just whether he could cope with an immediate Argentine offensive but the inhibitions that would be placed on his ability to move the British campaign along over the coming days. This frustration led him to order *Conqueror* to attack the *Belgrano*, at 0811Z. As he anticipated, as he had no authority over *Conqueror*, the order was immediately rescinded by FOSM at Northwood at 0904Z.

As he also anticipated, the episode was immediately brought to the attention of the Chiefs of Staff when they met at 0915Z. Summing up a short discussion, Lewin said he would seek the War Cabinet's agreement as soon as possible to extend the ROE for British ships and SSNs to allow attacks on all Argentine naval ships, submarines and auxiliaries outside the TEZ, as had already been authorised against the Argentine aircraft carrier. Lewin was to meet with ministers at Chequers that lunchtime. On arrival Lewin immediately explained the position to Thatcher. She brought together those ministers and officials who had been invited for lunch before the formal body met in the afternoon. The discussion took fifteen to twenty minutes. One of those present, William Whitelaw, later recalled it as 'one of the simplest decisions that I personally found myself involved in' once he understood the risk of losing contact with the *Belgrano* if *Conqueror* were not allowed to attack.[2] Parkinson found particularly compelling the question of what the politicians would say if they had refused the military request when the *Belgrano* could have been sunk, and the cruiser then went on to sink a British carrier with hundreds of casualties.[3] All were asked for their views before the Prime Minister gave her own but the issue was not controversial. In the only official report, the decision was said to reflect 'the latest intelligence about the movements and intentions of the Argentine fleet, and that of the new situation created by the military events of 1 May'.

Although the Chiefs had asked for auxiliaries to be included in the new ROE the immediate change only referred to warships. Attorney General

Havers, present at this impromptu meeting, made the point that the attack would be harder to justify if it took place a long way from the TEZ: Fieldhouse said that 'the patrol areas of the British units involved made that very unlikely to happen'. Acland reported back to the FCO the importance of this determination: 'Ministers had also taken into account the fact that, in the present military situation, it was unlikely that any warships would need to be engaged very far from the TEZ.' Pym was informed in Washington, and was reported to be 'fairly relaxed' about the extension. There are indications that it was described back to the FCO and then on to Pym as a general response to assessments about Argentine intentions rather than because the *Belgrano* was in *Conqueror*'s sights. The situation had changed. A military phase had taken over from the diplomatic. Both sides were looking to take the military offensive.

Almost immediately after Ministers agreed at 1145Z this was reported back to MoD who signalled CINCFLEET with the change at 1207Z. In half an hour the new ROE were being transmitted by Herbert to his SSNs. *Conqueror*'s communication problems meant that at first all that was known was that the ROE had changed: exactly how was unclear. The full message was not actually received by the SSN until 1710Z. Even so the FCO were impressed by the speed of the communication. Later one official compared the speed of transmission with past claims from the Navy, for example when seeking delays to the implementation of the MEZ, that such transmission could not be guaranteed in less than 12 hours (as in discussions of a temporary cease-fire). In an annotation one official observed that the speed of transmission seemed to vary in proportion to the aggressiveness of the instruction.

Argentine reversal

Up to the early hours (GMT) of 2 May, the British had interpreted Argentine intentions correctly. The Navy wanted to take the offensive and the various elements of Task Group 1 were moving into position. From the *25 de Mayo* Allara intended to use his Skyhawks to attack the British fleet and the *Belgrano* was part of a pincer. At this point, however, two developments changed the Argentine plans. First at 0100Z the wind dropped. Launching the Skyhawks required 40 knots over the deck. It now seemed unlikely that the Skyhawks could launch before 0900Z. The wind continued to drop, and the prospect now was of further delay and the aircraft taking off with reduced fuel and weapons loads. Nonetheless, the group continued to close on the British.

The second event was the arrival of the Sea Harrier at 0330Z, which had apparently spotted the carrier group. Allara's initial instinct was to persevere but at 0419Z, according to subsequent Argentine publications, Lombardo reported that there had been 'no further air attacks on the Malvinas', and that he did not know the position of the British carriers. 'The free-ranging

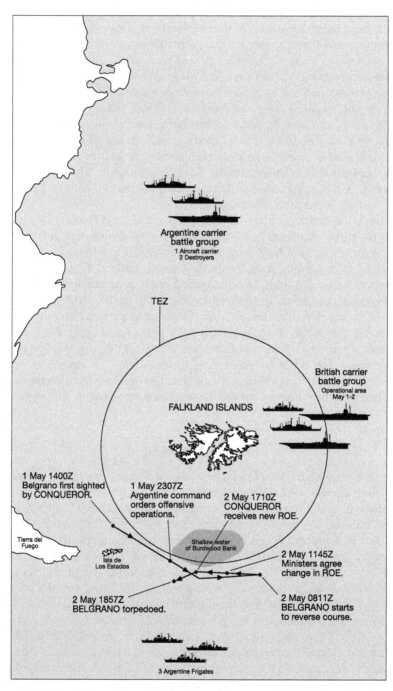

Argentine carrier
battle group
1 Aircraft carrier
2 Destroyers

TEZ

British carrier
battle group
Operational area
May 1-2

FALKLAND ISLANDS

1 May 1400Z
Belgrano first sighted
by CONQUEROR.

1 May 2307Z
Argentine command
orders offensive
operations.

2 May 1710Z
CONQUEROR
receives new ROE.

Tierra del
Fuego

Shallow water
of Burdwood Bank

Isla de
Los Estados

2 May 1145Z
Ministers agree
change in ROE.

2 May 1857Z
BELGRANO torpedoed.

2 May 0811Z
BELGRANO starts
to reverse course.

3 Argentine Frigates

Map 6 The sinking of the *Belgrano*

enemy still constitutes a strong threat to Task Force 79.' Taking all this into account, Allara decided that there was little point in carrying on, especially as the forecast gave him few reasons to expect better wind conditions. This conclusion he passed to Lombardo at 0445Z. The task groups were ordered 'back to their former positions.' He wanted to return to shallower waters to reduce the risk of falling victim to submarine attack. Just when he received this order is not known, but the Commander of the *Belgrano* did not actually begin to turn until 0811Z, completing the manoeuvre at 0900Z, by which time the cruiser was pointing in the direction of Staten Island. All other Argentine offensive operations were being frustrated that day: the Air Force had planned 19 attack sorties from the mainland but these were all cancelled because of poor weather conditions.[4]

Some of the relevant signals were intercepted by the British but not in time to influence the unfolding events. Those picked up included: Allara's initial reaction to the detection of enemy aircraft; his decision, on the assumption that he had been detected, to move away; and a much later warning from Lombardo that he could expect a British attack. They were not however distributed on the British side until the next day and had no influence on the day's events. The subsequent discussion of what was known was confused by a statement by Admiral Anaya, the Chief of the Argentine Navy, suggesting that the 2007 order was to withdraw when in fact it was to go on the offensive.[5] The details given here, based on Argentine publications together with *Conqueror*'s de visu reporting, show quite plainly that not until 0811Z on 2 May did *Belgrano* start to turn west.

For most of the Sunday morning Woodward had no inkling of any change in Argentine plans. After the earlier sighting, a Sea Harrier continued to search for signs of Argentine activity to the north and northwest. The fact that nothing was found was a positive indication, but the Task Force still retained its high state of anti-air readiness. Sunrise was at 1040Z (0740L). By 1100Z, with the light improving, Woodward was starting to conclude that the probability of an Argentine attack was diminishing. Into the afternoon preparations began to be made for the insertion of reconnaissance teams onto the Falklands.

In terms of later controversies the war diary now contains an intriguing conjunction. At 1600Z Woodward recorded that he 'now believed that the Argentines reversed their decision to attack the [Task Force] at approximately 0800 and are now retiring'. This was largely on the basis of the failure of an air attack to materialise when expected and of the Sea Harriers to find the Argentine Task Group. The Carrier Battle Group moved back towards the TEZ. Woodward, however, was by no means confident. He still held his position to the east, to reduce further the risk of successful Argentine air strikes. The SSN cover between the carrier group and the task group was to be doubled. Only when it became dark did he intend to move west again to insert more Special Forces into the Islands and attack

Argentine targets on the Falklands with naval gunfire. He was right not to be complacent for as his group moved back towards the Falklands two Exocet-armed Super Etendards took off from the Rio Grande base. It was not the weather that defeated this attempt to attack the British fleet but problems with refuelling. The two aircraft were forced to return to base.

To the north two SSNs were searching for the *25 de Mayo* group, on the assumption it was still moving closer to the Task Force. *Spartan* was in fact closer than *Splendid* but the target was still in *Splendid*'s allocated area. That evening a fleeting contact was made by *Splendid* but not sufficient to make positive identification and by early morning of 3 May it had been lost. Woodward knew that the *Belgrano* group was still being trailed, but not that it had reversed course at 0900Z. This was reported by *Conqueror* to Northwood at 1400Z, along with the *Belgrano*'s current position, just as the SSN was being informed about the changes in the ROE. *Conqueror*'s report of the change of course was received by Herbert at 1441Z, but it was not passed on to MoD, or to Woodward.

There was no reason to be surprised by the news. Concluding that an Argentine attack was not imminent was not the same as presuming that it had been postponed indefinitely. In terms of Woodward's original plan to flush out Argentine units he had succeeded enough with the Navy to have a fix on the *Belgrano*. If it was not attacked that day then it would be returning to the fray the next time the Argentine Navy positioned itself for battle, by which time *Conqueror* could well have lost its contact. Woodward did not know that his wish had been granted, and approval for the new ROE had already been agreed and transmitted to the SSNs. MoD did not signal the new ROE to surface ships until 1820. He therefore again requested the ROE release for *Conqueror* to attack the *Belgrano*.

At Northwood, Herbert knew of the cruiser's change in position, which would conform to Woodward's general analysis of immediate Argentine plans. As with Woodward he believed that the Task Force had to take its chances when it could, because the next day the chances might fall the other way. Even if he could have gained political authority at this point to rescind the new ROE and transmit them back to *Conqueror*, which was highly unlikely, there is no reason why he would have thought that sensible. The change in the ROE was seen as a necessary step that would have to be taken at some point, to enable the Task Force to engage an enemy that was clearly geared up for battle.

The attack

Conqueror had begun 2 May expecting to be following the *Belgrano* into the TEZ. By 0107Z it had been surprised by a change in course and remained uncertain as to which direction its quarry was intending to move for some time. Instead of moving into the TEZ it was skirting it, staying some 18 miles to the south but still moving east. The intelligence received at 0645 suggested that the Argentine group was going to move to attack RN units, through the TEZ. 'They won't make it', observed the Commanding Officer, Commander C Wreford-Brown. At 0900Z the group appeared to be avoiding the TEZ, and by 1144Z he had concluded that, contrary to his intelligence, it was now moving westwards, perhaps now aware of the risks of the Exclusion Zone. *Conqueror* returned to periscope depth at 1400Z to receive and transmit signals. It was taking the CO some time to make sense of his instructions.

Conqueror had been having considerable problems with communications equipment throughout its patrol, as a result of a damaged wireless mast, and in late April at one point it looked like it might be necessary to withdraw to get the mast changed. Wreford-Brown was aware of an order cancelling a previous order to attack (the original from Woodward – which he had not received) and that there appeared to be a new order to attack. The broadcasts from Northwood would only cease when all return signals from submarines indicated reception, so *Conqueror* remained at this depth until his instructions were clear. Now he was 'absolutely certain'. By the next transmission, at 1710Z, they were understood and this was reported back along with an intention to attack. Wreford-Brown chose the old Mk8 torpedo, in service since 1932, because as an impact weapon it had a better chance of penetrating the cruiser's armour and anti-torpedo bilges. The more modern Tigerfish, which was also available, had both impact and proximity fuses, and would have been used if it had been necessary to attack from a distance. Commander Wreford-Brown later described the build-up to the attack:

> I spent more than two hours working my way into an attack position on the port beam of the cruiser. It was still daylight. The visibility was variable; it came down to 2,000 yards at one time. I kept coming up for a look – but when at periscope depth we were losing ground on them – and then going deep and catching up. I did this five or six times. They were not using sonar – just gently zigzagging at about 13 knots. Twice I was in reasonable firing positions but found they had moved off a few degrees.

At 1813Z the SSN took up firing position and went to action stations. At 1857Z *Conqueror* attacked at a range of 1400 yards. Two hits were observed, although three explosions were heard. By 1930Z the initial report of the attack had been transmitted. This gave the cruiser's position, course and speed when attacked, adding 'successfully attacked *Belgrano*. Two hits with Mark Eights. Evaded to east.' The evasion was necessary because within a few minutes they were being attacked in turn with depth charges. From 2052Z to 2103Z more depth charges were heard.

On board the *Belgrano* some 200 men had been killed by the initial explosion, with fire spreading because doors and hatches, which might have contained the effects, had been left open. Another 850 took to life rafts as the cruiser began to sink. It sent out no signal of its own asking for help. The first signal from its escorts, indicating a problem, did not come until 1935Z, over half an hour after the attack, when the destroyer, *Bouchard*, reported that *Belgrano* was adrift without communications, believed to be damaged, adding that: 'We did not observe any explosions'. An hour later, a reconnaissance Squadron was being asked to provide anti-submarine air support for Task Group 79.3. The 'priority tactical objective' was 'to destroy the submarine in the area. You are to carry 4 torpedoes.' It only appears to have become apparent to the Argentine command just after midnight that the cruiser had sunk, and a proper rescue effort was launched. Three ships were sent to its aid, one of which made a visual sighting but later lost contact with the cruiser. The harsh weather and heavy sea conditions battered the crippled vessel and reduced the chances for survival of the crew as they abandoned ship. It took a day before the first survivors were picked up. In all 321 men of the *Belgrano* lost their lives.

Still unaware of the dramatic events to the south, at 2200Z an NGS Group (*Glamorgan*, *Alacrity* and *Arrow*) moved to bombard Stanley. As soon as he heard the news of the *Belgrano* at 2300Z, Woodward ordered the group to withdraw and rejoin. The reason was the risk they faced. There was evidence of a new Argentine surface build-up to the north-west. Woodward did not want what he considered to be the positive news about the *Belgrano* reduced by the loss of a British frigate inshore. This surface build-up later 'proved to be chimerical collection of false clues'. Just before midnight there was a second land reconnaissance party inserted by Sea King.

After attacking *Belgrano* and evading counter-attacks, *Conqueror* withdrew at high speed to the south-east and then, in accordance with the new ROE, circled to seek the destroyers once more in the area between Isla de Los Estados and Burdwood Bank. At 0700Z on 3 May, now feeling safe, *Conqueror* signalled a more detailed report. That afternoon it was directed to continue offensive operations against Argentine warships. Still unaware of what precisely had happened to the *Belgrano* and having failed to locate the destroyers, *Conqueror* signalled at 0145Z on 4 May (the evening of 3 May in the South Atlantic) that it was returning to the area where the *Belgrano* had been attacked to find them. Herbert responded at 0934Z repeating the previous order not to attack ships engaged in the rescue of survivors. Only later did the SSN report that *Bouchard*, which had been on the other side of the cruiser, might have been hit unintentionally. At 0740Z *Conqueror* detected *Bahia Paraiso*, acting as hospital ship. It trailed it and eventually at 1321Z made contact with a destroyer and a Boeing 747 aircraft. Later (1528Z) the Argentine tug *Gurruchaga* and possibly a second destroyer were detected. As it was assessed that they were all searching for survivors they were not attacked. *Conqueror* then moved north towards the TEZ.

22

SHEFFIELD

The official description of events came in a Parliamentary statement by John Nott on 4 May.[1] On 2 May 'at 8pm London time, one of our submarines detected the Argentine cruiser, '*General Belgrano*', escorted by two destroyers.' In explaining the action, he drew attention to the threat to the Task Force posed by Argentine units, the *Belgrano* group as part of this threat and that it was 'close to the total Exclusion Zone and was closing on elements of our Task Force, which was only hours away'. The Prime Minister also reminded the House about the statement of 23 April, which left open the possibility of Argentine forces outside the Exclusion Zone being attacked if they threatened the 'mission of the British forces'.[2] By changing the word 'attacked' in his brief to 'detected' in his statement, Nott created later problems for his Government. Other inaccurate details could be readily traced to the first hurried report of the engagement from *Conqueror*. An example of this was the statement that *Belgrano* was closing on elements of the Task Force. When Pym was notified (in Washington) of the attack on the morning of 3 May, he was told that the *Belgrano* had been hit about 30 miles outside the TEZ, but that: 'The MoD believe that the *General Belgrano* had just left the TEZ when the engagement took place'. At the same time FCO discovered from the Chiefs of Staff meeting that the *Belgrano* had not entered the TEZ and was heading in a south-westerly direction when the attack took place.

Curiously they noticed the muddle, not when Nott spoke to the Commons but when he addressed a meeting of Eurogroup ministers in Brussels on 5 May. The phrase 'closing on the Task Force' was used. A note went round the FCO trying to sort out their own recollections of the decision, including whether it had been taken as a general proposition about SSNs attacking Argentine warships outside the TEZ rather than a specific decision on the *Belgrano*. One commented that the confusion was 'symptomatic of the difficulty we face in keeping up with ministers, when short cuts are taken'. The inconsistencies and inaccuracies in Government statements did not in themselves cause any real difficulties at this stage. International opinion was already troubled enough by such a substantial loss of life, resulting from an attack outside the Exclusion Zone. Later, we shall consider the consequences of this for Britain's negotiating position, and, later still, the post-war controversy surrounding these events. In this chapter we shall assess the impact on Britain's military strategy.

Sobral to *Sheffield*

The sinking of the *Belgrano* was not the only attack on Argentine vessels over this period. The radar contacts of late 2 May, which had turned out to be so chimerical, had led to a Sea King helicopter being sent out to investigate during the morning of 3 May. It chanced upon a darkened ship, which fired at it, ineffectively. In response, Lynx helicopters armed with Sea Skua missiles were sent to join the Sea King, and one of these, from *Coventry*, was also fired upon as it approached the target. It sent two Sea Skuas back by way of response, and reported that the target was totally destroyed, although this was (correctly) denied by Argentina. There is no doubt that at just after 0500Z another Lynx flight, from *Glasgow*, 'approached target area to search for survivors of *Coventry*'s Lynx attack with no actual target expected', and came upon the patrol vessel, *Alferez Sobral*. This was a different ship: *Sobral* was grouped with its sister ship *Comodoro Somellera*, the first one to be attacked, for operational purposes as Task Group 50.[3] They were both converted tugs, serving as patrol vessels.

The Lynx was ordered to investigate further but not to engage. When it was fired at, however, Sea Skuas were sent back in response and the target was hit. Following this attack life-saving equipment was dropped by Sea Kings and an emergency message was broadcast with the position of possible survivors. A couple of days later the *Sobral* was reported to be still afloat. 'Precarious communications' had been established with the mainland, and it was travelling back to port under its own power, although badly damaged. Although the *Sobral* had been on the British 'hit list', and had fired first, Woodward was concerned by the discovery that it was on search and rescue duties, information that he did not want to be known due to the unfavourable press that would result.

The cumulative effect of these various actions was to underscore the Argentine difficulties. The weekend's engagements had highlighted a number of deficiencies. Buenos Aires heard that Stanley's air defences had shot down one of their own aircraft. Even if it could be repaired, the Stanley runway had been reduced to 15 metres width in centre, with possibly the tower damaged and aircraft hangars destroyed. The damage to the runway at Darwin was minor but two Pucaras had been destroyed, and two damaged at Stanley, with another Pucara taking a direct hit at Darwin. Ten men were dead and 25 wounded. Most importantly the events had exposed the vulnerability of the Argentine Navy. It had been necessary to move away the carrier, still affected by speed limitations and poor wind conditions, after detection by a Sea Harrier. Knowledge of British ship positions was poor, and there were evident problems in joint operations, with air force and naval commanders unable to operate in the same area lest they fire upon each other. Senior Argentine naval commanders also believed, incorrectly, that Britain had turned its attention to naval units because of access to satellite intelligence and the effectiveness of submarines while they could not get quick results on land. To these British advantages they lacked obvious responses. They had now lost the *Sobral* as well as the *Belgrano*, and had reason to suppose the odds were stacked against them if they ventured out too far. The key question was whether the Navy had any confidence left that it could beat the odds, and dared gear up once again for a major maritime encounter.

During the course of the week evidence accumulated suggesting to the British that caution was prevailing, and that the shocked Argentine Navy was unwilling to take large risks. By 4 May the Argentine fleet had moved closer to the mainland, possibly to get land-based fighter aircraft cover, and it seemed unlikely that for the moment it would move away from this cover. The next day it was apparent that the carrier had moved into shallow water very close to the mainland and well away from the TEZ. It did not appear to be confident of being able to go on the offensive. With its escorts it moved north, further out of harm's way. There were inevitable doubts about its ability to cope with British submarines, while its surface reconnaissance ability was now limited to 300 miles. It was restricted by a lack of resources, with its air attack capability reduced to six aircraft with a radius of 200 miles. Radar detection ranges on aircraft were limited to 80–100 miles. The destroyers which had been with the *Belgrano* were in port disembarking survivors and undergoing repairs (although the torpedo from *Conqueror* which had struck *Bouchard* had failed to explode it had caused damage to radar sonar and engines, while another destroyer had suffered storm damage). After another couple of days British confidence had grown; for now at least the Argentine surface fleet had withdrawn from the Falklands area.

Revenge

Bad weather had precluded most fixed-wing flying on 3 May. There was a scare with one of the reconnaissance teams on the Falklands, which believed that its position had been compromised. Attempts to provide a supporting strike and early extraction had to be cancelled, but the team carried on its work without interruption. Nor was there much Argentine air activity, although they did lose one Falklands-based Aermacchi, which crashed into the sea when returning to Stanley after failing to find British warships. There was considerable ASW activity by the Task Force, although neither Argentine 209 was close.

The next morning began, at 0820Z, with another Vulcan attack on Stanley airfield. The mission again ran smoothly, but the higher altitude adopted, to stay clear of Argentine Roland surface-to-air missiles, meant that the attack itself was less successful. This was not known for a few days until the weather cleared sufficiently for reconnaissance. The lack of feedback on runway condition was particularly frustrating. The Sea Harriers had no training on reconnaissance operations, and the capacity with the Task Force for interpretation was modest.

There were indications that the Argentine military were out for revenge, searching for the Task Force in the hope of mounting an air attack. This was going to depend on the Super Etendards. There had been concern that they would use Stanley airfield, and that was one reason for mounting the Vulcan attack, though the evidence that appropriate preparations were being made was flimsy. The latest estimate put the unrefuelled low-level radius of operation of the Super Etendard at 360nm. If operating from a mainland base this would bisect the Falkland Islands, but if it could refuel in flight then the radius of operation for an Exocet would extend a further 40nm. As the aircraft had a flight-refuelling pod this could not be ruled out, although the overall air refuelling capability was unknown. By 2 May a report had arrived that the five Super Etendards were operating out of Rio Grande, and also that they could not operate from the carrier because they lacked the latest inertial navigation system.

It was unclear how many were ready for action. While each had one Exocet installed, tests were not complete because of the withdrawal of technical support by the French. Only one aircraft had been fully equipped to launch AM-39 Exocet though 'all aircraft carried' such a missile. Nonetheless, the JIC concluded that, 'if these aircraft were fully modified they would pose the greatest air threat to the British Task Force'. The evening intelligence summary of 3 May, distributed to the Task Force, was relatively sanguine. 'Because French technicians may have had their setting to work interrupted there is some reason to believe that [the Exocet's] operational capability may be somewhat degraded.' (The Argentine media later claimed that Argentine technicians had made the final adjustments to the missile's systems not completed by the French contractor.) In principle, therefore, there was no reason for this particular threat to be discounted but the overall tenor of the assessments would not have left the Task Force at an unusually high level of alert. By 4 May it was recognised to be the most dangerous threat from the air, but the major concern was with the *San Luis*, which was still assumed to be operating in the close vicinity of the Falklands. The prevailing water conditions made it a submariner's paradise.

There was a further problem in that there were some similarities between the radar parameters of the Super Etendard and Mirage III and so it was possible to mistake one for the other. On 1 May there had been many false alarms, including a number of reports of imminent Super Etendard attacks that had turned out to be Mirage III, and had led to unnecessary expenditure of chaff and awkward emergency manoeuvres. This would inevitably colour future reports that Super Etendards were on the way. In addition, having anticipated heavy raids because of Argentina's aircraft losses on 1 May, nothing ensued. The two subsequent days were quiet, with no threatening aircraft within 200nm of the group. The weather had gone from one extreme to the other: either heavy seas with good visibility or calm seas with fog and visibility down to 100 yards. On the morning of 4 May, however, the sea was unusually calm while the visibility was 7–10nm. The Task Group was 40–50nm south-east of the Falklands. The three Type 42 destroyers were occupying air defence stations some 18nm west in front of the main body of the force. *Glasgow* (Captain A.P. Hoddinott) was in the middle with *Sheffield* (Captain J.F.T.G. 'Sam' Salt) on its left and *Coventry* (Captain D. Hart-Dyke) on its right.[4]

Two Harriers on combat air patrol were on station but were tasked by *Hermes* to search for the Argentine fleet some 120 miles to the southwest. This may have been one of the more significant consequences of a disagreement over the capabilities of the Harrier between the 800 Squadron on *Hermes* and 801 on *Invincible*, later publicised by the latter's leader, Lieutenant Commander N.D. 'Sharkey' Ward,[5] and accepted by Woodward. Woodward was a submariner and was dependent for his advice on the air campaign on the captain of the carrier, Lyn Middleton, who would in turn be getting advice from 800 Naval Air Squadron of Sea Harriers. This squadron had been formed prior to the introduction of the Blue Fox radar and took the view that the radar was useless. They also distrusted the aircraft's navigation system. This view survived the war and appears in a number of post-operational assessments that it was of 'little use' and regarded as a 'dinky toy'. From his pre-war work as Commanding Officer of the Sea Harrier Intensive Flying Trials Unit, Ward was convinced that the aircraft need not be limited to daytime use, but could be used at night and in poor weather. Although few crews had been trained to this level, his whole squadron had been trained by the time the carriers reached the South Atlantic. While he had tested the Blue Fox and judged it excellent, exceeding expectations, others had not been able to reproduce his results. Ward's maverick reputation led to his enthusiasm for Blue Fox being discounted. Ward later took the view that if the Blue Fox's capabilities had been understood the aircraft could have stayed on station because contacts could have been picked up from 100 miles. As it was they left as two Super Etendards approached the *Sheffield* group.

The presence of the Task Force in this area was known to Argentina, as a Neptune had picked up the radar emissions of one of the destroyers at about 1115Z (0815L) that morning. Within half an hour two Super Etendards, both armed with Exocets, had left Rio Grande in search, they thought, of *Hermes*. The previous Saturday they had tried to mount an attack but had been thwarted by problems with refuelling from a Hercules. This time there were no problems. Just after 1400Z they came across the three ships. It may be that the *Glasgow*'s release of chaff caused them to swerve towards *Sheffield*, but it was probably that this was simply the first ship they picked up. The two Exocets were released. One passed by into the sea, and the other hit the destroyer. After a quick look to confirm a hit they veered back to the mainland and returned safely.[6]

Glasgow correctly identified the threat and took appropriate counter-measures. The Captain, Paul Hoddinott, was expecting an Exocet attack as revenge for the *Belgrano*, had banned daytime use of his SCOT satellite communications system to ensure it did not blank out detections of enemy radar on the ESM equipment and was on full alert. One reason why *Sheffield* did not respond is normally held to be the unfortunate coincidence of the ship's SCOT satellite communications being used to transmit some messages so that it was unable, at the same time, to pick up the radar emissions from the incoming aircraft. This was the case, but it was not the only problem. Another unfortunate coincidence was that not only the *Sheffield*'s anti-air warfare officer but also three of his cell of eight were out of the room or out of position. Twenty minutes before the attack the officer had left the operations room, first to check the cloud base and then to get a coffee. This affected the way that the warning from *Glasgow* was received.

At 1356Z *Glasgow* intercepted three sweeps of the Super Etendard's radar and immediately reported its finding on HF and Ultra High Frequency (UHF), but the HF set on *Sheffield* was not manned at the time and the UHF set did not pick up the whole message. Two minutes later *Glasgow* made a further interception and then reported 'two low bogies, SW at 25 miles'. The ship went to action stations just after 1400Z and soon afterwards released chaff. The first *Glasgow* message had brought *Sheffield*'s operations room team to an enhanced state of alert, but key personnel in her anti-air warfare team remained absent from their stations, and returned too late to take appropriate actions. Because the SCOT was still transmitting, information from the ship's own ESM equipment was not available. It took time to switch off the SCOT, and before this was achieved it was apparent that an Exocet was on its way. This was only 15 seconds before impact.

The problems on *Sheffield* would not have been critical had *Glasgow*'s report been believed but instead it was assessed as a bombing run by Mirage III. Scepticism was not only found in *Sheffield*. The anti-air warfare co-ordination room in *Invincible* also disputed the warning and declared the contacts spurious. *Glasgow* argued back to no avail. If there had been agreement, or just a prudent recognition of the worst case, then *Invincible* could have alerted all ships. The disbelief on board *Sheffield* meant that the ship was not piped to action stations, the damage control state was not raised, and the captain was not called. Fifty seconds before impact two puffs of smoke were reported, but they did not realise that they were to be hit until the last moments. No chaff was released and no attempt was made to engage either the missile or the aircraft.

At 1403Z the single Exocet hit *Sheffield* at the starboard side, leaving a large hole and causing widespread minor shock damage and an immediate loss of fighting capability. Fortunately the warhead did not detonate. Nonetheless large fires still broke out and thick black smoke, mainly fuel but with the addition of noxious and toxic fumes from furnishings and other combustible material. Later it was wished that improvements in the habitability of the ship had not come at the expense of fire fighting and damage control. So fast did the damage occur that many key officers and senior ratings were unaware for some time of the extent of the damage and the location of fires. Many in the galley were killed instantly. The computer room crew of five men stayed at their posts until they were overcome by smoke. Of the crew of 281, 20 men died and 26 were injured. The ability to cope was severely hampered not only by the confusion within the ship but the loss of the firemain, which had been breached on impact. The fire-fighting parties, even when helped by *Arrow* and *Yarmouth*, were unable to make much headway. After an hour, with the fire still spreading, and concern growing that it might reach the Sea Dart Magazine, the captain ordered that the ship be abandoned. Woodward's first signal back to CINCFLEET stated: '*Sheffield* suffered internal explosion in Ops Room area in position 170 Port Stanley 70. Suspect torpedoed – no surface or air activity.' He corrected himself just under two hours later. On 7 May, to divert attention from *Yarmouth*'s task with *Sheffield*, and also 'to keep the Argentinians awake', *Alacrity* was sent to bombard Stanley. The weather remained poor so there could be little air activity.

Fieldhouse later recorded his view that while there were problems with the inexperience of some key officers, and *Sheffield* had been lulled into a false sense of security by the ineffectiveness of previous Argentine air attacks, sea-skimming missiles such as the Exocet presented a particularly dangerous and difficult threat. He therefore saw little to be gained by having any officers court-martialled, especially in the context of the eventual victory. The loss of the ship 'was an expensive warning and a foretaste of real Argentine capability'. The immediate lesson drawn by the Task Force commanders was that they must not pull punches: ships acting as pickets needed to have their SCOT strangled; tracks must be released immediately to link; spurious radar contacts must not lull the senses or engender a feeling of well-being through lack of collateral evidence; advice of a ship in contact should not be ignored; when a ship was unexpectedly damaged it was unwise to leap to conclusions as a second attack might be missed; the highest degree of readiness had to be maintained when in range of Super Etendard, and rocket firing panels must not be left unattended. Woodward judged that:

> we mismanaged the first attack fairly disastrously. *Glasgow* alerted correctly after an understandable hesitation to release to link on her ESM detection. AAWC (Anti-Air Warfare Control) rather pooh-poohed *Glasgow*, perhaps for lack of collateral; *Sheffield* who was

the obvious source of collateral was transmitting SCOT and provided none; there was a genuine feeling of disbelief which prevailed for a period of time after *Sheffield* was hit, witness *Yarmouth* and *Arrow* sardine bashing [i.e. anti-submarine warfare].

To add to a frustrating day, it soon transpired that all the bombs released by the second Vulcan attack on the airfield at Stanley had missed the runway. Furthermore, a Sea Harrier had been shot down in an attack on the Goose Green airstrip by anti-aircraft fire and the pilot killed. The attack was reported to have hit two Pucaras and damaged the airstrip. The news did not get better. On 6 May, two Sea Harriers from *Invincible* failed to return after descending below radar/radio cover in poor visibility to investigate an air contact reported at 1055Z. Both pilots were missing. The initial instinct from the military was that this news should not be reported because of the comfort it would give to the Argentines, and the correspondents with the Task Force were forbidden to mention it. The Chiefs did not want it to be known that ten per cent of the Task Force's combat aircraft had been lost in a single accident. To their irritation, the news was released in London after civilian staff in MoD argued strongly that any suggestion that news of casualties was being withheld would undermine Britain's position in the information war. At Downing Street, Bernard Ingham was also worried that the Argentines would claim that they had been responsible for their loss. More seriously the press had picked up evidence from a widely circulated MoD document giving routine notification of losses of aircraft due to accidents. Later Ingham also reported concern with allegations in the House of Commons press gallery that the story was being withheld because campaigns were on for local elections.[7]

Woodward's view the next day was that he should let *Sheffield* burn itself out, while using it as 'a tethered goat while she floats'. Whatever the value the hulk of the *Sheffield* had in attracting Argentine forces, however, was now spent and so it would have to be sunk or towed away. The preference from Northwood was to tow, as this could be taken to imply that 'she was not too badly damaged after all'. This was to be done by the *Yarmouth* until it was out of the TEZ and a tug could take over. Late that night the crippled destroyer was found, listing but without significant flooding, although the Exocet hole was barely three feet above the water. The calm weather of 9 May allowed for good progress but then that evening the wind speed picked up and the *Sheffield* began to take in water. By the next morning the list was much worse and there was little choice but to allow her to sink.

It would be unfair to say that either the Task Force commanders or the Government lost their nerve at this point, but these were certainly difficult days. Leach recalled that:

the waves of emotion that spread through Whitehall were almost tangible. Ministers and officials were deeply shocked and indeed it seemed that for many this was the first real comprehension that the country was at war.[8]

It was here that the wartime experience of the most senior officers made itself felt. Lewin had seen ships lost at sea: he steadied his staff by observing that 'there is no point in having destroyers unless you are prepared to lose them.' He told the War Cabinet about Operation PEDESTAL, the 1942 convoy that had lost two-thirds of its merchant ships but still saved Malta. When it was suggested that Cecil Parkinson be sent to the television studios to explain the unavoidability of casualties in war Thatcher looked to Lewin. 'No, no, they'll never believe a politician, CDS must do it.' He went to Northwood, emerged with Fieldhouse, and then spoke to the cameras for the first and only time during the campaign.[9] The military watched to see how the Government, and particularly the Prime Minister, reacted. There was general relief that in the face of the first serious casualties there was no change of course, but also that the Government and the country at large now realised the seriousness of the situation and the meaning of war.

Still the carrier

Woodward's immediate assessment back to Fieldhouse on 4 May was sour. 'Not a good day and a poor exchange for a clapped out cruiser and SAR tug and a job lot of spics flying ageing Canberras.' He made clear that he remained worried about future naval battles in addition to more Exocets, in that once the Argentine destroyers and frigates got among the islands they would be difficult to handle. On this basis the decision not to go for the *Belgrano* escorts had been unwise:

each of them is likely to return with four Exocet in due course and ruin another day what with my limited surface surveillance and the winter weather ... I request early political recognition that there is a war going on down here and that this is no time to allow Arg warships to start being treated as hospital ships.

In addition, and especially if it became clear that Argentina had more than five Exocet, 'a strike on Rio Grande will be essential for recovery of the Falklands'. These two concerns combined to limit his options in enforcing the TEZ. The eastern third could be controlled, the middle third terrorised, but the western third posed problems so long as 'the Args can freely use their southern airfields.' The conclusion: 'Some new initiative is going to be needed maybe even a high risk raid right inshore to the mainland.'

The JIC assessment of 5 May certainly made for disturbing reading. The attack on the *Sheffield* indicated that the Argentines may have managed to master in-flight refuelling for the Super Etendards and sort out the final technical difficulties in fitting Exocets. If two missiles had been fired the Argentines probably still had three remaining. More unpleasant, the *San Luis* would probably sink any British units it could find in the area where they would be involved in search and rescue operations following the attack on the destroyer. Intelligence also indicated that the Argentine submarine *Santiago del Estero* was not in its usual berth at Mar del Plata. This raised questions about its possible deployment and operational status. Previous reports had stated consistently that this vessel was not operational and possibly cannibalised. There had also been no information about the submarine *Salta* since 15 April, for which MoD was getting desperate.

Yet for the moment the problems were being caused more by the reluctance of the Argentine Navy to fight than some new-found boldness. By withdrawing, the enemy fleet had reduced the possibilities for inflicting further attrition. *Splendid* continued with its fruitless search for the carrier. During 3 May the emphasis began to change with the proposal to concentrate on the Type 42s rather than the carrier, whose distinctive radar transmissions would be easier to detect than those of the carrier they would normally escort. A signal at 0052Z to all SSNs on 4 May said that while the *25 de Mayo* remained the top priority, every effort should be made to attack other warships. Early on the morning of 4 May, *Splendid* reported that it was holding four sonar contacts close to the Argentine coast off Punto Deseado, one of which was 'heavy', and would attempt daylight identification. Visibility was not good during the day and, while this was probably the carrier group, there was no definite sighting. Argentine task groups now seemed to be patrolling within the 12 mile limit. By early on 5 May, Herbert could observe that: 'At present, the Argentinian units do not appear to have any intention of moving … outside the TML [Twelve Mile Limit].' The contacts reported by *Splendid* on 4 May indicated a potentially tricky problem, as they appeared to be in a bay claimed by Argentina as being within its territorial waters though it would be deemed outside by Britain. This complication required a view from the Attorney General, which was that so long as the carrier was more than 12 miles from the nearest point of land it could be attacked. By the next morning the issue was moot as it was clearly inside the limit and moving north. The Attorney General remained concerned about giving any instructions to *Splendid* when its target was moving north to the point where no threat could be posed to the British forces.

At a meeting of the mandarins' group on the morning of 5 May, it became evident that Whitelaw was concerned as well as Pym and Parkinson, at the possibility of an attack on the carrier at its present position close to or in Argentine territorial waters and moving north. Leach, who was present, argued that if the carrier was not immobilised then there might not be another chance. With international support wobbling, and concern growing over the mounting loss of life as a result of *Sheffield*'s demise, ministers believed that it would be disastrous if the carrier was sunk, especially if it was inside the 12 mile limit from the nearest point of Argentine land and moving away to the north. Havers argued that: 'even outside the 12 mile limit, an attack on the Argentine aircraft carrier might be difficult to justify legally if as a result of moving northwards she was much too far away to pose an immediate threat to British forces'. The Prime Minister consequently thought that no immediate changes to ROE for British forces should be implemented. This was the most dovish point in British thinking. The risk of political isolation and the pressure from the Americans was palpable. The War Cabinet and then the full Cabinet had been in discussions all morning about an unsatisfactory American plan that might have to be accepted. A cease-fire might be imminent. In these circumstances it seemed folly to push Britain's luck by attacking the carrier close to the Argentine mainland.

At a meeting Pym produced a paper, reflecting the latest intelligence on the carrier, noting that:

> we have good reason to believe that she is in, or very close to, Argentinian territorial waters, heading North and so away from the Falkland Islands and our Task Force, and that her attack capability is reduced to six aircraft with a radius of only 200 miles. Thus the carrier in her present posture can hardly be regarded as a direct or imminent threat to our Task Force.

He recalled the view of Havers that any attack in these circumstances would have a 'questionable' justification. Pym could see outrage, at home and abroad, a lost chance of a peace settlement, and the deliberate destruction of 'the prospects of an initiative to which we have just given our conditional agreement'. (The claim that was later made by the Government's critics about the attack on the *Belgrano*.) While it might be necessary to move at some point against the carrier, 'the instructions to the submarine concerned should be modified, at least until we know whether the Argentines are going to accept the Haig proposals'. So long as the carrier stayed in territorial waters or moved in a direction that did not signal hostile intent she should be left alone.

The assessment referred to in Pym's letter (which was new) caused a strong reaction from Havers, as he had been advising 'on the basis that she had a considerable number of aircraft with a strike range of 500 miles'. He backed Pym's line, arguing that in all circumstances a legal justification would require that the carrier only be attacked if she had 'approached our forces in such circumstances as to make her a threat and therefore a legitimate target'. MoD's initial reaction was nervous, pointing to the difficulties of monitoring at all times the capabilities of the carrier and its position. Regardless, Havers insisted that it had to be no more than twelve hours steaming from the Task Force. Accordingly on 6 May the ROE were amended to prevent attacks on the carrier when she was north of 44°S and west of a line parallel to the Argentine coast. This was initially put at a distance of 50–100 nautical miles but was then extended to 200. It was also agreed to send a message to Haig to the effect that at this delicate juncture in efforts for a diplomatic settlement Britain was exercising restraint in its search for the carrier (the new boundaries of the British area of action being described), while Argentine commanders were apparently not under similar operational restraints, as seen in the seeming readiness of the Argentine submarine to attack vessels picking up survivors from the *Sheffield*.

Although the Prime Minister at first accepted the draft she decided later against sending it. This was because of the discussion at the War Cabinet the next day, which produced a new decision. The military had found the new restrictions unfortunate. They believed that confining the Argentine carrier to the new area did not preclude an attack on the Task Force or on supply lines. They warned again about the problems of monitoring all Argentine fleet movements, with the risk that while they might be under surveillance one side of the line they could be lost as they moved to a more threatening position on the other. Furthermore, it now seemed that the Argentine Navy had taken fright after the loss of the *Belgrano*, and might now be inclined to stay within territorial waters. Lastly, the latest peace initiative was clearly not going anywhere and Britain had done enough to ensure that this was not deemed to be her fault.

The next day a minute was prepared from Nott to Thatcher, to remind the War Cabinet of the 'military imperatives' guiding decisions in this area. The problem was that the range of the carrier was not fixed but dependent upon the relative weights of the weapons and fuel being carried as well as their ability to refuel in-flight. Because the range could not be known with certainty, and the Skyhawks could accomplish a 500-mile range, this appeared to be the prudent radius of action to assume. In addition, if it was not being trailed by an SSN or monitored by regular maritime air surveillance, which was the case at that time, then it could cover a considerable distance undetected. At the speed shown in *Jane's Fighting Ships* this would be 250 miles in 12 hours; even at the limited speed of which the ship actually seemed to be capable, 200 miles could be covered. When a 500-mile radius was plotted against the likely position of the British carrier group, any position beyond the 12-mile restriction and up to the 35 degrees south latitude could be described as potentially threatening. Later MoD added the latest DIS assessment that the A4 could have an offensive radius of action of 600–700nm, even without in-flight refuelling.

The War Cabinet agreed a new approach. A warning was to be issued to Argentina through the Swiss to the effect that any of its warships or combat aircraft found more than 12nm from its coast would be liable to attack. After this was released all previous ROE limitations affecting the Argentine carrier would be cancelled. The new statement recalled the warning of 23

April to Argentine forces threatening 'to interfere with the mission of British forces':

> Her Majesty's Government has consistently made clear that the United Kingdom has the right to take whatever additional measures may be needed in exercise of its inherent right of self defence under Article 51 of the United Nations Charter. Her Majesty's Government will take all necessary measures in the South Atlantic in the self defence of British ships and aircraft engaged in operations and in re-supplying and reinforcing British forces in the South Atlantic. Because of the proximity of Argentine bases and the distances that hostile forces can cover undetected, particularly at night and in bad weather, Her Majesty's Government warns that any Argentine warship or military aircraft which is found more than 12 nautical miles from the Argentine coast will be regarded as hostile and are liable to be dealt with accordingly.

After allowing 24 hours for this warning to be acted on, changes to the ROEs were brought into effect to remove the restriction on attacks on *25 de Mayo* by SSNs imposed on 6 May and allow attacks on Argentine warships, submarines, and combat aircraft outside the TEZ and the 12nm limit.

Although the new warning was seen as extending the Exclusion Zone right up to the Latin American coastline, this was not quite what was intended as, unlike the TEZ, it only referred to Argentine warships and military aircraft. Nonetheless, the announcement immediately prompted queries from Chile and Uruguay as to how it might apply to them. In reply the Government drew their attention to the terms of the announcement. One difficulty was that these two countries claimed the waters out to 200nm but Britain did not recognise this. On the other hand there was no desire to get into an argument with them on this matter at this time. Accordingly, while appreciating the reluctance of the military to accept restrictions on their ability to attack Argentine warships in circumstances where they would already be violating this restriction, the FCO sought 24-hour notice of any attack within these areas. The Navy Department thought it highly unlikely that there would be any attacks in claimed Chilean waters and was prepared to accept a degree of extra restriction here. At a meeting on 12 May chaired by the Cabinet Office, the Naval Staff accepted the principle and an order for Fieldhouse was drafted. No attacks should be made inside the claimed 200nm territorial waters of Uruguay and Chile without this 24 hours' notice. On receipt of such notice there would need to be explicit authorisation before any action was taken. Assurances were issued to the Governments of these countries that Britain would not wish to mount attacks in sensitive areas so long as Argentine units were also not using these waters. There was certainly no intention on Britain's part to engineer an attack in these areas. In practice, as far as Uruguayan and Brazilian waters were concerned, the only issue would lie with the carrier, other than possibly a Boeing 707. With 707 flights, however, a 24-hour warning was impossible.

On 24 May Panama circulated a declaration signed by a number of Foreign Ministers about an alleged British decision to 'extend its naval and air military action to the River Plate.' A 1973 Treaty between Argentina and Uruguay had established a line at the mouth of the River Plate from Punta del Este to Punta Rasa de Cabo San Antonio. In response Parsons wrote to the President of the Security Council, pointing out that Britain had already made it clear to Uruguay that it had no intention of passing that line or infringing the sovereignty of Uruguay and that this had been accepted by the Government of Uruguay in a public statement on 24 May. This was despite the fact that Britain had reserved its position on the 1973 Treaty.

The announcement was also seen to herald an aggressive British intent. Henderson conveyed a warning from the Brazilian President that while many in South America had some sympathy with Britain's resistance to Argentine aggression, 'Britain would put itself in the wrong, and as a result inflame the whole American hemisphere, if it attacked the Argentine mainland'. A warning had also been received from the Colombian Ambassador, one of the more friendly to Britain, that an attack on the mainland could lead all Latin American countries to break relations with Britain. It was recognised that Venezuela, Peru, Panama, Bolivia and Nicaragua might break relations and preparations were put in hand lest they did so. Just before the landing, when pressed by Perez de Cuellar on rumours that Britain was preparing to attack the mainland, Parsons provided an assurance that this would not happen.

'Hacking the Shad'

The position with regard to surveillance aircraft had been left, since April, with a warning issued and a rule that would allow an Argentine aircraft identified both electronically and visually as being engaged in surveillance to be warned off, and if necessary attacked, so long as it was 40 miles from the nearest British unit. One difficulty with this rule was that an interceptor had to be available to give the necessary individual warning. This created problems with the ships moving from Ascension to the Falklands, as carriers were not escorting them. On 6 May *Canberra*, *Elk* and *Tidepool*, escorted by the *Argonaut* and *Ardent*, departed south from Ascension. The next day the *Norland* and *Europic Ferry* arrived at Ascension with 2 Para. There was just enough time for some disembarkation drills and an intensive programme of helicopter transfers, before *Fearless*, *Stromness*, *Norland*, *Europic Ferry* and *Atlantic Conveyor* (with 6 GR3 Harriers and 8 Sea Harriers loaded) moved off at 2000Z on 7 May, to be followed on 8 May at 0900Z by *Intrepid*, while Ascension engaged in phoney communications with ships to delay knowledge of their departure.

The Chiefs requested permission to use surface-to-air missiles to shoot down surveillance aircraft without warning and without identification by a Harrier. They argued that the Argentine 707 could be categorised as a long-range maritime patrol aircraft and so a combat aircraft within existing ROE and liable to be attacked. However, this did not solve the problem of identification. A lot of civil airlines crossed the South Atlantic between Africa and Brazil. If one of those came within surface-to-air missile (SAM) range of British forces, 'we should not want him shot down'. This after all had almost happened in April. To deal with this it was proposed that MoD issue an ROE caveat on the following lines: 'An aircraft which from its pattern of behaviour, flight path, radar characteristics or visual sighting is identified as an Argentine 707 or Hercules operating in the maritime surveillance role is to be treated as a combat aircraft within the terms of the ROE in force.' The risks were as before. There could never be complete confidence in the accuracy of non-visual identification. An internal FCO paper set out the dilemma, at a time when nerves were frayed:

> A successful submarine attack on British troop-carrying ships moving between Ascension and the Falklands would be a major blow risking many lives. The Chiefs of Staff undoubtedly have a responsibility to prevent this if at all possible. But we should not under-estimate the international outcry that shooting down an Argentine 707 would produce. The Argentines would undoubtedly claim innocent passage and it would be hard to show the contrary by convincing evidence of a kind we could disclose. If the incident was isolated we should be accused of over-reacting. A shooting down coming at the wrong moment politically would also wreck any diplomatic efforts under way at the time. This alone requires that the promulgation of any such Rule of Engagement would need to be thought about carefully in relation to ongoing diplomatic activity.

On this basis the War Cabinet did not accept Lewin's proposal and he was asked to present a fuller case. Fieldhouse informed Woodward that the application for 'Hacking the Shad' [shadower] had foundered at War Cabinet on grounds that the risk of misidentification was too high. A further attempt, he explained, would be made on 10 May. To strengthen their case, Fieldhouse required Woodward to describe if possible the flight patterns that Boeing 707s had executed, length of time of plots and the effectiveness of ESM [Electronic Warfare Support Measure] identification and interrogation on IFF.

Antrim's LSL group, moving slowly south following the recapture of South Georgia, was aiming to keep clear of the Argentine coast as it travelled to join the main amphibious group. *Antrim* had detected Argentine

C130s or Boeing 707s on surveillance. On 5 May, when it had first requested permission to engage them with Seaslug, the risk was not considered to be too serious. By 9 May the surveillance appeared more intense. Boeing 707 aircraft had been detected on three occasions by the *Antrim* over the past two days, and once visually identified passing within 10 miles. There was also a possible C130 detection. At one point they came across a Soviet bloc merchant ship. On 9 May, the amphibious group feared that it had been spotted a little more than half-way between Ascension Island and the Falklands.

Intelligence now assessed that all three Argentine submarines could be at sea, and that an Argentine surface picket group, of two frigates and a patrol boat, was operating 200 miles off Puerto Belgrano. If true, these would be the only Argentine surface naval combatants operating within the TEZ, and were probably searching for the amphibious group. In fact for Argentina the reconnaissance effort continued to be frustrating: they could find neither the carrier battle group nor the amphibious force and were having difficulty with the serviceability of their surveillance aircraft. There was not a lot they could do about the amphibious group at this time. The British, however, were still uncomfortable about being watched at all. Judging themselves to be at some risk, for example, *Antrim*'s group followed a diversionary and zigzagging course for a number of days. To provide some protection for the main amphibious group, one Sea Harrier was kept on deck alert in the *Atlantic Conveyor*, tanker support was maintained on call from Ascension as long as possible, and Nimrod surface surveillance sorties were flown to cover the likely time windows for the 707s.

A paper prepared for the War Cabinet meeting on 10 May noted that intelligence-gathering flights by 707 aircraft had continued with six recorded instances of flights over the previous week recorded by the *Antrim* group escorting the amphibious force from Ascension. In all cases the aircraft followed irregular and certainly non-commercial flight paths and had, in a number of cases, lingered for some time over the Task Force. The military now believed they had enough information on the radar signatures of the 707, and the use made of radar while engaged in surveillance, to support a positive identification. To this was added concern over the uncertain position of the *Santiago del Estero*, the second Guppy-class submarine, which American sources reported as having left port on 2 May. Lewin's notes for the War Cabinet meeting, under the heading 'Hack the Shadower', stressed the importance of surveillance information for an SSK, but had also noted that there was no hard evidence that an SSK had managed to reach the sea lines between Ascension and the Falklands. In fact by 10 May Woodward was able to signal 'threat reduction from the front line' as he now assessed the surface and submarine threats to the amphibious group as nil to one per cent, with the air threat very low. The carrier group was 'the biggest up threat picket you will ever get'. On this basis he was ready to let the amphibious group come to meet his group at the edge of the TEZ, rather than detaching forces to meet them. They were overflown on 11 May by two Soviet Bear aircraft and on the same day a possible submarine was detected which later turned out to be a whale.

Other ROE

Although it was hard to object to the demands from the Chiefs of Staff and the MoD for further relaxation of the rules of engagement in order to bring about attrition of the Argentine forces if the intention was to prepare for an opposed landing, at the senior levels of the FCO there was concern that the implications of this logic had not been properly thought through. The rapid change in international opinion following the *Belgrano* was a warning of how the diplomatic logic of sustaining support from key allies could be upset by following the military logic too slavishly. Was this logic to be followed to an attack on the mainland air bases or even a declaration of war? If there was such a tension between the political and the military requirements was there not a need to at least address alternatives to a landing, such as an intensification of the EZ? All these concerns, plus the anxieties that had been generated by the 7 May announcement, led to an effort to consolidate the ROE on 12 May. A number of difficult issues were addressed, such as the authority that had been given to sink without warning vessels engaged in re-supply. The ROE could not be interpreted, as far as the FCO was concerned, to allow for a hospital ship to be sunk without warning. Yet it was by no means clear that *Alacrity* knew what it was attacking when it engaged on 11 May in an incident discussed below.[10] The FCO was also concerned that the extension of the ROE to allow for any non-nuclear submarines to be attacked in an area south of 50°S opened up the possibility of an attack on a Soviet diesel submarine. The rules had to be adjusted to ease the prevention of an incident and Moscow could also be informed as before.

The difficulty with setting clear guidance was illustrated by the case of the *Bahia Paraiso*. On 14 May there was concern that the *Bahia Paraiso*, although designated as a hospital ship, might be employed for military purposes in contravention of the Geneva Conventions by being prepared to transfer food and weapons to the Argentine garrison, possibly sufficient for a 40 days' supply. It was agreed that the Argentines should be warned against such a move through the Swiss: if necessary Britain would stop, board and search her to confirm whether this was so, and explore whether the ICRC could mount an inspection. There would be obvious problems, however, if a hospital ship were sunk without clear evidence that it was being used inappropriately. MoD was concerned that if it did get through they should have the authority, as a last resort, to sink her. The FCO noted that there was no evidence that the *Bahia Paraiso* was preparing to dash to Stanley, and so existing instructions should stand. By early June the doubts on the role of the ship were still there, especially with regard to intelligence-gathering, but Argentina had agreed that an ICRC representative could travel on board and the British were keen that this should be arranged.[11]

After the San Carlos landings, MoD pressed again on the 12-mile limit. Following a Chiefs of Staff discussion on 27 May, with the news from San Carlos grim, the Chiefs discussed the issue and requested a paper for the next day's War Cabinet. With a number of British warships, two within 12 miles of the Falklands, the Chiefs of Staff concluded that the sanctuary allowed Argentina should be removed. Removal of the restriction would not only provide a number of targets but also inhibit Argentine forces from leaving their mainland bases. The targets would be any Argentine warship, submarine or naval auxiliary. It was not proposed that any further warning should be given. The concerns of the Chilean, Uruguayan and Brazilian Governments would continue to be respected. The FCO judged the argumentation in favour weak, and suspected that the 'real motive is transparently to retaliate for the recent sinking of British warships'. At most they were prepared to agree to a public warning that if any more British ships were attacked within 12 miles of the Falkland Islands Argentina would be rendered liable for an appropriate response within 12 miles of the Argentine mainland. The War Cabinet was unsure about how to proceed. They had two meetings without conclusion. The Prime Minister described it as a 'difficult problem.' It was assumed that any attack would only be carried out by SSNs. Nott later described the discussion:

> one of our nuclear submarines found the Argentine aircraft carrier lurking within Argentinean territorial waters ... and the rules of engagement did not permit an attack within Argentinean territorial waters. The Navy sought a change in the rules, although the shallow water would have posed a hazard to our submarine. Margaret Thatcher was keen to agree the change, on the basis that the aircraft carrier would present a continuing threat to our ships and to the Falklands even after we had recaptured them. I opposed the change, arguing against her and Terry Lewin on the grounds that action in South American territorial waters could bring in other countries on the Argentinean side just as we were about to achieve a victory. We did not agree the change.[12]

SECTION FOUR

23

THE PERUVIAN INITIATIVE

The *Belgrano* had been sunk during a hiatus in diplomatic efforts to settle the crisis, with the Haig effort concluded and other initiatives just starting to get off the ground. It was alleged after the war that the purpose of the attack on the Argentine cruiser was to stall these initiatives. This is not correct, and if it had been the intention it certainly failed. Diplomatic activity was as intensive during May as it had been during April. The allegation centred on an initiative taken by the Peruvian Government. This was abandoned in its early stages by the Argentine side on receipt of news of the loss of the *Belgrano*. By contrast the British, rather than exult in its collapse, desperately tried to give it life.

Peru had been interested in playing some sort of diplomatic role from early on in the conflict. On 11 April they circulated a proposal for a 72-hour truce, while American mediation was underway. This created some awkwardness in London as it implied a readiness to avoid too close an association with Argentina yet appeared to suggest that the Task Force should be halted while Argentina remained in occupation of the Falklands. Argentina accepted; Britain rejected. From late April the historian Hugh Thomas, Lord Thomas of Swynnerton, who was being consulted by the Prime Minister as a Latin American specialist, was in regular telephone conversation with Prime Minister Ulloa of Peru. There have been suggestions that this was an important, informal negotiating channel. Their discussions, however, were general in nature. Although he gained an indication of Peruvian anxieties and an interest in finding a diplomatic route out of the conflict, Thomas was not privy to the details of any British negotiating position and was not in a position to establish any new diplomatic links. When the Peruvians decided to act they went to Argentina, where they hoped for some influence, and to the United States, where they hoped to find some method of putting pressure on Britain. President Belaunde decided to take an initiative on 2 May. It seemed an opportune moment because of the previous day's military action, and also because of the availability of Pym in Washington.

The Foreign Secretary was visiting the United States ostensibly to expedite the material support that was to be provided following the Reagan

Administration's 'tilt'. Haig had not, however, given up on diplomacy. Before he met with Pym he consulted with Peru to identify the main elements of a new proposal. The basic ideas came from Belaunde but the Americans modified them in the light of their knowledge of the British position. According to Belaunde he spoke with Haig by phone for three-quarters of an hour on 1 May:

> I finally asked him please to dictate to me the essential points from Britain's viewpoint. Haig read them over to me, and I for my part told him what word was unsatisfactory and what conditions unacceptable for Argentina. We finally agreed on a plan which covered seven points, and I left it that I should call President Galtieri at once to put that formula to him.[1]

The basic elements would comprise:

1. An immediate cease-fire;
2. A mutual withdrawal of forces;
3. The involvement of third parties on a temporary basis in the administration of the islands;
4. Acceptance by both parties of the fact that a dispute over sovereignty exists;
5. Acknowledgement that the views and interests of the islanders must be taken into account in reaching a definitive settlement;
6. A contact group of Brazil, Peru, the FRG (Federal Republic of Germany) and the United States would be formed; and
7. A definitive agreement would have to be reached by 30 April 1983.

The advantage to Argentina of the new plan was that there would be no direct British role in the new administration, and that 'viewpoints and interests' was better than 'wishes.'

With the American Ambassador to Peru, Frank Ortiz, present, Belaunde contacted Galtieri and read the text to him. Galtieri was told that Belaunde was in direct contact with Haig, who would soon be in contact with Pym. He pressed for an Argentine acceptance of the formula even before the Haig-Pym meeting. The formula itself was vague, Belaunde admitted, but once accepted then negotiations to firm it up could begin at once in New York. Galtieri promised to study the proposal. Galtieri objected to the United States because of its recent 'public attitude'. Belaunde said that Canada had been mentioned as an alternative, but it had been suggested that it was even less acceptable, and that anyway the United States was balanced by Peru ('a country that's frankly on Argentina's side'). Brazil was the alternative. Although the Peruvian President urged against any attempt to amend the proposal, Costa Mendez had then rung to urge the expansion of the group to include Venezuela. The 'elimination of the US' from the contact group was 'fundamental' and there was a discussion about whether Peru could be included without the United States also being a member. Costa Mendez was less concerned about Canada. Later Haig reported that the British would object to Peru. Belaunde said 'Magnificent, we're on equal footing. We can both withdraw and look for two other countries.'[2]

The Argentine Foreign Minister also raised inevitable concerns about point (5), he wanted to change the phrase 'views and interests of the islanders' to 'views concerning the interests'. Belaunde promised to consider a redraft. Belaunde then worked with Ortiz on a redraft which was passed on to Costa Mendez. Belaunde knew that Haig had yet to meet Pym. Ortiz noted that Costa Mendez's change only involved one word, indicating his lack of familiarity with one of the most sensitive issues in this long diplomatic saga. Haig, who understood this only too well, wanted 'wishes' back in and they seem to have settled on 'aspirations'. Ambassador Wallace confirmed that the version of the plan that he received that evening contained the word 'aspirations'.[3] At 1230 Lima time (1330 Washington), the US Ambassador met again with Belaunde who told him that the Argentine Junta would be discussing the proposal that evening, and had given some positive indications, so long as there was no more violence from the British. He was told explicitly that Haig's observations on the first draft were made prior to any discussions with Pym. The Junta would meet that evening at 1900 (Argentine time). Belaunde had offered to ring back at 2000 to get a reply. Galtieri warned him not to be too optimistic and promised a reply at 2200.

The priority issues for Pym in visiting Washington were military co-operation and new forms of pressure on Argentina. On his arrival in Washington he had observed that whereas the previous week he had come to visit a negotiator, now he came to visit an ally. According to Henderson this remark 'made some members of the Administration wince'. The effect was not wholly unintentional.[4] This does not mean that he wanted to let go of the diplomatic initiative, or give the impression that Britain was simply letting military events take their course. He was however assuming, as were the Argentines, that the next focal point would be the UN and so part of his schedule was to visit the Secretary-General in New York to 'help in maintaining unity in the House of Commons.' When they met for two hours on the morning of 2 May Pym found Haig welcoming continued military pressure on Argentina, but with its influence on a diplomatic outcome clearly in mind. The Secretary of State's view was that a large-scale landing would be unnecessary once the British could demonstrate control over the TEZ. 'We could do all the damage we wanted to without a major assault.' As Haig remained concerned about the knock-on effects on the US position in Latin America, he still wanted a central role in any negotiations for a settlement. In this context he apprised Pym of the new plan, arguing that though a 'humiliation,' it might be acceptable to the Junta as Britain's military pressure increased. This, of course, assumed that Argentina's assessment of the events of 1 May was similar to his own.

Haig reported that President Belaunde had discussed the ideas with Galtieri earlier. There had been some indications this morning, via Costa Mendez, that a proposal along these lines might be acceptable to Argentina. Pym replied cautiously. The proposals were not even at drafting stage, and while they might be useful at an appropriate time, he doubted that Buenos Aires was yet ready to meet Britain's basic requirements. On the specifics of the proposal Haig reported that Argentina wanted Canada instead of the US on the contact group, but Pym said that the US would have to be there to guarantee a settlement. Pym also observed that Parliament was unlikely to accept a change in status quo over South Georgia now that it had been recaptured successfully. Haig accepted that it was too early to bring any greater precision to the discussions while Pym observed that he would 'wish to discuss this with the PM as soon as possible.'

Belaunde had no news until after Pym and Haig had lunched together at the British Embassy. By the time that he could report back to Haig, Pym was en route to the airport to fly to New York to meet the UN Secretary-General. As he realised just how far Belaunde had taken matters with Galtieri, Haig tried to talk on the phone again to Pym. As he needed to catch the plane, Pym asked Henderson to ring back. The Foreign Secretary was concerned that he was suddenly going to be presented 'with a communication from him, Haig, saying that the Argentinians had agreed and that it was now up to us to say that we did likewise.' There was much still to be clarified.

Haig promised restraint yet still insisted that he thought the initiative offered a great deal. An obvious problem area was the involvement of third parties in the temporary administration of the Islands, especially as Haig was now reporting that the preferred Argentine composition would be Venezuela and Canada, as well as Brazil, Peru, FRG and the US. Henderson observed that three Latin Americans would be unacceptable, as they would be able to block decisions to be taken by majority. Venezuela was particularly offensive. It had presented the Task Force as a threat to peace and an affront to Latin American dignity, and the crisis had highlighted its own claim against Guyana. Haig was reluctant to rule out Venezuela, but agreed that six was too many for the group. Henderson proposed Trinidad as a possible alternative. Haig said this might be acceptable. A report from the US Ambassador to Venezuela on his conversations with the Foreign Minister indicates that on 2 May the latter reported three conversations with Costa Mendez concerning a 'working group' to seek a solution.

Haig explained that it was his idea to give Argentina some 24 hours in which to send their Foreign Minister to a given place with full authority from the Junta to sign up. But Argentine compliance required, he warned, no further British military action in the meantime. Henderson replied that Britain would not agree to anything that inhibited it from maintaining the military pressure. The conversation concluded with Haig promising to get in touch as soon as he had heard again from Argentina. Henderson reported back to Pym that he had stressed the Foreign Secretary's main concern:

> You did not want to be rushed. You had not consulted London about them. Moreover there was another element of doubt in your mind. What was going to happen in practical terms if the parties agreed? How could we be sure that the Argentinians were going to stick by the scheme?

The press line was 'various ideas were discussed ... But no conclusions were reached. There was no question of accepting or rejecting anything out of hand.'

After Haig had spoken on the phone with Belaunde again, the Peruvian President then tried to reach Costa Mendez, whom he eventually found at 1730 local time on his way to the Junta meeting. Astonishingly, Belaunde felt able to tell Costa Mendez that Haig had informed him that Foreign Secretary Pym appeared prepared to accept the structure of the proposed agreement. New language was also suggested on the troublesome point (5) involving replacing 'wishes' with 'aspirations'. The difficulty over membership of the contact group was to be resolved by making it even vaguer – there was a reference to 'several countries designated by common consent.' Belaunde described the proposal as an 'Argentine triumph but not a UK capitulation.' The Argentine Foreign Minister was non-committal. The 'final decisions were in other hands'.

It appears extraordinary that Haig could have let Belaunde believe that Pym was on board. He was obviously aware of the limited information Britain could have received through him and the reservations expressed. He may have assumed that Britain's Ambassador to Peru was serving as the main conduit of information back to London. When Wallace met the Peruvian Foreign Minister, Dr Arias Stella, on the morning of 1 May, he was not given any indication of an imminent effort at mediation. He had observed that 'Argentina attached great importance to the attitudes and opinions in Peru ... Peru could usefully exert its influence ... in convincing Argentina to implement Resolution 502 without any preconditions as soon as possible.' In the ensuing conversation reference was made to Pym's forthcoming visit to Washington.[5]

During the afternoon of 2 May, Stella summoned Wallace to tell him about the initiative designed to break deadlock and bring about cease-fire. 'A way had to be found to allow the Argentines to climb down without too much loss of face.' Belaunde had attempted – unsuccessfully – to contact President Reagan in order to instil a sense of urgency 'and to take advantage of the presence of Mr Pym in Washington.' However Haig and Belaunde had spoken several times. On the specifics Arias reported that they had considered whether a token reference to the Argentine claim to sovereignty in the introductory part of an agreement might suffice to bring about the withdrawal of Argentine troops. He also discussed the composition of the group. Some procedural difficulties had arisen with regard to the inclusion of the US and/or Peru. Wallace was told, in confidence, that Belaunde would not mind if Peru was excluded, but Haig had already intimated that the US would not want to be excluded, as otherwise the proposal would not be acceptable to Britain.

Wallace was told that the English text of the seven-point formula 'had virtually been dictated over the telephone by Mr Haig,' and that Costa Mendez had approved it. General Galtieri had told President Belaunde that he was 'well disposed' towards it but that he had his 'senate' (i.e. the military Junta) to consult and convince. Arias said the Junta was meeting even at that hour to consider the terms and that a reply was expected hourly. He had reason to believe that Haig's proposals had been conveyed with the knowledge or at least the consent of Pym. Belaunde was anxious not to lose momentum. Washington had been told that if the formula were acceptable the signature of an interim document would take place in Lima. Wallace was warned to expect instructions tonight. Arrangements were already being made to stage a grand signature ceremony in Lima. On this basis, Belaunde did indeed hold a press conference at 1900 local time. He announced that Haig had telephoned him last night to put to him the seven-point plan. No details were revealed, but he insisted that the proposal would not involve capitulation by either side. The Argentines were considering it so the President hoped to be able to make an announcement either later that night or the next morning.

Arias indicated to Wallace that the announcement was made to put pressure on the Argentines, as it would create a risk for the Junta that a rejection might alienate the Peruvian Government and public opinion in Latin America. Wallace reported back to London Belaunde's anxiety to be seen to be an active and prominent peacemaker. This would help bolster his position against the Peruvian military, which he saw as a threat to the stability of his regime. 'In these circumstances we can hardly expect him to refrain from making further pronouncements on the subject, particularly if he receives positive Argentine reactions.'

To Pym the pace of events was becoming alarming. Wallace was instructed as a matter of urgency to get back to Arias and/or the President's office 'to ensure that no announcement is made which implies that we have agreed to these proposals or even had them formally presented to us.' He could at his discretion assure his interlocutors that Pym was grateful for the efforts the President was making. It had to be stressed that the first requirement was an Argentine withdrawal, properly supervised, and with effective guarantees that Argentina would implement whatever agreement was reached. Any interim agreements and the framework for negotiations for a definitive settlement must not prejudice the core principles behind the British position. Britain was prepared to work hard for a solution 'but cannot cut corners when matters of such importance are at stake.' In particular, Britain could not renounce its right of self-defence while Argentine troops 'maintain unlawful occupation of the islands'. As this was now 0330 in Lima, Wallace did not want to ring Arias lest he assume it to be good news. He could therefore react adversely if there had already been a positive reaction from Buenos Aires. He intended to contact Arias in the morning.

By the time that Wallace actually got to Arias to explain the British position the initiative was, to all intents and purposes, dead. In Buenos Aires, the Military Committee's meeting began at 1900. It has been reported that at 1930 Admiral Anaya announced the news of the loss of the *Belgrano*, although this seems rather early given what is known about the Argentine response times to the tragedy. When the news was confirmed the Junta was now unwilling to explore any negotiation involving the United States, assumed to be complicit in the British action, and preferred instead to explore an offer of mediation from the UN Secretary-General. At 0030 Galtieri spoke to Belaunde and expressed his feelings:

> the Argentine government will not, in the face of this military pressure, accept any negotiations relating to peace in the South Atlantic in these circumstances. We would rather die on our feet than live on our knees.[6]

Thus when Wallace met with Arias at 0630 the news of the Argentine decision was conveyed to him. The door had not been entirely closed but the Junta now claimed to need more time 'to review any proposals in light of most recent developments on naval front.' Galtieri in fact told Belaunde that there was nothing left to discuss. 'All that remained was to fight.'

Back to Haig

The Peruvian plan had no effect on British decision-making on the *Belgrano*, but the *Belgrano* had an effect on British decision-making on the Peruvian plan. On the Argentine side the incident eliminated enthusiasm for this deal; on the British side it made a deal more interesting. This was because of the severity of the immediate international reaction to the sinking of the ship and the considerable loss of life. Brazil described it as a violation of SCR 502. Mexico was milder, regretting that hostilities had broken out, while President Herrera of Venezuela condemned British aggression and called for a review by Latin America of policies of integration and collective security. He was said to be canvassing other Latin

American countries to break diplomatic relations with Britain. The British Ambassador to Bolivia having been summoned to the Ministry of Foreign Affairs (MFA) to receive a letter of protest, and having defended the action, observed that 'There is no doubt that the sinking of the *General Belgrano* and the reported casualties have had a profound effect on public opinion in Bolivia which has turned further against us.'

In Europe Spain issued a statement describing the attacks as a 'serious escalation in the conflict; more generalised British action would signify a great responsibility and an historic error'. The statement reaffirmed Spanish opposition to the use of force and deplored the fact that the colonial nature of the problem had been overlooked. Irish enthusiasm for a cease-fire resolution at the Security Council was sharpened. Elsewhere in Europe the reaction was more subdued, but diplomats commented on a definite change of mood, especially in Germany. Almost as soon as news began to filter through that the *Belgrano* had sunk with heavy loss of life, there were calls from the Washington Embassy and the Mission to the UN, anxious to find out if the rumours were true and warning of the presentational difficulties to come.

The first Henderson heard of the *Belgrano* was a telephone call from Haig on the evening of 2 May at about 0800 Washington time. Haig said 'Well you've sunk them. You better come down and see me about it.'[7] This began a series of pained conversations with Haig. Henderson was told of the bitter complaints from the Peruvian President, of the high price that might have to be paid in terms of a Soviet advance in Latin America, of the possibility of an American veto being needed to prevent anti-British sanctions being adopted by the OAS, of western opinion turning against Britain. Henderson reminded him of the Argentine naval manoeuvrings which formed the immediate background to the sinking, and that the Americans had also concluded that Argentine forces were determined to attack. Whatever the Argentine inflexibility that may supposedly come from this attack no flexibility had emerged during the three weeks when nothing had been done against them. Regardless Haig was after some diplomatic initiative from Britain: a promise to desist from further hostilities for some time if Argentina did the same. In the end the best bet appeared to be to re-float the Peruvian proposals, even though Argentina had claimed that they had been torpedoed.

After three telephone calls Haig asked Henderson for a meeting. The Peruvians were also prepared to persevere and he was now looking to see if Britain could accept this approach. At the same time he intensified his request that the British propose a cease-fire, lest they sink the whole Argentine fleet and cause chaos and the collapse of authority in Buenos Aires, alienating in the process all of Latin America. Henderson observed that 'after waiting three weeks while the Argentinians reinforced the Islands we were not in a mood to rush to an armistice just because the Argentinians were losing hands down.'

By now Peru was beginning to back away from what seemed to be a doomed enterprise. It is not the case that Argentine discussion with Peru came to a complete stop. On 3 May an Argentine delegation, including a number of the team that had been negotiating with Haig, arrived in Lima. They discussed the possibility of a joint Peruvian-Canadian mediation, or even an informal meeting in Peru of Argentine and British representatives empowered to find a solution. Ambassador Wallace reported that the Argentine emissaries had come to 'soothe Presidential feathers ruffled by terms of original Argentine rejection communiqué,' which had dismissed the plan as 'warmed-over Haig.' US Ambassador Ortiz continued his own discussions, even raising the idea of passing the issue of sovereignty to the World Court. None of these contacts were exactly promising.

Haig still pressed on, now ever more anxious to bring matters to a swift, but negotiated, conclusion. In the light of the *Belgrano* he wrote to Pym on 3 May:

> We are concerned that your military successes have not had the desired effect of making the Argentines more reasonable. Our assessment is that the fatalistic mentality characteristic of the Argentines is becoming stronger with each setback. Paradoxically – and tragically – the Argentines may well be waiting, and trying, for a military success of their own before making a serious move toward a settlement. Such a strategy would be consistent with everything we know about the Argentines.

He warned that as the military situation worsened for Argentina, Britain would find itself 'left with no alternative but a major long-term military burden.' In addition, international opinion would reflect a 'belief, however untrue, that British military action is the principal obstacle to a peaceful solution.' The risk was that Argentina would be able to avoid the onus of their responsibility for the diplomatic impasse. Strain was being put on the US as well, as it was asked to defend its decision to lend Britain full support in the face of an increasingly hostile hemispheric reaction. All this led Haig to a proposal for a joint US and Peruvian proposal. Both sides would be given 48 hours in which to accept or reject, with the understanding that no response would constitute rejection. This two-day period could begin at noon Washington time on Wednesday, 5 May. He further proposed that at that time Britain should announce that its forces would take no offensive action during this period, providing Argentine forces showed a corresponding restraint. Haig enclosed a suggested statement. This, he explained, was cast to avoid Argentine humiliation and therefore rejection.

The War Cabinet developed a number of responses to Haig. The link between a cease-fire and Argentine withdrawal would have to be firmly spelled out: Argentina must be kept out of any interim arrangements; predetermined outcomes must be avoided in later negotiations; there must be a voice for the islanders. For the moment, the idea of a restoration of British administration or a referendum seemed to be too provocative to Haig. Britain would withdraw to wherever it liked out of 200nm from the Islands, and the contact group would have a limited role. Following these deliberations, Pym replied to Haig on 4 May, observing that his ideas had some merit as well as deficiencies. However, while the military had to work within the existing ROE, Haig was to be 'reassured that nothing unprecedented is contemplated before we have come back to him in the light of his latest messages.'

After a further conversation with Haig that day Henderson reported back the minimal response from both the Argentines and Peruvians. Nonetheless, Haig still wanted to push ahead – if only to put Argentina on the wrong side of public opinion again. Otherwise there was going to be continuing 'attrition' in Britain's international support. Haig observed the American proclivity to rally round the underdog. Henderson retorted that he thought 'the American proclivity was to believe that nothing succeeds like success.' The conclusion of all of this was that while Haig was not wedded to a particular scheme, he did think it was urgent for Britain to come up with something to try to head off the inevitable emergence of opposition. Henderson added:

> Somewhat mysteriously he also spoke of the involvement of someone he described as 'a retired peer close to the Prime Minister' whom I have later identified as Hugh Thomas. This person has been in touch with Peruvian leaders and will be putting forward ideas to the Prime Minister which may or may not be helpful.

Thomas certainly had been in touch with the Peruvians the previous week but there is no evidence that he was ever in a position to act as a serious interlocutor, or thought himself to be so.

British proposals

The British in fact had been coming to similar conclusions to Haig themselves. They accepted the virtues of simplicity and that negotiations must not drag on. They would not agree to a cease-fire on the basis of an imprecise agreement, lest Argentina accept the proposal, and, relieved of military pressure, play for time in the negotiations and so prolong the occupation. A new version of the proposals was offered, with the seven points down to six, and the contact group reduced to four – Peru, Brazil, FRG, US. (Wallace had observed from Lima that it would help if there were still seven points in the plan when presenting it to the Peruvian Government, as it was almost certain to be leaked to the press.) This group should work by consensus with a rotating chair. The new proposal would take into account the possibility of no agreement by 30 April 1983.

In transmitting these ideas, Pym added a dramatic proposal for Haig's consideration:

> If you and the Peruvian Government were to call upon Argentina and Britain to accept within 48 hours an agreement in the terms I am enclosing, the British government would immediately announce that our naval forces in the South Atlantic had been given orders not to fire within or outside the TEZ unless directly threatened by Argentine ships or aircraft but that we would revert to earlier rules of engagement if Argentina failed to accept your proposals within 48 hours. We would need from you an advance assurance that Argentina at the same time would announce that the same orders had been issued to her forces and that her ships and aircraft would not be present in the TEZ in the 48 hour period.

Pym also sought a US guarantee of the security of the Falkland Islands, lasting from the seventh day after signature to implementation of a definitive agreement. For this to deter Argentina there must be no doubt about the guarantee.

This proposal came to Haig against the background of the news coming in about the successful Argentine attack on HMS *Sheffield*. Almost as soon as he got the British draft, Haig rushed round to see Henderson, having cancelled a meeting in New York. There was 'no doubt about his great anxiety'. All involved would be diminished if fighting continued with further loss of life. Haig expressed his view that it was 'now or never' if the fighting was to be stopped. The British draft would not work. There was not the slightest chance of Peru forwarding to Argentina anything that contained references to the former administration, the need for the wishes of islanders to be respected, and doubt that a definitive agreement could be reached.

Henderson observed that as yet there was no evidence that Argentina was prepared to be flexible. It had already rejected the Peruvian proposals. 'I asked him what, in the circumstances, he thought could be done, and this led him on to a prolonged analysis of texts, the outcome of which was a new set of points.' Nor was Haig able to be helpful on the idea of a US guarantee. This posed all sorts of difficulties, which could only be surmounted with a great deal of time. He had new language on this, which committed the US (and other contact group powers) to the non-introduction of Argentine forces. As Argentina would rather commit suicide than go back to the status quo ante he preferred to talk with less precision about the 'local administration,' and to discuss the islanders' 'aspirations and interests' rather than 'wishes.'

Haig urged the British to accept his latest proposals. 'He does not really think that we can go on drafting and counter-drafting.' If they were acceptable

London would respond by noon on 5 May and then Washington would transmit the text to Lima and request acceptance by noon, 6 May. Immediately, the US and Peru jointly would transmit the texts formally to the British and Argentine Governments and require approval in 48 hours. The British would say they had been received and considered, and that orders for a cease-fire for 7 May had been given, so long as Argentina was prepared to take similar action and had notified Washington and Lima. Once the cease-fire was in effect Britain would reply at noon 8 May accepting the proposals. If Argentina failed to accept then Britain would revert to previous ROE.

Haig followed up his meeting with Henderson with a forceful letter to Pym:

> I must tell you with a candour possible only between closest allies that the ideas you have conveyed can lead only to one outcome: Argentine rejection and therefore resumption of hostilities after 24 hour period, with the prospects for eventual settlement having been damaged in the process. Beyond that, we have no reason to believe that the Peruvian government would associate itself with your proposal. Indeed, our assessment is that even presenting it to them would drive Peru to a more pro-Argentine posture.

His new proposal:

> includes our best efforts to meet your concerns about a security guarantee. I will not deny that it is closer to the ideas we sent you than to those you sent us. The most important difference ... is not that ours abandon principle and reward aggression, for they do not, but rather that ours have a reasonable chance of acceptance provided that the Argentines are now of a mind to show greater flexibility.

While he was doubtful that Argentina would accept the American ideas he was certain they would not accept the British:

> I hardly need to say that we have left no doubt where we stand: the Argentines committed aggression: they have been inflexible in negotiations: and the US supports the UK, explicitly and concretely. We have never contemplated asking you to agree to anything that would undermine the rule of law, weaken our relationship, or be seen as less than a success for your country and your government. It was in this spirit that I must tell you that we are prepared to proceed on the basis of the revised version I am sending to you, but could not associate ourselves with your version.

A message was received from Reagan urging compromise.[8]

On 5 May first the War Cabinet and then the full Cabinet met to discuss the proposals. The position was difficult, with American pressure and wavering in the EC following the *Belgrano* and then the loss of the *Sheffield* denting national confidence in Britain's military position. The discussions lasted some four hours. There was general unhappiness about Haig's ideas, which certainly included the Prime Minister, but it was judged that some response was needed. His new proposals were more favourable to British interests than previous proposals. They caused difficulties, especially in relation to the interim administration, but Pym and Thatcher recommended acceptance. This would improve Britain's international position, and it was noted that opinion was moving against Britain since the *Belgrano*. If Argentina did not accept, and this was possible, then Haig should not allow his deadline to be extended as it had been at the end of April. In the Commons Pym observed that: 'The military losses which have now occurred on both sides in this unhappy conflict emphasise all the more the urgent need to find a diplomatic solution.' Here Britain had made a 'constructive contribution.'

After the meeting Pym replied to Haig. The proposals still fell short of what Britain wanted and would not be easy to defend. Cabinet had considered them against the background of issues involved. Because 'we share your strong desire to reach a negotiated settlement and avoid further bloodshed' the Government was prepared to accept the American proposals as a basis for proceeding. There were some caveats. The proposals should be headed 'Draft Interim Agreement on the Falkland Islands/Islas Malvinas' to make it clear that the Dependencies were excluded. It also had to be clear that all Argentine forces would leave the Falklands, and that the contact group would be:

> administering the government of the Falkland Islands in the interim period in consultation with the elected representatives of the population of the islands and ensuring that no actions are taken in the islands which would contravene this interim agreement.

Henderson was told that if Haig strongly objected to the phrase about elected representatives then he had discretion to drop it. However the Prime Minister, responding to President Reagan's latest message, was urging strongly that democratic countries such as the US and UK should agree on its inclusion. Henderson might therefore want to suggest that Haig discuss this matter with the President.

There would also need to be a specific moment when both parties stated formally to the US and Peruvian Governments that they accepted the agreement. Only then would instructions for a cease-fire be issued, to come into effect as soon as both parties could guarantee compliance by their forces. The British could accept an interval of 24 hours provided that Argentina would also undertake to abide by that. Britain would even support a shorter timetable. They would, however, also want a side letter confirming that the draft agreement incorporated a guarantee on the part of the US of the non-reintroduction of Argentine forces into the Falkland Islands pending a definitive settlement, and that Argentina should be informed that such a letter had been sent. Buenos Aires should be asked to give an answer by a precise deadline.

The Prime Minister had become anxious that she was dealing not only with Haig but also the White House. Having just been through a considerable effort to get the Americans to tilt in the British direction, they now appeared to be tilting back again. She drafted an irritated personal letter to President Reagan before thinking better of it and toning down the language before it was sent.[9] This letter was given the most limited circulation. Thatcher still complained about the constant pressure to which Britain was being subjected. She addressed the President as 'the only person who will understand the significance of what I am trying to say.' She began by stressing her loyalty to the US as a great ally, as both countries stood for the same principles. Yet now a settlement was being proposed that did 'not provide unambiguously for a right to self-determination.' Haig had rejected the British request that it be included explicitly because Argentina would not accept and that would preclude a settlement. Accordingly, 'I have tried to temper Al Haig's latest proposals a little by suggesting that the interim administration must at least consult with the locally elected representatives. It is not much to ask – and I do not think you will turn it down.' Yet she insisted that she wanted a peaceful settlement and an end to the loss of life, and to sustain the alliance between their two countries, and for those reasons would accept the latest proposals. She also welcomed American material military support and the importance of economic pressure if further military action could be avoided, and so urged 'a complete ban on imports to the United States.'

Haig was pleased that the proposal was being accepted and agreed that the Argentine Government must express their agreement in writing to the proposals, although he also believed that if Britain was to gain the advantage of coming out with the idea of a cease-fire they should do so immediately they got the proposals. No danger was seen in this if the actual coming into effect of the cease-fire had to await Argentine acceptance. The document was transmitted to Peru. When Ambassador Ortiz took it to Belaunde, who claimed to have been awaiting it eagerly, the President's first reaction was that it could not be made acceptable to the Argentines, especially as they were growing in confidence about their military position. The British had made a simple document complicated and reintroduced old points of contention. He promised to 'do his best', acknowledging the areas where the British had moved, but by late that night of 5 May it was apparent that the initiative was not going anywhere.

The end of the initiative

Belaunde once again spoke to Galtieri on 5 May. He reported that he had received through the US the British reaction to the document containing his proposals:

> In general, they accept it; they make it a bit more concise, because they reduce it from seven points to six, but they make some changes in editing. They leave the first part, for example – immediate cessation of hostilities. They talk of a mutual withdrawal, but also of a ... non-redeployment or non-reintroduction ... of all forces, that is to say a non-return of the forces during this period. They then go on at once to insist that the Contact Group be those countries originally mentioned – despite the fact that I had been very clear that this was not acceptable to you, above all in one case – and that its mission should be, first, to verify the withdrawal of forces, second to administer the government of the islands during the provisional period in consultation with the elected representatives of the islands' population – you see here they want to give prominence to the existing organisations, and make it certain that no action is taken on the islands that contravenes this interim accord – and, third to ensure that all the other terms of the agreement are respected.

He then asserted that the Americans would 'make them accept these accords in a discussion' but noted that the British were insisting on a very tight schedule for the discussion – 24 hours for giving orders and instructions for the cease-fire, 48 hours for the work, but only 12 hours, once the cease-fire had started, to reject or approve a previously presented but not necessarily approved document. Belaunde did not mention the stress on the 'wishes' of the islanders. At any rate Galtieri rejected the proposals.[10]

Haig telephoned Henderson at 2300 saying that Argentina was no longer interested in the US/Peruvian plan but was now committed to the UN route. The Argentines considered that they were securing growing international support, for example from Ireland, and that the European Community was cracking. The sinking of the *Sheffield* had greatly emboldened them, with the result that they were now convinced that they would triumph militarily and politically. Haig intended to wait for a formal answer from Peru and then, if it was negative as he expected, decide how to publicise the British readiness to support this effort. 'We will have to be sure,' Henderson suggested, 'that they do not pull their punches in attributing blame where it belongs for their breakdown.'

The next day Haig reported that the Peruvians had definitely turned down the initiative as Argentina was now going to the UN. Belaunde had spoken of the 'arrogance of the military leaders in BA whose military confidence was now soaring as a result of the attack on the *Sheffield*. Their aim would now be to isolate the UK and get a cease-fire at the UN without any commitment on withdrawal.' For the moment all Haig could do was to play it cool in Washington without much activity. His advice to Britain was to 'try to seal off the islands'. The Americans believed that Argentina 'had eight days of rations but thought that supplies were getting through in freighters. This should be stopped.'

In Lima Wallace had been told to present the proposals to Belaunde, telling him that Britain appreciated his efforts, and that this plan offered the best prospect of securing an early cease-fire and withdrawal before more lives were lost, even though it contained elements difficult for Britain to accept. He was also to explain that if the text was not acceptable to Argentina Britain proposed to disclose its lines to demonstrate to world opinion the seriousness of the efforts it had been making. Lest there be concern with the relationship between these ideas and those then being put forward by the Secretary-General in New York it was to be asserted that 'the Peruvian proposals are not only compatible with the Secretary-General's ideas but also provide essential clarity and precision in an imaginative and positive way.' Britain hoped that Belaunde would do his best to get Galtieri to accept.

When Wallace called on the President at 1015 (local time) on 6 May he was told that it was important that Peruvian authorship should not be ascribed to the proposals as Britain and the US had extensively modified them. The only Peruvian proposals were those of 3 May. Belaunde repeated the observations that the United States would be unacceptable to Argentina as a member of the group (which is why he had talked to the Canadians). Belaunde did nonetheless communicate Britain's ideas to Argentina, only for Galtieri again to reply that Argentina was already going to the UN.

The Americans at first did not seem to object to the publication of the proposals, although Henderson found Haig 'as difficult to follow as ever.' Later Haig seemed less keen, leading Henderson to complain that it would be unreasonable if he 'washed his hands of the whole matter and behaved as though it had never existed.' Britain had gone to enormous trouble to respond to American ideas. Haig appeared to be mainly concerned that the negotiating process was slipping away from his control. He had concluded that Argentina was not yet seriously interested in negotiation:

> They believe that time is on their side, that Britain's diplomatic support will dwindle and that with the onset of winter in the South Atlantic and possibly the sinking of another ship, we will buckle.

He judged that the Argentine intention, now aided and abetted by both Belaunde and Perez de Cuellar, was to get the US excluded from the process. Kirkpatrick's report back from her conversations with Perez de Cuellar would have added to his concerns. The Secretary-General observed that the US was not seen as a potential referee because of its partisan role, while the Peruvian proposal was discounted as the Haig proposals 'translated into Spanish.' Now he was being urged to take an initiative; Argentina had accepted this, 'several EC representatives, including France and Germany, have turned round on the question', and 'the opinion in the Security Council and in the UN has turned strongly against the UK, whom everyone feels is resisting settlement.'

24

BACK TO THE UN

> The Falklands Crisis continues to arouse intense interest amongst delegations here and we are not yet running the risk of boring our readership.

So wrote Parsons back to London at the end of April as the Task Force reached the South Atlantic and the Haig mission faltered. The atmosphere at the UN had become tenser in the expectation of military moves by Britain and diplomatic moves by almost anyone. Yet there had still been no initiative to activate the Security Council, and Parsons was not inclined to encourage one. Any move Britain tried to control would be seen at best as a cynical ploy, providing cover for military preparations, and control would be lost as soon as a resolution appeared demanding that all military operations be suspended. Until early May Argentina had also seemed content to keep the issue out of the UN, leaving the mediation to Haig before the brief flirtation with the Peruvian initiative. A meeting between Perez de Cuellar and Costa Mendez on 30 April had produced no proposals but promises that 'in their treatment of the islanders, Argentine generosity would know no limits.' Having just met the Argentine Foreign Minister, it was natural that the Secretary-General should also consult the British Foreign Secretary, a meeting scheduled in New York for 2 May, and also that he should say nothing more until he had done so. To avoid giving the impression that UN mediation was imminent, the British presented Pym's visit as a natural add-on to the main visit to Washington.

When the meeting took place on the evening of 2 May, the Secretary-General explained that he now considered it to be his duty to fill the gap left by Haig. He wished to set up some negotiating mechanism within the frame-work of SCR 502, if only to forestall dramatic and unhelpful initiatives from others. Members of the Security Council were getting increasingly restive. Pym promised that no doors were closed but reported, on the basis of his curious conversations with Haig earlier that day, that the US Secretary of State was also prepared to resume his efforts.

Perez de Cuellar handed Pym a confidential document that had also been given to Argentine Ambassador Roca. His assistant, Ahmad, introduced it. At its heart was a procedural formula that did not go into the substance of the issues in dispute and could be regarded as containing 'provisional measures' under Article 40 of the Charter. It attempted to circumvent the 'chicken and egg' problem resulting from Britain's insistence that the first step must be Argentine withdrawal and Argentine insistence that their case for sovereignty must first be accepted. The idea was that there should be 'simultaneity' between Argentine withdrawal, the redeployment of the Task Force, the lifting of sanctions and the beginning of negotiations. The UN was seeking responses by the two sides by 5 May, so that their scheme would come into effect on 6 May.

Pym responded that he was happy to consider proposals but the timetable seemed precipitate. UN mediation was an asset not to be wasted so it was necessary to find the right time, and he doubted whether Argentina would accept that the outcome of sovereignty should not be prejudged. Perez de Cuellar promised that if Britain accepted his formula he would use all his influence, including as a Latin American, to get Argentina to accept it too. Pym also explained that Britain could not accept a 'balanced' withdrawal of forces. Argentina had to go first, though there might be some optimal withdrawal of British forces, and Britain would also want arrangements for an interim administration agreed in advance. Parsons hoped that the positive meeting had a 'salutary affect on Ahmad who can no longer be under any illusion that his sketchy and ill-thought out ideas have much chance of acceptance.' He also felt that by not killing off the Secretary-General's efforts, time had been gained and any other efforts at the UN precluded.

Yet the view that only the UN could fill the vacuum left by Haig was getting stronger, and soon, on 3 May, the British delegation was starting to feel the backlash of the *Belgrano*. That morning Pym had a less than satisfactory meeting with the new President of the Security Council, Ling Qing of China. 'Little but platitudes to offer in reply ... no useful information ... singularly unproductive ... lacks self confidence ... missed the party line to which he can adhere when speaking for China.' On the credit side, his lack of assertiveness was also assumed to be helpful so long as the intention was to keep the issue out of the Council. The Secretary-General's initiative was keeping the Council at bay, but this benefit would be lost if yet another major incident at sea removed all restraints on Council members or else the initiative was allowed to lapse. Perez de Cuellar had asked for comments by 5 May and some sort of response was needed. Having first been inclined not to hurry, Parsons now considered that a relatively prompt reply was needed, so that Britain could be seen to be observing the diplomatic proprieties and not forgoing opportunities for a settlement.

The Peruvian complication

The Peruvian initiative was a complicating factor in all of this, as Haig wanted to keep the UN out of the act. Parsons hoped that he could be persuaded to relent, at least sufficiently to forestall more damaging initiatives by others in the UN. The pressure was building up. Parsons had hoped that an interim message to the effect that Pym was 'considering all the ideas … and hopes to get comments back to him shortly' would hold the line, but when he told the Secretary-General to expect such a letter, mention was made of 'encouraging noises' from Roca, the Argentine Ambassador. Meanwhile, despite attempts to convince Dorr that public proceedings of the Council would be so acrimonious that they would effectively kill the Secretary-General's initiative, Ireland was now proposing a Security Council session. The Soviet delegate Troyanovsky, who also wanted a meeting, accepted that it should not undermine the Secretary-General's efforts. Ling Qing felt obliged to respond to the extent of convening an informal meeting for the evening of 5 May.

Parsons was content with this. Listening to reports on the Secretary-General's initiative and discussing whether anything useful could be done was preferable to a formal and public meeting. He hoped to keep informal consultations going for a few days, provided that there were no more major military engagements. However, the prospects for the Peruvian initiative were unclear and so it was difficult to spin things out by offering proposals of substance. Should the Peruvian initiative collapse a full UN initiative was inevitable, and a confidential venture by Perez de Cuellar was preferable to a formal council meeting at which Britain might find itself vetoing an apparently mild resolution calling for a cessation of hostilities. Given the alternatives, it was becoming in Britain's interest to boost the status of the Secretary-General's efforts.

In London, the perspective was slightly different. The Government had decided that the Peruvian initiative was worth pursuing, not least because of the direct American involvement, and so Pym wanted to avoid responding to Perez de Cuellar in such a way as to encourage Argentina to look to the UN rather than to Haig. Parsons was instructed to make this clear to the Secretary-General:

> I should also wish you to make it clear that I am not in any way turning down his own ideas. I do not wish to foreclose any options and there could well be a place for action by the Secretary-General at a later stage. Meanwhile we shall need his help in making it clear that diplomatic activity is continuing.

This risked derailing Britain's UN strategy, especially as Costa Mendez was now saying that he was going to New York having accepted the Secretary-General's intervention. The close association with Haig might be justified if his latest venture had a future, but otherwise Britain might appear to be colluding with an American effort that seemed to be largely about excluding the UN from any role. Haig had spoken to Perez de Cuellar in rather dismissive terms. From Washington, Henderson appeared to share the wariness about the UN:

> On the face of it this looks as though the Argentinians see this UN manoeuvre as a good way of holding off increased military pressure by us, avoiding any action by them and winning world opinion to the idea that they, the Argentinians, are keen on negotiation. If they seriously want an early cease-fire and are ready to withdraw they will accept the US/Peruvian proposals.

On this basis it was wise to assume that Argentina wanted to shift to the UN solely to get a cease-fire without a specific commitment to withdraw.

The potential problems that might result if Argentina had the UN field to itself were illustrated on the evening of 5 May when the informal consultations took place. Parsons reported in a plaintive fashion:

> we were almost entirely isolated, no-one expressed support or understanding for the military action we are taking. Apart from me, only Guyana mentioned withdrawal. I was alone in resisting pressure to include in the statement a call for 'cessation of hostilities' or 'restraint'. I received no support from Mrs Kirkpatrick and De Nanteuil (France) was actively unhelpful.

The Secretary-General reported that Costa Mendez had accepted his proposal to bring about a settlement. Dorr observed that none of the three parts of 502 had been implemented. He thought that the 'Council should still consider how best to get an immediate end to the fighting without giving either side an advantage.' It was generally agreed – except by Russia – that a harsh debate in formal session would not help. Uganda and Spain, supported by Panama, the Soviet Union and Poland, urged that there should be a statement calling for hostilities to be 'frozen' until the parties had replied to the Secretary-General. Others, including France (several times) and 'the do-gooders', were less ambitious and proposed that the statement should appeal for 'restraint.' Parsons said repeatedly and very firmly that:

> there was no question of my accepting any such reference, which would simply mean that the Argentines were allowed to consolidate their position on the islands while we were prevented from exercising our right of self-defence. No-one supported me but the Council reluctantly accepted my position in order to obtain a statement tonight.

Parsons was not able to insert a reference to SCR 502. Panama was opposed and Russia would accept the reference only in return for a call for 'restraint'.

This disturbing experience led Parsons to warn 'how completely support for our position has been eroded since SCR 502 was adopted.' He believed Britain 'lucky to get away with tonight's harmless mouse without our isolation having the effect of turning the whole Council against us.' The position had not been helped by revelations about the Peruvian initiative. Perez de Cuellar appears to have known little of them, having been kept in the dark even by Peru, and had been 'rather upset' by Pym's emphasis on them in the House of Commons, feeling that 'he was being used.' Furthermore news had filtered back to New York of a briefing given by Julian Bullard of the FCO to the EC countries on the Peruvian proposals. Parsons observed that while the Secretary-General was meticulous about not leaking, his 'Community partners here include some of the worst gossips in New York and they are bound to receive reports of the briefing given by Bullard – if this traced to us will be upset'. Because of this Parsons had withheld the letter that had been sent by Pym as his interim reply to Perez de Cuellar because of its stress on the Peruvian ideas, and the dismissive approach taken to the Secretary-General's role, which could lead to an unfavourable contrast with the ostensibly positive response from Argentina.

Writing late from New York on 5 May, Parsons urged London to take note of the mood at the UN and find a more positive response to Perez de Cuellar, lest Britain was 'dangerously isolated here very quickly.' Rather than get Pym to follow Costa Mendez to New York, which would support the view that everything was switching to the UN, he wanted a substantive reply the next day that would affirm Britain's position but not cause embarrassment if published. It should give time for Peruvian ideas to succeed or fail, look positive and keep the ball in play 'but would contain conundrums which would give the Secretariat plenty to work on.'

His message had the desired effect. London accepted that activity might be moving inexorably to the UN even while still hoping for something from the Peruvian initiative. Hence, as requested, Pym sent a new version of his letter to Parsons. The draft explained that Britain was still considering the Secretary-General's ideas carefully and accepted the general approach they embodied. The British reply would explain its position and offer comments on elements needed for settlement. These would be shown to be fully compatible with the UN's views. As Argentina had started the present crisis, it was imperative that Resolution 502 be implemented, but to prevent further bloodshed Britain was willing to accept and immediately implement an interim agreement to prepare the way for a definitive settlement. The letter spelled out the position that Britain had reached through the discussions on the Peruvian initiative, concerning the relationship of a cease-fire, to Argentine withdrawal, to agreement on an interim administration and eventual negotiations.

As the UN mission was considering this draft, Henderson rang through with news of the death of the Peruvian proposals. This raised a new dilemma.

One of the positive aspects of the latest Haig exercise was the opportunity it provided to demonstrate once again that Britain was serious about negotiations in contrast to the intransigent Argentina. This required publicising just how far Britain had been prepared to go. It was now planned to publish Britain's final position to underline that point, but this was going to leave Perez de Cuellar unimpressed if he then received a letter from Pym that simply restated the same position.

Parsons therefore urged that any public statement avoided great detail. Meanwhile, out of the need to get some reply to the Secretary-General off at once, he did not amend the draft he had received other than to add a final sentence to deal with the sort of pressures he had recently experienced from his Security Council colleagues:

> You will understand that, until it is implemented, Britain will not accept a call for an unconditional cessation of hostilities which could have the effect of inhibiting its right of self defence as recognised by Article 51 of the charter.

The letter was a success. After meeting with Parsons for one hour from 1230, New York time, Perez de Cuellar immediately issued a statement, describing the British response as substantive rather than procedural. Ahmad's attitude in the meeting had, however, been 'unremittingly critical and hostile,' as he demanded to know whether the new British proposals were, in effect, the Haig/Belaunde proposals already put to the Argentines and rejected by them. Ahmad, he described as 'a sinister and malevolent influence. I gave him very short shrift today and am considering urgently the implications of his deplorable and totally partial performance.' Perez de Cuellar had accepted that even if this was the case it did not matter if they got the UN process going. Perez de Cuellar also squashed complaints from Ahmad that Britain had offered a 'phased' response instead of 'simultaneity,' had not given the Secretary-General a simple 'yes' or 'no,' and that Pym had not matched Costa Mendez in offering to come to New York.

At the very least the Pym letter had done the trick in terms of persuading Perez de Cuellar that there was now no need for a formal meeting of the Council. The informal consultations could go ahead as planned, as Roca, whom Perez de Cuellar had met an hour before Parsons, had conveyed the Argentine view that the UN was the only acceptable 'channel.' Parsons had already warned Jordan, Spain and Panama that if they proposed a further Presidential statement including the word 'restraint' they would get another all-night sitting, while the Secretary-General squared Dorr before the meeting. The President summed up supporting the Secretary-General. Council would continue to follow developments and when necessary either consult informally or hold a formal meeting, perhaps in order to give the Secretary-General a necessary mandate:

Dorr's incorrigible love of his own voice nearly undid this satisfactory result. He raised a quibble about whether the President's summing up conveyed enough encouragement to the Secretary-General to continue his efforts: Nuseibeh (Jordan) thought that Dorr was proposing a further Presidential statement and then started to offer language of his own.

On the brink of another marathon drafting session Parsons intervened to say he was sure that all had every confidence in the President and Secretary-General. The meeting adjourned. Parsons was now confident that he could get through the weekend.

Restlessness in London was still complicating his strategy. A Planning Staff paper, also distributed on 6 May, reflected concern that Pym's letter would not be enough to turn the diplomatic tide which had been running increasingly against Britain. Thoughts were turning back to the idea of a new UK initiative. The Prime Minister had expressed interest in the concept of a trusteeship, although this had evident disadvantages: it would be harder to preserve the position on sovereignty, take longer to negotiate, require complicated machinery, and could be got at by the General Assembly. Instead the plan followed what was now a rather familiar model: cease-fire linked to mutual withdrawal; immediate negotiations at the UN about interim administration (rather than trusteeship); negotiations on the future of the Falklands or a reference to the ICJ, resulting in a negotiated agreement on a binding ICJ ruling; negotiations without prejudice to outcome. They were looking for some way to get the ICJ to consider self-determination as well as legal title, so that Argentina would probably reject referral and was more likely to lose the case if it did not. Parsons sought to stamp on this idea. It was something for after the Secretary-General had failed, but it 'would be entirely wrong to launch an initiative of this kind while he is still in business.' This would be seen by him, and by the UN as a whole, 'as a blatant wrecking tactic which could only mean that we had never intended to take his efforts seriously and had now been forced to sabotage them because they were gaining momentum.' Here Parsons received support from Ambassador Fretwell in Paris who pointed out that France would see any UK initiative as an attempt to undermine the Secretary-General.

The proposed statement to the House of Commons on the Peruvian initiative posed a more serious problem. A number of paragraphs corresponded verbatim with Pym's message of 6 May. 'I cannot urge too strongly that it be changed,' he telegraphed London. The Secretary-General's staff – and especially Ahmad – would spot this and Perez de Cuellar would feel that he has been put in an impossible position, accused of 'being led by the nose by the British for their own purposes.' The conclusion would be drawn within the Security Council that Britain was not acting in good faith but just trying to gain time. This theme was already being played out in the media. 'I am bound to say,' Parsons warned, that if Pym spoke in terms of the draft statement then

> he will not only kill Perez de Cuellar's initiative, but lay us open to charges of having acted with cynical disregard for the UN. That will more than destroy such diplomatic advantage as we have gained hitherto, particularly today.

He suggested a brief outline. In the event Pym's statement to the Commons on 7 May was much fuller but he met Parsons' main objections. Pym stressed the need to link a cease-fire to the unambiguous commencement of a supervised Argentine withdrawal. Without mentioning any names he accepted that a 'small group of countries acceptable to both sides' could have a role supervising withdrawal, undertaking an interim administration 'in consultation with the islanders' elected representatives, and 'perhaps ... in negotiations for a definitive agreement on the status of the islands, without prejudice to our principles or the wishes of the islanders'.[1] Still after some propaganda advantage, London now wanted to give publicity to Pym's message to the Secretary-General. This Parsons also opposed, especially given Perez de Cuellar's care in avoiding leaks – he was not even going to release it to members of the Security Council.

It was clear that the Secretary-General was now anxious to get his own initiative moving and took his responsibilities seriously. When Mrs Kirkpatrick telephoned him, at Haig's request (she said), to tell him that other efforts (unspecified) were under way and that it would be a pity if the Secretary-General were to cut across them, Perez de Cuellar stated that he had stayed out of the game for three weeks to give Haig his chance, that he had come in now only very reluctantly, but that, once in, he was going to persevere and not allow anyone to cut across him. He was ready to abandon his effort unless he could get confirmation that the Argentines were prepared to leave the sovereignty question open, and, while worried by risk of another major military engagement, for the moment he accepted British good faith.

On the morning of 7 May Parsons met with Perez de Cuellar. He asked to see him alone without Ahmad. He explained to him that the previous agreement collapsed because Argentina had insisted that the transitional arrangements and the diplomatic negotiations had to be pre-judged at the outset by Britain accepting Argentine sovereignty. He also reported Haig's problem in dealing with reasonable civilians and an intransigent military in Argentina. While Ros, the Argentine Deputy Foreign Minister who had come to New York for the negotiation, might be reasonable 'we would not be impressed by anything which did not have Galtieri's signature on it.' This set a clear priority from the outset: to achieve a 'cast-iron agreement (i.e. signed by Galtieri in writing) on the transitional arrangements and the framework for the diplomatic negotiations' clearly without prejudice to the positions of both sides. Once that was agreed it would be possible to fill out the details on the wishes of islanders, contact group, UN umbrella, duration and so on. Parsons insisted that there was little point in addressing questions of withdrawal and cease-fire if they were then going to be scuppered by the Argentine pre-condition. He took heart from Perez de Cuellar's desire to avoid being used simply to get a cease-fire without any commitment to withdraw. Parsons gave 'him my word of honour that we were taking his initiative seriously' and negotiating in good faith. He then complained about Ahmad's interventions, which he had found to be unhelpful, distracting and tiresome. Perez de Cuellar said that he had already warned Ahmad. Apparently Kurt Waldheim, the previous Secretary-General, had trained him to give an appearance of toughness at meetings so that Waldheim, could display flexibility! Parsons thought that this was infantile. 'Ahmad was thoroughly chastised. ... I concluded by saying that Ahmad was lucky that I was an even tempered man.'

25

THE UN MEDIATION

The British Government was embarking on yet another negotiating effort with reluctance. A peaceful settlement was preferred to a violent one but not on any terms. Both the Haig mediation and the Peruvian initiative had ended up as negotiations between London and Washington with precious little Latin American input. The Government had been subjected to constant calls for compromise and restraint with no evidence of any Argentine interest in either. Having cast itself as the victim in the affair, the Government had surprised itself by how conciliatory it had been prepared to be to the sensitivities of the aggressor. Still Buenos Aires wanted more and it appeared that it would only be satisfied when Britain agreed that sovereignty over the Falklands was to be transferred. As this could not be agreed another round of negotiations appeared pointless. At the same time military action carried high political costs, and the Government had been chastened by the exclamations of international anguish provoked by the *Belgrano*. The loss of *Sheffield* had been chastening in a different way. This highlighted the military risks now being faced, and the War Cabinet understood that the Chiefs were by no means sure about achieving a successful landing let alone the repossession of the Islands.

For the moment the domestic political context pointed to a tough line but this could change quickly. A *Sunday Times* poll of 2 May, conducted before the recent burst of fighting, while generally supportive of the Government's stance, had shown the British people unprepared to see the lives of any servicemen (60 per cent) or civilians (66 per cent) lost, and clear that policy had to be decided not just on the wishes of the islanders (24%) but on the interests of Britain as a whole (72%). Against this background the presentational aspects of being seen to be trying to find a diplomatic way out were pressing, even if the efforts were bound to be futile, but there also had to be some hope that they would not be futile, that a way out of the impasse could be found.

These tensions were evident in a call made to Parsons by the Prime Minister on 8 May, as the negotiations were about to begin. It reveals Thatcher at one of the periods of greatest stress during the whole campaign.

Thatcher was not alarmed at Perez de Cuellar's role, as she had got to know and admire him during the Zimbabwe negotiations, and spoke of his 'tremendous integrity'. Nor did she suggest at all that she either wanted or assumed failure. If 'the worst comes to the worst and we have to go in and do something with force,' she remarked, 'then it's their young men against our young men and that's terrible.' She also acknowledged, presumably with reference to the *Belgrano*, that 'as events happened we did not make the best impression last weekend.' 'I feel deeply about many things,' the Prime Minister reported, 'first that our people there were living in self-determination and freedom before this started and one can't hand them over to anything less. But secondly that it is going to be the most awful waste of young life if we really have to go and take those islands.' She promised to do everything possible to see 'if we can stop a final battle.'

With the two previous negotiating exercises she had been able to stay in close touch with the talks but she was concerned that in this case she would be remote from the action. In this connection she wondered whether the Secretary-General might visit London, and Parsons thought he might, especially if he felt obliged at some point to visit Galtieri. The difficulties of negotiations conducted at such long range combined with the Prime Minister's lack of dedicated staff were evident after Parsons' first meeting with Perez de Cuellar. He sought a quick response from ministers but at that time Pym was outside Brussels while the Prime Minister was at Chequers. Thatcher could only offer conditional responses. On the withdrawal process she needed military advice; on the venue for negotiations and their terminal date she awaited FCO advice.

The negotiations began on the afternoon of 8 May. Perez de Cuellar, accompanied by Ahmad and Alvara de Soto (a Peruvian career diplomat who had joined the secretariat as Perez de Cuellar's special assistant) met first with Parsons, then with Ros, before meeting again with Parsons in the evening. Critical to the Secretary-General's undertaking was the concept that proposals were 'provisional measures without prejudice to the rights, claims or positions of the parties.' To this Britain readily agreed but a firm commitment was needed from Argentina. Argentina accepted the principle of simultaneity in toto. Britain wanted a more exact definition. Withdrawal, for example, would take time and there would have to be some sort of phasing. Until its completion, Britain would prefer not to suspend either the Exclusion Zone or the lifting of sanctions. There was no problem with the Argentine proposal that the procedures should start 24 hours after signature, and Parsons thought that his instructions would suggest 14 days to completion of withdrawal. On the terminal date for substantive negotiations, Argentina suggested 31 December 1982 (following Haig): Britain's position was 'perhaps one year'. Argentina wanted the final negotiations conducted by the Secretary-General or his representative in New York. Britain had suggested a contact group. Parsons said that his personal view was that New

York should be avoided because of the pressures that would be generated. On transitional arrangements, Perez de Cuellar assumed an interim administration that should be neither British nor Argentine; for Parsons that depended on how it was defined. Argentina favoured 'an exclusive UN role,' but what did this mean in relation to the different layers of administration: Governor, executive council and legislative council? More precision was needed on this matter. Was it intended that nominees should replace elected members and the Governor, as appeared to be favoured by Ahmad?

At 2130 local time Parsons met again with the UN team. He was told that Ros had proposed a short interim period with administrative arrangements that need neither affect individual rights nor prejudge the ultimate regime, but this meant that political structures would be kept in abeyance through this period. To be truly transitional, the arrangements would involve a clear-cut UN administration, with a presence from both interested parties. Parsons pointed out that not only would Britain not accept denying the islanders their own representatives, but also that Argentina had been more flexible in past negotiations. Perez de Cuellar could not know this as he lacked the details on past negotiations: Parsons promised to see what could be disclosed. More intriguing was the report that Ros had claimed that Argentina was not prejudging the question of sovereignty, though it was seeking appropriate terms of reference for a diplomatic solution. This would probably mean the insertion of language about General Assembly resolutions that tended to favour its case on sovereignty.

Parsons' analysis was that the Argentines were aware of the danger of the negotiations failing because of the sovereignty issue. That would be 'diplomatic game, set and match to us.' They were therefore looking for ways to oblige Britain to break off negotiations, which is why they were pushing on the interim administration. A total UN authority would obviously be very popular at the UN, so Britain would appear unreasonable if it refused this form of administration. If the Argentines were even more cunning, they would negotiate an agreement, get the cease-fire and an interim period under UN administration to terminate on a fixed date. Without automatic extension in the absence of agreement Britain would be accused of procrastination if it sought to gain one, and a Soviet veto might be used to prevent this. At the terminal date the UN, with no mandate to remain, would be obliged to withdraw, allowing Argentina to walk in again. They might engineer a General Assembly vote saying that the Islands should be decolonised and that sovereignty should pass to Argentina.

What then should Britain do? The first requirement was to continue to show a positive, sincere and urgent attitude towards the negotiations. Perez de Cuellar was 'behaving extremely well, and he is suspicious of the Argentines as I am. Our tête-à-tête sessions are invaluable.' This meant returning concrete replies to the questions, including a draft schedule for 'simultaneous' withdrawal, cease-fire, lifting of exclusion zones and economic measures. Ros's readiness to accept that the provisional measures were without prejudice to the rights, claims and positions of the parties could be pocketed. The focal point was going to be the interim administration. If Britain stuck by the idea of a contact group then Argentina could score heavily by making it a breaking point. For this reason Parsons proposed a shift in the British position to a more sympathetic consideration of the possibility of UN administration in the interim period to be carried out 'in consultation with the elected representatives of the population of the islands.' It would be helpful to go into the detail about such matters as whether the administrator would have a formal legal relationship with the representatives or just informal consultations. The next stage, following a British concession, would be to press for better language on the terms of reference for negotiations, if possible eliminating prejudicial references to General Assembly resolutions. This would put the ball right back into the Argentine court.

London took the advice. On 9 May Parsons was provided with a revised position. This not only covered mechanisms for a cease-fire and the withdrawal of forces (which must be equal and parallel, and not put Britain at a disadvantage), but also the delicate issues connected with the interim arrangements. A UN interim administrator could be accepted as the Governor, administering the Falkland Islands, though the Executive and Legislative Councils would still need to discharge their traditional functions. As it was unrealistic to set absolute terminal dates for the negotiations, when everyone knew that the parties, with the best will in the world, might not be able to conclude them, the Secretary-General's own expression of a 'target date' that had appeared in his proposals of 3 May would be supported. On that basis Britain could accept 31 December 1982. The agreement need not say directly that the negotiations might go on beyond the target date but it would have to insist that the interim arrangements would continue until an agreement on the future of the Islands was implemented. A hope was expressed that the negotiations would take place under the auspices of the Secretary-General and, as far as possible, in his presence. The preference was to get away from New York – if possible to Ottawa or Geneva.

The language on negotiations should be kept simple. If Argentina repeated its familiar ploy of inserting suitable sections from General Assembly resolutions, Britain would insist on references to self-determination or at least the purposes of the Charter, and this would lead to a complex and contradictory paragraph and endless wrangles about what it actually meant. Again the Government was happy with the original UN language of 3 May ('a diplomatic resolution to their differences'). As far as there being no prejudgement on sovereignty it was vital to get Ros on record, clarifying that any agreement reached in New York had to be backed by the Junta. Parsons was also warned that Britain intended to exclude the Dependencies, and it was searching for a security guarantee, although that need not necessarily be part of an agreement. Lastly, to help Perez de Cuellar, the Ambassador was permitted to hand over previous draft agreements. As the original Haig proposals contained many elements that Britain would not wish now to revive, it was best to stick with the draft that emerged out of the Peruvian effort.

Parsons took all this with him to his next meeting, on the afternoon of Sunday, 9 May. Some minor issues started to be sorted out. Was there any reason to delay the start of talks other than the need to assemble and prepare negotiating teams? Were there not verification issues about monitoring the withdrawal of naval forces? Should there be a post-deadline vacuum, how might a continuing role for an interim arrangement be described? All this, Parsons indicated, seemed pointless if Argentina continued to insist that the talks be prejudged. He drew attention to a Costa Mendez interview of that day in the US. His line appeared to be that while Argentina was not insisting that Britain should actually cede sovereignty before negotiations started, only that this is how they must conclude. Then their purpose became essentially how to deal with the interests of the islanders under Argentine sovereignty. If correct this was a major change in the Argentine position as reported to Perez de Cuellar. The Secretary-General agreed to ask Ros for clarification.

There were two discordant notes. The first was that Britain was only talking about the Falklands and not the Dependencies. These were quite a separate matter, with different titles and no settled population. The UN team had assumed that the Dependencies would be covered by the interim agreement. This had been the case in earlier negotiations. In particular, Ahmad referred several times to a joint communiqué issued in London and Buenos Aires on 27 April 1977 and conveyed to the Secretary-General in a letter dated 9 June 1977 for transmission to the special committee on decolonisation. It dealt with negotiations about 'future political relations, including sovereignty, with regard to the Falkland Islands, South Georgia and the South Sandwich Islands.' Similar letters and communiqués were circulated thereafter. The Prime Minister, who was most active in seeking their exclusion from further negotiations, had been advised by the FCO that while General Assembly resolutions referred only to the Falkland Islands without explicitly mentioning the Dependencies, there could be no confidence that a majority of Member States would support this. 'This note confirms my worst fears' annotated the Prime Minister. Rather than try and resolve this now, Parsons took the line that the Argentine invasion of the Islands 'created a new situation and that the precedent of earlier negotiations no longer relevant.'

The second discordant note had been struck by the *Narwhal* episode, which 'fluttered the dovecotes here.'[1] Argentina was putting it about that there had been an informal agreement that there would be no hostilities while the Secretary-General pursued his initiative. Parsons reminded both

Perez de Cuellar and Ling Qing, President of the Security Council, that Britain had made it absolutely clear that there was no question of suspending military operations, and he would expect their support if he was obliged to go public. At the same time he noted to London that the 'fortuitous lull over the past few days has been a great help here in enabling Perez de Cuellar to get on with his efforts.'

Later that day Parsons met again with Perez de Cuellar to be updated on the Argentine position. Unsurprisingly, Ros objected strongly to the exclusion of the Dependencies and expected a British military withdrawal from South Georgia. Second, he offered a complicated formula for withdrawal for the Task Force so that it was put outside three circles of 150nm radius from the co-ordinates that had originally been mentioned in the draft Haig proposals of 12 April – from the centres of Falklands, South Georgia and the South Sandwich Islands. Third, he sought provision for the withdrawal to be extended to 14 days if bad weather or other factors caused delay, and, to avoid the impression that the Argentine withdrawal was under duress, Argentina expected that the EZ and sanctions would be lifted as soon as the clock started ticking on withdrawal.

On what to do if the negotiations were incomplete by the target date, Ros had been unable to give a clear answer but had asked instead how long an extension Britain envisaged. Parsons' response was that it would be ridiculous for the agreement to include two target dates, one after the other. The British view was that it should be left to the Secretary-General to report, say in mid-December, on how much more time was needed if an agreement was not in sight. Argentina wanted the negotiations in New York, especially if the Secretary-General was to participate personally. Perez de Cuellar, conscious of a convention that the Secretary-General did not leave New York during the General Assembly, wondered whether somewhere in New York State might be sufficient. On the interim administration, Argentina continued to object strongly to any role for islanders even of an advisory character, as this would pre-judge the outcome of the negotiations. Parsons said that this was not acceptable. The Foreign Secretary had talked firmly about 'restoration of the traditional administration.' Any substantial change in the constitution of the Falkland Islands would require legislation and that would have serious parliamentary implications. Parsons also proposed a 'no-break' clause, asserting that 'this interim agreement shall enter into force until a definitive settlement of their differences has been reached and implemented by the parties.'

Argentina proposed that: 'the negotiations would have to solve the disputes between the parties, taking into account relevant General Assembly resolutions.' Parsons said that this would not do, especially in the light of Costa Mendez's remarks and similar statements that had caused the collapse of previous negotiations. Britain would have to insist on certain formulations to leave the integrity of the process beyond doubt. Having agreed that the Argentine position was unsatisfactory, Perez de Cuellar later asked Parsons to suggest some language. He could present this as his own to smoke out the Argentine position. Parsons (without instructions) offered the following:

1. As a first article in the agreement:

    i.   No provision in this interim agreement shall in any way preju-
         dice the rights, claims and positions of either party in the
         ultimate peaceful settlement of their differences over the
         Falkland Islands (Islas Malvinas)
    ii. No acts or activities taking place whilst this interim agreement
         is in force shall constitute a basis for asserting, supporting or
         denying a claim to territorial sovereignty over the Falkland
         Islands (Islas Malvinas) or create any rights of sovereignty over
         them.

2. As an article providing for the diplomatic negotiations:

    The parties undertake to enter into negotiations under the
    auspices of the Secretary General of the United Nations for a
    peaceful settlement of their differences and [some formula
    about the target date]. These negotiations shall be conducted
    without prejudice to the rights, claims and positions of either
    party and without prejudging the outcome.[2]

After agreeing to try this language on the Argentines, Perez de Cuellar raised the question of a quid pro quo. If this were accepted would Britain drop its insistence on islanders being in the interim administration? Parsons said not at all. It would be odd to agree not to prejudge the outcome and then deny any role for the islanders! The non-prejudice point was absolutely essential and needed to be cleared up before he could proceed with anything else.

Parsons had deliberately put the prejudgement issue to the fore to keep the ball in Argentina's court. He did not want to be caught on more contentious issues where Britain could soon find itself isolated, such as demands for an exclusive UN administration of the Islands. His basic strategy was still to avoid Britain being blamed for the breakdown by demonstrating a serious and constructive approach wherever possible. If Argentina was unable to come up with firm language on prejudgement then the mediation would fail, and it would not be Britain's fault. His tactics carried a risk. Supposing Argentina did accept a reasonable line on prejudgement. Then the pressure would certainly turn on Britain to accept UN administration, with the local bodies in abeyance, and withdrawal of British military forces from South Georgia in parallel with the Argentine withdrawal from the Falklands. If Britain dug in its heels on both issues, and so caused the negotiations to fail, 'we would be in an extremely isolated position in UN.' For the moment the only new concession he could see was to accept New York State as the venue for long-term negotiations. Otherwise, on the basis of a conversation with Henderson in Washington, there was some possibility that the US might be prepared to make a genuine effort to drive the Argentines off insisting on the South Georgia point, but he doubted whether they would concede both.

London was content to endorse Parsons' tactics. It fitted well with what was known from a variety of sources about the intransigent Argentine position. Keep up the pressure on the prejudgement issue, he was told, and insist that this must be reflected not only in the text but also in explicit Argentine statements. As for the Dependencies the line was that Britain's purpose in the present negotiations was to deal with the new situation created by the continued unlawful occupation of the Falkland Islands. The position now was as it was before the unlawful occupation. It was also vital to fight any idea that involving the islanders was inconsistent with not prejudging:

> You should also make what play you can with the thoughts that to exclude a people from the administration of their own affairs is hardly consistent with the spirit of the UN; and that we have developed the Councils in accordance with UN Charter obligations (at 73 (b)) and would be contrary to spirit of charter to dismantle them.

Fourteen days was long enough for withdrawal, but Britain could not accept the 'treacherously elastic' phrase 'bad weather or other factors.' With regard to its verification, declarations by each side of ships and forces in the zone, and daily declarations of what had been withdrawn, would help, but given Argentina's invasion 'it is a lot to ask that she should verify her own withdrawal.' The possibility of the use of surveillance aircraft from a neutral, such as Sweden, was raised. There was no problem with the Argentine suggestion of a 150nm radius, and there was discretion to go to 200nm if the issue was raised again. The lifting of zones from the start 'was under positive consideration in London, as was an agreement that Britain and other EC members could agree to lift economic measures'.

On the target date Parsons' instructions were to say that:

1. negotiations will start immediately to produce an agreement by target date of 31 December 1982;
2. the interim arrangements will remain in force until implementation of a definitive agreement about the future of the Islands;
3. The Secretary-General should report just before the target date about next steps.

The idea for starting long-term negotiations notionally from the start would be difficult and Parsons should maintain a reserve on it. New York State could be accepted but not New York City; Parsons was right to insist on all three signatures of Junta members, but a fall-back position would be a public declaration.

Argentina's concession

When Parsons met with Perez de Cuellar on the evening of 10 May he was handed an Argentine paper.[3] Although Ros had discussed it with Buenos Aires it had been drafted in New York and was therefore 'negotiable.' Ros had told the Secretary-General that he saw the paper as a 'package' so that all points could be discussed at the same time, but had been told at once that it would be unacceptable to Britain. This Parsons confirmed, declaring himself 'puzzled and disappointed' with a document that seemed out of phase with the talks the two of them had been having.

Nonetheless, Perez de Cuellar claimed that there had been one breakthrough. Argentina's paragraph 2 referred to: 'The agreement to which the parties commit themselves shall be without prejudice to the rights, claims or positions of the parties.' This, the Secretary-General argued, should meet Britain's concern on prejudging as it covered the whole exercise including the negotiating process. Ros, he explained, had not liked the British language because it implied that Argentina might cheat. The problem was different to this, Parsons replied. Argentina had said so often that sovereignty was not negotiable that Britain had to have absolutely clear evidence in the agreement that this was no longer their position. Was this to be a genuine interim administration or just a delayed transfer of sovereignty to Argentina? They had never suggested that they were claiming sovereignty, but rather 'they have it and that it has always been theirs.' The Article 40 language in the Secretary-General's aide memoire and in point 2 of the Argentine paper was not therefore enough protection. Unequivocal language, to the effect that the outcome of these negotiations would not be prejudged, was needed. De Soto produced language on the lines of 'all aspects of this interim agreement shall be implemented without prejudice to the rights, claims and positions of the parties,' but Parsons rejected this. Perez de Cuellar said he would go back to Ros.

There was some desultory discussion of the two most difficult issues for Britain, the Dependencies and the interim administration. Argentina seemed to be using language on withdrawal of forces from the Haig negotiation. As Parsons pointed out, Britain had not actually agreed this and it had been drafted at a time when the Task Force was still thousands of miles from the Falklands. The situation had now changed. The idea of using neutral aircraft for surveillance had been positively received, while Ros had spoken specifically about February 1983, and was not insisting on an absolute deadline.

None of this led Parsons to think that the essential tactics were wrong. Argentina was still not interested in reaching a negotiated settlement on terms which would be acceptable to Britain 'and that it is rapidly becoming a question of who wrong-foots whom when the negotiations break down.' On this basis his next ploy would be to confirm to Perez de Cuellar that he would not negotiate details of an interim arrangement until he was sure that this was not simply about a briefly delayed transfer of sovereignty and possession to Argentina. Once a specific formulation from Ros on non-prejudgement had been extracted, it would be referred to Britain for comments. Only then could Britain decide if it was worth continuing with the exercise.

The next morning, 11 May, Parsons' tactics were again endorsed by London. On a detail it was noted that only aligned countries, and Chile, had appropriate surveillance aircraft so it was best to stick to the United States for this role, and the Secretary-General should be urged to explore this possibility. On the interim administration, possible language might be that the UN administration be described as functioning 'in consultation with the executive and legislative councils in the islands.' The Legal Adviser believed that point 2 in the Argentine text could reasonably mean that the outcome was not prejudged, thereby creating the risk that it would not appear unreasonable if there was a breakdown, but clarity was essential. It was therefore proposed that this be expanded to:

> The agreement to which the parties commit themselves, including the negotiations to be undertaken pursuant to Paragraph 7 thereof, shall be without prejudice.

This would need to be accompanied by a statement to the Secretary-General that Argentina understood that the outcome of the negotiations was not being prejudged. On the interim administration Britain could agree in due course to both parties having observers and flying national flags but there would need to be a strict limit on Argentine personnel. On the target date, it would be preferable for the phrase 'to complete these negotiations by 31 December 1982' to be governed by 'with a view to completing' rather than 'the parties commit themselves.'

Having received his instructions, Parsons spoke with Perez de Cuellar. He was continuing with his strategy and it seemed to be working. The Secretary-General reported that he had warned Ros that detailed negotiation was contingent upon answering the question of non-prejudgement, and that with every day that passed Argentina's chances of getting a good agreement were diminished. It was no good acting as a gambler who refused to join the game unless his opponent conceded in advance, a characterisation Parsons considered to be so 'excellent' that he felt it necessary to warn London not to 'use it in public for Perez de Cuellar's sake.' With so little progress this meeting was brief, largely to report a difficulty with the concept of a target date. Argentina wanted to avoid an indefinite continuation of the interim administration while Britain would not allow renewal to depend on a new Security Council resolution.

On surveillance aircraft, of the capable countries only Canada might be acceptable to Argentina, while with regard to the freedom of transit and associated issues, Ros had drawn attention to the 1971 Communications agreement. Parsons left the meeting feeling that his tactics were working as planned.

Then came a bombshell. He was called back to see Perez de Cuellar to get an unexpected communication. The Secretary-General had what he thought to be good news. The Argentines had accepted that 31 December should be a target date and that the agreement should state that the outcome of the negotiations would not be prejudged. This was the text:

> The parties undertake to enter into negotiations in good faith under the auspices of the Secretary-General of the United Nations for the peaceful settlement of their dispute and to seek, with a sense of urgency, the completion of these negotiations by 31 December 1982, taking into account the Charter of the United Nations and the relevant resolutions of the General Assembly. These negotiations shall be initiated without prejudice to the rights, claims or positions of the parties and without prejudgement of the outcome.

This was a variation of Parsons' language, which Perez de Cuellar had represented as his own to Ros. Ros had reported that 'after consultations with everybody' Costa Mendez had instructed him to accept it. In his memoir Perez de Cuellar records Ros describing this as 'an extremely difficult decision which had not easily been reached' and his own belief that 'a crucial breakthrough had been achieved.'[4] Parsons could only say that this was an extremely encouraging development as it was now possible to look at other elements, although he reserved Britain's position on reference to General Assembly resolutions and still questioned as to whether Ros had the authority to state what he had stated. What would happen on 31 December? The media and Parliament would press the British Government.

There were other, more limited, concessions. On the interim administration the Argentines could accept that individual members of the Legislative Council could be used by the administration for advisory purposes, so long as the administration was also able to call on an equal number of members of the Argentine population for the same purposes. They wanted as few restrictions as possible on communications, transit of persons and acquisitions of property in the interim administration. More specifically, if not in this arrangement, they wanted obstacles to the acquisition of shares in the Falkland Islands Company to be lifted. Finally on zones of withdrawal, Argentina expressed the hope that agreement could be worked out on withdrawal distances for the Task Force, which could dispel any impression that Argentina was withdrawing under pressure because of proximity.

Parsons discussed a proposal from Ahmad to abandon the concept of circles when planning withdrawal, but instead identifying a certain line of latitude, within which British ships would move, and a certain line of longitude, within which Argentine forces would withdraw. Ahmad 'flashed a chart (including dependencies)' around which a rectangle was drawn. Parsons said that he thought this merited examination and he would get reactions from London. Perez de Cuellar was now keen to consolidate the progress but Parsons urged him not to do more until he heard from his Government.

One explanation for the Argentine concession was that it reflected concern that another attempt at a British landing was imminent and this represented an attempt to create the most difficult context for the British. It was still assumed that a serious landing had been attempted – rather than an elaborate ploy – on 1 May and that this had been repulsed. The increase in military activity noted from 9 May had led to an Argentine expectation of a major operation on 12 May.[5] As this reasoning bore little relation to London's actual timetable there was therefore here no corresponding assumption that any diplomatic moves were closely geared to imminent military action. The British were therefore taken by surprise, and had to assume that there could be some substance to the concession, based on the quality of a negotiating strategy backed by the threat of force.

'For better or worse our tactics have worked.' So wrote Parsons. The answer required had been extracted. There was no need to quibble on the General Assembly references, which were mild and only recommendations, for the more supportive Charter reference was also there. Britain had also achieved some flexibility on the target date and Argentina had scaled down their requirements on residence. They had also come off the demand for 200nm withdrawal and shown some flexibility about islander participation. Their strategy could no longer be explained by an attempt to prevaricate until 31 December in order to be able to walk in as the UN left. Argentina was either sincere or trying to put Britain in the position of breaking negotiations and being put on the wrong foot. The UN would now be looking for concessions from Britain, on either South Georgia or the Legislative Council. Parsons was clear where his priorities lay:

> If the negotiations broke down because we had refused to withdraw a small military garrison from a virtually uninhabited island where we had no garrison before the present crisis erupted, we would find ourselves abandoned by everyone here, even our friends and allies such as the old commonwealth and the ten. It would seem reasonable to everyone that we should withdraw our garrison from South Georgia and be prepared to negotiate, in the context of the Falklands negotiations, a separate agreement on South Georgia and the South Sandwich Islands perhaps on Antarctic Treaty lines.

The problem with islander participation was less serious as disproportionate representation for Argentina would seem unreasonable. Even so the great majority of the UN membership would, in Parsons' judgement, 'think us obdurate if we failed to reach some compromise on this question of circumstances of interim administration.' The pressure was now on London which had to face some tough decisions. He needed something by late 12 May and he hoped that it would be positive. Already the propaganda advantage might be swinging Argentina's way: a headline in the *New York Times* observed that 'Argentina eases terms for peace in the Falklands'.

On the Tuesday, the War Cabinet had been content with Parsons' general approach, geared to ensuring that any breakdown was clearly Argentina's fault, and that there was no need to seek to force the pace of the negotiations. Now on the Wednesday, perhaps not appreciating just how much might be assumed in New York to have changed following the Argentine concession, they discussed whether there need be any movement in Britain's position. The deliberations ranged over a variety of possible concessions but all posed political difficulties and the inclination was to stick with the established position, at least until there was more clarity on other aspects of the Argentine position but also on whether it would be possible to get a military guarantee from either the United States or a multinational force.

London took the view that the Junta had allowed for progress on the substantive negotiations with the aim of concentrating on trying to 'engineer changes in conditions on the islands during the interim period so as to considerably reduce the chances of any outcome unfavourable to them.' This had to be resisted. The Argentine text on prejudgement could be accepted at the end of the day, though it would be best to delete the references to the General Assembly, while the last sentence, though legally sound, could cause difficulties in presentation and there was no mention of the principle of self-determination. It was also easier to be confident about Argentine intentions if they ceased making statements in public which suggested that sovereignty was not negotiable. The Argentine proposals were unacceptable on the interim administration as the terms of reference were too wide. Furthermore, any Argentine withdrawal must include administrators, whether civil or military, that had been instituted on the Islands since the invasion, leaving the UN administrator as the officer administering the Government in the manner previously conducted by the Governor, acting through the established administrative personnel.[6] He must not have 'authority to make changes which might lead to a significant alteration in the character of life on the islands during the interim period.' To avoid there being any scope for Argentina to change the demographic character of the Islands, Britain would at most accept the application of the provisions of the 1971 agreement, and the joint consultative committee (constituting the Argentine Ministry of Foreign Affairs and the British Embassy) could be reconstituted.

A separate telegram on South Georgia recognised it to be a 'major stumbling block.' Not only was it British territory by title and possession, but also it would be needed during the period of withdrawal, as its anchorages were of value. During the interim arrangement, but also during the slightly longer term, it was intended to return the British Antarctic Survey to South Georgia and provide it with support using HMS *Endurance*. The administration would have to be transferred from the Governor to London. As at one time Argentina was able to contemplate their exclusion, Parsons should 'argue with the Secretary-General that it would be totally inappropriate for the Dependencies to be dealt with in the Interim Agreement under discussion.' They were Dependencies of the UK and not the Falklands and their history and circumstances were totally different. At the same time the British were not saying that the Dependencies should necessarily be excluded from the definitive negotiations. As an additional clincher it was suggested that as a sort of side deal, Britain would ignore the illegal Argentine presence on South Sandwich Islands if Argentina ignored South Georgia.

This was not the positive set of instructions for which Parsons had been hoping, and this time he did not have the option of ignoring unwelcome advice. He took these instructions that afternoon to the Secretary-General. 'I carried out these instructions,' he reported back. The UN team was 'stunned.' The Secretary-General's first reaction was that Argentina would withdraw their agreement to the previous day's formula on non-prejudgement and that the breakdown of his initiative was inevitable. He asked what he was supposed to say to Ros who was coming to see him in two hours. There would be nothing to pass on in return for what the UN team saw as the previous day's major concession. The Argentines would be 'bitter and disappointed' and might even break off the talks immediately. 'If we were genuinely interested in avoiding the "carnage" which would result from failure of his efforts, he could not understand why we had to take such a hard line.'

Parsons promised that the matter had been discussed extensively in London. The Secretary-General had to examine the matter from Britain's perspective. It was not Britain that had committed the aggression but it had still made a number of concessions from its position as set out on 6 May. 'A settlement could not be achieved in defiance of political realities in London.' Perez de Cuellar decided on reflection that the best way to avoid a breakdown was not to describe Britain's position to Ros 'bluntly.' He would not reveal the totality of the British position to Ros, in the hope that Ros would himself have something new to say. He nonetheless asked Parsons to convey his view that unless Britain moderated its position the whole initiative could collapse the next day.

There was some discussion of the concept of a box out of which forces must leave during the withdrawal, about which London was dubious,[7] on the idea that Argentine residents of the Falkland Islands should have equal representation with members of the Legislative Council in the advisory group, which it was explained came from the UN and had only been accepted by the Argentines, without enthusiasm, as a possible compromise, and on the possible situation after 31 December. On the Dependencies the UN team argued that Argentina was not necessarily thinking of a UN presence, but that Britain should withdraw and then allow their status to be negotiated separately from, but in same process as, the final settlement of the Falkland Islands.

Perez de Cuellar had only a fairly brief meeting with Ros, out of which came a private (Perez de Cuellar thought not on instructions) appeal to Britain to be transmitted through Parsons personally for military restraint while serious negotiations were continuing. Perez de Cuellar told Ros that Britain was generally satisfied, in the context of the overall agreement, with Argentine statements on non-prejudgement, but already had fresh misgivings because of a recent statement by Costa Mendez.[8] When Perez de Cuellar suggested a moratorium on public statements while negotiations continued, Ros started to complain about statements from London. He had nothing new to offer on the interim administration. In reporting back to Parsons, Perez de Cuellar reiterated that if he had exposed Britain's present positions to Ros, negotiations would have been terminated on the spot. He had taken care not to do so, thus buying London another day, and for the same reason had decided not to call Parsons back as he had little to say and reappearance would only excite speculation.

After this difficult day Parsons renewed his own efforts to extract more flexibility from London:

> You and your colleagues are now faced with an immediate strategic decision. If tomorrow I stick to the positions set out to Perez de Cuellar today and he puts them to the Argentines, as he will feel compelled to do, I agree with his assessment that the negotiations will terminate there and then. We can only keep the talks going if we are prepared to make fairly substantial concessions on the nature of the interim administration and on our military withdrawal from South Georgia (all in the context of satisfaction on the whole package).

While he was aware, and had explained to Perez de Cuellar, that Britain was not the aggressor nor was it inflexible, 'the plain if regrettable fact is that everyone here sees the situation quite differently':

> The majority of the membership sympathise with our reaction to Argentine use of force, but they believe (this includes a number of western delegations) that the Falklands should belong to Argentina provided that the interests of the islanders are safeguarded. At this stage, the dominant view here is that the Argentine position is becoming more moderate and that we should respond in order to bring an end to hostilities which are creating increasing concern world-wide.

The basic strategy that he had been following now threatened to backfire. It was now London rather than Buenos Aires that had been wrong-footed:

> Hence if we do not moderate position and negotiations break down tomorrow leaving a diplomatic vacuum accompanied only by intensifying military activity, we will be regarded as the culprits (the Secretariat will see to that). Support for our position, even from our allies and partners, will drain away as we cast vetoes against calls for a cessation of hostilities, probably accompanied by the clamour of an emergency special session of the General Assembly. I still have some shots in my locker to try to limit this damage but, if the diplomatic vacuum persists, they will become decreasingly effective.

Either Britain must make concessions or else set out its position in full for Argentina to reject. It would be better if they rejected it in toto rather than by reference to specific points.

Parsons proposed that as a minimum Britain should:

1. Agree to demilitarisation of South Georgia to accompany mutual withdrawal from Falklands, leaving basic BAS administration intact, freezing all fresh and other non-scientific activity (to deal with Davidoff contract) and agreeing that a separate solution to the Dependencies be included in diplomatic negotiations on the Falkland Islands.[9]
2. Agree that the UN administration should act in consultation with the elected representatives of the islanders, acting as a corporate body (unspecified), as regards the day to day affairs of the Islands and as regards the future of the islanders. Britain would accept that the operation of the existing institutions should be suspended (not abolished) during the interim period but insist that the UN administration should not make (or retain) any changes which would not be in conformity with the spirit of the laws and practices previously observed by the traditional local administration.

Parsons tried to avoid any mood music at all in talking to the press, sounding neither bright nor gloomy, but agreeing that discussions were on track. Perez de Cuellar sounded more upbeat, leaving the media to expect more responses the next day, and then 'perhaps one more round of discussion with each party and then I still feel that perhaps at the end of week we might have some really positive results.' When asked about the claims being made by Argentina on its concession on sovereignty, he said that the 'two parties have been so far as co-operative as possible.' As Britain had laid public stress on prejudgement, the Secretary-General's line suggested that Argentina accepted this position. All this was adding to Britain's difficulties. Ministers faced what they would consider the absurd position of being criticised for being too inflexible on the restoration of British administration and wishes of islanders. 'Our strategy today will therefore be to divert attention from the apparently stark simplicity of the argument over prejudging sovereignty to the notion that the negotiated package can only be judged as a whole.'

Back to London

The War Cabinet received with some anxiety Pym's report of Parsons' concerns on the morning of 13 May, and especially on the odium that Britain would incur if it were unable to modify its position on the nature of the interim administration and South Georgia. Ministers were torn between wanting to keep the UN discussions going, so that any failure should be Argentina's responsibility, and a conviction that they had no more substantial concessions to offer. At best they could see possibilities for adding one Argentine resident to the Councils and referring South Georgia to the ICJ. Meanwhile they were still worried about continuing statements from Costa Mendez about sovereignty, the danger of a political vacuum after 31 December and the possibility of US verification of withdrawal.

Being thrown into relief now was the basic issue of principle: could the wishes of a community as small as the Falkland Islands in all circumstances be the decisive factor? Even accepting that the demilitarisation of South Georgia was probably unacceptable, might it be possible to offer to withdraw the garrison currently ashore there? If, as the JIC assessed, Argentina was determined to prevent the return of a basically British administration to the Islands, and Britain had no more concessions to offer, how could the negotiations be terminated in circumstances which left the Argentines with most of the blame? The issues were difficult and Parsons was told to explain that over the coming day consultations would take place. This he did but this was not a ploy that could last indefinitely. Perez de Cuellar was appealing to Britain, as a founder member of the UN, to make the maximum concessions for peace. He feared the bloodshed that was to come. He was asking both delegations to provide their best position by 14 May and, once received, he would make his own evaluation within 48 hours for the two sides to consider. He did not wish to be used by either side 'as an instrument for endless manipulation.'[10]

The pressure for New York had to be set against contrary pressures at home. The strength of public opinion behind the Government, which had not been severely dented even by the loss of *Sheffield*, could well be endangered if a diplomatic sell-out was feared, or if any gap opened up between the Government's public pledges and the line being taken in negotiations. Some ministers felt strongly that the Government's supporters would not understand further concessions on the contentious matters. Not all agreed. These supporters might also be too ready to believe in a military settlement without serious penalties; others were more open-minded and would not want British lives unnecessarily endangered. Furthermore, public opinion might be persuaded to accept the kind of settlement being brokered in New York. Any attempt to secure the future of the Islands would require at some point negotiations in which Argentina was bound to play a part, while if negotiations failed now and Britain got the blame its international position would be compromised.

Already it was proving difficult to find the right words in public. Nott was reported, for example, when asked whether he ever envisaged the Falklands becoming sovereign Argentine territory, to have replied 'No, never'. As Pym noted this could be taken as prejudgement. Pym gave the approved formulation to the House on 13 May:

> We accept that negotiations about the future of the Islands can exclude no possible outcome but equally we insist that they must determine none. Nothing excluded, nothing prejudged. That is a reasonable position and one on which we shall not compromise.

When this was discussed that morning at the War Cabinet it was agreed that the line to be taken was that it was difficult to envisage the Falkland Islands becoming Argentine sovereign territory because it was difficult to believe that the Falkland Islanders would wish, especially in the light of their recent experiences, to live under Argentine rule.

This immovable local political logic now appeared to be coming against an almost irresistible international political logic. The moment was delicate. On 16 May there was a debate due in the EC on sanctions' renewal: the landing was planned for a few days later. In all of this American attitudes were crucial. The ground lost as a result of the *Belgrano* had been, to some extent, recovered as a result of the readiness to negotiate on the basis of the Peruvian initiative. Haig had extracted substantial concessions on 5 May but in return he had sent personal messages to NATO foreign ministers, reporting on how Pym had been helping in the attempt to get a cease-fire and a negotiated settlement and the need to reconfirm solidarity. After the Argentines rejected these proposals, alliance foreign ministers were informed of the joint approach made with Peru, the readiness of Britain to accept, Argentina's rejection, and that this was the basis of Britain's new negotiating position with the UN Secretary-General. A later message on sanctions was sent on 14 May explaining why support for Britain should not be weakened.

All this, along with continued practical military support, was welcome. At the same time there were plenty of indications that Washington was less than whole-hearted in its backing for Britain. The British were particularly disconcerted by a message Reagan sent to a variety of Latin American leaders on 2 May. In trying to balance the impact of overt support for Britain he had described Argentina as a 'state with which we share a common heritage and strong legal, moral and cultural links, from colonisation to nationhood.' He acknowledged Argentina's aspiration to confirm its 'historic claim of sovereignty over the Islands known as the Malvinas,' adding that 'no American believes that colonisation by any European power is to be accepted in this hemisphere.' The message referred to the President's understanding of the 'deep national commitment of Argentina to recuperate the Islands, and its frustration of long years of fruitless negotiations.'[11] The problem with Argentina's actions was only to ignore the rule of law for that of force. So incensed was the Prime Minister that when she entertained the American Ambassador at Chequers on 9 May she drew his attention to the quote, remarking that 'we had been a little bit dismayed to read what President Reagan had written.' She tore off a relevant piece of the telegram and handed it to the Ambassador, remarking that the extract seemed to condone aggression.

Nor was Haig any more forthcoming on the US guarantee, which the British had seen as critical to any settlement. At a meeting on 10 May, while observing that the UN could not provide a guarantee, he did not volunteer one from the United States. The trouble was that it would require the specific authorisation of Congress 'which would not be plain-sailing in the post Vietnam climate.' Under the Peruvian plan there was a stipulation that troops once withdrawn should not be reintroduced, while the contact group (with the US involved) would ensure that no actions were taken which contravened the agreement. In order to pin the Americans down a letter from Thatcher to Reagan was considered. Thatcher was unhappy with the draft, which appeared to suggest that she would accept a far from perfect settlement if the US was willing to play a part in deterring aggression. In further discussion Haig saw little difficulty about supervising Argentina's withdrawal. The problem came if there was no settlement and Argentina threatened to return. The best idea here was for the US to play a central part in the UN regime.

Furthermore, once a major Argentine concession appeared to be in the bag, the Americans were anxious to move to a full settlement. Haig might not approve of the UN process, as if it was an intrusion into his business, but success would serve American interests. As soon as the Argentines started putting it about that they had made a big concession on the prejudgement of sovereignty then, as reported to Parsons, Haig was on the 'phone to Perez de Cuellar offering to help'. The Secretary-General later recalled that Haig told him that 'he had been in direct touch with British Foreign Secretary Pym with suggestions regarding a schedule for the interim administration. He thought Ambassador Parsons would be receiving new instructions soon.'[12] Meanwhile Haig told Henderson that it was Perez de Cuellar who had called him, to tell him of the considerable concession by Argentina on sovereignty. This required something comparable from Britain that, it was hoped, Haig would try and extract. Henderson, in response, sought to play down the significance of the concession and play up past Argentine intransigence and the danger of transitional arrangements that could swamp the Islands. But Haig thought that some formula could be found to deal with the problem. Haig had just received a report from Vernon Walters, who had been in Buenos Aires and seen Galtieri and Lami Dozo. He had not detected any signs that they believed there had been any break-through on sovereignty, but confirmed the sense of a trade for more on the interim administration if matters were to be less definite on sovereignty. Haig agreed to ask Walters to explore with the Junta their flexibility on the South Georgia issue. This might help, but the American interest indicated that the diplomatic game was getting even more complicated. London's confidence in Walters had at any rate been dented by reports of his remarks to the American Enterprise Institute on 10 May; Walters had spoken of the crisis as 'a conflict of machismos' and 'a silly war and a conflict of egos.' Walters' own reports from his conversations suggested that while Galtieri understood US support for the UK, this had been overdone and that Weinberger's support for Britain had fed anti-Americanism. Galtieri remained bothered that the British would spin out negotiations so that Argentina would never get sovereignty, but also had promised that Argentina would seek support from all friends other than the Soviet Union. 400 men had been lost: 40,000 would be lost if necessary. Walters had denied claims that the US was providing satellite intelligence to the British and reminded them that they were fighting a great power. Walters found them flexible on pre-determined sovereignty and interim administration, but unyielding on access to the Islands for their nationals. They did not mention the Dependencies, suggesting this was not a high priority.[13] Meanwhile, through a friendly journalist the Washington Embassy was told how a White House official had described Walters' role in Buenos Aires as being to rein-stitute the American position by informing the Argentines that the US was prepared to follow a more even-handed approach if that would bring about a settlement, that US material support for the UK was not open-ended, and that any British attack on the Argentine mainland would be resisted by the US. Brazil was playing an important role in convincing the Americans that they had to appear more neutral if they wanted to repair their relations with Latin America.

This appeared to be reflected on 13 May, when Reagan telephoned Thatcher. He had received a call from the Brazilian President, regarded as a moderate, who had expressed concern about Britain launching a mainland attack, particularly against the five key Argentine air bases. In addition, Kirkpatrick, taking an opportunity while Haig was out of Washington in Europe, had reported on the Argentine concession. She had persuaded Perez de Cuellar to urge the President to contact Thatcher and Galtieri directly to urge them both to compromise.[14] This had suggested to the White House that with a quid quo pro from Britain there could be a settlement.

The Prime Minister was not in a receptive mood. While in public she had been cautious, in private she was becoming more anxious about the diplomatic trend. She had expressed her misgivings after reading the FCO draft letter for her to send to the US President: 'my views are hardening because I think that much of the compromise [treaty] will be totally unacceptable to our people.' So this conversation with Reagan became for Thatcher yet another exercise in dispelling misapprehensions. Reagan's starting point was that movement from the Argentine side meant that the two sides were quite close. No, the Prime Minister explained, they were not. She rehearsed the difficulties. When told of Brazilian worries about an attack on the mainland, she gave no ground, reiterating that only military measures helped diplomacy. No, the risk of Argentina getting closer to Moscow was not a strategic reason for Britain to offer compromises, but a reason why Britain should be supported. No, Britain could not hold off military action. No, Britain was not a Goliath to Argentina's David, especially at 8,000 miles. Though a difficult conversation, Thatcher believed it had been useful. At the same time if one of her closest political friends could be so misinformed then serious difficulties would be faced. Henderson worked on Judge Clark, encouraging calm. The Americans should not worry about any unpopularity in Latin America: that was 'the corollary of power.' He also warned about the adverse reaction some of Reagan's latest comments had attracted. Clark sought to reassure him that Reagan was completely on Britain's side.

This was the backdrop to the War Cabinet's meeting on 14 May to consider what appeared to be unpromising diplomatic options. The FCO's assessment was that it was still not clear whether Argentina's objective was to negotiate seriously or gain time while the weather worsened in the South Atlantic, but it was certainly getting itself into a good presentational position in order to blame Britain if the talks collapsed. The view remained that a settlement would be preferable to more military action, and that military action following a breakdown that could be blamed on Argentina was preferable to action following a breakdown that could be blamed on the UK. However if the break came it should be before major military action began, and so this would be a consequence of failure and not a cause. The real sticking point was not the Dependencies, where future concessions might be offered on military withdrawal if not full demilitarisation, but the interim administration. The UN administrator must not be able to 'make or permit any changes in the laws and practices in the Islands which would not conform with the spirit of those previously observed,' or allow the Islands to be flooded with Argentine people and businesses.

Pym reported that Parsons had skilfully played for time, but that Britain's options were now narrowing. If it were not possible to provide him with further instructions then Britain would be blamed for a breakdown of the negotiations. Alternatively minimum concessions might be offered on the interim administration and South Georgia to keep things going. Out of the anxious examination of these two unpalatable alternatives a third possibility had also come to the fore: to recall Parsons to London for early consultations. This might make it possible to hold the position in New York until his return but also enable Britain to regain the initiative, as once back in New York he could table a document setting out the kind of agreement Britain was willing to accept. This third option had obvious attractions as the best way to stop the negotiating process spinning out of control. The debate in Parliament the previous day convinced ministers that the Government's supporters would not welcome more concessions. They therefore decided that they had come to the end of the road in negotiations. Rather than send further instructions to Parsons, he was to be instructed to return for consultations. It would also make sense for Henderson to come to London. The aim would be to produce a comprehensive British document on a take it or leave it basis. Until it was ready, Perez de Cuellar would need to be dissuaded from formally putting forward proposals of his own.

After being told of the decision, Parsons saw the Secretary-General, to whom he 'spoke with considerable vigour and emotion.' He reported that he had been called back for urgent consultations at the highest level and would be back in New York by Monday morning. There was no question of these consultations being completed before then and the Secretary-General was urged not to present his paper until he returned. 'It was vital that my Ministers should be able to discuss the outstanding problems without further prejudice from any side.' Ros must be convinced that Britain was 'not playing games, that my return to London was not a ploy designed to buy time, and that it was in everyone's interest to sit tight and await my return.' He expressed concern that the Security Council might attempt to get Britain to accept a 'Presidential statement calling for military restraint or something of that kind.' These would be flatly refused. Any attempt to force Britain immediately into open Council would mean that he could not return to London and the Government would have to turn its attention to deal with the situation in the Security Council. The Secretary-General's initiative would almost certainly collapse and 'we would never know if it would have succeeded. He and everyone else concerned would have to live with this thought for the rest of their lives.'

Perez de Cuellar 'responded admirably to this oration.' He would not produce his paper until Parsons returned and he understood the need to hold everything over the weekend. He would see Ros privately and convince him to do the same. Ditto with the President of the Security Council. He also told Parsons that he had given Ros a hard time on the question of islander participation in the interim administration, arguing that it was inconceivable for any democratic country to accept that people should be robbed of democratic rights let alone accept parity between 2,000 and 30. It was possible to see that one representative of the business community might be included in the structure. Ros had taken this surprisingly well and Perez de Cuellar had been given to understand by another Latin American contact that Argentina might well move on this point. This provided some confirmation that the Americans had been putting pressure on Buenos Aires for a concession on the interim administration. The source here may have been Kirkpatrick. She had told Perez de Cuellar something of Thatcher's conversation with Reagan, and the difficulty posed by the determination of the House of Commons that there should be no more concessions and also that the White House expected a concession from Argentina on the interim administration.[15]

To help convince the Secretary-General that Britain was engaged in a serious exercise, the Prime Minister also rang him. Perez de Cuellar recorded the unexpected phone call:

> The Prime Minister appealed to me to keep 'her boys' from being killed. I sensed that this was the woman and the mother who was speaking to me – a very different person from the firm, seemingly belligerent leader of the British government. From this call I was certain that Margaret Thatcher was not, as so much of the press was reporting, hell-bent on war.

While it was clear that Britain was stepping up preparations for an invasion of the Islands, he felt that she was still prepared to accept a peace settlement. Nonetheless, the Secretary-General was, with his staff, 'surprised and disconcerted' by the recall of Parsons to London, 'since it inevitably meant a hiatus in the New York talks at a very sensitive and hopeful point and there was no time to spare.'[16]

Parsons reported that the consultation with the Security Council passed without 'mishap.' Perez de Cuellar was as good as his word and saw a number of 'do-gooders and troublemakers' individually before the meeting in order to make it quite clear that he too wanted the meeting to pass as uneventfully as possible. He described the hopes invested in his mediation, speaking generally but describing everyone as serious though with difficult differences. Parsons spoke paying tribute to Perez de Cuellar for his efforts, confirming negotiating in good faith and then said he had to return to London urgently for consultations. Everyone else spoke in favour of the Secretary-General. Dorr was 'his usual sententious self but this time his claptrap was harmless'. The only unpleasantness came from De Pinies (Spain) who asked to convey the position that a cease-fire should be maintained during the negotiations. No one else had asked for this. Parsons decided not to reply so as not to open up a debate. Though another hurdle had been cleared:

> there was no mistaking the members' nervousness about hostilities if and when the Secretary-General's efforts should fail. The Council is all set to support a simple cease-fire plus negotiations resolution in that event.

Britain's final offer

The discussion on 16 May at Chequers was vital to sustaining Britain's international position. It began at 1000 and did not finish until 1630.[17] The Prime Minister later recalled that:

> Tony Parsons and Nico Henderson were both closely involved in the drafting. We went over every point in detail, working as usual around the oblong table in the Great Parlour upstairs, remodelling the draft clause by clause. At hand were voluminous reference sources on the UN and the law relating to the administration of the Falklands.[18]

Other recollections suggest a less than harmonious day, with the Prime Minister in one of her more combative moods. Henderson reports that she 'veered the whole time to being uncompromising – she emphasised again and again the virtues of democracy, the evils of aggression, the concessions we had made to the Americans,' for example over the Multinational Force in the Sinai and observers to El Salvador. As for the FCO, they were accused of being 'wet, ready to sell out, unsupportive of British interests, etc, etc,' and: 'Did the Foreign Office have no principles?' While the FCO were 'content to be dishonest and consult with dishonest people, she was honest.' While Haig preferred unclear language, she insisted on clarity. 'This', Henderson added, 'was accompanied by a stern look in Tony's [Parsons] and my direction.[19] Nott also recalls a 'pretty aggressive' tone when he 'intervened in some exasperation'

> she then rounded on me and accused me of being rude to her! It is true, I had been. 'Those who live by the sword, die by the sword.' I am afraid these polite, civilised, intelligent mandarins as good civil servants were hardly able to retaliate, so it rightly fell to me.[20]

All agreed that the aim was not to draft a document that reached out to Argentina. As far as the Government was concerned offering the aggressor an interim administration and future talks on sovereignty went quite far enough. What was vital was that this offering was presented in its most reasonable form so that the UN, the United States and the countries of the European Community could appreciate just how far Britain had been prepared to go to prevent further bloodshed. It was this point the Prime Minister was persuaded to accept, though only after being convinced that however moderate the final document it would still be rejected by Argentina. Parsons had warned that while he had delayed the climax of the New York negotiations it remained important to retain the goodwill of the Secretary-General, to prevent him tabling unacceptable proposals of his own and also to demonstrate that Britain was negotiating in good faith. To the extent that this effort succeeded then there was always the possibility that Argentina might accept and the credibility of the FCO's own efforts following the Chequers meeting to some extent drew on this possibility. Parsons and Henderson argued that presentationally the provisions on the interim administration should lay more stress on local representative institutions than on the restoration of the colonial regime. This was relevant even with the Americans. It was thought that the Americans might help with South Georgia, but they would be reluctant to contemplate any form of guarantee of a settlement. The best approach to getting them to accept some responsibility for enforcement was judged to be through the verification regime. Thatcher later described the outcome as follows:

> We hardened our terms in respect of interim administration, ensuring something close to self-government for the islanders and denying any role to the Argentine Government. We excluded South Georgia and the other dependencies from the proposals altogether: South Georgia was back under British control and there could be no question any longer of including it in the negotiations. We made reference to Article 73 of the UN Charter, which implies self-determination, to make it clear that the wishes of the islanders would be paramount in long-term negotiations. The Argentine Government was required to give a response within 48 hours and there was to be no negotiation of the terms. This exercise also allowed me subsequently to explain each phrase to the House of Commons to allay their understandable fears that we might be prepared to yield too much.[21]

Pym had to hurry from Chequers to Luxembourg for meetings of both the EC and NATO, where he would see Haig. That Sunday evening the Foreign Secretary briefed the US Secretary of State on the results of Chequers. Prior to this meeting there had been some discussion of the tricky issue of whether Haig should be given an advance copy of the British text. There was concern about disclosure: once a copy was being passed around Washington it would soon leak out, and queer Britain's pitch as well as lead to calls for a premature debate in Parliament. Pym's staff worried that this left him in a difficult position, looking 'cagey and distrustful' and unable to return to the charge over the issue of a US guarantee. It was therefore agreed that he should have discretion. Haig was shown the draft as for his eyes only.

Of particular importance to the British side, as it had been throughout all the negotiating efforts, was a commitment to provide an American guarantee. Pym had raised it before with Haig along with Henderson, while the Prime Minister had raised it with Reagan. Haig had given the impression that he was favourably disposed to the idea and now confirmation was needed. The US was asked for 'an adequate number of men in addition to equipment to help the UN Administrator verify withdrawal and the non-reintroduction of forces.' This would help to deal with the interim period. The two countries 'would need to consult together again over longer term arrangements involving the US, if and when we get into substantive negotiations.' In practice Haig had always been cool on the issue of security guarantees, and remained so. He 'had not given much thought to the question of verification.' Now Haig responded that while there were limits to what action the US could take alone he might persuade others to join in, such as Brazil, Peru or France. He was confident Argentina would not invade again if an agreement had been reached.

On the details of the proposals Pym played down the Argentine concession on sovereignty, explained the problems with the interim administration and gained a positive response to the proposition that the US should encourage Argentina to ignore the issue of the Dependencies. Public opinion would not accept a departure from South Georgia, which, in any case, would be needed by the Royal Navy during any withdrawal period from the Falklands. In general there was no strong reaction from Haig. He appeared to find the text fair but had no view on its chances of acceptance. Back in Washington, Henderson was told to brief Haig's deputies, Stoessel and Eagleburger, but emphasise that there must be no leaks and great discretion until the Argentine reply had been received. He also promised that they would be given a copy of the proposals on 18 May with information on the Secretary-General's reactions.

The instructions to Parsons were to give the Secretary-General the draft agreement as soon as possible, as representing 'the absolute minimum acceptable to HMG.' There could be no amendments to it. He was to ask the Secretary-General formally to pass it to Argentina as the final British position. An additional letter confirmed that the Dependencies were to be excluded. He was to stress that the process could not 'drag on much longer' and so midday New York time on 19 May was set as the absolute deadline. The role of the United States in verification and enforcement was to be stressed. Parsons was to respond to any queries by saying that he was engaged in extensive consultations and instructed to continue negotiations. He was not to be drawn into the content of his instructions nor even hint at a British plan or deadline.

As he arrived back at John F Kennedy airport he remarked that his mood had not changed. Britain could not negotiate indefinitely: he was talking 'in terms of days, not weeks.' He went on to see the Secretary-General with whom he went over the background – the Argentine failure to comply with 502 and a series of good faith negotiations. Many concessions had been offered and after this document there were no more to be made. All Argentina had offered was a matching undertaking to put sovereignty to one side and a conditional agreement to withdraw. This was hardly a concession when Argentina was the aggressor. With great difficulty his Government had decided to put forward a draft interim agreement. No amendments were acceptable. After six weeks of negotiation the deadline was now 1200 on 19 May. 'Any appeals for further time, or any proposals for substantive amendment, would be interpreted as rejection of our proposals.'

Perez de Cuellar asked if the draft was confidential. Parsons replied that it was: 'I did not know what the chances there were of Argentine acceptance, but if the existence of the document, or the existence of a deadline, were leaked that would be the end of this exercise.' Could Britain not even contemplate minor amendments to help Argentina save face? Parsons would look at something minuscule but not substantive. Even 'the existing draft would be extremely difficult to defend in Parliament.' They went through the draft in detail. Perez de Cuellar would not pass judgement immediately. He could see, however, that it was 'more forthcoming' than he had expected. 'It covered all the proposals that I had made in my aide-mémoire of May 2 and included much of the language that had been developed during the proximity talks.'[22] His worry, as a Latin American, was that when he presented it as a British draft to the Argentines on a take it or leave it basis, they would inevitably reject it. He wondered whether he could present it as his, but Parsons warned that whether Argentina accepted or rejected the draft Britain would have to publish it 'and this would put him in a false position.' The Secretary-General accepted the warning of this pitfall. Parsons suggested that he should present it as a British draft, but one that was based on the negotiations that he had led and thus quite different to what would have appeared if he had not been involved. There were real concessions. He could say that he had imposed the deadline to stop the negotiations going on indefinitely. Later Perez de Cuellar regretted that he had not expressed more forcefully to Parsons his belief that Argentina would reject anything that appeared as an ultimatum. 'Pride now joined with shortness of time as an enemy of peace.'[23]

To Parsons' irritation, Ahmad made a 'characteristically unhelpful intervention' about the damage to Perez de Cuellar's reputation if he were to 'act as a postman' conveying an 'unreasonable ultimatum.' Perez de Cuellar would have to retain the right to report to the Security Council that the British position had been unreasonable. Parsons replied that if Perez de Cuellar said any such thing there would be no question of him playing any further role in this crisis. Perez de Cuellar ignored Ahmad. The two men then spoke alone, without any aides present. The Ambassador gave him the side letter about Dependencies, and explained the importance of avoiding this subject cropping up in the context of withdrawal. There was no question of Britain leaving South Georgia, and bilateral pressure was being brought to bear on Argentina to drop this question. When Perez de Cuellar pointed out that might be difficult, Parsons observed that in view of the Captain Astiz affair,[24] the Argentines might conclude that the less said about South Georgia the better.

Perez de Cuellar said that he thought the paper was perfectly reasonable and he admired the effort that had been made. He had some indications that

Argentina was a bit desperate and might like an agreement. 'His feeling was that they thought we could recapture the islands without much difficulty and that the only way to save themselves from ultimate humiliation was agreement before it happened.' He would see Ros that afternoon and transmit both the draft and the deadline. He accepted that the exercise could not be allowed to drag on beyond the Wednesday. It would be interesting to see if Ros came back with anything:

> To sum up, this first round went as well as could be expected, perhaps better. Perez de Cuellar's initial reaction suggested that our judgement of 16 May that our position would be regarded as basically reasonable if the break comes, was well founded.

Perez de Cuellar was going to say that the process of negotiation had had an effect. This was not the same as an ultimatum: that could have been put forward at any time over last ten days.[25]

On the evening of 18 May Parsons walked round to Perez de Cuellar's house (the only way he could see him without the press knowing). Perez de Cuellar reported that Ros had looked 'disappointed' when he read the British paper. Perez de Cuellar was already regretting that British tactics had made it difficult for him to produce a paper of his own, as he had expected to do by this stage of the process. Parsons explained that any 'median' paper would be unacceptable. If he produced a public paper (and Britain would publish its own) then Parsons would have to dismember Perez de Cuellar's paper in public and Ministers would lose confidence in him, as they would believe that he had acted to wrong-foot Britain or just cover himself in public. This would damage not only their friendship but also their ability to co-operate on other matters. Still the Secretary-General doubted whether he could allow the negotiations to peter out without anything coming from him. Parsons stressed that he did not want an appeal to cease hostilities. As for the Argentines, Parsons suspected that they would propose oral changes if only to avoid causing awkward problems for themselves domestically when the present document was made public. Perez de Cuellar thought it unlikely that they would settle for only small amendments.

The end game was still going to be tricky, Parsons warned London. He could now see that Perez de Cuellar would probably want to put some proposals to both sides, just to say that he had done so, but without any expectations of success. Meanwhile, waiting for the Argentine response, Parsons prepared draft resolutions, first authorising the Secretary-General to administer the Islands during the interim period and calling for a report setting out his proposals, and the second approving the report. He was also planning for a breakdown. His first thought was that as soon as the text was published in Britain on 20 May it should be conveyed to the President of the Security Council as a document of the Council, to show how far Britain had been prepared to go. On reflection he could see a risk in this, as it would then become the benchmark for a solution (as SCR 242 had for the Middle East) and be formally endorsed as the basis for settlement. This would be the last thing Britain would want once the Falklands had been retaken. He therefore decided not to circulate the draft formally but draw on it during debate in the Council and make copies available on request to other delegations.

The schedule was for Perez de Cuellar to report to the Security Council for informal consultations on the afternoon of Wednesday, 19 May. Parsons expected that the do-gooders would probably try and fill the vacuum by a formal meeting of the Council the next day in order to propose a draft resolution on 'motherhood' lines, calling for the implementation of 502, plus cessation of hostilities plus the opening of negotiations. To avoid the isolation that opposition would bring, he intended to table a draft resolution of his own at the outset, which would link any cease-fire with arrangements for Argentine withdrawal. He also suspected that Dorr would get bogged down on the pre-negotiation of his draft and would want to avoid a British veto. His own draft would probably fail for procedural or substantive reasons but it would still put him in a better position than otherwise to veto Dorr's motherhood draft. His own draft would have no provisions for an interim administration, and that would demonstrate the chance that Argentina had missed.

It was not only the Secretary-General who assessed the British offer as about as good as Argentina could reasonably expect to get. Kirkpatrick made her own effort to persuade her Argentine opposite number, Eduardo Roca, that the British proposal was 'not so bad', in that it offered the opportunity to declare a diplomatic triumph by declaring the establishment of a UN authority responsible for the Islands. To no avail. Late that Tuesday evening, 18 May, Ros saw Perez de Cuellar to give him 'ideas and views.' Argentina had followed Britain in providing a draft agreement and incorporating many of the positions reached during the proximity talks. It did not offer any concessions but instead 'presented a harder statement of the Argentine position than put forward orally.' The Dependencies were included; there would be no restrictions on Argentine movement into the Islands; British forces would be withdrawn to home ports; and there would only be one opportunity to extend the talks on the future of the Islands. After 30 June 1983 the General Assembly would be asked to determine the terms to which the final settlement should conform. Ros was told that this was obviously unacceptable and it would relieve Britain of all restraints.[26] To Parsons, who followed Ros, Perez de Cuellar did not disguise his deep disappointment at the Argentine reply, which he saw as an attempt to start a new negotiating process. He told Kirkpatrick also that the Argentine response had been 'terrible' and that they seemed to be putting faith in a General Assembly debate.

Parsons' initial response was that this was a crude attempt by Argentina either to gain more time or wrong-foot Britain over breaking the negotiations. Britain would not be able to avoid the latter charge: 'we are in a hurry and the Argentines are not.' He was relieved that, to his credit, Perez de Cuellar made no attempt to argue that the Argentine response could form a basis for negotiations, but he was worried that the failure could affect his ability to deal with other problems. Parsons said that his efforts had been heroic (and urged Pym to send in his own praise). For the next morning he wanted London to consider three tactical questions.

First, he understood that because of the Parliamentary debate, which was bound to consider diplomatic activity in the light of the next stage of military operations, he wanted to delay anything coming to the Security Council. He would therefore respond on Wednesday morning with a preliminary negative reaction but tell the Secretary-General that there would be no formal reaction until later when London had had an opportunity to study the Argentine paper. Second, Perez de Cuellar must be encouraged to prevent further procrastination on Argentina's part. He wished to remind him formally that when presenting the British text he had made clear that there was a deadline for an Argentine response of midday New York time on 19 May, and that an equivocal response from Argentina would be regarded as tantamount to a rejection. 'HMG regard the Argentine response as being exactly that. We therefore have no choice but to regard this round of negotiations as having ended.' Third, he needed press guidance. He could no longer say that the negotiations were continuing.

Events the next day, Wednesday 19 May, Parsons later observed, moved 'with bewildering speed.' When he read the Argentine text he assessed it to be much worse than he had been led to believe, even including prejudgement language. Argentina had reverted to its opening negotiating position. As Perez de Cuellar was desperate not to admit failure, his first in a major crisis, he might seek to extend the deadline in order that he might put forward two to three new points of his own as a last desperate throw. Parsons heard that Kirkpatrick had urged Perez de Cuellar to put forward a median paper, but that he had refused to do so, although this was largely out of suspicion of American motives. He had made a gloomy contingent report to the President of the Security Council who was proposing informal talks for Thursday afternoon. Yet, despite the widening gap between the two positions, Perez de Cuellar was reluctant to give up, although Parsons warned him that if he did not announce the end of his mission, Britain would have to do it for him.

From his own account it is clear that Perez de Cuellar was still anxious, looking for a way to bridge the two proposals. His staff began to develop a paper to do that. The suggestions he received leaned, to his mind, far too much towards the Argentine position:

> I felt strongly that the Argentine position was completely unrealistic and, under the circumstances, self-destructive. The British draft offered Argentina a fair chance of gaining sovereignty in the Falklands and the reality of a non-British administration of the

islands for an indeterminate period. The British military position was obviously very strong, and I was convinced that they were entirely serious in saying that they would accept no substantive changes to their proposal. Therefore it seemed to me that the best course – in the interests of peace and of both parties – was to devise suggestions that would offer some cosmetic satisfaction to soothe Argentine pride without changing the substance of the British proposal.[27]

His problem was not only that the Argentine position had hardened but also that the British position had been finalised, and they would not necessarily accept his changes as cosmetic. His first task was to see whether any side had sufficient flexibility to make it worth his while putting forward his proposals. At the same time Parsons' task was to bring matters to closure as soon as possible.

Ling Qing, possibly at Perez de Cuellar's prompting, decided to convene the Security Council for informal consultations for late afternoon. Because of this Parsons accelerated his programme for giving Perez de Cuellar Britain's formal response and proposed a working lunch with his full group of advisers. First he asked the Secretary-General formally to convey to Ros that Britain found the Argentine response totally unacceptable. Britain had drawn a line, following the Argentine failure to accept the draft interim agreement by the deadline of 12 noon. Then they reviewed the Secretary-General's continuing efforts to sustain his mission and the Ambassador's attempts to curtail them. Parsons appreciated the proposals for a median paper, with language 'not at all bad from our point of view', but Britain could not get into another endless process of negotiation. Perez de Cuellar had spoken to the Argentine mission and asked if it had any flexibility. He was told it had. Costa Mendez had urged Perez de Cuellar to speak to Galtieri, who, he claimed, 'was very flexible and had only authorised the latest tough Argentine reply because the UK proposals had been so tough and had attacked Latin honour.' He had encouraged the Secretary-General to send envoys to London and Buenos Aires. The Secretary-General thought this a good idea and tickets had been booked. Parsons squelched the idea as totally unacceptable. If he appeared to support Argentine procrastination there would be 'deep discontent in London.'

Perez de Cuellar acknowledged all that Parsons had said about the unimpressive aspects of the Argentine response, but he had to keep his options open. As requested he would telephone Galtieri: he could not refuse to consider any forthcoming response from the Argentine President. The Council would not accept that any last opportunity had been missed. After speaking to Galtieri he would ring Thatcher. Parsons warned that every round of negotiation had ended up with a last minute intervention by Galtieri claiming to be reasonable, but with no real concessions to produce a settlement. When Perez de Cuellar rang Galtieri he did not make much progress. The Argentine President 'seemed somewhat confused, as if he had been drinking,' and was being 'prompted by others on what to say'. The Secretary-General sought to persuade him that he should be pleased that Argentina had got to the position where there could be no return to the earlier situation on the Islas Malvinas. There were few indications that any progress was being made at all, for Galtieri complained about British deadlines, unreasonableness and an imminent military offensive. Nonetheless, Perez de Cuellar was thanked for his willingness to continue negotiations.

Then Perez de Cuellar spoke to Thatcher. He said that he appreciated the concessions made by Britain but a settlement was not in sight. He had just urged Galtieri to make further concessions and hoped for continued co-operation and understanding from London. When asked what Galtieri's response had been, Thatcher was told that it was an expression of interest in a peaceful solution with further comments in a few hours. She spoke of her gratitude for the Secretary-General's efforts, but the British view had now been clearly stated. Seven sets of proposals had now been discussed through mediators with the Argentine Government and the result had been the same each time. They always said they were flexible but their tactics were to confuse and delay. Britain had gone as far as possible, and now the Argentine response amounted to a total rejection. That is what Britain would say publicly the next day. When Perez de Cuellar reported that Galtieri said that the Argentine document was not final, she replied that a final document would never be forthcoming. The Secretary-General said he would convey to Parsons any further ideas he got from Galtieri. He could do as he thought fit, the Prime Minister said, but the British statement would be published the next day. More out of a weary courtesy than any conviction, she stated that Britain would look at 'totally fresh proposals' but for now had to stand firm, and then repeated her gratitude to Perez de Cuellar 'in whom we had great faith.'[28]

Perez de Cuellar read more into the final comment than intended. When he spoke to Parsons later he gave an unflattering portrait of Galtieri having difficulty reading from a prepared text and contrasted this with the friendliness of the Prime Minister. Unfortunately, reported Parsons, 'he had grasped the wrong end of the stick when the Prime Minister had said that she was prepared to look at fresh proposals.' He sought to explain that any new proposals had to be totally fresh. As far as Britain was concerned 'the current negotiating round was over.' This was the message that he had also conveyed to the informal Council meeting, where he had made it clear that Britain would not accept calls for restraint and moderation. His objective now was to keep the blame directed firmly on to Argentina. In this effort he was relying on help from the old Commonwealth (he was intending to meet the Australian Foreign Minister) and had even been 'brain-washing' Kirkpatrick. On the other hand, 'some of my Community partners are so untrustworthy that I will not brief them until Friday.' At midday London time (1700 New York) that Thursday, 20 May, the British Government intended to issue a short statement confirming the Argentine rejection. The issue would then be the subject of a full Parliamentary debate.

Parsons was then brought up sharp by the sudden production of a paper by Perez de Cuellar, sent to Ros and himself. The Secretary-General stated that there were only hours left to complete the substantive amount of agreement that had already been achieved. He also issued a press statement, referring to the need for a 'last urgent effort' and the need 'to work for peace without jeopardy to principle.'[29] This last phrase was to reassure the British that he was not interested in peace at any price. Parsons reported:

> The paper is cleverly drafted and is undoubtedly more favourable to us than to Argentina. But I fully realise that it has come too late, although his public hint at its existence (which may be amplified by leaks from the secretariat) is likely to give you difficulties in the Commons debate. I also accept that the Argentines are likely to accept it as the basis for negotiation, as it contains the seeds for weeks of further procrastination.

These could focus on the arrangements for withdrawal, whether Dependencies should be included in the diplomatic negotiations but excluded from the withdrawal process, as well as the formulas for both the long-term negotiations and the interim administration. 'To put it in nutshell, the paper would have formed a good basis for negotiations ten days ago, but it is nothing but an embarrassment to us now.' He therefore proposed that he tell Perez de Cuellar that his paper differed in important respects from Britain's bottom line though its positive aspects were recognised. It differed quite fundamentally, however, from the latest Argentine position, and so it would be necessary to see any Argentine comments before Britain went any further and this could not affect any military plans that Britain might have.

Yet in London Pym was inclined to accept the proposal as it was so close to the position in the British draft agreement:

> The significant problems are the omission of a requirement about non-reintroduction of forces and the vague suggestions of relaxation of restrictions on residence etc. Assuming that we could get the Secretary-General to reinstate a provision about not reintroducing forces, it would be impossible for us to argue convincingly that the proposals were intrinsically unacceptable to us: they are close in wording and very close in substance to what we ourselves proposed on 17 May. To argue that they were unacceptable because we could not hold back military action in the South Atlantic would of course be to invite strong international criticism and, I should have thought, considerable criticism in Britain.

My immediate recommendation therefore is that we should decide in principle to accept the substance of the Secretary-General's proposals. One of the advantages of this would be that it should greatly increase our chances of getting an American guarantee of the Falkland Islands in the interim period.

He wanted to spend the day addressing the Americans on that point while turning the Secretary-General's proposals into something more resembling a Treaty. He accepted that no delay could be caused to military operations and so any deadlines would have to be set in hours.

This idea did not get very far, although there was reluctance to reject it out of hand. The new proposals still represented a significant movement away from Britain's absolute bottom line, and offered no proposals about how to deal with the issue of re-introduction of forces. The most recent Argentine statement was more intransigent than ever. When the matter was discussed in War Cabinet on the Thursday morning it was apparent that there could be no question of holding up the landing because of these ideas. The Prime Minister was adamant that with troops about to land it would send a confusing and potentially demoralising signal if the UK accepted a proposal only for it then to be rejected by the Argentines. While the positive advantages of the UN proposals were understood, they were also incomplete and vague in several respects. So Parsons was instructed to make it clear that the search for a negotiated settlement would not interfere with military preparations and that Britain was not really interested in getting into any textual discussions. The original plan for the release of the rejection notice to the press was to go ahead, with an hour's delay so that Perez de Cuellar could be informed, and a full statement would later be released. Britain warmly appreciated the Secretary-General's efforts but after the Argentine response it was 'clear that further negotiation would be fruitless.'

After Parsons explained all this, Perez de Cuellar reported that he had been seeking to agree with Argentina a better reply to their unsatisfactory response. He accepted that he could not expect Britain to go forward unless he had detailed confirmation that the process was in line with its thinking. The main concern that he had was that Britain proposed to refer to the 'breakdown of the United Nations peace settlement.' Parsons apologised and said he would issue a corrected version. It was necessary, he explained back to London, to distinguish between that round of negotiations ended by Argentina's rejection and the Secretary-General's current efforts. He was very sensitive to the idea that his mediation was at an end. In the Commons in London that Thursday afternoon (20 May) the Prime Minister described the recent history of the negotiations. She noted that the latest proposals from Perez de Cuellar differed in certain respects from the British but also contained proposals that had already been rejected by Argentina. 'Even if we were prepared to negotiate on the basis of the aide-mémoire, we should first wish to see substantive Argentine comments on it, going beyond mere acceptance of it as a basis for negotiation.'

Perez de Cuellar spent the whole day waiting for an Argentine reaction to his aide-mémoire. By 2345 New York time he had still not received one. He told Ros that he had no choice but to inform the President of the Security Council that he could not continue his efforts. Ros had replied that he had been unable to get a response from Buenos Aires. It appeared that with the military pressure reaching a climax the Argentine Government simply could not organise a sensible response. The next day he would inform Ling Qing of his efforts and there would be informal consultations. By the time that the Secretary-General met with the Security Council informally on 21 May to report back on his failed mission the landings at San Carlos were well underway. The immediate proposal, from Ireland, was to call a formal meeting. There were then proposals for this to be in private but the Argentine Permanent Representative killed this idea by refusing to participate in a private session. A public session was agreed for the afternoon. There Perez de Cuellar gave a long, neutral, detailed account of his efforts since SCR 502, followed by Ros who spoke contrasting Argentine flexibility with British rigidity, followed by Parsons who did the opposite. Subsequent statements all asserted a desire for peace, varying in their readiness to apportion blame and call for a cease-fire.

SECTION FIVE

26

AMERICAN SUPPORT

The diplomatic efforts were important not only because of the need to maintain international support for economic pressure and military action and to prevent the imposition of an unacceptable settlement, but also to obtain material support for the Task Force and to prevent Argentina improving its position. In all of this the position of the United States was vital.

From the start of the conflict the Office of the US Secretary of Defense, Caspar Weinberger, had supported the British and had paid scant attention to the delicate line of impartiality along which Secretary of State Alexander Haig trod. No objections had been raised to the use of Ascension Island, and the provision of extra fuel to support the extraordinary British air re-supply effort based at Wideawake base. Intelligence information flowed. Awkward press coverage regarding this support had led Haig to seek to tone down the whole exercise but it had continued regardless. Even before the formal 'tilt' in Britain's favour on 30 April, discussions had been underway on the sort of exceptional supplies the British might welcome should the Americans be disposed to provide them.

Consideration of what these might be was prompted by a visit paid by Henderson, accompanied by his deputy and the Naval and Air Attachés, to Senator John Tower, Chairman of the Senate Armed Services Committee, on 19 April. Tower was strongly supportive of Britain and asked what help was required from the US. Henderson was not actually sure and so he ad libbed: intelligence and air support as the first priorities. As the question was likely to arise again he asked for better guidance. The Prime Minister added that she too would be grateful for views on this issue. MoD's initial response was couched in the most general terms. Ideas went no further than proposing that the Ambassador might aver, as if offering his own opinion, that help with intelligence, including US maritime reconnaissance information, would be most welcome.

Efforts were already underway to get access to more timely intelligence. The main priority here was extended imagery coverage. The Americans explained that the effort the British wanted was probably impractical, and would certainly be expensive both in terms of absolute cost and opportunity cost, in lost opportunities for important photographic targets, mostly in the Soviet Union. Less problematic were requests for clearance for six Stinger surface-to-air missile launchers plus 12 missiles. Special procedures would have to be invoked but Congress need not be involved. By 19 April it was reported that Presidential authority had been obtained to release the Stingers and night goggles. The Americans understood that if Haig's negotiating efforts failed, there would be further requests and they would want to help. US officials stressed the problems that would result if any word leaked out that the present equipment was being supplied. Only the most senior people on either side should deal with this subject.

There were reports that news of British dispositions were getting back to the US through intelligence connections, and this became evident from a report in the *Boston Globe*. This had led to claims that Northwood had been feeding false information to the Americans. When this was investigated it transpired that there had been no routine transmission of information to the Americans on the movement of British service ships. There were inevitably possibilities opened up to the Americans because RN ships made use of US communications, there had to be co-operation on 'water management' relating to British and American submarines and also in general intelligence provision. It was supposed that those American officers involved were under some pressure to report back to their superiors. Britain had passed no disinformation to the American authorities. There was not a lot that could be done about these connections. Any attempt to limit the position of American exchange officers could bring with it severe operational penalties, with serious long-term effects on Britain's intelligence system. Instructions were given to those in contact with American officers that comments should be confined to stressing the firmness of the Government's intentions and its readiness to use force if the need arose and not indulge in speculation about future intentions or plans. No US exchange officers would be serving in areas that would give them access to British operational plans.

The Prime Minister requested on 23 April early consideration of the attitude to take to offers of American assistance should the Haig negotiations fail. The main assumptions behind the resulting paper were that the United States would not commit forces to the hostilities; and that base facilities in South America would not be available to the United States for overt support of United Kingdom operations. Under existing arrangements the United States was providing substantial intelligence support for CORPORATE. The staff paper looked forward to increased strategic, tactical and technical intelligence cover of Argentine strengths, dispositions, intentions and deficiencies which would greatly enhance the prospects for a successful operation. They thought that real-time tactical intelligence would be particularly valuable. The most pressing communications requirement was the provision of secure speech equipment, as communications security needed improving.

It was not hard to generate a wish-list for operational support, short of direct participation in combat, including Maritime Radar Reconnaissance and air-to-air refuelling, particularly for Sea Harriers. At a later date, American air transport support, especially C5A (Galaxy), might be sought while amphibious shipping could greatly assist the transport of any subsequent reinforcements to Ascension Island. Medical support would back-up UK resources, which could be under extreme pressure during intensive operations. Increased US satellite and other meteorological coverage would be of considerable value in operational planning. As for weapons, equipment and material, the high-profile items would be Harpoon for Nimrod; Vulcan/ Phalanx Guns for *Illustrious*; AIM 9L Sidewinder missiles for Harriers, plus some very specific systems for submarines and special forces, as well as temporary accommodation and materials for extensions to the Stanley runway. The detail and ambition in the paper made the Chiefs of Staff nervous. After Leach commented about its wider implications, the sensitivities it raised for both countries led to an instruction that it be withdrawn.

On 30 April, the day of the Reagan tilt, it was assumed that overt US military assistance would be constrained by the terms of the Presidential announcement and that there was little prospect that the US would allow itself to be seen as engaging directly in operations or make ships or aircraft available on a lend/lease basis. The Chiefs of Staff were looking for areas that could be justified on the basis of existing arrangements and where Congressional approval would not be required. The initial approaches would cover intelligence, communications, indirect operational support, logistic support, and weapons, equipment and material supply. Where possible requests for assistance would be processed through normal channels, to avoid duplication and, in the case of weapons and equipment, to ensure that compatibility problems were minimised and full support services were included. A forthcoming NATO meeting provided an opportunity to take matters further forward with the Pentagon. For the moment it was easier to continue to develop wish-lists than to judge which of these wishes the United States would find it possible to grant.

On 2 May Pym and Henderson met with Weinberger, who made it clear that 'we would supply them with everything they needed that we could spare, and that we were able to do it very quickly.'[1] Support from the US Navy was particularly strong, evident in a visit paid by the Secretary for the Navy, John F Lehman, to Minister of State for the Armed Forces, Peter Blaker, on 4 May. Lehman saw few problems with intelligence, communications, logistic support and the procurement of weapons and equipment, and was ready to help accelerate the process if the usual channels for the supply of equipment appeared to be operating too slowly. In addition, he said he would not rule out the possibility of moving US forces, for example, one of the two Carrier Battle Groups currently in the Caribbean, to the South Atlantic as an indication of support. It appears to be at this point that the possible transfer of a US aircraft carrier was discussed. This was probably less definite than later suggested. Weinberger later indicated that the idea had not originated with him, and when asked about it he had said 'sure, no trouble', though he knew it would have been a lot of trouble, as did the British who never took the idea further. As American personnel would not be allowed to enter combat the offer could not really be followed through because the practical problems of training British personnel to take over the running of such a ship were too great.[2]

For the Americans an early resolution of the crisis was vital, as their support for the United Kingdom was 'very corrosive' as regards their position in Latin America, but that might mean accepting the need for even more support for Britain in the short term. There were also cold war benefits if the Alliance could demonstrate to the Soviet Union both political will and professional competence. Lehman also made it clear that after the war the Americans would be looking to more support from Britain for their Central American policies and also a review of the naval cuts proposed in the 1981 defence review.

Nott was to meet Weinberger in Brussels. His brief stressed as 'overriding needs', the provision as soon as possible 'of the equipment which would assist our operations while at the same time avoiding a long term imbalance in our war reserve stocks or long term distortion to our defence programme and priorities.' This could best be achieved through 'the loan or purchase of equipment from existing US stocks or production lines on the basis that any items used will be paid for but any items we do not in the event require will be returned.' In addition, while Britain would 'not wish to make requests which would lead to direct US involvement in the military operations in the Falklands area,' some 'indirect operational assistance away from the immediate operational area, such as maritime reconnaissance and air-to-air refuelling of our planes, would be of great value.' The British did not want to imply that CORPORATE could not be sustained without US assistance but that it would help Britain conduct operations with greater despatch and effectiveness, and bring about the earliest possible resolution of the conflict. Nott explained this to Weinberger and told the press that 'no assistance was needed at this time.'

When Nott wrote to Weinberger, seeking to agree terms – largely to pay only for what was used – he stated that the 'two immediate requests which we have in mind are for some 300 AIM 9L Sidewinder missiles and 2 Vulcan/Phalanx guns.' On the evening of 5 May Lewin met with his American opposite number, General David Jones, Chairman of the Joint Chiefs, and handed him a more detailed list of desired items. Early the next morning Nott again met Weinberger. Weinberger wanted assistance to be as rapid as possible with a minimum of bureaucratic formalities. He proposed that the most convenient arrangement would be for items on Lewin's list to be stored in the UK with only those items drawn from the store being paid for. Nott confirmed his satisfaction with these arrangements. The British list was immediately sent to Washington. On 12 May a text was agreed with the Pentagon. This confirmed the arrangement:

> that would have the United States transfer to US depots, whether in Britain or Ascension Island, such equipment as the UK might anticipate requiring during the conduct of its operations. The material whether pol [Petroleum, Oil, Lubricants], spares, or munitions – would remain under US control until the day the British determine they actually need it. At that point title would be transferred to the UK and payment would be forwarded to the Federal Reserve Bank. It was understood that you have agreed to cover the costs of the equipment that is transferred, as well as of transportation of that equipment. In such cases where a transfer would not be effected, the UK would still cover all transportation costs from and to their points of origination once these are determined.

On 13 May it was learned that although initial indications were that 100 AIM 9L would be made available and investigations were in hand for transportation, a Joint Chiefs Committee was now discussing the matter. A decision on the release of these US assets would be made by noon local time on Friday 14 May. Whatever agreement had been reached at the top of the Pentagon, at the desk level there were misgivings. Officials could not see the need for such items as 100 Sidewinder, with another 200 to follow, plus 200 Mk46 torpedoes, as existing stocks should be more than adequate to meet the threat. Either the British were using the conflict 'to build up our own long term stocks at the expense of American operational stocks' or were 'expending these weapons at a high rate with little success.' If the latter was the case the Americans wanted to know why. As one officer told British staff in Washington, there were already enough missiles with over a 50 per cent hit probability 'to knock down the whole Argentine air fleet.' With a maximum of three enemy submarines why were 200 additional Mk46 required?

The explanation for the Sidewinders was straightforward. There was no intention just to build up stocks. Britain's intention post-Falklands Crisis had always been 'sale and return' with unused weapons returned to the United States. The AIM 9L version provided a major improvement. Experience to date indicated that Argentine tactics were such that opportunities to fire were outside of the 9G envelope. The initial draft of the telegram for Washington also explained that in the face of potential massive Argentine air activity at the time of any invasion, we are 'working on a worst case assumption of 25 per cent loss of ships and aircraft in total operation'. Lewin minuted 'For God's sake don't tell US that!'[3] The two Vulcan/Phalanx anti-missile gun systems (for *Illustrious*) were delivered on 14 May; the first 100 Sidewinder missiles were delivered directly to Ascension Island the same day.

During May Britain procured some $120m of US material made available at very short notice (often 24 hours) and frequently from stocks normally earmarked for US operational requirements. This equipment had included the Sidewinder missiles, Vulcan/Phalanx, 4,700 tons of airstrip matting for Stanley airport once it had been recaptured, conversion of the SS *Stena Inspector* for use as a repair ship in the South Atlantic, Shrike missiles for use by the Vulcans, helicopter engines, submarine detection devices for use by the Sea King helicopters, temporary accommodation on a large scale on Ascension Island for British forces, Stinger ground-to-air missiles, as well as ammunition. Once procured they were flown immediately to the United Kingdom or to Ascension Island. Both Haig and Weinberger took a close interest in the processing of these requests, with Weinberger intervening to ensure that the larger and more difficult items were made available immediately at whatever the cost to US forces' requirements.

Weinberger set the tone from the beginning, but the arms relationship was reinforced at each stage by the thick web of personal contacts between Britain and the United States, with Lewin and his US opposite number, General David Jones, working together as old friends. Before British requests were made the likely response could be checked by an informal transatlantic phone call, based on deep knowledge about what was likely to be found in the US inventory. The Pentagon managed to dispense with some fifteen stages in the normal authorisation process, with daily meetings in Weinberger's office which came to be described as 'What-can-we-do-for-Britain-today meetings'. Where necessary State Department support was gained by going directly to Laurence Eagleburger. Weinberger described the process as a 'federal express' system.[4]

Satellites

With no pretence at even-handedness any more, there was no risk that any help would be given to Argentina – with one exception. In mid-April the Argentines asked the US authorities to conduct photographical reconnaissance over the Falkland Islands. On 21 to 23 April NASA duly programmed the civilian LANDSAT satellite to take the required pictures. Data was then fed by real time to the earth station in Argentina. Argentina possessed the ability to process the data by themselves as soon as it was transported by truck to Buenos Aires. The processing time could vary from several hours to two/three days. Late on 22 April Argentina then asked NASA for coverage of South Georgia on 24 and 25 April and of the open ocean to the west of the Island on 25 and 26 April. They asked for this on the basis of an established agreement with NASA. When the British queried what was going on, Haig explained to Pym while in Washington that the US had no alternative but to honour the agreement. On the other hand as far as he knew photographs taken from LANDSAT were not capable of providing intelligence of military significance because of their very low resolution.

While Pym acknowledged that this had to be a US decision he hoped some way could be found not to give the material to Argentina. Whatever the quality of the material they would be doing the Argentines a favour. The British were told that the Americans expected to have by early the next week data for the Argentines but they undertook to provide the same material to Britain. It was also confirmed that the past quality of pictures of this area had been poor. Then, in the light of British concerns, the Americans decided to use technical problems as a reason for not giving satellite material to Argentina. This was a decision that the Americans did not want to leak. The British view was that the longer the delay the better. While there was some disposition to support the American view that the picture quality was poor, there was concern that if the weather cleared then the fleet would show up and this would provide valuable intelligence. Representations were made in Washington that there would be grave consequences if a British ship was damaged as a consequence of information provided by the United States.

The issue then died down until 5 May when the State Department again informed the British Embassy that the Argentines had requested LANDSAT coverage of open sea areas from 7 to 12 May, then the Falkland Islands, and lastly South Georgia. Again Britain asked that the requests be rejected, but it was explained that US policy with LANDSAT was that this was a civilian programme without intelligence of military value. If a request was refused on the basis of Britain's allegations then the whole civilian space programme would be put at risk as it would encourage the view that LANDSAT had 'an espionage function, and no country could then allow such photography over its territory.' The British insisted that their overwhelming priority was the safety of their ships. They:

> could not underline strongly enough the incomprehension and resentment if the Argentines were given this intelligence in present circumstances. It would also convey an impression of easing of pressure at exactly the wrong moment.

As technical problems had been used as an excuse last time, why not do so again?

In London there was some anxiety lest too much bad feeling be created on this matter. Ships would only show up if conditions were ideal, unlikely at that time of year, and if there were sufficient concentration of vessels. But it was a risk that Britain would prefer not to take. It was also obvious that the Argentines had only put in a request because they did believe that they could obtain useful information. Although the State Department was inclined to agree that the Argentine request might be resisted because of the clear intelligence purpose, the next the Embassy heard was that the photography had taken place over the 7–12 May period and that the material had been transmitted to the Argentines. The Embassy was promised copies as soon as they were obtained. These revealed little.

Argentine arms acquisitions

The most substantial external help that Argentina was likely to receive would be additional supplies of weapons. The Defence Intelligence Centre (DIC) had been set up to provide continual coverage of all Argentine military activities, capabilities and intentions to serve both MoD and JIC needs. Within this Centre a number of specialist groups (for example on Argentine merchant shipping) were tasked to collect, collate and assess all relevant intelligence. The Arms Traffic Cell concentrated on Argentine attempts to procure arms and related equipment from foreign sources. The cell would be consulted before any assessments were made regarding Argentine arms supplies. It faced a constant battle to make sense of a mass of rumours, hints and innuendoes. Of particular concern was Exocet. Intelligence received suggested that on 13 May the Argentines had three AM39 Exocet missiles left. Aerospatiale confirmed that they had supplied only five such missiles to Argentina. The further five ordered by Argentina had not been delivered, nor those ordered by Peru (assessed between two and six). There was also technical advice that the sea-launched Exocet missile could not be converted for air launching. A check was done of the global distribution of the missiles. Sixty-five had been delivered to Iraq, although 45 had been used in the war with Iran; twelve had been delivered to Pakistan; thirty had been ordered by South Africa but none had yet been delivered as was the case with the ten ordered by Qatar.

Then came reports that four had been ordered by Peru and were due to leave France on 12 May by sea, with the probability that they would end up in Argentina. The French felt unable to cancel the delivery because they were under contract to Peru and the penalty clauses could lead to damages for late delivery, and they also did not want to lose credibility as arms suppliers and imply a lack of trust in Peru. They also took end user certificates seriously: Peru would know that if they disregarded the conditions they risked a complete cut-off of French arms supplies for the future. Yet there was evidence that Peru would pass the missiles on to Argentina and so, as a Peruvian Naval transport shuttled from one French port to another during May, constant reasons were found to prevent their release. It eventually became clear that the French had no intention of letting them get to Peru, and thus possibly to Argentina, while the conflict was underway. If they had been allowed to make the long sea journey to Peru, the British Government would have had to face interesting questions about whether they could be allowed to arrive.

There were regular reports of intermediaries acting for Argentina attempting to set up deals wherever they believed Exocets might be found.

According to Aerospatiale, 100 out of the 186 missiles ordered for export had been delivered. It was known that Argentine representatives in Paris were not only urging the Peruvian Naval Ministry to have the Exocets that had been ordered shipped to Lima by air, but were also dealing with, and promising money to, anybody who claimed access to Exocet supplies, including a dubious Panamanian-based company promising ten Exocets for $9.5 million. More probable go-betweens were Peruvian and Venezuelan contacts. None of these deals was consummated. John Nott later recalled the 'remarkable world-wide operation' to prevent Exocets being bought, and how he:

> authorised our agents to pose as bona fide purchasers of equipment on the international market, ensuring that we outbid the Argentineans, and other agents identified Exocet missiles in various markets and covertly rendered them inoperable, based on information provided by the French. It was a remarkably successful operation. In spite of strenuous efforts by several countries, particularly the Israelis and the South Africans, to help Argentina, we succeeded in intercepting and preventing the supply of further equipment to the Argentineans who were desperately seeking re-supply. [5]

A few missiles might have been available on the private market but MoD assessed the number was likely to be small. Consideration was even given to a British purchase of any missiles currently for sale if this appeared the only way of preventing them falling into Argentine hands. Of the other potential sources, the British Ambassador to Islamabad was assured on 30 May by a Director General at the Pakistani Foreign Ministry that they could account for all 12 they had received and it was inconceivable that they would part with any. Another eight had been ordered in 1979 and might be ready or nearly ready for delivery. The Pakistanis had been very co-operative in the matter and the cell assessed that this source could be ruled out. In addition, 35 for Qatar had been ordered in 1980 and surprisingly none had been delivered. Nonetheless none appeared to have illicitly left the factory despite the embargo. Iraq had been at war with Iran for nearly two years and it seemed unlikely that they would willingly part with any of their Exocets – let alone to Argentina. When approached by British diplomats they had been most co-operative and assured them that none would go out of their sight. One hundred had been ordered within the previous five months, but as few would have been held in stock, none was thought to have left for Iraq. However, one report of 26 May from a 'regular and reliable source' stated that nine had been captured intact by Iran and then offered to Libya and Argentina. Other reports had mentioned similar quantities as being sought by Argentina. It could not be ruled out that this number was on its way to Argentina.

There were at times reports of various other arms transfers to Argentina: that Brazil was to sell two or three Bandeirante maritime patrol aircraft, that

Venezuela was making available aerial fuel tanks for some Argentine Mirage, allowing them to increase their range and loiter time, and that Peru was being asked for five Mirage fighters. While Peru was under pressure to help Argentina, it seemed that President Belaunde had resisted this and other requests for Peruvian military support, including aircraft and helicopters, although there was evidence of some low level military assistance, such as aircraft spare parts and the loan of technicians. There were a number of indications that South American countries, particularly Peru, Venezuela and Brazil, would make substantial military assistance available should attacks be made on the mainland of Argentina. Ecuador supplied a large stockpile of artillery ammunition, later rationalised to Britain on the basis that the material was largely unserviceable.

Israel had in the past sold small patrol boats and second-hand French aircraft to Argentina, and was also conscious of the substantial Jewish community in Argentina and generally good relations with Latin America. There were numerous intelligence reports implicating Israelis, some with governmental connections, in attempts to sell arms to Argentina. Most reports involved the transmission of weapons, and parts for existing systems, through third parties. When confronted with these allegations by the British Government, Israeli diplomats denied them vehemently. The Israeli Ambassador reported that 'not a single military item had been supplied to Argentina since a decision taken by the Israeli Government early in the crisis' before the first demarche from the British Government, and that it was under pressure to reverse this from Argentina. The Israelis complained about increasingly being asked to check on rumours. Yet they were told that the sources were actual reports, requesting clothing, communications equipment, night vision sights information, and aircraft fuel tanks, and that the main reason for a lull in supply was because of Luxembourg closing down an intermediary operation. British troops entering Stanley at the end of the war came across Israeli equipment. Irritation with constant British pressure was one factor behind Israel's call on 24 May for a cease-fire. Another was probably just mischief making: by using language echoing western statements at times of conflict in the Middle East, Prime Minister Menachem Begin was saying that Britain had no more right to give Israel advice on how to secure its northern borders than Israel had to advise on the Falklands. The Jordanians, who were generally supportive, made the point that application of the principles of self-determination and the inadmissibility of occupying territory by force should be applied to the Middle East as well.

Libya had emerged as a major supplier of arms to Argentina, with an air bridge between Tripoli and Recife, Brazil, using B707–320C aircraft of the Argentine Air Force and Aerolinas Argentinas, which allowed direct flights carrying substantial loads. Up to ten flights were made, probably including Matra 550 Magic A-AM, SAM 7, ATGW, Mirage spares and fuel tanks, and ammunition. DIS was particularly concerned that Exocets or other anti-ship missiles might be carried. Clearance was given to the flights to transit Moroccan airspace, much to British irritation.

Consideration had also to be given to British sales to Latin America, especially those items that might find their way to Argentina. Care was taken because Britain did not want to be seen to be reneging on contracts or taking any provocative action. The normal response was foot-dragging (for example on the despatch of spares for Canberras to Venezuela), or explicit suspension of any talks (for example over torpedoes to Brazil) for the duration of the conflict. The question of the supply of naval equipment to German shipyards for installation in four frigates destined for Argentina was made more difficult because any compensation issues for the German yards would be affected by any disruption to the work. At any rate the British-made engines had already been delivered. Even more worrying, had the work been more advanced, would have been the six Corvettes and two submarines also ordered from Germany. In this case it was decided to rely on assurances from the German Government that the frigates would not be delivered to Argentina, either during the immediate crisis or subsequently.

27

CHILE

One of the most controversial of all questions relating to the Falklands Campaign was the degree to which Britain benefited from close co-operation with Chile. This question became particularly salient during 1999 when General Augusto Pinochet, who had been Chilean leader at the time of the Falklands, was arrested in London on the basis of a request from Spain for his extradition to face trial for crimes against humanity. Baroness Thatcher was especially energetic in his defence, not least because of his support for Britain in 1982. Pinochet himself spoke of how:

> When Argentine forces occupied the Falklands in 1982, I instructed my government to provide, within the context of our neutrality, whatever assistance we could to our friend and ally. I considered this a matter of Chile's national honour.[1]

The logic of co-operation was clear. Both countries had territorial disputes with Argentina and in both cases Argentina was behaving in an unacceptable manner, ignoring attempts at arbitration in the case of the Beagle Channel just as it had resorted to armed force in the case of the Falklands. The main bar to overt co-operation was Chilean reluctance to contradict hemispheric solidarity and British concern about the tension between its claim to be acting on behalf of democracy and Chile's dismal human rights record. Chile also had to reflect on Argentina's superior military strength when assessing the risks of supporting a British military build-up. For these reasons it was inevitable that any co-operation would be covert.

The possibility of co-operating with Chile was raised right at the start of the crisis. The military could see that Chile was the only possible source of a forward base close to the Falklands. Simonstown in South Africa, once a British base, had facilities that could ease the maintenance, repair and replenishment problems associated with a lengthy deployment but it was nearly 4,000 miles distant and would be even more politically unacceptable. When, on 2 April 1982, the first assessments were made of likely South American responses to the Argentine invasion the importance of Chile was soon highlighted. Questions started to be posed about whether Britain should request facilities and how to respond if they were offered by Chile. An early indication of a positive Chilean attitude was an offer to delay the hand-over of HMS *Norfolk* to the Chilean Navy, which was to be completed on 6 April. This was not seen as being that helpful because of the small size of the RN crew and her low stores, poor communications and lack of weapons. On the other hand, the Royal Fleet Auxiliary *Tidepool,* a tanker, also due to be handed over on 7 April, was fully manned, and if a full fuel load could be purchased from Chile, it would address problems of replenishment for the Task Force. The Chileans agreed to this and, after refuelling at Curacao, it sailed on 14 April to rendezvous with the Task Force and played a key role in the South Georgia operation.

There was one intriguing possibility for direct military action dependent upon co-operation with Chile. Tierra del Fuego, an island at the southern end of Argentina, was divided into western Chilean and eastern Argentine provinces. The Argentine province was sparsely populated but included an oil field producing 24,000 barrels per day and two airfields, at Rio Grande and Ushuaia. If it could be seized this would be a blow to Argentine national pride, providing a bargaining counter in any negotiations while at the same time making available useful military facilities that might otherwise be exploited against British forces. The island appeared at first sight to the Chiefs as an easier military objective for the Task Force than the Falklands. It would be less well defended and geared more to an overland attack from Chile than a British attack from the sea. There would be a reduced risk of civilian casualties and a greater element of surprise. A successful landing would, however, first require intensive operations against the Argentine Navy and land-based combat aircraft. And then, even if a British force could be established on the island, it would become vulnerable to attack from Argentine aircraft operating from mainland airfields. This then argued for covert operations by special forces to inhibit Argentine air attacks. So while the short-term risks appeared more manageable the longer-term problems were greater. The politics were also problematic. The collusion between the two countries necessary to make the operation work would cause a political storm.

Any airfield and port facilities could accelerate the build-up of British forces, ease support and re-supply problems and mitigate the Argentine geographical advantage. Against this there was a risk of becoming over-dependent on this help, lest it be withdrawn if regional pressures on Chile became irresistible. So, in general, proposals for co-operation concentrated on the acquisition of intelligence. In particular the Chiefs were keen to explore the possibility of basing the Nimrod Maritime Patrol Aircraft (MPA) in southern Chile. Otherwise this could only operate from Ascension. Targeting information from Nimrod would greatly increase the effectiveness of the SSNs that would soon be arriving in the South Atlantic. It could be described internationally as a reconnaissance aircraft, because it lacked offensive capability against shipborne or land-based fighter aircraft. Its Searchwater radar would allow it to stay safely outside the missile engagement zone of enemy warships.

Exactly how such co-operation might best be explored was a delicate matter. The British Ambassador in Santiago understood that he had to talk directly to the Chilean military. It was assumed that a quid pro quo would be required. Here thoughts turned first to the sale of Hunter aircraft, which had been of interest to the Chileans for some time. At the same time, the Chileans had a strategic interest in a quick British success against Argentina, as they were concerned that otherwise they would be attacked 'within three weeks' and were already raising military preparedness to meet this contingency.

It seemed unlikely from the start that facilities would be made available for British warships and aircraft engaged on offensive operations, because of the risk of retaliation by Argentine forces. Although the JIC took the view that Chile would agree to unarmed air reconnaissance Nimrod aircraft operating from Chilean airfields, the Ambassador was more cautious. For example, it seemed unlikely that a southern airfield would be made available. One that had been mentioned – on the island of San Felix – was still 1,900 miles from the area of operations, unless the Nimrod overflew Argentina. It would only be of value as the main operating base so long as more southerly airfields could provide refuelling facilities.

Ministers were unsure about how far links with Chile should be taken. In addition to the obvious political risks, the Foreign Office saw a:

> practical risk that if we put too many demands on the Chilean military and intelligence authorities … we may put at risk Chilean political agreement for those items of intelligence or practical co-operation on which we set most store.

There was also caution on the Chilean side, reflecting a growing awareness that Chile's wider continental interests would be better served if 'she does not stick her neck out too far'. The media appeared generally sympathetic to Britain, although public opinion was torn between satisfaction that arrogant and aggressive Argentina might at last be getting its comeuppance and anxiety about Latin American blood being shed. In Santiago there was still a real fear that if the Argentines were allowed to get away with this aggression at low cost, they would turn on Chile next. It was possible to envisage a hardening diplomatic strategy in the Beagle dispute, seeking every opportunity to amend the Papal proposal, as part of a generally much more forceful policy in the Southern Cone. Removing Britain from the scene while gaining control of access to the two ocean passages would give Argentina increased influence over the Antarctic territory.

At the same time the Chileans were understandably anxious that any hostilities between Britain and Argentina should not spill over their long and exposed border. If there was evidence of conniving at British intelligence gathering then Argentina might suddenly turn on Chile. Argentine troops had been concentrated in Rio Gallegos and Comodoro Rivadavia in excess of anything which might be needed for the Falkland Islands. To avoid pushing the situation beyond prudence, Ambassador Heath argued for carefully framed requests, certainly avoiding asking for anything that would involve either RAF or Chilean aircraft demonstrably flying into Argentine airspace from Chile. Otherwise there was a danger that 'any short-term military benefits will be outweighed by the long-term political consequences'.

The Chiefs were cautious for another reason. Would offers of assistance be honoured? Heath was confident that there would be no reneging. Very few were in on the secret and considerable efforts had been made to keep the Foreign Ministry ignorant, but President Pinochet appeared to support co-operation. There was a desire to bolster British resolve, but only in private. In public the stance would be more neutral. If any leaks occurred or rumours of Chilean co-operation with Britain began to circulate they would be at once denied. From the Government's point of view it also seemed best that as little attention as possible was given to co-operation with a regime widely condemned in Britain.

Some consideration was given to the possibility of sending a high-level emissary to Santiago to assist the Ambassador, but it was decided to leave the task to the man on the spot, who had the advantage of knowing well the local personalities. There might be a stronger case for sending a senior officer if high-level military advice was needed. In the event this requirement was met by the arrival in Santiago on 14 April of a new Air Attaché, a highly experienced officer with good Spanish. He became a key figure in all military contacts with Chile over the next two months.

In return for help Chile was looking for arms transfers. These were first discussed by FCO and MoD officials on 13 April. The most straightforward was a long-standing request for six Hunters. These had been earmarked and four were being disassembled at RAF Abingdon. A request for a further eight Hunters was problematic because most airworthy aircraft had been financed by the United States and the sale would need to be authorised by Congress. However, seven suitable aircraft had been identified, three of which were flying while the remainder were undergoing 'deep repair'. The Foreign Office had no political objection to a further sale. Blowpipe would be supplied over the coming two weeks. A more intriguing possibility had opened up out of a long-standing wish on the Chilean part to buy ex-RAF Canberra photographic reconnaissance aircraft. They had been offered three refurbished Canberras, but the price was judged too high. The RAF had subsequently offered to lend the Chileans some of Britain's own Canberras and to help them with the land survey tasks for which the aircraft were originally sought. This was the position before the invasion of the Falklands. After the invasion a proposal was made whereby one or more Canberra aircraft would be sold and flown to Chile by RAF crews who would train Chilean crews while carrying out photographic reconnaissance from an air base in southern Chile. The transfer of the aircraft would be on favourable terms, probably at roughly half the price originally quoted. This got as far as the aircraft and crews being selected and put on standby, but Chile turned down this scheme as it was certain that the aircraft would be identified and possible that they would be shot down.

Consideration was then given to supplying Canberras at a more attractive price, as a normal sale, but with some quid pro quo in terms of intelligence. On 16 April it was agreed that Canberras, and supporting Hercules, all with Chilean markings, would be sent on loan, trial or for purchase. The Hercules could be described as being purchased by Chile for her own transport force although Britain could take them back once the war was over. It was not possible for Nimrods to be sent as it would be too incredible to outside observers that Chile would be buying them. Nimrods would, however, be permitted to fly anywhere in Chilean airspace for transit and to land in an emergency. A radar would also be taken. Lastly, details of Argentine surface fleet movements would be made available for onward transmission.[2]

On 18 April, Lewin minuted Nott on progress. His main priority was timely intelligence on Argentine forces. Distance and geography had so far proved an insuperable handicap to providing Britain's own in-theatre intelligence gathering. Use of a suitable Chilean airfield would therefore give Britain a new and much needed capability. Because of the urgency of this requirement, there was little time to lose. Lewin, therefore, recommended that two Canberra PR9 aircraft and two Hercules were despatched to Belize that day, to be on station by 24 April, and that two additional Hunters along with other equipment should also be supplied. In turn Nott minuted the Prime Minister and his War Cabinet colleagues, recounting the background to these proposals and stressing the importance of proceeding. He noted that the Foreign Secretary had already agreed to the Canberra proposal in general terms. If questions were asked in public, Nott considered 'that the safest course is to treat all of these deployments as straightforward sales business.' The Chileans had been interested in buying Canberras for some time, and had bought Hunters in the past.

RAF crews would operate two Canberras in the South Atlantic for a hand-over period. A Hercules support aircraft would be deployed with them to a Chilean airfield. The Chileans wanted to announce its contract to buy Canberra reconnaissance aircraft, but London preferred to keep all collaboration covert, because of the need to ensure that any initial reconnaissance of the Falklands was kept secret as well as the potential political fallout in Britain. Initially the operation went according to plan, and by 26 April two Hercules had arrived in Santiago in disguise. The Canberras were now expected to arrive in Chile just after dawn on 30 April.

At this point wider political considerations intruded. First there was the collective resignation of the Chilean Cabinet, but this seemed best explained by economic issues, and had no connection with the Falklands dispute. Effectively this was no more than a cabinet reshuffle and the Cabinet was at any rate quite separate from the ruling Junta, made up of President Pinochet and four senior military officers. Then came information that the Pope had summoned the Chilean and Argentine Ambassadors to the Vatican to a private audience to urge them to reach a definitive solution to the Beagle dispute by 26/27 April. The Chileans were sending a senior figure from the Ministry of Foreign Affairs who would be flying to Rome immediately, but they did not think that the Argentines would show sufficient flexibility to enable a solution to be reached. Because of this, Pinochet had asked the commanders-in-chief to exercise restraint and not to sanction any activities which might be construed as provocative by Argentina for the time being. Heath surmised that, unless the Pope actually gave them an ultimatum, the Argentines would try to keep this exercise going for some time by hinting at minor concessions. The Chileans were also getting anxious about the possible impact on them if Argentina decided that the game was up over the Falklands and turned on Chile 'to reclaim national honour'. Argentine forces were still in positions threatening to Chile and on high states of alert, with the possibility even of Peru and Bolivia joining in an attack in the north. They were watching the Argentine Junta closely for signs of disunity, and any temptations to mount a diversionary attack against Chile. It was noted after the recapture of South Georgia that satisfaction at Argentina's discomfiture was balanced by apprehension that Chile should not be drawn into the conflict. Pinochet told the Press that he was 'concerned' by events in the South Atlantic, and the Foreign Minister ambiguously commented 'we sincerely regret that calls for peace have gone unheard'.

As the South Georgia operation was moving to its conclusion, the vote at the OAS was becoming imminent. The Chilean MFA had proposed a cautious stance but had apparently been overruled by Pinochet. Chile would abstain on 27 April, even though this would be regarded as an 'unfriendly' act. This reflected a growing conviction that Galtieri and his Government would not survive the conflict and that the internal crisis would preclude a foolhardy attack on Chile.

On 28 April, just after the OAS vote, Reuters reported what was said to be an official statement by the MoD spokesman in London to the effect that Chile had given its permission for RFA *Tidepool* to be detoured to join the British Task Force in the Falklands. Later it transpired that the issue had come up at an MoD news conference where it had been stated, in response to questions, that it was not known 'whether money has exchanged hands' but was known 'that the sale was going forward but the delivery has been postponed with the agreement of the Chileans'. The questions had arisen from a BBC TV report on 27 April that *Tidepool* had recently refuelled at

Curacao. Chile wanted an immediate denial: *Tidepool* had not been received by the Chilean Navy at the time she was ordered to turn around. The FCO's view was that it would be unwise to volunteer a formal denial as that could just create more interest. By this time the Chilean Government had published its own official denial. Chile believed that the question had been planted through a French journalist as a way of putting pressure on Chile after its OAS abstention, as the Argentines would have known of the ship's situation for some time.

The Chileans now warned that as soon as the Canberra operations were detected by either Argentina or the Press, the RAF men (18 officers and 24 SNCOs) who had arrived ahead of the aircraft would have to leave Chile immediately and thereafter not talk about what they had been up to. On 27 April, the *Daily Star* reported that:

> Britain's task force in the air is getting stronger by the day in prepa-
> ration for a battle for Port Stanley. Last week Phantom fighters
> secretly flew to southern Chile, via Ascension Island, from an RAF
> base in Suffolk. With them went six giant RAF Victor tankers to
> refuel them in the air ... Defence sources say the Phantoms will be
> more than a match for the Argentinians' 50 French Mirage fighters.
> Britain has quietly paid the Chileans for allowing our aircraft to use
> their vital base at Punta Arenas. The price – eight Hawker Hunter
> aircraft. The unmarked planes left RAF Brize Norton on Sunday
> aboard an American civilian Boeing 747.

The Embassy in Santiago was immediately approached by reporters, including the BBC, for comments. The details of the story were so untrue that Heath wondered whether this might even be deliberate Argentine disinformation. 'No doubt you will wish to consider whether a word on this in the right place might discourage similar trouble making.' Chile also denied as 'totally without foundation' reports claiming that RAF 'Phantom' aircraft would be allowed to land and refuel at Punta Arenas. A British statement was issued on 29 April. Heath now warned that Argentina would be seeking to discredit Chile's professed neutrality on the Falklands issue by more inspired questions asked through friendly journalists and he proposed the most carefully framed disclaimers.

By the afternoon of 29 April, the Canberras had still not received clearance from Chile. There had been yet another newspaper report, this time from Reuters, about Britain having permission to use aviation facilities in southern Chile. More delay saw the Ministry of Defence's enthusiasm for the operation beginning to wane, and plans were made to withdraw one Hercules. By the time that clearance was finally received for the Canberras to arrive on 3 May, the prudent course appeared to be an early departure of the Hercules and all personnel while Canberras were delivered in a slower time to Chile. The Chileans would have liked to have kept the Hercules, and were anxious to get the two Canberras as quickly as possible.

So by the start of May the first six Hunters were being delivered, an additional two were being sorted out, but no decisions had been made on any more (and a further 20 were apparently required). Two Canberras and spares, then in Belize, were on offer to Chile. The low price had been offered originally in anticipation of reconnaissance flights over the South Atlantic before the Task Force arrived. This had not proved possible and there was no longer a British requirement. Chile had expressed an interest in a radar to be based close to the Argentine border. This was on offer at a bargain price with support on its operation and maintenance. By the middle of May a draft letter of intent had been sent regarding the sale of the two Canberras, together with a quantity of spares and ground support equipment, and negotiations concerning the extra two Hunters had been concluded. In due course the RAF expected to be able to release further Canberras, although these would have to be sold at full market price.

In an interview conducted in 1999 but published in 2002, General Fernando Matthei, the Chilean Air Force Commander-in-Chief in 1982, described how he arranged with a 'secret agent' the provision of intelligence to Britain in exchange for military equipment, notably Hawker Hunter jet fighters, a powerful radar, and Canberra aircraft. Matthei recalled that after the war 'we kept the planes, the radar, the missiles. They received timely information, and we were all happy.' He also claimed that Pinochet was not fully informed of the deal, 'so in case the operation was discovered, he would be able to claim that he didn't know.' He described the creation of a well protected underground command centre in Punta Arenas, from where information on Argentine air movements from all sources was sent back to Northwood using a satellite communications system. Matthei's daughter had, in fact, already reported some of this in a letter to the *Sunday Times* at the height of the Pinochet controversy, noting correctly that her father's main contact had been an RAF wing commander (rather than a secret agent), and stressing the importance of Chilean monitoring of Argentine air activity, with information passed on via a direct satellite link to the Task Force. Through this means the South Atlantic fleet was given warning of any impending attack, enabling it to take countermeasures.[3]

Progress now began to be made elsewhere. It was now agreed that a Nimrod reconnaissance aircraft would be accepted at the airfield on San Felix, a remote island off the coast of Chile. From San Felix the aircraft could make several very valuable sorties, refuelling at night in the Chilean air base at Concepcion on the mainland coast, and then flying in Chilean airspace and out into the South Atlantic. The aircraft would be able to collect useful information from outside the cover of Argentine radar, and transmit it to the Task Force. The Nimrod would be supported by a VC10. The first sortie was flown early on the morning of Sunday, 9 May, a second on 15 May and a third two days later. Limited but significant information was obtained. By 18 May there was concern that it would be too risky to continue with the flights, as this would probably lead to the blowing of the whole operation, serious political problems and jeopardy to any future operations (not just with Nimrod). Woodward wanted the aircraft to fly on the nights 19–21 May, just in case the Argentine Carrier Group was at sea during those crucial days, but the Chilean desire to see this mission concluded was firm.

By 14 May it had become apparent that the Chilean request for a further 20 Hunters was proving difficult to meet: even sending five would be detrimental to the RAF. Nor was there any readiness to lease Hercules to the Chileans, although there was one supporting existing activities in Chile and it was allowed to stay for the time being, for Chilean use when available. Meanwhile, the Chilean connection was starting to attract attention in Britain. On 24 May the Prime Minister and other senior ministers received identical letters from MPs connected to the Chile Committee for Human Rights. Britain did not have at the time an embargo on arms sales to Chile, and the sale of the Hunters had been reported. To the standard letter a standard reply was drafted:

> It has long been our normal practice not to discuss details of Defence Sales business, and I am sure that you will understand that it would be quite inappropriate for me to depart from this policy on the basis of speculative press articles. But I can say that we have long-standing defence sales business with most South American countries and there is no embargo on Defence Sales to Chile. However, you can be assured that we do *not* supply to any country equipment which in our judgement might be used for internal suppression. I do not think the sale of equipment which does not fall within this latter category can be reasonably seen as an endorsement of Chile's internal policies. You will also be aware of our more general policy towards Chile, which is to have normal relations with her consistent with our interests, but in doing so to leave the Chilean government in no doubt that their record on human rights, like that in many other countries, has given rise to deep concern in the UK.

Britain did not wish to endorse Chilean human rights policy, and it also wanted to be sure that it was not implicated in any direct Chilean action against Argentina.

During the course of the war the presence of a strong Chilean force on the border had helped Britain if for no other reason than that it tied down two of Argentina's top Marine Infantry brigades: Chile had not suddenly disappeared from Argentine threat perceptions.[4] As the war drew to a conclusion there was some concern that Chile might seek to take advantage of Argentina's difficulties. A major exercise involving some 10,000 men appeared to have been put together in something of a hurry to start in early June. Heath suggested that he might be instructed to call privately on some senior Chilean figures to make it clear that Britain did not intend to be a party to any 'border incident' between Chile and Argentina. Although the FCO was still of the view that precipitate Chilean action was unlikely, Heath was allowed to make the contact to find out what was going on, providing he did not express any views on the substance. Heath reported back the Chilean view that reinforcements in the south had been deemed necessary because of uncertainty about Argentine intentions, especially if they held off Britain, but that now this was unlikely and Britain would be back in the Falklands, they were more relaxed and were standing down some units.

28

THE INFORMATION WAR

Good news, bad news and no news at all

Sir Frank Cooper had first briefed editors from the major media organisations on 7 April. He explained the concerns of MoD about the release of harmful information, and also warned about Argentine misinformation, such as exaggerated statements about the build-up of their forces on the Falkland Islands. MoD found the response positive, with some relief from the editors that there were no proposals for legal controls. But the concern at the possible fettering of editorial freedom was evident, particularly when it came to speculation about military intentions. Might this not, it was suggested, be as confusing to the Argentines as it was helpful? There was no way to stop the foreign press speculating. MoD suggested that as a general criterion, editors should imagine what they would want to see broadcast or in print if they had a son aboard the Task Force. It was implicit that the fact that this meeting had taken place would not be publicised.

As the Task Force sailed south with little happening operationally, defence correspondents had spent their time finding titbits of news to fill the newspaper pages and television time that the Falklands was soon commanding. MoD's policy was to help them by providing hard but approved news, while guiding them away from 'their wilder excesses', but the bar for approval was high. Nor was informal guidance helped by sole reliance on attributable briefings. Ian McDonald, who had favoured this approach, soon proposed to Nott that he should hold a daily non-attributable briefing, possibly with the FCO, together covering diplomatic and military moves. Even so the restrictions on operational news were going to mean that interest would have to be sustained with some relatively innocuous items. Nott remained resistant, despite pleadings from Ingham that it was unwise at such times to remove normal services from the press.

Cooper continued to urge restraint on the editors. He met them again on 20 April and gave examples of stories that MoD found worrying, such as the size of the amphibious force and reports on departures of ships from Ascension, and requested restraint over the reporting of military assistance provided by other countries to British forces, taking editors into his confidence over help from Senegal and Portugal. For their part the editors appeared generally satisfied with the existing arrangements but noted the variable standards of censorship, and the unfilled market for 'local boy' stories particularly in regional radio programmes and newspapers. Stories were still getting through, largely by using American sources. On this basis there was concern about detailed accounts of intelligence cover available to the Task Force in the *Sunday Times* on 18 April and even at Cooper's meeting he had been asked about reports emanating from the US about the possibility of an operation against South Georgia.

The haphazard procedures created tensions. Editors complained regularly to MoD about the treatment of correspondents while MoD worried that the level of speculation about British plans was greater than they had hoped, albeit sufficiently varied and conflicting to give Argentina little help. Later Michael Nicholson's disclosure of the name of the SSN which had sunk the *Belgrano* (which he had received from London) caused irritation as a breach of the rules, while a story in the *Daily Express* on 3 May referring to SBS teams was judged to be putting men at risk. Northwood grumbled regularly about irresponsible leaks and speculation, to the point where some senior figures considered removing the embarked press from *Canberra*. Clapp and Woodward came to their defence, acknowledging that useful intelligence was being disclosed by the media but largely not from the correspondents with them. They 'were controlled and therefore restless. But not a real nuisance.' They noted the foolish pressure they were often under from editors (for example to get down to South Georgia in 24 hours to interview troops). In general their reports were good for morale and helped keep public opinion on side, and resentment would be created if they were removed.

When Cooper met with the editors on 6 May he had a rougher ride than before. They claimed they were getting more news from Argentina and the United States, important information was being withheld and there were hints of manipulation, MoD statements were slow and unclear and couched in evasive and ambiguous language, and they were bereft of pictures or films. If only Argentine images could be obtained they would be the ones that would be used. Cooper in turn complained about reporting of assistance from third countries (which could put this in jeopardy), speculation by 'armchair strategists' about future operational plans and intelligence methods. A slightly different issue was the harassment of families of Service casualties.

Chastened by this encounter, Cooper accepted that the situation was unsatisfactory. There was still, he believed, a fund of goodwill but MoD was losing ground. If it was to be regained, the organisation must be more positive and respond more quickly. He argued for emphasising repeatedly the major successes, cosseting the defence correspondents and giving them more technical detail, and lifting the lid off Ascension, one area of considerable dispute. Reports from the Task Force needed to be regular, full even if unspectacular, and more should be done to squash rumours quickly. He understood the need for pictures and his staff were trying to find means of getting equipment to the Task Force. There were, he noted, no pictures as yet of South Georgia. Any that had been taken were coming back by sea.

McDonald also tried to warn the Chiefs of the dangers of losing the public relations war by forfeiting press goodwill. He got them to agree to a more positive attitude to the rapid release of factual information, routine reports from the Task Force Commander so that his staff were better informed, and more specialist background briefings on matters of topical interest, including the nomination of an approved panel of experts, who would be given background briefings and then be able to make authoritative comments when required. By the time this was established the media already had their favourite experts in place and so the panel had little impact. In their discussion on 7 May, having received a signal on the dissatisfaction of the correspondents embarked with the Task Force with restraints placed upon the release of their reports, the Chiefs considered it illusory for the correspondents to believe that they would receive, and be able to release, the first news of any incident involving the Task Force. They did however recognise that by and large the press was behaving responsibly and that the problems the correspondents were facing should be discussed with their editors.

For the tabloids the cause was both patriotic and just. By and large they rallied behind the flag. Yet even those elements that were ready to accept a role as cheerleaders for British forces were often exasperated by the lack of responsiveness from MoD's public relations team, both in London and in the Falklands. They felt that censorship was too heavy-handed, that the definition of operational significance was set too wide, and that the Government effort was basically unprofessional, unsympathetic to the demands of deadlines and the appetite for hard information to fill the pages and the airtime they were ready to devote to such unusual and historic events. If the hard news was not available then, the media argued, the Government should not be surprised if the space was filled by rumour and speculation.

Studies after the war confirmed that the official minders had taken a broad interpretation of their role, with whole stories scrubbed, rather than offending passages bracketed, and alterations made for reasons of 'taste and tone' (such as 'too many emotional adjectives') rather than security. Of 627 dispatches received by MoD during the conflict, 139 took more than 8 hours to be cleared, by which time the stories had often been broadcast. The crassest example of censorship cited was of a military PR officer who, faced with the sentence 'Only the weather can hold us back now', and aware that the weather had been identified as an operational factor, deleted it and suggested as a substitute 'politicians'.[1] The *Observer* journalist Patrick Bishop later complained about a report that suggested that the Task Force commanders had to take some blame for the *Sir Galahad* disaster being held up for four days on the pretext of 'inaccuracies' that he might want to correct, by which time it was out of date. Furthermore, from 21 May, after the landings, the vetting was taking place in London as well as the South Atlantic.

The dozen pressmen with the carrier group became extremely cross with their treatment. They were told little and what they tried to report was cut and held back, with potential scoops lost because news was first released by London. They had to check their reports with the Information Officers aboard almost all the ships carrying correspondents. The complaints were made known to Woodward who became irritated in turn at what he saw becoming a time-consuming distraction from his main responsibilities. One problem was that the PR man who had been allocated to him had been forced to withdraw at Ascension because of bad health and the Task Force commander lacked professional advice.

The problems this could cause were soon evident. Woodward held a briefing on-board *Hermes* for correspondents on 18 April, the majority of whom had by then joined the Task Force. The main aim at this time seems to have been to make them aware of the necessary restrictions and only talk about substance to the extent that it might unnerve Argentina. The ships now assembling near Ascension, they were to be told, would soon be ready to move to the Falklands area. *Hermes* would be presented in a determined war-like posture. After South Georgia, the message became confused. In an interview Woodward, aware of the potentially wide audience for his remarks, decided to be 'rather more sanguine – hopeful – than my personal feelings and knowledge might have suggested.' He was reported as telling correspondents that 'South Georgia was the appetiser. Now this is the heavy punch coming up behind. My battle group is properly formed and ready to strike. This is the run-up to the big match which, in my view, should be a walkover. I'd give odds of 20 to 1 on, to win.' Woodward's own recollection is that he was thinking mainly of encouraging those under his command, and that what he had actually said, after stating the odds, was that 'frankly, I'd really rather be given a walkover'.[2] One can see the two alternative interpretations of the word 'should'. As a result of this interview:

> I was advised by satellite communications verbally in straight English to tone down some of my opinions ... So in my next interview I did, like any good disciplined officer, obey the last order.[3]

This time when asked whether the war could be long he said 'it could last a few months which could seem like a long time' and when asked if people could get killed said 'there is bloodshed in most wars. I doubt this will be an exception.' The message was now that the Commander had promised a 'long and bloody' affair. So it was hard to hit the right note, even when not being very specific.

On 5 May, after some hectic days, he had further problems to report. There were tensions that arose when 'things are hot.' The officers were busy and the press wanted copy:

To imagine that we can possibly be bothered with political ... and security details when heads are being blown off nearby is to fail to make the mental switch from peacetime to war. While commanding officers can and will do their best, it can only be unreliable. Some other answer will have to be found.

In the War Cabinet the focus remained on operational costs rather than presentational gains. The problem, Thatcher observed to the War Cabinet, was that 'disclosures or even speculation in the media could assist Argentina's military efforts and thus endanger British lives'.

On this matter there was never a meeting of minds. Regular consultations with the media took place, and there was even agreement on sensible practice and actual progress, including the setting up of a television relay station at Ascension, but the management of the flow of information and the timing of announcements provided regular sources of friction. So difficult had relations become that when the *QEII* was due to sail, the director of public relations was reluctant to allow any more correspondents to embark, especially as there would have to be a scramble for a few places. Better he thought, and Bernard Ingham from No. 10 agreed, to have an official team preparing stories that could be released from London.

Policy was being made up in reaction to problems as they emerged. One officer complained in mid-May that there was widespread concern about 'information policy – or lack of it':

It is the fact of modern communications not the type of conflict which makes this essential. We can lose a war today quite as easily by failure of information policy as by failure of military competence or political will.

An effective policy would help rally and maintain public support, sustain the morale of the forces and erode that of the enemy while boosting international support. At the same time, it was noted, this policy would need to deny the passage of intelligence about political and military plans and capabilities to the enemy. The importance of the issue meant that policy should be approved at the highest political level and translated into clear instructions for its execution by all those involved, and not just left to the PR organisation to implement. 'If my thesis is correct, urgent action is now needed to retrieve the situation ... We have only nibbled at the problem so far.' It was surprisingly late in the day for documents such as this to be circulating among the senior commanders.

Eventually Nott was also lobbied by the editors. He soon identified the most pressing problem as the failure of the normal chain of command to keep those responsible in MoD informed in as speedy and full a way as they required for effective public relations action, and insufficient and inconsistent supervision of the embarked correspondents. By 10 May it was agreed that a signal should be sent to the Task Force explaining the importance of maintaining both national and international support through the media in the hope that officers of the Task Force would come to appreciate that the public relations battle was important to the overall success of the operation. Incident reporting had to improve and care had to be taken not to censor copy on grounds other than operational security. It was better that this be done on the ships rather than in London, because journalists sharing the operational dangers would appreciate the needs, while any censorship in London would lead to a loss of international credibility and accusations of media manipulation. This lobbying also led Nott to relent on unattributable briefings. Other than the conversations between Cooper and editors of the major news organisation, there were no background briefings for defence correspondents until 11 May. Lewin by now also accepted that the matter had not been well handled. Belatedly on 17 May he approached Cooper with a view to establishing within MoD an operations cell to handle public relations matters. Eventually on 18 May a News Release Group was established in the MoD.

Ingham's sense of the political aspects of the presentation of news, which included urging that more representatives of the media travel with the Task Force, also produced another source of tensions with more operational considerations. He wrote to Cecil Parkinson, who had a notional responsibility for these issues, on 10 May indicating the difficulties. Some of the correspondents had sent signals to their editors asking to be brought home because they were not being allowed to do a proper job. MoD had not given the issue a high enough priority and its procedures were too cumbersome. On 12 May a special group chaired by Parkinson met to consider how improvements might be made. It only met four times but it was later credited with clearing the air and improving co-ordination.[4] That day Cooper again met the editors, this time with Lewin present, and could report the measures that had been taken. Fresh instructions had been issued to the Task Force stressing the need for rapid reporting of operational incidents. Background briefings were now being provided, and black/white still photographs would soon be transmitted. He thanked them for restraint on reporting assistance from third-party countries and in not harassing the families of Service casualties. Lewin was able to add some hard fact by reporting the shooting down of two Argentine A4 aircraft one and a half hours earlier.

The situation changed again as the war moved from sea to the land. The Royal Marines and the Army, with twelve years of experience in Northern Ireland behind them, took the view that the only way to work with the press was to ensure that they were looked after by capable officers who enjoyed the confidence of their commanders and so could gain the trust of the journalists and make sure that they were properly informed. From this perspective, sending public relations officers – the 'minders' – was bound to fail. As civilians they often did not always understand things military and, lacking credibility with the press, lost control of them. The press had been desperate to get ashore with the landed forces, even those assigned to the Carrier Battle Group, and this meant that the Navy felt that their exertions during the last ten days of May were not fully appreciated. Some commanders, such as Clapp, believed themselves – and therefore their staffs – forbidden to talk to the press, which meant that junior officers were often talking without being fully aware of context. Even Northwood was not fully in the loop because the PR chain of command did not follow the operational chain of command. MoD information officers had direct access to MoD and bypassed CINCFLEET, who was not even told that a news release group existed in MoD until well after it had been established.

At a meeting early in June all members of this particular group expressed their 'extreme dissatisfaction with the current state of affairs'. One member wrote:

> In the last week or two the difficulties which we had experienced in the past about timely reports of incidents had become magnified. There had been hardly any occasions when we had been able to manage our PR on any important incident by considering in advance how we would present the news. In almost all cases we found ourselves reacting either to news on the tapes or from correspondence with the Task Force when we had no collaborating reports from our own people. As I write I have as yet seen no report of the incidents at Goose Green which resulted, we are told, in the deaths of some Argentine prisoners of war.
>
> I know that at the Chiefs of Staff meeting this morning, some concern was expressed about what was described as a provision of gratuitous information about our own losses to the Argentinians. But it was pointed out at the Group that the military representatives and DS11 are there precisely to exercise judgement about what should or should not be released on operational grounds. It is certainly not dominated by the PR world.

Stories were sent back to London by MARISAT and shore satellite communications. Black and white still pictures were sent by FAX, then fitted in selected ships. A second attempt to engineer the transmission of live television pictures came to nothing. Fieldhouse decided on 1 June that the use of the SCOT system for this purpose was unacceptable for operational reasons, as it was putting too great a load on an already overloaded and vital satellite communications system. Increasingly the flow of information from the South Atlantic reflected the close relationships that had developed between members of the media and the Task Force, which meant that command channels through London were often bypassed. MARISAT transmissions went directly to the broadcasting company in parallel with the MoD, allowing for voice reports to be broadcast on TV and radio while the information was still being circulated in MoD, even though the broadcasters had been asked to consult first before making use of any material. As a result, the Chiefs complained, the Defence Operations Staff were unable to brief them properly, and the Defence Public Relations Staff were 'unable to exercise an effective and balanced control'.

Content

There were issues of content as well as process. Politically the most serious of these, because it suggested a degree of equi-distance between the belligerents, involved a spat with the BBC. The Corporation had begun to irritate senior figures in the Government by mid-April. Of particular concern were displays of 'balance' that had Argentine and British claims given apparently equal credibility, though these concerns were not backed up when videos of television transmissions were examined. They revealed remarkably little disinformation, with appropriate attention being drawn to the use of Argentine material. Some MoD officials thought that the BBC and Independent Television (ITV) had given tremendous support by making available all their tapes, including material not transmitted, and were nervous lest excessive criticism of the media put at risk this unofficial arrangement. For its part the BBC was irritated by evidence that it was not always being told the whole truth (or the reasons why it was not getting the whole truth) and was also anxious when its independence was being put at risk, even to the point of disliking to be told that it had to share its film with other broadcasters under the pooling arrangements.

It also insisted that while it could not be insensitive to the public mood, it had to acknowledge those sections of the public unhappy with Government policy, as well as look after its own reputation for objectivity and impartiality. The Director General was conscious of pressures to conform to the national interest: but the issue of what constituted the national interest he thought to be less than clear-cut. The best way to get round the competing pressures, he thought, was to avoid provocation and aim for accurate and 'non-adjectival' reporting. If Buenos Aires made a claim they felt obliged to report it. Indeed, BBC news editors had sent express instructions on 26 April to their journalists not to use 'our' when they meant 'British'. This came after concerns had been expressed about a news headline containing the phrase 'We have warned the Argentines to stay clear of our fleet'. This was seen to risk the BBC's detachment and suggested that it was directly involved, as if the BBC had done the warning. The Editor of News and Current Affairs, Radio, warned that such use could make the BBC sound as a 'mouthpiece of government'. 'We are not Britain,' he explained, 'we are the BBC', so 'our' should be reserved for their own correspondents. The editor of Radio News told his staff that talk of 'our forces' was 'contrary to BBC style' and could give 'the impression that we are taking verbal sides – which we don't even do against (to quote Secretary of State Haig) "a bunch of thugs"'. Not all in the BBC management were happy with this. At least one senior executive observed that taken logically this policy might see 'British' removed from the BBC's title and that there was a risk that the Corporation would be seen to be putting itself above the crisis.[5]

The Prime Minister's exasperation was that such reports appeared to carry the same weight as statements from London. On 11 May the Prime Minister told the Commons that 'I know how strongly many people feel that the case for our country is not being put with sufficient vigour on certain – I do not say all – BBC programmes'.[6] The issue was discussed in Cabinet the next day, when the view was taken that it would be better if any criticism came from the general public, lest it be claimed that the Government was attempting to undermine the Corporation's impartiality. It was also noted that public opinion was still robust. Efforts to turn the public against the BBC were unlikely to succeed, as the rest of the press was ready to defend the Corporation against the Government; and the BBC were well placed to mount a campaign against alleged attempts at censorship. Polls generally gave the BBC high marks. One poll gave it 39 per cent for providing the best coverage of the war, ahead of all other news organisations, while in another about the same percentage said that the Corporation 'stood up best for Britain in reporting the crisis', again ahead of other organisations.[7]

Instead a more positive approach was adopted. The Government hoped that the extreme shortage of photographic material would soon be eased, and that 'care should be taken to derive maximum advantage from the release of pictures, which were expected to be available soon, on the arrival of Argentine prisoners in Ascension Island and on the repossession of South Georgia'. The first film from South Georgia was also due to reach London soon. The following day it was noted by the War Cabinet that: 'further difficulties had arisen over reporting arrangements for media representatives with the British Task Force'. The War Cabinet therefore contended that it was necessary to make it clear in public that no alternative arrangements would be possible.

It was not only the disclosure of information that mattered to the Government but also the constructions put on that information. It was bothered when the constructions were undermining, pleased when they were supportive. A *Sunday Express* story about Vulcan bombers being re-converted for in-flight fuelling with the capability of reaching the Argentine mainland led the Prime Minister to regret the publicity being given to Ascension's role while at the same time to observe that, although there was no intention of attacking the mainland, it might do no harm if the Argentines came to fear the prospect.[8] Later the Chiefs were not at all worried if it was reported that the Task Force could use Stingray or that RAF Harriers were being modified to enable them to use Sidewinder. Conveying any impression at all required some hard information, and ruling certain topics out could be frustrating for those who wanted to generate public support and add to the pressure on Argentina. The Air Commander, for example, was becoming irritated at the lack of publicity being given to the RAF role in what was largely a naval show. 'More had been written in Washington about Nimrods than has been written in the UK!'[9]

On 1 May, when fighting began in earnest, the Chiefs of Staff wanted to keep answers to queries as low key as possible, not even admitting the role of Vulcan aircraft. Curiously, they were bothered by the BBC report of the first Harrier operations, although Brian Hanrahan's line – 'I counted them all out and I counted them all back in' – might be said to have lifted the nation's spirits. Lewin wanted Cooper to represent to the BBC that such broadcasts were damaging. It was the case that this indicated to the Argentines that, although 601 Air Defence Group had damaged two Harriers, their air defence had failed,[10] but that had to be set against the presentational advantages of accurate reporting of an operational success, especially when Buenos Aires was claiming British losses.

The key test was the release of the news of the loss of *Sheffield*. Many in Northwood and the South Atlantic would have liked the news delayed: they wanted to trap Argentine forces coming to see what had happened. As always they were reluctant to give the enemy the satisfaction of knowing that they had cut into British capabilities. While this view may seem unrealistic in a media age, in operational terms it had merit. The Argentine airmen lacked a means of bomb damage assessment, and one way they could be sure of a hit was if this was confirmed by the British media. Indeed one source has suggested that if Britain had not announced the loss of *Sheffield* 'the Argentinians would have likely concluded that their Exocets were still malfunctioning and called off further attacks'.[11] Then there was the question of telling the families of those lost and injured, rather than having them worry after an announcement on the news.

But delay was impossible. A casualty reporting system had been established only as the Task Force sailed. Details of who was on board any ship at any time were bound to be incomplete, given the regular transfers of personnel, and it was difficult to be sure of the names of survivors. News was likely to come through from Argentina and, given the stir it had caused, out of the Navy. MoD did not want to be in a position of confirming a leak or a bad Argentine story, so McDonald took the initiative and reported the loss dramatically at a press conference that began at the start of the evening news on 4 May. Phones soon started ringing, the anxiety of the callers aggravated by the fact that the casualty information cell was not yet in place, and would have had no information to pass over even if it had been. Later stories of naval families in Portsmouth being harassed by reporters for their reactions did not help military–media relations. With the news out, Lewin's concern was that it was now necessary to counter the assertion that the attack on *Sheffield* had exposed a fatal flaw in Britain's naval defences. On 6 May, accepting that this allegation was both damaging and inaccurate, the Prime Minister asked that some counter be found. These were problems for the Government yet the speed – and candour – with which the announcement was made helped the credibility of later MoD pronouncements, particularly among foreign news agencies.

The presentational aspects of policy also had to take account of a great variety of more parochial agendas that influenced the information flow and content around Whitehall and Westminster and on to the media. These might have more to do with promoting the glory of a particular branch of the services, or calming an anxious backbench MP, than an overall information policy. Thus on 1 June the Chiefs observed that 'despite measures to improve security of information and control over reports, leaks were still occurring, not always from military sources'. As we shall see when discussing the post-landing operations, there was rarely a consistent media management policy and, arguably, because of the range of pressures facing the Government, nor could there have been.

Deception

A Special Projects Group (SPG) was charged with developing plans for deception and psychological operations. It had a small permanent staff, and part-time departmental representatives from various parts of MoD and close links with SAPU in the Cabinet Office and CINCFLEET's planning staff. The task of the group was to publicise Britain's capability, the effectiveness of its weaponry and its overall determination while, at the same time, acting 'to denigrate, discredit and demoralise the Argentines.' More specifically this would involve misleading Argentina as to the timing of attacks, the intention behind them and the quality of the intelligence assessments that had informed them. A major effort would be made to demoralise the Falkland Islands garrison. Some material could be sent out using official channels, such as the FCO and secret services, 'aimed at exacerbating Argentine inter-service rivalries, discrediting the junta and its members and drawing attention to economic problems and the dangers of Soviet adventurism'. It was understood that the BBC World Service could only be asked to carry hard fact and could not be used for psychological operations. There is no evidence that Fieldhouse ever gave these operations a high priority. A minute of 30 April, for example, observed that Fieldhouse did not share the enthusiasm of the SPG for a visit to Northwood.

Some early ideas for deception were gathered for the Chiefs of Staff meeting on 8 April. These did not betray great thought, and to some extent depended on the quality of the Argentine intelligence operation in Britain, as only then would misleading information of British options confided to a Sunday newspaper's defence correspondent be picked up. They might also notice suggestions that Australia and New Zealand might get directly involved, or advertisements for certain TA specialists, ostentatious orders for maps of false areas, movements of units to unknown destinations, dummy refuelling probes on Nimrod and increased activity at bombing ranges for Vulcans. A considerable amount of effort was put into persuading Buenos Aires that 'Argentine facilities on or close to the mainland are not safe.' The basic proposition was that 'if the hand of HMG is not revealed we need not be inhibited in suggesting courses of action totally opposed to our real intentions.' This appeared to fit in with Woodward's view that the carrier group should give the impression of heading toward the Argentine mainland in order to provoke movement of Argentine air units to more northerly bases. He also wanted to give the impression that the carrier group had an amphibious warfare capability so that a landing was possible from the group's arrival in the TEZ.

One proposal was to use the rumour channel in order to spread alarm, principally among insurance brokers, that Britain might resort to mining Argentine mainland waters. This developed after a report on BBC news on 10 April that the Argentines had mined the waters around the Falkland Islands. The ongoing Iran-Iraq war had demonstrated that even rumours of plans for mining had an immediate effect on insurance premiums for merchant shipping as well as the morale of crew members. The SPG therefore proposed publicising the idea that 'The British have a capability to mine the coastal waters of Argentina, and that this option is now under consideration.' It might be noted that the Argentine Navy relied exclusively upon shore-based facilities for repair, replenishment and maintenance and were therefore highly susceptible to mining operations, and also that the Argentine economy relied heavily on maritime trade. As this was not suitable material for an official spokesman, especially if further questioning was to be avoided, then the idea might have to be 'floated unattributably into the insurance market.' Although the military accepted the idea, the Foreign Secretary was opposed to doing anything to suggest that Britain was prepared to take action against the Argentine mainland or its ports, which was, apart from anything else, incredible in terms of available capability.

MoD was also cautious about taking this sort of activity too far. In part this was because it might jeopardise relations with the media. MoD had been trying to convince them that they would be playing 'the whole thing as straight as we can.' Confidence would be lost if the media felt that it was being used to relay false information. Another problem with alarming Argentines about British capabilities was that it could encourage the wrong reactions. This was the response, for example, to SPG proposals in late April to play up the purchase of Sub-Harpoon, a US anti-ship missile, and its deployment on British SSNs. At this time the Navy did not want to frighten off the Argentine Navy because it wanted to get a chance to cripple it early on in the hostilities. Other proposals to leak information, on the aerial refuelling capability of Nimrod, were also resisted by those responsible until they were sure that they were true.

Another high priority item was the preparation of leaflets for distribution over the Falklands. During the first phase, when there was still uncertainty about the future course of the campaign, three items were produced: a safe conduct pass, a message of inevitable defeat, which took the form of a message from Woodward to General Menendez, and a reassuring letter to the civilian population from the Governor. Later on extra items were produced, announcing the recapture of South Georgia ('Your valiant companions at arms recently on South Georgia have returned to their fatherland'), and the opening of Radio Atlantico del Sur (RAdS), discussed below. Although 12,000 copies of each leaflet were produced and reached *Hermes* in time for the landing, unlike the leaflet rounds that could be fired from the big guns of the world wars, a similar capability did not exist for modern field guns so they were never actually distributed.

After the conflict General Jeremy Moore professed himself to be unimpressed by efforts at psychological operations. He saw them as required not only to refute and discredit hostile propaganda, but also as an offensive weapon that might have helped reduce enemy morale and combat efficiency, promote dissidence and defection and support cover and deception operations, especially given the physical conditions under which Argentine troops were subsisting and their evident concerns about British capabilities. As there was no Psychological Operations group with the Task Force he was unaware of what had been attempted or achieved. He was aware of Radio Atlantico del Sur, but not of its programme content, target audience or effectiveness.

Project MOONSHINE

A proposal came forward from the SPG in late April to establish a means of broadcasting to the South Atlantic independent of the BBC. The idea was to provide truthful reports to the Falklands garrison about their predicament as well as pass on information to islanders and even instructions prior to an assault. The codeword was MOONSHINE. In contrast to BBC's Radio 4 type service to a wide Latin American audience, this alternative would be targeted at a 'lower social level to appeal to soldiers, families and those concerned with mainland base facilities' with 'ethnic music'. The news, drawn from international coverage, would be entirely on Falklands matters. It would broadcast for four hours each day. The BBC was prepared to provide help and advice so long as it could publicly distance itself. The station would use a transmitter based at Ascension, which would be requisitioned from the BBC under Clause 19 of the BBC's Charter. It would broadcast on a frequency as close as possible to the existing Argentine service, offering optimum reception in winter months and 'allocated to a minor third world country whose protests may be safely disregarded.' It would be called Radio Atlantico del Sur (Radio South Atlantic) and, somewhat optimistically, 'would seek for as long as possible to avoid any confirmation that it is British sponsored.' The cost was put at approximately £1,900 per week, going up to £4,000.

Bernard Ingham, the No 10 Press Officer, was unimpressed by the idea of playing 'downmarket dirty propaganda tricks through a requisitioned transmitter with the objective of sapping the morale of the Argentines.' The new station would have to compete with the BBC's established reputation and would become known as propagandist. Indeed it would suit the BBC's reputation to expose it. 'We would be a lot better off,' he suggested, 'if MoD put as much effort into ensuring a prompt PR response to South Atlantic events as it apparently puts into dreaming up moonshine.' This was written on 10 April, when Ingham suspected the project to be dead. Nonetheless, the War Cabinet decided on 2 May to ask the FCO to investigate what more needed to be done to step up the quality and quantity of broadcasts to Argentina and the Falkland Islands, and by 12 May the project was sufficiently developed for a paper to go back to the War Cabinet.

By this time the BBC's Spanish Service to South America was being received with approval by a growing audience, as was the 24-hour World Service in English, although an attempt was being made to jam it. The FCO approached the Voice of America (who broadcast in Spanish to Latin America for some five-and-a-half hours a day) to draw their attention to this problem and urge them to use the maximum amount of factual material about the Falkland Islands and British military operations. The Falkland Islands Service was also broadcasting daily and could be received along with the World Service. The Chilean authorities were also being asked to encourage their media to carry more British material.

This meant that Radio Atlantico del Sur could have a more military objective:

> maximising the use of radio to persuade Argentine troops (particularly conscripted troops) currently occupying the Falkland Islands to surrender with minimum resistance at the time when British troops land to re-occupy the islands.

During the first phase of its operation it would establish credibility, build up an audience, and work to increase the sense of isolation in the target group. After the invasion it would encourage Argentine troops to hesitate before firing and consider surrender. It would not attempt to demean or diminish loyalty to the flag, or argue against the sovereignty claim, or attempt to create dissension between officers and ranks, or even make excessive reference to the hardships caused by inadequate clothing or shelter. Instead it would refer to the long-standing friendship between British and Argentine peoples, the lack of training of the conscripts compared with British troops, the physical isolation of the Islands and its weather, lack of medical facilities, fear of British special forces, and disillusion with the Junta. While presenting itself as 'being neutral and apparently impartial,' it would not carry any Argentine claims for losses of men and equipment unless verified by British sources. The obvious objections were that the BBC might find it difficult to distance itself from this station, the Government would be rapidly identified as engaging in propaganda, and there could also be criticism that a frequency had been poached. By now the cost had gone up to £15K per week. It was also realised by this time that it would be futile to attempt to keep secret the British involvement.

The project was approved on 18 May and the first broadcast was made late the next day, just before the landing. It was announced as a means of giving the Argentine garrison accurate information on events and of world opinion, thereby reducing dependence on 'wildly inaccurate Argentine reports'. The news reporting would be 'strictly factual'; the station would 'not indulge in propaganda'. The statement stressed that no assistance was sought from the BBC or other established media. An initial broadcasting team had been recruited and trained, operating under the title of Media Assessment Team (MAT). In addition to a civilian station manager, a number of Spanish-speaking service personnel acted as announcers/broadcasters and also as translators, script writers and typists. A Military Editor had the final responsibility for ensuring the content of the broadcasts conformed to MoD guidelines. Two professional civilian journalists were employed as news editors to prepare the bulletins. The project lasted until 15 June, by which time 47 broadcasts had been made, three hours each evening between 2300–0200Z and an hour in the morning between 0830–0930Z.

The BBC monitored the station and were, unsurprisingly, unimpressed with its '[E]xtremely chatty, commercial radio style, bordering on vulgar.' All aspects were deemed unprofessional, with literal translations of English terms and grammatical mistakes. The judgement, which was not unique to the BBC, was that it was 'banal, weary and amateurish, surpassing sometimes the limits of good taste.'[12] There were Argentine attempts to jam the broadcasts but they seem to have been largely ineffectual, and probably cost more than the modest £40,000 the whole exercise cost the British taxpayer. There was also some anecdotal evidence that the broadcasts bothered the Argentine command. Some civilian transistors were confiscated to prevent Argentine conscripts listening in and it was reported that the Argentine military chaplain on the Islands had told his parishioners that it would be a mortal sin if they did so. (This may have had something to do with his daily morning broadcast coinciding with that of Radio Atlantico del Sur.) At one point the Argentine press agency was closed down for a few days for mentioning casualty figures drawn from this source. Other than that there were occasional indications that it was being listened to in Latin America, but its actual effect was hard to judge.

SECTION SIX

29

ENFORCING THE
EXCLUSION ZONE

During May a consultant astrologer, Peter Clark, issued a press release, which he sent to the Prime Minister. It is evident that she read it, for she corrected the grammar, but it is not clear whether she was perturbed by Clark's advice that her chart showed she would not enjoy a diplomatic solution or unqualified victory, and could look forward to disarray with her colleagues. Woodward's chart was bad for the coming weeks and Fieldhouse's not much better. The reasoning might have been dubious but, as with most such predictions, the gloomy conclusion could well have been reached by other means.

The first few days of May had brought home the realities of war. Both sides had been bloodied and had become conscious of the impact of military operations on the perceptions of the international community. Both were prepared for the next stage of the conflict but neither was quite sure what this would involve. Both supposed that it was likely to end with an attempted British landing on the Falklands and that the intervening days should be spent preparing for that event. The British had set a preferred date for the landing but were frustrated by the reluctance of Argentine forces to do battle. If the Argentines conserved their resources for the landing then the risks of the landing force being caught at its moment of greatest vulnerability would be severe, perhaps too severe.

The concept of operations

Woodward's mission, as stated in the planning directive signalled by CINCFLEET on 27 April, was 'to prevent enemy operations in the TEZ', in order to cut off supplies to the Argentine garrison, discredit the Argentine claim to sovereignty, provoke Argentine naval and air forces into action and to provide effective local sea and air control for the main landing. Enemy operations in the TEZ were now few and far between: this was not because the enemy was unable to conduct them but because he chose not to conduct them. The pre-programmed next step was to land on the Falklands, otherwise why bring along the amphibious force? There was not much time, however, to undertake the preparatory work for a landing – investigating the beaches, exploring the terrain on which fighting might take place and acquiring intelligence about the location and quality of Argentine positions, and their logistical arrangements. If Argentine forces continued to be held back it might not be possible at all to achieve the clear-cut air and sea superiority that had been assumed to be an essential precondition for a landing.

These considerations argued for more time, but delay caused its own problems as the over-worked ships and aircraft of the Task Force began to show the strain, and as the weather deteriorated. Even if it were possible to land, the deteriorating conditions could make the actual movement onto the beach and then out toward the Argentine positions slow and hazardous, hampering the effort to get ashore all the stores and fuel required. By sending 5 Infantry Brigade the British had added to the pressure on themselves, as it lacked its own beach landing capability. If it were to join the battle it would be wholly dependent upon the ability of 3 Commando Brigade to establish a beachhead that could receive them. Neither holding back nor advancing forwards appeared as attractive options. Returning to the UK was out of the question.

The events up to 5 May had not engendered a great sense of confidence in London. The political storm, and the intensive diplomacy, that followed the sinking of the *Belgrano* combined with the shock of *Sheffield*'s loss to undermine the resolution that had been acquired by the end of April. Firm decisions on the next step remained pending. The paper on options that had been tabled for the Chiefs of Staff Committee on 1 May was seen more as an aide-mémoire, requiring continual updating, rather than as a guide to action. It was not yet ready to be submitted to Ministers. By 6 May there was a revised paper setting out the military options, graded in ascending order of politico-military impact. Altogether 14 were identified. The fact they had not been narrowed down was in itself a sign of some uncertainty. A number using Special Forces were psychological in method or more aggressive in intent and could only be supplementary. Other options were largely irrelevant, such as repossession of the South Sandwich Islands, although militarily this would be straightforward so long as the weather held. Others, such as enforcing the Total Exclusion Zone, appeared vital whatever then followed. The Argentine garrison could be harassed from air and sea on the basis of available capabilities while a blockade could be viewed as part of the early preparations for an eventual landing. The land options began with the limited aim of establishing a secure military presence on part of the Falklands without attempting to evict the Argentines, which risked not bringing the issue to closure, and moved to the full and rapid repossession of the Falkland Islands, using both brigades, which risked heavy casualties and battle damage.

The more dramatic changes in military policy carried high political risks. Unrestricted attacks against Argentine naval units at sea, attacking Argentine mainland targets from the air, landing in Southern Argentina (Tierra del

Fuego), co-operating overtly with Chile, and mining or blockading main-land Argentine ports might lead to more serious negotiations and would enhance the chances of achieving other forms of military success. These would, however, be operationally challenging, politically controversial and could well result in adverse international reaction. One internal commentator, accepting that the options paper was not a set of recommendations but a guide to political discussion and decision, warned that some of the more drastic proposals 'involve the immediate loss of all political credibility and support throughout Latin America':

> South America is a region which has contrived to avoid general warfare (that is, involving the Armies, Navies and Air Forces of a number of states) for well over one hundred years; and they do not particularly admire our propensity to tumble into hostilities at the drop of a hat. The most hated country in South America is, or was, the United States; we had just about managed to live down the fact that we are so closely linked to them ('yanqui' and 'ingles' are the same word), but we have contrived in a few days to recover our old position at the top of the list of public baddies.

The Army and RAF remained anxious. The Chief of Air Staff expressed concern that he had yet to see from Fieldhouse an adequate concept of operations, certainly nothing that would allow the Chiefs to advise the Government on the feasibility of its implementation. Nor had they been given the concept for follow-up operations to an initial landing, although they had asked for one. If they were going to be asked to assess the prospects for a successful landing, they needed far better intelligence than had been gathered thus far. The unease was reflected when Lewin visited Northwood on 7 May to discuss the concept of operations with Fieldhouse. It was concluded that, for the time being, the blockade should be tightened, aircraft on the ground attacked and landings by special forces continued. Detailed planning for SUTTON, the landing operation, continued in greater depth and a separate planning cell was established. If a landing was a step too far then the only serious military alternative was to stay with the blockade in the hope that the plight of the garrison would oblige the Argentines to seek a diplomatic way out.

The risks with this option were different but still troubling. They required that the islanders shared the Argentine suffering, while the amphibious force was held back as if the Government was just waiting for something to turn up. All the time Britain's own military – and probably political – position would be weakened through wear and tear and pressure to bring the whole affair to closure. For the moment, keeping up the pressure on the garrison seemed to work best with the retention of the landing option, as it might oblige the Argentine Navy to take risks to get through relief.

Helpfully, the Junta had done itself no favours in the size and distribution of its forces on the Falklands. Visiting the Islands on 22 April, Galtieri agreed with his local commanders[1] that the British were most likely to land near to Stanley, in which case the Argentine reserves were inadequate. It was also agreed that a further regiment of infantry was needed, although the local commanders stressed the need to address the logistical issues that the extra men would raise. On his return to Buenos Aires, and without consultation, Galtieri decided to send an extra brigade. From 24 to 29 April, the three days before the TEZ became effective, the Patagonia-based III Mechanised Infantry Brigade, under Brigadier-General Omar Parada, moved to the Falklands. It had been intended that they would redeploy to reinforce defences against an opportunist Chilean attack. These troops had no experience of Falklands-type weather, lacked the right equipment and were bound to strain the support systems. Then they were sent to the more distant parts of the Falklands. The new arrivals added to the strain on the already stretched logistic resources, made worse by the tentativeness with which the EZ had been breached by merchant ships prior to the arrival of the Task Force and the limited capacity of the air bridge to Stanley airport. By attempting to cover all British options, Menendez had dispersed his reinforcing units. Argentine forces were thus deployed in West Falkland, where much of the new brigade was sent, in the Darwin area, where a 'Strategic Reserve' was created, and around Stanley where established defences were strengthened. The dispersed garrison was heavily reliant upon support helicopters and small craft. There was insufficient logistic support to sustain a protracted defence. These created possibilities for British forces of reducing the impact of much of the garrison, if the West Falkland force and the 'Strategic Reserve' could be neutralised.

The intelligence assessment for early May, which was broadly correct, put the garrison at 9,600 army personnel, of whom about 7,600 were on East Falkland and the remainder on West Falkland. There were in addition 1,700 Marines and 700 naval personnel. The largest group, six battalions, was in the Stanley area, and was under the command of HQ X Infantry Brigade. The bulk of the field and air defence artillery was also deployed in this area. On West Falkland two battalions were deployed under the command of HQ III Infantry Brigade. The deployments on West Falkland were less than the British anticipated: two battalions of III Infantry Brigade (together with its HQ staff), one (together with half the artillery group) at Port Howard and the other at Fox Bay. A third group was a battalion-sized strategic reserve, based 10 km north of Darwin.

The logistical headache facing the Army units was manifested in about two weeks of supplies. On subsistence rations, eked out, they could last until 18 May. Naval and Marine elements appeared to be in a better position, and were probably able to last to the end of the month, possibly longer. The poor inter-service relations led to two completely independent logistic systems, with the Army relying only on fishing vessels. An additional complication for the Argentine command was that the units on West Falkland had to be supplied from East Falkland. It had to be assumed that the Argentine military would not dare wait until they had only a few days' rations left before trying to re-supply. Exactly how they would do so was unclear.

Before the TEZ was established, and before extra troops had been sent by Galtieri to the Falklands, as many as twelve C-130, four F27/F28 and one Boeing 737 sorties were taking place on a daily basis. This was at a time when the garrison was being built up, but even so the reduced opportunities for airlift must have been causing General Menendez some headaches. For air supply, five airstrips were possibly available for use by C-130 Hercules transports operating from the mainland: Stanley, Dunnose Head, Darwin, Keppel Island and Pebble Island. Each Hercules could carry a maximum of 13,000lb. into the grass/beach airstrips and perhaps as much as 27,000lb. into Stanley airfield. Two sorties per day might be feasible for a single strip, which made for a maximum of ten per day. But this level was unlikely. Argentina was known to have seven Hercules, and there were reports of another three being deployed from Peru. There would, however, be distribution problems if the more remote airstrips were used, requiring helicopters and boats, and it did not seem that these were used for re-supply purposes. While flights might continue to get into Stanley, their level could not solve the garrison's re-supply problem. Attempts to supplement them with airdrops were unlikely to help, given that Argentina's capacity here was limited and unpractised. Sealift might be achieved using military transport vessels, commercial ships or, possibly, foreign flag vessels. Large cargo capabilities would have obvious advantages, but they would need air cover, as they would offer easy targets for the British.

Preventing re-supply

The Vulcan raids of 1 and 4 May had been designed to put Stanley airfield out of action but it was soon ascertained that they had not been a complete success. After the 4 May raid there were no early flights, and the damage appeared to be extensive enough for the airfield to be unable to sustain continuous use by large transport aircraft. It soon became clear that Hercules could use the airfield, along with light transports, and this would enable the Argentines to bring in urgent stores and evacuate the wounded or non-essential personnel. Over the following weeks British efforts to close this re-supply route must be considered unsuccessful, although the air link by itself was insufficient to meet Argentine needs. It appeared after the war that from 1 May only 70 tonnes of material and 340 personnel arrived.

On 7 May, *Broadsword* and *Coventry* were put in position to interdict Argentine flights to and from Stanley, as well as carry out naval gunfire support. They were told to stay by day in the area to the south of Stanley to await any incoming Hercules plus fighter escorts. To ensure that the enemy came into the missile trap Woodward instructed *Coventry* not to 'drive the enemy away with CAP' unless absolutely necessary. Early on 9 May they were alerted as a Hercules made a supply run into the airfield, but they were too far away to get at it. Later *Coventry* reported an air contact. This was another attempt to get a Hercules, with an accompanying Mirage escort, to the airport. Missiles were fired but missed: they still had a deterrent effect as the aircraft turned away. It later emerged that two of the escorting Skyhawks had collided and crashed whilst taking action to avoid an approaching Sea Dart missile. Then another wave of four aircraft was seen approaching. They also turned away when spotted.

The Argentine air warning radars at Stanley were picking up the Sea Harriers. This meant that the transport aircraft would only persevere with their mission when it was safe to do so, but if it was safe they could get through. Woodward wanted intelligence on the siting of these radars as he knew they were giving advanced warning of attempts to engage intruders: 'Furthermore attainment of air superiority is not possible while these radars are in operation'. Woodward felt that he 'had no real prospect of achieving this with my own resources other than further recce insertion'. He inquired whether MoD had any human intelligence possibilities. The reply came that the positions of AN/TPS43 radars were all in the Stanley area, with the presumed locations all based on debriefs of returning islanders. When, on 12 May, photographic reconnaissance was undertaken it became apparent that the runway at Stanley was usable by Hercules at a reduced width, even though no repairs had been undertaken. Aircraft were still flying in and out, though the local Argentine command was discouraging visits by senior officers from the mainland on the grounds that it was too risky and any seat would be needed for personnel evacuation. The next day, to drive home the point, another Hercules landed at Stanley at about 1955Z and took off fifteen minutes later.

This level of activity was still not enough to meet Argentine needs: many requests for supplies were being left unmet. The estimate now was that by stretching rations and using local resources the Army could survive beyond 18 May to 26/27 May but if the force was to be fed even on a reduced ration for ten days beyond that then some 75 tons of re-supply would be necessary. There was pressure on Buenos Aires for some emergency action to replenish the garrison, to which the Commander South Atlantic acceded. Evidence to this effect led to pressure on the British side to re-attack the airfield.

On 14 May Sea Harriers bombed Stanley airfield and associated military installations. All aircraft returned safely. Then on 15 May there was another Sea Harrier raid when twelve 1000-lb bombs were dropped. Photographic reconnaissance was frustrated by cloud. Further Vulcan raids were limited by the availability of Victor tankers at Ascension and the competing demands of Hercules store drops and Nimrod reconnaissance sorties.

Northwood did decide that a third Vulcan bombing attack on Stanley airfield should be planned for the night of 16/17 May. In the event it was postponed and then cancelled because there were insufficient Victor tankers available. Sea Harriers dropped six more bombs on Stanley airfield on 16 May, but a high altitude had been adopted to avoid anti-aircraft fire and the results were ineffectual. By midnight the airport was in use again as a Hercules flew in and out of Stanley. Two more attacks by Sea Harriers were conducted against the airport on 18 May, but again damage assessment reports indicated that the results were negligible.

There were reports on 17 May that the Argentines were planning to mount an aerial re-supply of Stanley that day. With fighter aircraft providing cover, transport aircraft would land provisions and munitions at Stanley airfield while other supplies would be air-dropped as ships attempted to break the maritime blockade. In the event there was no major re-supply effort and the conditions for the Argentine troops continued to deteriorate, with shortages of dry and waterproof clothing particularly pressing. The Argentine forces were now clearly suffering from an ill-considered deployment, with many more troops sent than could be adequately supported. They were being demoralised by worsening weather and the British blockade, and suffering from gastro-enteritis, influenza, and homesickness.

Narwhal

Argentine use of foreign-flag vessels might be problematic for the British, because of the political implications of an attack. However these would also take time to arrange and, while there was some speculation that Peru and Venezuela might be tempted to help Argentina in this way rather than by supplying military equipment or becoming directly involved with military assistance, the British readiness to enforce the Exclusion Zone probably banished any such thoughts. Fishing boats would provide smaller targets, but also smaller loads. This posed a complication for Britain, as there were possibly Polish and Soviet fishing boats inside the Exclusion Zone. To deal with this problem on 7 May MoD issued a statement:

> Her Majesty's Government will continue to enforce this Exclusion Zone which applies not only to Argentine warships and Argentine naval auxiliaries but also to any other ships, including merchant and fishing vessels, which are operating in support of the illegal occupation of the Falkland Islands by Argentine Forces.

The FCO were making arrangements to issue further advice to the Soviet and Polish authorities concerning the danger to their fishing vessels if they were still in the TEZ. The day after this announcement, Argentine military spokesmen insisted that the blockade would be defied, and that the Navy had resumed re-supplying its troops on the Falklands by air. Nonetheless, all the indications were that the Argentine Navy considered re-supply by sea to be too hazardous because of the threat of submarine attacks.

If Argentina was to attempt to move supplies by sea then fishing boats seemed as likely vessels as any. Fieldhouse sought a change in ROE to remove the requirement to warn off merchant ships before any action was taken against them, as this was inappropriate when the attack was likely to be carried out by Lynx helicopters armed with air-to-surface missiles. The Chiefs of Staff and then Nott accepted his recommendation. In fact the first contact was made by Sea Harriers – at 1130Z on 9 May, 50 miles south of Stanley. This was investigated and identified as the Argentine stern trawler *Narwhal*, which was suspected of intelligence gathering rather than blockade-running. It had been warned off ten days earlier so it could not claim innocence.[2] Having gained approval from Woodward, the aircraft attacked with their 1000-lb bombs. One missed. The other, incorrectly fused, penetrated the ship. With no damage observed, the Sea Harriers strafed the target with 30mm cannon. The *Narwhal* was now in trouble. The crew began to abandon ship, issuing a Mayday call and lowering liferafts, but they had not been manned before the next two Sea Harriers were on the scene. They noticed few signs of distress, and with *Narwhal*'s flag still flying, they also strafed it with cannon.

Woodward had wanted to capture *Narwhal* rather than sink her, both to avoid casualties and also, it was hoped, to acquire evidence of a naval and intelligence role. *Invincible* was told to prepare to board and capture *Narwhal* using SBS. At 1600Z, after what seemed to the Commander to be an interminable delay, the special forces stormed *Narwhal* from a Sea King 4. The crew, with 13 injured and one dead, soon surrendered and were airlifted to *Invincible*. A technical team was then sent aboard to investigate damage to see if it could be repaired and steamed clear of the TEZ. In the end it was left to sink. With some relief, documentation was found proving that it was not an innocent fishing vessel but engaged in intelligence gathering and with a naval officer embarked. Later Woodward judged that this incident 'could have been politically disastrous' but 'finally turned out well'. To end the day, at 1900Z *Coventry* used Sea Dart to shoot down a Puma, despatched from Stanley to see what had happened to the *Narwhal*. The fishing vessels *Constanza* and *Maria Alejanora,* consorts of *Narwhal,* could also be assumed to be engaged in the surveillance of British forces in the Falklands area.

The incident had not quite ended. Not only had the boat been holed below the waterline but all of the liferafts had been damaged, with only one small boat being sound. There was concern in Whitehall that Argentina could claim a 'grave breach' of the Second Geneva Convention, relating to wanton destruction.[3] Buenos Aires was making allegations and, while Whitehall doubted that there had been a breach, they were not disposed to give Argentina a propaganda advantage. It was therefore agreed also to ascertain the full facts. This had operational penalties, in using up a ship. The alternative, however, of transferring the prisoners to *Hecla* and then on to the *Bahaia Paraiso* had the additional disadvantages of transferring injured men at sea, not involving the ICRC. The eventual preference was for *Hecla* to go to Uruguay or Brazil with the prisoners, which would also take time. The Americans were later given evidence that the captain of the *Narwhal* had been asked to deny in public that he fired first on British helicopters and to claim that he was on a rescue mission.

Though there was no re-supply from the mainland by sea, the garrison was using boats to move supplies between West and East Falkland. Woodward knew that Falkland Sound was being used for this purpose and had ordered *Arrow* and *Alacrity* to locate, harass and destroy Argentine re-supply shipping. This was achieved on 11 May by *Alacrity*, but almost inadvertently, when it was sent on a hazardous mission down the Falkland Sound to confirm SAS reports that there had been no minelaying. It had no mine detection equipment and so if any mines were in place this would become known with an explosion. Woodward wrote in his diary: 'This latter has to be done if we wish to put the AW force in there in due course. Not a comfortable night.'

Alacrity entered Falkland Sound at 2300Z and in heavy rain moved slowly forward. If it met trouble any useful support was 130 miles away. Quite soon into its journey it detected a substantial radar echo at North Swan Island and raised its speed in order to close on the target. This appeared to have been alerted and so in turn made a dash to port. Efforts to illuminate the target failed but then it was attacked with gunfire and soon exploded. It was assumed that the local Argentine garrison at Port Howard on West Falkland would have been alerted by the noise, so a search for survivors was considered unwise. *Alacrity* moved sharply through the Sound unscathed and emerged at 0230Z, having made a satisfactory point about the lack of mines. It almost made a less satisfactory point about the continuing danger of Argentine submarines. It met up that morning with *Arrow*, after passing through the Sound, continuing to search for evidence of minelaying. The two frigates passed through the patrol area of the 209 submarine, *San Luis*, which gained contact. One torpedo was fired at the *Alacrity*: the weapon's guidance malfunctioned and it missed.[4]

The next day it became apparent that the victim of *Alacrity*'s attack was the Argentine Auxiliary Transport *Isla De Los Estados,* carrying vehicles and bulk fuel. It had been taken by surprise, and 21 men had been killed at once. The survivors were not rescued for another two days. The ship had been delivering supplies from Stanley to the Argentine garrison at Port Howard. The Argentines suspected that the British were landing commandos when they ran across the ship, and that they might also be trying deliberately to cut off West from East Falkland. The Argentines knew that the British were infiltrating reconnaissance units. Their own Special Forces were patrolling and setting ambushes. As nobody was found, the Malvinas Command came to doubt whether any British forces were still on the Islands.

At 1630Z on 15 May a reconnaissance sortie photographed a supply ship alongside the jetty in Fox Bay. There was no time for an air attack before dark but *Brilliant*, with an SBS unit embarked, was ordered at 2230Z to attack the ship, so long as it could confirm that she was not the hospital ship *Bahia Paraiso*. An SBS attack appeared too hazardous and so Lynx helicopters were to be used. When one approached Fox Bay it was forced to avoid heavy anti-aircraft fire. As it could not confirm that this was not the hospital ship the mission had to be abandoned. A Sea Harrier sortie the next day, 16 May, observed a merchant ship at anchor in Falkland Sound and was also able to identify the ship at Fox Bay as the naval transport *Bahia Buen Suceso* and not *Bahia Paraiso*. The first ship was the *Rio Carcarana* sighted at Port King. This had been unloaded but then ordered not to return to the mainland for fear of being intercepted. At 1630Z two Sea Harriers attacked it with four 1000-lb bombs and 30mm cannon, causing fires and sufficient damage to lead to her being abandoned. The crew was unharmed and escaped ashore. An hour later two more Sea Harriers attacked the *Buen Suceso*, using only cannon for fear that bombs would hit the adjacent civilian settlement. Having observed the first attack, the captain of the *Buen Suceso* had taken the precaution of ordering most of his crew ashore. The ship received many hits and fire broke out in the engine room. She could not be repaired locally, remained abandoned and, like the *Rio Carcarana*, was never used again.

30

THE AIR THREAT

During the course of May confidence that the naval threat was under control grew. Optimism on the air threat was much scarcer, especially among those who might be on the receiving end. The concern in the South Atlantic was that, having accepted a degree of local air superiority as an essential precondition for a landing, Northwood and the Chiefs were now taking a more relaxed view. In a 1949Z signal on 6 May, Thompson told Moore that he had always understood that there was a 'firm concept ... that sea and air battle must be won first before amphibious landing. Indeed recall these words used at meeting with CINC in *Hermes*.' If these conditions could not be met, Thompson felt that a landing should not be attempted 'unless we wish to risk losing large part of Brigade, possibly before we get ashore'. Thompson forcefully conveyed the fact that: 'Unpalatable though it may be, fact must be faced that amphibious operations cannot be successfully carried out in hostile air environment. This is not a new thought.'

His mood was not helped when later that day he read a signal from Woodward to Fieldhouse. The analysis was not promising. The discussion was prompted in part by proposals from Northwood for redistributing the landing forces out of *Canberra*. Fieldhouse was nervous about so many men being in one big ship. To get the right units and their equipment into the right ships prior to the landing required moving men at sea – cross decking. This was difficult enough in a calm and unthreatened environment, but carried great risk in stormy seas and with the risk of ships so occupied being caught by an air raid. Woodward felt that sheltered waters for cross decking operations just before the landing could not be guaranteed within the TEZ – 'only God can provide'. More importantly it was becoming increasingly apparent to the Carrier Battle Group Commander that:

> establishing sea and air control will be a protracted business for reasons of 50 per cent unsuitable weather for fixed wing flying due to inadequate visibility so far, and the need always to fight from a position of advantage in view of the numbers game. Thus air control over the Falklands will be almost impossible to achieve in

the next few days unless the weather changes and significantly increased attrition rates are achieved.

At the current rate of Argentine air activity the chances of getting successful attrition through CAP and SAM were 'bleak'. Attacking Argentine aircraft on the ground at their mainland bases 'maybe more profitable, but I do not have either the assets or ROE to achieve the task'. Consequently, he argued that: 'any landing in the short term will have to be organised primarily to meet a strong air threat throughout and only secondarily to land in the face of ground opposition simply since we cannot "assault" in the full sense of going in facing a multi threat'. Hence, Woodward suggested, cross decking on the scale required could only be achieved ashore under Rapier/Blowpipe cover after light 'assault' on an uninhabited area to prepare ground.

Thompson found this signal 'very disturbing'. He told Moore that cross decking must be carried out in sheltered water, which meant closing the Falkland Islands at night. He also had no intention of landing where strong ground opposition might be faced. Nor was he so sanguine about landing a Rapier Battery at night after light assault. He concluded that: 'Arg air cannot be hacked, prospects for follow up Bde look bleak too'. A telephone conversation with Moore left Thompson with 'the feeling, perhaps wrongly' that in some circles a landing was being contemplated in a situation where air superiority in the Amphibious Operations Area (AOA) could not be guaranteed. Although he was unsure that this included Fieldhouse and Moore, he developed his concerns at length, arguing that if air and naval superiority could not be achieved, going into the AOA with high risk ships such as *Canberra* ('with the bulk of my bayonets, all their first line ammunition in exposed positions on upper decks and 90 days rations embarked for the whole force') and *Elk* (with 20 days' combat supplies for the whole landing force embarked), should 'not in my view, even be contemplated'.

Yet, as things stood, that is precisely what was being contemplated if it really was impossible to engage in cross decking beforehand and the air threat could not be significantly reduced. These ships and the LSLs and LPDs would have to be taken into the AOA and kept there throughout:

The argument that we can establish a beachhead during the hours of darkness and be firm in all respects, including land based air defence, by first light does not hold water. The facts are that our off-load capability, I have deliberately not used the word assault capability, is still so limited that it is not possible to have assumed such a defensive posture in one night because:

A. All our 105mm light guns are in ships from which night operations by helicopter are not possible.

B. The nature of the ground and lack of roads dictates that the AD
    Bty [Air Defence Battery] must be inserted by helicopter straight
    into its fire positions; some 8–12 different locations. The Bty cannot
    be lifted out of its ship by night or inserted at night.

Thus was foreshadowed what was to be one of the most difficult issues
post-landing: Woodward's hope that Rapier air defences could relieve his
ships of what was bound to be a perilous air defence duty as soon as
possible after the landing. Woodward had no past experience of Rapier but
had been encouraged by the emphasis placed on the air defence missile in
the preparations for the landing. The land force commanders were aware of
its limitations, and also of the time it would take to establish the battery
ashore. This is one of those differences of perception that the lack of regular
conversations between the commanders made difficult to correct.

A beachhead could be established at night, Thompson continued,
'provided we arrive with all our assets', but then the dawn would find the
landing force without adequate land-based air defence. There would therefore be a reliance on the Battle Group to provide air defence and early
warning against an enemy whose route into the AOA could, depending on
the location of the beachhead, be over land for the last 150 miles. Thompson
therefore believed that before a commitment was made to a landing,
Woodward 'must say whether or not he can guarantee air and naval superiority from the moment we enter the AOA until the Args concede defeat'. If
air superiority was lost after the landing, 'we will be unable to maintain the
momentum of our operations, despite being reinforced by 5 Inf Bde'. The
added complication would then be the protection of their high value shipping such as the *QEII*. He concluded:

I am raising this matter because I consider that the politicians
should be quite clear that if we are ordered to land without air and
naval superiority, we risk very heavy casualties, possibly even before
any landing takes place. Indeed if, for example, Canberra is sunk,
any landing is out of the question. It is not my place to question the
political judgement of the risks involved. I do believe however that
it is my place to point out the military consequences that could flow
from deciding to do a landing and conducting operations ashore
without air and naval superiority.

Commodore Clapp, Commander Amphibious Warfare, reinforced
Thompson's message and warned of the extra demands that the air vulnerability would impose on Woodward's ships. On 7 May he signalled
Fieldhouse that, in his view, the enemy would be well aware of the complete
lack of air defence assets in the amphibious task group, the approximate position of TG 317.8 (the carrier group), the likelihood of TG 317.8 reinforcing

the amphibious task group at some stage and the 'fact that the whole war depends on survival of TG 317.0 [the amphibious group] main body'. The Argentines would therefore 'make extraordinary efforts to attack unde-fended TG 317.0 before TG 317.8 appears on scene. These efforts may include ad hoc air-to-air refuelling arrangements.' Support from the carrier battle group before the amphibious force reached radius 960nm from Argentine airfields was therefore 'of paramount importance'. He proposed that all air defence assets in TG 317.8 should support the amphibious force. If this was not possible, he required a minimum of one carrier and two Type 42s. He further proposed that Fieldhouse should task the intelligence organ-isation to examine the possibilities of Argentine air-to-air refuelling (AAR) and its effect on his assumed radius of action.

That evening Thompson spoke directly to Fieldhouse, urging that the landing be delayed until more had been done to deal with the threat. CINCFLEET's response, drafted by Moore, which came the next day, noted that he, Fieldhouse, had to weigh the risks of a landing, of which the air threat was but one, and find ways of reducing them. It was still possible that the landing might have to be delayed irrespective of the air threat. He judged, however, that the impact of the air threat could be reduced by landing at night as far to the east as possible, with diversion and deception used to confuse the enemy and delay his reaction to the reality of the landing. It should be possible to take out the majority of Argentine aircraft in the Falklands before the landing, and thereafter the Sea Harriers would play a critical role followed by surface-to-air missiles, provided they could be got ashore quickly. The first task would be 'to build a secure bridgehead, where sea/air re-supply can be conducted in safety. This must be followed by the establishment of a landing site ashore for helos and Harriers.'

Thompson remained unconvinced. On 14 May he apologised for 'banging on … in a most boring manner' about the lack of air superiority or even parity. They would do what they could, hoping to get Rapiers offloaded as a first priority and operational within hours, while hoping that the other air defences could cope. 'We are therefore bracing ourselves', Thompson concluded, 'for a very unpleasant first day which is price we will have to pay if invited to land before achieving basic prerequisite for amphibious opera-tions: a minimum of local air superiority.'

Cutting Argentine air capabilities

The extent of the Argentine air threat was still itself in some dispute. To what extent would their aircraft be operating at the extreme of their range? How dependent would they be on air and ground or airborne radars to find their targets? Was it the case that the A4s and Mirage could only operate in a clear environment? Could anything more than light aircraft and small transports operate from the airfields on the Falklands? How well could British air defences cope?

These questions would all be easier if a way could be found to reduce the air threat before the landing. Fieldhouse had identified the Falklands-based Argentine aircraft as accessible targets, and this was an area where pre-landing efforts showed some success. Pucaras and other small aircraft were known to be based at Pebble Island, posing a threat to British ships wanting to use the northern entrance to Falkland Sound. Planning for a Special Forces operation began around 7 May. As a result of the growing concern about the air threat, on 10 May Woodward and the SAS liaison officer discussed an early assault at a meeting on board *Hermes*. According to Woodward, he pressed for an early strike despite the SAS urging more preparatory work, possibly taking as long as three weeks, including the insertion of a recce team. He pointed to the lack of helicopter assets available the closer the date got to the landing and the urgency of dealing with the aircraft.[1] According to another source the Navy were resistant to making this a high priority, and were only persuaded by (fictitious) claims that an Argentine warning radar was also located on the Island.[2] At any rate a truncated programme of reconnaissance began that evening when a patrol was inserted using Klepper canoes. It was not possible to mount the raid on 13 May, as had been hoped, because the reconnaissance was not complete.

At 1800Z on 14 May the *Hermes*, *Glamorgan* and *Broadsword* set off once again towards Pebble Island as they had done the previous night. Early the next morning three Sea Kings carrying the raiding party were launched from *Hermes*. The party of 45 men of the SAS and a Royal Artillery forward observer landed on the south coast of the Island where they met up with the reconnaissance party. They reached the airstrip, seven km to the northwest, by 0700Z. The spotter ordered *Glamorgan* to illuminate the strip with starshell for about 5 minutes. The attacking group made for the aircraft on the runway, as naval gunfire provided covering support. One enemy unit on the airfield opened fire but was soon silenced. All eleven aircraft (six Pucaras, four Mentors and a Skyvan) were destroyed or put beyond use, as was ammunition and fuel stored nearby. The raiding party, including the original reconnaissance troop, retired to the landing point where they were picked up by four Sea Kings at about 0930Z and flown back to *Hermes*. This was a remarkably successful raid, conducted during a howling gale and without casualty, depriving the garrison of a number of aircraft and undermining morale, by demonstrating the capacity of special forces to mount operations on the Islands against units that were detached from the main forces.

The assessment after this raid was that three Skyvan light transports, two Navy Tracker early warning aircraft, nine Pucara counter insurgency aircraft, four Chinook, three Puma, and one Agusta 109 were left on the Falklands. There was no firm intelligence on the actual deployment of these remaining aircraft. The fixed-wing aircraft could be operated from any of four or perhaps as many as 20 of the small airstrips while the helicopters, on which the Argentine forces relied so much for mobility, were expected to be dispersed away from the airstrips. At Northwood, Curtiss continued to express concern that insufficient priority had been allocated to air reconnaissance, and that information was poor. On 17 May, this was picked up by Beetham, concerned that MoD had not received the full results of analysis of photographic reconnaissance missions, and in particular, no information on the serviceability of Argentine aircraft still reported as being at Stanley airfield.

The most drastic measure would be to attack Argentine territory or territorial waters. The political reluctance to go this far had been evident during the discussion of proposals to change the ROE to permit attacks on the carrier as it hugged the coast. Thompson was urging attacks against the mainland Argentine air bases, but here not only were the potential political costs substantial, and the subject of Latin American, US and UN representations, but also the military results could not be guaranteed. When the possibility was investigated the logistical demands appeared daunting. The bases would be equipped with radars so an incoming attack might be detected. Whether the Argentines could then do much with their fighter air defences, especially at night, was difficult to gauge. Point defences would certainly be in operation in the target areas and so flying below 8,000 feet would be advisable. The attacking aircraft would have to be operated either from Ascension or San Felix in Chile. From Ascension more than 20 Victor tankers (that is more than actually available) would be needed to support a single Vulcan flight with 21 × 1,000-lb bombs. Reducing the bomb load by two-thirds would bring the Victor requirement down to 11 tankers and allow for a possible diversion to Rio. Another way of reducing the tanker requirement would be not to fly at low altitude. San Felix was closer, so from there eleven tankers could support a fully loaded Vulcan, but the runway might not be able to support the tanker operations and the journey back to Ascension would be complicated because of the need to meet up with the tankers after overflying Chile and Argentina. Returning to San Felix with a full bomb load would require three Victors, or possibly two assuming high altitudes and low load. Even on the doubtful assumption that Chile could be persuaded to collude in offensive operations, getting all that was needed to San Felix, including the aircraft, would be problematic, to say the least, and time-consuming and the airport was of marginal standard. Also getting the necessary information for the attacks would require diverting effort from intelligence gathering over the Falklands.

This left a Special Forces raid as the only acceptable way of dealing with the mainland bases. The priority target had to be the Rio Grande airfield in Tierra del Fuego where the Super Etendards were stationed. Fieldhouse had requested the operation but political approval took time. On 13 May Lewin proposed a two-stage operation: first intelligence gathering and then offensive action. The second stage would have involved getting around 55 men close to Rio Grande in Hercules aircraft and, after they had destroyed the

Super Etendards, getting them out again (exactly how is unclear). On 14 May the War Cabinet gave approval to both stages. That day Fieldhouse signalled this to Woodward, adding that a 'bold move now could significantly tilt the balance in our favour during the critical landing phase.'

The method for inserting the men for the first stage reconnaissance became the subject of considerable debate, not least because of the reluctance to lose a Sea King (although according to Woodward also because the Director SAS believed that the plan to 'ditch' the helicopter literally meant it to be in the water so that his men would have to swim ashore). Another possibility would have been to get *Fort Austin* in very close so that the helicopter could return, but that would have put the RFA at risk and required Chile to turn a blind eye at an operation from within Chilean waters.[3] Eventually eight men from the Special Forces joined *Fort Austin* on 16 May and they were taken to *Hermes.* One Sea King would drop the men as close as possible to Rio Grande then proceed back across the Chilean border, before the crew would sink the helicopter and later give themselves up to Chilean authorities. When they had done their job, the Special Forces would exfiltrate by foot. Fieldhouse approved this plan, so long as the crew had a convincing cover story. With the weather closing in, Woodward would have liked to have sent the SAS reconnaissance team off on their mission after they had been brought on board following their long journey from the UK, but they insisted that they needed a day to recover. So it was that on 17 May, at 1800Z, *Invincible* and *Broadsword* detached from the Task Force with the team and a Sea King. Bad weather came in and the helicopter eventually came down on the Chilean coast 10 miles from Punta Arenas and 50 miles from where it was hoped to be.

The discovery of the burnt-out Sea King some 18 km south of Punta Arenas attracted public attention. The Chilean Foreign Minister summoned Ambassador Heath to deliver a note of protest at this discovery, which indicated 'that British units had entered Chilean territory and violated Chilean sovereignty'. The note asked for an explanation of the case and that no further incidents of this kind would occur. In private he was more understanding, given the circumstances in which Britain found itself. The discovery of the helicopter was by now news in London, and a press statement had been prepared referring to a 'reconnaissance mission' that had 'got into difficulties in bad weather and was lost, presumably while trying to reach Punta Arenas to make an emergency landing.' Heath delivered a note with the official explanation, a request for help in the search for the missing crew members, and stressing the Government's 'understanding and respect for the principles governing Chile's strict neutrality in this conflict' and regret for any inconvenience caused by 'this unfortunate incident.'

On 25 May the three Sea King aircrew were found safe and well. They were flown to Santiago the next day. By the time the crew reached the British authorities they had already been questioned by the Chilean police, and they told a story more or less conforming to the official British line, blaming engine failure. They had taken to the hills and destroyed the aircraft because they were unsure whether they were in Argentina or Chile. At a brief press conference a statement was read out, repeating the story and thanking the Chilean authorities for treating them well. Eventually, and with less publicity, the SAS men came out through Chile.

Even though this reconnaissance phase had failed and surprise had been lost, preparations continued for the second phase, in time to stop the Super Etendards having another go at carriers and *Canberra* prior to the landing. All accounts of this proposed operation indicate the apprehension with which those who would be responsible for its implementation now viewed it. In his memoir General Peter de la Billiere, the Director Special Forces, records that the attitude of the squadron was 'luke-warm', for which he blamed the squadron commander. Colonel Rose, CO of 22 SAS, was in the Falklands with the troops already deployed there. De la Billiere would have preferred him to stay in the UK but in his absence he took it upon himself to dismiss the squadron commander.[4] In the event, evidence of improved defences led to the operation being cancelled.

Lewin spent a considerable amount of time on this issue, exploring a variety of Special Force options. The problems were formidable. If the Super Etendards had been deployed to other airports, or were just better guarded, then more men would be needed. More men increased the risk of capture and a public relations fiasco. And then there was no guarantee of success. Another operation, using a diesel submarine to land men close to the base, was developed but became unnecessary because of the Argentine surrender.[5] The concerns about these operations were that they would have an impact on South American attitudes generally, possibly leading to sanctions, and that it would prejudice attempts to provide advance warning of aircraft leaving the southern airfields to attack the Task Force.

Throughout May the Argentines assumed that the British were thinking about an attack on their mainland bases, having taken note of an apparent allusion by Nott to such a possibility in early May, which the Interior Ministry Under-Secretary described as a 'new act of pressure'. When, on 7 May, the British extended the area of operations the Argentine assumption was that the *25 de Mayo* and Super Etendard aircraft were now the main targets, and the British might even be planning to neutralise some mainland airfields, including the Rio Grande airbase. The Argentines responded to the vulnerability of the carrier by disembarking the A-4Q Skyhawks, and thereafter, as we have seen, keeping it within the 12 mile limit. Buenos Aires also conducted a diplomatic offensive to ensure that the British were well aware of the political costs that would follow any attack on Argentine territory. This became one of the main events mentioned in assessments of wider Latin American attitudes as being most likely to lead to diplomatic and economic sanctions and even arms transfers to Argentina.

On 18 May, now days away from the landing, Curtiss produced a paper on how to reduce the enemy air capability over the Falklands, as he was not satisfied that the best actions were being taken. He was concerned that the targets being selected for air, naval gunfire and Special Forces concentrated too much on support facilities and not enough on vital equipment such as radars or air defence systems. He wanted to concentrate the minds of Fieldhouse and Woodward on the risks that were being run, more frustrating for him because there was little the RAF could do for the moment to help. In addition, the RAF's efforts to date, using Nimrod for long-range maritime surveillance, had been criticised by Woodward for the imprecision of their reports.[6]

Much effort was put into locating and destroying shore radars, by NGS, Special Forces and Vulcan raids with Shrike missiles, but none met with complete success and they remained a thorn in the side of friendly forces until the fall of Stanley, when it was discovered that the radars were mobile and frequently moved. A major factor throughout the month of May was the weather, which could never be entirely favourable to attacking forces. Heavy, low cloud and fog, frequently met at this time of year, prevented air attacks by Argentine land-based aircraft, but also inhibited the Task Force's aim of attacking the airfield and airstrips and other military locations on the Falkland Islands. Nor did it permit continued attrition of Argentine air assets. There were many days in the month when virtually no flying was possible and while this provided protection for the Task Group it also potentially provided cover for the Argentines to break the blockade.

Defences

If Argentine aircraft could get through then much would depend on the quality of the British defences. In the dogfights of 1 May Sea Harriers had clearly bested the Argentine Mirages and so there could be confidence on that score. There were relatively few Harriers available, however. Of the original 20 Sea Harriers three had been lost. Another eight were on their way, plus six Harrier GR3s in the *Atlantic Conveyor*. The original role for the GR3s was to replace Sea Harriers in the air defence role. It had been assumed in Northwood that once hostilities began losses could be expected of about one aircraft per day. For this reason, 1 Squadron RAF, under Wing-Commander Peter Squires, the only squadron that routinely did air-to-air refuelling was told to prepare its Harriers to operate in an air defence role. This required modifying the GR3s, for example to be handled on a carrier and to reduce the damage that might be caused by salt water and to prepare for aerial combat. They lacked air-to-air missiles and so had to be fitted for Sidewinder. Despite remarkable efforts to prepare the aircraft the equipment was still inadequate, particularly in inertial navigation and weapon aiming. Furthermore, because they were assumed to be replacements for lost Sea Harriers they only took 19 tradesmen, which meant that they would rely on the naval teams. When they shifted roles back to their normal reconnaissance and offensive operations this led to difficulties.

The other air defence systems had been granted only limited tests. Since 4 May there had been two significant bursts of activity. On 9 May *Alacrity* fired 93 rounds at six targets, including Moody Brook barracks, a troop concentration on the racecourse, and a major defensive position, all carefully circumscribed to avoid civilian casualties. A Skyvan aircraft at the racecourse was hit, as was an Iroquois helicopter at Moody Brook. This sudden burst of British activity may have convinced the Argentines that an invasion was imminent. At 1030Z four Skyhawks arrived at East Falkland but left without finding any targets or allowing time for interception. Four hours later three Daggers approached East Falkland, with a pair of Learjets apparently acting as pathfinders. *Coventry*, waiting to intercept Hercules, fired three Sea Darts at the Learjets at extreme range, but missed, and the enemy turned for home. There were three further raids during the day, although none were intercepted successfully, nor did any reach any British targets. As mentioned earlier, the only Argentine Air Force attrition suffered that day came because two Skyhawks collided on their way home. Later *Broadsword* picked up a slow-moving air track flying overland in the vicinity of Port Harriet. This was acquired when it came clear of land and the target (an Argentine Puma) was caught by a single Sea Dart. Against a slow-moving target, clear of land, and not engaged in a direct attack on a defending ship, Sea Dart had worked well.

On 7 May Woodward, as part of the dialogue regarding the problems of getting at the Argentine air forces, made a suggestion to Fieldhouse to attempt the 'short term forward deployment of the two Type 42s and the two Type 22s, preferably in poorish weather/visibility to keep any Arg attacking aircraft off the deck hence improving Sea Dart and Sea Wolf effectiveness.' By tempting the Argentine air force out this might just accelerate attrition. 'It does not escape me that the attrition could be confined to our own forces' but even then it would be as well to know the limits of these systems rather than discovering them 'halfway through the landing.' If enemy aircraft were caught then that would be good and if there was no engagement then at least it challenged the Argentine position in the western third of the TEZ. Much depended on whether a decision had been made to land, for if the Task Force was not going 'to press on, then I shall need to continue as at present keeping the options open by using more cautious means of little effectiveness and indecisive nature'. He had some ideas for more risky options, but for the moment 'I am feeling very like Aunt Sally,' to which Fieldhouse sent the rather flip reply 'Your Auntie must be very sexy'.

More seriously, Fieldhouse explained that London was 'still in the business of keeping options open':

Political handling still very much day to day if not hour to hour as the Junta twists and turns. *Sheffield* gave the thugs a great boost and I cannot agree even attrition achieves the aim hence my caution about expensive offensive action. However, don't get the impression acceptance of stalemate is imminent. Present intention is for presentation to Cabinet of landing plan after approval by COS (Chiefs of Staff) end next week.

He also gave Woodward an evaluation of the various high-risk options. He was not sure about the Type 42 missile trap, saw little value in more NGS activity – it was only 'good for your night frustration' – and was 'not yet' prepared to push for a Vulcan attack on the mainland airfields, although the special forces option was being pursued and more relaxed ROE for attacks on surface forces were being agreed. 'In summary tighten the air and sea blockade, attack a/c on ground and airfields in FI, step up offensive raiding and continue ASW all in whatever priority weather and other factors allow.'

On 12 May Woodward did attempt to draw Argentine forces out more, while getting in a bit more naval gunfire. *Brilliant* and *Glasgow* got into position to direct gunfire at Argentine air defences, supplemented by another Sea Harrier attack against Stanley airfield. The Argentines located the two ships, mounted an attack and used two groups of four Skyhawks from Rio Gallegos to attack them. The British ships were prepared for the attack. The plan was for the Type 22 (*Brilliant*) to acquire the targets and the Type 42 (*Glasgow*) to take them out with Sea Dart. *Brilliant* did its part but *Glasgow*'s Sea Dart suffered a defect when being launched and then its 4.5' gun misfired, as did its 20mm Oerlikon. *Brilliant*'s Sea Wolf, by contrast, operated without problems, destroying two Skyhawks while a third flew into the sea taking avoiding action. A bomb from the fourth missed *Glasgow*. With the second raid none of the systems on either ship worked allowing four Skyhawks to release their 1,000lb. bombs. One hit *Glasgow* but failed to explode. It entered on the starboard side just above the water line and exited port side at the same level. No fire was caused and there were no casualties other than one man shocked.

Bizarrely Argentine air defences had more success: as one of the aircraft flew back over Goose Green it was fired at in error and shot down. This, it was later discovered had been achieved by a Roland air defence missile. Although Argentina claimed that the Skyhawks had severely damaged both ships, *Glasgow* was able to move and neither its weapons nor sensors had been harmed. Repair work began at once. The Argentines now had a growing confidence about their anti-shipping capability, but also concern about the low level of their control of air space. To the British it was becoming clearer that A4s did not have a night attack capability but, ominously in terms of range, they might have in-flight refuelling.

In his War Diary Woodward observed that the probability of all defensive systems refusing to function 'should be very small indeed'. He wondered if the fact that the only bomb that hit *Glasgow* did not explode was also a 'low probability'. These experiences encouraged the view that sufficient Argentine aircraft were likely to pass through combat air patrols, SAM equipped ships and any land-based air defence batteries, to attack British ships and landing craft in alarmingly large numbers. On 13 May one RAF officer found it:

> Profoundly disturbing that some 6 raids by the Argentines have resulted in the loss of one ship and severe damage to another and that, conversely, we have only succeeded in destroying 4 enemy aircraft. This is an extremely unfavourable ratio and does not augur well for the future, particularly bearing in mind the comment [of outline concept of air operations] that the loss of either CVS [aircraft carriers] or LPD would preclude mounting OP SUTTON.[7]

Another expressed concern that the capability of Argentine aircraft was being 'underrated.' The Argentine aircrew had already impressed with their 'skill, determination and press-on spirit.' The Air Staff view was that if a mass attack of Argentine Air and Navy aircraft was mounted at the right moment, heavy damage would probably be inflicted on British forces. This challenged the Air Commander's confidence that 'considerable attrition can be expected from our CAP aircraft, SAM equipped ships and, once ashore, Rapier and Blowpipe.'

The experience of 9 and 12 May might have dented confidence in Sea Wolf and Sea Dart. A paper prepared by Vice Chief of the Naval Staff (VCNS), of uncertain circulation, gives some insight into how the engagements thus far affected views in London. The paper acknowledged that the number of engagements was a small sample, and that there had been problems. But 'sharp lessons have already been learned and there is no reason to doubt that these systems can cope adequately with the threats for which they were designed'. The analysis is striking for the lack of evidence on why *Sheffield* had failed to engage the Super Etendard or the Exocet. The failure of three Sea Darts from *Coventry* to shoot down a pair of Mirages escorting a Hercules was initially put down to them being fired at the limits of their range, and therefore still having a useful tactical value of forcing the aircraft to turn away. However evidence from *Coventry* indicated that range had not been the problem, but rather difficulties with both fusing and taking on multiple targets. It was noted that the current assessments were that there was a 92% probability of correct fuse operation, 75% successful missile flight and 51% probability for one missile against an aircraft, in combination producing only a 35% probability of a kill, leading to the recommendation to use a salvo of two missiles for each aircraft. With the attack on *Glasgow* on 12 May there appeared to have been a defect in the Sea Dart launcher logic circuits that prevented her from loading or perhaps moving the launcher. Yet, it was currently assessed, loading and firing material availability and performance was in the order of 90% and 98% respectively. 'There is no reason to suppose that this defect should recur.' *Brilliant* had used Sea Wolf on 12 May, and was reported to have splashed two A4s in the first raid, but the missile's operation during the second raid had been hampered by the problem of a multi-target situation leading to confusion in the system and a failure to acquire any targets.

Woodward and Clapp had no doubt that the defences on their ships would be hard pressed at the time of a landing, and once the bridgehead was established they would want to get them out of harm's way as soon as possible, leaving the land forces to look after themselves. Much would depend on Rapier. One Rapier group, with twelve clear-weather fire units, was already with the amphibious force. Fieldhouse doubted that this would suffice and asked for another all-weather Rapier Battery, as well as equipment to upgrade the clear-weather Battery already deployed to an all-weather capability, and a Tactical HQ to run the three Rapier sub-units. This was approved on 16 May. The reinforcements could not, however, reach the Falklands until 5 June. On 17 May more requests came from Northwood: one further light battery of close support artillery, to provide greater flexibility in the use of artillery and provide additional fire support to cause attrition on well prepared enemy defensive positions; and then an hour later came a requirement for American Stinger surface-to-air missiles to provide air defence for the landing force as soon as possible. Those responsible for meeting these requests found their sympathy strained: 'One wonders how many other 11th hour requests can be expected. Whilst obviously we must do what we can to help I wonder if COS CINCFLEET realises that each request is put to ministers and any more may look rather haphazard.'

The Stinger request reflected the continued anxiety about air attacks. It was now planned that the three Rapier batteries would provide cover for the anchorage, the beachhead, and the improvised airstrip. This left little flexibility in deploying suitable air defence for units in defence or operating against enemy positions on the Islands. Three Blowpipe troops were deployed but these would only provide limited point defence. The US Stinger could engage targets over a much wider range of profiles than Blowpipe and had a more sophisticated and reliable homing system. For these reasons, Fieldhouse was looking for 32 firing posts (four per infantry unit) with 10 missiles per post and 8 training rounds. The Army Department was sympathetic. It would be uncomfortable to rely so much on a limited number of Blowpipe missiles for point air defence away from the fixed cover provided by Rapier given the lack of natural cover on the Falkland Islands. Any helicopters would be vulnerable to air attack while on the ground. Stinger was easy to operate and had a longer range over certain profiles than Blowpipe. However, the Army was reluctant to show a lack of user confidence in Blowpipe, which was issued widely throughout the Army. This move might adversely affect Blowpipe sales, especially future sales of improved Blowpipe (Javelin), and even put the manufacturer, Shorts, at risk. Moreover unless Stinger was fired by someone fully trained in aircraft recognition (as were Blowpipe detachments) there was a real danger of engaging friendly aircraft. Specialist training would also be required. In some circumstances, including against head-on attacks and when electronic counter-measures were in use by the enemy, Blowpipe would be preferable.

The cost of 32 Stinger fire units and 320 live missiles estimated at approximately £13.2 million was not insignificant while, even with a rapid US response, the missile was unlikely to be in the Falklands before mid-June. On balance, therefore, on 19 May the Army Department recommended successfully against agreeing to this request. Anticipating this outcome, Fieldhouse submitted an alternative request for 24 Blowpipe fire units with crew and 10 missiles per units. This would require taking the missiles from British forces in Germany and it would still take them three weeks to reach the Falkland Islands. This the Army Department agreed.

31

TO SUTTON

Argentine passivity

By the end of the second week in May, Argentine commanders had a reasonably accurate grasp of British strategy – to attack and destroy targets of opportunity (as on 14 May at Pebble Island) and to infiltrate reconnaissance units (not that any had been positively detected), while preparing for an assault in a lightly defended area under protection of diversionary attacks elsewhere. They lacked, however, any detailed tactical knowledge of British dispositions, and had been rattled by the operations to cut off re-supply of West Falkland. They were aware of the imminent arrival of the amphibious force into the South Atlantic but poor reconnaissance undermined their hopes of attacking it before it reached the *Hermes* group.

The morale of the whole garrison was being aggravated by shortages of supplies, prolonged inactivity and heavy rainfall. Supplies were getting close to exhaustion and there was a sense of let-down at the passivity of Argentine naval and air strategy. Until the landing was underway, capabilities were to be held in reserve, with only really worthwhile targets to be attacked, but exactly what would be worthwhile was unclear as were the plans to cope with a landing, the command arrangements and the likely level of support from the mainland. Meanwhile by keeping forces in reserve, Argentina had allowed Britain the initiative. Their surface units operated with impunity near the Islands, even without direct carrier support.

For their own reasons the British also found Argentine passivity frustrating. The implications of this strategy were developed in a major JIC analysis, published on 12 May. Its starting point was that 'Argentina's overriding aim' was 'to ensure that Britain does not regain control over the Islands or any part of them'. The analysis suggested, correctly, that Buenos Aires felt itself under no pressure to take the military initiative by mounting full-scale air and naval attacks against the Task Force. This could change if the blockade seriously degraded the capability of the Argentine garrison, but Argentina believed British strategy to be based not on siege but invasion. Argentine forces would not be risked prematurely, but would be held back until the landing found the British at their most vulnerable. For now, and after the engagements of early May, they were reluctant to engage Harriers in aerial combat and were conscious of the British submarine threat. They therefore saw mainly risk in going for the British fleet by air or sea, and were unlikely to attempt to interdict the British supply ships at a distance from the Falklands Islands, even if they could work out where they were.

If this passive strategy delayed a British assault, that would allow more time for Argentine diplomacy to work and would support claims that only British escalation was preventing a negotiated settlement. Causing delay was a sufficiently important objective that evidence of an imminent British landing might well prompt Buenos Aires to take urgent diplomatic action in an attempt to cause a further delay, perhaps by offering apparently substantial concessions in order to obtain a cease-fire before Britain had re-established even partial control over the Islands. (This assessment needs to be kept in mind when considering the apparent breakthrough in the UN negotiations – and the British response – that took place at this time.) The other advantage of the passive strategy was that this might tempt the Task Force, frustrated by the growing wear and tear on its aircraft and ships, into taking risks in going after Argentine forces.

The main drawback with the passive strategy lay in the state of the Malvinas garrison. The JIC assessment, more optimistic (or pessimistic from the Argentine view) than Defence Intelligence, was that the army had adequate normal rations only until 13 May, while the naval group could last until 25 May. By drawing on combat rations both groups could last another five days. The JIC did not, however, draw from this the conclusion that the optimum strategy for the Task Force was simply to sustain the blockade. The task was demanding in itself and had its own potential for controversial escalation if submarines attacked merchant or fishing vessels, whether or not they were carrying military stores. The JIC took the view that maritime blockades had never been wholly successful and that Argentina would manage a partial break. In doing so some military losses would be acceptable and might even generate international sympathy.

Argentine passivity, at least by the Navy and Air Force, would end with a landing on the Falklands. The Air Force would certainly attack and the JIC doubted that the Argentine Navy would continue to hold back in these circumstances. That being said, in order to interfere with a landing, some surface units, as well as submarines, would need to be close to the Falklands as the assault force approached. If they left it too late the best their naval assets could manage would be interdiction of follow-up forces and the long maritime lines of communication. It was also assumed that a successful British landing could lead Argentina to undertake dramatic high-risk operations against prestige targets such as the *Canberra*. Army passivity might remain a more durable feature of the conflict. The Malvinas garrison would have little alternative to static defences of those areas they had decided to hold. Once Stanley fell, the remaining, smaller garrisons would have little inclination to continue to fight. But Stanley was defensible: overlooked by hills along which the Argentines had already established an outer cordon of defensive positions and an inner perimeter was probably under construction. Overcoming the garrison would require time and hard fighting, especially if Argentine morale held up.

Defence Intelligence, while not dissenting from the broad conclusions of the JIC estimate, took the view that it overstated Argentine strengths. It was doubtful whether the Argentines really were confident that they could 'prevent an outright military victory', given the stance of their fleet and the isolation of their garrison, which was suffering as a result of harassment, the weather and the blockade. More might have been made of the constraints on the Argentine Air Force and the Navy's fear of SSNs. While much had been made of the Argentine wish to 'defer the assault', there had been no indication that this was what was actually intended. The Royal Navy's tradition was never to shirk a fight, even in the face of overwhelming odds, if that is what the campaign requires and so they found the caution of the Argentines surprising. If Argentine naval strategy had been bolder then more ships would probably have been lost, but British operations would have become immensely more complicated.

The landing site

Finding the optimum landing site turned out to be remarkably uncontroversial. The operational parameters limited the options. In sorting out the possibilities for the landing, and also tasking the reconnaissance parties ashore, immense value was gained from Major Ewan Southby-Tailyour's specialist knowledge of the waters around the Falklands, gained by years of sailing and with a mariner's eye for a good landing spot. As early as 29 April San Carlos, with its sheltered waters and no chance of a swell, had emerged as the favourite both on *Fearless* and at Northwood. Thompson and Clapp had no doubt that it would be unwise to land on West Falkland. It might support a concept confined to a long-term presence without further action, but only because of the ease of the initial landing. After that there would be serious problems with air cover, as it would be nearer to the Argentine air bases and further away from the British carriers, while it would add to the difficulties of taking the fight to the Argentine garrison. At the other end of the spectrum a landing near Stanley would be a risk well worth taking if Argentine resistance were expected to be low. Clapp, who had responsibility for the relevant naval and land assets during the amphibious phase along with Thompson, kept this option open, just in case the Argentines might wish to give in, but a collapse in morale would be a bold assumption, and so planning continued to concentrate on San Carlos.

Woodward was aware that Northwood might require an enclave and was also conscious of the vulnerability of his carriers if they had to linger long within range of Argentine aircraft. He was also unaware of just how firm the *Fearless* group were in their preference for San Carlos. So he had been looking at a variety of sites, including Low Bay in Lafonia. To Thompson and Clapp this site was less hospitable to the landing force and with a complicated route to Stanley. Northwood was following the same logic as *Fearless*, so on 8 May Woodward was told that San Carlos was the most likely candidate, and this was confirmed with Clapp (who had been in regular discussion with Northwood on this issue) the next day. San Carlos had 'the overriding advantage of being sheltered from the elements'. Woodward also proposed a deception plan for Cow/Volunteer Bay because it was a logical landing place and the Argentines believed that the British landing would take place in this area. Clapp agreed but felt that the deception site should be Mare Harbour and East Cove (northern approach to Choiseul Sound): 'This is plausible area and well away from any perspective actual choice from Volunteer Bay NW to San Carlos.'

In his signal of 8 May, Fieldhouse explained that San Carlos was favoured because it should make 'the air and maritime protection of vulnerable amphibious shipping much easier.' Final confirmation would depend on there being no significant numbers of enemy troops: 'There can be no question of fighting our way ashore against entrenched opposition.' As for the other threats, 'an easily defended land-locked anchorage' could reduce those from submarines, while the surface fleet could be assumed 'isolated, or confined to harbour before operation starts'. The air threat was not discounted, but it would be less severe at night and to the east, and, at least, Exocet would not get into the anchorage. His conclusion was that the approach should largely be covert and the initial landing be in darkness, amphibious ships should stay in a reasonably protected harbour or stay out to sea by day, Sea Harriers' defence 'will be at a premium and the majority of Arg combat aircraft in Falkland Islands should be taken out prior to landing. SAM assets need to be deployed as early as possible.'

On 10 May San Carlos as a landing site was confirmed. Fieldhouse was also pushing to send a firmer instruction to 3 Commando Brigade to prepare to do more than sit tight once landed. The wording in the 15 April Chiefs of Staff directive 'to land with a view to repossession' had been too restrictive and too ambiguous. It suggested that the next step should not go too far, which is why it had been used to argue for holding back on extra ground forces, or establishing a presence with a view to further negotiations or preparing a beachhead from which future operations might be developed. Since the Chiefs of Staff meeting on 28 April Fieldhouse had argued that this implied the possibility of getting the Islands back without fighting for them and this was unrealistic. The aim should simply be 'to repossess the islands'. The signal on 8 May had made this clear but still retained a cautionary note:

> While 'Repossession' remains the ultimate aim it can only be achieved in stages. The first stage is to build a secure bridgehead, where

sea/air re-supply can be conducted in safety. This must be followed by the establishment of a landing site ashore for helos and Harriers.

Fieldhouse eventually got Lewin to agree on 12 May that the aim should now be 'to repossess the Falkland Islands as quickly as possible', but the appropriate conduct of the war post-landing still remained remarkably vague.

This became part of a discussion the Chiefs had at Northwood that day in order to prepare their recommendations for the War Cabinet, which could no longer be expected to be satisfied with lists of possible options. The Chiefs had before them yet another version of their own options paper. By now some of the softer supplementary actions were already in hand and in others the political restraints were no longer felt to be so pressing. In others some risks were appreciated more. It was, for example, understood that while Special Forces/Commando raids against the Argentine garrison could demonstrate British resolve, if they failed they could present the Argentines with a significant propaganda weapon. Most importantly, the paper acknowledged the developing problems with obtaining local air superiority, even though this was a pre-requisite to most of the options, hence the mention of possible operations to deny Argentina the use of its airfields at Comodoro Rivadavia, Rio Gallegos and Rio Grande. In a different way it was evident in proposals to keep the blockade in place for an extended period, by replacing *Hermes* and *Invincible* in August by *Illustrious*, whose in-service date was being brought forward, and exploring the reactivation of HMS *Bulwark*, a recently decommissioned carrier, or acquiring an ex-USN helicopter platform. This was, it should be recalled, just over a week before a landing was planned. All of these indecisive options carried severe penalties for a force that was likely to run out of time. At each stage of the campaign, going back was politically unthinkable, staying still logistically impractical, so the only option was to move on to the next stage, without any firm plan for the stage after that. In this same spirit, the Chiefs supported the determination of Lewin and Fieldhouse to press on with the landings.

On 12 May CINCFLEET issued his Operation Order 3/82 for Operation SUTTON. The mission was 'To repossess the Falkland Islands as quickly as possible'. Operations would be conducted in the following phases:

Phase I. CTG 317.8 to maintain blockade within the TEZ.
Phase II. CTG 317.8 to conduct SF recce and direct action ops prior to the main landing.
Phase III. CTG 317.0 [COMAW], with TU 317.1.1 [3 Commando Brigade] embarked, conducts main amphibious landing (including MCM Ops).
Phase IV. Land ops by TU 317.1.1 prior to arrival of CTG 317.1 (Commander Land Forces Falkland Islands) [CLFFI] and TU 317.1.2 [5 Infantry Brigade].

Phase V. Establishment CTG 317.1 (CLFFI) in *HMS Fearless* and landing of TU 317.1.2.

Phase VI. Repossession of the Falkland Islands by TG 317.1 (Landing Forces) supported by TG 317.8 and TG 317.0.

Local sea control/air superiority had to be achieved before Phase III was carried out, or initially landings must be conducted by night. Civilian casualties were to be kept to a minimum. Safeguarding civilian property was a lesser but important consideration. The earliest date for D-Day was put at 20 May. Tactical command of the amphibious task group was delegated to COMAW. In Phases III and IV, Brigadier Thompson was nominated as the Commander of the Landing Force and was responsible for operations ashore during the landing phase. Major General Moore was nominated CLFFI. On arrival Moore was to assume responsibilities of the Commander of the Landing Force for Phase V and VI and operational control of formations established ashore. Woodward would remain Tactical Air Controller. The codeword for the initiation of Phase III was PALPUS.

From Phases IV to VI the following sequence could be discerned for post-landing. Clapp and Thompson would get 3 Commando Brigade ashore, Moore would then join them with 5 Infantry Brigade, the Land Commander would establish his headquarters, and then 3 Commando Brigade would press on to repossess the Falklands. The order sent that day by Moore to Thompson stated that:

1. You are to secure a bridgehead on East Falkland, into which reinforcements can be landed, in which an airstrip can be established, and from which operations to repossess the Falkland Islands can be developed.

2. You are to push forward from the bridgehead area, so far as the maintenance of its security allows, to gain information, to establish moral and physical domination over the enemy, and to forward the ultimate objective of repossession.

3. You will retain operational control of all forces landed in the Falklands until I establish my headquarters in the area. It is my intention to do this, aboard *Fearless*, as early as practicable after the landing. I expect this to be approximately on D+7.

4. It is then my intention to land 5 Infantry Brigade into the beachhead area and to develop operations for the complete repossession of the Falkland Islands.

What actually was to be the role for 5 Infantry Brigade: as a reserve and garrison force or as a key element in offensive operations? Moore's view had always been that it would be necessary to use both brigades to defeat the enemy. Strictly speaking, if the standard formulas were used, he would need three brigades. Yet there was a degree of ambiguity in the signal for it did not clarify 5 Brigade's role in later operations. A more important ambiguity was that it was unclear just how far Thompson should push forward before Moore and 5 Infantry Brigade arrived. Repossession was the aim but the means to this end were still undeveloped. Thus a new sense of urgency was reflected in a revised war aim, but not in the phasing in the Operational Order for Sutton, or the more specific instructions to Brigadier Thompson.

Briefing the War Cabinet

There was little opportunity to explore these issues before the plan was presented to the War Cabinet on 14 May. Although Northwood provided MoD with some 42 copies of the plan, distribution was severely restricted to the Chiefs of Staff and their senior staff, and one copy each to a single service two star. No copies went to the Secretariat. Lewin was particularly adamant that the FCO should not receive a copy. The presentation of SUTTON to the War Cabinet took the form of three briefings. The first described the threat. By now a comprehensive collection effort had produced a much improved intelligence picture. The DIS assessment on the overall shape of the Argentine garrison was reasonably accurate. The Ministers were told that the Argentine surface ships would probably be held back in territorial waters, and would stay clear of the carrier task group out of fear of British SSNs, but that they might attempt a move against the troop ships. As the amphibious group moved into position, shore-based aircraft would become an increasing threat. There was not a lot to be done about this beforehand, for it could not be attacked at source, other than hope for opportunities to catch enemy aircraft. Woodward was trying to create such opportunities by launching forays by destroyers and frigates, under the protection of combat air patrols, into the range of Argentine aircraft in order to provoke them into responding. *Spartan*, backed by *Conqueror*, was in position to deal with any attempted naval breakout from port. The wide, gently sloping continental shelf prevented SSNs from operating close to shore especially as the water was crystal clear enabling patrolling aircraft to spot submerged submarines.

It was much more difficult to take the initiative against Argentine submarines, although a number of ASW sweeps had been undertaken. The amphibious group would need to take standard evasive techniques and rely on direct support from ships and helicopters, although that meant that there would be fewer ships available to apply pressure to the Argentines. Although the battle group had a limited range organic surveillance capability in the Sea Kings and Harriers (at the expense of other tasks), the Nimrod's radar range and target classification capability was essential. By using up to 18 tanker sorties per operation, the Nimrod radius of action could be extended to give up to five hours in the Falkland Islands area. Vulcans would be used if necessary against air defence radars in the Falkland Islands and, *in extremis* as a last ditch effort, against enemy mainland air bases. Two Vulcans were ready at Ascension for what would obviously be a high-risk contingency. To deny the Argentines information on Britain's own force movements the amphibious ships were operating in silence.

The second briefing described the choice of landing area, the approach to the Falkland Islands and the naval operations immediately before the landing. In order that those operations could be developed to put early pressure on the enemy, the landing had to be on East Falkland. Opting for West Falkland 'would be rather like doing so in Anglesey if your objective were Cardiff'. The criteria affecting the choice of beach were: good approaches for landing craft and helicopters; an easterly position to minimise the air threat; an area in which ships were least vulnerable to submarine attack and mines and which was suitable to be developed into a landing strip. The reasoning that had led to the choice of San Carlos was described. Of the other possibilities, Mare Harbour offered a good, sheltered landing but little cover and would be used for the deception plan, Berkeley Sound would be a bold move and would shock the enemy, but it was high risk because of enemy deployments and a minefield laid off the Sound.

The plan of approach would be for the separate elements of the amphibious group to join up and then alter course towards the Falkland Islands, using evasive routing with a super-imposed zigzag to confuse enemy submarines and reconnaissance aircraft. To provide protection, both missile and ASW capable units would reinforce it. It would get to within 50 miles of the carrier group on the edge of the TEZ three days before the landing (D–3) so that essential helicopter transfers of personnel, stores and equipment could take place. At this point the final decision on the time and place of the landing would be made, largely depending on weather and intelligence. From this point the first priority of the battle group would be to protect the amphibious group and prepare for the landing. Small groups of destroyers and frigates would close in on the Falklands to carry out bombardment and anti-submarine sweeps, with the aim of tying down the Stanley garrison, unbalancing and destroying outlying units, and reducing the threat in the amphibious objective area. These would be co-ordinated with deceptive operations designed to draw attention to the south-east of East Falkland. Whilst all this was going on, photo reconnaissance and Special Forces operations would continue, including covert surveillance of beaches and their approaches. Just prior to the landing the Special Forces would move on to the offensive.

A massed air attack by day was the prime, and most likely, threat to the landing. The assessment tended to the optimistic, more so than would have been found among the senior commanders in the South Atlantic. The presence of the amphibious group and the landing force would act as a magnet to the full weight of the enemy's air capability, but each sortie would manage barely ten minutes on task. San Carlos Water would provide good protection from Exocet missiles, while ships close inshore would have the benefit of the point defence missile systems as well as being under the Sea Harrier umbrella. Once the forces got ashore, more protection would be provided by land-based air defence assets. If, unexpectedly, the Argentine fleet broke out SSNs would fall back to strengthen direct support for the landing. Nimrods providing long-range warning should reduce the risk of one or two Exocet fitted units slipping out. The submarine threat could be limited so long as the Task Force remained in deep water to the east of the Falkland Islands. Sonar-fitted helicopters from the carriers and additional escorts would provide the ASW protection.

It was during the approach to a landing that the forces became the most vulnerable. The final run in would be made from 30 miles off shore and in darkness. Ships unessential to the landing would be held to the east awaiting re-supply requirements. Pickets would be re-deployed to the west overnight where by staying close to some of the many islets they could greatly reduce the threat to themselves from radar homing missiles, while continuing to provide long-range warning to the force. The priority tasking for the limited number of Sea Harriers had to be air defence under the control of pickets. Given this warning, local air control could still be achieved to ensure an adequate defence of the landing. As the logical position for Argentine submarines was the close vicinity of the Falkland Islands where shallow water made them difficult to find, there would be an active sonar search from the maximum number of helicopters and ships in the approaches and in the entrance to North Falkland Sound. Britain's own submarines would be drawn into the vicinity of the Falkland Islands to provide defence in depth against the surface threat. Initially escorts with sonar-fitted helicopters would be deployed to carry out an active sweep off the entrance four hours before the arrival of the amphibious group. They would be released to conduct bombardment in support of the landings on the arrival of the amphibious group. Because of the submarine threat and the numbers of units required to counter it, the area over which organic assets could carry out surface surveillance would by this stage be much reduced – and it had always been negligible. It was at this point that the Ascension-based Nimrod should be particularly valuable. (In the event sea surveillance was always inadequate.) In addition to Special Forces moving to the offensive a surface decoy group would also simulate an assault force to confuse enemy defences.

As the landing began the amphibious group would be inside the Falkland Sound, a haven free of enemy submarines and surface units. Special Forces would have played a vital part in ensuring the integrity of the haven and its approaches. The haven would be maintained by keeping the entrances closed. Units in the Sound would provide local air defence and gunfire support. At this point the forces would be vulnerable but it would take

Argentine forces time to react so the major enemy effort was most likely to occur during daylight following the landing. Any surface ships would be detected during their long transit from mainland ports. Submarines would have difficulty penetrating British defence. The force would be prepared for an air attack. As the operation continued Admiral Woodward would wish to withdraw his carriers to seaward where he could use speed and sea room to best advantage whilst carrying out further offensive operations. Naval operations would continue to support landing forces but the emphasis would gradually shift to a resumption of wider battle group operations once the situation ashore permitted.

The third briefing described the actual landing. The force consisted of three RM Commandos and two Battalions of the Parachute Regiment, supported by four batteries of close support artillery, a Royal Engineer Squadron, one battery of Rapier and two troops of Blowpipe and weapons plus logistic elements. The troop lift was said to be provided by twelve Sea King and 20 Wessex helicopters, plus eight Landing Craft Utility and twelve Landing Craft, Vehicles and Personnel (LCVPs). The actual numbers, it should be noted, were lower: one Sea King was soon to be lost in a cross-decking incident and only five Wessex were available. Nor were the four LCVPs from *Hermes* made available. Heavy lift was to be provided later by four Chinook helicopters, which would be invaluable in the logistic build-up ashore. Three of these were lost with the *Atlantic Conveyor* before their value could be exploited. The actual position would be much tighter than described to the War Cabinet.

The disposition of Argentine forces ashore was described, noting that the main enemy strength was in the eastern area. Reference was made to the Pucaras and air defence guns and missiles, and to the opportunities that could have been taken after six weeks to get established ashore and to prepare defended positions. A reserve, at battalion strength although unsupported by artillery, was available, with helicopter lift for up to two companies and so providing a potentially speedy response to a landing.

Of the 14 SBS patrols and 23 SAS patrols presently deployed with the Task Force, 13 had so far been committed to covert reconnaissance and intelligence gathering tasks. They had been operating since early May, all inserted by helicopter and, crucially, so far all undetected. Argentine patrols had been avoided through regular changes in position, the choice of unlikely spots and camouflage. This made possible a more accurate intelligence picture of the enemy's dispositions. Reconnaissance operations would continue until the landing.

As the landing took place, Special Forces would seek to destroy key enemy assets: radars, the Pucara ground attack aircraft, helicopters, air defence systems, fuel and ammunition; harass the enemy, cause dispersion of forces and reduce his morale; and deceive the enemy as to the location of the main landing. Assuming San Carlos, the amphibious group would enter

North Falkland Sound after last light with the key ships of the assault wave consisting of *Fearless, Intrepid, Canberra, Norland, Stromness*, the five LSLs and *Europic Ferry*. Some would move right into San Carlos Bay and the landing itself would then be carried out both by landing craft and helicopters. It was planned that the distance to run from ship to shore would not exceed ten miles, and with eight hours of darkness remaining after the approach up to four Commandos/Battalions with limited combat support would be ashore by first light. Provided that the landing continued at full pace the landing force would be well balanced before the day was out, and it would be thoroughly established ashore with seven days' logistic support after three days. The challenge of defending the amphibious force and the beachhead would begin almost at once. Presuming that could be survived, and the perimeter of the beachhead secured, then the support helicopters would move ashore to operate from a forward air base to be followed by a basic operating strip for the Harriers. The briefing stressed that although the landing of the Commandos in the early waves would be swift the subsequent build-up of logistic supplies, vehicles and ammunition would take some considerable time because almost everything which went ashore had to be lifted into its operational position by helicopter – movement by vehicles would be almost impossible except around the settlement areas.

Meanwhile, HQ Land Forces Falkland Islands (LFFI) had been established to control land forces in the Falkland Islands once the second brigade arrived. The core of this HQ was presently at Northwood. Once the initial landing on the Falkland Islands had become established, Lieutenant General Trant with a staff from SE District would assume the appointment of military adviser to CINCFLEET and Moore with his staff would fly to Ascension, there to join *QEII* for swift passage to the Falklands. On arrival there his HQ would cross deck to *Fearless* and establish itself there. 5 Infantry Brigade was due to arrive in the Falklands in the period approximately 29 May–1 June and land into the secure beachhead. It would be supported by 10 Sea King and 24 Wessex helicopters. Arriving slightly later would be a further six Harrier GR3, doubling the available numbers. When this build-up was completed Moore would have the balanced forces required for the repossession of the Islands. No description was provided of this next stage.

After the briefings, Fieldhouse endorsed the plan as presented as entirely feasible, with sufficient flexibility to cope with the unexpected and able to contain the various threats to the British force. Part of the flexibility was in the timing of D-Day, which for weather factors alone could not be precise at this stage. However, he argued for a final approach on the evening of 20 May with the landing in the early hours of the next day as being the first opportunity. This would require a decision to proceed during the morning of Tuesday 18 May. That decision could be delayed up to a week. The landing window was now therefore between Friday 21 and 28 May. CINCFLEET concluded:

In recognition that you will want to know the possible price of a landing operation, I have given a great deal of thought to this aspect, and it is of course, impossible to quantify. However, the combined air, submarine and surface threats with their various strengths and limitations, confirmed by experience, lead me to the conclusion that although we could suffer serious damage to ships of the landing force including perhaps the loss of a major unit, the plan we have conceived will nevertheless result in success at the least price. That is, in a viable landing force being put ashore. Furthermore, I am confident that in the face of today's opposition, under tight blockade, we can select a landing place where early opposition from shore will be negligible and thus allow the establishment of a sound and secure base from which further operations can be undertaken, should they in the event prove to be necessary. Neither is there any doubt in my mind that significant delay in landing will increase the possible cost in human life, not reduce it.

Final decision

Having been informed of the state of decision making, Woodward told Fieldhouse that he would need a decision, one way or the other, by 2130Z on 18 May (H-29 hours), the time when the amphibious group would need to start its transit. If he were to hold, the decision would need to be reviewed every 24 hours. Although initially it had been assumed that air superiority would be a prerequisite for a landing, by 17 May it was accepted that air control could not be achieved by the time the landing was planned to take place. The difficult judgement was made at Northwood that whilst losses due to an attack could be severe, SUTTON should still go ahead.

Unless Argentina accepted the final British proposals before the deadline expired at noon in New York (1700 London time) on 19 May, there could be no peaceful settlement to the dispute. The day before the deadline expired, on 18 May, the Prime Minister invited the War Cabinet to consider whether in these circumstances they were prepared to authorise the military repossession of the Falkland Islands. It was for the Chiefs of Staff to advise on the military feasibility of the operation. Their advice, presented first by the CDS, was that this was about the only option left that was feasible. There was no satisfactory settlement available to be negotiated nor was a long blockade viable. The recommendation was therefore that the landing should go ahead as soon as practicable. Once British forces were ashore they should press ahead in order to achieve either satisfactory conditions for a cease-fire and withdrawal or the surrender of the Argentine garrison. In making this recommendation they acknowledged risks: from the Argentine fleet, including submarines, and especially from air attack. Attrition of Argentine forces had been less than had been hoped. They judged the risks, and the expected consequential losses, to be militarily acceptable. So long as the landing force could get ashore it would have a very good chance of success. If political authority was given that day it could be countermanded up to the afternoon of 20 May should something unexpected happen on the diplomatic front. By then, unless hampered by bad weather, the landing forces would be inside the TEZ and the ships involved would be heavily loaded. If authority to proceed were suspended for any significant period at that stage they would need to withdraw and regroup.

Individually the Chiefs made their own submissions, all pointing to the same conclusion. Beetham was concerned that the Argentine Air Force had not been neutralised, and had shown that they could locate British ships on the move, by sinking one and almost sinking another. Once the landing had begun, British ships would be within range and in known positions. Faced with an all-out effort full air defence of British forces could not be guaranteed and some ships could be lost. He was confident that the landing forces would achieve success, though pockets of resistance could make total repossession protracted. In such circumstances, the process of attrition could take time while the TEZ would still have to be enforced to prevent Argentine resupply. Nonetheless, 'the point of decision had now been reached'. More softening up time would be an advantage, but delay created its own risks of further losses.

Leach was also more confident about being able to deal with the naval threats but was bothered by the lack of air superiority. The risk he judged acceptable, given the selected beachhead, British anti-aircraft assets and their planned deployment and sensible use of darkness. Two other factors were important. The longer British forces delayed the greater would be the attrition they suffered, not least from accidental causes. Furthermore: 'if Britain hung back now, the erosion of her national standing, both in general and as regards negotiations in the present crisis, would be profound and long-term'. This sense of the wider geo-political implications of the decision, as much as the immediate military practicalities, was also reflected in Bramall's submission. (Nott, who thought that the meeting went well, nonetheless noted how the Chiefs 'could not restrain their enthusiasm for making political comments'.[1]) Bramall noted that given luck, which would certainly be needed, the operation could turn out to be a great success; 'In that event, Britain's status in the world, the respect shown to her and the strength and credibility of her own deterrent strategy would be that much more enhanced for years to come.' Air superiority was, however, one of the modern principles of war and it had not yet been achieved. So the risks were higher than would normally have been considered appropriate in an operation of the present sort, particularly during the landing and build-up before troops were firmly established ashore. Once this had been achieved, the risks would decrease markedly. At some stage it should be possible to use what was expected to become a formidable and secure presence ashore as a means of achieving British aims and getting a lasting settlement. Bramall still hoped that this could be done without necessarily involving either major bloodshed around Stanley or the permanent stationing of land and naval forces in what strategically he regarded as entirely the wrong part of the world.

The legal submission, from the Attorney General, explained that since British territory was involved, the military operations now contemplated were legally compatible with the self-defence provisions of Article 51 of the UN Charter and with SCR 502. This compatibility would also extend to operations elsewhere provided they were in response to a serious threat to British forces.

The War Cabinet accepted the advice: the landing and repossession operations would go ahead unless it was clear that an acceptable diplomatic settlement was available by the afternoon of 20 May. They were now well aware that the air threat was a more dangerous factor than generally realised and this would need to be made clear to the full Cabinet, although because knowledge of the landing should be confined to the narrowest possible circle, this should be left to as late as possible. The loss of ships and equipment, it could be assumed, would matter less to public opinion, than the loss of British lives. Casualties, however, were hard to predict. It might be possible to achieve the desired result simply as a result of the landing, but the use of force to repossess the Islands completely could well be necessary. Leach later observed that he 'had fully expected to be asked how many ships I thought we would lose in action and what losses I would regard as the acceptable limit':

> I had speculated at length on this and reached the broad conclusions that we would probably lose about six destroyers/frigates and could, in the circumstances, afford to lose at least double that number. Where the assessment became more complex was over the possible sinking of one or both of the Carriers; here additional factors such as the state of the air battle, whether the landing and build-up had been successfully accomplished and the availability of helicopter and VSTOL operating sites ashore became relevant.

In the event, he was 'questioned on none of these aspects'.[2]

The decision was made: the landing and repossession operations envisaged in the plan put forward by the Force Commander and endorsed by the Chiefs of Staff were authorised by the War Cabinet. The operations should therefore proceed, unless the War Cabinet took a specific decision to the contrary, not later than on the afternoon of 20 May. It would be for the Force Commander to decide, in the light of local considerations, whether the landing should be made on the night of 20/21 May or later. On 18 May at 1145, the authority to execute operation SUTTON was given by the CDS. Weather permitting, the Task Force Commander in turn authorised a landing to take place at San Carlos Water overnight on 20/21 May. Fieldhouse had earlier spoken with Clapp to reassure himself that the amphibious group was ready to land 3 Commando Brigade and that they in turn were ready to be landed. He also confirmed with Woodward that he was ready and able to give a reasonable level of support to the amphibious group.

At 1000 on 20 May, the Prime Minister told the War Cabinet that 'though the weather remained an uncertain factor, the Force Commander had not altered his view on the timing of military operations. The authorisation he had been given still stood.' Within an hour the decision had been signalled to the Task Force. Clapp requested permission to proceed and Woodward approved. There was then a meeting of Cabinet who were told that Fieldhouse had been given discretion as to when to step up military operations. A landing in force would be necessary. The consequences of failing to achieve prior air superiority were explained, in terms of risks higher than would normally be considered appropriate for an operation of this sort. The Chiefs believed the risks to be manageable although they were likely to lead to casualties. It was also made clear that the Chiefs had not been denied authority to attack the Argentine mainland because they had not deemed it necessary to ask for it. The Cabinet unanimously backed the decision and expressed confidence in the armed forces.

That afternoon the House of Commons debated the issue. For the first time a vote was taken, forced by a number of dissident Labour MPs. The Government won by 296 votes to 33. One of the leading anti-war campaigners, Tam Dalyell, warned of 'a military defeat of the first magnitude.' The Labour Party had been careful not to oppose Government policy. From the start of the crisis public opinion had supported the use of force to regain the Falklands, with as many prepared for tougher action than the Government thought it prudent to take (such as raids against the mainland) as arguing that the action was disproportionate. In opinion polls, a steady two thirds of the population had been in favour of landing troops if necessary, even if the United States was critical. Only the sinking of the *Belgrano* led to evident unease. Although shares and sterling fell sharply after the Argentine invasion, they recovered. In other conflicts, for example Suez, public division and financial crisis played important roles. During the course of the Falklands the Government rarely had reason to doubt that it had public opinion on its side, and to the extent that it worried about a loss of support it was because it might have given the impression of being too eager for a diplomatic settlement.

Presentation

There would be no greater test of policy than the execution of SUTTON. MoD were desperate that not only should there be no hint of what was to come but that, even if it succeeded, news should not be released until well after the event. It was conceivable that British forces could establish a beachhead without the Argentines being aware of British intent. However, if success were to be trumpeted, it might well precipitate a last-ditch response from the Argentine Air Force. Such a reaction could take the form of a demented attack on the fleet or Ascension Island. One senior officer wrote: 'Better, I suggest, to let the news dawn slowly on the Argentinians from their own sources'.

When on 18 May the War Cabinet took the decision to land, Nott set out a paper on the public presentation of the Falkland Islands landing operations. There would be military and political advantages to be gained if Britain were able initially to disguise their scale:

> Militarily we should aim at creating the maximum uncertainty in the minds of the Argentine command. The potential benefits would be the holding back of a concerted Argentine air attack (the major threat in the landing phase) to await 'the main invasion'; the holding back of Argentine reserves on the Falkland Islands from all out commitment; and general confusion. The Argentine Aircraft Carrier and other naval forces might continue as now, withdrawn and irresolute.

Britain's landing operations should be presented initially as a further development of earlier raiding operations; 'and one more turn of the screw to encourage the Argentines to withdraw'. Subsequently when some ships had withdrawn, presence on the Islands, according to Nott, could be admitted as a way of bringing yet more pressure to bear on the Argentine garrison. Britain could then indicate that other landings might follow. This would require managing for a limited period reporting of military events in the South Atlantic. It would also require the co-operation of correspondents with the Task Force and the press here. Britain would need to avoid a public relations vacuum. Nott argued that: 'There was a reasonable prospect of this coming off and even a few hours of time gained would be valuable'. Actual fighting operations in and around the Falklands would be unaffected. Nothing would be lost, since Britain had the option at any time of announcing that it was carrying out 'full scale landing operations aimed at repossession of the Islands'.

On 19 May MoD signalled Woodward that for at least the first few hours after a major landing 'we shall want to do as much as we can to disguise from the Argentines the scale and true purpose of the operation'. To do this effectively, MoD needed the co-operation of the embarked press and media representatives. MoD wanted Woodward to brief them as follows:

> It will help a major landing to succeed, and minimise casualties, if the Argentine Garrison, and the Argentine Government, are in doubt for several hours that it has begun. They may hesitate to

commit forces to the point of decision: such as hold back land-based aircraft if they believe that the main landing will come later or somewhere else. We therefore need the help of the press and media representatives. It would be helpful if initial reports could indicate that this was another in a series of landings or raids (on a larger scale than before) to harass the Garrison and soften it up.

Once it became obvious what was going on press and media representatives would be free to report fully (subject to normal security restraints). They could then suggest that what had begun as a major raid had developed into a full-scale landing. On 20 May, MoD's Chief of Public Relations, Neville Taylor, told Frank Cooper that: 'we *must* have control over the initial report of a landing (and possibly first reports of subsequent operations)':

Quite apart from the fact that we shall all have some difficulty in ensuring that no single correspondent manages to get access to a communication channel we have no means of knowing how or when the Argentinian authorities will interpret first reports. It will be rather surprising if they have not already thought about the sort of announcement that they would make the moment there was a genuine report of an initial attack.

As it was essential that MoD controlled the timing of the first release of information on any landing, correspondents should only be allowed to process copy through military communication exclusively for MoD Press Office for passing on to London offices, and only after local vetting and when MoD had issued the first press release, the time of which would have been signalled. It was also deemed essential that correspondents did not have access to MARISAT before MoD authorities lifted restrictions. Even when this was done, correspondents were to clear text of broadcasts in the same way as written copy.

The situation as the landing took place and just after would be confused, so that early reports could well be inaccurate. Proposals were made to antici-pate the sort of announcements that might have to be made, especially if there were reverses. Cooper's view was that, whatever the PR or diplomatic penalties, information must not be given which would endanger British forces or reduce their effectiveness. In addition MoD must invariably tell the truth, correct errors and avoid deliberately misleading the media ('even if we some-times conceal certain points'). Credibility was MoD's greatest advantage over the Argentines, who had already proved themselves suspect to the media. On balance it was better to make a thin announcement early (particularly before the Argentines) than a fuller one later. MoD must also continue to make some initial reports on the record (and live to camera) since this was the best way of ensuring that statements were repeated accurately world-wide.

MoD had also to increase the volume of PR material released – particularly on operations. The coverage MoD received was directly proportional to the output it produced. The capacity of the world-wide media organisations would be filled somehow and, if not by Britain, then by the Argentines or ill-informed lay commentators. All announcements and briefings should show (either directly or implicitly) that military operations were being deliberately undertaken in support of broader government objectives and, especially, to reach a solution with the minimum use of force. MoD should not be afraid to announce bad news in the same way as good news. Only if there were genuine security concerns – which there often would be – should MoD conceal losses or delay their announcement. Internationally, British acceptance of losses was seen as a sign of steadiness and determination.

32

THE LANDING

In Britain and in the South Atlantic the risks to the landing force were analysed and re-analysed. The Argentines clearly knew that a landing was likely but not exactly where or when. Success required surprise. To achieve this good intelligence was required on Argentine preparations, while the enemy remained unaware of British preparations and, preferably, was looking elsewhere when the critical moment came. Intelligence gathering had not been easy. From 9 May, Nimrods had been mounting surveillance sorties from Ascension. The demands on tankers were extensive – requiring up to 11 Victors as the sorties moved further south. Vulcan bomber attacks and Hercules airdrops competed for the same resources. It was decided that for the moment, and until after the landing, the priority was to make sure that no Argentine warships were at sea, and, if any were, that there was sufficiently timely information for the SSNs to intercept them. On 16 May *Alacrity* travelled Falkland Sound again and could report back that there was still no hint of mining activity. Although Clapp was fairly confident that San Carlos would be free of mines, at least one of his captains thought that the lack of certain evidence meant that an unacceptable risk was being taken.

The British believed that the head of the Argentine Navy, Admiral Anaya, remained committed to defending the Falklands, regardless of the further cost in lives and equipment. The strategy appeared to be not so much one of stopping the British retaking the Islands as of imposing such costs that the Thatcher Government would fall. Rather than agree to an unsatisfactory negotiated settlement, the hawks in the Junta appeared to take the view that it was better to rely on London being unable to sustain either its military or diplomatic position over the long term. The contribution of Anaya's own force to this objective was less sure. The Argentine Navy was hardly taking a bold posture. The two Argentine Type 42s were going to be in port for refuelling and re-provisioning in the run up to the landing, while the Southern Task Group of two older destroyers was in Ushuaia. Three frigates had been at sea for some time, and at one point were well beyond the 12-mile limit, but they had been pulled back nearer the coast

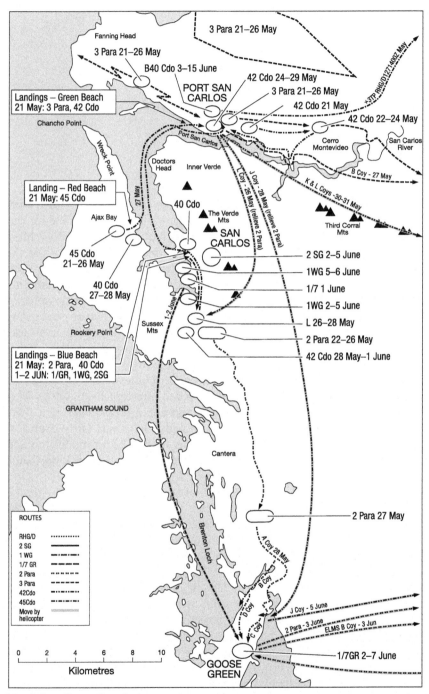

Map 7 Landing at San Carlos

where the rest of the surface fleet, including the carrier, had been operating. The cautious strategy was being followed, although the ships were being kept well supplied and could deploy quickly. The two Type 209 submarines had escaped detection so far but their impact had been limited and the threat had been downgraded. At most one submarine was on patrol. In fact the *San Luis* had returned to Puerto Belgrano on 17 May and needed maintenance and repairs before she could go on patrol again; the *Salta* was suffering from a series of defects and was not ready to deploy; the *Santiago del Estero* was permanently non-operational.

The Air Force was altogether better prepared. Its aircraft, deployed among the southern airfields, were well armed, and had been practising attacks against naval targets. They had considered the failure of the high-altitude attacks on 1 May and concluded that incoming aircraft should fly low to avoid the Harrier CAP and the ship's radar. By attacking in late afternoon they could come in from the west with the setting sun at their backs.[1] All operations over the Falkland Islands were to be carried out by a minimum of eight aircraft, arriving together. There were also to be periodic armed reconnaissance sorties over the Islands to seek active contact with British forces by day and night. There was a divided command, with attacks on ships to be controlled from the mainland while those on ground forces would be co-ordinated with the Southern Air Force. The Island commanders had been urged to continue supplying information on targets although the decision on what to attack would rest with the mainland commanders. The Air Force policy was only to mount strikes against ships in the vicinity of the Islands: the Argentine Navy's greatest hope was that an Exocet could be launched successfully, if possible against a carrier. At least three Exocet missiles were left and the international marketplace was being scoured for more. Inshore Exocets would be less of a worry than the Daggers and Skyhawks. Those in Britain who sought reassurance from these assessments noted that they would have to fly in daylight and at the limits of their range, although it was accepted that the A4 was capable of aerial refuelling.

The Army garrison, still put at about 11,000 men, was low in morale and supplies, cold, wet, and suffering from increasing sickness. The Special Force patrols had reported back on troops that appeared to be badly led, so that their defensive routines were poor and their main preoccupation appeared to be a search for food. The garrison had depleted local air support – some nine Pucaras and enough helicopters to lift two companies. Getting the measure of this force was not easy. One senior commander told his officers that the enemy was isolated and cold. 'The ratio of cas [casualties] in previous contacts with the RM may worry them. Some conscripts will be at the end of their year's service.' Yet despite these factors, including the role of conscripts, the general line was that the enemy would not fold up easily following British landings, or even after subsequent pressure. There was a cadre of well-trained officers and NCOs, and the troops were probably in positions with arms and ammunition able to make life and attacks very difficult for British forces, as well as being able to draw on some artillery backing. The prospect on land was of a protracted struggle and high casualties.

Final preparations

As the War Cabinet was deliberating in London on 18 May, the carrier battle group (TG 317.8) and the amphibious group (TG 317.0) had finally come together. The amphibious group had arrived overnight into a holding area on the eastern edge of the TEZ. To the irritation of the commanders news that the two had joined up leaked out. Again illustrating how operational and political imperatives could point in different directions, Nott thought the effect of the news helpful in demonstrating that military options had not been forgone for diplomatic reasons.

The amphibious force involved was of a 1950s design. The two LPDs – *Fearless* and *Intrepid* – each had four LCUs (Landing Craft Utility), each capable of getting 150 men ashore, and four LCVPs (Landing Craft Vehicle and Personnel). The Landing Ship Logistic (LSL), named after Knights of the Round Table, could land equipment and vehicles directly on to beaches through a bow door, but could also unload on to other vessels, including Mexeflotes which could be used as ferries. Under the command of Commodore Clapp on *Fearless*, the amphibious group comprised the two LPDs, five LSLs, *Canberra*, *Norland*, *Elk*, *Europic Ferry* and *Atlantic Conveyor*, supported by the RFAs *Stromness*, *Tidepool*, *Pearleaf* and the water carrier *Fort Toronto*, escorted by the *Antrim*, *Argonaut*, *Ardent* and *Plymouth*. They were joined by *Hermes* and *Brilliant* at 1100Z and remained in company, allowing Clapp and Woodward to confer, while *Fort Austin* and *Resource* joined the main body. This meeting was far more amicable than the previous encounter at Ascension. Woodward was now able to provide air cover to Clapp's group. Especially welcome were the extra Harriers. Six GR3s and an extra four Sea Harriers brought *Hermes*' total to 21. *Invincible* embarked another four new aircraft, bringing her Sea Harrier total to ten.

The plan had been for two Commandos, 40 and 42, and 3 Para, 2,000 men in total, to be taken into San Carlos together on *Canberra*. As noted earlier, Fieldhouse was nervous about so many men on a single ship, 'too many eggs could be placed in one basket'. On 18 May, Moore signalled from Northwood, to the exasperation of Clapp and Thompson, that it was 'unacceptable … that run in for assault be carried out with three units in one ship'. This required transferring two units from *Canberra* to other vessels. In the prevailing conditions it was hard to see how this could be done other than by finding sheltered waters, either at South Georgia or actually overnight in the Falklands. Nonetheless, the transfer was ordered irrespective of time delays.

At this point the weather intervened in an unusually helpful way, as 19

May turned out to be clear and calm, allowing 40 Commando to be trans-ferred to *Fearless* and 3 Para to *Intrepid* by LCUs. The movement of so many men and their equipment from one ship to another carried its own risks, a point tragically illustrated when the transfers were almost at an end as an 846 Squadron Sea King 4 taking SAS troops from *Hermes* to *Intrepid* ditched after what was reported to be a birdstrike. Eight survivors, including the two pilots, were picked up but the aircraft had turned over and sunk almost immediately. 21 SAS troops, including a number who had survived the glacier in San Georgia, and the RM aircrewman were killed. Also lost were the SAS's RAF Forward Air Controller and his laser designation equipment. The replacement target marker only barely arrived in time for the first ever use of a laser-guided weapon by the RAF just before the fall of Stanley. In noting that the weather had been kind, as otherwise the cross decking could not 'have been completed in twice the time', Woodward observed how 'the price has to be paid possibly due to equipment failure or pilot error but almost always in human life'.

Information on any Argentine units in the landing area depended on the patrols of the Special Forces. From 15 May it was known that an infantry company occupied Fanning Head, overlooking the main sea approach to San Carlos Water. The reported enemy strength was insufficient to trigger a change in the landing site but it was important now that this company be denied any impression of a special interest in the area. Because of this patrols to be inserted around San Carlos on 16 May were cut back. Then an SBS team that was being sent ashore from *Brilliant* saw torch flashes as they drew close to shore and had decided to abort the mission. If the Argentines stumbled across a patrol then the landing site would be given away. For this reason the site would have to be left unwatched until just before the landing. The final insertions did not take place until overnight 18/19 May using two Sea Kings. Plans also had to be developed for dealing with this company before they could interfere with the landings.

The deception plan had three aspects. Operation TORNADO was designed to convey the impression that the major focus of the British effort was close to Stanley. The area between Stanley and Choiseul Sound was to be bombarded for about four days in order to harass but also to deceive, to orientate Argentine commanders towards that area, as the likely landing spot. This was reinforced by spoof communications and air activity. The deception plan had started with a leak of strategic signals about a forthcoming opera-tion code name TORNADO, a reference to a 'large combined operation against mainland and Falkland Islands targets to be launched in near future'. The deception would be followed by air activity over the area, the insertion of an SBS patrol, who would talk to locals leaking the spoof and then leave some landing gear in the area, naval gunfire, further leaks on the inadequacy of naval air defences and then dummy insertions of reconnais-sance patrols, possible Vulcan strikes against mainland air bases, and a general sense of frantic activity all designed to create a sense of urgency around 20 May, the day before the real landing was planned. This had involved *Glamorgan* taking up a position off the Stanley peninsula and bombarding positions on Lively Island and at coastal points either side of the entrance to Choiseul Sound. A Wessex helicopter operated off the coast, and a communications deception plan was implemented. Second, D Squadron SAS was tasked to create a diversion in the Darwin area to occupy the attention of enemy forces in that area.

Third, as already noted, official comment in London encouraged the view first that nothing dramatic should be expected and then that a number of landings were under way. On 20 May Cooper told an unattributable briefing: 'Don't see this as a great World War II epic, a sort of great D-Day and everybody goes storming across the beaches and this, that and the other.' He predicted that 'the screw will be tightened at a variety of points – as and when the Commander thinks it's right.' He later defended his words on the grounds that the landings might have been delayed, because of weather, and because the intention was to have an unopposed landing, and so not like D-Day at all.[2] Parkinson recalls a conversation with an American journalist (whom he later discovered to be Carl Bernstein of the *Washington Post*) as he did an interview for the US ABC network early on the morning of 21 May. 'I am totally discreet', said Bernstein, asking to be told off the record if the British were about to go in. Parkinson used the agreed formula – 'there will be an intensification of activities from now on' – and was pleased to hear the journalist calling back to the US, on the authority of a Cabinet Minister, that the British would not be 'landing tonight.'[3]

The assault plan involved a silent landing in three phases. First a simultaneous beach assault by 40 and 45 Commando and then 2 and 3 Para would land to secure Port San Carlos Settlement and a defensive position on the reverse slope of Sussex Mountains. The third phase would see the artillery and air defence units brought ashore by helicopter to cover the beachhead. Only then would 42 Commando be brought ashore. They would then move out to observe and report all enemy ground and air movement especially at Douglas Settlement and Teal Inlet. The idea was to get this over as soon as possible so as to be able to cope with enemy attacks from the air or land. Critically, Thompson wanted to be in a good defensive posture ready to fight off enemy attacks in any form they might take: 'When we are firmly established and not before, we will patrol aggressively and mount operations to sap enemy morale and will to fight'. Thompson wanted to make clear that the landing was 'NOT an end in itself – merely the beginning.' Famously he finished off by writing: 'Will NOT be a picnic' but 'I feel absolute confidence that we will succeed'.

Thompson later changed the order of landing in order to block any threat from the Argentine garrison at Darwin and Goose Green. Now 40 Commando and 2 Para would land side by side in the first phase, allowing 2

Para to move quickly on to Sussex Mountains. 45 Commando would land later in Phase 2. The amphibious group would travel the last 100 miles to the entrance to the Falkland Sound in darkness. The landing would take place at 0630Z, leaving another five hours before sunrise to get as much as possible ashore.

The risk of being caught by Exocets had led Woodward to keep his carriers back, with Type 42s acting as pickets for added protection. It was still the case that no single event was likely to scupper the whole operation other than the loss of *Hermes* or *Invincible*. This reduced the amount of time Harriers could spend over the landing area to about half an hour and left the force dependent upon the frigates sent in to San Carlos Waters with the amphibious ships. At 1522Z on 20 May, Moore sent the following signal to all ranks of 3 Commando Brigade:

> As you prepare to land in the Falkland Islands, I wish you all well. Good to have the Red Beret alongside the Green again. We did so well together at Suez and we will do so again tomorrow I know. Best Luck.

Ashore

Fearless, *Intrepid* and *Yarmouth* led the group towards San Carlos, followed by *Plymouth*, *Brilliant*, *Canberra*, *Norland*, *Stromness* and *Fort Austin*. Behind came the five LSLs and *Europic Ferry* escorted by *Broadsword* and *Argonaut*. *Ardent* and *Antrim* had to rush to join the group, following earlier support for the diversionary operations. By 0400Z on 21 May, midnight local time, the force was in position. At the same time the two deception operations to alert the Argentines to activity around Stanley (bombardment by HMS *Glamorgan*) and Goose Green/Darwin (Special Forces raid and bombardment by *Ardent*) were underway. At 0740Z 3 SBS armed with machine guns and a mortar, backed by forward observers for naval gunfire from *Antrim*, and Captain Rod Bell, a Spanish linguist, landed to the east of Fanning Head to deal with the Argentine group from 25 Infantry Regiment positioned on Fanning Head. This dominated the entrance to San Carlos Water and offered opportunities to inflict severe damage on British forces as they landed, using mortars and anti-tank weapons. After naval gunfire and mortar fire was directed close to their position, the Argentines began to move away and they were urged to surrender. The offer was rejected. Subsequent fighting led to twelve Argentines being killed and nine taken prisoner. About 42 escaped.[4] As they withdrew to the east, they engaged a Sea King, which got away, but did bring down two Gazelles. Two pilots and one aircrewman were killed, one having been shot at in the water.

The actual landing took place in favourable circumstances on what Thompson later called 'an inspiring day'. The weather was calm and there was no opposition. The only problem was that a series of delays had led to the troops hitting the beach about an hour late at 0730Z, or 0330 in the morning local (Argentine) time. The delay was caused by a faulty satellite navigational system in *Fearless* which suggested that the command ship was going faster than was actually the case. First ashore were 2 Para, who were met only by a surprised Special Forces patrol who were apparently expecting the landing the next day, and then 40 Commando, which soon secured San Carlos Settlement and raised the Union Flag. There they came across 31 civilians, including 14 children.[5] At about 1100Z it was getting light as 45 Commando and 3 Para landed. The marines occupied the old refrigeration plant at Ajax Bay without trouble and 3 Para went ashore at Port San Carlos to protect the northern flank. They soon had a disturbing example of the need for coordinating all activity in the battalion area as patrols from A and C Companies came across each other and, assuming the other to be the enemy, together called in mortar fire, leaving some wounded. 42 Commando remained afloat as reserve. The landing craft, mexeflotes and helicopters soon began to move the follow-up troops and all the equipment, ammunition, fuel and stores ashore. Once the troops had been landed and the surrounding high ground taken, the next priority was to get the 12 Rapier firing posts established. They would be followed by the stores and the ancillary units that would be needed to create such vital facilities as the Brigade Maintenance Area, medical base, fuel farm and Harrier pad. Throughout the day preparation of defensive positions continued despite regular air raids, although the shipping in San Carlos was the main target. 2 Para had turned south and established a defensive position on Sussex Mountains, effectively blocking the route that any counter-attack from the Darwin area would have to take. 40 Commando moved east up onto the Verde Mountains.[6]

Air operations in support of the landing force began. One pair of GR3s from *Hermes* successfully attacked a helicopter park at Mount Kent, identified by one of the Special Force patrols, destroying a Chinook and a Puma. This was an important strike, reducing the Argentine ability to move reinforcements to critical areas. There was less luck for another pair intending to attack West Falkland. One had to return with a jammed undercarriage: a Blowpipe shot the other down over Port Howard. The pilot, Flight Lieutenant J Glover, ejected to become the only British prisoner of war. At Goose Green SAS observers saw six Pucaras preparing for take-off. They called in gunfire from *Ardent* onto the airfield. Only one aircraft got airborne and it was later shot down by an SAS Stinger, although not before it had reported on the activity in San Carlos Water. It was this report, combined with those from the troops retreating from Fanning Head, which led the Argentine headquarters to decide that San Carlos required closer investigation than the areas closer to Stanley and to Goose Green from where activity had also been reported. An Aermacchi was sent from Stanley and, having mounted an attack that caused minor damage to *Argonaut*, injuring three men in the process, returned with news of the ships in San Carlos Water. The landing was now known. Initially little was done by the Argentines with this intelligence, as there was still uncertainty over what was diversion and what was real. But this was the moment for which the Argentine Air Force had been holding itself in readiness and it was soon unleashed. The first Daggers left Rio Grande at 1225Z.

The British realised a strike was coming and the ships were on full alert. The first wave of nine Daggers was detected visually coming in low as they entered the Sound near Swan Island at 1325Z. They went for the two most accessible targets, *Antrim* and *Broadsword*. *Antrim* was damaged and temporarily out of action, with eight wounded and an unexploded 1000-lb bomb lodged in the after heads. *Broadsword* received cannon fire, wounding eight men and damaging its two Lynx helicopters. Another raid came in, with aircraft going straight for *Antrim*, which had little to fire back in return, with its Sea Cat out of action, while another went for *Fort Austin*, defended only by machine guns, only to be caught by a Sea Wolf from *Broadsword* before more damage was done. There was then relief for two hours, other than more reconnaissance by Pucaras from Goose Green, which led to one being shot down by a Harrier guided by *Brilliant*. *Brilliant*, with its more advanced radar, had moved to take over control of CAPs from the damaged *Antrim*. The next Argentine attack was in by 1600Z but turned into a fiasco. Of four A4s sent, two turned and the other two began by lining up to attack the crippled Argentine *Rio Carcarana*, assuming it to be a British transport.[7] One attacked the ship leaving the other, realising the mistake, to continue north until the *Ardent* was sighted and then attacked, but its bombs missed. Sea Harriers had arrived too late on the scene to interrupt the attack but went after the A4s in pursuit, only to come across four more heading east. When approached by the Sea Harriers, the A4s jettisoned their bombs and wing tanks but two were caught by Sidewinders.

There was then another lull before yet another, and altogether more serious, set of air attacks, which began at 1730Z. The first raid was assessed as a possible Super Etendard, leading to a number of ships firing chaff. A pair of Sea Harriers went to intercept and came instead upon four Daggers, one of which was shot down. The other three pressed on, preceded by five A4s, which had arrived undetected by flying in low over West Falkland and they soon attacked *Argonaut*. Only the failure of the two bombs that had hit her to explode spared the ship. She was nonetheless immobilised, with two men killed, and dropped anchor just in time to avoid going into the rocks by Fanning Head. A dozen more Argentine aircraft flew up the inlet attacking whatever was in their path, and whatever they could see through the smoke, including that deliberately created using Very pistols and rocket flares to distract them, facing a barrage of Blowpipe and small arms and also Rapiers from the first battery to get into action. Cannon fire hit the

Broadsword and *Brilliant*, causing some damage and casualties. The attack was limited by the success of two Sea Harriers in intercepting and shooting down with Sidewinder three incoming Daggers. Less satisfactory was *Brilliant's* Sea Wolf. Its radar would not lock on because the target was coming in diagonally rather than straight ahead.[8]

Eventually an Argentine attack succeeded. At 1755Z three Argentine Naval A4s sighted the *Ardent* patrolling three miles south-west of North West Islands. It had been on NGS duties and when these had been completed had been moved away into the mainstream of the Argentine air raids. Unable to get its Sea Cat launcher to fire, it was hit by three bombs, two of which exploded. It was then told to close San Carlos Water. Already in a bad state, and with few weapons operable, the ship could not resist a second wave of A4s, causing more bomb damage and casualties. Just after they had dropped their bombs, Harriers directed by *Brilliant* intercepted these A4s and all three were destroyed. *Ardent* was now in a bad way, listing and without steering. It was barely defensible, with no Sea Cat, and power off the 4.5' guns. When another attack came in there were only small arms available, including a machine gun taken over by the NAAFI canteen officer, John Leake, a former Army regular who fired at Skyhawks and managed to get one in the wing. Seven bombs had hit, with 22 men dead and 37 wounded. More air attacks were in prospect. Evacuation appeared the only prudent course although the ship still had main engines and had recovered steering and was under control, and it was later judged that further damage assessment might possibly have justified a further attempt at recovery. At 1830Z *Yarmouth* came alongside and took on the ship's company who were later transferred to *Canberra*. Overnight *Ardent* burned alone, sinking after twelve hours.[9]

Clapp signalled Woodward that: 'this seems to have been a stirring tale of verve and determination in adversity'. With considerable difficulty the unexploded bomb was removed from *Antrim* but it was now in no fit state to continue to support the amphibious force and returned to the carrier group. *Argonaut* was doing her best to patch up her damage and deal with flooding, attempting to stay operational despite having two unexploded bombs on board (from which she was not free for another six days).

The day had been testing for both sides. Argentina had made a strategic decision almost three weeks earlier to conserve its Air Force to attack a landing force, and had been prepared to throw almost every available aircraft in to the battle. By no means all the sorties planned even got to the Falklands, but some 45 did. Of these ten were lost (five Daggers, three A4Qs and two A4Cs), and a number of others were caught by small arms fire and out of action until they could be repaired. Two Pucaras had also been lost. While conserving itself for this battle, the Argentine Air Force did not appear to have planned for it. In particular they had come without their own escorts and had not identified the most important targets, that is the amphibious ships, but instead had attacked escorts as they came across them. In addition, although they were well aware of the problem they had not addressed the more technical issue of bomb fusing. Because of the attack profiles many bombs simply failed to explode.[10] Of seven warships sent in only two – *Plymouth* and *Yarmouth* – had escaped unscathed. The Argentines had caught one ship, *Ardent,* badly damaged another, *Argonaut,* and hurt three more, but they had made no difference to the actual landing and the vital process of getting equipment and stores ashore. All day *Canberra* – the 'Great White Whale' – had been anchored as close to the western shore as the depth and swinging room allowed and attracted no attack. A lot had been expected of the crew of the STUFT, and they had been understandably anxious before the landing of the risks they would be taking by sailing into the AOA.[11] Staff at Northwood had put in many hours trying to work out ways in which the ship could be spared the risks to which it was exposed that day and rebutting proposals that would have added to the risks (like continuing to use *Canberra* as a barracks once a beachhead had been established). Whenever it was necessary to convey the dangers inherent in an amphibious landing a picture was drawn of a loaded *Canberra* at the bottom of the sea.

The judicious placing of the civilian ships and the readiness of the escorts to draw the attack led to far less damage to the ships in this category than anticipated. British air losses on the first day were one Harrier GR3 and two Gazelle helicopters. At the same time, the Task Force overestimated their successes, assessing that three Pucaras, six Daggers and five Skyhawks had been caught, nine of the total by Harriers. On a fine day the damage to the British escorts was not in itself surprising, but there was reason to be concerned about Sea Wolf's lack of effectiveness when used inshore. More escorts were due to arrive – with *Antelope, Exeter* and *Ambuscade* available on 22 May, and the *Bristol* group's seven ships a few days away. Even so, Woodward's existing fleet was starting to look rather battered and he was aware that if he lost a modern Type 22, there was only one other replacement available in the whole RN.

None of this was particularly surprising to Woodward. A few days before the landing, he noted that while the Argentine Navy might be 'psychologically defeated', with the Air Force 'we have no trump card here like the SSN and though the SHARs have done well while we have been able to choose the killing ground, those days are nearly over with most of the Arg Air Force intact.' The 'exchange of attrition' was about to swing. He was frank in his expectation that he did not expect both Type 22s 'to survive the next few days as effective units.' Yet even if a carrier was lost all might be well so long as 'an adequate missile air defence enclave can be created ashore.' For this reason he 'put the utmost emphasis on the provision of more Rapier in the AOA within the next fortnight without fail, and I hope that will not be too late.' By comparison:

> the provision of a mobile radar is irrelevant unless it be essential to
> the operation of the Rapier system: I would expect to be able to

continue to provide warning radar cover from the ships necessary for harbour ASW defence and for the discouragement of minelaying.

His comment after the events of 21 May was in keeping. It would be 'easy to lose my cool,' he signalled, 'but the fact remains that we always knew and accepted that it would be more expensive to take on the Arg Air Force after the landing when we would no longer be able to choose the best conditions for geography and weather.' In defeating the enemy now the price had to be limited to the escorts while local air defence was established. Although Rapier was a visual system and without radar, somehow he hoped it could work as well for the land forces as Sea Wolf should do for the naval. 'Rapier remains the king of trumps, I just hope the pack does not turn out to be missing that card.'

He had not been disheartened by the missile's minimal initial impact: that could be explained by a short period ashore. By tomorrow morning, he noted in his War Diary, 'most of the Rapier batteries should be fully operational'. Clapp could then be left 'to his own local air defence' while the 'irreplaceable ships' were taken away. On balance he was positive, judging that the attack had cost Argentina:

> nearly 50 percent of their available aircraft and should at least set them back rather more than it sets us back. In fact they were both foolish in attacking the wrong ships and unlucky in damaging our older ones only.

The view in London was also upbeat. CINCFLEET signalled that evening:

> At the end of the hardest day's fighting we have known for many years you should all feel well satisfied that you have achieved the aim of establishing the beachhead. Our casualties are of course tragic, but in the circumstances they are much less than they might have been. The Argentine losses have been severe and you have established a moral ascendancy. Well done. Keep your guards up.

This was the view taken by the Chiefs the next morning, mightily relieved that the landing had been accomplished without massive casualties.

33

BOMB ALLEY

The Navy now found itself in an operating environment far removed from the one for which they planned during the Cold War. They were geared to dealing with Soviet submarines operating in the high seas (a bias evident in the predominance of submariners among the British high command). Preparations for anti-aircraft warfare were far less satisfactory. Few vessels carried dedicated anti-aircraft guns, although in the confines of San Carlos they would have been more use than missiles. The long-range Sea Dart was geared to dealing with missile-carrying aircraft, probably Soviet Bears and Badgers, coming over the open seas rather than actions close to the shore. The short-range Sea Wolf was still a relatively new system.

The evident problems coping with Argentine aircraft had been mitigated by the survival of the most vulnerable and important units, and in particular *Canberra*, but few would wish to gamble on such a prominent target surviving a second day. It was decided to get as much as possible out of the range of Argentine aircraft. If Buenos Aires grasped the sense of attacking amphibious ships, the next day could be much more difficult. It seemed prudent to get them out of the danger area. Although not yet fully unloaded, *Canberra*, *Norland*, *Europic Ferry* and *Stromness* left overnight. *Norland* and *Stromness* would return the next night after taking the stores required from the other two. This meant that 3 Commando Brigade's logistics had to become totally land-based earlier than anticipated. In particular, instead of the planned use of *Canberra* as a floating Main Dressing Station, this facility was established in short order at Ajax Bay, using an abandoned mutton refrigeration factory. A Brigade Maintenance Area (BMA) was established close by, making it possible to get ammunition, fuel and stores off the LSLs and STUFT. At the end of the first day, and despite the limited assets available, some 3,000 men and over 1,000 tons of stores had been safely landed. There was a lot more to be done, however, especially as the merchant ships could barely unload at a quarter of the rate of the RN's own amphibious ships.

As to how the landing force should be configured and the unloading organised on to the beachhead Woodward could leave matters to the two

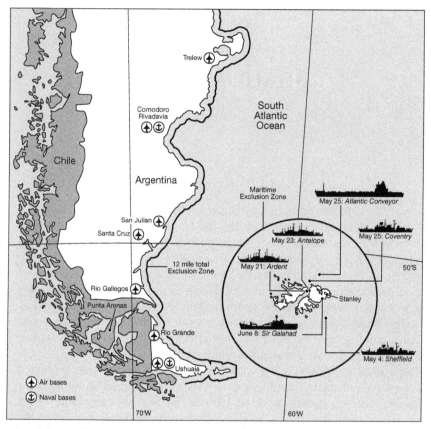

Map 8 Loss of British ships

relevant commanders, Clapp and Thompson, who had developed a close and effective working relationship. Thompson's Tactical HQ was ashore. Clapp would have preferred Thompson to continue to manage the landing operation together on Fearless, but Thompson both wanted to be with his men ashore and also to escape from the cramped and noisy headquarters on the ship. The space was so small that Clapp was having to work with a far smaller staff than he needed for the complex operations he was trying to manage. The main differences would be between Clapp and Thompson on the one hand and Woodward on the other. Personalities played a part, as did the lack of opportunities to talk directly and plan together. Problems of distance and differential priorities would test the ability of any commanders to appreciate each other's needs and co-ordinate their efforts. The basic source of the disputes, however, was the limited defensive resources available. The most testing issue of all was the provision of air cover. Sea Harriers had flown 54 sorties. With Sidewinder they had been extremely effective whenever they were able to get enemy aircraft in view. But because of the need to keep the carriers out of harm's way the aircraft were operating at the edge of their range, short on fuel and so pressed to get any engagements over quickly and then restrain themselves when tempted to chase too far from home.

Clapp and Thompson wanted Woodward to bring his carriers much further forward the next day, so that the Harriers could engage Argentine aircraft before rather than after they reached the Sound (although six of the ten mainland-based aircraft shot down on 21 May had been caught before weapon release). Woodward once again rejected this option. He would not 'risk half our long term air defence force by coming further forward'. *Broadsword* was also arguing for the adoption of a more offensive anti-air posture, after finding its Sea Wolf useless in circumstances of confined waters, so that targets could be intercepted as they closed from the west. Woodward agreed that *Coventry* would work with *Broadsword* as a 42/22 air defence combination at a point northwest of the Falklands, from where most of the raids appeared to be arriving. All this he still hoped was a stopgap until the Rapier batteries could relieve his escorts.

In the event Rapier was to be something of a disappointment.[1] However, even the sceptics would have hoped for more from the missile. It had suffered badly from poor loading and the journey south, and the units, when they did get ashore, were not well placed to deal with the aircraft coming in to attack ships.

22 May

Argentina claimed that on the day of the landing five British ships had been attacked and damaged, which was true, that two Harriers had been shot down, which was only half true, and that the landing had been resisted with many British casualties, which was not true at all. It was assumed that the Junta could rely on popular support so long as it could claim credibly to be fighting back against the British, but intelligence staffs in London hoped that as the extent of Argentine losses became apparent, calls for a political solution could gain strength. On 22 May, whatever the Argentine press was saying about the British beachhead being precarious, the Argentine command on the Islands knew that the enemy position was strong and included artillery and air defence, and that considerable and urgent air support would be required to dislodge it. As the Argentines were recovering from the previous day's exertions, with many aircraft needing repair, only two raids against the landing force were launched on 22 May and then quite late in the day. At 1120Z an Argentine Coastguard craft, *Rio Iguazu*, was spotted in Choiseul Sound and strafed. She was beached and abandoned, 12 miles from Darwin.[2]

Just after 2000Z two Daggers, shortly followed by three A4Bs, attacked ships in San Carlos after approaching from the south. One aircraft ditched its bomb load at the entrance and the second did not press home its attack. Nonetheless, the raids were hardly confidence boosting in terms of British air defences. Neither had been detected until the last minute nor successfully engaged by ship defences or Rapiers. Earlier that morning there had been another otherwise inconsequential incident that indicated the unreliability of the air defences. At 0645Z an Argentine Hercules was detected by *Invincible* at 175 miles but was away before Sea Harriers could intercept. *Coventry* detected the same aircraft. It was acquired for Sea Dart as it came within range but a launcher defect prevented firing. At 1540Z HMS *Cardiff*, approaching the TEZ about 1500nm north-east, had engaged a Boeing 707 shadower with a salvo of two Sea Dart at 30nm; one missile missed and one ran out of power just short.

This was discouraging, given that, with *Broadsword*, *Coventry*'s task was to patrol some 50 miles west of the northern entrance to Falkland Sound to use their Sea Dart/Sea Wolf combination to intercept and destroy incoming Argentine aircraft. Considerable progress was made that day in getting the 12 Rapier fire units into position, except that they had suffered with the sea passage and landing, and were days away from being fully operational. The first Rapier ashore on the bridgehead had not performed well: only one missile had been fired and it malfunctioned. The concern about Rapier was reflected in requests back to London for every available spare part, especially those known to suffer higher failure rates, to be got to the front line as soon as possible, even if this meant cannibalisation of UK-based Rapiers, and if necessary by air drop. Woodward's diary entry saw the quieter day as 'an invaluable opportunity to consolidate ashore while getting the RAPIER defence on line.'

The Sea Harriers were much more active over the skies, with 59 sorties flown. At 1730Z four GR3s attacked Goose Green, but found no Pucaras. Later at 2030Z, returning from an unsatisfactory photo-reconnaissance mission over West Falkland, a GR3 sighted the Falkland Islands vessel, MV *Monsunen*. This was being used by the Argentines for inter-island supply and Clapp decided that he could make use of the capability. He ordered that the boat be captured. *Brilliant* and *Yarmouth* embarked an SBS detachment, and then, rather later than intended, at 0330Z launched a Lynx to find the vessel, which it did on being fired upon at 0400Z. When the vessel failed to stop when ordered, *Yarmouth* fired rounds ahead of her. *Monsunen* then beached herself on the west side of Lively Sound. As it was unclear whether it was armed and had troops embarked, it was decided not to mount an assault but to leave her for later recovery.

West Falkland appeared to be used increasingly for re-supply, which would not be wholly surprising because of the easier access from the mainland, although there was no actual evidence of this from either observation by photographic reconnaissance or Special Forces. Nonetheless it was decided to attack one of the likely airstrips, Dunnose Head, at first light on 23 May using a GR3. In fact an SBS team had visited this but the report of no Argentine activity had not got through. A disagreement between Woodward and Clapp, who would have preferred an attack against the radar on Pebble Island, led to delays. Woodward appeared particularly exasperated by this. He signalled both Thompson and Clapp:

> Late change of plan this morning without any explanation or intelligence support resulted in lost opportunity for first light attack and confusion and frustration here. This is clearly unacceptable. Request you state reason and priority for mission in future. I may know something you do not. Your ground attack assets are ready and willing to help but they require notice, intelligence and all available targets details to obtain useful benefit.

This was, however, in part a reflection of the systemic problem in the tasking arrangements for the GR3s.

The system on board *Hermes* for tasking the RAF's Harrier GR3 effectively was inadequate. There was, as already noted, no RAF officer on Woodward's staff. Captain Middleton of *Hermes* was performing the role of air adviser. A squadron leader was sent as a liaison officer but was outranked in any debate. The air operations room on *Hermes* was at full stretch and was geared to defending the Task Force rather than mounting offensive air operations. There was no means for allocating the aircraft when faced with competing demands from Woodward, Middleton and the land commanders, none of which were eased by the regular difficulties with communications with *Fearless*, where Clapp, and later Moore, had their HQ. *Hermes* would become aware of requests from battalions to the land HQ for air support and start to prepare for the operations. They were supposed to wait for authorisation from the HQ. Sometimes they launched before the authorisation which then failed to materialise; sometimes they waited and the delay meant that the moment when they would have made the maximum impact had passed.

The attack on the Dunnose Head airstrip was heavy but pointless as there were no Argentines present. The main effect was to damage settlement buildings and injure the farmowner, Tim Miller, who lost an eye. An attack on Pebble Island airstrip destroyed several of the Pucaras already put out of action by the SAS raid. Reconnaissance missions elsewhere over West Falkland were more helpful, pinpointing the activity at Port Howard. Four Sea Harriers launched to attack Stanley at 2254Z. One exploded in a fireball one minute after take-off. *Brilliant* was detached to search the area but the pilot was not found. The other aircraft had problems releasing their bombs. More successful was an opportunistic attack at 1335Z by a combat air patrol over the Falkland Sound that saw two Pumas and an escorting Agusta A-109 gunship proceeding south along the western shore of the Sound in the vicinity of Shag Cove carrying ammunition. Their attack caused the leading Puma to crash into the hillside and explode. The Agusta landed but was set on fire by gunfire. The other Puma also landed and was engaged but damage could not be assessed.

It was of some comfort that the Argentine Navy still appeared to be failing to react to the British landing. The Argentine 209 submarines were still absent. Though the *San Luis* might return soon to the TEZ, it now seemed that the *Salta* had never even reached the area. The many opportunities to cause mayhem with so many British ships moving around a limited area had been missed. Nor was there much evidence that the Argentine Garrison was stirring itself to deploy against the bridgehead; lack of tactical airlift capability restricted the Commander's options to harassing attacks mounted from Darwin, holding back his main force as a reserve to defend Stanley. Because Menendez had not appreciated the full size of the San Carlos landing at five battalions, he had thought that another landing elsewhere was still a possibility, probably close to Stanley. He was placing his hopes in action against the carriers as a means of denying the British local air superiority. If they could be disabled then a whole series of options would suddenly be opened up. The Argentine Air Force was not unwilling to do this, and was holding Canberras and Super Etendards in reserve for the right opportunity. Their problem was in locating the carrier force.

23 May

The relative Argentine inactivity had been a matter of some relief in London. It was evident, however, that 23 May would be much more difficult, especially as the weather was clear for flying. Two Super Etendards were launched that afternoon from Rio Grande in search of the carriers but failed to detect them and had to return to base. Woodward had been aware that the Argentines might concentrate air effort against the carriers and for that reason had held back a Type 42 to protect his force rather than put a Type 42/22 combination forward. Instead four frigates, *Broadsword*, *Plymouth*, *Yarmouth* and *Antelope*, only just arrived, took up position at the entrance to San Carlos Water and Port San Carlos. The damaged *Argonaut* was anchored well up San Carlos Water.

It took until 1635Z for the first attack to arrive. Four A4Bs coming from the south were not detected until spotted by 2 Para as they crossed into Grantham Sound. They split into two pairs to attack the escorts from separate directions. Faced by a barrage of Rapier, Blowpipe and small arms they again concentrated on the most obvious rather than most important target, in this case *Antelope*. The attack came just twelve hours after the frigate had joined the Task Force. It had neither faced a large and co-ordinated air attack before nor learned about the problems of air defence in such a land-locked environment. One A4, having been caught by a Sea Wolf from the

Broadsword, and small arms from the *Antelope*, managed to release a bomb but then collided with *Antelope*'s mainmast and crashed. Another A4 was damaged. The frigate received two hits with 1000-lb bombs, but neither exploded. One man was killed and another seriously injured. After half an hour came three naval A4Qs, again without warning. This time both sides achieved little. Neither aircraft nor ships were hit. One of the aircraft was unable to release its bombs and had an accident when attempting to land at Rio Grande. The pilot was killed when he ejected.

Another raid of four Daggers came at 1805Z, but was ineffectual and led to one aircraft being shot down over Pebble Island by a Sea Harrier's Sidewinder.[3] *Antelope* was able to restore power and move slowly down San Carlos Water. Both unexploded bombs were located and work began to defuse them. Unfortunately, the delicacy of the situation had not been fully appreciated. When the first bomb to be tackled exploded, killing one member of the team and wounding another, the crew was caught by surprise. The resulting fire spread quickly leading to an order to abandon ship. It came none too soon. Not long after the last man left magazine explosions began. The frigate sank the next morning. The *Argonaut*, still with its unexploded bomb, had been berthed close to the *Antelope* but moved away after the first explosion. By that evening the *Argonaut* bomb had been isolated but not yet rendered safe.

Relief that many bombs had failed to explode led to anxiety that the Argentines might work out what to do about it. Up to this point reference had been made in briefings to the issue, starting with the hit on *Glasgow* on 12 May. After the landings, there were a number of reports of bombs failing to explode, including on *Antrim*. In a briefing American correspondents were told that the reasons for the failures to explode might be fusing, age or mode of delivery. The unattributable morning press briefing of 23 May referred again to the unexploded bombs that were still being rendered safe on board warships. That afternoon, however, following an anxious communication from Woodward, the Chiefs of Staff concluded that there should be no further mention of this issue because of the intelligence value to Argentina. The afternoon press briefing explained the change of policy and, thereafter, British reports spoke only of damage to various ships. This did not stop the speculation, based on information already in the public domain, possibly reinforced by briefings to American reporters, and then reinforced by the fate of *Antelope*.

The events of 23 May confirmed previous impressions. The confined waters of San Carlos were proving to be an extremely difficult air defence environment and none of the systems were able to work properly within it. Even then the British thought that they were doing better than was in fact the case. Two Argentine aircraft had been shot down that day, but British assessments were between four and seven. The main asset was undoubtedly the Sea Harriers. Their known presence was deterring Argentine pilots from pressing on and if they did so and were caught they were as likely as not to be shot down. They were also achieving impressive sortie rates – there were 50 on 23 May. But time was always short and they were used best when *Argonaut*, in the AOA, was able to task them. This argued for a return the next day to the 42/22 combination, even if it was still deemed imprudent to bring the carrier further forward. Although facing increasing shortages of escorts, as a result of mechanical problems and wear and tear as well as enemy actions, Woodward agreed to reinstate the Type 42/22, using *Coventry*, with the emphasis largely on the better use of Sea Harriers. He noted that evening in his War Diary:

> The weather, being good for flying, is costing both sides heavily. We are paying frigates for aircraft. I would prefer to pay RAPIER missiles for aircraft but time and the weather are not helping. There is a limit to this attrition process and I am not sure who will stop first. The onset of winter should help us now.

In a broader policy assessment signalled to his Task Group at the end of 23 May, Woodward recognised that destroyer/frigate losses looked bad particularly to those most directly involved but 'the twin aims of getting the beachhead solidly established and splashing the Arg Air Force are being achieved'. He went on:

> Attrition is what we are at, bloody though it be and the present method seems to be well on the way to defeating the Arg Air Force. Without that defeat, further operations cannot proceed. I remain open to better suggestions as to method.

He also assessed the Argentines' next moves, providing an interesting indication of the sort of nasty surprises he had been imagining, including the possibility of the Argentine Air Force being joined by the Peruvian (a prospect that had not figured highly in any of the London-generated assessments). More plausible as a danger was that the Argentine surface navy 'may have a large surge in it'. If so then the SSN force should be able to cope but if not then the carrier group would cover the retreating RFAs and MVs, leaving the inshore squadron 'safe in Sound'. If forced to retreat in that way, his ships 'would be back soonest but doubt Args could co-ordinate Air Force and Navy on record to date'. In addition there was still an Argentine submarine threat, particularly the *San Luis*. Woodward's policy meanwhile, was 'to continue to shore build up, splash Arg and if necessary Peruvian Air Force, remove Arg Army communications and isolate his supplies. Totally.'

24 May

There was more good flying weather on 24 May and San Carlos Water was still full of attractive targets for the Argentine Air Force. From the amphibious force there were two LPDs, five LSLs, plus *Fort Austin, Stromness, Resource* and *Norland*. Close by was the *Argonaut* with *Plymouth*, *Yarmouth* and *Arrow* on air defence duty. *Coventry* and *Broadsword* resumed the 42/22 combination patrol as a 'missile trap' outside the Sound, in a position that gave them the space for Sea Dart operations and the view for early warning and early attrition of raids. Meanwhile, the Argentine strategy for the day involved concentrating their attack into a half-hour period between 1345Z and 1415Z. Instead of approaching largely from the north and west as before, this time they would come largely from the south-east. More seriously they were determined to reach the amphibious ships. One group of Mirage acted to distract *Coventry* and *Broadsword*, without any intention of pressing forward an attack, while five Skyhawks flew in low over San Carlos Water. Woodward felt these pilots 'showed particular bravery'. They survived Rapier, Blowpipe, Sea Cat and small arms before hitting three LSLs, *Sir Galahad*, *Sir Lancelot* and *Sir Bedivere*. Bombs failed to explode on the first two and passed through the third. While the failure to shoot them down was frustrating, some consolation could be found in the thought that the effort to survive meant that the aircraft could not fly at the optimum height for effective attacks.

A second raid by four Daggers, at 1405Z, strafed *Fearless* and *Sir Galahad* with cannon shells. *Sir Lancelot* was again hit by a bomb striking the ship's side, causing some internal damage, but then bouncing off having failed to explode. As the aircraft left three were damaged but none were shot down. A second group of four Daggers coming in at the same time along the north coast of West Falkland was sighted near Pebble Island by a Sea Harrier patrol alerted by *Broadsword*. The Argentine aircraft jettisoned their bombs and tried to escape but three were shot down with Sidewinders. Ten minutes later another three A4Cs came in to attack, but hit nothing.

While all this was going on the unloading had continued, with vital airfield construction and fuel handling equipment getting ashore. Emptied of stores, *Stromness*, *Norland* and *Sir Percivale* could leave the danger area. The rush to get material ashore meant that storage on land was less than ideal and new headaches were being created for the logisticians. *Sir Lancelot* had almost finished unloading when hit but *Sir Galahad* was still full of ammunition. The evacuations necessary because of the unexploded bombs, and then the repairs, added to the delays. It took *Galahad* until 28 May before it became fully operational while *Lancelot* was not ready until 7 June, although it could still be used for accommodation and helicopter refuelling.

The fleet was getting depleted. In addition to the ships lost, *Glasgow* was considered in a sufficiently bad way to be ordered back to Ascension, while *Antrim* also left the group to carry out repairs and then collect General Moore from the *QEII* on 27 May. This left *Glamorgan*, *Brilliant*, *Exeter*, *Alacrity* and *Ambuscade* escorting the carriers, with the reinforcing *Bristol* group still two days away. So long as ships were still unloading then he would have to continue to provide escorts. Because of this Woodward recorded in his War Diary that he was becoming:

most unhappy with the Land Commanders' policy of keeping many ships inshore while they unload over several days instead of getting each one emptied quickly and taken out of harm's way. Does not seem to make very good sense from here!

It made sense from the perspective of Clapp and Thompson. Clapp describes their discussions that day:

We both wanted everything possible ashore, but Julian, understandably, wanted it ashore in the correct order and in the correct proportions. We had petrol in one ship, diesel in another, food in a third, ammunition in a fourth and so on. Personal gear spread across the fleet was also a serious problem. We felt we could only reduce the number of ships at anchor once the units ashore had at least a reasonable amount of equipment to make them feel partially equipped and able to sustain operations.

Clapp tucked the ships as close as possible under the eastern shore, with *Intrepid* to the north and *Fearless* to the south.[4]

The question was how much the enemy's air offensive capacity had also been depleted. Woodward remarked on the 'continued efforts and bravery of the Argentine air forces', especially as he believed that 'their efforts are met with near 50% losses on the day. It is hard to believe they can continue.' It was assumed that six to nine aircraft had been shot down, including three by Rapier, although the real figure was four in total with another six aircraft damaged. Some satisfaction was therefore felt that the air defence system was starting to work more effectively and that a rate of attrition was being imposed that could not be tolerated by the Argentines for much longer. The 42/22 combination had worked well in the control of the Sea Harriers although it had been too close to the land for effective Sea Dart operation. Woodward assumed that the Argentine attacks, while bravely executed, had been 'severely mauled'. There was growing confidence that the air battle was being won. Even Lewin thought 'we were nearly through.'[5]

25 May

On the basis of that increasing optimism, it was not surprising that 25 May turned out to be such a disappointment. This was Argentine Navy Day and had seemed as likely a day as any for the Argentine Navy to resume operations. There remained, however, still no sign that they were preparing to leave port. It was already clear that whatever was going to happen, the *25 de Mayo* would not be part of it. There had been no sign of the *Salta* (which had a problem with its torpedo tubes) and there were indications that the submarine force was facing communications difficulties. The only submarine at sea, *San Luis*, was thought to be sailing to the TEZ to arrive on 27 May. The main threat remained from the air. There were also grounds for hope that Argentine aircraft were experiencing engine-related and other wear and tear and problems, and that this must be affecting the high aircraft sortie generation rates.

The Argentine commanders were becoming doubtful about their ability to dislodge the British from their position at San Carlos. As they assessed the situation on 24 May they concluded that the beachhead was all but consolidated and that the British would use this as a base for all future operations. Although they urged Menendez to use his troops to contain the British land forces, they were still not expecting an overland move but rather a blockade of Stanley that would put pressure on the Argentine garrison without risking the local population. Accordingly their thoughts turned to the factors that could help sustain a blockade – the aircraft carriers and the logistic chain between Ascension and the Islands.[6]

On 25 May as the *Atlantic Conveyor*, *Europic Ferry* and *Elk* were prepared to go into San Carlos Water, Woodward signalled his anxiety about the risks this involved:

> the continued exposure of up to nine non-combatant ships of various kinds in Carlos Water while they are unloaded slowly in parallel, rather than one or two that could be emptied in 24 hours flat and returned to safety, appears to be nautical nonsense.

At least he wanted to get unnecessary ships out of harm's way. Clapp and Thompson agreed, so that *Stromness*, *Resource*, *Tidepool*, *Sir Bedivere* and *Fort Austin* were to leave that night while the *Elk*'s arrival was to be postponed. Releasing *Fort Austin* was a wrench for Clapp, as it contained anti-submarine Wessex helicopters. He accepted Woodward's view that the submarine threat was no longer high, although he remained concerned enough to have Falkland Sound searched whenever a Lynx was spare. To complicate any attack, the eight RFAs left were anchored nearer to the eastern side of San Carlos Water, with *Intrepid* at one end of the line, *Fearless* at the other and *Yarmouth* stationed to their south to protect them from attacks coming in from that direction. *Plymouth* and *Arrow* were inside Chancho Point while *Broadsword* and *Coventry* were outside the Sound, with a patrol line some 30 miles west of the previous day's in the hope that this would facilitate Sea Dart operations.

The optimum position for the frigate/destroyer combination had been discussed extensively as a result of what had been felt to be a successful day on 24 May. They had spent all daylight hours in clear weather conditions within sight of the coast yet had not been attacked while the Argentines went, this time, for the ships supporting the landing. They had been able to make good use of the Harriers but not full use of Sea Dart. It was therefore agreed that the next day the two ships should go slightly further north-west to allow *Coventry* a clearer look over the sea towards any threat developing from the west. This was a better position to use Sea Dart.

The defenders were helped this time by warning of an air attack from the mainland at 1120Z. Four A4Bs arrived over Falkland Sound at 1230Z but failed to make any attacks. One pair headed back close enough to be acquired by *Coventry*'s Sea Dart and one was shot down.[7] Another raid of four A4Cs came in at 1530Z, one of which was quickly brought down by a combination of Rapier and the *Yarmouth*'s Sea Cat and 20mm gun. Having achieved little, they went for home, and again a Sea Dart from *Coventry* caught one. Another aircraft, damaged in San Carlos, only reached home with difficulty. One pilot had ejected during this engagement and was captured. The frigate and destroyer were well aware that their position had probably been compromised and had steeled themselves for another attack. Just before 1800Z *Coventry* reported an air raid building up to the west of her and A4Bs made directly for the two ships. They knew that the attack was coming but did not pick up the incoming aircraft until they were almost upon them.

At 1817Z the first wave of three A4s were detected departing the coast over Pebble Island and heading towards the ships. A CAP gained contact and was intercepting but as the aircraft were within the missile engagement zone they were told to stay clear. In the event the low altitude caused problems for the Sea Dart so *Coventry* relied instead on its 4.5″ gun which had difficulty against a manoeuvring target. They went for *Broadsword*, with one bomb hitting the ship's side and flight deck after ricocheting up from the sea. It struck the Lynx and Mk44 but failed to explode. Because of an electronic fault, *Broadsword*'s Sea Wolf had failed to acquire the first pair. At about 1819Z the second raid crossed the coast. This time *Broadsword* locked on with Sea Wolf. Unfortunately, at that point *Coventry* did what it had done twice that day when engaging enemy aircraft, that is alter course to the south from an easterly heading to provide a finer aspect to incoming aircraft. The result was that *Coventry* crossed *Broadsword*'s line of sight and Sea Wolf could not be fired. *Coventry* was caught on the port side with cannon fire and three bombs, at least two of which exploded. Soon there were fires, smoke and flooding. Seventeen men were killed outright, and two died later. In the circumstances the evacuation was remarkably effective and *Broadsword*'s boats were quickly on the scene. *Coventry* capsized at 1924Z.

Even more serious in terms of the campaign was a second attack that day on the carrier force. *Exeter, Glamorgan, Brilliant, Alacrity* and *Ambuscade* escorted the two carriers, with *Regent, Sir Tristram, Sir Percivale, Fort Toronto* and *Atlantic Conveyor* in company. *Atlantic Conveyor* was intending to complete stores' transfers by helicopter before moving into San Carlos Water that night. Woodward had judged that it was less at risk spending a couple of hours extra in the afternoon with the Battle Group, which had not been attacked for a few weeks, than being caught while unloading at San

Carlos the next morning. At the time the CAPs were all devoted to the amphibious force. For the first time, through a combination of intelligent guesswork and observed aircraft movements from the radar at Stanley, the Argentines had come to a reasonable estimate of the Group's position. Two Super Etendards, with one Exocet each, flew from Rio Grande, refuelled, and then flew 270 miles to reach their targets.

Warnings that Argentine aircraft had left their bases normally helped to get ships to action stations, and one had been received this time. But as the enemy attack did not arrive at the expected time the ships were stood down. At 1936Z, *Ambuscade* and *Exeter* detected the Agave radar fitted in the Super Etendard. The Super Etendards detected three contacts ahead and two minutes later fired their missiles at the nearest radar echo before turning away back to Rio Grande. All ships took immediate, pre-planned countermeasures. *Ambuscade* fired chaff from her 4.5" gun to confuse the aircraft's target indication and a protective pattern of chaff from her 3" rocket launcher to decoy missiles. Other ships also fired chaff. *Brilliant* and *Ambuscade* detected the missiles being fired and more countermeasures were taken, with even more chaff being sowed by *Ambuscade*, who had good reason to believe itself to be the target. The two missiles veered towards the chaff pattern laid by *Ambuscade*. Having flown through or under chaff and not been triggered, the homing head on Exocet tends to look to its left for another target and that is where the two missiles both found *Atlantic Conveyor*. The ship had no defences and was caught in the starboard quarter. This was bad luck. Later it was judged that the missiles had initially acquired *Regent*, and only later turned to the larger ship. As *Regent* was carrying large quantities of ammunition, the consequences of its destruction might have been even more severe. The attack by the Argentines had been professionally executed but so had been the British response, although *Invincible* did attempt to engage the chaff launched by *Hermes* with six Sea Darts believing them to be hostile aircraft.

With major fires and dense black smoke spreading rapidly there was no opportunity for damage control and with so much hazardous cargo on board there was little choice but to abandon ship. Evacuation proved difficult, especially for those who had to take to liferafts. In addition to the three men who died on board, another nine died in the water, including the ship's captain, Captain Ian North. The loss of three Chinooks and six Wessex helicopters – another Chinook and a Wessex were airborne at the time – was a severe blow.[8] In addition there was tented camp for 4,500 men, and runway and fuelling equipment for the Harrier forward operating base. In the mistaken belief that the attackers might use Stanley as a diversion on their return flight, the airfield received gunfire from *Glamorgan* that night along with a Sea Harrier bombing raid. For Woodward, this 'bloody day' had been the 'worst so far for us'. He was gloomy about the deficiencies of his SAM systems and even more anxious to have only minimum shipping inshore. Two ships lost, another damaged, a loss of helicopters that would cause real problems and gaps continually being exposed in British defences. If a future gap meant that a carrier was lost then the whole campaign would be placed in jeopardy. Another day like this, he thought, and he would have to warn Northwood that he was losing the battle.

The mood was no better in London. In his memoir Admiral Leach described having been told to get to MoD Main Building because 'all hell seemed to have been let loose' and then on arrival coming across Nott who insisted that 'We can't go on like this, CNS, losing all these ships,' although the Defence Secretary denied to Leach that he wanted 'to call off the operation.'[9] The uncertainty and tension was reflected in the handling of this latest piece of bad news. Up to this point, major losses and casualties had been reported reasonably promptly and accurately. Even in these cases there were conflicting pressures, as attention had to be paid both to the sensitivities of the next of kin and the intelligence value of disclosure to Argentina. The potential for confusion in these conflicting requirements was illustrated when news that *Coventry* was sinking reached London at about 2030 local time on 25 May. Given the uncertainty it was decided to defer an interview that Nott was due to record for ITN's 'News at Ten' and instead give it live. Before he got to the studio he was asked by Lewin and Leach not to reveal the name of the ship, because they did not want Argentina to know right away that they had sunk a Type 42, although it would also seem that there was concern that without more details the effect would be to needlessly alarm all the families of *Coventry*'s crew.[10] At the same time the news came in of the *Atlantic Conveyor*. All Nott could do was to state that one of the Task Force ships had been badly damaged. The information was enough to cause anxiety among all relatives of those serving with the Task Force and it took until the next day for the position to be clarified and all next-of-kin to be informed. When he reported on the incident to the House, Nott acknowledged that the name of the ship should have been released the previous night.[11]

The gloom might have been even greater had it been appreciated just how much the extent of Argentine air losses at this point were being exaggerated. By the time of the landing the British assessed that Argentina had lost eleven combat aircraft (two Mirage, three Skyhawk and six Pucara) plus a Canberra, Puma and five small transport planes. This was recognised to be an insufficient number to prevent the Argentines from mounting a major effort against the landing force. The War Cabinet was told by Lewin on 22 May, that the previous day the Argentines had lost nine Mirage (Dagger) plus one probable, seven A4 plus one probable, two Pucara and four helicopters. This would have been a third of the combat aircraft taking part (41 in total). Woodward's estimate had been eight A4, plus one probable and one possible and three Mirage, but this later was revised to eight Mirage and five A4. The initial assessment to the War Cabinet of Argentine losses on 23 May was five Mirage plus one possible, with two A4, plus one probable and one possible, with three helicopters. That was later turned into six Mirage, plus one probable and one

Table 2 Argentine Air Losses: 21–25 May

	Dagger A	*A4B/A4C Skyhawk*	*A4Q Skyhawk*
21 May	5 (All SHAR)	2 (Both SHAR)	3 (All SHAR)
22 May			
23 May	1 (SHAR)	1 (SAM)	
24 May	3 (All SHAR)	1 (gunfire/shrapnel)	
25 May		3 (1 x multiple weapons/2 x Sea Dart).	
Total	9	7	3

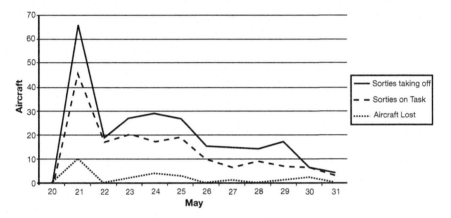

Figure 4 The Argentine air offensive

possible, or almost two-thirds of attacking aircraft (14). On 24 May out of 17 attacking Argentine aircraft, eight were said to have been destroyed – three by Sea Harriers, three by Rapier and two by *Fearless*'s Sea Cat. Again this produced a startling attrition rate – almost half of those taking part.

Thus the notes for Nott's statements to the Commons on 24 May suggested that the enemy had 'lost some 25% of his combat aircraft and, of course, some of his most experienced pilots,' as well as much mobility on the Falklands Islands. This was a 'best estimate,' according to DCDS(I), adding that: 'We suspect that in the event the Argentines lost more aircraft (on return flights to the mainland).' On 25 May, another four Skyhawk were believed to have been hit, plus one Aermacchi, and again constituting about half of the aircraft taking part. By 27 May the best estimate was that 20 Skyhawks had been lost to British forces and 17 Mirage.

In fact since 21 May ten Skyhawks and nine Daggers had been lost, in addition to the six Skyhawks, one Dagger, two Mirage 3s and a Canberra lost before. So the actual number was only two-thirds of the British assessment of Argentine losses, reflecting the familiar problem of optimism in claims, especially by those operating the various surface-to-air missiles. Nonetheless, it still meant that the Air Force (combined with Argentine Naval aircraft) as an effective fighting force was severely depleted and the strain was now beginning to tell. In addition eight Pucara, four Mentor, one Aermacchi, and three light aircraft had been lost, excluding accidents. The spirit of the Argentine pilots is perhaps explained by the fact that their assessment was that by 25 May they had sunk or disabled 19 British ships and shot down 14 Harriers, while the actual totals were five sunk, three damaged and five Harriers lost.[12]

Even so from the British perspective attrition at sea favoured Argentina: two Type 42 and two Type 21 frigates against one cruiser and one submarine. Against the *Atlantic Conveyor* were two patrol boats (*Sobral* and another), three transport vessels (*Rio Carcarana*, *Buen Suceso*, unidentified), and three others (*Narwhal*, *Monsunen*, unidentified). Argentina had lost about 500 killed and 200 wounded, with five in custody and 150 repatriated. At this time British losses were put at 76 military and three civilians killed, 33 military and seven civilians missing, about 132 wounded with one prisoner in custody and 92 repatriated.

While the loss of the *Atlantic Conveyor* complicated British plans, it was not quite the result Argentina had intended. They had been after the carriers and had now used up four Exocets in failing to do so. Moreover only one AM39 Exocet remained and efforts to obtain more from abroad had so far been unavailing. The problem therefore was that the air force and Naval air arm had run out of time and targets as well as out of steam. That evening the Argentine commanders accepted that their battle must now move on to the next phase. This moment of deep gloom for the Task Force, fully reflected in London, also marked the effective end of the battle of San Carlos. By the evening of 26 May, when Woodward had feared that he might be having an awkward conversation with Northwood, he realised that the position may have taken a turn for the better, and by the next evening he was confident of that.

Preventing re-supply

While the main effort had to be devoted to protecting the amphibious force, the days after the landing also saw an effort being made to prepare the way for the later repossession of the Falkland Islands. One necessity was still to disable the use of Stanley runway but this proved to be a continuing source of frustration. At 1130Z on 24 May, four GR3 Harriers and two Sea Harriers launched to attack on Stanley airfield. The attack was later assessed to have caused surface damage to the runway. One helicopter and a Pucara were also damaged. One GR3 was hit but managed to return safely to *Hermes*. These operations were inherently risky for Harriers. The alternative, already requested, was for a Vulcan raid, but these aircraft were being prepared for an anti-radar strike with the American Shrike missile. The best use of Victor tankers had also been deemed to be with the daily long-range Nimrod sorties.

One problem with these attacks was that the bomb fusing was incorrect, mirroring the problems the Argentines had faced when attacking ships. The reason appears to be differences between the GR3 and the Sea Harrier bombs, not appreciated by the RN armourers who did the fusing. They assumed the RAF instruction 'instantaneous' equated to the RN's 'direct action', but whereas the former required fusing at 40 milliseconds the latter could be up to 90 milliseconds. This may have resulted in the bombs bouncing so that they were not in direct contact with the runway surface when they exploded.

On the night of 24 May, for the first time since the landing, an Argentine air re-supply sortie reached Stanley. Although the Argentine garrison might be getting one flight in from the mainland to Stanley every night, this was quite inadequate for their needs. A number of units, especially in outlying areas, had almost exhausted their provisions. A telling sign was that no counter-attack against the bridgehead had yet been organised by the garrison. The pressure therefore had to be sustained. The next day, at 1417Z, two Sea Harriers and four GR3s tried a medium level attack against Stanley airport, but this again failed to damage the runway, as did two further attacks later in the day. The GR3 missions on 26 May included, at 1335Z, an attack on troop positions and vehicles at Port Howard, and, at 1730Z, another ineffectual attack on Stanley airfield, although the British claimed one Puma helicopter destroyed at Port Howard. At 1420Z the following day, two GR3s mounted another ineffectual attack on the airfield.

By 27 May there were only four ships to be protected, and by that night *Europic Ferry* and *Sir Geraint* could leave and *Sir Galahad* was almost finished unloading. Unlike previous nights, no new ships were taken in for unloading. All the guns, vehicles and the bulk of the immediate stores and ammunition were ashore, as were eleven Sea Kings, four Wessex and one Chinook. There had been progress with constructing a forward operating base for Harriers. *Sir Lancelot* and *Argonaut* were still struggling with their unexploded bombs. *Fearless*, *Intrepid*, *Plymouth*, *Yarmouth* and *Arrow* comprised the rest of the defence. Two Argentine raids turned back when they realised that they faced Sea Harriers. Woodward was still uncomfortable with the situation: 'The CAPs are not catching anything but are flying themselves to a standstill. Ships are rushing in and out until Blue on Blue gets uncomfortably close. Signal traffic is grinding to a halt.'

Only warships and the damaged *Sir Lancelot* and *Sir Galahad* remained in San Carlos Water. It took until the night of 27/28 May before the bomb stuck in *Argonaut* could be safely removed and lowered into the sea and then another two days for repairs before she could at last leave San Carlos. It is important to note, as the experience of *Antelope* confirms, how much worse things might have been not only if the Argentine bombs had exploded more often but if those that did not had not been dealt with so effectively. The *Antelope* bomb exploded as two Royal Engineers were persevering with a bomb they knew to be unsafe in unfamiliar surroundings, having already dealt successfully with one in *Argonaut*. The Fleet Clearance Diving Teams (FTCD) dealt with the second bomb in *Argonaut*, cleared explosive from the upper deck of the sunk *Antelope* and removed bombs from *Sir Galahad* and *Sir Lancelot*. This was painstaking work, often in dark, cramped and always dangerous conditions, pausing while further air raids were underway.[13]

During the morning of 28 May, *Glamorgan*, *Avenger* and *Alacrity* carried out NGS in the Stanley area at various targets. All units came under fire out to seven miles but there were no hits on the ships. The beachhead was now well established and all guns, vehicles and the bulk of the immediate stores and ammunition were ashore.

SECTION SEVEN

34

INTERNATIONAL OPINION

The British landing and the subsequent defence against relentless air attacks transformed the context for diplomatic efforts to resolve the conflict. The focus would be on mitigation of the impact of a land battle rather than prevention, and any cease-fire lines would now be drawn on the ground rather than at sea. In the light of the developing military situation proposals for new negotiations were soon drained of credibility. The British saw less cause for compromise the more pain they had to endure to retake land that had been illegally seized in the first place. At the same time international opinion could not be easily ignored. London's increasingly robust stance was apt to cause discomfort amongst its allies who felt that they were likely to suffer the consequences.

There is an aspect to contemporary strategy that is impossible to quantify yet is of considerable significance, and is normally summed up by the word 'legitimacy'. This is not quite the same as legality, although a backing in international law certainly helps, nor morality, although conformity with traditional 'just war' principles is also an advantage. It needs to be gained abroad as well as at home, so just because a course of action has popular support does not give it legitimacy. Rather it is an amalgam of legality, morality and democracy, and it is the task of a government in a conflict to create a sense of legitimacy around its actions and to cope with the consequences of a failure to do so.

The British Government had been very conscious of the legitimacy issue from the start. It barely attempted to make a strong case in terms of strategic or economic interests, avoiding claims to great benefit in terms of cold war rivalries or future oil wealth. Instead it had concentrated on key principles: self-determination for the islanders, the inadmissibility of force as a means of resolving disputes, the inherent right of self-defence under Article 51 of the UN Charter, and the importance of not rewarding aggression. On this latter point, for example, in early June the Prime Minister requested a comprehensive list of extant territorial disputes. The FCO managed to identify 90 (excluding Eastern Europe), of which some could well be influenced by the outcome of the Falklands, notably those in Latin

America – between Argentina and Chile, Venezuela and Guyana, and Guatemala and Belize. Britain had a direct interest in the last two, as Guyana was a member of the Commonwealth and Belize, claimed by Guatemala, was under British protection.

In making the case to foreign governments, therefore, the emphasis was on the precedent set if the Argentine occupation succeeded rather than the vital interests of the UK. Resolution 502 had played a large part in conferring an aura of legitimacy over Britain's action, while the various declarations of support by other governments and such concrete steps as economic sanctions supported the view that Britain was acting on behalf of a wider international interest. As the fighting became more serious, however, the issue inevitably moved away from Britain's cause to the means adopted by Britain in the name of this cause. The just war tradition argued not only that a war be undertaken to right a wrong, but also that the means employed should be proportionate. This is rarely straightforward. Any use of armed force has to take into account not only some notional relationship to the ends for which they are employed but also the means available to the opponent. There is an issue of proportion in relation to the threat. Moreover, there was also a question of when the principles at stake could be said to have been honoured: was it enough to get the Argentines off the Islands, if necessary through offering some concessions to their concerns, or must they be denied any face-saving compensation? Abroad the urge was to get a negotiated settlement as soon as possible; at home the urge was to see honour satisfied, whatever the damage to Argentine honour. How should the consequences of actions be included in the calculation? What was the price worth paying for success: in terms of lives, military capacity, resources and political goodwill, and how much should it matter if those costs were being imposed on those less directly involved?

From the start of April, when few appreciated the potential seriousness of the affair, to the end of May, when it was becoming a matter of real concern, international opinion developed in quite distinctive ways. National answers to these fundamental questions of principle varied considerably. Leaving aside the exceptional case of the United States, of Britain's traditional allies only the old Commonwealth gave essentially unconditional backing.[1] Canada, Australia and New Zealand all stood firm, with Prime Minister Muldoon of New Zealand even offering a frigate to enable the RN to release another vessel for Falklands duties. By and large the new Commonwealth was also supportive, with many of the smaller African and Caribbean countries appreciating the need to put regional predators in their place. Although the Indian Government adhered to its non-aligned position Indian public opinion appeared to be with Britain, while publicity about possible South African arms deliveries to Argentina helped reinforce black African support. Kenya and Guyana were particularly helpful in the Security Council.

Elsewhere there was a clear preference for doing as little as possible. Japan, for example, was rarely disposed to disrupting trade on a point of principle. Japan voted for SCR 502, although there were reports of some hesitation. Thereafter, although the Japanese Government claimed to have spoken firmly to Argentine representatives and to have warned of the possible economic consequences, they took no clear economic measures for several weeks. A letter of 12 April from the Japanese Prime Minister set out the Japanese view in general terms, and was amplified when the Japanese Ambassador told the FCO on the same day that no application for new commitments for export credit to Argentina was expected (although there was no willingness to make a public statement to this effect). A further message from the Japanese Prime Minister delivered on 27 April said that the Japanese Government would advise Japanese businessmen not 'unduly' to take advantage of the import ban imposed by the EC and other countries. A reply from Mrs Thatcher dated 28 April took up the reference to 'unduly' and asked Japan to consider imposing actual restrictions on trade. Japan's reluctance to do more was based on its economic interests in Argentina, including a large surplus on bilateral trade; the large numbers of Japanese nationals or people of Japanese origin in Argentina and elsewhere in Latin America; and claimed difficulties about taking specific action on imports in the absence of an explicit UN resolution, because of the restrictions of GATT and of Japan's domestic legislation.

Europe

In Europe France was in a critical position, as being both a leading member of the European Community, a fellow Permanent Member of the Security Council, and, from the start, Britain's staunchest ally. President Francois Mitterrand had ordered full support for Britain. This led at once to the embargo on arms and trade and support for 502. France provided valuable practical help to Britain's armed forces. Mitterrand appears to have been motivated by genuine gratitude at the stance taken by Britain during the Second World War and by the opportunity the crisis provided to demonstrate his socialist Government's reliability as a member of the western camp. It did not go down well in the Quai d'Orsay, where there were worries about the impact on relations with Latin America and an extension of Soviet influence. Mitterrand observed on 1 May: 'If there isn't a reflex of solidarity between England and France then between whom could such a reflex exist.' At the same time he made clear that support was for the duration of the crisis and no longer, and certainly did not extend to support for British sovereignty. He was also able to separate this from all other issues, taking the opportunity to move against Britain over EC issues on the budget and agricultural prices.

In Germany, by contrast, the response was more equivocal. It took until 7 April before Chancellor Helmut Schmidt spoke to Thatcher, although he had interrupted his Easter break to preside over an emergency Cabinet meeting the previous day. He reported that the Prime Minister's request for economic measures had reached him just in time. Schmidt had decided that he had little choice but to support Britain. Foreign Minister Genscher, accompanying President Carstens on a state visit to Brazil, did his best to get the Brazilians to intervene with the Argentines and offered to go to Buenos Aires to talk to them himself. The Germans joined enthusiastically in the NATO declaration of support; and despite their strong aversion to embargoes and their reluctance to set precedents which could later be used against them, they applied the arms embargo and agreed to the Community's import embargo with uncharacteristic speed. As the debate developed in the Community on sanctions during the first weeks of April, Pym rang Genscher to ask for Community sanctions to last for one month rather than fifteen days and he gained German support.

So far this had been an instinctive gesture of support for an ally, a Community partner and a close friend. At the same time the Germans were cautious about endorsing British policies. From the start the Embassy in Bonn warned that German support and understanding would begin to 'fall away at the first sight of blood'. A sense of the trouble which nationalism and a predilection for military solutions could cause led to unease when observing the surge of patriotic enthusiasm in Britain, fully aware of how unhappy others would be if Germans betrayed the same tendencies. The aversion to armed conflict ran deep, with the supposition always that there must be a better way. For those of this view, it would be best if military action were delayed while a better way was found, even if this meant putting to one side the issues at stake. As anticipated, after the *Belgrano* the position became difficult with Germany. The Ambassador was concerned that every effort be made to keep Genscher as fully informed as possible, second only to Haig. Yet the Ambassador to the European Community had got into trouble with Parsons because he had briefed fully member states on the various sets of proposals in play in early May so it was difficult to get the balance right. At some point the allies had to be asked to trust the UK to do the right thing. Some attempt was also made to indicate to the Germans that the British were not oblivious to the difficult issues involved. Whether the political, legal and moral stakes were worth the military investment was 'keeping a lot of us awake a good deal during this last month'.

Pym welcomed Genscher for an emergency meeting at Northolt on 6 May. He proposed that Britain should announce the terms of US/Peruvian ideas and then have a 48-hour cease-fire to give Argentina a chance to accept. The British view was that this was precisely what Argentina wanted as they could then procrastinate and Britain would be under pressure to continue. Given what had happened with the *Belgrano*, Pym also felt that he had better warn Genscher that it might also be necessary to go for the carrier. Genscher could see the dangers of letting the arguments among allies get out of hand. He observed to Pym, that '[Soviet Foreign Minister] Gromyko had predicted to the Yugoslavs that Falklands would lead to a crisis in confidence in NATO.'

The German interest in trade with Argentina was substantial as they took 28 per cent of all the European Community's imports from Argentina in 1980. There was also concern at the diversion of British forces from their NATO tasks. The Berlin parallel was invoked, including by the city's Mayor and the President: a country that could respond to aggression against one isolated outpost was likely to respond to a threat to another, although others denied any parallel between the Falklands and one of Europe's great cities. One senior diplomat in the Foreign Ministry (Auswärtiges Amt) took on the same role in British demonology as Kirkpatrick did in the US. He made the same observation that if Argentina really owned the Islands then their actions were not aggressive, and remarked to a number of interlocutors, as reported back to Britain, that it was ironic that Britain had divested Germany of her colonies at the beginning of the century and now expected German help in hanging on to her own. Argentina, in this view, was an old friend of Germany, having been the last to break relations during the Second World War and the first to open with the FRG.

In some ways the Italian position was the most interesting of all, and while it caused Britain a number of problems this could easily be explained by the political situation within Italy. According to the press the hostilities were 'absurd' and Britain's reaction to the Argentine invasion disproportionate, but the Italian Government was always careful to express sympathy for Britain's position despite the constraints it faced and it was known that Italy had condemned Argentina privately and directly. About half of Argentina's population was of Italian extraction. There were over one million Italian passport holders in Argentina who were entitled to vote in Italy's national elections and therefore formed an important lobby. Italy also had important commercial interests in Argentina and generally in South America. Against this background many Italians saw sanctions as contributing to the escalation of the conflict, providing opportunities for the Soviet Union and also causing adverse effects on long-term relations between Europe and Latin America. Lastly, there was a matter of political culture. British diplomats observed that Italian politicians tended to assume that there was no problem that could not be solved by negotiation. Political life was geared to a search for compromise even if this meant that big issues tended to be sidestepped rather than tackled head on. There had been a battle over sanctions within the governing coalition, who were desperate for an economic embargo of the shortest possible duration and a negotiated settlement. In mid-April an Argentine delegation had visited Italy to get the Government to put pressure on Britain and to block EC sanctions. Socialists had been sent to show that the cause was more than just the Junta's. They were then politely rebuffed. There were nonetheless regrets in Rome that the embargo had been agreed to for the sake of European solidarity. Coupled with this were doubts about the efficacy of sanctions, which it was claimed might make matters worse by hardening Junta attitudes

The relationship with Spain was potentially a source of greater difficulty. Spain supported the Argentine claim to the Falklands, and the Spanish press was jubilant at the Argentine invasion, while almost unanimously opposing a similar use of force against Gibraltar. The Argentine Junta represented exactly the sort of outmoded mentality which Spanish democracy was dedicated to opposing. Not surprisingly, therefore, Francoists were the more enthusiastic supporters of the Argentines. The Spanish Government did not want policy towards this dispute to interfere with its intention to join NATO in 1982 and the European Community later. Nor did it want the crisis to interfere with negotiations on the dispute over Gibraltar, although the pressures of the crisis led to a planned diplomatic initiative involving the two Foreign Ministers being postponed. The unavoidable role Gibraltar was playing in support of the Task Force did not help, however much this was played down. Whatever the feelings within Spain, no action, official or unofficial, was taken against Gibraltar. On 31 May, however, Spanish police arrested four men. They were Argentine naval officers in disguise, who admitted they had been sent to Spain to carry out acts of sabotage to create tension between London and Madrid. The main interest appeared to be blowing up ships in Gibraltar harbour. The officers, who carried mines, diving gear and small arms, were flown to Buenos Aires after a protest by Spain.

Most difficult of all was Ireland, the other European state in a territorial dispute with the UK, and also, like Spain, a temporary member of the Security Council. Irish attitudes were consistently exasperating to London, often compared with the assertion of neutrality during the Second World War, and the long-standing nationalist view that 'England's difficulty is Ireland's opportunity'. Reference was also made to the 300,000-strong Irish community in Argentina. Initially Dublin had disapproved of Argentina's use of force and supported 502. It even went along with EC sanctions, despite claims from the most Anglophobic sections of the community that this stance was inconsistent with Irish neutrality. The Irish were surprised, when claiming that they viewed the issue as an ex-colony, how many other ex-colonies, such as Kenya, Uganda and Guyana, supported Britain. Perhaps more important was the difficulty in identifying with the Falklanders: an intensely loyal but isolated British community facing a hostile neighbour was too redolent of the Unionist community in Northern Ireland. Furthermore, as with all countries, British military activity was viewed through a national lens. One – sympathetic – Irish citizen wrote to the British Embassy in Dublin:

For the Irish, war has never been a clear and uniting activity; on the contrary our wars have been insidious, neighbourly-murderous and never heroic. With us war has usually meant brother against brother. We can only envy the classic British infantry spirit, and envy still obfuscates our foreign policy.

The crisis did not come at a good time in Anglo-Irish relations. After the traumas of the IRA hunger strikes, there were serious divergences over Northern Ireland, but also on a range of EC issues. The announcement that a British submarine had accidentally sunk the Irish trawler *Sharelga* did not help. Then came the news of the *Belgrano*, leading to the Foreign Minister wondering to the British Ambassador whether he should shake his hand in public, while the Defence Minister told a local party meeting that Britain was now very much the aggressor in the South Atlantic. Taoiseach Charles Haughey, now in control of Falklands policy, disowned this statement but on 4 May he drafted a statement that marked a decisive shift, calling for the Security Council to get an immediate cease-fire and to seek withdrawal of EC sanctions. He then faced difficulty, as clarifications were required to bring this into line with SCR 502 and also with European solidarity. When the British asked for an explanation the Foreign Minister explained that sanctions had been supported to provide a balanced combination of economic, political and military pressure, but that balance had now been lost with the increase in military activity. At any rate until the middle of the month there could only be an informal review. The posture adopted was not without costs for Ireland. It encouraged views in Britain of the Irish as unreliable or hostile, and even led to calls for the boycott of Irish goods. At this point the £9.4 million worth of exports to Argentina looked rather puny when compared with £1.5 billion to the UK.

Maintaining sanctions

Many in the European Community had rationalised support for sanctions as a means of reinforcing diplomatic efforts to produce a settlement without recourse to further violence. It was widely assumed, even before the *Belgrano*, that Britain would have trouble arguing for renewal from the scheduled date of 17 May once fighting began. The character of the sanctions would have changed from supporting negotiations to supplementing armed force. Confirmation of the shift in opinion from mid-April to mid-May was found in votes in the European Parliament. On 22 April the vote had been 203 to 28 in favour of sanctions; by 12 May the figures were 132 to 79. There was also a further complication. Britain was arguing in the EC at the time on two other fronts: the size of its own budget contribution and farm price supports. While Britain insisted that there could and should be no linkage with these other issues other countries, vociferously Ireland but notably France, had no qualms about arguing that support should be reciprocated. A German official was quoted as saying 'solidarity is not a one-way street'.[2]

All these issues were on the agenda for what turned out to be a tough and unsuccessful meeting of Foreign Ministers on 8/9 May in Belgium. They agreed to meet again on 16 May, on the deadline for renewal. Although a meeting between Pym and French Foreign Minister Cheysson on 14 May had not resolved the linkage issue, the French were still working hard in support of Britain. It was assumed on 15 May that Mitterrand had bullied Schmidt when meeting in Hamburg into endorsing a joint Franco-German declaration of support 'as long as the conflict lasted'. Genscher reassured the British Ambassador that he would support sanctions if there was no political solution, although there were already hints that they might try to confine it to 15 days. Later Genscher was reported to have told the German Cabinet that he had agreed to extend sanctions only on the under-standing that the UK as well as Argentina would do everything possible to achieve a political solution. France and Germany worked to keep the Italians on board over sanctions. The Prime Minister, Spadolini, along with Foreign Minister, Colombo, was keen to maintain Community solidarity (a constant in Italian foreign policy) by renewing EC sanctions against Argentina, but his tiny Republican party commanded only three per cent of the Italian vote. The Christian Democrats and Socialists, the two largest coalition partners, were opposed. Had Spadolini gone ahead with a renewal of EC sanctions the Government could have collapsed. Italian companies had lobbied heavily on the basis that a prolonged application of sanctions could have damaged Italo-Argentine trade to the tune of hundreds of millions of dollars. Vague Argentine threats of nationalisation of Italian assets had also caused alarm.

By the night of 16 May the Foreign Ministers had reached no agreement. They gave themselves more time by deciding that the sanctions would not actually expire until the end of 17 May rather than the start. This set the scene for some frantic diplomatic activity. Thatcher spoke to Colombo, explained the importance of the decision, the need to uphold the rule of law and European solidarity, and drawing attention to Britain's fresh negotiating position at the UN. The UK, she explained, 'would be most upset if it appeared that Italy, a country from which Britain derived a lot of its law, was supporting aggression.' Colombo explained the risk of a political crisis in Italy. This Italian reticence provided Ireland with some cover. During the afternoon the Prime Minister, having been advised by Irish diplomats to appeal to his vanity, also spoke to Haughey, warning that a failure by the EC to agree on the continuation of sanctions would be a blow to the negoti-ations as it would persuade Argentina that there was nothing to fear internationally. Haughey told her that the British request created difficulties: he had supported sanctions to support a diplomatic settlement not a mili-tary solution. Nonetheless he hoped to find a formula which accommodated the Irish position without interfering with the course which the rest of the Community wanted to follow.

In addition Denmark had a legal difficulty if there was not unanimity. The EC Foreign Ministers' meeting (which took place in the margins of a NATO meeting, thereby allowing Haig to weigh in at times on Britain's behalf) had therefore to find a way to respect the majority wish while allowing the minority views. This was essentially to allow for an opt out but no circumvention. The Germans later claimed that they would have been happy with a 14 day extension and had Italian agreement but Colombo could not gain acceptance from Rome. Seven days was agreed.

This partly reflected unease with events in the South Atlantic, but it also reflected irritation with Britain's refusal to give way on the issues of the budget and farm price support. On 18 May, the other countries decided to press ahead with price increases, ignoring Britain's right to veto such decisions on the grounds that they were against vital national interests. The Prime Minister protested but with Falklands issues so pressing she took no retaliatory action. On the budget Britain had been pressing for a rebate of $1.1 billion, instead of the $810 million on offer. When the Foreign Ministers met again, on 24/25 May, to discuss the future of sanctions, Pym accepted $875 million.[3] These matters settled, the Foreign Ministers could agree on sanctions. Although a week earlier it had been doubted whether a further extension would be feasible as fighting intensified, the extra week had included the landing at San Carlos. The Foreign Ministers were now meeting against the background of British ships being bombed in San Carlos. Perez de Cuellar's statement of 21 May and the document published by London had demonstrated how far the British had been prepared to go in the search for a peaceful settlement. In these circumstances there was some reticence about being overly critical. Eight of the ten agreed to an indefinite extension of the import embargo, and although Italy and Ireland continued not to apply the Community regulation they undertook to prevent circumvention of its implementation in the countries applying the embargo. Denmark was not applying the Community regulation but instead passed national legislation imposing a similar embargo without time limit. The Norwegians, although not EC members, followed this by confirming that their own embargo remained in force. In Oslo there was officially 'unqualified' sympathy for Britain, reinforced by Norway's own close associations with the Antarctic region and even South Georgia.

The impact of sanctions

The importance of these various European views was particularly critical because of the need to sustain economic pressure on Argentina. When the issue was under EC review in mid-May, the JIC judged it too early to assess fully the effects of the crisis on the Argentine economy. It did appear that the Junta's economic strategy was in some disarray. Since the invasion there had been a major loss of confidence both internally and abroad. Nevertheless, it would still take time before the various measures adopted by the EC and other important trading partners had much effect, particularly as they did not apply to imports under existing contracts.

In the case of arms supplies, Argentina's ability to procure the more advanced equipment had been impaired. This had led to a very extensive search for equipment, spare parts and ammunition. Approaches had been made to military equipment suppliers in 30 countries, including Argentina's traditional suppliers in countries operating the embargo. Almost all enquiries were to private dealers, suggesting that the embargo was being effectively enforced. Any items from such sources would undoubtedly carry a cost premium, particularly as many of those being requested were sophisticated, such as missiles and spares for aircraft and helicopters. Assuming that the embargo held and Latin American countries maintained a largely neutral stance, the JIC predicted that Argentina would be prepared to accept communist arms for the first time, offered as they often could be on easy credit terms or under barter arrangements. In some respects the frantic activity set in motion by the Argentine Ministry of Foreign Affairs was counter-productive. The priorities were ill-considered and unclear, and a load of amateurs entering what was bound to be a sellers' market attracted numerous dealers of doubtful repute and some frauds, while undermining the role of the existing Argentine Arms Purchasing network.

The combination of the invasion and the likely effects of trade and other sanctions on Argentina's external financial position had been major factors in the growing concern in international banking circles about the country's creditworthiness. Despite repeated professions of confidence by the Argentine authorities, foreign lenders remained extremely worried that a growing shortage of foreign exchange could result in a failure to meet debt commitments. The regime fully recognised the need to retain banking confidence: interest and capital payments on existing debt had continued to be made to all but UK banks. Most lending banks had agreed to roll over short-term credits which had fallen due since the invasion although some lenders were charging higher interest rates. A number were actively seeking to limit their exposure to Argentina and were unwilling to replace longer-term loans falling due or would offer only short-term accommodation in exchange. Argentine borrowers had made a number of unsuccessful requests for new loans. There was no evidence to suggest that significant amounts of new money had been made available to major Argentine borrowers since 2 April. The attitude of American banks remained particularly important. Immediately after the invasion some did permit full drawdown of existing credit facilities but since the announcement of American measures against Argentina there was evidence that the stance of some lenders had hardened.

Faced with this situation, the Argentine authorities had implemented a series of measures aimed at stemming foreign outflows. There were now extensive controls on foreign payments, including a 45 day suspension of imports of luxury goods, prior Central Bank authorisation for all permitted foreign exchange transactions, the recall of existing import licences and an issue of 'external bonds' to replace cash payment of profits, dividends, royalties and technical assistance. On 5 May, the peso was devalued by almost 15 per cent to try to encourage exports and further restrict imports. The rate of levy on foreign exchange receipts from exports was also raised. It still seemed unlikely that the authorities had ended capital flight completely and delays in repatriating export receipts had further affected adversely the foreign exchange position. The best information was that after falling by around $400 million during March, the reserves fell by some $500 million in April. Although the Argentine authorities claimed an increase of over $100 million in the reserves during the first week of May this, even if true, was likely to be temporary. The situation remained precarious. Total foreign exchange reserves were now less than $2 billion. In addition there was some $1.5 billion of gold at current market values. In the early weeks of the crisis there was substantial precautionary switching of private Argentine foreign balances out of Western European and Caribbean centres into the US. Following the US declaration of support for Britain a large part of Argentine official and private balances were believed to have been moved again so as to avoid the possibility of any freezing action. Most of the Government's liquid official balances were suspected to be in Switzerland.

The Argentine banking system, already shaky, had experienced a substantial loss of deposits as many people responded to the growing uncertainty by withdrawing their holdings. The outflow was heavy during the first two weeks of the crisis. It then continued at a slower rate, reflecting continuing concern about the possibility of government action to freeze deposits or even nationalise the institutions. A number of financial institutions were known to be in difficulties before the present crisis and seven collapsed during its early stages, including two of the largest finance houses. Interest rates had risen sharply and would have risen further if the authorities had not relaxed reserve requirements in stages from 18 to 15 per cent. The number of pesos in circulation was reported to have risen by 50 per cent during April. The JIC stated that:

> The authorities had sought to reassure depositors and had made general appeals to patriotism but at the same time they had taken the somewhat risky step of announcing the progressive dismantling of the existing system of state guarantees for bank deposits in private banks.

There was evidence of hoarding of foodstuffs and heavy buying of other consumer items, notably motor cars. Lay-offs in key sectors – in particular, the car industry – had continued. The Government had asked companies not to suspend any more employees while the crisis lasted. However, not all the effects of the crisis would be adverse: the increases in consumer spending and probable reductions in imports, for example, could in the longer term help industrial output.

The authorities had adopted a series of fiscal measures to recoup at least part of the cost of the war. In addition to the higher export levies, the duty on petrol had been increased by 30 per cent together with other increases in indirect taxes, including on cigarettes and alcohol. These were unlikely to cover more than a small part of the additional costs facing the Government. At the same time, increases in money supply, higher interest rates, plus the effects of devaluation and the fiscal measures had all added to inflationary pressures. Export receipts were normally seasonally strong in the second and third quarters of the year, the peak period for grain exports, and so it was unlikely that there would be critical shortages of foreign exchange for some months, even if sanctions were maintained. In addition to its foreign exchange and gold holdings, Argentina could still draw on credit lines with other Latin American Central Banks and on non-conditional borrowing from the IMF. A gradual deterioration in the external financial position was the most likely, but a sudden foreign exchange crisis, resulting either from further capital flight or a collapse in banking confidence, could not be ruled out. Most banks wanted to avoid an Argentine default. Even if a single lender sought to declare a default, it was uncertain that major banks would follow suit. But even if the crisis ended quickly, it was increasingly likely that Argentina would have to seek some form of debt relief later in the year.

On the key political question the JIC had to conclude that 'there was no sign so far that economic factors had had a decisive effect' on the Junta's attitude to the crisis. As the Junta may have hoped in the first place, 'Popular attention seems so far to have been diverted away from economic grievances.' Its economic difficulties might continue, but there was no reason to suppose that there would be such a sudden sharp deterioration in the economy over the coming weeks that could have a significant impact on the Junta's handling of the crisis. The serious problems would not hit the economy until the later months of the year. The assessment was part of the analysis of options in the build-up to the decision on whether or not to land at San Carlos. At this level it was discouraging, and another argument in London for getting on with the military operations.

As the conflict moved into its final stage the pressures on Argentina began to tell. Economics Minister Alemann had visited Europe and the US to reassure bankers that Argentina would meet all debt obligations and that no thought was being given to request a moratorium or a loan from the IMF. These reassurances neither allayed bankers' fears nor opened new lines of credit. Although no country other than Britain had adopted formal financial measures against Argentina, the general malaise of the Argentine economy, the shock to confidence caused by the invasion and the impact of British measures had caused banks throughout the world to exercise greater prudence in their dealings with Argentina, and governments to take a cautious attitude towards granting new export credits. Their caution was reinforced as it became apparent that the Central Bank of Argentina was delaying loan repayments because of the time taken to process claims as attempts were made to reduce the outflow of foreign exchange and ensure that British lenders were not paid. This led to an increasing number of technical defaults on interest and principal payments overseas. Private borrowers were even less diligent at making loan repayments.

Adding to Argentina's problem were the financial difficulties of those who otherwise might have been inclined to help. The Soviet Union was after 270-day terms on all future purchases of Argentine grain, as it could not afford cash business. For all the talk about making advances in Latin America, Moscow delayed negotiating a new grain purchase contract to obtain the most advantageous terms possible. Argentina had expected to earn $500m between July and October in grain sales to the Soviet Union but now the receipts would not arrive until well into 1983. Venezuela appeared to be ready to offer economic aid to Argentina, including oil products at concessionary terms, but this was unlikely to amount to much. Venezuela was having difficulty securing a $2.5 billion syndicated loan and at least one European bank had decided temporarily to avoid making any new loans to Latin American countries. A number were already suffering from a fall in export revenues – due to depressed demand for their exports – and from high interest rates that had increased their debt service payments. A slowdown in lending to the region was beginning to develop before the Falklands crisis and probably would continue.

Furthermore Alemann's affirmations that Argentina would pay its overseas debts would be meaningless if he ceased to be in charge of the economy. He had to deny regularly that he was going to resign. By 8 June it appeared that he no longer controlled economic policy and expected increased inflation in the coming months as the result of war-induced military spending and abandonment of fiscal austerity measures. This would make it less easy for Argentina to find new long-term international loans to reduce its high proportion of short-term debt. The re-imposition of fiscal restraint after the war seemed unlikely because of the need to use public spending to rebuild political support. By 11 June Galtieri appeared to have been persuaded by business, labour and military groups to reverse Alemann's policies, although without actually publicly withdrawing support for him as this would accelerate the loss of confidence among Argentina's external creditors and prospective investors. So the prospect for economic policy after the Falklands was more state control, accompanied by more inflation and higher Government deficits.

In a final paper on the conflict's economic dimension produced by the FCO on 10 June, just four days before the Argentine surrender, the overall impression was that the EC's import ban had caused little significant damage to the European countries. This was largely because of the exemption of existing contracts and also because Argentine exports tended to be agricultural or other products that were not in short supply and could be obtained elsewhere without much additional cost. Argentina had retaliated by banning imports from the EC. As the economy was in a depressed state even before the crisis, it was hard to discern what difference this had made. Imports in the first quarter of 1982 were 51 per cent down on the same period of 1981 so those from Europe were already being hit. Nor had the ban been applied consistently. Exports to Argentina were largely in manufactures, which were normally supplied on longer-term contracts, so the effect of the ban would not be felt for some time. Also the regulations allowed the import of essential goods. The main contracts threatened were inevitably for military equipment. The Germans were hardest hit here because of the interruption of supplies for warships being constructed in Argentina. At risk was $1,242 million over eight years. French arms manufacturers were concerned about the long-term impact of the arms embargo on their future sales. Elsewhere Dutch firms had failed to secure a gas pipeline contract but for reasons unrelated to sanctions. There was no evidence that Italy, Japan or the US had picked up extra business because they had not banned imports.

Argentina's economic fortunes declined along with its military and political fortunes. The process was interactive. More military and diplomatic success would have provided the Government with the domestic support necessary to ask for sacrifices from the people and led its creditors to expect greater continuity in its policy and personnel. The sanctions regime would have begun to erode. So it is very difficult to know what would have happened had there been a military stand off and the economic pressures had continued to worsen for Argentina. In the event the pressures were not decisive.

The costs of war

The Prime Minister's original decision not to include the Chancellor of the Exchequer in the War Cabinet had the intended effect of removing financial considerations almost entirely from its deliberations. Whether this was the decisive factor in marginalising these considerations is uncertain. Another important aspect of the timing of the conflict was that it came as Britain was coming out of a deep recession, and the economic backdrop was increasingly positive. This meant that the Government's popularity was also starting to improve. In addition, after the initial shock, the position never seemed so dire to prompt a sterling crisis or stock market collapse. Indeed share prices reached new peaks. Unlike Suez the US was not trying to undermine the British position while the export markets affected in Latin America were not central to the balance of trade. If the economic conditions had been less propitious then, in or out of the War Cabinet, the Chancellor's voice would have been heard. As it was the Treasury had to watch as the

MoD shot well beyond its approved expenditure limits. After a period of desperately trying to keep the lid on public expenditure, notably in the defence field, this must have been painful for Treasury officials, but it was only to be expected, and many of the main costs of the war would only be borne later, as the lost equipment had to be replaced. The immediate costs were met out of the £2.4 billion contingency reserve within the Public Sector Borrowing Requirement. MoD gained agreement that the extra costs would not be met out of its established budget but from a separate account.

The costs incurred were largely political. In addition to the wear and tear on relations with the US and Europe, which concerned ministers during the war but never became critical, large geopolitical issues were raised internally and in discussions with allies. Without exception all advice from friendly governments pointed in the same direction: compromise and magnanimity in relation to Argentina, to the point of sparing it from a humiliating defeat. While this case was animated by issues of proportionality and the readiness to 'give peace a chance', most governments' concerns were more pragmatic in nature. A British victory, it was widely assumed, including by many in Britain, would have three unfortunate consequences: it would radicalise Argentina, alienate Latin America, and provide opportunities to the Soviet Union. The validity of these concerns was rarely challenged directly, although there was good reason during the conflict to believe that they had been exaggerated and based on scanty evidence. The third danger was only true if the first two were real, because what was being postulated was an historic shift in alignments. The Argentines would be so frustrated at having their territory snatched away from them once again that they would never forgive the British, nor their North American and European accomplices. They would seek every available means of continuing the struggle, however foolish and futile these may be, and become even more politically extremist. The rest of Latin America would follow in sympathy, convinced of the rightness of the Argentine cause and the inadmissibility of Britain's military response.

Latin America

Even as things stood in late May 1982 there were reasons to be sceptical of these assumptions. Indeed, despite the constant refrain from American diplomats about the threat to their position in Latin America, when one of Haig's team investigated the matter he found that there had been very little impact on the US's standing. At one level the concerns depended on ethnic stereotypes, of passionate Latin Americans, ready to give up everything on a point of honour. It supposed that the virulent anti-communism of recent years was extraordinarily superficial and could easily be thrown into reverse, as if this adventure went awry and ended in humiliation the right-wing Argentina Junta really would stagger into a communist embrace. It also supposed complete indifference to the economic aspects of the conflict, for western help would certainly be needed if Argentina was to sort out its shattered finances. As for the rest of Latin America, the gloomier analysis assumed a whole-hearted identification with Argentina, when the tensions between Argentina and the other countries of the region were well known. It was quite apparent that support was largely rhetorical, and that no Latin American country had been prepared to incur significant diplomatic, economic or military costs on Argentina's behalf. Moscow, and its local ally Cuba, did try to exploit the conflict but they were not very successful. Buenos Aires used contacts as a means of putting pressure on the west, but they were never going to lead to a move into the Soviet bloc.

Throughout May Argentina had been stressing that it was a responsible member of the western community rather than a potential convert to communism. The concern within the American, and also the British, intelligence community related more to the likely next Government. It was assumed that the new leaders would be highly nationalistic, reluctant to negotiate with the British, and increasingly inclined to blame the US for Argentina's defeat. Popular support for Argentina's claim would mean that even civilian leaders would have to sustain a nationalistic stance. Reports on 5 June that Argentina had signed a $100m trade agreement with Cuba, expanding an already growing commercial and political relationship with Havana, could also on the one hand confirm Washington's worst fears while on the other appear as a source of discomfort to a generally right-wing political and military elite. A picture of Costa Mendez (in Cuba to attend a meeting of the Non-Aligned Movement) embracing Fidel Castro had apparently irritated many officers. Even Costa Mendez was said to be unhappy about receiving assistance from communist countries.

The analysts well understood that something would have to be done about the economy and discontent with a repressive regime, but they underestimated the shock to the Argentine system that a defeat would bring, and the extent to which popular anger would be channelled internally, against the regime, rather than against foreign powers. The desire to get rid of military rule was also underestimated. Any government would eventually have to cope with the sort of recurrent economic failures prompted by the surge of inflation resulting from the abandonment of fiscal austerity measures. As the conflict wore on, at issue was not whether Argentina was rejecting capitalism but whether capitalism was rejecting Argentina.

Equally, all the economic and commercial arguments in Latin American countries were for strengthening rather than weakening relations with European countries, with whom there were close historical and cultural affinities, as well as important markets for their commodities and sources of finance and technology. Britain had played a role in the Latin American independence struggle, and in the region's economic development, while there were still sizeable British communities throughout Latin America. The responses to Argentine pressures had been slow and reluctant. Only Panama allowed its rhetoric to get out of hand, with chauvinistic comments about the Prime Minister, which many Panamanians deplored. British diplomats noted that they found little love for Argentina or for its military Government in the region, and that in private if not in public there was much condemnation of the Argentine aggression. American diplomats picked up the same messages: there was little sympathy for Argentina; the reason why a negotiated settlement was so earnestly desired was that they wanted neither side to win.

The basic interest in Latin America was to get the whole business over as soon as possible. The governments were aware of western concerns about realignment but, in using these concerns, they took care not to suggest that it was inevitable. Thus Peru warned that Britain's stance was making life difficult for pro-western governments, especially if London was determined to impose on Argentina an 'ignominious defeat and consequent humiliation', but that was not the same as wanting to break with Britain and the rest of Europe. They remained the weaker party in the relationship. Chile was officially neutral although in practice working closely with Britain. Brazil also had a recent history of quarrels with Argentina. When the Brazilian Ambassador called on Pym on 28 May, for example, he deprecated Argentine aggression and explained how much relations with Britain were valued, before worrying about the insistence on unconditional Argentine withdrawal and the consequences of Argentine humiliation. Brazil's draft cease-fire resolution submitted to the Security Council was, in its own terms, even-handed, while the Mexican Foreign Minister accepted in private discussion that Britain was the victim of aggression. Venezuela was the most active on Argentina's behalf, seeking endorsement for the withdrawal from London of Latin American Ambassadors but without getting very far. Peru and Colombia both remained interested in peace initiatives.

When Argentina moved to reconvene the meeting of the Consultative Organ of the Rio Treaty states on 27 May to consider further action there was confidence in London that a resolution which could achieve maximum consensus would not be able to demand mandatory collective measures against the UK under Article 8 of the Treaty. At most it would call upon states to adopt measures 'to assist Argentina [to] repel UK aggression'. On 29 May the Rio Treaty accepted a harsh resolution condemning the UK, calling on the US to cease supporting Britain and inviting Rio Treaty signatories to assist Argentina individually or collectively. Four countries – US, Trinidad, Chile and Colombia – voted against the Resolution. It had no consequences. It was only if Britain decided to undertake military action against the South American mainland, for example against Argentine air bases, that attitudes seemed likely to change 'drastically' and 'rapidly' in an adverse direction.

There was some unofficial action. Dock workers in Peru and Venezuela refused to handle British cargoes. The Peruvian Airport Authority Union also refused to handle British aircraft and cargoes and air traffic controllers blocked airfreight for Britain. There were reports that Venezuelan air traffic controllers were considering following suit. These actions were taken on the initiative of the unions concerned (encouraged by their fellow unions in Argentina) and not endorsed by their governments. Following a recommendation from the Embassy in Caracas it was decided not to raise the matter with the Venezuelan authorities, as exceptions had been allowed and, so far, the measures had been largely ineffective and applied selectively. These actions ended during May and there were no reports that similar measures were being adopted elsewhere. The Brazilian Government could declare any boycott by private organisations illegal if they so desired. The British Ambassador in Mexico City met the Head of the Dockers Union in Mexico's major port on 23 April and found that he could not have been more well-disposed to Britain. The FCO took the view that a boycott of British goods would need official backing to be fully effective and that this was unlikely. Boycotts of British vessels would not be of much consequence since circumvention would be easy. Ships could change flags of convenience or the lines could charter in foreign flag vessels.

The Soviet Union

Moscow was trying to use the crisis to ingratiate itself with Latin Americans, encouraging the media to denigrate British and American policies. During the Haig mediation it had warned Argentina that this was a smokescreen for American support for Britain and even that the US wanted to establish its own base on the Falklands. Its diplomats encouraged the exclusion of the US and Canada from the OAS, and promised to use its UN veto to help Argentina. The Americans saw Moscow seeking to capitalise on a major opportunity to improve its standing in Latin America. The British, however, doubted that Moscow would make much headway in improving its own position. It was known that the Soviet Union was keeping a close eye on developments in the South Atlantic, using a variety of satellites, reconnaissance aircraft as well as intelligence collection ships. The British assumed that, as likely as not, information gleaned was being passed to Argentina. There were no indications that Soviet equipment had been requested by Buenos Aires: such material would probably present severe technical problems for the Argentines. After the sinking of the *Belgrano* Moscow notified Britain that a number of its fishing ships were assisting the Argentine Navy in looking for survivors.[4] Britain took steps, successfully, to encourage Moscow to keep its nuclear submarines well away from where they might get caught up in British anti-submarine operations and the Soviet Union promised to keep their fishing vessels outside the EZ, although some did wander inside.

There was a strong Soviet protest to Britain stemming from the disruption of the Soviet/Argentine grain trade. Grain shipments were piling up in Argentine ports and insurance rates for ships operating out of these ports had been pushed up. Britain – and by extension the US – would be blamed by Moscow for domestic shortages of grain. The Americans were worried that Argentina might seek to obtain new weapons from the USSR after the conflict, on the grounds that they would be offered at bargain prices, western supplies had been restricted, and this would be a means of helping to pay for grain sales as well as increase Soviet influence. However, even Moscow was wary of getting too close to Argentina. It had been caught on the hop by the invasion, had avoided vetoing Resolution 502, and called for an Argentine withdrawal, even while condemning British colonial attitudes and describing the invasion as no more than an 'occupation.' It was well aware of the Junta's reputation among other leftist groups in Latin America, and had noted that third world support for Argentina was hardly overwhelming, a critical criterion for Soviet foreign policy.

The problem therefore was not that Britain was seriously jeopardising wider western interests in Latin America by pushing so strongly its national interests, but that it was widely assumed by its friends and allies to be doing so.

35

FINAL DIPLOMACY

After the landing these issues took up the bulk of Prime Ministerial time. Her files contain few discussions of rules of engagement or other military issues. On these matters she was now very much in the hands of the military. Instead they are full of reports from overseas embassies, telling of expressions of concern and anxiety, proposals for diplomatic initiatives and calls for generosity, extracts from newspaper editorials and conversations with opinion formers. From the point of landing, after which few governments appeared to harbour any thoughts of possible British defeat, the pressure for moderation grew palpably. It explains why the wait from the landing to Goose Green seemed interminable in Whitehall: how could Britain accede to calls for a cease-fire when there was no fire to cease except over San Carlos? Until now the Government had gone along with international concerns by offering compromises that would have caused real political difficulty at home had they been accepted by Argentina – and might not have been offered at all had such acceptance been likely. In the end the effort had been worthwhile for Britain because, although the aggrieved party, it appeared to have been more ready to compromise than the aggressor. The risk as the Junta contemplated the possibility of defeat was that they might soften their diplomatic position. For the same reason the British Government began to harden its own. As the land battle began in earnest the Government could not contemplate putting at risk gains achieved at such a high human cost on the basis of what they deemed to be a highly dubious political analysis of the detrimental effects of a decisive victory.

The impact of the changing military situation on attitudes to negotiations can be seen in the fate of the last Peruvian initiative. Lord Thomas remained in regular touch with the Prime Minister and was helping her stay in contact with moderate Latin American opinion. As the first Peruvian initiative came to an end he indicated that the Peruvian Prime Minister Ulloa would like to visit Thatcher in London. If so this was a potential intermediary with direct links to Argentina. On 11 May Thomas confirmed that Ulloa was visiting and that he had been in touch with both Perez de Cuellar and the Argentines who knew that he was coming. The brief for the meeting was defensive with regard to how seriously Britain had taken the Peruvian initiative: that it had failed because of Argentine intransigence rather than Britain military action. In terms of taking things forward it referred only to Argentine prejudgement of sovereignty and no cease-fire without Argentine withdrawal. In the event the meeting did not take place, largely because of the evident imminence of armed conflict.

On 20 May Thomas was contacted by Alvaro de Soto of Perez de Cuellar's office who said that agreement was close but that British action had preempted the Secretary-General's effort to put forward a working paper that represented a possible agreement. He had then intended to send a representative to Argentina to persuade them to accept it. Peru now wanted to develop its own initiative based on Perez de Cuellar's formula, which both sides were urged to accept. This was based on Belaunde's own experience of Ecuador in 1981 when without a document agreeable to both sides they did agree to a cease-fire and to certain points of agreement with the rest left for further negotiation.

Wallace spoke with the President on 21 May, who explained why he still had to try to get a settlement, although Wallace was more concerned about reported Peruvian military assistance to Argentina. Pym allowed a reply which essentially said that if Belaunde could persuade Argentina to withdraw then the prospects for a peaceful settlement would be transformed. After the landings Galtieri called Belaunde, and this led the Peruvian President to ask the US Ambassador to inform Washington that Argentina accepted Peru's latest peace formula in principle but would only accept the UN as the governing power on the Islands. This would last for six months or even one year during negotiations, after which the problem would be returned to the UN. Galtieri was concerned about the execution of the mutual withdrawal of forces, but was interested in the idea that forces on the Islands could withdraw to equidistant points, for example South Georgia for the British (although this was still claimed by Argentina) and Bahia Blanca for the Argentines. This was largely significant as indicating a wish to keep the US involved in the search for a peaceful solution. The President rang Wallace with the same news.

On 24 May Belaunde observed that his latest initiative had been received positively by Galtieri and courteously by Britain. He wanted more from Britain, however, and the next day rang Wallace, asking for news and offering another idea. With Colombian President Turbay he had a formula that would allow for the removal of the Argentine contingent followed by an equivalent British withdrawal. Peru would provide transport aircraft to help get off Argentine troops, thereby avoiding a bloody battle. He said Galtieri was well disposed to this. London quickly explained that such proposals could not now begin to meet British requirements. Turbay had sent his own message, composed before the British landings. This was judged by the FCO to have been sent with best of intentions and deserving of a full reply in response to its consistently moderate tone. Regardless, the time for this initiative had now passed. Previous efforts had petered out and had only been interesting as part of an effort to prevent the high-risk military operation which it had now been necessary to undertake. Editing the FCO's draft reply to Turbay, the Prime Minister took out references to 'hope that, even at this late stage, the way to a peaceful solution will be found.' Also excised was: 'remain ready to consider any proposal from any quarter which offers a real possibility of a satisfactory negotiated settlement of this crisis.'

More American pressure

It was easier to dismiss Peruvian and Colombian proposals than American. The attitude of the Reagan Administration was still causing the Government anxiety. Henderson recalls how at the end of the Chequers meeting on 16 May, Nott had 'protested about the American attitude. Did they realise the bitterness in the UK about them?' The Ambassador pointed out that all demands for intelligence and equipment had been met. Then the Prime Minister chipped in, referring with 'less than enthusiasm' to Reagan's recent telephone call 'urging us not to undertake military operations against the mainland'. She exclaimed once again against 'ingratitude'. Henderson, backed by Lewin, warned against taking this sense of grievance too far. After the meeting Nott agreed. The grievance was more against certain speeches and people than the overall US policy. Nonetheless, Henderson expressed concern that a visit Reagan was planning for June, after the coming Versailles summit of the group of seven leading industrialised nations, should not take place if feelings were still so strong. Thatcher reminded him that the Queen had invited Reagan 'and non-attendance would be rude.'[1]

In terms of material support the US had been more than generous, and diplomatic support had been provided when necessary, in keeping allies in line or defending Britain's position in forums as challenging as the Organisation of American States. Haig was called upon again to make a firm statement in support at the Rio Treaty meeting on 27–29 May. At the same time limits had been set to this support. Arms supplies to Argentina had been banned (in effect by closing loopholes in the earlier and not fully effective ban) and export credit cover had been withheld on new business. But Washington had resisted considering a ban on imports from Argentina and this had not been pressed. Constant requests during the various negotiations for some sort of guarantee against Argentine non-compliance had been side-stepped.

Most difficult, however, had been the persistent appeals to Britain to offer concessions to Argentina to pave the way to some face-saving settlement. These had often been requested not so much to produce a better outcome for the Falklands but to help Galtieri hold on to power, not a high priority in London, or to deflect Argentine irritation with Washington. Such requests reflected the warnings coming from the US Embassy in Buenos Aires. 'I scarcely need to say,' commented Ambassador Shlaudeman on 17 May, 'that a bloody battle on the Islands leading to Argentine defeat would produce grave consequences for US interests here and elsewhere in Latin America.' After the landing the more pro-Argentine Latin American countries, such as Venezuela, took every opportunity with American officials to raise spectres of resentment and rage against the US, Cuban and Soviet gains and intense nationalism.

On 23 May, Henderson reported on the Administration's post-landing assessment. This had also been reflected in the *New York Times* that day, and was believed to be widely embraced, including by many in Congress generally sympathetic to Britain. The gravamen was that Britain could win the war but without necessarily bringing about the complete capitulation of the Argentines. Any new Government in Buenos Aires would be revanchist, and attacks would continue indefinitely from the air, if necessary with borrowed aircraft and crews. This would impose an excessive long-term burden on Britain, provide opportunities for further Soviet and Cuban advances, and further damage US interests. Accordingly, now that Britain had made its point, a settlement of some sort was needed. Presented with these views Henderson retorted that 48 hours ago the concern apparently was that without military pressure little could be achieved. Now Washington was swinging in the opposite direction. Haig stressed that he was not intending to do anything that would be militarily or politically unacceptable, and he clearly had no ideas on what could be done, given that it would be unreasonable to expect the British to withdraw from the Falklands having just re-established some authority. He was warning of the pressures to come but was essentially after some sign that Britain was ready to negotiate. The next day a story appeared in the *Washington Post* suggesting that the US might cancel Reagan's visit to London if fighting was still underway lest it be too upsetting to Latin American friends. Mike Deaver of Reagan's staff rang Henderson to say this was not true, that the story was being officially denied, but it was the case that continuing fighting might require that some of the more glittering aspects be toned down – the banquet not televised, no ride with HM The Queen.

All this was very exasperating, Henderson acknowledged to London, but the importance of Latin America to the Reagan Administration had to be recognised even if at times it was difficult to understand. Henderson observed to his diary that:

> Mrs T has not yet consigned me to the Tower; but I am told that her voice drops two dangerous decibels when she goes through my telegrams during inner cabinet meetings. How much lower would it sink in patient but intolerant wrath if I included in my messages Al

Haig's plea that she should, at this juncture, even before we have overcome the Argentinian garrison, show magnanimity.[2]

With the Brazilians now being taken increasingly seriously as a natural collaborator on this issue, and the Americans anxious to keep them on side, there was a possibility that the two countries together might cook something up. The message did not improve the next day. A picture was being presented to Henderson of the whole Hemispheric system unravelling, as a result of Latin American solidarity with a probably Peronist successor Argentine regime hell bent on revenge. Previous reports that Galtieri would never deal with Moscow were now being discounted. Only so long as Brazil could be directly involved and Britain showed flexibility might this dire situation be avoided. The resultant ideas, however, involving mutual withdrawal, some American/Brazilian interim administration and discussions about the future had already gone down like 'a lead balloon' in London.

The next day, 25 May, Haig decided to try to work on Pym, assumed to be the most pro-settlement member of the War Cabinet. A letter was sent to the Foreign Secretary to be treated as personal and not for the rest of the War Cabinet, precisely because of the nervousness it might sow regarding American intentions. In passing it on, in a telegram not distributed outside of the FCO, Henderson explained that 'allowing for his cryptic tergiversations' Haig was basically on Britain's side, trying to protect his flank from the pro-Latinos in Washington. The fact that Henderson had been able to report his shifting views reflected his readiness to take Britain into his confidence. That did not make his letter any easier to take. A positive note was set by a promise that US support could be counted upon 'as you do what is necessary.' Then came the familiar warning about how Argentina might turn to the Cubans and the Soviets as a last hope of averting total humiliation, and how Galtieri might be swept aside by elements even more opposed to western interests. The expulsion of Argentine forces would not end the state of war, especially if Buenos Aires had been strengthened by communist support. Against this background, Haig urged on Pym that he persuade his colleagues to offer terms for a just and reasonable settlement. To encourage this he offered a concession of his own: a battalion-size force for the purpose of ensuring that there would be no violation of any interim administration preceding a final settlement. As Argentina would not accept a US only force, he wanted Brazil to be there as well. Brazil had just put forward a totally unacceptable text at the UN, but Haig urged London to use elements of it in their own proposal.

Pym's response was polite. He saw the risks as Haig described them and was grateful for the peacekeeping offer, but he drew attention to the mood in London. Now that a bridgehead had been established:

it would no longer be realistic to ask people here to accept the idea of an interim administration or mutual withdrawal from the Falklands.

They are just not political starters now. Too much has happened for there to be an alternative to repossession and the restoration of British administration.

Haig professed himself grateful for this frank account. Yet he, and the administration more generally, was now concerned that Britain wanted only a return to the status quo ante without any consideration of the possibility of a long-term negotiated solution. This was the basis for their gloomy prognostications on continued hostilities, with Latin America and, more ominously, the communists lining up behind Argentina. The London Embassy warned Haig that short of a major military setback Thatcher had little interest in negotiations and cease-fires, and was unlikely to be swayed by the possibility of an Argentine turn to the Soviets and Cubans. Minister Ed Streator wrote that:

> The only way we can see to sway her is to make clear soon that we cannot help guarantee an outcome that meets only British objectives and ignores Argentine aspirations. Even that may not work, particularly in the short run, since she can foot the bill alone for a while. And it may get her back up if we put it too baldly. But as she moves to get us on the hook, the point should be made to her.

To calm the Americans, and to prevent even less acceptable proposals being tabled, Henderson urged that London attempt at least to offer some suggestions for a settlement that might avoid an indefinite confrontation and could take advantage of Britain's improving military position. He was looking for a combination of self-government with a measure of internationalisation, perhaps drawing on the American and Brazilian offers to protect their defence and foreign policy interests. Britain would make proposals about the future status reflecting the wishes and interests of the islanders, but he assumed that there was still a role here for a contact group. The Prime Minister's own annotation, against this last point, was a large 'No'. When she turned to a telegram responding to Haig drafted by the FCO she removed references to any Argentine involvement on discussions of the future or on the economic development of the Islands.

The preliminary thoughts that Pym sent back reflected a compromise in London, drawing on Henderson's ideas but not offering Haig much to work with. The two major American concerns – communist interference and poor relations with Latin America – were noted more than endorsed. Britain had its own relations with Latin America, perhaps not as important as those of the US, and every effort would be made to restore them. That the long-term stability of the Islands required a secure environment was also accepted. At the same time it was vital that the Argentines understood the error of their ways and the importance of international law. The starting point had to be a return of British administration. Beyond that Britain could contemplate a change in the status of the Falklands if the islanders wished it, and a harmonious and co-operative relationship with the mainland would be in their interests. So at most there might be some sort of modified independence, within the context of a shared economic development package with Argentina, and backed by a US-Brazilian force.

When Henderson discussed this, the Secretary of State still urged that Argentina be offered something more than total humiliation. Rather than independence, anathema to Buenos Aires, the Secretary of State preferred to talk about self-government. When the Islands were retaken the Governor, as a symbol of colonial rule, would not return and there would be some sort of international umbrella that would deal with problems of security and future status. US forces would be present, only for the interim period until future status was settled, but the length of this interim period was not fixed. As for timing, he was anxious to get a move on but Henderson cautioned against putting anything forward until more military progress had been made, and also against consulting Brazil. Once they consulted with Argentina the whole business would get bogged down.

Haig was not inclined to wait as little could be done once the humiliation, the avoidance of which he now judged to be Argentina's prime objective, was complete. By the evening of 29 May he appeared convinced that the new initiative must come before Britain's final military push. Whether the Argentines would accept anything while its garrison at Stanley was intact and air and naval success remained possible he did not know, but it still made political sense to put them on the spot. Haig's plan involved:

1. General and permanent cease-fire and establishment of temporary British military administration; lifting of sanctions by Argentina, the UK and third countries;
2. Immediate introduction of peacekeeping force consisting of contingents from US and Brazil to verify cease-fire and ensure separation of forces;
3. Rapid withdrawal of Argentine forces;
4. Creation of contact group consisting of UK, US, Brazil and Argentina;
5. End of military administration and start of local self-government;
6. Phased withdrawal of British forces, with the peacekeeping force to assume responsibility for the security of the Islands for a limited period;
7. Negotiations, without precondition, on the definitive settlement of the dispute with assistance of other members of the contact group;
8. Undertaking by both parties not to take any action that would prejudice the outcome of the negotiations.

In this package he was looking to Britain to accept that the restoration of local administration did not include the return of a Governor; and that it was necessary not to espouse publicly the goal of independence or semi-independence. The agreement on withdrawal would have to say something about non-reintroduction of forces and he accepted that the contact group could stay indefinitely.

Henderson's response was lukewarm. It was unlikely that Britain would agree to withdraw its forces. Nonetheless, Haig asked for a reply by 31 May when he thought he might put proposals on a take it or leave it basis to Buenos Aires. He was clear that he did not want to fall out with Britain and understood why his ideas might be rejected, but he presented it as the best hope of preventing US-UK alienation from the continent. All London was concerned about was alienation from the US. If these ideas had come from any other quarter they would have been rejected out of hand. Because they came from Washington they had to be taken seriously, even though the political analysis underpinning them, and the prospect of any sort of Anglo-Argentine agreement at this stage, was doubted.

The difficulties were set out by the FCO's Planning Staff: the requirement to engage in such discussions before victory had been secured; the even-handed appearance; a contact group including Argentina as the only guarantor of good behaviour after British forces left. Having gone to the trouble of repossessing its own territory Britain would be accepting enormous restraints. With some effort they came up with an alternative package that might just be tolerable in London. Following a general and permanent cease-fire, and the lifting of all sanctions, there would be a temporary British military – not colonial – administration. When the military administration ended, a British officer would continue to be in charge and would introduce local self-government. Argentine forces would be withdrawn within two weeks. A contact group would be created, but consisting of the US and Brazil only. As an Argentine presence would not be acceptable Britain would accept exclusion. The functions of the contact group would be limited to approving decisions related to the purposes of the Agreement and not inconsistent with those purposes. The peacekeeping force would be responsible for the security of the Islands until the implementation of any long-term arrangement following negotiations, at which point there would also be a phased withdrawal of British forces. The negotiations on the definitive settlement of the dispute would be conducted, without preconditions, with the assistance of other members of the contact group. There would also be a clause about economic development. The optimum time for the release of the proposal would be just before Argentina's complete defeat, though this moment would be difficult to pinpoint. A US/Brazil proposal would be preferable as Argentina would not accept British proposals. However the Americans must be urged not to discuss anything with Argentina before they had agreed a position with Britain.

These ideas helped shape the first British moves on post-war administration, but beyond that there was little support in their pursuit. The best course was to disabuse the Americans of the idea that negotiations with

Argentina could now take place. Pym was to impress on Haig that the best way to organise an Argentine withdrawal would be through negotiation by the commanders on the spot.

Late on 31 May Reagan telephoned Thatcher to urge her to consider Haig's proposals lest Argentina's defeat be followed by a Peronist take-over. The previous telephone conversations between the two leaders had not gone well and Henderson had warned that another call might lead to more acrimony. On the other hand he had assumed that the Prime Minister would have been au fait with Haig's latest proposal, which she was not. The military action of the previous week had been tense and difficult, and had served to push diplomacy more to the background. Haig's latest plans meant that the Americans were attempting to snatch a hard won victory from Britain just as it was coming in to view. So when Reagan rang she was unprepared, although Downing Street had been warned that the call was coming. She explained, none too patiently, that Britain could not contemplate a cease-fire before Argentine withdrawal. Too many lives had been lost to consider handing over the Islands to a third party. Britain would repossess, restore order and then consider the future with the islanders. Reagan insisted that the world would know who had retreated but that failure to take the diplomatic initiative now would leave Britain having to prepare for future invasions. To this the Prime Minister responded that Britain had gone to the Islands alone, without outside help; she could not let the invader gain from aggression. How would the Americans react if Alaska were invaded and, as the invaders were thrown out, there were calls for the Americans to withdraw in favour of a contact group.

After the call she immediately rang Henderson on an open line to complain. She had been 'dismayed' by Reagan's attitude and wished the President to know how 'upset' she was at being presented with 'another peace initiative', one that was 'pure Haigism':

> We were prepared to negotiate before but not now. We have lost a lot of blood and it's the best blood. Do they not realise that it is an issue of principle? We cannot surrender principles for expediency.

Henderson persuaded her that it was vital that the President should feel free to talk to her when he chose but accepted that her general concerns needed to be understood. Almost immediately after this conversation the Ambassador was contacted by Haig. He was full of admiration for the Prime Minister but concerned that relations were entering a difficult phase – 'we can't accept intransigence'.[3] The President, while full of admiration for the Prime Minister's uninterruptible flow (to the point where he held up the phone to allow his aides to listen), had been frustrated by his inability to get a word in edgeways to transmit his admittedly complex message.

The next morning Henderson saw Judge Clark, again to emphasise how Britain had endured sacrifice and intransigence to get this far and could not suddenly pull out before the task was complete. Clark reported that Reagan had been disturbed by Thatcher's remark about going it alone, because the US was with Britain. But he was also concerned about the damage to American relations with Latin America and wanted to avoid further bloodshed and an Argentine humiliation. Yet, Henderson pointed out, Argentina had shown no interest in restraint and was still trying to acquire more weapons. They had plenty of opportunities to show restraint if that is what they wanted.

Henderson was so worried about the damaging implications of Thatcher's assertion about going it alone that he sent a long telegram explaining the problems faced by the US administration in giving the support it had done to Britain, despite pressure from the Latinos within the administration. 'They certainly feel that in terms of practical support and in ways that really matter they have done, as they could be expected to, a very great deal to assist us.' Because of the Administration's own reticence details of this help were not made public, although there had been many leaks, and so a balanced picture of American attitudes had not emerged. Henderson acknowledged Haig's disconcerting tendency to shift his position and his hyperactivity, but Britain knew about this precisely because he was prepared to confide. US assistance has to be worked for constantly.

Henderson was sent instructions to convey to Reagan British appreciation for all the material support received and the consciousness of Thatcher and Pym of the difficulties caused. But he also had to explain that, in response to Haig's various ideas, nothing could be done so long as the Argentines attached conditions to Resolution 502. The best option now was to get them to confront the choice themselves. The conversation was not easy. Haig was agitated by references in the British press to him being 'wet' because he had attempted to dissuade Britain from achieving legitimate objectives. He thought he had bent over backwards to acknowledge British concerns. Henderson did his best to mollify him.

On 2 June Lewin followed this up by writing to General Jones, the Chairman of the US Joint Chiefs of Staff, about the latest support. Satellite communication channels had just been made available at considerable cost to the Americans' own operations. Communication sets had been provided for British Special Forces on the Islands, there were secure speech facilities for the fleet and satellite weather information. Lewin wrote that he was 'greatly indebted' for all this. This facility was immensely valuable to Britain: 'just how much so, I will tell you when I can. You probably have a good idea anyway!' He added that the equipment provided, often at extremely short notice and from stocks earmarked for their own forces, had all been enormously welcome, and had been used effectively. Meanwhile, Lewin felt that Jones would be gratified by the success of the AIM 9G/L missiles and he hoped impressed with the Sea Harrier results. Stinger had secured at least one kill, though British forces had been running short of targets recently, and had some positive things to say about the first Shrike operation.[4] Lewin finished by writing: 'I would like you to know how much we all appreciate this help and especially the unhesitating way in which it is given'.

Materials were also provided so that the Prime Minister could express her gratitude for the material support during her coming Group of Seven summit at Versailles. MoD was also concerned that the scale of the American effort might not be fully appreciated by ministers. The Americans had been very helpful in setting up efficient arrangements for handling British requests, virtually all of which had been met in full. To minimise British expenditure on consumables, which might not ultimately be needed (munitions, spares etc.), they had agreed to hold stocks forward in US depots in Europe and on Ascension Island, with charges for the equipment being raised only as Britain drew items from store. The clandestine nature of the assistance did pose difficult presentational problems for both the US and Britain, but when the opportunity arose in direct meetings with the President warm thanks should be proffered.

There was a risk of a sharp deterioration in relations at a critical moment. The American press was reiterating the Administration's worries about the consequences for relations with Latin America and the possibility that a humiliated Argentine Government would be determined to seek revenge. The Prime Minister was being criticised, for example in a strong editorial in the *Washington Post*, for not standing up to her public opinion and explaining the advantages of negotiations. Britain was said to be showing a surprising indifference to 'the costs they expect their friends to bear'. Concern that the Prime Minister had been too sharp with the President, and that there was now real irritation in Washington with British ingratitude as well as intransigence, added to the importance of the planned meeting between the two leaders at Versailles. If there were similar exchanges with Mitterrand and Schmidt during the summit then the diplomatic position could become even more awkward, especially with a difficult UN vote imminent.

International comment

International comment tended to share the presumption that a negotiated, compromise settlement was always preferable to a decisive victory. One formidable indication of this came from the Pope. A visit to Britain had been long scheduled, and the Catholic Church in Britain had gone to great expense in preparing for it. There was no option to postpone; yet clearly the Pontiff was troubled by the conflict. Messages were also sent indicating that cancellation or delay would be seen as a political statement that could put British Catholics in an awkward position. He decided to come, although after the landing, on 22 May, he communicated to the Prime Minister his 'deep anguish' at events in the South Atlantic. 'I urgently appeal to you to act decisively in order to secure an immediate cease-fire that will open the way to a peaceful settlement of the dispute.' Thatcher replied reminding the

Pontiff that the conflict was not of Britain's making. She was ready for a cease-fire but not to reward aggression and negotiations had to be undertaken in good faith. Galtieri also sent a message to the Pope on 23 May that Argentina was ready to accept a cease-fire and to negotiate. The most sensitive aspect of this exchange was the visit to Britain planned for 28 May. To reduce any political impact he had decided to balance this with a visit to Argentina from 10 to 13 June, while promising that his visit would be 'strictly pastoral'. It was hard to be insensitive to Argentina as one of 22 countries in Latin America which together accounted for half of the world's Roman Catholic population.

The German press remained generally unsympathetic and apprehensive, seeing far more costs than benefits ahead as a result of the war, although the French press was more understanding. After the landings France retained its position that Britain was 'our friend' and defending its rights against Argentine aggression. It had been helpful on arms sales to Latin America, despite concerns that French companies were having future sales prospects blighted. By early June the Ambassador in Paris was expressing concern with the 'apparent assumption in Whitehall that the French are going to be co-operative whatever we ask of them and whenever and whatever way we put questions to them about arms supplied,' adding that 'British credit here is far from inexhaustible'. Foreign Minister Cheysson had remarked to American journalists that he was sorry that he had not heard the expression 'negotiation' from British mouths in recent days.

In Bonn, Chancellor Schmidt had started saying in public that 'German support is not a "blank cheque" for Britain' and was said to have told his Cabinet on 26 May that continued support for sanctions depended on Britain showing interest in a political solution. He welcomed efforts to revive UN mediation in the Falklands. While West Germany condemned the Argentine invasion they hoped to resume friendly relations with Buenos Aires 'as soon as possible'. Schmidt said that Bonn had 'perhaps a moral duty' to caution London against disproportionate military action. This notion that Bonn's 'limit' would be found if London used disproportionate force or took actions that precluded an eventual peace settlement of the crisis began to take hold. At the same time Schmidt was worried about souring relations with London, with whom in other respects disputes were few, if German parliamentarians made anti-British statements. Within the Auswärtiges Amt there were rumours of disagreements over whether British actions really were self-defence and consistent with Resolution 502 although the evidence for this was scanty. The advice from the Bonn Embassy was to ensure that the Germans felt that they were being fully consulted.

The Germans were starting to work with the French to preach moderation to Britain. Both had become attracted by American ideas for a truce to enable Argentina to withdraw and added their voices to those urging that the prospect of a negotiated settlement be kept open. On 1 June the Secretary-

Generals of the two Foreign Ministries (Guttman and Von Staden) met secretly and informally with Acland and Palliser, the current and former heads of the Diplomatic Service. Though briefed on the British position and on the lack of a serious Argentine interest in negotiations or even the preparation of its public opinion for major concessions, Paris and Bonn were pressing home the same message as Washington that day. Following the battle of Goose Green might not negotiations start again? There was a political moment to be seized, before the next big battle, and a small contact group might help resolve the difficulties in achieving the necessary breakthrough. The arguments put to the British were now familiar although often contradicted by their own evidence, as with the supposedly complete Latin American solidarity against Britain – there were already signs that Latin American countries were distancing themselves from Argentina now that defeat seemed more likely. Nor was it accepted that the alternatives to Galtieri were even more extreme, or that post-hostilities Argentina would be easier to deal with if it had not been humiliated and allowed some return on its original aggression. The opportunity was taken for Palliser to raise the issue of the potential French sale of Exocet missiles to Peru. It was made clear that this was a matter of crucial importance to the Anglo-French relationship in general and to the Prime Minister's own relationship with the President in particular. By the end of the day it was reported from Paris that the Peruvian Ambassador in Paris should be summoned tomorrow to the Quai d'Orsay to be informed (without any subterfuge in regard to technical difficulties etc. relating to the missiles) that the French Government had decided for political reasons that these missiles could not be supplied to Peru for the time being. Great appreciation was expressed, and it was agreed that the British had to keep the business 'as closely to ourselves as possible, irrespective of anything the Peruvians may say about it'.

Britain would not budge on the question of negotiations. A line still had to be prepared for the Prime Minister's meetings with Reagan, Schmidt and Mitterrand at the Versailles summit of the Group of Seven leading western states, scheduled for early June. The FCO proposed a policy that focused not on the wisdom or otherwise of an immediate ceasefire but more on the plans for the Falklands after repossession. This would stress that the British were anxious to devise arrangements to provide both for a stable future for the Islands and satisfactory relations with Latin America. They would not ignore the wider questions of concern to the allies, but they had to take full account of the wishes and interests of the islanders, ensure the security of the Islands and provide good prospects for economic development. In practice this meant at most a pause for a couple of years while rehabilitation took place and the islanders and everybody else gathered their thoughts. Awkward long-term questions could be set aside over this period. Other confidence-building measures might be a general commitment not to use force except in self-defence and to lift economic measures provided that Argentina also promised not to attack the Islands or British forces, leading eventually to reductions in the British military contingent, and later conferences.

From the start of June, after the costly battles at San Carlos and then Goose Green, the intention was to continue with the military campaign until it had been brought to a successful conclusion. This conclusion, it was anticipated, would be marked by an armistice arranged by the commanders on the spot, backed by some means for ensuring that the cease-fire covered operations from the Argentine mainland. It was assumed in this that Argentine POWs might provide a useful bargaining counter. There was now no intention to use the promise of wider political negotiations with Argentina to get a cease-fire. The Government had returned to its original objective of restoring British administration to the Islands, and this would continue until such time as their security and economic future could be guaranteed. There could be no cease-fire leaving any Argentine forces in place and in a position to procrastinate over withdrawal, nor any contact group involving third parties, nor a UN role in the administration of the Islands.

The political problem was how to get the Americans, and the other allies, to understand this while they still appeared to be hankering after a compromise settlement of some sort. Solutions possibly acceptable at an earlier stage of the crisis were no longer realistic in the light of British military exertions and losses. There was every incentive to avoid an open row with Washington. It was still thought at this time that American involvement would be needed in the longer term, both to help guarantee the security of the Islands and to contribute economically to their development. The main opportunity to get over the more robust British perspective would come with the summit to be hosted by France at Versailles from 4 to 6 June. Meanwhile, the most conspicuous sign of a loss of international support would be defeat at the United Nations.

Resolution 505

Over the same period as these troublesome discussions with allies there had been intense activity in New York as the British attempted to put off the day when they would be obliged to use their veto. The UN provided the context and the arena within which the allies hoped that Britain would demonstrate its moderation and magnanimity. In the event the critical vote came while the leaders of the western alliance were gathered together at Versailles.

It was no coincidence that the collapse of the Secretary-General's mediation and the British landing had come together. The publication of the British proposals may have irritated some close to Perez de Cuellar but had also reinforced the view that the British had not been unreasonable and this bought a bit of time. While the landing encouraged efforts within the Security Council delegations to get a cease-fire there was little interest in putting Britain on the spot by provoking a veto. Only Panama seemed to have this in mind, aiming, after the veto, to move to an emergency session of the General Assembly. This got little support. Ambassador Parsons was nonetheless worried that support for Britain was stretching thin. This was not simply because of traditional UN pacifism and a wish to see the organisation play a more central role but also because of a fear that the conflict was turning into a 'kind of cultural confrontation' between Latin America and Western Europe/North America that could impair the whole relationship between the two for some time to come. Argentine humiliation was thus seen to have wider implications, largely detrimental to western interests whatever the specific merits of the British case.

Initial ideas revolved around a resolution including a reaffirmation of 502, immediate cease-fire, mutual withdrawal, injection of a UN presence and some mechanism for longer-term negotiations. Parsons was making it clear that any ideas for mutual withdrawal were now non-starters. He had a private meeting with Irish Ambassador Dorr on 24 May, where he explained that it would be fine if the Argentines went quietly but Britain refused to get bogged down in interminable negotiations. Did Dorr really imagine that after all the 'human and material losses' suffered, Britain would pull back to be replaced by a UN administrator and a handful of observers? Still Dorr made it clear that while he wished to avoid a veto he was after a cease-fire plus additional efforts by the Secretary-General, based on his previous proposals. Mrs Kirkpatrick caused irritation with a speech which when shown in advance had appeared as a step back towards even-handedness, and when actually delivered was worse. In conversation she was unrepentant. On 25 May Eagleburger assured Henderson that Kirkpatrick's instructions were to veto the Irish resolution if it came to the vote in its current form. It became apparent from this conversation that the worst case would be a resolution falling just short of what Britain could accept as the American and French votes would be dependent upon the text. Parsons was worried that Kirkpatrick was starting to work more closely with the French Ambassador, whom he judged to be not wholly reliable. This was despite reports that Foreign Minister Cheysson wanted nothing to happen in the Security Council before British military operations were completed. The Americans thought that the French might abstain rather than become isolated with the US in supporting Britain.

The Irish draft was meeting some of its stiffer opposition from the neutral and non-aligned group who were irritated with Dorr for tabling a resolution that the British would have to veto, with all the risk of an even greater row breaking out in the General Assembly. The three African states plus Jordan and Guyana were working on amendments. In the light of this the Irish began to revise their text. Parsons took the line with other delegations that the draft placed unfair demands on the Secretary-General who would be asked to talk to the parties and get acceptable terms for a cease-fire over a few days. As Britain would only agree to a cease-fire with an Argentine withdrawal, he was being set a mission impossible. The amended draft was, however, apparently acceptable to the Latin Americans, including Argentina, and would not actually tie Britain's hands. Implicit in the wording was the assumption that military action would continue while the Secretary-General persevered with his hopeless task. Parsons was therefore inclined not to veto, if only to buy more time. This line was agreed in London, so long as he made a very strong explanation of the reasons for support, why a cease-fire required more than a verbal statement from Argentina and how changes to the situation since 21 May meant that there could be no parallel British withdrawal.

During 25 May Parsons negotiated successfully on the basis of the new Irish text, with the exception of one small amendment proposed by Perez de Cuellar that did not quite consign his mediation effort to history. He was hoping to get an early vote while the fragile near-agreement held and take what he could. The vote would have taken place that night but for delays caused by Costa Mendez, who had first been in intense discussions with Kirkpatrick and had then requested time to study the draft resolution. Parsons was happy for Argentina to be annoying everyone again. By the next morning Costa Mendez had accepted the draft and so the resolution would pass unanimously. Parsons was pleased with the outcome, and noted that this was largely due to the skill of the Ugandan delegate (Otunnu). 'It is ironic, in the light of my experience here, that our best support should have come from Africans, Asians and Caribbeans, with our partners and allies either useless or actively unhelpful.' Ireland had been perfectly prepared to push Britain to a veto.

Mission impossible

As Parsons had anticipated, Perez de Cuellar was unhappy. He told the Council: 'You've asked me to do this. I will try, but you should understand that what you are asking is practically impossible. A war is now underway, and it is simply not realistic to think in terms of achieving a cease fire.'[5] He was disinclined to serve as a vehicle for buying time and he knew how far apart the two parties were. On the Argentine side his task had not been made easier by the departure of Deputy Foreign Minister Ros back to Buenos Aires, while Costa Mendez was in Washington for the OAS meeting and the Argentine Permanent Representative was ill. On the British side Parsons judged him 'severely shaken by my public and private refusal to contemplate parallel withdrawal – the only negotiating card which he might have held.' Perez de Cuellar complained to Parsons that this had added to his difficulties. Given what he had heard from both sides he found it difficult to do anything other than report back within 48 hours that there was no possibility of mutually acceptable terms. Parsons doubted that it would be long before he was back in the Security Council facing a straightforward call for a cease-fire, and being blamed for refusing to entertain a mutual withdrawal of forces. The only way he could imagine buying more time would be to encourage Perez de Cuellar to send envoys to the national capitals. He had no reason to be optimistic.

Perez de Cuellar now shared the view that it was time for Britain to make the big concessions. Accordingly he looked to the Americans, Germans and French to put pressure on London to obtain greater flexibility. Cheysson does not appear to have done much more than to report to Pym that he had been asked to encourage British concessions, without making any attempt to argue for them. The German Ambassador to London tried a little harder. Without any flexibility the Secretary-General would have no chance, and he gave a vague hint that Britain's attitude might affect the continuation of economic sanctions against Argentina. The Secretary-General also contacted Haig who thought that a peacekeeping force might permit simultaneity of withdrawals, and promised to 'get busy'. However when Haig called back on 27 May he had made little progress, although he did report that there might be some modification in the British position.[6] This was the background to Haig's own efforts to get the British to keep thinking about a negotiated settlement, although typically the Secretary of State's own ideas had little role for the UN.

Perez de Cuellar had asked Britain for its views on the conditions for a cease-fire. In a long letter sent to Perez de Cuellar on 27 May, Pym explained again that a cease-fire had to be linked to an Argentine withdrawal, while British withdrawal would only follow the repossession of the Islands, restoration of British administration, reconstruction and consultation with the islanders. This did not leave much scope for negotiation but the Secretary-General was told that he, or an emissary, would be welcome in London if a visit was also planned to Buenos Aires. The British believed that matters had moved on, so even the Secretary-General's most recent proposals could not be described as 'contemporary'. The only basis for any 'glimmer of hope', as Perez de Cuellar read the message, was a reference to possible 'new international security arrangements.' This was not, however, much of a glimmer, especially in the light of the Prime Minister's uncompromising statements in the Commons. Parsons pressed home the message: the British wanted to be constructive, but nothing that happened in the UN was going to make much difference now to events on the ground.

It was not that he was getting anything more from Argentina. Perez de Cuellar made plans to fly in secret to Washington to meet Costa Mendez, but when he received an outline of the Argentine position he decided that this was pointless. This proposal, received on 28 May, was for a straight cease-fire followed by discussions on withdrawal. Perez de Cuellar sent a message that he expected a British response by 31 May.[7] By that day it was apparent that his efforts were not going to achieve anything. At an informal meeting of the Security Council that afternoon Panama pressed for an early formal meeting of the Council. However, this was postponed to give the Secretary-General more time. He now requested answers from the two sides to his own proposals by the afternoon of 1 June. His paper, passed to the two sides, proposed an immediate cease-fire, with the terms arranged on the spot by a UN representative, an inter-positional UN force, the withdrawal of all Argentine forces plus a token British withdrawal and resumption of negotiations on an interim agreement under his auspices.[8]

Parsons had already concluded that the UN had to be kept out of long-term negotiations, for there was a built-in majority sympathetic to the Argentine view on sovereignty. He explained to de Soto when he brought the proposal that Britain saw the UN as having essentially pre-judged the sovereignty issue. He still urged London not to assume that Perez de Cuellar was playing a double game – he just wanted to avoid bloodshed – and at least the latest initiative would gain a little time. The proposals were unacceptable but they would cause more problems to the Argentines than Britain and it was worth developing a reply that acknowledged the positive elements. The British response therefore largely took the form of requests for clarification. Might Argentina just attempt to use an inter-positional force to freeze the withdrawal process? What would be 'token' British forces? It was hard to see the relevance of another mediation effort. Any cease-fire would have to be arranged by the commanders on the spot while substantive negotiations could only come after the restoration of British administration.

The response disheartened Perez de Cuellar. The British may have denied any interest in humiliating Argentina but they did not share his team's interest in saving Argentine 'face.' He got Parsons to agree to ask London whether they would consider a UN presence to help stage-manage a cease-fire that would be arranged between field commanders; the gradual 'trickling in' of UN forces at a later stage in the Argentine withdrawal; restoration of British administration on an interim basis, perhaps with a military administrator rather than a colonial Governor. None of this was very likely. London reported these ideas to be neither practical nor desirable. When Argentina's own response to the UN proposals came in they were superficially positive, but the conditions added ruled them out of consideration.[9]

Two vetoes and an abstention

At the end of these deliberations Perez de Cuellar reported back to the Security Council on 2 June that there was no possibility of a cease-fire that was mutually acceptable. Parsons was aware of what was likely to happen next. He attempted to muddy the waters by circulating an illustrative British resolution and urging the FCO to work to call off the Spanish delegation through pressure on Madrid. Almost immediately, however, both Panama and Spain presented a resolution:

1. requesting an immediate cease-fire in the Islands
2. authorising the Secretary-General to use any means he judged necessary to put this into effect and
3. asking the Secretary-General to inform the Council within 72 hours of the implementation of this resolution.

The British line was that this was both unacceptable as well as impractical. The objective now was to restore life on the Islands to normality and that was inconsistent with meeting any Argentine conditions.

There was pressure for a vote on 3 June. On the assumption that the resolution would also get the support of China, the Soviet Union, Poland and Ireland, as well as Spain and Panama, and Britain could count on being joined by France, the US, Guyana and Japan, who would all abstain or vote against, Parsons urged intensive lobbying of the wavering delegations (Jordan, Togo, Uganda, Zaire). He was nervous that Kirkpatrick had spent the afternoon 'closeted with General Miret of President Galtieri's staff.' He was also anxious that De Nanteuil of France was recommending abstention and would need to be given firm instructions from Paris. The French delegation now seemed much less supportive than they had been two months earlier, and less likely to help, for example by bringing along Zaire and Togo. France claimed that the cooler stance was because Ambassador De Nanteuil as President of the Security Council had to show neutrality, but in private the line was increasingly that Britain was not being conciliatory enough. Within the UN context the French were concerned that the presentation of the conflict as one between the rich North and the disadvantaged South, would undermine their self-appointed role as a bridge between the two.

The non-aligned tried to improve this resolution and did so by gaining an amendment to the Spanish/Panamanian draft through an opening paragraph, which required implementation of both 502 and 505. Parsons said this would improve matters, as this meant, at least implicitly, that Argentine withdrawal was required, but he would need more time. When pressed later he said that he would still have to vote against as it stood but if certain, probably quite substantial amendments were put in to confirm a clearer link between the cease-fire and Argentine withdrawal, then this would change. Parsons was now under considerable pressure from the Spanish, French and American representatives, drawing attention to the symbolic misfortune of a British veto being exercised while not only the Versailles summit was underway but also the non-aligned summit in Havana. As Parsons was being stubborn, and the votes were still not there for the resolution, Spain agreed to postpone until the next day. In some ways, Parsons was disappointed that the vote had not been taken because it would probably have garnered less than the nine needed to force him to veto. The Argentines gave no hint that they were back-pedalling. For example they wanted the references to Resolution 505 to sustain past elements of the Secretary-General's negotiations, including the idea of an interim administration.

All this led the Americans to discourage the Argentines from persisting. They did not want to veto and had, according to Parsons, been 'begging and pleading with the Argentines, Panamanians, Spanish and other Latin Americans.' France also did not want to have to cast its veto. The vote was postponed. The Security Council was due to reconvene on 4 June. Parsons proposed that he should offer amendments to make the resolution acceptable. These basically involved saying Argentine withdrawal would 'commence immediately' and gave the Secretary-General a role in verifying withdrawal of Argentine forces. Otherwise, he was not sure the line could be held much longer.

The presentational value of demonstrating a desire to end the war without further loss of life was well understood, and had led to consideration of a personal message from the Prime Minister to General Galtieri, calling on him to avoid unnecessary bloodshed by agreeing to an unconditional withdrawal of Argentine forces from the Falklands before the final British assault on Stanley began. The War Cabinet discussed this idea on 3 June, with the imminent Versailles summit in mind. By now the advisability of such an Argentine course had become a regular theme in British statements, putting the onus for continuing the war on the Junta. The risk was that such a message could be used by the Junta to engage in protracted negotiations about the modalities of a withdrawal, with unacceptable conditions being proposed, and might even be used to draw the Prime Minister into a direct dialogue with Galtieri. For these reasons it was thought best to restate the general message without making a specific appeal.

This discussion helps explain the decision taken by the War Cabinet on 4 June not to propose amendments to the draft resolution. Parsons' ideas were still reflected in draft instructions from the FCO for consideration by the Versailles delegation on the morning of Friday, 4 June. These stressed the determination of ministers not to accept anything 'woolly and equivocal.' The outcome of the latest discussions at the Security Council had to be clean and quick, avoiding endless negotiations and imposing difficulties on the military commanders who had to judge the timing of any cease-fire. On the other hand the latest version of the resolution was cleverly drafted and could provoke rifts with the French and Americans. Some further amendments to render it more acceptable were therefore suggested, requiring their respective military commanders on the spot to enter into contact within 48 hours, but it would be left to Parsons to judge whether the circulation of these ideas would improve matters. When the delegation met to discuss the draft, ministers were concerned that even this suggestion went too far, and wanted to stick to the latest public line, which was that if Galtieri wanted to avert the battle he knew how to do so. The instructions were therefore simply to vote against the resolution rather than get involved in any more negotiations.

As far as was known the American instructions were to work closely with the British mission to make the resolution acceptable. If not they were to veto with Britain. The French were equivocating, nervous about the lack of any positive gestures from Britain and their new responsibilities as June's President of the Security Council. Over this period, however, active efforts were underway to change the instructions to the American delegation. The Argentines had warned the State Department about the damage that would be done to their mutual relations by casting the veto, denying Washington any future role in the resolution of the conflict.[10] Enders relayed this to Haig at Versailles, adding that he thought an abstention would be reasonable. At the same time, right-wing Senators, such as Jesse Helms, had also been arguing to Reagan that Latin American interests were getting neglected. Kirkpatrick was already pushing hard in this direction and had met with Reagan before he left for Paris. She now pointed to the movement of the Japanese and Irish in favour of the resolution. The delay in the vote that the Americans had requested on 3 June was to allow Reagan time to talk to Thatcher.

During 4 June it was clear that the Americans were unhappy about having to veto a resolution that confirmed the two past resolutions. Life was not made any easier by a request that they encourage the Japanese, who had suddenly decided to support the resolution, to abstain. Haig was coming to the view that as no effort had been made to improve the draft it was no longer appropriate for the Americans to vote against. The main British fury was reserved for Japan – having been led to expect an abstention, after a direct plea from Pym to the Japanese Foreign Minister and an apparently cordial discussion at Versailles, they found Japan siding with the opponents of the west, thereby obliging the UK to veto. Thatcher later reported having expressed her feelings to the Japanese Prime Minister 'in no uncertain manner.'

At the start of the day the assumption that Japan would abstain had led the Spanish to wonder whether the vote should be taken, but then instructions came from Versailles to the Japanese delegation to support the resolution, and Zaire followed. De Nanteuil tried to get the French delegation at Versailles to persuade Japan to change back but was not successful. As for Zaire, word went to Kinshasa that the positive attitude to development and military assistance that had followed support for Resolution 502 had now been dulled. The text stated that:

1. The Security Council, reaffirming its resolutions 502 (1982) and 505 (1982) and in the necessity to have all their parts complied with, asks the parties in the dispute to have an immediate cease fire in the region of the Islas Malvinas/Falkland Islands, and to start simultaneously the cease fire in compliance of resolutions 502 (1982) and 505 (1982) in their entirety.
2. Authorises the Secretary-General so that he may use the means that he judges necessary to indicate if this resolution has been complied with.

3. Asks the Secretary-General to present a report to the Council within the next 72 hours and to keep the Council informed on the implementation of this resolution in a period no longer than 72 hours.

The resolution was supported by Spain, Panama, Poland, Japan, Ireland, China, Zaire, Uganda and the USSR and opposed by the US and the UK. Countries abstaining were Togo, Guyana, France and Jordan. The vote had its own drama. Japan's explanation was 'brief and pained,' Ireland 'self-congratulatory drivel,' Guyana 'admirably robust,' Spain 'surprisingly mild,' Panama 'ranted on,' and France was 'limp.'

Kirkpatrick who delivered a curious speech about the failure of the UN and the horrors of war stole the show. She concluded:

Mr. President, the dilemma continues even in the process of voting this issue. I have been told that it is impossible for a country to change its vote once it has made it known but my government has asked me to put it on record that if it were possible to change votes, I should change it from a no to an abstention. Thank you.

Parsons noted later:

Fortunately any odium which might have attached to us for using our veto was diverted by the astonishing statement by Mrs Kirkpatrick ... This revelation left the Council and the media stunned and I was able to escape from the Chamber almost unnoticed by the press, the microphones and the television cameras as they engulfed Mrs. Kirkpatrick.[11]

Haig's new instructions had been sent through after the Security Council meeting had begun but reached her only after she had cast her vote. When Haig was later asked why he did not telephone Kirkpatrick directly he is said to have remarked that army commanders are not in the habit of giving orders direct to 'company commanders'. Henderson told Haig's deputy, Walter Stoessel, that he was furious that this came after Haig had told Pym that he would be supporting Britain and no contact had been made following the change of mind (although his attempt to do so may have caused the fatal delay). The UK record was that Haig phoned first at 2330 local time (Paris) just after the Foreign Ministers' dinner. Pym was then meeting with Thatcher, and Haig did not follow up the suggestion that he ring Pym there. Pym called back only after midnight. Haig then explained that the US had abstained because of the serious effect of a negative vote on relations with Latin America. He then rang back ten minutes later to say that the US had joined the UK in a veto. Pym welcomed this. Kirkpatrick later observed that the new instructions had arrived just a few minutes too late. The press picked up British dismay and Reagan's ignorance.

The confusion embarrassed the Americans, with one side furious for the veto and the other for the readiness to abstain. Reagan looked uncomfortable when questioned the next day about the incident while standing beside the Prime Minister. Even the British, for whom Kirkpatrick was something of a hate figure, realised that this was a mess largely of Haig's making, as he had changed his mind under pressure from Enders and Kirkpatrick. The Embassy also warned against the conventional western wisdom that her appalling behaviour meant that she would have to be sacked. They understood that her neo-conservative credentials were too important to Reagan to ignore. In the end it was Haig who was the main casualty of the in-fighting at the higher reaches of the administration.

Parsons remained cheerful. Given his early misgivings, he was pleased to have lasted for over two months without having to use a veto. Following the lacklustre performance of the resolution's proponents, Britain's position remained strong with third world delegations, and even many from Latin America were privately sympathetic. The Prime Minister sent him a personal and admiring message, acknowledging that he had argued for different tactics that might have gained more time but 'in the wider context, including the national mood in Britain and above all the military situation on the ground, I am sure it was better to reach the clear-cut result in last night's resolution.' She looked forward to more of his 'wise and entertaining telegrams.' Not long after Parsons got an even more surprising compliment. In a speech pointing out the ineptitude of Washington to deal effectively with the UN over many years, Kirkpatrick described Parsons as 'an enormously skilful diplomat' demonstrating 'what a Western democratic nation can do inside the United Nations' to make it responsive to their interests and policy goals. After their disagreements, Parsons appears to have been genuinely touched by this tribute.

Versailles

From the moment the world leaders began to assemble at Versailles on 3 June until late the next day the imminent UN vote dominated proceedings. Given the limits about what could be achieved at New York, the British strategy was to shore up support among its closest allies and dampen any criticism of its diplomatic stance. Critical to this was getting President Reagan on side. The key meeting took place on 4 June. The brief began with an expression of gratitude for American support, and then noted Argentina's consistent lack of real interest in a negotiated outcome. Thatcher was to explain how it was now difficult for Britain to make gestures before achieving full repossession. This stance, she was to argue, was consistent with recognising the need to improve the general western position in Latin America and to secure a good future for all. On the Islands time was needed to get things back to normal and to think about the long term, including possibly a greater degree of self-government, as well as economic development. The actual conversation lasted for an hour and was without anyone else present. The Prime Minister's report back to her colleagues indicated that she had stuck to the brief. The only deal now of interest to Britain, she explained to the President, would be 'a cease-fire, irrevocably linked to Argentine withdrawal within 14 days.' She had to make it clear to the President, who perhaps had not understood her point, that no proposal had yet been made along these lines. Reagan had expressed concern to her about the future course of events, after the retaking of Stanley. This included apparently some interest in decolonisation, leading him to push forward faster than Britain might choose towards full self-government, and even that it might become some sort of protectorate. Pym's discussions with Haig followed a parallel path. The Secretary of State was still expressing his view that Galtieri would continue with hostilities from the mainland as the best way of keeping his job, and was not sure, as the British hoped and Reagan had seemed to accept, that the return of prisoners would provide much leverage. He was still worried largely about the US position in Latin America.

When Reagan, contrary to the indications received by the French, publicly reaffirmed support for Britain, and suggested that the next step depended on the Argentine Government, this was assumed in Paris to be the green light for the battle for Stanley. Mitterrand, reporting his own conversation with Thatcher on 4 June, claimed that he:

> had not intervened with suggestions that military movements should be slowed down because we knew that in the first place it would have been pointless and in the second place it would have been contrary to the logic of events. This would remain so up to the recapture by British forces of Port Stanley.

He did however hope that a new logic would be launched after Stanley had been recaptured. This Thatcher agreed, but it would depend on Argentina.

After the summit Mitterrand stated that:

> We wanted to affirm our solidarity with Great Britain, who as it happens, had been the victim of aggression against both its national interests and its national pride, a solidarity which is natural. Great Britain must regain its right (doit retrouver son droit), it being understood that we shall do everything, once its right has been regained, so that peace triumphs over war.

He reiterated the core French position. Argentina was blamed for aggression and Britain was France's friend and ally.

The Prime Minister was heartened by evidence that Britain's most important allies accepted that Britain could and should retake Stanley. In a minute not shown to the Prime Minister, reflecting the discussions of officials with other delegations, it was observed that the other side of the coin was a conviction that, post-hostilities, Britain would be expected to be active in seeking the early lifting of economic sanctions. Slowly the diplomatic focus was shifting to the post-war situation. This was reflected in French arguments for magnanimity after rather than before Britain got back the Falklands. It pointed to pressure to come to find imaginative solutions to long-term problems, and also to gain release from economic sanctions and arms embargoes, especially if Argentina acknowledged that the war was over.

Neither the UN nor the US quite gave up. On 6 June, although unwell, Perez de Cuellar transmitted a confidential letter to both Galtieri and Thatcher. The British knew that there had been Argentine contact with his office earlier in the day. He warned of the conflict entering 'a new and extremely dangerous phase that is likely to result in a heavy loss of life on both sides,' and how this would 'gravely prejudice' the prospect for a future settlement. He called for a truce from 1100 on 7 June, with the military commanders meeting in the presence of a UN representative to agree a cease-fire by 11 June. At this point Argentine withdrawal would begin and the British would inform the Secretary-General of plans for the reduction of its forces. Then the two parties would enter into negotiations in good faith for a peaceful settlement of the dispute. There was no mention of an interim administration nor was the deadline on the negotiations firm. The objective was solely to save Argentine face. Parsons recommended polite rejection: it was all too late. When he went to explain that evening that the military situation on the ground was just too complex for an initiative of this sort, Perez de Cuellar had still not heard from Buenos Aires. Eventually a negative response was received. Parsons took the opportunity to draw attention to the disillusion in Britain with all mediation efforts. No serious compromises had ever been received from Argentina. The latest non-aligned movement meeting in Havana had endorsed an Argentine text allowing no scope for compromise. As late as 10 June the Secretary-General was exploring the possibility of getting the Pope to persuade Galtieri to accept his proposal. Parsons again had to explain that the time for such initiatives had long passed. Perez de Cuellar accepted this, while pointing out that he was still under an obligation, as a result of Resolution 505, to try because he saw trouble ahead as Argentina was unlikely to renounce its claim.

On 7 June Eagleburger of the State Department contacted Henderson after a long session with the Argentine Ambassador (Takacs). He reported a disturbing lack of Argentine realism on their ability to hold out and therefore an exaggerated view of their diplomatic leeway. Enders wanted to bring them down to earth by showing them Haig's tentative idea of 29 May.

Henderson was all in favour of convincing the Argentines of their parlous state but not of showing them old proposals rejected by Britain. Enders said he would do this only orally and then convey Britain's own misgivings before explaining that the only diplomatic option left was a cease-fire to allow for an orderly Argentine withdrawal. In the event Enders found it difficult to get Takacs out of the clouds. He claimed that the Argentine garrison was being re-supplied and that more British ships would be sunk while London was becoming progressively isolated politically. Eagleburger's next idea to introduce a dose of reality was to provide a military briefing to Takacs from the Chief of the US Army. Henderson discouraged this as it could prejudice British military security and, anyway, Buenos Aires knew exactly the military score, whatever the Ambassador may have been told.

The preference for a negotiated outcome was also evident at home. On 8 June Labour leader Michael Foot urged in Parliament a return to the Security Council with a British resolution, and he followed this up with a letter to the Prime Minister proposing that the basis for a long-term settlement be sought, in order to sustain international support over the short term but also because of the risk of persistent Argentine harassment of the Islands, which would make them a continued burden on Britain. If they were given no alternative to unconditional surrender then Argentina would persist leading to heavy casualties:

> Both for Britain's good name, and for the sake of the servicemen on both sides who may be killed and wounded, is it not worth giving an undertaking that discussions will reopen as soon as they complete their withdrawal.

The Prime Minister in reply used Mitterrand's statement after Versailles as evidence of the 'whole-hearted backing of our Allies', and stressed that no unconditional surrender was being demanded, in that any Argentine withdrawal could be undertaken with dignity and in good order without humiliation. Argentina had had every opportunity to agree terms with Britain but had insisted on the ultimate transfer of sovereignty as a precondition:

> Since our landings on the Islands and the losses which we have incurred it would be unthinkable to negotiate about the future of the Islands as if everything were still as it had been before. That would be a betrayal of those whom we have called upon to make such great sacrifices, even to give up their lives, because of the important principles at stake.

As to the future the islanders would be consulted, but they had to be allowed a breathing space to allow things to return to normal before they expressed their views.

As the final battle for Stanley began, allied governments had, by and large, been convinced that there was no longer any point in pressing London for some conciliatory gesture. The American media now encouraged Britain to avoid a post-war strategy which could leave Argentina still determined to regain the Islands. The *New York Times* was now starting to cast a sceptical eye about the 'calamitous' harm that was being done to US relations with Latin America. Even the German press appeared more reasonable, apparently impressed by the welcome the inhabitants gave to British forces and arguing that the best way for Argentina 'to save senseless losses' was to capitulate. If Argentina had hoped that political isolation was going to oblige London to accede to a compromise settlement it was disappointed. The only connection with the world beyond Latin America came from the Pope's visit, not long before the surrender. Although the Pontiff stressed the peace-promoting aspects of both his visits, Galtieri thanked him for his 'strengthening visit.' On TV the national flag followed the Pope's benedictory image.

SECTION EIGHT

36

THE CHANGING
MILITARY BALANCE

British diplomacy may have been progressively influenced by confidence in the eventual military outcome, but even after weathering the San Carlos storm, the Task Force commanders remained unsure about the battles to come. Exactly how much resistance could be expected from the Argentine Army was unclear. If they managed to impose significant delays then there was a risk that the wear and tear on the naval Task Force could still leave Britain with an inconclusive and untenable impasse, holding some of the Islands but unable to take them all. Key to all of this was the progress of the land battle, to which we are about to turn. Having described the diplomatic context in which this took place, it might be useful also to fill in the wider military context.

The 'lost' carrier

At the end of 28 May, warning was received of a coming series of Argentine air attacks but none materialised, probably, it was supposed, because of poor weather. Woodward wrote in his diary:

> The land forces are at last under way after a whole week. This, to a force which is watching the Exocet air launched threat grow in numbers and range, seems an age. To the land force, under air attack albeit directed at the ships, it probably seems just as long but better employed. Time, nevertheless, is running out and the naval covering force is nearing the end of its staying power. This moment is by nature, impossible to judge/predict accurately: it will manifest itself suddenly in the loss of a carrier through defective equipment or enemy action; whichever is earlier.

At least, with the forces now landed, and the Argentine Air Force apparently exhausted, he could look forward to making good some of the Task Force losses. More escorts were arriving, notably on 27 May, the *Bristol* group, including *Avenger, Active* and *Andromeda, Cardiff,* and lastly *Penelope* and

Minerva. To get these ships to the Task Force as soon as possible, tankers had been stationed along the route to reduce dependence upon the speed of the group's own tanker, the *Olna*, which arrived itself two days later. Meanwhile *Stena Seaspread* had been working non-stop as a repair ship and some of the veterans of the campaign, such as *Brilliant*, were sent to her for repairs, once reinforcements were available.

Evidence that the Argentines would like to interfere with British supply lines came on 29 May when the 15,000 ton *British Wye,* carrying fuel for the Task Force, came under attack by a modified C-130 Hercules well to the north-east of the Falklands. Eight bombs were released, one of which struck the tanker without exploding. The War Cabinet was initially under the impression that the tanker had nothing to do with the Task Force and wanted to make a protest. They relented, given that under British rules of engagement an Argentine vessel engaged in similar tasks would be considered fair game. A further problem was that it was policy not to give publicity to unexploded bombs. As Woodward was unable to provide air support to ships such as this, they set their course further east to stay out of range of further aircraft. Argentine C-130s attempted other attacks but without success. In the end they were deterred through fear of being caught by Sea Harriers (a C-130 was shot down on 2 June).[1]

One vital requirement was for more airpower. In terms of sea-based aircraft, losses thus far had largely been the result of accidents, which accounted for four Sea Kings, two Sea Harriers plus the two Wessex lost on South Georgia. One Sea Harrier had also been shot down at Goose Green. That meant 24 of the original inventory remained. Thirteen more Sea Harriers and six RAF GR3 Harriers, the most vital cargo on *Atlantic Conveyor*, had all been flown on to *Invincible* and *Hermes* before the ship was sunk. Six Wessex, which could carry 12 troops each, had been lost. Soon to arrive, however, were another 20 Wessex in *Atlantic Causeway* as well as ten Sea King Mk2. The real problem resulting from the *Atlantic Conveyor* was the loss of the three Chinook helicopters, along with ground support and other equipment, including two spare engines. Although a fourth Chinook had survived it lacked support equipment and could only continue to operate ashore so long as it did not require any essential spares. More Chinooks were not due to arrive until 10 June. While Wessex and Sea Kings were flexible and could undertake many tasks that Chinooks could not, the loss of the heavy lift capability meant that the LSLs and LCUs were bound to take the pressure of moving around the heavier items.

Once the *Atlantic Causeway* arrived safely, its Sea Kings and Wessex were based ashore at two sites, one at Port San Carlos and the other near San Carlos Settlement. Seven Wessex were kept afloat in the *Atlantic Causeway* as a reserve. Another four arrived on 7 June with the *Engadine*, on which many of the new aircrew were travelling. Many of the new aircraft had suffered during their sea passage and, with conditions so difficult, the land force commanders never felt that they had sufficient, especially as the needs of re-supply grew disproportionately as they moved further away from San Carlos. There was also a shortage of landing craft. The sheer weight of the unloading task in San Carlos, to which was added support of the forward units at Teal and Fitzroy and sundry other tasks from minesweeping to special force operations, added to this shortage. The eight LCUs, eight LCVPs and four Mexeflotes were at full stretch.

The Argentine Navy appeared to have given up completely, apparently convinced that the odds were heavily stacked against them. Serviceable units of the fleet had been steaming within the 12nm limit, and kept re-supplied so that they could deploy quickly if necessary, but confidence about venturing far away from coastal waters had been further sapped by a succession of mechanical problems. These also afflicted the submarines. Furthermore, before the end of May, Argentina had already played its strongest card with its last air-borne Exocet.

On 30 May a combined Super Etendard/Skyhawk mission was mounted against the carriers. This was the first time the Argentine Air Force and Naval Aviation had worked together. At about 1530Z two Super Etendards, one carrying the missile and the other providing radar back-up, took off from Rio Grande, followed by four A4Cs. The position of the carriers had been worked out using information on aircraft movements gathered by the radars at Stanley. As they got closer the Etendards took in more fuel from tankers. They detected several echoes ahead of them in the target area, and, at 1732Z, the missile was fired at what was believed to be *Invincible* 15 miles ahead. They then turned away to find their tanker.

The target identified was not *Invincible* but *Avenger*, then engaged on a Special Force assignment away from the carrier group and so well to the south of the other ships. *Exeter* was the closest, on picket duty with *Cardiff*, eight miles to the north, with *Regent*, *Glamorgan* and *Invincible* well to the north-east. The Etendard's radar was picked up at 1730Z by the *Ambuscade*, *Glamorgan* and *Cardiff*, leading them all to fire chaff as they prepared to engage. The *Avenger*'s chaff distracted the missile, which passed close to the ship but did no harm. Then in came the four A4s. One was caught by a Sea Dart, one of three fired from *Exeter*, while another was either hit by small arms fire from *Avenger* or debris from the explosion that had taken out the first A4. The other two dropped their bombs but missed and turned away to safety.

As far as the British were concerned this had been a costly and futile mission for the Argentines that had used up what might have been their last Exocet. Woodward noted in his diary for that day:

> The air launched Exocet threat remains the major headache. Again we had quite good warning, and this time the Argentinians had their A4s fly as interference. We heard later that both A4s failed to return

which cannot have greatly encouraged the rest. The 'interference' gambit partially worked in that our eye was taken off the Etendard.

In fact, the Argentine command had been told a completely different story, presumably the result of over-enthusiastic reporting by the two returning Skyhawk pilots combined with a craving for good news. They believed that *Invincible* had been struck by both the Exocet and the Skyhawks' bombs. The British denials were assumed to be deception, and they were convinced that there was a salvage/rescue operation underway and the reduction in air operations consistent with the loss of a carrier. Perhaps, they therefore thought, there were as few as 12–14 Harriers remaining, especially when taking into account other equally optimistic claims about the numbers of Harriers that had been shot down. Over the coming days they clung to the hope that Britain was maintaining a policy of not announcing the true magnitude of their losses.

It was actually not damage but the weather that was holding back flights from the carriers. The episode might have demonstrated an Argentine capacity for self-deception, but it also indicated a clear objective. Fieldhouse continued to fret about the carriers, postulating hypothetical and rather daring Argentine moves, well beyond recent activity, involving feints by a frigate and destroyer force to draw escorts away from the British carrier group and leave it more vulnerable to air attack. In the same spirit he worried about possible attempts to embarrass the British at San Carlos or to build up West Falkland as the Argentine stronghold.

Moore was unconvinced. He saw no value in taking on the Argentine garrison on the West Falkland, which would be a diversion of slender resources, while for the enemy 'to land further tps would not in my view achieve anything'. Buenos Aires would have to calculate that if it was possible for the British to land on East Falkland over 7,000 miles away they would 'not face undue difficulty in crossing Falkland Sound with an airfield at our back'. However far-fetched the scenarios might be, Fieldhouse did not want to take any chances. To guard against any desperate Argentine measures he therefore wanted to keep the carriers and other major surface units well to the east, while strengthening the defence of San Carlos against air and sea attack and emptying the harbour there as far as possible. He sought a small but quietly permanent presence on West Falkland and the Union flag flying on Pebble Island. Of importance in this effort was the construction of the Harrier forward operating base at San Carlos. This was completed on 28 May. Helicopters were refuelled there that day. Four aircraft could be parked there but not rearmed. On 2 June it was declared open and was immediately put to use by two GR3s, and the next day by two Sea Harriers. If anything the Sea Harriers found it more useful because it gave them extra time over the Falklands as they could refuel there before returning to the carriers, still being kept firmly out of harm's way by

Woodward. Consideration was given to opening up the Goose Green airfield but it could not be defended, because of a lack of spare Rapiers, while fuel supplies were problematic and the airfield itself was littered with debris.

Another area of concern was attrition in the Harrier GR3s, especially as the weather had also forced the cancellation of the second GR3 reinforcement flight from Ascension. The ground attack sorties carried out by the GR3s against Stanley airport and other targets took more of a toll than the combat air patrols. Of the original six GR3s, one had been lost over Port Howard on 21 May, another while supporting 2 Para's assault on Goose Green on 27 May and a third on 30 May after being hit by small arms fire while attacking sites connected with 42 Commando's move to Mount Kent. This loss reduced the available Harrier GR3 strength to three aircraft of which only two could be expected to be available at any one time.

The anxiety about a bold Argentine move to get Super Etendards with Exocet almost led to the loss of two more aircraft on 31 May. Sea Harriers from *Invincible* reported four possible Super Etendards at the eastern end of the Stanley runway. In a hurriedly organised raid, two Sea Harriers suppressed ground fire with four 1000lb bombs, whilst the GR3s attacked what turned out to be four Aermacchis. They had been parked on triangular stands which gave the impression, possibly intentionally, of a delta wing-form from the air. Both Harriers suffered battle damage but returned safely to *Hermes*. They were out of action for two days. Woodward noted crossly in his War Diary that this 'major flurry' had nearly cost two precious GR3s. '*Invincible* not top of popularity poll.' Two more GR3s arrived on 1 June followed by a further two a week later. A number of the aircraft received hits during later sorties but only one, on 8 June, was damaged so badly that it became unserviceable.

Although the intelligence staffs in London were now convinced that the last air-launched Exocet had been fired, Woodward, on the basis of some snippets of intelligence that he had seen, which in fact had been discounted by London, believed that Argentina could well have acquired more missiles from Latin American allies. This was another example of different parts of the British effort working with different assessments of Argentine capabilities. A couple of false alarms, for example, on 2 June, led to chaff being fired. There remained another sort of Exocet threat. The Argentines had improvised a means of firing the shipborne MM38 Exocet by fixing a pair of launch canisters onto a trailer which they towed to a point near the coast from Stanley during the night and then away again to be hidden during the day. The existence of this facility became apparent on 2 June when it was learned that there had been two Exocet firings from this installation the previous night. Of the two, one had remained stuck in the launcher and the other had missed its target (either *Exeter* or *Active*). The report led to *Active* and *Cardiff* being withdrawn.

Before the shore Exocet battery could be destroyed it had to be found. The weather prevented a Harrier search and visibility was so bad that a

Lynx helicopter flight on 3 June saw nothing. An attempt to locate the battery the next night using *Exeter*'s helicopter, fitted with a radar reflector decoy, flying slowly up and down south of the Stanley Peninsula to simulate a bombarding ship, failed to get results. The only consolation was that there were practical limits to its operational range because of the need for road transport and a firing arc completely clear of land. A danger zone was identified. So long as ships stayed clear of this zone they should be safe. The gunline south of Stanley would not now be occupied unless there was a task of such importance that it warranted substantial risk to a major unit.

The Exocet incident had confirmed the importance of the AN/TPS 43 (for warning of air attack) and Skyguard fire control radars at Stanley in providing intelligence on British movements and interfering with attempts to shut down the airfield. A considerable effort had gone into rendering the runway inoperable, especially after an Argentine air re-supply sortie reached Stanley on 24 May. There were regular strikes against the airport but they did not prevent occasional landings by the Hercules. The runway was occasionally hit but the main problem was that dropping 1,000lb bombs at low altitude had little impact. The radar at Stanley seemed to provide sufficient notice to the Argentine transports if they risked flying into danger, although a Harrier shot down one Hercules on 1 June. One successful flight a night was quite inadequate for Argentine needs, but for the British no flights would be better.

Further Vulcan raids against the airport had been requested but not provided. The best use of the Victor tankers appeared to be the daily long-range Nimrod surface surveillance sortie. Concern about radars led to consideration of use of the American Shrike anti-radar missile. BLACK BUCK 4 on 27 May was called off after five hours because of problems with refuelling. On 31 May BLACK BUCK 5 took off with four Shrike missiles. A Sea Harrier attack was co-ordinated with the raid to keep the radars turned on. Two Shrikes were launched, and one exploded – the first had detonated about 45 feet from TPS 43 antenna, inflicting significant damage – the second missile missed. The British were not sure how effective the attack had been – but thereafter it appeared to have had the effect of causing the Argentines to be more cautious in their use of the TPS 43 radar. It was intended to use Shrike by the GR3s. The operation was delayed as RAF engineers assembled the system from parts air-dropped to *Hermes* by a Hercules, but it was not quite ready when the Argentines surrendered. At this point the British became quite pleased that they had not destroyed the TPS 43 as it was put to use for their own air defence.

Another raid (BLACK BUCK 6) using Shrike on 3 June was hampered by the poor intelligence on the location of the radars. The TPS 43 was believed to be on Sapper Hill but was actually at the west end of Stanley. The secondary TPS 44 was believed to be on Wireless Ridge, but was actually at the east end of the town, while the Skyguard radars were highly

548

mobile. The weather was also poor, so there could be no Harrier decoy sortie to get the radars switched on. Two missiles were successfully fired at a Skyguard site without much effect. Then, when trying to get home, the Vulcan had to divert to Rio de Janeiro because of a broken refuelling probe. Although the Argentine military authorities drew attention to the fact that the aircraft had just bombed Stanley airfield, the crew had been told to say that they had been on a training flight from Ascension Island and had to divert when practising air-to-air refuelling. The British were also concerned that it was not public knowledge that Shrike missiles had been supplied by the US. In London it was unclear whether the Shrikes had actually been used. There would at any rate be clues as to their use, which the Brazilians (and indeed any television viewers with an expert eye) might well pick up. To get the aircraft back the Government agreed, on 4 June, that Lynx helicopter spares could be supplied to Brazil, within the terms of their contract, as soon as it was clear that the incident of this Vulcan had been satisfactorily resolved. This was to be regarded as a normal business arrangement and there should be no publicity. Brazil announced the next day, however, that it would retain the Vulcan until deciding how to respond to an Argentine request not to release it. A few days later British diplomats succeeded in persuading the Brazilians to let it go.

Argentine options

In terms of the land battle itself, the critical issue in the military equation was the response of the Argentine Army to the prospect of the coming fight, and the degree of future support they could expect from their Air Force. Buenos Aires was known to be dissatisfied with the Island garrison's some-what passive performance on the ground. The endemic inter-service rivalries had been sharpened by the contrast between the Air Force's heroic efforts against the San Carlos site and the Navy's apparent withdrawal from the battle, while the situation faced by the ground troops was deteriorating every day. Officers were taking orders only from their own service, and few seemed sanguine about the prospects for further resistance.

The state of the Argentine Air Force, and in particular exactly how many aircraft had been lost, was unclear. The British assessed that by 3 June the number was 80. Those that were left had problems of serviceability. In the absence of sufficient spare parts, some aircraft were being cannibalised to get others back into service. One problem caused by regular low-level air operations was that salt water was ruining the fighter engines. With many pilots also lost, the sharp tapering-off of Argentine air attacks did not seem surprising. By 10 June an Argentine Air Force source was said to have reported that between 1 May and 7 June his service had lost two Mirage III, eleven Mirage V (Daggers), sixteen A4B/C (excluding naval A4Qs), one Canberra, 14 Pucara and one C130. These numbers were in fact entirely accurate, but all that was noted was that this was a questionable source and the Mirage and A4 figures were less than British estimates although the Pucara numbers were two higher.

The best hope that the Argentines seemed to have, given that a successful defence of the Falklands was looking increasingly unlikely, was to gear military actions to achieving 'a tolerable negotiating position'. Regular reports came in suggesting that the mainland was exploring ways of reinforcing the Malvinas. The Argentine air bridge to the Falklands had certainly been more successful than appreciated by the British who were only aware of about 30 of the 73 sorties flown to the Islands from 1 May to 14 June and were not able to shoot down any, although a number were deterred from completing their journeys. Some five were aborted and there are doubts about the success of others. It was later concluded that a minimum of 46–53 medium/large transport aircraft landed at Stanley during this period. In all 854 passengers and some 505 tonnes of cargo were flown into Stanley, of which the most important item was probably the twin-launcher MM-38 Exocet system complete with five missiles whose first appearance was noted above. At least 264 people were evacuated back to Argentina. Extra Aermacchi (six) and Pucara (12) aircraft were also ferried to the Islands.

There were limits on what this effort could achieve in terms of reinforcement – Menendez had a total of only 159 vehicles of all types, including only ten light armoured cars. Fieldhouse was, however, bothered by any strengthening of the Argentine position on West Falkland. Prior to the landing, the garrisons at Goose Green and Fox Bay had been supplied using parachute drops. Further attempts were made, probably five times, after the landing to use this method again but they all appear to have been unsuccessful. It was erroneously assessed on 7 June that the West Falkland garrison had been augmented by an airdrop on 4 June, with reinforcements of at least two company strength, followed the next day by four support helicopters. Argentine press reports from 5 June spoke of 1,500 men taking up positions 'to open a second front to catch the British in a cross-fire.' Any move of this sort would have given the Argentines the capability to mount raids on the bridgehead and land lines of communication or reinforce Port Howard. This could be used for purposes of future diplomatic bargaining or else to make it possible for the Argentines to continue operations from West Falkland should they lose Stanley.

In fact the Argentines had attempted to get two Hercules to re-supply units in West Falkland by parachute drop but this failed. There were inherent limits to what could be achieved, with only five or six Hercules available, each of which could carry about 64 paratroopers, and ten F27s, which could each carry about 46. Any attempted air drop would face gusting winds, variable visibility as well as patrolling British aircraft. Pebble Island also appeared to be still garrisoned by the Argentines, with a usable air strip and Skyguard radar, and possibly two Sea King helicopters armed with Pescador missiles.

Special Forces kept up patrols on West Falkland to cover any Argentine reinforcements, backed by air and submarine reconnaissance. In addition to naval gunfire support a company of 40 Commando was kept at 12 hours' notice to move to West Falkland. Although suspicions persisted that the West Falklands garrison might be reinforced, all possible means of achieving this were being watched and nothing was observed. On 10 June the SAS team watching Port Howard was found and attacked, and the patrol commander, Captain G J Hamilton, was killed covering his signaller's escape when surrounded and heavily outnumbered. Hamilton had survived the Fortuna Glacier helicopter crash, the raids against Pebble Island and Darwin, and the early seizure of Mount Kent. The survivors were brought off by helicopter.

37

GOOSE GREEN

Other than the air attacks, the Argentine response to the British landing had been remarkably passive. Claims were being made that British forces were trapped on the beachhead but there was nobody there to trap them. In Buenos Aires there was some expectation that following the landings Darwin could be attacked but General Menendez appeared to be more concerned about developing a blocking line along the axis Long Island Mountain – Mount Kent – Mount Challenger. While the Navy observed that it had 'contributed its quota of blood' and the Air Force was testing 'its men and materiel on a daily basis', the Army was accused of having an attitude of 'static defence', which should it continue 'will make the men wilt in their own positions'. An offensive attitude was needed for purposes of morale if nothing else. Yet Menendez appreciated that he lacked intelligence, mobility and local air superiority. His men had no means of reaching the bridgehead safely and if they did they would be cut down by superior British firepower. Meanwhile by sending the bulk of his troops to the west he would leave Stanley vulnerable to a second landing using the extra forces coming on the *QEII*.[1] The position of the West Falkland garrison was becoming fraught, with rations running out – possibly completely by 10 June. At this stage, the Commander of the Argentine Garrison still believed he had to defend both East and West Falkland. The Navy also saw only danger in venturing out. Both 209 submarines had defects and could not get to the TEZ, although the British still assumed that they would and that a major Argentine effort to make all surviving submarines operational was underway. The best Argentine hope lay in disrupting the British force by air strikes. Whether intended or not, sinking the *Atlantic Conveyor* had undermined the mobility of the British troops and had also delayed establishing a Harrier base ashore.

The concentration of Argentine forces closest to San Carlos was at Goose Green. This was one of the most substantial settlements outside Stanley, situated at the neck of Lafonia. There 127 settlers lived. A track to the north led after five kilometres to an even smaller settlement, Darwin, with 25 inhabitants. An account by June McMullen reports how not long after the

Argentines had arrived the Goose Green residents felt that they were being used as hostages. In the first instance this was when helicopters were noted in among the houses, daring the Sea Harriers to risk killing civilians if they went for them. After the attack on the airstrip on 1 May the local people were herded out of their homes at gunpoint and put into the community hall. They were told it was for a meeting, so no provisions were taken for what turned out to be a long stay. 114 people had only two toilets and two washbasins to share, and only the floor to sleep on. 'As the Task Force got closer and closer,' she records, 'we got more and more worried. We were hostages and we didn't quite know what they would do with us, or how they would use us. We knew that they had shot a lot of people in their own country, so we thought they wouldn't be too worried about shooting us to get us out of the way.' After the landing on 21 May, they were aware of more Argentine troops in Goose Green. In preparation for a battle, holes were cut to allow people to get under the floorboards, which is where many spent much of the battle.[2]

The question of what to do about the Argentine garrison provided the focal point for the critical post-landing strategic debates among the British commanders. The decision to occupy the settlement led to real tensions between Northwood and Thompson. Then the actual conduct of the battle produced yet more controversy, in particular concerning the role of the Commanding Officer of the 2nd Parachute Battalion, Colonel 'H' Jones. As a result of all of this, the historiography of Goose Green has become highly charged. The first account of the battle came from the BBC's Robert Fox, who was with 2 Para, and provided a vivid early despatch that was circulated widely in Whitehall.[3] There was no equally compelling account from the Task Force – the Brigade Commander had not been present and the Battalion Commander was dead. Fox also offered numbers of some 1,500 for the Argentine garrison, of which some 250 had been killed. During the return journey from the Falklands, Captain David Benest of 2 Para was asked by the new CO to talk to all those involved in the Battalion's battles and produce as accurate an account as possible. This has never been published but remains the essential source for any student of the battle, and has been widely consulted. Benest did not have any better information than Fox on the Argentine garrison and casualties but he was candid about the conduct of the battle and the role of Colonel 'H' Jones. This account formed the basis of an enthusiastic book by General John Frost, a senior figure in the regiment, which reinforced the early views.[4] Although a number of further accounts were published, two – by Mark Adkin and Spencer Fitz-Gibbon – stand out, for the depth of their research. On some important issues they disagree, but on critical issues they converge.[5] Readers might at this point refer back to my comments in the introduction about the impossibility of definitive accounts of close battles.

Breakout from the beachhead

This period was one of the most confused in terms of the whole campaign and to understand why, it is necessary to consider the assumptions about the land campaign prevailing at this point. Each military move up to and including the landing itself had reflected a combination of political and military timetables. The military timetable was the more pressing, in that over time all the attritional factors of weather, wear and tear, equipment losses and extended supply chains would conspire to work against the British cause. For the first stages of the campaign this did not matter, for even moving the Task Force forward as fast as possible across the immense distances to be covered meant that there was ample time for serious negotiations. If anything, military progress served political purposes. It added a coercive element to diplomatic efforts, warning of the consequences of intransigence. The greater the progress the stronger the bargaining position should a cease-fire be agreed.

The military timetable also provided a framework for political decision-making. At each stage a decision had to be taken whether to press on – with sailing the Task Force, leaving Ascension, taking South Georgia, enforcing the Exclusion Zone, sending 5 Brigade, and then landing 3 Commando Brigade – and in none of these cases was there a compelling political case for holding back, certainly not one that would have justified disregarding the pressing military timetable. Even if there had been a compelling case for a pause in the military preparations, prior to a landing, there was no obvious place for the Task Force to bide its time. Until, that is, some Falklands territory had been re-occupied. Establishing a secure bridgehead had always appeared as the conclusion of the long opening stage of the campaign that had begun in early April. It was understood that the military issues would change once 3 Commando Brigade was safely ashore, but achieving that goal was going to be demanding enough. As we have seen, even up to the start of May there was a degree of equivocation over whether to send 5 Brigade. There was no consensus that satisfaction of the political aims really required a battle for Stanley, and that the orders for SUTTON of 12 May still left this matter open.

In fact the successful landing followed by the incessant Argentine air attacks had sapped the political will to continue to even pretend to seek a negotiated settlement. Instead the question was whether the Government would be able to resist pressure for the worst sort of cease-fire, one that left no stable basis for a durable peace in terms of either political agreement or a military balance. For this reason there was still a tendency in London to see the land battle as a continuation of the earlier campaign. Before the political hand was strengthened by distance covered; now it required territory recaptured. If there was not going to be a negotiated settlement, however, then the logic of the situation pointed inexorably towards the seizure of Stanley as the only way to be sure of achieving the restoration of British administration of the Falklands. The change in mood in London was bound to create a greater tolerance for a high-risk strategy in theatre. The military took some time to pick up on this. They were in the first instance preoccupied with a successful landing and had not given the same thought to the next stage. Nott had found a mid-May briefing at Northwood, in advance of that to be provided to the War Cabinet, to be one of the most unsatisfactory he received precisely because the whole focus was on getting ashore with nothing about how the Falklands would then be repossessed.[6]

Unfortunately there were no firm plans for how this was to be done. There were a number of reasons for this. Up to this point this had been a maritime campaign and taken forward by Admirals – inspired by the First Sea Lord, managed by the Chief of the Defence Staff, commanded by the CINCFLEET and implemented by the Flag Officer, First Flotilla and COMAW. Northwood had always been a fleet headquarters and never truly joint. The land commander, Major General Jeremy Moore, stayed with Fieldhouse at Northwood until the last moment. He left as soon as he knew that the initial landing had been approved. Though the quickest way to arrive would have been to fly from Ascension and parachute down to the Task Force, he was worried that the media might make too much of this image. More importantly, he had decided that he should arrive with another full brigade, because otherwise the command relationship with Thompson would have been awkward. He saw no advantage in having a General command a Brigadier. At any rate he knew Thompson, who had worked for him in a number of posts, extremely well and trusted him completely. Nonetheless, getting himself and his staff to the South Atlantic as fast as possible by ship was not really very fast at all. It is important to recall his orders to Thompson on 12 May which effectively told the 3 Commando Brigade Commander to secure a bridgehead that could take reinforcements and 'from which operations to repossess the Falkland Islands can be developed.'[7]

The role of 3 Commando Brigade once the bridgehead had been secured but before Moore arrived was unclear. On the one hand, to the extent it was safe, Thompson was to push forward 'to gain information, to establish moral and physical domination over the enemy, and to forward the ultimate objective of repossession.' On the other hand he was told that a week after the landing Moore himself would arrive with 5 Infantry Brigade, and would then 'develop operations for the complete repossession of the Falkland Islands.' This lack of clarity would not have mattered so much had Fieldhouse at one level and Thompson at another been able to talk directly with Moore prior to his arrival, but for reasons discussed below, he was essentially incommunicado.

Two days before D-Day, an outline plan for after the landing had been agreed at Northwood. It reflected no sense of urgency. Following an initial move to Darwin/Goose Green to destroy the enemy strategic reserve and to protect the right flank, an advance on Stanley would take place employing artillery, naval gunfire support and Special Forces. The enemy forces on West Falkland would be left to await their eventual surrender once Stanley had fallen. Moore, as land commander, saw no point in rushing ahead when three more battalions and helicopters would soon arrive. While on the *QEII* he developed his ideas for the next stage of the battle. These involved taking full advantage of his travelling companions in 5 Brigade. As he joined the *QEII* on the day of the San Carlos landings, Moore told 5 Brigade commanders that it was his intention 'to land 5 Brigade into the beachhead and then to develop operations, using both brigades to further dominate the enemy to such an extent that he cracks and gives up.' This was welcome news to the commanders: they were all anxious lest their battalions would be asked to pick up garrison duties in the wake of 3 Commando Brigade's triumphant but solo victory.[8]

What emerged from these discussions can best be described as the 'southern strategy'. The first assumption was that all available resources would be needed to overcome the Argentine defences. The second assumption was that these defences were expecting an attack to come from the south. One reason for this is that Argentine amphibious doctrine was derived from the American, which stressed getting as close as possible to the objective. That was the basis of the original Argentine attack on Stanley. Moore believed that this assumption should be encouraged by 5 Infantry Brigade approaching Stanley from that direction, so that the Argentines would then be less prepared to cope with 3 Commando Brigade as it approached from the west. The implications of this strategy and its implementation will be discussed below. For the moment all that is important to know is that it assumed well organised Argentine defences and sufficient resources on the British side to support the advance of both brigades.

This strategy reflected the views of neither Northwood nor 3 Commando Brigade. This did not mean that Northwood and 3 Commando Brigade were of like mind. Initially Northwood adopted an optimistic interpretation of the available intelligence, suggesting that the Argentines were unlikely to come and meet the British but intended to wait for them at Stanley. Fieldhouse had come to this view as early as 22 May, when he asked Thompson first for an outline of his intentions. It was the case, as was apparent to 3 Commando Brigade as well, that the problem was not the break out itself – there was nothing actually to break through. The problem was one of over-extended supply lines and vulnerable forward units. The practical problems posed by the limitations of helicopters and air defence cover meant that until there had been more attrition of enemy air assets Thompson and Clapp were loath to start attempting large-scale troop deployment by helicopters, especially by day. It took up to the equivalent of 70 Sea Kings to move one artillery battery plus ammunition to a new position.

Although at this stage Thompson's proposals were all in line with Northwood's main aim of going for Stanley, Fieldhouse concluded that

Thompson was being altogether too cautious, exaggerating the likely strength of Argentine resistance. Furthermore, delay would add to the political risks – a decline in support at home, in part caused by frustration at watching British ships get caught at sea while nothing happened on land, and pressure for a cease-fire internationally which could leave Britain in occupation of nothing more than a small patch of the Falklands.

Because of Moore's status a SCOT terminal had been fitted in *QEII* shortly before it sailed from the UK and was working well by the time the ship reached Ascension. Thereafter, technical difficulties rendered the terminal inoperable for most of the time. He was therefore left at a critical moment of the battle with sparse information and no method of talking directly to CINCFLEET or Thompson. The period in *QEII* was unsettling to say the least both for the Commander and his staff. He could receive and send signals, although he was only seeing a limited amount of traffic. What he read was enough to make him aware of the tensions. On 24 May he was signalled by Fieldhouse's new land deputy, Richard Trant, reflecting unease at the lack of movement out of the bridgehead. While acknowledging the difficulties Thompson faced, such as the Brigadier's concerns about air assets and the general soundness of his plans, the assessment from Northwood was that:

Enemy possesses neither will nor means to mount effective offensive ground operations, and that rapid and powerful action will bring about speedy resolution of overall situation. CTF 317's intention to deal with enemy in and around Stanley requires earliest possible development of D Sqn SAS operation by other forces. For example the establishment of strong forward positions from which, with support from artillery and OS, enemy's positions may be threatened if not eliminated. CINC would welcome an early indication of how quickly you see this occurring.

The reference to D Squadron SAS here is significant. They had reached Mount Kent, 40 miles away from San Carlos but only ten miles from Stanley, and on the basis of their patrols had concluded that the local Argentine position was weak. If they could be reinforced quickly, and further ground to their left taken, then all the key Argentine positions could soon be in artillery range. This prospect enthused the local SAS commander as well as Northwood.

In reply to Trant, however, Moore observed that by accepting the need to inflict attrition upon the enemy air force Northwood had acknowledged the 'limitation on speed with which ops too close with Stanley can develop'. He continued: 'Until we can make an assessment of how fast the attrition to en [enemy] air forces will take effect I find myself unable to give you any guess as to date when it would be prudent' to deploy artillery and infantry forces close to the enemy. He would be at the end of long lines of communications and yet the Argentine commando troops could direct close air support against British troops. Moore sought to reassure Northwood by concluding: 'I stress my aim remains to capture Stanley as soon as possible'. Also on 24 May he signalled Thompson to reassure him that he was not 'in sympathy with pressure to rush you'. He went through the various options being considered by Thompson and wondered gently whether there really would be 'unacceptable risk to our forces in pushing combined arms firebases forward (by which I mean east) of the rapier cover.' There would not be any real pressure on the enemy 'until we are close up to his main positions'.

He was concerned that the Admirals in London did not really understand the complexity of land operations and so assumed that it was all a matter of will, that rapid action would bring about a rapid resolution and that when it came to the crunch the enemy would not fight. He signalled back to Trant the next day that he had given further study to possibilities of closing with the enemy at Stanley. One option was to land 5 Brigade closer to the town – at Teal Inlet or Bluff Cove – but the risks posed by enemy air attack were too great. In addition, while evidence was thin on enemy determination, what was available, including from prisoner interrogations, showed that the Argentines were likely to fight. There was therefore no option but to plan to close with the main enemy force with at least one battalion in contact and another not far behind, and to recognise that this would require considerable maintenance and the ability to withstand a counter-attack. He communicated the same view to Thompson, whose latest signal had crossed with his, confirming that they were thinking along the same lines, and that they had to plan on defeating the enemy 'in the conventional sense' while taking advantage of any signs of sudden collapse. He had reminded Northwood, he assured Thompson, about the difficulties posed by continued Argentine air attacks. As these eased he was 'sure you will be ready to change gear and move into a more speedy operation'. Again he encouraged a move to the east – if possible a 'long leap' rather than a 'succession of small steps'.

The role of Goose Green

The issue between Northwood and Thompson/Moore was one of speed and risk-taking but not of direction. There was also some agreement about the role of the Argentine garrison at Darwin and Goose Green in the scheme of things. Moore had been prepared to mount a raid against this garrison, with the objective of destroying the airfield, hurting the enemy and then returning to the bridgehead. Thompson saw things in a similar way. If anything it was Northwood at this stage that was nervous that this raid could distract from the main thrust towards Stanley and risk a degree of unnecessary attrition. Thompson felt any large move required waiting for the extra forces. One reason why he was not thinking much beyond raiding rather than capturing the garrison was that the latter course would tie up a battalion, stuck guarding the re-captured settlement. Northwood certainly agreed that it would be unwise to tie up too many resources on these Argentine forces as they were not blocking any route to Stanley and their ability to make a nuisance of themselves was limited.

As 2 Para occupied Sussex Mountain, where they had been sent to prevent it being taken by Argentine units from Goose Green, they were the natural battalion to mount a raid on Goose Green. Plans were soon under development, to be executed by the night of 24/25 May at the earliest. The timing would depend on the speed with which artillery support could be brought forward: in order to avoid giving the game away this would have to be done at night. The early planning led to any ideas of an amphibious operation being abandoned, because the waters were too shallow. The advance would have to be on land. Then preliminary movements began at 1600Z on 24 May, when D Company, 2 Para set off to secure Camilla Creek House as the battalion assembly area. The raid was to be launched the following night.

That evening the plan changed. First, intelligence was received suggesting that the Argentine garrison was expecting an attack and had been able to put in position two 105mm artillery guns. Second, Thompson was concerned that the operation was going to stretch his helicopter assets, especially as the weather was poor, at the same time as he was trying to get the SAS to Mount Kent. Getting to this forward position was more important than dealing with the Goose Green garrison, especially as it did not actually pose a threat to the bridgehead. As an alternative for that evening a quick move against Camilla Creek House was envisaged, but this too was cancelled because of bad weather.

Early the next day, 25 May, Thompson reported his plan directly to Northwood. G Squadron SAS patrol had worked out that Mount Kent was surprisingly empty of Argentine troops. On the night of 24 May D Squadron had managed to get a reconnaissance team on this critical piece of high ground. The intention was to get the rest of the squadron to its lower slopes to secure a landing site. Meanwhile, SBS had been checking out Teal Inlet as a forward base en route to Stanley. Over the coming night he hoped to get his men to Teal Inlet and then move to Mount Kent and Mount Challenger in order to occupy the line surrounding Stanley. The idea was to get 42 Commando and a gun battery to Mount Kent, soon to be followed by the whole Brigade.[9] He wanted to head straight towards Stanley and dominate the high ground before the Argentine defenders realised that this was what they should be doing. Once artillery was in position the British position would be much stronger. Compared with this bold option, very much in line with Northwood's and Moore's thinking, taking Darwin and Goose Green was at best a secondary objective. Thereafter he was not planning on any more operations until there had been a further reduction in the Argentine air threat. Because the positions he wanted to occupy would be cold and wet, he intended to rotate forces away from them so that they could dry out before returning.

At this point news came in of that day's loss of the Chinook helicopters on the *Atlantic Conveyor*. This undermined all the Brigade's plans. Instead of the troops moving forward by helicopter they would have to walk, and that would only be possible if they could be properly supported. It would take Thompson three nights with his depleted stock of helicopters to get just 42 Commando with guns and ammunition forward, while the rest of the brigade walked. During this time the position on Mount Kent would be vulnerable, especially after the first night, when it would be occupied by only 42 Commando's tactical headquarters, one rifle company, the mortar troop and half a battery (three guns) with limited stocks of ammunition. That night there was further frustration as the bad weather made it impossible to fly helicopters and reinforce the advance party on Mount Kent. In these circumstances, Thompson was even less inclined to bother with Goose Green.

As he was digesting the news of the loss of the *Atlantic Conveyor* Thompson received a signal from CINCFLEET, supporting the plan for a quick move to the high ground around Stanley, and keeping Goose Green as a secondary contribution:

> Now that 3 Cdo Bde is established ashore the earliest opportunity must be taken to invest Port Stanley from positions on high ground west which dominate it. Enemy forces in Port Stanley must be dominated and harassed although I accept that decision to assault Port Stanley can await further developments. Major psychological advantage would be achieved by separate set piece operation to eliminate enemy in Goose Green/Darwin provided that this does not detract from investment of Port Stanley. My prime concern is to make best speed to invest Stanley.

Thompson, while aware of the pressure to go beyond the limited objectives originally set for him by Moore, might have been able to console himself that his plans for Mount Kent were in line with Northwood's intent. Unfortunately the loss of so many helicopters changed his calculations. When he discussed his options with his senior officers the next morning, he decided that with so few helicopters the move that had seemed so bold the previous day now seemed too dangerous. Thompson reverted to the view that he should wait for 5 Infantry Brigade to arrive – and more helicopters.

There were early indications that Northwood considered the field commanders to be too cautious. A signal from Trant on 26 May played down the air threat to land operations, suggesting that a combination of Blowpipe and confining movements to helicopter by night could ensure progress. Clapp and Thompson saw the threat to be much greater, once troops moved outside the air defence umbrella now established around the beachhead. They believed that Northwood was unrealistically sanguine about the enemy's capacity for resistance. They remained worried about air threats over land – not only from distant Skyhawks but also local Pucaras – and that when the moment came the Argentine land forces might display the same resolve and courage as the air forces. Once again they concluded that when a prior condition relating to air superiority – this time destroying all Falkland-based Argentine aircraft and breaking enemy lines of communication – was not fully met, the inclination was to relax the condition in order to get some tangible progress. These signals came in at the same time that Woodward was complaining about the number of ships in San Carlos Water. With no superior headquarters available to him Thompson had to look backwards as well as carrying out his primary role of fighting the forward battle. In the end Clapp replied for him. Clapp had urged Thompson to report more fully to Northwood about what he was up to, but had also been frustrated by Fieldhouse's failure to discuss the situation with him.

When Moore arrived he would be able to interpret the situation on the ground for London and the London perspectives for his commanders, but he was for the moment barely in the loop. The conversation therefore took place at great distances between people who did not know each other well or fully understand the other's respective difficulties. This became important following the loss of *Atlantic Conveyor* because London had drawn the opposite conclusion to Thompson. To the politicians and their senior commanders this loss confirmed that the campaign risked being stalled and that there had to be some movement. The politicians had had to endure a difficult week. The landing had taken place, which was good, but then there was just an interminable process of unloading while Argentine aircraft braved British air defences to attack ships, with some success, and this was less good. If their bombs had been fused properly it could have been much worse. Meanwhile nothing appeared to be happening to move the campaign to its next stage. Lewin, who had either forgotten or was unaware of Moore's 12 May orders to Thompson, had expected early movement and reported that to the War Cabinet. Bernard Ingham, the Prime Minister's Press Secretary, had told reporters that 'We're not going to fiddle around',[10] yet that seemed to be precisely what was going on. William Whitelaw later recalled the concern in Government. The beachhead at San Carlos was relatively small in terms of the whole of the Falklands. If British forces had got stuck in such a small area, 'we'd have had all sorts of troubles'. In particular, 'if we didn't get a move on all the proposals for ceasefires would become stronger .... So a break out was very important.'[11] While the politicians were not going to offer their own military plans, Lewin and Fieldhouse were savvy enough to understand the situation and the impatience. Besides they were also getting frustrated. Senior Army officers shared the concerns, musing on the inability of Marines to think beyond beaches.

The proposed raid on Goose Green, previously something of a sideshow, grew in possibilities as an opportunity to regain the initiative. A victory there would demonstrate to the British people that the reoccupation of the Islands was making palpable progress, to the Argentine commanders that the British forces were irresistible, and to the international community that there was no intention to pause to allow a cease-fire to be negotiated.[12] Northwood understood that the move to Mount Kent could not go forward to the extent previously planned, but waiting for 5 Infantry Brigade was not an option. Goose Green made sense.

Reflecting these pressures, Fieldhouse contacted Woodward and told him to go ashore and shout at Thompson until he moved out of the beachhead. Woodward, while also frustrated at the slow movement, refused, saying that he could not give orders to the land force commander on matters outside his authority. Thompson meanwhile was unaware of the strategic debate underway in Britain. His main explanation at the time was that his senior commanders were essentially ignorant of the nature of amphibious operations and the reality of land warfare. If he had been aware of the strategic debate then he would have had a better appreciation of the political importance now attached to this objective, and also the view among the Chiefs of Staff that a successful operation at this time would have a major psychological impact on Argentine forces. Moore, who was aware of such factors, had still not joined him and was out of touch. The War Cabinet also knew Moore, in whom they had confidence, but they did not know Thompson and were now steadily losing confidence in him.

At a troubled time, the Brigadier was made sharply aware of the Commander-in-Chief's perspective. Late on the morning of 26 May Thompson was called to speak directly to Fieldhouse over the Satellite Communication system, which had been set up at Ajax Bay, some distance from the headquarters. Thompson later described the conversation:

> The radio-telephone was as clear as if the call had been coming from next door. As clear and unequivocal were the orders from Northwood. The Goose Green operation was to be re-mounted and more action was required all round. Plainly the people at the back-end were getting restless.[13]

Just at the time when the loss of helicopter assets had reduced his options Thompson was being told to act as if they were plentiful by people who, on his assessment, could not understand the logistical difficulties he and Clapp faced. Clapp flew ashore to talk with Thompson. They agreed to end the amphibious phase. Operational control of most of the support helicopters was handed over to Thompson. Leaving Dingemanns on *Intrepid* to take control of the remaining offloading while supporting Thompson, Clapp rushed off to *Fearless* to get Moore to sort out the confusion in command and control.

There were ways of moving out. His planners had concluded that a walk to Teal Inlet, and from there to Stanley, was possible. The move would start with 45 Commando, which would aim to get to Douglas Settlement as soon as possible on 28 May. Before first light 45 Commando was ferried in LCUs from Ajax Bay to Port San Carlos and then began the 33 km march to Douglas. Later 3 Para departed for Teal, some 40 km distant. Meanwhile, 2 Para revived their plans for Goose Green and Thompson reported this back to Northwood.

Fieldhouse sent back an encouraging and positive signal, in the process revealing the political aspect to his thinking:

> On the diplomatic front it seems well nigh certain that the UN Sec Gens efforts to obtain a ceasefire will fail and the matter will return to the Security Council in the next very few days. In this case the pressure upon HMG to agree a ceasefire is likely to be very great and, without the let-out of bringing the Sec Gen into play again, this could indeed result in a ceasefire. Consequently it is imperative that we keep going at very best possible speed. With this in mind you should do all you can to bring the Darwin/Goose Green operation to a successful conclusion with Union Jack seen to be flying in Darwin. This will enable us to claim possession of Lafonia. Your liberation of Douglas and Teal, and the reinforcement of the D Sqn SAS base west of the main enemy position will allow us to claim with justification that we now control large areas of East Falklands. To complete the package you will understand how important it is to cover ground as quickly as possible to box him in Stanley.

A short Argentine air raid over San Carlos on 27 May underlined the importance of moving on. The weather over the Islands was overcast. San Carlos was almost empty of transport ships, and they were no longer the prime targets. Realising that they had failed to prevent the beachhead being established, the Argentines now belatedly turned their attention to its disruption. The first raid for some time using Canberras came at 1715Z when two aircraft dropped their bombs without much effect near 2 Para positions on Sussex Mountains. Just after 1930Z four A4Bs came low over Grantham Sound into San Carlos Water in two pairs separated by a few minutes and were able to drop their bombs on 40 Commando positions near San Carlos Settlement and on the BMA at Ajax Bay, killing six men and injuring another 30. The casualties would have been worse if the attacks had come half an hour earlier when the area had been full of men, and if more than a third of the bombs dropped had exploded. Notably, the field hospital was spared when two bombs hit its accommodation but failed to explode. If they had done so, undoubtedly killing the medical team, the casualties they were then treating and many more from the Logistics Regiment, the consequences would have been horrendous. Gun, mortar and other ammunition being loaded into helicopter nets ready to be lifted to 2 Para was also hit, along with anti-tank missiles and launchers. This carried on exploding all night.

The raid provided cover for two Argentine Pucaras to fly into Stanley. An attempt to escort two Hercules to re-supply units in West Falkland by parachute drop failed, but as with previous nights another Hercules did get in and out of Stanley. Two of the Skyhawks were hit by a combination of Rapier, Blowpipe, Sea Cat, 40mm and small arms. One caught fire and the pilot ejected over West Falkland: the other reached base badly damaged. Thompson, angered, signalled:

> Suggest we release above information to media stressing indiscriminate nature of Arg air attacks and total disregard for civilians. Both Argentines and ourselves have military personnel and equipment in settlements however our air and NGS attacks have been carefully targeted away from settlement buildings. This may avoid or reduce further attacks on civilian settlements.

The Argentine garrison

By the end of April Argentina had some 13,000 men in the Malvinas, the infantry component being eight regiments with between 5,000–6,000 men. Although Brigadier General Parada of 3 Commando Brigade was supposed to be in charge of all units west of the Stanley sector, including West Falkland, he did not actually get away from Stanley. The forces on West Falkland, 5 Regiment at Port Howard and 8 Regiment at Fox Bay, were effectively useless as they lacked the size, firepower and mobility to cope with any British operations on West Falkland, and had no means of moving across to East Falkland to help there.

Deployed at Goose Green was one company of the 12 Infantry Regiment, with companies from two other regiments, under Lieutenant Colonel I Piaggi, although the actual garrison commander was the senior officer present, Vicecomodoro (Wing Commander) W Pedrozo, in charge of the air base. The command relationship remained unclear and Pedrozo, to Piaggi's frustration, sought at times to assert his superior position. The command problems were compounded by a direct link to the senior command at Stanley, who interfered despite having no more information than that provided from Goose Green. There were 643 men in the Regiment of all ranks. Many were new conscripts and few had experience of anything approaching the harsh Falklands conditions. Piaggi's task was to hold the settlements and protect the airstrip in conjunction with the Air Force's AA gunners, and also to provide a reserve battle group. He was in no position to take the battle to the enemy, as he lacked vehicles and heavy equipment, and his communications were poor. He had been told to prepare for a seaborne landing, although those on the spot could see why it was both unlikely that the British would attempt such an operation and how difficult it would be for the Argentines to cope if they did manage to negotiate the waters and get ashore. Piaggi decided to put two companies in a position to watch the beaches while blocking the isthmus to any land attack. The more likely approaches from sea or land were mined.

The Goose Green airstrip had become operational for the Argentines on 15 April with the arrival of helicopters. Twelve Pucaras were sent there on 29 April. They had had a difficult time. Attempts to launch a number when fighting began in earnest on 1 May had resulted in a series of mishaps, and had been followed by an effective attack by Sea Harriers which had left the airfield in a mess, with one Pucara destroyed and three others damaged, two of which were never repaired. Five air force personnel had been killed and another 14 wounded, of whom a further two later died. Although the Argentine air defences got some revenge a few days later when Lieutenant Nick Taylor's Sea Harrier was brought down, for the moment the base was out of action. The three Pucaras that had been flying on 1 May were deployed instead to Pebble Island, where the SAS raid on 15 May later caught them. Four more had been sent to Goose Green to make up the losses before the Pebble Island raid but they were removed again after this raid because of Argentine anxiety that they were vulnerable to being caught in a similar fashion. The base was left with six functional aircraft. After two more were lost on 21 May it was decided to evacuate the base of all aircraft and helicopters. There was therefore no local air support available to the Argentines for the battle.

As the British made their way to Goose Green, Piaggi had been unable to strengthen his position. He had lost 60 men by sending them to Fanning Head. This detachment had been sent after *Alacrity* had sailed through Falkland Sound and sunk *Islas de Los Estados* in order to watch over the Sound's northern entrance. Although some escaped after being caught by the British in one of the preparatory operations for the San Carlos landings they were still lost to Piaggi. There was a further company of 12 Regiment just north of Mount Kent, 18 km west of Stanley, acting as a strategic reserve and guarding the helicopters based there, of which there was a limited supply. There were by this time only 19 in the Malvinas (two Chinooks, three Agustas, five Pumas and nine Hueys). In the attack on 21 May, a Chinook and two Pucaras had been lost at Kent, while a further three Pucaras and an Agusta had been lost on 23 May at West Falkland. Piaggi had been sent some artillery, two 105-mm howitzers on the *Rio Iguazu*, which had to be rescued when this ship was caught by Harriers and grounded. Only one of these could be made serviceable, although two more were lifted in by helicopters later, making for three artillery pieces, the same number as available to 2 Para.

Although, as discussed below, it was assumed later that the Argentines had reinforced Darwin because the BBC leaked the British plans this was not the case. Internal Argentine speculation that Darwin was likely to be attacked first began on 24 May. The Argentine debate at this stage was over whether it was best to counter the British on the ground, or go for the aircraft carriers and the logistic chain at sea which the Air Force still deemed to be Britain's main area of vulnerability. At the same time passivity on the ground appeared inappropriate and, on 25 May, Menendez at Stanley was ordered to abandon a static defence and move against the bridgehead before the British were able to land the reinforcements (5 Infantry Brigade) then en route. Menendez's forces, however, lacked the mobility to get to San Carlos and any attempt to try would leave Stanley's defences much depleted in the event of another British amphibious landing close by. As the British resolved to walk across the Island to engage the enemy the Argentine commander concluded that this could not safely be done by his troops in the reverse direction.

Instead it was decided on 26 May, the day Thompson was told to mount the attack on Goose Green, to patrol more actively, move some forces forward while sending airborne troops to reinforce the garrison at Darwin/Goose Green. Even this more modest plan soon appeared too risky because of the vulnerability of any Argentine forces in the open to British air activity. In the event 100 men were taken from Stanley by helicopter. They arrived as the battle was beginning. The other available reinforcements came from Mount Kent: 140 men plus artillery who arrived during the afternoon of 28 May, too late to influence the battle which was then coming to an end, but having vacated a critical position, one the British believed to be of key importance in their move towards Stanley.

Including 150 air force personnel who played no part in the battle, there were altogether 1,007 Argentines in the area on 28 May. At the start of the battle, however, the actual combat strength available to Piaggi was about 550 men, comparable to that of 2 Para.[14] Much was later made of the differences between the Argentine conscripts and the British professionals. This can be overdone. Not only did many of the conscripts fight bravely but also many of the British professionals were as young and inexperienced in warfare.

The British had known from mid-May that there was a garrison of some size at Goose Green, and that it could be in a position to cause difficulties to the landed British forces. Numbers were put at anything between 300 and 500 men. The Pucaras and air defences had already made their presence known. This was one reason for the diversionary raid conducted by the SAS on 21 May. It was also known that there were a number of aircraft based there and there were AA gunners in place, sufficient to have shot down a Harrier on 4 May. There was no decent air imagery available so what was known depended on what had been seen – the famous 'Mark One Eyeball'. The SAS observation post that had been established in early May had a partial view and could only identify about one company. The raid on 21

May confirmed the impression of a rather light defence, likely to crumble if pushed hard. Putting together the intelligence was hampered by a number of factors that generally affected the early stages of the land campaign, including Thompson's intelligence staff being denied information because they lacked the necessary security clearances.

Around 22 May as first plans were being formulated there were grounds for supposing that Goose Green was largely an Air Force garrison, possibly with as many as 300 personnel. The idea that it was defended only by about a company of infantry was starting to be challenged, as a result of the SAS starting to raise their numbers on the basis of their visits and the level of Argentine communications activity. A debriefing of an Argentine NCO captured that day by 3 Para also supported the view that 12 Infantry Regiment was there in force. Some documents showed that this amounted to three rifle companies, plus a reconnaissance platoon and support and logistic elements. This suggested a total strength of about 450, excluding the Air Force personnel. Concern has been expressed that 'an unhealthy competition had developed between the long-term, mundane and steady growth of intelligence by Brigade HQ and the exciting but relatively short-term information gained by the SAS.'[15] Patrols by other units had been discouraged because of the SAS involvement in the area, and there were complaints that the SAS did not provide full enough reports to others. It should be noted, however, that the Commanding Officer 22 SAS recalls telling Jones that he should expect more or less equal Argentine combat forces to his own. According to van der Nijl, by the time that Jones was told that the operation was on again, the assessment was that up to 1,000 Argentines might be available to defend the isthmus.[16]

First plans

On 26 May at 1515Z, HQ 3 Commando Brigade issued a Warning Order to 2 Para:

1. Darwin/Goose Green Ops to start tonight as before.
2. Outline. Night 26/27 move 1 Coy to secure Camilla Creek House on foot. Night 27/28 move 1/2 Bty at last light to Camilla Creek House. Assault Darwin/Goose Green before first light.

Thompson later questioned his own approach to this battle, speaking of himself in the third person:

> There is no doubt that at this stage Thompson should have taken his own tactical headquarters, 2 Para and a commando, probably 40 Commando who were the nearest, and mounted a two battalion attack. He should also have taken at least one of his two troops of

Scorpion and Scimitar light tanks (CVRT). This force, particularly
with light armour, would have taken the position in half the time
and with far lower casualties than was the case. In the event, 2
Para were left to carry out this daunting task virtually on their
own.[17]

Is Thompson being too hard on himself? It is by no means clear that the
problems eventually faced at Goose Green resulted from a deficit of senior
officers, although extra firepower and numbers would have made a significant
difference. One issue, not taking the light tanks, represents a simple
misjudgement. The terrain was erroneously believed to be unsuitable and
there was a general lack of confidence in the ability of the vehicles to cope.
The real problem was the attitude to the battle, whose strategic importance
Thompson had not fully appreciated and which he saw as a diversion from
his main effort. He was aware of his orders and the impatience they
reflected, but not the reasoning behind them. This battle would have been
easier if he had committed his Tactical HQ and another battalion but it
would also have added extra delay to the primary task of 'investing' Stanley.

This strategic tension was aggravated by a further ambiguity in the operational concept. Thompson had thought of the action in terms of a raid,
which in principle might leave the Argentine garrison bloodied but still in
place, but Northwood had discussed the objective in terms of 'eliminating'
the enemy garrison, which had raised the stakes. The uncertainty was
reflected in Thompson's orders to 2 Para. These were to 'carry out a raid on
Goose Green isthmus to capture the settlements before withdrawing in
reserve for the main thrust in the north'. Capturing the settlements meant
more than just a raid, and more than a raid was implied by an attack of the
planned size and logistical complexity. The Commander, 2 Para, Colonel 'H'
Jones, who had been much more enthusiastic about the operation from the
start and then frustrated when it had been called off, was focused more on
the 'capture' aspects of the plan than the raid. Even though Thompson had
not allocated extra resources, Jones' ambition was reflected in his orders to
his company commanders. The objective was now to capture Goose Green.
Once that had been achieved he confessed himself uncertain as to whether 2
Para would stay there or not.

On 26 May C Company, 2 Para, walked to Camilla Creek House, which
they found to be empty, and established a base. By the next day Jones had
information from his own patrols that allowed a reasonable, and by now
much more pessimistic, sense of the enemy positions. The intelligence picture
available was quite good, with some 14 Argentine positions identified. But it
was being put together hastily and, because it was changing, with residual
uncertainty about its reliability. The main conclusion he drew was that before
the objective could be reached a substantial number of Argentine positions
would have to be passed and, given the openness of the terrain, the more of

this journey that could be accomplished at night the better. He had in mind an optimistic 14 km, optimistic largely because there was no obvious way to outmanoeuvre the enemy and so the assault would have to be direct.

An early start was required if there was any hope of taking full advantage of the night. It would need to begin at last light on 27 May and be as complete as possible before first light the next day. Speed being so important, loads had to be light. Other than three 105mm guns brought forward by helicopter, with 200 rounds per gun, everything else had to be carried, and this inevitably limited the amount of firepower, including mortars and machine guns. The force comprised the Battalion's three rifle companies, the patrol company reinforced by the assault pioneer platoon, the support company with the GPMG Sustained Fire (SF) kits, Milan missiles and the two 81mm mortars that had been brought on the operation, plus the reconnaissance troop of 53 Independent Squadron RE. Two companies of 45 Commando were to be on notice to provide extra support if required. Air defence would be provided by two Blowpipe detachments, one of which would stay at Camilla Creek House to protect the guns while the other advanced with the Battalion. In addition to 2 Para's own artillery, *Arrow* would direct gunfire at the Argentine position, until it was obliged to move away from an exposed position before first light. Harrier strikes would be available between dawn and dusk, weather permitting.

The BBC leak

While preparing for the coming night's exertions, at 1400Z (1000 local), the rather astonished Paratroops heard on the BBC World Service that they had just completed the move they were then preparing to make. Their feeling that they had been badly let down by the media was not helped by the sight of Argentine helicopter activity around the garrison they were about to attack.

Few in the Task Force were aware of the full frenzy of media speculation in Britain. Official statements made no mention of Darwin and Goose Green. After reporting on Monday, 24 May that the bridgehead had been firmly established and the surrounding areas were being patrolled, nothing at all had been said on the Tuesday, while on Wednesday, 26 May, presumably reflecting assurances from Northwood, Nott had told the Commons that 'our forces on the ground are now poised to begin their thrust on Port Stanley'. He briefed Conservative Party backbenchers that evening. It also seems that Northwood had got ahead of themselves as well, with relief that there was movement at last leading to an exaggeration of its speed. Evidence that Northwood was very much in the dark about the timing and course of the battle comes in a conversation between Moore, now on board *Antrim* on the last stage of his journey to the Falklands and in touch with events, and Trant on the evening of 27 May at 2045Z. When Trant referred to '2 Para taking Darwin/Goose Green now he hoped (they had heard nothing so assumed all was well!)', Moore warned him that 'they would not wake up tomorrow morning and find these units [including 45 CDO and 3 Para] had secured their objectives'. But the assumption that all was well may already have permeated the inner circle in London. That day the War Cabinet indicated some awareness that the political pressures might be going too far. After observing that it was important to make the earliest possible progress with the operations on land, it was reaffirmed that only the military commanders could take specific operational decisions. The Prime Minister refused to go into details during Parliamentary Questions but said that 'our forces on the ground are now moving from the bridgehead' while all MoD would add was that 'they are not hanging around'.

Robert Fox, the BBC's man on the spot, entirely innocent of any leaks, felt the initial brunt of 2 Para's outrage, with Jones threatening to sue John Nott and the Prime Minister if necessary.[18] Whether or not this 'tirade' was to be taken seriously, Jones was not alone in his instincts. At least one public relations source at MoD was later to tell the BBC that these statements, and perhaps particularly Nott's briefing, were the source of the speculation. On receipt of the news Thompson decided not to abort the operation, but expressed his dismay at the leak. Fieldhouse replied, 'Equal horror expressed here. Have made representations at highest level.' In their conversation at 2045Z, Trant also told Moore of the 'considerable ire' at Northwood. Moore expressed his anger 'at hearing that the Secretary of State had as good as stated publicly the H-hr, axis of advance and objectives of my units'. If this was repeated, warned Moore, 'I would cease reporting our intentions in advance'. Moore made a note to himself to send a formal and recorded signal 'next time it happens'. So strongly was the view held at Northwood that the culprit was the Secretary of State, that Lewin was obliged to write to Fieldhouse exonerating Nott, praising his support for the Task Force, while observing that 'most armchair strategists were openly speculating that Darwin/Goose Green should be taken first and it seems more likely that the Argentinians came to the same conclusion in time to reinforce the garrison'.

It certainly did not take much strategic insight to work out that Darwin and Goose Green represented a tempting target for the Task Force, and speculation that it was about to be taken (or indeed already had been taken) began on Monday, 24 May, took hold by the Tuesday and was rife by the Wednesday. A reported remark from the backbench meeting that there could be successes to report, even within 24 hours, implied very strongly that the speculation was correct as there was nowhere else so obviously in reach of land forces. The potential involvement of 2 Para soon leaked out. At 1300 London time on 27 May the BBC's defence correspondent was quoting sources as saying that 'there is something quite big going on. They're saying for example that the 2nd Parachute Regiment has moved South towards Darwin area.'[19] That is what was reported on the World Service and heard by 2 Para.

The report had been picked up by the Argentine command, but if anything it was dismissed as part of an effort at intimidation.[20] In practice, as already noted, the broadcast had little impact on Argentine plans, but 2 Para could not know that. There was real concern that any element of surprise had been lost. The immediate result was that Jones ordered dispersal from Camilla Creek House, lest the enemy engage in aggressive patrolling and start to direct artillery fire in their direction. This made co-ordination for the later battle even more difficult. Jones was already anxious about the threat posed by the artillery and had sent two patrols to try to find the guns, taking with them a reserve forward air controller (FAC). The designated FAC, an experienced RAF officer aged 50, had been evacuated after collapsing with the effort of carrying his heavy equipment over difficult terrain. The patrols failed to find the guns but were able to observe Argentine positions. When they were spotted and sought to withdraw they asked for artillery support, but that was refused, as it would have revealed the location of the guns. Harrier strikes, which had earlier been delayed by bad weather, were now coming in for support, although their impact was less than it might have been because the reserve FAC had returned to Camilla Creek House and was still on his way back to his patrol having been told that the Harriers were coming. The strikes, at 1440Z, did make it possible for the troops to withdraw safely, but otherwise had little effect. One of the two Harriers was hit, although the pilot, Squadron Leader Iveson, ejected safely and managed to hide until after the battle.

News of this exchange of fire came back to Piaggi just after the BBC broadcast and led him to send off his own patrol, travelling in a Land Rover, to explore possible British activity around Camilla Creek House. Having just left the House to return to join their patrol, the FAC's party came across the Argentines and ambushed and captured them before any communication could be made back to Piaggi. The interrogation of the prisoners confirmed that the Argentine force was ready for an attack.

The battle for Goose Green

It is perhaps important here, in view of subsequent controversies, to consider the dilemma that Colonel Jones faced. He had embarked on his mission expecting to face a smaller enemy force than the one he now believed to be confronting him, and the effective position of 2 Para had just been broadcast, literally, to the whole world. He had brought only two 81mm mortars and a limited amount of ammunition for a quick action. The improving intelligence and the World Service report led 2 Para to signal back that: 'the task is a lot harder and amount of goods given are not sufficient, could 8 Bty bring some more.' As the three guns of 8 Battery were brought in, the number of rounds per gun was increased from 200 to 320.

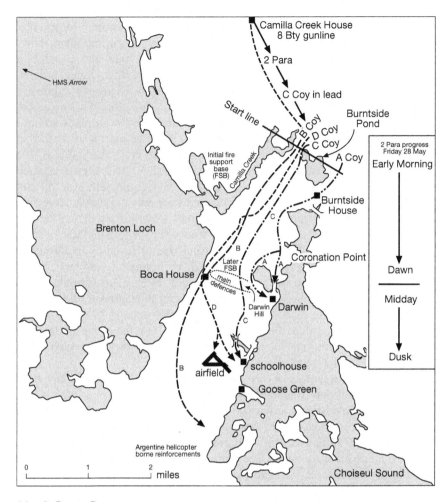

Map 9 Goose Green

The terrain was unfamiliar, it would have to be covered at night, so co-ordination was bound to be difficult, and at speed, to take advantage of the darkness while it lasted. The detail of the Argentine deployments was sketchy yet this could make an enormous difference in terms of the fate of the men of 2 Para as they pressed forward. Whatever the SAS might have thought about the quality of the Argentine defenders there was no track record to study. This was to be the first major land engagement of the war. In such unfavourable conditions, few would have quibbled if he had decided that common prudence argued for the attack to be delayed, while reinforcements were brought forward from the bridgehead, or even cancelled altogether. Jones, fully imbued with his regiment's spirit, but conscious of the consequences of failure, hesitated. He then took the decision, steeled himself and his men to go forward, and issued orders.

The 'O' Group meeting, delayed because of the BBC leak and with little time before the end of daylight and the preferred start of battle, was rushed. Jones was in a hurry, anxious to move even while his company commanders were still digesting the information they had received. Essentially they had to move down a corridor – five miles long and one mile wide. There were three ridge lines approaching the isthmus and the Argentines controlled each one of them. There has been some dispute about whether it was known that the Argentines had taken a position atop Darwin Hill, the most significant high ground and, along with Coronation Point (incorrectly supposed, on the basis of the Sea Harrier's observation, to be a strong Argentine position), the most critical of the early objectives. The answer is that the Darwin Hill position was known, but that the planning, which had largely been completed the previous day, had not fully taken it into account. The intelligence briefing was hurried along by an impatient Jones and so the full significance of this deployment was not fully appreciated or discussed.

2 Para at this point involved some 620 men. Of this less than half were assigned to the cutting edge of the three rifles companies (A, B and D), making for about 300 in total, with C Company, in charge of reconnaissance, a support company with the artillery providing fire support, and the HQ Company responsible for logistics. The night attack would be silent to start with until Argentine positions were reached, and then as noisy as possible to disorient the defenders. The plan, which was complex, envisaged a move down the isthmus in six stages. It would begin with C Company clearing the route forward, protecting the start-line and also taking out a suspected gun position at the north-east tip of Camilla Creek, then A and B Companies would clear the first Argentine positions, respectively at Burntside House and overlooking Camilla Creek. A and D Companies would move on to the next positions, respectively at Coronation Point and down the west coast of the Creek, so that B Company could then pass through D Company to take Boca House, with D Company providing backup if necessary to ensure that this position was taken. The penultimate stage would be for A, B and D Companies to make their way up to Darwin and Goose Green while C Company cleared the airfield, with the final stage seeing Darwin and Goose Green taken with C Company moving well to the south to Bodie Creek. Jones concluded his orders, on what basis it is unclear, by saying that: 'All previous evidence suggests that if the enemy is hit hard, he will crumble.'

As planned the attack began at 0200Z 28 May. *Arrow* moved to the southern end of Grantham Sound to provide NGS if required. Between 0200Z and 0500Z she fired 120 rounds controlled by a Naval Gunfire Forward Officer (NGFO) well forward with the battalion. Fire was at extreme range, accurate, and reported as having seriously weakened the enemy's initial resistance.

The ship was prevented from firing between 0600Z and 0800Z by a gun defect, but then fired more high explosives and some starshell at Goose Green airfield. At 0920Z the bombardment ceased and the ship had to leave for San Carlos for its own safety.

At 0230Z A Company moved against the enemy position at Burntside House, but the Argentine platoon withdrew without resistance, although the Paras did face some accurate artillery fire. Four civilians were relieved to be safe after a harrowing experience of bullets passing through their house as they lay on the floor. On the right flank B Company, led by Major John Crosland, advanced at 0311Z against two Argentine positions. Resistance again was weak, apparently because of the naval gunfire, and the positions were overwhelmed with up to eight Argentines killed. Progress had been slower than hoped. D Company had missed its position, but was ordered by Jones to move forward against Argentine positions bypassed by B Company. There they faced more substantial resistance, with only the battalion's two 81mm mortars and three light guns available now to provide supporting fire. Nonetheless, D Company, commanded by Major Phil Neame, managed to clear these, though losing three dead, with B Company pushing on to take their original objective. At 0827Z the battle was described in a signal back to Brigade headquarters as 'a bit chaotic but going well. Almost on Green'. The reference here, however, was to a colour coded report line down the isthmus – not Goose Green itself.

A Company had managed to get past Coronation Point, surprisingly unopposed, and a platoon was sent to establish a fire base at the tip of a point overlooking Darwin Settlement from the north. The remaining two platoons circled west around the bay. Although the original plan had been for A Company to wait when it reached Coronation Point, the advance had been delayed. Major Dair Farrar-Hockley, Officer Commanding, wished to press on while it was still dark to take what was now recognised to be a significant Argentine position ahead of him, but was told to hold until Jones and his Tactical HQ could join him to assess the position.[21] The Main HQ, regimental aid post (RAP) and defence platoon now moved up to some 1500 metres north of Darwin from where they could co-ordinate the evacuation of casualties and prisoners and organise the re-supply of ammunition. Initially there had been delays in evacuating and treating the wounded, although the success rate in keeping them alive once they had been evacuated was remarkable.

While good progress had been made only now were the main Argentine defences being approached. Piaggi was intending to hold the British back until reinforcements, which he had been promised, could be flown in. Despite urgings from Stanley, he was reluctant to risk a counter-attack with inadequately trained troops. Instead his men occupied all available trenches and bunkers. They would be difficult to dislodge. Firepower might facilitate this process, but this was proving difficult to bring to bear: *Arrow* was leaving, the weather would not allow Harrier strikes, so that the only support came from the three guns of 8 Battery. Their operations were hampered by the close proximity of British and Argentine forces. The enemy's artillery was also causing problems with general movement and re-supply of ammunition.

The momentum was being lost. When Jones eventually joined A Company he realised that it needed to press forward and now urged Farrar-Hockley to do so. By this time the hours of darkness were coming to an end, and the advantage was bound to switch to the defenders.[22] Soon two of the Company's platoons were struggling to gain a foothold on Darwin Hill. B Company was unable to assist as they had now come across strong opposition from the ridge north-east of Boca House, and had taken casualties including one killed.

The battle had reached a critical stage. Piaggi felt able to report back to Stanley that the British attack had been halted. When reports emanated from London to the effect that Darwin/Goose Green had already fallen, Buenos Aires denied them, claiming that the battle was going very well for Argentina. If they had been able to move fresh units into the battle at this point, particularly in support of the hard pressed troops defending Darwin Hill, then the outcome might have been different. As it was the British were being held up rather than forced back. Jones was nonetheless frustrated, aware that time was working against him. His men had been pressing forward, but even after successful engagements with the enemy, the platoons had taken time to sort themselves out, do what they could for the dead and wounded, regroup and work out what to do next. The attack had long since lost its rhythm and synchronisation. Argentine artillery was being directed effectively; it was proving impossible to direct the British artillery towards suitable targets.

Jones was not short of advice on alternative options: D Company proposed a flanking movement into the western beach; B Company also saw the Argentine vulnerability on the right if the position at Boca House could be taken; C Company might be able to direct some fire against the Argentine defenders on Darwin Hill. Support Company with Milans and GPMGs were ready to bring them forward to blast away through enemy defences. All suggestions were dismissed. Jones was unable to reappraise the overall situation and so, concerned about any further delays, he concentrated on what he could control and focused on the obstacle ahead of him, the enemy position on Darwin Ridge leading towards the Hill. He did not want the other Companies to move forward until A Company was able to do so. He had told A Company to remove the obstacle but this had yet to happen and so he decided to join them to see what could be done. By now, at 0930Z, the fight for Darwin Hill had been going on for about two hours.

Farrar-Hockley's inclination was to win this engagement through putting superior fire onto the enemy positions. He felt that this approach was starting to work. Jones wanted quicker results, both to make up for past delays and to reduce the risk of A Company being caught in an Argentine counter-attack. He proposed various forms of direct attacks, few of which seemed feasible because of the weight of enemy fire. Eventually, it was agreed that a small group of about 15 men led by the A Company Commander should make an assault. The Battalion Adjutant (Captain Wood), who had been following Jones, decided to participate. They were repulsed by intense enemy machine gun fire, killing three, including Captain Wood. At this point Jones decided to lead from the front. With some members of his Tactical HQ he moved into a small gully, from where he could see an enemy position close by. Armed with a sub-machine gun, he charged off towards the nearest enemy trench but was exposed to enemy fire from other trenches. Having been shot once he picked himself up and carried on firing but close to his target, he was hit again. At 1030Z his loss was immediately transmitted back – 'Sunray's down!' He died before he could be evacuated.

This moment became the stuff of legend. None of those who had served with Colonel 'H' Jones were surprised by the action that he took. While other commanders might have felt that their place was further back, better placed to gain an overall view of the course of the battle and the options available, he was always going to lead from the front and, where necessary, by personal example. He almost reached the enemy position without being noticed and if he had put it out single-handedly and survived then the story now being told would be different but still the stuff of legend. There was undoubtedly an inspirational quality to his heroism. Where caution is due is in regard to the claim made for this action, notably in the citation for his posthumous Victoria Cross, that this 'devastating display of courage ... completely undermined' the Argentine 'will to resist,' allowing for the 'momentum of the attack' to be regained rapidly. The immediate impact on the battle was modest, and probably affected the Paras more than their opponents. There were many more hours of fighting to come. The Argentines had, after all, just cut down three other men who had also been trying to take the ridge. As David Benest, who wrote 2 Para's first in-house history, later commented, the real contribution of 'H' Jones lay not so much in his act of great personal bravery but in the decision, just hours before battle was due to commence and with every reason to believe that the odds were stacked against his battalion, to press ahead in the conviction that his men 'could, would and indeed had to deliver a positive outcome – even without him, a possibility he had always acknowledged.'[23]

In the end what made the real difference to A Company's attack was fire-power, in the form of 66mm anti-tank rockets, one of which scored a direct hit on the Argentine trench from where Jones had been killed. Soon white flags began to appear and a cease-fire was ordered. The battle for Darwin Ridge had cost 2 Para six dead, including three officers (Jones, Wood and Farrar-Hockley's second-in-command, Captain Dent) and eleven wounded. The Argentines had lost 18 dead and 39 wounded, more than half of the 92 men present. Two Scout helicopters bringing in extra ammunition and intending to return with casualties, including Jones, were caught at around

1100Z by two Pucaras, who had been trying unsuccessfully to attack the gun line. One of the Scouts was shot down, killing the pilot and severely wounding the observer, while one of the Pucaras crashed returning to Stanley.

When the Battalion Second-in-Command, Major C Keeble, at Main HQ heard that Colonel Jones had been killed he took over command. Thompson accepted assurances from Keeble that 2 Para would win. He had to let the officers on the spot get on with the battle. Nonetheless, back at San Carlos, 42 Commando, no longer expecting to get to Mount Kent, was readied to move forward carrying as much ammunition as they could manage. Meanwhile Keeble quickly received assessments of the position from the Battery Commander at Tactical HQ, and A and B Company Commanders. He decided to look hard at the right flank. Crosland, commanding B Company, was now told to assume command until Keeble reached him. The fire base was set up to the rear of A and B Companies. Support Company with its extra firepower was taken towards B Company to overlook the confusingly named Boca House (there was no house). D Company, now recovered from their night attack, came to support B Company as envisaged in the original plan, crawling along the shelving to the beach on the extreme right and then, using GPMG and artillery fire, they began to take substantial numbers of prisoners. With substantial firepower, including Milans, now directed towards Boca House the position fell at 1110Z. Twelve Argentines had been killed in the bombardment. The emerging lesson of the battle was that intensive and accurate firepower was the key to breaking enemy resistance at key positions.

More progress had been made, and the point at which the British operation could have been damaged by a serious counter-attack had passed, but it was still not possible to get the Harriers in or to bring in more supplies via helicopter. The enemy was still occupying vital ground. With access to the settlements now possible, A Company was ordered to consolidate on Darwin Hill, while on its east shoulder, overlooking Goose Green, a new fire base could be established. One of A Company's platoons was detached to C Company who were to pass through to seize the bridge north of Goose Green. Meanwhile, Major Neame, who had been told to wait by Jones, now persuaded Keeble (on the spurious grounds that they might be caught on the beach by an incoming tide) that his D Company should swing east and, using cover, close in on Goose Green.

By 1600Z, midday local time, the battle had been going far longer than initially planned. The Argentine defences had proved to be tougher, and their artillery fire more discouraging, than anticipated. Instead of cutting through Argentine lines it had been a hard slog, using up ammunition and causing casualties. The connection with the rear had become increasingly important, both for purposes of re-supply and casualty evacuation, but resources were limited, resulting in painful and demoralising waits for many of the injured. Were it not for the captured Argentine land rover, which had been ferrying mortar shells to the support company, there would have been no motorised transportation at all. Helicopters were scarce and one of the Scouts that had been assigned to the battalion had been shot down, as related earlier. Later more were assigned, but 2 Para's own medical team initially had to cope under enormous pressure, which they did impressively.

Largely based on the original plan, Keeble now wanted A Company to hold Darwin Hill, having released one of its platoons to C Company, which was to move to the airfield, while D Company would get closer to the settlement. B Company had been intended to stay back but instead, after reorganising itself at Boca House, was now to swing around the airfield to seize the high ground to the south of the settlement. The aim was to press forward the advantage recently gained. But this had to be achieved without substantial fire power: indeed the mortar line (of only two 81mm mortars of the eight available) were now at the edge of their effective range, coordination between the different companies and the tactical HQ was poor, with inevitable confusions resulting, including the eventual intermingling of C and D companies. At one point D Company had to ask B Company to stop firing on Argentine positions that were already showing white flags. Argentine artillery was still firing, and, placed close to the settlement's buildings, could not safely be taken out. New defensive positions had been set on what still could pass for the higher ground, ever closer to the Goose Green settlement, but with a clear view of any troops coming in their direction. The defence still had some coherence and capability.

So as 2 Para moved forward intense fire of all types came in on them, including from the anti-aircraft guns. Progress was still slow. C Company, without covering fire and in open ground, took heavy casualties moving down the forward slope to the bridge, with one killed and eleven wounded, including Company Commander, Major R Jenner. It was now about 1830Z. B Company, fortunately, found its move to the airfield more straightforward. D Company came upon a minefield. They were diverted away from the airfield and the settlement, and then came under fire from the school and the area around the airport flagpole. 12 platoon from the Company, led by Lieutenant J Barry, was sent to deal with this position. He apparently saw white flags near the flagpole, and informed HQ that he was intending to investigate. A message that he should wait failed to get back to him. When he approached the Argentines he found they did not wish to surrender. According to Aldea, an Argentine platoon commander answered in English: 'Son of a bitch! You've got two minutes to return to your lines and then I give the order to open fire.'[24] When a British machine gun opened up from Darwin Hill, the Argentines opened fire, killing Barry and two others and leaving another wounded. The rest of his platoon immediately overran the position. This news reached London later and CINCFLEET reported: 'Long fire fight some 10 hours. Initially firm resistance then enemy started playing dirty. White flags were put up and when troops moved forward they were fired upon!' This incident, a product of the fog of war, and some disregard of normal procedures, undoubtedly sharpened the determination of

the British troops, in this and subsequent actions. At the same time a ferocious and confused battle for the school area developed, involving a
combination of C and D Company platoons. The Argentines eventually
abandoned the burning building under intensive fire.

Argentine efforts were focused on reinforcements. Menendez in Stanley
decided to throw in the only reserve available into the battle, which was at
Mount Kent. Using all available helicopters, 140 men were taken from
Mount Kent to Goose Green. A correct realisation that this might be too
late led to second thoughts and the order being rescinded, but by this time
the men had left. Their arrival was spotted by B Company, which quickly
engaged the new arrivals with artillery. Then, tired and concerned about low
ammunition, the Company moved back from the settlement and onto the
high ground into a blocking position.

The other card that the Argentines could play was to employ their light
aircraft. They had turned around two of three extra Pucaras that had flown
into Stanley from Argentina, and joined them with two Navy Aermacchis.[25]
At 1900Z (1500 local) they attacked. One Aermacchi was shot down by
Marine Strange of 3 Commando Brigade's Air Defence Troop serving with
D Company. The Pucaras dropped napalm, which missed. One was caught
by ground fire and crashed. The pilot was captured. The ineffectual Argentine
air attack was soon followed, at last, by a more effectual Harrier strike, taking
advantage of improved weather, directed against the Argentine artillery and
the AA gunners. Demoralised by the violent blasts of the cluster bombs, the
Argentine forces abandoned their guns, leaving the garrison not only without
air defences but also any effective form of artillery. Soon B Company arrived
from the south. The airfield was now outflanked, the anti-aircraft guns were
neutralised and Goose Green was surrounded. Milan was being used against
enemy bunkers, machine guns and snipers were harassing any attempts to
move in the settlement, while the artillery was shelling the enemy's
remaining artillery. At 1919Z it had proved possible to move the company
from 42 Commando by helicopter to Camilla Creek House carrying two
mortar bombs per man. By that time 100 or so enemy prisoners had been
brought there and the Marines were initially tasked to guard them. The
balance of advantage had now turned in favour of 2 Para, although it is not
clear that this was appreciated by the forward companies, who were tired,
depleted, short of ammunition and unsure of the overall position.

Piaggi had a fresh reserve, but the chances for further relief were now
slim. His air defences were down and he was hemmed in. The Argentines
were not sure of the strength of the force facing them, but some suspected
that it could be as many as 800. Keeble's assessment began with the fact
that Goose Green had not yet been captured. Both sides had taken heavy
casualties. When he spoke to Thompson, he not only got a promise of reinforcements, but also an understanding that 'Goose Green could be
destroyed, if necessary, should the Argentines not surrender in the morning'.

Whether Keeble could have proceeded on this basis without making some effort to ascertain the circumstances of the inhabitants must be doubted. At any rate directing fire onto the settlement ceased to be an option when the inhabitants of Darwin, who had been liberated, told the paratroopers that 112 civilians were locked up in the Community Centre in Goose Green, where they had been since 1 May. Although he was prepared to go forward the next morning to take personal control of the battle, for the moment all Thompson could do was brief Northwood on its progress and ask that the hospital ship, *Uganda*, be moved closer to take the casualties.[26] A number were collected during the night by a skilfully flown Scout helicopter.

The presence of the civilians argued in favour of a direct approach to the Argentines to encourage them to release the civilians before the start of any siege. Overnight Keeble drafted an ultimatum to the enemy commander:

To: The Commander Argentinian Armed Forces
Darwin/Goose Green Area

From: The Commander British Armed Forces
Darwin/Goose Green Area

Military Options:
We have sent a POW under a white flag of truce to convey the following Military Options:
    That you surrender your force to us by leaving the township forming up in a military manner, removing your helmets and laying down your weapons. You will give prior notice of this intention by returning the POW under the white flag with him briefed as to formalities no later than 0830 hrs local time.
    You refuse in the first case to surrender and take the inevitable consequence. You will give prior notice of this intention by returning the POW without his flag (although his neutrality will be respected) no later than 0830 hrs local.
    In any event and in accordance with the terms of the Geneva Conventions and Laws of War you shall be held responsible for the fate of any civilians in Darwin or Goose Green and we in accordance with those laws do give you prior notice of our intention to bombard Darwin/Goose Green.

Signed: C KEEBLE
COMD BRITISH FORCES
DARWIN/GOOSE GREEN AREA

In case a negative response was received more ammunition and weapons could be brought forward, with the fresh troops of 42 Commando. Air support would be available from first light. A 'firepower demonstration' was planned in the event of the ultimatum being rejected. Four GR3s were tasked to attack an area visible to the Argentines to bring home what to expect if real targets had to be attacked.

These preparations turned out to be unnecessary. The Argentine commanders had come to the conclusion that they could not hold out indefinitely. They initiated contact through the civilian managers at Goose Green and Port San Carlos on the Island civil radio net.[27] At first they raised the possibility of a cease-fire to facilitate the evacuation of civilians. Replying by the same means, the enemy was informed of the imminent arrival of an ultimatum being carried by two captured Argentine Warrant Officers. When these men returned soon after dawn Keeble, joined by the Brigade Liaison Officer, the Battery Commander, the RM interpreter, and two reporters, walked to the airfield to meet the three Argentine commanders. After 'fruitful' discussions with 2 Para and having consulted their superiors in Stanley, they agreed to a dignified surrender at 1450Z. At 1642Z, HQ 3 Commando Brigade signal log recorded: 'The Union Jack has just been raised over Goose Green Settlement'. The 112 civilians were released unharmed. 2 Para had achieved its mission at a cost of 16 killed and 36 wounded, with around another 30 having minor injuries. A Scout pilot and a Royal Engineer Commando sapper had also been killed. If the Argentine commander, whose forces had been pushed back, but were not yet defeated, had decided not to surrender the casualty list would have been much higher, and could well have included many civilians.

The BBC journalist Robert Fox, who had followed the battle closely, and had been present at the surrender, sent back a report which described how 250 Air Force personnel had come out, and stood to attention before being harangued by an officer and then singing the national anthem. He reported that then came some 800 army personnel. British troops found the settlement in an absolute mess, with some evidence of looting and hoarding of food by officers. There were other reports, widely quoted and certainly believed in London, that some 250 Argentines had been killed, with some dark hints that little mercy had been shown because of the death of Jones. This was also conveyed by the use of the term 'mass grave', which was used in a BBC television report concerning the burial of personnel from 2 Para. These perceptions, not surprising after a long, ferocious and often confused battle, were wrong. A total of 961 prisoners were accounted for including 81 held at Camilla Creek House, although the counting process was possibly less precise than the number suggests, with reports of some 50 Argentine bodies found and buried. Aldea gives figures of 45 Argentine dead and 90 wounded.[28]

A Company occupied a defensive position above Darwin Settlement and the Officer Commanding, Support Company, assumed responsibility for managing the civilian population. D Company elements and the machine gun platoon provided the guards and prisoner escorts for the work parties and were fortunate in having covered accommodation. That night helicopters started ferrying in Bergens and rations as snow started to fall.

In congratulating the acting Commanding Officer of 2 Para on their success Fieldhouse made clear the relief felt at Northwood (and in the MoD) that positive action by the land forces was at last apparent: 'you have kindled a flame in land operations which will lead to the raising of the Union Jack in Port Stanley'. This spirit of optimism was reflected within the brigade; their Sitrep stated 'spirits high from 2 Para success and splendid example of offensive action'. From conception to completion the battle had an improvised quality and was not a model to follow for the future. A less resilient battalion could well have been defeated, especially if it had been fighting a bolder enemy. Indeed, the lessons learned about the importance of night fighting and the role of firepower were reasons why Thompson developed a more positive sense of the battle's value. It signalled determination and opened up the southern route to Stanley. Hew Pike, Commanding Officer of the sister battalion, 3 Para, later described Goose Green as 'the moral turning point', in that before 'we understood that we had to win, whilst after it, we knew that we would.'[29] This was the battle's objective envisaged by those who had been pressing from London for action.

The time for a quick push to Stanley based solely on 3 Commando Brigade had passed, although the movement of the Argentine heliborne reserve away from Mount Kent did reduce the risks to 42 Cdo and the SAS Squadron on Mount Kent. Matters had not progressed to the point where Thompson had committed Moore to any particular course, and the move into Goose Green had not been his choice. Northwood had urged it on him more for short-term than long-term reasons. Nonetheless, the re-capture of the settlement set up the southern strategy and, in doing so, reinforced the preference Moore had already developed.

38

3 COMMANDO BRIGADE

For the Government the victory at Goose Green came as a major relief. It confirmed that the initiative and momentum was still with British forces. It had also, however, demonstrated that the enemy was no pushover. The thought of the political consequences of bloodied paratroopers being obliged to withdraw after robust Argentine resistance, especially after the settlement's liberation had been advertised in advance, indicated just how much depended on every battle, well beyond the immediate military value. The growing drama of the story added to the political stake. Fox's report, the first account of what had actually happened, was widely circulated around official London as it was transmitted back from the South Atlantic. It conveyed a sense of just how tough the battle had been. It established 'H' Jones as the first authentic hero of the campaign, but also raised some disturbing thoughts about its ferocity, with the suggestions of 250 Argentine dead. The reports of napalm being discovered indicated just how nasty the battle might become in the future.

The complex interaction between the military and political aspects of the campaign was bound to affect the presentational aspects of the war, as consideration had to be given not only to the quantity and quality of the information disclosed but also the interpretations put on it. If the Chiefs wanted their interpretations to prevail they had to reveal far more information to back them up than their instincts and sense of prudence would allow. The Chiefs of Staff meeting on 30 May on the one hand noted the 'extreme dissatisfaction' coming from the Task Group on the press leaks over Goose Green, and on the other the need to counter Argentine claims, apparently preparing their people for losses, which suggested that it was the backing of the US that was giving Britain the advantage. The Chiefs decided that special briefs should be prepared to show that 'direct US help was small and that it was our forces who were at a disadvantage, forced to conduct operations 8,000 miles from the UK and opposed by a shore-based air force superior in numbers to our embarked aircraft.' Yet at the same time, the Chiefs and also the War Cabinet picked up on the propaganda advantages of the capture of napalm at Goose Green. The Prime Minister took the view that:

Accurate press reports of bad behaviour by the Argentines on the Falklands could have a useful impact on British and world opinion; e.g. their possession of napalm, their abuse of the flag of surrender and the mass incarceration of civilians at Darwin and Goose Green.

In general from this point on, the media were going to have modest pickings. After the dramas of bomb alley and Goose Green, the next task was to get troops in place for the assault on Stanley and the commanders were clear that there must be no further revelations about the position of individual units or the general progress of the advance.

The next step

With Goose Green taken, British intelligence estimated overall Argentine strength in the two West Falkland garrisons of Port Howard and Fox Bay at 1,000 each, and between 6,500 and 8,000 at Stanley. There was uncertainty over Argentine forces in the Stanley area because the strengths of individual Argentine infantry regiments were unknown. They had been assumed to be between 840 and 1,000 but, given 'recent intelligence and experience,' it was suggested on 4 June that they could be as low as 600. By 7 June, Moore's HQ judged that the best estimate was of an overall strength of 8,000 with a bayonet strength of 5,000. In fact by the end of April Argentina had some 13,000 men in the Islands, the infantry component being eight regiments with between 5,000–6,000 men. The elite Marines and experienced officers and NCOs had the burden of holding together the mainly conscript force. They were equipped with 150mm and 155mm artillery, air defence weapons, APCs and perhaps some self-propelled anti-tank guns and so, in principle, should be able to inflict heavy casualties in any direct British assault against the capital.

By and large they were deployed for a positional defence, with some forward observation posts and patrols. Stanley was viewed 'as the prize' and had, from the Argentine perspective, the advantage of being protected by defensive positions in the surrounding mountains. The British assessment had suggested that most of the possible positions were occupied but it was already clear that this was not actually the case. This was not surprising to the British commanders who understood that their opposite numbers would want to defend both the high ground perimeter of the Stanley area as well as retain a firm grip on the town and airstrip. Faced with the choice they would rather not spread their forces too thinly but would instead occupy key features in strength, accepting the risk that these positions would not be mutually supporting. This was the case: the Argentines only had enough troops for just over a third of the 48 kilometres of their defence perimeter along the high ground surrounding Stanley.

The British were less inclined now to deride the fighting qualities of their opponents. Goose Green was said to have 'served to dispel certain misconceptions about enemy'. Being a largely conscript force they were not considered to be as well trained or effective as British troops, but 'they believe in their cause and they can fight hard'. Some trenches had been poorly constructed but their machine guns had been well sited and their mortar and artillery fire was accurate. Nor was there much support for earlier reports that the Argentines were inadequately clothed for the conditions and had insufficient rations. Nevertheless, re-supply from the mainland was becoming steadily more difficult, as was that from Stanley to the distant garrisons, so 'their logistic problems are likely to increase'. Shortages of fuel and ammunition were starting to develop. As stated in the conclusion of the estimate of 31 May, the Argentines were 'likely to defend Stanley area with determination – they should not be underestimated'. A supplement to this intelligence summary reported that the whole coast north of the Murrell River was largely clear, which meant that 'the most likely line of defence against an approach to Stanley from north is now high ground to the south of Murrell River. This would reduce the overall area which the enemy has to defend but renders him more vulnerable to an approach from north.' The Argentine command assumed that the British would want to get the whole affair over as soon as possible, as the stresses and strains of the operation had already exacted a considerable cost. They even thought that this might lead to a seaborne assault against Stanley co-ordinated with an overland attack with marines and paratroopers already ashore.

The period leading up to the final battles for Stanley had certainly been governed by a determination, for practical and political reasons, to get the whole affair over as soon as possible. At the same time quite different practical and political factors imposed constraints on what could be done and the speed with which it could be achieved. In some cases they were the same: wear and tear on the ships, some of which had been at sea for two months, and fatigue amongst many members of the Task Force, and in particular air crew. The loss of a major warship was still seen as one of those events that might give Argentina heart and unnerve British opinion. For this reason consideration had to be given at all times to their safety from either air attack or land-based Exocet. Politically ministers wanted to bring the war to closure but only when Argentine forces had been defeated and not as a result of international pressure in favour of a cease-fire. All this had led to the land forces being urged to press ahead with an attack, even though the resources that would enable them to do so were limited. The problems did not revolve around the capabilities of the fighting forces but their ability to move forward safely, and to co-ordinate their efforts as they did so. The weather was appalling and those troops in the open faced conditions that were apt to cause as many casualties as the enemy. Problems with command and communication were at times chronic. There was therefore something of a race between what was believed to be the progressive demoralisation of Argentine forces and the strains on the Task Force.

The next steps were the responsibility of Moore. He had transferred to *Antrim* from the *QEII* on 27 May, when good communications had been restored, and to *Fearless* on 29 May, where he could establish his headquarters in the facilities recently vacated by HQ 3 Commando Brigade (who had found it too cramped and noisy) and stay in close touch with Clapp, who became his naval adviser and was to coordinate support of land operations with Woodward. Clapp found this new position challenging: on the one hand he did not feel well informed about the land force's plans, while his staff was less suited to questions of tasking Harriers and naval gunfire than logistic support and air defence. The next day Moore took over full control of the land battle. During the final stages of his journey he had at last communication with the key players and was starting to assert his authority. The most perplexing issue, for which there was no simple remedy, was the fact that neither of the two brigadiers chosen for him appeared to enjoy Northwood's confidence. He had only learnt while on *QEII* that the 5 Brigade's pre-embarkation exercises in Wales had gone badly and that there were questions about Brigadier Tony Wilson's competence; then he got strong hints from London that the civilian and military leadership were despairing of his other brigadier, and might even consider him a touch 'yellow'. He had a mandate to sack Thompson if on arrival he concluded that the commander of 3 Commando Brigade was not up to the job. He had become aware of Wilson's sense of insecurity, especially about his Brigade's role, but he understood enough about Thompson and his predicament not to suspect that his previous confidence would turn out to be unfounded.

Northwood was certainly relieved that it had someone in place who understood the constraints under which they were operating and also how to communicate back to them, in terms that politicians would understand, the situation on the ground. His first full telephone conversation with Trant late on 27 May concluded with a suggestion that this be a daily occurrence. Moore made clear that he thought this a bad idea, because of the time it would take up, but prepared his subsequent signals back with a wider audience in mind than just Fieldhouse and his staff. His first requirement was to make his own assessments of what was going on and to remind those who had not been accustomed to including him in their signals that it was now time to start doing so – one of his first signals to Thompson was a rocket. 'I have for the first time today received a reasonable picture of your position,' he noted, 'but this has only been because my sig staff have intercepted a message not addressed to me.' Before telling Thompson to ensure that all future SITREPS were sent to him, and contained 'a full picture rather than short bald statements', he had reminded him that: 'It has been increasingly difficult to protect you from ill-informed criticism while I have been totally devoid of real information.'

He was also trying to get more realism into all planning. He was aware, for example, that some in the Task Force assumed that Stanley could be captured by 7 June. His observation to Trant was that he hoped nobody in Northwood thought that there was a 'snowball's chance in hell' of that occurring. As he prepared to meet directly with 3 Commando Brigade for the first time he asked for time to see the Falklands 'before I start pontificating' and urged that Trant keep 'interfering busybodies off my back!' He wondered whether 'instant strategists' might be a more polite phrase. Soon he had concluded from the evidence of Mount Kent that Argentine forces lacked the 'stomach' to fight in the 'high, arid, bitterly cold area' beyond their outer defensive perimeter around Stanley.

At 0415Z on 1 June, Moore issued his first Operation Order, LFFI OpO 1/82, with the mission: 'To secure Port Stanley'. This confirmed the southern strategy. While 3 Commando Brigade advanced on the Teal Inlet – Malo Bridge – Mount Kent axis, 5 Infantry Brigade would move along the southern axis starting at Camilla Creek House and then going to March Ridge, Fitzroy, Bluff Cove and Mount Challenger where they would link up with 3 Commando Brigade. In the next phase they would consolidate against enemy defensive positions before beginning a final phase of the attrition of the enemy main force leading to the capture of Stanley. The southern route was important because that was the line most anticipated by Argentina. From this line the most direct approach could be made either from the beach or over the rudimentary road, and so that is where the Argentines had concentrated their defensive efforts. The more they were kept looking in this direction, the less they might appreciate the developing 3 Commando Brigade attack along the northern route. If nothing was happening to the south General Menendez was bound to look in 3 Commando Brigade's direction. Prior to Moore's arrival this brigade had already begun the move north. Whatever the varied motives behind the operation, by re-taking Goose Greeen, they had set up the southern route.

The one unit that was not to move north was 40 Commando. They were taking responsibility for the bridgehead area, when the first Argentine air attack on the beachhead itself came on 27 May. The next day had been spent cleaning up after the air raids, and searching for a small enemy group who had clashed with A Company the previous night. On 29 May A Company were preoccupied coping with Argentine prisoners taken at Goose Green. Thompson's intention had been to move the battalion to Douglas or Teal Inlet, and he sent orders to this effect on 30 May. It was expected that units from 5 Infantry Brigade would relieve them. However, on 31 May, this move was cancelled and late on 1 June 40 Commando received an order from Moore's HQ to stay back to defend the bridgehead. This infuriated the Commanding Officer, Lieutenant Colonel M Hunt, who went to see Moore to try and get him to reconsider his decision. Later he wrote:

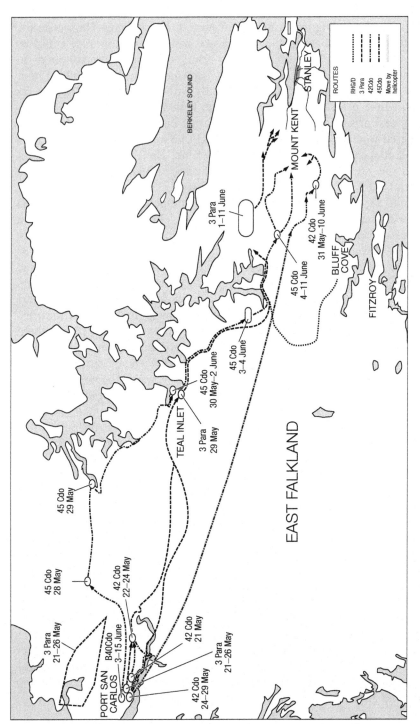

Map 10 Movement of 3 Commando Brigade

[I]t was not my opinion that the units of 5 Inf Bde would be so well prepared for the task (later proved to be so in my view) and anyway I did not consider that this comparatively static task was making the best use of Commando troops. Having listened patiently to me, not surprisingly, General Moore did not change his plans. There was considerable resentment in the Commando at this decision and it was to be reinforced later after 1 WG suffered appalling and sad casualties at Bluff Cove when rather than being relieved by 40 Cdo the unit, in fact, reinforced the battalion with two rifle companies.[1]

There were two reasons for the decision. The first was that the task was considered by all the senior commanders to be an important one, reflecting their continuing concern that the Argentines might attempt something bold from West Falkland, and that in any contingencies the greater experience of the marines to the army in the use of helicopters and landing craft would be essential. The second was that the relative positions of 40 Commando and the Welsh Guards meant that to move all the Marines (rather than the two companies later transferred) would have involved not only 40 Commando's headquarters being transported forward but also the Guards' HQ being transported back, adding to the pressure on scarce helicopter resources.

Mount Kent

As we have seen it had always been intended to get 42 Commando to Mount Kent to take over from D Squadron SAS. Late on 27 May the commando was told to prepare to get elements there with a half battery of guns. The idea was to lift first one company group to consolidate the position and then a second company and Tactical HQ, with the guns to follow. Then, in the late afternoon of 28 May, J Company of 42 Commando had to be flown to Camilla Creek House to reinforce 2 Para. There they stayed for four days, helping handle the numerous prisoners taken. Weather delayed the move of the remainder of the commando to Mount Kent. While waiting for reinforcements the SAS were facing attacks from Argentine patrols. These were the result of one of Menendez's bolder moves. Looking beyond his defensive perimeter, he had decided on 28 May to assemble available Special Forces with a 'plan to plant a north-south screen to strike at the British logistics line of communication and to capture British soldiers.' This plan would prove difficult to implement. Many of the Argentine troops had not long been in the Islands and were poorly prepared for this task. Even when they could gather intelligence, their communications were often inadequate to report back their findings.[2]

On the evening of 28 May, 42 Commando was tasked to seize Mount Kent the following night, 29/30 May. Lieutenant Colonel Nick Vaux, the CO, planned to take his tactical headquarters, K Company, this mortar troop, and half a battery of guns. Half-way to the objective, snow blizzards forced the helicopters to return to Port San Carlos, and the operation was re-scheduled for the next night 30/31 May. It was on this night that two of the Argentine Special Force patrols tasked by Menendez, both quite large, reached Mount Kent. They were ambushed by the SAS and in a fierce battle two Argentines were killed and five captured, with three SAS wounded. The fight was still underway as the leading elements of 42 Commando arrived. But the fly-in continued unabated.[3] The SAS soon had the situation under control, and, having handed over Mount Kent to 42 Commando, were able to withdraw to San Carlos to prepare for future operations. Enemy positions located during 30 May near Mount Kent and further to the east were successfully engaged by two GR3 sorties. Unfortunately during the second sortie one of the two Harriers was hit by enemy small arms fire. The pilot made a creditable effort to fly his aircraft back to *Hermes*, but half-way back he had to eject into the sea. He was rescued by an SAR helicopter.

The move to Mount Kent had been viewed with misapprehension by some in 42 Commando – well into enemy territory and vulnerable to air and artillery attack once discovered. Yet while the move was a logistic challenge the enemy had not worked hard to hold this critical position. When L Company and the remaining elements of Support Company arrived the following night they were pushed forward at once to Mount Challenger where they could dominate the main road from Stanley to Bluff Cove. An intensive patrolling programme was started while 45 Commando and 3 Para marched across the Island to join 42 Commando. An observation post was soon established on Mount Kent, from where naval gunfire from *Alacrity* could be controlled, leading to over 100 salvos being fired from early on 1 June against enemy positions on Wall Mountain, Mount Harriet, Goat Ridge, Two Sisters, Mount Longdon and Moody Brook.

45 Commando's move to Douglas had begun after first light on 27 May. Initial optimism about helicopter availability having been dispelled, there was no option but to walk, carrying basic battle equipment and bergens, weighing some 120lb, with a limited amount of the heavier equipment carried in tracked Arctic warfare vehicles. The heavily laden troops moved only with great difficulty over the soft boggy peat and high clumps of tussock grass. Progress was very slow and there were several minor injuries. Eventually a request was put back to the Brigade Headquarters: 'Hels required if we are to get to the objective on time, what is state of play as regards hel availability'. The reply came back: 'None available'. The request had come at a difficult time, when the helicopter shortage was unusually acute with all general duty support helicopters temporarily unserviceable, and those able to operate at night primarily dedicated to Special Forces operations and moving the guns to support 2 Para at Goose Green. Later one Sea King was sent to support the battalion.

It took until late on 28 May before the Marines reached Douglas, clear of the enemy, where the locals welcomed them, provided accommodation in buildings and transport help using civilian tractors and trailers. The whole of 29 May was spent consolidating the position and resting. By 0030Z on 31 May, they had reached Teal Inlet and once again islanders were very helpful in providing accommodation. Later that day they were visited by Thompson, who complimented the rate of advance on foot, but raised hopes by suggesting that the next leap forward, to the Mount Kent area, would probably be by helicopter.

Unfortunately, bad weather on 1 and 2 June prevented flights. With no prospect of helicopter support, the Commanding Officer, Lieutenant Colonel Whitehead, decided to continue his move on foot the following morning. Although the weather looked more promising on 3 June, the demands of 5 Infantry Brigade were now diverting most helicopter assets. Once again Whitehead decided to move out on foot, and by 1700Z on 4 June the commando was complete in its patrol base just to the west of Mount Kent. Preparation of defensive positions in the appalling weather was not made any easier by the fact that helicopters could not even fly the bergens forward that evening. HQ 3 Commando Brigade, somewhat unsympathetically, warned 45 Commando not to keep choking up the system with its requests for helicopter support: 'your task will be acknowledged when and if hels available'.

During the night of 4/5 June the first patrols began to explore the enemy position on Two Sisters. This established that there were no mines on the track running east from the Murrell Bridge or across country south-east from the bridge towards Two Sisters. The next night an enemy patrol of five men was engaged killing three and wounding others. Two observation posts had by now been established. On 6 June, however, one of these was compromised by an enemy patrol. This led to a fight which left nine enemy dead, with only one minor casualty among the Marines, but required the party to withdraw under cover of friendly artillery fire, which killed and wounded further Argentine soldiers. The Argentines appeared very disorganised and employed no artillery in support.

3 Para

The original intention was that 45 Commando would be followed by 3 Para, who would move through Douglas to secure Teal Inlet. This plan was changed on the advice of the civilian manager at Port San Carlos who pointed out a more direct route to Teal Inlet. Again steady but slow progress was made on 27 May by foot across difficult terrain. During the afternoon 3 Para had an unexpected visitor – Stanley Councillor and ex-Chief of Police, Terry Peck. He had escaped Stanley on a motorbike and evaded the Argentines for five weeks. He provided intelligence on enemy positions, including possible minefields. He was recruited as a scout and later flown to Teal Inlet to rejoin 3 Para.

The Commanding Officer, Lieutenant Colonel Pike, did not wish to risk air attack in the final advance on Teal Inlet. The walk was taking its toll, with a number of exposure cases reported, and so he decided that the daylight hours of 28 May should be spent some 8–9 km west of their objective while the rearmost elements caught up. Lack of helicopter support meant that it was not possible to bring forward fire support for an assault on enemy positions. Before last light on 28 May this issue became less pressing when the SBS patrols in the Teal Inlet area reported it to be clear of enemy. The battalion continued its advance, and by arrangement met the SBS, which accompanied Tactical HQ and the two leading companies into Teal Inlet at 0230Z 29 May. Soon Thompson received a signal confirming that 3 Para had secured Teal Inlet and that they had now 'gone firm' and would be 'digging in at dawn'. The biggest concern at this stage was the tiredness of the soldiers and the condition of their feet. It was remarkable that in spite of the distance covered, in excess of 40 km, and the difficult terrain, only 15 men had been injured by the march. Some idea of what was involved can be gathered from the description by a soldier with 3 Para of the clothing he wore from leaving *Canberra* until arriving at Stanley:

> Long johns and long-sleeved vest 'Extreme Cold Weather' were covered by lightweight green trousers and a civilian fibre-pile jacket (I shared a common distaste for Army 'KF' shirts and had left mine behind on *Canberra*). On top of that I wore an Army pullover and a camouflaged 'windproof' smock and trousers. In addition I sometimes wore the quilted jacket under my smock and occasionally donned quilted trousers. I wore two pairs of 'Arctic' socks and I strapped a pair of civilian waxed canvas gaiters over my 'DMS' boots. To keep my spare socks warm and dry I carried them in the front pockets of my lightweight trousers. I wore the issued 'head-over' around my neck. My helmet (with red beret tucked inside) was usually replaced by an Arctic issue cap when I considered the threat to my skull to be minimal. I carried leather combat gloves and wore them when I was dry.[4]

At 1800Z, Thompson advised 3 Para to prepare to move to Estancia House, where an estimated 200 plus enemy were believed to be located. Pike was concerned that his troops were not ready for the attack, tired after their exertions, and with inadequate support weapons, ammunition supplies and communications. The orders were therefore changed to securing Teal Inlet until 45 Commando arrived and clearing the surrounding area before a later move to take Estancia House. The next day, 30 May, a couple of helicopters were found to re-supply the battalion, move its remaining mortars and other support weapons forward and bring the Patrol (D) Company to join the rest. At 1430Z the battalion set out for Estancia House, with a following convoy of tractors carrying mortars. After two hours A Company accepted the surrender of an enemy observation post composed of very cold and wet Argentine Air Force soldiers, who had been in the area for a few days having been sent from Stanley to observe the area. By the end of the day the battalion was close to the objective.

The plan had been to remain firm during the day of 31 May but then word came back from the Patrol (D) Company that there was no enemy at Estancia House. The battalion advanced silently, confirmed that the enemy was absent, and by 2240Z the house was secure. The troops began to take advantage of the comparative comfort of their new surroundings. The Mountain & Arctic Warfare (M&AW) Cadre had located an enemy patrol using Top Malo House, some nine km south of Teal Inlet. This patrol was another part of the special forces screen that Menendez had been trying to establish. They had taken to the House after some gruelling time in the open. After the cadre was reinforced, the House was raided successfully at 1300Z on 31 May by 19 men, in a short fierce fight against a trapped enemy, who lost two dead with seven wounded. Five more were captured. Three marines were wounded. As van der Bijl notes, this signalled the end of the attempt to establish a screen. Of the 170 men earmarked by Menendez for the operation about 50 made it into the field and of these, 32 were soon killed, wounded or missing.[5]

On 1 June, tractors and other vehicles from the other settlements arrived, led by Mrs Trudi Morrison, and volunteered to help. They were set to work moving ammunition, rations and stores up to the companies on the mountain. Having taken this objective with comparative ease, 3 Para began preparations to patrol the next one, Mount Longdon, although no attack was expected for another couple of days. It would be co-ordinated with 45 Commando's planned move to take Two Sisters. Orders from Thompson on 2 June were to engage in aggressive patrolling as far as the east end of Mount Longdon, securing any unoccupied positions. No major advance was to take place until full support had arrived. Although an attack had been planned for 3 June it had now been held up by the need to switch the main helicopter effort to cope with the consequences of 2 Para's unplanned advance to Fitzroy which is discussed in the next chapter. The message, as recorded in 3 Para's log, read: 'Concern that en might launch counter attack. They are [2 Para] now in a sit whereby they may need all the SP they can get ... 7 Bty will register tgts along the track to try to stop any Argie advance. CO 3 Para should be aware that any helo SP promised tomorrow and any arty SP for his attack tomorrow night may have to be switched to 2 Para if the situations warrants it, i.e. if they appear to be cut off.' 3 Para was therefore not to be too adventurous in its planning. Pike was still not disposed to hold things up. He outlined to his officers a plan to take Mount Longdon. Intensive patrolling began, often as close as 50 metres to enemy positions, and soon confirmation was received of approximately two companies of

Argentine infantry in occupation (actually there was only one). Fire support was put in position. At 1600Z the battalion began its advance to contact, intending at the very least to establish a patrol base at the west foot of Mount Longdon and possibly taking out the objective during darkness. After making good progress, by 1655Z the enemy was engaged, although they soon went to ground.

Thompson at this stage was mainly concerned that 3 Para clear routes to Longdon for later use as well as prepare the way for 45 Commando to get to Two Sisters. The paratroopers, however, were getting more ambitious, seeing an opportunity to exploit their position. At 1718Z, 3 Para's log recorded that: 'Aggressive ptls may end up taking out obj during darkness'. The leading company continued to make good progress but soon enemy small arms, mortar and artillery fire was being received, especially from Two Sisters on the right flank. Thompson signalled at 1824Z:

> I am concerned that you are pressing on too fast, I do not want you to get into a situation you cannot get out of. You are therefore to stay where you are and dig in. You can carry out your future intentions but you are not to move the whole of your C/S (call-sign) forward; you are to patrol forward only. When you have consolidated you are to send locstat soonest. You should dig in well when you stop.

On receipt of this, Pike stopped the advance and ordered the battalion to consolidate its position on a defensive reverse slope just west of the Murrell Bridge some 6 km from Mount Longdon. All companies started to dig in and make their positions secure. Thereafter 3 Para began an extensive patrol programme. Early on 6 June there was a clash by a bridge over the Murrell River, when an Argentine patrol was ambushed with five killed, although the paratroopers then had to leave quickly as mortar and machine gun fire came down on them from Mount Tumbledown. There was more skirmishing the next day, suggesting that Argentine forces in this area were better trained and motivated than others encountered.

The costs of delay

The delays in mounting the attacks against the defences around Stanley, while waiting for 5 Infantry Brigade to be brought forward, were frustrating. They also carried risks. The Argentines were aware that the British had occupied these forward positions and on 4 June they mounted raids using six Daggers against targets in the Mount Kent and Green Patch Settlement, while four Pucaras from Stanley also dropped bombs in the Mount Kent area, as did four Canberras much later. None of these hit anything and there were no British casualties. Although the British were aware of the Daggers it was not possible to attempt any interceptions.

Thompson was worried at the vulnerability of his position, and in particular his re-supply point and brigade HQ at Teal Inlet. Getting Rapier detachments forward had been painfully slow. He signalled to Moore at 0140Z on 5 June that not only had the promised air defence Rapier not yet arrived but also the BBC had announced that this area is 'the HQ of the force attacking Stanley'. 'If the enemy believe this,' he continued, ' this location is an undefended prime target for air attack on the San Carlos scale.' He asked for Harrier air cover until the Rapiers arrived. Moore supported this in a signal to Woodward, while hoping to get the air defences in position by the end of the day. Later the same day he was bemoaning references on the BBC World Service to 45 Commando leaving Teal Inlet in a massive helicopter lift forward. 'Sorry to bang on but could press officers at Ajax Bay and *Fearless* be ordered to delete mention of units, place names and movements from press copy.' He added: 'Mentioning place names may have been OK in WW2 in context 21 Army Group advancing on Paris but 21 Army Group had air superiority! Sorry if this denies politicians the pleasure of moving pins on their Childs Atlas maps of the world.'

The delays also caused confusion. It had been intended to mount the attacks on the night of 5/6 June. The Navy had geared itself up to this task, taking into account the risk to ships providing gunfire support from ground-based Exocet. This risk had already led to limits being placed on general activity close to shore, and not just in the area to the south of the Stanley peninsula. There were also concerns that Berkeley Sound might be mined. Given the importance of the coming attacks, however, four bombarding ships – *Cardiff, Yarmouth, Active* and *Arrow* – had been allocated. When Moore postponed the attack he signalled Woodward cancelling the four NGS ships, although he did suggest that one ship might usefully carry out harassing fire in the Tumbledown-Moody Brook area. Communications broke down, as Woodward was unaware of the postponement, and, when he signalled for confirmation that the gunfire was still required, he heard nothing back. Only after he had detached the ships did he get Moore's signal. He recalled *Active* and *Arrow*, but sent *Yarmouth* and *Cardiff* to go to their station off Fitzroy, the latter under orders to interdict any Argentine re-supply sorties. Before it could get within Sea Dart range one C130 had landed at Stanley and taken off again. They fired a number of rounds between 0245 and 0550Z. It was while this was going on that a 5 Infantry Brigade Gazelle was mistaken for a possible Argentine Pucara and shot down. The confusion this night also led to the LCUs taking the Scots Guards from *Intrepid* off Lively Island being illuminated by British warships.[6]

39

FITZROY AND BLUFF COVE

Getting 5 Infantry Brigade into position was proving to be a prolonged and painful process. From the point when its deployment to the South Atlantic had been first mooted its position had been problematic. It had been cobbled together after losing the two parachute battalions, and almost the Gurkhas because of the political sensitivities believed to be associated with their use. The addition of the 2nd Battalion Scots Guards and 1st Battalion Welsh Guards was controversial because they had come from public duties (although the Welsh Guards had recently had a tour in Northern Ireland). One officer in the Scots Guards later recalled that his men had focused their training on the two crucial areas of shooting and fitness.[1] Another later observed that though the men were fit 'tactics were very rusty.'[2] To raise levels of fitness and to weld the Brigade together as a coherent fighting unit they were sent off to Wales for exercises, which were conducted at the platoon and company rather than battalion level. The results were not encouraging. With so many units that had never worked together before the disjointed performance was not surprising. Nonetheless it led to questions being raised about the suitability of Brigadier Tony Wilson, although not sufficiently to alter the normal reluctance to change a commander at such a critical time. Brigadier John Waters went on the *QEII* to serve as Moore's deputy but also as a possible replacement Brigade Commander should a need arise. He was already the reserve commander for 5 Infantry Brigade. As Moore's deputy he would be able to take the lead on crucial but time-consuming issues involving logistics and prisoners and, should something happen to Moore, take over his role. The Gurkhas were commanded by Lieutenant-Colonel David Morgan, the Welsh Guards by Lieutenant-Colonel Johnny Rickett and the Scots Guards by Lieutenant-Colonel Michael Scott.

As soon as the *QEII* had sailed from Southampton on 12 May, 5 Infantry Brigade established a training schedule to make maximum use of the time available to increase the troops' physical fitness and general readiness for war. Poor weather limited what could be achieved. In addition, they might have stopped at Ascension Island, where stores could be re-organised, use made of the field firing ranges and further time given to fitness training and practical battle skills. Instead at 1540Z on 19 May a signal was received ordering the *QEII* to proceed direct to the Falkland Islands without stopping at Ascension. The previous plan of cross decking with MVs *Baltic Ferry* and *Nordic Ferry* was postponed. The intention was to increase the momentum of the campaign, and also to get Moore and his staff to the front line as soon as possible. By 21 May they were on the *QEII*, having transferred by helicopter from HMS *Dumbarton Castle* and Ascension.

Later that same day the *QEII* met up with *Atlantic Causeway* and crossdecked stores until 0800Z on 20 May. Once completed the *QEII* headed south at best speed to rendezvous with the ferries in the South Atlantic at South Georgia. Then at 0957Z on 24 May, HQ CLFFI decided that the planned cross decking with the ferries would not now take place. The *QEII* was to proceed direct to South Georgia (ETA on 27 May) where cross decking into RN shipping would take place in calm waters. The Brigade would then go to the Falklands and meet with the ferries en route. The *QEII* was to stay well out of Argentine surveillance range. London had decided that it was not acceptable to risk the *QEII* in the battle zone. This, however, carried its own risks, including delay, especially if the weather was unkind.

On 26 May the cross-decking of the 3,000 men and their immediate equipment from *QEII* to *Canberra*, *Norland* and *Stromness* began at South Georgia, while the *Baltic Ferry*, *Nordic Ferry* and *Atlantic Causeway* carrying the brigade's heavy equipment went directly to a safe position until they were required to unload. The ship had been routed to avoid attracting Argentine attention. Leach later recalled his concern 'at 0700 on the Today Programme one morning' when he heard a reporter say, 'I am standing on the upper deck of the *QEII* watching 5 Infantry Brigade transfer to the *Canberra* and the *Norland* against the magnificent glacial backdrop of South Georgia'.[3] There had been concerns that a submarine would attempt to disrupt this process, but this was now assessed as a false alarm.

It took time to manage the transfer, first because *Stromness* was held up picking up survivors from *Coventry* and *Atlantic Conveyor*, and then because there was some confusion over which units were to go on *Canberra* (eventually 2 Scots Guards and 1 Welsh Guards) and which to *Norland* (1/7 Gurkha Rifles). Fortunately good weather and calm seas allowed the cross decking to be completed late on 28 May, but bad weather thereafter slowed the ships down. When they arrived at the edge of the TEZ they had to loiter, because other supply vessels, such as the *Atlantic Causeway*, had to be unloaded first. *Norland* was able to unload as planned on the night of 31 May/1 June but *Canberra* had to wait until the next night. The Battalion War Diary recorded the arrival of the Welsh Guards: 'Slightly bewildered after twenty-two days at sea they staggered ashore from LCUs weighed down by enormous bergens, all their webbing, a lot of ammunition and the whole outfit topped by the archaic steel helmet.'

The initial orders were 'to establish 5 Infantry Brigade in San Carlos Settlement – Sussex Mountains area prior to move on southern flank'. Once disembarked the two guards battalions remained in concentration areas in San Carlos, while the Gurkhas relieved 2 Para at Darwin/Goose Green and one company of 40 Commando on Sussex Mountains. The subsequent off-load from *Baltic Ferry* and *Nordic Ferry* was later described in the Brigade's own report as a 'logistic horror story'. Reasons for this included the inability to rectify at Ascension problems posed by the rushed original loading in Britain; insufficient helicopters because of the opportunity created by the Argentine vacation of the Mount Kent/Mount Challenger area and the need to get Marines there to fill the gaps; the risks of having both ferries in San Carlos together; and the limited time and capacity for off-loading at night.

From 20 May Moore had become the Task Group Commander (CTG 317.1) with both 3 Commando Brigade and 5 Infantry Brigade under his command. Moore was anxious not to be seen to be favouring the Royal Marine brigade (which is why he avoided wearing his green beret) and went out of his way to treat both brigades fairly. If anything, the poor communications afflicting *QEII* meant that he was able to talk much more with Wilson than Thompson. On 21 May Wilson told his staff that, unless the Argentines gave in, so that 5 Infantry Brigade would garrison the Islands, the options open were either to reinforce through the existing bridgehead or to mount a separate attack in a different area. It was clear that his preference was for the latter option. One difficulty was that 5 Infantry Brigade was carrying insufficient logistic support with them and had brought with them almost no additional means of moving men, material and equipment. En route Wilson proposed to Moore an equal allocation of the existing helicopter support assets between the two Brigades as a means of allowing 5 Infantry Brigade to advance separately and so support the southern strategy. Clapp describes Wilson arriving 'clutching a promise' of 'parity with 3 Commando Brigade over the availability of assets'. His demands for helicopters yielded little. The Marines seemed to be getting preferential treatment. The problem was that 3 Commando Brigade were then in the middle of a series of moves that required the air transport. There was nothing to be gained by their sudden reallocation.[4]

To Fitzroy

A controversial piece of private enterprise brought 5 Infantry Brigade back into the picture. Reassigned to 5 Infantry Brigade, for a while 2 Para were on their own, waiting for the rest of the Brigade and its commander to arrive. The manager of the Darwin settlement suggested that before they moved forward they should check with the manager at Bluff Cove to see whether the enemy was around, and also whether the bridge connecting the Cove to Fitzroy Creek was still standing. The lines from Burntside House were down

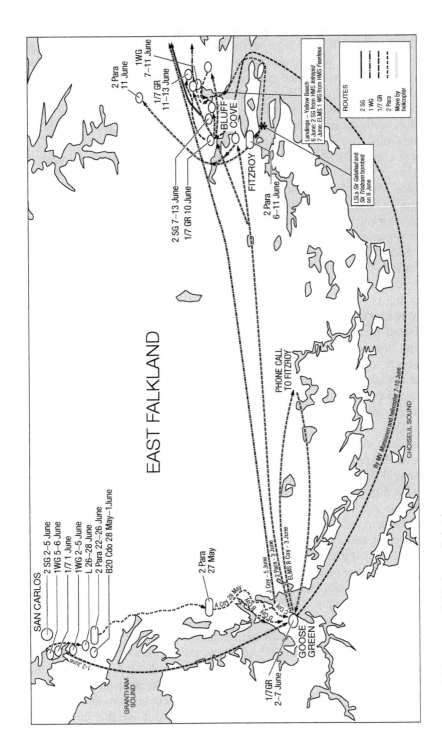

Map 11 Movement of 5 Infantry Brigade

and so the next settlement was Swan Inlet House, some 25 km to the east of Darwin. Keeble, still in charge of the battalion, developed a plan to get there. On 30 May, Wilson arrived with his own plan to advance to the Mount Pleasant sector, which could only be achieved by walking or flying. The advantage of Bluff Cove was that it was accessible by sea. From 2 Para, hardened to Falklands conditions and by no means in awe of their Brigadier, came dissent.[5] By 2 June Wilson had acknowledged the logic of the Paras' plan.

It was executed that day. A small force was taken by helicopter to Swan Inlet House, which they found to be empty. The telephone line was intact and when Fitzroy Settlement, some 30 km further east, was contacted, the Manager's young daughter answered it. Her father was able to report that there was no enemy at that time in either Fitzroy or Bluff Cove. On receiving this intelligence, Wilson effectively commandeered the Chinook helicopter, which had arrived at Goose Green to collect prisoners of war, to take as many troops from 2 Para and as much equipment as could be carried to Fitzroy and Bluff Cove to secure them. Further reinforcements were flown in that night. Nobody else had been told of the move, and the Chinook's radio was broken. The sudden arrival of a Chinook setting down troops was therefore of great interest to a 3 Commando Brigade patrol which had been watching the area. They assumed that the Chinook must be Argentine and were about to bring down artillery fire on the landing troops when they noticed British Scout helicopters

Over the next day they were joined by the remainder of the Battalion and 29 Battery, and then by two troops of the RHG/D who drove in from the north. This was all taking place as 2 Para were joined by their new commanding officer, Lieutenant Colonel D Chaundler, who had arrived after a 'swift and eventful journey from the UK involving a parachute drop into the sea!' He was concerned at the way that his battalion, still recovering from a hard battle and with inadequate rations, had been moved. It was not until 4 June that there was a sufficient helicopter lift to bring up re-supplies and the bergens, which included badly needed sleeping bags. With no enemy in the vicinity, and a number of relatively comfortable sheep shearing sheds to occupy, the paratroopers were, however, soon grateful for an opportunity to recover from their exertions and also to address minor medical problems, mainly incipient trench foot.

At 2300Z on 3 June, Wilson briefed his staff on the new situation, explaining that his original plans had been overtaken by events in the capture of Fitzroy and Bluff Cove. In order to maintain the momentum of the advance he intended to move the whole Brigade there and eventually abandon Goose Green. He hoped to use MV *Monsunen* to ferry the Welsh Guards, Gurkha Rifles and the Brigade HQ to Fitzroy in that order. The Scots Guards would move to Fitzroy on an LSL round Lafonia and helicopters would be used to move all available personnel and equipment forward if weather conditions permitted. His overriding priority was to reinforce Fitzroy and Bluff Cove to ensure that those already there could withstand a counter-attack. In a later report Wilson claimed that by this move he had obtained a great leap forward for the Brigade of some 55 km and denied Argentine units access to valuable positions that could have hampered the advance of the land forces. The contrary view is that by creating this forward position he had divided his force and created a new and demanding logistics and command requirement that distorted priorities. Once 2 Para had been established in the Fitzroy/Bluff Cove area it was imperative to bring the rest of the Brigade and its logistic support forward as quickly as possible. Moore's report to Fieldhouse on 2 June welcomed that a leading element of 5 Infantry Brigade was established in so forward a position, but also pointed to the need this created for the Brigade now to 'close up and get themselves balanced'.

It soon became apparent that the men could not march to Fitzroy. One consideration was that the Guards were not as well suited for a march of this kind as were the Commandos and the Parachute Battalions. Moore later acknowledged that, as 5 Infantry Brigade had not 'been doing the level of training that 3 Cdo Bde had, it was a worry'. This was not, however, the main problem. The men were fit enough, if not as fit as the others. The problem was the amount of equipment they had to move without helicopter or vehicle support, and the need to be prepared for battle on arrival at their destination. The difficulties were illustrated by the experience of 1st Battalion Welsh Guards who had only landed in San Carlos on 2 June from *Canberra* and had yet to get to Darwin. When they had arrived at San Carlos they were moved on foot to an assembly area some 6 km from the landing point, taking with them a quantity of heavy equipment. They could not use Land Rovers, although some had been landed, because of the boggy terrain. The initial plan was to march over the Sussex Mountains to the Darwin/Goose Green area. There were no helicopters available and while Snocat vehicles were, and could take the heavier equipment, there was no petrol for them. Civilian tractors, the next best option, failed as they became bogged down. Leaving the kit behind for later transportation carried the risks of going into battle unbalanced. The advance was slow and cumbersome. At 0020Z on 4 June the march commenced and by 0220Z the Commanding Officer, Lieutenant Colonel J F Rickett, had decided to turn back. At a rate of 1 km/hour the march was pointless.

It was still necessary to complete the deployment of 3 Commando Brigade while poor weather was reducing flying time all round. When helicopters were available the first priority was to bring forward ammunition, guns and equipment rather than troops. On 3 June, Moore and Clapp decided that the only option was to take the men by sea. Clapp signalled Woodward at 2110Z on 3 June that he intended to land the two Guards battalions in the Bluff Cove area at first light 6 June, with 2 Scots Guards and half of 1 Welsh Guards travelling in *Intrepid* and the rest of the Welsh

Guards in *Sir Tristram*. He requested two escorts to provide anti-aircraft co-ordination, combat air patrol control, and naval gunfire support. Later Clapp explained that he had in mind a normal movement of troops and assets by sea along a coastline already in British hands rather than a full-scale amphibious operation. This did assume, however, continued protection from bad weather and combat air patrols and acceptance that the loss of one of the ships involved, provided it had been emptied, would not affect the course of the war.[6]

Woodward was unhappy and signalled back to Clapp at 1051Z on 4 June:

> As keen as anyone to finish job fast but shore based threat and, in good weather, resurgent Arg air threat could expose 2 x Bns and 3 or 4 major naval units unnecessarily. Args are unlikely to repeat D-Day mistake of going for escorts. Hence conclude Amphib Op should be contingent on suitable clag [bad weather] and preferably night landing. By all means plan on 6 Jun but be prepared for indefinite delay for weather. Consider more robust plan might be to move troops forward by foot/helo accepting that this may take to 6/7 Jun and providing logistic support by one/two relatively inconspicuous LSLs as at Teal. Extremely reluctant to interfere your business and will provide escorts you wish, but suggest you reconsider first.

Clapp who was unhappy both with 5 Infantry Brigade's unfamiliarity with amphibious operations, including the need for them to be managed by the naval commander, and also about the development of the southern route, precisely because it would lead to such problems, could now see no other way of proceeding. He signalled back at 0029Z on 5 June that: 'current met [meteorological] and military situation dictate Guardsmen, guns, ammo and stomachs go all the way from Buckingham Palace to Bluff Cove by sea'. He wanted *Arrow* to escort *Intrepid* and *Avenger* to escort *Sir Tristram* both to arrive before first light on 6 June. Woodward remained reluctant to risk ships in this way. He suggested at 1104Z that *Sir Tristram* should be 'left to her own salvation' during 6 June. He agreed to provide CAP cover over Bluff Cove and, if essential, *Yarmouth* could be made available for *Sir Tristram*. On 5 June the two battalions began to embark on to *Intrepid*. After the Scots Guards were on board, the embarkation of the Welsh Guards was stopped and then reversed. 'Order and counter order were rife.' The Commanding Officer flew out to HMS *Fearless* to impress upon Moore the battalion's readiness and exasperation at not knowing why plans kept changing.

The reason lay in Northwood. Fieldhouse was also unhappy. The plan indicated that 'a proportion of the move would be by day', and the ships could be vulnerable to enemy artillery and sea mines, resulting in 'Guardsmen swimming'. He suggested instead an insertion via Teal or the south-eastern corner of Salvador-Water. Moore's reply acknowledged the risks of a sea move but argued that if the CINC wanted to get the Stanley battle started then they had to be accepted. Moving by helicopter and foot would mean a five-day delay at minimum, with almost certainly a penalty to 3 Commando Brigade's ammunition stocks and the physical and mental state of the troops. Alternative landing spots would also mean that the freshness of 5 Infantry Brigade would be lost, as well as the strategy of persuading the Argentines that the main thrust was coming from the south. Fieldhouse was unconvinced. The balance of political risks was now changing. Before he had been worried that the international calls for a cease-fire, and uncertainty in the Government, would bring his campaign to a stuttering halt. Now he was more confident: 'PM has held out resolutely for victory not ceasefire.' In this she was supported by public opinion. What might undermine her position and turn public opinion would be a 'catastrophe at sea with large loss of life':

> Thus while I agree risk involved in the operation maybe acceptable in military terms, the political risk is not. Your excellent progress to invest Port Stanley has eased pressure for immediate victory in that area. I therefore accept the delay that any alternative to Bluff Cove could impose, albeit that I hope it might be less than 5 days you mention. Perhaps by LCU to SE corner of Salvador Water, time for deployment of 5 Bde and log build up – FSP could be reduced. Therefore please drop this plan.

This left both Moore and Clapp frustrated. Moore explained Fieldhouse's concerns about the political impact of a major loss at sea: 'I think CINCFLEET saw *Intrepid* with two battalions on board as just such a loss and he therefore felt it was a risk too large to be acceptable.' In acknowledging the signal, Clapp sought advice on the acceptability of using LSLs as logistic suppliers with a few troops embarked as at Teal Inlet. Fieldhouse replied at 1825Z on 5 June that this was a decision to be made by Commanders in the field. A new plan was therefore devised.

One issue in this debate was whether the moves might be discovered either through observation by any Argentine troops in Lafonia or on Lively Island or through what appeared to be an Argentine radio intercept capability. Bluff Cove and Fitzroy were out of artillery range, but the sea approaches were not out of the range of the land-based Exocet. Clapp had assessed all this while drawing up his plan: the issue was whether the level of need justified the degree of risk involved. He noted that LSLs had used Teal Inlet to build up 3 Commando Brigade's forward maintenance area without interference by the enemy. The significant difference, however, which was not appreciated at the time, was that 3 Commando Brigade held the high ground that overlooked Teal Inlet, namely Mount Estancia, Mount Kent and Mount

Challenger. In contrast, it was the Argentines who, from positions on Mount Harriet and Mount William, could see the masts of ships in Fitzroy.

In the end the only way to meet Fieldhouse's concerns was to put the battalions ashore by LCUs from a stand-off distance in darkness. Under the new plan, sent by signal on 5 June at 1910Z from Moore, there would be a complex series of moves that would see the Scots Guards get to the area of Lively Island on *Intrepid* that night, from where they would be moved in four LCUs to Bluff Cove, while *Intrepid* returned to San Carlos before first light. A similar operation would be repeated for the bulk of the Welsh Guards the next night, while the remainder of those to be removed would be taken in stages to Darwin where they would eventually embark on MV *Monsunen* for passage to Bluff Cove.

The proposed movements were complicated enough without the added confusion caused by poor communications and the lack of an overall in-theatre commander. There were now five separate decision centres that had to be co-ordinated: Fieldhouse at Northwood, Woodward on *Hermes*, Moore and Clapp at San Carlos, 5 Infantry Brigade HQ at Darwin, and 2 Para, with some elements of the Brigade HQ, in the Fitzroy/Bluff Cove area. Even with Moore and Clapp together on *Fearless*, communication had been imperfect: Clapp had not been briefed on Moore's southern strategy, which under-pinned this major effort. In addition, individual ships could only operate according to the information and orders transmitted to them. Communications between the divided Brigade Headquarters depended upon a manpack re-broadcast station on Pleasant Peak. On 5 June, as discussions continued about how best to move the rest of the Brigade forward, one of the station's two sets developed a technical fault, while 2 Para's vehicle radio sets were unusable as they were low on fuel. To deal with this problem 5 Infantry Brigade decided to despatch a helicopter carrying an officer and sergeant from the Signals Squadron with the necessary equipment and fuel. In doing so they did not take account of the likelihood that one of the Task Force ships would be in the area. They did tell Moore's staff in *Fearless* what was planned but too late for ships to be notified. The ships in the area, including *Cardiff*, were unaware that a helicopter was about to fly, and also appeared to have lacked a clear picture of the disposition of Argentine forces which would have confirmed that there were none in the area west of Bluff Cove/Fitzroy. At 0358Z, while bombarding Argentine shore positions, *Cardiff* detected a slow-moving aircraft flying in the direction of Stanley. Having no reason to assume that this was anything other than hostile, *Cardiff* fired two Sea Darts, the second of which hit causing the helicopter to crash and all four occupants to be killed. Because of the initial assumption that this was caused by an Argentine patrol, Gurkhas were sent out to find the enemy, which could have led to another blue-on-blue as they came across the signals group already on Pleasant Peak.[7] The communications problem was eventually eased by taking a vehicle system to Pleasant Peak where it managed to stay

604

operational for the duration of the campaign, but the situation remained unsatisfactory and over the next couple of days this had more fateful consequences.

There had almost been another tragedy as a result of miscommunications on the night of 5/6 June as the new plan for moving troops to Fitzroy by sea was implemented. A crucial figure in all of this was Major Ewen Southby-Tailyour, who had already played a critical role in planning the landing because of his unique knowledge of the coastline. He was tasked to manage the process of getting the battalions safely ashore, but was anxious, as he informed Clapp, because the operation was so rushed and navigational error as much as enemy action carried substantial risks. Clapp had agreed that *Intrepid* would launch the LCUs loaded with Scots Guards near Middle Island or Elephant Castle, which promised a difficult but manageable four-hour trip to Bluff Cove. Captain Dingemans of *Intrepid*, however, had been unhappy with the operation from the start, and had not been reassured by Clapp's insistence that the risks were not great. Dingemans remained impressed by Fieldhouse's concerns about the political consequences of the loss of the LPD. *Intrepid*, he told Southby-Tailyour, after he boarded, was not 'politically, allowed further east than Lively Island.' This was the maximum range for Exocet. The Captain was unimpressed by the Major's concerns about the possible loss of 600 Scots Guards at sea on four unprotected and small LCUs without decent navigational aids. Clapp refused the request of an escorting frigate (as he was concerned that this would draw attention to the movement) which meant that if any warships turned up they could be assumed to be Argentine.[8] After his difficult exchanges with Southby-Tailyour, Dingemans signalled to Moore at 2338Z on 5 June his surprise that Southby-Tailyour had been briefed about the operation only half an hour before cross decking to *Intrepid* in order to navigate the LCUs. He continued:

Whilst the operation will go ahead as planned tonight with an element of surprise on our side and sufficient escorts to protect the LPD a repetition tomorrow night at the same time over the same route with a second battalion exposed in open waters in undefended and unescorted LCUs is viewed with grave misgivings.

If safety was the priority, he suggested, then at least consideration should be given to the movement of the Welsh Guards (the second battalion lift mentioned in the signal above), by whatever means available to Darwin and then from Darwin overnight using the LCUs now at Bluff Cove. Alternatively helicopter assets could be temporarily diverted from supporting 3 Commando Brigade. Dingemans continued to press his view with Clapp, whose response was that using the LPDs remained the best way of getting troops into position for the assault on Stanley, and that the planned journeys were no more risky than staying at San Carlos.

At about 0430Z on 6 June the four LCUs left *Intrepid*, with 150 troops crammed in each with kit and some Land Rovers. Then the sea was calm. Southby-Tailyour had been told incorrectly that there were no British ships in the area, for orders had changed. He did not know that when he picked up two ships on radar, and when his LCUs were illuminated. They were illuminated because *Cardiff* and *Yarmouth* were still unaware of the troop movements underway and they were lucky that this option had been chosen by the ships rather than high explosives. He decided to try to move into shallow water to outrun them but they were still closing when they flashed the word 'friend' by flash lamp, to which he replied 'to which side' and was thereafter left alone (no attack but no assistance either). The weather then worsened. Southby-Tailyour later described the 'very miserable night the Scots Guards had spent – some of them had spent 7½ hours in the well deck of these craft the last 3 or 4 hours of which they were soaked to the skin.' Without the Major's knowledge of the area it could have been much worse.

The arrival of this bedraggled group, including many severe cases of exposure, led to the Scots Guards being given the warmer accommodation while 2 Para were moved back to Fitzroy as the Brigade reserve and to defend the Brigade Administrative Area, which was to be established there. The paratroopers were themselves still feeling the strain. 5 Infantry Brigade's War Diary noted that 2 Para was in 'poor physical shape having been in the open since 2 Jun and still tired after Goose Green battle. They have a large number of cases of trench foot.' Other than a brief interlude at Goose Green they had been in the open since 21 May. In order to get to their next resting place 2 Para used three of *Intrepid*'s LCUs to get to Port Pleasant, off Fitzroy Settlement. To do this, and after some argument, they counter-manded Southby-Tailyour's orders to the LCU coxswains to wait at Bluff Cove. The first attempt to move the men failed because the weather was too bad for the short route. They returned to Bluff Cove. After another argument, they took the long route, this time successfully. One LCU was not used for this journey and was left at Bluff Cove. The conditions now prevented the others getting back. All this had taken place without the knowledge of the higher command. The consequences of this unilateral action were severe.

At this stage the plan for the next night was that the Battalion would be split between *Sir Tristram* and *Intrepid* and that all four of the LCUs would sail about midnight to meet *Intrepid* and bring off the four companies of Welsh Guards to Bluff Cove. At this point the main plan changed again. Moore's HQ sent a signal to 5 Infantry Brigade at 1215Z on 6 June stating that:

> 1 WG complete is to emb[ark] in *Fearless* for passage to Lively Island, R/V with LCUs and landing at Bluff Cove a.m. 7 Jun. 100 troops of FBMA who were to have emb in *Intrepid* are to be emb instead in *Sir Tristram*. 60 tps previously briefed to move in LCUs tonight to Cantera House are also to emb in *Sir Tristram*. Time of

emb of all tps into *Fearless* and *Tristram* will be 061600Z from Blue 2 Beach to be cfm once Sitrep on 2 SG landing has been received and assessed.

There were three reasons for the change of plan. First, *Fearless* was achieving faster speeds and would still be able to return to the protection of the transport area under cover of darkness. Second, a rendezvous point further north reflected a new interpretation of the Exocet envelope. Third, the new point would cut the journey time on the LCUs to shore. *Fearless* only had two LCUs of her own – one had been left at San Carlos with a defect and another because it was involved in general unloading – and so it needed to be met by two of those supposedly waiting at Bluff Cove if the battalion was to move as one.

That morning Southby-Tailyour had attempted but failed to communicate directly with Moore or Clapp and so had decided to return to *Fearless* to establish contact. On doing so he discovered the change in plan that would have the Guards delivered by *Fearless*, and also a new point for the rendezvous so that the LCUs would not have such a long journey back to shore with the troops. He returned to Bluff Cove by Sea King to organise this, but he too was now caught by the awful weather covering the Falklands. He could only find one LCU, but he presumed the other three could not be too far away. He was unaware that they were at Port Pleasant. He managed to get 2 Scots Guards to send a signal to Darwin and then on to Clapp, that the weather was unsuitable for the LCUs to sail, but it was also unavoidably ambiguous on the number of LCUs available. In fact the signal did not get through to *Fearless* until nearly 0100Z. With the weather then moderate, it offered no firm guidance on whether or not to expect the LCUs.

By 0250Z, *Fearless*, escorted by *Avenger* and *Penelope*, had reached the rendezvous position but there was no sign of *Intrepid*'s LCUs. After a fruitless search for the lost LCUs it was decided to send two of the Welsh Guard companies to Bluff Cove in the two *Fearless* LCUs but take the other two companies back to San Carlos, to be delivered the next day by some other means. The journey of the two LCUs this time took less than three hours.

Meanwhile, on the evening of 6 June, *Sir Tristram* had loaded with stores and ammunition from San Carlos, adding a Mexeflote and a reduced Amphibious Beach Unit for the unloading. The idea was that she would carry the four Rapiers as well as the Field Ambulance Team, which would have allowed this to be the last run by an LSL. However the weather made it impossible to bring the Rapiers forward and the Field Ambulance Team did not board. *Sir Tristram* was still fully loaded, with more, in fact, than could be off-loaded in a day. She arrived off Fitzroy in darkness on 7 June. With six LCUs available to help, unloading went generally smoothly. In addition *Monsunen* was able to bring D Company 1/7 Gurkha Rifles and the echelon of 2 Para to Fitzroy, while helicopters ferried supplies from San Carlos. The unloading of *Sir Tristram* could not quite be completed and the Captain signalled that he would not be able to sail for another 24 hours.

At last it seemed as if the forward movement of 5 Infantry Brigade could be completed. The plan for the night of 7/8 June was that the two companies of Welsh Guards would be moved, plus four Rapier fire units and elements of 16 Field Ambulance. Rather than follow the pattern of the previous two nights, this time *Intrepid* was to meet up with her four LCUs and bring them back to San Carlos where they were needed, while *Sir Galahad* would take the Welsh Guards, the Field Ambulance and the Rapier overnight to Fitzroy where it would unload the next day. There would be two LCUs and a Mexeflote, plus some helicopters, available for this to be achieved reasonably quickly. Clapp only realised on the morning of 8 June that two LSLs would be operating together in daylight that day, and before air defences could be established. If he had realised that *Sir Tristram* had been delayed leaving, he might have held *Sir Galahad* back. But its cargo was vital, and could not be transported by any other means. Furthermore at San Carlos the weather was still filthy. Some risks had been taken at Teal Inlet, at least initially, and it would be a relief to have this awkward operation finished. Already the movement to and fro between San Carlos and Bluff Cove had led to postponement of Moore's plans for a 3 Commando Brigade attack on the night of the 5/6 and now further delay appeared inevitable, leaving men caught in what Moore had described to Fieldhouse on 7 June as 'the worst weather, from a soldier's point of view, since we came here. Absolutely filthy with a high wind and driving rain resulting in serious worries about the effect on our troops – especially those high up in the mountains.' The Royal Army Medical Corps (RAMC) reported that day on the poor physical condition of the troops, many of whom were suffering from exposure and trench foot. Unless the campaign was brought to a swift conclusion there could be serious health problems.

Although it was Clapp's intention that *Sir Galahad* should go directly to Fitzroy, where the stores were needed and the ship would be safer, the initial briefings and warning signal received by the Captain of *Sir Galahad* had, unfortunately, mistakenly implied he was expected to take his ship with the Welsh Guards to Bluff Cove and to land the main 5 Brigade stores at Fitzroy. He, on studying his charts, realised that an LSL could not be taken into Bluff Cove, and requested clarification. A widely circulated signal from Clapp at 1318Z, which went to 5 Infantry Brigade and *Sir Tristram*, described the moves to Bluff Cove, but a later signal, not so widely circulated, instructed *Sir Galahad* to sail for Fitzroy. When the constant and rapid changes of requirement combined with a variety of minor delays sailing time was moved back to 0200Z 8 June at the earliest. In view of this, but with everyone now on board, the Captain of *Sir Galahad* signalled at 0015Z 8 June to Clapp that he intended to remain at San Carlos overnight. Clapp's staff, in consultation with Moore's, discussed this and they decided to order *Sir Galahad* to sail in accordance with earlier instructions and to proceed direct at best speed to Fitzroy. Sea Harrier air cover was to be requested if they arrived after first light. Unfortunately this signal, which was the best opportunity to bring everybody, including 5 Infantry Brigade HQ and the units already at Fitzroy and Bluff Cove fully informed on the most recent developments, was not widely circulated.

The ship did not anchor in Fitzroy beside *Sir Tristram* until 1130Z, less than half an hour before sunrise. Because *Sir Tristram* had been placed (as recommended) under a cliff, *Sir Galahad* had to anchor in an exposed position. The arrival came as a complete surprise to those at Fitzroy, who were preoccupied with unloading *Sir Tristram*, although the brigade HQ at Darwin had known about the sailing. The re-broadcast station on Pleasant Peak was not yet fully operational. With 5 Infantry Brigade's radio vehicles yet to be transferred from Darwin, Southby-Tailyour had agreed the previous night to send one LCU to Darwin during the night of 7/8 June to collect them. At the time he had no idea that *Sir Galahad* was to arrive in Port Pleasant the next morning. So his efforts to rectify a problem that had left him uninformed aggravated the difficulty caused by an example of the communications problems – the unexpected arrival of the LSL.

While *Sir Galahad* went where she had been told to go, it was not where the Welsh Guards expected to be. Bluff Cove and Fitzroy were close on the map but by no means adjacent. Rather they were either side of a deep-water inlet. The Guards wanted to go to Bluff Cove where they would find the rest of their battalion and did not wish to march what they assumed to be 15 miles from Fitzroy to Bluff Cove. They might have been more relaxed on this score had they known that this had been reduced to six miles as a result of a temporary footbridge constructed at the site of the Fitzroy Bridge which had been blown by the Argentines. Moore, unlike the Guards, was aware of this fact which is why he had been relaxed on the actual point of embarkation. Meanwhile neither the main 5 Infantry Brigade HQ at Darwin nor the advanced HQ at Fitzroy had any clear picture of the planned movements for *Sir Galahad*, and communications between the two elements remained poor. The Major in charge of the Welsh Guards assumed that this night's operation would be the same as that of the previous night.

No preparations had been made for the timely off-load of the new arrival. *Intrepid* had removed her four LCUs that night and, as noted, another was off getting better radio communications. The available LCU and the Mexeflote were loaded with ammunition from *Sir Tristram*. In this confused situation intense discussions soon began about how best to unload. These were not helped by ambiguities in the line of command among the officers directly involved. The only area without controversy was the value of getting Rapier ashore, and this was quickly achieved by a Sea King. The Mexeflote and the LCU began to take ammunition from *Sir Tristram* but the state of the tide would not let them get to the beach until 1300Z. They did, however, get alongside *Sir Galahad* about 1200Z to enable around 100 men to get to shore atop the ammunition. Even at this stage things might have been better had 5 Brigade's liaison officer for amphibious warfare not been immobilised with a bad back and stuck on *Fearless*. Southby-Tailyour attempted to fill the gap by inviting the Welsh Guards to disembark (there is some dispute as to whether they were ordered) but they did not do so. The officer-in-charge's orders were for his men to stay with their equipment and to go to Bluff Cove. They had been messed around for three days and he wanted to be sure that they would now be taken by sea to where they were supposed to be.

Although the sky was clear the risk of an Argentine air attack was not to the fore. If the Welsh Guards had experienced the first days after the San Carlos landing their attitudes might have been different but they had missed that stage of the war. Since 25 May the Argentine Air Force had been frustrated by the weather and so had had little chance to show the aggressive spirit that had caused so much consternation after the landing at San Carlos. Nor were the other sources of delay appreciated – the time to get advice from 5 Infantry Brigade's Forward HQ at Fitzroy because of the tortuous communications involved or that once the Mexeflote and LCUs had left it would take so long for them to return.

At the same time the officer in charge of the Field Ambulance did want to get his unit ashore and insisted that it should be a priority. A plan had been devised to land the 16 Field Ambulance by Mexeflote and to take the Welsh Guards by LCU in two trips to Bluff Cove, but when the first asset to arrive back at *Sir Galahad* at 1500Z was the LCU, the officer in charge of the Field Ambulance insisted that it should be used to get his men ashore. In the event this meant that when the attack came, they were able to treat the wounded more effectively than would otherwise have been possible. Embarked in *Sir Galahad* were two companies, each of 120 men (Prince of Wales' and No. 3), plus 1 Mortar Platoon, 'A' Echelon and Engineers Troop, of 35, 45 and 40 men respectively. The equipment included 300 Mortar ammunition (HE and smoke), 66mm rockets, mine clearing equipment, 10 cases Hexamine, and an electrical generator. After 16 Field Ambulance had disembarked at 1530Z the LCU was instructed to proceed to the jetty in Fitzroy to collect fuel and rations, known to be in short supply at Bluff Cove. This caused a further delay in the eventual embarkation of the Welsh Guards. The LCU arrived back at *Sir Galahad* at 1610Z. In a final twist, a hydraulic failure of the ramp lowering equipment on the LCU meant that stores had to be moved for unloading by crane. Eventually, the Welsh Guards commenced loading into an LCU at 1630Z.

The attack

How serious was the risk of air attack judged to be? Woodward was certainly not complacent but his main concern had been San Carlos. There, on 6 June, could still be found the *Nordic Ferry* (now nearly empty), *Elk* (still with most of the 105mm ammunition on board), *Blue Rover*, *Sir Tristram* (loading for Fitzroy), *Sir Geraint* (loading for Teal), *Sir Galahad* (waiting to load), and *Sir Lancelot* (now repaired and temporarily the home for the SAS). Unloading in Teal was *Sir Percivale*. At Teal Rapier was now operational but Rapier units had yet to deploy to Fitzroy. Although that night the *Blue Rover* and *Nordic Ferry* left, the *Baltic Ferry* replaced them with more 5 Infantry Brigade stores and ammunition along with the *Norland*, coming in to embark the rest of the Goose Green prisoners. Reviewing all this activity Woodward signalled his concern: 'The enemy may well have in mind one last major attack' – but it was San Carlos that worried him. Moreover, he now had another problem. His engineers on *Hermes* had been warning him for two weeks that the boiler needed cleaning to maintain power and this task would take three to four days. So long as his forces were on the offensive this may not matter, but it could make a serious difference if the Argentine fleet came out and he had to retreat quickly to give the SSNs space to sink Argentine ships. Also thinking ahead he knew that *Illustrious* might not be available until September while the airstrip at San Carlos kept on being put out of action by a variety of mishaps. He therefore judged that the boiler cleaning had to go on. The number of Harrier patrols was maintained by passing those from *Hermes* through *Invincible* when they needed re-fuelling.

It was on 6 June that the Argentines first became aware of the reinforcement operation in the Fitzroy/Bluff Cove area.[9] Then, on 8 June, a sighting of a 'British landing craft' was reported at 1515Z. There would have been Argentine raids that day without this sighting but it provided a focal point for Argentine efforts. That meant that the San Carlos area was left alone, although inside the inlet there were still many ships at anchor. If they had wanted to interfere with the build-up at Teal Inlet they were now too late. LSLs were no longer needed to bring in 3 Commando Brigade supplies. If the first Argentine sortie had been against a real target, and this had become known, then the disembarkation from *Sir Galahad* might have been expedited. The British, however, were quite unaware that two Skyhawks, acting on faulty intelligence, had already attacked non-targets on Broken Island, south of Pebble Island, at 1300Z.

Now with the accurate intelligence about the landing craft at Fitzroy, four Mirage 3s and eight A4Bs were sent from Rio Gallegos, and six Daggers from Rio Grande. The makeshift early warning system in operation, including the submarine *Valiant*, led the British to expect a major raid around 1700Z, a little later than it actually arrived. Argentine tactics were to use the Mirage 3s as a diversion, hoping to draw off any Harriers, while the Daggers and the A4Bs would fly low, hoping to stay undetected. As they came in the Mirages were detected and the other aircraft were not. Around 1650Z they reached the southern entrance to Falkland Sound. The Daggers turned north and came upon *Plymouth* off Chancho Point, engaged in naval gunfire support; the Skyhawks flew over Bluff Cove and then as they circled south over the sea spotted the two LSLs in Port Pleasant.

Plymouth had been warned of a possible air raid and had decided to stop firing its guns. It was returning to San Carlos as five Daggers armed with bombs and cannon appeared. They were engaged with Sea Cat and 20mm guns, in two cases apparently successfully, although in fact all aircraft returned home safely. *Exeter* sent Sea Harriers to chase them but they were too far away. Four bombs hit *Plymouth* but none exploded, although one caused a depth charge on the flight deck to explode. It managed to get back to San Carlos Water and with some assistance from other ships extinguished all fires. There were five casualties, one of which was serious.

Just before 1700Z *Exeter* had raised a general alarm but by the time the air defence teams in the two LSLs at Fitzroy began to prepare themselves it was too late. Only two of the four Rapier fire units ashore were operational but one had a temporary defect and the other was in a poor position. There were no surface escorts present. The two Harriers that might have been able to help were fruitlessly chasing the Daggers after their attack on *Plymouth*. Just after 1700Z the Skyhawks flew into Port Pleasant from seaward. Three bombs hit *Sir Galahad* on the starboard side and while none exploded they immediately caused fierce fires. These were soon out of control. There was little to be done but abandon ship. Helicopters and every vessel available, including lifeboats, were used to get men ashore, often at great risk because of the possibility of being caught by exploding ammunition. The coxswain of the Mexeflote helped up to thirty men escape by inverting a life raft on the deck for use as a landing cushion when they jumped. Field Ambulance personnel still on board treated the injured. Three Sea Kings and one Wessex helicopter winched men to safety as they hovered feet above the burning ship, with minimal visibility because of thick smoke and ammunition constantly exploding. The Commanding Officer of the Welsh Guards later described the bravery of the pilots as 'magnificent to behold'. An Advanced Dressing Station (ADS) was set up ashore and dealt with 135 casualties in the space of 3 hours.

Sir Tristram was also hit by two bombs, neither of which exploded, although a third that hit the water close by did so. Two of the crew were killed in the attack. While the position on *Sir Galahad* was hopeless from the start, that on *Sir Tristram* was not. But with senior officers stunned by the turn of events, the fire spread further than necessary and at about 1750Z, as the evacuation of *Sir Galahad* was completed, the captain ordered that *Sir Tristram* also be abandoned. Eventually the fire burnt itself out but the stores, including ammunition, were eventually recovered. Unlike *Sir Galahad* she was not beyond repair.

That evening there was another Argentine raid, following a similar pattern, with Mirage 3s in a diversionary role. Again there was some notice and two pairs of Sea Harriers were launched to greet the four incoming Skyhawks. The Argentine aircraft survived Rapier, Blowpipe and small arms as they flew past Bluff Cove and then, at the entrance to Choiseul Sound, picked out the *Fearless* LCU. Contrary to instructions, but in light of the pressure to get the Brigade HQ vehicles to Bluff Cove, it was travelling in daylight. It was hit by one bomb, which did not explode, but killed three marines and two naval ratings. Twelve men were rescued by helicopter. The craft remained afloat but when *Monsunen* later attempted to tow her towards Port Pleasant she sank. This time the Skyhawks did not escape: three were shot down with Sidewinders by the first combat air patrol.

Woodward's reaction was that 'the lessons of yesterday should not have needed relearning after D-Day. Our CAP may not arrive in time and our shipborne close in AAW weapon systems are inadequate to meet the near *Kamikaze* tactics of the Arg Air Force who are no doubt kept coming by totally false information.' This led him to instruct that, as a general rule, ships were not to deploy beyond Rapier or main battle group cover in daylight or reasonable flying weather without his express permission or in dire emergency.

The attacks caused the death of 39 Welsh Guards, one member of Field Ambulance and two Royal Engineers, plus five of the crew of *Sir Galahad* (including two Chinese) and two of *Sir Tristram* (both Chinese), making 49 in total. A further 115 were wounded of whom about 75 were suffering relatively minor injuries, mostly burns, but the remaining 40 were serious. The Task Force had effectively lost two Companies of Guards and a mortar platoon, a troop of sappers with vital equipment and the majority of the equipment of the Field Ambulance. The survivors were flown back to San Carlos.

Moore spoke directly to Fieldhouse on the phone as soon as he heard of the attack, the first time he had done so since arriving at the Falklands. He pointed out that the position was not disastrous and at worst the delay to the final assault would be four days. The fit Guardsmen were re-equipped and taken under command of 40 Commando. At the same time, two companies of 40 Commando were released to come under the command of 1 Welsh Guards, but the rest, despite Thompson's urgings that they all be brought forward, were to continue to protect the San Carlos base. The incident had been terrible in itself, but now 5 Infantry Brigade was fully deployed forward at Fitzroy and Bluff Cove. More weight, nonetheless, had to be put on 3 Commando Brigade's attack, and for this reason the Welsh Guards, along with 2 Para, were put under Thompson's command. The overall effect was to delay by two days the assault on Stanley. If the attacks had come at the start of the transfer process then the impact would have been more severe, but coming at the end it meant that the completion of a difficult process, although marred by a tragic finale, was in practical terms a success.

At a cost of adding to anxiety at home, the Government agreed to a request from the Task Force commanders to hold back the full details of the casualties to encourage the mistaken belief in Buenos Aires that the blow had set back the British far more than was in fact the case. The Argentines believed that future British operations had been hampered because of the loss of some heavy vehicles, supporting arms and provisions as well as many men. This piece of news management came when relations with the media were still strained. After Goose Green very little information had been allowed out from the Falklands – the Chiefs were even cross when the fact that 5 Infantry Brigade was ashore was divulged as that removed any Argentine concerns about a second landing. Suspicions had been growing that MoD would give priority, when transmitting pictures, to the residents of San Carlos offering a Marine a cup of tea, rather than the explosion on HMS *Antelope* (although this became one of the most famous of the war). In addition, the problems of looking after the correspondents became even greater once they had been able to get ashore, especially as there were more opportunities for private enterprise, at which Max Hastings was particularly adept, by thumbing lifts on helicopters and cultivating individual officers who might be looking for sympathetic coverage of their unit's exploits. While the release of details about individuals was supposedly prejudicial to operational security, especially if they were captured and interrogated, publicity could also boost morale, especially after the event. It was noted later that while the report on Fitzroy from ITN's Michael Nicholson referring to a 'day of extraordinary heroism' was released immediately, that from the BBC's Brian Hanrahan, which arrived at the same time, had its release delayed. Hanrahan had referred to a 'setback for the British', and his description of survivors coming off unhurt 'but badly shaken after hearing the cries of men trapped below' was removed.[10]

It was understood that before the event too much information could help the enemy. Goose Green's dramatic impact gave 2 Para a degree of notoriety that other battalions might envy. Unflattering comparisons between the Guards' battalions that had arrived with 5 Infantry Brigade and the hardened marines and paras caused additional resentments. The SAS, normally content for their activities to remain secret, were less sure in this case. After the loss of 18 of their men in a helicopter accident on 19 May, the regiment was keen to have some positive publicity for some of their achievements.[11] Hastings accompanied 42 Commando up to Mount Kent and wrote an article about how the SAS had, with the RM, established strong positions overlooking Stanley. The article was ready for dispatch on 31 May and the SAS, keen to have it published in time for a memorial service for those killed to be held on 1 June, uniquely transmitted the piece using their communication systems so that it arrived back in good time. References to the SAS were still deleted by MoD. A few days later MoD did agree to the publication of another article by Hastings, delivered via the normal means, which recounted the SAS's exploits in South Georgia and the Falklands. The longer the conflict went on the more nerves were apt to get frayed.

This was the context to the first MoD press statement on 9 June indicating that casualties from the attacks on *Sir Tristram* and *Sir Galahad* had been heavy and that 'early reports indicate a number of killed and injured.' Early the next morning reports from Buenos Aires had military experts saying that the Argentine air attacks were likely to cause serious delays to the expected British attack on Stanley, and that '500–900 troops' had been killed or wounded in the attack, an estimate that was later cut to only 350–400. That afternoon, Nott told the Commons that:

> Having consulted the military authorities, I am not prepared at this stage to give the total numbers of our casualties, and to do so could be of assistance to the enemy and put our men at greater risk. Meanwhile next of kin are being informed and I shall give further information as soon as is reasonably possible.

Downing Street was clearly unhappy at the implications for morale at home, of the sort of speculation that was starting to develop, and released figures of about 43 killed and 120 wounded. MoD refused to comment on these figures. Other speculation continued, especially after radio hams picked up reports from a Falkland Island farmer who was an eyewitness of the Fitzroy attack and estimated the casualties to be 220 dead and 400 wounded (these were close to the first estimates sent back to Moore's HQ). This figure was widely reported on 12 June. The next day, after Nott had been able to announce that Mount Longdon, Two Sisters and Mount Harriet had been taken he confirmed the Downing Street figures, 43 men killed and 46 wounded, plus 7 officers and crew of the LSLs killed and 9 injured. In announcing these he explained:

> it was important for success of the land operation that the Argentinians were not able to assess exactly when, how, or in what strength we would attack. It is clear that the Argentinians greatly overestimated the extent of the casualties and damage resulting from their air attack ... We wished them to remain uncertain about our strength on the ground and our capability to mount an early attack.[12]

Battlefield casualty evacuation

The attack had highlighted the importance of the treatment of injuries. In the planning for land operations, it had been recognised that casualty evacuation was not possible overland due to the lack of roads and the difficult terrain, and could not be relied upon by air due to uncertain flying conditions and enemy activity. It was necessary therefore to provide surgical facilities close to the battle area if lives were to be saved. An Advanced Dressing Station (ADS) with 1 Field Surgical Team were to be established in the Forward BMA at Teal Inlet in support of 3 Commando Brigade, while

16 Field Ambulance would form an ADS with surgical facility at Fitzroy in support of 5 Infantry Brigade. The Main Dressing Station would remain at Ajax Bay, and SS *Uganda*, with No 1 Surgical Support Team, would anchor in Berkeley Sound daily at first light to receive casualties. The Surgeon Commander at Ajax Bay, Rick Jolly, initially reported that relationships between the various groups attached to the Medical Squadron were 'unpredictable', particularly over the matter of rivalry between the Marines and Paras. However, Jolly quickly defused the situation by summoning the whole group and stating: 'we have to work together because there are 5,000 potential customers out there who don't care who looks after them, just as long as they get fixed up properly'. Working under the threat of two unexploded bombs in their building from late May, it was a testament to the professionalism of the Medical Squadron that all injured British personnel who reached Ajax Bay alive went out alive.[13] Over 1,000 casualties were received in the MDS and the forward stations at Teal and Fitzroy, of which 650 were the result of combat. Of these only three subsequently died. In all 202 major operations were performed at Ajax Bay, with another 108 at Teal, Fitzroy and SS *Uganda*. Approximately 30 percent of the casualties treated were Argentine. The problems faced often had little to do with the enemy but resulted from the cold, wet and windy conditions and the boggy peat ground of the Falkland Islands. Fifty-seven cases of cold injury were reported to the Field Record Office but the figure could possibly have been higher.

Casualty evacuation was by helicopter, often after ammunition had been taken in on the inward journey. With 3 Commando Brigade was the Air Squadron, with six Scout and nine Gazelle helicopters, while 656 Squadron Army Air Corps operated six Scouts and six Gazelles. The Air Squadron records that in one 24 hour period, 85 casualties were evacuated, while during the whole campaign an estimated 400 casualties were evacuated by the Army Squadron from forward positions.[14] Evacuations at night required use of passive night goggles with which there had been little training. Throughout the campaign one Wessex helicopter was dedicated to the Main Dressing Station for casualty evacuation and medical re-supply and other helicopters were used on an opportunity basis. The arrangement worked well. Pilots, using PNG, evacuated casualties at night and undoubtedly many lives were saved because of this. For the assault on Stanley three dedicated Wessex helicopters were attached to each Advanced Dressing Station (ADS) under local control. This was the maximum number available, but was also considered sufficient to deal with the anticipated casualty load, and allowed flexibility of operation with evacuation to each ADS or to the Main Dressing Station, or to the Hospital Ship as dictated by local circumstances. Returning helicopters brought back medical stores.

After the raid on *Sir Galahad*, which caused losses of men and stores for 16 Field Ambulance, it was re-equipped with one spare set of Surgical Support Team stores and other items from the Para Clearing Troop and the

Medical Squadron. An injured surgeon and anaesthetist declared themselves fit for limited duties. On 10 June the reconstituted Field Ambulance was returned to Fitzroy and the ADS was fully established in time for the assault on Stanley. On 10 June also the Mini Support Surgical Team embarked in HMS *Intrepid* was landed at Ajax Bay to reinforce the Main Dressing Station. In the event fewer casualties resulted than had been forecast and, once established, casualty evacuation was conducted very satisfactorily. Many memoirs of the conflict pay tribute to the role of the chaplains, in circumstances where there were substantial and unusual spiritual needs to be met, and the support required by those dealing with injury and death.

40

TAKING THE HIGH GROUND

The battle for Stanley was about to begin. The Argentine commanders had exhausted their options and could now only reinforce their defences. On 9 June Menendez's Chief of Staff had reached Buenos Aires for consultations. He described the problems of supply but played down difficulties of morale. Galtieri later claimed he had only been asked for 'ten thousand pairs of bootees and long underpants as a change of clothes'. The President pushed for more offensive action, urging that with 'a will and imagination' a counterattack could be mounted. Menendez's plan, which was only marginally less realistic than that proposed by Galtieri, involved using West Falkland as a base to attack the British position at San Carlos and Darwin. Meanwhile the forces at Stanley would take the initiative against the British units moving towards them. All this, however, required more from the Argentine Navy and Air Force, who would have to gain some sort of local superiority around San Carlos and Darwin, than they were able or prepared to deliver. The fact that these plans got as far as they did indicates that the Argentine command was losing its grasp of the situation. All options suffered from a basic lack of intelligence, firepower, air strength and mobility. They could not move sufficient forces into position to catch the British unawares. By considering only ambitious operations they had missed a number of modest but potentially significant possibilities. In the event the discussion of the various plans in Buenos Aires led to an order from Galtieri to Menendez to fight to the end and not surrender.[1]

So in practice all that they could do was hope that the British advance had been dealt a serious blow at Fitzroy, and to wait for the British to come to them, confident at least that their troops were in a decent shape and had, at least for the moment, adequate supplies. A certain amount of patrolling had been undertaken and they had a reasonable notion of British movements, but they were in no position to exploit any intelligence because of a lack of transport. This passivity suited the British but it also left them wondering how best to reduce the preparedness of the Argentine defences. The southern strategy, and the commotion at Fitzroy, had succeeded in persuading the Argentines not to pay as much attention as they might to 3

Commando Brigade, but decisions still had to be made on the best way to breach the outer defensive perimeter.

Thompson had been developing his position on the basis of the southern strategy: 5 Infantry Brigade would keep the Argentines looking in their direction while 3 Commando Brigade prepared to come in from the north-west, attacking Mount Harriet, Two Sisters and Mount Longdon. By 7 June, the Brigade HQ had been established on the slopes of Mount Kent. Thompson informed Moore at 0105Z that day that his brigade should have completed reconnaissance and be ready to attack the three objectives on the night of 8/9 June. At about first light on 8 June Moore cancelled 3 Commando Brigade's plans for the coming night. They were postponed first until the night of 10/11 June and, then by another 24 hours, to the night of 11/12 June. The reasons for the delays holding up 3 Commando Brigade lay partly in the difficulties being faced by 5 Infantry Brigade. They were largely influenced, however, by logistical considerations. Moore had discussed the problem of the necessary ammunition supplies with the commanding officers of the two gunnery regiments. They had about 300 rounds per gun; they wanted about 1000 rounds. With the helicopter lift available it would have taken four days of flying to get that amount of ammunition forward, and experience suggested that because of bad weather, that could easily turn into a whole week. And then, of course, more ammunition was being expended during that period so the time required could easily reach nine days. Balancing the eagerness to move to the final battle and ensuring that there was sufficient ammunition involved a fine judgement. Moore decided that the gunners would have to make do with 500 rounds, accepting that this would make for a very tight situation (in the event at the end of the final battle some guns had barely six rounds left). So the start of the operation was postponed so that the extra supplies could be brought forward.

The first delay on 8 June also reflected a developing disagreement about strategy. Wilson argued for making a narrow breach through the outer perimeter at Mount Harriet, in an attack directly along the Fitzroy-Stanley track. Once the breach had been made all battalions and commandos would pour through, one after the other, and put their whole weight against the inner perimeter. Thompson was unhappy with this. He thought that the whole point of the southern strategy had been to encourage the enemy to assume that the obvious line of attack was being followed, without actually following it. The risk of a narrow front was that Argentine positions on Mount Longdon would be left alone, well placed to observe British moves and direct fire against them. Waters thought that Wilson's approach at least needed careful consideration. Moore took the view that he needed his brigadiers to sign up to an agreed strategy, but he had always assumed that a broad approach would be needed because of the vulnerability of any forces pushing forward on a narrow front to enemy firepower based in the surrounding hills. All the high ground would need to be taken.

These issues were addressed on 8 June at a conference between Thompson, Wilson and Waters on *Fearless*. As they discussed the issues news came in of the loss of *Sir Galahad* and that changed the balance of the argument. The attack left 5 Infantry Brigade in a weaker position and led Moore to place more reliance on 3 Commando Brigade. The brigades were to be regrouped with 2 Para and 1 Welsh Guards (less the two companies who had suffered casualties at Fitzroy plus two companies from 40 Commando who had replaced them) coming under the command of Thompson. Wilson, bothered with a severe head cold and now suspecting that Moore was favouring his fellow Royal Marines, saw his brigade's units being transferred and its role being diminished. He later observed:

> I think we started to suffer to some extent from what appeared to be cap-badge rivalry, when it seemed that most of the resources were being allocated to the other brigade. And therefore my people started to feel that they were not only deprived, but had been, shall we say, cast into the role of the Cinderella of the Falklands.[2]

The reality was that Moore had come to share the doubts about Wilson as a commander. He was sure that Thompson could manage three battalion battles simultaneously, although this would be an enormous responsibility, but he did not want Wilson to be fighting more than one at a time. Moore's operational order, OpO 2/82, issued on 9 June, now envisaged a phase one, in which the enhanced 3 Commando Brigade would commence a night attack on Mount Harriet and Two Sisters, to be followed by 5 Infantry Brigade's attacks on Tumbledown Mountain and Mount William. Phase three would be to secure Sapper Hill. These attacks would be reinforced by naval gunfire support at night with air support during the day. Longdon was still not included but Moore gave Thompson 'discretion on whether or not to attack Longdon'.

Wilson would now concentrate 5 Infantry Brigade in the Bluff Cove area until 3 Commando Brigade was secure on its objectives at Mount Longdon, Two Sisters and Mount Harriet. The Gurkhas and Scots Guards would then patrol forward vigorously against Tumbledown Mountain and Mount William. If necessary they would mount full attacks on these features from the southwest. Early on 10 June, one Gurkha company moved forward from Bluff Cove close to Mount Challenger to establish a base from which to carry out aggressive patrolling against Mount William. This task was cancelled and the company withdrew. In doing so it was noticed by Argentine observers who directed considerable quantities of shell fire against it. Meanwhile the rest of the Gurkhas moved forward, carrying mortars and anti-tank weapons over very rough ground, to a new defensive position forward of 1 Welsh Guards. There were some problems between the two battalions as a result of poor radio contact and liaison and a clash was only narrowly averted. The Welsh

Guards' War Diary complained that: '1/7 GR were very difficult to deal with as they did not know the location of their fwd posns, nor did they answer to their C/S'. The Gurkhas spent 11 June consolidating their position. This was initially under enemy 155mm shell fire that wounded four men and only slackened after counter-battery fire was directed in return.

On 10 June Moore had been obliged to respond to a report that Argentine forces might attempt a heliborne attack or parachute drop on West Falkland, which led him to request Woodward to keep aircraft on stand-by, and then a report that four Pucaras had bombed and strafed 3 Para on the northern slopes of Mount Kent before returning to Stanley. No damage had been caused but Moore was worried that the airport was still in use and requested another Black Buck raid on the morning of 12 June. The raid was mounted but was ineffective. At 2120Z on 13 June, Woodward reported to CINCFLEET that: 'PR of Stanley airfield today shows BLACK BUCK 7 bombs dropped on identical line to BLACK BUCK 2 without damage to the target'.

Air and naval suport

One lesson from Darwin/Goose Green was that a lack of artillery and insufficient ammunition had almost resulted in a dire outcome. In the future there was to be much more fire power right forward with the rifle sections, including machine guns, 66mm, 84mm and Milan. Another was that fighting in daylight in open terrain allowed the enemy to see British forces approaching, even when several miles away. They would then be vulnerable to machine gun and artillery fire. The Argentines had more and better night visual aids but the British were better trained for this sort of fighting. Night, wrote Thompson later, 'is still the infantrymen's friend.'

If the idea was to put down maximum fire power on the enemy then this required artillery and the Navy's guns. Thompson found air support too weather dependent and 'so sparse as to be a bonus and nothing more'. In his post-conflict report, he observed that the 'five 105mm light gun batteries were perhaps the battle winning factor.' By bringing down concentrated, accurate fire the enemy's morale was 'crushed' and that of the British troops raised. One of the preparations en route to the South Atlantic had been to train everyone to know how to call for fire and correct it. At times the gunners were bringing down fire within 50 metres of their own troops.

Naval gunfire was always going to be problematic because even when committed there were all sorts of reasons why it suddenly might become unavailable. The vulnerability of ships also meant that the Navy was reluctant to commit ships to this task except for the duration of an actual attack. Thompson argued that gunfire support prior to an attack had an important psychological impact, degrading enemy morale while wearing him down and restricting his freedom of movement. It also was good for the morale of

British troops and conserved artillery ammunition. He argued on 5 June for naval fire every night. 'We must mallet enemy from now on.'

Woodward still had to consider the risks, especially if his ships had to take new positions. On 7 June the MSAs *Cordella*, *Junella* and *Pict* joined the Task Force from South Georgia. Woodward sought an 'early MCM check of Berkeley Sound and approaches plus adjacent harbours before committing ships in support of the battle for Stanley'. Clapp was concerned that the MSAs, with their wire sweep and limited acoustic capability, could not by themselves reduce the threat to an acceptable level and meanwhile ships should remain in 'well tried waters'. There was no evidence of Argentine minelaying anywhere except off Stanley and frequent coastal passages and use of Falkland Sound, Port Salvador and later Port Pleasant increased confidence that the Stanley field was the only one. Nonetheless, Woodward wanted to get ships into Berkeley Sound. He therefore replied to Clapp:

> the present circumstances require the acceptance of risk to find out if Berkeley Sound is mined. The employment and possible loss of an MSA for this purpose is infinitely preferable to that of a frigate, LPD or hospital ship. The earliest deployment of an MSA/MSAs into Berkeley Sound is therefore required preferably at night.

This was accepted.

During this time the SBS and SAS had been working independently to gather information on enemy dispositions along the intended routes of both brigades. On 1 June G Squadron SAS had moved into the Mount Vernet area close to Long Island Mount. This soon led to a clash with an SBS patrol in the same area, which had been dropped off by a Sea King some miles from where it should have been, leading to the death of one SBS man.[3] The patrols were moved further east in order to identify a suitable base area. The entire ridge line of the Murrell River north of Stanley was found to be clear of major enemy forces. Having briefly deployed into this area, the lack of any substantial enemy presence led to the Squadron withdrawing on the night 6/7 June, leaving two patrols on Beagle Ridge observing the landings by transport aircraft at Stanley airport and the enemy's dispositions on Wireless Ridge. When the main battle came they would be joined by a party that would control naval gunfire with great efficiency against targets behind the main Argentine defence line. There they stayed, undetected, until after the surrender, providing a remarkably accurate picture of the Argentines' situation.

The gunfire planned for 9 June was cancelled the previous day well before the attack on *Sir Galahad* and *Sir Tristram* because 5 Infantry Brigade was not ready. On the night of 10 June, *Active* on the southern gunline fired 84 rounds at a company position on Mount Harriet, an ammunition dump near Moody Brook, and another troop position on Mount William, and this was effective. Less so was that by *Arrow* to the north. Meanwhile *Cordella* and *Pict* were inside Berkeley Sound carrying out their MCM task. No mines were found and they reported back that there was low risk to ships engaging in naval bombardment.

Early on 11 June, a Wessex 5 from Teal attacked the Town Hall and police station on Stanley's waterfront with one AS12 missile and great accuracy after the SAS had established that it had some military headquarters function. Another missile malfunctioned and hit the water uncomfortably close to the hospital ship *Bahia Paraiso*. The helicopter escaped as it came under fire but the Argentine defences managed to shoot down one of their own helicopters. At 1130Z, four Sea Harriers braved Argentine air defences around the airport in order to deny it to Pucaras for the coming battle. They tossed twelve 1,000lb VT-fused bombs onto Stanley airfield. Eleven exploded as planned on or above the runway causing fires and damaging a Pucara in the dispersal area, but they did not stop other Pucaras using the runway later that day or C-130s every night.

By the time the battle was ready to start that evening, *Yarmouth*, *Avenger* and *Glamorgan* were on the southern gunline in direct support of 3 Para, 42 Commando and 45 Commando, while *Arrow* was in Berkeley Sound to cover the airfield and other targets near Stanley, controlled by the spotter on Beagle Ridge. Ships were to be ready for the first call for fire by 2359. They had to wait until called to fire their guns, as the initial advance of the attacking troop would be silent. Expenditure per ship was limited to about 300 rounds because of the availability of ammunition for re-supply and barrel life of some guns. Over that night they would fire a total of 788 rounds, by far the heaviest bombardment of the war so far. The gunfire, with land-based artillery, was directed at reported troop positions on Mount Harriet, Mount Longdon, Wireless Ridge and west of Stanley. One bombardment at 0425Z on 11 June detonated an enemy ammunition dump on Mount Harriet.

The results were impressive, marred by a stray round landing in Stanley, killing two civilians and wounding some others. A third died three days later. John Smith wrote in his diary, that night 'was the most incredible, frightening one yet. Hundreds of shells were fired, which screamed and whistled over the town for hours on end – it's non-stop.' By 0530Z on 12 June *Arrow* had completed its task, and *Glamorgan* and *Yarmouth* stopped just over half an hour later. *Avenger* remained on the gunline.

At this point *Glamorgan*, anxious to get back to the carrier group, crossed the south-west corner of the Exocet danger area, and at 0637Z the shore-based Exocet missile hit her. The incoming missiles had been detected by both *Avenger* and *Yarmouth*, and also by *Glamorgan*, allowing it time to fire Sea Cat and turn hard away to present a stern aspect, probably just enough to prevent catastrophic damage. The missile struck the top edge of the flight deck port side. When it detonated a large hole was blasted in the flight deck and a small one in the crew's galley deck below. The ship continued to steam and quickly left the Exocet danger area. The *Yarmouth* and *Avenger* closed to assist, but *Glamorgan*'s fire fighters tackled the blaze effectively. The steam plant was undamaged and so Captain Barrow decided to return to the Task Force with the two frigates in company. The fires had been extinguished by 1000. Thirteen men were dead and 15 injured. The SeaSlug and Sea Cat systems had been knocked out, and the helicopter lost, but everything else was serviceable. Woodward signalled: 'While I am very sad at the casualty list, I am glad to note that you are the first warship in the world to survive an Exocet attack'.

Mount Longdon

During 11 June the land forces made their own preparations for the evening's operations. The last of the companies required was brought up by helicopter. Left to the rear was one company of 40 Commando at San Carlos at 12 hours' notice to establish a presence on West Falkland, two Welsh Guards companies being re-equipped, also at San Carlos, and a company of 1/7 Gurkha Rifles at Darwin. Moore and his Tactical Headquarters had deployed to Fitzroy, leaving the Main HQ in *Fearless*.

Thompson's plan was that 3 Para would first advance on to Mount Longdon and then 42 Commando would attack Mount Harriet from the south while 45 Commando would attack Two Sisters from the north-west. If these positions were successfully taken and the opportunity existed, Thompson told the Commandos and the battalions to prepare to exploit forward, so 3 Para would look to Wireless Ridge and 45 Commando to Tumbledown, supported by 42 Commando. As they did not have a role in securing a start line, 2 Para were to move down the axis between 3 Para and 45 Commando, and be ready to support either. If 45 Commando went forward they were to be ready to clear and hold Two Sisters. 1 Welsh Guards were to secure the start line for 42 Commando and remain in reserve, prepared to reinforce the assault on Mount Harriet and to clear and hold the mountain if 42 Commando exploited forward. Arrangements were made for casualties to be evacuated south to Fitzroy using 5 Infantry Brigade facilities as well as 3 Commando Brigade's own Field Ambulance at Teal Inlet. Thompson gave H-Hour for phase one as 0001Z on 12 June and for phase two 0030Z for 42 Commando and 0100Z for 45 Commando. As the units prepared to move Moore sent them the following message at 1317Z on 11 June:

> As you prepare for battle I send you all my best wishes. I know that none of us expects a walkover. There will be hard fighting but the reputations of all units in this formation are that they fight hard and they win. I know that all of you are keen to uphold those reputations and I am confident that you will do so. The Navy has got us here and will, as you all know, continue to give all the support it can. May God go with you.

On 10 June Colonel Pike gave out his orders to 3 Para for the coming battle. He stressed that the battalion was to move as far east as possible towards Stanley: 'We were to exploit to the full our opportunities. If a Parachute Battalion couldn't do it then nobody could. It was now the time to pressurise the enemy.'

Assessments of the strength of the enemy had vacillated. A couple of days earlier, various approaches had been explored by patrols with civilians, including Peck, serving as guides. They concluded that 'there may not be as much on the Mount Longdon feature as had been once believed'. The next night there was further reconnaissance and an observation post was established to observe the enemy's rear positions. By 11 June the best intelligence was that they would be facing the Argentine 7th Infantry Regiment, probably three companies totalling some 800 men, who would be well dug in, with good defences, backed by three 105mm guns at Moody Brook and 155mm on Sapper Hill. Pike observed that the enemy had been gearing themselves up for an amphibious assault from the south, possibly confirmed for them by 5 Infantry Brigade's landing at Bluff Cove. After the battle, information gleaned from enemy prisoners indicated that the position had been held by some 220 men, 60–80 of whom were from 7th Infantry Regiment; of the rest 100 were Marines, with the remainder being small packets from other units.[4] Later a sergeant in 3 Para cast a professional eye over how the defenders could have made life more difficult for the British and turned the rocky ridge into a fortress. Their positions, however, were poorly sited and constructed, without barbed wire or sandbags. The minefields had not been laid properly nor had they patrolled to get the measure of their opponents. Even so, this was such a natural defensive position that, however poor the preparations, the Argentine units would be hard to displace.[5]

This would be the first serious battle since Goose Green. Little had happened since then to convince 3 Commando Brigade that they were fighting a particularly capable opponent, but the Argentines had demonstrated some fighting spirit at Goose Green and there could be no certainty that they would break quickly under pressure. The plan was to advance south-east from the start line with A Company on the left, directed against the north-east spur of Mount Longdon (Wing Forward), B Company on the right, to move in the dead ground eastwards to tackle the summit (Fly Half and Full Back), and C Company in the rear, to support either company or pass through them to subsequent objectives on Wireless Ridge. Pike later noted that the long, narrow and broken summit of the feature dictated that only one company could effectively fight along it at a time:

Outflanking was not a sound option, because of known further enemy company positions on Wireless Ridge (to the east) and a large minefield to the south. The summit of the feature also dominated the very open ground around it for several thousand metres, adding to the hazards of such movements, even by night.

As the track east from Mount Kent was also needed by 45 Commando for their attack on Two Sisters, the vehicle-borne part of the company, the Mortars and some of the Milans, could not advance until later. The other weapons, six machine guns and five Milan firing posts with 15 missiles, were to be manpacked forward.

The attack was to rely on stealth rather than softening up the enemy through preliminary bombardment. This drew on what had been a successful pattern of patrolling, during which units had managed regularly to move close to Argentine positions without detection. As there was a long distance to cover before Longdon would be reached, the troops would be extremely vulnerable to artillery fire if they had been noticed by the Argentines. Pike was concerned that prior bombardment would have alerted the defending forces, although others took the view that there would be no particular reason for the Argentines to assume that this was any different from previous shelling. Leaving aside the positive reasons for attempting to advance by stealth there really was no alternative. Thompson had to manage three attacks that night and there was not enough ammunition for preliminary bombardments on all objectives (some support was made available to 42 Commando). If it was used up in a bombardment to soften up the enemy then there would not be enough left to cope should this process turn out to have been insufficient. If the enemy proved to be stubborn when engaged then extra fire support could become vital. It would be too late to be told that there was nothing left to fire. There are indications that some of 3 Para's officers would have preferred to have the enemy hit hard before the infantry moved in, but not that they made their concerns known to Pike.[6] At any rate the decision was Thompson's and reflected the scarcity of supplies as much as a tactical judgement.

The Battalion moved out just after last light, aiming for silence until contact with the enemy was made. Movement was slow. The Murrell River could only be crossed using a lightweight bridge, and then some platoons got lost. The start line was crossed only 15 minutes late. Major M Argue, the Officer Commanding, B Company, decided to change direction so as to approach the objective direct from the west thus moving well south of the intended route and well to the right of A Company. He believed that: 'if this had not been done and a wider northern route used, more casualties would have been received both from AP mines and enemy gun fire from flank positions'. The initial advance went well: Argentine sentries were 'either badly sited or asleep – and were certainly not using their radar and numerous night-vision devices.'[7] As the platoons began to climb up the feature, a mine wounded one man. The explosion alerted the enemy: the full advantage of surprise was now lost. The attack went 'noisy' and artillery fire began, largely ineffective because of the good cover afforded by the rocks. A Company, meanwhile, met no opposition and was able to get to the top of the ridge, where it came under fire from positions at the eastern end of the main feature. By 0128Z all units were engaged with the enemy (see map on p. 628).

Soon A Company was pinned down by sniper fire, and had to wait until the way was cleared out by B Company. Several machine gun positions were knocked out by 5 Platoon of B Company using anti-tank weapons and hand grenades, while 4 Platoon engaged targets further to the east. Further south, 6 Platoon had unknowingly by-passed an enemy position that now fired into their rear, killing four men and wounding eight before the position was cleared. The Platoon Commander requested that he be allowed to go firm so that he could reorganise, recover casualties and treat them. This was granted, although he was warned that he might need to provide support for 4 or 5 Platoon in dealing with their immediate problem. Both these platoons were in an area vulnerable to a well-sighted Argentine position, from which they faced machine gun and sniper fire. A burst of fire killed one man of 4 Platoon and wounded six more, including the Platoon Commander. At this point Sergeant Ian McKay, taking control of 4 Platoon, determined to take out the Argentine position. He led four men, all of whom were killed or wounded, but he succeeded in knocking out the trenches supporting the machine-gun 'sangar'. Before he could attack this last position he was killed. For this brave action he was later awarded a posthumous VC. It succeeded in reducing the firepower facing B Company, and van der Bijl has this attack turning the tide in favour of 3 Para,[8] though further attacks were repulsed and more casualties were sustained.

A Company was still pinned down by enemy fire from the top of Mount Longdon. Several snipers were successfully engaged until B Company was so close that the firing had to stop while the companies joined. They brought together their firepower, but artillery was proving ineffective while naval gunfire support from *Avenger* was of marginal benefit. Seeing for himself the parlous position of his men, Argue decided to withdraw 5 Platoon and the remnants of 4 Platoon to a safe distance to allow them to regroup and for more effective shelling of the enemy position, which was then achieved. There was a possibility of sending C Company on a flanking movement, but it was not clear what they would face and they could not expect artillery support because they would be out of range, and one source suggests doubts about the company commander's ability to cope.[9] In spite of the strong enemy fire, B Company reported to Pike at 0330Z that: 'there are a few well sited auto wpons but believe little resistance left. Do not think it necessary for C/S 3 [C Company] to pass thro us yet. We will keep knocking the enemy bit by bit.' Nonetheless, enemy artillery and mortar fire was hitting A and C Companies with increasing accuracy. The enemy positions were bombarded intensively and B Company advanced again, clearing a position at a cost of one man killed and one wounded before coming under heavy fire from both flanks, leading to another three men being wounded. Argue was now concerned that his numbers were becoming

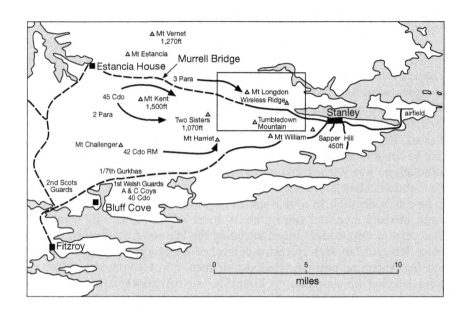

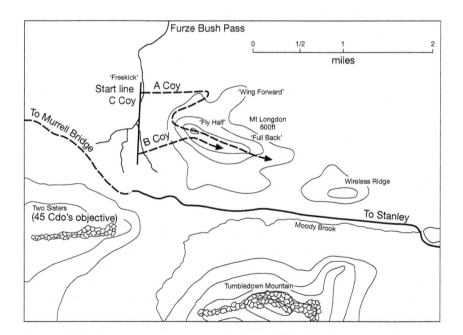

Map 12 Mount Longdon

critical. Aware that A Company could not make progress from where they were on the northern slopes, Pike ordered them to pull back and move through the western end of Mount Longdon, and then pass through B Company. This eased the pressure on B Company, although it continued to take substantial 105mm artillery bombardment, leading to a fatal casualty and four injuries. Argentine resistance was yet to be broken. By early morning the Company had taken 50 per cent casualties and medical teams were severely stretched.

At 0725Z Pike could report to Thompson that B Company had taken its objective, with considerable casualties, and that A Company would pass through and take the east end of Mount Longdon by first light. Pike noted: 'There is fierce resistance on feature and it is difficult to pinpoint the exact locations of the enemy positions amongst the rocks'. Thompson was becoming concerned that 3 Para was being fought to a standstill. He told 3 Para that: 'We are going to reinforce you with 2 PARA but need to know which flank you want them on and how you will tie up with them'. A patrol from D Company was dispatched to rendezvous with 2 Para and guide them up and through C Company.

A Company, commanded by Major D Collett, now carried the assault forward. An initial attempt to outflank the enemy from the north failed in the face of heavy fire from machine guns and snipers. The Company moved back and round to the western end of Mount Longdon. As it passed through a suspected minefield a mine injured one man. A Company moved into the rocks on the northern side of the western crest. A Company wanted to avoid the fate of B Company and decided on a slow advance over the ridge, with heavy supporting fire from the Support Group, methodically clearing positions, to reduce the risk of being attacked from the rear. The fire had to be halted when it began to threaten A Company. Soon some enemy could be seen withdrawing to the east and Argentine positions were gradually cleared. A Platoon moved forward to take over and hold the extreme eastern end of Mount Longdon, a long, narrow forward slope running towards Wireless Ridge.

At 1028Z, Collett told Pike that his company was now on what was described as 'a very extensive position' with support weapons. Soon 3 Para could report that Mount Longdon itself was secure and that C Company was moving east towards Wireless Ridge to take out a particularly trouble-some position. Daybreak came as A Company reorganised, fortunately with a heavy mist. This hid, at least for some time, the position from the surrounding enemy-held features. Collett later recalled: 'The sight of groups of young soldiers, tired, grim-faced but clearly triumphant, moving through the mist to check the enemy dead, with bayonets still fixed, will remain forever vivid in the memory'. The assault had lasted some ten hours and cost 18 men killed and some 40 wounded. Over 50 enemy dead were counted and a similar number were taken prisoner.[10]

At 1150Z 3 Para reported a good view of Wireless Ridge and an opportunity to move forward, but Thompson cautioned against 'getting caught out on a limb'. Collett later acknowledged that: 'any further advance eastward in daylight would have been at great cost from both direct and indirect fire on and behind Tumbledown'. The snipers and rocket launchers on Mount Tumbledown were well sited to harass 3 Para and this forced them to dig in only on the northern slopes. Pike reported at 1515Z, that 'Mt Longdon under continual heavy shell fire and we are sustaining further casualties'. A further four men were killed and several more wounded by this fire. Retaliation came in the form of artillery fire directed against enemy positions, although there were more targets than could possibly be engaged. As the position stabilised, 3 Para began to prepare for its next task, the capture of the Moody Brook area. H-Hour would be 0400Z on 15 June.

Two Sisters

At the centre of 3 Commando Brigade's attack was 45 Commando's assault against the twin peaks known as Two Sisters. It was held by B Company of the 6th Argentine Infantry Regiment and a reinforced C Company from the 4th.[11] In the days leading to 11 June, units from the commando had gradually moved forward. On the night of 8/9 June the Commanding Officer, Lt. Colonel Whitehead, had deployed two strong patrols onto the peaks. They had to withdraw as a result of enemy fire. Further patrols over the night 9/10 June led to an enemy patrol being ambushed and a machine gun post destroyed. More seriously, a combination of lost communications and bad weather led to a clash between groups of Marines, resulting in four killed and three wounded. These patrols did identify a likely approach from the east foot of Mount Kent found to be clear of mines.

The attack on Two Sisters would begin when X Company, 45 Commando, would come in directly from the west, seizing the western peak, known as *Long Toenail*, thereby capturing the enemy's attention, and enabling Y and Z Companies to attack the eastern part of the feature, called *Summer Days,* from the north-west. The entire commando would then regroup and assault Mount Tumbledown. As with Mount Longdon the idea was for the attack to begin silent with artillery and mortars coming in later. Unfortunately, poor ground conditions, the heavy carriage of Milan Firing Posts and navigational errors meant that X Company was delayed, and at 0416Z on 12 June Whitehead, conscious that he had to take advantage of the night, decided to advance without waiting for X Company to complete its attack. Nonetheless, X Company caught up and soon secured its first objective. As the attack went 'noisy', they moved as fast as possible, and without effective fire support, up the ridge to the west.

The intense activity as X Company reached its objective and drove away the defending Argentine troops, may have distracted the units defending the other peak (Summer Days). Meanwhile Y Company also captured its first objective at 0530Z and, with Z Company, pushed on. Enemy machine guns were well sited among the rocks and they held up both X and Z Companies. They were soon targeted by enemy mortar and artillery fire, including 155mm shells. They called in artillery and mortar fire. Effective support was also coming in from *Glamorgan*, which fired 261 shells during the battle, before leaving to its own encounter with a land-based Exocet. To avoid being pinned down by enemy fire, and fully exploiting their own firepower, Z Company charged forward. This limited Y Company's options until Z Company had reached their objective. With the two peaks now secure, Whitehead, well forward, ordered Y Company to move between them. This spirited assault by the leading elements meant that by 0640Z all three companies had reached the top of the ridge. More enemy positions were soon eliminated, and by 0818Z the final objective on Two Sisters was occupied. Soon the whole position was considered secure.

The enemy defences on Two Sisters had revolved around six machine gun strong points, some containing .50 heavy machine guns. Only the more experienced Argentine troops had defended what was potentially an extremely strong position. The Marines concluded that 'although some enemy will stand and fight quite bravely, majority of them will run when confronted by aggressive and determined troops'. Their casualties had been kept down to four men killed and ten wounded. Argentine dead were put at ten with another 50 wounded and 54 taken prisoner.

After the commando had regrouped Whitehead offered to press on to Tumbledown. Thompson preferred to wait. Ammunition needed to be brought forward for the guns. Mount Harriet was not yet taken, while Argentine positions on Tumbledown were presumed to be strong. Instead the battle was followed by another two days of patrolling (12 and 13 June). On 13 June, the commando was told that its next task would be to secure Sapper Hill and then to support the Welsh Guards in their attack on Stanley Common (see map on p. 632).

Mount Harriet

Mount Harriet was the responsibility of 42 Commando. The Marines had engaged in aggressive patrolling in preparation. This was hazardous, often carried out in appalling weather and observed by enemy patrols. There were a number of engagements, as the Marines sought to harass the enemy with direct and indirect fire. One action on the night of 8/9 June resulted in up to six enemy soldiers killed.[12] These important patrols led to a reappraisal of the initial plan, which had been to move across from Wall Mountain to Mount Harriet. This was clearly what the Argentines expected and the ground was probably mined. The patrols were told instead to investigate the possibility of a right hook from the line of the track, which would be more

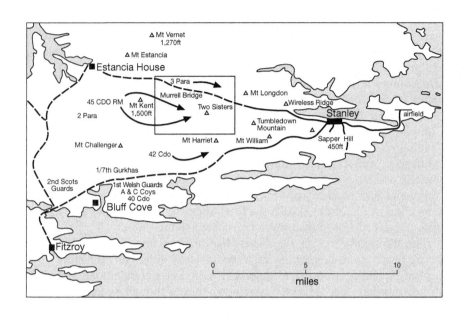

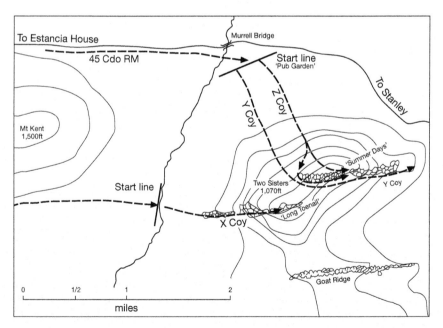

Map 13 Two Sisters

likely to surprise the defenders. Eventually a suitable mine-free route was identified south of the track. The enemy positions appeared to be concentrated on the north and east slopes of Mount Harriet. By 9 June, the Commanding Officer, Lt. Colonel Nick Vaux, felt that he had a sufficiently clear picture of enemy defences and patrolling was concluded.

The enemy position on Mount Harriet was considered to be very strong, in something of a natural fortress, possibly the toughest nut of all to crack.[13] Here were to be found two strong rifle companies of the 4th Infantry Regiment, supported by a reconnaissance platoon and heavy mortars. Vaux's plan depended on catching the Argentine defences by surprise by attacking from the rear. Welsh Guards were to secure the start line for 42 Commando, and to that end late on 10 June the Blues and Royals used their light tanks to ferry a platoon to locate and clear the area. There then followed a series of signals indicating that the platoon had been delivered to the wrong place, some way from its objective, and was disoriented. It had to return to battalion HQ. The next evening, after last light, the Reconnaissance Platoon with a Milan Firing Post, moved forward to secure the forward position and start line. A troop of J Company had already gone ahead to mark the route and drop off two Milan Sections, one immediately south of Mount Harriet near the track to the west and the second to the Stanley-Goose Green track to the east. It was supposed to meet up with the Welsh Guards although it did not find them until well after the planned time, causing some anxiety about the potential for another friendly fire incident and irritation at the delay. Vaux had been unconvinced that it was wise to have such a late attachment of Welsh Guards to an action for which they had not sufficient time to prepare (see map on p. 635).

Guides from J Company also led K and L Companies, who had moved forward from Mount Challenger, along the cleared route. Uniquely, because of concerns about supplies, 42 Commando was allowed diversionary fire, to deceive the enemy as to the point of attack. Some 40 salvos of gunfire from *Yarmouth* were brought down on the western end of Mount Harriet as K Company crossed the start line at 0200Z, while other salvos hit enemy positions between Mount Harriet and Goat Ridge to the north. For some twenty minutes K Company moved quietly and speedily up the steep slopes without drawing fire. The Argentines were taken almost completely by surprise and the leading elements of K Company were within 150 metres of the summit before the startled enemy showed any reaction. Helped by supporting artillery fire, K Company cleared the enemy positions. Vaux later recorded the 'overwhelming advantage' provided by over 1,000 shells or bombs, 'all of them instantly, precisely laid to cover movement, suppress defensive fire, break up resistance.'[14] By 0240Z 42 Commando could report that the east end of Mount Harriet was secure although under heavy enemy machine gun fire. Four 120mm mortars were captured as well as several prisoners, mostly young conscripts. L Company advanced on the western end of

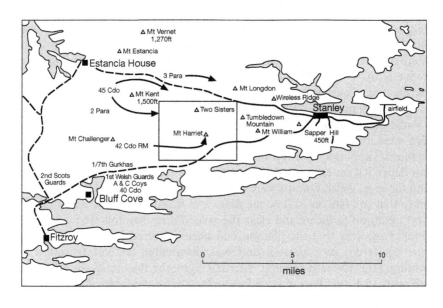

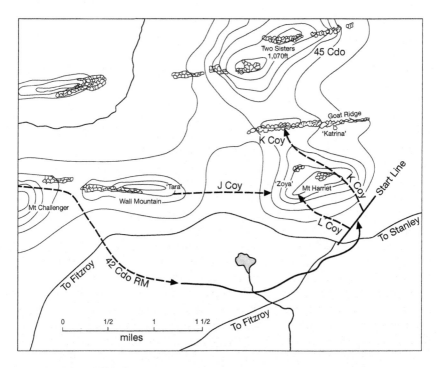

Map 14 Mount Harriet

the feature shortly after 0300Z, again supported by accurate and intense naval gunfire. This time resistance was more serious, and it came from a number of strong enemy positions, with machine guns and snipers, backed by artillery and mortar fire. The return fire from L Company was also landing at times uncomfortably close to K Company. Nonetheless, after sorting this out and methodically clearing Argentine machine gun positions using Milan, the Company was able to get to the western end of Mount Harriet, by which time it had acquired numerous prisoners.

At 0600Z Vaux modified the plan, ordering L Company to maintain their momentum by pushing straight on to Goat Ridge while K Company consolidated on the east end of Mount Harriet in preparation for a counter-attack. One hour later, L Company was still fighting through isolated posts and clearing out snipers. At least one machine gun position had been destroyed by artillery fire and another by a Milan. J Company and Vaux's Tactical HQ moved forward with the Rifle Companies in the hope of getting to Tumbledown, pushing through a minefield in order to do so, but in the event it took until 1030Z before the whole position was secured. As many as 300 prisoners now had to be processed, including a Lieutenant Colonel carrying valuable intelligence material.

Casualties had been relatively light, with two killed and 13 wounded. The Argentines lost ten killed and 53 wounded. A strong position had been taken as a result of an imaginative plan. The Argentine troops had evidently left in haste, apparent from the debris of personal possessions as well as good-quality equipment. The stubborn resistance exhibited elsewhere was absent as a result of the British coming from an unexpected direction with intensive supporting fire. Another symptom of the disarray this caused lay in reports from K Company of several incidents of Argentine officers and NCOs firing at their own men as they tried to surrender (encouraging the marines to target these officers). Soon 42 Commando was helping the 2 Scots Guards observe the enemy's positions on Tumbledown, and on 13 June it was ordered, with 45 Commando, to prepare to reinforce or exploit 5 Infantry Brigade's attack on Tumbledown and Mount William the coming night. Moore had spent a frustrating time for much of the battle, with his communications down, unable to evaluate progress. Now, relieved, he could prepare for the final to Stanley.

41

THE FINAL BATTLE

The islanders

The closer the battle got to Stanley the more the civilian population was at risk. There was some discussion about whether to seek to arrange special protection for the islanders so as not to inhibit the British military advance. Under Article 17 of the 4th Geneva Convention (protection of civilians) Argentine forces were obliged to 'endeavour to conclude local agreements for the removal from besieged or encircled areas, of wounded, sick, infirm, and aged persons, children and maternity cases, and for the passage of ministers of all religions, medical personnel and medical equipment on their way to such areas', while under Article 34 hostage-taking was prohibited, and under Article 49, they should 'not detain protected persons in an area particularly exposed to the dangers of war unless the security of the population or imperative military reasons so demand.'

It was, however, difficult to raise these issues directly with the Argentines, as it would provide an opportunity for procrastination and the political implications of encouraging a move out of Stanley were mixed. Nonetheless, the conclusion from a meeting of senior civilian and military officials in London on 7 June was that the UK had a duty under the Convention at least to consider asking the Argentines to allow some, if not all, of the civilians to leave Stanley. All that was done for the moment was to draw Woodward's attention to the relevant articles. There was no requirement to give instructions to him in one direction or the other, but there was a need to ensure that the British had fulfilled their obligations under the Convention.

It was unclear what could be done to render the islanders safer. Encouraging congregation in one building, such as the cathedral, would risk an even greater catastrophe if a stray shell hit it. Any evacuation would be hampered by the vulnerability and scarcity of helicopters. The Government could only assume – or hope – that from the time that British forces had begun attacking the airport and various targets in and around Stanley in early May, the civilians would have been able to practise safety drills and that shelters would have been organised. The incarceration of civilians in a single building at Goose Green did not give confidence, however.

The Argentines assured the islanders that they were concerned about their safety. Residents were under a sunset to dawn curfew. This meant effectively they must stay inside from 1800 to 0630 local time. Group activities were discouraged and a total blackout was enforced. Although most people appeared to be living in their own houses during the day, they moved to stone shelters for the curfew. A group of islanders established themselves on 24 April, with an Argentine representative present, to help and advise Stanley residents on how best to prepare for an eventual conflict. Action taken included stone buildings allocated as shelters; Stanley town divided into six areas, each with an appointed warden; and the establishment of 'safe houses' where people could spend the night if they felt unsafe in their own home. These more robust buildings were marked with a civil defence sign, although the islanders were correctly concerned that the markings required by Argentina meant very little to British observers.

Air and sea power

On the morning of 12 June the Argentine High Command were said to be claiming that a British assault force, consisting of some 4500 men, was being contained at Mount Longdon and Mount Harriet, as well as reporting, more accurately, a frigate being badly damaged by a land-based missile. The truth could not be withheld from the Argentine garrison and it was assumed that they must now be disheartened. Their fresh rations had supposedly expired on 10 June. There were reports that there had been no bread for a month, and that many Argentine troops suffered from 'protein deficiencies, advanced malnutrition and the beginnings of serious psychiatric problems'. Air strikes against the British land forces had been ineffective so far, while attacks on ships could do little to reverse a rapidly deteriorating tactical situation for Argentine ground forces.

The final maximum air effort against the advancing British troops took place on 13 June, comprising 18 sorties. The far more extensive Sea Harrier combat air patrols now possible made the Argentine task even more difficult than before. Thus, at about 1450Z, the first formation of four Daggers turned back without releasing weapons. They did come across *Cardiff*'s Lynx, which was caught by surprise but the pilot managed to escape the attack through skilful manoeuvring. Then at 1510Z seven A4B Skyhawks (an eighth having aborted early) came over Berkeley Sound, and attacked the Mount Kent area from the east, dropping bombs on and around the 3 Commando Brigade HQ. Moore and Thompson were consulting at the time. Bombs landed uncomfortably close to the two commanders but with the peat muffling the explosions nobody was hurt. Three light helicopters were damaged. The Skyhawks also fired cannon at two airborne transport helicopters but again no serious harm was done. Although they were engaged by Blowpipe and small arms, and later by Rapier, and suffered some damage, they all got back to base. The attack was generally inconsequential but it indicated what might have been if the Argentines had thought harder about their air attack priorities, and also if the 3 Commando Brigade O Group had not been postponed for a couple of hours. Otherwise a far larger group of senior officers would have presented attractive targets. Concluding that the position of his headquarters had been compromised, Thompson decided that it had to be moved, a time-consuming task over rough terrain and with nightfall approaching.[1]

At 1855Z another two pairs of Daggers approached Falkland Sound but turned away when Sea Harriers came towards them. As they did so a pair of Mirage 3 fighters that had been on a diversionary mission also turned away. Later that night came the final Argentine air raid. A pair of Canberras, escorted by a pair of Mirage 3s, dropped bombs harmlessly in the Mount Kent/Two Sisters area. A Sea Dart from *Cardiff* took out the leading Canberra while the other escaped, as did the two Mirages. That night a final C130 managed to land and, after a delay, get away from Stanley. Another was deterred because of the presence of a combat air patrol. On 14 June it appeared that HMS *Penelope*, then escorting the *Nordic Ferry*, had come under an Exocet attack from a Super Etendard using the cover of Mirage. It fired chaff and assumed the missile had self-destructed after diverting. It was later judged that there had been no attack.

Early on 12 June, at 0850Z, there was the last Vulcan raid on Stanley airfield – BLACK BUCK SEVEN. The intention was to attack the airfield parking and storage area with VT fused air-burst bombs, but impact fusing was set in error, and the 21 bombs fell wide of the target. Later, three pairs of GR3s, operating direct from *Hermes*, made attacks on gun positions and troops in the open in the vicinity of Sapper Hill. Several of the aircraft received minor damage from AA fire. On 13 June came the last GR3 raid. This time it was decided to make another effort with a laser guided bomb. At 1500Z an infantry position on Mount William received a direct hit, and at 1900Z a 105mm gun position in the Moody Brook valley took another. At last, just as the campaign was coming to an end, the command and control systems were working well to get the most out of the GR3's ground attack capabilities.

In terms of naval gunfire support, problems were starting to develop with a shortage of both ships and ammunition. Woodward was becoming extremely concerned about his 4.5″ ammunition stock, with only some 2,500 Mk8 rounds remaining. There were better stocks of Mk6 but *Plymouth* and *Glamorgan* were now damaged and *Antrim* was in South Georgia, so these could only be used by *Yarmouth*. Moreover after the attack on *Glamorgan* it was now thought prudent to extend the Exocet danger area. The approach to the southern gun-line had become even narrower. At the same time, because the efforts on 11 June had been so successful the remaining Argentine targets were all within range of the northern gun-line. It was therefore decided to position all ships providing naval gunfire support in Berkeley Sound.

On the night of 12 June 186 rounds were fired by *Arrow* and *Active* at targets behind the front line around Moody Brook, Sapper Hill and the Racecourse. They included two Argentine battery positions that were hit. At 1507Z on 13 June Moore told Woodward that 5 Infantry Brigade's attack on Wireless Ridge, Tumbledown Mountain and Mount William would take place the coming night, with H-Hour set at 0100Z. The attack initially would be silent but could go noisy at any time. Four NGS ships were requested from 2359Z to 0600Z, and if possible for later. Moore recognised that the southern gun-line might be unusable because of the Exocet threat but he hoped that the northern line could handle three ships with a reserve ship at 20 minutes' notice. Woodward's diary recorded just how difficult it was becoming to meet these requests: only three ships without a major operational defect; almost half the destroyer/frigate force with 'near zero capability.' He concluded 'Frankly, if the Args could only breathe on us, we'd fall over!'[2] The four NGS ships – *Avenger, Yarmouth, Active* and *Ambuscade* – were to operate again from Berkeley Sound, and again 300 rounds per ship were allocated. Woodward warned that there could only be one more comparable operation after this night, at least using Mk8 rounds. The option of using Mk6 stocks had been extended by the return of *Plymouth*.

On the morning of 13 June the artillery engaged 42 targets and 1,620 rounds were fired. In support of the final attacks and the advance to Stanley, a further 5,500 rounds were fired onto 40 targets. The naval bombardment did not really get going until almost 0300Z and lasted for four hours, but it was the heaviest of the war with 856 rounds providing close support for the advancing troops, and attacking known enemy gun and troop positions. If the Argentines had not surrendered there would have been little to spare for subsequent operations. In retrospect it was regretted that so much scarce ammunition had been used up prior to this moment in harassing attacks. When the campaign ended there was barely enough ammunition left for a further two days' bombardment, and further supplies weeks away.

In position

The encirclement of Stanley was to be completed by 5 Infantry Brigade. Critical to the plan was the seizure of Tumbledown, the task of the 2 Scots Guards, as 1/7 Gurkha Rifles advanced to Mount William, followed by 1 Welsh Guards moving through to take Sapper Hill. At the same time 2 Para of 3 Commando Brigade, supported by Special Forces, would take Wireless Ridge.

The Scots Guards and the Gurkhas had expected to be flown forward to their assembly areas after first light 12 June, but available helicopters had been replenishing 3 Commando Brigade with artillery ammunition and so movement was delayed. At 1600Z Wilson held an orders group with the

Commanding Officers of the Scots Guards, Gurkhas and 4 Field Regiment. Having visited Thompson's HQ he was now confident that all their objectives had been secured so that the enemy was not in a position to interfere with his brigade's advance. For that reason he wanted to move immediately. There was an obvious advantage in doing so, not least the possibility that his brigade might be able to make the crucial breakthrough to Stanley. There were however risks in rushing forward. There had not been proper reconnaissance and there was uncertainty about the Argentine strength. In addition, the support helicopters were still at full stretch moving forward troops, guns and ammunition for the next phase of the battle, and bringing back wounded and prisoners. During the day it became evident that 5 Infantry Brigade would not be ready to attack that night and also that more ammunition must be brought up to 3 Commando Brigade positions. Although many in 3 Commando Brigade were unhappy about the delay, not least because they were being shelled, Moore agreed to a 24-hour postponement. In permitting the delay, Moore was particularly influenced by the problems being faced coping with the large number of prisoners taken during 3 Commando Brigade's attacks. He signalled Fieldhouse that night, requesting 'your speedy advice on the resolution of POW repatriation which is out of all proportion to the slender land force available resources not totally committed to battle'. Those Welsh Guards and Gurkhas not involved in 3 Commando Brigade operations assisted in the processing of the prisoners who were eventually evacuated to the 'cage' at Fitzroy. Some limited intelligence was provided. When late on 12 June, 42 Commando delivered 120 prisoners from Mount Harriet to the Welsh Guards, the sole officer with them could offer little concrete information, except his opinion that defeat was inevitable and that West Falkland would follow Stanley in surrendering.

The company commanders and artillery representatives from 5 Infantry Brigade took advantage of the delay to examine their objectives from the recently taken vantage points on Mount Harriet and Goat Ridge. Shortly before last light helicopters flew the Heavy Machine Gun Platoon and some rations – the first for many men for 48 hours – forward to the Gurkhas. Soon after 1200Z on 13 June the Scots Guards started to move by helicopter to an assembly area just west of Mount Harriet. The battalion dug in under sporadic enemy shell fire that caused one minor casualty. The Gurkhas started to move forward by helicopter at 1640. A number of groups were dropped in the wrong place and the remainder of the daylight hours were spent in reorganising the battalion, a process hampered by occasional, but at times heavy, enemy artillery and mortar fire.

The Welsh Guards reverted back to 5 Infantry Brigade on 13 June to support the coming night's attacks, although there was some confusion as 3 Commando Brigade apparently thought that the battalion was staying with them. Thompson intended to airlift the Welsh Guards north of Tumbledown Mountain so that it could act as a reserve during the first three phases of the planned rolling advance on Stanley, and then, in the fourth phase, move to capture part of Stanley Common to the east of Sapper Hill. After the Commanding Officer of the Welsh Guards, Lt. Col. Rickett, had accepted these orders, Wilson briefed him with alternative plans. The battalion was to act as reserve while the Scots Guards seized Mount Tumbledown and the Gurkhas took Mount William and would then clear the ground south of Mount William. The Reconnaissance Platoon was immediately tasked to confirm a sighting of three enemy companies south of Mount William. The ground turned out to be clear. As Rickett was about to hold his orders groups, his second-in-command came back with the alternative orders from 3 Commando Brigade. Rickett attempted to get some clarification as to which set of orders he should act upon and, having failed to do so, decided to proceed with Wilson's plan.

At 2300Z 1WG moved off towards its assembly area and then to its forward position. Its route had previously been cleared and used by 42 Commando, but it strayed slightly and two minefields were encountered. They walked in single file without incident, until one of the Marines (attached from 40 Commando) trod on a mine and lost his foot. His troop commander edged forward to assist him and in doing so stood on a mine himself and blew off part of his foot. Both men had to be evacuated by helicopter. As enemy fire came down on the battalion, the Engineer Reconnaissance team with the lead company was painstakingly clearing more mines. This took some five hours. It reached its forward position at 0700Z. Neither the Scots Guards nor the Gurkhas called for assistance and the battalion remained uncommitted. At 0915Z, it left the assembly area and withdrew to its previous location, which was less exposed. There Rickett attempted to clarify the battalion's position and get his attachment to 5 Infantry Brigade agreed. Meanwhile, the Reconnaissance Platoon returned confirming that the three enemy companies believed to be south of Mount William did not exist. The battalion was now advised that no move before 1400Z was expected.

Tumbledown

The plan developed by 2 Scots Guards and approved by Wilson to capture Tumbledown Mountain involved three companies launching the attack from the west, but preceded by a diversionary company attack from the south. A full attack from the south appeared too dangerous (especially if, as originally envisaged, in daylight) for the approaches were well defended, including by minefields. If successful, this operation would mean that all other features would be dominated by Tumbledown's height (229 metres as against Mount William's 213 metres and the 138 metres of Sapper Hill) and so be rendered untenable.

The Argentine 5 Infantry Marine Battalion held these three features with 703 men. They were conscripts, but from the class of 1962 and so more experienced than the new recruits, and supported by heavy machine guns and six 105mm guns. The Marines were better looked after than their army comrades and had undergone some training in night fighting. This was recognised in British assessments, where the Marines were described as being of 'higher calibre than soldiers already encountered'. Just before the battle, three companies from infantry regiments were attached to the marines. They enjoyed excellent overhead protection in the caves, which had been dug out from under the rocks, and the defensive positions were well arranged. Nor were they going to be taken by surprise. The British attack was expected for the night of 13 June as a result of the pattern and direction of artillery bombardment. The Argentine hope was that if the British could be resisted until the dawn they would be obliged to withdraw.

The Scots Guards were fortunate in being taken by helicopter from Fitzroy to their assembly area. The delay in launching the attack also meant that the plan was well understood at all levels of command. The Commanding Officer's plan required G Company to secure the most westerly rock of the mountain's spine. The Left Flank Company would then move through to clear the slopes and ring contour on the middle summit. The Right Flank Company would then pass through to secure the final ring contour on the summit of the main feature. Once this third objective was secure, the Gurkhas would pass through and establish a fire base on Tumbledown Mountain to support two separate company attacks to capture the north-east spur of Mount Tumbledown and Mount William respectively.

The Argentine positions suffered from British shelling and, on the morning of 13 June, the first laser-guided bomb was successfully delivered by Peter Squires' Harrier GR3. A diversionary attack along the most obvious attacking route was also planned, to be conducted by a force of some thirty men under Major Richard Bethell supported by four tanks of the Blues and Royals. The diversion was due to start at 1230Z but, by that time, no enemy locations had been found. Instead it began that evening. The Scorpion and Scimitar light tanks drove east along the road to attract the enemy's attention and fire. This plan was rapidly curtailed when the lead tank went over a mine, fortunately without casualties. There was still no enemy reaction and so the force had to move on, which it did until it came across a possible enemy sangar. As the assault groups got close to it, snoring was heard, indicating a certain lack of preparedness, and other sangars became visible. These were soon taken out but the many other Argentine positions in the area now opened fire, immediately killing two Guardsmen and injuring four others. It took time for the assault groups to deal with their casualties and direct supporting fire to the enemy trenches, although once this was done the results were impressive. After two hours of fighting the troops began to leave, two getting caught by anti-personnel mines as they did so. Bethell and another were injured by a grenade. By 0430Z on 14 June the infantry had reached the tanks and they withdrew to behind 42

Commando's positions on Mount Harriet. 5 Infantry Brigade's War Diary recorded that:

> Although at first this appears to be a fiasco, it subsequently turned out that the enemy were expecting an attack from the south and this diversion confirmed their expectations and caused them to concentrate on observing to the south and not to the west whence came the real attack.

Although this did not cause any reserves to be redirected, the Argentines were not paying attention as the Scots Guards moved forward.

While this was going on, at 0100Z, G Company had advanced against the background of the noise from the diversionary attack. The sky was lit by starshells fired from the outskirts of Stanley and an artillery battery near the mouth of Moody Brook. Still there was no enemy reaction and the first objective was reached only for it to be found to have been abandoned. The next objective, a machine gun post, was also deserted. As planned, Left Flank Company now advanced through G Company. At this point, 0230Z, Argentine fire opened up. G Company supported with automatic weapons for as long as it was safe for Left Flank Company for them to do so, in the process drawing enemy mortar and shell fire onto their positions.

General John Kiszely later described the attack of the Left Flank Company he was then commanding as a Major:

> [V]ery little went according to plan for us and almost everything that could go wrong did. The enemy – the 5th Marine Battalion – were well dug-in and waited until we were about 100 metres away before opening fire with every weapon they had. In the ensuing fire-fight, half my company headquarters got separated, both forward platoons were pinned down and every time they moved forward, took casualties. We continued to be shelled and mortared, and were unable to 'win the firefight'. Contrary to expectations, the enemy were standing and fighting. The artillery, key to our ability for fire-and-manoeuvre, had a major problem getting on-target. [3]

A number of men were killed and progress through the rocks and crags was slow and painful, not helped by the cold and a gale with wind speeds of up to 40 knots. A breakthrough came when the enemy's communication cable was located and then followed, leading to several sangars and sniper positions, which were then destroyed. Resistance remained fierce, with some of the enemy 'shouting and singing' as they directed fire against the approaching British troops. Matters were not helped by the battalion's mortars sinking into the peat. The Battery Commander was concerned that poor communications made it difficult to locate the Scots Guards' positions, while naval gunfire was not accurate enough to be risked against enemy positions in these circumstances. The NGFO Officer felt that 2 SG Tactical HQ, which remained behind the start line throughout the battle, was too far away from the leading companies to exert positive control.

Wilson pressed the CO, Lt-Col Michael Scott, for progress, complaining that the delay was holding up his formation's entire attack. An officer from the Gurkhas, listening in, waiting to get his own men moving, recalls an intense dialogue. 'The Guards' CO kept his cool and his superior's aggressive questions and hopeful suggestions slowly petered out.' When Wilson came back later the radio was turned off.[4] After three hours of battle, at around 0530Z, Left Flank was still pinned down in atrocious weather. There was no useful way of employing reinforcements from behind, and 2 Para, by then fully occupied on Wireless Ridge, was in no position to help. There was little option but to move forward with available assets. Scott discussed the position over the radio with Kiszely and agreed to advance by getting artillery rounds on target in front of advancing troops, who could follow up with grenades and rifles. Soon four to five enemy sangars were taken. The fighting became close and intense, as the company sought to maintain the momentum of their attack, with Argentine troops being killed by grenades, rifles and bayonets while others gave themselves up. One section commander was shot dead and another man wounded, but still the company moved forward, taking a number of sangars and bunkers at the point of bayonet. As each position was cleared and prisoners held the number of advancing troops was reduced. By the time the summit of the mountain was reached there were only seven men, and of these three, including the Platoon Commander, were immediately cut down by a burst of machine gun fire. At about 0800Z Kiszely found himself holding Tumbledown Mountain with three other men. It took almost 15 minutes before others joined them. A small enemy counter-attack was driven off, although more casualties were taken in the process. As they were being evacuated, the stretcher party received a direct hit from a mortar bomb, killing two and wounding eight. Over 30 Argentine bodies were subsequently recovered and 20 prisoners were taken. The Argentine Commander had been frustrated. His calls for more ammunition to help him resist and even push the British back, had been met by Stanley with orders to withdraw.

At 0905Z with this objective now secure, Right Flank Company, which had remained stationary for over five hours, could take the lead, moving to capture an objective known as '2nd Company', because it was believed that up to one enemy company held the area. They reached Left Flank Company's forward position at about 1000Z. Kiszely briefed the Officer Commanding, Right Flank Company:

En MG and some snipers in the area of the rocky outcrops 2–300[m] ahead ... I can't progress. Enemy are very determined

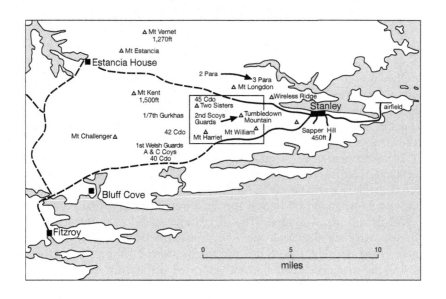

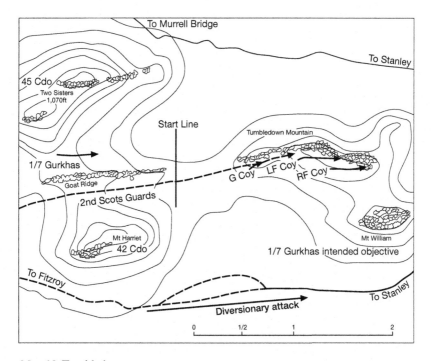

Map 15 Tumbledown

84mm & 66mms don't move them. Only co-ordinated fire support and attacks do. You have to close right close in to beat them. You have only little darkness left. I will show you ground.

The plan was to go round the right flank, with supporting fire from Left Flank Company's area. With only anti-tank weapons and no artillery support the initial assault was successful, and this was soon followed up by assaults by small teams against identified enemy positions on and around a ridge of rocks. By 1200Z this engagement was over, with seven enemy dead and 14 more prisoners. A counter-attack was under preparation by the Argentines when the remaining units were ordered to withdraw under the cover of artillery fire. The whole battle had cost the Scots Guards eight men killed and 35 wounded.[5] Seven of the dead were from Left Flank Company as were 21 of the wounded. The Argentines had lost 16 dead and 45 wounded. Artillery fire could now be directed with great accuracy on to targets in the Stanley area. Soon the enemy started leaving their trenches and walking around. When this was reported a cease-fire was ordered at about 1215Z.

Mount William

During the course of the battle the Gurkha battalion had been moving to be 'ready to go when the word is given' once Tumbledown had been taken. They were then kept behind the Scots Guards to enable them to pass through at the right moment. Because Tumbledown was taking longer than hoped, Moore and Wilson were concerned that if they were held back for too long the Gurkhas might be caught in daylight on ground dominated by the enemy. The Gurkhas were itching to get moving for the same reason. At 0635Z they caught up with the Scots Guards and were then ordered to press on regardless to the north of Tumbledown to their objective. As they advanced eight men were wounded by shell fire and this led to a short delay. When, after first light, the top of Tumbledown was reached it became apparent that the enemy were withdrawing from the Mount William area. The Commanding Officer ordered the two companies to press on and take their objectives as soon as possible. B Company advanced towards the north-east spur of Tumbledown Mountain under cover of some 50 rounds of artillery fire while the Battalion's mortars engaged Mount William. A further delay came at 1355Z when some small arms fire was mistakenly directed against B Company from Scots Guards, fortunately only wounding one man. D Company's advance on Mount William was delayed by the discovery of a minefield. There was little actual opposition and at 1705Z the Gurkhas reported Mount William secure. At this point Wilson was prepared to let the Gurkhas continue their advance but then as Moore took control of the developing situation, they were ordered to wait.

It was assumed that one reason for the Argentine retreat was the fearsome reputation of the Gurkhas. There had been international concerns about the mercenary status of the men from Nepal, and fanciful stories about vicious acts, with heads cut off with Kukris. The fanciful stories continued after this campaign, with stories of Argentine troops running away in the face of a Gurkha advance.[6] The fact that the Gurkhas were not engaged in any major fighting, but could be shown to have influenced the final outcome, was judged to be politically the optimum outcome.

Wireless Ridge

For the operations of the night 11/12 June, 2 Para had been held in reserve, prepared to support either 3 Para's or 45 Commando's attacks. From 1825Z, the battalion was moved by helicopter to Bluff Cove Peak. A troop of light tanks from the Blues and Royals had joined them some days earlier after a remarkable journey across the mountains to Fitzroy. They then had, in effect, to go back again as 2 Para moved to get into position for the final battle. At 2300 the battalion moved across the Murrell Bridge, skirting the minefields on the other side and into position. At about 0730Z on 12 June Brigade HQ ordered a move forward to reinforce 3 Para, because of the heavy losses being sustained on Mount Longdon. Before they reached the front, however, 3 Para had secured their objectives, and so the battalion moved on to an assembly area in Furze Bush Pass. There they dug in. That night, on extremely short notice, they were ordered to attack Wireless Ridge, but the action was postponed until the following night to fit in with 5 Infantry Brigade's delayed schedule. As preparations were being made during 13 June, 2 Para came under attack from the seven Skyhawks. No damage was done but the attack caused some delays. More seriously, new intelligence revealed that Wireless Ridge was better defended than had been thought, requiring some revision to the plan. The position was held by the 7th Infantry Regiment, with four companies occupying all the key objectives that had been set for 2 Para.

Unlike the other battalions fighting in mid-June, 2 Para had known battle, and this would pose special problems of motivation. One officer was later quoted, explaining the problems of the second battle:

When you're on the start line for the first battle, it's just like the movies and you're John Wayne. Especially if you have young troops. They are just ready and anxious to dash off and do some killing. Then when the blood and guts and the gore come home, then you know what battle is all about. Not only if you get hit but it's when you hear the dreadful noise of those incoming shells. No one can tell you what battle is like. You simply have to be there. And it's not a movie. Then when you have to get the men moving again for the second battle, that's your test of leadership and that's when you find out who is a man or not.[7]

One lesson learned by 2 Para was that battle was much easier with plentiful firepower, and that lesson was applied at Wireless Ridge. This was to be the first, and in the event the only, attack of the campaign that would be noisy rather than silent. One reason for this is that this was the only attack of the night for which Thompson had responsibility and he was therefore able to devote his artillery resources to it. These resources had also been replenished as a result of the various delays in launching the attack. Lt. Col Chaundler, the recently-arrived Commanding Officer, knew what his men had been through, and just before the battle he reminded himself of just how disagreeable it could be to be on the receiving end of heavy firepower when he went to the peak of Longdon to observe Argentine positions, a time when it was still under artillery fire. He believed that the enemy would crack under a heavy barrage. He later observed that:

> It was hardly surprising that the impact of fire support was gener-
> ally underestimated. Before the campaign none of us had either
> seen or experienced the effects of bombardment with large quanti-
> ties of high explosives.[8]

The noise accompanying the four-phase night attack would be provided by two batteries of 29 Commando Regiment RA, HMS *Ambuscade*, the mortars of both 2 and 3 Para, the Machine Guns Platoon and, for the first time, the light tanks of the Blues and Royals.

There was in addition to be a diversionary raid conducted by SAS D Squadron against the Cortley Hill area of Stanley, to the east of Wireless Ridge. At 0100Z a mortar base plate and machine gun position was to be established on the high ground 1000 metres west of Blanco Bay to provide fire support, while 17 Troop with six SBS men crossed Port William Water to their objective – the fuel depot. This raid is now described as diversionary, and it might have had that effect. It nonetheless caused some misgivings with Thompson and Chaundler, neither of whom had asked for it. While Special Forces were operating to their east, 2 Para's own operations were restricted, because of the risk of 'blue-on-blue' incidents, and this inhibited intelligence gathering. Furthermore, the SAS objective was to destroy a fuel depot, and it was unclear whether this was the timeliest target when the Argentines were on the verge of defeat and spare fuel might come in handy. Third, if the SAS got into difficulties the Paras might have to provide reinforcements.

As the Special Forces approached Cortley Hill, they faced heavy auto-matic fire and had to withdraw immediately, their three Rigid Raiders all hit and three men wounded.[9] At the same time the Squadron firebase was neutralised by enemy artillery and infantry. The SAS party got ashore on the

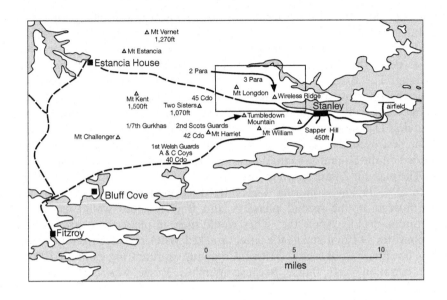

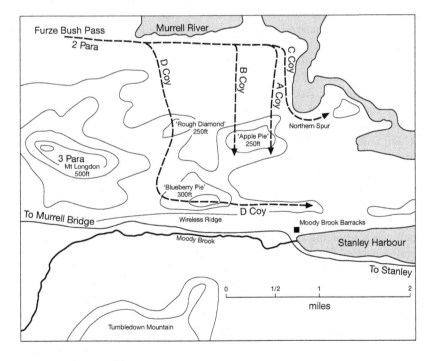

Map 16 Wireless Ridge

banks of the Murrell River to the east of 2 Para, whose attack by then was in full swing. Help was requested from 2 Para, but Thompson was unwilling to distract the battalion when it was already engaged in a difficult operation, to extricate the SAS from what he considered to be a mess of their own making. The Brigade Air Squadron eventually flew a night-time mission, over the ongoing battle, to pick up the wounded. At 0300Z an artillery battery was called in against the enemy guns and they were soon silenced, enabling D Squadron to make their withdrawal. The main target had not been destroyed, but a diversion of sorts had been achieved: enemy fire landed on the Squadron's initial position for an hour after it had departed.

The plan for 2 Para's own attack was that it would open in the first phase with D Company capturing a recently discovered enemy position in the north-west. In the second phase A and B Companies would capture a feature named as 'Apple Pie'. They would then, in phase three, provide fire support for D Company as the latter attacked Wireless Ridge from the west. The last phase would see C (Patrol) Company capture Ring Contour 100 on the battalion's left flank. Because Wireless Ridge was overlooked by Tumbledown, and there was no certainty that this would be taken, it was necessary to take the last ridge line in darkness.

When it came to launching the attack, 2 Para had been operating with little sleep for three nights, and now faced a blizzard as well as Argentine troops. As Chaundler was standing on the start line, about to launch the battalion attack, a marked map sent from Brigade Headquarters was thrust into his hand which showed that there were two companies on Wireless Ridge, and a minefield across his intended axis, between the start line and Apple Pie. He deemed that it was too late to do anything about the mine-field, accepting the risk involved in walking through it, and ordered the attack to begin. As he did so, it began to snow. D Company reached its first objective by 0140Z, finding a few enemy dead. Most had withdrawn. A and B Companies began their advance, with the Argentine troops seen to be running away in front of them. They came across several radios (still switched on), and telephone lines, supporting earlier speculation that this was a Regimental Headquarters. Fewer problems were posed by the trenches, which were easily taken, than by constant Argentine shelling onto their old positions. With their own naval gunfire not yet available, *Yarmouth*, which was supporting the Scots Guards, was borrowed briefly to engage two enemy batteries. Their fire was neutralised, allowing C (Patrol) Company, whose attack had been brought forward, to clear Ring Contour 100 to the east, and again they came across abandoned tents and kit.

D Company was now ready at the west end of the main ridge, a long spine broken in the middle, with each section 800 metres in length. The tanks and the Machine Guns Platoon moved up to provide covering fire. The first feature was taken unopposed, and then the second feature was effectively suppressed by the concentrated firepower from all sources – tanks, machine guns, Milan and ships. The Scimitars and Scorpions of the Blues and Royals found plenty of targets, with enemy positions being given away by use of torches and even the lighting of cigarettes. The gunners were able to observe clearly almost all enemy activity through their night sights. The only mishap came when two vehicles fell into 155mm craters.

Once again, before the advance, a heavy bombardment by all available weapons was applied. This time an artillery shell landed near D Company killing one man and wounding another. The assault, when it started, still faced considerable resistance (including heavy machine gun, recoilless rifle, artillery and mortar fire) causing casualties. The enemy was withdrawing but fighting at the same time as D Company closed, until suddenly the Argentine troops broke and ran, harassed off the ridge by machine gun fire and pursued by D Company. Now D Company came under heavy artillery and small arms fire from Tumbledown Mountain and Mount William, which had not yet been captured by 5 Infantry Brigade. The enemy were believed to be regrouping in the darkness further along the ridge and also to the south in the area of Moody Brook. At 0600Z, 2 Para were given permission by Thompson to go to Moody Brook Camp below the ridge to the south to 'beat it up', with the proviso that: 'they must return to high ground by first light' (see map on p. 649).

Shortly before first light there was a curious but unexpected counter-attack of about platoon strength coming from the Moody Brook area. This was easily repulsed by small arms, mortar and artillery fire. Its failure appeared to have left the Argentines completely demoralised, and they could soon be seen withdrawing in large numbers from Moody Brook, Mount William, Tumbledown Mountain and Sapper Hill. It was now only the Argentine artillery and mortar fire that was causing problems. Slowly the resistance crumbled, and A and B Companies and the light tanks were ordered forward onto Wireless Ridge. Thompson reached the ridge in time to watch Scout helicopters firing SS11s at an artillery battery across the valley from Moody Brook, after a planned air strike had been cancelled due to the weather.

Against what was assumed to be an original strength of about 500, up to 100 Argentine soldiers may have been killed. Only 17 were taken prisoner as the rest fled. The battalion suffered three dead and 11 wounded. The contrast with 2 Para's struggle at Goose Green was marked. All the lessons hard learned at the start of the campaign had been applied, with the determination of the paratroops this time fully complemented by naval gunfire (288 rounds were fired), field artillery and the light tanks. Thompson later judged the Battle of Wireless Ridge to be a true 'all arms' affair.

651

42

SURRENDER

The last skirmish

The intelligence summary for the morning of 14 June concluded that although a few hotheads might still dream of the arrival of significant assistance from West Falkland or from the mainland, with forces in contact, the Argentine Command in Stanley would have a reasonably realistic grasp of the facts; British artillery fire was effectively hitting Argentine positions, and the airfield was under consistent and heavy fire and unusable.

Thompson's plan for the final push against Stanley, OpO 4/82, envisaged another night attack with 3 Para capturing the Essro Building position and moving to the forward edge of the racecourse. 45 Commando would take Sapper Hill and then move to the road north-east to south-west from Stanley, while 42 Commando would take Stanley Common, stopping 600m east of the objective. The second Stanley Common defensive position was to be taken by the Welsh Guards (who over Wilson's objections were to join 3 Commando Brigade). They would then move on to 44 Easting. It soon became apparent that the planned attacks would not be necessary.

As the battles of Wireless Ridge and Tumbledown came to their successful conclusion, reports came back to the brigade headquarters of an enemy in disarray. At 1225Z 2 Scots Guards reported that: 'large no of troops withdrawing from Mt William to Stanley. It looks as if others are about to surrender. Am under regular artillery fire. Large no of enemy withdrawing Moody Brook – possible 300 moving off Sapper Hill to Stanley.' Initially these groups were engaged with artillery fire but this was soon halted and at 1250Z, 3 Para, 42 and 45 Commando were placed at 30 minutes' notice. An air strike onto Sapper Hill was cancelled.

B Company, 2 Para, came off Wireless Ridge through Moody Brook onto the high ground on the other side of the valley. A Company followed onto the Port Stanley Road with D and C Companies behind. Troops were ordered to fire only in self-defence. The Blues and Royals moved east along Wireless Ridge to provide covering fire if necessary. As 2 Para pushed on further than expected, 3 Para sent its forward company to follow as 45 Commando were told to move forward when ready. By 1513Z it was apparent that enemy resistance was all but over. Many troops stood up, threw down their weapons and surrendered. Chaundler had been piling up firepower to pound the retreating Argentine troops but he ordered a cease-fire as it became clear that any further bombardment would be tantamount to the slaughter of a defeated enemy. As he was standing, watching the retreat, Chaundler was rugby-tackled to the ground by Thompson, anxious to prevent 2 Para losing another Commanding Officer to enemy fire. Only then did he appreciate the extent of the Argentine retreat.

Thompson asked Moore whether 3 Commando Brigade should continue advancing. The reply was 'Yes – to the 39 Easting'. The Brigadier recommended that, as speed was now essential, the Welsh Guards stay with 5 Infantry Brigade and press on, as he now intended to do with his Brigade. The final advance was not without its confusions. Thompson intended the two paratroop battalions and 42 Commando to move into Stanley while 45 Commando took Sapper Hill. He then intended 2 Para to move there to allow him to get his Tactical HQ forward and take command of the next phase.

However, Sapper Hill had also been the objective earlier set by Wilson for the Welsh Guards. At 1330Z Moore ordered them to secure Sapper Hill but not to press on to the east until he had firm evidence of an enemy collapse. To this end the two companies of 40 Commando with the Welsh Guards were sent to take up an attacking position south-west of Mount William. Unfortunately, at 1545Z, they were landed by helicopter in the wrong place close to an enemy position just west of Sapper Hill and two men were wounded by enemy fire. This led to a final skirmish with several Argentines killed.[1] After this there was unopposed progress up the Stanley Road, staying clear of the heavily mined verges and adjacent fields. 'As the Battalion approached the summit of Sapper Hill,' the War Diary recorded, 'hope became certainty as more and more deserted enemy positions were passed.' Backed by a troop of Blues and Royals they secured Sapper Hill at 1657Z without opposition. The last obstacle before Stanley was now in the Brigade's hands. 45 Commando's leading elements arrived on foot some 30 minutes later, rather surprised to find the position already occupied. In different circumstances the confusion could have been dangerous.

To the north 3 Para and 42 Commando advanced to join 2 Para near Stanley racecourse, now the designated limit of exploitation. Units were warned to maintain vigilance and normal operational procedures until the negotiations in progress had been completed. Contrary to orders, but with Argentine forces evaporating in front of them, 2 Para walked on. Most of their radios had been turned off, to avoid being stopped, but Thompson who was following close behind, found one connection that worked and ordered 2 Para to stop, which they did close to the racecourse. The only person who carried on walking was the journalist Max Hastings, thereby gaining the scoop of a lifetime.[2] Hastings had already served, almost single-handedly, to throw into relief all the problems with media policy after the landing. Moore later observed that it could have been an embarrassment if someone, including a journalist, had had to be rescued from enemy fire while negotiations were in progress.

In fact, the lack of challenge Hastings faced suggests that Stanley could probably have been taken without too much trouble without any formal negotiations. This might have prevented some of the damage caused by Argentine troops during the last hours between when they knew they had been beaten and had formally surrendered. The main advantage of a negotiated outcome was that the transfer of control should be more orderly and Argentine forces on West Falkland could be included.

At 1810Z Moore signalled Fieldhouse that 3 Commando Brigade with 1 Welsh Guards under its command had pressed forward to 39 Easting (outskirts of Stanley). It was now apparent that the Argentines were not prepared to fight: 'Large numbers stood about, threw weapons down and surrendered'. He reported that at 1505Z on 14 June the Argentine Garrison had indicated a willingness to talk. At 1530Z orders had been given for British ground troops to fire in self-defence only. At 1715Z Woodward signalled to his ships that the situation was very delicate as the mainland reaction to the surrender negotiations was not known. No naval attacks were to take place without further orders, but the Argentine air threat remained and had to be countered.

Negotiations

The form an Argentine surrender might take had been under discussion since Goose Green. On 28 May Woodward wondered whether it might make sense to issue a call to Argentine troops to surrender. The Argentine commander, General Menendez, would be invited to surrender directly by Major General Moore without involving the Argentine Government. A proposed message from Moore to Menendez was drafted, explaining how British forces had Argentine forces dominated and surrounded so that further resistance would only result in substantial extra casualties:

> I call on you, therefore, as one military man to another, to lay down your arms now, with honour to avoid unnecessary bloodshed. This action will be understood by your countrymen and would not lessen the high regard in which the Argentine Armed Forces are held or the military reputation which you have maintained throughout the present conflict. You and your forces would return to your homeland.

The statement went on to propose that 'practical steps' be taken 'to make the necessary arrangements under a local flag of truce.' A further document would then cover the means of notifying outlying troops, laying down of weapons and equipment and the corralling of Argentine troops. Because of the sensitivity of the POW issue, the Prime Minister sought to preserve the

Government's freedom of action by removing the implicit reference to early repatriation. The prospect of repatriation she thought best to appear in leaflets which could be dropped to the Argentine garrison.

The timing of such a call was difficult. It should not be premature:

> if the Argentine garrison is not under sufficient pressure to comply it is likely to be rejected out of hand. If rejected it would be difficult to re-start the process and there could be more rather than less fighting.

Moore's view when the idea was first mooted – in late May – was that such a call would be unlikely to have much effect.[3] Yet there might be other tactical purposes. If pressure built up in the UN Security Council for a cease-fire and Britain found itself isolated, a call for surrender might serve as evidence of a desire to avoid further hostilities.

When the moment was opportune, Fieldhouse envisaged a series of stages in which Britain first applied pressure, and then made an approach taking care not to place Menendez in a position where he subsequently and publicly 'has to eat his words'. This had begun with Argentine forces being bottled up at Stanley and he expected (erroneously) that leaflets would be dropped inviting surrender, but without expecting an early response. He envisaged the possibility of a pause between each tightening of the screw to allow an approach to be made, but it would be militarily unsound and unacceptable to pause in mid-stride, when active operations of an indivisible nature were in progress. He observed to Moore that 'Militarily, we must remain balanced at all times. How we might first make contact with him, on what pretext, is a problem.' If Menendez had a mind to negotiate he would be on the lookout for a pretext, if he did not initiate something himself. 'Your ideas on the bait to be offered are interesting, to which might be added, provision of supplies and medical help to civilians, evacuation of wounded/sick Args from Stanley, or even search, collection and evacuation of wounded on the battlefield.' The terms would also be crucial: the objective was the cessation of fighting and subsequent withdrawal of all Argentine forces from all of the Falkland Islands. Fieldhouse recognised the possibility that in the first instance 'we might have to settle for Port Stanley only because, to hold out for the surrender of all Arg forces FI-wide and thereby incur heavy casualties in fighting in and around Stanley, including possibly civilians, would probably be unacceptable to HMG.' Parallel to local negotiations an approach via diplomatic channels to the Junta might be profitable but that was a matter for the Government at the time: it might just result in the Junta bracing Menendez to refuse to negotiate. To ensure close consultations in any negotiations required between Northwood and Moore, vital because of the political considerations, 'good, and well nigh instant comms from me to you would be essential. Land based SATCOM well forward could achieve this.'

Discussions had also been going on among the senior officers conducting the land battle. As the final battle approached, Moore was of the view that enemy psychology was such that he would 'fight hard until his "military honour" is satisfied and then surrender willingly enough'. This logic developed into the determination to overwhelm at least one major enemy position, so there would be no doubt about a clear British victory. A 'small nibble or pressure' would not work. The question then would be how this point would be recognised and how communications with the enemy would be arranged. A variety of ploys had been considered, including the use of captured Argentine officers as intermediaries.[4] In the event the organisation of the surrender reflected the thinking of Lieutenant Colonel H M Rose, Commanding Officer 22 SAS Regiment. His model for organising a surrender reflected the tactics used by the SAS to persuade terrorists to surrender without bloodshed. Once Moore had two brigades on the high ground west of Stanley the situation would be akin to laying siege to an isolated stronghold, with the civilian population serving as hostages. Rose teamed up with Captain R Bell RM, who had been born in Costa Rica and had acted as interpreter during the surrender talks at Goose Green. They believed that the Argentine Commanders could be susceptible to surrender proposals if appropriately phrased. This was confirmed in discussions on board *Fearless* with an Argentine officer captured at Goose Green, out of which themes emerged relating to Argentine pride, humanitarian sensibilities and desire to be part of the western world. Their conclusion was that some communication should be established as soon as possible and that once the defensive lines around Stanley had been overcome, this should be used to point out the hopelessness of the Argentine position, while acknowledging the bravery of the forces, and the need for a surrender to avoid further loss of life.[5] Moore agreed this strategy, after having checked with Northwood.

As telephone contact with the Argentine Headquarters could not be established, the civilian medical net, based in the hospital in Stanley, was employed, as the Argentine occupation force had not closed this down. On 5 June, Bell came up on the net, explained his status, and got through to an Argentine officer, Captain Melbourne Hussey of the Argentine Navy, the chief administrative officer on Menendez's staff. Hussey insisted that he had no authority to talk to the British but accepted that it would be sensible to maintain a line of communication between the two HQs, and agreed to listen everyday at 1300 local time. Hussey did listen everyday and reported what was said back to Menendez. Bell also promised to maintain a 24-hour listening watch so that the Argentines could call him at any time they wished. The daily messages were then sent but no response came.

On 12 June, after the battles of the previous night, a message was sent, suggesting Britain had a humanitarian interest in avoiding civilian casualties but also in avoiding 'the destruction of the Argentine forces in the Falklands'. The message asserted that Argentine forces 'now have little hope of inflicting a defeat on the British.' It concluded by observing that the British appeal would undoubtedly be heard, because of the means used. 'If you fail to respond to this message and there is unnecessary bloodshed in Port Stanley, the world will judge you accordingly.' Still no response. Nor the next day when a similar message was sent, this time with more emphasis on the hopelessness of the Argentine position. The next day, 14 June, after Moore had ordered British forces to hold fire as Argentine units rushed back to Stanley in retreat, the message was repeated again, pointing again to the dire Argentine situation. ('There is nowhere that is not covered by British artillery fire'.) Indications of a readiness to talk had come shortly before the final battle was due to start when a 'neutral zone' was established in Stanley with the agreement of both countries. Bell's messages concluded by acknowledging 'that the International Red Cross has designated the stone built Cathedral as a refuge and neutral zone for civilians'.[6]

At this point the Argentines had not surrendered. Thompson and Chaundler heard that the Argentines had hoisted a white flag over Stanley as British forces were closing in, an arresting image that was soon repeated in the House of Commons by the Prime Minister, but as they searched with their binoculars none could be seen. At this point the only white flag that had been put out was from a civilian and not by the Argentine forces. Early that morning, however, Menendez had concluded that the remaining defensive lines were unlikely to hold. He rang Galtieri to explain that further resistance would just mean more Argentine casualties. The shocked President, still out of touch, was unwilling to admit the possibility of surrender. He asked, plaintively, about 'sectors of the Argentine Army and the Navy Marines that must organically still exist, still resist in the rear of the first English units.' He urged Menendez to 'use all the means at your disposal and continue fighting with all the intensity with which you are capable.' The Commander explained that he had no means at his disposal, no troops, no high ground, no ammunition. Having given his President this gloomy prognosis, Menendez did soon receive permission to begin negotiations, although with a rather unrealistic mandate.[7]

Dr Alison Bleaney, who knew of the use of the medical net, urged Captain Hussey on humanitarian grounds to make contact with Rose and Bell. Just after 1300 local time, Hussey came on the net and stated that he wished to arrange a meeting between the opposing sides to discuss a possible ceasefire. Then the South Atlantic Command authorised negotiations. Rose and Bell flew by helicopter from *Fearless*, following a pre-described route to the football field behind Government House, after Hussey confirmed that Argentine forces would hold fire. Hussey met Rose and took him to the Secretariat Building, arriving at about 1930Z (1530 local time – a bit later than had been agreed). There Menendez and his staff were waiting. Through the negotiations, Rose was able to use the SAS communications link to stay in touch directly with Fieldhouse at Northwood and *Fearless*. Rose explained that the British Commander demanded an unconditional surrender with honour of all Argentine Forces in the area.

Rose, having been reminded of the importance of the issue by Fieldhouse, also insisted that the West Falkland garrison must be included in the arrangements. Having been told that British troops were already on West Falkland, Menendez left the room for about ten minutes, to talk to his officers, after which he agreed to the point, while warning that this could not be implemented during the hours of darkness. It was agreed that all Argentine troops would move to the area of the isthmus south-west of Stanley airfield and lay down their arms, where a dump would be established. It then became apparent that the disconnected Argentine chains of command meant that Menendez would be unable to surrender the Navy and Air Force. Menendez then contacted Galtieri to obtain assurances on the control of these other forces. A further difficulty then arose on how the POWs should be shipped out. That this had to be done urgently was not doubted. It was becoming apparent that there would be some 11,000 prisoners for whom there were no tents and little water.

The administrative details were then finalised. It was agreed that the formal surrender would be 'low key' with no press present.[8] At 2030Z, Rose sent Moore the following message:

> General Menendez has agreed to a ceasefire in W & E Falkland. DTG Ceasefire effective now. 1 PNG hel will deliver surrender document to Fitzroy at 2200 and the General will arrive at Stanley to sign at 2330. Menendez has reservations about Argentinian Navy & Air Force but will speak to General Galtieri. Troops are moving to the airfield and leaving their weapons at the W end of the isthmus. W Falkland – no further action till first light. The Argentinians will co-operate in the admin of PW. They will also give a deep water harbour and RE Sp with the minefield & loc of mines. Do you accept?

It was then decided to call in General Moore from his HQ to receive the surrender. Moore was extremely nervous about the final negotiations. If it was handled badly then Menendez might walk away and resume fighting in circumstances that would be likely to lead to civilian casualties. He was particularly concerned about the demand for 'unconditional' surrender which he suspected would offend the Argentine sense of honour and which he had concluded was, for all practical purposes, actually irrelevant. Aware of London's demands he dealt with the problem in a traditional way by going incommunicado as he entered his discussions with Menendez, determined to strike out the offending word if Menendez objected – which he did.

Moore arrived in a very heavy snowstorm at about 2330Z. Some time after midnight GMT he signed the 'Instrument of Surrender' with Menendez.

However, to avoid any future misunderstanding over dates and time zones, it was dated 2359Z on 14 June 1982, and was effective from that time. Even without the word 'unconditional', the surrender was total and comprehensive with regard to Argentine personnel and equipment on East and West Falkland and all the outlying islands. At 0200Z 15 June Moore signalled back to London:

> Major General Menendez surrendered to me all the Argentine armed forces in East and West Falkland together with their impedimenta. Arrangements are in hand to assemble the men for return to Argentina, to gather their arms and equipment and to mark and make safe their munitions. The Falkland Islands are once more under the government desired by their inhabitants. God Save the Queen.

The next day 40 Commando HQ and two troops flew to Port Howard on West Falkland by helicopter and took control without any difficulties.

Stanley

Towards noon on 14 June, Terry Spruce, the Falkland Islands Company manager, called everyone together to give a situation report. The population had been advised by the Argentines to remain indoors and Argentine troops were milling about everywhere. John Smith takes up the story in his diary:

> In the afternoon, at about 2.30, Vice-Comodoro Bloomer-Reeve called in to inform Terry Spruce that definite negotiations were progressing for a surrender; these would take time; we were to be patient and all remain in the store ... It was highly dangerous to be on the streets, probably more dangerous that at any other time, but there was no way of letting people know what was happening other than to go out and tell them ... An uncanny stillness had fallen over the town. It took some time for it to sink in that the firing had at last stopped; the silence seemed just as deafening. The air was still; the smoke and smell drifted like a mist. It was very cold; the mud was freezing on the streets ... Argentine troops huddled in groups, bewildered and uncertain as ever ... At about 10.20 we were having a cigarette and a mug of tea discussing the excitement of the day when there was a knock at the back of the door ... Terry Spruce opened up and in walked Patrick Watts, followed by a small British soldier who said, "Hullo, I'm Jeremy Moore. Sorry it's taken rather a long time to get here". Told us that a surrender had just been signed. More British officers then crowded in. The reaction was fantastic. People cried, others cheered; others just stood mesmerised, all by candlelight among the bags of flour and crates of food. He

introduced his officers and then it got through to us. We are free, liberated.[9]

The surrender negotiations were closely followed in London through satellite communications. At 2212 BST the Prime Minister rose in the House of Commons to announce that the negotiations were in progress, and next afternoon made a full statement that began:

> Early this morning in Port Stanley, 74 days after the Falkland Islands were invaded, General Moore accepted from General Menendez the surrender of all Argentine forces in East and West Falkland together with their arms and equipment. In a message to the Commander-in-Chief Fleet, General Moore reported: "The Falkland Islands are once more under the Government desired by their inhabitants. God Save the Queen".

Southern Thule

The Argentine Navy had maintained personnel on Southern Thule since 1976, causing considerable political difficulties for the British Government. Nott enquired on 7 June whether any plans existed for the removal of this Argentine presence. Once the Falkland Islands had successfully been recaptured, the MoD felt that the illegal Argentine presence on Southern Thule would be 'untidy politically'. To allow it to continue would cloud the required distinction between Falkland Island Dependencies and the Antarctic Treaty area and could complicate negotiations after a cease-fire. There was little up-to-date information on the size of the Argentine presence. The most recent indication was obtained in January 1981 when the Argentine icebreaker *Almirante Irizar* re-provisioned the base. There was, however, an assessed strength of 41 personnel. It was unlikely that any military personnel would have anything other than light infantry weapons.[10]

At 2335Z on 14 June, CINCFLEET issued a Warning Order for the repossession of Southern Thule. The next day Woodward suggested that *Endurance* try and establish communications with the Island and pass a message saying that *Endurance* would collect all personnel otherwise 'Southern Thule will be attacked/taken by overwhelming force'. Woodward nominated *Endurance*, *Olmeda*, *Yarmouth* and two Wessex 5s for the task, although the commander at South Georgia argued on 15 June that *Endurance* should do the task alone, in view of likely opposition and more particularly likely weather/ice conditions, supported by the tug *Salvageman*, 16 Marines from M Company, 42 Commando, with a Wessex 5 helicopter and Blowpipe. Later that day *Endurance* did establish communications with Southern Thule, to be told that the ship was in Argentine waters and that Southern Thule was a scientific station. *Endurance* replied that to avoid further bloodshed Southern

Thule should be given up with the complement embarking in *Endurance*, the alternative being an attack by overwhelming force.

The next day Woodward agreed the deployment of *Yarmouth* and *Olmeda*. Another message was sent to the effect that the Argentine party were on the island without permission and that events in the Falkland Islands had demonstrated British resolve. Fieldhouse was concerned that any plan to use *Endurance* alone was too risky and that 'overwhelming force' would be best provided by all ships proceeding to Southern Thule. *Endurance* by itself could not provide gunfire support if this became necessary. The message ended: 'it is necessary to remove Args from Southern Thule now – as opportunity may never occur again without major opposition from world opinion'. At 1541Z he signalled his Operation Order for the recovery of Southern Thule and the codeword KEYHOLE was allocated to the operation. On 17 June at 0230Z *Yarmouth/Olmeda* departed from the carrier group to South Georgia where they picked up the commandos. *Endurance* sailed in company with *Salvageman* at 1600Z and at 1350Z on 19 June they arrived at Southern Thule.

A reconnaissance party was inserted. The Argentines were aware that the British were in the area and were soon encouraged to believe this was a substantial force by spoof messages transmitted by helicopters from *Endurance*. They were seen to be destroying material on the ground. At 0400Z on 20 June all ships rendezvoused north-west of Southern Thule. *Endurance* gave the Argentines until 1130Z to surrender. The Argentine party accepted this just before the deadline and white flags were shown. At 1224Z the eleven Argentines present surrendered to the reconnaissance party and M Company, 42 Commando, landed. After a formal surrender ceremony at 1800Z a search was conducted of the South Thule base, furnishing evidence that it was part of an Argentine meteorological network.[11]

43

AFTER VICTORY

There could be no rest after 15 June, not least because there could be no certainty that the cease-fire would hold, or that some diehard Argentine elements might not try a last desperate attack, shocked by Menendez's abrupt surrender. The fleet had to stay on a high alert until there was confidence that the Argentines had no more fight left in them.

The campaign had been demanding, requiring that troops endure dreadful and physically draining conditions with brief but intense and often vicious moments of combat. Now they had to switch to the post-war tasks of managing prisoners and generally helping put the Falklands together again. Most arrived at Stanley hungry and with little food and water of their own. The small town, with many houses destroyed, could barely cope with the influx. The filtration plant had been damaged during shelling and there was no fresh water. Not surprisingly a degree of looting went on, largely but not solely from Argentine stores. The combination of the lifting tension and the arrival into Stanley of the troops did not always produce the best behaviour. Thompson later recalled:

> I had to get the COs in and line them all up to read the Riot Act.
> Careful and diplomatic work by 3 Commando Brigade's police sorted
> it out – MPs from outside would certainly have caused a riot. I
> banned everyone from the streets of Port Stanley – including myself.

A curfew was imposed and the only pub was put out of bounds.[1] Most islanders were reluctant to be too harsh because of their gratitude at liberation and their awareness of what these young men had been through, but at times their tolerance was tested.

Most of the men wanted to get home, but it was evident that the Falklands would have to be garrisoned for some time. In addition to Argentina deciding to have another go, there were problems such as dealing with poorly laid minefields. The Argentines had laid about 25,000 mines in about 119 minefields that covered a total of twelve square miles of the Falklands. Those laid on beaches were being covered by shifting sands and others had sunk in peat.[2] Wilson, reflecting concerns that he had brought with him from Britain, raised the issue in a long report to the Chief of the General Staff, sent on 16 June. As Commander of 5 Infantry Brigade he reported his concern that having played a major part in the war, if his Brigade was left in a garrison role while 3 Commando Brigade returned to the UK there would be an 'explosive situation'. Not that he was necessarily intending to take his Brigade straight home. After reporting on the excellent shape and morale of his troops, he continued, with what irony it is hard to say, that 'it has been put to me that you might now consider taking advantage of our superb battle fitness to take out Guatemala on our way home and so solve the Belize problem. We are looking for further business.'

In the event 3 Commando Brigade battalions did leave first, with the Paras on *Norland* and most of the Commandos on *Canberra* departing on 25 June, followed later by some companies of 45 Commando on *Stromness* and most of the Brigade HQ, guns, vehicles, light helicopters and so on, on *Fearless* and *Intrepid*. Infantry Brigade battalions sailed on *Norland* and *Uganda* on 18/19 July. Kiszely observes that his battalion was 'singularly unimpressed when we were told we would be the last to go home', yet later mused that this gave his men time to unwind and 'to get the battlefield out of our systems', perhaps helping avoid many of the stress-related problems.[3] The bulk of the Task Force ships returned during July, often to enthusiastic welcomes, although it took until September before *Invincible* was able to get home, as she had to wait until *Illustrious* was fitted out and ready to provide air defences.

Prisoners and cease-fires

As the land campaign approached its climax the War Cabinet's main fear had been of an incomplete victory and in particular a partial cease-fire, not applying to the Falklands as a whole, and Buenos Aires refusing to accept defeat. Just before the fall of Stanley, Pym sent messages to the Foreign Ministers of all the states that had applied economic measures, warning that it could be necessary to maintain the measures until Argentina agreed to cease all hostilities. Britain would be ready for a complete end to hostilities: Argentina would be asked to concur without delay. It was assumed that the allies would be comfortable with this approach. If Argentina accepted then Britain could terminate the Exclusion Zone, promise not to use force except in self-defence, obtain the lifting of economic measures and return Argentine POWs. Pym proposed to work through Washington, to offer this package, to take effect within the minimum possible time after the final cease-fire. Washington might see an opportunity to offer aid to Argentina in reconstructing its economy after the conflict as a way of making a start in mending fences with Latin America.

What had to be made absolutely clear was that there was no question of Britain negotiating about the Falklands as if nothing had happened. Britain now had no interest whatever in proposals for an interim administration prior to talks on the future status of the Islands. The Prime Minister was particularly adamant on this point. While waiting for news of the final night's attacks, she noted that friendly governments should be firmly discouraged from even thinking in these terms. The Argentines had been unwilling to settle on terms at all possible for the UK, and now they had lost their chance. Any Argentine withdrawal would be as a consequence of British military action in exercise of the right of self-defence, and not at all voluntary in compliance with Security Council Resolution 502. The only diplomatic dialogue she could envisage would be with the US Government about arrangements to repatriate Argentine POWs, and she was not even sure about Pym's proposals for discussing a comprehensive cease-fire.

The pressure of events would not allow Britain complete freedom of manoeuvre. The problem of POWs in particular raised issues of practicality as well as principle. The demands of handling, administering and guarding large numbers had become apparent after Goose Green. A cage in which to keep prisoners was constructed at San Carlos but this soon proved to be inadequate for the numbers involved. Following a general surrender of Argentine forces on the Islands there could be as many as 10,000 prisoners. The Geneva Convention of 1949 would not require their return until the formal end of hostilities but the problems of managing such large numbers created an incentive for repatriation even prior to a general surrender. On the other hand, if hostilities were continuing, even if the risk was confined to air or sea attacks from the mainland, evacuation by sea would tie up Task Force ships. Furthermore the return to active service of certain categories of prisoners, for example pilots and Special Forces, would be unwelcome, while other returning prisoners might give the Argentines useful intelligence about Britain's own deployments and strength. While the prisoners were held, there were useful opportunities for interrogation. For these reasons, MoD judged that:

> it would not be difficult to defend a decision to hold Argentine prisoners for longer than we have done so far. The holding of prisoners against a general cease-fire could exert some salutary pressure on the Argentines, although it would require careful presentation.

If prisoners were to be held for any length of time, however, it would be necessary to comply with the very stringent provisions of the Geneva Conventions: evacuation as soon as possible to camps far enough from a combat zone to be out of danger, and not to ships except in transit. Their conditions should be as favourable as those for British forces. They would need to be clothed, fed and given medical attention. Unfortunately there were no facilities on the Falkland Islands which met the requirements, especially with the onset of the Southern winter. In addition, it would not look good if Britain abandoned the norm of early repatriation of prisoners that had already been established by both sides. Presentationally, early repatriation would appear as a humanitarian gesture. It might even do no harm if demoralised Argentine soldiers took back reports of British strength. This led MoD to conclude that the military interest would be best served by continuing to repatriate Argentine prisoners prior to a general surrender of Argentine forces on the Islands. This would, however, be subject to intelligence or other operational requirements in particular cases. Differential treatment was not excluded by the Geneva Conventions. There was also some understanding that it might be useful to hold on to a number of prisoners until there was a complete cessation of hostilities.

As a result of these deliberations, the prisoners taken at Goose Green had been put on ships, mainly the ferry *Norland*, and sent to Montevideo once the Uruguayan Government agreed and arrangements were made to ensure the safety of *Norland* on the return journey. That left about 300 Argentine POWs in the Falkland Islands, of which about 50 were considered to be in a special category for intelligence or specialist reasons. There seemed to be little choice but to bring them to Britain. It was militarily essential to remove POWs from the Falkland Islands as soon as possible and it would be impracticable to set up POW camps on Ascension Island, St Helena or Tristan da Cunha.

As the military campaign concluded different considerations began to apply. Just before Stanley fell Pym considered the role of the prisoners as a diplomatic card. He concluded, in the light of the stringent provisions of the Geneva Conventions, that 'the prisoners should provide a significant element of leverage, though not a really strong one, over Argentina'. He thought it would be desirable to keep back all the Argentine prisoners while negotiations for a general cease-fire continued. If those negotiations dragged on and the retention of all prisoners proved logistically impossible, Pym contended that there would be arguments for returning only a proportion to Argentina so as to maintain some bargaining power.

When the surrender actually came, practical problems soon came to dominate the policy debate. The prior British estimate of the numbers involved was 8–10,000 men, but Menendez gave the impression that he commanded some 15,000 and it was assumed that he should know. The eventual count was 11,848. Whatever the number, the condition of the prisoners was poor: the British blockade had been so successful that the Argentines only had food for three days and very little tentage. In view of the bad weather and lack of shelter there was every incentive to get them home as soon as possible. Some 5,000 of them were embarked on 17 June on *Canberra* and another 1,000 in *Norland*. Equipment captured included 44 Argentine aircraft and helicopters and two long-range warning radars. Most of the aircraft were damaged but six of the helicopters were taken into British service.

There were two complicating factors that encouraged keeping some back, in addition to those who were worth interrogating. One was the need to secure the release of Flight Lieutenant Glover, the only British prisoner held by the Argentines. There had been another – an SAS man captured near Port Howard – but he was released after the West Falkland garrison surrendered. Three British journalists were also being held in Argentina. Sir Michael Beetham, the Chief of Air Staff, expressed concern that the problem could develop from the other direction. If the Argentines knew that Britain was holding a number of prisoners they could decide to hold on to Glover as their counter. For this reason he wanted every effort to secure Glover's release before news leaked out of Britain's intention.

The other reason for holding on to some prisoners was to encourage Argentina to agree to a cessation of hostilities. A message was therefore sent via the Swiss:

> Following the ceasefire in the Falkland Islands, there are a large number of Argentine personnel who will wish to return as soon as possible to their homes and families in Argentina. The British Government is prepared to start the process of repatriation as soon as possible, provided that they receive confirmation from the Argentine Government that there is now a total cessation of hostilities between the two countries and that Argentina is ready to accept the return of Argentine prisoners of war and others from the Falkland Islands and dependencies direct to Argentine ports on British or other ships or aircraft. The British Government would also require confirmation of safe passage for any ships and aircraft used for this purpose. Furthermore once confirmation of the total cessation of hostilities is received, the British Government proposes that the economic measures and exclusion zones instituted by both parties should be lifted and at the same time the British Government would be ready to ask those countries who have imposed economic measures against Argentina to bring them to an end. As soon as an affirmative response is given to these proposals the detailed arrangements for repatriation of Argentine personnel can be notified.

The Argentine reply was that it was inconceivable that any British ship should enter an Argentine port, and that in any case the 'infrastructure' in Argentina for the reception of the soldiers was not ready. There were indications that the prisoners already returned had not yet been allowed by the Argentine authorities to get back to their homes, perhaps indicating anxiety on behalf of the authorities about the stories they would have to tell about the conditions they had endured. Although the Argentine Government argued that a *de facto* cessation existed, the new Foreign Minister, Aguirre Lanari, repeatedly took the line that a *de jure* cessation of hostilities was unacceptable because it imposed a new 'condition' without any sign of the British Government being ready to negotiate on sovereignty. The Argentine Government would not declare a formal end to hostilities in the South

Atlantic until the British Government lifted its 'air and sea blockade' around the Islands. This was what the War Cabinet had feared.

On 18 June the ICRC reported that it had obtained guarantees of safe conduct for *Canberra* and *Norland*, unarmed and unescorted, to put the prisoners ashore at Argentine ports, and for Argentine hospital ships to take sick and wounded prisoners, of which there were about 400, from Stanley. Within a few days all but the special Argentine prisoners were repatriated. There were indications that an Argentine military stand-down was in progress except for the airfield of Rio Grande. Instructions had been issued to British forces to open fire only in self-defence, except against Argentine warships entering the TEZ without due warning: but these instructions were not being made public. Getting clear statements from Buenos Aires was now hampered by the collapse of the Junta. For the moment nobody was in a position to say that hostilities were at an end. According to van der Bijl, who describes tense and difficult dealings with a number of the prisoners, by 20 June 10,250 Argentines had been repatriated through Stanley and Ajax Bay. Remaining were 593 Special Category prisoners, including the Argentine Commander, Major-General Menendez, thirty-five engineers on parole (helping with mine clearing) and 200 conscripts.[4]

It was still proving difficult to get any response from Buenos Aires, even after a moderately cordial message had been conveyed on 3 July. However when the journalists were released in late June, there was talk of a *de facto* cessation of hostilities and on 6 July the Argentine Foreign Minister telephoned the UN Secretary-General to say that his Government had decided to release Flight Lieutenant Glover. The Government therefore decided to issue a statement to the effect that all this added up to a cessation of hostilities and that all prisoners would be released. An approach was also made to the Argentine Government about the disposal of the bodies of Argentine servicemen killed in the Falklands (eventually a substantial cemetery was built for them near Goose Green). By 14 July all the Special Category prisoners had been repatriated.

Ending sanctions

On 22 June the Prime Minister announced to Parliament the lifting of the 200-mile TEZ and its replacement by the Falkland Islands Protection Zone (FIPZ) of 150 miles. Argentine authorities were asked to ensure that their civilian ships and aircraft did not enter the FIPZ unless by prior agreement with the British Government. Argentine military units continued to be excluded. At the Toronto meeting of the IMF on 14 September 1982, the Argentine and British Governments agreed to lift all financial restrictions that had been imposed as a result of the conflict. Blocked accounts in London and Buenos Aires were unfrozen, and financial institutions in the UK were once again free to lend to Argentina (paving the way for British participation in a

January 1983 IMF loan). On the Argentine side, however, the agreement was only partially implemented and a number of restrictions remained in place:

- Argentine Government-appointed overseers in British company subsidiaries remained in place;
- British companies were required to seek special permission to repatriate dividends, royalties and service fees;
- British companies were excluded from public sector contracts, including those funded by the World Bank.

In addition to these financial restrictions, the embargo on trade between the UK and Argentina remained in place. British ships were banned from Argentine ports, as Argentine ships were in Britain, and the Aerolineas Argentinas operating permit in the UK remained suspended. The Argentine Government had terminated the UK-Argentine Air Services Agreement on 3 June 1982, even though it was part of the agreement to provide one year's notice of termination.

Meanwhile, the failure of Argentina to confirm the cessation of hostilities meant that Britain wanted sanctions to stay in place. Other European countries, however, were already moving to lift them. On 20 June the EC Foreign Ministers decided to do so, against British objections, although they did agree to maintain an arms embargo. The British had no objections to informal talks taking place between individual members of the Community and Argentina, but would not accept a formal agreement with the Community on any subject until there was satisfaction that Argentine discrimination against the UK across the board had ceased. The EC Commission endorsed this line, saying that contact between the Community and Argentina would be necessary but could not be institutionalised while Argentina did not have equal relations with all member states.

It was evident that a number of countries, including the US, France and Germany, would become increasingly reluctant to maintain the arms embargo, and the problems encountered over the renewal of economic sanctions against Argentina showed the dangers if Britain tried to overplay its hand. The best approach seemed to be to concentrate on the most sensitive items and ask to be kept fully informed about sales, and to be vigilant in policing end-user certificates. For example, the French Government would now send Exocets to Peru – the order was fulfilled in August – but it claimed to have secured an undertaking that they would not be diverted. There would be more serious difficulties with the supply of British equipment to Germany for incorporation into frigates being built for Argentina in a German shipyard if British firms were prohibited from supplying the equipment in accordance with their contracts. Pym proposed that the remaining equipment should now be delivered to Germany on the basis of an understanding with the Federal Government that the frigates would not be delivered to Argentina without prior agreement with the UK. In the event the first frigate was delivered in late 1982, with the two TR1700 submarines following in 1984. In 1986 Rolls-Royce was refused permission to supply spares for the ships.

A contract to supply 24 Hawk trainer aircraft to Venezuela had been signed in March before the Falklands crisis, but its implementation had been delayed by the crisis, and in May the President of Venezuela had stated that the contract would be frozen. The two main arguments against the sale were the possibility that the aircraft might be used by Venezuela against Guyana or that Venezuela might make the aircraft available to Argentina if hostilities were resumed over the Falklands. But the Venezuelans had repeatedly indicated their intention to seek a peaceful solution to their dispute with Guyana, and were unlikely to direct the aircraft to Argentina. The French had offered the Alphajet in place of the Hawk. Pym therefore recommended that the contract should go ahead. The Hawk contract with Venezuela was of great importance to British Aerospace. It would maintain 6,000 jobs and avoid large-scale redundancies. There was a similar problem over the supply to Venezuela of the balance of 20 bomb carriers for Canberra aircraft from an order placed well before the Falkland crisis. The risk of diversion to Argentina seemed small, and he recommended that this contract also should be allowed to proceed. He took the view that the Germans, the French, the Italians and possibly the Russians would supply South American countries with arms if the UK was reluctant to do so and it would be better if these countries possessed British equipment with which British experts were familiar and over which the Government could exercise some degree of control.

Thanksgiving

The question of the return of the British dead was a sensitive one. Past practice had always been to bury the dead where they fell, but families were given a choice. The bodies of the servicemen killed in action could be buried in a military cemetery on the Falklands or repatriated for burial to the UK. Families of those whose bodies were buried on the Falklands or had died at sea would be offered the opportunity of visiting the Falklands at public expense. Most elected to have the bodies returned to Britain for burial. In late October Nott attended a ceremony at the permanent cemetery for the 16 war dead, including Lt Col Jones VC, whose families had chosen for them to remain in the Islands, at a site at San Carlos overlooking 3 Commando Brigade's landing point. After a helicopter salute and a piper's lament, another 65 bodies sailed for home on RFA *Bedivere* (one to Hong Kong). A wreath was thrown into the sea in memory of those – 174 – who had died at sea. In February 1983 a cemetery for the Argentine war dead was consecrated at a site by Goose Green. It took until 1991 before the first significant visit of Argentine relatives to the site. In the Falklands a number of memorial sites mark the lost lives of the conflict. In Stanley a 'Liberation Monument' was erected just outside the Government offices. It was unveiled on 14 June 1984, exactly two years after the Argentine surrender. It took until 1999 for a memorial chapel to be opened in Britain (at Pangbourne School in West Berkshire).

Those involved in prosecuting the war were awarded the South Atlantic Medal. Further awards for gallantry and exceptional service were also announced in the *London Gazette* of 11 October 1982. (See appendix.) The construction of the list still causes irritation, not because of those who were recognised (for example the two posthumous VCs for Colonel 'H' Jones and Sergeant Ian McKay), but because of those who were not, often despite being recommended by their commanding officers. After the war there was also some surprise that service in the Falklands appeared to be disregarded in promotion terms, especially in the Navy, on the grounds that it would be unfair on those unable to attend.

The South Atlantic Fund was established for donations to meet the needs of the armed forces, associated civilian personnel and respective dependants who had suffered distress due to the conflict. By the time it was closed at the end of 1992 it had received £15.25 million, made up of more than 400,000 separate donations, and had been able, as a result of investments, to disburse £16.6 million leaving a residual sum of £3 million to be handed over to the single service benevolent funds who would use the funds to meet future needs.

To mark the end of the conflict a thanksgiving service was held at St Paul's Cathedral at the end of July. This added to the growing sense of irritation with some hallowed British institutions. The FCO and the BBC were already in bad odour and now the Church of England was to join them. It was said of Margaret Thatcher that while with the Foreign Office she disliked the institution but tended to like the individuals within it, her attitude to the Church of England was the opposite.

The problems arose in fact less from the attitudes of the Church towards the conflict than the Archbishop of Canterbury's determination to make the service inter-denominational. This meant securing the direct participation of Cardinal Hume, who was naturally influenced by the Pope's recent pleas for reconciliation, and Dr Kenneth Greet, Moderator of the Free Church Federal Council, who had recently published adverse comments on the campaign in the *Guardian*. There was some relief in Government that the Moderator of the General Assembly of the United Reform Church turned out to be a 'robust' lay person with 'no pacifist leanings'.

The expectation of Ministers was indicated by the initial title: 'A Service of Thanksgiving for the liberation of the Falkland Islands and in remembrance of the fallen'. The proposals from the Church side moved matters in a different direction. These involved inserting a reference to reconciliation in the title, including the Lord's Prayer in Spanish and an excerpt from the Pope's recent address at Coventry. In addition Cardinal Hume argued strongly

670

that the world 'liberation' should be removed from the title because of its connotations in Roman Catholic theology, especially in South America. Most seriously Greet was opposed to the participation of members of the armed forces reading lessons, while even Cardinal Hume was also said to have misgivings, to the point where it might lead to some church leaders staying away.

Ministers were appalled. Nott later summed up their sentiments:

> No one was more in favour of reconciliation with Argentina than I; we could all say prayers privately, if we wished, for the dead and maimed of both sides; but this was a service for the veterans of the war and, in particular, the families of the British dead. It almost seemed as if our disagreements on the form of worship were more about the Church of England's own war against Margaret Thatcher and her policies than about comforting the families of our dead.[5]

As delicate negotiations began between the Government and the Dean of St. Paul's, Nott expressed the view that it would be better to abandon this service and convene instead one under military auspices in Horse Guards Parade. Without going that far, the Prime Minister made known that she was prepared to go public in Parliament and the press if there was any attempt to bar members of the armed forces from making a contribution. At the same time she was wary about giving the service too political a content and readily agreed that with the gathering uncertainties surrounding the event she would be well advised not to participate so directly. Here she might have been influenced by the Dean's suggestion that she read as a lesson Micah, chapter 4, verses 1–4, which was not exactly 'Iron Lady' fare.[6]

Eventually sufficient common ground was reached. The service was to be called simply 'The Falkland Islands Service.' It was agreed that the final theme, after thanksgiving and remembrance, would be peace and reconciliation, to be led by Greet. His proposed contribution, longer than all others, was cut back, thereby removing references to nations building defences against poverty, hunger and disease rather than each other, although a reference to their eradication remained, and a special blessing of the United Nations. One lesson was read by the Chaplain to the Fleet while two junior members of the Task Force led the congregation from one section of the service to the next with appropriate sentences of scripture.

The other difficulty lay in whom to invite once members of the Task Force and their families had been catered for. It had been expected that the representatives of foreign governments would be invited, with the United States, New Zealand and Nepal having a particular claim because of the material help they had provided, but the problems of space and diplomacy created problems. Many governments had provided support and it would be invidious to ask only a few, while some exclusions, for example, Ireland would be seen as pointed (especially as Irish citizens had fought with the British forces). In the end it was decided that the occasion would be purely domestic. The Archbishop of Canterbury's sermon, which stressed the reconciliation theme, did little to ease the Prime Minister's irritation with the episode. Even some churchmen were uneasy about expressing thanks only for the war's end without addressing the reasons, commensurate with just war theory, why it was fought or giving meaning to the sacrifices.[7]

She found much more satisfactory the victory parade on 12 October when over 1,250 individuals involved in the Task Force marched from Armoury House to Guildhall, with about 30,000 spectators. There was a fly past of helicopters and aircraft. A small pacifist demonstration made little impact: more upset was caused by an initial reluctance to allow wounded servicemen in their wheelchairs to have a prominent position. The occasion, reminiscent of past military parades through the City of London, was taken to represent a resurgence in the British character. At the Guildhall the Lord Mayor told those from the Task Force that they represented 'what is best in Britain'. The Prime Minister reflected on the inspirational quality of the events of the past months: 'Doubt and hesitation were replaced by confidence and pride that our generation too could write a glorious chapter in the history of liberty.'[8]

SECTION NINE

44

FORTRESS FALKLANDS

Before the war the British Government had been faced with two options, neither of which was attractive, and policy had been to avoid the choice. One option was to negotiate a deal with Argentina to hand over the Falkland Islands and the Dependencies in return for some protection for the islanders. A promise, regularly repeated, to the islanders that their wishes would be paramount made the negotiating option look increasingly hopeless. British governments were not beyond ruthlessness in such situations, especially when wider economic and political interests argued for a deal, but in this case the islanders, though small in number, were articulate and well organised and it was not hard to imagine the outcry if they were to be handed over to a disagreeable Argentina regime. The other option was to invest in the Falklands and defend them against any aggressive Argentine action. Successive governments balked at the cost and the diplomatic consequences of so firmly ruling out a negotiated solution.

The policy of prevarication with both the islanders and the Argentines, which resulted from the inability to choose, was untenable. If Argentina had left well alone, in all probability the Falklands would have continued to decline in population and economic prospects, and at some point some deal with Buenos Aires would have appeared as the best way out. Impatient, the Argentine Government forced the choice, intending to present the British Government with a fait accompli. They failed, however, to close off all realistic responses. The responses available to London may have appeared disproportionate in terms of cost and effort, and eventually lives, to the assets in dispute, but they did not appear disproportionate when considered in the light of the affront to British pride and principles posed by the Argentine invasion. If there had been no military counter available then the Malvinas would now be part of Argentina. This would also have been the result of a failed military response. Once the British Government determined to send the Task Force it had decided to deny Argentina the Malvinas, and once the matter had been decided by force of arms then the Falklands were going to remain British.

Arguments about sovereignty rumbled on, but the terms of the debate had now changed. At one level the war meant that the question was investigated far more critically than had been the case before, with the House of Commons Foreign Affairs Committee declaring itself unable, to the Government's vexation, to reach a conclusion on the quality of Britain's claim.[1] While successive governments had held to a consistent position on the strength of the British claim, and continued to do so, it was evident that over the years doubts had on occasion been expressed on their robustness. There was some alarm when it was discovered that a collection of relevant documents, confirming this point, had been accessible to the Argentines during their occupation of Government House. They contained some potential diplomatic ammunition to be deployed against Britain but, remarkably, did not appear to have been disturbed. More alert had been academics and journalists who had found documents which had made their way into the Public Record Office, and from which they had culled statements that suggested official doubts about how the Islands came under British control in 1833. For a while these documents were recovered from the PRO, but after this was noticed in Parliament, it was decided that they had to be returned.

At the same time the successful campaign and the eviction of the Argentines was bound to be seen by public opinion as a great victory, leading to the return of the Governor (albeit under a new name), the traditional local administration restored and the Falkland Islands and the Dependencies garrisoned and protected, perhaps indefinitely, and even without American support, against renewed Argentine aggression. So the price of victory was 'Fortress Falklands'. The prospect was greeted without enthusiasm in Whitehall and in the armed services. Many had hoped for some sort of diplomatic outcome precisely to avoid the diversion of economic and military resources to maintaining a distant and tiny outpost of a former Empire in a hostile environment. Argentina had forced the choice, and the choice was that there was to be no deal with Argentina.

It was a more difficult choice than it would have been prior to the war in terms of the need to recover from the destruction and traumas of the occupation and the campaign, and in the belief among Britain's allies and partners, which turned out to be mistaken, that it would be impossible to repair relations with the rest of Latin America without some conspicuous nod in the direction of Argentina's territorial aspirations. At another level the choice was much easier. The war had ensured that it was presented in stark terms, and as Argentine behaviour had comprehensively ruled out one course, the only thing to do was to follow the other with vigour. There may have been wavering during April and much of May, but as soon as 3 Commando Brigade landed at San Carlos, the Government's policy was to retake the Islands and then hold on to them.

Hiding the choice

The war did not change the geography of the Falklands and nor did it lead Argentina to abandon its claims. It could keep up the threats of air raids, naval attacks and even commando-style raids in order to make the British victory as pyrrhic and as expensive as possible. The policy would be to deny Argentina the opportunity to aggress again or flood the Islands with their people against the wishes of the islanders, and to foster economic development. Somehow this was to be achieved with as modest as possible additional expenditure, and somehow the Americans had to be associated with the outcome and be involved in providing assurances of security for the Islands. Indeed it was assumed, in a briefing for the first major War Cabinet discussion on the post-repossession options on 26 May, that 'our freedom of action will be limited by the attitude of the United States Government and of American public opinion.'

Reading the assessments prepared for that meeting, it is striking how little grasp officials had of the sheer scale of the new commitment. They were working with the pre-war assessments and estimates, and were largely concerned with the level of assistance necessary to render the Falklands viable rather than a transformation of the Islands' economy. Among senior military officers as well as civil servants, the logic of the Fortress Falklands option appeared to point to prohibitive costs. The Assistant Chief of Defence (Policy), reviewing the papers prepared for the War Cabinet meeting, took the view that an alternative logic had to be developed:

> After a suitable period of time, negotiations on the sovereignty of the Falkland Islands must be progressed either through the United Nations or some other third party. Agreement must be reached with Argentina in the medium term if HMG is not to be involved in a long term major commitment in the South Atlantic otherwise the cost and overstretch of maintaining a garrison in the Falkland Islands must have a major effect on our commitment to NATO, particularly for the Royal Navy.

Victory makes a difference. The extent of Britain's intensified commitment was underlined by visits first from FCO Minister Cranley Onslow on 3–8 October 1982, and then John Nott on 22–25 October 1982. Most dramatic of all was the surprise visit by Mrs Thatcher on 8–12 January 1983, the first ever by a British Prime Minister, accompanied by Sir John Fieldhouse, by now promoted to Chief of Naval Staff. Not surprisingly, the Prime Minister was given a rapturous welcome. Hunt later recalled:

> Perhaps the most emotional moment of all came when the Islands' Financial Secretary, the Honourable Harold Rowlands, conferred upon Mrs. Thatcher the freedom of the Falkland Islands at a public

reception in Stanley Town Hall, attended by practically all the civilian residents of Stanley ... He echoed the sentiments of all Falkland Islanders in expressing his pleasure at being able to thank Mrs. Thatcher in person for the liberation of the Falkland Islands. He described the occasion as the greatest moment in his life. He thanked her not only for the liberation of the Islands but also for the rehabilitation and development of the Islands. He pledged Islanders to build a better future and thus to ensure that the battle had been worthwhile and that the men whose lives had been lost would be remembered. I am assured that Mrs. Thatcher's reply received the most enthusiastic reception ever witnessed in the Falkland Islands. The biggest cheer came when she said, 'Today again the Union Jack flies over Port Stanley, and may it ever fly there'. This had particular significance for me as it was in the same Town Hall that on 2 April General Garcia told me that the Argentines would stay on the Islands forever.

The price of victory was bound to be high, in terms of both paying for the campaign and looking after the Islands over the long term. Their extent came through clearly in a paper prepared by Cabinet Office officials in November 1982 for the OD's sub-committee on future arrangements for the Falkland Islands. Total costs until 1988 would approach £4 billion, of which

Table 3 Costs of Falklands campaign and r econstruction

	1982/3	*1983/4*	*1984/5*	*1985/6*	*1986/7*	*1987/8*	*Total*
Campaign	700	190	310	280	190	120	1790
Garrison*	200	530	440	330	250	250	2000
Rehabilitation	10	5					15
Compensation	3.5	1.5					5
Mine Clear ance**		2					2+
Economic Development	2.5	10	8.5	4.5	3.0	2.0	30.5
Total	916	738.5	758.5	614.5	443	372	3842.5

£ million in 1982/ 3 prices

*including airfields and 'detriment minimising' measures

** judged unquantifiable after 1983/4

less than half could be attributed to the campaign, and less than one percent would be devoted to future economic development.

Governance

While sure of the need to confirm Britain's commitment to defend the Falklands and respect the wishes of the islanders, the FCO was nervous about establishing any new constitutional arrangements that could be taken by international (and especially American) opinion to imply a return to a straight 'colonial' regime on the Falklands. Nor was there any interest in the Islands or in London for the independence option. There would be the very practical difficulties of obtaining international recognition for a new state whose sovereignty would be contested from the start and would not meet any stringent test of viability. Moreover the experience of 1982 had confirmed to the islanders their dependence on Britain in both military and economic terms.

Any new framework had to leave room for other countries to be associated with the UK in the role of protecting power as well as acknowledge that this was a population too small to fit the normal pattern of constitutional development. A four-stage process was therefore concocted for the return of a British administration. First the Financial Secretary would be sworn in as officer administering the Government. Then the Governor would return. There was no alternative to this, as Hunt had the confidence of the islanders and understood the requirements for rehabilitation, even though it would be criticised by other governments as evidence of a determination to return to the *status quo ante bellum*. To ease this, at the same time an announcement would be made that this was (a) only on a provisional basis; and (b) would be followed by the appointment of a Special Commissioner, a more senior figure with broader responsibilities, and moves towards greater self-government, the latter to be discussed with the islanders. Finally, self-government would be introduced, limiting the Special Commissioner's role to exercising the British Government's responsibilities for foreign affairs and defence.

Eventually, a form of dual management was agreed with a civil and military commissioner. Hunt returned, with the civil responsibilities of Governor; but on military matters he would accept direction from the Commander, Land Forces, Major-General Moore. In effect Hunt and Moore would act as civil and military commissioners working together. An Order in Council gave effect to these arrangements. The arrangement was implemented but did not survive for long. The titles of civil and military commissioners lasted until 1985. The title of Governor was restored as part of a new Constitution of the Falkland Islands. This was a personal decision of the Prime Minister's. A request for the restoration of the title had come from the Legislative Council, who saw this as a means of demonstrating a return to normality. The FCO was opposed, as indeed were most of her advisers, out of concern that this would be seen as a reversion to an old-fashioned colonial administration. 'He will be called Governor', Thatcher noted, 'whatever title you decide to give him', adding 'What is wrong with that?' The senior military officer became the Commander, British Forces in the Falkland Islands rather than Military Commissioner.

This new constitution was published on 20 March 1985, presented to Parliament on 28 March, and entered into force on 18 April. It guaranteed the islanders' right to self-determination, a guarantee specifically sought by Councillors and to which the Argentines inevitably took particular exception. The Islands were divided into two political constituencies – Stanley and the Camp, while the Dependencies (South Georgia and the South Sandwich Islands) were formally separated from the Falkland Islands on the grounds that the legal claim was quite distinct and without a population they did not need elaborate constitutional arrangements. On this latter matter there were many misgivings, not least among the islanders who felt a close bond with the territories and felt that the separation might be a first step towards their eventual surrender as a sop to the Argentines. A link was maintained by having the Governor retain responsibility for the administration of the Dependencies.

Economic development

As the fighting concluded the first task was to help the Islands recover from the ordeal. As soon as Rex Hunt returned to the Falklands, a Rehabilitation Committee was established, which included Moore and Clapp. A census was organised, a helicopter service was established to the outlying farms and essential supplies were delivered. There was still a lot to do. Major-General Sir David Thorne later wrote of his first impressions on arriving as the new Military Commander in July 1982:

> The road to Stanley, already showing signs of excess wear, was littered with enemy weapons, equipment and ammunition in disorderly heaps. Stanley itself had suffered from a total swamping of its infrastructure; power, water and sewage services had all collapsed in the face of excess demand. There was no effective bakery or laundry, and accommodation was in such short supply that most servicemen were living on board the ships in the harbour. The stores were also, in the main, afloat, but there was no proper pier or unloading point.[2]

Conditions in the Falkland Islands were gradually restored. Civilian houses were made habitable, and water supplies provided. Attention was given to dealing with the mines laid indiscriminately by the Argentine occupation force.

Consideration of how best to develop the Islands' economy over the long term was the main subject of a paper prepared by Rex Hunt in late May for the War Cabinet, and which prompted responses from the FCO and the Department of Trade. The broad conclusions were generally accepted, although Hunt was the more optimistic. It was agreed that the wool industry would remain the basic platform for economic development. This could be improved through greater productivity and the further subdivision of large farms into smaller owner/occupier holdings, which would also have the advantage of providing the islanders with a direct stake in the economy. Further diversification would require exploiting the Islands' other resources – inshore fishing, salmon ranching, frozen meat production, kelp harvesting – but this would involve substantial investment. The measure which turned out to be the salvation of the local economy – licensing of deep-water fishing by third parties, following the establishment of a fisheries zone – was recognised in an FCO paper as a source of 'useful additional revenue' but carrying considerable costs of enforcement. Oil would make an enormous difference, but reserves had yet to be identified and the security issue would still loom large.

Hunt also accepted that 'Argentina will be able to continue to prevent any development of the Islands' deep-sea fisheries and possible offshore oil deposits for the foreseeable future.' Development, therefore, would only succeed if islanders, immigrants and investors could be assured of a stable and peaceful political future. To the FCO that still required an arrangement 'which at least has Argentine acquiescence':

> While the Islanders might survive a Fortress Falklands situation, some or many would likely leave, outside investors would understandably fight shy, and the cost to HMG of maintaining the Islands would be substantial.

Thus the post-war prospects at first appeared to be almost as gloomy as the pre-war, with the trends of economic decline and depopulation picking up where they had left off on 2 April 1982. Without a political settlement, access through Argentina would remain blocked, and alternative communications to other points on the South American mainland would probably be denied. Poor communications would not help gain investment and would be an obvious bar to some of the new options, most obviously tourism. A Department of Trade paper, picking up on the late May discussions, and produced in early June, looked at the costs of a weekly air link with the mainland. Available options pointed to costs of a few millions a year to operate, of which only a small amount could be recovered from fares or freight charges. Then there would be the problem of getting other governments to agree, setting in place new operational arrangements and accepting the need for an open-ended subsidy.

Prior to the conflict, aid to the Falklands had been running at about £1 million per annum, an amount high in per capita terms but insufficient to stimulate the economy. In the new circumstances any funds for reconstruction and development would have to come from the Government. Hunt was clear that:

> The Falkland Islands can survive and indeed prosper without Argentina; but they will need more help from Britain than they have received in the past. If after the cessation of hostilities Britain makes clear to the world that she is prepared to continue to defend the Islanders' right to stay British, I believe that we can reverse the population drift and attract private investment for development.

His view, therefore, was that the removal of political uncertainty and initial British assistance was the key. Thatcher declared Hunt's paper to be 'excellent.' If that was the policy then the most effective way of communicating it was an early demonstration of Government intent. This could be achieved by sending Lord Shackleton back to the Falklands to update his report, and this he was prepared to do. On 28 May, Lords Shackleton and Buxton visited the Prime Minister when the former was confirmed in his mission.

The second Shackleton Report was presented to the Prime Minister on 27 July 1982 and an unclassified version was published on 13 September. Little had happened since 1976 to support the local economy. The 20 per cent fall in the price of wool produced an even larger question mark against the Islands' economic viability. Without continued support or development the collapse of the local economy was forecast. Nothing had transpired to alter Shackleton's prescription for economic recovery, and his proposals would not have surprised anyone who had read his earlier report:

- The construction of a new runway for Stanley airfield, as an absolute priority, at an estimated £35 million;
- £35 million investment for economic development over five years;
- £40 million investment in the exploitation of fishing resources around the Falkland Islands and South Georgia;
- the transfer of farms from major (absentee and private) landowning companies to islander farmers, to halt the drain on resources from the Islands in the form of remittance of profits;
- the establishment of a Falkland Islands Development Agency to allocate development loans and grants;
- a 200-mile fishing limit around the Falkland Islands, South Georgia and the Dependencies, plus support for a survey of possible shellfish and salmon ranching industries;
- the development of a tourist industry involving the promotion of activities with wildlife tourist operators and the building of a new hotel in Port Stanley.

The report estimated that if these recommendations were carried out the economy of the Islands could expand by between 75–90% and provide employment for an additional 200 people. This would increase the population by a possible 500 to a maximum of 2,300 civilians to offset the three per cent fall in population between 1975–1980. The main difference with 1976 was the political context. Instead of being asked to explain the economic facts of life without a settlement to the islanders (which he had then refused to do) Shackleton was now explaining to a receptive Government what had to be done to sustain the Islands economically without a settlement.

When the new Cabinet Sub-Committee considering the future of the Falklands (OD(FAF)) met on 6 September 1982, the Prime Minister described the new Shackleton Report as excellent but noted that full implementation of its proposals would be very expensive. The more radical ideas, notably the proposal for compulsory purchase of land belonging to the Falkland Islands Company, which owned 45 per cent of the total, and to other absentee landlords, were challenging for a Conservative Government. There was resistance to the idea that, as a matter of principle, tenant farmers had a statutory right to buy land from their landlord and also the risk that the Government might be left holding the land if insufficient purchasers came forward. As the Government was not going to sign a blank cheque, the expectations of the islanders had to be kept realistic.

By late November the sub-committee had proposals for economic development based on Shackleton's report. His proposal for the establishment of a Falkland Islands Development Agency (FIDA) was accepted, albeit in a more restricted form. His proposal for the compulsory acquisition and transfer of land was unrealistic, and unlikely to solve the real problem of stemming the outflow of farm profits from the Islands. Instead the FIDA would acquire land as it became available on the open market and then sell or lease it to islanders on soft terms. In the event within six years local land ownership had moved from 24 per cent to 73 per cent, and the old quasi-feudal system had been broken.

The FIDA would be looking to encourage the development of private enterprise, initiative, and an inflow of skilled labour to the Islands. The main difficulty with regard to these and other proposals was that standard economic criteria for the appraisal of development projects could not be applied to the Falklands; the Government was committed to their economic development and a failure to meet this commitment could result in a large-scale exodus of the Islands' population. The package of development aid proposed was estimated broadly to cost £31m over six years. This far exceeded any provision made in the overseas aid budget, and so required new funds from the Treasury. The area that proved the most controversial, and took longest to implement, was the establishment of a 200-mile fisheries limit. This is dealt with below.

One area where the effort was far more limited than originally envisaged was that of mine clearance. The Prime Minister indicated as the war ended that clearing the Falklands of mines would be a high priority. In the event this proved to be a more forbidding task than at first envisaged, largely because of the haphazard way that they had been laid by the Argentines. In August 1983 work stopped because no existing system appeared to be capable of detecting the mines. The existing minefields were fenced off and warning signs erected. A programme to develop more effective equipment was established and, while by early 1986 progress had been made in its development, with successful trials of remotely controlled vehicles that could deal with exposed (but not hidden) mines, there was reluctance in the Ministry of Defence to procure a system at a cost of some £25 million that would be of limited value in European contingencies and for which there was no military need in the Falklands. The standards for successful mine clearance were exacting: even a small failure rate would be unacceptable. It would take until the end of the 1980s before full clearance could start and possibly another ten years before it could be completed. The FCO thought the work should go ahead but they had no funds of their own to support it. The minefields remained fenced off but uncleared.

Garrison

In parallel with discussions on the economy were discussions on how to garrison the Falklands following repossession. In practice these were the main drivers of British policy. A large and permanent military base, as Shackleton recognised, was bound to have a major impact on the local community, while major investments that could not be supported out of development assistance could find justification in military need. Discussions about the future garrison had begun on 5 April almost as the Task Force was being sent to the South Atlantic. The military challenge was identified as it had been before the war and as it would be after: a slight risk of re-invasion, a greater threat of low level harassment operations and some possibility of air attacks. These risks would increase progressively as Argentine losses were made good. In equipment terms the levels followed pre-war analyses – a couple of warships, an RM Commando or Infantry Battalion Group of 800 plus men, some decent air defences including radars, Rapiers and up to six Harriers, and a variety of helicopters. That would still produce a force at a level about twice that of the Falkland Islands population. If the Argentine forces survived the war intact, the numbers could be higher, putting pressure on local accommodation and the public utilities, which might also have been damaged during hostilities. It would also be sensible to keep an SSN on station. Even then early reinforcement would be necessary, so the airfield would have to be upgraded to take transport aircraft, involving new facilities in every area.

With the war over, the JIC concluded that Argentina's determination to achieve sovereignty over the Falkland Islands had not diminished. The political situation would remain confused and unstable, although with little public support, or from elsewhere in Latin America, for more military action for the moment. It would take time to rebuild a force large enough to mount an invasion and recent experience should have a substantial deterrent effect. More likely would be harassment of the Islands and Dependencies and threats to Britain's lines of communication. These might be at a very low level, sufficient to undermine local morale and add to the problems of maintaining a garrison. Having been surprised once, the JIC did not want to promise that Britain would not be surprised again, especially if a Junta remained in control. Submarine or air attacks could take place without warning.

On 13 July the Chiefs considered the future position. Lewin noted that the proposed garrison size of some 4,200 looked unbalanced against the population to be defended of 1,800 if not against the potential threat. A new Commander British Forces Falkland Islands (CBFFI) would soon be taking over and it was agreed that his views would be critical to the final decisions. There was already concern about the detrimental impact on NATO requirements. It was also agreed that a vital element in any deployment was improved intelligence and early warning, as well as air defences. On 28 October 1982 the new CDS, Sir Edwin Bramall, presided over a Chiefs' meeting attended by Nott, who had recently returned from his visit to the Falklands. Bramall acknowledged the problems of balancing the needs of deterrence with the many other calls on defence resources and the impact a garrison in the Falkland Islands would have on their ability to meet commitments elsewhere. At the time naval forces in the area included five destroyers and frigates, and, according to the RN, one might be reduced through the introduction of three patrol craft. The Harrier force was to be reduced to four aircraft, which led the RAF to propose that eight Phantom aircraft be based at Stanley for air defence purposes. The Army was reluctant to lose the Rapier battery at San Carlos as a third line of defence, and argued that it should be retained.

On 1 November OD(FAF) received the final proposal from the Defence Staff. This recommended a garrison in the near term consisting of around 3,100 personnel on the Islands. Anything less would involve unacceptably high military risks, at least until a better airfield had been built. Some £900 million over three years was to be added to the defence budget to meet garrison costs, but that figure had been agreed before the Chiefs had considered the matter and had assumed a garrison of no more than 2,000. The estimate now was that the garrison would cost just under £1,300 million over three years. Some of the capital and running costs would be totally dedicated to the South Atlantic forces, other expenditure might be implemented in such a way as to minimise the detriment to Britain's NATO commitments by investing in extra equipment and manpower. At best this would amount to £360 million of the total. At the same time the garrison capital costs included £220 million for the airfield. Building works in the adverse conditions of the Falklands would always be expensive. The upshot of this was that the increment to the defence budget left a gap of over £100m a year in the cost estimates. The result of this was that some of the extra manpower and equipment intended to compensate for those diverted to the Falklands would have to be forgone, with corresponding damage to Britain's military capability in the NATO area. It was still the case that some of the investment planned for the garrison (particularly four DC 10 tanker/freighter aircraft) as well as the 'detriment minimisers' would be valuable additions to general defence capability, so Nott would have to consider whether savings could be made elsewhere in the main defence programme.

By this time there was also more confidence that Argentina was even less likely than before to return to force to settle the dispute, and was now relying largely on diplomatic means. The risk still remained of various forms of limited action should frustration grow in Buenos Aires, and the problem of inadequate warning would always be there. Upon reading the November JIC paper which reached this conclusion, the Prime Minister expressed an interest in whether or not offensive operations by Britain might be a reasonable response to any Argentine military adventures: 'Their shipping and bases are now vulnerable, as we have considerable forces in or near the Falklands'. This led to a considerable debate, the results of which were reported to the Prime Minister by the new Defence Secretary, Michael Heseltine, in February 1983.

The task had been to identify possible responses to Argentine harassment that could be launched within 48 hours of the Argentine action. They should be proportionate, directed at the particular form of harassment employed, and as positive as was consistent with the UK's international obligations. The options were to attack an Argentine ship, provided a suitable target was at sea and in a known position, mount an air attack on the Argentine mainland targets using Phantoms or Harriers, but this would be of limited military effectiveness and would detract from their air defence tasks, or take harassment measures against Argentine merchant shipping and fishing boats. If more offensive options were to be created then it would be necessary to base Buccaneer aircraft at RAF Stanley, maintain a diesel-powered submarine (SSK) permanently on patrol around the Falklands, base a Special Forces Unit there, stockpile mines, station Hercules minelaying aircraft, Nimrod reconnaissance aircraft, Vulcan aircraft at the Falklands or Ascension, and station additional warships in the area. All these measures would allow for more reliable and effective 48 hour responses, against the mainland, warships, and ports, as well as an extension of the Falkland Islands Protection Zone (FIPZ), notified to Argentina on 21 July 1982 as replacing the Total Exclusion Zone. These deployments, while feasible, would add significantly to the size and cost of the garrison (and its impact on Britain's NATO contribution) to the point where it might become unsustainable. Yet once Britain had enhanced the garrison any later reduction might send the wrong signals to the Argentines. Equally, if there were no enhancements the existing garrison would have a very limited response capability.

Heseltine took the view that it was not worth developing a response to remote threats, but he was concerned that an attack might be mounted on one of the ships stationed to the west of the Falklands enforcing the protection zone and on radar picket duty. Anti-missile defences had been improved but the ships were still potential targets for a surprise Argentine air attack. The risk would be reduced but not eliminated when a westward-looking shore radar capability was in place from April. The most appropriate response to any attack, he suggested, would be to use Buccaneer aircraft against an Argentine warship at sea or in port, or on the Argentine airfield that launched the raid. That would require as many as eight Buccaneers at Stanley, straining further the limited local facilities and reducing further Britain's NATO force levels. Alternatively two Buccaneers might be deployed temporarily to the Falklands in order to demonstrate capability and resolve. 'Subject to the views of my colleagues, I believe the penalties involved in a permanent deployment outweigh the benefit from the additional insurance; but that it would be worth making a deterrent deployment.'

The framework for Britain's rules of engagement in the South Atlantic was based on the 150nm radius FIPZ. Outside this area British forces were permitted to engage Argentine units only in self-defence. Within the FIPZ, British forces could attack all combat units: the act of crossing the boundary line was deemed to be an act of hostile intent against British forces or territory. In December 1983 an Argentine submarine deployed much further south than usual, and Heseltine authorised a temporary change in the ROE to minimise the risk of the submarine being sunk should it stray into the FIPZ accidentally. In the event the deployment passed off without incident. A 'warning zone' 30nm in from the edge of the FIPZ was established in which unidentified submarines could be harassed but not attacked unless they unmistakably demonstrated hostile intent. Once a submarine penetrated further than 30nm inside the FIPZ it could then be attacked, since such a significant incursion was unlikely to be accidental and could, in itself, reasonably be deemed to indicate hostile intent. This change applied only to submarines but led to Heseltine asking the Chiefs of Staff to re-examine the ROE to ensure that they met the threat from Argentina while minimising the risk of an 'accidental' engagement. Out of this came a recommendation that the warning zone concept should be extended to include Argentine surface combatants and combat aircraft, both of which could be unmistakably warned-off by visual means. A warning zone 30nm deep would still leave the Commander British Forces with adequate room and time to engage Argentine combat units that had aggressive intent, and kept the risks of a successful attack on British forces at a low level. The Commander was later given additional discretion to identify potential targets close to, but outside, the FIPZ boundary. This had the added advantage of further extending the range of response to a potential incursion, as British forces could first identify potential intruders outside the FIPZ, then harass within the warning zone, and finally attack in the Central Zone. Publicly Britain's position would remain unchanged and the 1982 warnings to Argentina giving notification of the FIPZ would remain in force. The FCO had wanted British forces only to fire with warning against Argentine combat units in the Central Zone although MoD's view was that an incursion into the Central Zone was 'unlikely to be by a mistake', and that British forces had to 'retain the discretion to fire without warning'.

Mount Pleasant airport

Central to all plans was an improved air base. The existing airfield at Stanley was only a temporary facility and Ministers were publicly committed to improving it. During the discussions prompted by Hunt's paper in late May, the arguments in favour of an improved runway and facilities at Stanley appeared compelling. The Department of Trade was relaxed, as the charges would be against the defence budget. Going back to pre-war analyses the cost was put at about £16 million, to be compared with the cost of establishing an air service which would require a huge and continuing Government subsidy. Shackleton doubled the potential cost – to £35 million – but this was still a small proportion of the eventual cost.

The reason was that rather than a civilian airfield with possible military applications, the proposal was soon for a military airfield that could also serve as a civilian airport. The demands would be substantial. The airfield was needed as an operating base for the garrison aircraft, an airhead to accept reinforcements in the event of indications of a re-invasion attempt, for which no more than 14 days' warning could be expected, and a terminal for air roulement of the garrison and logistic supply. Without an airfield it would not be possible to deploy Phantoms for air defences, nor conduct effective airborne reconnaissance or reinforce within the likely warning time. In the event of a heightened risk of an Argentine invasion, the Government would be obliged to build up a larger garrison and accept a standing naval presence of Task Force dimensions.

Engineering surveys of the possible options for providing a Falklands airfield were carried out by the Property Services Agency (PSA), with the assistance of the Royal Engineers, based upon a requirement stated by the RAF. The forbidding Falklands winter meant that construction would take up to three years. The intended location was Mount Pleasant, between Stanley and Darwin on land belonging to the Falkland Islands Company. The likely cost was put at £375–450 million. This was a stunning figure. MoD officials argued that: 'unless we foresee a military commitment on something like the present scale well beyond 2–3 years, it would be wasteful to sink major funds in new permanent facilities'. Nott was also nervous.

Writing to CDS in October, he accepted that a case had to be prepared for a new airfield, but, given the cost and the potential for cost overruns, he also wanted 'more radical alternatives' to be explored. The numbers involved were very large in relation to the strategic importance of the Islands and the capacity of the islanders to absorb such a huge influx of military personnel. With an eye on the prospects of greater pressure on the defence budget in the future, Nott wanted some thought given to 'second best' options which would provide a reasonable deterrent to renewed Argentine aggression against the Falkland Islands without requiring the construction of a new airfield. In the case of land and air forces, Nott felt:

> we need to look at ways of reinforcing which do not depend upon a huge new airfield – and which might conceivably enhance our 'ready reaction' capability for 'out of area' contingencies generally. In the naval case we need to pare back to the bone the *deterrent* force needed in the South Atlantic.

He did not have an answer to the problem himself but a conviction that: 'We must try to think the unthinkable – not merely to repeat the safest solutions and to identify all of the reasons why an alternative approach is not possible and/or prohibitively expensive'.

In practice, the key question was whether to make do with a tactical airfield, along the lines of the temporary post-war construction, or a strategic airfield of sufficient length and strength to take wide-bodied jets. This would ease emergency reinforcement and reduce the cost of roulement because civilian aircraft could be used. It could recover its cost over a period through savings in the annual costs of supporting the garrison. Consideration was given to making do with minimum improvements to the existing airfield at RAF Stanley. These had been put together using AM2 runway matting, but that was narrow and vulnerable to air attack, and would need continuous maintenance and full refurbishment within three years. The support facilities and accommodation had been improvised and would not last for more than five years. Nor was the Stanley site ideal for airfield construction, especially now that it was ringed with minefields. It would also be difficult and possibly dangerous to maintain air operations while the construction work was in progress. The alternative site had been surveyed at Mount Pleasant. The terrain was easier than at Stanley, there was access by sea and good supplies of material were available. There was a convincing engineering case for building on a 'greenfield' site. It would take 28 months to complete if all went well, compared to 37 months at best at Stanley.

For all these reasons the Chiefs recommended to Nott that there should be a permanent strategic airfield built at Mount Pleasant with a main runway with a minimum length of 8,500 feet and a secondary runway. The capital costs were provisionally estimated at up to £200m, and they were already in the defence budget. In conveying this to Thatcher, Nott supported the case for a strategic airfield, although he added that he was 'not persuaded that we should decide now to construct all of the facilities proposed and to select the Mount Pleasant option'. His main concern remained the problem of persuading public opinion that such a large facility should be built at such a large cost. It was also important to weigh carefully the impact of such a project on the Islands where the focal point had traditionally been Stanley, although he recognised that 'there might be attractions for the Islanders in keeping the military and the airfield out of sight'. (In the event the separation probably contributed to keeping civil-military relations cordial.) Finally, the military arguments were not all one-way. Care had to be taken not to leave Stanley undefended with all the focus on Mount Pleasant. Nott therefore recommended that the Government should proceed carefully and clarify all the options. The decision was nonetheless confirmed to build a strategic airfield at Mount Pleasant. When announced by Michael Heseltine, Nott's successor as Defence Secretary, on 27 June 1983, it was stressed that this would 'give a powerful boost to the economy and infrastructure of the Islands', thereby linking the decision to the economic and developmental objective of improving links with the outside world.

Unusually the project was committed on time, with the first stage ready for opening in May 1985 and the second runway completed in spring 1986. By this time, although the new civilian Government in Argentina had done nothing to indicate tolerance of the status quo, and had made no concilia-tory gestures towards the islanders, force had been ruled out as a means of resolving the dispute. There was always concern that there could be another military coup, in that there was some discontent among the officer class as colleagues were tried for their roles in the 'dirty war' waged under the Junta, but the civilian Government appeared to have consolidated itself, and there was clearly no popular appetite for a return to military rule. The Beagle Channel dispute had at last been solved. Although the Americans took the view, in the context of discussions with Britain over resumed arms sales, that the Argentine forces were at only 30 per cent of their pre-conflict level of equipment and 60 per cent of manpower, the British view was that the two brigades' worth of arms and equipment lost in the war had been replaced, some older ships had been paid off and replaced with more modern types while the combat aircraft lost in the war had been largely replaced to a level of around 120, with acquisitions of more Super Etendard aircraft, Exocets and Mirage, including improved air-to-air refuelling.

Against that, training and operational readiness was poor, and the old inter-service rivalries remained. It was on this basis that the JIC in July 1985 described the threat of a re-invasion as practically non-existent, and assessed that even if policy changed in Buenos Aires there would be at least 14 days' notice. The threat of an unauthorised hit-and-run attack was also very low, and any such attack mounted would be more politically embarrassing than militarily serious. The British reinforcement plan would, on a worst case, take 23 days to implement, but by putting forces on a reduced notice in the UK, a battalion could get to the Falklands in two days. Once the Mount Pleasant Complex was completed in 1987, complete reinforcement should be down to nine days. The core of the defence plan for the Falklands, therefore, would then be to make sure that the Complex could be defended under all circumstances to allow time for support to arrive.

MoD and the Chiefs were looking for ways to bring down the costs of the garrison. In October 1982, just after the war, the Falklands garrison ashore had been established at 4,778 personnel. This was soon reduced to 3,400 and it was hoped that the new base, facilitating quick reinforcement, would allow for cuts of more than 500 – still well above a civilian population of just over 1,900. There was in addition a small garrison on South Georgia of 41 personnel. With the runway it would be possible to bring in four Harriers, four Phantoms, eight Buccaneers and 3,000 Army personnel within nine days. By 1987 there was also a land-based early warning radar programme with the Falkland Islands Patrol Vessels improving in-shore surveillance. It was now possible to withdraw all of the Harriers and two of the nine Phantoms that had been stationed at Stanley, as well as two of five Sea Kings.

While the air base only existed because of the defence case, as the opening ceremony approached, the Foreign Secretary, Sir Geoffrey Howe, hoped that over time civilian operations would gradually gather momentum, and the airfield could be presented to the islanders as not only 'a reaffirmation of our commitment to their security, but also a contribution of our commitment to their long-term prosperity'. Latin American opinion, he hoped, would find it hard to object to the second of these objectives. 'Argentina is bound to react sharply whatever the exact form of the opening ceremony' but there was no need to encourage allegations that Britain was engaged in the 'militarisation' of the Falklands or using them as a 'strategic base'. The inauguration of the Mount Pleasant Complex (MPC) produced the expected hostile reaction from the Argentine Government, leading to an emergency session of the OAS Permanent Council in Washington.

By 1988 the MPC was providing the headquarters of British Forces Falkland Islands. The new Falkland Islands Interim Conservation and Management Zone (FICZ), discussed below, was being enforced and the JIC was still assessing that Argentine forces lacked the capacity to re-invade although lesser actions could not be precluded. Current deficiencies in Argentine capabilities were unlikely to be remedied. The aim now was to sustain a steady state deployment, reached on 1 April 1987, of an ashore garrison of 1,900 with another 550 at sea. Running costs, which had reached £200 million at their peak in 1983/4, were down to under £100 million per annum. By this time it was estimated that the total cost of the campaign, including costs of replacing equipment and stores, was £1.8 billion.

45

NEGOTIATIONS

As the Government reviewed its international position after the war it had reason to be satisfied. From many governments, notably from the Commonwealth, came effusive letters of congratulations. On 18 June 1982 the Prime Minister had received a personal message of congratulations from President Reagan:

> Your victory was both a brilliant military feat and a defense of our shared principle that disputes are not to be resolved by aggression. The minimum loss of life and the generous terms of withdrawal were also in the finest British tradition.

There had been arguments with a number of countries and some, for example with Ireland, had left an unpleasant aftertaste. The war also ended with a minor spat with Germany who accused Britain, rather bizarrely, of pushing ahead to remove EC sanctions unilaterally. Actually all that had been communicated to Argentina was that Britain would ask for sanctions to be lifted when hostilities had ceased. There was further irritation with suggestions, at a time when it appeared that Britain would link the return of prisoners to a long-term deal, that prisoners would be allowed to die of exposure to achieve political ends. Most galling, according to one senior diplomat, was the constant 'nauseating' repetition of the phrase 'magnanimity in victory'.

There was never any reason to suppose that a war would make the dispute easier to resolve, although this came as a disappointment to those without a direct connection who had hoped that it might. Britain's American and European allies had accepted the need for a modicum of solidarity during the war but once it was over they expected the problem with Argentina to be sorted out so that everyday business could get back to normal. Having taken no notice of the dispute before April 1982 they wanted to be able to forget about it after June. Support for London had been rationalised on the basis of the unacceptability of Argentina's methods not its goals, where views were more neutral. With the fighting over they were not going to endorse British colonial rule. The US was still anxious to mend their Latin American fences. In his letter of 18 June Reagan pushed for political activity:

> A just war requires a just peace. We look forward to consulting with you and to assisting in building such a peace. It must of course take into account the sacrifices of your men in battle. Its elements in my judgement must include enhancement of the long-term security of the South Atlantic, mitigation of Argentine hostility and improvement in the relations of both our countries with Latin America.

President Mitterrand advised that within twenty-four hours of repossession Britain should show magnanimity and demonstrate an intention to think positively about the longer-term future.

Western governments understood the political realities. They knew that London was not going to just hand over the Falklands to Argentina. They were less understanding of Britain's reluctance even to talk to Argentina and its determination to maintain an arms embargo. There were, after all, the stirrings of democracy in Buenos Aires. A negotiation would help democracy take root and calm nationalist passions. And would not a democratic government be altogether more reasonable? Surely two reasonable governments ought to find some way of sharing their interest in such a modest piece of land.

London found such advice disingenuous. After their ordeal the wishes of the islanders were more paramount than ever. They would be as suspicious of any conciliatory gestures as the Argentines would be likely to misinterpret them as weakness, hoping that Britain was wilting under international pressure. It would be best to let the air clear and tensions relax. No available deal could meet British political needs, Argentine aspirations and the concerns of the international community. London had investigated every possible constitutional arrangement available for the Falklands – condominium, partition, lease-back and many others – and none of them offered an easy way out. Moreover, as British diplomats attempted to explain, after all the heartache and sacrifices it was wholly unrealistic for a British Government, let alone the islanders, to even contemplate negotiation with Argentina. Parsons speaking to Perez de Cuellar neatly summed up the British attitude, as was so often the case:

> I would not mince my words. Britain and the islanders had gone through a very testing experience. There had been an unprovoked invasion. The Argentines had refused or evaded all attempts to get them to implement SCR 502 peacefully. We had had to fight. We had suffered significant human losses and losses of material in making a monumental effort which had caught the imagination of

the whole country. The islanders had had an appalling experience, details of which were now beginning to emerge. We had been obliged fully to defeat the Argentine in the field in order to repossess the islands. Even then the Argentines had shown an indifference to the wellbeing of their own troops which had further revolted British opinion.

Against this background it was absolutely and totally out of the question that we should sit down to diplomatic negotiations with the Argentines through any third party in order to discuss the future of the Islands or anything else. This represented not just the firm view of my government but the strongly held view of the British people as a whole.

Not long after the Argentine surrender, on 23 June, the Prime Minister visited Perez de Cuellar in New York and left him in no doubt that the Government was not prepared to be drawn into a further round of negotiations. When she met President Reagan and Secretary of State Haig on the same day they did not bother trying to press her on talking to Argentina. On 14 July Thatcher told Parliament that she saw 'no prospect of entering into negotiations with Argentina at present' and had no 'intention of negotiating sovereignty'.

The unusually decisive conclusion to the campaign did not fit those models of international conflict which always assumed that the most likely, and often the best, outcome would be a negotiated fudge based on a cease-fire agreed before the battle had run its course. Resisting this assumption had at times appeared risky in itself, particularly during the more difficult days of early May. Then there was anxiety that pursuit of military victory would come at the cost of diplomatic isolation. But enough had been done during the campaign to demonstrate a readiness to find a political solution to reassure the international community. The compromises might have been offered on the assumption they were unlikely to be reciprocated, but many at the time believed that Argentina missed out on some real opportunities and few have subsequently revised this belief. If the Junta had seized their chances, Britain would not have been able to restore its administration after the withdrawal of Argentine forces, nor been able to do much in the short term to boost the morale of the islanders or offer hope for the future. The promised negotiations would have been extremely difficult for the Government, with an undefeated Argentina in a strong position and the US pressing hard for a conciliatory approach. The diplomatic aspects of the campaign had thus been successful for Britain, obviously not in terms of helping avoid the bloodshed, but in terms of creating an international appreciation that Britain had truly relied on armed force as a last resort.

The campaign had also provided an insight into the views of many of those who might have been expected to sympathise with Argentina in an anti-colonial struggle. Rhetorical public support for Argentina had rarely translated into anything very practical, and was often contradicted in private. This was true even in Latin America, and raised a question for post-war policy. One of the presumed political costs of the campaign had been antagonising Latin America, and so there was an issue about the effort that needed to go into mending fences. At the end of July 1982, Pym wrote to the Prime Minister on this matter. Britain 'must try to cultivate a closer political relationship in order to buttress stability, encourage democracy and develop a community of interest', as well as exploit the commercial opportunities. Rather than the war alienating Britain from the continent it was arguable that there was a greater respect for Britain's military and diplomatic capabilities:

> We want to counter hostile propaganda and anticipate Argentine diplomatic moves against us. We want to be able to assess the dangers to our other interests and commitments and to cultivate those countries most capable of being helpful.

One difficult area was the human rights record of many of these countries. Another was the role of the military, although Pym felt that this was a 'force that must be cultivated', notwithstanding 'the possibility of their providing military support for Argentina and the dangers of aggravating local tensions complicate the issues'. High level visits were the most visible and effective means of demonstrating British interest, although if they were to make a real impact they would need to be backed by modest offers of new aid activities.

Thatcher was unconvinced that the Latin Americans would be over-impressed if they were pursued too hard, and now had enough experience of the local military to be wary of any efforts at their cultivation. The international economy did not require more subsidies being dispensed at this time, and if aid was to be the main agenda item when British Ministers visited, then the net effects could be harmful. She was also unsure about the wisdom of moving so quickly. Nott's view was even more strategic. Before the war neither he nor his officials had attached a high priority to the South Atlantic, and while it was now understood that the Falklands had to be garrisoned, Latin America could not be a high priority. Apart from Antarctica's longer-term potential, there were no fundamental strategic interests at stake, nothing to learn from South American military doctrine, equipment or intelligence. Sales would remain the dominating feature of Britain's defence relationship with the continent. Nott continued:

> If I may venture a view as an ex-Trade Minister, I believe it is not only in defence terms that Latin America is a low priority area. In nearly all countries of the region, there are too many factors which

make for instability. Society is too stratified; the church is too strong. Tensions between extremes of poverty and wealth are likely to grow. And they will no doubt be exacerbated as immigration of the poor into the towns increases. With these considerations in mind, I believe we should keep our political relationship at a low key and without diverting too many resources.

These cautious responses led the FCO to point to the evidence being amassed to show how the Argentines were actively seeking to unite Latin America behind them on the Falklands issue, and to invoke the concept of regional solidarity at the UN as well as within the OAS and the Non-Aligned Movement: 'We must not simply leave the field open to the Argentines'. The diplomats were concerned that the hard work that had been necessary to maintain relatively balanced Latin American attitudes during the conflict was not appreciated, and that a falling off now would be noticed, especially when other western countries were likely to be increasing their efforts in order to repair the damage caused by the conflict to relations with Latin America. The greater commitment to the Falklands had created new interests. Shackleton had pointed out that Britain's chances of maintaining and developing the Falklands economy depended to a critical degree on restoring regular communications with the South American mainland. This would not be easy to achieve – 'but we shall not be able to keep this possibility open if our attitude to the region as a whole is interpreted as one of indifference or disdain'.

Back to the UN

It was still the case that however much there might be admiration, grudging or otherwise, for the robust stance taken by Britain, the international preference for diplomatic solutions had not diminished. In order to demonstrate the inadmissibility of force as a means of resolving disputes, it was considered vital to show the progress that could be made in direct negotiations. Furthermore, while few third world countries were wholly convinced by the efforts taken by Argentina during the war to turn the dispute into an 'anti-colonial' cause they were not inclined to assert the opposite. Argentina could still garner support in the Non-Aligned Movement, the OAS and the UN Committee of 24. The military failure did not result in diplomatic exhaustion. Instead Argentina went back to square one, and to the forum which had always yielded the best results and which, in 1965, 1973 and 1976, had provided resolutions that gave some authority to its position – the UN General Assembly.

On 1 October 1982 Argentina, with others, tabled a draft resolution in the Assembly, calling for the Governments of the UK and Argentina to resume negotiations in order to find, as soon as possible, a peaceful solution to the sovereignty dispute. It also called for the UN Secretary-General to undertake a renewed mission to assist the parties, and to submit a report to the General Assembly at its 38th session (i.e. after twelve months) on the progress made on the implementation of the Resolution. No reference was made initially to the islanders: eventually their interests were mentioned but not their wishes. Only those steeped in the symbolism of the dispute appreciated the significance of the distinction. The Resolution went to the Assembly on 4 November and was adopted by 90 votes for, 12 against, and 52 abstentions – the largest turnout ever recorded for such a vote. Those opposed, with Britain, were largely from the Commonwealth. The majority of Britain's allies abstained, with the exception of the United States and also Greece, who supported the resolution. Thus the US (and for that matter Israel) voted with the Soviet bloc and the radical non-aligned. The moderate non-aligned largely abstained.

The origin of the Resolution had been a personal initiative by the Mexican Foreign Minister. Not surprisingly London was displeased because it considered calls for negotiations pointless. Argentina was also unhappy. The war had not yet dimmed its commitment to the Malvinas or its rhetorical expression. It wanted a strong anti-colonial resolution. The Argentines began, however, to see the Resolution's possibilities and decided to pick it up. By mid-August they had received support from sufficient countries for the Resolution to be certain to be tabled. The British decided that rather than let the non-binding Resolution pass and then ignore it, they would fight it all the way, with an intensive lobbying effort both in the UN and in capitals. Problems were seen with a counter-resolution, which could be subjected to embarrasing amendments, or spoiling amendments to the original Resolution, as the British could not commit themselves to the improved resolutions if the amendments were passed. Sir John Thomson, the new Ambassador to the UN, suggested an amendment, using Article 73 of the charter, the most sympathetic to self-determination. The Government decided in the end that this risked a loss of control of the exercise. Pym wrote to Thatcher on 18 October that:

As far as possible amendment of the Resolution is concerned, we have concluded that simple attempts to insert references to self-determination or the non-use of force into the resolution would be likely to fail ... On balance, my conclusion is that we should steer clear of sophisticated UN tactics and go for a straight negative lobbying exercise, accepting that the Latin American resolution will nevertheless pass and remain on the record to our future disadvantage. In my view this should be done through messages from you and me to our opposite numbers in a wide range of friendly countries. These would say simply that the Argentine-inspired Resolution on the Falkland Islands is deeply offensive to us, both because of its prejudicial comments on colonialism and its references to the decisions of the non-aligned movement and because it is a blatant and hypocritical attempt by Argentina to achieve by diplomatic means what she has so recently failed to achieve by force. Having seen previous negotiations with Argentina unilaterally broken off and followed by an unprovoked armed attack on the Islands, in defiance of international law and international opinion, the British people would simply not understand how any friendly and responsible government could vote for such a Resolution.

The Prime Minister agreed. A worldwide lobbying campaign began, with the Prime Minister writing almost 50 letters to heads of government. The effort proved sufficiently successful for the Argentines to include some cosmetic but well-drafted changes at the last minute. These had been drafted, it was reported, with American help. Against this background, the British mission to the UN felt they had done rather well, with Commonwealth help, to avoid losing more heavily on a watered-down draft.

Once again American behaviour exasperated the Prime Minister. In September discussions, first Enders and then Eagleburger explained that relations with Latin America had to be got back in order. They understood that Britain could not be expected to negotiate with Buenos Aires: they did hope that Britain would present itself in a reasonable light. Looking ahead to the General Assembly they had no intention of opposing a resolution that did not pre-judge sovereignty. The British suggested that the Americans were over-stating the importance of their stance in terms of Latin American opinion. The FCO was optimistic that some headway was being made with the new Secretary of State, George Shultz, who had replaced Haig, but to no avail.

On 25 October the Prime Minister wrote to President Reagan asking him to ensure that the United States did not support the Argentine resolution. His reply expressed the view that the most recent Argentine draft was more moderate, did not pre-judge sovereignty, referred to the cessation of hostilities, rejected the further use of force and acknowledged the principle of self-determination. He also reaffirmed what had been to many of Britain's allies a central proposition: opposition to the use of force as a means of solving disputes suggested that peaceful methods should be encouraged. The option of negotiations or other means of peaceful settlement should not be foreclosed. He ended with a sort of reassurance:

Margaret, I know how you have anguished over this conflict from the beginning. Your courage and leadership throughout have been a source of deep personal inspiration to me. I count it as a privilege to have been able to support you and Britain at this critical moment. You may be absolutely confident that I would do it all again the same way.

698

The response was less warm. 'I received your message about the Falklands just as I was going into a meeting of my Cabinet this morning,' she replied. It had been discussed with colleagues. 'I must tell you at once that we are utterly dismayed at its contents.' She explained again how American support would encourage the Argentines in their ambitions, that the formula on self-determination was a mockery, and that references were made to earlier resolutions which pre-judged the issue. She was grateful for the 'staunch support' given over the Falklands, but then Britain had also 'supported you at the UN and elsewhere in matters of prime concern to the United States.' She urged Reagan to think again on a matter of 'prime concern' to Britain:

A vote by the United States for the resolution would be received here with incomprehension. Worse, it would be seen as an affront to the Government and the people of Britain and to me personally. I cannot believe that you would consider delivering such a blow to the right of self-determination which means so much to the democracies of the free world. I had greatly hoped that you would vote against this hypocritical text. But if you cannot, I must ask you, with all that we have done together in mind, at least to abstain.

To no avail. Enders reportedly had been active in persuading the Argentines to water down the draft and when the decision to support the new version had been made, Mrs Kirkpatrick wasted no time in making sure that this was generally known. After the vote the Washington Embassy complained to Eagleburger to underline the strength of British objections both to the way the Americans had proceeded – 'hypocrisy and deception' – and to the substance of their decision:

[W]e had been assured all along that the Americans would not work actively with the Argentinians for a Resolution which the US could accept. We now had clear evidence that they had on the contrary done just that. Another objection was that we had not seen a text of the revised draft until after we had received the President's message telling the Prime Minister of his decision to accept it.

The British were furious that the Americans had not given them the opportunity to express their views before the President made his decision. 'This was no way to treat an ally.' Pym relayed that he felt personally deceived.

A year later, another UN vote and the Americans had not relented. It would have been inconsistent for them to do so, especially with Argentina now on the road to democracy. For that reason the new Foreign Secretary, Sir Geoffrey Howe, decided not to use up political capital pressing the Americans to change their position. He raised the matter with Shultz on 14 July, who only promised to consult closely. Howe took the view that it was pointless 'to use up credit with the Americans unproductively' so long as the Americans did not vote for 'anything worse than last year'. He just let it be known to Washington that he was 'disappointed and distressed' at the attitude of such a close ally, especially as he considered that it would encourage Argentine intransigence. With the move to democracy, the Americans also were prepared to recertify Argentina as being eligible for arms sales, although they promised not to sell equipment that could be used to reoccupy the Falklands.

The Argentine aim appeared to be to achieve at least the 90 votes they got the previous year and preferably a significant increase, so they refrained from a tougher resolution. During the actual UNGA debate on 15 November the British Ambassador declared that the British Government was 'ready for, indeed eager for, a return to normal relations' with Argentina. He stressed that the British Government would reject any Argentine Resolution calling on Britain to negotiate over the Islands' sovereignty. The final Resolution was adopted by 87 votes for, 54 abstentions and 9 against – in some ways again a victory for British diplomacy given the Argentine objective. The Greeks this time switched to abstention.

This vote took place after the Argentine elections in October 1983 but before the inauguration of the new President, Dr Raul Alfonsin. In one respect this represented one of the most important, and benign, consequences of the war. Rarely anticipated in the gloomy musings from Britain's allies, but also in intelligence assessments, was the withdrawal of the Junta from government and the subsequent election of a relative moderate. After General Galtieri's resignation, his successor, General Reynaldo Bigone, promised open elections. Alfonsin's party, the Radicals (UCR/Union Civica Radical), took 52 per cent of the vote, as against 40 per cent for the Peronists, and so enjoyed an outright majority in the Chamber of Deputies. During the conflict Alfonsin had condemned the British decision to re-take the Islands by force as 'an aggression of the North against the South' but he was also critical of the Junta's decision to invade. He described the Argentine military occupation of the Falkland Islands as 'an illegal act by an illegitimate government in a just cause'. His election platform, like the Peronists', was committed to recovering the Falkland Islands by peaceful means. The President-elect took the position that negotiations between the two Governments, through the good offices of the UN Secretary-General, were the most appropriate path for solving the dispute.

It was understood in London that a plea from a democratic government for negotiations would gain even more support among the international community, and even in Britain, where the high cost of maintaining the garrison was attracting adverse comment. It might be possible to talk on issues other than sovereignty, but there was no evidence that any Argentine government would have an interest in doing so. Although the possibility of secret talks to explore possible contacts was raised, including by Sir

Anthony Parsons, now working in Downing Street, the Prime Minister could only see danger in such a course, especially when the fact of contacts inevitably leaked. There had to be an explicit cessation of hostilities before there could be any resumption of diplomatic relations. Nonetheless, the day before President Alfonsin's 10 December inauguration, the Prime Minister wrote saying that 'I wanted to let you know that, although we have many differences, we can all take pleasure in the restoration of democracy in Argentina, believing it will bring freedom and justice to all your people. Today brings new hope to your country.' Alfonsin replied, acknowledging the message but also the differences, adding 'In this regard it would be useful to recall an old English proverb: where there's a will, there's a way.' In his inaugural address, the new President still referred to Argentina's 'unalterable objective' to secure the 'recovery and definitive affirmation of [Argentina's] right to its sovereign territorial integrity' and condemned the 'installation of the military and nuclear fortress' on the Islands. This left the Prime Minister unimpressed, and although the FCO was pressing for an approach through the Swiss to see if talks about some sort of normalisation of relations could be set in motion, she preferred to wait until the new Government had established itself and ministers had further opportunities to discuss the issues.

After the inauguration, on 3 January 1984, Argentina issued a communiqué appealing for renewed negotiations between the two Governments. Once again it was the interests, rather than the wishes, of the islanders that were highlighted. They could now be 'served and guaranteed by the National Constitution and the democratic principles, rights and guarantees in effect in Argentina, as well as by any statutes and safeguards that might be eventually agreed to.' While refusing to enter into talks on sovereignty, the next day the Prime Minister offered to lift the 150-mile FIPZ around the Islands if the Argentine Government announced a formal end to hostilities in the South Atlantic. She envisaged early talks on restoring normal commercial relations, followed by a restoration of diplomatic relations, but there would be no discussions on sovereignty.

The new Argentine Foreign Minister, Dr Dante Caputo, showed little interest in an offer made on television, but Alfonsin was more positive, calling the Prime Minister's comments a 'step forward'. This indicated a tension in Argentina between those who argued that a campaign of diplomatic attrition would gain the Falklands and those who believed that normalisation was a precondition for successful negotiations, and so better that it should start early. So Britain now had a Government in Buenos Aires with whom it might be possible to deal, but then again might not. The issue was posed in terms of the possibility of normalising relations without conceding on the sovereignty issue. When the Cabinet's Defence and Oversea Policy Committee discussed this on 25 January 1984, the memorandum presented by the Foreign Secretary proposed to continue with the 'dual track' policy of aiming for normal relations with Argentina, while at the same time standing firmly by a commitment to the islanders. There need be no hesitation on an early approach geared to a realistic, step-by-step approach to the normalisation of bilateral relations, so long as there was also no ambiguity on the sovereignty issue. At most there could be '... an arrangement whereby each side made a short statement on sovereignty for the record and agreed not to revert to it again during the talks'.

It was also important that while the talks had to be confidential, they could not be secret, given the effect any later revelations might have on the islanders. After the meeting Howe reported to Parliament that Britain was seeking more normal relations with Argentina, and that the first step would be through the mediation of the Protecting Powers. The next day the Swiss were asked to approach the Argentine Government. The possibility of talks at an official level was raised. These would exclude sovereignty but address the lifting of trade and financial restrictions. They could also consider arrangements for the return of the Argentine dead from the Falkland Islands or, failing that, for a next-of-kin visit, plus restoration of the Air Services Agreement between the UK and Argentina, and the resumption of cultural, scientific and full sporting contacts and the upgrading of official relations.

The Argentine Government reply on 16 February agreed on the importance of normalising relations and accepted British proposals as a 'positive' step, but still insisted that any dialogue had to move towards negotiations on Falklands sovereignty under UN auspices. They were in favour of a 'preliminary and open exchange of ideas', including the agenda items suggested by the British, but adding the 'lifting of the FIPZ', an end to the 'fortification' of the Islands, the construction of the 'strategic' airfield at Mount Pleasant, the 'warlike concentration' of military forces in the area, and the withdrawal of 'nuclear weapons or artefacts' from the region. In the light of the outcome of these informal discussions, there should be formal negotiations on sovereignty involving the UN Secretary-General, taking as their starting point the framework that had been agreed in the Joint Communiqué of 26 April 1977. On 1 March the Defence Committee discussed how to respond. Howe's paper stressed the simplicity of the aims of allies, who wanted to get back to business as usual, especially now that the Junta had gone. He also thought that public opinion at home was getting more bothered at the long-term cost (a judgement that earned a firm, annotated 'No' from Thatcher). There was no problem in getting Argentine agreement to the British agenda items but considerable problems with Britain agreeing to Argentina's. One way perhaps to deal with this was to allow the Argentines to state their position on sovereignty, so long as it could then be pushed to one side. The Prime Minister was opposed to the issue even being mentioned lest the wrong conclusions be drawn. Talks could only proceed on a condition of silence on this matter. At the end of March Howe tried again, and this time gained consent. If the Argentines raised sovereignty and their other issues then the British would simply offer rebuttals. At least then the Government

702

would not appear to be on the defensive and could show international opinion that an effort at dialogue was being made.

By the end of June preparations were ready for a meeting in Berne on 18–19 July. The Swiss had agreed, and the Argentines appeared to accept, that the discussion of sovereignty was to be confined to a single exchange. The Prime Minister had reservations that the choreography would be as promised but the meeting could go ahead. A statement was prepared for the first stage of the meeting and probable later publication, not addressing the Argentine claim but instead rebutting the expected Argentine position that sovereignty was a proper subject for negotiation. The terms of the British rebuttal were communicated to the Swiss, for onward transmission to Buenos Aires.

The eventual meeting was not a great success, confirming Thatcher's misgivings. The choreography was soon lost. Unfortunately, and no doubt trying to be helpful, the Swiss who had been frustrated by the continuing argument over the formula, had decided that some 'constructive ambiguity' would help, and so transmitted the British statement to the Argentines neither in Spanish nor in English but in French. The result was that the Argentines were expecting a much more flexible British position on sovereignty (although even the French version should not have led them to expect too much). When the British delegation attempted to move onto their agenda items dealing with bilateral relations, the Argentines refused to go further until a mechanism was agreed for addressing sovereignty. They then broke off the talks, leading the British to accuse them of violating their agreed basis, not only in pursuing the sovereignty issue but then in ignoring the confidentiality provisions.

The Argentine account complained that the British delegation said they were 'not prepared' when, according to the script, they were supposed to say that they were in 'no position' to discuss sovereignty.[1] As relevant to the Argentine position may have been the delicate stage in negotiations underway at the same time with the Chilean Government over the Beagle Channel. Alfonsin might have been worried about the impact of appearing too concil-iatory on hard line nationalist opinion. Charles Powell, in the Prime Minister's office, observed that her instinct that 'the Argentinians would behave duplicitously is borne out.' The line that it was Argentina's fault was plugged, not that this helped a great deal as Britain's position that sovereignty must not be discussed had little sympathy elsewhere.

At the end of 1984, Argentina came back with informal proposals for a phased resumption of talks, which would include at some point discussion of the political status of the Islands and their inhabitants. The previous false start left the British Government determined not to attempt any more conversations with the Argentines without far greater clarity on what was to be discussed. On the other hand, as Howe had noted in a memorandum to the Prime Minister, the evident readiness to establish more normal relations with Argentina had played well at the UN, with allies, and at home. The current policy had been endorsed by the Parliamentary Foreign Affairs Committee. Pressure was also building up from British companies who wanted to resume trade with Argentina. So a constructive response to Argentina made sense. He proposed that the Government's approach should be to identify single subjects, including individual components of the Berne package, in which Britain could seek to make progress when conditions were ripe. Britain would 'remain committed to normalising relations through confidence-building measures, but there must be no linkage between this and discussion of sovereignty'. It was also clear that the Protecting Powers were acting only as channels of communication and not as mediators.

One opportunity for developing this approach came not in any direct talks, but at the multilateral Paris Club, which dealt with the problems of debt-ridden countries. On 15–16 January 1985 it was due to discuss rescheduling the Argentine debt. Howe suggested that this might be an opportunity to suggest to the Argentines that the two sides should lift all commercial and financial restrictions. However as this could be seen as a complicating factor in the multilateral setting, it was agreed that the most sensible setting would be subsequent bilateral negotiations under the auspices of the Paris Club, likely to start in March, where lifting of commercial restrictions could be presented as being in the long-term interest of the Argentine economy. Rather than reply directly to the Argentine proposal, therefore, Ministers decided to wait until after the first multilateral Paris Club meeting, when Britain could demonstrate that it was playing a constructive part on debt rescheduling, and then promise to approach the bilateral sessions in the same spirit. A further concession could be an offer to accept a suitably prepared party of Argentine next-of-kin to visit the graves of their dead buried in the Falklands. The Falkland Islands Councillors appeared to be ready to accept this, and it would appear as a positive humanitarian gesture. It would help if there were parallel action through the Catholic Church so that Argentina would also have to accept this as a humanitarian issue.

The formal British note sent, via the Swiss, on 25 January 1985, failed to elicit a positive response from Argentina, as it still ruled out discussions on sovereignty. Whatever view the Argentines were taking, there were concerns that the ban on Argentine imports would be difficult to defend under the Treaty of Rome and could be subject to legal challenge. If the embargo had to go it was best that the maximum presentational benefit be extracted. Howe urged that any announcement did not refer to the legal issues but instead to Britain's 'readiness to make the running in trying to restore more normal relations with Argentina'. There were also some practical advantages to be gained by allowing British firms access to Argentine raw materials. Presentationally the move had the desired impact. In addition, as Britain was not imposing restrictions on Argentina, the European Community would view any Argentine restrictions against Britain as discriminatory and therefore unacceptable.

Argentina was also caught by surprise and responded, according to Howe, in a 'characteristically curmudgeonly' manner. Two days after the announcement, on 8 July 1985, the Argentine Government took note of the move but did not reciprocate, merely hoping that the gesture expressed a 'true negotiating will', and once again invited negotiations on all issues including sovereignty, proposing that they might start within the next sixty days. It was not considered worth re-iterating the British objections to this approach. When the sixty-day period was up, on 12 September, yet another Argentine communiqué expressed a wish to approach the next UN General Assembly with negotiations already in progress, and condemning the 'flagrant indifference' shown by Britain to past Assembly resolutions.

The trade announcement did not make that year's General Assembly vote any easier. The British position was becoming more difficult, as key European partners began to back the Argentine drafts. Admiration for Alfonsin was growing while few could see the problem with talking about sovereignty for that did not in itself require putting it up for transfer or ignoring the wishes of the islanders. For the 1985 debate, the Argentines concentrated on a soft sell. They omitted the word 'sovereignty' and then criticised the British for seeking to insert 'self-determination.' Argentina gained 107 votes, 16 more than the previous year, with 41 abstentions. Only three countries – Belize, Oman and Solomon Islands – voted with Britain as against nine the previous year. Three members of the EC – France, Italy and Greece – had switched from abstention to support for Argentina. Nor was the Commonwealth immune from the drift. Australia and Canada also voted for the resolution. This was widely interpreted as a victory for Argentina, especially after an energetic British lobbying effort, and led to a decision for the next year to downgrade the significance of the vote. In 1986, with a similar resolution, Argentina moved another seven countries from abstention to a positive vote, including the Netherlands.

As the debates took on a routine quality, and the US and European states repaired their relations with Argentina and Latin America more generally, the heat had gone out of the issue. This was once again becoming increasingly a private British-Argentine affair, with other countries uninterested in using up political capital either way to influence matters. In Britain too the Government's position was criticised for its obstinacy. Business leaders were said to be concerned that they were missing out on Argentina's economic reconstruction. There were concerns about the cost of the garrison. In 1983, as a counter to the Falklands lobby and to promote a peaceful settlement, the South Atlantic Council was formed with Conservative MP Cyril Townsend and Labour's George Foulkes to the fore. The Leaders of the Labour Party and the Liberal Party held highly publicised meetings with President Alfonsin during a European tour. Mr Neil Kinnock MP met the Argentine President in Paris on 18 September 1985, and Mr David Steel MP in Madrid on 6 October. Both meetings resulted in the issuing of Joint

Communiqués which supported the idea of re-opening negotiations on 'all aspects of the dispute', which had now become the Argentine line. Soon after this second meeting, on 10 October 1985, President Alfonsin held his first British television interview. He announced that he would welcome a meeting with the Prime Minister, but that talks would have to have an open agenda dealing with every problem. The opportunity for talks at a lower level soon arose. When FCO Minister of State, Mr Timothy Eggar, offered to meet four visiting Argentine parliamentarians in London on 20 February 1986 'without preconditions' for an exchange of views, the Argentines declined the offer.

Arms sales

The question of arms sales by Britain's allies to Argentina was as much an indicator of the revival of their overall attitude to the continuing dispute as an Argentine threat to the Falklands. There were some indications before the Junta handed over power that they were trying to restock the military's depleted arsenal, and that this was having some success, even in the face of Britain's energetic campaign to discourage potential suppliers and their good reason to be already discouraged by the country's parlous financial position. President Alfonsin was pledged to reduce the role of the armed forces in the Argentine economy as well in its political life. He did not seek to place major new contracts and spending on the military went down in 1984 to four per cent of GDP, down from six per cent the previous year. At the same time he was presented as a much more deserving beneficiary of western support, and over time the British accepted that it was useful for their allies to develop a dialogue with the Argentine military establishment, and allow this to extend to some training, assistance and military supplies. Efforts became concentrated on preventing the acquisition of equipment that could be used in an offensive against the Falklands or British forces in the South Atlantic.

Inevitably the most difficult area was equipment ordered prior to the conflict. In 1984, for example, it became apparent that more air-launched Exocets had been delivered to Argentina, and that meant that all 14 Super Etendard aircraft could be armed. This issue was relevant also in terms of payment. This was a time when loans were being negotiated to help Argentina out of its financial mess and British banks were participating. As it was, an outstanding $1 billion of a loan of $1.5 negotiated the previous year was being held back until Argentina proposed a programme which would satisfy the lenders' conditions. Another persistent issue concerned American A4 Skyhawk fighter aircraft in Israel but which had been paid for by the Argentines.

In late 1983 the US Secretary of State agreed to consult with the British on arms sales to Argentina. Each time the US did so, the British insisted that the Argentines could not be trusted until they had agreed to a formal cessation of hostilities and given up pressing on sovereignty, so that any enhancement of their military capability must be viewed with dismay. Washington increasingly felt this to be unimaginative. From late 1985 they argued that improved security relations with Argentina could be part of an effort to restructure and depoliticise the armed forces. This dialogue could not progress 'if all decisions on supplying military equipment were to be deferred to an indefinite future'. Argentina would start seeking equipment elsewhere, such as Peru or China. The US view was that 'if Argentina had to acquire equipment from external sources, it would be better if such equipment came from sources actively urging restraint.' In the event the US embargo on the sale of military effort was not lifted until 1994, when Argentina ordered 36 A-4Ms from US surplus. The last five of the original Argentine Skyhawks continued in service until they were retired in March 1999.

46

DIPLOMATIC FISHING

The inability of the Argentine Government to budge from its position made it impossible to move forward on the negotiation of other issues. Yet other issues had to be addressed, of which the most important was fishing. When the 1982 Shackleton Report had proposed a 200-mile fisheries limit this was roundly derided in an inter-agency assessment. Three problems were seen. First, the proposed limits would be contested by Argentina. Second, highly expensive exploratory fishing projects were proposed without any evidence that large-scale commercial operations would be viable. Third, enforcement would require specialised vessels and aircraft and would add significantly to the cost. Officials spoke of an initial outlay of £100 million and annual operating costs of £50 million. When announcing decisions on Shackleton's recommendations the Government simply said that this proposal required further study.

Thereafter it was stated that the matter was under consideration, but, as Howe noted in a paper for the Defence and Oversea Policy Committee, by December 1983 this line was 'wearing thin'. The previous month the Executive Council had formally requested a zone, claiming that revenue from licences and joint ventures could amount to as much as 30 per cent of the Islands' present budget. Those interested in fishing projects insisted that a proper system of management and control of stocks was already needed. There was concern that stocks of certain species were being depleted because of intensive fishing by other nations. Howe agreed that for this reason alone, matters could not be allowed to drift. However he was, at this time, also hoping for something out of the process which eventually led to the ill-fated Berne meeting, and he was reluctant to risk such a provocative move as a 200-mile limit, with the additional burden of policing it. The main offenders in over-fishing were Russians, Poles and Spaniards who were unlikely to cooperate in a regime derived from a contested British claim to sovereignty. Howe's preferred method was therefore to approach Argentina with a view to establishing a Regional Fisheries Administration. This would have to carry all the normal caveats on sovereignty. It seemed to make sense to make this approach through the Food and Agriculture Organisation (FAO) to explore how a regime might be run.

When the matter was discussed at the OD (FAF) Committee, MoD expressed its concern that the costs of policing even a regime agreed with Argentina would be prohibitive. The area of surveillance would be twice that currently covered. Even a token force of patrol vessels would cost £5 million per year to run (after capital costs) – in excess of the projected revenue of £3 million. Joint enforcement arrangements risked providing Argentina with information about British military deployments. With any political process with Argentina still at an early stage, an approach seemed premature. The Committee decided on more study, including the implications of a possible Argentine decision to announce its own zone.

The failure of the Berne process appeared to rule out discussions on the multilateral route, yet the costs of unilateralism still appeared prohibitive and the problem of what to do about fishing in the waters around the Falklands did not go away. After a year had passed Howe came back again with a proposal for a multilateral fisheries management regime in the South West Atlantic, covering a wider area than that over which the UK claimed jurisdiction. It would be established through the FAO, although this would still at some point require Argentine acquiescence and possibly co-opera- tion. Multilateral action would not only be preferable in conservation terms, and less open to challenge by the fishing nations, but also would avoid raising any sovereignty issues. Pressure was also coming from the Falklanders. Rex Hunt's October 1985 valedictory as Civil Commissioner contained a strong argument for a zone. A joint venture, negotiated by the Falkland Islands Government, between Coalite and the Japanese Company Taiyo, provided for two years' exploratory fishing. This would, however, cut across any effort to establish a multilateral regime and, for this reason, the FCO, faced with pressure from Coalite to approve the scheme, had been prevaricating. On the other hand the proposed venture would provide more information on fishing stocks and the basis for any future licensing system, and so Howe wanted to change the terms of the joint venture to make it more compatible with his preferred approach, although the effect was to make it unattractive to the parties.

In December Howe proposed to Thatcher, who agreed, that a multilat- eral regime should still be sought but preparations had to be made to pursue the unilateralist option. MoD remained unhappy about the legal issues raised and the consequential international opprobrium, especially if Britain was seen to be undermining the work of the FAO and putting off reconciliation with Argentina. So great might be the reaction that it would become even harder to hold the line on arms sales. Any zone was likely to be challenged, probably by Argentina, and Britain's stretched maritime resources would be stretched even further, not to mention the problems caused if enforcement came to require opening fire on unarmed vessels. And who was going to pay for all this? Minister of State John Stanley took the view that:

It would be extremely unwise and damaging – both diplomatically and in defence terms – for HMG to assume what would be a major new defence task in preserving the integrity of a unilateral EFL, and then be forced to abandon it within a few weeks because of insufficient RN and/or Fishery Protection resources. Better not to take on the task at all than be forced to abandon it in a few weeks.

Another year passed and still no progress on the multilateral approach. The FAO did agree to approach all concerned and to study the situation, but this work would not be completed until June 1986 at the earliest. Argentina showed some interest in the FAO initiative but then decided to opt instead for a network of bilateral agreements. This cast doubt over the feasibility of the multilateral approach. Meanwhile, the 1986 fishing season threatened to see the stocks depleted further, with squid the main target of Japanese and Korean vessels. This was despite optimism at the start of the year about assurances from the Governments of these countries that their fleets would show voluntary restraint. Although unilateralism still seemed expensive and risked even a confrontation with the Soviet Union, it was now becoming apparent that this option could not be so readily dismissed as in the past.

The pace was forced by Argentina. In May 1986 an Argentine warship sunk a Taiwanese fishing vessel, more than 200 miles from the Argentine coast but within 200 miles of the Falklands. It was outside the 150-mile FIPZ but in waters where the UK could claim jurisdiction. Such a vigorous assertion of the Argentine territorial claim and the readiness to use force demonstrated that the tendencies that had led to trouble in 1982 might not have gone away. Britain deplored the loss of life and the Argentine 'attempt to pursue a sovereign claim by force'. More progress was made by Buenos Aires with the Soviet Union and Bulgaria, with whom agreements were signed in July 1986, and which allowed fishing in the disputed waters within 200 miles of the Islands. Britain responded by making clear that this agreement had no validity in international law, a position dismissed by Argentina.

By September 1986 there was no choice but to declare a unilateral fisheries zone around the Falklands Islands. There was now more confidence that countries would acquiesce (the Soviet Union was under moderate leadership) although Argentina might try and mount a challenge. Howe's proposal was received with some misgivings, with MoD still worried about enforcement and the Treasury about cost. The estimates presented at the start of 1985 put the maximum sustainable yield from a zone at around 210,000 tonnes, generating probably some £1.85 million in licences each year and at most £3.1 million. MoD estimates, assuming that a unilateral regime would demand considerable enforcement, saw a requirement for three vessels at £13 million each plus an aircraft at £10 million, followed by £12 million per annum running costs. The islanders argued for a more modest form of self-policing, which the FCO thought would lack credibility and would still cost more than £3 million per year. All this had to be set against an annual Falkland Islands budget of £5 million, already close to deficit. By late 1986, the position had not improved, although it was pointed out that the low revenue estimates assumed a five per cent licence fee though Argentina charged 15 per cent. To manage the budget, therefore, the proposal was to make do with a civil force of one vessel and one aircraft, but assuming military back-up if necessary. There was then an issue of rules of engagement when a vessel, particularly if Argentine, refused to comply. By early October it had been agreed that the enforcement of the new Falkland Islands Conservation and Management Zone (FICZ) would be a civil task. There would be no increase in planned military force levels and any military assistance in enforcement would be subject to military priorities and repayment. Two ships would be on station, one in each of the main fishing areas, for at least the first three months of the new regime and aerial surveillance would be increased in intensity. There remained concern about getting the civil force in place and also what to do if Argentine vessels probed the zone and refused to leave when asked. Arresting Argentine vessels would be provocative and there were no obviously safe options for such tricky circumstances.

On 29 October 1986, after prior notification to interested governments (including Argentina), the Government announced the introduction of the FIPZ to enter into force on 1 February 1987. The boundary was set to coincide with the existing FIPZ, except for the omission of a small segment in the south-west where a median line with Argentina would cross into the FIPZ. Britain also claimed an entitlement to a zone for fishery and continental shelf purposes extending to a maximum of 200nm from the baselines, although this outer area (later called the 'doughnut') was not subjected to a fishery regime under Falkland Islands legislation. While it might have been unfortunate that unilateral action had to be taken, and no progress had been made on normalisation of relations, the blame for this was laid at Argentina's door. Every initiative, Sir Geoffrey told the Commons, has been rebuffed:

> We have suggested measure after measure to enable us to normalise relations with Argentina. The Argentine Government have made it repeatedly clear that the only matter on which they wish to commence discussions is that of sovereignty.

A political storm was expected and one ensued. The Argentine Government immediately refused to recognise the new zone, saying that it involved 'maritime areas over which the Argentine Republic exercises full sovereignty and jurisdictional rights'. Army leave was halted, although the evidence was that the main effort would be to use the incident to gain diplomatic advantage. On 11 November the Permanent Council of the OAS passed a Resolution, sponsored by Uruguay, asking the British and Argentine Governments 'to use all possible opportunities for negotiations and to refrain from taking actions introducing changes in the already delicate situation'. To the Government's irritation it was supported by the US Government, which in return made little secret of its irritation with Britain for what it considered a provocative step in an area where it was still trying to claw back the ground lost as a result of its support for Britain during 1982. In Britain the Labour Party warned of a dangerous escalation. The press pointed to the policy's apparent dependence on Argentina being, to use Howe's words, 'sensible' – but this was precisely what Argentina had not been in the past. Britain's allies were unhappy with the revival of this anomalous issue. 'For Britain it is becoming rather lonely,' observed the *Financial Times*, 'an offer of direct and unconditional talks would not come amiss.'[1] Argentina did use the controversy to promise a formal end to hostilities in exchange for lifting the zone, but did so (through a statement to the press) in a way that was easy for the British Government to dismiss. The annual vote at the General Assembly went decisively in Argentina's favour – 116 to four, with 34 abstaining (compared with 107 to four the previous year). Undoubtedly the Government found the diplomatic pressure uncomfortable but it was already well aware after four years of the 'surely it would not do any harm to talk' type of argument, that it was really quite easy to ignore. Allies and partners queried why Britain cared so much for its sovereignty over these Islands; the corollary of this was that they certainly were not going to get too embroiled in an argument with Britain over an equally baffling Argentine claim.

Despite the initial fuss the policy was soon a great success. The fishing nations, whose attitudes were in the end the most crucial in this matter, did not object. By the end of the year 500 applications had been received, over twice the number of licences that were to be issued in the first half of 1987. Only two applications came from Britain where few firms owned appropriate vessels. So the official estimates turned out to be too gloomy. In the first year of operation, fishery patrol boats and a Dornier surveillance aircraft did cost £4 million, but no call was made on military resources and licence income was received from 220 vessels, adding £14 million to the budget. This, as the Governor noted, 'transformed at a stroke the financial outlook of the territory'. While there had been only modest growth in GDP per head in constant prices from 1980 to 1986, from 1986 to 1987 it more than doubled, and then it doubled again over the next year. Government revenues over the 1985/86 financial year were about £6 million; for 1988/89 they were projected to reach £35 million. Not all of this was due to fishing: the transfer from overseas to local ownership had sustained many of the farms at a difficult time. Governor Jewkes' valedictory in November 1988 noted that financial aid was no longer required from Britain, and that the problems for the local community were now those of absorbing new immigrants and accepting changes to their traditional way of life.

Breakthrough

The transformed economy gave a new sense of confidence to the islanders, a rising population, and the prospect of long-term viability. The argument that only co-operation with the mainland could secure the future of the Falklands was dispelled. The potentially positive impact of the unilateral action was soon evident. Howe's October 1986 statement had left open the door to Argentina by offering discussions on fishery issues. When it became apparent that London was not going to back down on its fisheries zone, Buenos Aires made an indirect approach through the US Government proposing discussion of fishery topics, in particular conservation and humanitarian issues, such as sea and air rescue. When the issue was discussed in July 1987, the Prime Minister remained sceptical of any approach from Argentina, yet acknowledged that as it appeared to follow Britain's own suggestions for discussions on practical matters it could not be dismissed out of hand. It took until early 1988 for a reply to be received via the Americans to a generally positive British response. The Government's formula for a statement reserving respective positions on sovereignty was accepted but this was combined with a request for direct talks.

The position was complicated by the announcement of military manoeuvres on and around the Islands over 7–31 March 1988, to practise reinforcement of the reduced garrison using Mount Pleasant Airfield. Although less than 1000 troops and a small number of aircraft were involved in exercise FIRE FOCUS, it led to an angry Argentine reaction, American irritation at a lack of consultation (it coincided with a planned visit by the Vice-Chairman of the Joint Chiefs to Argentina), and sufficient storm elsewhere in Latin America for it to be considered prudent to cancel a planned ministerial visit to Brazil. Argentina even attempted, unsuccessfully, to take the matter to the UN Security Council. The timing, which had nothing to do with the discussions on fisheries, was nonetheless viewed in Buenos Aires and, for that matter, Washington, as a response to the latest proposals to achieve a breakthrough on these talks. On 6 April Secretary of State Shultz sent Howe a strongly worded message, arguing that much misunderstanding might have been avoided if the UK had 'availed itself of the informal channel of communication to Argentina which has been provided by the US since the Falklands conflict.' He also suggested that the timing was poor, derailing an initiative by Alfonsin to declare an end to hostilities as well as other steps to normalise relations.

The FCO was looking for a way to calm the situation, and so wished to respond favourably while not agreeing with direct talks. It was hard, however, to see whether a proposal for an exchange of technical information on fisheries, suggested to the Americans in a 'non-paper' of July 1988, was going to prove attractive. Then, in August 1988, an opportunity came. Shultz was to visit Argentina and the Americans suggested that this was an opportunity to explore options for improving British-Argentine relations.

British conditions for direct talks remained avoiding sovereignty and acknowledgement that there were two maritime jurisdictions. The question was whether Argentine assurances through the Americans would suffice. In September the Argentine Foreign Minister was elected President of the UN General Assembly. The Foreign Secretary decided that it would be best on balance to pay a courtesy call when he visited the Assembly, as a snub would be noticed. The Prime Minister noted that 'I utterly recoil from this and so I think would the relatives of all those who lost their lives in the Falklands. Argentina has not announced a cessation of hostilities.'

Shultz had not given up. Argentina had responded to the British 'non-paper' of July with one of its own. To the British this seemed unimpressive – nothing on either of the two key reassurances requested – but the American saw a readiness to engage in a responsible manner, and extracted promises that any talks would contain no surprises. With the Americans pressing for a gesture, it was agreed that a meeting could take place between the Argentine Foreign Minister, in his capacity as President of the Assembly, and the UK Permanent Representative to the UN, Sir Crispin Tickell. This took place in Geneva on 14 December 1988, and appeared to have made progress. It did seem that the Argentines now acknowledged the possibility of practical talks on bilateral issues while sovereignty was not discussed. Tickell suggested assurances should be sent through the Americans. The Prime Minister remained wary of the dialogue being conducted via the Americans – 'I have been through that before'. In the event Argentina could not confirm their assurances in writing. By this time new presidential elections were imminent, on 14 May 1989, and it was decided to wait.

Just before the election, there was another indication of the durability of the established arrangements for the Falklands when, on 16 January 1989, the MV *Indiana I* arrived in Montevideo on her maiden voyage from Stanley to re-establish links with the mainland. It was registered in the Bahamas and while the ownership included British and other companies with fishing interests in the area, the ultimate owner was the Falkland Islands Government. Argentina protested vigorously, and even encouraged the local dockers' unions to refuse to unload the ship. While Britain denied that a ship with a commercial purpose and an irregular schedule could be considered a ferry service, the event confirmed the failure of Argentina's policy of keeping the Falklands isolated.

Since the war Argentina had managed to isolate Britain diplomatically, in that the Government's policy was widely seen to be intransigent and unyielding. Yet by every practical indicator it was British policy that was succeeding. The FICZ had been established successfully and the Islands could look forward to a more confident and prosperous future. Provisions for their defence had now reached a steady state. At no point had Britain suggested the slightest wavering on its claim to sovereignty or its willingness to even discuss the matter further with Buenos Aires. The Argentine strategy of wearing down British resistance was failing. The more sympathetic Liberal and Labour parties had failed to make headway at the polls. Public opinion in Britain was supportive of improved relations with Argentina and probably ready even for concessions on the Falklands, but it had long ceased to consider either matter a high priority.[2]

Despite all this, expectations of a radical reappraisal on the Argentine side were not high. They were thought to have suffered a further setback when the relatively unknown Dr Carlos Saul Menem of the Partido Justicialista (Peronists) won the presidential election. His campaign had been highly nationalistic, and even included a speech envisaging more bloodshed in the continuing struggle for the Malvinas. The language later moderated but the 'recovery' of the Islands remained a persistent theme. The JIC's view was that Argentine forces were insufficient to mount another invasion, and it would take time and much money to acquire such a capability. Nonetheless, so concerned was London that before the inauguration a message was sent through the US Government assuring Menem that any threat to the Falklands would be met with firmness, while also re-iterating the possibility of talks on practical matters. The Prime Minister did send a personal message to Menem on the inauguration day in July, but it was terse: 'I congratulate you on your inauguration as President of Argentina, in accordance with the result of democratic elections, and wish you success.'

It was therefore a pleasant surprise that the day after the inauguration on 8 July 1989, Menem and his new Foreign Minister, Dr Domingo Cavallo, announced that they wished to see improved relations with Britain and proposed direct Argentine/British talks within the framework of the UN that would not necessarily deal with sovereignty. The reason for this bold step was an awareness that the previous Government's policy was not getting anywhere and that the continuing dispute with Britain was limiting Argentina's ability to improve its links with the West, essential for a restoration of the country's economic and political fortunes, and also its own ability to take advantage of the lucrative opportunities for revenue from the South Atlantic fisheries. The new tone was welcomed by Britain, as was a proposal, delivered on 13 July 1989, for direct talks with British officials on a basis which would not prejudice the sovereignty position of either side. Restrictions on British imports were lifted on 1 August. 'Talks about talks' took place on 16–17 August at the UN between Sir Crispin Tickell and the Special Representative of the Argentine Government, Sr Garcia del Solar, and it was agreed to hold a substantive meeting in Madrid in mid-October. A 'diplomatic package' provided for the ending of restrictions on both Interests Sections and for direct access to Foreign Ministries for the first time since the conflict.

London recognised the need to take advantage of this opportunity while it lasted. The economic situation in Argentina was as dire as ever and would eventually limit Menem's political room for manoeuvre. It was noted that at the September 1989 meeting of the Non-Aligned Movement, Menem had taken care to confirm Argentina's 'inalienable right' of sovereignty over the Islands, asserting that these would eventually be recovered through bilateral negotiations, while at the same time ensuring that the NAM resolution was not over-critical of Britain's stance. At the end of 1989 the JIC assessment was that a breakdown of law and order was possible, and that this could lead to Menem's dependence on the military. Still it seemed that, for the moment, Menem's diplomatic strategy enjoyed military support. Even more reassuring was the judgement that in the event of a political turn for the worse, Argentine forces were insufficient to pose a serious threat to the Falklands.

Against this background the talks progressed. On 28 September 1989, the new Foreign Secretary, John Major, met his counterpart, Dr Cavallo, in the margins of the UN General Assembly in New York and then on 17–19 October 1989, talks were held in Madrid, led by Tickell and Garcia del Solar. They drew on the sovereignty 'umbrella' formula as used during the 1970s to confirm that nothing that was to transpire in their discussions should be interpreted as changing, supporting or denying either side's position with regard to sovereignty or territorial and maritime jurisdiction over the Falkland Islands, the Dependencies and the surrounding areas.

The Joint Statement met British objectives. Sovereignty was not discussed and it was agreed that financial discrimination against British companies would be ended, while air and sea links and consular relations would be resumed. It was possible to get round the Argentine failure to announce a cessation of hostilities, and agree to hold specialised talks on fisheries and military confidence building measures. The FIPZ would remain in place, other than for a slight enlargement of the territorial sea around the Islands and that of South Georgia from 3 to 12 nautical miles from baselines. Further talks would take place in February 1990, in Madrid, to discuss progress and the restoration of full diplomatic relations. In return Cavallo expressed satisfaction with the prospect of much better relations with the European Community and the US, and a reduced British military presence. The new developments were greeted with inevitable suspicion in the Falklands, where all eight members of the Legislative Council, elected on 11 October 1989, publicly declared that they would not support closer links between the Islands and Argentina. However, having been reassured on the sovereignty issue by a full briefing from the Governor and a message from Major, the islanders accepted the merits of an improvement in UK/Argentine relations.

By the time of the second round of Madrid talks progress had been made in all areas and diplomatic contacts were now regular and productive. There was no vote pushed at the UN General Assembly, consular relations were resumed on 22 December, as were commercial relations (including direct flights between the UK and Argentina). A high level British trade mission visited Argentina, and working groups on fisheries and CBMs had met. Argentina wanted to see the abolition of the FIPZ. A Joint Statement of 15

February agreed that the unilaterally imposed FIPZ would be replaced by a mutually agreed system of confidence building measures (Interim Reciprocal Information and Consultation System – IRICS). A new system would monitor and control military movements. All military units approaching coasts closer than 70 nautical miles (by air) and 50 nautical miles (by sea) had to give 48 hours' advance notice of their intention to do so. In the case of combatant units, a movement that posed a military or political difficulty could only proceed on the basis of mutual agreement. In addition, a system of advance notification of 25 days for larger deployments over a wide area of the South Atlantic was agreed.

The statement also proposed the resumption of diplomatic relations, continuation of the fisheries and CBMs working groups, abolition of visas, preparation of an investment promotion and protection agreement, co-operation in the fields of drugs and the environment, and a visit by Argentine relatives to the military cemetery on the Islands, on carefully prepared terms. In the margins of the talks, the Argentine Government even agreed that it might be prepared to allow RAF aircraft to use airfields in Argentina, and would not pressure the Brazilian and Uruguayan Governments to deny diversion facilities. The final symbolic moment came on 19 February 1990, when diplomatic relations between Britain and Argentina were resumed. President Bush wrote to the Prime Minister on 20 February marking the end of a 'lengthy and difficult period in Great Britain's relations with Argentina'. After noting the benefits to the hemispheric relations of the US, he concluded: 'I am certain the future historians will note the positive results that arise from a nation standing up resolutely for what it believes.' Even, he might have added, at times against the advice of its closest ally.

The Interests Section reverted to an Embassy on 26 February. The first Argentine Ambassador to Britain since the 1982 conflict, Sr Mario Campora, arrived in the UK on 11 May 1990. Britain's Ambassador, Mr Humphrey Maud, arrived in Argentina on 15 July 1990.

SECTION TEN

47

THE FRANKS REPORT

A number of aspects of the Falklands Campaign became the subject of official inquiries. This final section considers these inquiries in the light of the evidence and analysis contained in this book. Their impact was shaped by the fact of victory. Public opinion was more forgiving than it might otherwise have been of the handling of both the underlying dispute and the particular crisis which led to the war. Nor did the various shortcomings in military capabilities have the political effect they might have done if the forces had suffered an embarrassing defeat. The only charge that the Government found it difficult to refute was that it had deliberately forgone a chance for peace by sinking the *Belgrano*, although this was the most poorly founded of the charges. In this chapter I consider the first charge, of missing the warning signs of imminent war. This was addressed by the first of the major inquiries into the conflict – the Franks Report. In Chapter 20 of the first volume, covering the origins of the conflict, I questioned the Report's conclusions: in this chapter I explain why it turned out the way it did.

On 8 April 1982, though the Task Force was sailing and Haig was beginning to shuttle, the political aftershocks of the Argentine invasion had not quite subsided. The only ministerial resignations had come from the FCO and it was therefore supposed that that was the Department most to blame and most in need of a thorough overhaul. Jo Grimond, the former Liberal leader, asked the Prime Minister if she would 'order an inquiry into the conduct of the Foreign and Commonwealth Office in recent years and the sufficiency of the advice and information supplied to Ministers.' The Prime Minister, not known for her affection for the FCO, refused 'so wide an inquiry', but took the opportunity to acknowledge that at some point there was bound to be a demand for an investigation into why the Argentine invasion was allowed to happen and why it came as such a surprise. Accordingly she told the House that she favoured 'a review of the way in which the Government Departments concerned discharged their responsibilities in the period leading up to the Argentine invasion of the Falkland Islands.' She would inform the House in due course about the form the review should take.[1]

From the start three aspects of the review were clearly established. While there was an issue of why Argentine intentions and capabilities had been so seriously misjudged there was a larger issue of a failure in policy and that required a consideration of how the Falklands problem had been handled by successive governments. This large policy question was bound to move well beyond particular administrative or individual failings. That could argue for a Select Committee Report, but the Government were loath to encourage such an approach, because of the danger that it might become mired in partisan controversy and, more seriously, because of the security concerns raised by passing on to MPs the intelligence material necessary for a full analysis. Nor did the other familiar format of a Tribunal presided over by a senior judge appear appropriate. Such tribunals normally met in open session, which would create problems on the intelligence side, would tend to put individuals in the dock, as they would be subjected to cross-examination, and would normally take an inordinate amount of time. Moreover as Government held all the information there was no need for a special tribunal to collect it.

By 15 April, the Cabinet Secretary, Robert Armstrong, had already concluded that the only sensible way forward would be to put together a small group of Privy Counsellors – initially he thought three would be sufficient – to sift through the evidence. They could be trusted with the intelligence, understand the policy processes and deliberate expeditiously. There would be one member from each of the main political parties and they would be presided over by a more impartial figure. The question was whether this should be a senior judge or a distinguished academic. Armstrong did not initially think a former civil servant would be considered sufficiently impartial. Lists of names began to circulate.

Debate was further stimulated by a minute from the Foreign Secretary in early May, which set down the terms that were, in the end, largely followed. The review, he wrote, should 'cover all relevant departments and agencies of government' and would 'need full access to all relevant documents, including intelligence.' The issues now were how far it should look back – at least, said Pym, to the 1976 Shackleton incident and withdrawal of Ambassadors – the size of the group, which he still put at three, and the profession of the chairman. The Lord Chancellor was opposing the use of a judge because of the political sensitivity of the inquiry. The former civil servant route still did not seem promising because the list of former civil servants who were also Privy Counsellors contained only two names and one was needed for another inquiry while the second, Lord Franks, was aged 77. Other candidates could be admitted to the Privy Council if necessary, however, and that was certainly to be required if an academic was chosen.

Towards the end of May there were some discussions among senior ministers. There was little enthusiasm for the review, a term much preferred to 'inquiry', and doubts about its utility. Nonetheless it was recognised to be unavoidable and there was agreement that the form in which it was already being discussed was the most suitable. The inclination was to encourage as long a view as possible, pushing back the starting point to 1965 when the Argentine claim was raised afresh and Whitehall first concluded that the Falkland Islands were not in the last resort defendable. This was the basis on which on 21 June 1982, less than a week after the Argentine surrender, the Prime Minister wrote to all party leaders, recalling her answer to Jo Grimond's question and conveying the views reached by the Government on the form that a review would take. It would need to satisfy parliamentary and public opinion, and involve a small group with access to all relevant material able to devote a considerable amount of effort to the task. The proposal was for three Privy Counsellors, two of whom might be former ministers. As to the Chairman, a senior judge would not be appropriate because the questions were not 'justiciable' and had a high political content, nor a retired civil servant because the records of government would be under investigation. The inclination therefore was for an academic, and probably an historian. They would look back as far as 1965 and would be asked:

> To review the way in which the Departments concerned have under successive Governments discharged their responsibilities in relation to the Falkland Islands, with particular reference to the period leading up to the Argentine invasion of 2 April, 1982, and to report.

The Prime Minister met with the leaders of all opposition parties, concluding with the Labour opposition on 6 July 1982. By this time the group had been expanded so that it involved two Conservatives and two Labour former ministers. The enthusiasm for academics had waned, and two former civil servants now presented themselves: Sir Patrick Nairne and Lord Franks as chairman. The latter was chosen after the Prime Minister had regretted in conversation to Armstrong that he was no longer available, and was surprised to discover that he was still very much alive. His age had not impaired his faculties and his record of public service was substantial. Moreover he had the advantage of an affinity with the Liberal-SDP Alliance, which meant that there was not complete dominance by the main parties. A civil servant from the Home Office, Anthony Rawsthorne, who had no previous Falklands connections, was appointed as a secretary. The Labour Party's main concern was with the reference back to 1965, wary that the Prime Minister was hoping to deflect blame from the most recent period by having the policies of earlier administrations picked over. She agreed, however, that the priority was the events leading to the Argentine invasion. In the event they started from 1965, with the report gathering in detail as it approached 1982.

On 12 July the Prime Minister was able to write to Lord Franks inviting him to Chair the review and to announce this to Parliament. In addition to Sir Patrick Nairne, the Committee comprised Lord Barber and Lord Watkinson for the Conservatives, and Lord Lever and the Rt. Hon. Merlyn Rees for Labour. The remit was now:

> To review the way in which the responsibilities of Government in relation to the Falkland Islands and their dependencies were discharged in the period leading up to the Argentine invasion of the Falkland Islands on 2 April 1982, taking account of all such factors in previous years as are relevant; and to report.

It had changed in two significant respects. First, it was to be up to the Committee how far back they wanted to go, and second, it was the performance of the Government as a whole that was to be reviewed, and not just that of individual departments.

As the Prime Minister explained in her letter to Lord Franks:

> The review is intended to be an investigation of the performance of institutions and systems, and of the handling of the issues by departments separately and collectively. In other words it is to be a review of the way in which the governmental machinery operated in relation to the Falkland Islands over the relevant period.

She expected the Committee 'to identify any areas in which the machinery failed to function effectively or where errors of judgement occurred; and to draw lessons for the future conduct of affairs', but 'the form of the inquiry, and the pressure for an early report, imply an assumption that its primary objective will not be to attempt to assign responsibility and allocate blame to individual officials.' She did not want to tell the Committee how to go about its business, but suggested that if it was likely that it would be commenting adversely on the performance or judgement of particular individuals then they should have a chance to respond to any particular criticisms prior to publication. All information would be made available, although previous Prime Ministers were being asked to agree that papers from their administrations could be consulted. While it was the 'Government's firm intention to present the Committee's report to Parliament in full, as it is submitted', they would wish to protect 'information made available to the Committee whose disclosure would be prejudicial to national security or damaging to the international relations of the United Kingdom.' These would be the only grounds on which any proposals for deletions could be considered.

Within Whitehall the relevant departments were told to assemble a collection of papers with a covering note. This should be 'to present a self-contained account of its own handling of the issues, identifying all the documents relevant to the decisions taken or advice tendered by it.' They were reminded that the Prime Minister had stated that the Committee would have unrestricted access, including to intelligence materials' and that 'every single bit of evidence should go before it'. In discussions within the Cabinet Office it had been acknowledged that it would be 'unethical (and almost certainly impracticable) for Departments to agree in advance on a fully co-ordinated story for presentation to the Committee' but that the Committee would need some help in interpreting the material. The Committee took evidence in private, seeing all the key figures. While records were kept of the evidence sessions none were kept of its drafting process. Its report was produced on schedule and agreed unanimously.

When the report was published in January 1983,[2] it was widely seen to have let the Government off the hook, but also spared the previous Labour Government embarrassment. One issue, for example, was whether the Committee should point out that there was no evidence to support former Prime Minister Callaghan's contention that he had used covert sources to warn Argentina that Britain was sending two frigates and a submarine to the South Atlantic in late 1977. The first draft read: 'We have had no evidence that the Argentine Government were informed of this deployment'. Lever changed 'were informed' to 'became aware'.[3] Yet it was Callaghan in the Commons debate on the report who provided one of the most damning critiques:

> for 338 paragraphs the Franks Report painted a splendid picture, delineating the light and shade. The glowing colours came out. When Franks got to paragraph 339, he got fed up with the canvas that he was painting and chucked a bucket of whitewash over it.[4]

This is what this key, and most carefully drafted, paragraph 339 states:

> Against this background we have pointed out in this Chapter where different decisions might have been taken, where fuller consideration of alternative courses of action might, in our opinion, have been advantageous, and where the machinery of Government could have been better used. But, if the British Government had acted differently in the ways we have indicated, it is impossible to judge what the impact on the Argentine Government or the implications for the course of events might have been. There is no reasonable basis for any suggestion – which would be purely hypothetical – that the invasion would have been prevented if the Government had acted in the ways indicated in our Report. Taking account of these considerations, and of all the evidence we have received, we conclude that we would not be justified in attaching any criticism or blame to the present Government for the Argentine Junta's decision to commit its act of unprovoked aggression in the invasion of the Falkland Islands on 2 April 1982.

To what extent was Callaghan's charge of a whitewash fair, and did the Government, as was alleged at the time, in some way influence the conclusions?

It was of course the case that the choice of Privy Counsellors was unlikely to produce a highly radical analysis, but there is no evidence that Ministers attempted to exercise any influence on the Committee's proceedings except, unavoidably, when subjecting themselves to examination during the course of the evidence sessions. By and large departments were scrupulous in adhering to the guidelines.

It was always understood that there would be some excisions in the final version as a result of security concerns and the need to protect sources.[5] The intelligence community wanted this to be interpreted extremely restrictively, certainly without mention of the Joint Intelligence Committee. Franks asked the Cabinet Secretary to explain why the Government 'does not avow' JIC and the assessments staff. The arguments were presented in a classic defence of official secrecy: confidence in confidentiality improves the quality of decision-making; once the committee system of government is exposed collective responsibility would be undermined; selective disclosure, whatever the particular merits, undermines the general policy; any discussion of intelligence procedure leads inevitably into the taboo area of intelligence collection; much might have appeared in the press, but such disclosures were often inaccurate and dated, any authorised disclosures were bound to be more credible and would also pose for governments the challenging task of where to draw a line when asked for further disclosures.[6] Lord Franks was unconvinced. The final draft prompted concern among the Cabinet Secretariat and the intelligence agencies 'at the high profile given to intelligence and the content of specific intelligence reports in the paper.' This 'marked a significant departure from previous practice' even though the JIC's existence and descriptions of its machinery were already to be found in the press. Attempts to dissuade the Committee from disclosure persisted until the last moment.

This is not to say that the intelligence community did not influence the Committee's conclusions. As I noted in Volume One, the Committee appeared to have accepted the conclusions of an internal study conducted by a senior figure from the intelligence community in May 1982. This study argued that it was not until 31 March that the Junta decided to invade and that this was to a considerable extent a response to the political situation in Argentina. This view, if correct, would mean that there was little that the British Government could have done to prevent the invasion and rendered virtually irrelevant issues connected to the quality of British crisis management in March 1982. Within Whitehall this view did not command universal acceptance as it failed to distinguish between the decision to set in motion an invasion and that to give the final go-ahead. This limitation was also recognised within the Cabinet Office where this report was described as being 'within a category of its own':

> It contains many facts but also a Part IV, Conclusions and Recommendations. It is also *ex post facto* in so far as it was written

after the invasion. I also detect uneasiness that one Government Agency should be allowed to put in material which allows value judgements and even recommendations for changes in procedures, something which it is surely the review's task to pronounce upon. There is even a whiff of exculpation about it, at least in the eyes of certain people.

While at first it was thought that Lord Franks would find the material of value for his own purposes, he ordered copies for all members of the Committee and it seems that the analysis was found to be persuasive.

It was not only the conclusion that the British were caught out by such a late decision that was welcomed by the Government. The report drew attention to the extent to which successive governments had been prepared to negotiate about sovereignty and had considered the Islands indefensible with *Endurance* only of limited value. The main area in which the Government was vulnerable was the lack of discussion of policy outside of the FCO and especially among Ministers, as well as the lack of military contingency planning. The Home Office was irritated by the slighting references to the Nationalities Bill. To have given British citizenship to the islanders would have invited Hong Kong and other Dependencies also to have done so, although it was noted that in the exceptional circumstances of the conflict, the Government had agreed to give technical support to a Private Bill introduced into the Lords by Baroness Vickers that would confer British citizenship on all Falkland Islanders. The Treasury meanwhile suggested that the Chief Secretary's negative response to the Foreign Secretary's request for additional financial provision to provide alternative transport links could be explained by his belief that there were already sufficient funds in the FCO budget.

The amount of detail provided by the review ensured that conspiracy theories, particularly those based on advanced knowledge of Argentine plans, could be discounted, while there was sufficient for those who wished to develop an alternative account of recent events. As noted in Volume One such an alternative could address the failure of the Government to pay proper attention to the Falklands issue and to consider the implications of policy decisions on Argentine attitudes, and to appreciate the full consequences of the strategic weakness that had been allowed to develop when they were suddenly confronted by the South Georgia crisis in March 1982. Britain had found itself at war as the result of many policy decisions, rarely in themselves unreasonable, stretching back over many years. As Alex Danchev has observed, the Committee found itself in 'the unusual position of reviewing a putative diplomatic failure in the light of a decisive military success.'[7] The national humiliation of the Argentine occupation had been reversed. After the requisite political points had been made, the complex question of whether war could have been avoided could be left to historians.

48

LESSONS

For many years Britain had struggled against the view, which it was hard to refute, of a former great power in decline, withdrawing from its international commitments and falling behind economically. Few would have been confident, after the recourse to the IMF of 1976 and then the deep recession from which the country was only starting to emerge, of a reversal in economic fortunes. Many would wonder whether the country could, or should, be revived through an impressive demonstration of military prowess. This was not a means by which productivity could be raised, infrastructure restored, or public services improved. Yet, with all these qualifications, Britain's allies could applaud the same sort of stubbornness in the British character for which many had been grateful 40 years earlier, which led to taking on dictatorships and challenging aggression. After all that had been said about the softening effect of the consumer culture, a western country had shown that it had the mental, as well as physical, toughness to take risks and accept casualties. 'The lesson of the Falklands', observed Mrs Thatcher, speaking at Cheltenham on 3 July, a few weeks after the 'great victory', was:

> that Britain has not changed and that this nation still has those sterling qualities which shine throughout history. This generation can match their fathers and grandfathers in ability, courage in resolution.

Those defeated by the war included the 'waverers and the fainthearts' who 'believed that our decline was irreversible'. Now it could be seen that 'We have ceased to be a nation in retreat.' The 'Falklands Factor' for a while became part of British political life, strengthening the Government's hand as it pushed through economic reforms and helping it to gain a substantial victory in the May 1983 General Election. It was perhaps because of this victory and the close association thereafter between the Falklands and 'Thatcherism' that those who disliked the phenomenon most, especially in the media, were so keen to characterise the war as evidence of narrow nationalism and pointless violence.[1]

The basic surprise with the campaign was that it had taken place at all, far away from the European theatre, which dominated defence provision, and against an unexpected enemy. The second surprise was that in such unpropitious circumstances things had turned out so well, although it might also be pointed out that Argentina was by no means the most sophisticated or numerically strong enemy the British could expect to fight, and the nature of the combat played to Britain's strengths. The result had never been a foregone conclusion, and those who had fought the war, perhaps more so than those who conducted later analyses, were all too well aware of how a more intelligent and organised, or in some cases just more lucky, enemy might have been able to produce a much less satisfactory result for Britain. The deficiencies in British capabilities caused few surprises. Many were well known when the campaign started and enhancements and improvements were already in the plans. Only years of financial stringency had denied them to the forces.

Wars, as one of the post-conflict reviews noted, 'have a habit of occurring at a time and place other than those expected in formal policy assessments or scenarios'. They have to be fought with the forces and equipment in hand, not what was planned for the future. The Falklands was exactly the sort of war that Britain's forces had not planned to fight. It had been many years since a requirement to reinforce dependent territories had justified any force enhancements, and it had been assumed that in most contingencies of any major size, when British communities were at risk, there would be allies at hand. Indeed, only in the context of a wider western effort, probably in support of the US, were major operations out of the NATO area contemplated. The intelligence and logistic capacity to mount operations far from home had been run down. Large aircraft carriers had been abandoned. It was entirely fortuitous that the Ascension Island base had been available, at 3500 miles from the operational area still close enough to provide an air terminal, an operational airfield, a communication facility, and a training area. So long as they were politically tenable, even isolated island bases had their value. In the end, therefore, there was just enough left to be able to mount the operation but in many respects it was a close run thing. The logistics achievement, in getting fuel, ammunition, spares, and all the other essential stores to the South Atlantic, and, once there, to distribute it to the fighting units, was remarkable.

The war was fought with the military assets available to Britain at the start of the campaign and a few others that could be rushed into service during its course. In this sense it vindicated a policy that had been put under severe challenge with the progressive contraction of the defence budget, namely the determination to maintain a 'balanced' force, with a little bit of everything, rather than concentrate on a few specialised areas in an alliance division of labour. It was possible to cope with an alternative contingency to the one for which most planning took place, requiring armoured warfare and intensive air campaigns close to home, because sufficient long-range naval and, to a more limited extent, air capabilities had been maintained. It helped that the enemy was of Argentine rather than Soviet dimensions. Against a more substantial force the risks would have been too great. As it was they were on the margins.

While MoD did not accept, in its first public post-war reflections, that anything had happened to change the 'broad strategic thrust' of British defence policy, in practice this could not be the case. Not only had the Royal Navy been able to rehabilitate itself, and its carriers, as vital to the nation's security, but attitudes at home and abroad to Britain as a military power changed. One official recalled the growing alarm among senior officers as they realised that they might actually have to fight a war apart from the Americans. The fact that they did so successfully gave them a credibility to which they could previously only aspire.[2]

Even so in some critical areas the effort was highly dependent upon American help: not causing problems with the use of Ascension Island and providing fuel, the provision of specialist equipment and in particular Sidewinder missiles, not to mention the regular provision of intelligence material and access to satellite-based communications, without which it would have been extremely difficult to conduct the war sensibly and effectively.

In general the political management of the campaign had worked well. The line of command at the highest level had been clear and was respected. The Government was not required to adjudicate between competing forms of military advice and by and large showed itself ready to back the judgement of the Chief of the Defence Staff and the Task Force commanders. There had been moments when the full implications of military moves had not been fully appreciated and at other times the political assessment of the implications had been too slow. The exercise of political control through rules of engagement was adequate and worked best during the early stages of the campaign. They were not always easy to follow, and consumed considerable amounts of time on the parts of staff, senior officials, Chiefs of Staff, and Ministers, often on the minutiae. Existing maritime ROE documentation was adapted using caveats, exceptions and suffixes, and thus tended to lack logical consistency. The early declaration of a Maritime Exclusion Zone around the Falklands had turned out to be a successful tactic, gaining Britain the initiative, demonstrating purpose, and legitimising British actions. It had worked, in that Argentine forces largely respected it. On the down side, it had created unrealistic expectations of a tight blockade and encouraged the view that it could be considered a combat-inclusive zone, so that Britain was perceived to have acted improperly according to its own rules when it sank the *Belgrano* outside it.

Far more problematic were the command arrangements in the South Atlantic, with uncertain lines of authority and command between Woodward, Clapp and Thompson. According to Fieldhouse's naval assistant at the time, the arrangement reflected the CINC's view that they were 'tactical commanders whose roles would be driven logically by the phases of the campaign.' Yet it was unrealistic to expect Northwood to be able to take account of all the factors in play in the theatre of operations, while Woodward was not in a good position to exercise authority over the land commanders and had enough to worry about without getting involved in the conduct of their campaign. The system broke down as Thompson had to cope with direct pressure from London when he was also trying to cope with a nightmarish logistical situation. He believed that a three-star commander could have shielded him from this sort of pressure. What was needed, he later argued, was a commander that would spend time:

> visiting his groups, learning their problems and strengths, maintaining a clear operational concept, boosting morale and guiding overall tactical balance in-theatre, and especially keeping the HQ in Northwood off our backs.

Once he arrived in the South Atlantic, Moore was able to play the necessary role. The problem was that for a crucial period he was travelling and largely out of touch. For the rest of the time any Admiral would have problems commanding the land forces while a General would have been equally poorly placed to handle maritime issues. Apart from anything else, until the landing he would probably have been sharing the flagship with Woodward, which would have created different sorts of problems. This was before the development of the practice of truly joint headquarters, which would have improved the coordination between the naval and land forces and also provided a better in-theatre grasp of the relevant air power issues.

Another set of difficulties was connected with the coordination of so many disparate activities in unfamiliar settings. This book includes many examples of poor communications, more so than poor command decisions, having disastrous and at times fatal consequences. It seems plausible that some of this might have been mitigated by a senior headquarters with an operational overview. Against this an extra tier of command could have slowed down decision-making and might not have been able to avoid many of the more localised incidents. Here many of the problems can be attributed as much to the problems of units who had not worked much together before the campaign and the lack of time for the headquarters staff (particularly with 5 Infantry Brigade) to sort out its working procedures.

The great success was in naval air power, without which the operation would have been unthinkable. The real difference was made by the large flight deck of *Hermes*, operating up to 21 Harriers, nine Sea King, two Lynx and two Wessex, compared with the ten Harriers, nine Sea King and one Lynx on *Invincible*. The ability to maintain the aircraft in such testing conditions had been impressive, as had been the ability to switch roles. On one occasion *Hermes* was able to launch 12 Sea Harriers to attack Stanley and Goose Green and one hour after their return to re-launch the same aircraft on air defence tasks. In addition, Sea Skua, a new missile barely through its trials and carried by Lynx helicopters, had achieved hits with all of its eight firings, engaging and sinking Argentine vessels. Naval gunfire had also proved its value, although issues of gun reliability and ammunition consumption had been raised. The other factor that had made the campaign possible was the reprieve of the two LPDs, *Fearless* and *Intrepid*.

The distances involved had placed enormous demands on sea and airlift. CORPORATE involved the most intensive air transport effort since the Berlin airlift. It was undertaken by the Hercules and VC10 air transport force, which chartered Belfast aircraft for extra large loads. By the end of the campaign Britain had moved 5,500 personnel and 6,300 short tons of equipment through Ascension; and undertaken over 40 Hercules supply drops around the Falklands each involving a 25-hour round flight. Remarkably, less than five per cent of tasks were delayed due to aircraft unserviceabilities. The distances had made air-to-air refuelling essential. By using all the available Victor forces, Hercules could be used for airdrop sorties to the Task Force, Harrier reinforcements could be delivered directly to the carriers, the Black Buck raids could be mounted, and isolated long-range reconnaissance missions could be conducted.

The sealift was if anything more remarkable, using to the full 22 ships of the Royal Fleet Auxiliary, and heavily dependent upon the ability to take up ships from trade (STUFT). On 45 merchant ships were carried 9,000 personnel, 100,000 tons of freight and 95 aircraft to the South Atlantic. Some 400,000 tons of fuel had to be delivered through the extended supply chain. Ships from over 30 companies were used, and the processes of acquisition and conversion had all passed remarkably smoothly. As it happened, the operation occurred at a time of a general slump in world trade and by itself still caused an acute shortage of British Flag, British crewed vessels. It also depended upon a substantial merchant fleet, and trends in British shipping were not encouraging if such an exercise had to be repeated.

The major concerns had been in air defences. Until 1978 the RN's carrier, *Ark Royal*, would have been able to launch airborne early warning (AEW) aircraft but this was no longer in service. In a NATO setting AEW could be provided by shore-based aircraft, but out at sea the lack was keenly felt. This allowed Super Etendards to penetrate into Exocet missile launch range. It was just as well that the enemy had been unable to use electronic countermeasures. This gap was the more noticeable because of the inadequacies of most shipborne warning radars close to land. The Sea Harrier aircraft performed exceptionally well, exceeding expectations; nonetheless their dominance in air-to-air combat was undoubtedly helped by the fact that they were attacking fighter-bombers, with minimum fuel in daylight. There does also seem to have been a lack of communication on air warfare techniques between the two squadrons, for example over whether the Harriers' Blue Fox radar had a look-down facility. Of the missiles, Sea Dart had a strong tactical influence on the Argentine air operations, especially following simulated attacks against their own Type 42s, but its actual performance in terms of reaction times and its radar had been disappointing. We shall discuss the performance of Rapier more below. Initially it came out of the campaign with a strong reputation even though it had initially been unreliable as a result of the long sea voyage and the lack of second-line support. It had also been hampered by the low altitude of enemy air attacks, often coming out through valleys shrouded in mist and in poor light. Sea Wolf had appeared more effective, but this point air defence system was only on a few warships. On land Blowpipe missiles had been unreliable, although this was in part because they were designed to attack targets head on rather than crossing, which is how most appeared.

Six ships were lost and 11 were damaged. If a further 13 bombs that hit ships but failed to explode had done so then the record would have been even grimmer. The losses of ships had led to public debate about the 'lack of survivability' of warships. Their loss, and the near loss of many more, was due to an unfortunate combination of factors – the need to operate in range of the Argentine mainland against an opponent who understood the RN's defences, the gaps in those defences and then some characteristics of the ships that limited their ability to absorb damage. It was not only incorrect fusing of the bombs that spared more ships, but also the skill and bravery of the bomb disposal teams. Furthermore, whatever the problem of surviv-ability they did their job, which in the circumstances of the landing meant acting as bait, in that the damage to the amphibious force was far less severe and only one civilian ship, *Atlantic Conveyor*, was lost, and then because of the diversion of an Exocet. Thus *Coventry* had been overwhelmed by numbers: the Type 21s were on duty in the narrow confines of Falkland Sound, unable to take advantage of their manoeuvrability and their weapons systems. If there were lessons in future ship design it would be in finding better ways to contain fire and smoke. Chaff decoys also showed their value and would be relatively easy to add to most ships, including otherwise unarmed RFAs. The limited defences available underlined the courage of those on those ships, notably but not solely LSLs, that regularly accepted great risks to move essential supplies.

In some ways the dog that had not barked had been the Argentine submarines. This was not for want of trying: *San Luis*, for example, fired a torpedo at a totally unaware *Arrow* but missed. It later transpired that there was a problem in its torpedo control system. The RN had, under the influ-ence of comparatively narrow NATO scenarios, become a predominantly deep-ocean ASW force, focusing on the detection of SSNs by passive acoustic systems. In the South Atlantic, the threat was from small, quiet SSKs, under conditions which were difficult and unfamiliar to the ASW teams, and the sonars in use had not all been reliable. As a result many false alarms were generated by marine life, bottom contact and the environment generally. This led to considerable nugatory weapon expenditure and post-war concerns that even when no contact was being made with submarines, established stock levels were inadequate. The fact that after the sinking of the *Belgrano*, there was no further involvement of the Argentine surface fleet in the sea battle was testament to the value of the SSNs, in addition to their role in intelligence gathering, and the advantage they had shown by being able to arrive early and establish the Maritime Exclusion Zone. They posed a threat which the Argentines were never able to measure let alone oppose. While little real evidence of ASW weapon performance was available, as in for example the choice made by the captain of *Conqueror,* the Tigerfish torpedo retained its reputation for unreliability. Many depth charges had been used in response to sonar noises, often leading to attacks on whales. Some 200 anti-submarine torpedoes had been launched with no effect. On one occasion, on 12 May, *Antrim*'s Wessex Mark III did launch a torpedo at what it was sure was a submarine (and so probably Soviet) shadowing the amphibious force as it steamed to the South Atlantic. It should be said that there is no corroboration for this and certainly nothing was hit.

There were problems with both strategic and tactical intelligence. As the resources allocated to the collection effort were so very limited, Britain's database on Argentine forces and Falklands topography was inadequate. Although Britain received substantial assistance from the American agencies, considerable time was needed to build up an informed assessment capability. There was no intelligence contingency plan and it took some time to re-organise the DIS to be capable of providing timely analysis and briefing from the increasing amount of information received. Nonetheless, assessments in several critical areas were correctly made. The relationship between the tactical and strategic intelligence was less satisfactory, as relevant information had not always been made available to brigades and units. At one point the captain of *Uganda* sent a telegram complaining that a delay in sending him classified information meant that his ship 'had apparently sailed through a minefield off Stanley'.

The difficulties faced in putting Stanley runway out of action would have been even more worrisome had Argentina managed to extend it (which the British managed to do quite quickly after regaining it). The reasons for this failure do not appear to lie in simple neglect, because preparations were made. Rather it was something to do with shifting Argentine logistic priorities, including looking after the expanding ground force, for the landing mats were at one point loaded on to a Falklands-bound ship, only to be unloaded.

Ground attack operations, particularly against the runways, had only moderate success. There was also a basic tactical lesson to be learned, in that two of the three Harrier GR3s shot down were lost while making multiple pass attacks. The risks of multiple passes were well known, and in these cases one was to help out 2 Para and the other because of a direct order. All such risks could be reduced with good information about targets as well as the systems to destroy them. Out of this experience came a determination to acquire an effective Airfield Denial Weapon. Additional needs identified were for improved quality of certain troops' clothing and personal equipment, and adequate mine clearing equipment.

The success of the land actions hinged on night operations, aggressive patrolling, surprise and concentrated fire power. In this regard the five 105mm gun batteries had been of great value, not least in their ability to bring down accurate instant fire at night and in poor visibility, and at the call of relatively junior commanders. Moving artillery forward and keeping it supplied with ammunition was a constant challenge. Because of this, naval gunfire support – with 4.5" guns firing some 8,000 rounds – made a vital difference. They were also helped by superiority in helicopters, although numbers were still tight. At the time of the landing Clapp had available five Wessex Mk 5 and 11 Sea King Mk 4, which were largely needed to offload stores, and only some of which could occasionally be allocated to Thompson. After the disastrous loss of *Atlantic Conveyor* only one Chinook was added. By the start of June another 14 Wessex Mk 5 had been added. There were also four, and eventually ten, Sea King Mk 2. These were designed for anti-submarine warfare but lent by Woodward to help with the movement of men and equipment. They were often the only way that key supplies could be moved. In addition to the logistics feat in maintaining such a long and busy supply line to the Falklands, was the feat in keeping the forward troops supplied. Over 9,000 tons of stocks were moved around the Falklands. The constant and varied demands on helicopters at times exceeded the capacity of the command and control systems to cope.

Morale and performance were also helped by the impressive contribution made by doctors and medical staff both in the field and on board ship. A survival rate of over 90 per cent of all casualties was achieved, in line with that achieved by US forces in Vietnam and well above Second World War rates. The major factor was the success in getting patients into surgery in under six hours from the time they sustained their injuries, making full use of helicopters and the hospital ships.

One controversial area concerns Special Forces. The reconnaissance operations they undertook were of considerable importance and the raid on Pebble Island made a significant contribution to reduce the enemy's local air power. But the land commanders also found their readiness to act outside the standard command structures a nuisance. Moore wrote a caustic note at the end of the campaign detailing what he saw to be the problems. One was that too many senior officers, especially from the Royal Navy and RAF, had an inadequate understanding of what Special Forces could achieve. This led to what he described as 'fatuous expectations, culled one suspects from avid reading of Boy's Own or Beano'. Another problem was that there were too many Special Forces around, especially after the main landing. He had found it useful to be able to send a number of the Special Forces to West

Falkland to prevent pressure for 'non-productive diversion of effort' (an example of which was the attack on Cortley Point). Lastly, while communications with the home base were good ('at times too bloody good') those with neighbouring forces had not been good at all.

What then was the basis for success in the land campaign? The enemy did not lack courage. Wilson observed in his 16 June report, after complaining that intelligence had misrepresented the situation:

> The enemy was not inept and frightened. Nor was he badly equipped and starving. His use of air was audacious. His defensive positions were well sited and well constructed. He fought with skill and bravery. Some units resisted almost to the last man.

That being said, Argentine forces had not coped well with pitched battles. Undoubtedly, some Argentine units had fought well and most fought bravely, but many had been poorly led and let down by inadequate tactical doctrine, inter-service squabbling, a highly stratified command structure with little vertical bonding, and poor command and control.

This leads to the basic lesson that was timeless and in many respects encouraging. There was no alternative to well-trained and motivated forces. All reports spoke of the professionalism shown by all ranks. The comparative performance of British and Argentine ground forces showed up the difference, which was more than just volunteer forces versus conscripts, or for that matter bravery versus cowardice. A US Army sociologist, Nora Kinzer Stewart, later summed up why British forces had fought as well as they had. It was partly that the cause was considered just and the best troops were sent. But she noted how, contrary to Argentine evaluations, these troops were not 'battle-experienced veterans.' Half of the enlisted men had an average age of 20 (and a visit to the cemetery at San Carlos will confirm the youth of many of those that died), while few of the officers had participated in modern battles, as opposed to the lower-intensity operations in Malaysia and Northern Ireland.

Kiszely recalls the surprises of combat, for which training provided no preparation. One was the noise of battle:

> Incoming artillery and mortar rounds, grenades exploding near you, have your ears ringing, and at times you become almost completely deaf. You realise this only when you shout at someone to do something, and it's quite clear they can't hear you. The only way to get your message across is to run over to them, grip them by the arm, and shout into their ear. Then there is the effect in the dark of immensely bright flashes of light as the shells and grenades explode. You are blinded, and just as your eyes get accustomed to the dark again, the same thing happens. You also tend to become over-focused on the enemy immediately to your front. The result of all

this is disorientation and confusion. At the same time you have a mass of information, much of it contradictory, coming in to you over the radio nets, such as casualty reports. Not just exercise casualties, but real people – your family. And yet there is no time for emotion, that can wait; and hardly time for much fear, you're too busy, and you're responsible for so many people's lives.

He stresses the importance of group cohesion but also notes the absence, on both sides, of one factor common in war that can help a group cohere – a deep hatred of the enemy. In terms of morale the impact of firepower was also critical: 'Seeing 1,000 pound bombs crashing into Tumbledown was almost as psychologically significant to us as it was to them, even if these bombs killed no-one; the side capable of delivering such a big bang looked to be the bookies' favourite.'[3]

To explain the 'high morale, esprit, and cohesion' of the British at war, Stewart explains how:

Soldiers and NCOs were confident that their officers were well versed in battle tactics. British NCOs are trained to accept responsibility at all levels of command. An open organizational climate with little regard for privileges of rank and accompanied by good humor led to continual adaptation in the fluid and ever-changing battle and spelled swift success on the battlefield.[4]

Long-term effects

An important question to emerge from the Falklands arises from the contrast between the small number of psychiatric casualties initially reported and the substantial numbers later alleged. Very few cases of battle shock were reported. The initial figure for psychiatric casualties was put at only two per cent of all wounded, although it was soon suggested that the true figure was eight per cent.[5] This was still a historically low figure. There were a number of plausible explanations for this: the long sea voyages there and back made it easier at first to adjust to the possibilities of combat and then to return to an environment far removed from the privations and stress encountered during combat; morale was high in a successful campaign involving short battles largely conducted by elite units and enjoying public support. Some variations were also noted. For example the survivors from *Sir Galahad* and *Sir Tristram*, though badly shaken, recovered rapidly following 24 hours' recuperation in ships in San Carlos Water and then returned to duty, while survivors from ships in the Task Force who could not be so returned suffered from much more protracted symptoms and required more psychiatric support.

Later studies suggested that the early figures were underestimates. The symptoms of post-traumatic stress disorder (PTSD) appeared to have been delayed.[6] The most important evidence that the psychiatric impact had been severe came in a 1987 study, published in 1991, comparing a sample of veterans from an infantry battalion with a control unit from the same division, which had not been involved in the conflict. The Falklands veterans described more general symptoms, with half of them reporting symptoms of the PTSD complex. Twenty-two per cent were rated as having the complete syndrome. Suffering was not correlated with age, rank or length of service but with the intensity of combat experience.[7] Although these subjects were still functioning effectively in the military, and do not appear to have been leading abnormal lives, they indicated the difficulty of the emotional adjustments following a return from battle.[8]

Denzil Connick, who had been wounded while serving with 3 Para on Mount Longdon, went on to form the South Atlantic Medal Association (SAMA) 82. This continues to provide support to veterans. In 2001 Connick was quoted as saying that: 'Apart from the suicides there are more Falklands veterans compared with any other section of the community in prison, jobless, alcoholics, divorced and abusing drugs. Their lives are a shambles and they drink and use drugs, treat their families badly, steal to fund drinking and drugs, get caught and go to prison.'[9] At this point the suicide rate was put at almost half of the number of those who died during the conflict, which would be less than 125. The next year, however, SAMA was claiming that the numbers of suicides exceeded those who been killed during the war. Soon the figure of 264 was being cited as a reliable statistic. Yet all SAMA had said was that the group was 'almost certain' of the numbers, adding that: 'Nobody knows the official figures for suicides – that is one of the problems.' Connick's starting point was based on the loss of an average of 10 veterans per year since the conflict ended, making 'for 200 veterans who have committed suicide and that is bound to be a conservative estimate. … I am almost certain there will be dozens more that we do not know about and the figure is likely to be more than 255.'[10] By 2003 the British Association for Counselling and Psychotherapy was claiming that 300 veterans had killed themselves.[11] The correct figures do not seem to be known and cannot be extracted from any available data set (which would not be the case for later conflicts). Any statistics would then need to be compared with the suicide rate in the population at large, and among service personnel.

In 2002 a group action with which some 2000 veterans were associated, including a number from the Falklands (notably Welsh Guardsmen who had been aboard *Sir Galahad*), reached the High Court. The claimants argued that MoD had not given them adequate support to cope with post-traumatic stress disorder. The Ministry insisted that treatment of service personnel with suspected PTSD was 'in line with contemporary best practice'. In May 2003 Mr Justice Owen ruled against the claim. He did not doubt the reality and severity of the disorders suffered by the veterans, and that some cases had not been well treated, but he found no evidence of systematic negligence. In fact the cases covered by the Falklands came under those prior to May 1987 which were covered by Crown Immunity.

Rapier kills

One of the most sensitive areas when it came to assessing weapons performance was that of British air defence missiles. We have seen how during the hectic days after the landing at San Carlos reports from the defenders tended to exaggerate the number of 'kills'. We might also note that the number of kills achieved is only a limited guide to performance. Much depends on the conditions under which a missile is deployed and the threat faced. Thus the disappointing results from Rapier in its first deployment after the landing resulted from the batteries being placed in inappropriately high locations. In addition, there could be positive strategic benefits even when few aircraft were shot down. Given that they had purchased some of their own, the Argentines were surprisingly ignorant of the shortcomings of Sea Dart, and their aircraft treated it with respect, flying in at low altitudes. This helped them evade the missile but impeded the efficient delivery of their bombs.

During the course of the campaign claims had been made for both missiles, but particularly for Rapier, that were overstated. Navy Department figures circulated just after the war credited Rapier with eight kills, while the Army Department had an estimate of eleven. The Defence Staff was using a figure of nine. The analysis undertaken illustrates the problems of being sure what had been shot down and by what weapons. Thus a 'probable' of 23 May was not included; a more confident claim of that day might have been an A4 or Mirage; two Rapier hits were claimed on 25 and 27 May, but there was only evidence of one on each day, and one of these was also claimed by a 40 mm gun on *Fearless*. No Rapier hits were claimed by the Army Department for 7 June, but as sources claimed that two Skyhawks had been shot down at Teal Inlet that day these were included in the tally. On the other hand a Rapier hit claimed by the Army for 8 June was credited by other sources to ground fire.

By the time the White Paper on the Lessons of the Falklands was produced in December 1982, all the missiles were given high marks, and the claims for Rapier had moved up from nine to 14 confirmed, with another six probable. This produced a remarkable achievement of 49% kill ratios, expressed as total kills (including probables) as a percentage of total valid firings.[12] Not surprisingly the missile was described as having 'performed well.'[13] This was a judgement shared with allies. The preliminary US analysis of March 1983, the main concern of which was to dispel notions that the conflict had revealed the unique vulnerability of surface ships, used the White Paper's figures and described Rapier's performance as 'particularly noteworthy', with 'a credible kill ratio of 49 per cent.' There was some inflation elsewhere. The original figures for Sea Dart and Sea Wolf, eight and five kills respectively, survived the first post-war analyses into the White Paper, although Sea Cat rose from six to eight, and as with Rapier, this was a missile where later analysis suggested that a more accurate number would be one.

Initially there was confidence in the figures, reflected in Ian MacDonald's testimony to the House of Commons Defence Committee in November 1982, as demonstrating MoD's commitment to accurate reporting. Gradually, however, it became apparent that the figures were problematic and attempts were made to refine them for later operational analysis. For example a meeting in February 1983 was still seeking more information on all the claimed Sea Dart kills. The issue of the accuracy of the claims for kills only attracted attention with the publication in 1983 of *Air War South Atlantic*, a well-researched book by two air historians, Jeffrey Ethell and Alfred Price. Having checked with Argentine sources, they challenged MoD's claims.[14] They argued that Britain's surface-to-air missile and gun systems had achieved far fewer kills than claimed. In the case of Rapier they acknowledged only one confirmed kill. As at the time the Defence Committee was undertaking a study of weapons performance in the Falklands, this led to questions from the Committee to MoD, sent on 29 February 1984. The view taken by DIS officials at the time was:

> Our answers should support the figures published in the DWP [Defence White Paper] but in such a way that any subsequent changes can be defended if, as seems likely, the MOD figures do have to be adjusted. The OEG [Operations Evaluation Group] which is reviewing the air campaign will report in November. Not until then will we know how accurate the MOD figures are. The Ethell and Price figures are probably not going to be far out, so we must be careful on the way we comment on them.

This was the position adopted in reply to questions from the Committee. The Government did not resile from the *Cmnd 8758* figures, but acknowledged uncertainties to be clarified in a detailed analysis of the air campaign, not to be completed until late 1984.

The study to which MoD referred was undertaken for the Defence Operational Analysis Establishment (DOAE). This involved a detailed reconstruction of the air war, and took into account Ethell's own research. It purported to have identified all air sorties, most losses and all firings of missiles by armed forces. The findings were that far fewer Argentine aircraft were in fact shot down than the White Paper had claimed (only 41 certain kills, as against 72 confirmed and 14 probables). Within the total only five Argentine aircraft might have been shot down by Rapier, and, as originally noted by Ethell and Price, only one of these was certain, with two probables and two possibles. Similar discrepancies arose over other weapon systems, notably Blowpipe (one to two confirmed kills as against nine confirmed and two probable in the White Paper) and Sea Cat (zero to one against eight confirmed and two probable in the White Paper). Some compensation could be found by looking at aircraft damaged, although the evidence here was uncertain, which suggested that at the top end of wide ranges as many as eight aircraft might have been damaged by Rapier, six by Blowpipe and four by Seacat. The main reason for the discrepancy, not unfamiliar to historians of these matters, is that a number of incidents recorded as separate kills were in fact single incidents where several weapons were fired at one aircraft.

This confirmation that MoD had exaggerated, however unwittingly, the capabilities of Rapier was deemed to be political dynamite. It was observed that if this assessment became publicly known it 'could have a serious adverse effect on sales' prospects for Rapier, which is the staple revenue-earner for BAe's Dynamic Group. There is therefore a lot at stake commercially; hence the high classification of this minute, and the restriction on copying.' It was judged to be prudent not to repeat the White Paper claims, certainly not in relation to any future sales, and attention had to be paid to the prospectus for a BAe offer of shares, as it was being privatised. Its statement on the Falklands – 'A number of British Aerospace's guided weapon systems were successfully deployed by the Falklands Task Force' – was considered fair. The Defence Policy Staff also suggested that any conclusion which appeared to cast doubt on the effectiveness of Rapier would, if publicly known, tend to weaken deterrence. It should therefore be treated as highly classified and sensitive.

There the matter might have rested had not the Defence Committee decided to return to its own work on weapons performance in the Falklands and asked in the summer of 1985 for an update on MoD's studies. When this was discussed that October it was recognised that the findings would be hard to hold back, but MoD were anxious that there should be no rush to publication, not least until the shortcomings revealed in the DOAE study had been identified and remedied. This required persuading the Committee, through a quiet word with the Chairman, Sir Humphrey Atkins, not to disclose 'the most interesting and important evidence they had managed to unearth.' The companies involved – BAe and Shorts – would be told about the revised assessment.

For whatever reason, the Committee's report left the issue alone. It noted the discrepant claims and then observed that:

> After so long a passage of time, there seems little to be gained by detailed examination of such discrepancies. The number of aircraft shot down provides one measure of an anti-aircraft system's efficiency, but it is by no means the only measure; many factors must be taken into account in making an overall assessment of a

weapon's performance. These include practicality and ease of use, reliability, maintainability, cost, and the question of whether the very presence of the system forces the attacker to adopt more difficult or dangerous tactics. It is also inevitable that there will be uncertainties about precisely which weapons did what. In the final analysis, assessments of performance must be based on the experience of those most closely involved. They are unlikely to endorse a weapon that does not work well, or to complain unduly about one that does.[15]

49

THE *BELGRANO*
CONTROVERSY

The most important controversy in the years after the war concerned the sinking of the *Belgrano*. At the heart of the controversy was the conviction of a number of journalists and MPs that the sinking was more political than military, designed not so much to torpedo a 44-year old cruiser, which posed little threat at the time, but instead to torpedo a new Peruvian-led opportunity for peace, which was showing signs of real promise. On 21 December 1982 Tam Dalyell MP (Lab Linlithgow) alleged in the Commons that the Prime Minister:

> coldly and deliberately gave the orders to sink the *Belgrano*, in the knowledge that an honourable peace was on offer and in the expectation – all too justified – that the *Conqueror's* torpedoes would torpedo the peace negotiations.[1]

It should be evident from this study that this allegation is simply not true.

From May 1982 to the end of February 1985, Defence Ministers and the Prime Minister answered some 205 written and 10 oral questions on the sinking of the *Belgrano* and related issues. In addition there were several statements and full-scale debates on the subject, and exchanges in other debates. The intensity of the questioning only concluded when the issue was examined by the Select Committee on Foreign Affairs.[2]

The starting point for this challenge to the Government's record lay in statements made by the Defence Secretary and the Prime Minister immediately after the attack on the *Belgrano*. These were, in a number of respects, inaccurate. As this became apparent, allegations of a cover-up came to be added to those already tabled on the events themselves. This produced some of the more bizarre aspects of this case, taking in missing logs from the submarine, the trial of a senior civil servant under Section Two of the Official Secrets Act, and even a suggestion of murder.

As with most controversies of this nature much of the debate surrounded the question of who knew what when. In this, three questions of fact became important. First, what movements had the *Belgrano* made prior to being attacked and did these tend to undermine the claim that when attacked it posed a threat to the Task Force? Second, when and in what form was crucial information relayed to London, about the attack, and about the parallel developments in Washington and Lima concerning the new peace initiative? Here time zones were a source of regular confusion. Third, what was the best intelligence about Argentine intentions at the time, and how did this feed into the decision-making process?

First statements

The origins of the confusion were described earlier.[3] In his first statement to Parliament Nott described the extent of the exchanges on 1 May and the consequent dangers to the Task Force. He also explained how the next day 'at 8pm London time' a submarine 'detected' and then attacked the *Belgrano*, escorted by two destroyers, 'close to the total Exclusion Zone' and 'closing on elements of our Task Force, which was only hours away.' The fact that this was outside the TEZ was bound to be controversial and was picked up at once by Shadow Foreign Secretary, Denis Healey, who asked whether there had been breaches of either political control or injunctions to use minimum force. In the discussion Nott suggested that two torpedoes had been fired, put the distance outside the Exclusion Zone at about 30 miles and indicated that there were problems communicating with the submarine. The Prime Minister also drew attention to the statement of 23 April, which left open the possibility of Argentine forces outside the Exclusion Zone being attacked if they threatened the 'mission of the British forces.'[4]

A number of details were wrong: three not two torpedoes were fired; when attacked the *Belgrano* was not closing on elements of the Task Force but had turned away; it had been detected the previous day. The confusion of the time of attack with that for detection (8pm London time) appears to have been a straightforward mistake by Nott. He does not now recall how 'attacked,' the word used in his brief, became 'detected.' There is no evidence that this error was noted at the time, but on the matter of closing on the Task Force, new and more accurate language was introduced by the Defence Secretary on 13 May.[5] When engaged, he now reported, the *Belgrano* group 'had been closing on elements of our Task Force' with which it 'could have been within striking distance ... in a matter of some five to six hours, converging from a distance of some 200 nautical miles.' The changes of tense made this more true, but gave no clue that the *Belgrano* had been steaming away from the Task Force when actually hit. Moreover, the bulk of the Task Force was between 290 and 315 miles from *Belgrano* when sunk, and the nearest any ship, probably *Coventry* on picket duty, could have been was 30 miles less than this. It could only have closed at a speed almost treble the one at which it was actually travelling (30 knots as against 11). Nott also stated that the cruiser was attacked because it was 'manoeuvring into a position from which

744

to attack our surface vessels' and under 'certain rules of engagement that we had already agreed', although it was the rules that were changed because of this assessment. It was however fair to say that when the decision was made, as far as Ministers knew the ship was closing on the Task Force. What care went into the preparation of these reports is unclear. They were all put together in a hurry, reflecting imperfect means of communication with the South Atlantic, the confusions of battle and a highly pressured decision-making process, with many difficult issues still pending. For these reasons a number of immediate descriptions of events in the South Atlantic as reported to the Commons turned out to be wrong (including the 'white flags over Stanley'). The Prime Minister later expressed her doubts to Dr David Owen that 'as events unfolded in early May with the Task Force under threat', it was reasonable for Ministers to:

> devote their time solely to establishing in detail the circumstances surrounding individual operations which had already taken place; their principal concern had to be to look ahead and to seek to anticipate events.

Yet little effort was made to correct inaccurate statements in the two main official publications on the war, the Government White Paper on the lessons of the war, and Admiral Sir John Fieldhouse's official despatch. Both retained the claim that the *Belgrano* had been detected on 2 May. Fieldhouse had apparently queried this, but, so it was later explained, consistency with earlier statements was not the issue, only that a change would reveal sensitive intelligence and operational information, relating to the tracking capacities of SSNs.[6]

The inaccuracies with regard to detail soon came to haunt the Government as, after the war, unofficial accounts began to be published. Interviews with crew soon revealed that detection was the previous day, including one in early 1983 with the Commanding Officer of *Conqueror*.[7] It was also evident from a lecture by Woodward, in which he had spoken of how early on the morning of 2 May, '*Belgrano* still had *Conqueror* on her tail,' and that the cruiser had been picked up the day before.[8] Although the confusion between the time of attack and detection was clarified in a parliamentary answer on 15 December 1982,[9] it took until May 1984 before the earlier sighting (and of the oiler rather than the cruiser) was acknowledged.[10] The claim on the striking distance of the *Belgrano* from the Task Force was maintained until late October 1984. The original statement was based on naval staff assessments that the two groups could have converged at 40 knots (that is 20 each). Lord Lewin used a maximum speed for *Belgrano* of 30 knots in newspaper articles.[11] The reluctance to acknowledge what was already in the public domain was rationalised in terms of 'political credibility' and the tendency for each answer simply to raise more questions.

The reference in Nott's statement on 'closing' had been based on an understanding of the *Belgrano*'s intentions rather than the actual course. There is no evidence that the cruiser's change of course was well known in MoD and Navy circles in May 1982. It only came to the attention of Defence Ministers, but not the Prime Minister, in November 1982 when a Parliamentary Question was asked. In an answer on 29 November 1982, Peter Blaker (Minister, Armed Forces) stated that when attacked *Belgrano* was on a course of 280°.[12] In a famous television exchange on *Nationwide* during the General Election Campaign of 24 May 1983 Mrs Diana Gould asked: 'Why when the *Belgrano* was outside the Exclusion Zone and actually sailing away from the Falklands, did you give the orders to sink it?' Thatcher replied that *Belgrano* was not sailing away from the Falklands, and apart from the fact that she was clearly discomfited by the question, it also appeared that this was incorrect, in the light of the disclosed course of the *Belgrano* of 280° towards Argentina and that she had been sailing in a westerly direction for 11 hours. In fact, she was only 35 miles outside the TEZ when attacked and the Falklands lay just east of north of her position. The Prime Minister may not have become aware that the *Belgrano* had changed course at 0900 London time, well before its attack, until issues of disclosure were being discussed in detail in March 1984 and possibly not until the material had actually been leaked that summer. The standard position taken by the RN on this issue was that the precise course at this time was irrelevant, as the ship could just as easily change course again. Closing speed was also irrelevant, for should the *Belgrano* escape *Conqueror*, she might still be able to use the night and/or bad weather to get in amongst the British carrier battle group.

Scandal

As the various discrepancies in the original account were revealed, it came to be argued by the Government's critics that a cover up of substantial proportions was underway. These largely depend on assumptions about the speed with which commands and information were transmitted and assimilated into the decision-making process at different levels. After the war a number of the signals sent by Argentine units over this period were disclosed.[13] At issue was whether these had been intercepted and decoded by Britain. This was a matter upon which the Government of the day and its successors were reluctant to comment in line with standard practice. One consequence of this was to encourage extravagant claims by those engaged in the controversy, assuming that one Argentine unit could not send a signal to another without it being intercepted and decoded almost immediately. As the controversy went deeper, ministerial statements accepted that important decisions were informed by high-quality intelligence. If the cruiser had really been sunk to torpedo the Peruvian initiative then the timing and content of diplomatic communications from Lima were also crucial. It took until 1984 before the nature of these were revealed by the Government, and although they were conclusive in demonstrating the lack of impact of the initiative on the decision, they had very little impact on the controversy.

One reason for this was the actions of the official dealing with these issues, Clive Ponting, the recently appointed (9 March 1984) Head of DS5. Soon he was part of the team responding to a series of questions from Tam Dalyell, Shadow Defence Secretary Denzil Davies and George Foulkes MP. Heseltine decided that he needed a full account of what had happened, and so his Private Secretary, Richard Mottram, wrote to Ponting on 22 March asking for the full story of May 1982 with a detailed chronology, covering the ROE, nature of intelligence, precise sequence of events, Peruvian initiative, and intelligence on the Argentine return to port. He was happy to have it in log form with the relevant documents and also wanted a draft reply to Dalyell. The resultant document, which was classified TOP SECRET, became known as the 'Crown Jewels'.

Heseltine met with officials, including Ponting, on 30 March 1984 on how best to respond to the questions without damaging security. On 2 April, Heseltine conferred with the head of 'the appropriate intelligence agency,' along with other intelligence experts. Their concern was that once it was confirmed that the *Belgrano* had reversed course 'the focus of attention would be on the intelligence assessment which led to the decision to sink the ship and allegations about Argentine orders to recall her fleet as part of the so-called Peruvian peace initiative.'[14] Nonetheless the reply to Davies from Thatcher was fuller than either Heseltine or Ponting had suggested. This letter described the risks to the Task Force, the time of detection, the rationale for the attacks, the ministerial agreement to changes in the rules of engagement and the orders to *Conqueror*, as well as the alleged link with the Peruvian initiative. Thatcher explained that she was only prepared to go into such detail now as 'with the passage of time, those events have lost some of their operational significance.'

In a minute of 4 April, Ponting considered the consequences of the admission in the letter to Davies that the *Belgrano* had been sighted on 1 May. He noted that since this information had been reported by *Conqueror*, and her report of the position and course at the time of sinking had already been given, it was hard to see how the same information for other times should remain classified. Release of such further details, however, would show the reverse of direction of the cruiser, and that would require establishing when the SSN was in communication and what information was passed. The next day Dalyell wrote to the Prime Minister. In a minute of 8 April, Ponting now noted that 'in general the arguments put forward by Dalyell and his supporters [about a connection between the sinking and the Peruvian peace initiative] can be refuted'; but he was troubled by the ROEs, which he felt were 'the most difficult area presentationally'. What had struck him was that British actions had gone beyond what Argentina might have expected from the warning issued on 23 April:

The details of these ROEs, as exemplified by the stern chase and attack on *BELGRANO*, the attempt to sink the CVA and *all* other Argentine warships outside the TEZ do not sit easily with the terms of warning given on 23 April.

His view now was that the materials required for the answers to Dalyell were not classified and should not be denied to Parliament. John Stanley, Minister of State at MoD, having seen this, pointed out that this new advice was inconsistent with the line agreed for Thatcher. Heseltine therefore decided to reply on general lines:

Your purpose in asking the questions you put to me is to pursue your campaign that the *Belgrano* was attacked in order to destroy the prospects for peace negotiations rather than for the military reason that she posed a threat to the Task Force. I do not believe that there is any point in prolonging this argument by a further round of detailed correspondence.

This drove Ponting to write an anonymous letter to Dalyell on 24 April. The letter[15] explained to Dalyell that he had not got answers to his letter of 19 March:

against the advice of officials but in line with what John Stanley recommended. None of the info is classified and to get answers you should put the questions down as PQs. The answers will be quite interesting. In addition you might like to consider another linked question. Did the change in the rules of engagement on 2nd May refer only to the *Belgrano* or did they go wider? When were the rules of engagement changed to allow an attack on the *25 de Mayo*? Was this on 2nd May or was it earlier? If so, when? You are on the right track. Keep going?

During May Dalyell twice wrote again to Heseltine with detailed questions. By this time the Foreign Affairs Committee, which had been exploring the progress towards restoration of diplomatic and commercial relations between Britain and Argentina, and the prospects for a negotiated settlement of the dispute, began to get interested. On 28 June the Clerk asked for a note on changes to ROE during the war. This caused immediate difficulties as it could not be both unclassified and informative, especially as some of the ROEs were still in force. Michael Legge, Head of DS11, sent advice to Stanley on 6 July, which he had discussed with Ponting. In addition to the other difficulties, Legge added that 'a full list of changes would provide more information than Ministers have been prepared to reveal about the *Belgrano* affair.' To illustrate this point he drew attention to the fact that the change of 2 May was not restricted to the *Belgrano* 'but included all Argentine warships over a large area,' and that while previous changes and public warnings had been simultaneous, 'there was a delay until 7 May before the appropriate warning was issued for 2 May change.'

As this was precisely the issue that Ponting believed ought to be ventilated in public, on 19 August 1984 he sent to Dalyell three documents at the Commons in a plain envelope. In addition to his letter of 24 April these included a copy of the Legge memo to Dalyell, which had been classified 'confidential', along with his draft answer disclosing answers to the MP's questions that had never been sent, which Ponting himself had judged to include only unclassified material. Unfortunately for Ponting, Dalyell then passed them to Sir Anthony Kershaw MP, Chairman of the House Foreign Affairs Committee, who in turn, on 27 July 1984, passed them on to Heseltine. Their provenance was quickly established, and, after an investigation by MoD police, an admission was obtained from Ponting that he was the culprit. Ponting was arrested on 16 August under the Official Secrets Act. The draft reply to Dalyell appeared in the *New Statesman* on 24 August.[16]

The consequence of this material entering the public domain through such an informal route was that the Government accepted that it had to get out a full account of the events leading up to the sinking of the *Belgrano*.[17] In addition, a BBC TV *Panorama* investigation, broadcast on 16 April 1984, confirmed that an Argentine submarine had fired a torpedo against a British ship on 1 May and that a Super Etendard aircraft with Exocet had been launched on that day but failed because of problems with in-flight refuelling. It included Admiral Lombardo apparently agreeing that the *Belgrano* was involved in a pincer movement and had been ordered into the TEZ. It also demonstrated the limited state of the Peruvian initiative at the time the *Belgrano* was sunk.[18]

The result of all this, as Ponting may have intended, was to shift attention away from the now discredited notion that *Belgrano* was sunk to scupper a promising peace plan to the more specific claim that it was not a threat when sunk, raising questions about what the War Cabinet knew when authorising the change in the ROE, and the general handling of changes in the ROE over this period. Questions now were also being raised over the management of the affair. There were allegations that Parliament had been misled. The decision to prosecute Ponting was criticised, given that he had not leaked documents of high classification and could claim to have been acting in the public interest (as he did successfully at his trial). It was alleged that he had been prosecuted at the insistence of Heseltine, though it had been a DPP decision.

In the course of Regina v Ponting the 'Crown Jewels' were made available to the Court. The Foreign Affairs Committee then sought access to the 'Crown Jewels'. The precedents were awkward. On the one hand they had been seen by jurors and court officials, and had been disclosed to parliamentarians before. On the other hand there was a long-standing convention that information on matters of security and intelligence was not disclosed. The Permanent Under Secretary of MoD recommended that the Committee see the document under strict conditions, as refusal would create a political storm. Although Heseltine's instinct was to refuse, in the end they were seen and provided the basis of the Committee report. The Committee concluded: 'the classified evidence we have seen and other evidence authoritatively and conclusively shows that no intercepted orders for a withdrawal of Argentine forces reached the British Government before the sinking of the *Belgrano*'.[19]

At this point a further complication arose. On 17 October an official reported that she, and the staff of the Flag Officer Submarines, had been unable to find *Conqueror*'s log. The Prime Minister had been asked by Foulkes to place this log in the library and had refused as it was classified,[20] but agreed that the Foreign Affairs Committee might ask for sight of it. It would contain little of interest as operational incidents were recorded in a separate report of proceedings, which had been used in the 'Crown Jewels'. Its absence was, nonetheless, potentially embarrassing – 'at best, we shall look foolish.' A cover up would be claimed. In November 1984 Heseltine reported to the Commons that the report of the board of inquiry, convened by CINCFLEET on 25 October, had failed to locate the missing logs or identify a proven explanation for their disappearance. It had been ascertained that proper procedures for custody and disposal of logs had not been followed for some time.[21] A police inquiry was closed a year later without results. A check at the time indicated that a number of logs from other ships had not been handled as they should have been.

Soon Paul Foot of the *Daily Mirror* was reporting the flap about *Conqueror*'s log. The *Observer* on 11 November claimed that the log had been removed two years earlier by a member of the crew, and that the newspaper had been able to inspect extracts. The *Observer* had muddled up the log with a quite different document. Lt Narendra Sethia had kept a diary on board *Conqueror*. Although he had not sanctioned publication he suddenly became aware, from his new home in the Caribbean, that extracts had appeared in print. On 3 October 1983 he wrote to the Director of RN Public Relations, insisting that this was not his responsibility. He remained loyal to the RN and aware of the Official Secrets Act. He had previously asked for help in getting the diary published in book form, but, having received no reply, had given the manuscript to a friend, who had also been serving in *Conqueror* at the time, for his opinion. His friend, embittered by the *Belgrano* controversy, had shown it to Dalyell. Extracts were soon appearing in newspaper stories and television documentaries. Dalyell claims to have been given the diaries in September 1982 and used these to check facts against the official account.[22]

While British Belgranauts searched for evidence that contradicted the official line, an American defence journalist soon realised that the real significance of publication of the Sethia diary lay in what it indicated about British interceptions of Argentine communications, collaboration with Chile, equipment problems and entry late in the war inside Argentina's twelve mile limit. Once these had been published in the US, British officials were concerned that the material would soon get a wide audience.[23] The published extracts of the diary confirmed that *Conqueror* had been expecting the *Belgrano* to turn into the Exclusion Zone, when it would have pounced, and that the crew were frustrated when it steamed parallel to the zone 'quite unconcernedly'. It showed that neither the *Belgrano* nor its accompanying destroyers ('equally decrepit') were taken that seriously, and conveyed the drama of the receipt of the order to attack even though the cruiser was still outside the zone. The attack itself was vividly described, a 43 second wait before the explosions are heard, 'shouting and cheering' in the control room, and then anxiety in the face of exploding depth charges. Sethia recorded feeling 'scared, almost trembling, sweating and nauseated' by the whole series of events. It confirmed that when the *Conqueror* returned to the scene, it was told not to attack the hospital ship or destroyer as she was assisting the search for survivors.

Sethia, who had good reason to feel aggrieved, eventually filed suit against the *Mail on Sunday*, the *Sun* and the *Observer* for printing extensive portions without his permission and for libelling him by suggestion that he was responsible for taking the missing log. He was successful in his actions in late 1987 and received substantial damages. The cases resulted in further difficulties for the Government as the defendants sought to use the Defence Secretary's views on the content of Sethia's diary as evidence of his irresponsibility. An Under Secretary eventually represented him in court where he was cross-examined by the plaintiff's counsel to the effect that the affidavit and Public Interest Immunity Certificates from the Defence Secretary exaggerated any damage to national security. By the very nature of the claims being made by MoD it was rather difficult to substantiate its concerns in court by releasing yet more information. In a final bizarre twist in 1988, indicating how conspiracy theories encourage the steady suspension of belief, an allegation was made in the *Daily Mirror* that a civil servant had claimed while on a training course in November 1985 that he had witnessed the destruction of the log. The civil servant in question was soon embarrassed by revelations which appeared to have had more to do with alcohol than fact (he was in no position to have witnessed such a thing, as his role was with the UK Land Forces monitoring centre). A denial failed to satisfy the Belgranauts who insisted that their source was definite about the original claim.[24] Other assertions were made: from Dalyell that an Argentine family claimed that a Soviet submarine had picked up four survivors from the *Belgrano*, although arrangements had been made in April to warn the Russians to keep their surface vessels and submarines well clear of the South Atlantic to avoid the risk of inadvertent encounters.[25]

The most unpleasant aspect of the developing proclivity for conspiracy theories concerned the murder of Mrs Hilda Murrell, a widow, in March 1984. The attack was quite vicious and involved sex and theft. She was a known opponent of nuclear power and her nephew, Cdr Robert Green RN, had retired from the Navy just after the Falklands. During the war, Green served as Staff Officer (Intelligence) to CINCFLEET at Northwood. He acted as a watch-keeper during CORPORATE but had not been involved in any significant way with the transmission of orders to *Conqueror* on the *Belgrano*. The argument that there were political motives for her murder appeared in the *New Statesman* on 9 November 1984, when the writer Judith Cook suggested that this lay in her opposition to the Sizewell B nuclear power station. This depended on discrepancies in the police evidence, none of which turned out to be serious. This was followed by Dalyell in an adjournment debate on 19 December 1984. He told the House: 'I am informed that the intruders were not after money, not after nuclear information, but were checking to see if there were any *Belgrano*-related documents of Commander Green in the home of his aunt.' Green later developed theories of his own involving a bungled abduction attempt by the nuclear industry and involving numerous organisations held together by freemasonry and possibly Satanists. Once launched, the conspiracy theory, which had absolutely no foundation, led to three television documentaries, two books, several stage plays, two parliamentary debates and endless columns of newsprint, all investigating the proposition that this lady was a victim of the secret state.[26]

Giles Shaw, the Minister of State at the Home Office, wrote on 28 December categorically denying any evidence of involvement of intelligence agencies in her death. Dalyell was interviewed by West Mercia police, in charge of the murder enquiry, and provided no new evidence. Shaw later conveyed the essence of the police report to the Home Office: that there was evidence within the house of a thorough and systematic search, and of a struggle between Mrs Murrell and her assailant. The telephone had been disconnected, by snatching out some wires rather than any sophisticated means, and there were signs of some attempted sexual activity.[27] A cold case review of the killing in 2002 led in 2003 to a builders' labourer from Shrewsbury (who would have been 16 at the time of the murder) being charged with her murder and he appeared in court in March 2004. I have dealt with this case at some length because it illustrates the fevered speculation and sheer irresponsibility to which the *Belgrano* controversy led.

By way of postscript to this section I should note that in February 1984 I was asked by the *Times Literary Supplement* to review the book by Gavshon and Rice, which developed the conspiracy case most fully. As I did so, it became apparent that the core theory – that a credible peace plan developed by Peru was deliberately undermined on 2 May by a Prime Ministerial order to sink the *Belgrano* – not only lacked evidence but made impossible assumptions about what the British could know and the speed with which senior politicians might know it. The review[28] led to parliamentary questions by Mr Dalyell to check on whether I had been in conversation with either the FCO or MoD on the matter (I had not). Later, with my Argentine colleague Virginia Gamba, I was able to reconstruct the affair in more detail and we both became convinced that the conspiracy theory did not hold up. In particular we were able to check the Argentine signals, and in the course of this it became apparent that the assumption that the British might have known about an Argentine order to withdraw as early as 2007 on 1 May reflected a confusion by Admiral Anaya, as the order at this time was in fact one to initiate offensive operations.[29]

Reviewing this controversy, it is hard to avoid the conclusion that the Government's reluctance to acknowledge that the first descriptions of events had, for understandable reasons, been inaccurate, allowed the assumption to grow that some scandalous secret was being protected, although the reluctance of those who made these allegations to allow that they might have been mistaken is also remarkable. That being said, it was probably unavoidable that an attack which left so many dead and which had, at the time, shocked many at home and abroad, would be subject to intense post-war scrutiny. For the Government there was undeniable frustration that, having managed successfully a difficult conflict and then, courtesy of the Franks Report, avoided some of the anticipated blame for the mismanagement of the crisis which led to the conflict, it found itself caught up in endless controversy over this one incident and a series of bizarre tangents.

ENVOI

One of my aims through this Official History has been to take the claims and counter-claims made about the origins and conduct of the Falklands War and test them against the available evidence, including the substantial quantities of archive material that I have been able to view. For this reason I appear to have expended many words on what was a relatively short war, and one that was in many respects uncomplicated, with only two belligerents fighting at the end of tenuous supply lines. It is perhaps of scant comfort to readers who have reached the end, to learn that there are areas I still wish that I could have covered in greater detail. I have decided to resist the temptation to conclude with more reflections, save for one. Immediately after the Falklands campaign was successfully concluded I wrote an account of the conflict for an American journal and noted its curiously 'atavistic' quality and how in a war in which the physical elements such as terrain and climate loomed as large as the technical ones, the traditional military virtues – of training, stamina and professionalism – could be decisive. At the end of 1982, in a paper for the British International Studies Association, I suggested that in its political aspects the Falklands might turn out to be a precursor of things to come, in the role allotted to the United Nations, the importance of the principle of self-determination, and a line-up that was neither East-West nor North-South, that is it reflected but was not dominated by either the cold war or anti-colonialism. At the time this was greeted with a degree of scepticism, but in retrospect this argument seems justified. Furthermore, with the end of the cold war and the prospect of further great power confrontations, new types of international conflict have demonstrated the continuing importance of the traditional military virtues. So while in many respects this conflict still stands out as an anomaly in recent international history, the last war of a past imperial era, in others it can now be recognised as one of the first of the coming post cold-war era.

APPENDICES

DRAFT AGREEMENTS

Original US draft tabled by Haig on 12 April

On the basis of United Nations Security Council Resolution No 502 and recalling relevant United Nations General Assembly resolutions, Argentina and the United Kingdom have agreed on the following steps, which form an integrated whole:

- All military and security forces shall be withdrawn from the islands and agreed surrounding areas within a short period of time, but not later than two weeks from the date of this agreement.
- After the date of this agreement and pending a definitive settlement, no military or security forces shall be introduced into the islands or surrounding areas. All forces that have been deployed in connection with the current controversy shall be returned to their normal operating areas.
- The United Kingdom, Argentina and the United States shall each appoint a representative to constitute a Special Commission which shall provide observers to verify compliance with the obligations in the preceding paragraphs.
- On an interim basis, all decisions, laws and regulations adopted by the local administration on the islands shall be submitted to and expeditiously ratified by the Special Commission, except in the event that the Special Commission deems such decisions, laws or regulations to be inconsistent with the purposes of this agreement or its implementation. The traditional local administration shall continue, including the Executive and Legislative Councils, which would be enlarged to include representatives of the Argentine population resident on the islands. The Special Commission shall fly the flag of each of its constituent members at its headquarters.
- Henceforth travel, transportation, communications and all trade between the mainland and the islands shall be facilitated and promoted, and the Special Commission shall make specific recommendations.

757

- Within a short period of time, but not later than two weeks from the date of this agreement, steps shall be taken to terminate the economic and financial measures adopted in connection with the current controversy, including restrictions relating to travel, transportation, communications, and transfers of funds between the two countries. Likewise, the United Kingdom shall request third countries that have adopted similar measures to terminate them by that date.
- 31 December 1982, will conclude the interim period, and during this period the conditions of the definitive status of the islands shall be negotiated, consistent with the Purposes and Principles of the United Nations Charter.

Final Haig plan, 27 April 1982

1   On the basis of United Nations Security Council Resolution 502, and the will of the Argentine Republic and that of the United Kingdom to resolve the controversy which has arisen between them, renouncing the use of force, both governments agree on the following steps, which form an integrated whole:

2.1 Effective on the signature of this agreement by both governments, there shall be an immediate cessation of hostilities.

2.2 Beginning at 0000 hours local time of the day after the day on which this agreement is signed and pending a definitive settlement, the Republic of Argentina and the United Kingdom shall not introduce nor deploy forces into the zones (hereinafter "zones") defined by circles of 150 nautical miles radius of the following coordinate points (hereinafter "coordinate points"):

    a)   LAT. 51 DEG 40' S
         LONG. 59 DEG 30' W

    b)   LAT. 54 DEG 20' S
         LONG. 36 DEG 40' W

    c)   LAT. 57 DEG 40' S
         LONG. 26 DEG 30' W

2.3 Within 24 hours of the date of this agreement the United Kingdom will suspend enforcement of its "zone of exclusion" and Argentina will suspend operations in the same area.

2.4 Within 24 hours of the date of this agreement Argentina and the United Kingdom will commence the withdrawal of their forces in accordance with the following details.

2.5 Within seven days from the date of this agreement, Argentina and the United Kingdom shall each have withdrawn one-half of their military and security forces present in the zones on the date of this agreement, including related equipment and armaments. Within the same time period, the United Kingdom Naval Task Force will stand off at a distance equivalent to 7 days' sailing time (at 12 knots) from any of the co-ordinate points, and Argentine forces that have been withdrawn shall be placed in a condition such that they could not be reinserted with their equipment and armament in less than 7 days.

2.6 Within 15 days from the date of the agreement, Argentina shall remove all of its remaining forces from the zones and redeploy them to their usual operating areas or normal duties. Within the same time period the United Kingdom shall likewise remove all of its remaining forces from the zones and shall redeploy such forces and the naval task force and submarines to their usual operating areas or normal duties.

2.7 In accordance with its Letter of Acceptance of even date, the United States shall verify compliance with the provisions of this paragraph, and the two Governments agree to cooperate fully with the United States in facilitating this verification.

3. From the date of this agreement, the two governments will initiate the necessary procedures to terminate simultaneously, and without delay, the economic and financial measures adopted in connection with the current controversy, including restrictions relating to travel, transportation, communications, and transfers of funds between the two countries. The United Kingdom at the same time shall request the European Community and third countries that have adopted similar measures to terminate them.

4. The United Kingdom, and Argentina shall each appoint, and the United States has indicated its agreement to appoint, a representative to constitute a Special Interim Authority (hereinafter "the Authority") which shall verify compliance with the obligations in this Agreement (with the exception of Paragraph 2), and undertake other responsibilities as are assigned to it under this Agreement or the separate Protocol regarding the Authority signed this date. Each representative may be supported by a staff of not more than 10 persons on the islands.

5. Pending a definitive settlement, all decisions, laws and regulations hereafter adopted by the local administration on the islands shall be submitted to and expeditiously ratified by the Authority, except in the event that the Authority deems such decisions, laws or regulations to be inconsistent with the purposes of this agreement or its implementation. The traditional local administration shall continue, except that the Executive and Legislative Councils shall be enlarged to include: (a) two representatives appointed by the Argentine Government to serve in Council; and (b) representatives in each Council of the Argentine population whose period of residence on the islands is equal to that required

of others entitled to representation in proportion to their population, subject to there being at least one such representative in each council. Such representatives of the resident Argentine population shall be nominated by the Authority. The flags of each of the constituent members of the Authority shall be flown at its headquarters.

5.2 Pending a definitive settlement, neither government shall take any action that would be inconsistent with the purposes and provisions of this agreement or its implementation.

6.1 Pending a definitive settlement, travel, transportation, movement of persons and, as may be related thereto, residence and ownership and disposition of property, communications and commerce between the mainland and the islands shall, on a non-discriminatory basis, be promoted and facilitated. The Authority shall propose to the two signatories for adoption appropriate measures on such matters. Such proposals shall simultaneously be transmitted to the Executive and Legislative Councils for their views. The two signatories undertake to respond promptly to such proposals. The Authority shall monitor the implementation of all such proposals adopted.

6.2 The provisions of paragraph 6.1 shall in no way prejudice the rights and guarantees which have heretofore been enjoyed by the inhabitants on the islands, in particular rights relating to freedom of opinion, religion, expression, teaching, movement, property, employment, family, customs, and cultural ties with countries of origin.

7. December 31, 1982, will conclude the interim period during which the signatories shall complete negotiations on removal of the islands from the list of Non-Self-Governing Territories under Chapter XI of the United Nations Charter and on mutually agreed conditions for their definitive status, including due regard for the rights of the inhabitants and for the principle of territorial integrity, in accordance with the principles and purposes of the Charter of the United Nations and in the light of the relevant Resolutions of the United Nations General Assembly. The negotiations hereabove referred to shall begin within fifteen days of the signature of the present agreement.

8. In order to assist them in bringing their negotiations to a mutually satisfactory settlement by the date stipulated in the preceding paragraph, the Authority shall after consultation with the Executive Council make specific proposals and recommendations as early as practicable to the two signatories, including proposals and recommendations on:

8.1 The manner of taking into account the wishes and interests of the islanders, insofar as islands with a settled population are concerned, based on the results of a sounding of the opinion of the inhabitants, with respect to such issues relating to the negotiations, and conducted in such manner, as the Authority may determine:

Issues relating to the development of the resources of the islands, including opportunities for joint cooperation and the role of the Falkland Islands Company; and

Such other matters as the two signatories may request, including possible arrangements for compensation of islanders, or matters on which the Authority may wish to comment in light of its experience in discharging its responsibilities under this Agreement.

The signatories have agreed on the procedures in sub-paragraph 8.1 without prejudice to their respective positions on the legal weight to be accorded such opinion in reaching a definitive settlement.

9. Should the signatories nonetheless be unable to conclude the negotiations by December 31, 1982, the United States government has indicated that, on the request of both Governments, it would be prepared at such time to seek to resolve the dispute within six months of the date of the request by making specific proposals for a settlement and by directly conducting negotiations between the Governments on the basis of procedures that it shall formulate. The two Governments agree to respond within one month to any formal proposals of recommendations submitted to them by the United States.

10. This agreement shall enter into force on the date of signature.

Peruvian initiative: First Peruvian draft, 2 May 1982

- An immediate cease-fire;
- A mutual withdrawal of forces;
- The involvement of third parties on a temporary basis in the administration of the islands;[1]
- Acceptance by both parties of the fact that a dispute over sovereignty exists;[2]
- Acknowledgement that the views and interests of the Islanders must be taken into account in reaching a definitive settlement;[3]
- A contact group of Brazil, Peru, the FRG and the United States would be formed; and[4]
- A definitive agreement would have to be reached by 30 April 1983.[5]

Peruvian initiative: Final UK version, 6 May 1982

Draft Interim Agreement on the Falkland Islands/Islas Malvinas

- An immediate cease-fire, concurrent with:
- Mutual withdrawal and non-reintroduction of all forces, according to a schedule to be established by the contact group;

- The immediate introduction of contact group composed of Brazil, Peru, the Federal Republic of Germany and the United States into the Falkland Islands on a temporary basis, pending agreement on a definitive settlement. The contact group will assume responsibility for:
- Verification of the withdrawal;
- Administering the government of the Falkland Islands in the interim period in consultation with the elected representatives of the population of the islands and ensuring that no actions are taken in the islands which would contravene this interim agreement; and
- Ensuring that all other provisions of the agreement are respected.
- Britain and Argentina acknowledge the existence of differing and conflicting views regarding the status of the Falkland Islands.
- The two governments acknowledge that the aspirations and interests of the Islanders will be included in the definitive settlement of the status of the islands;
- The contact group will have responsibility for ensuring that the two governments reach a definitive agreement prior to 30 April 1983.

Proposed UK interim agreement, 19 May 1982

The Government of Argentina and the Government of the United Kingdom of Great Britain and Northern Ireland

Responding to Security Council Resolution 502 (1982) adopted on 3 April 1982 under article 40 of the Charter of the United Nations,

Having entered into Negotiations through the Good Offices of the Secretary-General of the United Nations for an Interim Agreement concerning the Falkland Islands (Islas Malvinas), hereinafter referred to as "The Islands",

Having in mind the obligations with regard to non-self governing territories set out in Article 73 of the Charter of the United Nations, the text of which is annexed hereto.

Have agreed on the following:

Article 1

- No provision of this interim agreement shall in any way prejudice the rights, claims and positions of either party in the ultimate peaceful settlement of their dispute over the islands.
- No acts or activities taking place whilst this interim agreement is in force shall constitute a basis for asserting, supporting or denying a claim to territorial sovereignty over the islands or create any rights of sovereignty over them.

Article 2

- With effect from a specified time, 24 hours after signature of this agreement (hereinafter referred to as Time 'T'), each party undertakes to cease and thereafter to refrain from all firing and other hostile actions.

Argentina undertakes:
- To commence withdrawal of its armed forces from the islands with effect from time 'T';
- To withdraw half of its armed forces to at least 150 nautical miles away from any point in the islands by time 'T' plus 7 days; and
- To complete its withdrawal to at least 150 nautical miles away by time 'T' plus 14 days.

The United Kingdom undertakes:
- To commence withdrawal of its armed forces from the islands with effect from time 'T';
- To withdraw half of its armed forces to at least 150 nautical miles away from any point in the islands by time 'T' plus 7 days; and
- To complete its withdrawal to at least 150 nautical miles away by time 'T' plus 14 days.

Article 3

- With effect from time 'T', each Party undertakes to lift the exclusion zones, warnings and similar measures which have been imposed.

Article 4

- On the completion of the steps for withdrawal specified in Article 2, each Party undertakes to refrain from reintroducing any armed forces into the islands or within 150 nautical miles thereof.

Article 5

- Each party undertakes to lift with effect from time 'T' the economic measures it has taken against the other and to seek the lifting of similar measures taken by third parties.

Article 6

- Immediately after the signature of the present agreement, Argentina and the United Kingdom will jointly sponsor a draft resolution in the United Nations under the terms of which the Security Council would take note of the present Agreement, acknowledge the role conferred upon the Secretary-General of the United Nations therein, and autho- rise him to carry out the tasks entrusted to him therein.

- Immediately after the adoption of the Resolution referred to in para- graph (1) of this article, a United Nations administrator, being a person acceptable to Argentina and the United Kingdom, will be appointed by the Secretary-General and will be the officer administering the govern- ment of the Islands.

- The United Nations administrator shall have authority under the direction of the Secretary-General to ensure the continuing adminis- tration of the government of the Islands. He shall discharge his functions in consultation with the representative institutions of the Islands which have been developed in accordance with the terms of Article 73 of the UN Charter, with the exception that one representa- tive from the Argentine population normally resident on the Islands shall be appointed by the United Nations Administrator to each of the two institutions. The Administrator shall exercise his powers in accordance with the terms of this Agreement and in conformity with the spirit of the laws and practices traditionally obtaining in the Islands.

- The United Nations Administrator shall verify the withdrawal of all armed forces from the islands, and shall devise an effective method of ensuring their non-re-introduction.

- The United Nations Administrator shall have such staff as may be agreed by Argentina and the United Kingdom to be necessary for the performance of his functions under this Agreement.

- Each Party may have no more than three observers in the Islands.

Article 7

- Except as may be otherwise agreed between them, the Parties shall, during the currency of this Agreement, reactivate the Exchange of Notes of 5 August 1971, together with the Joint Statement on communications and movement referred to therein. The Parties shall accordingly take appropriate steps to establish a special consultative committee to carry out the functions entrusted to the special consultative committee referred to in the Joint Statement.

Article 8

- The parties undertake to enter into negotiations in good faith under the auspices of the Secretary-General of the United Nations for the peaceful settlement of their dispute and to seek, with a sense of urgency, the completion of these negotiations by 31 December 1982. These negotiations shall be initiated without prejudice to the rights, claims or positions of either party and without prejudgment of the outcome.

Article 9

• This interim agreement shall enter into force on signature and shall remain in force until a definitive agreement about the future of the islands has been reached and implemented by the Parties. The Secretary-General will immediately communicate its text to the security council and register it in accordance with Article 102 of the Charter of the United Nations.

Done in .... in the English and Spanish languages in a single copy

Unofficial translation of Argentine paper of 18 May 1982

The Government of the Argentine Republic and the Government of the United Kingdom of Great Britain and Northern Ireland, hereinafter referred to as 'the parties',

In response to the provisions of Security Council Resolution 502 (1982) of 3 April 1982, and taking into account the Charter of the United Nations, Resolution 1514 (XV), 65 (XX) and other resolutions of the General Assembly of the United Nations on the question of the Malvinas (Falkland) Islands, have accepted, in accordance with Article 40 of the Charter of the United Nations, the assistance of the Secretary-General of the United Nations and have engaged in negotiations and arrived at the following provisional agreement relating to the Malvinas, South Georgia and South Sandwich Islands, hereinafter referred to as 'the islands' for the purposes of this agreement.

1. The geographical scope of the area within which the withdrawal of troops is to be carried out shall comprise the Malvinas, South Georgia and South Sandwich Islands. The withdrawal of the forces of both parties shall be gradual and simultaneous. Within a maximum period of thirty days, all armed forces shall be in their normal bases and areas of operation.
2. With effect from the signature of this agreement, each party shall cease to apply the economic measures which it has adopted against the other and the United Kingdom shall call for the same action by those countries or groups of countries which, at its request, adopted similar measures.
3. Supervision of the withdrawal of forces of both countries shall be carried out by specialized personnel of the United Nations, whose composition shall be agreed with the parties. The interim administration

of the Islands while the negotiations for final settlement of the dispute are in progress shall conform to the following provisions:

The Administration shall be exclusively the responsibility of the United Nations with an appropriate presence of observers of the parties;

The said administration shall perform all functions (executive, legislative, judicial and security) through officials of different nationality from that of the parties.

Notwithstanding the provisions of 2 (A) and (B), and in order not to cause unnecessary changes in the way of life of the population during the period of the interim administration by the United Nations, local judicial functions may be exercised in accordance with the legislation in force on 1 April 1982 to the full extent compatible with this agreement. Similarly, the United Nations interim adminis- tration may appoint as advisers persons who are members of the population of British origin and Argentines resident in the islands, in equal numbers.

The flags of the parties shall fly together with that of the United Nations.

During the period of interim administration, communications shall be kept open, without discriminatory restrictions of any kind for the parties, including freedom of movement and equality of access with respect to residence, work and property.

Freedom of communication shall also include the maintenance of freedom of transit for the state airline (Lade) and for merchant ships and scientific vessels: In addition, telephone, telegraph and telex communications, Argentine television transmissions and the state petroleum (YPF) and gas services shall continue to operate freely.

The customs, traditions and way of life of the inhabitants of the islands, and their social and cultural links with their countries of origin, shall be respected and safeguarded.

4. The parties undertake to enter immediately into negotiations in good faith under the auspices of the Secretary-General of the United Nations for the peaceful and final settlement of the dispute and, with a sense of urgency, to complete these negotiations by 31 December 1982, with a single option to extend until 30 June 1983, in order to comply with the Charter of the United Nations, Resolution 1514 (XV), 65 (XX) and other relevant resolutions of the General Assembly of the United Nations on the question of the Malvinas, South Georgia and South Sandwich Islands. The negotiations shall be held in New York.

5. The Secretary-General of the United Nations may be assisted in the negotiations by a contact group composed of representatives of four states members of the United Nations. To that end, each party shall nominate two states and shall have the right to a single veto of one of

the states nominated by the other. The Secretary-General of the United Nations shall keep the Security Council assiduously informed of the progress of the negotiations.

6. If the period specified in Point V (1) above expires without the attainment of a final agreement, the Secretary-General shall draw up a report addressed to the General Assembly of the United Nations, in order that the latter may determine, as appropriate and with the greatest urgency, the lines to which the said final agreement should conform in order to achieve a speedy settlement of the question.

Secretary-General's Aide Memoire, plus attached formulations of 19 May

Aide Memoire

The Secretary-General believes that, at this critical point in the exchanges which he has been having with the parties concerning the continuing crisis, it is useful to set down those issues on which agreement seems to exist and those on which differences remain.

In the Secretary-General's judgement, the two parties are in essential agreement on the following points:

- The agreement being sought is interim in nature and will be without prejudice to the rights, claims or positions of the parties concerned.
- The agreement will cover a) a cease-fire, b) the mutual withdrawal of forces, c) the termination of exclusion zones and of economic measures instituted in connexion with the conflict, d) the interim administration of the territory and e), negotiations on a peaceful settlement of their dispute.
- The initiation of these various parts of the agreement will be simultaneous.
- Withdrawal of forces will be phased and will be under the supervision of the United Nations observers.
- The interim administration of the territory will be under the authority of the United Nations. The United Nations flag shall be flown. Argentina and the United Kingdom will establish small liaison offices, on which their respective flags will be flown.
- The parties will enter into negotiations in good faith under the auspices of the Secretary-General of the United Nations for the peaceful settlement of their dispute and seek, with a sense of urgency, the completion of these negotiations by 31 December 1982, taking into account the Charter of the United Nations and the relevant resolutions of the General Assembly. These negotiations shall be initiated without prejudice to the rights, claims or position of the parties and without prejudgement of the outcome. The negotiations shall be held in New York or at a mutually acceptable location in the vicinity thereof.

Those points on which full agreement must still be achieved, in the Secretary-General's judgement, are the following:

- Certain aspects of the interim administration of the territory.
- Provision for the extension of the time frame for completion of negotiations and the related duration of the interim administration.
- Certain aspects of the mutual withdrawal of forces.
- The geographic area to be covered by the terms of the interim agreement.

It is evident from this review that the extent of agreement is substantial and important. If it can be incorporated in the text of an interim agreement, the requirements of Security Council Resolution 502 would be met. The Secretary-General is deeply concerned, however, that unless the remaining points are resolved in the very immediate future, all that has been accomplished will be lost and the prospects for the early restoration of peace will be frustrated.

In the desire to be of assistance to the parties in overcoming these differences, the Secretary-General is appending to this aide memoire two informal papers containing formulations which, in the Secretary-General's view, might satisfactorily meet the objectives of the parties with regard to an interim agreement. These formulations deal with the time frame of diplomatic negotiations and the form which the interim administration of the territory under the authority of the United Nations might take.

With regard to the question of the geographic area covered by the terms of an interim agreement, the Secretary-General would suggest, as a practical approach, that the status of the dependencies be included within the scope of the negotiations foreseen on a diplomatic settlement on the same basis as was provided in the joint communiqué issued by Argentina and the United Kingdom on 26 April 1977. In this understanding, and without prejudice to the issue of the status of these islands, the force withdrawal and interim administration provisions would not be applicable with regard to the dependencies.

The Secretary-General would suggest that the United Nations be entrusted with the modalities of mutual force withdrawals which will be simultaneous and phased. Their responsibility would be undertaken with a view to completion of the withdrawals within a two-week period.

The Secretary-General wishes to emphasize that the time left for agreement must be measured now in hours. It is, therefore, his earnest hope that the parties will find it possible to agree to the proposed formulations and suggestions as a means of reaching the agreement which cannot, without great peril, be longer delayed.

The Secretary-General feels obligated, in the interests of peace, and the preservation of human lives, to make clear that this might be the last chance for agreement through negotiations.

Formulation on Terms of Reference for Negotiations on a Diplomatic Settlement

- The parties undertake to enter into negotiations in good faith under the auspices of the Secretary-General of the United Nations for the peaceful settlement of their dispute and to seek, with a sense of urgency, the completion of these negotiations by 31 December 1982, taking into account the Charter of the United Nations and the relevant resolutions of the General Assembly. These negotiations shall be initiated without prejudice to the rights, claims or position of the parties and without prejudgement of the outcome. The negotiations shall be held in New York or at a mutually acceptable location in the vicinity thereof.
- Should the Secretary-General, after taking account of the course of the negotiations and the views of the parties, determine that the achievement of a negotiated settlement will not be possible within the time frame envisaged, he may establish a new target date which will be in keeping with the urgency of a diplomatic solution to which the parties are committed by this agreement.
- The Government of Argentina and the Government of the United Kingdom of Great Britain and Northern Ireland should be bound by the provision of this agreement until the negotiated settlement provided for above comes into effect.

An Interim Administration Formulation

- The United Nations representative shall assume, on behalf of the United Nations, full and exclusive authority to administer the territory. He shall discharge his functions in consultation with the representative institutions in the islands with the exception that one representative from the Argentine population normally resident on the Islands shall be appointed by the representative to each of the two institutions. The United Nations representative shall exercise his powers in accordance with the terms of this agreement and in conformity with the laws and practices traditionally obtaining in the islands.
- The United Nations flag shall be flown in the territory.
- The Government of Argentina and the Government of the United Kingdom will, in consultation with the United Nations representative, establish small liaison offices to maintain contact with their representative.

The flags of the Republic of Argentina and the United Kingdom may be flown on their respective liaison offices.

- During the period of interim administration, all communications and other co-operative arrangements in the economic, social, cultural and scientific-technological fields in effect on 31 March 1982 shall continue and be promoted further, as appropriate.
- Relaxation of restrictions on residence and the acquisition of property will be considered, keeping in mind the necessity to respect and safeguard the customs, traditions and way of life of the inhabitants of the islands.

BRITISH UNITS IN THE FALKLANDS WAR

Naval and Maritime

Table 4 Royal Navy Ships

Type	Ship	Commissioned	Displacement Full Load (tons)	Captain	Date entered operational area
Carriers					
	Hermes	1959	28,700	Capt. L.E. Middleton	25/4/1982
	Invincible	1980	19,500	Capt. J.J Black, MBE	25/4/1982
Guided Missile Destroyers					
'County Class'	Antrim	1971	6,200	Capt. B.G. Young	17/4/1982
	Glamorgan	1966	6,200	Capt. M.E. Barrow	25/4/1982
Type 82	Bristol	1973	7,100	Capt. A. Grose	23/5/1982
Type 42	Cardiff	1979	4,100	Capt. M.G.T. Harris	23/5/1982
	Coventry	1978	4,100	Capt. D. Hart-Dyke	20/4/1982
	Exeter	1980	4,100	Capt. H.M. Balfour, MVO	19/5/1982
	Glasgow	1979	4,100	Capt. A.P. Hoddinott, OBE	20/4/1982
	Sheffield	1979	4,100	Capt. J.F.T.G. Salt	20/4/1982
Frigates					
Type 12	Plymouth	1961	2,800	Capt. D. Pentreath	17/4/1982
	Yarmouth	1960	2,800	Cdr A. Morton	25/4/1982
'Batch II'	Argonaut	1967	3,200	Capt. C.H. Layman, MVO	13/5/1982

(continued on next page)

Table 4 (cont.)

Type	Ship	Commissioned	Displacement Full Load (tons)	Captain	Date entered operational area
Leander	Minerva	1966	3,200	Cdr S.H.G. Johnston	23/5/1982
	Penelope	1966	3,200	Cdr P.V. Rickard	23/5/1982
'Batch III'	Andromeda	1968	3,100	Capt. J.L. Weatherall	23/5/1982
Type 21	Active	1977	3,250	Cdr. P.C.B. Canter	23/5/1982
	Alacrity	1977	3,250	Cdr C.J.S. Craig	25/7/1982
	Ambuscade	1975	3,250	Cdr P.J. Mosse	18/5/1982
	Antelope	1975	3,250	Cdr N.J. Tobin	18/5/1982
	Ardent	1977	3,250	Cdr A.W.J. West	13/5/1982
	Arrow	1976	3,250	Cdr P.J. Bootherstone	20/4/1982
	Avenger	1978	3,250	Capt. H.M. White	23/5/1982
Type 22	Brilliant	1981	4,400	Capt. J.F. Coward	20/4/1982
	Broadsword	1979	4,400	Capt. W.R. Canning	25/4/1982
Patrol Submarine					
	Onyx	1967	2,030 (surface)	Lt-Cdr A.O. Johnson	28/5/1982
Fleet Submarines					
Valiant	Conqueror	1971	4,000 (surface)	Cdr C.K. Wreford-Brown	16/4/1982
	Courageous	1971	4,000 (surface)	Cdr R.T.N. Best	30/5/1982
	Valiant	1966	4,000 (surface)	Cdr T.M. Le Marchand	16/5/1982
Swiftsure	Spartan	1979	4,200 (surface)	Cdr J.B. Taylor	12/4/1982
	Splendid	1981	4,200 (surface)	Cdr R.C. Lane-Nott	19/4/1982
Amphibious Assault Ship					
	Fearless	1965	12,120	Capt. E.S.J. Larken	13/5/1982
	Intrepid	1967	12,120	Capt. P.G.V. Dingemans	13/5/1982
Offshore Patrol Vessels					
	Dumbarton Castle	1982	1,450	Lt.Cdr N.D. Wood	
	Leeds Castle	1981	1,450	Lt Cdr. C.F.B. Hamilton	

(*continued on next page*)

Table 4 (cont.)

Type	Ship	Commissioned	Displacement Full Load (tons)	Captain	Date entered operational area
Survey (Ambulance) Vessels					
	Hecla	1965	2,733	Capt. G.L. Hope	9/5/1982
	Herald	1974	2,733	Capt. R.I.C. Halliday	15/5/1982
	Hydra	1966	2,733	Capt. R.J. Campbell	14/5/1982
Antarctic Patrol Vessel					
	Endurance	1956 (RN 1968)	3,600	Capt. N.J. Barker	In Theatre
Deep Armed Team Sweep Trawlers					
	Cordella		1,238	Lt. M.C.G. Holloway	18/5/1982
	Farnella		1,207	Lt. R.J. Bishop	18/5/1982
	Junella		1,615	Lt. Routledge	18/5/1982
	Northella		1,238	Lt. J.P.S. Bishop	18/5/1982
	Pict		1,238	Lt. Cdr. D.G. Garwood	18/5/1982

Table 5 Fleet Air Arm Squadrons deployed

Squadron	CO	Aircraft	Deployed
737	Lt. Cdr. M.S. Tennant	2 Wessex III helicopters	Antrim/Glamorgan
800	Lt. Cdr. A.D. Auld	12 Sea Harriers	HMS Hermes
801	Lt. Cdr. N.D. Ward	8 Sea Harriers	HMS Invincible
809*	Lt. Cdr. T.J.H. Gedge	8 Sea Harriers	Hermes/Invincible
815	Lt. Cdr. R.I. Money	24 Lynx Helicopters	various
820	Lt. Cdr. R.J.S. Wykes-Sneyd	9 Sea King Mk.II ASW	Invincible
824	Lt. Cdr. I. Thorpe	7 Sea King Mk.II ASW	'O' class tankers
825*	Lt. Cdr. H.S. Clar k	10 Sea King Mk.II ASW	San Carlos
826	Lt. Cdr. D.J.S. Squier	9 Sea King Mk.V ASW	Hermes
829	Lt.Cdr. M.J. Mullane	12 Wasp Helicopters	various
845	Lt. Cdr. R.J. Warden	21 Wessex V Helicopters	various
846	Lt. Cdr. S.C. Thornewill	13 Sea King Mk.IV ASW	various
847*	Lt. Cdr. M.D. Booth	24 Wessex V Helicopters	various
848*	Lt. Cdr. D.E.P. Baston	12 Wessex V Helicopters	various
899	Lt. Cdr. J. Gunning	5 Sea Harriers	Yeovilton

* Indicates squadron specially formed for Task Force operations.

Table 6 Fleet Clearance Diving Team

FCDT 1, Lt. Cdr. B.F. Dutton
FCDT 3, Lt. N.A. Bruen

Table 7 Royal Fleet Auxiliaries

Type	Ship	Commissioned	Displacement Full Load (tons)	Captain
Fleet Oilers				
'O'	Olmeda	1965	33,240	Captain A.P. Overbury
	Olna	1966	33,240	Captain J.A. Bailey
Tide	Tidepool	1963	25,930	Captain J.W. Gaffrey
	Tidespring	1963	25,930	Captain S. Redmond
Rover	Blue Rover	1970	11,520	Captain J.D. Roddis
Support Oilers (Chartered)				
	Pearleaf	1960	18,797 (deadweight)	Captain J. McCull och
	Plumleaf	1960	19,200 (deadweight)	Captain R.W.M. Wallace
	Appleleaf	1979	33,750 (deadweight)	Captain G.P.A. MacDougall
	Bayleaf	1982	33,750 (deadweight)	Captain A.E.T. Hunter
	Brambleleaf	1980	33,750 (deadweight)	Captain M.S.J. Farley
Fleet Reple nishment Ships				
	Regent	1967	23,000	Captain J. Logan
	Resource	1967	23,000	Captain B.A. Seymour
	Stromness	1967	16,800	Captain J.B. Dickinson
'Fort'	Fort Austin	1979	22,750	Commodore S.C. Dunlop
	Fort Grange	1979	22,750	Captain D.G.M. Averill
Helicopt er Support Ship				
	Engadine	1967	8,960	Captain D.F. Freeman
Landing Ships (Logistic)				
	Sir Bedivere	1967	5,674	Captain P.J. McCarthy
	Sir Galahad	1966	5,674	Captain P.J.G. Roberts
	Sir Geraint	1967	5,674	Captain D.E. Lawrence
	Sir Lancelot	1964	5,550	Captain C.A. Purtcher - Wydenbruck

(*continued on next page*)

Table 7 (cont.)

Type	Ship	Commissioned	Displacement Full Load (tons)	Captain
	Sir Percivale	1968	5,674	Captain A.F. Pitt
	Sir Tristram	1967	5,674	Captain G.R. Green
Royal Maritime Auxiliary Service				
Tug	Typhoon	1960	1,380	Captain J.N. Morris
Mooring Vessel	Goosander	1973	1,200	Captain A. MacGregor

Table 8 Ships Taken up from Trade

Type	Ship	Commissioned	Deadweight (tons)	Captain
Auxiliary Fleet Support				
Hospital Ship (liner)	Uganda	1952	5,705	Captain J.G. Clark
Minesweeper Support (passenger/cargo)	St Helena	1963	2,264	Captain M.L.M. Smith
Mooring Vessel	Wimpey Seahorse	1982	2,085	Captain M.J. Slack
Repair Ship	Stena Inspector	1980	4,835	Captain D. Ede
	Stena Seaspread	1980	4,835	Captain N. Williams
Salvage Tug	Irishman	1978	686 (Gross register)	Captain W. Allen
	Yorkshireman	1978	686 (Gross register)	Captain P. Rimmer
	Salvageman	1980	1,598 (Gross register)	Captain A.J. Stockwell
Logistic Support				
Support Oiler	Anco Charger	1973	25,300	Captain B. Hatton
	Balder London	1979	33,750	Captain K.J. Wallace
	British Avon	1972	25,620	Captain J.W.M. Guy
	British Dart	1972	25,620	Captain J.A.N. Turner

(*continued on next page*)

Table 8 (*cont.*)

Type	Ship	Commissioned	Deadweight (tons)	Captain
	British Esk	1973	25,620	Captain G. Barber
	British Tamar	1973	25,620	Captain W.H. Hare
	British Tay	1973	25,620	Captain P.T. Morris
	British Test	1973	25,620	Captain T.A. Oliphant
	British Trent	1973	25,620	Captain P.R. Walker
	British Wye	1974	25,620	Captain D.M. Rundell
	Eburna	1979	31,375	Captain J.C. Beaumont
	GA Walker	1973	30,607	Captain E.C. Metham
Base Storage Tanker (Ascension)	Alvega	1977	57,372	Captain A. Lazenby
Base Storage Tanker (S Georgia)	Scottish Eagle	1980	56,490	Captain A. Terras
Fresh Water Tanker	Fort Toronto	1981	31,745	Captain R.I. Kinnear
Stores Ships				
Refrigerated Stores	Avelona Star	1975	11,092	Captain H. Dyer
	Geestport	1982	9,970	Captain G.F. Foster
Military Supplies	Laertes	1976	13,450	Captain H.T. Reid
Ammunition	Lycaon	1976	13,450	Captain H.R. Lawton
Naval Stores	Saxonia	1972	12,182	Captain H. Evans
Transports				
Aircraft Transports (Roll-on/Roll-off Container Ships)	Astronomer	1977	23,120	Captain H.S. Braden

(*continued on next page*)

Table 8 *(cont.)*

Type	Ship	Commissioned	Deadweight (tons)	Captain
	Atlantic Causeway	1969	18,150	Captain M.H.C. Twomey
	Atlantic Conveyor	1970	18,150	Captain I. North
	Contendor Bezant	1981	17,993	Captain A. MacKinnon
Despatch Vessels				
	British Enterprise III	1965	1,197	Captain D. Grant
	CS Iris	1975	2,150	Captain G. Fulton
Personnel and Vehicle Transports				
Roll-on/Roll-off Ferry	Baltic Ferry	1978	8,704	Captain E. Harrison
Liner	Canberra	1961	9,910	Captain W. Scott-Mason
Roll-on/Roll-off Ferry	Europic Ferry	1975	2,784	Captain C.J.C. Clark
Roll-on/Roll-off Ferry	Nordic Ferry	1978	8,704	Captain R. Jenkins
Roll-on/Roll-off Ferry	Norland	1974	13,000	
Liner	Queen Elizabeth II	1969	15,976	Captain N.C.H. James
Roll-on/Roll-off Ferry	St. Edmund	1974	1,830	Captain M.J. Stockman
Roll-on/Roll-off Ferry	Tor Caledonia	1974	9,882	Captain A. Scott
Falkland Islands Merchant Vessels				
Coaster	Forrest	1967	140	
Coaster	Monsunen	1957	240	Lt. I. McLaren

The land forces

HQ 3 Commando Brigade (Brigadier J. Thompson, RM)

29 Commando Regiment Royal Artillery (Lt-Col. M. Holroyd-Smith)

29 Battery, 4 Regiment RA (Major A. Rice)

59 Independent Commando Squadron Royal Engineers (Major R. Macdonald)

40 Commando RM (Lt-Col. M. Hunt)

42 Commando RM (Lt-Col. N. Vaux)

45 Commando RM (Lt-Col. A. Whitehead)

2nd Battalion Parachute Regiment plus attached units (Lt-Col. H. Jones, KIA 28 May; Lt-Col. D. Chaundler from 2 Jun)

3rd Battalion Parachute Regiment plus attached units (Lt-Col. H. Pike)

9 Parachute Squadron Royal Engineers (Major C. Davies)

Commando Logistics Regiment RM (Lt-Col. I. Helberg)

3 Commando Brigade HQ and Signals Squadron RM (Major R. Dixon)

3 Commando Brigade Air Squadron (Major P. Cameron)

2 Medium Reconnaissance Troops, B Squadron, the Blues & Royals (Lt. M. Coreth)

T Battery 12 Air Defence Regiment

Air Defence Troop

1 x Raiding Squadron RM (Capt. C. Baxter)

Mountain and Arctic Warfare Cadre, RM (Capt. Rod Boswell)

2, 3 & 6 Section Special Boat Squadron, RM (Major J. Thomson)

D & G Squadrons, 22nd SAS Regiment (Lt-Col. M. Rose)

3rd Commando Brigade Air Squadron (Major C.P. Cameron) with 12 Gazelles and 6 Scouts

3 x Tactical Air Control Parties

4th Assault Squadron Royal Marines

Air Maintenance group

Rear Link Detachment 30 Signal Regiment

3 x Mexeflote detachments 17 Port Regiment Royal Corps of Transport

5 x Landing Ship Logistics Detachments 17 Port Regiment

3 x Surgical Support Teams

Postal Courier Communications Unit Detachment of 1 PC Regiment

Detachment RAF Special Forces

Detachment 47 Air Despatch Squadron RCT

Detachment 49 EOD Squadron 33 Engineer Regiment

Y Troop Detachment (Communications)

Commando Forces Band (Stretcher-bearers)

HQ 5 Infantry Brigade (Brigadier A. Wilson)

2nd Btn Scots Guards (Lt-Col. M. Scott)

1st Btn Welsh Guards (Lt-Col. J. Rickett)

1/7th Duke of Edinburgh Own Gurkha Rifles (Lt-Col. D. Morgan)

656 Squadron of Army Air Corps (Major C.S. Sibun) with 6 Gazelles and 6 Scouts

97 Battery, 4th Regiment Royal Artillery

HQ 4 Field Regiment Royal Artillery
21 Air Defence Battery, Royal Artillery
16 Field Ambulance
81 Ordnance Company
Forward Air Control Party
5 Infantry Brigade Provost Unit RMP (Provost Marshall Capt A. Barley, RMP)

Other Army units:
49 Field Regiment RA
137 Battery, 40 Regiment RA
16th Air Defence RA
148 Commando Battery
11 Field Squadron, RE (Major Hawken, RE)
33 Engineer Regiment
Military Works Force RE
10 Field Workshop REME
14th Signals Regiment
202 Signals Squadron
602 Signal Troop (Special Communications)
10 Field Ambulance RAMC
2 Field Hospital RAMC
Joint Helicopter Handling Support Unit (407 Troop RCT)
29 Transport and Movement Regiment RCT
91 Ordnance Company, Royal Army Ordnance Corps (Major R.B.P. Smith)
421 EOD Company, Royal Army Ordnance Corps (Major A.C.D. Welch)

Royal Air Force

Table 9 RAF Squadrons deployed

Squadron	CO	Aircraft	Deployed
44/50/101	Sqdn. Ldr. A.C. Montgomery	6 Vulcan	Ascension
1 (F)	Wg. Cdr. P.T. Squire	10 GR.3 Harriers (+4 after conflict)	Hermes
18	Wg. Cdr. A.J. Stables	7 Chinook (3 sunk before arrival)	San Carlos
55/57	Gp. Capt. J.S.B. Price	23 Victor tankers	Ascension
42 (TB)	Wg. Cdr. D.L. Baugh	5 Nimrod MR1	Mainly Ascension
120/201/206	Wg. Cdr. D. Emmerson	7 Nimrod MR2	Mainly Ascension
47	Sqd. Ldr. A.M. Roberts	Hercules	Ascension
24/30/70	Sqdn. Ldr. M.J. Kempster (4–17 Apr) Sqdn. Ldr. J.R.D. Morely (18 Apr–11 May) Sqdn. Ldr. M.J. Kempster (12 May–23 July)	Hercules	RAF Lyneham
10	Wg. Cdr. O.G. Bunn	13 VC-10	RAF Lyneham/ Ascension
202	Sqd. Ldr. R.A. Cross	1 Sea King	Ascension
29 (F)	Sqd. Ldr. P.R. Morley	2 Phantoms	Ascension
3 Wing HQ Unit RAF Regiment	Wg. Cdr. T.T. Wallis		
15 Field Squadron RAF Regiment			
63 Squadron RAF Regiment	Sqdn. Ldr. P.G. Loughnorough		

1 ACC Radar
Tactical Communications Wing
Tactical Supply Wing
UK Mobile Air Movements Squadron
Ordnance Demolition Unit
Mobile Met Unit
Mobile Catering Support Unit
HQ 38 Group TACP (MAOT)

CASUALTIES

Table 10 Dead/missing presumed dead up to 15 June

	RN	*RM*	*Army*	*RAF*	*Civ*
HMS Sheffield	19				1
HMS Ardent	22				
HMS Argonaut	2				
HMS Antelope	1		1		
HMS Coventry	18				1
SS Atlantic Conveyor	3				9
Sir Galahad			42		5
Sir Tristram			3		2
LCU (HMS Fearless)	2				
HMS Glamorgan	13				
Aircrew	5	3			
Sea King Accident		1	19	1	
Falkland Land Battles		22	58		
TOTAL	85	26	123	1	18

Grand Total = 253

Table 11 3 Commando Brigade Group – summary of casualty lists up to 23 June

Unit	KIA	WIA	IIA	Other Illness	Casualty Total	Remarks
40 Cdo RM	1	6		2	15	2 Trench Foot
42 Cdo RM	2	24	5		48	10 Trench Foot 1 Frostbite
45 Cdo RM	12	23		2	58	2 Trench Foot
2 Para GP	18	39	21	3	105	PARR: WIA & KIA 18 Trench Foot 7 Frostbite
3 Para GP	22	56	45	7	98	8 Trench Foot 1 Frostbite
Cdo Log Regt RM	1	7	13	2	11	
Bde Air Sqn RM	4	2	1	1	8	
M&AW Cadre	–	3	1	–	3	
59 Indep Cdo RE	4	7	–	–	12	Includes 49 EOD
HQ & Sigs Sqn RM	–	2	1	1	5	Includes 1 RSRM
4 Field Regt (29 Bty)	–	–	2	1	2	
29 Regt RA	–	4	1	–	9	1 Trench Foot
32 Regt RA, 43 Bty	–	2	5	1	4	1 Trench Foot
12 Regt RA (T Bty)	–	–	1	–	3	3 Trench Foot
11 Fd Sqn RE	–	–	3	–	2	1 Trench Foot
Blues & Royals	–	–	2	–	1	
RAF Special Forces	–	–	1	–	1	
SBS	1	1	1	–	3	
SAS	1	4	1	–	5	
846 Naval Air Sqn	1	1	–	–	2	
9 Para Sqn RE	1	2	–	–	3	
Totals	68	183	122	25	398	

KIA. Killed in Action – includes two men from 3 Commando Brigade who died of wounds.
WIA. Wounded in Action – directly attributed to bullet, shrapnel, mines etc.
IIA. Injured in Action – breaking limbs whilst on patrol etc.
Illness. Defined as those that would have been contacted anyway.

Table 11 5 Infantry Brigade – summary of casualty lists up to 23 June

Unit	KIA	WIA	IIA	Other Illness	Casualty Total	Remarks
2 Scots Guards	8	39	10	4	61	2 Trench Foot
1 Welsh Guards	39	28	8	1	76	
1/7 Gurkha Rifles	–	8	–	–	8	
16 Field Ambulance	3	4	1	–	8	
4 Fd Regt, 97 Bty	–	1	3	–	4	
49 Fd Regt RA	–	1	1	–	2	
Support RA (RSA)	–	3	–	1	4	
656 Sqn AAC	2	1	–	–	3	
63 Sqn RAF	–	–	–	1	1	
81 Ord Coy RAOC	–	–	1	1	2	
HQ 5 Inf Bde	2	–	–	–	2	
9 Para Sqn RE, 1, 3 & 4 Tp	3	1	1	1	6	
Totals	57	86	25	9	177	

Killed in action

Private Richard Absolon
Petty Officer Michael Adcock
Air Eng Mech Adrian Anslow
Mne Eng Mech Frank Armes
Able Seaman Derek Armstrong
Rifleman Raymond Armstrong
WO2 Malcolm Atkinson
Staff Sgt John Baker
Lt Commander David Balfour
Lt Commander Richard Banfield
Able Seaman Andrew Barr
Lieutenant James Barry
Lt Commander Gordon Batt
Corporal William Begley
L/Corporal Gary Bingley
Able Seaman Ian Boldy
Petty Officer David Briggs
Petty Officer Peter Brouard
Private Gerald Bull
L/Corporal Barry Bullers

Corporal Paul Bunker
L/Corporal Anthony Burke
Corporal Robert Burns
Private Jason Burt
Chief Petty Officer John Caddy
Marine Paul Callan
Mne Eng Paul Callus
L/Sergeant James Carlyle
Petty Officer Kevin Casey
Bosun Chee Yu Sik
L/Corporal Simon Cockton
Private Albert Connet
Catering Assistant Darryl Cope
L/Corporal Anthony Cork
Private Jonathan Crow
Sergeant Philip Currass
Lieutenant William Curtis
Guardsman Ian Dale
Sergeant Sid Davidson
Marine Colin Davidson

A/Petty Officer Stephen Dawson
Guardsman Derek Denholm
Captain Christopher Dent
Elect Fitter Dis Leung Chau
Private Stephen Dixon
A/Wpns Eng Mech John Dobson
John Dobson Merchant Navy
Private Mark Dodsworth
Cook Richard Dunkerley
Guardsman Michael Dunphy
Butcher Dis Sung Yuk Fai
Cook Brian Easton
Sergeant Clifford Elley
Sub Lieutenant Richard Emly
Sergeant Roger Enefer
Sergeant Andrew Evans
Corporal Kenneth Evans
Guardsman Peter Edwards
Chief Petty Officer Anthony
    Eggington
Lt Commander John Eyton-Jones
Petty Officer Robert Fagan
L/Corporal Ian Farrell
C/Sergeant Gordon Findlay
Corporal Peter Fitton
Chief Petty Officer Edmund
    Flanagan
Private Mark Fletcher
A/Ldg Cook Michael Foote
Mar Eng Mech Stephen Ford
Major Michael Forge
Frank Foulkes Merchant Navy
Petty Officer Michael Fowler
Lieutenant Kenneth Francis
WO2 Laurence Gallagher
Sapper Pradeep Gandhi
Guardsman Mark Gibby
Guardsman Glenn Grace
Guardsman Paul Green
Private Anthony Greenwood
L/Corporal Brett Giffen
Cook Neil Goodall
S/Sergeant Christopher Griffen
Marine Robert Griffin

Guardsman Gareth Griffiths
Private Neil Grose
3rd Eng Officer Christopher
    Hailwood
Wpns Eng Mech Ian Hall
Captain Gavin Hamilton
A/Steward Shaun Hanson
Corporal David Hardman
Corporal William Hatton
David Hawkins Merchant Navy
Flt Lieutenant Garth Hawkins
Able Seaman Sean Haywood
Lieutenant Rodney Heath
Air Eng Mech Mark Henderson
2nd Eng Officer Paul Henry
Able Seaman Stephen Heyes
L/Corporal Peter Higgs
Air Eng Mech Brian Hinge
Chief Radio Officer Ronald Hoole
Corporal Stephen Hope
Guardsman Denis Hughes
James Hughes Merchant Navy
Guardsman Gareth Hughes
Sergeant William Hughes
A/Sergeant Ian Hunt
Private Peter Hedicker
Private Stephen Illingsworth
Mne Eng Art Alexander James
Guardsman Brian Jasper
Private Timothy Jenkins
C/Sergeant Brian Johnston
Sapper Christopher Jones
Private Craig Jones
Private Michael Jones
Lieutenant Colonel Herbert
    (H) Jones
Corporal Philip Jones
Sailor Kam Yung Shui
Guardsman Anthony Keeble
L/Sergeant Kevin Keoghane
Laundryman Lai Chi Keung
Laundryman Kyo Ben Kwo
Ldg Mne Eng Mech Allan Knowles
Private Stewart Laing

Wpns Eng Mech Simon Lawson
Chief Petty Officer David Lee
Sergeant Robert Leeming
Marine Eng Mech Alistair Leighton
L/Corporal Paul Lightfoot
Corporal Michael Love
L/Corporal Christopher Lovett
Corporal Douglas MacCormack
Marine Gordon Macpherson
Cook Brian Malcolm
Guardsman David Malcolmson
Guardsman Michael Marks
Naval Airman Brian Marsden
Ldg. Cook Tony Marshall
Marine Stephen McAndrews
Air Eng Mech Allan McAuley
Corporal Keith McCarthy
Air Eng Kelvin McCullum
Corporal Michael McHugh
Corporal Andrew McIlvenny
Sergeant Ian Mckay
L/Corporal Peter Mckay
Corporal Stewart McLaughlin
Private Thomas Mechan
Corporal Michael Melia
Private Richard Middlewick
A/Ldg Mne Mech David Miller
L/Sergeant Clark Mitchell
Guardsman Christopher Mordecai
3rd Eng Off Andrew Morris
A/Ldg Seaman Michael Mullen
L/Corporal James Murdoch
Lieutenant Brian Murphy
Ldg P.T. Inst Gary Nelson
L/Corporal Stephen Newbury
Corporal John Newton
Guardsman Gareth Nicholson
Petty Officer Anthony Norman
Captain Ian North Merchant Navy
Marine Michael Nowak
Lieutenant Richard Nunn
Major Roger Nutbeem
Staff Sgt Patrick O'Connor
Cook David Osborne

A/Wpns Eng Mech David Ozbirn
A/Petty Officer Andrew Palmer
Private David Parr
Guardsman Colin Parsons
L/Corporal John Pashley
Mne Eng Mech Terence Perkins
Guardsman Eirwyn Phillips
Marine Keith Phillips
Seaman Po Ng
Guardsman Gareth Poole
Staff Sergeant James Prescott
Private Kenneth Preston
Corporal Stephen Prior
L/Air Eng Mech Donald Pryce
Guardsman James Reynolds
Cook John Roberts
Lt Commander Glen
     Robinson-Moltke
Craftsman Mark Rollins
Sergeant Ronald Rotherham
Guardsman Nigel Rowberry
Marine Anthony Rundle
L/Cook Mark Sambles
L/Corporal David Scott
Private Ian Scrivens
Lt Commander John Sephton
Craftsman Alexander Shaw
Seaman Shing Chan Chai
L/Cook Anthony Sillence
Sergeant John Simeon
Private Francis Slough
Corporal Jeremy Smith
Private Mark Holman-Smith
L/Corporal Nigel Smith
Corporal Ian Spencer
L/Radio Op Bernard Still
Guardsman Archibald Stirling
Able Seaman Matthew Stuart
Steward Mark Stephens
Mar Eng Art Geoffrey Stockwell
L/Corporal Anthony Streatfield
Stewart John Stroud
Chief Petty Officer Kevin Sullivan
Cook Andrew Swallow

L/Corporal Philip Sweet
A/Weap Eng Art David Strickland
Able Seaman Adrian Sunderland
Corporal Paul Sullivan
Corporal Stephen Sykes
Sapper Wayne Tabard
Guardsman Ronald Tanbini
L/Corporal Christopher Thomas
Guardsman Glyn Thomas
L/Corporal Nicholas Thomas
Guardsman Raymond Thomas
Chief Petty Officer Michael Till
Lieutenant David Tinker
Mne Eng Mech Stephen Tonkin
A/Cook Ian Turnbull
Corporal Andrew Uren
Petty Officer Collin Vickers
Ernest Vickers Merchant Navy
Corporal Laurence Watts
Guardsman James Weaver
Guardsman Andrew Walker
Petty Officer Barry Wallis

Corporal Edward Walpole
L/Corporal Christopher Ward
WO2 Daniel Wight
A/Ldg Marine Eng Mech
    Garry Whitford
Master at Arms Brian Welsh
Ldg Cook Adrian Wellstead
Private Philip West
Sergeant Malcolm Wigley
A/Wea Eng Art Philip White
A/Ldg Mar Mech Stephen White
Guardsman David Williams
Mne Eng Mech Gilbert Williams
Apprentice Ian Williams
Cook Kevin Williams
Marine David Wilson
Corporal Scott Wilson
Captain David Wood
Lt Commander John Woodhead
Doreen Bonner
Mary Goodwin
Susan Whitley

EQUIPMENT LOSSES

Table 13 Air attacks against British ships

Aircraft type	Attack DTG	UK unit attacked	Ship damage assessment	UK lives lost
A4B	12 May	Glasgow	Moderate	0
	21 May	Broadsword	Minor	0
	21 May	Ardent	Minor	0
	21 May	Argonaut	Major	2
	23 May	Antelope	Fatal	2
	24 May	Sir Galahad	Moderate	0
	24 May	Sir Tristram	Moderate	0
	24 May	Sir Bedivere	Minor	0
	25 May	Broadsword	Moderate	0
	25 May	Coventry	Fatal	19
	27 May	UKLF	-	4
	08 June	Sir Galahad	Fatal	48
	08 June	Sir Tristram	Major	2
	08 June	LCU F4	Fatal	6
A4C	24 May	Stromness	Minor	0
A4Q	21 May	Ardent	Fatal	22
Super Etendard	04 May	Sheffield	Fatal	20
	25 May	Atlantic Conveyor	Fatal	12

(*continued on next page*)

Table 13 (*cont.*)

Aircraft type	Attack DTG	UK unit attacked	Ship damage assessment	UK lives lost
Mirage 5	01 May	Glamorgan	Minor	0
	01 May	Arrow	Minor	0
	21 May	Antrim	Major	0
	21 May	Broadsword	Minor	0
	21 May	Brilliant	Minor	0
	08 June	Plymouth	Major	0
C-130	08 June	British Wye	Minor	0

Table 14 Air losses

Aircraft	Date	Squadron	Cause	Casualties
Sea Harrier	4 May	800 NAS	Shot down	Lt Taylor RN killed
Two Sea Harrier	6 May	801 NAS	Collision	Lt Curtiss and Lt Cmdr Eyton-Jones RN killed
Sea Harrier	23 May	800 NAS	Accident	Lt Cmdr Batt RN killed
Sea Harrier	29 May	801 NAs	Accident	Pilot ejected safely
Sea Harrier	1 June	801 NAs	Shot by SAM	Pilot ejected safely
Harrier GR3	21 May	1 (F) Squadron	Shot by SAM	Fl Lt Glover ejects, injured and captured
Harrier GR3	27 May	1 (F) Squadron	AA gun	Sqdrn Ldr Iveson ejects and is rescued
Harrier GR3	30 May	1 (F) Squadron	Small arms fire	Sqdrn Ldr Pook ejects and is rescued
Harrier GR3	8 June	1 (F) Squadron	Engine failure	Pilot unhurt
Two Wessex HU5	22 April	845 NAS, (RFA Tidespring)	Lost on Fortuna Glacier	No casualties
Wessex HAS.3	12 June	737 NAS	Destroyed when HMS Glamorgan hit	No casualties

(*continued on next page*)

Table 14 (*cont.*)

Aircraft	Date	Squadron	Cause	Casualties
Sea King HC4	23 April	846 NAS	Accident	Pilot rescued but PO Aircrewman Casey lost
Sea King HAS.5	12 May	826 NAS	Engine failure	All crew rescued
Sea King HAS.5	17 May	826 NAS	Altimeter problems	All crew rescued
Sea King HC.4	18/19 May	846 NAS	Deliberately destroyed by crew in Chile	All crew rescued
Sea King HC.4	19 May	846 NAS	Crashed into sea	20 passengers killed
Two Gazelle	21 May	3 CBAS	Small arms fire	Pilot Sgt Evans RM killed in first and Lt Francis RM and Crewman L/Cpl Griffin RM in second
Gazelle	6 June	656 AAC	UK SAM	Pilot Sgt Griffin, Crewman L/Cpl Cockton and two passengers killed
Lynx HAS.2	21 May	815 NAS	Lost with HMS Ardent	No casualties
Two Lynx HAS.2	25 May	815 NAS	Lost with HMS Coventry and Atlantic Conveyor	No casualties
Scout	28 May	3 CBAS	Shot down by Pucara	Lt Nunn RM killed

BRITISH GALLANTRY AWARDS[1]

The South Atlantic Medal was awarded to all personnel who took part in operations in the South Atlantic for the liberation of South Georgia and the Falkland Islands. To qualify, the recipient had to have at least one full day's service in the Falkland Islands or South Georgia, or thirty days in the South Atlantic operational zone, including Ascension Island. Additionally, those who qualified under the first condition were awarded a rosette to wear on the medal ribbon. The breakdown of medal awards was: Royal Navy 13,000; Royal Marines 3,700; Royal Fleet Auxilliary 2,000; Army 7,000; Royal Air Force 2,000 and Merchant Navy/Civilian 2,000.

Victoria Cross – Posthumous

Lt Col H Jones OBE, CO 2nd Battalion The Parachute Regiment
Sgt I J McKay, 3rd Battalion The Parachute Regiment

Royal Navy, Royal Marines, Royal Fleet Auxiliary and Merchant Navy

Distinguished Service Order

Capt M E Barrow RN, CO HMS Glamorgan
Capt J J Black MBE RN, CO HMS Invincible
Capt W R Canning RN, CO HMS Broadsword
Capt J F Coward RN, CO HMS Brilliant
Capt P G V Dingemans RN, CO HMS Intrepid
Commodore S C Dunlop CBE RFA, CO RFA Fort Austin
Lt Cmdr B F Dutton QGM RN, CO Fleet Clearance Diving Team 1
Capt E S J Larken RN, CO HMS Fearless
Capt C H Layman MVO RN, CO HMS Argonaut
Capt L E Middleton ADC RN, CO HMS Hermes
Capt D Pentreath RN, CO HMS Plymouth
Capt P J G Roberts RFA, CO RFA Sir Galahad

Lt Cmdr I Stanley RN, Flt Cmdr, No.737 NAS, HMS Antrim
Lt Col N F Vaux RM, CO 42 Cdo RM
Lt Col A F Whitehead RM, CO 45 Cdo RM
Cmdr C L Wreford-Brown RN, CO HMS Conqueror
Capt B G Young RN, CO HMS Antrim

Distinguished Service Cross – Posthumous

Lt Cmdr G W J Batt RN, No.800 NAS, HMS Hermes
Capt I H North Merchant Navy, CO Atlantic Conveyor
Lt Cmdr J M Sephton RN, HMS Ardent
Lt Cmdr J S Woodhead RN, HMS Sheffield

Distinguished Service Cross

Lt Cmdr A D Auld RN, CO No.800 NAS, HMS Hermes
Lt A R C Bennett RN, No.846 NAS
Lt Cmdr M D Booth RN, CO No.847 NAS
Cmdr P J Bootherstone RN, CO HMS Arrow
Lt N A Bruen RN, CO Fleet Clearance Diving Team 3
Lt Cmdr H S Clark RN, CO No.825 NAS
Cmdr C J S Craig RN, CO HMS Alacrity
Lt Cmdr J A Ellerbeck RN, Flt Cmdr, No.829 NAS, HMS Endurance
Fleet CPO (Diver) M G Fellows BEM, Fleet Clearance Diving Team 1
Capt G R Green RFA, CO RFA Sir Tristram
Lt R Hutchings RM, No.846 NAS
Capt D E Lawrence RFA, CO RFA Sir Geraint
Lt Cmdr H J Lomas RN, No.845 NAS
Lt K P Mills RM, RM Detachment, HMS Endurance
Sub Lt P T Morgan RN, HMS Argonaut
Cmdr A Morton RN, CO HMS Yarmouth
Lt N J North RN, No.846 NAS
Capt A F Pitt RFA, CO RFA Sir Percivale
Lt Cmdr N W Thomas RN, Nos.899/800 NAS, HMS Hermes
Lt S R Thomas RN, No.801 NAS, HMS Invincible
Lt Cdr S C Thornewill RN, CO No.846 NAS
Cmdr N J Tobin RN, CO HMS Antelope
Cmdr N D Ward AFC RN, CO No.801 NAS, HMS Invincible
Cmdr A W J West RN, CO HMS Ardent

Military Cross

Capt P M Babbington RM, 42 Cdo RM
Maj C P Cameron RM, CO 3 CBAS

Lt C I Dytor RM, 45 Cdo RM
Lt C Fox RM, 45 Cdo RM
Lt D J Stewart RM, 45 Cdo RM

Distinguished Flying Cross – Posthumous

Lt R J Nunn RM, 3 CBAS

Distinguished Flying Cross

Capt J P Niblett RM, 3 CBAS

Air Force Cross

Lt Cdr D J S Squier RN, CO No.826 NAS, HMS Hermes
Lt Cdr R J S Wykes-Sneyd RN, CO No.820 NAS, HMS Invincible

Distinguished Conduct Medal

Cpl J Burdett RM, 45 Cdo RM

George Medal – Posthumous

Second Eng Offr P A Henry RFA, RFA Sir Galahad

George Medal

AB (Radar) J E Dillon, HMS Ardent

Distinguished Service Medal – Posthumous

PO MEM(M) D R Briggs, HMS Sheffield
Cpl Aircrewman M D Love RM, No.846 NAS

Distinguished Service Medal

Colour Sgt M J Francis RM, coxswain LCU F1, HMS Fearless
Ldg Aircrewman P B Imrie, No.846 NAS
Sgt P J Leach RM, RM Detachment, HMS Endurance
PO J S Leake, HMS Ardent
Sgt W J Leslie RM, HMS Broadsword
PO (Sonar) G J R Libby, HMS Conqueror
Chief MEM(M) M D Townsend, HMS Argonaut
CPO (Diver) G M Trotter, Fleet Clearance Diving Team 3

CPO Aircrewman M J Tupper, No.846 NAS
LS (Radar) J D Warren, HMS Antelope

Military Medal

Acting Cpl A R Bishop RM, 45 Cdo RM
Sgt T Collings RM,
Sgt M Collins RM, 42 Cdo RM
Cpl M Eccles RM, 42 Cdo RM
Cpl D Hunt RM, 45 Cdo RM
Mne G W Marshall RM, 45 Cdo RM
Cpl S C Newland RM, 42 Cdo RM
Cpl H Siddall RM, 45 Cdo RM
Cpl C N H Ward RM, 42 Cdo RM
Sgt J D Wassell RM, M&AW Cadre RM

Distinguished Flying Medal

Sgt W C O'Brien RM, 3 CBAS

Queen's Gallantry Medal – Posthumous

Colour Sgt B Johnston RM, coxswain LCU F4, HMS Fearless

Queen's Gallantry Medal

Chief Eng Offr C K A Adams RFA, RFA Sir Galahad
Lt J K Boughton RN, No.825 NAS
MEA(M)1 K Enticknapp, HMS Ardent
Third Offr A Gudgeon RFA, RFA Sir Galahad
PO Medical Asst G A Meager, HMS Sheffield
Lt P J Sheldon RN, No.825 NAS
Third Eng B R Williams Merchant Navy, Atlantic Conveyor

British Army

Distinguished Service Order

Maj C N G Delves, Devonshire and Dorsets
Maj C P B Keeble, 2 Para
Lt Col H W R Pike MBE, CO 3 Para
Lt Col M I E Scott, CO 2 Scots Guards

Distinguished Service Cross

WO2 J H Phillips, 49 EOD Sqdn RE

Military Cross – Posthumous

Capt G J Hamilton, Green Howards, D Sqdn 22 SAS Regt

Military Cross

Maj M H Argue, 3 Para
Capt T W Burls, Parachute Regt
Maj D A Collett, 3 Para
Lt C S Conner, 2 Para
Maj J H Crosland, 2 Para
Maj C D Farrar-Hockley, 2 Para
Maj J P Kiszely, 2 Scots Guards
Lt R A D Lawrence, 2 Scots Guards
Capt W A McCracken, 29 Cdo Regt RA
Capt A J G Wight, Welsh Guards

Distinguished Flying Cross

Capt S M Drennan AAC, 656 Sqdn AAC
Capt J G Greenhalgh RCT, 656 Sqdn AAC

Distinguished Conduct Medal – Posthumous

Pte S Illingsworth, 2 Para
Gdsmn J B C Reynolds, 2 Scots Guards

Distinguished Conduct Medal

Cpl D Abols, 2 Para
Staff Sgt B Faulkner, 3 Para
Sgt J C Meredith, 2 Para
WO2 W Nicol, 2 Scots Guards
Sgt J S Pettinger, 3 Para

Conspicuous Gallantry Medal – Posthumous

Staff Sgt J Prescott, 49 EOD Sqdn RE

Military Medal – Posthumous

Pte R J de M Absolon, 3 Para
L/Cpl G D Bingley, 2 Para

Military Medal

Cpl I P Bailey, 3 Para
L/Cpl S A Bardsley, 2 Para
Sgt T I Barrett, 2 Para
L/Cpl M W L Bentley, 2 Para
Sgt D S Boultby, 17 Port Regt RCT
Cpl T Brookes Royal Signals
Cpl T J Camp, 2 Para
Pte G S Carter, 2 Para
Gdsmn S M Chapman, 1 Welsh Guards
Cpl J A Foran, 9 Para Sqdn RE
Sgt D Fuller, 3 Para
Pte B J Grayling, 2 Para
Cpl T W Harley, 2 Para
Bdr E M Holt, 29 Cdo Regt RA
Sgt R W Jackson, 2 Scots Guards
L/Cpl D J Loveridge, 1 Welsh Guards
Sgt J G Mather,
Sgt P H R Naya, 16 Field Ambulance RAMC
WO2 B T Neck, 1 Welsh Guards
Gdsmn A S Pengelly, 2 Scots Guards
L/Cpl L J L Standish, 2 Para
Sgt R H Wrega, 9 Para Sqdn RE

Royal Air Force

Distinguished Service Cross

Flt Lt D H S Morgan RAF, Nos.899/800 NAS, HMS Hermes

Distinguished Flying Cross

Wing Cdr P T Squire AFC RAF, CO 1(F) Sqdn RAF
Sqdn Ldr R U Langworthy AFC RAF, 18 Sqdn RAF
Sqdn Ldr C N McDougall RAF, Vulcan aircrew
Sqdn Ldr J J Pook RAF, 1(F) Sqdn RAF
Flt Lt W F M Withers RAF, Vulcan aircrew

Air Force Cross

Wing Cdr D Emmerson RAF, Nimrod aircrew
Sqdn Ldr R Tuxford RAF, Victor aircrew
Flt Lt H C Burgoyne RAF, 47 Sqdn RAF
Sqdn Ldr A M Roberts RAF, 47 Sqdn RAF

Queen's Gallantry Medal

Flt Lt A J Swan RAF, CO No.1 EOD Unit RAF
Flt Sgt B W Jopling, 18 Sqdn RAF

NOTES

INTRODUCTION TO THE SECOND EDITION

1 In this regard I was pleased to see the publication of the *Board of Inquiry into the circumstances leading to and attending the disablement and later sinking of HMS* Sheffield *between 3rd and 11th May 1982.* <http://www.mod.uk/DefenceInternet/AboutDefence/CorporatePublications/BoardsOfInquiry/LossOfHmsSheffield BoardOfInquiry.htm>
2 *Guardian*, 22 November 2005; *Sunday Times*, 20 November 2005; *Sunday Times*, 27 November 2005.
3 I deal with this issue in more detail in the 'Review symposium on Sir Lawrence Freedman's *The Official History of the Falklands Campaign*' in *Political Studies Review* 5 (1), 2006.
4 One interesting point for historians. What I describe as Admiral Woodward's War Diary is not recognised as such by the Admiral, although he agreed the sentiments were familiar. It turns out that this was compiled, unsupervised, by three Midshipmen in the Flag Operations Room in *Hermes* based on what they saw and heard. As such it was not strictly speaking an official document but it remains nonetheless a fascinating one.

1 AT WAR

1 Admiral of the Fleet Sir Henry Leach, *Endure No Makeshifts* (London: Leo Cooper, 1993), pp. 212–13
2 This time is given by John Smith, *74 Days: An Islander's Diary of the Falklands Occupation* (London: Century Publishing, 1984), p. 20.
3 *Ibid.*, p. 22.
4 See Martin Middlebrook, *The Fight for the 'Malvinas': The Argentine Forces in the Falklands War* (London: Viking, 1989), pp. 21–24.
5 Graham Bound, *Falkland Islanders at War* (London: Leo Cooper, 2002), p. 54.

2 RESPONSE

1 John Nott, *Here Today: Gone Tomorrow: Recollections of an errant politician* (London: Politico's, 2002), p. 261.
2 *The Falklands Witness Seminar* (Strategic and Combat Studies Institute: The Occasional no. 46, 2004), p. 7.
3 Alan Clark, *Diaries: Into Politics* (London: Weidenfeld & Nicolson, 2000), p. 313.
4 Nott, *op.cit.*, p. 267.

5 *Ibid.*, p. 268, Alan Clark, *Diaries:*

> I asked a long, sneering question about the failure of intelligence. I made a point of addressing it to Peter Carrington whom, with my very long memory, I had not forgiven for snubbing me at a 1 December 1980 meeting, in the Grand Committee Room. As my irony developed, people in the Committee Room started sniggering, Notters answered it, while Carrington sat staring at me in haughty silence.

6 Peter Carrington, *Reflect on Things Past* (London: Collins, 1988), pp. 368–371.
7 Nott, *op.cit.*, pp. 277–8.
8 House of Commons, *The Falklands Campaign: A Digest of Debates in the House of Commons, 2 April to June 1982* (London: HMSO, 1982), p. 5. This volume contains the most important debates.
9 *Ibid.*, pp. 8–9.
10 Anthony Barnett, *Iron Britannia: Why Parliament Waged its Falklands War* (London: Allison & Busby, 1982), p. 48. A similar point is made by G M Dillon, *The Falklands, Politics and War* (London: Macmillan Press, 1989), p. 136.
11 Margaret Thatcher, *The Downing Street Years* (London: Harper Collins, 1993), p. 184.
12 Peter Hennessy, *The Prime Minister: The Office and its Holders Since 1946* (London: The Allen Lane Press, 2000), Chap 16.
13 One official noted 'future historians will not get the whole story from OD (SA) and Cabinet minutes.'
14 John Nott, *Here Today*, p. 246.
15 Speech by Lewin quoted in Richard Hill, *Lewin of Greenwich: the Authorised biography of Admiral of the Fleet Lord Lewin* (London: Cassell & Co., 2000), p. 344.
16 *Ibid.*, p. 355.
17 When Labour MP Tam Dalyell alleged on *Panorama* on 10 May that CAS had advised against the dispatch of the Task Force, Nott wrote to him asserting that there was no truth in the assertion and asking Dalyell to withdraw it.
18 Cited in Denys Blakemore, *Channel Four: The Falklands War* (London: Sidgwick & Jackson, 1992), p. 64.
19 Hill, *Lewin of Greenwich*, p. 358.
20 Nott, *Here Today*, p. 246.
21 Hill, *Lewin of Greenwich*, p. 358.
22 Nott, *Here Today*, p. 279.
23 Julian Thompson, *No Picnic*, 3rd edition (London: Cassell, 2001), p. 17.
24 Martin Middlebrook, *Operation Corporate: The Story of the Falklands War 1982* (London: Viking, 1985), p. 181.
25 House of Commons, First Report from the Defence Committee, Session 1982–3, *The Handling of Press and Public Information During the Falklands Conflict*, London: HMSO, December 1982. Vol. 1, Report and Minutes of Proceedings, Volume 2, Minutes of Evidence.
26 See Derick Mercer, Geoff Mungham and Kevin Williams, *The Fog of War* (London, Heinemann, 1987).
27 Commons, *Handling of Press*, Minutes of Evidence, Q 1179.
28 Mercer *et al.*, *The Fog of War*, p. 108.
29 Admiral Sandy Woodward with Patrick Robinson, *One Hundred Days: The Memoirs of the Falklands Battle Group Commander* (London: Harper Collins, 1992), p. 109.
30 Mercer *et al.*, *The Fog of War*, p. 59.
31 Commons, *Handling of the Press*, Minutes of Evidence, Q.955.

32 Leach, *Endure No Makeshifts,* p. 218.
33 Nott, *Here Today,* p. 263.
34 Dissatisfaction with the media aspects of the campaign remained high throughout, so that this became the first topic for a post-mortem by the Parliamentary Select Committee on Defence after the conflict and led to MoD commissioning academic studies.

3 RESOLUTION 502

1 Woolly Al transcript (BBC TV Programme).
2 Thatcher, *The Downing Street Years,* p. 187.
3 *Ibid.*
4 Nott, *Here Today,* pp. 260–1
5 Both wrote accounts of their activities during the crisis: Sir Nicholas Henderson, 'America and the Falklands', *The Economist* (12 November 1983); Sir Anthony Parsons, 'The Falklands Crisis in the United Nations, 31 March–14 June 1982', *International Affairs,* Vol.59: No.2 (Spring 1983).
6 The appeal, released at 1700 on 1 April, stated that:

> The Secretary-General, in view of the apparent tension now existing between Argentina and the United Kingdom, has spoken to the Permanent Representatives of both countries to the United Nations, and urged them to continue to use diplomatic means to resolve the outstanding issues between the two countries.

7 Cited in Michael Charlton, *The Little Platoon* (London: Blackwell, 1989), p. 200.
8 Of the fifteen members of the Security Council, five are Permanent and ten are drawn from the rest of the membership for two year periods. To win a Security Council vote it is necessary to have the support of at least nine members. Even then a vote against by one of the Permanent Members means that the resolution is lost.
9 This also ruled out the British tampering with their own resolution. A possible recourse to the International Court of Justice suggested itself in Whitehall as one possible diplomatic escape route. Consideration was given to getting this raised, although it would annoy both France and the Soviet Union. This idea does not seem to have been taken very far.
10 According to Baroness Thatcher, he began the conversation by asking 'What can I do for you Prime Minister?' Thatcher, *The Downing Street Years,* p. 183.
11 Oscar Cardoso, Ricardo Kirschbaum, and Eduardo van der Kooy, *Falklands: The Secret Plot* (London: Preston Editions, 1983), p. 113.

4 THE TASK FORCE

1 Nott, *Here Today,* p. 274.
2 The *Canberra* with a reduced P & O crew of 416 had a naval party of 100 under an RN Captain; the *Elk,* with a crew of 23, had a commander and 16 others.
3 Forces stationed at Gibraltar included the Guardship *Ambuscade;* HMS *Rooke* – the RN shore establishment, administering naval personnel and RN ships refitting; HMS *Calpe* – the RN Reserve HQ Unit. There was also a surveillance troop Royal Artillery (two radars deployed); one Fortress Specialist Team Royal Engineers including HQ troop, power station troop and Field troop; a line troop Royal Signals; one infantry battalion; the Gibraltar Regiment (a territorial unit at 12 hours' notice for full-time employment) consisting of Infantry company,

artillery troop (four L40/70 defence guns), artillery troop (two 105mm Pack Howitzers); Fortress HQ Staff and Postal Courier and Communications Unit. Lastly, there was a unit of some 420 RAF personnel providing airfield facilities for aircraft using the airhead and a base for the support of maritime operations. All were armed for ground defence purposes.

4 The only problem for Britain was that it had failed to negotiate a bilateral safe-guards agreement with the IAEA as required under Article 13 of the Treaty, and was brought into force for the UK by virtue of ratification of Protocol 1. This was not because there was anything to hide – Britain had no nuclear installations in the Falklands – but because of Argentine sensibilities.

5 Protocol II of the Treaty of Tlatelolco committed Britain to abide by provisions of the Treaty with respect to territories to which the Treaty applied; since Argentina had *not* ratified the Treaty, this Protocol did *not* protect it from nuclear attack. Indeed, Article 3 of Protocol II specifically required the nuclear weapon states not to use or threaten to use nuclear weapons against 'Contracting Parties'; it was clearly an intention of the Treaty that it should not protect states *not* Contracting Parties – in the way that Argentina was not a Contracting Party.

6 *New Statesman* (31 August 1984).

7 See the denials by Lord Lewin and Sir Henry Leach. Rodney Cowton, 'Nuclear option in Falklands denied', *The Times* (24 August 1984).

8 Duncan Campbell and John Rentoul, 'All Out War', *New Statesman* (24 August 1984). See also Paul Rogers in *The Belgrano Enquiry, The Unnecessary War* (London: Spokesman Books, 1988).

9 *Official Record, House of Lords*, 27 April 1982, vol. 429, c. 778.

10 *New York Times*, 1 July 1988.

11 *The Arms Control Reporter*, 23 June 1986. There were reports during the campaign that the Soviets had told the Argentine Ambassador in Moscow that the British force was carrying nuclear weapons.

12 David Tinker, *A Message from the Falklands* (London: Junction Books, 1982). Gareth Parry, 'Task Force Ships "carried live nuclear weapons to the Falklands"', *Guardian*, 2 November 1982.

13 *Official Record*, 23 July 1982, Vol. 28, c. 340.

14 See Rob Evans and David Leigh, 'Falklands warships carried nuclear weapons, MoD admits', *The Guardian*, 6 December 2003.

15 United Kingdom of Great Britain and Northern Ireland, *Defence: Use of Wideawake Airfield in Ascension Island by United Kingdom Military Aircraft*, 29 August 1962. The UK was supposed to give the local American commander 24 hours' notice of the arrival of a single aircraft and 72 hours of anything more.

16 Despatch by Admiral Sir John Fieldhouse, GCB, GBE, Commander of the Task Force Operations in the South Atlantic: April to June 1982, 14 December 1982, Supplement to *The London Gazette* of Monday, 13 December 1982, p. 16111.

17 AVM Ron Dick, contribution to Roger Miller, ed., *Seeing Off the Bear: Anglo-American Air Power Co-operation During the Cold War*, Proceedings, Joint Meeting of the Royal Air Force Historical Society and the Air Force Historical Foundation, USAF 1995.

18 Captain Bob McQueen, *Island Base: Ascension Island in the Falklands War* (London: Whittles Publishing, 2005), p. 14.

19 *Ibid*, p. 13. McQueen acknowledges the 'deterrent, psychological effect of the raids'.

5 FIRST ASSESSMENTS

1 *Signals of War*, p. 132.

2 Nott, *Here Today*, p. 305.
3 In addition, a number of Skyhawks managed to get back to Argentina after being badly damaged without having to ditch though remaining coupled to KC-130 tankers.
4 One Sea Harrier was brought down by a Blowpipe on 21 May.

6 RULES OF ENGAGEMENT

1 When the UK announced the MEZ on 9 April, the Argentine Ambassador to the UN, Roca, denounced this as a blockade and so an act of aggression as defined in Article 3 (c) of General Assembly Resolution 3314 (XXIX). The response was that this was not aggression as Britain was not the first to use force and could not blockade its own territory.
2 The Deputy Legal Adviser also pointed out that in any planning which took place in relation to the Falklands, Britain had to bear in mind the relevance of the Antarctic Treaty, which stressed under Article I, that Antarctica should be used for peaceful purposes only. Any measures of a military nature were prohibited. Article IV was the Article protecting rights on, or claims to, territorial sovereignty.
3 Evidence of Lord Lewin, in House of Commons Foreign Affairs Committee, *Events Surrounding the Weekend of 1–2 May 1982*, Third Report Session 1984–85 (London: HMSO, 1982), pp. 77, 78. See also R.P. Bartson and P.W. Birnie, 'The Falkland Islands/Islas Malvinas Conflict: A Question of Zones', *Marine Policy* (January 1983).
4 Hill, *Lewin of Greenwich*, p. 362
5 See Thatcher, *Downing Street Years*, pp. 189–90; Nott, *Here Today*, pp. 288–90.
6 See below pp. 145–7.

7 NON-MILITARY PRESSURE

1 Sir Ian Sinclair, in Iain Dale, ed., *Memories of the Falklands* (London: Politico's 2002), p. 125.
2 Export licences can be revoked by administrative action without any right of appeal or financial compensation on the part of the firms concerned.
3 The list included aircraft; arms and related material; ammunition; military stores and appliances and para-military equipment; atomic energy minerals, materials, facilities, equipment and appliances; and certain industrial equipment and material of strategic importance. Because of controls on the supply of strategic goods to communist states, the list also included inter alia a wide variety of goods such as metal working machinery, chemical and petroleum equipment, some electrical power generating equipment, electronic equipment, scientific instruments, certain metals, minerals, chemicals and petroleum products. The Order did not control, however, other goods that could conceivably assist Argentina, for example, most civil ships, mobile generating equipment, civil vehicles and motor cycles; nor crude and refined hydrocarbon oils. Exports to third countries made with the intention of subsequent re-export to Argentina would be an offence under the Act, but there were obvious practical difficulties in enforcing this.
4 Rolls Royce also had a contract for the supply of marine gas turbine engines to a German firm who were building ships for the Argentine Navy. Although the bulk of this order had already been delivered, eight gas generators were due to be delivered from May-July 1982. This issue was resolved by the Federal Republic of Germany's decision to introduce its own embargo on arms exports to Argentina.

Equally, the supply of components for Puma helicopters would need to be caught under the French ban rather than the British. With the Puma being exported to a number of different countries, it would clearly be impracticable to identify any particular components, which might be destined for Argentina.

5 This did not provide full exchange control powers of the kind needed to prevent British residents from making voluntary payments abroad. To deal with these payments would require the reintroduction of extensive exchange control arrangements, at considerable expense. As a ban on imports was in place, it seemed unlikely that there would be good reason for UK residents wishing to make any substantial payments to Argentina, or incurring significant obligations.

6 Those that were made involved instructions from UK companies in Argentina designed to get money out of their Argentine balances and into UK parent or similar hands to prevent them being blocked by Argentine instructions, irrevocable letters of credit, bills of exchange, etc., in which the only losers from refusal of permission would be the ultimate UK recipients or the intermediate UK financiers; *de minimis* payments to prevent hardship for individuals dependent on balances in this country (including British employees, returning British residents from Argentina and Argentine residents in this country with no other source of funds); other very minor tidying up cases.

7 On the question of releasing Argentine funds to pay British exporters, the Chancellor was considering a proposal for funds to be released to settle contracts completed before 3 April, but had not excluded the possibility of settling contracts completed after that date. The War Cabinet was not averse to some exports to Argentine customers continuing, providing payment could be obtained.

8 The designation of this grouping has been at times the Common Market, the European Communities, the European Community and recently the European Union. In 1982 the European Communities would have been the most appropriate term but I have opted here for the less cumbersome European Community.

9 House of Commons, *The Falklands Campaign*, pp. 74–5.

8 AGAINST BRITAIN

1 Ian Strange, *The Falklands Islands* (London: David & Charles, 3rd edition, 1985), pp. 267–269.

2 Michael Bilton and Peter Kosminsky, *Speaking Out: Untold Stories from the Falklands War* (London: Andre Deutsch, 1989), pp. 247–249.

3 Smith, *74 Days*, p. 42.

4 See for example John Smith's diary entry for 18 April: 'We are all wondering where the Task Force is … The following conclusions were reached. At 12 knots, would take approx 28 days – should be here in a couple of weeks. At 18 knots, would take approx 21 days – will be here next Monday. At 24 knots, would take approx 13 days – they will either turn up about supper time, or have already gone past', Smith, *74 Days*, p. 76.

5 Strange, *The Falklands Islands*, pp. 251–253.

6 *Ibid.*, pp. 254, 257.

7 Smith, *op. cit.*, p. 49.

8 Strange, *op. cit.*, pp. 259–260, 264–266.

9 In cases where an Argentine purchaser wished to pay a British exporter, he would not be permitted to do so using funds deposited in the UK. The Bank of England would discriminate in the granting of permissions so that payments could be made for pre-zero exports and for trade conducted under irrevocable letters of credit.

10 There was no precedent for joint military action against an extra-regional country but the Rio Treaty could provide a suitable umbrella for individual states to provide military assistance.

11 Inter-American Treaty Of Reciprocal Assistance (Rio Treaty), Article 8:

> For the purpose of this Treaty, the measures on which the Organ of Consultation may agree will comprise one or more of the following: recall of chiefs of diplomatic missions; breaking of diplomatic relations; breaking of consular relations: partial or complete interruption of economic relations or of rail, sea, air, postal, telegraphic, telephonic, and radiotelephonic communications; and use of armed force.

9 OPTIONS FOR A SETTLEMENT

1 On the background to the lease-back option see Volume One.

2 A hand-written addition to his instructions from the FCO: 'It would also be useful if they referred to other forms of third party settlement. You could then undertake, in the course of your statement, that we would consider this favourably.' It is not clear that this was sent.

3 State Department press guidance of 13 April 1982 noted that the President had known of the dinner beforehand and had not objected. The public line was that her attendance was 'appropriate' and that very day the US had 'made it clear publicly and privately that we strongly disapproved the Argentine use of force'. Privately State Department officials insisted that they were dismayed by the dinner. The main solace was that at the dinner, after praising the Argentines, Mrs Kirkpatrick had reportedly said that the only thing they were incapable of doing was governing themselves, thereby offending them as well.

4 In *Pilgrimage for Peace: A Secretary-General's Memoir* (London: Palgrave, 1997), p. 381, Perez de Cuellar acknowledges the British distrust for the head of his Task Force, Rafeeuddin Ahmad. 'Ahmad led the Task Force with great efficiency, and his counsel was almost always impartial. But being a Pakistani, he could not help but be hostile to colonialism in any form.' At one point it seemed as if Brian Urquhart, the British Under Secretary General for Special Political Affairs, might be put in charge of the Secretariat's monitoring work on the crisis. He was disqualified for his nationality as was the other Under Secretary General for Special Political Affairs, Diego Cordovez, for being Latin American (Ecuadorian).

10 HAIG'S FIRST VISIT

1 Haig cited in Charlton, *op. cit.*, pp. 159, 160.

2 Alexander Haig, *Caveat* (London: Weidenfeld & Nicolson, 1984, p. 270.

3 For further material on the Haig mission see David Gompert, 'American Diplomacy and the Haig Mission', in Alberto R. Coll and Anthony C. Arend, *The Falklands War: Lessons for Strategy, Diplomacy and International Law* (London: Allen & Unwin, 1985).

4 In his discussions with Haig on 6 April Costa Mendez had offered a joint Argentine-British administration in the Islands during the interim period while arrangements were made for formal transfer of sovereignty. He saw this as lasting for a few months and might help save some face. He had not, however, seen any value in getting third parties involved, except possibly the United States. The Administration of small islands and a small population should not be too

difficult. Lawrence Freedman and Virginia Gamba-Stonehouse, *Signals of War: the Falklands Conflict of 1982* (London: Faber, 1989), p. 169.

5 Thatcher, *The Downing Street Years*, p. 103.
6 Haig, *Caveat*, p. 280.
7 *Ibid.,* p. 282.

11 HAIG'S SECOND VISIT

1 In her memoirs Baroness Thatcher notes Rex Hunt's line to the media that when the Prime Minister had said she sought the return of British Administration, she meant what she said, and added 'there were many times in the coming negotiations when I wondered whether I would indeed secure Rex Hunt's return to the Falklands.' Thatcher, *The Downing Street Years*, p. 187.
2 Later Robert Wade-Gery of the Cabinet Secretariat added that Haig claimed to have told Argentina that if they reneged on proposed agreement US would impose economic sanctions, and also that Buenos Aires was being kept posted by the Soviets on the movement of the Task Force (which it was not).
3 Thatcher, *The Downing Street Years*, p. 195.
4 Nott, *Here Today*, pp. 291–2.
5 The Argentine version is that it was Haig who initiated the phone call. Haig, *Caveat*, p. 283 claims that it came from Costa Mendez, which is what he told the British at the time. Haig may have rung Buenos Aires earlier.
6 The Foreign Secretary, Defence Secretary, CDS, Sir Anthony Acland and Mr Coles supported the Prime Minister. Haig was supported by US Ambassador John Louis, General Walters, Thomas Enders and David Gompert.
7 Thatcher, *The Downing Street Years*, p. 198.
8 *Ibid.*, p. 198.
9 We note in *Signals of War* that on the Argentine side there is no record of a concession either being discussed or offered. All Costa Mendez told the Military Committee was that Haig had been more positive and thought that it was still worth pursuing the negotiations.
10 They had brief a tête-à-tête and were then joined by Walters, Enders, Gompert, Funseth and Gudgeon on US side, with Acland, Sinclair, Ure and Fall on the UK side.
11 Caspar Weinberger. *Fighting for Peace*, (London: Michael Joseph, 1990), p. 144.
12 Haig, *Caveat*, p. 285.
13 The second paragraph of the statement now read as follows:

> From the outset of this crisis, the United States has viewed its role as that of assisting the two sides in finding a peaceful solution. Our ability to do this is based on our longstanding relations with both the United Kingdom and Argentina. We have been careful to maintain these relationships in order to preserve our influence with both governments. Failure to live up to existing agreements – or going beyond them – would obviously jeopardize our ability to perform the role both countries wish us to perform.
>
> Since the onset of the crisis, the United States has, therefore, not acceded to requests that would go beyond the customary patterns of co-operation based on existing bilateral agreements. That will continue to be our stand while our efforts are underway.

14 *House of Commons Debates*, pp. 73–77.

15 Consideration was also given to a draft 'agreement constituting the special Commission.' Most of the points raised were not of big principle. It was acceptable that flags should be flown 'in such a fashion that no flag permanently occupies a position of precedence.' Otherwise one might have Britain on one side of the American flag and the Argentine on the other, giving the impression that neither side had better claim to sovereignty than the other. There was some argument over how important all this was. Sinclair stressed the question of attitude towards toleration of majority voting in Special Commission; and the fact that Parliament would have to refrain from legislating for the Falkland Islands during this interim period, apart from initial changes to law effected by order in Council.

16 Thatcher, *The Downing Street Years*, pp. 199–200.

17 *Ibid.*, pp. 201–2.

18 Cardoso *et al.*, *op. cit.*, pp. 172–4.

19 See *Signals of War*, pp. 199–200.

20 Haig, *Caveat*, pp. 286–7.

21 Transcript of recording of Haig's meeting with Galtieri obtained by BBC for *Panorama*, 16 April 1984.

22 *Caveat*, p. 288.

23 This episode is further discussed below in the context of the operation to retake South Georgia.

24 *Ibid.*, pp. 289–90.

25 Thatcher, *The Downing Street Years*, pp. 203–4.

26 See chapter 26 below.

27 Rattner, 'US Handling of Falkland Crisis Stirs Deep Resentment in Britain,' *New York Times*, 17 April 1982.

12 THE HAIG MISSION CONCLUDES

1 The British proposed to the Americans a draft letter of assurance from President Reagan to the Prime Minister. This would state that:

> Have no doubt that the US presence on the Islands during the interim period will serve as an effective guarantee of the implementation of the agreement and against any use of force to frustrate it. We shall leave the Argentinians in no doubt that any challenge by them to the provisions of the agreement, particularly those relating to the withdrawal of Argentine forces and their non-reintroduction, will be seen as a challenge to the Government of the United States and responded to accordingly.

> Once negotiations between the parties have been concluded and the definitive settlement has been achieved, the United States will have only such responsibilities in respect of the implementation of the definitive settlement as it shall have specifically accepted in response to the requests of the two signatories. It will, however, be prepared to respond positively to any such requests; and notwithstanding the above, it will continue to regard any use of force to frustrate or overturn the provisions of the definitive settlement as a challenge to the United States government to be responded to accordingly.

2 Parsons argued that an observer force would be preferable to a peace-keeping force. There could be objections from the Russians about being asked to support

an agreement negotiated outside of a UN framework, and also concerns about the financial implications, but the general view would be one of delight that the UN had a role. He noted that a peace-keeping force provided at best some deterrence but certainly no guarantee against aggression.

3 Nicholas Henderson, *Mandarin: The Diaries of an Ambassador, 1969–1982* (London: Weidenfeld & Nicolson, 1994), p. 454. Haig was also cross that Clark leaked some of his negotiating stance.

4 Haig, *Caveat*, p. 290.

5 Para 6.1 (a) to read:

> two representatives appointed by the Special Interim Authority on the nomination of the Argentine representative on the Authority from among the Argentine population resident on the islands to serve on the Executive Council.

Para 7.1. First sentence after mainland to read

> mainland and islands shall be promoted and facilitated on the basis of non-discriminatory measures to be proposed to the two signatories by the Special Interim Authority.

6 Henderson, *Mandarin*, p. 456.

7 Thatcher, *The Downing Street Years*, pp. 206–8.

8 *The Falklands Witness Seminar* (Strategic and Combat Studies Institute: The Occasional no. 46, 2004), p. 29.

9 *Ibid.*, p. 207.

10 Haig, *Caveat*, p. 292. Baroness Thatcher acknowledges that Britain had been exploring a Mexican offer to provide a venue for negotiations. Thatcher, *The Downing Street Years*, p. 210. On 6 May President Portillo attempted to arrange face to face talks between Galtieri and Thatcher, and claimed to the British Ambassador to have secured the former's agreement. On 12 May the Prime Minister replied, warmly thanking the President for his concern, but expressing her reluctance to undercut the UN effort then underway. Portillo was content with this reply and agreed to Thatcher's urging that his proposal and the subsequent discussion should not be made public.

11 *House of Commons Debates*, p. 147.

12 See below page 165.

13 Later it was reported that he had also said that Argentina would have accepted Haig's proposals but for the British action on South Georgia. The reference to the request for a delay may be linked to the proposal that both parties refrain from action in the Exclusion Zone while the deliberations concluded, but the status of this was uncertain to say the least.

14 Louise Richardson, *When Allies Collide: Anglo-American Relations During the Suez and Falkland Crises* (New York: St. Martin's Press, 1996), pp. 139–141.

13 AFTER HAIG

1 After the war Parsons was appointed to No. 10 as the Prime Minister's Foreign Policy adviser.

14 OPERATION SUTTON

1 Woolly Al (BBC TV) transcript interview. See also Hill, *Lewin of Greenwich*, pp. 355–6.
2 The Mexeflote rafts could carry 55 tons of stores. They played a critical logistical role during the campaign because of the lack of berthing facilities in the Falklands in moving men and equipment, but also, on occasions, as buffers between ships and, even less often, as landing pads for helicopters.
3 Woodward, *One Hundred Days*, 2nd ed., p. 117.
4 Michael Clapp and Ewen Southby-Tailyour, *Amphibious Assault: Falklands: The Battle of San Carlos Waters* (London: Leo Cooper, 1996), p. 57.
5 See Thompson, *No Picnic*, pp. 17–18.
6 Part of this may have been confusion resulting from Clapp seeking to respond to an earlier request from Fieldhouse for some choice materials on amphibious warfare. The mix-up may have convinced Fieldhouse that the pressure was getting to Clapp. See also Clapp and Southby-Tailyour, *Amphibious Assault: Falklands*, p. 71.
7 There is some confusion about the timing. In her memoirs Thatcher has the meeting on 16 April, but there is no record of a meeting then and the description of the substance does not fit. Nott appears closer with the morning of 22 April, but he does not mention (and nor does Thatcher) 25 April when it is clear that a meeting did take place. One problem was that this meeting had been regularly rearranged. There was an intelligence briefing for the War Cabinet on 16 April. Thatcher, *The Downing Street Years*, p. 201. Nott, *Here Today*, p. 300.
8 Thatcher, *The Downing Street Years*, p. 201.
9 *The Falklands Witness Seminar* (Strategic and Combat Studies Institute: The Occasional no. 46, 2004), pp. 35–6.
10 Nott, *Here Today*, p. 299.
11 *Ibid.*, p. 306.

15 THREATS TO THE TASK FORCE

1 See below pp. 238–9.
2 Nicholas van der Bijl and David Aldea, *5th Infantry Brigade in the Falklands* (London: Leo Cooper, 2003), pp. 50–1.
3 According to Woodward, *Hundred Days*, p. 151, the word was taken from a country parson who did not like to use ruder words when he fell off a bicycle.
4 Woodward, *One Hundred Days*, pp. 102–4.
5 Van der Bijl and Aldea, *5th Infantry Brigade*, p. 51.

16 RETAKING SOUTH GEORGIA

1 Nott, *Here Today,* p. 297.
2 PARAQUAT is the use favoured by Roger Perkins, who blames the original corruption on a typographical error. Roger Perkins, *Operation PARAQUAT: The Battle for South Georgia* (Chippenham, 1986), pp. Vii, 110. Although most signals within the Task Group used PARAQUAT, and the original name slipped out of use, official documents used PARAQUET and this is employed here.
3 General Michael Rose, 'Advance Force Operations: The SAS,' in Linda Washington, ed., *Ten Years On: The British Army in the Falklands War* (London: National Army Museum, 1992), p. 56.
4 While 13 BAS members had been at Grytviken, along with 22 marines, another 13 members were at various camps, including the Misses Buxton and Price at St. Andrews Bay. The Swiss had been asked on 15 April to inform Argentina of the

disposition of all personnel so that they would not be at risk when winter came in, although they would be fine until well into June. On 14 April word came back that the Grytviken party was on an Argentine warship, but it was assumed unlikely that the others were on board. Communication with the separate field parties was maintained through the BAS Survey station at Signy Island in the South Orkney Islands.

5 Clark, *Diaries*, pp. 322–3.
6 Sir George Gardiner, in Dale, ed., *Memories of the Falklands*, p. 128.
7 Clark, *Diaries*, p. 324.
8 Nott, *Here Today*, p. 297.
9 *Ibid.*, p. 301.
10 *Ibid.*, p. 297.
11 Nott suggests that Sir Michael Palliser raised this issue on 21 April, and then in the form of whether or not to inform Henderson. This does not fit the archival record.
12 *Ibid.*, p. 299.
13 See p. 167.
14 Admiral Lombardo commanded a new South Atlantic Operational Theatre, established on 7 April. His Chief of Staff was Rear Admiral Alberto Padilla. General Julio Ruiz was put in charge of Land Forces, Brigadier A.C. Weber of Air Forces and Admiral G. Allara of Naval Forces.

17 PARAQUET IN TROUBLE

1 At the same time Young found the wider political comment provided by the BBC as helpful background to the ROE signals, which would otherwise have been read in a vacuum. He later observed that more extensive briefing on the diplomatic negotiations would have been 'a useful adjunct' to the policy statement included in the ROE. 'This greater awareness would have served to increase local confidence that the Task Group was implementing the given Rules with the same intent as they were issued.'
2 Perkins, *Operation PARAQUAT*, p. 156.
3 In this event, the Ambassador would have to be warned that in such a case he would receive very little notice. Although a cover story of a training flight was proposed, the Ambassador was advised to come clean about a reconnaissance mission, as the authorities would inevitably search the aircraft.
4 Nick Vaux, *March to the South Atlantic: 42 Commando Royal Marines in the Falklands War* (London: Buchan & Enright, 1986), p. 42.
5 The deliberations on Fortuna are outlined in Perkins, *Operation PARAQUAT*, pp. 124–6.
6 For a graphic account see *Ibid.*, pp. 131–142.
7 In her memoirs Thatcher states that she received this news just as she was to leave No. 10 to speak at a charity dinner. Thatcher, *The Downing Street Years*, p. 205. Nott, *Here Today*, p. 302, seems to suggest that better news became available during the meeting ('towards the end of the meeting ... we felt that the thing was not all lost') but this appears to be referring to the 1610Z signal which already mentions that some had been rescued. This brought some relief.
8 See p. 219.

18 THE BATTLE FOR SOUTH GEORGIA

1 Perkins, *Operation PARAQUAT*, p. 158.
2 *Ibid.*, p. 168.

3 *Ibid.*, p. 175.
4 Thatcher, *The Downing Street Years*, pp. 208–9. She was further irritated when this was interpreted as an injunction to rejoice in the war.
5 See David Brown, *The Royal Navy and the Falklands War* (London: Leo Cooper, 1987), p. 105 and *Signals of War.*
6 After reporting this affair, Young convened a Board of Inquiry. Artuso was buried in the Grytviken cemetery with full military honours on 30 April. The guard, bugler and pall-bearers were provided by *Antrim*, and the ceremony was attended by the *Santa Fe*'s Commander and a number of the crew. The Chiefs of Staff would have preferred the incident to be played as low key as possible, but the Geneva Convention obliged the British to provide the names of all prisoners of war and report any such incident to the Protecting Power as soon as possible.
7 The paper also dealt with Britain's obligations under the Convention. The Second Geneva Convention set down a duty for ships to search for and rescue shipwrecked survivors without delay after a naval engagement. But at the same time, it was generally recognised that there was no rule that the Commander of a warship must engage in rescue operations if, by doing so, he would expose his vessel to attack. There was also a raft of reasons why submarines would not normally be able to rescue survivors: the time taken to surface, the difficulty of recovering personnel from the sea and their own vulnerability while surfaced. So while the decision on whether or not survivors should be rescued had ultimately to be one for the local commander, his clear duty was to make every effort to do so unless there were overriding operational reasons to the contrary and even then he should do everything possible to alleviate the distress of survivors by such measures as leaving life rafts at the scene or alerting other vessels or aircraft. After rescue, accommodation in HM surface ships was limited and in SSNs practically non-existent. Survivors would have to be transferred elsewhere as soon as operationally feasible. Until this could be done, vessels carrying prisoners should remain on station. Seriously sick or wounded prisoners must be repatriated once they were fit to travel. The most practical arrangement would seem to be that they should be transferred to a hospital ship as soon as possible and then repatriated to Argentina through Ascension. In accordance with the Third Geneva Convention 1949, the detaining authority should ensure that those who died in captivity were honourably buried in accordance with rites of religion to which they belonged, graves respected and marked so as to be found later. The conclusion was that in order to conform strictly to the Geneva Conventions at all times, and to minimise logistic problems, prisoners should be repatriated as soon as possible consistent with (a) their possession of intelligence useful to the enemy becoming stale and (b) the requirement for interrogation to be carried out.
8 Further reading on this subject can be found in Guy Bransby, *Her Majesty's Interrogator* (London: Leo Cooper, 1996).
9 Extensive material and documents were recovered from the *Santa Fe* and exploited; but many crates were sent to *Hermes* and none of these were examined until after the war.

19 THE CARRIER ISSUE

1 However Lewin told his biographer that: 'We had a certain amount of difficulty in persuading ministers that the *25 de Mayo* was a ship with guns with a range of 250 miles ... The Attorney General, with six years' wartime Fleet Air Arm experience, in fact carried the day on my behalf.' Hill, *Lewin of Greenwich*, p. 366.

20 HOSTILITIES

1 Rose, *'Advance Force Operations'*, p. 58.
2 Nott, *Here Today*, p. 300.
3 Captain Chris Craig, *Call for Fire: Sea Combat in the Falklands and the Gulf War* (London: John Murray, 1995), p. 47.
4 For background see J. S. B. Price, 'Operation Black Buck', in McQueen, *Island Base*, pp. 35-43.
5 Rodney Burden, Michael Draper, Douglas Rough, Colin Smith and David Wilton, *Falklands: The Air War* (London: Arms and Armour Press, 1986), p. 20.
6 Craig, *Call for Fire,* p. 60.
7 Major General Sir Jeremy Moore and Rear Admiral Sir John Woodward, 'The Falklands Experience', *Journal of the Royal United Services Institute* (March 1983), p. 28.
8 Despatch by Fieldhouse, *London Gazette*, 13 December 1982, p. 16113.

21 THE SINKING OF THE *BELGRANO*

1 Freedman and Gamba-Stonehouse, *Signals of War.*
2 Bilton and Kosniinsky, *op. cit.,* p. 299.
3 *The Falklands Witness Seminar* (Strategic and Combat Studies Institute: The Occasional no. 46, 2004), p. 32.
4 *Falklands: The Air War*, p. 22.
5 Testimony to the Rattenbach Commission, *Gente*, 8 December 1983, p. 90. This mistake was repeated in Desmond Rice and Arthur Gavshon, *The Sinking of the Belgrano* (London: Secker & Warburg, 1984) and skewed their analysis, and much subsequent commentary that followed their lead. As discussed in *Signals of War*, no other Argentine account supports Anaya's suggestion.

22 *SHEFFIELD*

1 *Official Record*, 4 May 1982, cols. 30–7.
2 *Official Record*, 4 May 1982, cols. 14–18.
3 Middlebrook, *The Fight for the 'Malvinas'*, p. 118.
4 *Sheffield* was the first of the class 42 destroyers, ordered in 1968 and laid down the following years at Barrow, launched in 1971 and commissioned in February 1975. It had been with the SPRINGTRAIN group, arrived at Ascension on 10 April and then was one of the advance group, sailed on 14 April at some 25 knots, entering the TEZ on 1 May.
5 See Commander 'Sharkey' Ward, *Sea Harrier over the Falkland: A Maverick at War* (London: Leo Cooper, 1992).
6 One source, however, suggests that the Argentines were unsure of success, and could not confirm a hit because of the lack of a reconnaissance capability until informed by the BBC. 'Had the British not announced the loss, the Argentinians would have likely concluded that their Exocets were still malfunctioning and called off further Exocet attacks.' Dr James Corum, 'Argentine Airpower in the Falklands War,' *Air & Space Power Journal*, Fall 2002, p. 69.
7 Evidence, p. 394.
8 Leach, *Endure No Makeshifts,* p. 217.
9 Hill, *Lewin of Greenwich,* p. 370.
10 See p. 429.

11 On suspicions see Clapp and Southby-Tailyour (who claim that it smuggled an Exocet missile into Stanley), *Amphibious Assault: Falklands*, p. 202.
12 Nott, *Here Today*, pp. 294–5.

23 THE PERUVIAN INITIATIVE

1 Gavshon and Rice, pp. 82–3. Haig's account is muddled on timing, but he notes that 'Speaking over an open line, we worked all day on a new draft'. Haig, *Caveat*, p. 293.
2 Gavshon and Rice, pp. 85, 87; *Signals of War*.
3 House of Commons, Third Report of the Foreign Affairs Committee, Session 1984–5, *Events of the Weekend of 1st and 2nd May 1982* (London: HMSO, 1985), p. 66.
4 Henderson, 1983, p. 55.
5 Evidence to Foreign Affairs Committee, Qs 305, 306.
6 Gavshon and Rice, p. 118.
7 Woolly Al transcript.
8 Thatcher, *The Downing Street Years*, pp. 216–17.
9 *Ibid.*, p. 217.
10 Gavshon and Rice, pp. 123–5.

24 BACK TO THE UN

1 *Official Record*, 7 May 1982 Vol.23 Col.394.

25 THE UN MEDIATION

1 For details see below, pp. 427–9.
2 These were taken from Article 40 of the Charter, and from Israel/Jordan armistice agreement (based on Article 40) and from Article IV (2) of the Antarctica Treaty.
3 Argentine Paper:

- This agreement is concluded within the framework of the Charter of the United Nations and taking into account Security Council Resolution 502 (1982) and the relevant resolutions of the General Assembly.
- The agreement to which the parties commit themselves shall be without prejudice to the rights, claims or positions of the parties.
- The geographical scope of this agreement shall comprise the three archipelagos considered by the United Nations.
- The Government and administration shall be the exclusive responsibility of the United Nations. The observers of the parties may fly their respective flags.
- There shall be freedom of transit and residence for citizens of the parties, who shall enjoy the right to acquire and dispose of real estate.
- The withdrawal of forces shall be effected under the supervision of the United Nations.
- The parties shall commit themselves to undertake in good faith negotiations under the auspices of the Secretary-General with a

811

view to peaceful settlement of the dispute and, with a sense of urgency, to complete these negotiations by 31 December 1982.

4 *Pilgrimage for Peace*, p. 373.
5 *Signals of War*, pp. 336–7.
6 The new proposed draft read:

    a.   A United Nations administrator, being a person acceptable to Argentina and the United Kingdom, will be appointed by the Secretary-General and will be the officer administering the government of the islands.

    b.   The United Nations administrator will have authority under the direction of the Secretary-General to ensure the continuing administration of the government of the islands. He shall discharge his functions in consultation with the executive and legislative councils in the islands and shall act through the competent officials and institutions of the traditional local administration. He shall exercise his powers in accordance with the terms of this agreement and in conformity with the spirit of the laws and practices previously observed by the traditional local administration.

7 In the UN draft this was described as: 'A zone bounded by straight lines connecting the following four co-ordinate points: 48 degrees South 63 degrees West, 48 degrees South 23 degrees West, 60 degrees South 22 degrees West, 60 degrees South 63 degrees West.' The southern boundary was thus the same as the northern boundary of the Antarctica Treaty area. The UN proposal was for two stages: in the first half Argentine forces would withdraw west of 63 degrees W and UK north of 48 degrees S. In both cases withdrawals would be described as being 'en route to their usual operating bases or areas.' In the second phase the rest of Argentine forces and civilian personnel not present in the Islands on 31 March would be withdrawn and British forces would go north to 33 degrees S.

8   On briefing the national cabinet on the diplomatic negotiations that are being carried out, Foreign Minister Nicanor Costa Mendez stated that all negotiations must lead to recognition of Argentine sovereignty over the Malvinas Islands. This was disclosed at the reporters' hall at the end of the meeting by Rodolfo Baltierrez, public information secretary of the Presidency.
    BBC Monitoring report from Argentina of 1604Z 12 May

9 Parsons had concluded that his instructions were unreliable when, having made the point to the Secretary-General that the dependencies were of the UK he discovered that, according to Halsbury's Laws of England, they were established as dependencies of the Falkland Islands in 1908 by Letters Patent.
10 *Pilgrimage for Peace*, p. 376.
11 There is unfortunately no record of this statement in the Public Papers of President Reagan. The word 'recuperate' suggests a translation from a statement delivered in Spanish.
12 *Pilgrimage for Peace*, p. 374.
13 Henderson received a report on these lines on 14 May. Another report was of a conversation between the American Ambassador to the OAS and the Argentine Ambassador to the US. The latter said that his government had deliberately de-

linked sovereignty from the negotiating process. He also claimed that Argentina had been observing an effective cease-fire since the *Sheffield*, that 10 civilians had been killed, and that Argentina would ask the US to stop the British continuing with hostilities if they did not get a peaceful settlement.

14 *Pilgrimage for Peace*, p. 375.

15 The Secretary-General also heard from Haig, ringing from Turkey, unhappy about Reagan's involvement. Perez de Cuellar explained how he thought the President might help, and like many others involved he was also worried about the imminence of a British attack on the Argentine mainland. Haig gave his view that the President should only be involved when he could get results. Not enough stumbling blocks had been removed. The Secretary-General suspected that Haig was really unhappy about Kirkpatrick's 'interference in his business.'

16 *Pilgrimage for Peace*, p. 376.

17 Present were the War Cabinet, Attorney General Havers, Lewin, Parsons, Henderson, Cooper, Wade-Gery, Palliser, Acland, Sinclair (FCO Legal Adviser), and the Deputy Secretary of the Chiefs of Staff.

18 Thatcher, *The Downing Street Years*, pp. 222–3.

19 Henderson, *Mandarin*, p. 462.

20 Nott, *Here Today*, pp. 293–4; Henderson, p. 463.

21 Thatcher, *The Downing Street Years*, pp. 222–3.

22 *Pilgrimage for Peace*, p. 378.

23 *Ibid.*, p. 380.

24 See pp. 258–9.

25 As this was going on there was a discussion between Perez de Cuellar's and Parson's staff, especially with regard to the tension between the draft's stipulation that the administrator's staff must be agreed by Argentina and Britain, and the Secretary-General's powers to appoint staff, including the 150–200 men who would be verifying the non-reintroduction of forces. In the normal way the arrangements including nationality would be approved through the Security Council's endorsement of the Secretary-General's proposals with informal consultations beforehand, and then expenses apportioned. Would this formulation mean that Argentina and Britain would pay expenses? The Secretary-General's draft agreement also had provisions about privileges and immunities of the UN administrator and staff. The British had no instructions on these points, but it was thought that they could be managed by omitting 'agreed by Argentina and the UK' in exchange for assurances that they would be consulted in advance about acceptability and nationality of all UN officers, and expenses would then be of the UN and apportioned on peacekeeping pattern.

26 *Pilgrimage for Peace*, p. 380.

27 *Ibid.*, p. 381.

28 *Ibid.*, pp. 384–5.

29 *Ibid.*, p. 384.

26 AMERICAN SUPPORT

1 Weinberger, *Fighting for Peace*, p. 146.

2 The issue is dealt with in Thatcher, *The Downing Street Years*. Henderson, *Mandarin*, p. 443, says the offer was made at a garden party at the British Embassy. Weinberger does not mention the offer although he does refer to the British Embassy gardens as the location for his discussions with Henderson and Pym on 2 May. *Fighting for Peace*, p. 146.

3 MoD was also puzzled by the reference to 200 Mk46 torpedoes. No such request had been authorised by Lewin but 50 boxes of Mk46 tubes were requested on 12 May.
4 Richardson, *When Allies Collide*, pp. 128-9.
5 Nott, *Here Today*, p. 305.

27 CHILE

1 General Pinochet's Statement, 9 November 1998.
2 Paolo Tripodi describes the equipment on offer as Hunters, long-range radar, anti-aircraft missiles, Canberras and a 'Photographic Reconnaissance Unit', of which the latter was probably the most important as Chile lacked any equivalent units at that time. 'Chile's Role During the Falklands War', *The Journal of Strategic Studies*, 26:4 (December 2003), p. 116.
3 The authoritative information from Chilean sources is covered fully in Tripodi, *op.cit. Associated Press*, 24 March 2002, *La Tercera*, Santiago. *Sunday Times,* 29 November 1998. She suggests that the day the 'long-range radar was taken out of service for overdue maintenance' was the day of the attack on *Sir Galahad* and *Sir Tristram*. Baroness Thatcher mentions the same incident, without giving a source, in her book, *Statecraft* (London: HarperCollins, 2002), p. 267, in which she confirms the help given by Chile to Britain during the campaign. The Chilean question is discussed in Nigel West, *The Secret War for the Falklands* (London: Little Brown & Co, 1997).
4 Tripodi, *op.cit.*, p. 118.

28 THE INFORMATION WAR

1 Mercer *et al.*, *The Fog of War*, pp. 170, 174.
2 Woodward, *One Hundred Days*, p. 154.
3 Defence Committee, Minutes of Proceedings, pp. 301–2.
4 The studies were published as Valerie Adams, *The Media and the Falklands Campaign* (London: Macmillan, 1986), as well as Mercer *et al.*, *The Fog of War*.
5 I am indebted to Jean Seaton for BBC material.
6 Official Report, 11 May 1982, c. 598.
7 Cited in Yoel Cohen, *Media Diplomacy: The Foreign Office in the Mass Communications Age* (London: Frank Cass, 1986), p. 138.
8 It was at any rate about to become known that the Vulcans were being given conventional bombing practice in Scotland.
9 It was agreed on 14 April that publicity should be given to Royal Air Force Harrier pilot training, particularly at RNAS Yeovilton.
10 Nick Van der Bijl, *Nine Battles to Stanley* (London: Leo Cooper, 1999), p. 81.
11 James S. Corum, 'Argentine Airpower in the Falklands War: An Operational View', *Air & Space Power Journal* (Fall 2002)
12 I am indebted to Jean Seaton for BBC material.

29 ENFORCING THE EXCLUSION ZONE

1 General Menendez did not take charge of the Malvinas Joint Command until 26 April. Under him were General Americo Daher (9th Infantry Brigade) his Chief of Staff; General Oscar Joffre (10th Infantry Brigade), commander of the Puerto Argentino Group of Forces; and General Omar Parada (3rd Infantry Brigade) of the Malvinas Group of Forces.

2 This incident is described in Craig, *Call for Fire*, pp. 54–6.

3 Article 51 defines grave breaches as 'wilful killing ... wilfully causing great suffering or serious injury to body or health, and extensive destruction and appropriation of property not justified by military necessity and carried out unlawfully and wantonly'. Article 50 provides that parties must search for and prosecute persons alleged to have committed such breaches and Article 53 provides that any party can request an enquiry into an alleged breach.

4 Craig's account of the journey is in *Call for Fire*, pp. 76–82. Craig sees no reason to doubt the Argentine account.

30 THE AIR THREAT

1 Woodward, *One Hundred Days*, pp. 276–7.

2 There was no radar on Pebble Island when it surrendered on 15 June. It is probable that a portable surveillance radar was present when the airfield was in commission, but removed to Fox Bay after the raid.

3 Woodward, *One Hundred Days*, p. 316.

4 General Sir Peter de la Billiere, *Looking for Trouble: SAS to Gulf Command* (London: Harper Collins, 1994), pp. 346–7.

5 The proposed operation is described in David Reynolds, *Task Force: The Illustrated History of the Falklands War* (London: Sutton, 2002), pp. 193–201. This account suggests that from 1 May the five Super Etendards had been moved each night to a nearby town for protection. On the apprehension among those involved see the account by Richard Villar, in Dale, ed., *Memories of the Falklands*, pp. 168–170.

6 See Woodward, *One Hundred Days*, p. 290.

7 This was before news came in that three not two of the A4s that attacked *Glasgow* were lost.

31 TO SUTTON

1 Nott, *Here Today*, p. 310.

2 Leach, *Endure No Makeshifts,* p. 217.

32 THE LANDING

1 Dr James Corum, 'Argentine Airpower in the Falklands War,' *Air & Space Power Journal*, Fall 2002, p. 69.

2 Defence Committee Report, Minutes of Evidence, pp. 432–3, 22.

3 *The Falklands Witness Seminar* (Strategic and Combat Studies Institute: The Occasional no. 46, 2004), p. 63.

4 Other sources suggest the SBS group killed 18 and captured nine. See also Hugh McManners, *Falklands Commando* (London: William Kimber, 1984), ch. 7.

5 3 Para reported the number as 35 adults and 7 children.

6 Despatch by Fieldhouse, *London Gazette*, 13 December 1982, p. 16115.

7 A similar mistake was made on 23 May when British helicopters engaged the deserted ship with Sea Skua until told not to expend further effort on her. The ship sank that day.

8 Fortunately *Brilliant* had a specialist computer engineer from Marconi on board who managed to re-wire and re-programme Sea Wolf so that it could recover from the damage.

9 For an account of the *Ardent*'s experience, from the perspective of the crew, see Mark Higgitt, *Through Fire and Water: HMS Ardent: The Forgotten Frigate of the Falklands* (London: Mainstream Publishing, 2001).

10 According to one Argentine airman, the problem was that the fuses needed enough delay so that 'the first bombs did not explode underneath the last of the three aircraft as it came over' while not so much that 'the bomb had time to arm and to explode inside the ship's hull when it hit its target'. The problem was not solved until just before the war ended. Brigadier Horacio Mir Gonzalez, 'An Argentinian Airman in the South Atlantic', in Stephen Badsey, Rob Havers, Mark Grove *et al.*, *The Falklands Conflict Twenty Years On: Lessons for the Future*, (London: Frank Cass, 2005), p. 7.

11 See for example Clapp and Southby-Tailyour, *Amphibious Assault Falklands*, pp. 112, 18.

33 BOMB ALLEY

1 See Thompson, *No Picnic.*

2 Its cargo of two 105mm guns was recovered by the Argentine air force two days later and delivered as originally intended to the Goose Green garrison.

3 The situation report that evening referred to the *Broadsword*'s Sea Wolf accounting for one Mirage and *Antelope* and *Plymouth* accounting for another with 20mm guns. Another Mirage 'possibly splashed'. It also stated that 'a simultaneous raid Sea Harriers on combat air patrol splashed 2 Mirage'.

4 Clapp and Southby-Tailyour, *Amphibious Assault Falklands*, pp. 170, 177.

5 Hill, *Lewin of Greenwich*, p. 372. It is not clear when this judgement was made: this seems the most likely day.

6 *Signals of War*, pp. 362–3.

7 For some reason these were subsequently assessed as either Pucara or Aermacchi on reconnaissance.

8 Van der Bijl and Aldea suggest that while Clapp had wanted to land the helicopters earlier, Northwood had told him to keep the helicopters safe for 5 Infantry Brigade. I have no evidence of this. Given the desperate need for helicopters at the time, and Northwood's anxiety that 3 Brigade press forward, this seems unlikely. *5th Infantry Brigade in the Falklands*, p. 45.

9 Leach, *Endure No Makeshifts*, pp. 217–18.

10 *Ibid.*, pp. 217–18. A note by CDS also suggests that the motives were more to do with protecting the next of kin. They had three minutes to decide and thought they would be spreading small amounts of anxiety rather than grim news to *Coventry* next of kin.

11 House of Commons Defence Committee, First Report, 82–83, vol. II, p. 430. Leach observes: 'Nott had been right, Lewin and Leach wrong.'

12 Corum, 'Argentine Airpower in the Falklands War'.

13 On the exploits of FCDT, see Bernie Bruen, *Keep Your Head Down: A Falklands Farewell* (Sussex: The Book Guild, 1993).

34 INTERNATIONAL OPINION

1 Edmund Yorke, 'The Commonwealth response to the Conflict', in Stephen Badsey, Rob Havers, Mark Grove *et al.*, *The Falklands Conflict Twenty Years On: Lessons for the Future* (London: Frank Cass, 2005).

2 Cited in Lisa L. Martin, 'Institutions and Cooperation: Sanctions During the Falkland Islands Conflict,' *International Security*, 16:4 (Spring 1992), p. 166.

3 *Ibid.*, pp. 169–171.
4 On 12 May the Soviet Union offered to hand over some bodies it had found and requested instructions for delivery and assurance of security for vessels. According to press reports a Polish fishing vessel earlier had rescued two Argentine Canberra crewmen.

35 FINAL DIPLOMACY

1 Nott, *Here Today,* pp. 293–4. Henderson, *Mandarin*, p. 463.
2 Henderson, *Mandarin*, pp. 465–6.
3 *Ibid.*, pp. 466–7.
4 This is discussed below, pp. 548–9.
5 James S. Sutterlin, 'The Good Offices of the Secretary-General', in Diane B. Bendahame and John W. McDonald Jr., *Perspectives on Negotiation: Four Case Studies and Interpretations* (Washington D.C., Center for the Study of Foreign Affairs, Foreign Service Institute, US Department of State, 1986), p. 86.
6 *Pilgrimage for Peace*, p. 386.
7 The formal reply was delivered on 31 May.
8 *Pilgrimage for Peace*, p. 386.
9 *Ibid.*, pp. 388–9.
10 *Signals of War.*
11 Parsons, *International Affairs*, p. 176.

36 THE CHANGING MILITARY BALANCE

1 Van der Bijl and Aldea, *5th Infantry Brigade*, pp. 51–2.

37 GOOSE GREEN

1 *Signals of War*, pp. 363–4.
2 Bilton and Kosminsky, *Speaking Out*, pp. 256–259.
3 Fox, *Eyewitness Falklands* (London: Methuen, 1982).
4 John Frost, *2 Para Falklands: The Battalion at War* (London and Sydney: Sphere Books Limited, 1983).
5 Mark Adkin, *Goose Green* (London: Cassell, 1992); Spencer Fitz-Gibbon, *Not Mentioned in Despatches: The History and Mythology of Goose Green* (Cambridge: The Lutterworth Press, 1995). Fitz-Gibbon is particularly concerned with the historiography of the battle, illustrating at great length how the various accounts differ, and also with promoting a particular, and not wholly convincing, view of how such battles should be fought.
6 Leach, *Endure No Makeshifts*, pp. 209–211; The Falklands Witness Seminar (Strategic and Combat Studies Institute: The Occasional no. 46, 2004), p. 44.
7 See p. 450.
8 Van der Bijl and Aldea, *5th Infantry Brigade*, pp. 45–6.
9 Thompson, *No Picnic*, pp. 70–71.
10 Robert Harris, *Gotcha: The Government, Media and the Falklands Crisis* (London: Faber, 1994), p. 117
11 Bilton and Kosminsky, p. 301.
12 John Wilsey, *H Jones VC: The Life and Death of an Unusual Hero* (London: Hutchinson, 2002), pp. 248–250, records the impressions of General Sir John

Stanier, Commander-in-Chief UK Land Forces, that without movement it might be necessary to recover 3 Brigade from the beaches. This possibility may well have been raised but it was certainly not being seriously considered at that time. Fieldhouse's concerns were as much political as military. Wilsey also reports that Stanier proposed, after discussions with Trant, a battalion sized attack on Goose Green. This may have reinforced Fieldhouse's inclinations but the option had been in play for some days.

13 Thompson, *No Picnic*, p. 81.

14 One well informed article puts the Air Force contingent at 202. It also says that there were 684 Argentine Army personnel together with a half of a 105mm howitzer battery of the 4th Airborne Artillery Group. Air defence was provided by a battery of 20mm Rheinmetall pieces manned by Air Force personnel, and two radar-guided 35mm anti-aircraft guns from the 601st Air Defense Artillery Group. David Aldea, 'Blood and Mud at Goose Green', *Military History*, April 2002, p. 45. Robert Bolia puts the numbers of officers and men from the infantry regiments at 554. Robert Bolia, 'The Battle of Darwin-Goose Green', *Military Review*, July-August 2005, p. 46.

15 Van der Bijl, *Nine Battles*, p. 115.

16 Van der Bijl, *Ibid.*, p. 124.

17 Thompson, *Ready for Anything: A History of the Parachute Regiment* (London: Weidenfeld & Nicolson, 1989), p. 322.

18 Robert Fox, *Eyewitness Falklands*, London: Methuen, 1982, p. 156.

19 HCDC, Defence Committee, First Report, 1982–3, vol. II, 425–6.

20 Middlebrook, *The Fight for the 'Malvinas'*, p. 180.

21 There is some controversy about this point. Wilsey argues that Jones had ordered A Company to press forward (in Wilsey, *H Jones VC*, pp. 266–7). On this he relies a lot on Fitz-Gibbon, *Not Mentioned*, pp. 60–63 (although he does not mention Fitz-Gibbon's generally critical assessment of Jones as a commander). This view depends largely on working back from the CO's irritation with A Company for not being further forward when he reached them, but that may have reflected his surprise that the position was more difficult than he had thought. Jones would not have been the first commander in such circumstances to take out his frustration on a subordinate. There is no doubt that Farrar-Hockley believed that he had been asked to wait.

22 Adkin, *Goose Green*, p. 218, suggests that the Argentine position at Darwin Hill came as something of a surprise. It had, however, as he notes, been mentioned in the original 'O' briefing and Farrar-Hockley was aware of it. It is not clear whether it was fully appreciated by Jones until the engagement actually began.

23 Review of Wilsey, *H Jones VC*, in British Army Review, 2002.

24 Aldea, *op.cit.*, p. 48.

25 Many accounts say Skyhawks.

26 Thompson, *No Picnic*, p. 81.

27 For an account of how this was done see Eric Goss, in Dale, ed., *Memories of the Falklands*, pp. 19–20.

28 Van der Bijl refers to 145 Argentine killed and wounded, including 48 infantry, two AA gunners, and five pilots. Aldea gives a figure of 55 Argentine dead, including four Air Force and one Navy pilot. Aldea, *op. cit.*, p. 49. Aldea does not include pilots.

29 Brigadier Hew Pike, 'The Army's Infantry and Armoured Reconnaissance Forces,' in Washington, ed., *Ten Years On*, p. 40.

38 3 COMMANDO BRIGADE

1 Following the surrender of Stanley Hunt drafted a letter to Moore bringing his attention to these feelings, at the time running high, and which continued for some time thereafter. But, following discussion with Thompson it was decided that nothing could be gained by such action. However, it was agreed that Hunt's feelings should be recorded in the Commander's Diary.

2 Van der Bijl, *Nine Battles*, p. 144

3 The move is described in Nick Vaux, *March to the South Atlantic* (London: Buchan & Enright, 1986), chapter seven.

4 Graham Colbeck, *With 3 Para to the Falklands* (London: Greenhill Books, 2002), pp. 90–1. Colbeck notes that the boots were blamed for the foot injuries, but doubts that any boot available at the time could have prevented wet feet for long.

5 Van der Bijl, *op. cit.*, p. 153.

6 See below p. 606.

39 FITZROY AND BLUFF COVE

1 Lieutenant General J. P. Kiszely MC, 'The Land Campaign: A Company Commander's Perspective', in Badsey *et al.*, *The Falklands Conflict Twenty Years On*, p. 100

2 McManners, *The Scars of War*, p. 107.

3 Leach, *Endure No Makeshifts,* p. 219.

4 Clapp and Southby-Tailyour, *Amphibious Assault Falklands*, pp. 210–11.

5 Van der Bijl and Aldea link the tension between the two to the distinction between Restrictive Control, the standard for the British Army at the time, by which the Commanders issue detailed orders which the units apply, and Directive Control, which had long been the paratroopers' preference, by which broad guidance is issued by commanders but implementation depends on the assessment by the local commanders of the situation they faced. In this case the tension was aggravated by Wilson's credibility with the Paras, going back to a 5 Brigade exercise 'Green Lanyard' in February that year. *5th Infantry Brigade*, pp. 70–1.

6 Clapp and Southby-Tailyour, *Amphibious Assault Falklands*, p. 226.

7 These were 5 Infantry Brigade's first casualties. Initially this was thought to have been 'a hostile missile' and it was recorded as a loss to enemy fire, even though there was circumstantial but not metallurgical evidence that it could have been a Sea Dart. By 1985 questions were being raised by the House of Commons Defence Committee who were encouraged to handle the matter sensitively 'out of a wish to avoid distress to the next-of-kin of the men who had died'. Studies in 1985 however removed the metallurgical doubts and it became evident that the Sea Dart explanation was correct. Although senior figures still felt that the interest of the next-of-kin would best be served by the old explanation, in 1986 the loss of the helicopter was publicly acknowledged to be a 'blue-on-blue' incident.

8 Ewen Southby-Tailyour, *Reasons in Writing*, pp. 262–275.

9 Some journalists in London had pieced together the story and would have published details of the movements by ship to Fitzroy had they not been urged to hold back by the head of Army public relations, thereby preventing the media getting the blame for the subsequent attack. Mercer *et al.*, *The Fog of War*, pp. 80–1.

10 Cited in Cohen, *Media Diplomacy*, p. 151.

11 Max Hastings, *Going to the Wars* (London: Macmillan, 2000), p. 317.

12 House of Commons Defence Committee, First Report, 1982–3, vol. II, 418. This was one more soldier killed than the Army estimate.

13 See Rick Jolly, *The Red and Green Life Machine: A Diary of the Falklands Field Hospital* (London: Century Publishing, 1983).

14 Marion Harding, 'Unsung Heroes,' in Washington, ed., *Ten Years On*, p. 64

40 TAKING THE HIGH GROUND

1 *Signals of War*, pp. 390–4.

2 Quoted in Blakeway, *The Falklands War*, p. 152. The debate is covered in van der Bijl.

3 The story is told in McManners, *Scars of War*, pp. 231–2.

4 Argentine Forces on Mount Longdon included B Company, 7th Infantry Regiment; 1st Platoon, C Company, 7th Infantry Regiment; Platoon, 10th Engineer Company; 4th Airborne Artillery Group (Pack Howitzers); D Battery, 3rd Artillery Group (155mm) and Platoon, Marine 12.7 Machine Gun Company. See van der Bijl, *Nine Battles*, p. 242.

5 Colbeck, *With 3 Para to the Falklands*, p. 179

6 Christian Jennings and Adrian Weale, *Green-Eyed Boys: 3 Para and the Battle for Mount Longdon* (London: Harper Collins, 1996), pp. 122–3.

7 Colbeck, *With 3 Para to the Falklands*, p. 179

8 Van der Bijl, p. 174

9 Jennings and Weale, *op. cit.*

10 Van der Bijl gives figures of 17 killed, most from B Company, and 31 Argentine dead, with 50 taken prisoner and at least 120 wounded. Vincent Bramley, who had been Lance Corporal in 3 Para, wrote a book about Mount Longdon – *Excursion to Hell* – which made allegations of some nine instances of killing and three cases of beating up of enemy soldiers while surrendering, wounded or already captured. As, if true, these would be grave breaches of the Geneva Wounded or PW Conventions of 1949, the Ministry of Defence had to investigate them thoroughly. Metropolitan Police officers carrying out the investigation looked into a number of allegations, including one that an A Company soldier shot and killed an Argentine prisoner who was part of a group burying the Argentine dead. Although there were witnesses to this incident there was not sufficient evidence to support a prosecution. The critical incident is described in Jennings and Weale, p. 163. They give a figure of 29 Argentine dead.

11 Enemy forces on Two Sisters included C Company, 4th Infantry Regiment; 2nd and 3rd Platoons, A Company, 4th Infantry Regiment; B Company, 6th Infantry Regiment; Section, Mortar Platoon, 4th Infantry Regiment; 3rd Artillery Group (Pack Howitzers) and B Battery, Marine Field Artillery Battalion (Pack Howitzers). See van der Bijl, *Nine Battles to Stanley*, p. 242.

12 Van der Bijl and Aldea say that this claim is 'unsubstantiated'. They also note that Argentines appeared to have believed that they had killed some 30 British soldiers in these exchanges, *5th Infantry Brigade*, p. 173

13 For further reading see Vaux, *March to the South Atlantic*, chs. 11–12.

14 *Ibid.*, p. 177.

41 THE FINAL BATTLE

1 Thompson, *No Picnic*, p. 148.

2 Woodward, *One Hundred Days*, pp. 468–9.

3 Kiszely, 'The Land Campaign'.

4 Mike Seear, *With the Gurkhas in the Falklands: A War Journal* (London: Leo Cooper, 2003), p. 252.

5 Van der Bijl says 9 killed and 43 wounded, *Nine Battles*, p. 203.
6 For an attempt to get the record straight from the battalion's perspective see Seear, *With the Gurkhas in the Falklands.*
7 Cited in Nora Kinzer Stewart, *Mates and Muchachos: Unit Cohesion in the Falklands/Malvinas War* (New York: Brassey's, 1991), p. 91.
8 Reynolds, *Task Force*, p. 236.
9 It appeared that the fire had come from an Argentine hospital ship somewhere in the eastern part of Port William.

42 SURRENDER

1 According to Van der Bijl and Aldea, the Argentine command mistakenly took this for a full heliborne assault and that accelerated the decision to surrender, *5th Infantry Brigade*, p. 217.
2 Hastings, *Going to the Wars*, pp. 372–9. The arguments continued after the fighting was over. An article by Hastings in the *Evening Standard* on 23 June, entitled 'How the Admiral Upset the Army', described some of the grumbles common amongst senior land officers irritated by Woodward's reluctance to risk his carriers to provide better air support after the landing (a decision which many acknowledged later to have been warranted) and such issues as the fitness of the Guards' Battalions. Brigadier Wilson fumed back on behalf of 1 WG, in a telegram replete with references to suffering 'the totally ill-informed opinions of third grade incompetents' and being 'pilloried by fools'. 'Hastings would not last one night in Stanley now', the Brigadier added – possibly correctly given the views of those of his colleagues who believed that his success had come at their expense.
3 Moore may have been influenced by the fact that he had been given an intelligence picture of the wrong General Menendez, of which there were a number in the Argentine Army. The one he believed himself to be fighting was a somewhat tougher warrior than the one he was actually fighting.
4 For a flavour of the discussions see Fox, *Eyewitness Falklands*, pp. 231–4.
5 The story is told in H.M.Rose, 'Toward an Ending of the Falkland Island War,' *Conflict*, vol. 7, no. 1 (1987)
6 The zone comprised the Cathedral and the area bounded by Ross Road and John, Dean and Philomel Streets. The zone intended to give shelter to the wounded and sick whether combatant or non-combatant, non-combatant civilians and unarmed Argentine military personnel responsible for organisation, administration, control and food supply of the zone. The UK would regard involvement of Argentine personnel in activities connected with military operations as a breach of conditions of the establishment of the neutral zone. The zone was not to contain military material or supplies except arms taken from wounded inside the zone.
7 See *Signals of War*, pp. 402–6.
8 This was much to the later irritation of the House of Commons Defence Committee who felt that the opportunity to record an historic moment had been lost.
9 Smith, *74 Days*, pp. 240–243. Moore's recollection is that he said 'Sorry it's taken 3½ weeks'.
10 Van der Bijl gives a figure of '100 troops and scientists', *Nine Battles*, p. 216.
11 Van der Bijl says nine. *Ibid.*, p. 216. Later that year an Argentine flag reappeared and was again replaced. 'Brun' Richards, the naval gunfire support officer who was landed on the island before the surrender, also suggests nine Argentines were removed, and also refers to general suspicions of *Endurance* trying to win battles on its own. 'Operation Keyhole', *Journal of the Royal Artillery*, March 1984.

43 AFTER VICTORY

1 Cited in McManners, *The Scars of War* (London: Harper Collins 1994), p. 95.
2 Van der Bijl, *Nine Battles*, p. 58.
3 Kiszely, 'The Land Campaign', in Badsey *et al.*, *The Falklands Conflict*, p. 107.
4 *Nine Battles*, p. 224. Contemporary documents put the numbers at 560 special category and 25 engineers, but van der Bijl was on the spot.
5 Nott, *Here Today*, p. 317.
6 'And he shall judge among many people, and rebuke strong nations afar off; and they shall beat their swords into plowshares, and their spears into pruning hooks: nation shall not lift up a sword against nation, neither shall they learn war any more.'
7 On the debate surrounding the service, see George Boyce, *The Falklands War* (London: Macmillan, 2005), pp. 211–14.
8 See the discussion of the victory parade in Klaus Dodds, *Pink Ice: Britain and the South Atlantic Empire* (London: I.B. Tauris, 2002), pp. 172–4.

44 FORTRESS FALKLANDS

1 This is addressed in Volume One.
2 Major-General Sir David Thorne, 'The Legacy,' in Washington, ed., *Ten Years On*, p. 81.

45 NEGOTIATIONS

1 Guillermo Makin, 'Nature of Anglo-American diplomacy, 1980–1990', in A. Danchev (ed.), *A Matter of Life and Death: International Perspectives on the Falklands Conflict* (Basingstoke: Macmillan, 1991), p. 229.

46 DIPLOMATIC FISHING

1 'Risks around the Falklands,' *Financial Times*, 5 November 1986.
2 Peter Willets and Felipe Noguera, 'Public attitudes and the future of the Islands', in Danchev (ed.), *A Matter of Life and Death*. There were remarkable similarities in popular attitudes in Britain and Argentina except for the question of future ownership of the Falklands with two-thirds of the Argentines considering the return of the Islands to Argentina as the only solution, while only a third of the British population were as definite about future British sovereignty.

47 THE FRANKS REPORT

1 *Official Record*, Column 416, 8 April 1982.
2 Report of a Committee of Privy Counsellors, *Falkland Islands Review*, January 1983, cmnd 878 (hereinafter referred to as *The Franks Report*).
3 Alex Danchev, *Founding Father* (Oxford: Clarendon Press, 1993), p. 179.
4 *Official Record*, 26 January 1983, col. 945.
5 One important non-intelligence issue was the extent to which Nicholas Ridley discussed lease-back with the Argentines during the course of 1980. This episode is discussed in Chapter 11 of Volume One. The discussions had been undertaken on the basis that they would not be disclosed. Lord Franks was informed and agreed that this confidence could be respected, especially as Ridley had not

diverged from the position that any deal would have to be agreed by the islanders.

6 This is based on a draft letter.

7 Alex Danchev, 'The Franks Report: A Chronicle of Unripe Time,' in Danchev, ed., *International Perspectives*, p. 129. See also Danchev, *Founding Father*.

48 LESSONS

1 On the attitudes towards the war displayed in literature and plays see the excellent discussion in Boyce, *The Falklands War,* chapter 1. The extent of the 'Falklands Factor' in the General Election became a matter of dispute. One view is that there was a boost to the Government, perhaps at as much as six per cent at the time of the 1983 election, but then declining. Others put it much lower, attributing the rise in government popularity to evidence of economic recovery. For a sense of the debate see two articles in the *British Journal of Political Science*, vol. 20 (1990): H.D. Clarke, W. Mishler, P. Whiteley, 'Recapturing the Falklands: Models of Conservative Popularity, 1979–1983', and D. Sanders, H. Ward and D. Marsh, 'A Reply to Clarke, Mishler, and Whiteley'.

2 See Vice Admiral Sir Jonathon Band, 'British High Command during and after the Falklands Conflict' (p. 32), Major General Julian Thompson, 'Force Projection and the Falklands Conflict' (p. 86) in Badsey *et al.*, *The Falklands Conflict*. See also Stephen Prince, 'British Command and Control in the Falklands Campaign', *Defence and Security Analysis*, 18/4 (December 2002).

3 Kiszely, 'The Land Campaign', in Badsey *et al.*, *The Falklands Conflict*, p. 103.

4 Nora Kinzer Stewart, *Mates and Muchachos*, pp. 133–4.

5 J. Price, 'The Falklands: rate of British psychiatric casualties compared to recent American wars', *Journal of the Royal Army Medical Corps*, 1984; 130:109–113; P. Abraham, 'Training for battleshock', *Journal of the Royal Army Medical Corps* 1982; 128:18–27. I am indebted to Professor Simon Wessely for some of the material in these paragraphs.

6 G. Jones and J. Lovett, 'Delayed psychiatric sequelae among Falklands War veterans', *Journal of the Royal College of General Practitioners* 1987; 37:34–35.

7 L. S. O'Brien and S. J. Hughes. 'Symptoms of post-traumatic stress disorder in Falklands veterans five years after the conflict', *British Journal of Psychiatry*, 1991, 159, 135–141. A later study, which suggested up to sixty per cent of PTSD, appears unreliable because it used only volunteers and lacked controls. R. Orner, T. Lynch and P. Seed, 'Long-term traumatic stress reactions in British Falklands War veterans', *British Journal of Clinical Psychology,* 1993; 32(4): 457–459.

8 For a sensitive discussion of the problems faced by returning veterans see Chapter 13 of McManners, *The Scars of War*. For personal accounts see Simon Weston, *Wallking Tall: An Autobiography* (London: Bloomsbury, 1989), and John Lawrence and Robert Lawrence MC, *Tumbledown: When the Fighting is over: A Personal Story* (London: Bloomsbury, 1988).

9 Audrey Gillan, 'Falklands war veterans have high suicide rate,' *Guardian*, 6 June 2001.

10 In 1997 a question was asked in Parliament about the suicides of Falklands veterans. The answer noted that there had been 329 confirmed suicides by serving personnel since January 1982, but these did not distinguish Falklands veterans, and there was no information on ex-service personnel.

11 http://www.bacp.co.uk/members_visitors/media/current/255_soldiers.htm. The web story cited does not support this figure.

12 Out-of-envelope, non-feasible and certain other engagements terminated, e.g. for safety reasons, were discounted since they were not relevant to the assessment of system performance.

13 *Cmnd 8758*, p. 22.

14 Jeffrey Ethell and Alfred Price, *Air War South Atlantic* (London: Sidgwick & Jackson, 1983).

15 House of Commons, Fourth Report from the Defence Committeee, Session 1986–87, *Implementing the Lessons of the Falklands Campaign*, Report and Appendices, together with the Proceedings of the Committee, 6 May 1987, para 32.

49 THE BELGRANO CONTROVERSY

1 Tam Dalyell MP, *Thatcher's Torpedo: The Sinking of the Belgrano* (London: Cecil Woolf, 1983), pp. 22–3. The most substantial presentation of the argument is contained in Desmond Rice and Arthur Gavshon, *The Sinking of the Belgrano* (London: Secker & Warburg, 1984).

2 House of Commons, Third Report of the Foreign Affairs Committee, Session 1984–5, *Events of the Weekend of 1st and 2nd May 1982* (London: HMSO, 1985).

3 See p. 299.

4 *Official Record*, 4 May 1982, cols. 14–18.

5 *Official Record*, 13 May 1982, cols. 1029–30.

6 Secretary of State for Defence, *The Falklands Campaign: The Lessons*, Cmnd 8758 (London: HMSO, 1982); Supplement to the *London Gazette* (London: HMSO, 8 October 1982). *Guardian*, 1 February 1985; Prime Minister, *Official Report*, 12 February 1985, col. 164.

7 The Sunday Times Insight Team, *The Falklands War: the full story* (London: Sphere, 1982), p. 157. The interview had first been published in the *Western Evening Herald* in November 1982, without attracting notice. The published book was Geoffrey Underwood, *Our Falklands War* (Maritime Books, 1983).

8 Major General Sir Jeremy Moore and Rear Admiral Sir John Woodward, 'The Falklands Experience', *Journal of the Royal United Services Institute* (March 1983), p. 28.

9 Lords, *Official Record*, 13 July 82.

10 *Official Record*, 15 May 1984, col. 91.

11 *Times*, 2 October 1984; Jane's Fighting Ships of 1981/2 had put it at 32.5 knots when new, and while, in May 1982, it was 44 years old, its captain had given the maximum cruising speed as 18 knots, which was not incompatible with a higher maximum speed. During 1 to 2 May its speed however had been between 11–14 knots.

12 *Official Record*, 29 November 1982, col. 103: 'Throughout 2 May, the cruiser and her escorts had made many changes of course.' This statement was repeated many times later.

13 Cardoso *et al.*, *Falklands: The Secret Plot*; Rice and Gavshon, *The Sinking of the Belgrano*; *Signals of War*.

14 *Official Record*, 18 February 1985, col. 744 (737–824).

15 Transcribed by MoD from *News at Ten*, 11 February 1985 interview. See *Official Record*, col. 748.

16 Duncan Campbell and John Rentoul, 'All Out War', *New Statesman*, 24 August 1984. The author of Peter Greig, 'Revelations', *Granta*, No.15 (Spring 1985) clearly had access to some of these materials.

17 Prime Minister's letter to George Foulkes MP, 25 September 1984, reproduced in *Official Record*, 22 October 1984, cols. 469–472.

18 Lombardo complained that his remarks had been quoted out of context. *Tiempo Argentino,* 26 August 1984.

19 *Third Report of the Foreign Affairs Committee*, p. 182

20 *Official Record*, 8 October 1984.

21 *Official Record,* 30 November 1984, cols. 593–4.

22 *Official Record*, 18 February 1985, cols. 775–6. However later he claimed to have read them first in the autumn of 1983. *Official Record*, 7 March 1988, col. 1232.

23 Walter Pincus, 'British Got Crucial Data in Falklands, Diary Says,' and 'Tension and Elation Aboard a Sub at War: Diary Record Life on HMS *Conqueror*,' *Washington Post*, 23 and 24 December 1984.

24 The claimed source, a friend of Dr A. W. Williams, MP for Carmarthen, who raised the issue, was easy to identify. For journalistic inability to let a matter drop see Paul Foot, 'Wanted Missing Belgrano Witness,' *Daily Mirror*, 21 April 1988.

25 *Times*, 1 July 1985. *Official Record*, 12 July 1985.

26 Nick Davies, 'Death in the time of conspiracies', *The Guardian*, 21 March 1994.

27 *Official Record*, 17 January 1985, cols. 173–5.

28 Lawrence Freedman. 'Storms over the South Atlantic', *Times Literary Supplement*, 9 March 1984.

29 *Signals of War*, p. 440.

DRAFT AGREEMENTS

1 Peru version: introduction of third parties to administer the islands temporarily.

2 Peru version: Two Governments acknowledge the existence of conflicting views with respect to the islands.

3 Peru version: Acknowledge the need to take into account the aspirations and interests of the islanders in the final solution. US version: 'the two governments acknowledge that the aspirations and the interests of the Islanders must be taken into account in the definitive settlement (*solucion*) of the problem.'

4 Peru version: The third party or contact group would be composed of Brazil, Peru, West Germany and the US Alternative (Spanish text) would read: the third parties or contact group which would intervene immediately in the negotiations to implement this agreement would be composed of various countries to be designated by mutual agreement. US version: The contact group that would become immediately involved in the negotiations to carry out this agreement would be composed of Brazil, Peru, the Federal Republic of Germany, Jamaica, Venezuela and the United States.

5 Peru version: The final solution would be reached no later than 30 April 1983 under the guarantee of the contact group. US version: adds 'or which the countries listed above will have responsibility.'

BRITISH GALLANTRY AWARDS

1 URL: http://www.naval-history.net

BIBLIOGRAPHY

PRIMARY SOURCES

Despatch by Admiral Sir John Fieldhouse, GCB, GBE, Commander of the Task Force Operations in the South Atlantic: April to June 1982, 14 December 1982, Supplement to *The London Gazette* of Monday, 13 December 1982.

Report of a Committee of Privy Counsellors, *Falkland Islands Review*, January 1983, Cmnd 878 (*The Franks Report*).

Secretary of State for Defence, *The Falklands Campaign: The Lessons*, Cmnd 8758 (London: HMSO, 1982).

House of Commons, *The Falklands Campaign: A Digest of Debates in the House of Commons, 2 April to June 1982* (London: HMSO, 1982).

House of Commons, First Report from the Defence Committee, Session 1982–3, *The Handling of Press and Public Information During the Falklands Conflict*, London: HMSO, December 1982. Vol. 1, Report and Minutes of Proceedings, Volume 2, Minutes of Evidence.

House of Commons Foreign Affairs Committee, *Events Surrounding the Weekend of 1–2 May 1982*, Third Report Session 1984–85 (London: HMSO, 1985).

House of Commons, Fourth Report from the Defence Committee, Session 1986–87, *Implementing the Lessons of the Falklands Campaign*, Report and Appendices, together with the Proceedings of the Committee, 6 May 1987.

SECONDARY SOURCES

Abraham, P., 'Training for battleshock', *Journal of the Royal Army Medical Corps*, (1982).

Adams, Valerie, *The Media and the Falklands Campaign* (London: Macmillan, 1986).

Adkin, Mark, *Goose Green* (London: Cassell, 1992).

Aldea, David, 'Blood and Mud at Goose Green', *Military History*, (April 2002).

Badsey, Stephen, Rob Havers, Mark Grove, ed., *The Falklands Conflict Twenty Years On: Lessons for the Future* (London: Frank Cass, 2005).

Barker, Captain N.J., *Beyond Endurance: An Epic of Whitehall and the South Atlantic* (Barnsley: Leo Cooper, 1997).

Barnett, Anthony, *Iron Britannia: Why Parliament Waged its Falklands War* (London: Allison & Busby, 1982).

Bartson, R.P. and P.W. Birnie, 'The Falkland Islands/Islas Malvinas Conflict: A Question of Zones', *Marine Policy* (January 1983).

Bicheno, Hugh, *Razor's Edge: The Unofficial History of the Falklands War* (London: Weidenfeld & Nicolson, 2006).

Bilton, Michael and Peter Kosminsky, *Speaking Out: Untold Stories from the Falklands War* (London: Andre Deutsch, 1989).

Bishop, Patrick and John Witherow, *The Winter War: The Falklands Conflict* (London: Quartet Books, 1982).

Blakemore, Denys, *Channel Four: The Falklands War* (London: Sidgwick & Jackson, 1992).

Bolia, Robert, 'The Battle of Darwin-Goose Green', *Military Review* (July-August 2005).

Bound, Graham, *Falkland Islanders at War* (London: Leo Cooper, 2002).

Boyce, George, *The Falklands War* (London: Macmillan, 2005).

Bransby, Guy, *Her Majesty's Interrogator* (London: Leo Cooper, 1996).

Brown, David, *The Royal Navy and the Falklands War* (London: Leo Cooper, 1987).

Bruen, Bernie, *Keep Your Head Down: A Falklands Farewell* (Sussex: The Book Guild, 1993).

Burden, Rodney, Michael Draper, Douglas Rough, Colin Smith and David Wilton, *Falklands: The Air War* (London: Arms and Armour Press, 1986).

Campbell, Duncan and John Rentoul, 'All Out War', *New Statesman* (24 August 1984).

Cardoso, Oscar, Ricardo Kirschbaum, and Eduardo van der Kooy, *Falklands: The Secret Plot* (London: Preston Editions, 1983).

Carrington, Peter, *Reflect on Things Past* (London: Collins, 1988).

Charlton, Michael, *The Little Platoon* (London: Blackwell, 1989).

Clapp, Michael and Ewen Southby-Tailyour, *Amphibious Assault: Falklands: The Battle of San Carlos Waters* (London: Leo Cooper, 1996).

Clark, Alan, *Diaries: Into Politics* (London: Weidenfeld & Nicolson, 2000).

Clarke, H.D., W. Mishler and P. Whiteley, 'Recapturing the Falklands: Models of Conservative Popularity, 1979–1983', *British Journal of Political Science*, vol. 20 (1990).

Cohen, Yoel, *Media Diplomacy: The Foreign Office in the Mass Communications Age* (London: Frank Cass, 1986).

Colbeck, Graham, *With 3 Para to the Falklands* (London: Greenhill Books, 2002).

Corum, James, 'Argentine Airpower in the Falklands War,' *Air & Space Power Journal*, Fall 2002.

Craig, Captain Chris, *Call for Fire: Sea Combat in the Falklands and the Gulf War* (London: John Murray, 1995).

Dale, Iain, ed., *Memories of the Falklands* (London: Politico's, 2002).

Dalyell, Tam, MP, *Thatcher's Torpedo: The Sinking of the Belgrano* (London: Cecil Woolf, 1983).

Danchev, Alex, *Founding Father* (Oxford: Clarendon Press, 1993).

De la Billiere, General Sir Peter, *Looking for Trouble: SAS to Gulf Command* (London: Harper Collins, 1994).

Dillon, G.M., *The Falklands, Politics and War* (London: Macmillan Press, 1989).

Dodds, Klaus, *Pink Ice: Britain and the South Atlantic Empire* (London: I.B. Tauris, 2002).

Ethell, Jeffrey and Alfred Price, *Air War South Atlantic* (London: Sidgwick & Jackson, 1983).

The Falklands Witness Seminar (Strategic and Combat Studies Institute: The Occasional no. 46, 2004).

Fox, Robert, *Eyewitness Falklands* (London: Methuen, 1982).

Freedman, Lawrence, *Britain & the Falklands War* (Oxford: Basil Blackwell Inc, 1988).

Freedman, Lawrence and Virginia Gamba-Stonehouse, *Signals of War* (London: Faber, 1989).

Freedman, Lawrence, 'Storms over the South Atlantic', *Times Literary Supplement*, 9 March 1984.

Fitz-Gibbon, Spencer, *Not Mentioned in Despatches ... The History and Mythology of Goose Green* (Cambridge: The Lutterworth Press, 1995).

Frost, John, *2 Para Falklands: The Battalion at War* (London and Sydney: Sphere Books Limited, 1983).

Gompert, David, 'American Diplomacy and the Haig Mission', in Alberto R. Coll and Anthony C. Arend, *The Falklands War: Lessons for Strategy, Diplomacy and International Law.*

Greig, Peter, 'Revelations', *Granta*, No.15 (Spring 1985).

Grove, Eric, *Vanguard to Trident: British Naval Policy since World War Two* (Annapolis, MA: US Naval Institute Press, 1987).

Hastings, Max, *Going to the Wars* (London: Macmillan, 2000).

Haig, Alexander, *Caveat* (London: Weidenfeld & Nicolson, 1984).

Harris, Robert, *Gotcha: The Government, Media and the Falklands Crisis* (London: Faber, 1994).

Henderson, Sir Nicholas, 'America and the Falklands', *The Economist* (12 November 1983).

Henderson, Nicholas, *Mandarin: The Diaries of an Ambassador, 1969–1982* (London: Weidenfeld & Nicolson, 1994).

Hennessy, Peter, *The Prime Minister: The Office and its Holders Since 1946* (London: The Allen Lane Press, 2000).

Higgitt, Mark, *Through Fire and Water: HMS Ardent: The Forgotten Frigate of the Falklands* (London: Mainstream Publishing, 2001).

Hill, Richard, *Lewin of Greenwich: The Authorised Biography of Admiral of the Fleet Lord Lewin* (London: Cassell & Co., 2000).

Jennings, Christian and Adrian Weale, *Green-Eyed Boys: 3 Para and the Battle for Mount Longdon* (London: HarperCollins, 1996).

Jolly, Rick, *The Red and Green Life Machine: A Diary of the Falklands Field Hospital* (London: Century Publishing, 1983).

Jones, G. and Lovett, J., 'Delayed psychiatric sequelae among Falklands War veterans', *Journal of the Royal College of General Practitioners* (1987).

Kinzer Stewart, Nora, *Mates and Muchachos: Unit Cohesion in the Falklands/Malvinas War* (New York: Brassey's, 1991).

Lawrence, John and Robert Lawrence MC, *Tumbledown: When The Fighting is Over: A Personal Story* (London: Bloomsbury, 1988).

Leach, Admiral of the Fleet Sir Henry, *Endure No Makeshifts* (London: Leo Cooper, 1993).

Makin, Guillermo, ' Nature of Anglo-American diplomacy, 1980–1990', in A. Danchev (ed.), *A Matter of Life and Death: International Perspectives on the Falklands Conflict* (Basingstoke: Macmillan, 1991).

Martin, Lisa L., 'Institutions and Cooperation: Sanctions During the Falkland Islands Conflict,' *International Security*, 16:4 (Spring 1992).

McManners, Hugh, *Falklands Commando* (London: William Kimber, 1984).

McQueen, Captain Bob, *Island Base: Ascension Island in the Falklands War* (London: Whittles Publishing, 2005).

Mercer, Derick, Geoff Mungham and Kevin Williams, *The Fog of War* (London: Heinemann, 1987).

Middlebrook, Martin, *The Fight for the 'Malvinas': The Argentine Forces in the Falklands War* (London: Viking, 1989).

Middlebrook, Martin, *Operation Corporate: The Story of the Falklands War 1982* (London: Viking, 1985).

Miller, Roger, ed., *Seeing Off the Bear: Anglo-American Air Power Co-operation During the Cold War*, Proceedings, Joint Meeting of the Royal Air Force Historical Society and the Air Force Historical Foundation, USAF 1995.

Moore, Major General Sir Jeremy and Rear Admiral Sir John Woodward, 'The Falklands Experience', *Journal of the Royal United Services Institute* (March 1983).

Nott, John, *Here Today: Gone Tomorrow: Recollections of an errant politician* (London: Politico's, 2002).

O'Brien, L. S. and S. J. Hughes, 'Symptoms of post-traumatic stress disorder in Falklands veterans five years after the conflict', *British Journal of Psychiatry* (1991).

Orner, R., T. Lynch and P. Seed., 'Long-term traumatic stress reactions in British Falklands War veterans', *British Journal of Clinical Psychology*, 32(4)(1993).

Parsons, Sir Anthony, 'The Falklands Crisis in the United Nations, 31 March – 14 June 1982', *International Affairs*, Vol.59: No.2 (Spring 1983).

Perez de Cuellar, Javier, *Pilgrimage for Peace: A Secretary-General's Memoir* (London: Palgrave, 1997).

Perkins, Roger, *Operation PARAQUAT: The Battle for South Georgia* (Chippenham, 1986).

Price, J., 'The Falklands: rate of British psychiatric casualties compared to recent American wars', *Journal of the Royal Army Medical Corps*, 1984.

Prince, Stephen, 'British Command and Control in the Falklands Campaign', *Defence and Security Analysis*, 18/4 (December 2002).

Reynolds, David, *Task Force: The Illustrated History of the Falklands War* (London: Sutton, 2002).

Rice, Desmond and Arthur Gavshon, *The Sinking of the Belgrano* (London: Secker & Warburg, 1984).

Richardson, Louise, *When Allies Collide: Anglo-American Relations During the Suez and Falkland Crises* (New York: St. Martin's Press, 1996).

Rogers, Paul, *The Belgrano Enquiry, The Unnecessary War* (London: Spokesman Books, 1988).

Rose, General Michael, 'Advance Force Operations: The SAS,' in Linda Washington, ed., *Ten Years On: The British Army in the Falklands War* (London: National Army Museum, 1992).

Sanders, D., H. Ward and D. Marsh, 'A Reply to Clarke, Mishler, and Whiteley', *British Journal of Political Science*, vol. 20 (1990).

Seear, Mike, *With the Gurkhas in the Falklands: A War Journal* (London: Leo Cooper, 2003).

Smith, John, *74 Days: An Islander's Diary of the Falklands Occupation* (London: Century Publishing, 1984).

Strange, Ian, *The Falklands Islands* (London: David & Charles, 3rd edition, 1985).

The Sunday Times Insight Team, *The Falklands War: the full story* (London: Sphere, 1982).

Sutterlin, James S., 'The Good Offices of the Secretary-General', in Diane B. Bendahame and John W. McDonald Jr., *Perspectives on Negotiation: Four Case Studies and Interpretations* (Washington D.C., Center for the Study of Foreign Affairs, Foreign Service Institute, US Department of State, 1986).

Thatcher, Margaret, *The Downing Street Years* (London: Harper Collins, 1993).

Thompson, Julian, *No Picnic*, 3rd edition (London: Cassell, 2001).

Thompson, Julian, *Ready for Anything: A History of the Parachute Regiment* (London: Weidenfeld & Nicolson, 1989).

Tinker, David, *A Message from the Falklands* (London: Junction Books, 1982).

Tripodi, Paolo, 'Chile's Role During the Falklands War', *The Journal of Strategic Studies*, 26:4 (December 2003).

Van der Bijl, Nicholas and David Aldea, *5th Infantry Brigade in the Falklands* (London: Leo Cooper, 2003).

Van der Bijl, Nick, *Nine Battles to Stanley* (London: Leo Cooper, 1999).

Vaux, Nick, *March to the South Atlantic: 42 Commando Royal Marines in the Falklands War* (London: Buchan & Enright, 1986).

Ward, Commander 'Sharkey', *Sea Harrier over the Falkland: A Maverick at War* (London: Cassel)

Weinberger, Casper, *Fighting for Peace* (London: Michael Joseph, 1990).

West, Nigel, *The Secret War for the Falklands* (London: Little Brown & Co, 1997).

Weston, Simon, *Wallking Tall: An Autobiography* (London: Bloomsbury, 1989).

Willets, Peter and Felipe Noguera, 'Public attitudes and the future of the Islands', in A. Danchev (ed.), *A Matter of Life and Death: International Perspectives on the Falklands Conflict* (Basingstoke: Macmillan, 1991).

Wilsey, John, *H Jones VC: The Life and Death of an Unusual Hero* (London: Hutchinson, 2002).

Woodward, Admiral Sandy with Patrick Robinson: *One Hundred Days: The Memoirs of the Falklands Battle Group Commander*, 2nd edition (London: HarperCollins, 1992, second edition 2003).

INDEX

831

CPSIA information can be obtained
at www.ICGtesting.com
Printed in the USA
BVOW06s1735250817
493062BV00003B/12/P